Herbert H. Lehman

Herbert H. Lehman

A Political Biography

DUANE TANANBAUM

Published by State University of New York Press, Albany

For information, contact State University of New York Press, Albany, NY
www.sunypress.edu

Production, Diane Ganeles
Marketing, Michael Campochiaro

Library of Congress Cataloging-in-Publication Data

Names: Tananbaum, Duane, 1949–
Title: Herbert H. Lehman : a political biography / Duane Tananbaum.
Description: Albany, NY : State University of New York Press, [2016] | Includes
  bibliographical references and index.
Identifiers: LCCN 2016007754 (print) | LCCN 2016009110 (ebook) | ISBN
  9781438463179 (hardcover : alk. paper) | ISBN 9781438463193 (e-book)
Subjects: LCSH: Lehman, Herbert H. (Herbert Henry), 1878–1963. |
  Governors—New York (State)—Biography. | New York (State)—Politics and
  Government—1865–1950.| New York (State)—Politics and government—1951–
  | Legislators—United States—Biography. | United States. Congress.
  Senate—Biography. | Liberalism—United States. | United States—Politics
  and government—20th century.
Classification: LCC F124.L53 T363 2016 (print) | LCC F124.L53 (ebook) | DDC
  328.73/092—dc23
LC record available at http://lccn.loc.gov/2016007754

10 9 8 7 6 5 4 3 2 1

Contents

Illustrations

Preface

You think you choose the subjects of your books. But sometimes, in ways you don't know, the books choose you.[1]

In the 1930s and early 1940s, New Yorkers chose their leaders wisely, electing Fiorello La Guardia as Mayor of New York City, helping send Franklin Roosevelt to the White House, and voting four times for Herbert Lehman to be their Governor. All three men believed that government should help people in need, and, guided by that liberal philosophy, they led New Yorkers and the nation through the Great Depression and the world crises that dominated those years.

As Lehman was concluding his fourth term as Governor in late 1942, Franklin Roosevelt called his old friend and colleague to Washington to head the State Department's new Office of Foreign Relief and Rehabilitation Operations (OFRRO) that was tasked with providing aid to nations that were liberated from the Axis powers. After a trying year in the morass of the State Department and White House bureaucracies, Lehman was named the first Director General of the United Nations Relief and Rehabilitation Administration (UNRRA) in November 1943. Lehman remained in that position until early 1946, when he resigned in protest over the Truman administration's failure to take stronger action to deal with the growing threat of worldwide famine.

In 1949, at age seventy-one, Herbert Lehman was elected to the United States Senate after a hard-fought campaign in which he endorsed "the welfare state." In the Senate, Lehman was one of the first to stand up against Senator Joseph McCarthy's reign of terror, and he was the only Senator up for re-election who opposed the McCarran Internal Security Act of 1950, which threatened the rights and liberties of the American people. Re-elected to the Senate in 1950, Lehman fought for civil rights, immigration reform, and other liberal causes, and his devotion to principle led Eleanor Roosevelt and others to describe him as "the conscience of the Senate."[2] Retiring from the Senate in 1956, Lehman, despite his advanced years, led a movement to reform New York politics by reducing the power of Tammany Hall leader Carmine De Sapio and the party bosses.

Despite his important role in American political life from the late 1920s through the early 1960s, Herbert Lehman has been largely ignored by scholars and forgotten by the general public. Allan Nevins's authorized biography of Lehman, entitled *Herbert H. Lehman and His Era*, was published in 1963, but despite the subsequent opening of numerous archives and manuscript collections, there has not been a full-length study of Lehman since Nevins's book.[3] In writing a new biography of Herbert Lehman, it seemed redundant to focus on Lehman's personal and family life or the German-Jewish milieu from which Lehman came, all of which Nevins had covered in detail. Thus, after a chapter on Lehman and Lillian Wald that explores Lehman's lifelong devotion to serving others, this book concentrates on Lehman's political career and his interactions with the key figures in his political life, especially Al Smith, Franklin Roosevelt, Harry Truman, Joseph McCarthy, Lyndon Johnson, and John Kennedy. In approaching Lehman in this way, this study sheds new light on New York politics from the 1920s to the 1960s and improves our understanding of the relationship between FDR's New Deal in Washington and Lehman's "Little New Deal" in New York. Lehman's experiences in OFRRO and UNRRA exemplify the bureaucratic conflicts that sometimes undermined Franklin Roosevelt's policies and programs, and they demonstrate the difficulties in maintaining American support for multinational efforts. The chapters on Lehman's Senate years make clear Lehman's commitment to his liberal principles, especially civil rights and immigration reform, despite the obstacles in getting the Senate even to consider such measures in the 1950s. Lehman's interactions with John Kennedy and his fight against bossism in New York show how Lehman, even in his eighties, continued to fight for liberal reforms nationally and in New York.

Herbert Lehman did not always achieve his objectives. In New York, the Republicans controlled at least one house of the State Legislature for all but one year of Lehman's governorship, enabling them to block or delay some of Lehman's initiatives. At UNRRA, his plans to feed the hungry people of Europe and Asia were often undercut by higher military priorities, shortages of supplies and shipping, and the unwillingness of the Truman administration to require the American people to make sacrifices to help prevent starvation overseas. As a Senator, Lehman found himself frustrated by that body's archaic rules and the dominance of Democratic leader Lyndon Johnson and Southern conservatives. In New York, De Sapio and the bosses stood in the way of Lehman's efforts to persuade the Democratic Party to nominate statesmen rather than politicians. Lehman often succeeded in New York by appealing directly to the people, and he had some success in OFRRO and UNRRA by appealing directly to Franklin Roosevelt. As a senator, however, Lehman refused to compromise his liberal beliefs, and he frequently had to content himself with keeping issues like civil rights and immigration in the forefront of the nation's political consciousness so that reforms could be enacted in the future. Ironically, it was President Lyndon Johnson, who did so much to block such measures when he and Lehman were in the Senate together, who won congressional approval of civil rights legislation and immigration reform as part of his Great Society in 1964–1965.

This book relies heavily upon Herbert Lehman's words as expressed in his public speeches and private correspondence. Words were crucially important to Herbert Lehman in his efforts to educate and arouse the public, whether it was to overcome the New York State Legislature's reluctance to implement the Social Security Act, alert the American people and his Senate colleagues to the danger posed by Senator McCarthy, or make the case for civil rights legislation. Lehman had not spent his whole life in politics; he saw public office as an opportunity to serve others, and his wealth and his prestige meant that he did not need the job or the income or the acclaim that went with it. As a result, Lehman refused to tailor his views to what was popular. His honesty and his integrity were the keys to his political success; people knew that he meant and believed what he said, that he was not just another politician saying whatever was necessary to win an election.

My reliance on Lehman's words also reflects the scarcity of colorful stories and anecdotes about him. In 1944, Jacob Marcus of Hebrew Union College asked Carolin Flexner, Lehman's longtime personal assistant, for copies of any of Herbert Lehman's letters that reflected, in "a lighter vein," Lehman's involvement in human interest matters. Flexner regretfully replied that "everything that Governor Lehman has ever done has been of human interest, but none of it is in a lighter vein." William Shannon, a columnist for the *New York Post*, attempted to write a biography of Lehman in the early 1950s but gave up the effort in 1955, explaining that Lehman's friends and family had "volunteered warm expressions of respect and affection . . . but very little in the way of anecdotes or crisp, dramatic details." Allan Nevins had to deal with similar difficulties in writing his book a few years later. Actually, Lehman's career was filled with dramatic moments, including his confrontation with Tammany Hall over the gubernatorial nomination in 1932, his opposition to FDR's court-packing plan in 1937, his battles with Senator McCarthy, his coming to blows with Republican Senator Homer Capehart of Indiana after a radio interview, and his challenge to De Sapio and the bosses who controlled the Democratic Party in New York. But Lehman shared his sense of humor mostly with family members, believing that government was serious business. As a result, his earnest demeanor, his honesty and integrity, and his belief that it was the government's responsibility to help those in need characterized and dominated his years of public service.[4]

In many ways, it seems like I spent a large part of my life preparing to write this biography of Herbert Lehman. I still remember my mother's high regard for Herbert Lehman, who was Governor of New York during her teen-age years. Even though she never met Lehman nor had any personal contact with him, my mother, like many Jews of her generation, was confident that if there was a problem, she could somehow appeal to Lehman, who would help in some way. While earning my PhD at Columbia University in the 1970s, I did research in the Lehman Papers for my dissertation, and I worked for three years as an archivist at the Herbert Lehman Papers and Suite at Columbia, where the Lehman Papers were then housed. My familiarity with the Lehman Papers proved to be invaluable in writing this book, although the papers themselves are now housed off campus and the Special Files of the Herbert Lehman Papers have been digitalized and are available online. In 1980–1981, I was one of the American Historical Association's first Congressional Fellows, and working for the Senate Committee on Foreign Relations gave me a better understanding of how things really work in Congress that was very helpful in understanding Herbert Lehman's Senate years.

In 1986, I was hired to teach United States History at Lehman College, City University of New York. Lehman had originally been the Bronx campus of Hunter College, but it became a separate unit within CUNY in 1968–1969 and was named in honor of Herbert Lehman in the hope that his life and career would inspire the students and faculty. In 2002–2003, then–Vice President of Institutional Advancement Anne Johnson approached me about presenting a scholarly paper on Herbert Lehman at the college's upcoming symposium com-memorating the 125th anniversary of Lehman's birth. Feeling somewhat stymied on a project that I had been working on for many years, I agreed, and thus I renewed my "acquaintance" with Herbert Lehman. I did not think of doing a book right away, but I quickly realized that a new biography of Lehman was needed, one that would utilize all the relevant manuscript collections that had been opened since the publication of Nevins's book, and one that would place Lehman's career in historical perspective. At that point, I could feel this book choosing me. I found the idea of doing a biography very appealing in its simplicity and its finite nature: the subject is born, lives, and then dies. What I failed to appreciate was that Herbert Lehman's life was not that simple. His political career had four distinct phases: New York State politics in the 1920s and 1930s, international relief at OFRRO and UNRRA, national affairs in the U.S. Senate, and New York reform politics. And in order to write this book, I had to be knowledgeable about all these areas. I was already familiar with the national issues that occurred during Lehman's Senate term, but the other areas required substantial research before I could start writing.

Over the past decade, I have incurred many debts in the research and writing of this book. Vice President Johnson retained her confidence in me even when, two weeks before the Lehman College Symposium in 2003, I ripped up the paper I had prepared and started work on a different one that was better suited to the occasion. Lehman College President Ricardo Fernandez has been truly committed to keeping Herbert Lehman's memory and legacy alive for Lehman College students and has been supportive of this project from its inception. Mario Dellapina, the current Vice President of Institutional Advancement, and Frederick Gilbert, the Assistant Vice President of Institutional Advancement and Executive Director of the Lehman College Foundation, helped me secure funding to facilitate the publication of the book. I thank Wendy Lehman Lash and the Edith A. and Herbert H. Lehman Foundation for that funding. Herbert Lehman's great-nephew William Bernhard and his wife Catherine Cahill contributed funds to help secure the rights to certain photographs, as did John L. Loeb, Jr., another of Herbert Lehman's great-nephews.

A Shuster grant from Lehman College and a series of Professional Staff Congress–City University of New York grants helped finance some of the research for this book as well as the rights to use some of the photographs. A one-semester sabbatical from Lehman College helped free up time to work on the book.

Grants from the Franklin and Eleanor Roosevelt Institute, the Harry S. Truman Library Institute, and the John F. Kennedy Library facilitated my research for this project. The archivists at the Franklin D. Roosevelt, Harry S. Truman, John F. Kennedy, and Lyndon Baines Johnson Libraries were all very helpful in locating relevant materials.

The Herbert Lehman Papers at Columbia have had a number of curators since William Liebmann—the "boss" to those of us who worked under him—first organized and opened the Lehman Papers and Suite at Columbia. I thank all of them, as well as the rest of the staff of the Rare Books and Manuscripts Division of the Columbia University Libraries, for all their help. Marlene Subit made available to me the many books on Zionism and Judaism in the Sinai Free Synagogue Library in Mount Vernon, New York. The Mount Vernon Public Library remains a hidden treasure trove of older books on American history, while the Westchester County Library system makes it possible to access newer works.

My thanks also go to Lauren Post and the estate of Rollin Kirby Post for permission to use some of Rollin Kirby's editorial cartoons, to *The Jewish Advocate* for permission to reproduce an ad from John Kennedy's Senate run in 1952, to the Herb Block Foundation for the right to use a few Herblock cartoons, to Helene Berinsky for permission to use one of Burton Berinsky's photographs, to Matthew Lutts of AP Images for his help in locating relevant photographs, and to the Houghton Library at Harvard University for permission to quote from the J. Pierrepont Moffat Papers.

William vanden Heuvel and Norman Sherman kindly shared some of their memories of Herbert Lehman with me, as did Lehman's great-niece, the late June Bingham Birge. Al Smith biographer Chris Finan clarified some points for me on the 1928 gubernatorial election in New York, and Professor Michael Green of the University of Southern Nevada helped me better understand Nevada Senators Pat McCarran and Howard Cannon. Professor Green also brought to my attention Booth Mooney's story about Lyndon Johnson wanting to be more "sincere," like Herbert Lehman.

The staff at the Leonard Lief Library at Lehman College, including Janet Munch in Special Collections, Eugene Laper in Interlibrary Loan, Angelina Brea and Olga Torres in Circulation, and Edwin Wallace in Periodicals, among others, provided invaluable assistance in getting me the books and other materials I needed for this project, as well as helping me when I encountered the inevitable difficulties with the microfilm copier machine. My friends and colleagues in the History Department at Lehman constantly offered their support and encouragement, and Cindy Lobel showed me how to print out newspaper articles from ProQuest in a way that actually made the text large enough to read the articles. She also put me in touch with her sister-in-law, Judith Kafka of Baruch College, and they both pointed me toward important sources on racial problems in Northern cities in the late 1950s. Stephen Petrus contributed significantly to my knowledge about the reform Democrats in New York in the late 1950s and early 1960s. Vincent Prohaska, Kathy Brown, Lenore Schultz, Teddy Meyrowitz, Maryann Gerbacia, and the late Woody Greenhaus helped me keep my sense of humor and perspective and smile at life's absurdities.

Michael Rinella and James Peltz of State University of New York Press demonstrated great patience in waiting for this manuscript and moving forward with its publication despite its length. I appreciate the helpful suggestions offered by David Woolner of Marist College and the Roosevelt Institute and the other reviewer for State University of New York Press who had to make their way through an even longer version of this study. I also thank Dana Foote for copyediting the manuscript and Diane Ganeles for shepherding the book through the production process.

As a student, I had the privilege of working under two exceptional teachers and scholars who inspired me by their examples. Walter LaFeber of Cornell University and William E. Leuchtenburg, then at Columbia University, showed me that great teaching and distinguished scholarship can go hand in hand, and I remain thankful for their guidance and tutelage over the years.

My biggest debt, of course, is to my family. My parents' love and support helped me realize I could achieve whatever goals I set for myself, and my sister Pee Gee Coyle and her husband Phil always made us feel welcome when we returned to my native Buffalo, New York. My brother and sister-in-law, Harvey and Rona Tananbaum, provided me with all the comforts of their home when I did my research at the Kennedy Library, and my brother-in-law and sister-in-law, Jim and Kathie Ehrenreich, did the same when I visited the Truman Library. My niece Kelly Ehrenreich and my sons Rob and Willie Tananbaum facilitated my research in various digital sources. I probably have not set a good example for Rob and Willie on the importance of brevity in writing, but I do appreciate their encouragement as I have worked on this project and used their bedroom for books and filing cabinets that had overrun their natural habitat in the living room. I also appreciate the help of my daughters-in-law Samantha Tananbaum and Beka Breitzer in resolving various computer issues that arose while I was working on this book.

Finally, and most importantly, my greatest debt is to my wife Joan, for whom my love and gratitude go way beyond anything I can put into words. She has been a wonderful editor and proofreader for every page of this book, including the endnotes when they were in small print, and her love, patience, support, and encouragement at every step along the way have enabled me to bring this project to its conclusion.

CHAPTER I

"A Dearly Beloved Friend"

Herbert Lehman and Lillian Wald

With the exception of my wife and my parents, no one has had as great an influence on my life [as Lillian Wald].[1]

Herbert Lehman was born in New York City in 1878, the son of Jewish immigrants who had come to the United States from Germany. His father, Mayer Lehman, was one of the founders of Lehman Brothers, which had become one of the nation's leading investment banks, and the family lived very comfortably among the city's wealthy German Jewish community. Herbert's parents set an example of helping others with their strong support of Mount Sinai Hospital and Temple Emanu-El in New York, and they instilled in their children a sense of duty to aid those less fortunate than themselves. Herbert Lehman's concern for the welfare of others was nurtured and strengthened by Lillian Wald, who Lehman described as "a great and wonderful woman" who "always saw more ways in which to be helpful and to render service in the community than any other person" he had known. Eleanor Roosevelt later attributed Lehman's activities as a "humanitarian . . . to his close association with Lillian Wald when he was young."[2]

Lillian Wald was born in Cincinnati, Ohio, in 1867, the daughter of German and Polish Jews who had come to the United States in 1848. Wald and her family moved to Rochester, New York, in 1877, where they prospered

---

Chapter title quotation: Herbert Lehman to Leo Arnstein, November 29, 1940, Herbert Lehman Papers, Special Correspondence Files, Lillian Wald.

1

and became part of the local Reform Jewish elite. Inspired by a nurse who had aided her pregnant sister, Wald came to New York City in 1889 to enter the nursing program at New York Hospital, from which she graduated in 1891. She spent a year working as a nurse in an orphan asylum and then a year studying at the Women's Medical College in New York. As part of her studies, she was sent to teach immigrant mothers on the Lower East Side the rudiments of public health. Appalled by the squalid living conditions in the tenements there, Wald sought and received funding in 1893 from Jacob Schiff, a financier and leader of New York's wealthy German Jewish establishment, to open the Nurses' Settlement, which the *New York Times* later called "the first non-sectarian public health nursing system in the world." The Nurses' Settlement soon evolved into the Henry Street Settlement House and the Visiting Nurse Service of New York. Henry Street differed from most settlements in its emphasis on and utilization of trained nurses to care for residents of the community.[3]

When Herbert Lehman was fourteen years old, a school tour of the Lower East Side made a lasting impression on him. Sixty-five years later, he still remembered "the poverty and the filth and bleakness" that he saw and felt in the streets and the admiration and respect he had for "Lillian Wald because she lived down there." Jacob Schiff or a member of his family introduced Lehman to Lillian Wald and the Henry Street Settlement House, and Lehman began volunteering there in the late 1890s, when he was home on breaks from Williams College.[4]

The Henry Street Settlement House quickly became the focus of Herbert Lehman's efforts to help others. After graduating from Williams in 1899, Lehman went to work for J. Spencer Turner Co., a textile firm, and he joined a number of friends who were already active at Henry Street. At Lillian Wald's request, Lehman organized a club for neighborhood boys between the ages of twelve and fourteen. For the next four years, he led the "Patriots," a group of about fifteen boys from the Lower East Side. They usually met at the settlement house for an hour or two and then went out for ice cream sodas. Lehman later recounted how his attempt to teach the boys about democracy succeeded only too well. After Lehman "had talked a lot about democracy to these kids and the importance of the ballot," each boy voted for himself for club president.[5]

Lehman's Patriot boys later recalled that Lehman was "utterly devoid of that patronizing attitude" that they "sense[d] in some of the other Settlement workers." They were impressed by his "absolute sincerity and honesty of purpose" and his desire "to encourage and spur young people onward and upward," and they were grateful for having "received a grounding in ethics at an age when habits of thought and action usually influence one's whole future." Lehman remained in touch with many of the boys for the rest of their lives, helping a number of them get an education, a job, or a start in business, and at least one of the boys named his firstborn son after Herbert Lehman.[6]

A warm friendship quickly developed between Herbert Lehman and Lillian Wald as they worked together to bring about needed social reforms. Wald was always concerned about the welfare of children, and as she later wrote in her autobiography, she was appalled that the federal government had more information and seemed more "concerned . . . with the conservation of material wealth, mines and forests, hogs and lobsters" than with "the conservation and protection of the children of the nation." In the early 1900s, she joined with Florence Kelley, Jane Addams, and other reformers to advocate the creation of a federal children's bureau within the Department of Labor. As Wald explained in a letter to the *New York Times*, "the bureau would be a clearing house, a source of information and reliable education on all matters pertaining to the welfare of children, and it would investigate and report upon the questions pertaining to them now nowhere answered in complete or unified form." Herbert Lehman told Wald that he was "very strongly in favor of such a Bureau," believing "that through this alone real effective child labor supervision can be had." Lehman understood "that in order really to do effective work in this field, there must be federal action rather than State legislation," and he was eager to do what he could "to further the movement . . . either in work or by contributing." Wald's and Lehman's efforts came to fruition in 1912 when the Federal Children's Bureau was established.[7]

Lillian Wald and Herbert Lehman opposed racial discrimination and advocated equality for all Americans. Wald was one of the signers of the "call" that went out in 1909 for a biracial group to meet and focus attention on the problems of African Americans, leading to the formation of the National Association for the Advancement of Colored People (NAACP). When the new organization met in New York, Wald volunteered to host a reception for its members, both blacks and whites, at Henry Street. As she recalled in her autobiography, she dismissed warnings that the settlement house would receive unfavorable publicity because "as soon as white and colored people sit down and eat together there begin to be newspaper stories about social equality." She assured everyone that there would not be enough room at Henry Street for anyone to sit down to eat. Wald served as a member of the NAACP's General Committee and its board of directors, and Herbert Lehman later sat on the NAACP's board for more than thirty years, generously contributing both his time and his money to the cause.[8]

The one issue on which Lehman and Wald strongly disagreed was American involvement in World War I. As chairman of the American Union Against Militarism, Wald met with President Woodrow Wilson on a number of occasions to urge that the United States not get involved in the war in Europe. Herbert Lehman, on the other hand, believed that the United States should actively oppose Germany and the Central Powers. Long before American entry into the conflict, he joined a group of men doing military drills on Governor's Island, using broomsticks for rifles. In February 1917, Lehman asked Francis Sayre, a friend from Williams College who was Woodrow Wilson's son-in-law, to inform the President, or "whoever is in charge of organizing the necessary additional government machinery, that if my services can be used in any capacity, either here or abroad, I should be very glad indeed to put myself at the disposal of the government." Lehman stressed that he was "seeking no office," but he believed that "in the emergencies which will arise in the near future, the government will need men of experience and training," and he was "willing to make whatever personal sacrifice is necessary." Lehman tried to impress upon various Wilson administration officials that his experience in the textile and banking industries especially qualified him for service in the Quartermaster Corps.[9]

Once the United States entered the war in April 1917, Lehman quickly dropped his interest in the Quartermaster Corps and sought instead to enlist for officers' training, but the Army was reluctant to offer him a commission because of his age and lack of military experience. Wanting to get involved as soon as possible and not knowing when he would hear anything definitive from the Army, Lehman went to work for the Navy Bureau of Supplies and Accounts as a civilian in May 1917, helping to procure needed supplies. In August 1917, Lehman was commissioned as a Captain in the Army and assigned to the General Staff Corps to oversee contracts for textiles and other necessary commodities. After the Armistice, Lehman served on the Board of Contract Adjustment and the War Claims Board, both of which dealt with problems caused by the abrupt cancellation of contracts when the fighting ended. Lehman rose to the rank of Colonel, a title he proudly used until he was elected to high civilian offices, and he was awarded the Distinguished Service Medal for his work "in the settlement and adjustment of terminated obligations."[10]

Although Henry Street was always near and dear to Herbert Lehman's heart, his philanthropic activities extended far beyond the Lower East Side. During World War I, he was one of the founders of the American Jewish Joint Distribution Committee (JDC), an organization funded mostly by American Jews of German descent to unify and expand efforts to help European Jews displaced by the war. Lehman was one of the younger members of the JDC, which was led by Jacob Schiff and then Felix Warburg. The JDC raised $16.4 million during the war to relieve the suffering of European Jews, and its leaders hoped that their mission could be completed and the organization disbanded once the war ended. But they soon realized that the Jews' distress in Eastern Europe would continue, and, after the war, they shifted the JDC's focus from relief to rehabilitation. Herbert Lehman served as chairman of the JDC's Reconstruction Committee, which allocated millions of dollars for various projects in Eastern Europe in the 1920s and 1930s, and he later recalled that his experience with the JDC's Reconstruction Committee was "great training" for his "later activity in UNRRA."[11]

Lillian Wald "appreciate[d] the great work" Lehman was "doing for the Jewish War Relief," but she hoped he would also have the time to serve on the board of Henry Street, joining Jacob Schiff and all his other friends "who are on the Directorate of the Henry Street Settlement." In November 1916, Herbert Lehman and his wife Edith contributed $5,000 to a $1,000,000 fund-raising drive to help Henry Street "increase its facilities and to care for children who were crippled in the epidemic of infantile paralysis." A few months later, Lehman formally joined the Henry Street Board, emphasizing to Wald, "There is no activity in the city which has interested me more than yours, and there is none with which I have been affiliated, both in work and in sympathetic interest, for a longer period."[12]

Lehman took his responsibilities as a member of the board at Henry Street very seriously. He offered to resign from the board when he went to work for the military in Washington during the war, but Wald and the other directors refused to accept his resignation, granting him instead a leave of absence until "the happy days of peace" would allow Lehman to resume his "active participation." In 1919, Lehman was appointed to Henry Street's Finance Committee, and he looked forward to sharing in the work when he returned to New York that autumn. Lehman used his business and banking expertise to review financial statements and recommend new accounting systems and budget procedures for Henry Street. In 1924, he expressed concern over a potential decrease in contributions, and in 1926, he suggested that Wald "personally strongly urge every Director to be present at what will undoubtedly prove to be a very important meeting" at which "the whole subject of finances should be exhaustively discussed." Lehman also helped support a summer camp near Lake Mahopac that Henry Street established "to give as many as possible of these children a breath of fresh air, a chance to see the sun on flowers and fields, . . . to take them away from the cruelty of the Summer's heat in the city." Lehman remained on the Board of Directors of Henry Street and the Visiting Nurse Service, albeit in a much less active role, during his tenure as Governor of New York and later when he was a U.S. Senator.[13]

Lillian Wald realized early in her career the importance of politics and elections for achieving social reforms and improving working and living conditions for the inhabitants of the Lower East Side. She cheered in 1928 when Democrats nominated Al Smith for President and Franklin Roosevelt for Governor of New York, but she took special pleasure in the nomination of Herbert Lehman for Lieutenant Governor. In a letter to the *New York Times*, she detailed Lehman's long involvement with Henry Street, tracing his progress from "the young man who accepted duty as a club leader . . . to the directorate of our settlement." She recalled that Lehman had "exercised a remarkable influence over the younger men with whom he was associated." He had "recognized their ambitions, their need of sincere fellowship; and when a friend was needed, he never failed."

She emphasized that Lehman "has never lost his sensitiveness to social conditions and has participated in the efforts to meet their problems." In mediating labor disputes or confronting other societal problems, she noted, Lehman always showed "the same qualities of disinterested and intelligent comprehension." In Wald's opinion, Lehman's example of service to his fellow man in peace and in war "should stimulate our youth and encourage the older folk."[14]

The lack of adequate housing for working people in New York had long concerned Lilian Wald. As she explained in a letter to Lieutenant Governor Herbert Lehman in February 1929, social workers such as herself sought, as a bare minimum, "removal of all outside toilets (there are many in the yards here); a separate toilet for every family, if not now, at some time prior to 1935; better fire protection; prohibition of cellar dwellers; and by 1935, or possibly 1940, prohibition against occupying a room that does not have a window opening directly to outer air." She emphasized that these were reasonable, "not revolutionary demands."[15]

Wald's efforts to improve New York's housing culminated in 1929 when she persuaded Lieutenant Governor Lehman to join with Aaron Rabinowitz, a Henry Street "boy" who had succeeded in the real estate business and was now a member of the State Board of Housing, to purchase land on the Lower East Side to construct model housing. When Rabinowitz failed to secure financing elsewhere, Lehman contributed $325,000 of his own money toward the project, with Rabinowitz putting up a similar amount, and the Bowery Savings Bank issuing a mortgage for $900,000 to cover the rest of the costs. Under the leadership of Sidney Hillman, a longtime resident of Henry Street, the Amalgamated Clothing Workers Union organized the sale of the apartments on a cooperative basis. Rabinowitz noted that "it has been a life ambition of Miss Wald that model housing should be developed in the heart of the Lower East Side" and that he and Lehman were "glad to gratify this desire without profit" to themselves. Wald called it "one of the happiest experiences in all my happy life," and Lehman hoped the project would "serve as an incentive to similar developments on the East Side and elsewhere in the city." When the Grand Street development opened in the fall of 1930, it received architectural awards, the *New York Times* hailed it as "a landmark in the history of housing development in New York City," and Arthur H. Sulzberger of the *Times* exclaimed after seeing the buildings: "to say that they are thrilling is but to mildly express the effect that they had on us."[16]

Lillian Wald paid very close attention to Herbert Lehman's political career. After Lehman was renominated by the Democrats in 1930 for a second term as Lieutenant Governor (until 1938, Governors and Lieutenant Governors in New York served two-year terms, and until 1954, they were elected individually, not as a team), Wald told Lehman how glad she was that he was "willing to serve again." She told Lehman, she understood "what tremendous responsibilities you have, but I think that it is most generous and consistent for you to serve the state as an official as you have served the city as an individual for so many years." Wald fondly recalled the "many, many wise and unselfish and truly distinguished contributions" Lehman had made in areas such as "protection for children" and "justice for the laborer." She also led a large group of social workers who strongly endorsed Franklin Roosevelt and Lehman for re-election so that they could continue to implement "forward-looking social legislation." Wald and her colleagues particularly noted Lehman's role as FDR's "helpmate," describing Lehman as "a man of rare worth and experience in the realm of social work." They emphasized Lehman's "personal service to the educational, philanthropic and social service organizations of the state," including "his recent undertaking to improve housing conditions in the congested New York area."[17]

In 1932, Wald employed all of her resources to ensure that Herbert Lehman received the Democratic nomination for Governor. Knowing that Tammany Hall leader John Curry preferred someone who would be more cooperative with Tammany on patronage and other matters than the scrupulously honest and independent Lehman, Wald met with Curry and other leaders, urging them to support Lehman. She even withheld her support from Franklin Roosevelt and the national ticket temporarily, confiding to a friend in mid-September, "I am all for Roosevelt, for he has done well, but I am not allowing my name to be used, despite pressure, until I see Herbert Lehman nominated." In a letter published in the *New York Times* on the eve of the Democratic State Convention, Wald and fellow social workers John Elliott and Mary Simkhovitch welcomed Lehman's willingness to place his "outstanding business ability and financial acumen . . . at the service of all the citizens of the State." They emphasized, "Colonel Lehman's single-mindedness, his generosity, his intelligence, his experience in serving the people, together with his great ability, make him in our opinion the outstanding candidate for the Governorship in these exacting times." With strong support from Wald, Franklin Roosevelt and Al Smith, Lehman won the nomination, and Wald worked for his election through the Democratic Party's Women's Campaign Committee.[18]

Wald took great pride that so many people connected with Henry Street were "helping shape social legislation" in Washington, Albany, and New York City in the 1930s. In December 1934, after Wald reported to Herbert Lehman her great pleasure at being a guest at the White House, Lehman noted, "It certainly must have been a great satisfaction to you to see so many of the Henry Streeters in the Administration." When Lehman appointed Susan Brandeis, the daughter of Supreme Court Justice Louis Brandeis, to the New York State Board of Regents, Wald agreed that Brandeis's "intelligence and courage and background, not excluding her residence at Henry Street," made her an excellent choice. Wald was "very certain that our various forms of government are extensions of Henry Street influence!" She asserted, however, that "the proudest banner that waves, floats over the Executive Mansion in

Albany." Wald emphasized in her 1934 autobiography that, "since his college days," Herbert Lehman had "devoted himself with unstinting generosity to causes, and in his elective office has demonstrated the importance of trained intelligence and social vision in the great affairs of the state." In the midst of the Depression, he had provided the people of New York with "a markedly effective administration."[19]

Lillian Wald never fully recovered her health after a series of illnesses in the early 1930s, spending most of her last decade at the "House on the Pond" in Westport, Connecticut, and yielding the role of Head Worker at Henry Street to Helen Hall. Nevertheless, she maintained her active interest and involvement in Herbert Lehman's political career. In 1934, she endorsed his re-election as Governor, declaring that "he had not disappointed the social service workers who supported him two years ago." Two years later, when Lehman announced that he would not run for a third term as Governor, Wald, "with the rest of New York, and perhaps of the United States," deplored Lehman's decision, but she "recognize[d] the limit of one's right to impose upon a man who has done so well." She knew Lehman would not be leaving public life unless he had no choice, and she emphasized that his "unique example of an able man in an important office, who is not a politician and does not use a politician's technique, is priceless." Despite her seeming willingness to accept Lehman's decision, Wald served as one of the honorary chairmen of the "State-wide Citizens Committee for Lehman" that was formed in June 1936 to try to persuade "Governor Lehman to reconsider his decision not to run for re-election." Like the rest of Lehman's friends and supporters, Wald cheered when Lehman changed his mind and agreed to run for re-election, joining other prominent social workers who endorsed his re-election. When Lehman ran again in 1938, Wald urged voters to support him, asserting that "State administration under Governor Lehman means better living and working conditions for the people we know as consumers, workers, and neighbors."[20]

Herbert Lehman and his wife Edith remained in close contact with Lillian Wald, visiting her frequently and remembering her birthday and other special occasions. In 1933, on the fortieth anniversary of the founding of Henry Street, Lehman recalled that he "became a club leader thirty-four years ago and a director seventeen years ago." He noted that his "close association with the settlement and with Miss Wald during all these many years have built up a great store of affection and admiration for both." Despite the press of his duties as Governor, Lehman helped raise funds for Henry Street and the Visiting Nurse Service, declaring in 1934 that "no philanthropic or social undertaking is more necessary or better conducted than the Henry Street Visiting Nurse Service." Lehman urged people to support this wonderful organization that, under Lillian Wald's leadership, "has brought health or relief to countless of our citizens, making a contribution to the community which is unsurpassed."[21]

In March 1940, as Wald's health continued to fail, Governor Lehman spoke to the three hundred nurses of the Henry Street Visiting Nurse Service. The Governor declared that "the advances in public health nursing in New York State, as well as in the country as a whole, are in very large measure due to the work of the Henry Street nurses, and to the farsightedness of Miss Wald." He highlighted their efforts in bringing tuberculosis, syphilis, and other diseases under control, pointing out the lives and the dollars that had been saved by their work, and he called for an expansion in the number of public health nurses employed by the state and local communities. "When pain and anguish wring the brow," Lehman observed, "it is the ministering angel rather than the master of arts who is welcome in the home." Lehman was gratified to learn that Wald had been able to listen to a radio broadcast of his remarks and that they had given her "great pleasure and satisfaction."[22]

When Lillian Wald passed away on September 1, 1940, Herbert Lehman was among the many who paid tribute to this remarkable woman. Lehman mourned the passing of his "very dear friend," noting that he "had the great privilege of following her leadership for more than forty years in many civic activities." Miss Wald, the Governor declared, "was one of the outstanding women of our day and was an inspiration to the entire country. She was beloved by everyone who knew her." According to Lehman, Wald's "wonderful work in public health, nursing and in countless welfare activities brought comfort and health and security to hundreds of thousands of people throughout the State and nation who bless her memory. Her great service to humanity will ever be her monument."[23]

Herbert and Edith Lehman maintained their close connection with the Henry Street Settlement even after Wald's death. In March 1943, Lehman and other "Henry Oldtimers" who "call themselves the 'grown-up sons of Mother Henry' in memory of Lillian D. Wald," sponsored a ball to raise money for Henry Street. Later that year, Lehman regretted that "the great pressure of my work in connection with the organization of the United Nations Relief and Rehabilitation Administration" made it impossible for him to attend the "Fiftieth Anniversary Celebration of the founding of the Henry Street Visiting Nurse Service." Lehman recalled fondly his "long association" with Henry Street and his "affection for and admiration of Miss Lillian D. Wald," whose memory he would "always cherish." It would have given him "much satisfaction," Lehman noted, to see "once again my friends of the Henry Oldtimers" and join them "in paying tribute to Miss Wald and the splendid nursing service she created."[24]

Like many Americans, Herbert and Edith Lehman suffered a grievous loss during World War II when their son Peter, a pilot in the U.S. Army Air Force, died when his plane crashed during a training flight over England in 1944. In memory of Peter, the Lehmans donated the money for a new building at Henry Street, to be called Pete's House, which would serve as a youth center and allow

Henry Street to expand its efforts to lure neighborhood youngsters away from gangs and into more constructive activities. According to Helen Hall, who had succeeded Lillian Wald as Head Worker at Henry Street, the new building was "the most exciting thing that has happened to Henry Street in years." She later wrote that "it was a joy to work with the Lehmans for they were interested in every detail" as they planned and built Pete's House. When the costs for the fully equipped photography studio, the carpentry shop, and the art rooms put the project way over budget, Herbert Lehman told Hall not to worry, "that he wanted us to have just what we needed and in the quality that would last." At the official opening of the building in November 1948, Herbert Lehman emphasized that he and his wife were "greatly blessed" that they were "able to present this youth center to the Henry Street Settlement, which has so long and so well served the people" of New York City, and they hoped that Pete's House would be a place where "young people of all faiths and races and national origins can meet in friendship and good-will." The *New York Times* spoke for many New Yorkers when it proclaimed that "the Lehmans have earned the gratitude of the city. . . . They have made a valuable and lasting contribution to the lives and characters of our city's future citizens."[25]

Lehman's election as a U.S. Senator in 1949 and his re-election to a full six-year term in 1950 forced him to curtail his involvement with Henry Street temporarily, but he resumed his active role after he left the Senate. In 1958, for example, Lehman and others appealed for contributions so that Henry Street could augment the minimal psychological, social work, and psychiatric services offered by the public schools, and in 1959 Lehman hailed Henry Street's comprehensive program "to study prevention and control of juvenile delinquency" on the Lower East Side. A few weeks later, he and Mrs. Lehman hosted a breakfast kicking off a special campaign to raise $175,000 for Henry Street in just four weeks. Herbert Lehman became the honorary chairman of the Henry Street Settlement, and Mrs. Lehman remained actively involved with Henry Street after her husband's death in 1963.[26]

Lillian Wald had a major impact on Herbert Lehman, reinforcing his social conscience and awareness, his sense that one had a duty to make the world a better place. It was at Henry Street that a young Herbert Lehman first contributed his time and effort to bettering the lives of those less fortunate than himself. His long association with the American Jewish Joint Distribution Committee, the NAACP, and the countless other philanthropic and charitable organizations to which he generously contributed both his time and his money grew from seeds planted by his parents and nurtured by Lillian Wald at Henry Street. Lehman was unable to attend the public memorial service held for Wald at Carnegie Hall in November 1940, but in the telegram he sent that was read to the gathering, Lehman summed up his feelings toward the woman who was his "friend for more than forty years." The Governor emphasized that it had been his "high privilege" to follow Lillian Wald's "leadership and ever to be inspired by her courage, vision, and perseverance." He reiterated his high regard for this "pioneer in the solution of social problems and in public health . . . who worked tirelessly in behalf of the downtrodden, the underprivileged, and the handicapped." Lehman would always "cherish the memory of her beauty of soul, of mind, and of spirit," and he stressed that "her noble life must ever serve as an inspiration to all of us." Lillian Wald certainly inspired Herbert Lehman, who followed her example and devoted much of his own life to serving others through philanthropic endeavors and government service. Through his lifetime of public service, Lehman truly honored the memory of Lillian Wald, "a great soul" and "a dearly beloved friend."[27]

CHAPTER 2

"On a Chinese Laundry Ticket"

Herbert Lehman and Al Smith

It was because of my deepest admiration for Governor Alfred E. Smith, and through the inspiration of his humane and enlightened leadership, that I first became interested in public life, and it was at his suggestion that I accepted public office.[1]

At first glance, Herbert Lehman and Al Smith had very little in common. Lehman came from a wealthy uptown Jewish family, while Smith was born into a working-class Catholic family in lower Manhattan. Lehman attended the exclusive Dr. Julius Sachs's School for Boys and then graduated from Williams College, while Smith attended his local parish school at St. James Roman Catholic Church. Because of his father's illness and death and his mother's poor health, Smith took a job selling newspapers, and then he quit school before he finished the eighth grade so that he could work full-time at the Fulton Fish Market to help support the family. Smith spent most of his adult life in politics, first being elected to the New York State Assembly in 1903, while Herbert Lehman worked in the textile and investment banking businesses for almost thirty years before running for Lieutenant Governor of New York in 1928. Al Smith was a protégé of Charles Murphy, and the Tammany Hall Democratic machine, while Lehman's relations with Tammany were often contentious. Smith was colorful, quick with a humorous quip or anecdote; Lehman was always

---

Chapter title quotation: Al Smith quoted in Josephson and Josephson, *Al Smith*, p. 442.

serious, almost to the point of being dull. Nonetheless, in the 1920s Lehman became one of Smith's strongest supporters and Smith brought Lehman into New York State politics.[2]

I

Herbert Lehman and Al Smith shared an allegiance to the Democratic Party and the belief that government should help people overcome the problems resulting from industrialization, urbanization, and immigration. Lehman's father and uncles had settled in Montgomery, Alabama, when they first came to the United States in the late 1840s and had naturally gravitated to the Democratic Party, which dominated Southern politics. When the family moved north after the Civil War, Mayer Lehman remained a loyal Democrat, and in 1878, he named his newborn son Herbert in honor of Hilary Herbert, a Montgomery attorney and close family friend who was elected to Congress in 1876 and went on to serve as Secretary of the Navy in President Grover Cleveland's cabinet. Herbert Lehman later described his parents as "very, very strong Democrats" and he recalled that "all though my boyhood I used to hear graphic stories about how Tilden had been gypped out of the Presidency [in 1876]. The Presidency had been stolen by Republicans in the election of Hayes." One of Herbert Lehman's earliest memories of his father dated back to 1884, when Mayer Lehman had "marched in the [Grover] Cleveland procession, carrying one of those tallow torches" and ruined his new coat. Mayer Lehman's only deviation from the Democratic Party came in 1896 when, according to his son, "he supported McKinley and 'sound money'" rather than William Jennings Bryan. In 1900, when Bryan was again the Democratic candidate against McKinley, Herbert Lehman cast his first presidential vote for Bryan, but, as he later recalled, "not with any great enthusiasm."[3]

During the Progressive Era, Herbert Lehman strayed from his Democratic roots, preferring Theodore Roosevelt, who tried to rein in what Lehman later called "the economic buccaneers" of that era, over conservative Democrat Alton Parker in 1904. When the Democrats returned to Bryan as their candidate four years later, Lehman refused to support him in his race against Republican William Howard Taft.[4]

Herbert Lehman's first active involvement in New York State politics and his first encounter with Tammany Hall leader Charles Murphy occurred in 1910, when the newly married Lehman was elected as a delegate to the New York State Democratic Convention in Rochester. Lehman "was all fired up with enthusiasm" over what he expected to be his role in helping "to pick out the nominee for Governor." Even after "the word was passed around that the nominee was going to be John A. Dix, who at that time was Democratic State

Chairman," Lehman "still thought that my vote would be counted, that my name would at least be called." But when the roll call reached New York County, Lehman was startled to hear Tammany leader Murphy announce that "New York County casts all of its votes for John Dix." Lehman learned firsthand that Boss Murphy and Tammany Hall *were* the Democratic Party in Manhattan.[5]

Al Smith rose rapidly through the ranks of Tammany Hall and became one of the Democratic leaders in the New York State Assembly, where he and Herbert Lehman first crossed paths during the controversy surrounding Governor William Sulzer in 1913. Sulzer had enjoyed Tammany support in winning election to the State Assembly and then the U.S. House of Representatives, where he had championed progressive reforms, including the establishment of a Department of Labor, direct election of U.S. Senators, and a federal income tax. Recognizing the strength of the reform movement and not wanting to jeopardize their chances for a Democratic victory in a year when New York Republicans, like the national party, were split between Teddy Roosevelt's Bull Moose Progressives and William Howard Taft's Old Guard Republicans, Charles Murphy and Tammany acquiesced in Sulzer's nomination for Governor in 1912 despite their concern that the mercurial and ambitious Sulzer, if elected, could not be relied upon to do the Hall's bidding.[6]

During his time in Congress, Sulzer had condemned anti-Semitism in Russia, winning acclaim and support from Jewish leaders in New York. Impressed by Sulzer's progressive views and his efforts to help Russian Jews, Herbert Lehman realized that he could use his wealth to further causes and candidates that he believed in. Lehman emphasized to Sulzer that the voters needed to be made aware of Sulzer's "full record of accomplishments," and Lehman offered "to help defray the expenses of such a campaign of publicity." Sulzer appreciated Lehman's support, explaining to Lehman confidentially and somewhat cryptically that "you can help me very materially, and you know exactly what to do and how to do it, what to say and how to say it, and a word to the wise is sufficient." Lehman, who was still somewhat naïve when it came to political matters, spent $7,000 to reprint and distribute fifty thousand copies of a book of Sulzer's speeches, and he also gave Sulzer $5,000 in cash.[7]

After he was elected Governor, Sulzer stressed his independence from Tammany Hall. He refused to appoint the Hall's men to key positions and began an independent investigation into waste and corruption in state government. The final straw for Tammany came when Sulzer insisted that the State Legislature enact a bill providing for direct primaries to choose candidates for state offices, which would have severely reduced Tammany's influence. When the lawmakers rejected the measure, Sulzer condemned Murphy and Tammany Hall for blocking the bill, called the Legislature back into special session to reconsider his proposal, and organized a Direct Primary Campaign Committee to pressure the legislators. Herbert Lehman assisted Sulzer in this battle with

Tammany, offering to help finance Sulzer's corruption inquiry if the State Legislature refused to appropriate the necessary funds and serving as treasurer and a major financial backer of the Direct Primary Campaign Committee.[8]

Lehman continued to support Sulzer, but Tammany veterans and Murphy allies in the Legislature, including Assembly Speaker Al Smith, turned the tables on Sulzer and formed a Joint Investigating Committee of the State Legislature to determine whether Sulzer had diverted campaign funds to his personal use. Lehman worried that his generous support of Sulzer's campaign might be a problem, but the Governor reassured him that "so far as I know, there is no law covering the matters to which you refer. . . . The laws to which you call attention relate only to candidates for office," and Sulzer pointed out that he was not yet an official candidate at the time when Lehman had made his contributions. The Joint Investigating Committee subpoenaed Lehman to testify, which he did on September 4, 1913, detailing the finances of the Direct Primary Campaign Committee. Lehman was the group's largest contributor, having lent the committee $5,500 that had not been repaid, most of which had gone to reprinting Sulzer's speeches and preparing pamphlets on the issue.[9]

When the Joint Investigating Committee completed its inquiry, Speaker Al Smith and the State Assembly filed formal impeachment charges against the Governor to be heard by a special court composed of the members of the State Senate and the State Court of Appeals. Following Sulzer's earlier advice, Lehman emphasized to the impeachment court that he had paid vendors directly for reproducing and mailing Sulzer's speeches, and he claimed that his cash gift to Sulzer was not a campaign contribution and did not have to be reported because he had made it before Sulzer had received the nomination for Governor and become an official candidate. Nonetheless, observers were shocked when Lehman testified that he had given Sulzer $5,000 for his "personal uses, without any conditions," in "either $500 or $1,000 bills." Lehman asserted that Sulzer "was a man of straightened circumstances," and Lehman "did not care what he did with his money, whether he paid his rent, or bought himself clothes, or paid for his office or any other expenses which he might incur." Despite Lehman's testimony on his behalf, Sulzer was convicted of using campaign contributions for his personal benefit and removed from office.[10]

II

Herbert Lehman's and Al Smith's paths began to converge in the early 1920s. Smith had been elected Governor of New York in 1918, but he had been defeated when he sought re-election two years later, a victim of the national Republican landslide in 1920. In 1922, New York Democrats again nominated

Smith for Governor, and as Lehman later recalled, it was around this time that he recognized Smith "as a coming young professional politician with a liberal point of view." Despite Smith's affiliation with Tammany, he and Lehman had many friends in common, including Lillian Wald; Smith aide Belle Moskowitz and her husband Henry, a social reformer and civic activist in his own right; and Joseph Proskauer, an attorney who wrote speeches and formal statements for Smith and counseled him on legal matters. Lehman later noted that he "was too busy in Washington to pay much attention" when Smith was first elected Governor in 1918, and he was "preoccupied" with his "own business and with many charitable and civic undertakings" when Smith was defeated in 1920 and then elected again in 1922. But Lehman remembered being very impressed when he heard Smith address a League of Women Voters dinner in 1922 and call for public development of electric power from the St. Lawrence River, explaining the issue to the mostly female gathering "so simply that they, and even I, could understand what he was talking about."[11]

By 1924, Herbert Lehman was firmly committed to Al Smith and looked forward to playing an active role in Smith's campaign to win the Democratic presidential nomination. As a Jew, Lehman understood that Smith's Catholicism made him a controversial candidate for national office at a time when the Ku Klux Klan was at its height in the North as well as the South, denouncing and terrorizing Catholics and Jews as well as African Americans. As Lehman later recalled, "we were in the midst of a bitter Ku Klux Klan situation, and I was outraged at the things that the Ku Klux Klan was doing and stood for." Lehman believed that the Klan's position "with regard to minority religious groups was evil," and he knew that the Klan "would become a great issue in the 1924 campaign, notably in the 1924 convention." Certain "that there would be a fight on the racial issue and religious issue," Lehman "wanted to get into it," so he "worked closely with the group that was behind Al Smith."[12]

Lehman tried to do everything he could to help Smith in his pursuit of the 1924 Democratic presidential nomination. In April 1924, shortly after Smith became an official candidate, Lehman assured George Van Namee, the Governor's former secretary, that "if there is anything that I can do to further his candidacy I hope you will call on me. I hope that you will bear this in mind and will assure the Governor that I am entirely at his disposal." Van Namee passed Lehman's letter on to Smith, who was very appreciative of Lehman's "kind offer" and promised to be in touch with Lehman "in the near future." A few weeks later, Lehman was thrilled to receive an invitation from Franklin Roosevelt, Smith's campaign manager, to join the committee that Roosevelt was establishing to work for "Governor Smith's nomination and election." Lehman replied that he would be "very glad indeed to serve on this Committee" and hoped that Roosevelt would "call on me for any service that I can render."

Lehman emphasized in a handwritten note at the bottom of his response to Roosevelt that he would be "very glad to help in defraying the expense of the Committee," and he also asked for one hundred copies of a pamphlet of Smith's speeches "for distribution among friends in other states."[13]

Much to Lehman's disappointment, another assignment from the Governor prevented him from playing a significant role at the 1924 Democratic National Convention. In May, about a month before the convention was scheduled to open in New York City, Lehman received a call from Governor Smith, who was concerned that fifty thousand members of the International Ladies' Garment Workers' Union were threatening to go on strike when their contract expired on June 1. The Governor wanted to avoid a strike, which would be embarrassing to him during the Democratic Convention, so when talks between the union and management broke down, Smith persuaded both sides to accept his appointment of a mediation commission "to investigate and make recommendations." Herbert Lehman was surprised when Smith asked him to serve on the commission because, as Lehman later recalled, he knew "very little about the needlework industry," although he was "quite familiar with the sweatshop conditions and with the other evils of worker-employer relationships." Moreover, as Lehman explained to the Governor, he was reluctant to serve on the commission because he wanted "to be very active in your behalf in the pre-convention activities and at the convention." Smith assured Lehman that the commission would not interfere with Lehman's desire to work for Smith's nomination and attend the convention, predicting that "this potential strike threat will be over long before that. . . . This thing will be all straightened out without a strike."[14]

The Governor was half right. The commission averted a strike, but its work continued through and beyond the Democratic Convention. In early July, both sides accepted the commission's recommendations, which included the establishment of "an impartial board to settle disputes." As Lehman later noted, his work on this commission was "a forerunner of my long association with mediation, and notably mediation in the needlework industry." As late as 1958, Lehman was still busy, as he told Hubert Humphrey, "mediating the strike in the dress industry here in New York."[15]

As Lehman had feared, his involvement in the garment industry dispute limited his activities on behalf of Smith during the Democratic National Convention. He served as a liaison to the Massachusetts delegation, which he later described as a pretty easy assignment. He "visited" and "entertained" the delegates "and talked to them about Al Smith. It didn't take much persuasion. . . . They were always pretty strongly for Smith." But despite the best efforts of Lehman and others, the Democrats in 1924 were not yet ready to nominate a Catholic from the streets of New York for President, and the convention eventually nominated John W. Davis on the 103rd ballot. Nonetheless, as Lehman told Franklin Roosevelt, he believed that it had been "a great fight in a good cause" and he was "happy and proud to have shared in it." Lehman's involvement in Smith's campaign brought him "into contact frequently and more or less intimately with a good many of the [Democratic] leaders, particularly those from New York City," and he soon became a vice president of the National Democratic Club.[16]

Denied the presidential nomination, Smith and his supporters reset their sights on maintaining his governorship. Herbert Lehman was among "twenty-one leaders in the fields of labor, education, welfare, economics, business and philanthropy" who endorsed Smith's re-election, praising the Governor for his efforts "to protect the lives, health and welfare of working men, women and children" in New York State. Lehman served as treasurer of the Governor's re-election campaign and contributed $10,000 to the Independent Citizens' Committee for Governor Smith, the largest single contribution and almost 10 percent of the total $116,671.51 that the committee raised on Smith's behalf. He also gave $2,000, which again was the largest single contribution, to the New York State Democratic Committee. Smith easily defeated Theodore Roosevelt, Jr., by more than one hundred thousand votes, becoming the first Governor in almost one hundred years to win a third term.[17]

By 1926, Lehman later recalled, he had "gotten very close" to Smith, who asked him to chair the Independent Citizens' Committee for his re-election that year. According to Lehman, "prior to that time, the position had been more or less of an honorary position . . . pretty much of a figurehead. But I didn't treat it that way." Lehman "gave up his business for six weeks or so, and was down at headquarters continuously." He "had a very considerable voice in the conduct of the campaign, both upstate and even in New York City," and he took the lead in responding to many of the charges Republican gubernatorial candidate Congressman Ogden Mills hurled at Smith. Lehman refuted Mills's claim that the state had increased its indebtedness by $465 million during Smith's tenure as Governor, showing that the total state debt was less than $250 million and asserting that "the figures given by Congressman Mills are so grossly inaccurate that one must conclude that either he has not, as claimed by his friends, a good head for figures, or is deliberately trying to mislead the voters of this State." When Republicans attacked Smith's plans to have the state develop its hydroelectric resources as "socialistic," Lehman angrily retorted that Mills's "reference to Governor Smith as a Socialist and to the Governor's 'half-baked socialistic ideas' shows clearly that the Congressman has no issues except those of misrepresentation and scandalmongering [sic]." If Smith's support of equal rights and opposition to special privileges could be construed as socialism, Lehman concluded, "I thank God for it and am proud to be arrayed under its banner." With Lehman running the campaign, Smith was re-elected to a fourth term as Governor by 260,000 votes.[18]

Lehman's superb job directing Smith's re-election campaign led the Governor to propose Lehman for the chairmanship of the New York State Democratic Committee. Current chairman Edwin Corning had just been elected Lieutenant Governor and was expected to resign the chairmanship in early 1927, and Smith thought Lehman would be an excellent choice to reinvigorate the state party organization and start laying the groundwork for Smith's campaign for the Democratic nomination for President in 1928. As the *New York Times* noted, Lehman's ascension to the chairmanship would "give this committee a responsible, active head, who is expected to be of much value to the Governor in developing Smith sentiment among Democratic leaders in other States." The *Times* also reported that Lehman's selection "will be likely to heal a tendency toward jealousy among different groups of the Governor's advisors by giving him an official position, which will make him the natural custodian of the Smith boom in its early stages." However, Tammany Hall was angry at the Governor because of his appointment of Robert Moses, a Republican, as Secretary of State, and Lehman later recalled that Tammany opposed him for the state committee chairmanship because he "was more independent than they liked" and lacked "practical political experience."[19]

Lehman was not eager to take the position, but at Smith's urging, he gave it serious thought, and at one point he seemed ready to accept it. However, Lehman encountered Democratic National Committee member Elisabeth Marbury at Carnegie Hall one night, and she advised him not to take the position. Lehman later described Marbury as "a very outspoken woman with good judgment, who had always been very friendly to me," and she warned him that "all you're going to get out of it is a kick in the pants." Lehman did not know that Marbury's advice was based on her belief, as she explained privately to Norman Mack, a Buffalo newspaper executive who was her colleague on the Democratic National Committee, that it "would be a grievous mistake" to make a Jew the chair of the state committee. Marbury emphasized that

> Jews are not any more popular upstate than are the Catholics. There is an idea here that the Governor is being closed in by the Semitic race due to certain influences. A great deal of criticism is going around here in high quarters which will not help him in the presidential campaign. Surely there is someone of wealth and position for the state position who is not a Jew.

Not suspecting Marbury's real motivation, Lehman appreciated her advice and turned down the chairmanship, and Democrats eventually decided to retain Corning as their chairman, even though he was now the Lieutenant Governor. Putting a positive gloss on the episode, Eleanor Roosevelt confided to Lehman's niece Elinor Morgenthau that Smith had decided "to reserve Mr. Lehman for more useful things."[20]

III

Despite their disappointment at the Democratic National Convention in 1924, Al Smith and his supporters were determined to win the Democratic nomination in 1928. As early as January 1927, a headline in the *New York Times* proclaimed "Smith Offered to Nation as Presidential Candidate at Democratic Rally Here," and in March 1927, Texans Albert Burleson and Thomas Gregory, both of whom had served in Woodrow Wilson's cabinet, endorsed Smith's candidacy. By this time Lehman was part of Smith's inner circle, and Lehman later recalled that those around the Governor "were very certain that Smith could and should be nominated in 1928." Lehman visited Colorado, Wyoming, Idaho, New Mexico, and Arizona on Smith's behalf in 1927 and "met with a very friendly reception almost everywhere." In January 1928, Lehman told the *New York Times* that at the recent Jackson Day dinner in Washington, "Alfred E. Smith was the man most talked about," and that many Democratic leaders agreed that "Smith was the only man who could lead the Democratic Party to victory" in the presidential election that fall. Lehman later went to California to help organize Smith forces there, discovering that "San Francisco was much more friendly to Al Smith than Los Angeles was." Just before the California primary on May 1, 1928, Lehman made sure that two hundred thousand pamphlets expounding Smith's record were distributed to California Democrats, helping Smith win a key victory there.[21]

Herbert Lehman considered the 1928 campaign "one of the most sordid and the meanest within my recollection." He was "appalled at the many evidences of prejudice and discrimination which developed," and he later recalled that "the question of religion entered into the campaign very strongly and in a manner that was deeply disturbing and distressing and . . . caused a great many wounds." Attorney Charles C. Marshall attacked Smith's religion and his candidacy in April 1927, asserting in an open letter published in *The Atlantic Monthly* that if Smith were elected President, his Catholicism would take precedence and interfere with his constitutional duties as chief executive. Judge Proskauer drafted Smith's response, which was published in the following issue of *The Atlantic* under the title "Catholic and Patriot." Smith reiterated his belief "in the worship of God according to the faith and practice of the Roman Catholic Church," but he emphasized that there was "no power in the institutions of my Church to interfere with the operations of the Constitution of the United States or the enforcement of the law of the land." He stressed his belief "in the absolute separation of Church and State and in the strict enforcement of the provisions of the Constitution that Congress shall make no law respecting an establishment of religion or prohibiting the free exercise thereof." Smith hoped to "join with fellow Americans of all creeds in a fervent prayer that never again in this land will any public servant be challenged because of the faith in which he has tried to walk humbly with his God." Herbert Lehman considered Smith's response "a masterpiece" and "was in full sympathy in everything he wrote," but Smith's essay did not put the religious issue to rest; anti-Catholic bigotry reared its ugly head time and time again during the campaign.[22]

In the period leading up to the 1928 Democratic National Convention, Lehman and a few other key supporters of Al Smith contributed huge sums of money to the Governor's campaign. As Lehman later recalled, both he and his wife contributed generously to Smith's campaign in 1928 because they believed it was important to combat "the evil forces of religious bigotry that were aroused in this country" by Smith's candidacy. Lehman contributed $10,000 to Smith's pre-convention campaign in October 1927 and another $10,000 in early 1928 to help the Democratic Party eliminate the deficit it was still carrying from the 1924 campaign. Smith's great success in raising funds led the Republican-controlled U.S. Senate to create a Campaign Fund Investigating Committee, which summoned Lehman and other Smith supporters to Washington to testify. Like the others, Lehman explained to the committee that it was his "love and affection for the Governor" that had led him to contribute so generously to Smith's campaign. Lehman emphasized that his contributions were voluntary and had not been solicited, his business interests did not have city or state contracts, he did not expect anything in return for his contributions, and he planned to give more once Smith secured the Democratic nomination for President. As the *New York World* observed, if the committee hoped to embarrass or derail the Smith campaign, its efforts backfired because Lehman and the others "were quite plainly delighted at the chance to come forward and tell the world what pleasure they took working for Al Smith."[23]

The 1928 Democratic National Convention met in Houston, and for Herbert Lehman, the only drama came when he realized that a rabbi had not been included among the clergy offering invocations for each session. Lehman worried that "the omission, if allowed to go throughout the convention, might be severely and properly criticized by my coreligionists," and he asked Henry Morgenthau, Jr., to bring the situation to the attention of Franklin Roosevelt, who was the floor manager for the Smith forces and would be presiding over the final session of the convention. Roosevelt encountered what he later called "amusing difficulties in Houston in trying to locate the rabbi," requiring "the aid of the police and Fire Department." According to Roosevelt, "apparently, the rabbis in Houston, like the Catholic priests, were backward about coming forward." When Roosevelt was ready to gavel the convention to order, a rabbi had not yet been found, but the authorities had located "a willing Baptist to meet the emergency." Just as Roosevelt was about to introduce the Baptist clergyman, he later jested to Morgenthau, "your good rabbi was led in handcuffs, delivered over to me and the day was saved."[24]

After the convention, Al Smith asked Bernard Baruch to head the Democratic National Committee's Finance Committee, but when Baruch turned him down, preferring to help the campaign unofficially, Smith turned to Herbert Lehman. Even though Lehman had what he later described as "the thankless job of trying to raise the sinews" of the campaign, Eleanor Roosevelt described him as "the nicest, calmest person at h'd'q't's!" Lehman later recalled that "it was very difficult to raise money," most of which "came from just a few people. The businessmen, of course, outside of a small group, were unwilling to contribute to the Democratic Party. . . . We were in this great period of prosperity and they wanted no change." Lehman and his wife contributed $135,000 to the Smith campaign, and their school-aged children, John, Peter, and Hilda Jane, each contributed a modest sum as well. Democratic National Committee Chairman

Figure 2.1. Herbert Lehman (*far left*), Democratic National Committee Chairman John Raskob (*second from left*), and other Al Smith backers gather in Albany, August 22, 1928. Courtesy of the Herbert H. Lehman Papers, Columbia University.

John J. Raskob gave $110,000, Smith friend and New York contractor William Kenny contributed $100,000, and Baruch donated $26,590. Lehman later recalled one especially effective tactic that was sometimes used to persuade reluctant donors to contribute to the campaign: they were taken to a room at headquarters that was "called the 'Chamber of Horrors,' in which on the walls we had any number of cartoons and editorials, news items, of the most vicious character." When "we had somebody who was a little bit hesitant, who we thought would be outraged by the religious issue being brought in the way it was, we'd take him into this room. He usually came out pretty well convinced." Under Lehman's and Raskob's leadership, the Democrats raised more than $5 million for Smith's campaign, by far the most they had ever raised for a presidential race.[25]

Lehman believed that Smith went into the 1928 campaign against Republican nominee Herbert Hoover with "three strikes" against him: "The dominant one was the religious issue. The other was the Prohibition issue. . . . And the third was the feeling that he did not have the experience or the knowledge or understanding of national or international issues." According to Lehman, "it was a hard, mean, vicious campaign—utterly vicious and stupid." Smith's opponents "spread one report that if Smith became President, they were going to build a tunnel from the White House to the Vatican."[26]

The low point in the campaign, Lehman recalled, came when Smith and his advisors, including Lehman, decided that Smith should "carry the fight, in regard to the Ku Klux Klan and the religious issue, right into enemy territory" by delivering a major speech in Oklahoma City, a hotbed of Klan activity. Smith openly and angrily confronted the religious bigotry and the scurrilous rumors and innuendo that were circulating against him, condemning them "as a treasonable attack upon the very foundations of American liberty." He defended his religious beliefs, and he denounced the efforts of those who inject "bigotry, hatred, intolerance and un-American sectarian division into a campaign." Smith complained that the Ku Klux Klan had "the effrontery to refer to themselves as 100 per cent Americans," arguing that the Klan's assertion that Smith's religion disqualified him for the presidency demonstrated its leaders' ignorance of the decision by the framers of the Constitution to prohibit any religious test for office. He attacked one of the Klan's favorite tactics, declaring that "the world knows no greater mockery than the use of the blazing cross, the cross upon which Christ died, as a symbol to instill into the hearts of men a hatred of their brethren while Christ preached and died for the love and brotherhood of man." Smith also noted that Assistant Attorney General Mabel Walker Willebrandt, who was responsible for enforcing Prohibition, had urged Methodist ministers in Ohio to ensure that their parishioners voted against Smith, and he charged that the Republicans' silence after her sectarian appeal signified approval of such tactics.[27]

After listening to the Governor practice the speech at the Executive Mansion in Albany, Herbert Lehman was so impressed that he advised Smith not to "change a word of that speech . . . it's a knock-out, a wonderful speech." Lehman had high expectations for the speech, and he invited some friends over to listen to it on the radio. Once Smith started, however, Lehman "was almost in tears" as he realized Smith was giving "an entirely different speech, . . . a really poor speech, both in contents and delivery." Although Smith told Mrs. Moskowitz that the crowd had been cheering him during the speech, and the *New York Times* reported that Smith had received a very warm and favorable reception from the audience, Lehman was told by others in the Smith campaign who were there that "the hostility of the audience" had negatively affected Smith and the speech. The *Times* noted that Smith might have been affected by "a blazing cross in a near-by field [that] had greeted" Smith's train when it entered Oklahoma. Joseph Proskauer, who was traveling with the Governor, recalled that "we could see the fiery crosses of the Ku Klux Klan burning in the countryside, and, as we stepped down from the cars we were confronted by groups of thin-lipped, evil-looking, sneering men, and we heard rumors of violence." The presence at the back of the stage of the Reverend Dr. John Roach Straton, pastor of the New York Calvary Baptist Church, who had called Smith "the deadliest force against moral progress in America today," and Dr. Mordecai Ham, a local Baptist preacher who had voiced similar sentiments, might also have thrown Smith off his game. Straton had rented the same hall to attack Smith the following evening. Lehman later explained that Smith, "perhaps more than most politicians, relied on the friendliness of his audience. If the audience responded, he could let himself go," but in this instance the unfriendly surroundings had clearly affected him.[28]

IV

Smith and Democratic Party leaders knew that it was essential to carry New York if Smith were to have any chance of winning the presidency, and they believed a strong Democratic ticket for New York State offices was the best way to ensure a Smith victory in the Empire State. Smith's first choice as his successor in Albany was Owen Young, the chairman of General Electric, but Young was not interested in running for public office. According to James Farley, Secretary of the New York State Democratic Committee, when party leaders met with the Governor in August, they all agreed that "because Smith was a Catholic, it was imperative to choose a non-Catholic for the Governorship to balance the ticket." Farley suggested Franklin Roosevelt, but Smith rejected the idea, believing that Roosevelt was not up to the job physically or intellectually. "It was apparent," Farley noted, "that Smith wanted Lehman." New

York State Attorney General Albert Ottinger, a Jew, was favored to win the
Republican nomination for Governor, and Smith feared that Ottinger would
make significant inroads among Jewish voters in New York City unless the
Democrats responded with a Jewish candidate of their own. Smith had always
been impressed with Lehman's intelligence, integrity, and administrative abilities, and he was confident that Lehman would continue the liberal policies
that Smith had instituted in New York. Smith's advisors worried, however, that
nominating a Jewish candidate for Governor would be almost as bad as selecting
a Catholic; it would confirm Protestants' fears that Smith was anti-Protestant
and, if elected President, would not appoint Protestants to high positions in his
administration. Eventually, Smith and the Democratic state leaders agreed that
nominating Franklin Roosevelt, an upstate Protestant who was not associated
with Tammany Hall, would be the best way to aid Smith's campaign for the
presidency, and, with great difficulty, they prevailed upon Roosevelt to accept
the nomination. Herbert Lehman agreed to run for Lieutenant Governor, as
he later explained, to help Al Smith and the Democrats' efforts "to combat
the bigotry and discrimination against a great public servant whose religion
was not my own."[29]

    Although not a great public speaker, Lehman proved to be an effective
candidate for public office, and his brother Arthur Lehman, a Republican, joked
that Herbert's "nomination almost persuades me to be a Democrat." More
seriously, Lehman later recalled that he and Roosevelt "covered the southern
tier of counties, . . . came back to New York [City], and a couple of weeks
later . . . went through the Mohawk Valley." Most of their appearances were
outdoors, causing "a great strain on the voice . . . because very frequently the
loudspeaker went out of commission." Lehman's speech in Binghamton was
his "very first public speech," and he later confessed that he "made probably
the poorest speech that any candidate ever made. I forgot my lines completely . . . [and] lost my place several times." Although Lehman was very disappointed in his performance, the audience seemed satisfied with his remarks.
Judge Sam Rosenman, who traveled with Roosevelt and Lehman during the
1928 campaign, later recalled the reason for Lehman's

> great influence with the voters even in those early days as a compara-
> tively young man. When Herbert Lehman said something you got
> an impression of sincerity which has rarely been duplicated. . . . He
> was able to convey to his listeners the fact that what he was saying
> had nothing to do with political advantage, but was something
> which he really intensely felt.[30]

Lehman's campaign for Lieutenant Governor may have encountered an
incident of the same prejudice and bigotry that was haunting Al Smith's presi-

dential bid. The Ku Klux Klan was strong in the Southern Tier of New York State, and the Klan was just as virulently opposed to Jews as to Catholics. Although there was no report of such an occurrence in the press, Lehman later recalled that after his first campaign speech in Binghamton, he was told that "they did burn a cross on the hill there." Other than the incident in Binghamton, which he did not witness personally, Lehman did not remember any heckling or disturbances during his speeches or religious attacks directed against him in the 1928 campaign.[31]

Some Jewish leaders resented the Republicans' nomination of Ottinger for Governor as a blatant appeal to Jewish voters and urged their coreligionists not to vote along sectarian lines. Samuel Untermyer, a prominent New York City attorney who was active in Jewish circles in New York, asserted that Ottinger was "a stalking horse to attract the Jewish votes that would otherwise go to the Democratic national and state tickets as a protest against the despicable campaign that is being waged against Governor Smith by the un-American forces of religious bigotry—simply because he is a Catholic." According to Untermyer, Ottinger's lack of involvement "with any important Jewish movement, either in the city, state, or nation, or with the Jewish cause itself, except around election times and as a vote-getting bait," stood in sharp contrast to Colonel Lehman's leadership and involvement "with all the great Jewish local, national and international movements, . . . giving constantly and generously of his valuable time and of his money to all these movements throughout the world." Similarly, Rabbi Stephen S. Wise of the Free Synagogue congratulated Lehman on his nomination and jokingly proposed the following campaign slogan: "Better a first class Jew in the second place in the State than a second class Jew in the first place in the State."[32]

Election Day brought bittersweet results for Herbert Lehman. Although it was clear by then that Smith was going to lose to Herbert Hoover, the Democratic National Committee had rented the cavernous armory on Park Avenue and 34th Street to listen to the election returns. Lehman recalled that when he arrived early in the evening, "there were only a few hundred people" present, and that Smith just sat there, "surrounded by not much more than a corporal's guard of his friends and associates and admirers, listening to these reports, and one was worse than another. It was perfectly hopeless, early as it was—perfectly hopeless by 9:00 o'clock surely. The crowd, of course, never came. They just couldn't bear to hear the bad news officially reported." Lehman "stayed with Governor Smith a long time. It was a very sad evening." The final blow came when they learned that Smith had not even carried New York State.[33]

In terms of his own and Roosevelt's candidacies, Lehman later recalled that "election night was a terribly exciting and difficult evening." Lehman was optimistic; candidates for Governor and Lieutenant Governor ran individually, but many people voted for the straight ticket, and Lehman expected that FDR's popularity upstate, combined with his own strength in New York City, would enable Roosevelt to defeat Ottinger and Lehman to triumph over his Republican opponent, Charles Lockwood, a former state legislator from Brooklyn. But with Hoover carrying the state, the elections for Governor and Lieutenant Governor were neck and neck. According to Lehman, "there were a number of mistakes in reporting that had to be corrected and which changed the picture from time to time. At first it looked as if Roosevelt was beaten and I was elected, and I felt very badly about that. I couldn't conceive of my being Lieutenant Governor with Ottinger. I had no feeling against him, but he just didn't attract me." As more returns came in, the lead swung back and forth. Lehman "left downtown headquarters at about 5:00 in the morning, convinced that I was beaten." He still had a slight lead, but "there were 1,500 election districts out of about 9,000 still outstanding, and we all thought that all 1,500 were upstate and therefore would be very strong Republican districts, and that it would wipe out the small numerical lead which I still had at the time and give my opponent a comfortable margin." When they got home, "dog-tired," Lehman and his wife left a note on their bedroom door instructing their children: "Don't wake us. Daddy has been beaten, but he doesn't feel badly." Lehman was shocked a few hours later when "my brother-in-law called me up to congratulate me." It turned out that one-third of the missing election districts were "strongly Democratic" areas in New York City whose votes offset the more numerous but less populated upstate Republican districts. Final returns showed Lehman carrying New York City by a margin of 515,000, enabling him to win the state narrowly by approximately fourteen thousand votes out of more than four million cast. Roosevelt's plurality in New York City trailed Lehman's and Al Smith's, but FDR's better showing upstate brought him into the Governor's mansion by a margin of twenty-four thousand votes.[34]

A few weeks after the election, Lehman expressed optimism for the future of Al Smith and the Democratic Party. Smith was "a great governor," Lehman asserted, who "will never retire" from public life. Smith had "brought politics closer to the people by speaking in a language which they understood," and he had helped make the Democratic Party "the real liberal party." Looking at the election more objectively many years later, Lehman concluded that although he had "worked harder for Al Smith than he had ever worked for any of his own campaigns," it was probably a good thing that Smith had not won the election. Lehman realized that "Smith wasn't ready for the presidency," that he had no "experience at all in international affairs and very little in national" matters. In retrospect, Lehman believed that Smith "wouldn't have been a match for the problems that were going to have faced him if he did become president," and his election "would have killed any later possibility of a Catholic being president, because his failure would have been blamed on his Catholicism" rather

than "the limitations of his background and his education," which would have
been the real culprits.[35]

The ultimate amateur

V

Once Franklin Roosevelt became Governor, his relationship with Al Smith
quickly deteriorated, which placed Herbert Lehman in the awkward position of
serving as Roosevelt's Lieutenant Governor while remaining friendly with Smith,
the man who had brought him into politics. At a farewell dinner in Smith's
honor at Albany, Smith vowed "to keep close to the public affairs of this State
and be ready and eager to come up here and participate in any civic duty that
presents itself in the promotion of the welfare of the State and the people who
live in it." But Roosevelt, as Lehman later recalled, was determined "to run
his own show" and demonstrate that he was up to the job of Governor. FDR
seldom called upon Smith for advice and counsel, replaced Robert Moses with
Edward Flynn as Secretary of State, and chose not to retain Belle Moskowitz
as Secretary to the Governor.[36]

In 1932, Franklin Roosevelt won the Democratic nomination for the
presidency, and, after four years as Lieutenant Governor, Herbert Lehman hoped
to succeed him as Governor of New York. Lehman's prospects were complicated,
however, by the growing split between FDR and Al Smith, who had belatedly
sought the Democratic presidential nomination, too, and by opposition from
Tammany Hall. Lehman felt a certain loyalty to Smith, who had been instrumental in Lehman's entry into politics and government, and it was only after
Smith had assured Lehman that he had no intention of seeking office again
that Lehman had become actively involved in Roosevelt's campaign for the
presidency. But Tammany boss John Curry and Brooklyn Democratic leader
John McCooey, who was a close ally of Curry, were angry that Roosevelt had
allowed the Seabury investigation to proceed, exposing Tammany's corrupt hold
over New York City government and leading Mayor Jimmy Walker to resign,
and they blamed Roosevelt for denying Smith another chance to run for the
presidency. Moreover, they knew that Lehman as Governor would be just as
independent from and unsympathetic to the wishes of Tammany as Roosevelt
had been. So Curry and McCooey sought to deny Lehman the Democratic
nomination for Governor, first by supporting Albany Mayor John Boyd Thacher,
who had the backing of the Albany Democratic machine, and then by proposing
the nomination of U.S. Senator Robert Wagner for Governor and designating
Lehman for Wagner's Senate seat.[37]

But Curry failed to reckon with Al Smith's loyalty to Herbert Lehman.
Smith did not let his growing jealousy of Roosevelt undermine the tremendous
regard he had for Herbert Lehman, who had done so much for him in the

1920s, including donating large sums of money to Smith's campaigns and running for Lieutenant Governor in 1928 to strengthen the Democratic ticket and improve Smith's chances to win the presidency. Smith thought the idea of running Wagner for Governor and Lehman for Senator was "ridiculous and would be flying in the face of Providence," pointing out that "the people of the State know that Lehman will make a good Governor; they don't know what kind of a Senator he would be. They know Wagner is a good Senator; they don't know what kind of a Governor he would be. What explanation could they make to the people of the State?" Smith made it clear that he planned to nominate Lehman for Governor at the State Democratic Convention, and to drive the point home, Smith warned Curry that if Lehman were not the nominee, Smith would run for Mayor of New York City in 1933 and deprive Tammany of its main source of patronage and influence. When Curry wondered what ticket Smith would run on, Smith retorted that he would run "on a Chinese laundry ticket" if necessary. Smith believed that Lehman, not a Tammany candidate, was necessary to continue the programs and policies that he and FDR had instituted in Albany over the past decade.[38]

Determined to run for Governor, not Senator, Herbert Lehman rejected Curry's scheme. Franklin Roosevelt, State Democratic Chairman James Farley, Secretary of State Edward Flynn, and other supporters informed Lehman about Curry's plan and urged him to confront the Tammany boss and make it clear that he would not accept the nomination for Senator. Curry was conferring in his hotel room with McCooey, Senator Wagner, and others opposed to Lehman's candidacy when, as Lehman later described it, he "decided to go up and barge in on the meeting unannounced." Max Steuer, a Tammany lawyer, glibly informed Lehman that everything was all "sewed up now," that Lehman was "going to be nominated for the U.S. Senate, and Bob Wagner is going to be nominated for the governorship." But Lehman made it clear that he "expected to be nominated as Governor" and would "not take the nomination to the U.S. Senate." Steuer asserted that there was nothing Lehman could do to block this strategy, pointing out that "we nominate the Senator before the Governor. . . . If you're nominated," Steuer asked, "what are you going to do about it?" Lehman insisted that he would decline any nomination for the Senate and that when "the nominations are called for, for the governorship, my name will be placed in nomination." With that, Lehman left the room. One hour before the convention was scheduled to convene, Curry called and conceded, telling Lehman, "You win. You'll be nominated for Governor."[39]

A rebellion in the ranks of Brooklyn delegates to the convention helped persuade Curry to surrender. As Lehman later recalled, Hymie Schorenstein and some of the district leaders from Brooklyn told Brooklyn Democratic leader John McCooey that "regardless of any pressure or instructions from the top, they would, if necessary, break away from the organization and vote for" Lehman.

FIGURE 2.2. "Too Much Smith!" by Rollin Kirby, October 1932. Original cartoon in the Library of Congress. By permission of the Estate of Rollin Kirby Post.

The Brooklyn leaders recognized Lehman's popularity among their constituents, and, according to the *New York Times*, they feared that his rejection by the bosses "would be construed as due to racial and religious prejudice," which might lead to challenges to their leadership next year, especially in "some of the districts with large Jewish populations." Lehman had "no doubt in my mind that this revolt made an impression on McCooey, and possibly on some of the other County Leaders, and was helpful in compelling them to accept me as the nominee."[40]

Herbert Lehman hoped that Curry's efforts to deny him the gubernatorial nomination would harden him as a politician, but it did not. Lehman later recalled that when he returned to his wife in their hotel room after the meeting with Curry, he "stalked in, shook [his] finger under her nose and said: 'Make me one promise. Keep me a little vindictive.'" But he noted that even though Mrs. Lehman "frequently reminded me of this incident," he "never learned my lesson very thoroughly" and did not think he "ever was really vindictive towards those who had sought to injure me."[41]

Lehman did have one humorous moment at the convention. After the drama of his meeting with Curry and the other bosses, Lehman, in his excitement, forgot his ticket to the convention—the convention at which he was going to be nominated for Governor. Lehman realized his error while "riding down in the hotel elevator" but was assured by one of the other passengers: "'Don't worry, you'll get in all right.'" And Lehman did get into the convention without any problem and, upon entering the hall, he "received a heart-warming reception."[42]

At the convention, Al Smith shook hands and reconciled with Franklin Roosevelt, and he formally nominated Herbert Lehman for Governor. Smith castigated the national Republican administration for failing to stem the nation's economic collapse, and he listed all his accomplishments as Governor of New York: reorganization of the state government; establishment of the executive budget; development of the state's highways, ports, waterpower, and parks; and taking care of "the poor, the aged, the weak and the afflicted." Now, Smith emphasized, he was

> looking for the logical man to protect this program from Republican invasion, . . . the man that has the background, that has the understanding sympathy, that has the experience and has above all other things an appeal to thoughtful people, . . . a man in this time of stress that will be able to stand up on the bridge of this ship of state and bring her into a harbor of safety and a haven of repose, a man who stands behind that program . . . [that] is going to be attacked by the forces of reaction.

After searching his heart, his mind, and his conscience, Smith had found that man: "the Hon. Herbert H. Lehman."[43]

Lehman appreciated Smith's efforts to help him secure the nomination for Governor and welcomed the opportunity to continue the liberal policies that Smith had pioneered as Governor of New York. In his acceptance speech to the convention, Lehman took "particular satisfaction" in the support he had received from Smith, emphasizing that "it was because of my deepest admiration for Governor Alfred E. Smith, and through the inspiration of his humane and enlightened leadership, that I first became interested in public life, and it was at his suggestion that I accepted public office the first time four years ago." Lehman reiterated Smith's record of accomplishments as Governor, as well as Roosevelt's success in preserving and extending such programs as aid to the elderly, unemployment relief, protection for industrial workers, and conservation of the state's hydroelectric power resources, and he promised to "fight to carry on this program of good and progressive government."[44]

Al Smith campaigned actively for Herbert Lehman in 1932, accepting "the post of honorary chairman of the Independent Citizens' Committee for the Election of Herbert H. Lehman and M. William Bray." Smith's prominence in Lehman's campaign was needed, according to the *New York Times*, "to offset any appeal to racial prejudice" by the Republicans, especially among Catholic voters who might be opposed to Lehman because of his religion. Smith's campaign activities for Lehman would also help prevent any attempt by Tammany Hall to "knife" or deny votes to Lehman during the election. Smith made major addresses on behalf of Lehman and the Democratic ticket upstate in Buffalo and Troy and downstate at the new Tammany Hall and Madison Square Garden. Smith told a packed house at the Brooklyn Academy of Music that when he left Albany in 1929, he "felt safe and secure" in handing over the state and the reforms that had been enacted despite Republican opposition "to somebody that could carry on and improve upon them." Now, Smith wanted control of the state "handed further on from Governor Roosevelt to Colonel Lehman . . . [to] preserve for the people of the State the benefits that were secured for them after such a long, a hard and a bitter struggle."[45]

In his own campaign appearances, Lehman emphasized his business and government experience and promised to continue the progressive policies initiated by Governors Smith and Roosevelt. He attacked his opponent, World War I hero "Wild Bill" Donovan, and the Republicans for waffling on Prohibition, which Lehman and the Democrats wanted to repeal, denied Donovan's charges of waste and extravagance in state government, and called for public development of the state's water power resources. Lehman pledged to work toward enactment of unemployment insurance and extension of workmen's compensation, and he vowed to mobilize "every resource of the State to give complete assurance that no one shall go cold, unsheltered or hungry." Lehman repeatedly cited his close ties with Al Smith, asserting that "the State of New York owes and will owe a perpetual obligation" to Smith "for that leadership that assured for this State the nation's most progressive governmental program and code of legislation in behalf of all the people." At the final campaign rally in Madison Square Garden, Lehman again praised Smith as a man who "needs no introduction, for his name is engraved in everlasting letters in the hearts of the American people. He will live for all time as a truly great American leader of liberal thought," Lehman proclaimed.[46]

On election day, Herbert Lehman won a smashing victory, defeating Donovan and capturing the governorship by a record 840,000 votes, the largest victory margin for a Democrat in New York State history up to that time. With the nation in the throes of the Depression and people blaming Hoover

FIGURE 2.3. "Lieutenant Governor to Governor," by Rollin Kirby, November 1932. Original cartoon in the Herbert H. Lehman Center for American History, Columbia University. By permission of the Estate of Rollin Kirby Post.

and the Republicans for the economic collapse, 1932 was a very good year for Democrats in New York and all over the nation, but Lehman led all Democrats in New York State, running ahead of both Roosevelt and Senator Wagner. Lehman carried New York City by almost one million votes and came within one hundred thousand of carrying Upstate as well. As the *New York Times* noted, Lehman's unique "combination of heart and mind," business and government experience, and humanitarianism explained "the extraordinary vote which he polled." Lehman's election, the *Times* confidently concluded, showed that "ability and high character and unselfish devotion to the public good are sure of approval by the American people."[47]

Al Smith and Herbert Lehman were colleagues in arms in the fight to institute progressive reforms and make New York State's government more responsive to the needs of its citizens. Lehman formally entered politics at the behest of Smith, contributing large sums of money and managing Smith's campaigns, and Smith, in turn, encouraged Lehman to run for Lieutenant Governor in 1928, and he fought Tammany Hall to ensure Lehman's nomination for Governor in 1932. Although Smith and Lehman later disagreed about Franklin Roosevelt's New Deal and its extension of federal authority, they worked together to ensure that New York State met its responsibilities and obligations to improve the lives of New Yorkers.[48]

CHAPTER 3

"That Splendid Right Hand of Mine"

Lieutenant Governor Herbert Lehman and Governor Franklin Roosevelt

I've always felt that a very great part of the contribution that I may have made in the State came largely from the training that I had under him [FDR] for four years. It was a wonderful, wonderful experience—wonderful training.[1]

Herbert Lehman believed that "Franklin Roosevelt was the greatest man of my time." According to Lehman, Roosevelt "had what it takes to be great—vision and courage." What is often overlooked, however, is the vital role that Herbert Lehman played in Roosevelt's success in making New York State's government responsive to people's needs during the early years of the Great Depression. Roosevelt often referred to Lehman as "that splendid right hand of mine," and he made good use of his Lieutenant Governor's talents and abilities in governing New York from 1929 through 1932.[2]

I

Herbert Lehman and Franklin Roosevelt both came from wealthy families, the Roosevelts having been part of America's landed gentry for many genera-

---

An earlier (and much briefer) version of the chapters on Lehman and Franklin Roosevelt was published as " 'I Can Leave the Combination of My Safe to Colonel Lehman': Herbert Lehman and Franklin Roosevelt: Working Together to Improve the Lives of New Yorkers and People All Over the World," *New York History*, LXXXVII, 1 (Winter 2006): 88–133. Chapter title quotation: "Governor Roosevelt's Address," *New York Times*, October 5, 1932, p. 17.

tions, while the Lehmans made their fortune in banking and commerce during and after the Gilded Age. Lehman and Roosevelt were both interested in public service, and even before they met for the first time in 1917, they worked independently for many of the same candidates and causes. They both supported William Sulzer for Governor in 1912, based on his strong progressive record in Congress, and they continued to support him during his brief tenure as New York's chief executive until he was impeached and removed from office in 1913. In 1916, Lehman and Roosevelt both served on Judge Samuel Seabury's campaign committee in his unsuccessful race for Governor against Republican incumbent Charles Whitman. Nationally, Roosevelt was one of Woodrow Wilson's earliest supporters in New York, and the new President rewarded him with the post of Assistant Secretary of the Navy in 1913 and gave him a voice in filling postmasterships and other patronage positions. Lehman originally favored Senator Oscar Underwood of Alabama for the Democratic presidential nomination in 1912, but by 1916 he was wiring his uncle in California to advance the money needed to guard the ballot boxes to ensure that California Republicans did not steal away Wilson's re-election victory.[3]

Herbert Lehman and Franklin Roosevelt first worked together in the Navy Department during World War I. The United States entered the war in April 1917, and in mid-May Lehman secured a position as a textile consultant with the Navy's Bureau of Supplies and Accounts, which he described as "the equivalent of the Quartermaster's Department in the Army." Lehman's business and banking experience proved invaluable to the Navy, where he frequently needed Secretary of the Navy Josephus Daniels's or Assistant Secretary Franklin Roosevelt's signature on various papers. "Even then," Lehman later recalled, Roosevelt "showed a great deal of ability and drive and a great deal of boldness, cut red tape without any hesitation at all. . . . Roosevelt had no hesitation at all about getting things done even if it meant cutting corners." Lehman "found it much easier to get FDR's signature" than Daniels's; Daniels would often ask Lehman to leave the papers for him to review, but Roosevelt would quickly sign them if Lehman assured him that everything was in order. Roosevelt tried to help Lehman secure the naval commission Lehman so desperately wanted, but to no avail, and their working relationship ended when Lehman received an Army commission as a Captain in August 1917. He was assigned to the War Department's General Staff Corps, where he eventually rose to the rank of Colonel and earned the Distinguished Service Medal.[4]

In the 1920s, Lehman and Roosevelt both devoted their efforts to helping Al Smith win the governorship of New York and pursue the presidency of the United States. Lehman, Roosevelt, and Smith agreed that the government had an obligation to provide safe working conditions in factories, better housing for people living in slums, and help to those who needed assistance. Lehman's efforts on Smith's behalf have already been discussed. Roosevelt seconded Smith's nomination as a favorite son candidate for the presidency at the Democratic National Convention in 1920. Four years later, when Smith was a serious contender for the presidency, Roosevelt served as his campaign manager and gave the nominating speech for Smith, memorably describing him as "the Happy Warrior." In 1928, Roosevelt acted as floor manager and again delivered the nominating speech for Smith, and Lehman chaired the Democratic National Committee's Finance Committee. After the Houston convention, Lehman congratulated Roosevelt "on your wonderful nominating speech," describing it as "the greatest speech of its kind to which I have ever listened," and Roosevelt responded in kind, telling Lehman "how very glad I am that you are to direct the finances." The growing friendship between Lehman and Roosevelt during their work together on Smith's campaign led Roosevelt to insist that it was "silly for us to keep on calling each other by our last names," and Lehman warmly responded, addressing his next letter to "my dear Franklin."[5]

Democratic Party leaders believed that Franklin Roosevelt was their strongest candidate to retain the governorship in 1928 and help Al Smith carry New York in the presidential election. Smith disagreed, asserting that Roosevelt lacked the physical strength and intellectual prowess needed for the job, but when Owen Young, the chairman of General Electric, refused to run, and none of the other possible candidates, including Herbert Lehman, garnered much support within the party councils, Smith concurred that Roosevelt was the best choice to oppose Republican Albert Ottinger. Smith and the others hoped that Roosevelt's appeal in strongly Republican Upstate New York would help minimize the GOP's margin north of New York City, offsetting Republican gains among the city's Jewish voters, who were expected to support Ottinger, a fellow Jew. But Roosevelt was not interested in running for Governor in 1928. He was intent on continuing his therapy at Warm Springs, Georgia, to regain the use of his legs, crippled by polio since 1921, and he also wanted to watch over his substantial financial investment in Warm Springs. Moreover, Roosevelt and Louis Howe, his chief political advisor, believed that 1928 was not going to be a good year for the Democrats, since Herbert Hoover and Republicans nationally would claim credit for the prosperity most of the nation was enjoying; they preferred to wait until 1932 for FDR to make his political comeback. FDR stayed far away from the New York State Democratic nominating convention in Rochester, attending instead to his treatments at Warm Springs.[6]

As Roosevelt had planned, Democratic leaders at the convention in Rochester had a difficult time reaching him on the phone at Warm Springs. Only after a reluctant Eleanor Roosevelt agreed to place the call were Smith and the others able to contact Roosevelt directly. Smith employed every argument he could think of to persuade Roosevelt to accept the nomination for Governor, appealing to him both personally and on the grounds of party loyalty and stressing Smith's need to have the strongest possible nominee for Governor backing him up on the ticket. John Raskob agreed to help with any financing necessary for Warm Springs, and Herbert Lehman agreed to run as the Democratic candidate for Lieutenant Governor, which would ease the burdens of the governorship on FDR and allow him to spend as much time as he needed in Warm Springs. Even though candidates for Governor and Lieutenant Governor ran separately at that time, Lehman's presence on the ticket, the leaders hoped, would minimize Jewish defections to Ottinger. Roosevelt finally relented and agreed that, if chosen by the convention, he would accept the Democratic nomination for Governor.[7]

Roosevelt was pleased to be running on the same ticket with Lehman. As he stated to the press, he was "particularly happy that my running mate is such an old and valued friend as Colonel Herbert Lehman." Roosevelt fondly recalled their service together in the Navy Department during the war and noted that Lehman "will be of tremendous assistance to the next administration, if we are elected, in helping me conduct the administrative affairs of the State government on a sound and business-like basis." The *New York Times* observed that it was

> a fine thing for the State when a man of Colonel Lehman's range
> of experience, covering as it does not only large business interests,
> but even larger undertakings in charitable and philanthropic work
> for all sorts of men, women, and children, is ready to respond to
> the call for public service. His name on the ticket should be of
> great value both to Mr. Roosevelt and to Governor Smith.

In a telegram to Lehman, Roosevelt expressed confidence that "this Army Navy team," as he referred to Lehman and himself, "ought to win," and joking with reporters about Lehman's wealth and integrity a few days later, Roosevelt noted that if he had to leave the state for any reason, "I can leave the combination of my safe to Colonel Lehman, knowing that it will be in safe hands."[8]

Despite press reports mentioning him as a potential candidate for Governor or Lieutenant Governor before the convention, Lehman later claimed that when he went to the convention, he "had no idea" he "was going to run." Lehman pointed out that his wife was not even there when he was nominated, "the only convention she ever missed," and "she's never forgiven me entirely since then." Lehman recalled that he "was so anxious to see the State remain under a liberal Democrat, which I knew Roosevelt to be, that I think I probably would have done almost anything that he asked me to do."[9]

Roosevelt and Lehman campaigned together all across New York State. The formal campaign period was relatively short, only from mid-October until the election in early November, but Lehman later recalled that Roosevelt "was tireless in the campaign." As opposed to Smith, who had "confined his campaigning to the New York Central mainline," meaning Buffalo, Rochester, Syracuse, Schenectady, Albany, Poughkeepsie, and New York City, with "a few intermediate stops at industrial centers," Roosevelt competed for the rural vote, "tour[ing] the country districts," delivering "8 or 10 or a dozen speeches in the course of a day, particularly when he toured the rural sections." Lehman related how Roosevelt organized "a caravan that traveled all over the State, 6 or 7 cars, with a bus for the newspapermen, and mimeographing machines to give out copies of his speeches, and he'd time it so that he would arrive at the same place for lunch to which local leaders were invited." Roosevelt and Lehman defended Smith's record of progressive legislation, assailed Republican obstructionism in the State Legislature, and denounced Republican attacks on Smith because of his religion and his identification with New York City.[10]

A few days before the election, Roosevelt sent Lehman his "affectionate regards" and emphasized "how confidently I look forward to our two years in Albany together." Lehman replied with a telegram on Election Day in which he predicted that FDR was "going to be elected by a tremendous vote" and "look[ed] forward with keenest pleasure to our association during the next two years." Roosevelt's strength upstate combined with Lehman's popularity in New York City to carry them into office by small margins over their Republican opponents, Albert Ottinger and Charles Lockwood. Ottinger's religion helped shrink Roosevelt's margin among Jewish voters in New York City compared to the totals amassed by Lehman and the other Democrats on the ballot, but those gains were more than offset by Roosevelt's strong showing in Protestant areas upstate. Given the easy victory for Republican presidential candidate Herbert Hoover over Al Smith, Lehman was convinced that "nobody but Roosevelt could have carried the State that year."[11]

II

Although Franklin Roosevelt considered Herbert Lehman a political neophyte and sometimes treated him as such, Lehman later recalled that he was "the first Lieutenant Governor who really became an important member of the Governor's official family." Previous Lieutenant Governors had been content to preside over the State Senate and carry out a few other mostly ceremonial duties, but Roosevelt, according to Lehman, "really turned over anything he possibly could to me, and I was in constant consultation with him." Lehman believed this was because Roosevelt "had confidence in my ability to carry on, and also it might very well have been that he foresaw that someday I'd succeed him and wanted to train me for the position." Roosevelt and Lehman were sworn into office by Herbert's brother, New York State Court of Appeals Justice Irving Lehman, on December 31, 1928, so they could deal with any crisis that might arise on January 1, and they quickly developed a strong working relationship. Wanting "the benefit of Colonel Lehman's great ability in financial and budget matters," Roosevelt included Lehman as part of his Cabinet meetings with department heads, as well as his "Turkey Cabinet"—his sessions with Democratic legislative leaders to align their objectives while munching on cold turkey. When FDR traveled to Warm Springs for therapy on his legs, or campaigned for the presidency in 1932, he and Lehman made sure they were not out of the state at the same time because that would make George Fearon, the Republican Majority Leader in the State Senate, Acting Governor. Roosevelt presented Lehman with a copy of the official volume of his papers and addresses from 1929, inscribing it: "My colleague and friend Herbert H. Lehman who has been my right hand and contributed so greatly to the contents of this volume."[12]

Lehman's conscientious, almost compulsive, attention to detail complemented Roosevelt's focus on the big picture. According to Lehman, Roosevelt "never took his troubles to bed with him . . . and he didn't worry about his decisions. . . . When he made a decision, that was it, for better or for worse." Lehman recognized that this was "a trait which I never was able fully to cultivate, because I always took my troubles to bed with me, and I always worried until the problems were solved." Eleanor Roosevelt agreed with that assessment, recalling that Lehman "will go through far more tortures than Franklin went through. Once having made up his mind, that won't end it. He will think about it all night, and he will worry about it the next day, and will talk to everybody about it, and it will go on being a worry after there is no use worrying, because he's done it, you see." She remembered that when FDR met with Lehman and Louis Howe to discuss a banking problem, Lehman's constant pacing so irritated FDR, who of course was confined to a wheelchair, that when Howe, who had not moved during the conversation, went to answer the telephone, FDR snapped, "Louis Howe, can't you sit still?" The remark "was really addressed to Herbert," but the Governor "couldn't tell Herbert that." After Lehman left, FDR confided to his wife that "Herbert is not going to be able to work tomorrow. But we've made our decision and I cannot see why he must continue to worry." When FDR was asked once during his governorship whether he worried about things, he replied, "I let Herbert do the worrying for me."[13]

New to the formal corridors of power in Albany, Lehman learned quickly. On one of his first days as Lieutenant Governor, the *New York Times* reported, he "attempted to explore the labyrinth" that was the State Capitol, but he promptly got lost and needed the help of a Capitol guard to return to his office. But by April 1929, Roosevelt was entrusting him with important responsibilities. Expecting the Republicans "to try to analyze and criticise [*sic*] every possible expenditure made in the departments, commissions, etc.," Roosevelt sought to utilize Lehman's business experience by placing him in charge of "a very careful check-up of our own on the actual business administration of the departments." FDR instructed Lehman to investigate state purchasing practices and "the progress of all construction work." He also wanted Lehman to conduct "a general survey of departmental administration," which he thought could be "conducted without stepping on anybody's toes," to look for "better cooperation and prevention of duplication between departments" and examine "the question of employees' efficiency, necessary employees, etc." Lehman's "preliminary survey" could then be turned over to "a special Advisory Commission of three leading business men to make a full report on insuring administration efficiency." As Jewel Bellush noted in her study of Lehman's lieutenant governorship, Roosevelt was utilizing "Lehman's most important resource—his experience in business administration," and Rexford Tugwell agreed that the task "actually brought into use the genuine talents of the Lieutenant Governor."[14]

Roosevelt received a detailed report on state construction projects from the Superintendent of Public Works, but the press of other duties seems to have prevented Lehman from undertaking the efficiency study that Roosevelt had proposed. Roosevelt's paralysis made it difficult for him to travel, and he began to utilize Lehman as his eyes and ears to inspect state facilities, much as he often did with his wife Eleanor. Just two weeks after asking Lehman to scrutinize the state's administration, Roosevelt requested that the Lieutenant Governor visit the state's mental hospitals. Lehman found the facilities to be in "shocking condition, because of the age of the buildings, the physical condition of the buildings, and the degree of overcrowding." Roosevelt and Lehman determined that a $50,000,000 bond issue was needed to construct new hospital facilities to remedy the overcrowding, but they understood it would be difficult to get the Republican State Legislature to agree to such a proposal. To build support for expanding and modernizing these facilities, Roosevelt instructed Lehman "to make a survey of the hospitals and to give publicity to the shocking situation."[15]

Lehman knew that the best way "to secure any effective publicity of the facts was to take newspapermen with me whenever I inspected these hospitals." When he visited Hudson Valley Hospital in Poughkeepsie, Lehman was struck by "the hopelessness of the thing, . . . seeing many of these people sitting around, perfectly hopeless, just staring into space, not doing a thing, not interested in anything." After his visit, Lehman later recalled, he "was sick for a week after." At Brooklyn Hospital, Lehman noted that the original building from 1854, which was still in use, was "in very bad repair and . . . a serious fire hazard." The "certified capacity" of Central Islip State Hospital was 4,248 beds, but Lehman reported that "the net population of the hospital is 6,017," and he was dismayed at discovering "in the wards row after row of from thirty-five to forty beds placed one immediately next to the other, without an inch of space between. The patient could enter or leave only by climbing over the other beds or the foot of his bed." Conditions were even worse at the Manhattan Hospital for the Insane, located on Ward's Island. According to the *New York Times*, an all-day visit to the facility, including "the ward containing the most violent of the women inmates," left Lehman "considerably disturbed." He stressed that "such overcrowding as we witnessed here today must greatly affect the curative treatment of patients. There is no privacy, and the very close proximity in which patients are thrown excites them and makes treatment difficult, particularly in the disturbed wards." Lehman was "convinced that if the people of the State knew the actual situation they will neither permit nor tolerate the continuance of such outrageous conditions," and he was pleased that the reporters who accompanied him "wrote very helpful and objective stories" that did not exaggerate the conditions, in part because "you couldn't have exaggerated them very much because really they were awfully bad." Lehman's tour and the resulting publicity helped bring about the passage of the $50,000,000 bond issue in 1930, which provided funds for the expansion and modernization of existing facilities and the construction of new ones, and Lehman worked closely with the Republican legislative leaders to begin this work as quickly as possible.[16]

Roosevelt especially relied on Lehman in dealing with various bank failures. The City Trust Company collapsed in February 1929, shortly after the death of its president, amid rumors of improper activities by the bank's directors. The situation came to a head in April, when Roosevelt was at Warm Springs and Lehman was Acting Governor. As Lehman explained in a letter to Roosevelt, he had assumed that the normal regulatory and criminal processes would be sufficient to deal with the City Trust matter until he discovered that Banking Superintendent Frank Warder, an Al Smith appointee, "had applied for a passport and arranged to go abroad." Lehman feared "that any further temporizing would lead to added suspicion and aggravate the situation," so he had named Robert Moses, who had served as Secretary of State under Al Smith, to head the investigation into the bank's collapse and any possible involvement of the State Banking Superintendent. Ignoring Roosevelt's intense dislike for Moses, Lehman blithely asserted that FDR would agree that Moses "was courageous and of great ability" and "was so familiar with the departments of the state government that he would be less likely to disrupt things than would a brand new man." In response, Roosevelt noted that Lehman "must have had a horrid time in regard to the banking situation," but he made no comment on Lehman's selection of Moses, an appointment that led FDR's political advisor Louis Howe to wonder if Lehman remained part of Al Smith's team rather than FDR's. Lehman quickly allayed such suspicions in a conversation with Howe, as Howe dutifully reported to his boss. Criminal charges were brought against Banking Superintendent Warder and various officers of the City Trust Company, but Moses's recommendations to strengthen the State Banking Law and protect thrift accounts in commercial banks the way savings bank accounts were safeguarded went unheeded. Lehman contributed $1,000,000 of his own money to a fund to guarantee that depositors at the City Trust Company did not lose their life savings.[17]

In the fall of 1930, Roosevelt and Lehman tried unsuccessfully to prevent the closing of the Bank of United States, which, despite its name, had no connection with the U.S. government. The bank's leading officers were later found guilty of conspiracy and other criminal charges, but Lehman believed that the bank's main problem was a crisis of liquidity, with "too large a proportion of their money in mortgages and frozen assets." He thought it could have been saved if other, larger banks had been willing to help by "taking over some of these unliquid assets for cash," and Lehman, Roosevelt, and State Banking Superintendent Joseph Broderick did everything they could to persuade other banks to merge with the Bank of United States or use some of their own shrinking capital to rescue the imperiled institution. On more than one occasion a tentative agreement was reached, only to fall apart a few hours later. The night before the bank's closing, Lehman recalled two years later, he met with "nearly all of the leading bankers" of New York, "including Governor [George] Harrison and other representatives of the Federal Reserve Bank. Until nearly 3:00 o'clock in the morning," Lehman "appealed to them to save the situation," but to no avail. Lehman came under tremendous pressure from the bank's mostly Jewish depositors, who begged him to put together a reorganization plan like the one he had worked out to save the mostly Italian clients of the City Trust Company, but he was unable to do so. As Lehman explained in 1932, he "took steps immediately to see whether something could be done to reorganize and reopen" the bank, and he was willing to do what he could, "regardless of financial sacrifice, but the amount involved was too large and the financial situation of the whole country already too greatly strained." He could not persuade others to join him in saving the bank. Depositors lost somewhere between 10 and 25 percent of their money, but the Republican State Legislature still refused to enact serious banking reforms along the lines advocated by Robert Moses in 1929 and now, belatedly, endorsed by Governor Roosevelt.[18]

The most serious crisis Lehman faced as Lieutenant Governor occurred in December 1929 when he demonstrated his ability to make tough decisions—life and death decisions—under pressure. Roosevelt was delivering a speech in Chicago, meaning Lehman was Acting Governor, when inmates at Auburn Prison killed the prison's chief keeper, who was the second in command, and took Warden Edgar Jennings and eight guards hostage, threatening to kill them too unless the prisoners were released. Although Lehman was concerned about the warden's safety, he believed that the warden's "situation was no different from that of a soldier in wartime," and he declared that "the warden will have to take his chances. There will be no compromise." Lehman "wanted to avoid bloodshed" if he could, but he refused to give in to the prisoners' demands. As he explained the next day, he knew these were "hardened criminals who were willing to face death in their attempt to get out with the warden and these guards at their mercy." Lehman "ordered the state police to send down a detachment of men from Oneida," about ninety minutes away, and he called into service "a company of National Guard militia stationed at Auburn . . . to guard the prison walls so that the convicts could not make a break." When the prisoners rejected an ultimatum to surrender, Lehman ordered the state troopers and the militia to retake the prison and rescue the hostages. The inmates "were well armed" and "in the ensuing fight several of them were killed," but the hostages were all saved. The following day, Lehman reiterated his belief that "there was nothing else I could do consistent with duty. . . . And yet for two hours that seemed endless I was almost borne down by the weight of responsibility thrust upon me as a result of the position I was occupying temporarily." As for the hostages, Lehman "felt all the time that they were going to be killed," and he emphasized, "no one can picture the relief I felt when word came that they had been rescued."[19]

The riot at Auburn was the second serious incident there that year, and there had also been a disturbance at Clinton Prison in northern New York in July in which three guards had been killed. These violent confrontations dramatized the need to expand and modernize the state's prisons to curb the overcrowding and to reform the prison and parole systems to treat inmates more humanely. Roosevelt and Lehman had been studying the issue since the Clinton uprising, meeting with experts in the field, and Lehman believed that "now that public interest has been aroused this is the best time to make provision for improved housing for prisoners and a better and more enlightened care in handling" of prisoners. In the aftermath of the trouble at Auburn in December, Lehman revealed the Governor's prison reform program. When the State Legislature convened in January, Lehman announced, Roosevelt planned to ask for money to expand the capacity of the state's prisons, increase funding for prisoners' food and clothing, and transfer some of the more "amenable" prisoners to "road or construction camps," which would reduce some of the congestion in the prisons and provide the inmates with "healthful out-of-door work." While stressing the need to maintain "order and discipline," Lehman warned that "to force men in confinement, who have very little or no hope, to spend their hours and days in idleness is dangerous to the men, to prison morale, and to the community to which they will later return." He "look[ed] forward to the time when the state will have equipped every inmate of our prisons with a useful trade, so that when he again returns to the outside world he will have at least a chance to make an honest living." Lehman also called for the current Parole Board, made up completely of corrections officials, to be replaced by a three-person, fulltime board of professionals, with the necessary staff to look at each case individually. In January, the State Legislature quickly appropriated funds to establish the prison camps and increase spending on prisoners' food and clothing, and a bond issue later that year included money for enlarging and modernizing the prison system. The lawmakers also reformed the parole system along the lines Lehman had outlined. As Bernard Bellush noted in his study of FDR's governorship, the approval of the new, more enlightened parole system came about largely because of the "unceasing efforts by Lieutenant Governor Lehman, who more than any other official of prominence at the Capitol had shown consistent interest in the parole problems."[20]

Governor Roosevelt also utilized Lehman's expertise in dealing with labor disputes in the garment industry. Lehman had been involved in mediating and settling such clashes since Governor Smith had appointed him to the Advisory Commission in the cloak and suit industry in June 1924, a position that Lehman retained as the commission continued its efforts over the next few years. Lehman believed that strong unions were necessary to maintain the peace in this often chaotic industry, and when the International Ladies' Garment Workers' Union (ILGWU) was on the verge of bankruptcy in 1928, Lehman provided a $25,000 interest-free loan to help the union survive. In July 1929, Roosevelt asked Lehman to try to settle a strike by thirty thousand cloakmakers, and the Lieutenant Governor met with representatives of the employers and the ILGWU. Through what both sides described as his "untiring efforts," Lehman persuaded them "to organize a joint board of control to supervise the maintenance of standards and agreements and to discourage the manufacture of garments in non-union or sub-standard shops." Lehman took great pride in his role in making this strike, which lasted thirteen days, "the shortest in the garment industry since 1910," and he hoped "that the agreements reached will serve permanently to stabilize the industry and to give greater security to the workers."[21]

In late 1929, with a strike in the dressmaking industry looming early in the new year, Roosevelt was urged to convene a conference of all the interested parties, but Lehman advised Roosevelt "that it would be a mistake . . . to intervene officially or unofficially . . . at the present time." The Lieutenant Governor believed that "it is probable that a strike will occur sometime in January or February," but he warned that "the situation is still in the talking stage," and that any intervention now would be ineffective. When the dressmakers did go out on strike in February 1930, both sides accepted Roosevelt's suggestion that Lehman try to mediate the dispute. Employing a series of all-night bargaining sessions, Lehman beat his own record, helping settle the strike after an eight-day stoppage. A management spokesman attributed Lehman's success as a mediator to his "unlimited patience, diplomatic tact, abundant resourcefulness, and timely and helpful suggestions," and the New York Times printed a summary of Lehman's schedule showing the many late hours he put in settling the strike, noting that it was a good thing that "he is not restricted by union rules" and did not "charge the state for overtime."[22]

Unlike the chief executives of many states during this period, Roosevelt and Lehman preferred mediation to using the National Guard or the State

Police to break strikes. In May 1932, for example, when Mayor L. E. Youngs of Johnson City (just outside of Binghamton) asked Acting Governor Lehman to send in "about thirty state troopers" to deal with a strike at the Endicott-Johnson shoe factories in the area, Lehman spoke with the Mayor on the phone and concluded that no such action was necessary. Lehman emphasized that Youngs had conceded that "no overt act has been committed, that the peace has not been disturbed, and that there is no injury to life and property." Moreover, the Mayor had not asked for help from the Broome County Sheriff. Lehman refused "to order State police to Johnson City unless and until" he had "definite evidence that the local peace authorities of the village and county are unable to care for any situation that may possibly arise."[23]

As the Depression deepened. Lehman continued to use his good offices to promote collective bargaining and labor-management stability in New York. In October 1931, he invited representatives of the Cloth Hat, Cap and Millinery Workers International Union and the Women's Headwear Group of manufacturers to meet with him in Albany as part of his effort to encourage "employers and workers alike to join forces for a constructive program." After months of hard negotiating, the industry's first collective bargaining agreement was reached, and Max Zaritsky, the president of the union, emphasized that Lehman had "rendered a conspicuous service to both sides and to the industry" by helping them reach an accommodation. In July 1932, Lehman prevented another strike by garment workers by persuading both sides to accept his recommendations that workers continue to be paid on a weekly basis rather than reverting back to the piece-work system, and that limitations be imposed on the role of contractors and jobbers. Representatives of the industry, the union, and the jobbers all praised Lehman's efforts, with union counsel Morris Hillquit noting that Lehman "has managed to attain an object generally considered unattainable," a "peace without victory for all parties concerned."[24]

III

There was some question in 1930 as to whether Herbert Lehman would run for a second term as Lieutenant Governor. As the *New York World* noted, the Lieutenant Governor had "lifted a routine job out of routine mediocrity and made it a vital and helpful agency of the State." However, Lehman was suffering from recurrent attacks of appendicitis, an ailment that had recently caused the deaths of State Assembly Democratic leaders Maurice Bloch and Peter Hamill, and he felt a responsibility to return to Lehman Brothers to help the firm weather the storm of the Depression. When the *New York World* suggested in early May that Lehman was not going to run, Lehman quickly refuted the story, informing Roosevelt that he had "come to absolutely no conclusion in

the matter because I have not even given it any serious thought" and promising to discuss the matter with the Governor "before coming to a conclusion
of any kind." Roosevelt urged Lehman to keep the team together, appealing to
Lehman's great sense of duty and his desire to serve the public. The Governor
conceded, "you and I both have many reasons why we should not run again
this autumn—perfectly good personal reasons and probably wholly in accord
with our own personal desires. Nevertheless," Roosevelt stressed, "you and I
both have the same kind of sense of obligation about going through with a task
once undertaken, and, frankly, the only reason either of us would run again
is that sense of obligation to a great many million people who may insist that
we shall try to carry on the work for another two years."[25]

Lehman could not resist such an appeal, and by late July he and Roosevelt were discussing campaign strategy. Roosevelt noted that "reports from
the up-State counties are without exception extremely encouraging. . . . If the
election were tomorrow," he predicted, "you and I would both run at least ten
votes to the election district better than we did before." Since there were 8,397
election districts in New York State, Roosevelt's forecast, if true, would mean a
gain of more than eighty-three thousand votes. FDR also asked if Lehman had
any suggestions "in regard to a campaign manager for the Roosevelt-Lehman
Committee," wanting someone of stature like Norman Davis, an experienced
diplomat and Democratic political strategist since Woodrow Wilson's days,
rather than "a Democratic politician." Lehman did not have any specific ideas
for a campaign manager, but he recalled that in 1926, when he had managed
Al Smith's campaign, he had "worked from early morning until late at night,"
and he believed the campaign needed "a practical and experienced manager who
is willing to work himself almost to death," someone more like the late Maurice
Bloch, who had served in that role in 1928. Lehman questioned whether Davis
"had enough experience to manage a campaign or would be willing to give
himself to the work as much as will be necessary." The Lieutenant Governor
recommended "that Howard Cullman should be made the official for raising
money" because "he did almost all of the work two years ago." Cullman did
serve as the campaign's treasurer and chief fundraiser, and he succeeded in raising
$211,488, much of it from members of the Lehman family. James Farley, who
was elected New York State Democratic Chairman at Roosevelt's insistence, ran
the campaign, while Frank Polk, whose resume was similar to Davis's, headed
the Roosevelt-Lehman Citizens' Committee.[26]

During the campaign, Roosevelt extolled Lehman's contributions to his
administration, often citing the Lieutenant Governor's business background to
answer Republican charges that the Governor was wasting taxpayer's money. At
a luncheon in Manhattan sponsored by the Independent Citizens' Committee
for the Re-Election of Roosevelt and Lehman, Roosevelt asserted that he was
"more fortunate . . . than any other Governor" because he had a Lieutenant

Governor "who is not only fully as capable of running the government as well as I am, but probably a good deal more so." Roosevelt emphasized that "all of the problems that come before the State government are handled by us jointly," and he was "able to refer a great number of business and social matters to Herbert Lehman, because he is not only one of the greatest business men in the State, but he has also done more along the lines of social welfare than almost anybody else in the State, and he knows his subject." When Roosevelt had to be out of the state, he could "sleep well at night" because he knew that "Herbert Lehman [was] in charge." In a radio address officially opening his campaign for re-election, Roosevelt stressed that in his efforts "to give a thoroughly business-like administration to the State," he had benefited from the assistance and advice of his Lieutenant Governor, "a man trained in industry and banking and social welfare." As opposed to every previous Lieutenant Governor, who had "merely fulfilled his constitutional function of presiding over the Senate," the Governor explained, Lehman "works at my side in the constant effort to improve business efficiency in all of the departments." This "teamwork," Roosevelt maintained, had "saved the State many millions of dollars, or, put in another way, has enabled the State to get vastly more for every dollar expended than ever before." Lehman's continued presence in Albany, Roosevelt declared, was "an absolute necessity," and he urged voters to support "the present ticket as a whole and not piecemeal," warning that he "would be very much lost up there without Col. Lehman and the State would be very much lost without Col. Lehman." He could not conceive of going back to Albany "without that other Governor, Herbert H. Lehman."[27]

Trying to capitalize on the scandals that were rocking Tammany Hall and New York City Democrats, Republicans nominated U.S. Attorney for the Southern District of New York Charles Tuttle for Governor and State Senator Caleb Baumes of Newburgh for Lieutenant Governor. Baumes was best known as the author of the "so-called Baumes law," which mandated a life sentence for an offender convicted of a fourth felony regardless of the circumstances. As opposed to the Republicans' focus on "law and order" issues, Roosevelt and Lehman emphasized the "progressive humanitarian program of government" begun in New York under Al Smith and expanded by FDR, the repeal of Prohibition, and the economic problems the nation was experiencing under President Herbert Hoover. Lehman and Roosevelt charged that the "lack of leadership at Washington has brought our country face to face with serious questions of unemployment and financial depression," and they warned against entrusting similar leaders with power in Albany. Roosevelt and Lehman also used technological advances to their advantage during the campaign, with many of their speeches broadcast over the radio and "three motor vans, equipped to show talking pictures of the candidates," touring the state. With the Depression getting worse, 1930 was a good year for Democrats all over the nation, and New York was no exception. Roosevelt and Lehman won re-election by 725,000 and 565,000 votes, respectively, and Roosevelt's strong showing immediately propelled him into the ranks of serious contenders for the Democratic presidential nomination in 1932.[28]

IV

Roosevelt's and Lehman's second terms as Governor and Lieutenant Governor focused on helping New Yorkers cope with the effects of the Depression. As Lehman later recalled, "there was a general feeling—which was probably shared in the early months of the Depression by Roosevelt and myself and by other people too—that this was a problem that the states should be able to handle themselves." No one foresaw "the degree of the unemployment, and the degree of suffering that later developed." By late 1930, however, the Roosevelt administration realized the gravity of the situation as "unemployment became a very serious problem." A few weeks after their re-election, Roosevelt asked Lehman to "act as a committee of one to survey and speed up as far as possible all of the public works of the State." Roosevelt hoped in this way "to employ several thousand additional men during the winter months." He also requested

FIGURE 3.1. Lieutenant Governor Herbert Lehman taking the oath of office from his brother, New York State Court of Appeals Judge Irving Lehman, as Governor Roosevelt and others look on, December 31, 1930. Courtesy of the Franklin D. Roosevelt Library.

that Lehman "look over the preliminary draft of the budget and take up with the departments and the Department of Public Works the question of how many construction items could be made to help in the unemployment situation if the Legislature were to anticipate the appropriations in January instead of waiting until March." Lehman immediately met with state public works officials and announced that "for the purpose of aiding in the relief of unemployment," the state would speed up seeking bids and letting contracts on $17,000,000 already appropriated by the Legislature for highway and bridge construction and other projects. He also recommended that Roosevelt ask the State Legislature to assign top priority to appropriations for road-building, park maintenance and development, and other construction activities when the lawmakers convened in January, rather than waiting until later in the session to pass such measures. Lehman conferred with the Republican leaders of the Legislature on November 25, 1930, and they "agreed on a plan whereby the State Architect is authorized to proceed at once" to draw up plans for "a $20 million hospital building program," which would create jobs for five thousand men. They also decided to increase highway construction funds by $5,000,000 to create another one thousand jobs.[29]

Such measures were only stopgaps, however; as Lehman told the New York State Conference of Mayors in June 1931, "unemployment relief will unquestionably be a serious problem in the Fall and Winter of 1931 and 1932 in almost every city." Lehman later recounted how the Roosevelt administration realized "that this situation was of very great proportions, and that we had to set up a real organization to handle it." The Lieutenant Governor played a key role in formulating the Roosevelt administration's proposal in August 1931 to establish a Temporary Emergency Relief Administration (TERA)—which would be authorized to spend $20,000,000 to create jobs for the unemployed and provide relief for those in need—and increase the state income tax by 50 percent to pay for it. Lehman took the lead in pressing the State Legislature to approve the Governor's plan, urging its adoption before a joint hearing held by the Senate Finance and Assembly Ways and Means Committees. When the Governor and the Legislature appeared deadlocked over the measure, Lehman helped bring about a late-night conference among all the parties in his suite at the DeWitt Clinton Hotel in Albany. The meeting began at 9:00 p.m. and lasted until 2:00 a.m., when a compromise was finally reached. With the creation of the TERA, New York under Roosevelt and Lehman became the first state in the nation to enact a comprehensive unemployment relief program to help its citizens during the Depression.[30]

In 1932, Democrats nominated Franklin Roosevelt for the presidency. Herbert Lehman was one of the first major financial contributors to FDR's presidential campaign, but he was less active in helping Roosevelt in 1932 than he had been in working for Al Smith in 1928 because he had to preside over New York State while Roosevelt was out campaigning. Lehman traveled to Montgomery, Alabama, where his father and uncle had originally settled, to speak on FDR's behalf, telling Roosevelt that "it may be helpful if they hear about your work and accomplishments at first hand from an associate rather than through the public records," and he worked with Roosevelt on a series of radio addresses focused on their record in New York State that were later turned into campaign pamphlets. Although the New York delegation to the Democratic National Convention in Chicago was controlled by Tammany and a majority of its members supported Al Smith, Lehman strongly declared his support for Roosevelt for President during the group's caucus and when the delegation was polled on the floor of the convention. In a speech to Tompkins County Democrats a few weeks later, Lehman praised Roosevelt's leadership and predicted that he "is going to be elected by the greatest vote next November."[31]

Franklin Roosevelt believed that Herbert Lehman's experience as Lieutenant Governor for the last four years uniquely qualified him to be the Democratic candidate for Governor in 1932. Roosevelt and his supporters also hoped that Lehman's presence on the ticket would facilitate a reconciliation between Roosevelt and Al Smith, who would be more likely to support the entire Democratic slate if Lehman were on it. Moreover, reminiscent of Smith's desire to have Roosevelt run for Governor in 1928 to improve Smith's chances of carrying the state in his bid for the presidency, Roosevelt wanted Lehman on the ticket with him in 1932 to increase the likelihood of winning the state in his race for the White House. Roosevelt and his advisors remembered that in 1930 Lehman had "received the largest plurality ever given to a candidate for public office in New York City," and they understood that "Lehman's appeal in New York City would aid greatly in swinging groups there into line for the whole State." To boost Lehman's chances for the governorship, Roosevelt announced in mid-July that he was asking Lehman to fill in for him and conduct the annual inspection tour of state facilities. Lehman set off on a three-day tour in late July and followed up with a ten-day journey in August, garnering attention and publicity in upstate areas where he was not as well known.[32]

On August 4, 1932, Herbert Lehman formally declared his candidacy for the Democratic nomination for Governor, and Franklin Roosevelt immediately endorsed him. Lehman explained that many friends as well as members of the press kept asking whether he intended to seek the governorship, so he believed it was time to announce his candidacy. He emphasized, however, that he would "not open headquarters, or engage in any pre-convention campaign at the present time." Rather, he preferred "to stand on my record of the past three and a half years as a public official." Roosevelt declared, "Lieut. Gov. Lehman should be the candidate of our party for Governor of New York this Autumn" because he "knows the government of this State inside and out." "In these times of financial stress and budget and tax problems," Roosevelt asserted, Lehman's "splendid business training and wide experience with public finance" and his "personal experience in and complete familiarity with the affairs of State government in Albany are not only desirable but almost essential qualifications in a candidate." The Governor credited Lehman with helping to develop the administration's policies to provide "cheap electricity in the home, farm and small shops of the State by means of State development of water power; . . . old-age security against want; . . . unemployment relief; . . . adequate housing for the wards of the State; . . . [and] liberalization of the workmen's compensation laws and labor laws of the State." Roosevelt noted that "in the handling of social problems and peaceful adjustments of industrial disputes, Lieut. Gov. Lehman has for many years been recognized as without equal in our State." He praised Lehman's "great integrity and ability" and expressed confidence that "the leaders and the rank and file" of the Democratic Party would recognize his "splendid qualities" and nominate him for Governor.[33]

Unfortunately, not all of the New York State Democratic Party leaders cared about Lehman's superb qualifications to be Governor. State party chairman James Farley, Bronx boss Edward Flynn, and a few other leaders supported Lehman, but Boss Curry of Tammany Hall and his ally, James McCooey of Brooklyn, blamed Roosevelt for forcing New York City Mayor Jimmy Walker to resign amid scandal, and they sought to take revenge by denying Lehman the nomination for Governor. In addition, the O'Connell brothers, who controlled the Democratic Party in Albany County, were pushing for Albany Mayor John Boyd Thacher to be the party's gubernatorial nominee. In early September, Roosevelt promised Adolph Ochs, the publisher of the *New York Times*, that he would attend the State Democratic Convention and "battle bitterly and openly for the nomination of Herbert." He emphasized that "only an utter madness on the part of a handful of people who would rather commit suicide than give in" would prevent Lehman's "nomination and election."[34]

For a brief time, it seemed like the Tammany leaders had come to their senses. On September 8, Roosevelt's good friend and Dutchess County neighbor Henry Morgenthau, Jr., who was also State Conservation Commissioner and the husband of Herbert Lehman's niece Elinor, told Lehman that events were proceeding "in a manner distinctly to your advantage," and he hoped that would continue to be the case "up to the final point when I feel sure they are going to nominate you." The following day, the State Democratic Committee pledged "its active and loyal support" to Roosevelt in the fall campaign, and Roosevelt met with Curry and McCooey at the Executive Mansion. By mid-September, Roosevelt confided to Felix Frankfurter, "it looked as if the New York City crowd will find it more and more difficult to turn down Herbert, and both Herbert and I feel much more confident of his nomination." Roosevelt told Frankfurter that he was planning to address the State Democratic Convention and had warned Curry "that the subject of my address would depend largely on the decision he makes during the next three weeks." Lehman's prospects looked good on September 25 when the *New York Times* reported, "Tammany Is Seen Turning to Lehman."[35]

Relations between Roosevelt and Tammany suddenly deteriorated again a few days later, however, when the Democratic Party in Manhattan endorsed Republican State Senator Samuel Hofstadter for a seat on the State Supreme Court rather than Samuel Rosenman, Roosevelt's former counsel, who had been appointed to fill a vacancy on the court. According to the *Times*, Tammany's rejection of Rosenman "served notice that, while it may be supporting Mr. Roosevelt for President, it intends to be complete master of the situation in New York City." Tammany's actions also called into question whether it would support Roosevelt's choices for state office, including Lehman for Governor. Worried that Tammany and the Brooklyn organization might oppose Lehman at the convention, Roosevelt tried to maneuver around Curry by phoning Brooklyn leader McCooey directly and asking him to support Lehman, but McCooey would not commit himself, adding to Roosevelt's and Lehman's growing concern.[36]

As delegates to the Democratic State Convention prepared to convene in Albany in early October, Roosevelt reiterated his strong support for Lehman. Roosevelt was returning from a campaign trip out West and would be arriving in Albany just prior to the convention, where, according to a report in the *New York Herald Tribune*, he would "fight to the last ditch for the nomination of Lieutenant Governor Herbert H. Lehman to succeed him as Governor." In another phone call to McCooey on the eve of the convention, Roosevelt hoped that an intraparty conflict could be avoided, but he warned that if a battle developed over Lehman's nomination, he would "fight until the other man was dead."[37]

Realizing that he needed a stronger candidate than Thacher if he were going to deny Lehman the nomination for Governor, Curry came up with the idea of nominating U.S. Senator Robert Wagner for Governor and Lehman for Senator. That way, Curry hoped, Jewish voters and other strong supporters of Lehman would be mollified and vote for the Democratic ticket, but the Executive Mansion in Albany would be in more friendly hands. Roosevelt, James Farley, and Ed Flynn all urged Lehman to confront Curry and the others who opposed his nomination, and Lehman did so, barging uninvited into Curry's hotel room to tell them in no uncertain terms that he would be nominated for Governor, not Senator. Just before the nominations began, Curry capitulated and dropped his opposition to Lehman, who was nominated unanimously by the convention.[38]

Lehman's victory allowed Franklin Roosevelt to discard his speech attacking Tammany and focus instead on Lehman's qualifications for the governorship when he addressed the convention later that evening. Roosevelt emphasized that a Governor had "to be an expert in all the range of human knowledge and human progress, prisons, paroles, hospitals, crippled children, agriculture, old-age pensions, unemployment, highways, water power, public utilities, budgeting and finance." In Herbert Lehman, Roosevelt stressed, New Yorkers had "a man who has the knowledge, a man who knows every nook and cranny of the State, who knows every principle of the details of government, a man who understands how to run things in a business way, but more important than that, a man with an understanding heart, a man to whom social justice is not an unknown word." Roosevelt promised that after campaigning in a few other states, he would be back in New York to "work heart and soul for the election of Herbert H. Lehman for Governor," and he looked forward to January 1, 1933, when he would "turn over the reins of the government of the State of New York to that splendid right hand of mine, Herbert H. Lehman."[39]

FIGURE 3.2. Franklin Roosevelt and James Farley congratulate Herbert Lehman on his nomination as the Democratic candidate for Governor as Mrs. Lehman looks on, October 4, 1932. AP Images.

In accepting the nomination for Governor, Lehman paid tribute to FDR, emphasizing that he had been privileged to work with Roosevelt "during these last four years—years which have been very busy and replete with experiences and broad training." Under Roosevelt's leadership, Lehman declared, the state government had extended its role "into many new activities affecting the economic and social well-being of all the people of the State," adopting "a system of old-age security against want," a "program of unemployment relief, . . . measures for the protection of workers in industry, . . . and for the conservation of the State water power resources." Lehman was inspired by Al Smith's and Roosevelt's accomplishments, and he hoped and prayed that he would "have the ability and the wisdom to carry on the work that they have initiated."[40]

Despite the demands of his own campaign, Roosevelt made sure to help Lehman in the fall of 1932. They had lunch together at Roosevelt's home in Hyde Park a few days after the state convention and then attended a local gathering at which Lehman recalled his long association with FDR, going back to their days together in the Navy Department in 1917. Lehman emphasized Roosevelt's "vision, courage and knowledge," and his "capacity for hard work," and how difficult it would be to follow in Roosevelt's footsteps. FDR, in turn, expressed his pleasure that he would be "succeeded by a man who knows the State, . . . a man who is a humanitarian, who can think in terms of the average citizen." In mid-October, Roosevelt spoke in Rochester and Buffalo, urging people to vote for Herbert Lehman, "a man who translates his humanity into deeds and actions, . . . a man who understands this State, and a man who will carry on what has become a tradition in this State, a government that is aimed at progressive and liberal policies and won't stand still." Roosevelt also announced his intention as President to consult with the nation's governors, and his hope that when he called Albany he would be able to say, "Hello Herbert. I wish you would run on down to the White House and have supper. I have got a lot of problems that are common problems to the federal government and the State of New York. I want you to come down and talk it over with me, and see if we can't be of mutual help to each other."[41]

Roosevelt and Lehman closed out the campaign in early November with rallies at the Brooklyn Academy of Music and Madison Square Garden. Once again, Roosevelt called for the election of his "long-time associate and friend," Herbert Lehman, the man who was "best qualified" to be Governor of New York, and Lehman paid tribute to "a leader rich in statesmanship and sound in economic ideas—lofty in ideals and possessed of human and sympathetic understanding, the next President of the United States—Franklin Delano Roosevelt."[42]

In November 1932, with New York and the nation reeling from the effects of the ever-worsening Depression, Franklin Roosevelt easily defeated Herbert Hoover for the presidency, and Herbert Lehman triumphed over William Donovan in the gubernatorial race. Nationally, Roosevelt received 6.8 million

Figure 3.3. Governor-elect Lehman and President-elect Roosevelt congratulate each other on their election victories, November 8, 1932. AP Images.

votes more than Hoover and carried forty-two states with a total of 472 electoral votes, and he beat Hoover by almost six hundred thousand votes in New York. As impressive as Roosevelt's victory was, Lehman surpassed Roosevelt's victory margin in New York, winning by 840,000 votes, the largest plurality for a Democrat in state history up to that time. The *New York Times* observed that as Lieutenant Governor under FDR, Lehman had demonstrated "a passionate interest in non-banking subjects—public education, public health, public recreation, the protection of women and children, the protection of old age, [and] the care of the mentally afflicted," as well as the ability to carry on "this work by sound business methods." Lehman's election, the *Times* declared, was "both a tribute to him and a sign that the people know how to appreciate and reward a faithful and able public servant."[43]

CHAPTER 4

"The New Deal in Washington Is Being Duplicated by the 'Little' New Deal at Albany"

Governor Lehman and President Roosevelt, 1933–1936

Lehman was naturally a New Dealer, . . . he was just as naturally
a liberal as Roosevelt was, and it was a natural thing for him to
follow the lead, and take on the New Deal things and put them
into the state.[1]

I

After the elections of 1932, Herbert Lehman and Franklin Roosevelt
worked to ensure a smooth transition in Albany. As Eleanor Roosevelt noted,
"The work of the governorship was familiar to Mr. Lehman, so he took over with
complete confidence." Lehman reappointed all of Roosevelt's cabinet, including Industrial Commissioner Frances Perkins and Conservation Commissioner
Henry Morgenthau, Jr., both of whom were rumored to be in line for positions
in FDR's administration. Morgenthau later conceded that he "was already planning to go to Washington at that time . . . and was not in Albany much at
all." He remembered Lehman once teasing him: "Don't you think you might
show up in your office once in a while?" When Harry Hopkins offered to resign
as head of the state's Temporary Emergency Relief Administration (TERA) to
give Lehman "a perfectly free hand" in appointing members of the TERA,

---

Chapter title quotation: Russell Owen, "The Man Behind the 'Little' New Deal," *New York Times
Magazine*, March 15, 1936, SM 4, 21.

Lehman informed Hopkins that "I greatly desire you to remain as Chairman," emphasizing that Hopkins had "done a splendid piece of work, which would be handicapped by your withdrawal at this time." Roosevelt relinquished to Lehman the "No. 1" New York State license plate that had adorned FDR's car for the last four years, and new Lieutenant Governor William Bray inherited Lehman's old "No. 2," relegating FDR to "No. 3," and pushing Al Smith down to "No. 4." Preparing to vacate the Executive Mansion, Roosevelt joked that he had "left Herbert a few pencils, an old pen, half a card of matches and some rubber bands," claiming that "everything else is mine and I am taking it away."[2]

Many of the festivities scheduled around Lehman's inauguration were cancelled or scaled back when Lehman's sister Clara Limburg died on December 30, 1932. But Herbert Lehman took great pride that his brother, New York State Court of Appeals Judge Irving Lehman, swore him in as Governor at midnight on December 31 in a small ceremony in New York City. Lehman's formal inauguration on January 2, 1933, was considered a major event because, in addition to Lehman's speech, it featured remarks by Franklin Roosevelt, the first President-elect to speak at his successor's inauguration as Governor of New York. Lehman's and Roosevelt's speeches were broadcast nationwide on radio, and Al Smith was also present for the occasion.[3]

As Governor, Herbert Lehman was exceedingly conscientious, almost to a fault, working late into the evening and resuming early the next morning. Samuel Rosenman later recalled that Lehman "took his problems to bed with him and to mealtimes, . . . and even after they were decided, he wanted to relive them. . . . Two or three days after he'd made a decision, [Lehman] began to discuss it and see whether he was right or wrong." New York State and Democratic National Chairman James Farley complained that "you never could get him to make a decision on a matter of policy or patronage while you were with him." Lehman would "always say, 'Well, I'll think it over, and we'll look into it.' Then maybe a day or two or three later, he'd do it or he wouldn't do it." As opposed to Al Smith, who had basically commuted to Albany from New York City, and to FDR, who had spent considerable time in Warm Springs and campaigning nationally for the presidency, Lehman moved his family into the Executive Mansion and made it their primary residence, and Mrs. Lehman even wrote a brief "autobiography" of the building. Lehman refused to accept any speaking engagements outside the state, and when the Legislature was in session, he rejected any invitations that would take him out of Albany. Lehman also declined any social engagements on the nights when prisoners were scheduled to be executed, nor would he drink any alcohol that evening, ensuring that he was available to deal with any last-minute appeals or emergencies.[4]

Governor Lehman relied heavily on a few key aides. When he was Lieutenant Governor, he had hired Joseph Canavan, a former editor at the *New York World*, to handle his schedule and his mail, and Canavan continued as

FIGURE 4.1. Governor Lehman with his predecessors, President-elect Franklin Roosevelt and Al Smith, at Lehman's inauguration as Governor, January 1, 1933. AP Images.

Lehman's secretary until November 1934, when Lehman appointed him to the State Parole Board. A few months later, Lehman selected Walter Brown, the head of the Associated Press bureau in Albany, as Canavan's successor. Keenly aware that he was not a lawyer, Lehman knew that he needed to get the right person as his legal counsel to advise him on the mass of bills that would be coming across his desk as Governor. At the recommendation of Harvard Law School professor and New Deal talent scout Felix Frankfurter, Lehman chose Charles Poletti to fill this vital post. Lehman quickly came to value Poletti's legal and political acumen so much that he invited the young attorney to move into the Executive Mansion. As always, Edith Lehman remained her husband's most influential advisor. Believing in the power of words to persuade people, Lehman spent long hours working on his messages to the Legislature and his other speeches, writing many of them himself but also receiving help at times from Canavan, Poletti, Samuel Rosenman, and others.[5]

Lehman's relations with Tammany Hall remained tenuous. The Governor worked closely with his department heads—too closely in the opinion of Industrial Commissioner Frances Perkins—but he did not interact much with Lieutenant Governor William Bray, Attorney General William Bennett, or State Controller Morris Tremaine, all of whom had closer ties to the Democratic political organization. More concerned with competency than politics, Lehman refused to appoint Tammany hacks, but he approved recommendations that came to him through party channels if he felt that the person was qualified. Bronx Democratic leader and Democratic National Committee member Edward Flynn stayed on as Secretary of State and became a key political advisor to Lehman. The Governor adopted a policy of replacing Republican officials who died with qualified Democrats, but much to the dismay of Democratic leaders, he reappointed Republican officials whose terms had expired if they had served the state well. Of course, since the Democrats had controlled the governorship for the last ten years, there were not very many Republicans in such positions. Lehman sought the input of the bar associations when it came to making judicial nominations, but he made sure not to give the lawyers a veto over such appointments.[6]

On January 4, 1933, Governor Lehman addressed the state's serious problems in his first annual message to the Legislature. He noted the cumulative effects of the Depression, now in its fourth year, and the growing toll it had taken on "the health and well-being of our citizens, the mental and moral effects upon them, [and] the strain upon the treasury of the State and upon its activities." Anticipating the repeal of Prohibition, which Lehman considered "one of the most damaging legislative enactments in the entire history of the country" because it had resulted in "brutal and flagrant lawlessness on the part of racketeers" and "a disregard for law among our young people and their elders," the Governor called for the enactment of legislation for the sale of beer and a tax on it to raise needed revenue for the state. Lehman advocated fiscal restraint, but he warned against budget cuts that would hurt school children and other groups the state needed to serve. He pointed out that 25 percent of the state's workforce was unemployed, and though New York, under Franklin Roosevelt's leadership, had been one of the first states to recognize "in a practical way its duty and responsibility to help sustain by emergency work relief, or by actual home relief, the thousands of men and women who are willing to work but who can find no jobs," Lehman emphasized that "the strain on State, local and private resources" had "reached its limit." New York would have "to look to Washington for assistance," where "the new federal administration," coming in March under Franklin Roosevelt, was "definitely committed to the policy that the federal government has the ultimate responsibility for the continued promotion of the public welfare and for the relief of unemployment distress."[7]

The banking crisis presented Franklin Roosevelt with his most immediate challenge as he prepared to assume the presidency on March 4, 1933, and it also required strong action from Governor Lehman. Banks in most states were already closed, and financial institutions in New York were under tremendous pressure as panicky depositors rushed to withdraw their funds. On the evening of March 2, Lehman met with representatives of the New York banks until 3:00 a.m. He had planned to attend Roosevelt's inauguration in Washington on March 4, but as the banking situation worsened on March 3, he realized he needed to stay in New York to deal with the crisis. As Lehman later recalled, he wanted to have legal advisors present when he met with the bankers again on the evening of March 3, but "the Attorney General, the Counsel to the Governor, and all of their assistants had left for Washington," so Lehman asked Robert Moses to attend the session, only to discover during the meeting that Moses "was not a lawyer, had no legal experience, and knew nothing about the banking crisis." Lehman thought, "it was a great joke on me to have invited as my legal advisor a man who knew nothing whatsoever about the law." The Governor believed that the banking problem was national in scope and required action by the outgoing Hoover administration in Washington, but when it became clear that Hoover was not going to act, Lehman understood he would have to step into the breach. After conferring with President-elect Roosevelt, and in response to a specific request from the Federal Reserve Bank of New York and the Clearing House banks that transferred funds between banks, Lehman proclaimed a bank holiday at 4:20 a.m. on March 4, closing New York banks through March 6 and giving FDR a little breathing room.[8]

On March 5, as one of his first official acts as President, Roosevelt proclaimed a national bank holiday and called Congress to meet in special session on March 9, at which time it passed the Emergency Banking Bill the administration had drawn up to resolve the crisis. Roosevelt's decisive actions, along with his clear explanation of them in his Fireside Chat on March 12, restored people's confidence in both the federal government and the banks, and when the first banks reopened on March 13, more money was deposited than withdrawn. Lehman congratulated the President on the "tremendous impression everything you have done thus far has made on the public," asserting that Roosevelt's "leadership has been a real inspiration to the people," and that "even the people who were most opposed to you before [the] election and, as a matter of fact, since then, are now in the main one hundred per cent in your corner. You have done a great job," Lehman emphasized, "and I know that you are going to keep it up."[9]

Governor Lehman and President Roosevelt maintained their close relationship during Roosevelt's first term in the White House, but there were a few instances when their interests clashed. Frances Perkins later recalled that when she met with Lehman a few days after his inauguration as Governor to make sure that Lehman wanted her to stay on as New York State Industrial Commissioner, Lehman assured her, "I want you to go on very much. I count on you. I depend on you. I'm very anxious to have you stay." Perkins looked forward to working with the new Governor, noting, "Lehman was fully committed—politically, intellectually and, I guess, spiritually. It was part of his religious code," so "you didn't have to begin the process of educating him to the desirability of some of these social progress measures, as we had to do with both Smith and Roosevelt." After working for Lehman for two months, however, Perkins concluded that "it wasn't going to be as much fun to work for Governor Lehman as it had been for Smith and Roosevelt . . . because Lehman was a fuss-budget" who "used to telephone two or three times a day" to check up on matters that he had referred to her. Perkins was relieved when Roosevelt appointed her Secretary of Labor, the first woman to serve in a President's Cabinet. When she informed Lehman that Roosevelt wanted her to come to Washington, the Governor was disappointed but not surprised. Perkins and Lehman agreed that she would remain in New York for a few more weeks to "finish up various projects" and would be sworn in as Roosevelt's Secretary of Labor a few weeks after the rest of the Cabinet, but on March 4, 1933, immediately after Roosevelt's inauguration, presidential aide Stephen Early called Perkins and explained that Roosevelt "wants everybody to swear in tonight at the White House." Early emphasized that "the crisis is so frightful that the President thinks we must have the full Cabinet, that the people will feel better and less disorganized if there is a full Cabinet in operation." Perkins immediately wired Lehman her resignation as State Industrial Commissioner, apologizing for being "unable to carry out our plan of one more week in which to confer and clean up matters pertaining to my office in New York."[10]

Lehman put up more of a fight when Roosevelt sought to appoint Harry Hopkins as head of the new Federal Emergency Relief Administration (FERA). When newspaper reports in early May 1933 indicated that Hopkins was going to be nominated to lead the FERA once it was established by Congress, Lehman objected, explaining to Roosevelt that "it would be a great blow to relief in New York State for Harry Hopkins to leave at this time." Despite Lehman's protests, the President told Lehman on May 19 that he had just asked Hopkins "to take over for a month or two [the] administration of [the] public relief measure," and that Hopkins "has consented to come down and get [the] work started." Roosevelt explained that because of the great need resulting from the Depression, he needed to "get a man on the job immediately," and he claimed that there was "no one else available." The President stressed that it was "very difficult [to] find a man fitted [for] this special work" and that he "felt Hopkins could get away for a month or two without interfering" with Lehman's program in New York. Roosevelt promised to discuss the matter with Lehman when they met the following week.[11]

Furious that Roosevelt had ignored his objections, Lehman correctly predicted that Hopkins's service in Washington could not and would not be temporary. Lehman argued that "there is no one on board now" who could replace Hopkins "without seriously crippling the work in New York State which is after all the most important in size and in need of any state in the union." Lehman emphasized that the President had "the entire country from which to make a choice," and he begged Roosevelt to "reconsider your decision and advise Harry Hopkins to stay in New York." Lehman reiterated his arguments against Hopkins's appointment when he met with the President and stayed overnight at the White House a week later, but his protests fell on deaf ears, and Hopkins headed to Washington to take charge of the FERA.[12]

Some of Roosevelt's advisors, including Harvard law professor Felix Frankfurter, questioned Lehman's commitment to liberal principles and his willingness to fight for them. For example, Lehman supported the general concept of a state minimum wage bill for women and children, but he worried that such a law would put New York businesses at a competitive disadvantage with their rivals in neighboring states. Frankfurter and others explained to Lehman that the companies exploiting women working as maids and waitresses and in laundries were not in competition with out-of-state firms, and they persuaded him to propose a minimum wage law for women and children. When the State Legislature enacted the bill, President Roosevelt congratulated Lehman on this "great forward step" and publicly called upon the governors of the other industrial states to follow Lehman's example. Frankfurter shared with the President his hope that such "nationwide recognition" would "encourage Herbert Lehman to realize that fighting has its rewards as well as its joys."[13]

Lehman strongly supported Roosevelt's efforts to pull the nation out of the Depression through programs such as the National Recovery Administration (NRA). To enable people to show their support for the NRA, the Governor declared the afternoon of September 13, 1933, a holiday so that workers and employers could attend a parade celebrating the NRA's efforts. Lehman hailed the massive gathering of 250,000 marchers, cheered by 1.5 million onlookers, as "the greatest New York has ever seen," and "proof that the NRA is going over." In remarks to the Merchants Association of New York that same day, Lehman asserted that 97 per cent of employers and 40.2 percent of families in some upstate areas had subscribed to the NRA codes or pledged to patronize businesses that subscribed to the NRA rules. Such action, Lehman emphasized, was "but the first step in the President's program to put men and women back at work, to give them a living wage, to increase their buying power, and through this increase to bring about recovery." As he traveled around the state, the Governor declared, "I sense and see a new hope, a new confidence, a new enthusiasm. People are coming out of their lethargy and their discouragement, and are again facing the future with some feeling of security."[14]

In New York State, Lehman sought to expand on the policies of Al Smith and Franklin Roosevelt and use the power of the state government to help people cope with the Great Depression, but he was hampered in his efforts by having to deal with a Republican majority in at least one house of the State Legislature in every year except 1935. Nonetheless, as Robert Ingalls has detailed in his book, *Herbert H. Lehman and New York's Little New Deal*, Lehman and the State Legislature enacted into law measures to provide unemployment insurance, relief for the unemployed, assistance to those who were unable to work, public housing, cheaper utility rates, and help for farmers. Some of these measures anticipated federal programs that soon followed; others implemented legislation already enacted in Washington. Lehman nicely summarized the relationship between New York under his leadership and the federal government under Franklin Roosevelt, as well as illuminating his relationship with FDR, when he reported to the President in December 1933:

> At the recent extraordinary sessions of the Legislature, we enacted a lot of legislation to make our State laws conform to federal statutes, and to insure the complete cooperation of the State with the federal government in your plans for national recovery. I think we have already covered the field pretty well but if there is any other legislation which you desire, and which will help us in any way to cooperate to the utmost degree with the federal government, please let me know and I will try my best to get it through.[15]

In addition to their political ties, Lehman and Roosevelt maintained a close personal relationship during this period. The Lehmans hosted the President-elect and Mrs. Roosevelt at the Executive Mansion for tea in February 1933, and the Lehmans enjoyed visiting the White House on their way south in late spring 1933. Lehman also saw the President frequently at Hyde Park. When Lehman suffered a bout of appendicitis in September, the President was among the first to call to express concern and send flowers. Lehman underwent surgery in October to remove his troublesome appendix, and though his recovery was interrupted by a bout of pleurisy, his condition was not fatal, as was rumored at one point, and Lehman was finally released from the hospital in late November. President Roosevelt, who was all too familiar with physical disabilities, was glad to know that Lehman was "sitting up again," commiserating that Lehman had "certainly had a long siege of it." The President knew "it is not much comfort to suggest that it was sent from heaven to give you a rest," but he hoped that Lehman would not "try to get back into harness too quickly" but would give himself a "little chance to get your strength back."

Lehman did spend a few weeks relaxing at Atlantic City before returning to Albany in mid-December to work on the budget and other problems for the coming year. He assured the President that he was "entirely recovered" from his recent illness and actually felt better than he had "for a long time." In May 1934, Herbert and Edith Lehman were thrilled to be the guests of honor at a White House dinner.[16]

Lehman's constant efforts to obtain more federal funds for relief programs in New York became the main bone of contention between Lehman and President Roosevelt in these years. As Lehman later recalled, the state's "resources had been pretty well exhausted . . . and people were becoming very restless about it." While New York was "very glad to have the federal assistance, as is always the case, we felt that we weren't getting our full share, that other states were being given relatively preferential treatment over New York." In January 1934, Lehman emphasized to Roosevelt his "very keen desire to continue to cooperate with you and Harry Hopkins in every possible way in making your civil works program fully effective," but he cautioned that "the discontinuance

Figure 4.2. Governor Lehman confers with President Roosevelt at Hyde Park, August 6, 1933. AP Images.

or substantial reduction" of appropriations for the Civil Works Administration (CWA) "might lead to serious social and economic consequences." Lehman asserted that the state was "already doing as much as it possibly can," having "been forced to take over a larger and larger part of the municipal expenditures because of the withdrawal of federal aid for home relief." According to the Governor, New York was now spending on home relief alone "vastly more than was heretofore spent by the State of New York for home and work relief combined." Lehman considered the situation to be critical, and he volunteered to meet with Roosevelt at any time to discuss the matter. In a letter to Harry Hopkins, Lehman was much more explicit, warning that

> the unemployed of this State have been led to believe that they would be given continuing work by the Federal Government. In their minds the Federal Civil Works' activities . . . are closely connected with the relief program. If, therefore, the men and women who have been given work by the Federal Civil Works' program were deprived of their jobs, unrest might, I fear, assume serious proportions.

A week later, Lehman released to the press his earlier letter to the President as well as a new telegram in which he reiterated his hope that Roosevelt would "make every effort to obtain from the Congress appropriations sufficient in amount to continue the civil works program for the unemployed . . . until such unemployment can be absorbed by industry or through your public works program."[17]

Lehman's missives provoked a reaction in Washington, but not the one he had hoped for. Presidential aide Stephen Early complained to Judge Samuel Rosenman, a close friend of both Lehman and Roosevelt, that "telegrams addressed to the President are not ordinarily made public by the senders unless the White House is asked for such permission." In this case, Early noted, Lehman's telegram "evidently was given out in Albany that afternoon, even before it was received at the White House. . . . It did not reach the President until after he had read it in the newspaper. . . . Frankly and confidentially," Early stressed, "the reaction here to the Albany publicity was not good." Early maintained that the President was "doing everything he possibly can to continue the C.W.A. and at the same time keep within the necessary budget limitations," but "even requests from Governors for appropriations of monies in amounts exceeding the budget limitations cannot be considered and acted upon overnight." He cautioned that "the pressure of publicity, put on a man as busy as the President, is not likely to help . . . particularly when the publicity appears before the request is received and given consideration." Early hoped that Rosenman would "suggest to the Governor's publicity advisers that they, in the future, give the President a chance to read the telegrams from Albany, to consider the requests contained therein, and not first see them in the columns of newspapers." Rosenman agreed that Lehman's communication to the President "never should have appeared in the press," and he was willing to transmit a copy of Early's letter to Lehman and his staff. However, "in view of the personal relationships involved," Rosenman wanted "to speak to the President about it first," and Roosevelt instructed him to "take the matter up orally" when he next saw the Governor. Early lamented that this "will not be as effective as sending him the letter," but he recognized that, "under the circumstances, it is all we can do."[18]

At times, Lehman's efforts to capitalize on his special relationship with Roosevelt did result in additional aid for New York. In mid-March 1934, for example, Lehman and New York's legislative leaders traveled to Washington to meet with Harry Hopkins and the President to voice their concern that the termination of the CWA would leave five hundred thousand families, consisting of 1,750,000 people, in need of unemployment relief in New York. As Lehman related to his niece Elinor, who was married to Secretary of the Treasury Henry Morgenthau, Jr., the Governor and the legislators had met with Hopkins and then had gone to the White House and conferred with the President for almost two hours. "We were occupied continuously," Lehman reported, "in working out a plan for relief in this State and in preparing a statement for the press." Lehman emphasized to Hopkins and Roosevelt that New York had $48,000,000 left from a previous bond issue to deal with the problem, and municipalities were contributing another $5,000,000 each month to help ease the situation, but more money was needed. Much to Lehman's delight, Hopkins and Roosevelt promised to make an additional $100,000,000 available to New York's Temporary Emergency Relief Administration to pick up the slack once CWA funds dried up. Hopkins explained publicly that New York would receive this special help because its needs were the most pressing and because "it has gone to bat in doing its utmost to take care of its own problems better than any state in the Union."[19]

II

Herbert Lehman did not want to run for re-election as Governor in 1934. Mrs. Lehman was concerned that "the worries and problems of . . . public office" were taking too great a toll on her husband, as manifested in his appendicitis the previous year, and the Governor was ready to return to private life. At a meeting with Roosevelt in early May and in a subsequent letter, Lehman explained that much as he would like to go along with the President's wishes, he preferred "not to be a candidate for Governor this fall." Lehman emphasized that "this had been a difficult decision to make," and he had made it "not impulsively but after mature and thoughtful consideration over a period of several months." He had "served the State for the past six years, . . . served it loyally and well," Lehman declared, but as Roosevelt could well understand, serving as Governor of New York had required great sacrifices by Lehman and his family, and the strain had left him "in need of a rest." Lehman felt that he could withdraw at the end of his term knowing that he had achieved many of the goals that he and Roosevelt shared.[20]

Roosevelt and New York Democratic leaders refused to accept Lehman's decision as final. The President worked on Lehman when the Governor and his wife were in Washington for a White House dinner in Lehman's honor on May 17. William Kenneally, the acting leader of Tammany Hall, guaranteed that there would be no repeat of 1932 when Boss Curry and Tammany had opposed Lehman. This time, Kenneally promised, Lehman would have Tammany's full-fledged support, and he expressed confidence that Lehman would "receive from the people an overwhelming approval of his stewardship as Governor of the State of New York." New York State and Democratic National Committee Chairman James Farley told Roosevelt that Lehman "should be forced to run because he wanted the nomination [in 1932] and won it through the influence of the President against the objection of the Tammany crowd." According to Farley, Lehman "owed it to the President to run again, because if he didn't, it would cause an embarrassing situation in the state," where there was no obvious candidate to replace him. Farley and Roosevelt agreed in mid-June to put all their efforts behind "insisting upon Lehman running again," and the President promised to "bear down upon" Lehman when they met at Hyde Park the following week. Roosevelt kept up the pressure, and eventually Lehman relented and agreed to run for re-election to continue his efforts to confront "the many economic and social problems" still facing New Yorkers. When Lehman wired Roosevelt to tell him of his decision, Roosevelt immediately responded: "You have made me very happy. I congratulate the people of our State on your unselfish decision."[21]

The Governor's race in New York in 1934 gave voters an early opportunity to register their opinions on both FDR's New Deal in Washington and Lehman's "Little New Deal" in New York. New York Republicans adopted what the *New York Times* described as "a platform condemning the Roosevelt New Deal and denouncing the Lehman administration at Albany" and nominated Robert Moses as their candidate for Governor. Lacking any real issues on which to criticize Lehman, Moses ran one of the nastiest, most vile political campaigns New York State had ever seen, resorting to personal attacks on Lehman's character and integrity. As Moses himself characterized it, his campaign featured "striking from the shoulder, mincing no words, . . . with a healthy instinct for the jugular and solar plexus." He charged that a Lehman-appointed investigation of the State Insurance Department was an attempt "to sprinkle cologne

on a manure heap," accused the Governor of "feebleness" in keeping the State
Insurance Superintendent in his post, complained that Lehman was "a weak
man in a weak administration," and asserted that Lehman had "lied to the
people of the State" about problems in the milk industry. Moses claimed that
Lehman was "too close to the federal administration," that he was "ready to
go along with whatever they propose at Washington," and that he was locked
in the "terrible grip" of Tammany Hall. Although Moses's own ancestors were
Jewish, he invoked anti-Semitic stereotypes by calling Lehman "a miserable,
sniveling type of professional man . . . who is ashamed of his profession," a
"contemptible banker," a "money lender."[22]

Lehman was shocked by Moses's campaign tactics; as Carolin Flexner,
Lehman's longtime assistant, later recalled, "Moses was the only person in
the world who ever called Herbert Lehman a liar." The Governor had always
respected Moses's intelligence and integrity and his ability to get things done,
and he had even persuaded the Legislature to enact a bill allowing Moses to
retain his position as New York State Parks Commissioner while also serving as
the head of the New York City Parks Commission and the Triborough Bridge
Authority. Despite being hurt and angry at Moses's unfounded personal accusations, Lehman wisely decided that his best strategy was to ignore Moses and
run on his record as Governor, stressing the need to continue the work begun
by Al Smith and Franklin Roosevelt before him, and the close ties between his
administration in Albany and FDR's in Washington. In formally accepting the
Democratic nomination in mid-October, Lehman praised the New Deal, which
had "translated into action the liberal and progressive ideals of the Democratic
party," and he emphasized, "as your candidate for Governor, I endorse with
enthusiasm the program of national recovery."[23]

Franklin Roosevelt disliked Moses and he was pleased when Moses won
the Republican nomination because he was confident that Lehman would easily
defeat him. After Moses was nominated, the President and Democratic Chairman James Farley discussed how they could best aid Lehman's campaign. FDR
joked that Moses "had done a pretty good job in the parks in Long Island"
and thought "it might be a break if he were to get lost in one of them," while
Farley hoped that someone would take Moses "for a walk in Central Park and
give him a ducking in the Reservoir." More seriously, Roosevelt and Farley
decided that FDR would announce his support for Lehman at a press conference on November 2, just a few days before the election. At his meeting with
reporters, Roosevelt warmly endorsed Lehman's re-election, reminding everyone,
"Lehman served as my Lieutenant Governor for four years and in that capacity earned my admiration as a public official and my warm regard as a man."
As Governor, Roosevelt emphasized, Lehman "has made good. He has shown
courage, energy, fine administrative and executive qualities, and, above all, a
deep interest in and understanding of the welfare and needs of the citizens

of the State of New York." Accordingly, Roosevelt declared, "on returning to my home to cast my ballot as a citizen of the State of New York, I have no hesitancy in making it known that I expect to vote for Governor Lehman and that I hope he will be re-elected."[24]

Lehman won re-election in 1934 in a landslide, defeating Moses by more than eight hundred thousand votes. The Governor carried Moses's own election district on the Upper East Side of Manhattan, and, as Mrs. Lehman had predicted, he even outpolled Moses in heavily Republican Upstate New York. The President declared that "Herbert's victory was well deserved," while James Farley proclaimed that "this election is convincing proof that the people of the State of New York are certain to have a most excellent administration of State affairs for the next two years." After the election, Lehman demonstrated that he still had not learned to be vindictive. Ignoring the wishes of Roosevelt, Farley, and many others, Lehman allowed Moses to continue as State Parks Commissioner for the remainder of Lehman's years as Governor.[25]

III

Herbert Lehman hoped that the President would attend his second inaugural as Governor on January 1, 1935. "It would be a great thing," Lehman wrote to Roosevelt, "if you and Al [Smith] and I could repeat the schedule of 1932." But in 1932, Roosevelt had been President-elect with no official responsibilities until March 4, 1933. This time, as the President explained to Lehman, he had "to deliver the annual Message to the Congress on January third" and had "to send in my Budget Message on January fourth," meaning that "from Christmas on I shall have to be working steadily." Roosevelt emphasized that although "there is nothing [he] would rather do" than come to the inauguration, he had "reluctantly decided[d] that a trip is impossible." Lehman was "very sorry indeed" that the President and Mrs. Roosevelt could not make it to the inauguration, but the Governor understood that the President had his "hands full" and that it was not possible for Roosevelt "to leave Washington at that time." Lehman stressed that Roosevelt was "doing a wonderful job" and prayed that the President would "have the strength to carry it through." Cabinet members James Farley and Frances Perkins represented the Roosevelt administration at Lehman's inaugural, and the President sent a telegram wishing he "could have been with you today not only for old times' sake but because of the splendid service you continue to render."[26]

Lehman's overwhelming victory over Moses combined with the popularity of Franklin Roosevelt's New Deal to produce a Democratic majority in both houses of the New York State Legislature for the first time in twenty years, and the Governor looked forward to the enactment of liberal social and labor legislation in 1935 that the Republicans had previously blocked. In Washington, Franklin Roosevelt and Congress adopted the Works Progress Act (WPA) to create millions of jobs for the unemployed; the Social Security Act to provide assistance to the elderly, the unemployed, the sick, and mothers with dependent children; and the Wagner Act to guarantee workers the right to join unions and bargain collectively. In Albany, meanwhile, Lehman and the State Legislature improved New York's Workmen's Compensation plan, reduced the working hours of women and children, increased the compulsory school age from fourteen to sixteen, imposed limits on the use of injunctions in labor-management disputes, and established a state unemployment insurance program that Lehman described as "the most progressive and enlightened piece of social legislation enacted in this State in many decades." Reviewing the legislature's accomplishments, Lehman called it "the greatest session in years," noting that the lawmakers had approved all but two of his major proposals, rejecting only his recommendations on reapportionment and his call for ratification of the federal child labor amendment. Very uncharacteristically, Lehman bragged that "never before was the program of any Executive so completely carried into effect." Lehman's success in winning approval of all these measures led Secretary of Labor Frances Perkins to observe "how perfectly remarkable . . . the whole session of the Legislature was," telling Lehman she was certain that "it was entirely due to your excellent leadership which has hardly been equaled by anything I have ever seen." Similarly, Felix Frankfurter told Lehman that "the legislative achievements in Albany this past session were chiefly attributable to the care with which you planned the legislative program, and the courage with which you pursued it. The various social enactments . . . transcend local problems and are of significance far beyond the boundaries of New York." George Meany, the head of the New York State Federation of Labor, later credited Lehman with bringing about the passage of "more legislation of social significance and of importance to the workers" than any other Governor in any other state, asserting that Lehman's achievements as Governor during this period ranked with those of Lyndon Johnson in winning approval of the Great Society in 1964–1966.[27]

When Congress appropriated almost $5,000,000,000 for the WPA, Lehman was determined "to procure for the State and its municipalities their full share for highway construction, elimination of grade crossings, slum clearance, low-cost housing, sewage disposal plants, water-works and other public improvements." Lehman later recalled that "our relationships in relief work were generally very close with Roosevelt and with Harry Hopkins," the head of the WPA, but that did not mean "that we didn't have a lot of arguments about it. We always felt that we should have been given more, and we weren't particularly in sympathy with the manner in which things were being done." In a series of meetings in September 1935, Lehman, Roosevelt, and Hopkins eventually agreed that the federal government would continue to provide funds for those who remained on home relief until work was found for them. When Lehman returned to Washington in November and December, seeking additional relief funds for New York, an exasperated Roosevelt "tried to make it perfectly clear" to the Governor that "Congress has given me a specific sum of money and that I must put three and a half million persons to work out of this." Roosevelt explained that he had "no discretion by which I can increase this fund," and that "New York has and is receiving its equitable share of the total sum both in the number of men put to work and the dollars themselves. The federal government," the President stressed, "is discharging its obligations in New York State in the fullest manner."[28]

In July 1935, Lehman mobilized the full resources of the state government to deal with severe flooding in the Southern Tier region that caused an estimated $25,000,000 in damages, but he also called upon his friend in the White House for assistance. The Governor sent in National Guard units and utilized unemployed workers receiving state aid to restore water purification systems, but after touring the area and seeing firsthand the damage to crops and livestock, Lehman asked the President to "authorize the AAA [Agricultural Adjustment Administration] or some other appropriate federal agency to extend immediate relief," and he sought the help of Civilian Conservation Corps (CCC) workers in the area as well. Roosevelt immediately ordered the Department of Agriculture, the Federal Emergency Relief Administration, and the WPA to do what they could, and when the CCC's Director of Emergency Conservation Work claimed that his agency did not have the authority to work on privately owned land, the President cut through the red tape and overturned the ban on using CCC personnel, ensuring that all available men could be deployed to protect the region from further soil erosion.[29]

Torrential rains caused further damage in the Southern Tier in 1936, and when the President toured the flood-ravaged area in mid-August, he made sure to include Lehman on his inspection trip from Chautauqua to Binghamton. After meeting with Lehman and other New York State officials, the President reversed an earlier decision that flood control projects would be delayed for a year, announcing the immediate allocation of $2,568,000 for the CCC, the WPA, and the War Department to begin work on three new dams in the Binghamton area, survey potential sites for additional dams, and improve flood control channels in the region.[30]

Lehman and Roosevelt suffered a major disappointment in the 1935 elections when the Republicans regained control of the New York State Assembly. Democratic control of both houses of the State Legislature in 1935 had presented Democrats with a rare opportunity to reapportion the state's legislative districts to remove the upstate bias that Republicans had built into the system in 1917. However, in what Lehman later denounced as "one of the stupidest things that Tammany Hall has ever done," Tammany Democrats joined with Republicans in rejecting the Governor's redistricting plan because it increased Brooklyn, Queens, and Bronx representation at the expense of Manhattan's. With neither Lehman nor Roosevelt on the ballot in 1935 to boost Democratic turnout, Democrats retained control of the State Senate, but Republicans captured eighty-eight of the 150 seats in the still gerrymandered State Assembly. Although Lehman, Roosevelt, and Democratic Chairman James Farley all noted that Democratic Assembly candidates actually received four hundred thousand more votes than their Republican opponents, Republican State Chairman Melvin Eaton pointed out that the eight hundred thousand vote margin for Lehman and the Democrats in 1934 had been halved to four hundred thousand for Assembly Democrats in 1935, asserting that "this decrease in majorities of nearly 50 per cent in one year most certainly attests [to] the wide swing away from the New Deal, and its increasing unpopularity gives every evidence the State will be safely in the Republican column in 1936."[31]

IV

By 1936, Herbert Lehman was determined to return to private life. As early as May 1935, the *New York Times* reported that Lehman would not seek another term as Governor, explaining that after four years as Lieutenant Governor and what will have been four more years as Governor, Lehman and his wife were "firm in their desire to devote themselves to other things besides politics and its accompanying life after 1936." But the *Times* noted the possibility that "President Roosevelt, anxious to roll up a big vote in his home State," would "stress the danger of party strife that would develop over selection of another candidate, turn on his best smile, and ask Mr. Lehman for the good of the party in State and nation to run again." A few days later, Lehman tried to quiet the speculation by publicly declaring that he had not discussed his "future political plans with any one, either political leaders or members of the press," including President Roosevelt. Lehman emphasized that he was "certainly not giving any consideration or thought whatsoever" to whether he would "be a candidate for renomination in October 1936, more than fifteen months away." Republican State Chairman Melvin Eaton charged that Lehman was "afraid" to run again, alleging that "the Governor is a timid man who is willing to campaign when everything is with him and he is on the crest of a wave. But when things begin to look doubtful, as they certainly do today, he has no taste for a real political battle." According to the *Times*, however, "persons closely allied with the President in political affairs"—presumably James Farley—expected that a reluctant Lehman would eventually yield again to Roosevelt's entreaties. Missy LeHand, the President's private secretary, reported to an upstate Democratic leader in June 1935 that Roosevelt "still hopes that Governor Lehman will be the candidate," and a few months later, Farley reiterated publicly his conviction that "Governor Lehman will be renominated and re-elected."[32]

In a face-to-face meeting at the White House on March 6, 1936, Lehman informed Roosevelt of his intention not to be a candidate for re-election that fall. Nonetheless, there were widespread reports in the press in mid-March that Lehman, who was regarded as the Democrats' strongest candidate by far because of what the *New York Times* characterized as his "great strength in New York City and a friendly feeling toward him up-State," had agreed to Roosevelt's request that he run for another term as Governor. The *Times* noted that Lehman's candidacy "would be a great aid to President Roosevelt in carrying New York State, and the forty-seven electoral votes of New York might decide the Presidential election." Because of all the speculation in the newspapers, Lehman wrote to the President on March 17 to "reiterate, in all sincerity, that I have not in the slightest degree changed my mind and that I intend to withdraw this fall." Lehman planned to "make my position publicly known whenever I think the time is opportune."[33]

Franklin Roosevelt refused to accept Lehman's decision as final. The President wanted the strongest possible Democratic ticket in New York in 1936 when he would be running for re-election, and immediately upon receipt of Lehman's letter, Roosevelt confided to Secretary of the Treasury Henry Morgenthau, Jr., that he was "greatly disturbed" by Lehman's plan not to run again. Roosevelt instructed Morgenthau to try to "get pressure to bear from any source you can" to persuade Lehman to change his mind. The President emphasized that Lehman "simply cannot be permitted to withdraw," that "the State and its citizens need him as Governor." Roosevelt feared that "a mess would be caused by trying to find a successor" to Lehman, and he went out of his way at the Jefferson Day dinner in New York City in April to highlight New York's "good fortune in the loyal, competent and unselfish service of its present Governor, Herbert Lehman," who "has continued to extend and strengthen the humane laws for which this State has been noted." Roosevelt hoped that Lehman would "continue his splendid work for at least two more years."[34]

Lehman delayed announcing his decision not to run for re-election because he did not want to become a lame duck while the State Legislature was considering his social security program and other important measures. The Governor had submitted an eight-point program to the Legislature on March 3, which lowered from seventy to sixty-five the age at which people could receive old-age pensions and provided state funds for the blind and dependent or crippled children, with the money coming from an increase in the state's liquor tax. As the *New York Times* reported, Lehman's social security program was "patterned on, and designed to dovetail into, the national Social Security Act originating with President Roosevelt and a Democratic Congress," and it would furnish the matching funds the state needed to spend to qualify for federal money for these programs. But as the *Times* also noted, New York Republicans, who controlled the State Assembly, viewed the Governor's plan "as the nearest thing to the New Deal in the State's wide curriculum of humanitarian legislation, and they are sworn to fight the New Deal wherever possible." The Governor appealed repeatedly to the Assembly to pass his social security program, which was a vital part of his "little New Deal" for New York, and he even made a statewide radio broadcast to arouse public support for the measure. But Assemblyman James J. Wadsworth, delivering the Republican response, denounced the Governor's plan as "just another New Deal boondoggle," and the Republicans kept the Governor's proposal bottled up in the Assembly's Rules Committee, refusing to allow it to come to the floor for a vote. They planned to make social security a major campaign issue in the fall against both Roosevelt and Lehman. When asked for his reaction to Wadsworth's speech, Lehman declared that "no comment is necessary on the speech of a man so heartless as to refer to the care of the blind, the crippled, the sick, the penniless, the old people and helpless children as boondoggling." The Governor believed "that attitude tells the whole story of the opposition to the social security program."[35]

Early in the morning on May 20, 1936, Herbert Lehman placed a phone call to the President, only to be told that Roosevelt was still in bed. Roosevelt returned the call "as soon as he got up," at which time Lehman informed the President that he was going to announce his decision not to run for re-election. According to James Farley, Roosevelt "tried to persuade Lehman not to make the announcement at this time," believing that the fifty-eight-year-old Lehman was overreacting to the death of his sixty-two-year-old brother Arthur a few days earlier, but Lehman refused to delay his announcement. Farley noted that "the President seemed terribly sore about it."[36]

Later that day, Herbert Lehman announced that he would not run for re-election as Governor, hoping that a public declaration would dissuade Roosevelt and others from trying to change his mind. Lehman was frustrated with the Republican State Assembly, which had adjourned without even voting on his social security program, and he knew that the Democrats' failure to reapportion the New York State Legislature in 1935, when they had controlled both houses, meant that the gerrymandered Assembly was likely to remain in Republican hands for the foreseeable future. The Governor, and even more so Mrs. Lehman, were also concerned about his health and well-being after eight hard years in Albany. Not only had his brother Arthur just died, but his seventy-two-year-old sister Settie Lehman Fatman had passed away in February. Mrs. Lehman believed that "the Governor has earned a rest" and she was "extremely glad" that her husband was "not going to run again." Herbert Lehman later recalled that after Arthur Lehman's death, "I felt that I owed it to my family, and to my brother's family, to go back into private life." The Governor distributed a statement to reporters in which he explained that "for almost eight years I have given to the work of the State all my time and all my strength." He had "greatly enjoyed these years of public office," and he was "deeply moved by and appreciative of the expressed desire of my friends that I should again stand for re-election." But he believed "that the time has come when I may ask release from the cares and responsibilities of the Governorship. Accordingly," Lehman declared, "I shall not be a candidate for re-election this Autumn."[37]

Despite Lehman's repeated insistence to Roosevelt that he would not run for re-election, the Governor's decision caught the President and his advisors by surprise. Roosevelt had always assumed that he could convince a reluctant Lehman to seek another term for the good of the state and the nation. Just two days before Lehman's statement, the President and James Farley observed that New York Republicans "had made a terrible mistake" in opposing Lehman's social security program. Roosevelt and Farley believed that Lehman and Democratic Assembly candidates "would have an excellent issue because of the Republicans' attitude on Social Security and they could win on it."[38]

The President, Mrs. Roosevelt, James Farley, and others immediately set out to persuade Lehman that his presence on the ballot was necessary for the Democrats to succeed nationally and in New York in 1936. When asked for his reaction to Lehman's announcement, FDR let it be known through a spokesman that he hoped that Lehman "would reconsider his decision . . . [and] change his mind." The *New York Times* reported that Farley and state Democratic leaders were considering formation of "a 'draft Lehman' movement," and Lehman was "deluged by messages demanding that he run again." At a press conference on May 22, the President reiterated his hope "that Governor Lehman would reconsider his decision to retire from politics, and become a candidate for re-election," asserting that "the people of New York State need him." Eleanor Roosevelt emphasized to Lehman "how dreadfully I feel about your announcement." She understood that the death of his brother, added to the Governor's previously expressed determination not to run again, "made this decision almost inevitable," but she wanted Lehman to know that she did not think that "any one can possibly take your place." With Lehman's departure, she predicted, "it is practically inevitable that New York State will be lost to the Democrats, including the presidential vote." When Maurice Davidson, a New York City attorney and a key member of the "good government" group that had helped elect Fiorello La Guardia as Mayor of New York City in 1933, informed the President that he and others were forming an "Independent Citizens' Committee . . . to prevail, if possible, upon Governor Lehman to reconsider his stand with regard to a third term," FDR repeated his hope that Lehman would change his mind because "the State of New York needs his fine services."[39]

It was not just the President and his advisors who believed that Lehman's presence on the Democratic ticket in New York in 1936 was crucial for the Democrats' success. *New York Times* columnist Arthur Krock described the Governor's withdrawal as "a body blow to the administration the effects of which will have to be determined later by the ringside physicians of politics." Krock noted, "Lehman has proved himself one of the greatest vote-getters in New York State political history, having polled half a million and a million votes more than Mr. Roosevelt and Alfred E. Smith in their State campaigns." Lehman's presence on the ticket, Krock observed, "draws votes to the whole party list which otherwise would not be drawn." Moreover, Krock argued, "the implication of support for the New Deal from a business man of Mr. Lehman's standing in the role of a fellow-candidate is invaluable to a national government under the fire of conservatives." Lehman's absence from the ballot, Krock claimed, threw into doubt the results not just in New York, but in the nation as a whole. Similarly, an editorial in the *Times* asserted that Lehman's decision had forced Democrats and Republicans "out of the electoral calculations which they had complacently made, and led them to reach again for pad and pencil in order to do some fresh figuring on the campaign outlook." According to the *Times*, "persons high in the Democratic board of strategy" had concluded "that it was exceedingly doubtful whether the President could carry his own State, without the aid of Governor Lehman as a running mate." The *Times* reported that most observers now believed that New York had moved from the Democratic column in the presidential race "to the list of doubtful states since the vote-getting Governor Lehman has decided not to head the State ticket next Fall," and that the Republicans had an opportunity "of recapturing control of the State government, electing a Governor and other State officers and defeating President Roosevelt in his home commonwealth." Interviewed years later, Mrs. Roosevelt, Samuel Rosenman, and Lehman aide Charles Poletti all remembered the widespread fear at that time that Lehman's absence from the Democratic ticket might cause the President to lose New York State and the election.[40]

Lehman did not accept the conventional wisdom that his withdrawal would have a significant effect upon the state and national races in 1936. He was confident Roosevelt and the Democrats would carry New York and that the President did not need him on the ballot to win the election. The Governor emphasized to Eleanor Roosevelt his eagerness "to help in every way" that he could, assuring her that his "time and efforts will be entirely at Franklin's disposal." Similarly, in an interview on the eve of the Democratic National Convention, Lehman stressed his intention "to make an active campaign for the re-election of President Roosevelt" and his confidence that FDR "will carry the State of New York by a very substantial majority."[41]

V

As the Democratic National Convention in Philadelphia in late June 1936 drew near, Herbert Lehman came under tremendous pressure to reconsider his earlier decision not to run for re-election as Governor. Rabbi Stephen S. Wise of the Free Synagogue in Manhattan expected that Roosevelt would carry New York regardless, but he believed that Lehman's presence on the ticket "would make that result in New York State certain," and he urged Lehman "to stand once more firmly and valiantly at the President's side, . . . to hold up the hands of the Leader whose continuance in office alone can ensure the preservation of those ideals of the democratic life in which we believe." Maurice Davidson and former State Supreme Court Justice John Mack of Poughkeepsie, a close friend of the President, organized a "State-wide Citizens' Committee for Lehman," with Lillian Wald as one of its honorary chairs. Mack announced that the committee was "exerting every effort to persuade Mr. Lehman to run" because they believed "he is the strongest candidate" and because "he would add strength to the national ticket." The New York Young Democratic Club unanimously adopted a resolution urging Lehman "to reconsider his decision not to be a candidate for re-election," declaring that Lehman's "record as Governor was such that all citizens of the State of New York could be proud" and asserting that Lehman's "consent to be a candidate of the Democratic Party would greatly assist the re-election of Franklin D. Roosevelt as President of the United States." The Executive Committee of the Queens County Democratic Committee importuned Lehman to run again, as did upstate Democrats from Erie County and suburban Democrats from Westchester County. James Farley told reporters that pressure was being brought to bear on Lehman not just by politicians, but also by businessmen and others who wanted the Governor to seek another term.[42]

Much of the attention at the Democratic National Convention focused on whether Lehman could be persuaded to run for another term as Governor of New York. Lehman's desire to do everything he could to ensure Roosevelt's re-election had left an opening that the President, Farley, and other Democratic leaders moved quickly to exploit, especially after Al Smith publicly declared his opposition to Roosevelt's re-election. The President and his advisors hoped that Lehman's presence on the ticket would offset any defections in New York resulting from Smith's hostility. Delegates from thirty-five states signed a petition urging Lehman to run again, and there were reports that a formal resolution might be adopted by the convention exhorting Lehman to seek another term as Governor. There was no precedent for a national party convention involving itself in a state race, but the New York Times noted that Lehman was "the man whom President Roosevelt would vastly prefer as standard bearer in the Democratic fight within his own state, which might tip the scale for or against his own re-election." Asked directly whether he would run if the convention formally asked him to reverse his earlier decision, Lehman showed that he was beginning to waver when he replied, "No comment."[43]

Roosevelt and Farley masterfully choreographed events at the 1936 Democratic National Convention to increase the pressure on Lehman to continue as Governor. They arranged for Lehman to give the main speech seconding Roosevelt's nomination for the presidency, which triggered what the *New York Times* described as "a series of tumultuous uprisings," second only to the cheers for Roosevelt himself. Farley had planned the lengthy demonstration, which was led by the New York delegation and included representatives of other states as well, waving banners and placards proclaiming "Lehman Must Run" and "New York, Draft Lehman." As Turner Catledge observed in the *Times*, the convention, "with two prolonged demonstrations for Governor Herbert H. Lehman and another for President Roosevelt, . . . attempted by a frank show of its enthusiasm to tie together the personalities of these two leaders for the campaign" and "add what they all considered a 'dynamo of strength' to the Democratic ticket next fall." Later that evening, FDR sent Lehman a telegram emphasizing that the "wonderful tribute to you came from the hearts of every State and you richly deserved it."[44]

As Roosevelt and Farley had hoped, the outpouring of support and affection for Lehman at the convention began to soften the Governor's resolve. Lehman told reporters that he was "deeply moved by the reception given me here this evening," which "surpassed anything I ever saw at a national convention. It was swell." When asked whether the convention had changed his determination not to seek re-election, Lehman refused to answer, a departure from his earlier insistence that his decision was final and an indication that he might be reconsidering. Even Mrs. Lehman, who had been so relieved by her husband's decision to withdraw from political life, had been thrilled by "the great tribute that has been paid him" at the convention and realized that it altered the situation. Lehman later recalled that even though he knew that the demonstration was less spontaneous than it had seemed—that it "had been, to a certain extent, inspired and encouraged by political leaders"—he was "touched by it, and gratified too."[45]

Roosevelt knew that Lehman was weakening, and he continued to work on the Governor as they traveled together from the convention back to Hyde Park, where they discussed the governorship for more than three hours. When Lehman had informed the President that he would not be a candidate for re-election, he had thought that Roosevelt agreed that Lehman's withdrawal would not affect the President's re-election chances, and that Roosevelt "was entirely satisfied with the national outlook generally." But the President now impressed upon Lehman "the *political importance*" of Lehman running again and warned that Lehman's retirement would imperil all the social welfare legislation they had worked to enact in Albany over the last eight years. Roosevelt later told Secretary of the Interior Harold Ickes that he had used every argument he could think of, including telling Lehman how important it would be to Jewish Americans if Lehman equaled Al Smith's record of being elected governor three successive times. The President complained to James Farley that Lehman wore out "fifteen dollars' worth of carpet" pacing at Hyde Park while trying to make up his mind, but Roosevelt was elated when Lehman finally consented to run if the President would formally ask him to do so, which would give the Governor a reason for reversing his earlier decision.[46]

Roosevelt quickly drafted both private and public letters asking Lehman to reconsider his decision not to run again for Governor. In the private note, which was handwritten and delivered to Lehman by state troopers, the President explained that the accompanying public letter was "clumsily expressed because it comes more deeply from my heart than I can adequately express on paper," and he apologized that "it isn't really strong enough about all the grand things you have done these four years." But, the President emphasized, "the more I look at it from every angle the more I'm convinced of the *very great importance of your running*—important to the social security of the whole nation in all that that implies." Roosevelt also noted that political considerations were important, too, and asked Lehman to telephone him with "any suggestions or amendments" the Governor wanted to make in the public letter.[47]

In his public letter, Roosevelt asked Lehman, for the good of the state and the nation, "to reconsider your statement that you would not run again." The President "fully appreciate[d] . . . and sympathized" with "the valid personal reasons" that had led Lehman to withdraw from the Governor's race, but he feared that if the state government came under Republican control, "many of the excellent laws put on the statute books during your four years as Governor would be repealed, weakened, or enforced by people who had their tongues in their cheeks." Under Lehman's leadership, Roosevelt asserted, New York had been a pioneer and a model for other states and the nation in the passage of "social legislation such as fair wage laws, unemployment insurance, old age pensions, [and] care of the destitute," as well as "legislation affecting public utilities and conservation and, in general, the lives of the average citizen." But all of this could be in jeopardy if the Democrats lost the governorship in the election. The President argued that Lehman's candidacy was important not just to New York, but to the entire nation, for other states often followed New York's example. He emphasized that the "magnificent and richly deserved tribute" that Lehman had received at the Democratic National Convention "shows what the other states think of your fine and successful leadership." He assured Lehman that reconsideration of his earlier decision "would make me very happy—more than that, it would make millions of people all over the United States very happy."[48]

On June 30, 1936, Herbert Lehman acceded to Roosevelt's wishes and announced that he would run for one last term as Governor. Ever since he had made his decision not to run for re-election, Lehman declared, he had "been deeply touched and stirred by the many expressions of confidence and friendship" he had received from all over the country. Lehman stressed that "regardless of personal considerations," he could "no longer resist the pleas" of those in his party with whom he had worked closely for many years in "the fight for equal opportunity and social security." As Lehman explained to his nephew Arthur Goodhart, "I realized that in loyalty to causes very dear to me I could not possibly refuse to at least offer myself for service to the people."[49]

Roosevelt and Democrats throughout the state and the nation rejoiced at Lehman's decision. New York State and National Democratic Chairman James Farley described the President as "elated over Governor Lehman's decision," and Roosevelt released his letter to Lehman to the press, emphasizing to reporters that Lehman's decision made him "very happy." The President stressed that Lehman's candidacy "will be a good influence for the carrying out of our program of social legislation in the broadest sense," and Farley asserted that Lehman "has made a remarkable record during his two terms and the next two years will enable him to carry out his program so necessary to the citizens" of New York. Farley was confident that "both Roosevelt and Lehman will carry New York State by greater majorities this year than they did in 1932." Felix Frankfurter congratulated the President on his handling of Lehman, noting that his "persuasion of Herbert Lehman has of course had psychological effects much beyond the immediate New York contest."[50]

New York Republicans derided Lehman's about-face, asserting that the pressure on Lehman to run was a sign of Roosevelt's weakness and Democrats' despair. State Republican Chairman Melvin Eaton charged that "after the thoroughly organized circus at Philadelphia and at the direction of President Roosevelt, Governor Lehman has consented to run for an office which he says he does not desire." Eaton argued that Lehman's "vacillation during the past six weeks and his final surrender despite his protests have not left him in a favorable light before the people of the State," and he claimed that "Republicans will enter the campaign with renewed strength and confidence" in their ability to defeat both Lehman and Roosevelt. New York County Republican leader Kenneth Simpson was even more critical of Lehman's change of heart, asserting that "the Farley-Roosevelt machine is in a panic, so a tired, unhappy Governor must be flogged back into the race." Simpson belittled Lehman's candidacy as evidence of the "desperation of the machine, hoping in vain to save the pivotal State of New York for Roosevelt at any cost."[51]

VI

Despite the Republicans' professed optimism, the *New York Times* reported that within hours of Lehman's announcement, the odds on Wall Street on the presidential election had risen from even money to 9 to 5 in Roosevelt's favor. *New York Times* columnist Arthur Krock estimated that Lehman's name on the ballot would attract fifty thousand to one hundred thousand additional voters in New York who would support the entire Democratic ticket and could provide the margin of victory for President Roosevelt in a close election. Similarly, James A. Hagerty reported in the *Times* that Lehman's decision to run again boosted "President Roosevelt's chance of carrying his home State of New York, . . . thereby adding to the prospect of his re-election." According to Hagerty, Republican presidential nominee Alf Landon needed to carry New York to win the election, but Lehman's presence on the Democratic ticket made that outcome highly unlikely. Hagerty predicted that "Lehman's candidacy will add at least 100,000 to the Roosevelt vote in New York City" because "many persons who otherwise might not register will do so to support Governor Lehman and his social-security program," and "virtually all of these also will vote for President Roosevelt."[52]

Many of these additional votes for Roosevelt and Lehman came through the vehicle of the American Labor Party (ALP), a new political entity established with Roosevelt's blessing by labor leaders Sidney Hillman of the Amalgamated Clothing Workers, David Dubinsky of the International Ladies' Garment Workers' Union, and Alex Rose of the Millinery Workers. Roosevelt saw the ALP as a means of weaning working-class Jewish and Italian voters away from their traditional ties to the Socialist Party while respecting their reluctance to vote for Tammany Democrats. Secretary of Labor Frances Perkins later recalled that Dubinsky had explained to her the rationale behind the formation of the new party:

> Our people are all Socialists. I've taught them for years to vote under the Socialist symbol. I can never teach them to vote under the Democratic symbol. We've been warning them for years to never vote for Tammany Hall. "Never vote for Tammany Hall. Tammany Hall is against the working man. Never vote under the star [the Democratic Party symbol on the ballot]." Now I can't teach them to vote under the star all of a sudden. I've got to have them vote under something that's got labor in it.

Democratic Party leaders Jim Farley and Ed Flynn had strong reservations about creating a new party, even if its purpose was to boost Roosevelt's and Lehman's vote totals. But the President, encouraged by New York City Mayor Fiorello La Guardia, who needed a political base for his own re-election campaign in 1937, overrode their concerns and gave his blessing to the ALP. Roosevelt and Lehman accepted the new party's endorsement, and they each received nearly three hundred thousand votes on the ALP line in the November election.[53]

Roosevelt's and Lehman's labor support extended beyond the needle workers who comprised the core of the ALP. William Green, president of the American Federation of Labor, urged delegates at the State Labor Federation's convention "to rally behind the Governor and march to the polls in November as one man to insure his re-election." Green proclaimed that Lehman, who had "made so many sacrifices for the working people, ought to be re-elected by the greatest majority given to any Executive." George Meany, president of the State Labor Federation, made the case for President Roosevelt, asserting that "no man in our nation's history has ever accomplished more for our common citizenry and no man is better qualified to lead the way in the direction of a better day for those who toil." The New York State Federation of Labor unanimously endorsed both the President and the Governor for re-election.[54]

Educators, too, supported Lehman and Roosevelt. Dr. George Ryan, chairman of the Educators' Committee for the Re-election of President Roosevelt and Governor Lehman and a former president of the New York City Board of Education, claimed that "President Roosevelt and Governor Lehman saved the schools of this State, the former by giving us money to erect sorely needed new buildings and the latter by insisting upon adequate appropriations of State aid to education." Ryan asserted that the "Roosevelt administration through the allocation of federal funds has made possible the erection of 195 school buildings in New York State, whose cost totals $76,970,634," while Governor Lehman "resisted all attempts to make drastic cuts in State appropriations to help pay the cost of conducting our educational program." According to Ryan, "Governor Lehman is one of education's staunchest friends and the schools of this State will forever be indebted to him for his determination to maintain educational standards."[55]

New York Republicans linked Governor Lehman and his policies with President Roosevelt and the New Deal, seeking to make the state election a referendum on national issues. At the Republican State Convention in September 1936, State Senator Benjamin Feinberg of Plattsburgh asserted that "it is impossible to discuss the impending State election without simultaneously discussing the national election . . . because the New Deal in Washington and in this State are one and the same." Feinberg denounced Roosevelt and Lehman as "administrative Siamese twins" who had "disregarded the scientific relativity between deficit and credit, between budget balance and budget collapse," and had "pursued policies of imposing ever-increasing tax burdens upon the people." According to Feinberg, the President and the Governor had "consistently sought to substitute propaganda for facts, deficits for deeds, administrative chaos for order, class appeals for government in the public interest, patronage for the proprieties, and bombast for needed action." At a Republican campaign rally in Brooklyn, Republican gubernatorial candidate William Bleakley belittled Lehman, describing him as a "robot Governor; one who responds to the political influences of the New Dealers in Washington," and GOP vice presidential candidate Frank Knox characterized "New York State as the New Deal colt tagging along behind its Washington mother, with the same habit of 'dashing in and passing laws without looking at the Constitution.'" Knox asked voters to "keep in mind what it costs to have a big New Deal in Washington and a smaller New Deal in Albany and a quintuplet New Deal in the five boroughs of New York City."[56]

Roosevelt and Lehman welcomed the association between the President's New Deal and the Governor's "little New Deal." On September 19, 1936, at a dinner hosted by the New York Young Democratic Club, Lehman defended the President against the charge that he was "fostering class feeling," noting that similar accusations had been made against Thomas Jefferson, Andrew Jackson, and Theodore Roosevelt. Lehman's experience, "both as a business man and as a public official," led him to conclude that such charges "may not be based so much on dislike of class feeling as it is on selfish opposition to the reforms advocated." He emphasized that it was impossible to "advocate and favor the recognition of and respect for the rights of labor . . . without disclosing the actual conditions under which our workers toil, without reviewing the pitiful wages that are paid to some of our women in industry and the long hours they have to work, without mentioning the advantages that large business organiza-tions possess as against unorganized workers." He stressed that there were "very fundamental differences between the two major parties in their philosophy of representative government," differences that had been clearly demonstrated in the last session of the State Legislature when the Democratic-led State Senate had passed his social security program unanimously, but the Republican leaders in the Assembly had "refused to allow the Social Security Bill even to come out of committee." Lehman called on people to reject "the Bourbon philosophy supported by virtually all of the responsible Republican leaders in this State" that was blocking the enactment of laws reflecting the Democrats' belief "that the functions of government went far beyond institutional care or the mere clothing and feeding of the indigent." In contrast to the Republicans, Lehman proclaimed, the Democrats believed "that it was the duty of government ever to strive toward securing greater social security for its people."[57]

The 1936 New York State Democratic Convention in Syracuse renomi-nated Governor Lehman and the entire Democratic state ticket by acclamation. In addressing the delegates, Lehman put to rest rumors that he was tired of being governor and would resign after the election, promising to serve the full two-year term. The Governor took pride in having reduced New York's deficit by almost one-half while maintaining "unabated the high quality of the services the State renders its people." Lehman noted that "during the past four years, in spite of militant opposition," he had "secured in this State the enactment of a program for the protection of the underprivileged and for the safe-guarding of the wage-earner that has no parallel in the history of any country." However, Lehman warned, "that program is now under ruthless attack of reactionary forces" and "can be maintained only if the Democratic Party is retained in office." If he were re-elected, Lehman promised, "social progress and sound administration will continue to be the foundation upon which the government of this State will stand."[58]

President Roosevelt delivered his first political speech of the campaign at the New York State Democratic Convention, adding excitement to what otherwise was a dull affair. Roosevelt's presence signified that the Democrats, too, saw the New Deal as the main issue in the state as well as the nation, and, as the *New York Times* noted, the President's appearance "aligned his national campaign . . . with the race for re-election to be conducted by Governor Lehman." Lehman introduced the President to the convention delegates and a national radio audience, describing him as "the man who changed despair to hope and confidence, and restored prosperity in our country." Roosevelt, in turn, praised Lehman to the hilt, telling his listeners that "the great tradition of a liberal, progressive Democratic Party has been carried still further by your present Governor, Herbert H. Lehman." The President stressed that Lehman

FIGURE 4.3. Governor Lehman and President Roosevelt campaign with members of the American Legion in Syracuse, New York, September 30, 1936. Courtesy of the Herbert H. Lehman Papers, Columbia University.

had "proved himself an untiring seeker for the public good; a doer of social justice; a wise, conscientious, clear-headed and businesslike administrator of the executive branch of our government."[59]

Lehman waged his usual vigorous campaign, emphasizing in particular his determination to see his social security program enacted, and President Roosevelt made a number of appearances in New York State in which he linked his own policies in Washington with Lehman's initiatives in New York. Addressing an enthusiastic crowd outside the Executive Mansion in Albany, Lehman introduced Roosevelt as "a great and beloved Governor of the State and a great and beloved President of the United States," and Roosevelt expressed his delight in returning to Albany, "a place that has meant so much in the lives of Mrs. Roosevelt and myself, especially when there are in the Executive Mansion two people of whom we are very, very fond, Governor and Mrs. Lehman." The President stressed that "we cannot afford to have any change in the occupants of the Executive Mansion for the next two years," explaining that he was "looking forward in the next two years at least, perhaps four years, to coming up to Albany with my wife to spend the day and visit with Herbert Lehman and his wife."[60]

On the eve of the election, W. A. Warn reported in the *New York Times* that "The Nation's Eyes Are on New York," where the campaign "has been fought almost exclusively with the New Deal at Washington and the 'little' new deal at Albany under Governor Lehman as the outstanding issue." Warn noted that "interest in the New York State election became country-wide and acute from the moment the Democratic National Convention, in its grandest gesture, proceeded to 'draft' Governor Lehman as a candidate for a third term . . . to make certain that Mr. Roosevelt would emerge a victor from the battle for the State's electoral votes." Warn could not predict which way the election would go, but he speculated that New York State, "with the largest city in the country and a small army of industrial workers," would "muster liberal supporters of the Roosevelt policies in sufficient numbers" to ensure FDR's and Lehman's re-election.[61]

If the 1936 election was a referendum on Roosevelt's and Lehman's leadership of the nation and the state, voters responded with an overwhelming endorsement of the New Deal and the "little New Deal." Lehman had been confident all along that Roosevelt would be re-elected by a large margin, but the Governor was "delighted" by "the huge pluralities" Roosevelt "received all over the country," carrying every state except Maine and Vermont, and triumphing in New York by a record-breaking margin of more than 1.1 million votes. The Governor believed that FDR's "magnificent victory" would enable the President "to carry on his splendid work in behalf of all the people of the nation."[62]

Herbert Lehman defeated William Bleakley by almost 529,000 votes, a comfortable win, but much smaller than the record-setting pluralities by which Lehman had won in 1932 and 1934, and much less than FDR's huge victory margin. Bleakley, an Irish Catholic from Westchester County, proved to be a more formidable candidate than Donovan or Moses, Lehman's two previous opponents, and he received a quarter of a million more votes in New York than Republican presidential candidate Alf Landon. This time Lehman received no help with Catholic voters from Al Smith, who was distressed over what he viewed as Franklin Roosevelt's taking the nation down the road toward socialism and communism. There were even rumors that Smith had helped the Republicans choose Bleakley as the strongest candidate to run against Lehman, although the GOP kept waiting in vain for Smith's expected endorsement of Bleakley. Running against a Catholic candidate and without the benefit of Smith's support, Lehman suffered defections from Catholic voters who were upset by his veto of a bill to provide free bus service for children attending parochial as well as public schools. Carolin Flexner, Lehman's longtime assistant, later recalled a priest in Troy who refrained from telling his parishioners whom to vote for, but as the people were leaving the church, he would remind them, "My friend Bleakley is a very fine man." Father Charles Coughlin, the fiery right-wing radio priest, had denounced Lehman's veto of the school bus measure as "the high-water mark of bigotry," and Arthur O'Leary, the president of the Catholic Laymen's League of Orange and Rockland Counties, had written a twenty-three-page letter, later circulated in pamphlet form, charging that Lehman's rejection of the school bus bill "was convincing proof that he believed in and, as Governor, actually put into practice the fundamental communistic tenet upon which all pagan and anti-Christian religious persecution is based, that the State must be the enemy of religion." O'Leary argued that "the American principle of freedom and education—inseparably connected as it is with freedom of religion"—superseded "allegiance or obligation to parties or political leaders," and that New Yorkers "have a patriotic duty to do our utmost to see to it that Governor Lehman retires to private life without further endangering that liberty of education and of worship which Christianity and Christian civilization established in Europe and brought to our land."[63]

By the end of 1936, Democrats and Republicans alike saw Herbert Lehman and Franklin Roosevelt as a team, the President's New Deal in Washington inspiring the Governor's "little New Deal" in Albany. They had not ended the Depression, but both men took pride and satisfaction in their accomplishments over the last four years as the federal and state governments had provided jobs and assistance to those in need. Their re-election in 1936 showed that the people of the state and the nation agreed with Lehman and Roosevelt that the government had a responsibility to help individuals buffeted by economic forces beyond their control. With lopsided Democratic majorities in Congress, Roosevelt looked forward to carrying the New Deal forward, while Lehman was eager to resume the battle with the recalcitrant Republican majority in the State Assembly that had opposed him on social security and other needed legislation.[64]

CHAPTER 5

"The End of a Beautiful Friendship"?

Lehman and Roosevelt, 1937–1939

Up to that time the two men had been Damon and Pythias, David and Jonathan and Castor and Pollux reduced to an essence.[1]

I

Herbert Lehman hoped that Franklin Roosevelt would attend his inauguration as Governor on January 1, 1937, especially since Roosevelt had played such a key role in persuading Lehman to run for re-election. In early December 1936, Lehman wrote to the President, asking him to "make my inauguration perfect by being with us and making an address." Roosevelt complained to aide Marvin McIntyre, "Governor Lehman begs me to go to his inauguration," and the President asked that Lehman be told "confidentially that I most certainly will if I possibly can." The President warned that "no story on it" should be released to the press "to avoid possible disappointment." Roosevelt informed Lehman, "I want and hope to come to Albany for the inauguration," but "from Christmas until early February I face a very tiring schedule," including not only "the Annual Message on January 3rd and the Budget Message on January 4th, but all the plans for the new Inauguration day, January 20th and, about the same time, a series of other messages to Congress." The President stressed that it was "only the physical aspect of the whole time which makes me hesitate about

---

Chapter title quotation: Arthur Krock, "In the Nation: Possible Effects of Governor Lehman's Letter," *New York Times*, July 20, 1937, p. 22.

a special trip away from Washington," but he promised to discuss it with Mrs. Roosevelt and assured Lehman that his "every intention is to come!" Lehman understood "how terribly busy" the President would be, but emphasized that it would "mean a great deal to Edith, to me and to our family, and it will also give the people of Albany and the State the keenest pleasure to have you here."[2]

Distressed that he could not get a definite answer from Roosevelt about the inaugural, Lehman wired the President on December 28 that they had "delayed in making the final arrangements" until they heard from him. Later that day, Roosevelt informed Lehman that although he had "been trying to arrange matters for Albany on January first," he reluctantly had to "agree with everyone else in the White House and Executive Offices that it would be folly . . . to attempt the trip." Pressing engagements in Washington on December 31 and January 2 would require him to take the night train to and from Albany, and it would just be too taxing on him physically. Roosevelt was "really deeply disappointed," because even though he had been present for Lehman's first inauguration, he had not been there for the second one in 1935. The Lehmans were "very sorry" that the President would not be attending the inauguration, but they did "not want to put any extra burden" on him or Mrs. Roosevelt. The President did send a telegram congratulating Lehman, which Secretary of State Edward Flynn read during the inaugural ceremony.[3]

In shaping his legislative program in 1937, Lehman gave priority to measures to implement the New Deal emanating from the Roosevelt administration in Washington and to solidify and extend the little New Deal in New York. Lehman's "first order of business," was his social security bill, which the State Senate again passed unanimously. This time, the Republicans in the Assembly, influenced by the election results, allowed the measure to come to the floor, where it was approved 115 to 20. The Governor "greatly rejoice[d] in the passage of the Social Security Bill," which he characterized as "a great step forward for the benefit of the handicapped and underprivileged men, women, and children of the State." He believed that the bill's enactment represented "a great victory for democratic government" because the people of New York had made their opinion known on this issue by supporting him for re-election. In his statement upon signing the law, the Governor emphasized that the bill aligned the state program with the federal program and would enable New York to receive more than $20,000,000 in federal funds. Any additional costs incurred by the state, Lehman explained, would be offset by savings for local governments.[4]

As he had done every year since he became Governor in 1933, Lehman called upon the State Legislature in 1937 to ratify the pending amendment to the U.S. Constitution to end child labor. The amendment had been passed by Congress and referred to the states for their approval in 1924, but strong opposition from farmers, business, newspapers, and the Catholic Church had blocked the measure in New York. Moreover, Al Smith, who had endorsed the amendment when he was Governor, had now gone over to the opposition, claiming that the amendment would give "the federal government complete control over the lives and daily habits of every person in the country below the age of 18." Lehman admitted to Lillian Wald that Smith's "opposition has unquestionably influenced a great many people." In 1936, a few of the amendment's opponents even resorted to anti-Semitic attacks, charging that the measure, "which Jewish Governor Lehman tried to railroad through the New York State Legislature . . . following previous action by Illinois under Jewish Governor Horner," was an attempt "to sabotage the U.S. Constitution."[5]

President Roosevelt supported Lehman's efforts to persuade the State Legislature to ratify the child labor amendment. At a time when the Governor and the President enjoyed considerable influence because of their recent re-elections, they persuaded Bronx Democratic leader Edward Flynn and Brooklyn leader Frank Kelly to support the measure despite the Catholic Church's opposition. Lehman and Roosevelt pushed so hard for the amendment that when it was approved by the Democratic-controlled State Senate in early February 1937, Republican State Senator Benjamin Feinberg charged that "Simon Legree" had "whipped the boys" in the Legislature into line. The Governor hailed the Senate's action, telling reporters it was "one of the happiest days of my life" because he had "been fighting for this thing since I was a young man." The President wired Lehman to express his pleasure at the Senate's action, reiterating publicly his strong support for this amendment "to protect the rights of childhood." He hoped that New York would soon be among the states to ratify the measure.[6]

Lehman's and Roosevelt's delight at the Senate's approval of the child labor amendment proved to be short-lived. When the Republican-dominated Assembly Judiciary Committee scheduled a public hearing on the measure in mid-February to slow down its momentum, the Governor emphasized to Secretary of Labor Frances Perkins that there was "no certainty of the bill passing in the Assembly," and he urged that "all proponents of the resolution present their side of the case as fully and forcefully as possible" to the Assembly. The President pitched in, sending a telegram to the Governor that was read at the hearings. Noting the State Senate's approval of the amendment, Roosevelt asked the Assembly to "take similar favorable action as quickly as possible." Mrs. Lehman hosted a luncheon at the Executive Mansion for supporters of the amendment, and the Governor made a special radio appeal on behalf of the measure. But much to Lehman's and Roosevelt's dismay, Catholic clergy across the state opposed the bill, condemning it, in the words of Bishop Edmund Gibbons of Albany, as "an unwarranted invasion of parental rights and a menace to the real welfare of millions of children throughout the entire nation." The opposition of the Catholic Church led a majority of Assembly Democrats to join with almost all of the Republicans to defeat the amendment in the Assembly by a vote of 102 to 42, after which Lehman described himself as "deeply disappointed."[7]

Lehman also called in 1937 for the enactment of a new minimum wage for women and minors to replace the New York State law that had recently been declared unconstitutional by the U.S. Supreme Court. The Governor stressed that "a large proportion of women employed in factories and stores in New York City are earning wages of less than $10 a week," leaving them "unable to support themselves," with the result that "their wages have to be supplemented by payments from relief bureaus." Republicans disingenuously called for the measure to include men, supposedly to help it meet constitutional muster, but Lehman warned that the inclusion of men would actually call into question the bill's legality by removing it from the realm of protective legislation for women and children that had previously been upheld by the Supreme Court in some instances. The Governor agreed with President Roosevelt that federal legislation was needed to provide wages and hours protection for men, asserting that only a law applying to all states could "release industry and labor as a whole from cutthroat competition based on labor sweating." When the Supreme Court upheld a Washington State minimum wage law for women in late March, Lehman quickly sent a new minimum wage bill for women and minors to the Legislature, which promptly enacted it into law.[8]

II

By 1937, Franklin Roosevelt, Herbert Lehman, and many others were increasingly frustrated by the conservative majority on the Supreme Court which had invalidated New York's original minimum wage law for women and nullified much of Roosevelt's New Deal. During the 1936 campaign, Lehman called for amending the Constitution if necessary to allow the states to pursue the "philosophy of progressive government," and in his message to the Legislature in January 1937, the Governor promised, "If it develops by decision of the Supreme Court that there is no effective means other than by prompt constitutional amendment" to enact legislation "to give our working women a decent wage," then he would urge prompt changes in the state and federal constitutions. But President Roosevelt, very much aware that the child labor amendment approved by Congress in 1924 was still languishing in the states, thought that a constitutional amendment would take too long and the outcome would be too uncertain, especially with the Social Security Act and the National Labor Relations Act among the legislation pending before the court. Moreover, the President believed that the problem lay not in the Constitution, but in the way a narrow majority of the justices were interpreting the nation's charter. The President stressed in his State of the Union address in January 1937 that "the vital need is not an alteration of our fundamental law, but an increasingly enlightened view with reference to it. Difficulties have grown out of its interpretation," Roosevelt explained, "but rightly considered, it can be used as an instrument of progress and not as a device for prevention of action." After summarizing what the executive and legislative branches of the government had done to meet the crisis of the Depression, Roosevelt argued that the American people also wanted "the judicial branch . . . to do its part in making democracy successful. We do not," he concluded, "ask the courts to call non-existent powers into being, but we have a right to expect that conceded powers or those legitimately implied shall be made effective instruments for the common good."[9]

On February 5, 1937, Roosevelt proposed legislation to "reorganize" the federal courts, allegedly to make them more efficient. The President asked for the authority to appoint, with Senate approval, additional justices, up to a maximum of six, for each Supreme Court Justice who reached the age of seventy and did not retire. Since six of the present justices were already over seventy, the proposal would allow the President to nominate six new justices immediately, who would quickly be approved by the huge Democratic majority in the Senate. Roosevelt's opponents denounced the bill as an attempt by the President to "pack" the Supreme Court with liberal justices who would rule in favor of the New Deal and expand the federal government's role in regulating the nation's economy.[10]

Despite Herbert Lehman's great friendship with and admiration and respect for Franklin Roosevelt, Lehman was willing to oppose Roosevelt when he thought the President was wrong, and as Lehman later recalled, he believed from the start that the President's court-packing plan "was an unwise proposal." Perhaps because his brother Irving Lehman was a judge on New York's Court of Appeals, the state's highest court, Herbert Lehman had an especially high regard for the separation of powers among the executive, legislative, and judicial branches of the government. Herbert Lehman's concern about unchecked executive power had led him to oppose New York City Mayor Fiorello La Guardia's request for what Lehman had denounced as "dictatorial powers" to deal with the city's fiscal crisis in 1934. As Lehman had explained to Lillian Wald at that time, he "felt terribly strongly with regard to the governmental principle involved," because he did "not believe that any man should have the powers alone" that La Guardia had sought. In 1955, when Lehman was a U.S. Senator, that same principle led him to oppose the Formosa Resolution because he feared that it gave President Dwight Eisenhower "a blank check" that he could use to involve the United States in a war in Asia.[11]

Lehman refused to comment publicly on Roosevelt's court-packing plan, hoping to discuss the matter with the President in person during an upcoming visit to the White House, but when state business prevented him from traveling to Washington, Lehman explained his concerns in a letter to the President. Although he shared Roosevelt's "disappointment that many important measures have been declared unconstitutional by a narrow and unconvincing vote of the

Supreme Court," Lehman believed that the President's goal of a more balanced
Supreme Court did not justify the remedy Roosevelt had proposed. Lehman
cautioned that "a mere enlargement of the Court will not remove the possibility of narrow decisions in the future," and he advised that "nothing should be
done which is merely an attempt to meet an immediate situation at the expense
of orderly and deliberate processes of government." He warned the President
that "whatever gain might be achieved through liberalizing the decisions of the
Court would be far more than balanced by the loss of confidence which would
result from the enactment of your proposals."[12]

Ignoring Lehman's private plea, as well as opposition to the plan from
many others who had supported the New Deal up to this point, Roosevelt
refused to abandon his court-packing proposal. Not even Supreme Court decisions narrowly upholding the Wagner Act and the Social Security Act, conservative Justice Willis Van Devanter's announcement of his upcoming retirement,
and the death of Senate Majority Leader Joseph Robinson (D-AR) could change
the President's mind. The only concessions that Roosevelt made were agreeing
to raise from seventy to seventy-five the age that would allow the appointment
of additional justices and limiting such appointments to one per year. Otherwise, he remained adamant about enlarging the Supreme Court so he could
add liberal justices.[13]

After wrestling with his conscience for months, Lehman reluctantly decided to go public with his opposition to the court-packing plan as the Senate
was about to vote on the measure. Charles Poletti, the Governor's counsel, later
recalled spending many hours with the Governor and Mrs. Lehman discussing
whether Lehman should speak out against the bill. According to Poletti, the
issue was "torturing" the Governor, who was "torn between disapproval of the
recommendation of the President and at the same time his sincere devotion
to the President," but Lehman "felt that it was important to his own integrity
that he have a public declaration of his position." The Governor later recounted
simply that he was "increasingly concerned" that "it was going to be very
close in Congress," that the bill would pass, giving the President "the power of
reorganizing the Supreme Court." Lehman explained that he "had come out
publicly" against the measure because he "thought it was necessary . . . to help,"
so far as he could, in defeating the proposal.[14]

Lehman announced his opposition to the court-packing plan in a letter
to Senator Wagner, who had not yet taken a position on the proposal. Much
to Wagner's annoyance, the Governor's letter was released to the press on July
19, before Wagner had even received it, and it put pressure on the Senator
to come out for or against the measure. Lehman noted that "the President is
already familiar with my views" that the enactment of his court plan "would
not be in the best interest of the country." The Governor shared Roosevelt's
"disappointment that important legislative measures have been declared uncon-

FIGURE 5.1. "Why Herbert!" by Rollin Kirby in the *New York World-Telegram*, July 20, 1937. By permission of the Estate of Rollin Kirby Post.

stitutional by a slim and unconvincing margin in the Supreme Court," but he emphasized that "the orderly and deliberate processes of government should not be sacrificed merely to meet an immediate situation." Lehman stressed that "whatever immediate gains might be achieved through the proposed change in the court would . . . be far more than offset by the loss of confidence in the independence of the courts and in governmental procedure." He believed that the New Deal "represented the greatest step forward in social reform that any nation had undertaken for many years," but he feared that passage of Roosevelt's court bill "would create a greatly dangerous precedent which could be availed of by future less well-intentioned administrations for the purpose of oppression or for the curtailment of the constitutional rights of our citizens."[15]

Lehman's public opposition to the court-packing bill caused quite a storm in Washington. On July 20, the *New York Times* ran a banner headline, "Lehman Calls Court Plan Dangerous," on the front page and featured nine separate stories plus an editorial about the letter. James Farley and other administration spokesmen tried to minimize the potential impact of the Governor's letter, but Lehman's public stand against the bill made it easier for other liberals and New

Dealers to oppose the measure. Senator Burton Wheeler (D-MT), who was already leading the opposition to the bill, pointed out that Lehman "has been one of the outstanding liberal leaders of the country and a particularly close friend of the President," yet his "views on the court plan are identical with those expressed by us who are opposing it," and Senator Joseph O'Mahoney (D-WY) asserted that Lehman's letter "sets at rest any contention that opposition to the bill involves either any lack of sympathy with the general aims of the administration or lack of personal loyalty to the President." Few people in public life were more closely associated with Roosevelt and the New Deal's social policies than Herbert Lehman, and as the *Times* noted, this was Lehman's "first opposition to any major proposal in President Roosevelt's program since their personal and political friendship began in 1928." A few days after the release of Lehman's letter, the Senate voted to send the court bill back to the Judiciary Committee, from which it never returned. The court-packing plan was dead, and according to Turner Catledge of the *New York Times*, Lehman's letter was "among the final thrusts which spelled doom" for the President's proposal.[16]

Roosevelt and his closest aides were furious that Lehman had gone public with his opposition to the court-packing plan; in their view, Lehman had failed what they saw as a crucial test of loyalty to the President and his program. Farley and Roosevelt agreed that "Lehman had 'butted' into a situation wherein he had no right at this time" and that the Governor's letter was "out of order." The President confided to Felix Frankfurter that he was "hot all over regarding Herbert Lehman's letter. Some things just aren't done—they violate the decencies of human relations and offend the good taste and the decorum of friendship." Roosevelt complained that it was not "cricket" for Lehman to come out publicly against the proposal at this late date, when the Senate was about to vote on it. Unnamed administration officials quoted in the *New York Times* described Lehman's letter as "gratuitous" and "a stab in the back," and Secretary of the Interior Harold Ickes wrote in his diary that "the letter from Governor Lehman to Senator Wagner proved to be extremely harmful. It was a devastating shot directed with deadly aim just at the right time."[17]

The President and his advisors were particularly annoyed by Lehman's public opposition to the court-packing bill because they believed it stemmed from Lehman being angry at Roosevelt. Ickes recorded in his diary a conversation with the President during the court fight in which Roosevelt claimed that Lehman resented the President pressuring him to run for re-election in 1936 and then failing to attend his inauguration in Albany. According to Ickes, "someone, the President doesn't know who it was, told Lehman that he had been played for a sucker, that all Roosevelt had wanted of him was to help him out in New York State and that the demonstration" at the Democratic National Convention "had all been staged in order to overcome his resistance to the idea of running again."[18]

There is no evidence to support the President's belief or Ickes's contention that the Governor was motivated by personal pique rather than principle in opposing the President's court-packing plan. Lehman was disappointed that Roosevelt had not attended his inauguration, but he understood why the President could not be there, and their interactions over the following few months do not suggest that the Governor held a grudge against the President. Lehman went to Washington for the ceremonies and festivities when Roosevelt was inaugurated for his second term in January 1937 and congratulated the President on his "stirring and inspiring" address. The Lehmans were "delighted" to receive a medal from the President commemorating the inauguration, and the Governor served as "Honorary Chairman for New York for the Birthday Ball for the President" later that month. The Lehmans looked forward to staying over at the White House in late February after a birthday party for Elinor Morgenthau, but they had to cancel at the last minute when the Governor had to remain in Albany to work on the child labor amendment and other pressing state matters. In a speech before the Albany County Democratic organization in early March, Lehman compared FDR's re-election to that of Thomas Jefferson, asserting that "Jefferson's victory was significant as the first success of liberalism over the forces of reaction [and] President Roosevelt's re-election marked a vitalization of liberal government," and he congratulated the Roosevelts in June on their son's marriage. None of these interactions is particularly significant in itself, but together they show that Lehman and Roosevelt continued to be on good terms even after the President's failure to attend Lehman's inauguration. As Charles Poletti later explained, Lehman "wasn't conscious of the timing" of events in Washington, and once he made up his mind to speak publicly, "he just shot out" the letter to Senator Wagner.[19]

The President and Ickes also believed, correctly, that Mrs. Lehman had played a key role in her husband's decision to oppose the President's court-packing plan, but they erroneously attributed her position to her being mad at Roosevelt for not letting her husband retire from the strenuous job of being Governor. Mrs. Lehman was certainly her husband's closest advisor on most issues, and she clearly had wanted him to withdraw from public life rather than running for re-election, but there is no reason to believe that her opposition to the court-packing plan stemmed from personal reasons. At the beginning of the controversy, Mrs. Lehman sent a "personal" letter to Senator Wagner in which she voiced her strong opposition to "so radical a change in our structure of government." She warned that "we, who have confidence in our present leader in the nation, might conceivably live to rue the day that we had failed to raise our voice in protest of vesting such wide additional powers in the hands of one man." Charles Poletti later confirmed Mrs. Lehman's major role in the Governor's decision, noting that she had been present when the issue was discussed "for weeks and weeks and weeks" at the Executive Mansion, and that the Governor had reached his final decision to send the letter to Senator Wagner and release it to the press when he and Mrs. Lehman were alone on vacation. President Roosevelt later conceded, perhaps inadvertently, that Mrs. Lehman's stand was based on principle when he told Ickes that Mrs. Lehman had bragged that her husband's letter to Senator Wagner had "saved the Supreme Court and, with it, our constitutional form of government."[20]

Besides his wife, Herbert Lehman probably consulted with his brother, New York State Court of Appeals Justice Irving Lehman, about the President's court-packing plan. The brothers were very close and spoke "each Sunday morning to compare notes and to check up on what had occurred in the interval," and Herbert Lehman later recalled that even after Irving became a judge, "he always maintained his great interest in politics. He and I used to discuss a great many things. We were always on the same side—we always looked on things pretty much the same way." After the Governor sent his letter to Senator Wagner, Irving Lehman congratulated him on his "timely and courageous message" and had "little doubt that it had very considerable influence" in defeating the President's proposal and "preserving the independence of the court." Irving emphasized that "no one had a right to stand aside" in this "very great crisis if he could help materially in averting it." The court bill's supporters might resent the Governor's involvement, but Irving understood that "in view of the strength of your convictions, you could not do otherwise and you have reason to be well satisfied with its result."[21]

New York Times columnist Arthur Krock speculated that the split over the court-packing bill might mark "the end of a beautiful friendship" between Herbert Lehman and Franklin Roosevelt, who, until then, "had been Damon and Pythias, David and Jonathan and Castor and Pollux reduced to an essence." Lehman later recalled that their disagreement over the court bill "ushered in a low point in my relationship with the President," who "was disappointed that I had come out publicly against his position," and Samuel Rosenman, a confidant of both men, related that the dispute led to "a very distinct coolness for a considerable period of time. Roosevelt not only was hurt but he resented it." James Farley later wrote that Lehman's letter "had put his friendship with Mr. Roosevelt 'on ice,'" and Eleanor Roosevelt noted that in the aftermath of the court-packing controversy, "there was a certain amount of coolness for a little while between Herbert and Franklin . . . a kind of tension between them." Over the next twelve months, there were no invitations to the Lehmans to visit the White House, and Lehman and Roosevelt did not appear together in public except when Lehman attended a White House luncheon as part of a group of seventeen governors.[22]

Lehman's opposition to the court-packing plan led Secretary of the Interior Ickes, the leaders of the American Labor Party, and others to question Lehman's liberalism. Ickes was convinced that Lehman was "a conservative," and

Alex Rose, executive secretary of the ALP, accused Lehman of lending "aid and comfort, as well as material support, to the reactionaries." Ignoring Lehman's liberal record as Governor, *The Nation* suggested that Lehman's objections to the bill came from "his friends in the banking fraternity," and the editors at the *New Republic* charged that "Lehman, like many other Democrats, is and always has been a conservative, as one could expect from his career in a Wall Street banking house." They alleged that Lehman had "supported President Roosevelt out of party loyalty and personal friendship" rather than a strong belief in liberal principles, and they claimed that "like many conservatives," Lehman "was willing to accept a certain amount of social legislation designed to cover up some of the more glaring inequalities created by private capitalism," but he would not support "a plan that cuts really deep." The *New Republic* asserted that Lehman's opposition to the President's court bill "illuminates as clearly as anything else in recent times the fact that Democrats are not necessarily progressives and that we still need a realignment of parties in this country to conform with political reality."[23]

III

Roosevelt and his aides did not quickly forgive or forget those who had crossed them on the court-packing plan, including Herbert Lehman. A month after the proposal's rejection, Assistant Secretary of the Treasury Stephen Gibbons relayed to the President a report that Lehman, immediately upon winning re-election in 1936, had allegedly asked about ships leaving the United States on January 2, 1939, when his new term would be finished. The Governor supposedly did not care about the destination "as long as he got out of the country." Gibbons claimed that this anecdote helped explain Lehman's public opposition to the court plan, and he believed that Lehman "is more to be pitied than censored, as the pride of Lucifer himself could hardly create a more distorted psychology." Roosevelt considered this "a grand story," but he disagreed with Gibbons's conclusion that Lehman was finished with politics, noting that "a little bird tells me that the editorial approval of the gentleman's statement on the court plan has puffed the gentleman up so that the gentleman may be a candidate again in 1938!" A few months later, when James Farley suggested that "Governor Lehman might want to run again," Roosevelt agreed, asserting that "Mrs. Lehman likes to be first lady of the State." But Roosevelt alleged that Lehman "spends a lot of time [at his vacation home] in Westchester and doesn't work like he did." When the *American Hebrew* magazine asked for a tribute it could use in a special issue in March 1938 celebrating the sixtieth birthday of "Herbert H. Lehman: American," White House assistant Stephen Early wanted to bury the request in the files, but he forwarded it to Missy

LeHand, the President's personal secretary, realizing that "there may be others with more generous, bighearted and forgiving dispositions than mine." Roosevelt told Early to explain to the editor that he could not "send a congratulatory message properly through a magazine or paper but that on the 28th of March" he would "doubtless send a telegram of congratulations direct to the Governor." On Lehman's birthday, the President did send a brief note extending his "hearty congratulations and all good wishes for a happy birthday."[24]

Herbert Lehman hoped to secure the Democratic nomination for the Senate in 1938, but the rift between the Governor and the President helped prevent that from happening. As the 1938 elections approached, Lehman was even more determined to leave the governorship than he had been in 1936, and there was talk again of Lehman and Senator Wagner trading positions. Lehman was very interested in running for the Senate; as he explained to Lillian Wald, he knew that "the work of a Senator is extremely hard and taxing," but he believed it would "not impose the same degree of strain and unending responsibility as the governorship, while the opportunities it offers for service are not substantially less." He was also concerned, as he later recalled, that the nation was "drifting nearer and nearer to war . . . that war was inevitable," and he believed that in the Senate he could help ensure that the United States was "giving help to our Allies and taking steps towards adequate preparedness."[25]

Secretary of the Interior Ickes and others did not look favorably on the possibility of Lehman and Wagner switching places. Lehman's opposition to the court-packing bill had convinced Ickes that the Governor was not in sympathy with the New Deal, and Ickes believed that the proposed swap "would be replacing a fighting liberal with a conservative and it would not be so good either for the Senate or the administration." The editors of *The Nation*, who had always questioned Lehman's liberalism because of his banking background and alleged ties to Tammany Hall, agreed that "drafting Wagner for the governorship and running Lehman for the Senate in Wagner's place . . . would replace a strong liberal in the Senate with a man more to the liking of the financial interests." But Senator Royal Copeland's death in June 1938 opened up New York's other seat in the U.S. Senate, meaning that Lehman could run for the Senate without displacing Wagner.[26]

As James Hagerty observed in the *New York Times*, "The only doubt about Governor Lehman's nomination for Senator, if he should desire it, was said to be the difficulty of obtaining the approval of President Roosevelt." When Lehman formally announced his candidacy for the Senate on June 21, declaring that "if my party desires me to be a candidate for the office of United States Senator to succeed Senator Copeland, I will accept the nomination," Hagerty noted that "the nomination of Governor Lehman for Senator is known to be unsatisfactory to President Roosevelt." However, Warren Moscow reported in the same newspaper that most people in Albany believed that "there is no one in the party, including President Roosevelt himself," who could deny Lehman the Senate nomination. According to the Associated Press, Lehman's candidacy "created something of a sensation" in Washington, where observers wondered what the President would do about "the senatorial aspirations of the man universally credited with dealing one of the strongest blows at the Roosevelt court reorganization bill."[27]

Lehman had informed James Farley at Senator Copeland's funeral that he was going to announce his candidacy for Copeland's Senate seat, and Farley had passed the news on to the President. According to Farley, Roosevelt was irritated that Lehman had not given state Democratic leaders an opportunity to discuss the situation before declaring his candidacy, complaining, "the Governor should have had more confidence in us and should have come to us with his desires." FDR and Farley realized there was little they "could do beyond seeking to persuade Lehman to sit tight and not rock the boat," and they considered Lehman's announcement precipitous, coming before Copeland was even settled in his grave.[28]

An editorial in the *New York Times* hailed Lehman's candidacy, asserting that "certainly no man in public life in the State of New York is better equipped by experience and by temperament and by character for membership in the Senate of the United States." But Mayor Fiorello La Guardia and some of the leaders of the American Labor Party disagreed and urged President Roosevelt not to endorse Lehman's nomination. La Guardia had feuded with Lehman for years over New York City's finances and its relations with the state and was interested in the Senate seat for himself, while some of the leaders of the ALP hoped to increase their leverage by forcing the Democrats to accept an ALP candidate for the Senate nomination, possibly Sidney Hillman, the president of the Amalgamated Clothing Workers and one of the party's founders. Neither La Guardia nor the ALP leaders referred specifically to Lehman's opposition to FDR's court-packing plan, but they did so by implication when La Guardia, who had always questioned whether Lehman was a "real progressive," emphasized that "the essential need is for persons who will support good, sound, progressive policies in Washington, Albany, and New York." David Dubinsky, whose International Ladies' Garment Workers' Union had been saved by a no-interest loan from Lehman in 1928, was more circumspect in his remarks, mentioning no names but declaring that the ALP "is in sympathy with the New Deal and is ready to support outspoken New Dealers." For some people, Lehman's opposition to the court bill disqualified him from the ranks of the "outspoken New Dealers."[29]

President Roosevelt was not enthusiastic about Lehman's bid for a Senate seat, but conventional wisdom held that he would acquiesce in Lehman's nomination for political reasons. According to the *New York Times*, Farley realized and would explain to the President that "the Governor would add strength to the Democratic State ticket," warning that "a Democratic defeat in his home state . . . would be accepted throughout the country as a forerunner of Democratic defeat in the 1940 election." But Roosevelt made no public comment on the situation in New York. On June 22, when reporters asked Lehman whether he had heard from the President since announcing his candidacy the previous day, Lehman said he had not talked with Roosevelt before declaring his candidacy and had not heard from the President since the announcement. Two days later, the President laughed off the press's efforts to get him to comment on Lehman's candidacy. On June 25, the *New York Times* reported that according to FDR's "close political advisers," the President was "ready to endorse" Lehman for the nomination "when the situation in New York crystallizes and the party leaders are in agreement as to the entire ticket, including the candidate for Governor," but no such endorsement of Lehman's Senate candidacy ever came.[30]

Lehman's candidacy experienced a roller-coaster ride of highs and lows in the next few weeks. First, Mayor La Guardia removed himself from consideration for the Senate so he could continue what he described as his efforts to provide the people of New York City with "a nonpartisan, nonpolitical and scientific administration." But La Guardia pointedly refused to endorse Lehman's nomination. On the contrary, the Mayor's assertion that "the people of this State desire a progressive to represent them, one who has the courage of his convictions and who understands conditions," was widely understood as an attack on Lehman, as was his contention that "any official in a responsible position who thinks of another office or a coming election is like a one-armed driver of a high-powered car driving full speed with a charming companion. His mind cannot be fully on his work."[31]

Any relief Lehman felt at La Guardia's withdrawal was short-lived, however, as the Governor's liberalism and his candidacy continued to come under attack from the left. In early July, the *New Republic* complained that the Governor's candidacy "meant that Mr. Lehman and the relatively conservative Democratic elements about him meant to continue their undivided control of the State machine," and the leaders of the American Labor Party endorsed a slate of candidates that included Sidney Hillman for the Senate rather than Herbert Lehman. *The Nation* welcomed Hillman's possible candidacy, asserting that "Lehman's conservatism makes his inclusion on a labor ticket anomalous despite a good record in supporting labor legislation," and the *New Republic* reported that ALP strategists had shunned Lehman because they believed that the President "meant to wage war on Democratic conservatives, particularly those who had opposed the reorganization of the Supreme Court," including Herbert Lehman. David Dubinsky, remembering all that Lehman had done for the ILGWU, immediately deplored the ALP's action, pointing out that "though we may not have agreed with all Governor Lehman has done or said in the last year, he is undoubtedly a staunch and sincere friend of labor, with an admirable labor record." He wondered how the ALP could ignore Lehman's "record and valuable services." Luigi Antonini, state chairman of the ALP, agreed that "Governor Lehman has proven himself to be a staunch friend of labor" who would certainly be endorsed by the ALP if he were to run for re-election as Governor. But Lehman's Senate candidacy was more complicated, Antonini explained, because "the American Labor Party is committed to support of the New Deal." Antonini noted that "Lehman has been a supporter of President Roosevelt except on the one issue of reorganization of the Supreme Court," and that because of Lehman's stand on that matter, "there have been reports that President Roosevelt is opposed to the election of Governor Lehman to the Senate." Antonini claimed not to "know whether there is any truth in these reports."[32]

Not only did Roosevelt fail to squelch reports that he was opposed to Lehman's candidacy, he seemed to go out of his way to provide further evidence of what the *New York Times* called the "breach between the President and the Governor." On July 5, 1938, Governor Lehman proudly proclaimed that the New York State budget had been balanced and that he had eliminated the $100,000,000 deficit he had inherited. A few days later, while campaigning in Kentucky for Senator Alben Barkley, who was locked in a close primary race against Governor A. B. Chandler, the President minimized Chandler's accomplishment in balancing Kentucky's budget. But rather than confining his remarks to the situation in Kentucky, Roosevelt belittled Lehman's achievement in New York as well, mocking "your Governor, my Governor and a good many other Governors [who] are able to go before their people and announce proudly that they have balanced budgets. More power to their arms!" Roosevelt pointed out the problems he had faced as Governor, when he "could get no assistance from Washington" and had been "compelled to create State deficits—to put the State treasury into the 'red'—in order to feed the destitute and give work to the unemployed; in order to care for the thousands of people who had become dependent on the State for food and shelter." In contrast, the President emphasized that his New Deal had "put a national shoulder under national problems" and instituted "work relief paid for by the Federal Government . . . which took the support of men, women and children off the backs of communities." According to FDR, it was only "because of that help from the national government" that "many of our States . . . my own State of New York—and your own State of Kentucky among them," have "got back into the 'black' again." Lehman refused to comment on the President's speech, but Republican State Senator Thomas Desmond characterized the President's remarks as another example of the deteriorating relationship between Lehman and Roosevelt.[33]

IV

As the 1938 elections drew closer, the President finally took the initiative to repair his relations with Governor Lehman. At Roosevelt's behest, Bronx Democratic Chairman and New York Secretary of State Edward Flynn met with Lehman in late August, noting that the President had written Lehman a while ago, inviting him to Hyde Park, but Lehman had never responded. The Governor made it clear that the only correspondence he had received from the President in recent months had been an acknowledgment that Roosevelt had received the copy of the Executive Budget that Lehman had sent him, on which the President had written, "I do hope to see both you and Edith this summer." Regardless, Flynn explained that the President wanted Lehman to call for an appointment so the two of them "could discuss the political situation."[34]

Offended that Roosevelt had resorted to "an intermediary" rather than contacting him directly, Lehman wrote the President a very blunt letter in which he tried to clear the air between them. Lehman lamented, "the impression is widespread both in New York State and elsewhere that there has been a breach between us" because Lehman had opposed the President's court-packing bill. Since that time, Lehman noted, "there have appeared in the press many articles to the effect that you had taken great offense at my action and that our relations were no longer friendly." Lehman stressed that he had "neither done or said anything, nor left anything unsaid or undone that might stimulate these rumors," but Roosevelt had done nothing to contradict or dispel such reports, and the President's silence had "added fuel to the fire." Lehman was especially disappointed that after all their years working together, the President had not even expressed his "good wishes" when Lehman had announced his Senate candidacy, and Lehman had been told that Roosevelt did "not look with favor on my candidacy." Lehman believed that his record entitled him to Roosevelt's support, and he assured the President, "I will always be ready to come to see you at Hyde Park or Washington at your request or on your invitation." But Lehman emphasized that the invitation had to come from Roosevelt; otherwise, "the impression would be created that I had done so for the purpose of enlisting your help in my candidacy." Lehman hoped that the President would "understand the spirit in which this letter was written," and he sent his "kindest personal regards" to the President and Mrs. Roosevelt.[35]

Roosevelt realized that it was time to put Lehman's opposition to the court-packing bill behind them; he knew that the Governor's presence on the Democratic ticket was vital if the party were to retain its hold on statewide offices. New York's elections also carried national implications for the future. As the *New York Times* noted, Republican victories in the Empire State "would encourage Republicans throughout the country to hope for a victory in the presidential election of 1940." Roosevelt knew that he and Lehman would both be attending the ceremonies in Poughkeepsie on September 17 to celebrate the 150th anniversary of New York's ratification of the U.S. Constitution, and picking up on Lehman's suggestion in his recent letter, the President invited the Lehmans to join the Roosevelts at Hyde Park for lunch that day. Roosevelt hoped that "after all these years it goes without saying that you are very welcome at any time." The Governor immediately replied that he was "very glad indeed to accept" the President's invitation. The crisis in Czechoslovakia prevented Roosevelt from meeting with Lehman that day, but the planned get-together demonstrated that the wall between Roosevelt and Lehman had been taken down. The Governor made sure to pay tribute to Roosevelt in his remarks in Poughkeepsie, regretting that the European crisis had kept the President in Washington and announcing that he had sent a telegram extending to the President "the hearty wishes and greetings of his fellow-citizens of the State of New York." Meanwhile, Roosevelt's aides let it be known that Lehman "remains in the President's view essentially a New Dealer at heart."[36]

Roosevelt and New York Democratic leaders wanted Lehman on the ticket in 1938, but they wanted him to run for Governor again, not Senator. The President had looked far and wide for a viable Democratic gubernatorial candidate, but with no success. Roosevelt had first tried to interest Postmaster General and Democratic National Chairman James Farley in running for Governor, but Farley had rejected the suggestion, arguing that he could not afford it financially and that his wife did not want to live in Albany. The President had then sought to advance Assistant Attorney General Robert Jackson for the position, but as Mayor La Guardia reported to the President, "Jackson is not at all known . . . he is not identified with any particular achievement or standing," and "he would require a great deal of building-up, hand-shaking and getting around." The Mayor warned that "the mere discussion of Jackson among politicians, before and after cocktails, brings out possibilities of Herbert." The idea of Governor Lehman and Senator Wagner swapping positions resurfaced, but Wagner refused to give up his seniority in the Senate, where he hoped to complete work on "a number of important legislative projects." In a conversation with Farley, Roosevelt recalled how he had prepared for his successor as Governor by doing "everything possible to put Lehman in the limelight," including sending him "to different places throughout the State so he could be better known," and he lamented that "the trouble with the Democratic Party now is that they haven't built anyone up, particularly upstate."[37]

Democratic leaders realized by this time that Lehman was the only Democrat who could defeat Thomas Dewey, the ambitious, young, racket-busting prosecutor who was the likely Republican candidate for Governor of New York in 1938 and a possible Republican presidential nominee for 1940. Roosevelt, Farley, Flynn, and the others warned Lehman that a Republican Governor serving for four years (the state constitution had recently been amended to lengthen the Governor's term of office) could undo much of the good work that Al Smith, Roosevelt, and Lehman had accomplished in Albany. But Lehman resisted all their efforts, and when he left to attend the Democratic State Convention in Rochester in late September, he later recalled, there was not "the slightest doubt in my mind that I would run for the Senate."[38]

Farley and other party leaders started working on Lehman as soon as the Governor arrived in Rochester. After conferring with Ed Flynn, Brooklyn leader Frank Kelly, the O'Connells from Albany, and other chieftains from across the state on the train en route to Rochester, Farley was convinced that "there was nothing else to do but renominate Governor Lehman, despite his wishes to retire to run for the Senate." According to Farley, they all agreed that Lehman would be the Democrats' strongest candidate because "the arguments that Dewey might offer against Lehman would not hold water inasmuch as Governor Lehman appointed him and the Lehman record is something he cannot touch or talk against." Farley arranged for the leaders to meet with Lehman upon the Governor's arrival in Rochester, and although they expressed sympathy for Lehman's desire to leave the governorship, they warned that Dewey's election "would upset all the good that had been done by the Democratic Administration since 1922" and argued that Lehman "should run to carry out his social welfare program." As Farley noted, however, none of their arguments "seemed to have any effect," and they agreed to resume their discussions the next day. As the meeting concluded, Farley predicted to Lehman that "the delegates would take the matter out of the hands of the leaders, and no matter how the Governor felt, he would be drafted by them." When Farley asked if Lehman had any objection to Farley telling the press that he was "personally . . . of the opinion that the convention will draft Governor Lehman," Lehman said he could not prevent Farley from doing so, as long as Farley made it clear that Lehman had not approved any such statement. Farley saw this as the first hint that the Governor was weakening and would eventually accede to the party's desire that he run again. They "were getting closer to the nominations," Farley noted, and Lehman "did not close the door." Farley also thought it was a good sign when Lehman agreed to hold their next meeting at ten Thursday evening, leaving little time to find another candidate if Lehman were going to decline.[39]

The Democratic leaders, led by Farley, pulled out all the stops in their effort to persuade Lehman to accept renomination. They dispatched various Jewish leaders and social welfare advocates to meet with Lehman to urge him to run, and the Monroe County Democratic organization staged a rousing reception for Lehman when he arrived at the train station, followed by a torchlight procession to his hotel. When Farley mentioned Lehman by name during the convention's opening session, a fifteen-minute demonstration ensued, with placard-carrying delegates marching and cheering, "We want Lehman!" The Governor later recalled that Farley was "the main man—who persuaded me to run again in 1938."[40]

Farley conferred by phone with President Roosevelt, briefing him on the meeting with Lehman and Farley's growing confidence that "we could get him to make the race." When Farley asked whether the President "would wire Lehman, if we wanted him to do so," Roosevelt "said he would gladly do so, but he thought it would not be good judgment." Lehman agreed with the President; when Farley asked if he wanted the President to call, the Governor made it clear that he "did not want to be beholden to Roosevelt, and if he did run, it would be on his own, without any drafting." Wanting to have further ammunition ready to use with Lehman "as a last resort," Farley raised with the President the possibility of appointing Herbert Lehman's brother Irving to the vacancy on the U.S. Supreme Court resulting from the recent death of Justice Benjamin Cardozo. Roosevelt had great respect for Irving Lehman's distinguished record as an Associate Justice of the New York State Court of Appeals and told Farley that "nothing would give him any greater pleasure" than elevating Irving Lehman to the Supreme Court. However, the President explained that "the appointment would have to go West" because there were no justices from states west of the Mississippi River. Moreover, Roosevelt asserted that Irving's age—he was in his mid-sixties—precluded such an appointment because it would make the President's "argument regarding the age of the jurists look foolish."[41]

When Lehman met with Farley and the party leaders again Thursday evening, Farley was confident that the Governor would yield. Lehman raised certain conditions that would have to be met if he were to run, the most important of which was his insistence that Charles Poletti, his former counsel whom he had appointed to the New York State Supreme Court the previous year, replace Lieutenant Governor William Bray on the Democratic ticket. Lehman had never developed much of a relationship with Bray, and he wanted a Lieutenant Governor in whom he had confidence, one who could relieve some of the heavy burdens of the job, much as Lehman had done for FDR. Mrs. Lehman was then invited to the meeting because everyone realized that her acquiescence would be essential if the Governor were to run. As Lehman later described it, Farley "really put the heat on" him "and on Mrs. Lehman, who had to make the decision" with him. The conference broke up around midnight, without Lehman making a commitment, and they all agreed to meet again Friday morning at nine, just five hours before the nominations were scheduled to begin.[42]

By this point, as Mrs. Lehman told the press, she had become "reconciled—completely" to her husband's renomination. She admitted that she was less than "jubilant" about how events had transpired, but she understood that "the Governor's decision, in view of the circumstances, was the only possible one to make." As she explained, "I care too much, like all the citizens of the State, about the record which I have seen grow during the past six years, to want to see it placed in jeopardy. And you get to the point where you feel that perhaps your own inclinations and preferences are not the most important things."[43]

Herbert Lehman finally consented to run for Governor one last time, and he based his decision in large part on the Republican nomination of Manhattan District Attorney Thomas Dewey for the governorship. During their meeting the previous night, Farley had made certain that Lehman was aware of Dewey's speech to the Republican convention in which Dewey had attacked Lehman's honesty and integrity, charging that in New York, "any Democratic Governor is, perforce, the good-will advertising, the front man, the window dressing for what is in part, at least, a thoroughly corrupt machine." Trying to link Lehman to Tammany Hall and corruption scandals in New York City, Dewey had alleged that "the objectives of respectable Governors have been dangled as bait before the people by an organization whose sole purpose was politics for profit." Dewey's remarks infuriated Lehman, who resented these attacks on his character, especially since it was he who had appointed Dewey in 1935 "as special prosecutor to act against racketeering and corruption in office in New York City." The Governor also believed that Dewey, who had just been elected to his present position in 1937, owed it to the people of Manhattan to remain as District Attorney for more than one year. Departing from political tradition, Lehman referred to Dewey by name during his acceptance speech to the Democratic convention, pointing out that Dewey "had no record of accomplishment in the fields of social or labor problems or in their relation to business and government." Lehman asserted that there was no indication that Dewey was "familiar with either the fiscal or social problems of government of a great State of 13,000,000 people," and he maintained that Dewey lacked the "experience or training" necessary for the governorship. As Lehman later recalled, he "was very fearful that if Dewey was elected he would undo a great many things, much of the progress that we had made, that President Roosevelt and I had made, in the previous fifteen or twenty years." Farley and the others had convinced Lehman that he was "the only man who could beat Dewey."[44]

With the Governor renominated for another term, President Roosevelt made it clear to all that the rift between him and Lehman was now completely healed. At Farley's suggestion, Roosevelt sent a telegram to the Democratic convention in which he proclaimed his happiness at "the willingness of Governor Lehman to accept renomination." The President "realize[d] the personal sacrifice which this involves," but he was "certain that the people of our State will continue to approve the forward-looking, businesslike and clean government" Lehman had provided. FDR congratulated the convention on "insuring the continuation of liberal democratic government in my own State." The *New York Times* reported that at a press conference later that day, "The President was lavish in his praise of Governor Lehman," declaring that Lehman "had been a perfectly splendid Governor during his six years in Albany." The *Times* noted that although the President "did not join publicly in the 'draft-Lehman' movement," he had discussed the matter thoroughly with Farley, and that "it was with the President's approval" that Farley had urged Lehman to accept renomination for another term as Governor. When syndicated columnist Raymond Clapper alleged that Roosevelt had "become very bitter about Governor Lehman" and had accepted the Governor's renomination only because Lehman was seen as a means of stopping Dewey's presidential ambitions, White House aide Stephen Early immediately informed Clapper that "at all times (despite the Court letter, etc.), the President has said that Governor Lehman should run for renomination." Roosevelt's "statements to this effect," Early emphasized, "were made long before Senator Copeland died or before Dewey gained prominence as a possible Republican nominee for the governorship." The President had always believed, Early claimed, "that because of Governor Lehman's splendid record in Albany, he would run victoriously if he would accept the nomination for another term."[45]

After the convention, Robert Jackson summed up the feelings of those close to FDR, stressing to Sam Rosenman that "the friends of the President have reason to feel extremely happy at the result." Jackson thought that "Lehman was the most certain and perhaps the only man who could stop the Dewey movement," and he believed that Lehman's acceptance speech, which could only have come from the man who had appointed Dewey, had "completely deflated the Dewey movement."[46]

When Lehman had originally announced for the Senate in June 1938, the American Labor Party had refused to endorse him because his opposition to the court-packing bill had led party leaders to question whether he could be counted on to support FDR and the New Deal completely. State ALP Chairman Luigi Antonini had suggested at that time, however, that if Lehman were to run again for Governor, the ALP would certainly support him. The ALP had backed Dewey for District Attorney in 1937, but its leaders realized now that a Dewey victory over Lehman, in the words of the *New York Times*, "would be hailed throughout the country as repudiation of the Roosevelt policies in the President's home State and possibly make the District Attorney, of whose views on labor and social welfare legislation they have no knowledge, the Republican nominee for President in 1940." At the ALP convention in early October, the ILGWU's David Dubinsky recalled how Lehman had repeatedly mediated labor disputes in the garment industry, and he described the Governor as "the outstanding champion of liberalism in this great Empire State, one who so ably defended the interests and welfare of all groups of our citizens, one who enjoys the absolute confidence of the working masses of our State, one who represents so marvelously the progressive, courageous and forward-looking spirit of our times." The delegates agreed, and the ALP nominated Lehman for Governor by acclamation.[47]

The editors of *The Nation* and the *New Republic* were ambivalent about Lehman's nomination for another term as Governor. The *New Republic* cheered his withdrawal from the Senate race in favor of Representative James Mead, "a *thoroughgoing* New Dealer," but they worried that Lehman "as New York Governor, . . . could have a 'moderating' influence on New Dealers at the 1940 Democratic convention." *The Nation* was more enthusiastic about the Governor's re-election, noting that Lehman "lacks any flair for the histrionic, but by sheer devotion to the public services has won an extraordinary public esteem," especially among "the workers of the State." While the editors still wondered what had motivated "his attack on the President's court plan," which seemed "for a time to push him into the arms of the conservatives," they predicted that such heresy would now prove valuable in winning support from "Republicans who are impressed with his businesslike conduct of affairs at Albany and pleased with his anti-administration stand on the Supreme Court issue last year." *The Nation* also warned that a defeat for Lehman and the Democrats in Roosevelt's home state would be seen as "a serious setback for the New Deal" and "a blow from which Roosevelt could scarcely recover."[48]

V

In contrast to the President's active role in several 1938 Democratic primaries, in which he tried with little success to purge some of the party's more conservative senators and representatives, Roosevelt played only a minor part in the general elections. Despite pleas from party leaders, Roosevelt refused to campaign for the Democratic candidates for Governor or Senator in Pennsylvania, and he made it clear in early October that he "did not plan to make any campaign speeches outside his own State." That suggested to the *New York Times* that Roosevelt did plan to make "one or more speeches on behalf of the New York State Democratic ticket and the candidacy of Governor Lehman in particular." At a press conference on October 4, Roosevelt explained that he had no specific plans to speak in New York, but he did expect to meet with Governor Lehman to discuss the campaign.[49]

The President offered unsolicited advice to the Lehman campaign on a number of occasions. In a memorandum to the Governor, FDR passed on an upstate Republican friend's suggestion that Lehman and the Democratic ticket should try to appeal to farmers and consumers by adopting the slogan of "five cent milk at the farm, and ten cent milk on the street." The President realized that "this may be a pretty difficult thing to carry into effect," but he thought it could be accomplished "over a period of two or three years." When another friend predicted that Dewey would not carry Upstate by a sufficient plurality to win the state in this nonpresidential election year, Roosevelt hoped that his calculations were correct and suggested that "the best line that can be circulated in up-State New York—especially among Republican or Independent voters—is

'I propose to vote for Dewey—to continue as District Attorney for the balance of his term.' "[50]

Roosevelt understood that Lehman's re-election as Governor was anything but assured. As one observer reported confidentially to the President, although "Lehman would be the betting favorite in this election, and Dewey the long-shot," there were "various new factors to be taken into consideration." Unlike so many failed Republicans in New York in recent years, Dewey was not running against the New Deal; instead, Dewey was "campaigning as a 'liberal,' labeling the Democrats as 'radical,' and . . . concentrating on crime and corruption as his selling-points." Lehman, "the old champion," was described as "pretty well played out," as evidenced by the fact that "although he had been 'drafted' to aid the President's campaign" in 1936, he had "trailed Roosevelt in the State" by a substantial margin. More importantly, Dewey's "histrionic ability on the radio," which gave him "a direct appeal to the people, and especially to women," was contrasted with Lehman's unexciting delivery and estimated Crossley rating—a measure of how many listeners a radio broadcast had—"of about 0.0000002." This prognosticator predicted that Dewey would defeat Lehman or come very close to doing so.[51]

The President assured Jim Farley that he wanted "to do all he can" to aid Lehman's re-election, and at his press conference on October 14, Roosevelt revealed that he would be meeting with Lehman at Hyde Park the following week to discuss the campaign. The *New York Times* noted that this would be Roosevelt and Lehman's first meeting since the Governor's "attack on the administration's plan to reorganize the Supreme Court—a criticism which many administration officials credit with having turned the tide against the court plan." Later that day, Press Secretary Stephen Early announced that Roosevelt would speak on a radio hookup from Hyde Park on the Friday before the election, explaining that "while the President's remarks primarily will concern the voters of New York State, they will be sufficiently extensive in range to interest the nation as a whole."[52]

Lehman's meeting with Roosevelt at Hyde Park on October 18 made the front pages, but not because of their two-hour discussion of the Governor's campaign. When reporters confronted Lehman shortly after the meeting, they focused not on New York State matters, but on the Governor's support for the New Deal. According to the *New York Times*, Lehman "appeared surprised and somewhat puzzled that he should be called upon to answer questions concerning his attitude toward the national administration," questions that *Times* columnist Arthur Krock suggested had been planted by White House aides. But the Governor made it clear that he had not compromised any of his beliefs to win FDR's approval. Despite repeated attempts by reporters to get him to give a blanket endorsement to the President's policies, Lehman declined to do so, declaring that he was "going to discuss many issues during the campaign" and that "my speeches will reflect my attitude toward the many issues involved." When reporters asked whether Lehman's campaign was going to be based on his support of Roosevelt and the New Deal, and whether his refusal to endorse the New Deal in total meant that he opposed it in part, Lehman just reiterated that people would have to "wait and see," that his views would be made clear during the campaign.[53]

The Governor's refusal to declare his wholehearted support for Roosevelt and the New Deal dominated the news coverage of Lehman's campaign for the next few days. The editors of the *New York Times* emphasized that in the New York gubernatorial election, "the question at issue is not one of endorsing the National Democratic Administration," but "whether the people of this State should not take advantage of their present opportunity to retain the services of a conscientious, self-reliant public servant who has administered a great trust with deep care, marked success and a fine fidelity to principle." However, even in the *Times*, the headline read: "Lehman Silent on the New Deal after His Talk with Roosevelt," and the *New York Daily News* proclaimed that "Lehman Refuses to O.K. New Deal at F.D.R. Parley." A few days later, when Senator Wagner was asked after meeting with the President whether "Democratic candidates for State office should declare their support of the Federal Administration and of the President in their campaign speeches," he tried to calm the troubled waters by responding, "I think they should and I think they do." A reporter persisted, pointing out Lehman's apparent reluctance to support the President and his policies, but Wagner refused to take the bait, praising Lehman as "a great liberal and a great humanitarian . . . [who] has been an excellent Governor." Wagner noted that he himself had "voted against some of the measures proposed by the Administration in Congress. But that does not mean that I do not support the New Deal and the President."[54]

Dewey expected the support of Mayor La Guardia, his running mate in 1937 on the Republican, ALP, Fusion, and Progressive Party lines, but the Mayor, not wanting to offend the President who had provided so much federal aid to New York City, instead proclaimed his neutrality in the gubernatorial race. Farley urged the President to get "a little rough" with the Mayor, to "positively bear down on him" to endorse Lehman, advising FDR to remind the Mayor of all the assistance he had received from the Roosevelt administration. The President met with La Guardia at Hyde Park a few days after Lehman's visit, but the Governor's reluctance to embrace every aspect of the New Deal gave the Mayor a way out of his dilemma. Speaking with the press after conferring with the President, La Guardia criticized Lehman's failure to endorse the New Deal, asserting that "the Governor should have answered those questions and let the voters know where he stood." When asked directly whether he supported Lehman's re-election, the Mayor finessed the issue, declaring that he would "endorse and support every candidate for the Senate and the House who can be depended upon to support the present National Administration." He maintained that "support of the National Administration is a factor not only in this State campaign but in the nation as a whole."[55]

Roosevelt did what he could to minimize the growing controversy. The President instructed Missy LeHand, his private secretary, to advise a supporter "not to believe all the silly stories you read in the papers." Following Roosevelt's directive, LeHand emphasized that "the President is wholeheartedly for the re-election of Governor Lehman and the other candidates on the Democratic ticket and has said so many times." Lehman finally put the issue to rest in a speech in Oneonta on October 22 when he called upon New Yorkers to elect Democratic Senators "to strengthen the hands of President Roosevelt in his humane legislation."[56]

Lehman faced numerous obstacles in his bid for a fourth term as Governor in 1938, including voters' displeasure with the New Deal at a time when the economic recovery had faltered, and growing concern that Roosevelt, in trying to pack the Supreme Court and purge conservative Democrats, was seeking to centralize too much power in the White House. Dewey attacked Lehman's efforts to implement the New Deal in New York, charging that "the Governor should be more than a branch manager in a chain store system of national politics." The indictment and trial of Tammany district leader James Hines on charges that he was connected to the Dutch Schultz gang, followed by allegations of widespread corruption in Brooklyn District Attorney William Geoghan's office, fed into Dewey's accusations that the Democratic political machines were in bed with "the criminal underworld." Lehman was also threatened by large-scale defections from Catholics, who were upset that Lieutenant Governor William Bray, a Catholic, had been dropped from the Democratic ticket and replaced by Charles Poletti, Lehman's former counsel. An endorsement from Al Smith would have helped Lehman minimize his losses among Catholic voters, but Smith rejected Farley's and Lehman's requests that he speak on the Governor's behalf. Finally, there were also rumors that if Lehman were re-elected, he planned to resign shortly after his inauguration, leaving Poletti as Governor.[57]

Lehman dealt decisively with all these issues and more during the campaign. He quickly disposed of the concerns about his willingness to serve as Governor. In contrast to Dewey, who was seeking to leave the Manhattan District Attorney's office to which he had just been elected in 1937, the Governor pledged that if he were re-elected, "I shall, God willing, carry on the duties of that office with all the strength and power that is in me for the full term for which I am elected." Lieutenant Governor Bray agreed to help buoy Lehman's backing among Catholics, dining with the Governor at the Executive Mansion, publicly declaring that he "was whole-heartedly supporting" Lehman "and the entire Democratic ticket," and introducing the Governor at a campaign rally in Utica, Bray's hometown. Poletti assuaged some concerns about his religious background and his political beliefs when he responded to the Reverend Edward Curran, president of the International Truth Society, who had questioned both, assuring the priest that he rejected "both reactionary and radical government" and that he "believe[d] profoundly in the worship of God." Poletti explained that his parents, who were part of an Italian American immigrant community in Vermont, had not raised him in any faith, and that an Italian Baptist missionary had baptized him and several other boys in the neighborhood at the age of twelve. Lehman moved against criminal elements in Brooklyn, superseding District Attorney Geoghan for the third time to ensure a far-reaching investigation into the rackets and any ties between criminals and politicians. The Governor repeatedly emphasized his experience and his record over the past ten years, asserting that "the issue in this campaign is simple and clear. Do the people of this State wish the continuation of a proven liberal, progressive, humane and efficient government, or do they wish to yield to the seductive promises from a party whose record in this State belies its promises?" The Governor and Poletti also rejected any support from the Communist Party, which had withdrawn its nominees for state offices and urged its members to vote for the candidates of the American Labor Party, including Lehman and Poletti. When Dewey disparaged the governorship under Lehman as "a mere bookkeeping job," Lehman proudly accepted the description and seized the opportunity to compare his own financial experience with Dewey's lack thereof. "Where would the State be today," Lehman asked, "if the Governor had not had full understanding of the financial problems which Mr. Dewey likes to call 'bookkeeping?'" Lehman hated "to think what would happen to the State if its administration was turned over to a Governor who belittles the importance of sound finance."[58]

As Election Day neared, Roosevelt and his advisors agreed with the *New York Times* that a Dewey victory "would be accepted throughout the nation as a personal defeat for the President and a forerunner of a Republican victory in the presidential election of 1940." Alarmed at poll results that showed Lehman and Dewey "running neck-and-neck," the Roosevelt administration stepped up its efforts on behalf of the Governor. Trying to boost Lehman in upstate rural areas where Dewey was running especially well, Secretary of Agriculture Henry Wallace characterized Lehman as a "100 per cent New Dealer" on agricultural issues who had coordinated his programs with the national government, resulting in the "enormous benefit which farmers and consumers of New York State have reaped from the federal programs of soil conservation, milk marketing, cattle disease eradication and the buying and distribution of surplus farm products."[59]

Worried that Lehman "may win by not more than 150,000" and that Wagner might lose, the President asked Assistant Secretary of State and La Guardia confidant A. A. Berle whether he "could get La Guardia to give some

FIGURE 5.2. Governor Lehman shakes hands with Mayor La Guardia after their joint radio appearance, November 6, 1938. AP Images.

help." Under pressure from the White House, La Guardia inched toward a formal endorsement of Lehman, but he never could quite get the words out. The Mayor went out of his way to pick up the Governor at his Manhattan home to ride together to Councilman B. Charney Vladeck's funeral on November 2, and citing sources "close to the Mayor," the *New York Times* reported the next day that La Guardia had "definitely decided to support Governor Herbert H. Lehman." Speaking at an American Labor Party rally on November 4, La Guardia referred to Lehman as "our great Governor of New York," and the next day he praised an FDR radio address for Lehman as "a very splendid statement on behalf of a progressive Governor." Asked by the press if he would be "more specific in endorsing a candidate for Governor," La Guardia growled, "What do you want me to do? Draw you a picture?" Two days before the election, the Mayor and the Governor appeared together on a radio show discussing the proposed amendments to the state constitution, at which time the Mayor "readily posed for photographs shaking hands with Governor Lehman." As Arthur Krock noted in the *New York Times*, despite his reluctance, the Mayor had little choice but to back Lehman, however grudgingly and belatedly, if he wanted to keep his credentials as a New Dealer and retain the support of the ALP for his future political career. Dewey may have expected the Mayor's support, but his constant criticism of the New Deal during the campaign made it impossible for the Mayor to support him; to do so would have jeopardized the Mayor's cozy relationship with the President and the federal aid that flowed to the city as a result of that connection.[60]

On Friday, November 4, President Roosevelt delivered a national radio address in which he urged his fellow New Yorkers "who are interested in preserving good government and American democracy to vote for Herbert H. Lehman." Without mentioning Dewey by name, Roosevelt criticized the Republican candidate's youth and inexperience. The President recalled that when he was Assistant Secretary of the Navy in 1918, he had declined to run for Governor because "he did not think it quite right to abandon in mid-stream an important public job that I had undertaken." Roosevelt was only thirty-six years old then, the same age that Dewey was now, and the President realized in retrospect that he had lacked "the experience and knowledge of public affairs" necessary to govern New York State. FDR warned that "a social or an economic gain by one administration . . . may, and often does, evaporate into thin air under the next one," and he emphasized that New Yorkers "cannot take the risk of supplanting seasoned leaders like Governor Lehman with men, no matter how sincere, who have yet to win their spurs or prove what they really know or where they really stand in the fight for social justice." Over the last sixteen years, Roosevelt asserted, New York had enacted "a magnificent liberal program," and Lehman's re-election was necessary to "maintain, preserve and improve the great body of social legislation already on the statute books of the State—unemployment insurance, workmen's compensation, social security, help for the needy and the underprivileged." Herbert Lehman appreciated the President's kind words, and James Farley claimed that Roosevelt's "magnificent address . . . put the finishing touches" to Dewey's campaign. George Gallup, director of the American Institute of Public Opinion, later noted that the President's speech was "generally credited with tipping the scales in favor of Lehman in that extremely close race."[61]

During the last few days of the campaign, Dewey, Roosevelt, and Lehman all deplored the introduction of prejudice and anti-Semitism into the race. Republican leaders, including Lieutenant Governor candidate Fred Bontecou, were urging people to "Vote American," to "Save Our State for Americans," and to "Keep the American Way," which Lehman and the Democrats interpreted as attempts to dissuade voters from supporting the Jewish Governor. In a statement on November 3, Dewey regretted that "whispers concerning racial and religious prejudices have been injected into this campaign on both sides" and declared that "the man or woman who votes for a candidate because of his race or religion or votes against him for such a reason is a disgrace to American citizenship." Asserting that "there are some things more important than being elected Governor, and one is a spirit of religious and racial good-will," Dewey repudiated "any support based on racial or religious prejudice" and emphasized that he "would rather go down to defeat than be elected by any votes based on race or religion."[62]

Despite Dewey's denunciation of racial or religious appeals, Democrats feared that the "anti-Semitic whispering campaign" upstate might cost Lehman the election. In his radio broadcast on November 4, President Roosevelt exhorted voters to choose their candidates "without regard to race, creed or color," and Lehman noted the next day that Republican leaders were still using the same anti-Semitic slogans. The Governor stressed that "the perils of toying with bigotry for political advantage must be recognized and rejected by the rank and file of party workers and each and every voter throughout the State. Only in that way," he asserted, "can the cornerstone of our liberties be kept clean of the corroding acid of intolerance." Lehman emphasized that he had never, and did not now, "seek the support of any one on the ground of race or creed," and he asked for support solely on the basis of his "record as Governor" and his "unflagging devotion to those principles of true Americanism which are dear to the voters of this State."[63]

Nationally, Republicans picked up eight Senate seats, eighty-one House seats, and thirteen governorships in 1938, but in New York, Governor Lehman narrowly won re-election. The only Democratic Governor elected north of the Mason-Dixon line and east of the Mississippi River, Lehman defeated Dewey by 67,506 votes. The Governor carried New York City by 681,369 votes, barely offsetting Dewey's strong showing upstate where he outpolled Lehman by 616,975 votes; the 419,979 votes Lehman received on the American Labor Party line provided his margin of victory. Lehman's plurality trailed those compiled by Senator Wagner and the other statewide Democratic candidates, who faced much weaker opponents. As the *New York Times* noted, "Dewey's personal popularity brought him more than 200,000 votes from people who voted solely for him and apparently did not cast a ballot for any other candidate for any other office whatsoever." According to the *Times*, Lehman had successfully overcome the cumulative impact of Dewey's

> personal crusade against organized crime, . . . the fresh interest
> kindled by a new personality, . . . the natural tendency of the pen-
> dulum to swing against the continued success of any party which
> has been in power over a long period of years, . . . the renunciation,
> by Mr. Dewey and his colleagues, of the old Republican position of
> unfailing opposition to progressive legislation, and their willingness
> to identify themselves with the objectives of Governor Lehman's
> own social program.

And La Guardia's reluctant backing of Lehman, even if it was worth considerably less than the two hundred thousand votes City Hall sources had predicted, certainly helped in such a close election.[64]

As Arthur Krock observed in the *New York Times*, if not for New York, the election "would have been a disaster for the Democrats and the New Deal." Roosevelt and the Democrats suffered serious setbacks nationally with the defeat of such New Deal stalwarts as Governor Frank Murphy in Michigan, but the President took some solace in the results in New York. White House secretary Marvin McIntyre reported that the President "heard the New York returns with a big grin on his face. He was very happy." FDR called Lehman to congratulate him and was greatly pleased that Senator Wagner and James Mead, who had both campaigned primarily on their support of the New Deal, won New York's two Senate seats. The only sour note came from Secretary of the Interior Harold Ickes, who had not forgiven Lehman for opposing the court-packing bill. Ickes wrote in his diary that "Lehman would not have been re-elected if the President had not come out for him the Friday night before the election." Ignoring Dewey's strength as a candidate, as opposed to the weakness of the Republican Senate aspirants, Ickes publicly asserted that Lehman "just squeaked through and the liberals ran far ahead of him" because of the Governor's refusal to endorse the full agenda of the New Deal. But Ickes soon learned that the differences between Lehman and Roosevelt were minor compared to the distance between the New Deal and the coalition of Republicans and conservative Democrats that formed in Congress after the 1938 elections to block further liberal reforms.[65]

VI

Personal, political, and social contacts between Herbert Lehman and Franklin Roosevelt increased significantly in 1939, further evidence that the rift between them over the court bill had healed. When the President attended the opening of the World's Fair in Queens in April 1939, Governor Lehman was among the small group that dined with him, and when twenty-four governors and their wives lunched at Hyde Park in June, Mrs. Lehman was seated at the President's table. The social highlight of the year was the picnic that FDR threw for the King and Queen of England at Hyde Park at which hot dogs were the main course, and again the Lehmans were seated in places of honor, the Governor sharing a table with the King, the President's mother, and Elinor Morgenthau, while Edith Lehman was seated with the President, the Queen, and Secretary of the Treasury Henry Morgenthau, Jr. The Governor also had the great pleasure in 1939 of signing into law "the bill permitting 'one Franklin Delano Roosevelt of Hyde Park, Dutchess County, New York,' to build a library at Hyde Park," jurisdiction over which would be transferred to the federal government when the Franklin D. Roosevelt Library was established.[66]

Lehman and Roosevelt both confronted hostile legislatures in 1939. Although Democrats still maintained nominal control of Congress, conservative Democrats joined with Republicans to block most of the President's initiatives. Lehman tried to help ward off major cuts in WPA funds, warning the Senate Appropriations Committee that "any reduction in the Federal appropriation which would require the dropping of needy employable persons from the Federal Works Progress Administration rolls more rapidly than they can be absorbed by industry" would "cause great suffering and misery." Nonetheless, an economy-minded Congress cut $150,000,000 from Roosevelt's request for WPA funds, voted to investigate the WPA and the National Labor Relations Board, stripped the President of his authority to devalue the dollar, rejected his proposed $3.86 billion in loans for housing and other programs, and refused to revise the neutrality laws.[67]

In New York, even though the Democrats had swept all the statewide races in 1938, Republicans had retained their majority in the State Assembly and had captured control of the State Senate as well. Senate Majority Leader Joseph Hanley declared that Republicans were "determined that this nation should not be choked to death and killed under a burden of excessive and unnecessary expenditures," and Republican Assemblyman James Wadsworth argued that "the people no longer want service after service, appropriation after appropriation, tax after tax." Reflecting these sentiments, Republican legislators accepted the Governor's suggestion to raise the liquor tax to help meet a projected budget deficit, but they rejected Lehman's proposal to increase business and real estate taxes, imposing a cigarette tax instead. Believing that economy was going to be a major issue against the Democrats in the 1940 presidential election, the Republicans cut $25,000,000 from the Governor's proposed budget for state agencies and aid for schools and highways. Lehman challenged the legality of the reductions in funding for state agencies, asserting that the Legislature's use of lump-sum appropriations for each agency rather than reducing, striking out, or inserting items on a line-by-line basis "would destroy the executive budget" process established under Al Smith and successfully defended by Franklin Roosevelt in 1929. When the State Court of Appeals upheld Lehman's position, he hailed the decision as "a great victory for governmental procedure within the Constitution," and President Roosevelt immediately wired Lehman: "Delighted you won budget case by unanimous vote. Congratulations." However, the Republican Legislature refused to restore any of the cuts and merely repassed them as specific line items, satisfying the state's constitutional requirements.[68]

By the middle of 1939, Herbert Lehman and Franklin Roosevelt had weathered the worst storm in their long political relationship. It had taken more than a year, but they had finally moved past the Governor's public opposition to the President's court-packing plan, and Lehman had been re-elected to an unprecedented fourth consecutive term as Governor of New York. The two men hoped to continue implementing and expanding New Deal programs in Washington and the little New Deal in New York, but they both faced recalcitrant legislators reluctant to go along with such measures. Moreover, Lehman and Roosevelt both recognized that the growing threat posed by Nazi Germany and fascism in Europe would occupy more and more of their time and attention in coming years.

CHAPTER 6

"Fighting for Freedom, for Security, and for the Dignity of Man"

Lehman and Roosevelt, 1933–1942

I felt certain that what was happening in Germany would in time be bound to involve the world in another war, in which we ourselves would participate, and I was convinced that Roosevelt had great concern about the matter too.[1]

I

Herbert Lehman and other leading American Jews feared the worst after Adolf Hitler and the Nazis came to power in Germany in 1933, and the Governor tried to use his influence with President Roosevelt to help German Jews suffering under the Nazi regime's persecution. Irving Lehman, who was one of the leaders of the American Jewish Committee, spoke to the President on March 14 about the Nazi attacks on Jews and Jewish businesses and asked Roosevelt to rescind Herbert Hoover's 1930 tightening of immigration restrictions. Roosevelt raised the issue in a Cabinet meeting in early April, but the State Department remained concerned that most immigrants were "likely to become a public charge."[2]

In response to increased violence against Jews in Germany, Rabbi Stephen S. Wise and the American Jewish Congress organized a massive protest rally at Madison Square Garden on March 27 and invited Governor Lehman to

---

Chapter title quotation: Herbert Lehman quoted in "Nazi Punishment Seen by Roosevelt," *New York Times*, July 22, 1942, pp. 1, 4.

address the gathering. Like many of the successful Jews of German American descent who led the more conservative American Jewish Committee, Lehman believed that quiet diplomacy was preferable to mass meetings, and leading Jews in Germany urged him not to participate in the meeting, reporting that they were not being mistreated but warning that the rally might incite retaliation against them. Consequently, Lehman at first declined Wise's invitation, saying that he was "working in many directions on this thing" but that "it would be a mistake" for him to attend the meeting. Wise asserted that "it would be a much greater mistake" not to attend the rally, but Lehman expressed "great doubts as to whether it is a wise thing to do." Wise emphasized that what was planned was "an orderly, dignified representative dominantly Christian protest meeting under our auspices," and he cautioned that "if we do not have this meeting there will be Socialist Jewish meetings, Communist Jewish demonstrations." Lehman agreed that "it should be a dominantly Christian meeting," and he promised "to think it over," but he also hoped that Wise would "not make a public question of this" by announcing that Lehman would not be attending. The Governor subsequently decided to speak at the rally, but when state business prevented him from leaving Albany, he addressed a mass meeting there instead at which he called upon the German people to return to "the principles of civil and religious liberty" rather than being "deluded by falsehood and misrepresentations" and "appeals to bigotry."[3]

As promised, Herbert Lehman, and his brother Irving, pursued the matter in other, more quiet ways. On March 30, the Governor called President Roosevelt, interrupting the President's dinner, to urge him "to forward, via government channels, a stiff message of protest from the Jews of America." The President replied that the State Department had already warned the German government that its actions might negatively affect the American public's attitude toward Germany. After meeting with Reichsbank head Dr. Hjalmar Schacht in May, the President assured Irving Lehman that "at last the German government now knows how I feel about things," and that "it is probably better to do it this way than to send formal notes of protest because, frankly, I fear that the latter might result in reprisals in Germany." In mid-June 1933, Governor Lehman opened the American Joint Distribution Committee's campaign to raise $2,000,000 to help German Jews suffering under Nazi persecution, and in September Irving Lehman met with the President and then with Secretary of State Cordell Hull, Secretary of Labor Frances Perkins, and others to discuss the problems German Jewish refugees were encountering in their efforts to obtain visas to come to the United States.[4]

When Nazi Germany adopted the Nuremberg laws stripping Jews of their citizenship in the fall of 1935, James G. McDonald, League of Nations High Commissioner for Refugees (Jewish and Others) Coming from Germany, and Felix Warburg, a noted Jewish philanthropist, hoped that President Roosevelt would respond by authorizing "a more lenient interpretation of present regulations" that were making it "difficult or impossible" for German Jews to obtain visas to come to America. McDonald and Warburg believed that Herbert Lehman was the best person to approach the President about the problem, and the Governor immediately wrote a letter to Roosevelt in which he "very strongly endorse[d]" the request to liberalize "the very stringent regulations with regard to the immigration quota from Germany." The Governor stressed that "conditions in Germany . . . appear to be getting worse continually," and he pointed out that even though the annual immigration quota from Germany was twenty-five thousand, State Department policies and procedures had limited German immigrants to 2,500 per year. Lehman proposed that the number should be doubled, emphasizing that the people trying to flee from Germany were "very much the type of men like my father, Carl Schurz, and other Germans who came over here in the days of 1848 and who later were among our best citizens." The Governor suggested that the Secretary of State be instructed "to make certain that our diplomatic and consular representatives show sympathetic interest in permitting immigration of German Jews into this country, providing, of course, they fulfill the immigration requirements in every particular." Lehman emphasized to Roosevelt that "the matter is of such importance that I feel justified in taking it up directly with you," and he hoped it would receive the President's "personal consideration and favorable action." Two weeks later, when he had not yet received a reply, Lehman wrote to Roosevelt again, urging the President to give his "approval and support" to increasing the number of German Jews admitted to the United States.[5]

In a response drafted by the State Department, Roosevelt asserted that there was neither a specific immigration quota nor an "arbitrary limitation" for Jews wishing to leave Germany for the United States. The President reported that "nearly all immigration quotas have been considerably under-issued during the past four years," including the German quota, but he stressed that "a very large majority of immigration visas under the German quota are issued to Jewish applicants," and that the number of immigration visas issued to natives of Germany had increased from 1,798 in 1933 to 5,117 in 1935. Roosevelt explained that the State Department had instructed American consular officers to give "the most considerate attention and the most generous and favorable treatment possible under the laws of this country" to "persons who are obliged to leave the country of their regular residence, and who seek to escape from the conditions in that country by coming to the United States." These orders, he noted, had been discussed in person with "the principal consular officers stationed at Berlin, Hamburg, and Stuttgart." The President thanked Lehman for calling this situation to his attention and assured the Governor that it was his "earnest desire that all consideration and justice shall continue to be shown to the type of immigrants in whom you are interested."[6]

Six months later, when nothing had changed, Lehman wrote to the President again, reminding Roosevelt of their previous correspondence concerning the problems German Jews were experiencing in obtaining visas to come to the United States. Lehman recalled that Roosevelt had "taken the matter up with the Department of State" and had assured him "that difficulties would be reduced to a minimum in cases of people worthy of admission to our country." The Governor enclosed letters and memoranda he had received from Felix Warburg and Sir Herbert Samuel, former British High Commissioner for Palestine, showing that the same problems continued to block people seeking to leave Germany, and Lehman hoped that "every effort will be made to make possible the obtaining of visas for those who, in the opinion of our authorities, will make worthy citizens of the United States."[7]

The President's response, prepared again by the State Department, was more sympathetic in tone than in content. Roosevelt reported that additional personnel had been assigned to clear up the backlog that had developed in processing visa applications in Stuttgart, but he warned that consular officials would continue to grant visas only "when the preponderance of evidence supports a conclusion that the person promising the applicant's support will be likely to take steps to prevent the applicant from becoming a public charge." The President asserted that "the Department of State and its consular officers abroad are continuing to make every effort to carry out the immigration duties placed upon them in a considerate and humane manner," and he noted that they were "issuing considerably more immigration visas to German Jewish applicants at the present time than was the case last year or in recent previous years." Roosevelt assured Lehman of his "sympathetic interest" in this question and his appreciation that Lehman had brought the matter to his attention.[8]

Not content to rely solely on an exchange of letters, Lehman followed up his note to the President by discussing the matter with him personally. After his meeting with the President, Lehman reported to Warburg that Roosevelt "feels great sympathetic concern in the situation and will do everything within his power to be helpful." Lehman's efforts eventually bore fruit. As Richard Breitman and Alan Kraut note in their study of American refugee policy in this period, "there is no evidence that Roosevelt issued any instructions to the State Department about immigration to the United States, but careful observers could see which way he was leaning," and by the end of 1936, "shifting currents within the State Department" resulted in a more liberal interpretation of the "likely to become a public charge" clause and "a substantial increase in the immigration of German Jews to the United States."[9]

In March 1938, in response to Germany's annexation of Austria and the widespread seizures of Jewish property and arrests and expulsions of Jews from Vienna that followed, President Roosevelt authorized Secretary of State Cordell Hull to invite the nations of Europe and the Western Hemisphere "to cooperate in setting up a special committee" to facilitate the emigration of political refugees from Germany and Austria. In its official announcement of the initiative, the State Department made clear that "no country would be expected or asked to receive a greater number of immigrants than is permitted by its existing legislation," but the Department stressed that "the urgency of the problem" required a "speedy cooperative effort under governmental supervision if widespread human suffering is to be averted." The President endorsed the initiative wholeheartedly, citing America's heritage as "a haven for the politically oppressed of all nations," and though he emphasized that Christians would also benefit from the cooperative effort, he acknowledged that its "main purpose . . . was the relief of Jews in Germany and Austria."[10]

Herbert Lehman welcomed the President's involvement in seeking a solution to the growing crisis. The Governor emphasized in a letter to "my dear Franklin" how much he welcomed the President's and the Secretary of State's "splendid" position "with regard to the admission to other countries of refugees from the dictatorship-ridden countries abroad." Lehman had "no doubt" that the President's attitude would "be of great practical value," and he was confident that it had "given new inspiration and hope to many hundreds of thousands of people." Even though Roosevelt had not yet reconciled with Lehman over the Governor's opposition to the court-packing bill, the President appreciated Lehman's "letter of commendation relating to the refugees" and hoped that "we can help many of them." Roosevelt "only wish[ed] we could do more." The President's initiative resulted in the Evian Conference in France in the summer of 1938, which accomplished little when the United States and Latin American nations refused to admit additional refugees.[11]

As the Nazis stepped up their persecution of Jews and America's doors remained mostly closed, Lehman became more concerned that Palestine remain open for those Jews who were able to get out of Germany. Lehman wrote to Roosevelt in October 1938 about press reports and confidential information he had received suggesting that "the British government is planning to abandon its pledge to facilitate the establishment of the Jewish National Home in Palestine and that . . . it may halt Jewish immigration into Palestine." Although he was "not a member of a Zionist organization," Lehman emphasized that it was essential that Palestine "continue to offer a haven of refuge for the tens of thousands of Jews whom hatred and intolerance have made homeless." Lehman urged that the American government "indicate to the British government the extraordinary anxiety which prevails on this subject among virtually all American Jews," and he implored Roosevelt to use his "influence to prevent any decision by the British government that would add to the suffering of the Jewish people at this time." The Governor noted that "it would be a tragic anti-climax to what you tried to achieve through the Evian conference if, at this moment, Great Britain should stop Jewish immigration into Palestine and repudiate its obligations assumed in the Palestine Mandate of the League of Nations."[12]

Roosevelt responded to Lehman immediately, reiterating his "sympathy in the idea of establishing a National Home in Palestine" and emphasizing that the U.S. government had kept the British fully informed of American interest in Palestine. He explained, however, that the United States could not prevent changes in the British mandate in Palestine; it could only deny the applicability of any changes to American interests there. The President stressed that he had frequently reminded the British government of his "abiding interest in the welfare of the refugees in Europe" and his "belief that all nations should cooperate in the task of alleviating the suffering of these unfortunate people," and he pledged that the United States "will leave no stone unturned" in its efforts "to persuade the British Government to adopt a liberal policy with regard to the refugees." Roosevelt assured Lehman that "everything that this government can appropriately do to alleviate the situation of these thousands of unfortunate human beings will be done." However, British policy in Palestine and saving European Jews were not Roosevelt's highest priorities, and the American government did not protest in May 1939 when the British issued a White Paper severely limiting Jewish immigration into Palestine.[13]

II

Ever since the Nazis had come to power in Germany, Herbert Lehman had feared that "what was happening in Germany would in time be bound to involve the world in another war, in which we ourselves would participate." The Governor believed that "as early as 1938," Roosevelt, too, was "certain in his own mind that we were bound to be involved in the war," but as Eleanor Roosevelt later recalled, "Franklin couldn't very well move until he thought the people were ready to go with him." Realizing that "the American public was not prepared to go to war," the President, according to Lehman, set out "to educate the American people with regard to the situation, and show them the real danger . . . which we and the rest of the free world" faced. Reviewing New York City's huge Army Day parade in April 1939, Lehman emphasized the need for preparedness in New York State and the nation to meet this growing threat, declaring that "preparedness, instead of being an incentive toward war, is our greatest safeguard for peace." A few weeks later, speaking at the opening of the New York World's Fair, Lehman lamented that nations had not yet learned "the secret of living together in understanding and friendship, in tolerance and in good-will." Lehman prayed that the "World of Tomorrow" would be "a world in which men will seek to help their neighbors, not to harm them; a world of which the keystone will be justice, equality and tolerance; a world in which right will ever be the master of might."[14]

When World War II broke out in Europe, Herbert Lehman agreed with President Roosevelt that the best way to defend the United States at this time was to provide military aid and equipment to Britain and France. The Governor was one of the founding members of the Committee to Defend America by Aiding the Allies, which was established in May 1940 to build public support for "aiding with our supplies and wealth the nations now fighting to stem the tide of aggression." A few weeks later, Roosevelt used Lehman to signal his support for such assistance. After lunch at the White House on June 6, the Governor explained that he had come to Washington "to urge strongly that our government furnish the Allies promptly with all the planes, equipment and supplies which the President felt could be spared without jeopardizing our national defense." Lehman asserted that "England and France are fighting not only for their own liberties but for the liberties of a freedom-loving world," and that a Nazi victory would endanger "our country, our liberties and our entire way of life." The Governor reported that "the President listened but made no comment" as Lehman had voiced these concerns, but the *New York Times* pointed out that "rarely, if ever, do White House visitors express themselves as forcefully as did Governor Lehman without at least tacit approval of the President." Four days later, Roosevelt made his own position clear, pledging that the United States would "extend to the opponents of force the material resources of this nation." In late July and early August, when the Committee to Defend America by Aiding the Allies and others called for the United States to sell or transfer to Great Britain ships dating from World War I, Edith Lehman wrote to the President, exhorting him to do everything in his power "to facilitate the release of sixty recommissioned destroyers to Britain without further delay."[15]

Lehman continued to support Roosevelt's efforts to ensure that the nation was prepared should it become involved in the war. When the President proposed a selective service bill in August 1940, Lehman agreed that a peacetime draft was "the only possible way by which we can secure man power sufficiently large for our national defense within any reasonable length of time." Lehman accompanied the President in mid-August to observe the First Army's maneuvers in northern New York, which the *New York Times* described as "the largest military exercises ever held in the United States." Both men were shocked at the army's "lack of equipment," which resulted in soldiers "drilling with drain pipes instead of regular trench mortars and broomsticks instead of machine guns."[16]

III

Just as Herbert Lehman had followed Franklin Roosevelt as Governor of New York, some people saw him as a logical successor to FDR as President. In an interview shortly after Lehman's re-election as Governor in November 1938, Alf Landon, the Republican presidential nominee in 1936, praised Lehman as "the outstanding Democratic candidate for the Democratic nomination for President in 1940," and a Gallup Poll in late 1938 showed that 9 percent of

Democratic respondents favored Lehman as the party's presidential candidate in 1940 if Roosevelt did not run again. In subsequent surveys, Lehman's support quickly dropped to 3 percent in March 1939, 2 percent in May, and less than 1 percent in June. Lehman was neither surprised nor disappointed at these results. Remembering vividly the religious bigotry that had derailed Al Smith's candidacy in 1928, Lehman knew that such hatred and hostility would be magnified against a Jewish candidate, and he never seriously considered seeking the presidency in 1940 or at any other time.[17]

Lehman strongly supported Franklin Roosevelt for a third term as President in 1940. As Lehman later recalled, he "was very anxious" for Roosevelt to run again "because of the war in Europe." Lehman believed that FDR "was the only man who could really educate and prepare the country" for what Lehman saw as "an inevitable conflict in which we would be engaged." Accordingly, when Representative Martin Kennedy (D-NY) asked Lehman to join in a movement to designate James Farley as "New York's favorite son for the presidential nomination," Lehman ignored the request. Rather than see New York support Farley, who opposed FDR seeking a third term, the President suggested that the state's delegation to the 1940 Democratic National Convention cast its votes for Governor Lehman. The President stressed that this would be "a decent thing to do for the leader of the Democratic Party in the State of New York who for eight years has been its thoroughly successful and able Governor." Roosevelt's real motive, however, was to prevent the New York delegation from committing to Farley or any other candidate until the President made up his mind whether to run again.[18]

Leading up to the Republican National Convention in late June, Thomas Dewey appeared to be the likely Republican presidential candidate, and Herbert Lehman did all he could to help FDR by weakening Dewey. At Roosevelt's request, Lehman met with the President at Hyde Park on April 9, and despite the Governor's insistence to the press that they discussed "fishing—not politics," the election likely came up during their time together. Ten days later, Lehman attacked Dewey, charging that in the Republican-controlled New York State Senate and Assembly, "legislation was enacted or killed, depending on how it might affect the fortunes of a particular presidential candidate." According to the Governor, Republican leaders, acting on Dewey's behalf, had forced the lawmakers to pass "a completely unbalanced budget" authorizing "expenditures far in excess of prospective receipts; to cut needed appropriations for relief; and to defeat virtually every progressive measure that was introduced." Lehman noted that "even bills to outlaw the 'dirty business' of wire-tapping and unlawful search and seizure were killed" (Dewey had used such tactics in his criminal prosecutions), and the Governor warned that "these same Republican leaders who have betrayed and failed the people of New York now seek the power to administer the affairs of the nation." In June, when Dewey criticized

Roosevelt's appointment of Republicans Henry Stimson as Secretary of War and Frank Knox as Secretary of the Navy "as a direct step toward war" and an act of "weakness and desperation," Lehman rushed to the President's defense, publicly congratulating him on "the selection of these two outstanding men."[19]

Lehman believed that Roosevelt's re-election "was essential beyond any description, for the good of the country and for the good of the free world," and on the eve of the Democratic National Convention, the Governor formally endorsed the President for a third term, urging Roosevelt to accept the draft that was likely to come at the convention. Lehman served as chairman of the New York delegation at the convention and enjoyed the "high privilege and great pleasure and pride" of seconding Roosevelt's nomination for the presidency, praising the President "for his ability, for his capacity, for his loyalty, for his vision and for his patriotism."[20]

Besides ensuring Roosevelt's renomination, Lehman's main concern at the convention was that the platform include a strong plank pledging assistance to Britain and other victims of aggression. At a meeting with Senator Wagner, the chairman of the Resolutions Committee, and in a subsequent phone conversation with the President, Lehman advocated that the Democrats promise to supply the Allies with all aid short of war. But noninterventionists, including Senators Burton Wheeler of Montana, Pat McCarran of Nevada, and David Walsh of Massachusetts, dominated the subcommittee that was writing the platform, and they rejected the efforts by Lehman and others to insert language that would have committed the Democrats to providing aid " 'short of war' to countries seeking to throw off Nazi or Fascist domination." Instead, after asserting that "the world's greatest democracy cannot afford heartlessly or in a spirit of appeasement to ignore the peace-loving and liberty-loving peoples wantonly attacked by ruthless aggressors," the platform qualified its promise of assistance by pledging "to extend to these peoples all the material aid at our command, consistent with law and not inconsistent with the interests of our own national self-defense, all to the end that peace and international good faith may yet emerge triumphant." Moreover, the platform took on an even stronger isolationist tint when it declared that "we will not participate in foreign wars, and we will not send our Army, naval or air force to fight in foreign lands outside of the Americas, except in case of attack." Lehman's disappointment over the platform's limited promise of help to the Allies was quickly dispelled when the President, in his speech accepting the nomination, vowed to continue "openly to oppose by every peaceful means the spread of the dictator form of government." Roosevelt warned against "appeasement and compromise with those who seek to destroy all democracies everywhere, including here," and he promised to provide "material aid" to the Allies. As the *New York Times* noted, the President, in his remarks, annulled "the strong non-interventionist tone of the party platform."[21]

Herbert Lehman played an important role in Roosevelt's bid for re-election. The President had promised in his acceptance speech not to engage in "purely political debate," which meant that surrogates were needed to campaign and give speeches on his behalf. Republican candidate Wendell Willkie, needing to carry New York if he were to win the election, campaigned all across the state, from Jamestown to Brooklyn. To counter Willkie's efforts in New York, Ed Flynn, who had succeeded Farley as the chairman of the Democratic National Committee, announced in early September that Lehman would be among those carrying "a heavier load than usual" in the President's re-election campaign.[22]

Speaking at the New York State Democratic Convention on September 30, 1940, Lehman delivered what the *New York Times* described as "one of his most effective addresses." Lehman asserted that "Franklin Roosevelt now stands as a symbol of militant democracy arming to defend itself and to defend its belief in the dignity of man throughout the world," and the Governor argued that Roosevelt had demonstrated that "our democracy can provide decent standards of civilized living, while our press can remain free, our speech can remain free, our homes can remain free, our religion can remain free." Lehman lauded Roosevelt for the economic and industrial improvements that had been achieved in America "without the surrender of a single principle of individual liberty, . . . without yielding one inch to the forces of reaction which would tear down the banners of enlightened democracy we have come to know in the new world."[23]

Lehman ignited a major controversy when he declared in his speech that "nothing that could happen in the United States could give Hitler, Mussolini, Stalin and the government of Japan more satisfaction than the defeat of the man who typifies to the whole world the kind of free, humane government which dictators despise—Franklin D. Roosevelt." Picking up on a theme first raised by Democratic vice presidential candidate Henry Wallace at the Democratic National Convention, Lehman claimed "that to the whole world, including the enslaved nations," Roosevelt was "a symbol of democracy and freedom" whose defeat would "weaken the resistance of free nations and blast the last hope of millions of conquered people who love liberty just as do you and I, but who now bear the heavy yoke of tyranny." Roosevelt's re-election, Lehman stressed, "would mean a stronger unity in American purpose, a beacon of hope to oppressed people throughout the world, a stronger physical defense in America, a sounder, tougher fiber for the American people." He spoke "heatedly of these things," Lehman explained, because he felt them "deeply."[24]

Willkie immediately denounced Lehman's remarks, charging that "the innuendo of this statement is false, malicious and subversive." The Republican candidate was "shocked that a man of Governor Lehman's character and responsibility should stoop to a kind of politics that can only jeopardize the safety and welfare of the American people in a critical hour." Willkie emphasized that he had gone out of his way "to give unity to certain important aspects of our foreign policy . . . [and] to avoid any risk of any suspicion in foreign minds of a disagreement in this country on our fundamental attitudes toward aggression and toward aid to Britain." But Lehman's comments, he charged, "tend to destroy the unity of this country and they challenge in flagrant fashion the principles upon which" Willkie had conducted his campaign. According to Willkie, Lehman, "as Governor of New York and an intimate friend of the President and in his personal character of an American citizen, has a threefold and grave responsibility," and he asked Lehman to make it clear that he did not "impute to me any other attitude than that of a defender of democracy."[25]

Lehman stood by his remarks, declaring that his statement was "true and accurate," that he had said exactly what he meant to say. The Governor maintained that his speech did not "in any way impugn Mr. Willkie's patriotism or his devotion to American democracy," and that "such an interpretation" was "a complete distortion" of his statement. Lehman reiterated his contention that "President Roosevelt, by action and by word, is the outstanding symbol of democracy throughout the civilized world and that he typifies the kind of liberty which the dictators hate," and Lehman suggested that a perusal of the "dictator-controlled newspapers of foreign lands" would prove his point. Lehman warned that "if Mr. Willkie were ever to be elected President, he would have to deal with the same miscellaneous assortment of appeasers and extreme isolationists in his own party that he has had to deal with as a candidate." According to Lehman, "the real leadership of the Republican party" was forcing Willkie "to compromise his own best judgment" and renege on his earlier support for Roosevelt's foreign policies. "Even conceding Mr. Willkie the best of intentions," Lehman asserted, "the cause of democracy would greatly suffer through a defeat of Mr. Roosevelt."[26]

The *New York Times* objected to Lehman's comments, arguing in an editorial that Lehman's accusation was "unjust because the record shows that Mr. Willkie has been just as straightforward as Mr. Roosevelt in condemning Hitler and everything he stands for," and "reckless because it attempts to arrogate patriotism for the Democratic ticket." The *Times*, which had endorsed Willkie, resented Lehman's attempt "to create the impression that the issue of this campaign is the choice between Mr. Roosevelt and Hitler," and warned that Lehman's comments were "capable of doing great harm to the very cause which Governor Lehman has at heart . . . by dividing the American people" and leading other nations to misinterpret a Willkie victory. *New York Times* columnist Arthur Krock noted in early October that the last time a political party had appealed for votes in wartime on the specious grounds that a victory for its opponents would be welcome in the enemy's capital had been in 1918, when Woodrow Wilson and the Democrats had claimed that a Republican victory in that year's congressional elections would be welcome news in Berlin.

Although the parallel was not exact, since the United States had been at war in 1918 and President Wilson had not been on the ballot, Krock observed that the tactic had backfired on the Democrats in 1918 and might be "politically perilous" again in 1940. Krock was still complaining in a column on October 30 about what he called the "Wallace-Lehman argument" that a Willkie victory would be seen "in the Axis capitals" as "a victory for 'appeasers.'"[27]

Others quickly joined the fray over whether Lehman's speech had been a low blow. New York Republican Assemblyman Abbot Low Moffat, who had clashed with the Governor numerous times over budget matters in Albany, complained that Lehman had branded "every American who opposes a third term for any President a Nazi," and he asserted that "there is not one jot or tittle of difference between the two parties in their complete opposition to Hitler." Moffat charged that Lehman must be "moonblind" because he failed to see that "the inordinate growth of presidential power [and] the breakdown of our democratic traditions," such as presidents not seeking a third term, represented "a more insidious threat to our democracy." Similarly, Joseph Proskauer, one of the leaders of the American Jewish Committee, a close friend of Al Smith, and a Willkie supporter, criticized Lehman's speech, claiming that Willkie "has no more sympathy with the bigotries of Hitlerism than the Governor or myself," and warning that Roosevelt's "violation of the precedent against the third term" posed the real threat to democracy. The *New Republic*, on the other hand, defended the Governor, arguing that "the effect of our election on foreign opinion is vital, and Mr. Lehman was not unfair in calling attention to it." Over the next few days, the *New York Times* printed numerous letters to the editor on both sides of the dispute, one reader emphasizing that "you nowhere in your editorial assert that Governor Lehman's remark is not true," while another reader congratulated the *Times* for condemning "such offensive utterances as that made by Governor Lehman."[28]

President Roosevelt soon joined the discussion, taking great pleasure in reading aloud to reporters excerpts from an article published in the *Times* on October 4, 1940, which reported from Rome that "the Axis is out to defeat President Roosevelt, not as a measure of interference in the internal policies of the United States but because of the President's foreign policy and because of everything for which he stands in the eyes of the Italians and Germans." Roosevelt did not specifically refer to the controversy over Lehman's speech, but everyone realized that the President had called attention to the story because it supported Lehman's contention that Roosevelt's defeat would please America's enemies.[29]

New York City held the key to Roosevelt's chances of carrying New York State and its forty-seven electoral votes, which seemed in jeopardy when various polls in late October showed Willkie ahead in the state. The President had agreed in mid-October to deliver a number of political speeches, and when he campaigned in New York City on October 28, he made sure that Lehman, who had always run strongly in the city, was at his side as he visited all five boroughs. Along with the President, Lehman addressed a huge rally at Madison Square Garden that night, challenging the thesis that Willkie was "a great businessman" who would "increase industrial production" and "step-up the output of defense material—that he alone can provide increased employment." Lehman emphasized that Willkie had never been "a manufacturer or producer," but was merely "a very successful, a very resourceful and a very clever corporation lawyer, who has served for years as the head of a large—and I have no doubt profitable—public utility holding corporation." The Governor reminded the audience of "the terrible situation which existed at the time former President Hoover went out of office" and "the far-reaching and spectacular gains that have been made since those bitter times—gains in profits, gains in employment, gains in morale." The American people, Lehman proclaimed, "know that the credit for saving the country belongs solely to Franklin D. Roosevelt." The President, in his remarks, chastised the Republicans, especially "Congressmen Martin, Barton, and Fish," for their opposition to various defense measures.[30]

As the campaign wound down to its final days, the *New York Herald Tribune* declared that "New York Vote Is Key in Election," the *New York Times* reported that "the outlook in New York State is for the closest election since 1928, when Franklin D. Roosevelt won his first election as Governor by the margin of 28,000 votes," and Dr. George Gallup of the American Institute of Public Opinion revealed that his surveys showed Willkie with a narrow lead in New York. In a last-ditch effort to counter the trend toward Willkie, Lehman made speeches on FDR's behalf at rallies sponsored by the Milkdrivers' Union, the Women's and Children's Apparel Industries Committee, the American Labor Party, the Brooklyn Democratic organization, the Independent Voters Committee, and the Motion Pictures Division of the Democratic National Committee. The Governor spoke in venues ranging from Madison Square Garden to the Mother Zion Baptist Church in Harlem and the Shriners' Mecca Temple in Manhattan, repeating his attacks on "the motley crew of appeasers and extreme isolationists in and out of Congress who are the leaders of the Republican Party." The Governor proclaimed that "Franklin D. Roosevelt is the very symbol of democracy here in this country and wherever free people live," and he warned that Roosevelt's "defeat would be a tragic blow" in the "fight for freedom."[31]

Like many leading American Jews, Herbert Lehman opposed efforts to make religion the determining factor when citizens entered the voting booth. Lehman agreed wholeheartedly with Rabbi Stephen S. Wise of the Free Synagogue of New York, who delivered a sermon entitled "An American's Duty on Election Day" in which Wise condemned "the Republican National Committee and 'its Jewish puppets'" for "pretending there is such a thing as 'the Jewish vote.'" Wise asserted that "a Jew who votes for a candidate, whoever he be, is not a Jewish voter, and is not casting a Jewish Vote," and he explained that a preponderance of American Jews supported Roosevelt not because they were Jews, but because "the President is a symbol, as no other living personality, to all the world, of the democratic hope." Rabbi Wise warned that "if the time has come when the Jews of America may, through threat, be moved to vote for one candidate or another on the ground that their Jewish interests are involved, then it will not be needful for Hitler to assume sovereignty in our land, for this country will, by this token, have been reduced to a chattel of Hitlerism."[32]

When Benjamin Buttenwieser, who was married to Herbert Lehman's niece Helen, objected to Rabbi Wise's criticism of Willkie's Jewish supporters, Lehman could barely conceal his anger. The Governor denounced Buttenwieser and the Republicans for "injecting the religious issue into the campaign in the most scandalous manner." Lehman found it ironic that Buttenwieser was upset about Rabbi Wise's sermon but had failed to mention the adjacent article in the *Herald Tribune* that included Buttenwieser among a group of prominent "Jewish Leaders Backing Willkie." Lehman noted that most of the people listed as Willkie supporters "are normally Republicans and have probably never in their lives voted for a Democrat," and he complained that they were identified only by "their connections with Jewish organizations." The Governor criticized "the wide publicity given by the Republican committee to the creation of a Jewish Division at National Headquarters and the distribution of literature, advertisements, buttons, etc. in Yiddish," and he emphasized that "the whole program of distortion, of racial appeal by the Republican committee, has not only been a dangerous one, but one which merits forceful condemnation."[33]

Buttenwieser tried to turn the tables on Lehman, charging that the Governor and the Democrats had been the first to introduce race and religion into the campaign with their assertions that Hitler wanted to see Roosevelt defeated in the election. According to Buttenwieser, such statements constituted "a thinly veiled but perfectly obvious appeal along racial and religious lines." Buttenwieser argued that it was necessary to show that there was not a monolithic Jewish vote that would be cast for Roosevelt, and that "a release such as the one listing Jewish leaders backing Willkie" that had so upset Lehman might "prove most helpful" in achieving their common goal of "preventing the diabolic growth of anti-Semitism." He also expressed his disappointment that when "the diabolical development of the religious issue in this campaign" first surfaced, Lehman, the "one Jew in America above all others . . . who could have crushed it once and for all and thereby have rendered his country and his co-religionists one of the greatest services in its and our history," had failed to offer an "unequivocal condemnation of the raising of any religious or racial issue in any form in political affairs."[34]

Rather than being mollified by Buttenwieser's reference to their common interest in stopping anti-Semitism or Lehman's status as the "leading Jew in America today," the Governor took great offense at the suggestion that his speech to the New York State Democratic Convention had "raised any religious or racial issue." Lehman complained that the *New York Times*, Joseph Proskauer, and others had "deliberately distorted the intent of these remarks to make it appear that an appeal to racial or religious groups had been made," and the Governor quoted extensively from his speech to show that his "remarks were addressed to all Americans regardless of race, religion or national origin." Lehman pointed out that he was "so averse to any appeal by Jews to the Jewish voters" that he and Edith had "refused even to appear before distinctively Jewish groups" because "even a semblance of an appeal along religious lines was hateful to us."[35]

Herbert Lehman was greatly relieved when Franklin Roosevelt was re-elected to a third term as President in 1940. Lehman's efforts on Roosevelt's behalf helped the President carry New York City by more than seven hundred thousand votes and New York State by 233,000 votes. As had been the case with Lehman's victory in 1938, the votes that Roosevelt received on the American Labor Party line proved decisive. Nationally, FDR received almost five million more popular votes than Willkie, and he won 449 electoral votes compared to eighty-two for Willkie. At 1:00 a.m., when the results were clear, Lehman went on the radio to "congratulate the entire nation on the re-election of President Roosevelt," and a few weeks later, when the state's electors gathered in Albany to cast their official votes for the President, Lehman hailed Roosevelt and his victory "as a symbol of democracy throughout the world."[36]

As pleased as he was at FDR's re-election, Lehman worried that the campaign had left a bitter residue that would make it hard to unite the nation to face the growing threat posed by the Axis powers. In his first public comments after the election, the Governor emphasized that "this is no time for recrimination; it is no time for triumph and gloating." Lehman called upon all Americans to "wipe out all hard feelings, all suspicion, all hatred, and join together to maintain peace, to safeguard our country, and to make it a haven and a symbol of democracy, here and wherever free people live." Privately, Lehman urged the President to meet with Willkie to discuss "the best means of securing the wholehearted cooperation for national defense of all the people of the nation." Lehman believed that such a gesture would be seen as "magnanimous and statesmanlike," and that it would demonstrate even to the President's most bitter opponents his "deep-seated desire to serve the interests of the nation as a whole." Willkie allayed many of Lehman's concerns after the election when he reiterated his support of providing military aid to Great Britain and endorsed the general idea of Roosevelt's Lend-Lease proposal. Roosevelt and Willkie did meet at the White House in January 1941, when Willkie was about to leave on a trip to England, but there is little reason to think that Lehman's suggestion had anything to do with the get-together.[37]

IV

Lehman devoted most of his efforts as Governor in 1941 to the enactment of state measures to complement defense legislation that FDR was pushing through Congress. Like FDR, Lehman focused on security in his annual message, asserting that "total defense is the only answer to total war." Specifically, he called upon the Republican-controlled State Legislature to establish the State Council of Defense as an official state agency, create legislative committees on national defense to receive and coordinate specific bills, expand local defense councils, protect the jobs of men drafted into the armed forces, require the state and municipalities to pay the salary difference for state and municipal employees conscripted into the military, authorize the courts to protect draftees against eviction or foreclosure, allow men in the armed forces to register and cast absentee ballots, strengthen state laws against sabotage and conspiracy, and regulate the manufacture, sale, possession, and use of explosives. Republican lawmakers approved most of these measures, but they rejected money for guarding state armories and for a defense contingency fund to be spent at the Governor's discretion, claiming that the Governor's thinking had been clouded by "intense emotional alarm" rather than guided by "sane business judgment."[38]

When President Roosevelt proposed his Lend-Lease plan in January 1941 to provide all possible aid to Great Britain, Herbert Lehman immediately endorsed the President's initiative. The Governor described England "as our first and possibly our last line of defense" and warned that "if Great Britain falls, we cannot hope to keep the war from our shores." He emphasized that "oceans can no longer protect against the impact of military and economic warfare or social revolution," and he declared that "if we in this country want to stop Hitler, if we want to aid Britain in bringing this ruthless mutilation, both spiritual and physical, to an end, we must do so now while we still can." Lehman stressed that "a concrete policy has just been put forth to meet the emergency of the present crisis," and he asserted that "we must stand a united nation behind the President and see that with a minimum delay this policy is put into effect."[39]

Herbert Lehman watched with growing concern as the Nazi war machine conquered most of Europe, threatening the survival of the continent's Jews, including numerous Lehman relatives. The Governor worked with family members in New York to create the Mayer Lehman Charity Fund to finance the immigration of relatives and guarantee that they would not become "a public charge," but it became more and more difficult to get these people out of Europe. In one case, after trying to work through Secretary of State Cordell Hull to secure exit visas for Mrs. Lehman's cousins, the Duschnitz family, to leave unoccupied France for the Dominican Republic, Lehman appealed directly to President Roosevelt for help. The President explained that "our representatives abroad do not ordinarily intercede with foreign officials in behalf of persons who are not American citizens," but he assured Lehman that the U.S. Ambassador to the Vichy government had been contacted and asked to "render any assistance he may deem appropriate." Two weeks later, Roosevelt reported to Lehman that the American Embassy had been actively trying to help the Duschnitzes for months, but the French Ministry of the Interior had refused to issue the necessary exit permits because of "administrative confusion and fear that the surrender of the Duschnitz family might be requested by the German authorities." The President deplored "the unfortunate situation in which the family now finds itself," but he made it clear there was nothing else he could do. Lehman was "sorry to hear" FDR's "discouraging report," but he "greatly appreciate[d] the interest" that the President had "shown in this very unfortunate case." Unlike most such cases, this one had a happy ending. Through Lehman's efforts with the U.S. government, and the tireless endeavors of Lehman assistant Carolin Flexner with Jewish groups and refugee agencies, the Duschnitz family was able to leave France for the Dominican Republic in the summer of 1941, and six months later they received visas to come to the United States.[40]

Members of the extended Roosevelt and Lehman "families" joined forces in July 1941 to rally support for England. As the *New York Times* reported, "Governor Lehman's 4-year-old German boxer, Budget, presided with dignity and grace" when more than three hundred dogs delivered "a noisy sendoff to the New York State 'Barkers for Britain' campaign, a canine auxiliary of Bundles for Britain." While the dogs cavorted on the lawn of the State Capitol, "Mrs. Lehman read a telegram from President Roosevelt's famous Scottie, Falla, commissioning Budget as New York State chairman of Barkers for Britain." The gathering raised more than $150 selling bronze medallions to the dogs' owners for fifty cents.[41]

As American and German ships became involved in an undeclared naval war on the Atlantic in the fall of 1941, Governor Lehman reiterated in his Columbus Day address the need for national unity and support for the President. "We must stand as a unit," the Governor declared, "behind the President of the United States in his foreign policy. That is the only way we can insure our safety and the preservation of our liberties; it is the only way we can restore liberty to the enslaved peoples of the world." In late October, as the clashes between American and German ships continued, Lehman called on Congress to comply immediately with the President's request to repeal remaining restrictions in the Neutrality Acts, warning that "it is no exaggeration to speak of the danger to the United States in terms of days."[42]

The only real difference of opinion between Lehman and Roosevelt in 1941 involved the New York City mayoral election in which the Governor backed the Democratic candidate, Brooklyn District Attorney William O'Dwyer, and the President endorsed Mayor La Guardia, who was running for re-election on the Republican, Fusion, and American Labor Party tickets.

A lifelong Democrat, Lehman believed that there were fundamental differences between the Democrats and the Republicans, a belief that had been strengthened by his frequent battles with Republican legislators in Albany. Lehman had supported the Democratic candidates against La Guardia in 1933 and 1937, and, not feeling that he owed the Mayor anything for his last-minute and halfhearted support in the 1938 gubernatorial election, Lehman saw no reason to help the Mayor now. The Governor planned to limit his involvement in the campaign to two speeches on O'Dwyer's behalf, and his comments endorsing O'Dwyer were tepid at best, characterizing him as "an honest, capable and conscientious public official" who would "give the people of New York City an efficient, honest, independent and progressive administration." Lehman conceded that La Guardia was "a hard worker and a patriotic man," but he criticized the Mayor for continuing as chief executive of the city after Roosevelt had appointed him national Director of Civilian Defense, asserting that no "man can simultaneously discharge the duties of those two difficult and important positions."[43]

Just a few days after Lehman's endorsement of O'Dwyer, President Roosevelt, never a friend of Tammany and the City Democratic machine, publicly backed La Guardia, emphasizing that the Mayor had provided the city with "the most honest" and "the most efficient municipal government" that Roosevelt could recall. National Democratic Chairman Ed Flynn of the Bronx, Roosevelt's handpicked successor to James Farley, regretted the President's abandonment of the Democratic Party that had supported him so many times in the past, but Herbert Lehman refused to comment directly on the President's support for La Guardia. The Governor cautioned, however, that "if members of a party are to repudiate well-qualified nominees of their party . . . the party system, as we have known it in this country for 150 years, will disappear," to be replaced by "little personal machines, . . . selfish factions, and . . . racial and national blocs."[44]

During the last week of the mayoral campaign, La Guardia suddenly injected Governor Lehman and his brother Irving, now the Chief Justice of the New York State Court of Appeals, into the middle of the fray. On October 27, the Court of Appeals canceled a special election that had been set for November 1941 to choose a new State Controller to replace the recently deceased Morris Tremaine. Governor Lehman had appointed Purchasing Commissioner Joseph O'Leary, a member of the American Labor Party, to fill the vacant controller's position, and the court's decision meant that O'Leary would remain in that post until the regular state elections in November 1942. Inexplicably, La Guardia charged that the court's ruling was somehow evidence of a corrupt deal between Herbert and Irving Lehman, with the Governor and his brother having allegedly "double-crossed the double-crossers." According to the Mayor, the Governor had tricked the Democratic leaders who supposedly had forced Lehman to appoint O'Leary. La Guardia claimed that "Herby Lehman" had "punched himself and knocked himself out," and that Democratic leaders were complaining about "that dope Herby." The Mayor's charges made no sense; it was Lehman who had compelled the bosses to accept O'Leary as the Democratic candidate in the now-canceled election. But what the Mayor's accusations lacked in logic they made up for in invective, as the Mayor called the Governor a "goniff," a Yiddish word for thief, for his supposed role in the alleged conspiracy with his brother Irving to fix the outcome of the controller election case.[45]

Infuriated by what he termed La Guardia's "shameless and scurrilous attack," the Governor denounced La Guardia for accusing him "of being a thief and a double-crosser and a fixer," and for accusing "the Court of Appeals of being corrupt and taking orders" from him. The Mayor's verbal excesses, Lehman charged, were not merely "an eccentricity, but a deliberate technique to intimidate those who oppose him." But Lehman refused to be "intimidated," or to allow such "abuse and misrepresentation" to stand, asserting that once again the Mayor's "intemperate tongue willfully distorts the truth." Even though the Governor's integrity, as well as that of the court headed by his brother, were beyond reproach, they had found themselves the subjects of a deliberate, malicious attack by the Mayor seeking "to vent his personal spleen . . . in the mistaken hope of gaining political advantage." The Governor condemned La Guardia's "evil and dangerous" assault "at orderly government and at our democratic processes," and he asserted that "these shameless and sinister attacks" demonstrated that La Guardia was "unworthy of being Mayor of the City of New York."[46]

As Lehman, O'Dwyer, and other leading Democrats pounded away at the Mayor for impugning the Governor's honesty and integrity, La Guardia tried to remove his foot from his mouth, claiming that his name-calling had been directed at the Democratic Party bosses, not the Governor. But the incident highlighted the Mayor's lack of self-control and the negative side of his combative personality, and an election that had been expected to be a cakewalk for the Mayor was suddenly transformed into a competitive race. The *New York Times* reported a few days before the election that the Mayor had seemed to be sailing toward re-election by a comfortable margin of around two hundred thousand votes until his spurious comments about the Governor and the Court of Appeals ruling. La Guardia's remarks breathed new life into the Democrats, who hammered away at the Mayor for his unbridled attack on Lehman. The mayoral election ended up being the closest one in New York City in thirty-six years; La Guardia won, but by only 134,000 votes. The *Times* immediately attributed the drop off from earlier predictions to the Mayor's "reckless name-calling," asserting that he had "turned some of his friends into enemies by his attack upon Governor Lehman." City Controller Joseph McGoldrick, who was re-elected with a larger plurality than La Guardia, estimated in an interview ten years later that La Guardia's senseless attack on Lehman cost the Mayor 250,000 votes, and McGoldrick speculated that had it come earlier in the campaign, it could have cost La Guardia the election. After the ballots had been counted, Lehman put his anger aside long enough to extend to the Mayor his "best wishes for a successful administration."[47]

V

When Japan attacked Pearl Harbor on December 7, 1941, Governor Lehman moved quickly to coordinate New York's response with the federal government's actions. Lehman immediately instructed mayors across the state "to take all steps necessary to prevent sabotage in defense plants, public utilities, waterworks, bridges and all other places of strategic importance in your jurisdiction." Fearing that some Americans might seek revenge against targets close at hand, Lehman also directed local officials "to protect all Japanese nationals residing in your city." Concerned about "the possibility of enemy action against New York State while attention is being diverted elsewhere," the Governor ordered state police to assist in carrying out federal orders grounding all civilian air traffic. He convened a meeting of the State Defense Council on December 10, and in a radio address later that day, Lehman denounced "baseless rumors . . . that air attacks were imminent," urged people to remain calm, and reassured New Yorkers that the State Guard that had been established when New York's National Guard units had been called up was "on the alert for any call to service." When the President requested that American industry operate seven days per week to meet the nation's needs for arms and munitions, Lehman met with Republican leaders and labor officials and won their support for waiving any state laws restricting hours of employment for the duration of the war. Similarly, Lehman took the lead in state efforts to conserve steel, rubber, and construction materials by ordering the State Motor Vehicle Department to issue only rear license plates in 1942, recommending the adoption of a forty-miles-per-hour speed limit, asking that state and local officials be given "the necessary power to enforce rationing regulations and to prosecute violators," and putting on hold $340,000,000 in state construction projects. The Governor even gave up tennis and donated his rubber-soled tennis shoes to a scrap-rubber drive. Lehman also provided strong and visible support for war bond drives, making a statewide radio appeal in which he asked everyone to do their part for the war effort by investing 10 percent of their income in war bonds and directing that 20 percent of his own salary be deducted for that purpose.[48]

Lehman lunched with the President at the White House on April 7, 1942, and according to the Governor, they discussed "defense matters." They also discussed the possibility of Lehman being appointed to a federal post, and a few days later the *New York Times* reported that "President Roosevelt was planning to call Governor Lehman to Washington to assume a high position in the national war effort." The *Times* noted that "Lehman has already volunteered his services to his country in whatever capacity he may best be able to serve during the war," and that "if the President were to call him to Washington there is no doubt that the Governor will immediately accept the call as a patriotic duty." When asked about the story, Lehman refused to comment, and the President, according to the *Times*, "said he had never heard of the idea except for newspaper stories."[49]

Even though the Governor denied that he had discussed New York State politics during his meeting with the President, the possibility of Lehman giving up the governorship to take a position in Washington had obvious repercussions in New York since 1942 was a statewide election year. If Lehman were to relinquish the governorship, Lieutenant Governor Charles Poletti would succeed him. Lehman wanted to see Poletti elected Governor in his own right,

Figure 6.1. "Ready to Step In," by Jerry Costello, *Albany Knickerbocker News*, April 1942. By permission of the *Albany Times Union*.

but Poletti had little support among the party regulars who would control the nomination. Democratic State Chairman James Farley told Poletti that he did not "have a chance in the world to be nominated" because although he had been "baptized as a Catholic," he had "drifted from the Church," and there were "a lot of bigoted Catholics who would resent that." Farley favored James Bennett, a Catholic and a former leader of the American Legion who had been New York Attorney General since 1931. Farley believed that Bennett had graciously "stepped aside" when Lehman had been persuaded to run again in 1936 and 1938, and that Bennett, in contrast to Lehman, "had always been a strong party man." Many observers saw the clash between Farley on the one side and Lehman and Roosevelt on the other as a struggle for control of the Democratic Party in New York State and its delegation to the 1944 Democratic convention, at which Roosevelt was expected either to seek a fourth term or try to designate his successor. Farley later described the battle over the 1942 Democratic nomination for Governor as "the most important political fight" he "ever engaged in."[50]

Lehman and Roosevelt were not enthusiastic over Bennett's candidacy and Farley's role in it. Roosevelt and Farley had split over the President's decision to run for a third term in 1940, and even though Roosevelt had originally recruited Bennett to run with him on the Democratic state ticket in 1930, he feared that Bennett "could not win" the governorship because he had never been in the forefront of liberal causes and would not win the support of the American Labor Party. Many on the left had never forgiven Bennett for presiding over a 1936 rally in support of Franco's fascist forces in Spain, and the *New Republic* had warned back in 1938 that labor would not support a conservative Democrat like Bennett for Governor. Lehman later recalled that he and FDR "were very anxious to have a real progressive succeed me, so that the continuity of progressive Governors could be continued." Lehman believed that "Bennett had been a good conscientious Attorney General, and was a fine gentleman, personally, but he certainly had not been a vigorous progressive in any sense . . . he was not to any degree a leader of the progressive movement of government." There had been some talk about U.S. Senator James Mead of Buffalo as a possible gubernatorial candidate, but Mead declared that he had no interest in the position, and in mid-April speculation focused on Owen Young, who had retired after heading General Electric for many years. Thomas Dewey, who had shown himself to be a very formidable candidate in his race against Lehman in 1938, was seen as the almost certain Republican nominee for Governor in 1942, and Democrats knew it would take a strong candidate and a united party to defeat him.[51]

By May of 1942, the Democrats were anything but united, and some believed that the only way to bring them together would be to persuade Herbert Lehman to run for yet another term as Governor. The *New York Times* reported on May 4, 1942, that "New Deal supporters of President Roosevelt," realizing that Bennett was close to wrapping up the Democratic nomination for Governor, were waiting for word from the White House to launch "a 'draft Lehman' movement." Most of Bennett's support was premised on Lehman not being a candidate, and Bennett had "told friends he would contest the nomination against any candidate but the Governor." Lehman was seen as the only candidate who could bridge the gap between the more conservative elements in the party, headed by Farley and Bennett, and liberals led by the President.[52]

The only problem with this strategy was that Lehman was adamant this time about not running again for governor. With the U.S. now fully involved in the war, Lehman later recalled, he was "very eager" to leave Albany for a position in Washington directly connected to the war. According to Charles Poletti, Lehman believed that Washington "was the hub of things and he ought to be down there, with his experience" in World War I, in business, and in government. To squelch any further talk about drafting him to remain as Governor, Lehman met with the Albany press corps on the morning of May 7, 1942, and declared: "I shall not be a candidate for re-election. If nominated I will not accept the nomination. When my duties as Governor are over I expect to devote all my time and energy exclusively to the war effort." Lehman had tried to phone the President earlier that morning, wanting Roosevelt to hear the news directly from him rather than from the press, but when he failed to reach the President, Lehman sent a telegram instead, explaining that the announcement was along the lines he had discussed with the President when they had met in April.[53]

As Warren Moscow noted in the New York Times, the Governor's Sherman-like statement "bars any 'draft Lehman' movement, and leaves the question of his successor wide open." Lehman later regretted using such "uncompromising and categorical terms" in declaring that he would not run again, believing in retrospect that he had committed "a serious political mistake," because "the minute I made that statement, of course, I gave away my strongest weapons of influence in the choice of my successor." The Governor probably overestimated his power within the New York State Democratic Party to name the party nominee, but he always thought that if he "hadn't come out with this unequivocal statement, I possibly—probably—could have had controlling influence in the selection of my successor."[54]

This time, the President had no choice but to accept as final Lehman's decision not to seek another term as Governor, but that did not mean he was happy about it. Roosevelt told Lehman he would have preferred that Lehman "continue on as Governor for the rest of your life—you have been wonderful," but the President understood that "some consideration must be given to the personal equation. That is only fair." He warned that "there will be much insistence that you run again," and he looked forward to meeting with Lehman soon to discuss "New York State politics" and Lehman's "getting into the war work after the first of January." The Governor met with the President in Washington on May 20 to discuss his "future participation in the war effort," and the *New York Times* reported a few days later that "President Roosevelt will call Governor Lehman to Washington, probably within a month, to assume a high position in the nation's war machine," most likely in the supply area, similar to his duties during World War I. It proved to be much more difficult than anticipated to find the right position for Lehman, however, and the Governor announced in late May that he expected to remain in Albany until the end of his term.[55]

Lehman's removal of himself as a candidate for re-election opened the door for Attorney General Bennett, who had already secured support from James Farley and many of the leaders of the New York State Democratic Party. However, Lehman and Roosevelt remained opposed to Bennett's nomination, and they searched desperately for an alternative, but with no success. Owen Young refused to enter the race, and Senator Mead continued to deny any interest in running for Governor. The President met with Farley at the White House on June 6, 1942, and even though FDR raised questions about Bennett's ability to win the support of the American Labor Party and "certain elements" within the Democratic Party, Farley came away with the impression that Roosevelt "would not oppose Mr. Bennett's nomination for Governor if it appeared that the state organization wanted him." With Roosevelt's blessing, Farley leaked to James Hagerty of the *New York Times* the details of how Roosevelt had initially suggested Bennett as the Democratic candidate for Attorney General in 1930, and Hagerty, based on his conversation with Farley, predicted that the President would support Bennett "actively and request his endorsement by the American Labor Party."[56]

This semblance of Democratic unity lasted less than a week before Herbert Lehman threw a monkey wrench into the proceedings. Alarmed at reports that the Democrats might balance a ticket headed by Bennett by replacing Lieutenant Governor Poletti with a Jewish candidate, Lehman hurried down to Washington to confer with the President on June 11. Lehman reinforced the President's reservations about Bennett, and after his meeting with Roosevelt, Lehman announced that "the President assured me that he has not expressed a preference for any candidate." The Governor made it clear that he "hoped that Lieutenant Governor Charles Poletti" would succeed him, emphasizing that he and Poletti had "worked very closely together for ten years" and saw "eye to eye on State problems." The Governor described Poletti as "the strongest candidate and as the best-fitted man to be Governor of the State," and he pointed out that as opposed to Bennett, Poletti would be assured of the backing of the ALP.[57]

Confusion reigned for the next few weeks as Lehman and Roosevelt tried to block Bennett's nomination. In Washington, Roosevelt confirmed at a press conference that "he had not endorsed any candidate for the Democratic gubernatorial nomination in New York," and leaders of the American Labor Party in New York made clear their opposition to Bennett's candidacy, calling instead for the selection of "an outstanding liberal, a New Dealer, for the governorship of New York." Bennett's supporters attributed both of these events directly to Lehman's meeting with the President, but instead of sulking or conceding, they kept adding to the list of county organizations committed to Bennett, and by mid-June they had won the support of more than enough delegations to guarantee Bennett's selection at the Democratic convention. Democratic National Chairman Ed Flynn, who also headed the party in the Bronx, conferred with the President and then predicted that Roosevelt "probably will wait and see what happens" rather than endorsing any particular candidate. Roosevelt's and Lehman's efforts to prevent Bennett's nomination continued to be plagued by the lack of a viable alternative as Senator Mead reiterated that he was not interested in running for Governor.[58]

While Roosevelt claimed that he was "too busy being President" to get involved in New York State politics, Lehman took the lead in trying to prevent Bennett from winning the nomination. Lehman still hoped that the Democrats would turn to Poletti who, like himself, was an ardent supporter of the President's domestic and foreign policies. Representatives of the state's C.I.O. unions gave Lehman a standing ovation when he warned that New Yorkers "cannot afford to elect mediocrities." Without mentioning any names, Lehman made clear his preference for Poletti over Bennett or Dewey when he called for the election of "true liberals in thought and in act." Both parties' gubernatorial candidates, Lehman stressed, should be "men on whom we can count to support the war effort of our President wholeheartedly, militantly, and with courage," men who "possess an enlightened social viewpoint" and who have demonstrated "that they have the courage to fight for what they believe." Lehman sent a copy of his speech to the President, marking certain passages which he thought FDR would especially enjoy, and the Governor was pleased when the labor leaders adopted a resolution opposing the candidacies of both Bennett and Dewey and calling instead for the election of "a true and tried liberal and a proven supporter of President Roosevelt's administration."[59]

Lehman remained committed to Poletti, but the President and others opposed to Bennett finally persuaded Senator Mead to challenge Bennett for the Democratic gubernatorial nomination. With Roosevelt orchestrating events behind the scenes, Senator Wagner, Assistant Secretary of State Adolf Berle, Henry Morgenthau, Sr., and other New York Democrats closely associated with the New Deal released a pair of letters in mid-July in which they appealed to Mead to run for Governor, stressing the need for a candidate "who has given concrete evidence of ability to understand the needs of this country without having to have them blasted into him by a Japanese or German bomb, . . . a man familiar with the program of the national government, so that he can ably and wholeheartedly support, with experience and vigor, the leadership of the President of the United States." Bennett was described as "a splendid American who has served the people well," but Wagner and the others emphasized that Mead's "unblemished record of support for the President's foreign policy, before and since Pearl Harbor," as well as his ability to attract support from independent voters and working people, would make him the strongest possible Democratic candidate. In a prearranged scenario, Roosevelt met with Mead at the White House on July 22, after which the Senator announced that he had agreed to seek the Democratic nomination for Governor, and the President announced that if he were a delegate to the New York State Democratic Convention, "I would cast my vote for Jim Mead."[60]

Governor Lehman declined to answer when asked to comment on the President's endorsement of Mead, hoping that a deadlock between Bennett and Mead would allow Poletti to emerge as a compromise candidate. Within a week, however, the Governor realized that Poletti had no chance, and, following Roosevelt's lead, Lehman threw his support behind Mead, characterizing the Senator as "a liberal in thought and in action" who "will give to the people of the State of New York a continuation of the high type of government to which they have become accustomed over the past twenty years." Lehman noted that Mead had "upheld the President of the United States whole-heartedly in all matters pertaining to the war effort—both before and since Pearl Harbor," and that Roosevelt had "publicly expressed his confidence in him and a preference for his nomination." The Governor denied reports that in return for his support of Mead, he had been promised that Poletti would be chosen again for Lieutenant Governor, and that Lehman would succeed Mead in the Senate.[61]

On August 18, the eve of the New York State Democratic Convention, party leaders and Herbert Lehman met to agree on a slate of candidates. Farley and most of the county chairmen still supported Bennett for the governorship, and they remained confident that they had sufficient votes to nominate him. Lehman and FDR, wanting a more liberal candidate, still backed Mead, but their forces at the gathering were clearly outnumbered. During the meeting, Lehman received a call from William Hassett, FDR's secretary, who read a letter that the President wanted Lehman to share with the others. Roosevelt disingenuously denied taking "any active part whatsoever" in the party's deliberations, claimed to have "no quarrel with my old friend, Jim Farley," and emphasized that "the question of nominating a Governor" was in no way "a fight for control in our State." Roosevelt reiterated that "I like and admire Jack Bennett, . . . an old friend of mine," but the President worried that the Attorney General "would not be a strong enough candidate against Dewey." FDR predicted that "Bennett's nomination would cause serious defections in the normal Democratic vote," especially among "the great majority of the Independents" and the American

Labor Party. Although he still believed that Mead would be the Democrats' strongest candidate, "rather than see the party split up" by "a bitter Convention fight" between the Mead and Bennett forces, the President offered "to accept any good compromise candidate that you gentlemen agree on." Unless the Democrats were united, the President warned, the state would be turned over to "the reactionary isolationist control of Tom Dewey." Roosevelt's pleas fell on deaf ears, however, and Farley and the other party leaders remained committed to nominating Bennett for Governor.[62]

Delegates and observers cheered Governor Lehman when he delivered the convention's keynote address, highlighting FDR's leadership in guiding the nation through the Depression and the war. Lehman's honeymoon with the delegates and the galleries proved to be short-lived, however. The Governor and the President pushed for a compromise candidate right up to the beginning of the voting on August 20, but Farley would not budge, so Bennett and Mead were both nominated by their supporters. Farley had selected the Hotel St. George in Brooklyn as the site of the convention to guarantee a crowd friendly to the Brooklyn-born Bennett, and when Lehman rose to deliver the main seconding speech for Mead, the *New York Times* reported, his remarks on behalf of Mead "brought boos of derision." Lehman later recalled that "the booing and the jeering was quite whole-hearted at the time," and that "it left a very bad taste in the minds" of many people across the state. This was the only time Lehman could remember "that both Franklin Roosevelt and I were booed at a Democratic convention." Lehman and other Mead supporters insisted that individual delegates be polled, but Bennett still won the nomination by a convincing margin on the first ballot in what was widely interpreted as a triumph for Farley and a defeat for Roosevelt and Lehman. It was a Pyrrhic victory, however. Lehman had always believed that Bennett would have a difficult time defeating Dewey under the best of circumstances, but after such a divisive convention, Lehman knew that Bennett had no chance to be elected.[63]

Lehman took some solace out of the convention when Charles Poletti was renominated for Lieutenant Governor. At first, Lehman was surprised that Poletti had agreed to run on the same ticket as Bennett, but at that time the Lieutenant Governor was still elected separately from the Governor, and Democrats thought that Poletti, who enjoyed labor and liberal support, might sneak in even if Bennett were defeated. Moreover, as Poletti later explained, Democratic leaders hoped that his election as Lieutenant Governor might "prevent Dewey from ever running for President, because he would have had to turn the State over to me as Lieutenant Governor."[64]

Once Bennett won the nomination, the focus shifted to whether Lehman and Roosevelt would support him. As the convention concluded, Lehman approached the platform, and the delegates hoped he was going to endorse Bennett's candidacy enthusiastically. Instead, Lehman merely congratulated Bennett and wished him well. A few days later, as Lehman and Roosevelt had predicted, the American Labor Party officially rejected Bennett, nominating New York attorney and self-described "New Deal Democrat" Dean Alfange as its gubernatorial candidate and adopting a platform calling for full-fledged support for the President and his domestic and defense policies. Lehman quickly returned to the Democratic fold, announcing at a press conference on August 28, "I will, of course, support Attorney General Bennett and the rest of the Democratic ticket, and I very much hope for their success." Bennett's supporters were elated by the Governor's endorsement and eagerly awaited word from the White House. In late September, Eleanor Roosevelt attended a gathering of Democratic women in New York, and even though she did not mention Bennett by name, her exhortation to the party faithful to "work for the election of all the candidates" was seen as an indication that the President would endorse Bennett, or at least call for the election of the Democratic ticket. FDR finally issued a statement on October 4 in which he declared that "of the three men in the race for the Governorship of New York, I shall cast my ballot for John Bennett because I believe he is the best qualified." The Bennett camp welcomed what many others considered to be the President's rather tepid endorsement, citing it frequently during the campaign, hoping it would rally disaffected Democrats to Bennett's candidacy.[65]

As Election Day neared, Roosevelt and Lehman stepped up their efforts on Bennett's behalf, having decided that any Democratic Governor was preferable to Dewey, who would immediately become a leading contender for the Republican presidential nomination in 1944. But even with Lehman's and Roosevelt's belated assistance, Bennett lost to Dewey by almost 650,000 votes. Republicans made impressive gains all across the nation. Pollster George Gallup noted "the phenomenally low turnout of voters" and concluded that "the light vote delivered by political machines in metropolitan areas was a great factor in decreased Democratic strength," as "was the fact that some 5,000,000 men are under arms." In New York, Dewey won despite receiving 179,000 fewer votes than he had garnered running against Lehman in 1938; Bennett's total was almost nine hundred thousand votes below what Lehman had received four years earlier. Dewey clearly benefited from the split in the Democratic ranks, as Alfange, the ALP candidate, received four hundred thousand pro-FDR, pro–New Deal votes that would have gone to a more liberal Democrat than Bennett. Lehman later recalled that many voters, "remembering the affront that had been shown to Franklin Roosevelt and to me" at the Brooklyn convention, just stayed home rather than voting for Bennett. As Lehman and Roosevelt had feared, Dewey's strong showing immediately elevated him to the forefront of Republican presidential candidates for 1944.[66]

VI

At the same time that Lehman was trying to influence the New York gubernatorial election in 1942, he also worked with the President on other matters as well, such as using his close ties with Roosevelt to try to reduce unemployment in the New York metropolitan area caused by the decline in non-war industries. The diversion of resources and raw materials needed for the war and the rationing of certain commodities proved to be particularly damaging to New York's factories that produced civilian and consumer goods. Lehman conferred with city, state, and federal officials and called upon the President to increase New York's share of federal contracts and to utilize existing factories and labor in the city rather than building new production facilities in other parts of the country. Roosevelt instructed federal officials to discuss the issue with Lehman and Mayor La Guardia, and over the next several months, New York's share of war contracts increased from $77,000,000 in May to $222,000,000 in August. By November, the Governor declared his satisfaction with the help New York had received from the War Department, the Navy Department, the Federal Manpower Commission, and other federal agencies in creating or finding jobs for half of the estimated four hundred thousand workers in New York City who had been unemployed in July.[67]

Lehman continued to be concerned about the plight of European Jewry. As reports filtered in of Nazi atrocities in Europe, the American Jewish Congress and various other groups organized a mass rally at Madison Square Garden in July 1942. The purpose of the gathering, Rabbi Stephen Wise explained to Lehman, was to express "the sorrow of American Jewry and indeed of our whole country over the mass murder of Jews and non-Jews in the Central and East European countries and urging that the United Nations make it possible for the large Jewish population of Palestine to defend itself." Wise hoped that Lehman, "as the chief magistrate of our State," would participate in the meeting and denounce "the crimes committed by the Nazis throughout Europe." Although Lehman supported public condemnation of Nazi atrocities, he opposed the creation of a Jewish Army in Palestine, and he was reluctant to appear at a rally where the two issues would be intertwined; therefore, he initially declined the invitation, claiming that other commitments required him to remain in Albany. But Rabbi Wise would not take no for an answer, begging the Governor to "reconsider . . . and, if humanly possible," to rearrange his schedule so that he could attend. Wise warned that the "great public meeting" would expect Lehman to be there and would be "profoundly disappointed" by his absence. Reluctantly, Lehman realized that as one of the leaders of the American Jewish community, he had no choice but to attend the rally.[68]

In addressing the gathering, Lehman explained what was at stake for every American, describing the war as a conflict between "all the free peoples of the world fighting for freedom, for security, and for the dignity of man," and "the Nazi tyrants and their jackals, determined to foist on the entire world a system of cruel slavery which they boast will last for a thousand years." The Governor emphasized that "there must be no appeasement or compromise measures in this fight for freedom. Either we destroy the Nazi, the Fascist, and the Japanese war lords, or they destroy us. Either their way of life disappears or ours disappears. There can be no compromise between slavery and freedom." Lehman heard "scattered hisses and boos" when he rejected the call for a separate Jewish Army in Palestine, recommending instead that Palestinian Jews "be permitted to fight side by side with their British and American friends, in behalf of our common cause—the defense of democracy, of freedom and of security."[69]

In a telegram to the rally, President Roosevelt declared that all Americans "share in the sorrow of our Jewish fellow-citizens over the savagery of the Nazis against their helpless victims," and he promised that "the perpetrators of these crimes" would be held to "strict accountability in a day of reckoning which will surely come." Roosevelt hoped that "the Atlantic Charter and the just world order to be made possible by the triumph of the United Nations will bring the Jews and oppressed people in all lands the four freedoms which Christian and Jewish teachings have largely inspired." Roosevelt and Lehman both made it clear in their remarks that they believed that the best way to help European Jewry was to defeat the Nazis rather than taking specific steps to rescue European Jews.[70]

In late September 1942, Governor Lehman looked back with pride on all he and the people of New York had done for the war effort. He noted the creation of the State Guard to replace the National Guard when the latter had been called to active duty; the organization of local defense councils which, after December 7, 1941, had become war councils and had conducted numerous blackout and air raid drills; and the establishment of procedures to mobilize police, fire, and medical personnel all across the state in times of emergency. According to the Governor, New York was "girded for total war. Its people are ready to show the world that democracy can function as promptly and effectively in war as in the peace and victory we are sure to win."[71]

When Herbert Lehman announced that he would neither seek nor accept another term as Governor, he expected the President would soon appoint him to a war-related job in Washington. Lehman's departure for Washington was delayed, however, as Roosevelt found it difficult to find just the right position for him. Initial speculation focused on an appointment as a Major or a Lieutenant General to work in military procurement, similar to his duties during World War I, but other possibilities included "supreme federal arbiter of wages"; "director of wage stabilization"; chairman of a proposed Economic Stabilization Authority "with broad powers to coordinate federal policies on prices, wages, taxes, savings, and credits"; and "economic 'czar,'" charged with "limiting all wages, salaries and farm prices . . . to hold down the wartime cost of living." In late August, Herbert Lehman confided to his brother Irving that he had "not heard from the President for some time. I know he has some definite work that he wants me to do but he has not as yet told me what it is." According to James Farley, Roosevelt knew that "as Governor of New York, Lehman is entitled to a decent place," but the President moved slowly in appointing Lehman "because of the criticism that there are too many Jews in the administration." But when Roosevelt chose James Byrnes rather than Lehman to head the newly created Office of Economic Stabilization, Byrnes's long experience in Washington as a Congressman, Senator, and Supreme Court Justice was the determining factor in the President's decision, not Lehman's religion. Even the *New Republic*, which noted that "labor leaders and liberals . . . would have preferred either Governor Lehman of New York or Supreme Court Justice William O. Douglas," conceded that Byrnes "was the most effective legislative agent who ever represented the President."[72]

A few weeks later, Roosevelt asked Byrnes about appointing Lehman as "Food Coordinator in the Department of Agriculture," where he "would be responsible for the production and processing of the food itself, and would carry out requisitions put in by Army, Navy, WPB, etc." Byrnes preferred Milo Perkins, the head of the Board of Economic Warfare, for Food Administrator, and he suggested that Lehman could replace Perkins in the Board of Economic Warfare, "and while in this job could plan for relief in occupied countries." Working from Byrnes's suggestion that Lehman should be involved in relief work in some capacity, Roosevelt finally found the right spot for Lehman—to lead the new Office of Foreign Relief and Rehabilitation Operations in the State Department that would be charged with assisting refugees and inhabitants of nations freed from Axis rule. In that position, Lehman would help to carry out Roosevelt's vision of a world in which nations and people worked together to end fascism and provide the basic necessities needed to recover from the devastation of the war. And Lehman's humanitarian work with the Joint Distribution Committee during and after World War I, as well as his administrative experience as Governor of New York, made him the perfect choice for this position.[73]

CHAPTER 7

"Governor Lehman . . . Doesn't Know the Way Things Are Done in Washington"

Lehman, Roosevelt, and OFRRO, 1942–1943

It is indeed fortunate that one with Herbert Lehman's humanitarian instincts and varied experience in administrative work is now in association with our Department of State, further serving his fellow man as Director of Foreign Relief and Rehabilitation.[1]

I

Shortly after Thomas Dewey's election as Governor of New York, President Roosevelt invited Herbert Lehman to lunch at the White House on November 11, 1942. Lehman was eager to participate in the war effort, and Roosevelt had been searching for months for just the right position for him. The *New York Times* speculated that Lehman would serve in the supply area in a role similar to his duties during World War I, but the President and administration officials realized that Lehman's expertise could better be utilized on what Vice President Henry Wallace described as "the job of feeding and clothing the hungry peoples of Europe when the Army went out of the picture." During their meeting, Roosevelt offered Lehman the opportunity to head the new Office of Foreign Relief and Rehabilitation Operations (OFRRO) being created in the State Department, even though in typical Roosevelt fashion, the President had never mentioned Lehman's possible appointment to Secretary of

---

Chapter title quotation: Henry Wallace quoted in Blum, ed., *The Price of Vision*, p. 251.

State Cordell Hull. Hull first learned that Lehman would be working in the State Department when the President called to inform him during Roosevelt's meeting with Lehman. The Governor immediately accepted the President's offer, emphasizing to Roosevelt that this position "appeals to me tremendously and I know that my experience in administrative work as well as my deep interest in and long contact with social problems will enable me to do an effective job."[2]

On November 21, 1942, the White House announced Lehman's appointment as Director of Foreign Relief and Rehabilitation Operations in the Department of State. The official statement explained that Lehman would organize "American participation in the activities of the United Nations in furnishing relief and other assistance to the victims of war in areas reoccupied by the forces of the United Nations." Lehman was "greatly honored" in his appointment by the President, fully realized "the scope and importance of the work and the great responsibilities involved," and believed that Roosevelt's "program of relief and rehabilitation" would "render an immediate and effective further contribution to the winning of the war and to the solution of post-war problems."[3]

Lehman's appointment in the State Department was expected to be temporary. Assistant Secretary of State Dean Acheson was working with his counterparts from Great Britain, China, and other nations to create the United Nations Relief and Rehabilitation Administration (UNRRA), an international agency that would provide assistance to people in North Africa, Europe, and Asia when they were liberated from the Axis powers, and it was anticipated that Lehman would be the head of UNRRA once it was established. Allied military successes meant that relief operations would be needed in North Africa before UNRRA had been created, however, so Lehman and OFRRO would direct American relief and rehabilitation planning and activities until UNRRA was ready to take over.[4]

Franklin Roosevelt derived special pleasure from appointing Lehman to head OFRRO, and subsequently UNRRA, because Lehman was a Jew. In explaining his choice to Samuel Rosenman, the President stressed that Lehman was "a fine administrator and executive with experience in this kind of work," but he then added:

> After all that Hitler has done to the Jews of Germany and of every nation he has conquered, I think it would be wonderful, poetic justice if we could get a Jew to head the agency which is going to feed and clothe and shelter the millions whom Hitler has robbed and starved and tortured—a member of the group Hitler first selected for extermination. It would be a fine object lesson in tolerance and human brotherhood to have a Jew head up this operation, and I think Herbert would be fine.

Similarly, an official of the British Embassy in Washington reported that at the time of Lehman's appointment, Roosevelt was overheard saying, "I want to see some of those Goddamned Fascists begging for their subsistence from a Jew," and Eleanor Roosevelt later recalled that her husband "thought it was very amusing—he thought it was particularly appropriate for a Jew to be Director of UNRRA, as far as Germans are concerned." Maurice Perlzweig, political director of the World Jewish Congress, believed that "the appointment of a Jew to an office which is going to play a decisive role in the reconstruction of Europe is a fact of the most far-reaching significance," but he gave Roosevelt way too much credit when he asserted that Lehman's appointment showed that Roosevelt, "more than any statesman living, . . . appreciates the full moral horror of anti-Semitism and is determined to make no sort of compromise with it."[5]

Lehman's appointment as head of OFRRO was widely cheered. Eleanor Roosevelt was "delighted" at Lehman's appointment, knowing of "no one who could be more valuable in this important work," and the *New York Times* asserted that Lehman's "liberal and successful administration" of New York State for ten years, his unique combination of "the practical experience of a sound business man with the vision of a proved statesman," his deep sympathy "with the problems of oppressed minorities everywhere," and "his close and friendly association with President Roosevelt," made Lehman the perfect choice for this important position. Secretary of Labor Frances Perkins was pleased that Lehman was willing to undertake this new service for humanity, which she saw as a natural outgrowth of the Governor's many years of work "dedicated to human betterment," and Joseph Proskauer of the American Jewish Committee noted that "this really is a case where the office and the man fit perfectly." Edith Lehman confided to her brother Frank Altschul that she was "thrilled at the reaction to the President's appointment of Herb and cannot imagine a more fitting job for him," and longtime Lehman aide Carolin Flexner later recalled that this was an especially appropriate position for the Governor "because his prime interest is in people, . . . not in the rich people, but in the suffering people."[6]

Roosevelt and Lehman conferred at the White House on November 25, and the President made it clear that he was eager for Lehman to assume his new position as soon as possible. So, after serving as Governor of New York for ten years, Herbert Lehman resigned as the state's chief executive effective December 2, 1942. In a statewide radio broadcast that he described as both "a farewell and a report to the people" of New York," Lehman emphasized that "government is for the people" and that it needed to "concern itself with the solution of human as well as material problems." Proud as he was to be handing over to his successor a surplus in the state treasury of $75,000,000, Lehman's "greatest satisfaction" came from his role "in enacting enlightened and beneficial social labor legislation." The Governor stressed that New York State "has given equal protection and equal opportunity to all of its citizens, regardless of economic or social status," and he "pray[ed] that that policy will continue," asserting that "no healthy, strong communal life can exist if any group or class of our citizens is exploited or denied equal rights and opportunities with their fellows."[7]

Before proceeding to Washington to be sworn in as the head of OFRRO, Lehman stopped in New York City to meet with former President Herbert Hoover, who had directed American relief efforts during and after World War I and had hoped for a similar assignment now. Hoover had written to congratulate Lehman and to offer "any assistance" that he could, based on his previous experience, but Hoover also confided to a friend his belief that this was "a rotten appointment from any point of view," presumably because of Lehman's close relationship to Roosevelt and his lack of experience in international affairs. Hoover complained to Lehman about the Allies' refusal to meet "the urgent need of food supplies during this winter to the women, children and the unemployed men in the occupied democracies—Belgium, Holland, Norway, and Poland." Secretary of State Hull had repeatedly explained to Hoover that it was the German government's responsibility "to replace the stocks of food removed from the occupied countries," and that any food sent to Europe would "release labor now required for food production to be used in furtherance of the German military effort." Lehman listened politely as Hoover detailed his proposal to distribute food aid to Europe through neutral nations, but he refused to make any commitment. After their luncheon, Hoover revealed his program to the press and Lehman refused to comment when asked about Hoover's plan.[8]

Hoover's repeated calls to send food through the Allied blockade to prevent starvation in Nazi-occupied Europe continued to be a thorn in the side of both Lehman and President Roosevelt. Thomas Reynolds, who headed OFRRO's public information office, warned Lehman about Hoover's efforts "to snatch the leadership in the relief problem in any manner possible," noting that "the outstanding relief issue in the public mind at the moment is the pressure drive and debate being led by Hoover for extension of relief through the blockade." The President resented what he considered to be Hoover's grandstanding, and he forwarded to Lehman a letter making all sorts of outrageous accusations about Hoover's actions as a mining engineer and during his relief efforts in World War I, including the claim that the Germans had executed English nurse Edith Cavell to prevent her from revealing that Hoover was shipping relief goods intended for Belgium to Germany instead. Lehman read the letter "with great interest," then returned it to the President for his files. Despite Hoover's importuning, Britain insisted on maintaining the blockade inviolate rather than making any exceptions for food relief, so Lehman and OFRRO were unable to send any assistance to the civilian populations in Nazi-occupied Europe.[9]

Lehman was sworn in as the head of OFRRO at a White House ceremony on December 4, 1942, attended by the President, Secretary Hull, and various administration officials and family members. An official letter from Hull notified Lehman of his appointment as "Director of Foreign Relief and Rehabilitation Operations in the Department of State" at an annual salary of $10,000. Roosevelt declared his "special confidence" in Lehman's "ability to discharge the manifold duties which lie before you," and he assured Lehman, "your new associates, and your old, in the Federal Government welcome you to Washington, and hold themselves ready to work with you to the end that the four freedoms may spread through all the earth." In accepting his appointment, Lehman promised "to give due attention to the problems of the many millions among our Allies who have suffered severely from the horrors of war, not in one continent or region alone but wherever they are found in need and to such extent as capacity to be of assistance exists."[10]

FIGURE 7.1. President Roosevelt congratulates Herbert Lehman on his appointment as head of the Office of Foreign Relief and Rehabilitation Operations, as Edith Lehman looks on, December 4, 1942. AP Images.

II

As Governor of New York, Herbert Lehman had often needed to over-come the venality of Tammany Hall and the opposition of a Republican-con-trolled State Legislature, but none of those experiences prepared him for the internecine warfare he faced in the Roosevelt administration and the State Department, where everyone was supposedly on the same side. The New Deal was notorious for its tangled lines of jurisdiction and authority, with different officials and agencies pursuing complementary or conflicting goals, and this pattern was reflected in the administration's handling of foreign relief issues. Arthur Krock of the *New York Times* quoted Democratic National Chairman Ed Flynn describing Roosevelt's management style in the following way: "The boss either appoints one man to do the work of four, or four men to do the work of one. Often he does both." Vice President Henry Wallace, who chaired the Board of Economic Warfare (BEW), was constantly at loggerheads with the State Department and quarreled incessantly with Secretary of Commerce Jesse Jones, who also headed the Federal Loan Administration (FLA) and the Recon-struction Finance Corporation (RFC), which controlled most of the funds the BEW needed to carry out its activities. Foreign relief efforts were not immune from these problems. After reading the State Department's "preliminary draft of a proposed United Nations Relief and Rehabilitation Administration" in June 1942, Wallace concluded that "this is a matter of the utmost importance" and requested "a chance to discuss it" with the President "before a final decision is reached." Roosevelt complained to Hull that "I know nothing about this," and he met with Wallace and Hull to talk about UNRRA on September 2, 1942.[11]

Lehman's appointment was designed in part to clarify responsibility within the administration concerning foreign relief and rehabilitation, but chaos still prevailed. Ironically, while a member of the House of Lords in Britain called for the appointment of a "British Lehman" to direct plans for helping Europe after the war, Assistant Secretary of State Dean Acheson thought that the Presi-dent, in appointing Lehman, had "tossed a lighted firecracker" into an already "explosive situation." Lehman later recalled that his appointment had come "as a surprise and perhaps as a shock to Hull, who in theory had to make the appointment," since Lehman was to be a State Department employee. Com-pounding the confusion, two days before Lehman's swearing in, Undersecretary of Agriculture Paul Appleby was "temporarily loaned to the State Department" to head a new Office of Foreign Territories, which was supposed to "imple-ment the pertinent policies of the government in harmony with the Atlantic Charter and the Declaration of the United Nations." The announcement of Appleby's new position noted that "there will of necessity . . . be close col-laboration between the functions of Governor Herbert H. Lehman of New York as Director of Foreign Relief and Rehabilitation Operations and the functions of the Office of Foreign Territories," but it was unclear how they would work together. Lehman's authority was further undermined on December 6, two days after his swearing in, when Secretary of Agriculture Claude Wickard was named Food Administrator with "full responsibility for and control over the nation's food program." Among other tasks, Wickard was to "collaborate with other government agencies in feeding the peoples of foreign countries," and any disagreements between Wickard and any such agencies would be referred to the President. According to the *New York Times*, Wickard would "work closely" with Lehman, who would "direct food distribution to liberated peoples *under* Mr. Wickard's supervision" (emphasis added).[12]

The President tried to clarify Lehman's authority in a memorandum to Hull on December 11. As Roosevelt envisioned it, Lehman, as the head of OFRRO, "would have complete charge of all of our foreign relief activities" and would report directly to the Secretary of State. The Governor would "co-ordinate all foreign relief activities," and his responsibilities would include "supervision of all of our own relief work abroad until the war is finished," and setting up, "as circumstances permit, a United Nations relief program which he, Governor Lehman, would head up." Roosevelt thought that "the simplest way of getting administrative control of this within the State Department would be to have Appleby [head of the new Office of Foreign Territories] report through Lehman" to Hull, while the President ensured that "Lend Lease and Red Cross and any other governmental agency" involved in relief activities "coordinate their work through Governor Lehman." The President suggested that Hull "issue appropriate instructions in the State Department to make sure that all matters of relief come to you through Governor Lehman," while Roosevelt would "take care of the other agencies in such a manner as you and Governor Lehman think best."[13]

After two weeks in his new position, Lehman reported to his brother-in-law Frank Altschul, "The job is even more complex that [*sic*] I had anticipated," but "I find it intensely interesting, and I think I am making some progress." In a speech to the Albany Chamber of Commerce, Lehman noted proudly that although he had only been at OFRRO for a short time, food aid was already en route to liberated areas in North Africa. By the end of December, Lehman confided to his brother Irving, "The work is very hard indeed and because of its countless ramifications . . . is more difficult than anything I have undertaken for a long time. It is, however, most interesting and I think I am making some headway. Everybody has been very nice to me and appears to desire to cooperate." A week later, Lehman was still optimistic that everything would work out, telling Altschul that the new job was "full of interest and also full of problems" that kept Lehman's mind "on the go twenty-four hours a day." Lehman hoped that "little by little" things would "get straightened out" so that he could accomplish some of his goals "reasonably soon."[14]

Despite Lehman's confidence, confusion continued to surround his status within the Roosevelt administration. Shortly after Lehman's arrival, the State Department drafted an executive order reasserting its authority over "all matters concerning our international cooperation in the immediate present and after the war, involving political, economic and financial elements," and another directive stipulating that the Director of OFRRO should be responsible for "supervising and integrating the activities of the various departments and agencies of the government . . . for the relief abroad of victims of war." But Director of the Bureau of the Budget Harold Smith blocked the State Department's attempt to affirm its jurisdiction in this area, warning the President that the proposed edicts were "very sweeping in their implications and raise the question of the operations of the Board of Economic Warfare, Lend-Lease, Coordinator of Inter-American Affairs, and various corporations under the RFC." Smith argued that "the orders, as drafted, would not serve in any way to clarify responsibility for the various foreign economic and relief operations," and he advised that "perhaps this is the time to raise the question as to the merger of these operations into one organization." He recommended that Roosevelt "refer this matter to Budget for some study and comments." The President accepted Smith's suggestion, telling the Budget Director to "study the proposed orders and talk with the Secretary of State about this," meaning that Smith had successfully parried State's attempt to proclaim Lehman's and the Department's predominance in this area.[15]

Lehman and OFRRO won some of the constant bureaucratic turf wars, but most of their victories were fleeting. The British Embassy reported to London that Paul Appleby, the head of the State Department's new Office of Foreign Territories, had developed "happy relations with his new colleagues," including Lehman, but that Appleby had concluded that "Lehman's insistence on including rehabilitation, in its widest aspects, as well as relief, within his sphere of competence," had rendered Appleby and his position superfluous. "Rather than indulge in the fashionable pastime of jurisdictional border warfare, whereby rival officials spend their time in appeals to the President to defend them against encroachment and for the recovery of lost powers," Embassy officials noted, Appleby "preferred to leave the field of battle and make a dignified withdrawal to his own Department of Agriculture." They predicted that "the struggle for power in the field of reconstruction is likely to be very bitter, and the State Department in its present mood would do its best to prevent even a moderate New Dealer from capturing genuine control of this field." The British diplomats had Appleby in mind when they wrote those words, but they could also be taken as an indication that Lehman was in for rough sledding.[16]

In early February, the State Department submitted a revised executive order "defining the powers and duties of the Director of Foreign Relief and Rehabilitation Operations in the Department of State." But Budget Director Smith questioned whether the directive would "improve the relationships among the several agencies concerned," and Attorney General Francis Biddle pointed out that the document had not been cleared by some of the agencies "likely to be directly affected by the order." The Attorney General reported to the President that Lehman "feels quite strongly that the basis of his powers should be clarified and defined along the lines of the proposed order," and that the Governor was "willing to rely on your judgment as to whether or not the order ought to be cleared with the Board of Economic Warfare and the Lend-Lease Administration before you sign it."[17]

The President thought the proposed executive order was "all right," but that "everyone would be happier if it were cleared through all channels." However, Smith warned in early March that it did not make sense to designate OFRRO as the overall coordinator of "foreign economic, relief, and supply matters in all areas occupied by this country" when OFRRO was intended to be responsible "for only a part of the operations to be coordinated, and in view of plans to make OFRR [sic] a United Nations organization." Smith also cautioned that the proposed order would complicate matters for the Army, which was "gravely concerned over the task of dealing with a large array of civilian agencies here, in North Africa, and on new fronts." Unless immediate consolidation occurred combining all these programs, including OFRRO, into a single agency, Smith suggested that the State Department, not OFRRO, be assigned "the responsibility for coordinating the war programs of American civilian agencies abroad."[18]

Roosevelt forwarded Smith's comments to Harry Hopkins and James Byrnes, asking them to discuss the matter and then talk with him about it. Byrnes, the Director of the Office of Economic Stabilization who was sometimes referred to as the "assistant president," believed that "all foreign economic functions" should be centered in the State Department; however, he realized that such action "would require a reorganization within the Department" that was "not possible within the near future." He recommended that the executive order not be signed "if Lehman is planning to transfer his work to a United Nations Relief organization within a measurable time" because issuing the directive "would not effect a real consolidation of related activities" and "might complicate rather than simplify Lehman's relations with existing agencies when later he becomes the head of United Nations Relief."[19]

As Lehman's assistant Carolin Flexner later recalled, the Governor "had a most frustrating time" with the bureaucratic bickering and delays, and he finally appealed directly to the President for help in resolving his status. In a letter to the President on March 13, Lehman pointed out that he had been on the job at OFRRO for three months, but, despite his "urgent requests," he was still waiting for an executive order defining his "responsibilities and authority." Lehman complained that his dealings with other agencies and with foreign governments had "grown increasingly difficult and complicated" while his own organization was "becoming confused and discouraged." The Governor empha-sized that "the problem of foreign relief and rehabilitation is not only one of the most important but one of the most difficult tasks confronting us," noting that even "under the best of circumstances the planning and administration of relief and rehabilitation will tax to the utmost the ability and energy of any organization." He asserted that "if the program is to be conducted with any degree of success it must have the full and carefully coordinated support of all governmental authorities as well as of the public." Lehman was about to embark on an official visit to London "to discuss with the British and other authorities questions of mutual interest and concern regarding relief and rehabilitation," but without "official recognition" of his "authority and responsibilities and some agreement on the policies of this government," he feared that his trip might not only be "fruitless but might conceivably lead to misunderstandings and serious embarrassment." For all these reasons, Lehman hoped that Roosevelt would issue an executive order covering his work.[20]

Roosevelt asked Byrnes to prepare a response to the Governor's letter, but Byrnes decided to talk with Lehman rather than trying to explain his concerns in writing. Byrnes spoke with the Governor on March 17, and as he reported to the President, he believed that he had "raised doubts" in Lehman's "own mind as to the wisdom of the Executive Order," pointing out that Lehman "would in a few months be heading up the United Nations' relief work" and "might then wish quite a different American set-up than that proposed in his Order." Instead of a presidential directive, Byrnes suggested Roosevelt send Lehman "a letter outlining his authority pending the working out of more definite plans with our Allies," and Byrnes began working on such a missive.[21]

The President also asked Judge Samuel Rosenman, an old friend of his and Lehman's who often served as an unofficial advisor on legal matters and had helped draft numerous executive orders, for his advice on how to handle the situation. Like Byrnes, Smith, and Biddle, Rosenman believed that "the conflicts and overlapping" jurisdiction in this area would continue "until all of the civilian agencies engaged in the foreign field are put together under one responsible head." Theoretically, Rosenman argued, the State Department should be in charge of such activities, but he realized "that would be impossible under the present set-up in the State Department and would require thorough reorganization there." As for Lehman and OFRRO, Rosenman advised against issuing the executive order that the Governor had requested because "it would be almost impossible to draft language which would not on its face run into some of the BEW, Lend-Lease, Treasury, Agriculture, and Army activities."[22]

Byrnes and officials in the Bureau of the Budget composed a letter that Roosevelt signed and sent to Lehman on March 19, 1943. "Pending the working out of final plans with our allies," the President defined "the scope and duties" of Lehman's "work as Director of the Office of Foreign Relief and Rehabilita-tion." Roosevelt authorized Lehman "to plan, coordinate, and arrange for the administration of this government's activities for the relief of victims of war in areas liberated from Axis control through the provision of food, fuel, clothing, and other basic necessities, housing facilities, medical and other essential services; and to facilitate in areas receiving relief the production and transportation of these articles and the furnishing of these services." In carrying out these activities, Lehman was to "utilize the facilities of the various government departments, agencies, and officials which are equipped to assist in this field," and Lehman's supremacy over competing civilian agencies was made clear when he was given the power to issue to these departments and officials "such directives as you deem necessary to achieve consistency in policy and coordination in administration." Lehman's actions in specific areas abroad were "subject to the approval of the U.S. military commander in that area," and, "in matters of general foreign policy," he was to "be guided by the directives of the Secretary of State." Finally, Lehman was to coordinate his efforts with America's allies and any United Nations organization "established for providing relief and rehabilitation to victims of war." Roosevelt assured Lehman "of my full cooperation and that of federal agencies in fields related to your own" in meeting the "grave responsibility and challenging opportunity to facilitate the progress of the war and to relieve the deep suffering of those under Axis domination."[23]

The President's letter departed from the State Department's original proposal and weakened Lehman's authority in significant ways. The draft order had given equal weight to relief and rehabilitation, but Roosevelt focused mainly on Lehman's responsibilities for relief, barely mentioning rehabilitation. The State Department had suggested giving Lehman broad administrative power, but the President merely authorized Lehman to "arrange for the administration of this government's activities." Moreover, a presidential letter carried much less force and legal authority than a formal executive order.[24]

Nonetheless, Lehman welcomed Roosevelt's letter clarifying his role. Mrs. Lehman explained to her brother that "Herb's job still remains full of problems and difficulties," but she believed that "the atmosphere has been considerably cleared since the President's letter of March 19th, which sets forth so clearly and so strongly the duties and responsibilities of the office to which he appointed Herb. Had this been done earlier," she noted, "much conflict could have been avoided." Herbert Lehman later recalled that the challenges he had faced at OFRRO "in setting up a working organization with adequate powers" helped prepare him for the "problems and difficulties which arose later" when UNRRA was established in November 1943.[25]

III

Bolstered by the President's letter, Lehman traveled to London in April 1943 "to procure all the information available on problems connected with relief of victims of war in areas liberated from Axis control." Britain and other nations eager to coordinate their efforts with the United States and to create the United Nations Relief and Rehabilitation Administration had been urging such a visit ever since Lehman's appointment in December, but the Governor had not wanted to undertake such a trip until his authority had been clarified. In London, Lehman met Sir Frederick Leith-Ross, who headed the Inter-Allied Relief Committee; British Prime Minister Winston Churchill and Foreign Secretary Anthony Eden; numerous American and Allied military and diplomatic officials, including Greek, Russian, and Chinese representatives; and leaders of various governments-in-exile. He lunched with King George VI at Buckingham Palace and conferred with Queen Wilhelmina of the Netherlands, King Peter of Yugoslavia, and King Haakon of Norway. Lehman also met with his son Peter, who was stationed in England and had recently transferred from the Royal Canadian to the U.S. Army Air Force. Speaking with the press in London, Lehman reported that his trip had given him "a much clearer idea of the magnitude of the task and the requirements and difficulties involved in his position," and that he was "tremendously impressed" by the "careful and systematic work" already undertaken to determine "what the people of Europe would need to keep them from perishing of starvation and to get agriculture and industry going again." U.S. Ambassador John Winant noted that no one had "done a more thoroughly workman-like job on any mission assignment" than Lehman, who had gained "the confidence and respect" of all those with whom he had met. Winant stressed that Lehman's visit had "lifted the consideration of this problem on the part of the British from one of secondary importance under the supervision of a civil servant to a major problem of cabinet policy status."[26]

Returning to Washington in early May, Lehman tried to build on the authority he had gained from the President's letter and the acclaim he had won during his trip to England. On May 8, Lehman sent the President and the agencies and departments involved in foreign economic activities a twelve-point "Statement of Policy for Relief and Rehabilitation in Future Liberated Areas" delineating what he saw as his and OFRRO's primacy in this field. Invoking the President's name frequently, Lehman noted "the grave responsibility" that had been conferred on him by Roosevelt's letter of March 19, and his confidence "that this responsibility can be discharged with the full support of the President and with the cooperation of the federal agencies" engaged in related activities. He appreciated that "the President and the individual agencies" had "generously given me their assurances" of cooperation, pointing out that the main reason OFRRO had been created "was to 'facilitate the progress of the war' by concentrating in a single agency responsibility for relief and rehabilitation, and civilian supply related thereto, during the period following liberation. Such a concentration," Lehman explained, "simplifies the problem of the Army by assuring the existence of a single civilian supply line and administration," reducing "to the minimum all duplication of effort," and eliminating "the administrative confusion which exists when several agencies operate in the same field, and the danger of contradictory policies in dealing with foreign governments." Lehman asserted that centralizing authority in this way "provides the only means by which goods which will inevitably be in short supply can be allocated on a practical and equitable basis to the peoples requiring assistance" and would "make easier the transition to any United Nations relief organization that might hereafter be established."[27]

Relying heavily upon Roosevelt's letter, Lehman's own "analysis of the economic operations in North Africa," and his "many discussions here and in London with responsible officials, American and Allied, military as well as civilian," Lehman recognized that "for an initial period after any area is liberated from the Axis, the military authorities must, of course, have complete control over and responsibility for the administration of civilian relief and rehabilitation," and that OFRRO's role during this time would be "to serve the military authorities, as they may request, in planning for and carrying out these operations during this initial period." But later, "when the responsibility for the administration of relief and rehabilitation passes from military to civilian hands," Lehman believed that it was his "responsibility as Director of the Office of Foreign Relief and Rehabilitation Operations to control, so far as the activities of the United States Government are concerned, the entire civilian supply for the particular liberated area during the relief and rehabilitation period." Lehman realized that other civilian agencies also had important roles to play, that "the problem of financial and currency control," for example, was "a function of the Treasury Department," and that "the development and procurement of strategic and critical materials and the gathering of economic intelligence are among the functions of the Board of Economic Warfare," and he pledged that OFRRO "will work in close cooperation" with such agencies "so that the necessary coordination can be achieved, both in the planning stage and in operations." But the Governor emphasized that "to fulfill the responsibilities" placed upon him by the President, "the Office of Foreign Relief and Rehabilitation Operations must and does take responsibility for the formulation of requirements and plans for the relief and rehabilitation of civilian populations in liberated areas and for all coordination thereof."[28]

Unbeknownst to Lehman, at the same time that he was trying to consolidate his authority in relief and rehabilitation matters, others within the administration were attacking the limited ascendancy he had gained. I. F. Stone had reported in *The Nation* back in February that "the State Department has executed a successful encirclement of former Governor Herbert H. Lehman and will control his Office of Foreign Relief and Rehabilitation Operations. . . . Not only is Lehman subject to Hull, but it now appears that his field representatives will be subordinate to diplomatic officers." Now in mid-May, Jerry Kluttz wrote

in the *Washington Post* that the State Department was about to win "an under-
cover fight for foreign and postwar control" at the expense of other agencies,
including "Governor Lehman's Relief and Rehabilitation." According to Kluttz,
this would be "an important victory, with plenty of implications," and "the
matter is now up to the President and some sort of an order is expected soon."
When asked about his source, Kluttz informed a member of Lehman's staff that
"he got this squib of information from someone in the White House" who "told
him that the White House would move to 'nip in the bud' a developing interagency conflict over post-war operations." Kluttz warned that "some kind of a
White House order was in prospect within the next week or so, and . . . that
the decision was to be made in favor of the Department of State rather than
in favor of the OFRRO as a segment of the Department of State."[29]

Kluttz's information was correct. A few days earlier, Budget Director
Smith had asked the President to sign a letter addressed to Secretary of State
Hull "fixing clear responsibility for leadership and coordination in the State
Department and restating the relevant basic functions of the interested agencies." In the letter, the President instructed the Secretary of State to "appoint
for each area which may be liberated a Director for Economic Operations
acceptable to the Office of Foreign Relief and Rehabilitation Operations, the
Board of Economic Warfare, the Office of Lend-Lease Administration and the
military." This Director "would be a single source of contact and assistance on
civilian agency activities in the economic field to the military commander for
the area," and he would enjoy "full authority to direct the representatives of
the United States civilian economic agencies." The President also told Hull "to
establish an inter-departmental policy committee under the chairmanship of a
Director for Foreign Economic Operations" that would include representatives
of OFRRO and other agencies within and outside of the State Department,
the purpose of which would be "to coordinate in Washington our economic activities relative to liberated areas and to provide an appropriate channel
for military-civilian cooperation." The President acknowledged that the State
Department had "already taken measures to integrate and unify the economic
operations of the several agencies," but he stressed that "stronger measures are
needed and the Chairman of the proposed inter-departmental policy committee
should be given sufficient status and staff for the job." Under this new set-up,
OFRRO would be "responsible for distributing relief goods and services, and
goods to facilitate the production of basic civilian necessities," and it would
"provide technical advice and services with respect to relief and the production
of civilian necessities."[30]

As requested, Roosevelt signed the letter, and Smith reported a few weeks
later that he "discussed the letter with Secretary Hull (who found it entirely
acceptable), but because of certain developments," the Budget Director had
decided "not to deliver it formally, nor to make its contents known to the other

agencies." The main "development" had been Lehman's twelve-point statement, which had gone in a very different direction from the one Roosevelt, Smith, and Hull were pursuing. Smith pointed out that Lehman had circulated his plan to the other departments "without prior notice to us or any of the agencies," and that the Governor's proposal was "inconsistent" with the President's letter "in a number of respects, particularly with regard to coordinating responsibility and operations in the liberated areas." The Budget Director noted that the issuance of the President's letter to Hull at the same time that Lehman was circulating his statement "would have occasioned much embarrassment for Governor Lehman and further confusion in the already tangled interagency relations," so, instead, he had "conferred at length with the principals involved" to see if agreement could be reached on a slightly revised letter. In the meantime, Roosevelt met with Lehman at the White House on May 18, at which time the Governor strongly objected to the new policy outlined in the letter to Hull, complaining that "it puts some State Department man directly over his relief people."[31]

Roosevelt sent Lehman's twelve-point statement to the Secretary of State, asking him to prepare a response for the President to sign. Cordell Hull was a skillful infighter who held the position of Secretary of State longer than any other person in U.S. history, and he met with Roosevelt on May 18 to discuss the problem of relief and rehabilitation and other overseas economic activities. Hull brought with him a memorandum drafted by "six of the most capable and appropriate members of the State Department," which placed Lehman and OFRRO in a subordinate place by minimizing the significance of relief and rehabilitation. The Department maintained that "as long as the war lasts, relief and rehabilitation cannot take precedence over the various phases of economic warfare," and "when the war is over relief and rehabilitation must be considered as part of the larger pattern of economic reconstruction, which will also involve the restoration of international trade, the development of the world's raw materials, the creation of international financial mechanisms and numerous other complex operations." Almost as if Lehman and OFRRO were somehow outside of the State Department rather than within, the Department offered "to place its facilities at the disposal of OFRRO to assist it in every appropriate way in the discharge of its responsibility." Subtly twisting the knife in Lehman's back by bringing up OFRRO's lack of any clear legal basis or status, the Department "recognized that the responsibilities charged to the other departments and agencies by Acts of Congress or by Executive Orders are theirs alone and are not to be carried out by the State Department." At the same time, however, the Department needed to retain the ability "to discharge its responsibilities, i.e., to see to it that not only the political policies but also the broad economic policies of this government in the international field are adhered to by all agencies of this government operating abroad" and to coordinate the activities of various agencies to ensure that the end result was "an orderly and coherent foreign policy."[32]

On June 3, 1943, President Roosevelt issued a series of letters to Secretary of State Hull, Secretary of the Army Henry Stimson, Secretary of the Navy Frank Knox, Secretary of the Treasury Henry Morgenthau, Jr., Lend-Lease Administrator Edward Stettinius, OFRRO Director Lehman, and Vice President Wallace, who headed the Board of Economic Warfare. The President enclosed the "Plan for Coordinating the Economic Activities of U.S. Civilian Agencies in Liberated Areas" that Smith and the Bureau of the Budget had prepared, and he emphasized to Lehman and the others that the document "has my approval as a positive approach to the establishment of adequate inter-departmental machinery." Roosevelt explained that he had asked the Secretary of State "to undertake full leadership in the coordination here and abroad of the relevant civilian agency activities," and he stressed that "the time for preparation is short and the need for the best of interagency cooperation is pressing." The President was sure he could count on everyone's "wholehearted assistance" in carrying out this program.[33]

The President's letter to Secretary Hull outlining the general assignments and responsibilities of each agency made it clear how far OFRRO had fallen from the high perch that Lehman had envisioned just a few weeks earlier. The new plan rested on the premise that "there must be one central point in Washington for the coordination of interrelated activities of the several U.S. agencies operating abroad," and that "leadership in providing this coordination rests with the Department of State." OFRRO would be merely one of seven agencies represented on the "Interdepartmental Committee for Economic Policy in Liberated Areas (Policy Committee)," to be headed by an Assistant Secretary of State, and a separate Coordinating Committee. The "Area Director," appointed by the Secretary of State "with the approval of the Policy Committee," would "provide over-all direction and coordination to the economic activities of U.S. civilian agencies" in areas liberated from Axis control. OFRRO would be "responsible for the relief and rehabilitation of victims of war in certain liberated areas" to be designated by the President, and "Governor Lehman should distribute relief goods, and goods to facilitate the production of basic civilian necessities, whether they be given away, sold, or bartered." OFRRO would "also provide technical advice and services with respect to relief and the production of civilian necessities, and should facilitate the restoration of agriculture, housing, and transportation." In undertaking this work, the President wanted OFRRO "to make full use of available personnel and facilities of other agencies" and to work closely with Lend-Lease officials because, "so long as Lend-Lease funds are used to finance the Relief and Rehabilitation program, allocations of goods by the allocating agencies should be made to Lend-Lease for the account of the Office of Foreign Relief."[34]

Lehman clearly lost this round in the bureaucratic infighting. A headline in *PM*, a progressive New York City newspaper, proclaimed that "Hull Wins Power Over Foreign Relief from Lehman," and I. F. Stone reported that the State Department had "succeeded in relegating former Gov. Herbert H. Lehman and his Office of Foreign Relief (OFR) to a very minor role." Stone pointed out that "OFR's function under this setup will be little more than that of an operating agency to hand out relief," and as for Lehman, Stone observed that "it is difficult to imagine a man of his ability and stature content with the minor role he will have under the Interdepartmental Committee." However, despite his disappointment in OFRRO's reduced status in the new arrangement, Lehman assured Roosevelt that OFRRO would "carefully and fully carry out" the President's directives, and he informed Secretary Hull that he would represent OFRRO on the Coordinating Committee.[35]

An overly optimistic Budget Director Smith informed the President on June 7 that "the difficulties which have arisen in connection with governmental organization in the foreign economic field among Lehman and the State Department, Lease Lend [sic], BEW, etc., have been pretty well resolved by the recent letters you signed dealing with the subject." Smith reported, "The reactions I have thus far received from those letters and the definition of functions which they provide have been most favorable." But the Budget Director failed to realize that agencies would pay lip service to the President's new policy while working to undermine it. As Assistant Secretary of State Dean Acheson, who headed the Interdepartmental Committee, later noted, he was expected to administer a structure that only cartoonist Rube Goldberg could have contrived, and it proved impossible to coordinate policies among all the different agencies and departments involved. Despite Smith's assurances that everything had been settled, a month later Hull sought to meet with the President to discuss "the relationship that should exist between the Department of State and other agencies of this government engaged in activities abroad, if we are to assure that the foreign policies of the United States shall be administered in a unified and coherent manner." At a meeting a few days later, James Byrnes reiterated that the State Department was in charge of foreign policy, but he refused to issue any specific instructions to the agencies and departments, and the bureaucratic battling continued unabated. Lehman's longtime assistant Carolin Flexner remembered that the State Department "was tremendously jealous" of its authority, and Hull and the others saw Lehman as "an outsider." Even worse, she recounted, were the constant clashes with Lend-Lease Administrator Edward Stettinius and Secretary of Commerce and Federal Loan Administrator Jesse Jones over supplies needed for relief and rehabilitation. She recalled that "Lehman had a devil of a time . . . he was awfully frustrated."[36]

IV

Despite the turmoil within the Roosevelt administration, Acheson continued to meet with British Ambassador Lord Halifax, Soviet Ambassador Maxim

Litvinov, and Chinese Ambassador Wei Tao-ming to negotiate a formal agreement to create the United Nations Relief and Rehabilitation Administration. On May 25, Secretary of State Hull informed the President that "complete agreement has been reached with the British Government, the Soviet Government, and the Chinese Government" on a draft charter for UNRRA, and he recommended that if Roosevelt approved the proposed compact, planning should begin for a conference to be held in July at which the agreement would be officially adopted by forty-four nations. Two weeks later, the President approved the draft agreement, which was then submitted to other nations for their consideration prior to convening a formal conference.[37]

Recognizing that American funds for UNRRA would have to be appropriated by Congress, Roosevelt met with congressional leaders to brief them on the draft agreement the day before its release to other nations and to the press. Secretary of State Hull, Assistant Secretary Acheson, and Lehman attended the meeting on June 9 along with the President, Vice President Wallace, Speaker of the House Sam Rayburn (D-TX), House Majority Leader John McCormack (D-MA), House Minority Leader Joseph Martin (R-MA), Acting Senate Majority Leader Lister Hill (D-AL), and Senate Minority Leader Charles McNary (R-OR). During the session, the operating mechanisms for UNRRA were explained, and it was noted that Lehman was expected to become the new organization's Director General. The congressional leaders expressed their general satisfaction with the setup, Rayburn and Martin telling reporters afterward that they understood the need to provide relief to people liberated from Axis rule.[38]

A problem quickly developed, however, over whether the proposed UNRRA agreement was going to be submitted to the Senate for approval as a treaty. The administration had not planned to ask for formal congressional consent; as Secretary Hull explained to Senator Arthur Vandenberg (R-MI), "It has been decided, after consultation with the majority and minority leaders of both houses of Congress, that the United States' participation in the establishment of this United Nations' administration should be through an executive agreement." But Vandenberg immediately objected to what he called "a preview of the method by which the President and the State Department intend to bypass Congress in general, and the Senate in particular, in settling every possible international war and postwar issue by the use of mere 'executive agreements.'" Vandenberg complained that the administration "intended that there should be no interference with this world-wide prospectus as it might be conceived by Roosevelt, Lehman, Hopkins and Co., until that long last moment when Congress would be confronted with a 'fait accompli,'" at which point "it would be next to impossible for Congress to do anything except acquiesce." Hull warned the President in early August that "the establishment of the United Nations Relief and Rehabilitation Administration is imperiled" because "Congress feels that it has not been adequately consulted," and the President agreed to try to mollify legislators' concerns by assuring them "that after the UNRRA agreement has been negotiated and signed," he would "recommend the introduction of a bill authorizing the appropriation of funds as Congress may from time to time determine for United States participation in the relief and rehabilitation of foreign liberated areas in association with other nations." As Hull explained, "this will provide opportunity for full discussion by Congress of the entire United Nations relief plan."[39]

Herbert Lehman continued to be frustrated by the bureaucratic infighting in Washington. In mid-August 1943, the War Food Administration (WFA) informed Lehman that it was cancelling food allocations that had already been assigned to OFRRO because the Army was taking responsibility for feeding people in liberated areas for the next six months. The Army, tired of dealing with competing civilian agencies providing food relief in North Africa, had decided to undertake such activities itself. But according to a report in the *New York Times*, Lehman was concerned that the stripping away of food reserves already promised would make it impossible for OFRRO to "make comprehensive long-term plans," and he worried that the task of feeding large numbers of people would later be turned over to OFRRO "at a time when there would be very little food available." The Governor and his aides feared that unless they proceeded "vigorously with plans for the future," OFRRO's place "in the international relief field could easily be subordinated."[40]

Reluctantly, Lehman realized that he had no choice but to appeal directly to the President again, and on August 30, 1943, he sent Roosevelt a ten-page letter in which he outlined all the problems he and OFRRO had endured in trying to plan and implement relief and rehabilitation efforts in liberated areas. Lehman apologized for bothering the President, who he knew was "continuously faced with many highly difficult issues." He assured Roosevelt that he had tried to settle his problems without burdening the President, but "certain questions of major policy affecting this nation's plans for the relief and rehabilitation of areas liberated from Axis control have become compelling and are of such paramount importance" that he needed to bring them to the President's attention.[41]

Lehman summarized the history of his problems within the bureaucracy, reminding the President that at the time of his appointment, "you, the public and I all understood that my assignment included all liberated areas and that 'relief and rehabilitation' would be the principal economic job to be done in liberated areas." The Governor had left New York to assume his new responsibilities immediately, but "almost from the first day" that he arrived in Washington, questions had arisen with other agencies concerning his "authority and responsibility." Lehman had sought an executive order clarifying his responsibilities, but "representatives of some of the other interested agencies" had prevented such a directive from being issued. Instead, the President had sent his letter of March 19, 1943, which had helped to clarify the situation, and Lehman had used it as the basis for his talks in England with the British government and leaders of the various governments-in-exile. Returning from England, Lehman had circulated his twelve-point statement, which he believed "was exactly in line" with Roosevelt's directive, but Lehman's plan had been rejected "by one or two of the agencies." Roosevelt had issued his new instructions on June 3, "which provided for the coordination by the State Department of all economic activities in liberated areas," but Lehman pointed out that the President's order had "greatly diminished" Lehman's authority as set forth in Roosevelt's letter of March 19. Nonetheless, Lehman had "fully and faithfully" complied with the President's directive "in every case where prospective action was along the lines of coordination and not of active operations."[42]

The Governor complained, however, that since June 3, "*the constant efforts to reduce the scope of my work have little by little whittled away my authority to carry out the responsibilities imposed upon me.*" He lamented, "*today I can do nothing of any importance that is not subject to the veto of two or more agencies.*" Lehman found himself in an impossible position where although his responsibilities were "*very great,*" his "*independent authority*" was "*virtually nil.*" He lacked direct control over any funds, was "*unable to count on any substantial reserve supplies of food or clothing or equipment for future use,*" and was "*unable to plan intelligently or with any degree of accuracy*" because there was "*constant conflict and misunderstanding with regard to the areas or extent*" in which OFRRO was to operate. Moreover, Lehman was now "*threatened with the loss of authority*" over OFRRO's "*field operations*" and "*the preparation of* [its] *supply requirements*" (emphasis in the original).[43]

Lehman believed that much more was at stake than his own power and prestige. His main concern, he explained to Roosevelt, was "*for the success of this government's program for liberated areas and for what a successful program may contribute to winning the war and to securing a stable peace.*" Specifically, Lehman noted that America's "long-term program for liberated areas has been planned in anticipation of the formation of a United Nations Relief and Rehabilitation Administration," which would have to control needed provisions "during a period of urgent shortages of supply and shipping of all the civilian goods going into the whole of the liberated areas." Lehman stressed the importance of UNRRA succeeding in its mission to relieve human suffering, warning that "*failure in this first attempt to create an operating United Nations organization would certainly prejudice later attempts to establish other and more permanent organizations.*" Lehman emphasized to Roosevelt "that the time has come to return to your original conception that the 'relief and rehabilitation' of *all* the liberated areas is a single, unitary job," and that "pending the establishment of UNRRA, . . . clear authority should be given to some *one* agency of this government to control, administer, or arrange for the administration of this government's part in the job." He argued that "this authority was given to

OFRRO," and "it is only logical that that authority should be returned to the organization that you designated to plan for and prepare to undertake the same functions that UNRRA is expected to assume" (emphasis in the original).[44]

Lehman was "still most eager" to do the job that he had been assigned, asserting that "nothing is of more importance both as a weapon of war and as the guaranteeing of the right kind of peace." But for Lehman or anyone else to succeed, "the appropriate conditions must be created and adequate support provided." Lehman called for "a clear statement that during the relief period OFRRO is responsible for the administration of relief and rehabilitation, including control of the export and import of all civilian supplies in areas liberated from Axis control as long as there exists a shortage of shipping or of supplies." In addition, Lehman recommended that OFRRO be authorized "to prepare relief and rehabilitation programs for liberated areas without interference except for necessary coordination with the programs of other agencies," and that "adequate recognition" should be given to "the need for setting aside supplies for relief and rehabilitation by the various agencies controlling the allocation of supplies so that some reserve supplies can be assured when they are needed." OFRRO should have access "to funds to finance the procurement of supplies within amounts agreed upon without being subject to policy supervision by the financing agency," and it should be allowed "freedom to control relief and rehabilitation operations in the liberated areas within the limitations of the foreign policy defined by the Secretary of State, subject in a period of military occupation to the control of the military commander in the particular area." Lehman emphasized that Roosevelt knew him well enough to know that the only power that interested Lehman was the authority to carry out the job that Roosevelt had given him.[45]

The Governor sent a copy of his letter to the Secretary of State, offering to discuss its contents with Hull at the latter's convenience, but Hull had the State Department prepare its own six-page memorandum to the President instead. The Secretary waited until the Saturday afternoon of Labor Day weekend to try to reach Lehman, who had already gone home to New York. Hull sent Lehman a copy of the Department's response for his "strictly personal and confidential information" and asked to meet with Lehman when the Governor returned to Washington.[46]

In a note transmitting the Department's memorandum to the President, Hull blamed Lehman for the State Department's failure to coordinate American economic policies overseas. He claimed that the Department "has been working for a considerable period of time with other agencies in the foreign field such as R.F.C., Lend-Lease, O.E.W. and others," and that the Department had "established a relationship with these agencies which on the whole has been effective and cordial." Lehman and OFRRO, however, had rejected "these same procedures," even though they would "in no way interfere with the operations to be carried on by Governor Lehman abroad." The Secretary asserted that Lehman's letter "appears to indicate that he feels he will not be able to work in partnership with the State Department in these foreign operations," and that Lehman was asking the President "to set aside the procedure" set forth in the President's letter of June 3. If Roosevelt insisted, then Hull, "in the interest of harmony," would "be glad to acquiesce" in the President's decision to accept Lehman's proposals and "relinquish this important part of the control of [the] foreign policy of this country," but the Secretary would "regret this result" because he believed that the procedures described in his accompanying memorandum were "administratively sound," had passed "the test of experience, and in no way interfere[d] with the responsibilities of the economic agencies which operate abroad." Hull claimed that he had "made every effort to avoid having this matter come to an issue," but he warned that he could not carry out the responsibilities the President had previously given him "if the present uncertainty of authority and inability to arrive at decisions continue.[47]

The formal State Department memorandum reiterated many of the arguments the Department had raised in May. The Department acknowledged "the heavy responsibilities which have been placed upon the Office of Foreign Relief and Rehabilitation Operations" and declared "its earnest desire to facilitate in every appropriate way the work of Governor Lehman in his carrying out of these responsibilities." The Office of Foreign Economic Coordination called for in the President's letter of June 3 had been established, and the Department claimed that it had tried "to be as helpful as possible to OFRRO and not to infringe on its prerogatives." The Department asserted that it had already assisted Lehman by "arranging the correlation of his supply arrangements with those of the British military and civilian authorities and with the War Department in such a way as to make possible appropriate allocations by the Combined Boards."[48]

The State Department noted, however, that "the work of OFRRO, important as it is, is by no means the only activity of this government which will be carried on in the areas to be liberated; and relief and rehabilitation, even on the widest interpretation, is by no means the totality of economic problems." It then listed the same ten issues it had cited in May to show that "the interrelation of relief and rehabilitation with multiple other matters involves the whole economic policy of this government abroad and requires the coordination of all such activities," and it warned that "to separate the operations of OFRRO from the rest of the many-sided economic operations of our government abroad would be comparable to making one branch of the Armed Forces independent of the overall strategic direction." The State Department stressed the need for "a unified economic program abroad," which could only be achieved if "one department coordinates our manifold activities," and it cautioned, "we cannot have a consistent policy in our foreign relationships if the Department of State is excluded from day to day contacts with operations in the economic field."

As for the issues Lehman had raised concerning UNRRA, the Department asserted that any such discussion was premature and should await UNRRA's formal establishment.[49]

Rather than yielding any ground, the State Department tried to use Lehman's letter as an opportunity to increase its authority and control over foreign economic activities. The Department believed that the basic plan outlined in the President's letter of June 3 "is sound and should not be changed," but that "there is a need for clarification of the authority of the Department of State thereunder." Given the difficulty of obtaining unanimity, the Department recommended that it "should have the power, after the fullest hearing of the views of the interested agencies, to resolve the differences of opinion by making a decision." In addition, it suggested that whenever the Department concluded "that some given economic proposal would affect the foreign relations of this government, or its post war policies, the Department should have the power, after making the fullest and most cordial attempts to reach a unanimous agreement, to make a decision which is binding." In other words, the State Department sought from the President the power to resolve all conflicts with or among agencies and to make the final decisions on any issues that it determined involved the nation's foreign policy. The Department did promise, however, "to continue its practice of not assuming responsibility for the operations of the other agencies and of attempting with the utmost patience to reach agreement before resorting to the power to decide."[50]

Lehman and his staff were flabbergasted at what seemed to be the State Department's deliberate distortion and misrepresentation of his letter to the President and the Department's unmitigated grab for power. Handwritten comments in the margins of Lehman's copy of the State Department's memorandum questioned the Department's assertion that it had provided considerable assistance to Lehman and OFRRO and complained that issues such as currency exchange rates and trade were extraneous to the matter at hand, observing that "not one of these subjects has even been under discussion, much less debate, between OFRRO and the State Department." Lehman and his staff agreed that American economic activities required coordination and that OFRRO's operations "should not and could not" be separated from other American economic initiatives, but they pointed out that Lehman had not "even remotely suggested that OFRRO be free from 'effective coordination,'" just that it "should be free from inefficient and complicating operational interference." Noting that Lehman and OFRRO had long sought the clarifications the State Department was now seeking in its authority, OFRRO claimed that rather than OFRRO or even interdepartmental conflicts causing delays, the problems were the result of "the State Department's inefficient and outmoded approach," and thus the Department's "efforts should be frustrated." If unanimity could not be reached, OFRRO recommended that decisions be made by majority rule, wondering why the State Department should have the authority to "set itself up as the sole arbiter." As for the Department's promise not to poach on the activities of other agencies, OFRRO noted that giving the State Department control over any issue that the Department claimed involved foreign affairs would be "tantamount to saying *all* decisions of any measure are up to the State Department," and warned that "there will be no operations of other agencies left which the State Department could [not] take on for itself."[51]

Newspaper articles began to appear in early September suggesting that Lehman and OFRRO were losing the bureaucratic turf wars. On September 3, the *New York Times* reported that a plan would be implemented shortly that would give the State Department "complete control" over the activities of the Office of Economic Warfare, Lend-Lease, and OFRRO. The *Times* explained that the change was intended to give better direction and coordination to American international economic activities, but the article noted that there was "some doubt . . . whether ex-Governor Herbert H. Lehman is willing to subordinate OFRRO to the State Department to the extent desired." OFRRO's position in the proposed reorganization was described as "ambiguous," with the possibility raised that "OFRRO may be squeezed out of all but nominal existence" between the Army's responsibility for initial control over liberated areas and the State Department's "final coordinating power over relief and rehabilitation." As for Lehman, all these changes would mean that "the job which would remain for him would not be the one he thought he had accepted." A few days later, when asked about the State Department's appointment of an area director to head relief and other economic efforts in Italy and the Department's increasing authority over OFRRO, Lehman refused to comment. Vice President Wallace noted in his diary that one of Lehman's associates had observed that the Governor "is not a very good fighter" and "doesn't know the way things are done in Washington."[52]

At this point, Lehman and OFRRO were the least of Roosevelt's problems with the State Department, which was in complete disarray. Secretary Hull and Undersecretary Sumner Welles had feuded for years over Roosevelt's tendency to turn to Welles, an old and trusted friend, on important matters, while relegating Hull to the background, and Hull was morally outraged by Welles's homosexuality. The Department's organization along geographic lines made it difficult for officials to take a broad view when issues arose, and Roosevelt's frequent use of Harry Hopkins and others outside the Department for diplomatic missions and advice on foreign policy further eroded morale. By August 1943, the situation had become untenable, with stories in the press charging that "conflicting personalities, lack of a cohesive policy, and a resulting impairment of the efficiency of the Department of State at a time when it must assume tremendous burdens relating to the effectiveness of the coming peace" had led to "great concern . . . in high quarters over the ability of the

State Department, in its present organizational condition, to fulfill the added tasks imposed by the President." Hull finally gave the President an ultimatum, threatening to resign if Welles were not removed from the Department, and Roosevelt reluctantly complied with the Secretary's demand in late September.[53]

V

"Assistant President" James Byrnes saw Welles's departure as an opportunity to remedy the longstanding confusion and duplication in American economic activities overseas. Byrnes suggested, and Roosevelt agreed, that Lend-Lease Administrator Edward Stettinius would replace Welles as Undersecretary of State, and that the Offices of Lend-Lease Administration, Foreign Relief and Rehabilitation Operations, and Economic Warfare would be merged into a new Office of Foreign Economic Administration (FEA). This new agency would be directed by Leo Crowley, who had headed the Office of Economic Warfare since its formation in July, it would operate out of the Executive Office of the President rather than the State Department, and it would inherit all the "functions, powers, and duties" previously carried out by its predecessors. It was hoped that Crowley's appointment to oversee all of the nation's foreign economic programs, including OFRRO, would end what Byrnes later described as "the intolerable situation abroad where several agencies were competing to lend, lease or give away something."[54]

As for Herbert Lehman, FDR accepted Byrnes's suggestion that the Governor be moved out of the State Department and be made a special assistant to the President "with directions to organize immediately the United Nations Relief Administration, which is due to meet on November 9." Byrnes emphasized that this was what the President "originally had in mind" for Lehman. In his autobiography, Byrnes complained that "characteristically, the President, disliking to give a friend bad news, turned to me when he had signed the order and approved the press release and said, 'Now Jimmie, I am doing this with the understanding that you will personally explain it to Herbert.'" But Byrnes also stated, "Governor Lehman, who had a deep affection for FDR, readily appreciated the necessity for his transfer and so my task on this occasion was not a difficult one."[55]

The White House announced the shakeup on September 25, 1943, including Lehman's appointment as "Special Assistant to the President for the purpose of perfecting the plans for the meeting of representatives of the United Nations" at which UNRRA would come into being. Roosevelt also revealed his intention to urge Lehman's appointment as Director General of UNRRA when the new organization convened in November. As the *New York Times* noted, Lehman's duties in his new job as Special Assistant to the President were similar to the responsibilities he had carried out at OFRRO, and when Lehman became the head of UNRRA, he "would continue in essentially his present functions, but as head of a United Nations Relief and Rehabilitation agency . . . instead of chief of a purely American agency aimed at the same end."[56]

In a letter to OFRRO staffers two days later, Lehman put the best face possible on the organization's demise, asserting that OFRRO's merger with "other agencies of the government concerned with economic activities abroad in the Foreign Economic Administration" would lead to "more efficient administration of our manifold economic activities and the more efficient prosecution of the war." He emphasized that OFRRO's work "making plans and actually engaging in relief and rehabilitation operations" would "be carried on by the staff of OFRRO and the other interested civilian agencies as one part of the total economic job now merged in the Foreign Economic Administration . . . until such time as the United Nations organization is established." Lehman stressed that it would be his "privilege and duty as Special Assistant to the President to lay the foundations for American participation in the United Nations Relief and Rehabilitation Administration," and that FEA Director Leo Crowley had promised "his complete cooperation and that of his staff in this undertaking." Lehman and Crowley quickly agreed that OFRRO staff members would continue to carry out their current work while preparing for the upcoming meeting at which UNRRA would come into being.[57]

Determined to avoid the battles that had occurred within the State Department bureaucracy, Lehman immediately sought to define his authority in his new position and clarify his relationship with his old bosses and rivals in the State Department. Lehman prepared a memorandum for the President in which he asserted his primacy over the Secretary of State, stipulating that the Special Assistant to the President was "to formulate and approve, in collaboration with the Secretary of State, all plans relating to the policy of this government vis-à-vis UNRRA, subject to the approval of the President." According to Lehman, the State Department would "continue to handle all negotiations with other governments, and will make the necessary physical arrangements for the UNRRA Conference and for the first meeting of the UNRRA Council," but the President's Special Assistant would "represent and speak for the President in all negotiations within the U.S. government as to the policies to be established relating to UNRRA, the representation of this government on UNRRA, and the plans for the establishment of UNRRA, for its interim financing, and for the first meeting of the UNRRA Council." The Special Assistant would also "exercise general oversight and supervision over all these matters."[58]

Roosevelt asked Samuel Rosenman, who had just resigned his judgeship to become the President's Special Counsel, for his thoughts on Lehman's memorandum. Roosevelt had previously asked Rosenman to look at the proposed executive order back in March, and now he wanted Rosenman's opinion before responding to the Governor. Rosenman recast the document into a memorandum to be signed by the President, but more importantly, he gave more emphasis to the Secretary of State's authority. Instead of burying the reference to the Secretary of State deep in the text of one of the points raised in the second page of the memo, Rosenman elevated him to top billing at the very beginning of the document, so that it now read that "the Secretary of State and the Special Assistant to the President in charge of UNRRA shall, in collaboration, and subject to the approval of the President," undertake the various duties and responsibilities Lehman had outlined for himself. Assistant Secretary of State Dean Acheson had approved Lehman's original memo, but no one else in the State Department had seen it, and Rosenman noted that "it is barely possible that the Secretary of State may object." Rosenman thought that any such opposition would be groundless, pointing out to the President that "Governor Lehman is acting as Special Assistant to you and is really acting for you in the premises." As long as Lehman acted in "collaboration with the Secretary of State," as Rosenman had emphasized in the revised memo, Rosenman did not see any problems. He did advise, however, that Secretary Hull should be shown the memo before the President signed it.[59]

The President instructed Rosenman to show the memo to Undersecretary of State Stettinius instead, and the State Department insisted on more changes, further eroding Lehman's position once again. Lehman's draft had emphasized the primary role of the President's Special Assistant, to be exercised in collaboration with the Secretary of State, while Rosenman's text placed the Secretary of State first but made it clear that he and the President's Special Assistant were to work together as equals. The State Department, however, rewrote the document so that it transferred to the Secretary of State all the functions and responsibilities that Lehman had originally defined as belonging to the Special Assistant, providing only that the Secretary of State should carry out such duties "in collaboration with the Special Assistant to the President in charge of UNRRA." In other words, the document had been transformed from one that gave Lehman, as the President's Special Assistant, the lead role, and the Secretary of State a collaborative and secondary position, to one in which their places were reversed. Once again, Lehman had been stripped of any authority and was relegated to a supporting position. However, with the birth of UNRRA just around the corner, Lehman decided it was not worth fighting the State Department anymore, so he reluctantly gave his approval to the Department's version of the memo, which the President signed and issued on October 19.[60]

With such demeaning treatment from the State Department continuing, Lehman worried that the President was not devoting sufficient attention to relief and rehabilitation matters. Eleanor Roosevelt shared Lehman's concern, and in late October 1943, she invited Herbert and Edith Lehman and Francis Sayre, who had been Lehman's deputy at OFRRO, and Mrs. Sayre to dine at

the White House to discuss "the plans for the international relief and rehabilitation administration which is to be set up soon." Mrs. Roosevelt wanted
to provide Lehman and Sayre with "a chance to tell F[ranklin] some of their
troubles" before the meeting in early November at which UNRRA would be
formally established. As she confided to a friend afterward, Lehman and Sayre
felt that "no one is fighting for them or telling the country about their needs,"
and they had to "fight here with local demands" for "stores of food, clothing,
seeds, farm machinery." UNRRA, with its forty-four member nations, would
be "our first test on working together," and Mrs. Roosevelt observed, "we are
not even sure what our own Congress & our own agencies will do." Lehman
greatly appreciated Mrs. Roosevelt's interest in UNRRA and stressed that "its
success will largely depend on the support it receives from the different departments and agencies of our own government." He promised "to keep in touch"
if difficult problems arose.[61]

Meanwhile, plans proceeded to create UNRRA as the first functioning
United Nations organization. On August 31, Hull informed the President that
a revised draft of the UNRRA agreement had been circulated to British, Soviet,
and Chinese representatives, and the new text was shared with other nations and
released to the press on September 23. Hull suggested that the final agreement
be signed at a White House ceremony so that Roosevelt could "take an active
part in the launching of this first United Nations organization with operating
functions," and the Secretary hoped that the President would use the occasion to deliver "a major address . . . regarding the hope of a better world and
the significance of this gathering of the representatives of the United Nations
to plan for the taking of concrete steps toward the relief of victims of war."
Roosevelt quickly agreed that the signing ceremony should take place in the
East Room at the White House, and that he would address the group. Herbert
Lehman looked forward to this "deeply historic" occasion when UNRRA would
be formally established, both because he had high hopes that UNRRA would
succeed in carrying out its humanitarian mission, and because he hoped his
move to UNRRA would free him from the bureaucratic morass of the Roosevelt
administration.[62]

As Governor of New York for ten years, Lehman had grown accustomed
to being the final decision-maker. In Washington, however, his voice was one
of many competing for the President's attention. Much as Roosevelt may have
wanted to help his old friend, the President could not afford to alienate Secretary of State Hull at a time when the Secretary's popularity and prestige in
Congress and in the nation were at their peak. Roosevelt saw Hull's presence
in the Cabinet as essential in winning support for American participation in
a postwar organization to keep the peace, so when forced to choose between
Hull and Lehman, the President had sided with the State Department rather
than OFRRO every time. Hull was a wily veteran of the bureaucratic wars

while Lehman was a neophyte in Washington, and the only weapon Lehman had in his arsenal was his special relationship with Roosevelt, which allowed him to appeal directly to the President when the situation became unbearable. The Governor did just that on a number of occasions, but Roosevelt, realizing that the Secretary of State was much more important than Lehman in achieving his long-range goals, could offer only limited support. Lehman's problems had to take a back seat to higher priorities.[63]

CHAPTER 8

"Freedom from Want"

Lehman, Roosevelt, and UNRRA, 1943–1945

Roosevelt of course was always very friendly to UNRRA. He backed me up so far as he could in almost anything I asked. . . . He was very sympathetic and very helpful.[1]

I

On November 9, 1943, representatives of forty-four nations gathered in the East Room at the White House to establish the United Nations Relief and Rehabilitation Administration. The President wanted the ceremony held at the White House to demonstrate his commitment to UNRRA, and other nations sent high-level delegations to show their support. Speechwriters Robert Sherwood and Samuel Rosenman, State Department officials, and Herbert Lehman and his staff all worked on Roosevelt's speech, which was broadcast nationwide. The President welcomed the coming together of so many nations "united by a common devotion to the cause of civilization and by a common determination to build for the future a world of decency and security and, above all, peace." Roosevelt emphasized that "nations will learn to work together only by actually working together," and he noted that in UNRRA, the United Nations were taking "the first bold steps toward the practicable, workable realization of a thing called freedom from want."[2]

Chapter title quotation: "President's Address to the Relief Conferees," *New York Times*, November 10, 1943, p. 4.

After signing the UNRRA agreement, the delegations traveled by special train from Washington to Atlantic City where the UNRRA Council met for the next few weeks to flesh out the details of how the new organization would finance and carry out its mission. On November 11, 1943, as one of its first acts, the Central Committee of UNRRA, consisting of representatives of the United States, Great Britain, China, and the Soviet Union, unanimously nominated Herbert Lehman for election as Director General of UNRRA, and the Council of all forty-four nations immediately concurred.[3]

As Director General of UNRRA, Lehman promised to do everything in his power to help bring hope and relief to the oppressed and starving people of

FIGURE 8.1. "A Big Job for the New Chef," by Jerry Doyle, November 1943. Original cartoon courtesy of the Herbert H. Lehman Center for American History, Columbia University.

Europe and Asia. He assured the Council of his "complete and sincere devotion to this task," and he promised to "act as a representative of all the member governments, neither seeking nor accepting instructions from any individual government." Evoking FDR's Four Freedoms, Lehman declared that "freedom from gripping want is a basic component of any enduring peace," and he stressed that "if the world is to have any hope of lasting peace and a stable economy," then nations had to "co-operate whole-heartedly to the end that the liberated peoples are restored as rapidly as possible to a self-sustaining basis." He warned that "the fate of all United Nations' efforts to assure a world of security and of lasting peace may well be largely influenced by the success of this, their first joint action in relief and rehabilitation."[4]

Observers hailed the selection of Herbert Lehman to lead the new organization. The *New York Times* asserted that "the work of the UNRRA is both a crusade and a business" whose "direction demands a warm heart and a clear head," both of which Lehman possessed in great abundance. The *Times* believed that "no candidate for the post could have come more earnestly to the task" of feeding and clothing those in need, "none could have been more keenly aware of the manner in which these acts of mercy are tied in with our 'long-range economic security,'" and "none could have been more fittingly trusted to work toward the final objective," which Lehman himself had described: "A world of free men engaged in free enterprise, an economy producing and consuming to the full extent of its needs." Similarly, Czechoslovakian Foreign Minister Jan Masaryk declared that "we have a good vehicle in UNRRA," and he emphasized that "we have a good driver in Herbert Lehman."[5]

On the same day that Lehman was elected Director General of UNRRA, Roosevelt secretly left Washington to confer with Allied leaders in Cairo and Teheran. But to conceal FDR's absence from the capital, the White House released a steady stream of presidential announcements, messages, and proclamations over the next few weeks, including a message issued on November 15 in which Roosevelt asked Congress to enact legislation implementing the UNRRA agreement. The President explained that he was not asking Congress to vote on a specific sum of money at this time, but he was requesting that Congress authorize the use of American funds for UNRRA, with specific appropriations bills to follow. In response to the President's request, Representative Sol Bloom (D-NY), chairman of the House Foreign Affairs Committee, immediately introduced H.J. Res. 192, "a bill to authorize appropriations to enable the United States to participate in the work of the United Nations Relief and Rehabilitation Administration."[6]

American officials and agencies pledged their support for Lehman and UNRRA, leading the Governor to believe that he had escaped from the bureaucratic morass of the Roosevelt administration now that he was at UNRRA. Secretary of State Hull hoped that Lehman's "able leadership and untiring efforts" would lead to a successful beginning for UNRRA in the meetings at Atlantic City, and Leo Crowley, head of the Foreign Economic Administration, assured Lehman of his "wholehearted cooperation in the great task that you have undertaken." The heads of the Combined Production and Resources Board, the Combined Raw Materials Board, the Combined Food Board, and the Combined Shipping Adjustment Board, appreciating "the importance of organizing the flow of supplies" and "the needs of liberated areas," promised their "closest cooperation toward the solution of the complex and difficult problems" that Lehman faced. By the end of November, Lehman felt "more than pleased" with the way things were going for UNRRA. He thought that "the definition of the scope of UNRRA's activities" was "quite satisfactory," and he was relieved that the Council had not done anything "which would tie the hands of the Director General in carrying out the administrative work which needs to be done."[7]

It soon became apparent, however, that Lehman had not broken as far away as he had hoped from the infighting in the Roosevelt administration. Lehman and Crowley had agreed back in October that when the UNRRA Council met in Atlantic City, Lehman would "take a substantial part of the OFRRO staff" with him "to serve as technical experts and advisers," and that Lehman would later bring most of these people into UNRRA when it was established. Crowley was fully in accord with this plan and had agreed to do anything necessary to facilitate it. Nonetheless, Arthur Krock reported in the *New York Times* in mid-November that "the steps taken by the administration toward a coordinated foreign economic policy with smooth operation" under Crowley and the FEA had not succeeded. According to Krock, "border raids by UNRRA . . . into vague areas of FEA's appointed domain and that of the State Department are believed to be impending, made almost inevitable by the looseness of the new set-up." Based on previous such incidents, Krock warned, the likely result would be "counter-invasions" and controversies that "the President will be obliged to resolve." To avoid such conflicts, according to Krock, some in the administration were considering a proposal that called for "the appointment of a plenary committee to manage all aspects of foreign economic activity and to assure that operations are conducted within the framework of policy." Such a committee would be "headed by a representative from the State Department and include members from FEA, UNRRA," and other agencies. Others allegedly preferred a plan under which "as the conquered territory of the Axis is reclaimed, the work of the American units of UNRRA would be supervised on the ground by FEA in order to make certain that relief and rehabilitation measures were responsive to local public opinion and were being conducted within the foreign policy framework by effective agents." Under such a structure, FEA would have the authority "to nominate new agents when it decided that changes of personnel were necessary," and FEA supervision would ensure proper "distribution of the supplies which the FEA collects for UNRRA."[8]

No record exists documenting Lehman's response to Krock's column, but one can assume that the Governor was furious. Krock was on excellent terms with Secretary Hull and often received information that the State Department wanted to make public, but the "solutions" that the administration was allegedly considering ignored the fact that UNRRA, unlike OFRRO, was an international organization and thus could not be under the supervision of the FEA or any other agency of the U.S. government. But the column sent a strong signal that Lehman's struggles with the American bureaucracy were not yet behind him.[9]

Other evidence pointed to the ambiguous relationship between UNRRA and various agencies within the U.S. government. In early December, John L. Loeb, who was married to Lehman's niece Frances and worked for the Treasury Department, warned Lehman that the FEA was planning "to screen UNRRA's programs and requirements, consider their impact on [the] U.S. economy, etc.," rather than acting "as UNRRA's advocate." When the State, War, and Navy Departments all pledged their cooperation with UNRRA in early January 1944, Francis Sayre, who had joined Lehman at UNRRA, showed his skepticism, noting: "I hope they mean it."[10]

II

As Roosevelt biographer James MacGregor Burns has written, once UNRRA was established "under the quiet, devoted leadership of Herbert Lehman, the President's main role was to help win funds from Congress and to define the jurisdictional line between UNRRA and other relief activities, such as those of the Army and the Red Cross." Recalling his days at UNRRA many years later, Lehman stated emphatically,

> Roosevelt of course was always very friendly to UNRRA. He backed me up as far as he could in almost anything I asked because he, too, was the chief of staff. All the military said, "Well now, look here, you can't let UNRRA have twenty million bushels of wheat because we need that or may need it, for our own needs. We can't surrender it. You can't give X number of tons of shipping because we may need that to supply our armed forces abroad. Or we can't release this man or that man for service in UNRRA because he still is needed for service in the Army." Roosevelt accepted that, in the main, but on the whole he was very sympathetic and very helpful.[11]

When the House Foreign Affairs Committee opened its hearings on Representative Bloom's resolution authorizing American participation in UNRRA on December 7, 1943, the Roosevelt administration strongly endorsed the bill and American involvement in UNRRA. Secretary of State Hull submitted a letter to the committee in which he noted that the UNRRA Council had "elected a distinguished American, the Honorable Herbert H. Lehman, to be Director General," and when Representative Edith Rogers (R-MA) stressed that "the important thing to do is to get the best possible Director here," Assistant Secretary of State Acheson replied that "we have got the best possible Director General in Governor Lehman." FEA Administrator Leo Crowley assured the Committee that UNRRA's need for American food and other supplies was not likely to lead to increased rationing of scarce commodities, and that he expected that American contributions to UNRRA would be disbursed through the FEA, which would enable Crowley and the FEA to prevent the "diversion of American food and other supplies to UNRRA when they might be needed more for the domestic economy or other war purposes."[12]

Crowley's testimony reassured committee members who were pleased "to know that matters were in such solid and capable hands." But Herbert Lehman was upset that Crowley had left "the impression that sovereignty lay with FEA." According to British Embassy officials, Lehman complained to Acheson, who "tried to take the line that Lehman was now a great international official, placed high above any servant of the United States Government and would perhaps do best to ignore the Committee's summons as in his new capacity he was not bound to appear." British officials noted that "Lehman was neither mollified by the elevation ascribed to him, nor did he take kindly to the advice to ignore Congress."[13]

Lehman realized that Congress controlled the purse strings and would have to appropriate funds for UNRRA, so he wisely disregarded Acheson's suggestion and appeared before the committee in his new capacity as the Director General of UNRRA. British officials reported that Lehman "came off well" as he outlined what he considered to be UNRRA's three guiding principles: that UNRRA intended "to help people help themselves"; that UNRRA's limited resources "must be used only to meet the most pressing needs" and "not be dissipated in financing long-range reconstruction projects, however sound and praiseworthy these may be"; and that "the success of UNRRA must be measured by the speed with which it is able to liquidate itself; the sooner it becomes unnecessary, the greater will have been its accomplishments." UNRRA's success, Lehman stressed, would show the world that "international cooperation is possible, that common interests can be stronger than separate differences. Having done it once, the United Nations will have more confidence that they can do it again. The habit will have been formed."[14]

In his budget message to Congress on January 13, 1944, President Roosevelt "outlined the financial requirements for victory." Besides the obvious need for men and supplies to fight the war, Roosevelt emphasized "the necessity of initiating the restoration of civilian life and productivity in the liberated areas." In such areas, he explained, "relief must, of necessity, be a military problem at the outset," but he promised that "this job will be turned over to civilian administration as soon as feasible," and he stressed that it was "for this reason the United Nations Relief and Rehabilitation Administration has been created." The President noted that "appropriate committees of Congress are now considering enabling legislation that will permit the United States to make its proportionate contribution."[15]

In mid-January, the House Foreign Affairs Committee favorably reported H.J. Res. 192 to the floor. The bill limited America's total contribution to $1.35 billion, which equaled the 1 percent of national income for 1943 that UNRRA had suggested for countries that had not been invaded. The legislation specified that the money was to be used for relief and rehabilitation, not permanent reconstruction projects, and required the President to make quarterly reports to Congress on UNRRA's expenditures and operations. The committee's report characterized UNRRA as "the first civilian operating agency of the United Nations" and emphasized that American participation in UNRRA was "essential if the United States is to carry out in the field of international action those responsibilities of world leadership which are imposed upon us by the deepest interests of the security and prosperity of the United States."[16]

The House of Representatives took up the UNRRA authorization bill on January 20, 1944. Representative Hamilton Fish (R-NY) led what the *Washington Post* described as "a small-but-loud group of House members, critical of administration policy," who tried to cut the American financial commitment in half, but Representative Charles Eaton (NJ), the ranking Republican on the Foreign Affairs Committee, and other Republicans from the committee joined Chairman Bloom in defending the bill and urging its adoption. Representative John Vorys (R-OH) wished that Herbert Hoover had been appointed as the head of UNRRA, but he confessed, despite "starting out with a prejudice against former Governor Lehman, I now feel that he will do an excellent piece of work administering this bill."[17]

As the House was debating the UNRRA bill, Lehman sought to arouse public opinion in support of the new agency. On January 30, the *New York Times Magazine* published an article entitled "Half a Billion Hungry People" in which Lehman explained the need for UNRRA. He described the dire conditions in Europe, where hunger "is today the great fact of life," and he explained that to meet this emergency, UNRRA would provide "those goods and services which are needed for immediate relief after the military period: essential consumer goods—food, fuel, clothing, shelter and medical supplies." UNRRA would help to establish a "program of health and welfare services" and try to "reunite families, to repatriate exiles and prisoners and forced laborers, to bring the more than twenty millions of displaced persons in Europe back to their homelands." But seeking to reassure the American people about the costs involved, Lehman emphasized the limited nature of UNRRA's commitment, noting for example that rehabilitation would "apply only to such industries and transportation as are essential to relief." Lehman stressed that "a great work lies before the United Nations," and he was "determined" that UNRRA would fulfill the expectations of "millions of suffering people in the occupied countries [who] look to UNRRA with great hope, look to it as their only hope."[18]

On January 25, 1944, the House of Representatives approved the UNRRA authorization bill by a vote of 338 to 54, sending the measure on to the Senate, where the Foreign Relations Committee held hearings on February 9 and 10. Acheson reviewed the UNRRA agreement's specific provisions with the Senators and stressed that Congress retained the authority to approve or reject appropriations for UNRRA, and Lehman emphasized that UNRRA was intended to be a temporary agency to deal with the relief and rehabilitation crisis that would follow the liberation of occupied countries. The Director General did not "envisage the creation of a vast international bureaucracy which will take over and perform at great administrative expense functions which can and should be performed by others." Senator Vandenberg welcomed Lehman's assurances of UNRRA's limited role, wanting to ensure that other nations did not believe erroneously "that Santa Claus has arrived." At the end of the hearings, the Foreign Relations Committee voted 16 to 1 to recommend the resolution favorably to the full Senate, where Vandenberg helped shepherd it through to passage. The Michigan Republican defended UNRRA and the resolution as the best protection against the "dreamy launching of some philanthropic postwar spree" and emphasized that "Congress has complete authority under this agreement to stop appropriations at any time, or to lay down rules as to how this money will be spent." The Senate approved the resolution with some minor changes by a vote of 47 to 14, and the *Washington Post* characterized the Senate's action as "a tribute to the confidence felt in the ability and sound judgment of former Governor Lehman of New York, who is the Director General of UNRRA." The House and Senate quickly reconciled their differences, and the President signed the bill into law on March 28.[19]

III

Herbert Lehman's religion created problems for UNRRA with some members of Congress. Lehman could barely contain his anger when Dean Acheson told him that Senator Tom Connally (D-TX), the chairman of the Foreign Relations Committee, had asserted that Lehman, as Director General of UNRRA, had "appointed an unfair proportion of Jews to important positions" and would show preference to his fellow Jews "in furnishing relief." In a letter to Connally, Lehman declared that "any fair analysis would disclose that both charges are entirely untrue and unfounded." Of the twenty key appointments he had made, Lehman emphasized, "just two are filled by Jews." Lehman was proud that "many members of my Faith have sought to take part in what they, along with all right-thinking people, conceive to be a great human enterprise," but he emphasized that he had not and would not "permit religious or racial origin to affect employment in UNRRA." He had "sought to make UNRRA a truly international organization representative of many faiths and nationalities," and he had insisted that "the sole requisites for employment be character, competence, experience and an understanding of the problems and ideals of the organization which was brought into being for the sole purpose of helping to restore to suffering humanity some of those necessities of life, without which people cannot exist, and to help restore to the world a future of hope, dignity and security." Lehman took even greater umbrage at the suggestion "that among the millions of needy and starving the world over," he would "single out for primary consideration" those of his own faith. The Director General believed that his record over the years, especially his many years of public service, "would have given the lie to any such ugly thought," and he noted that he had never been subjected to such charges "even in the heat of a campaign, by those whose political, religious or ideological philosophies" differed from his own. Lehman could "not be true" to himself or to the work he had begun if he "allowed such an accusation to remain unchallenged," and he stressed his "utter revulsion at the thought that the success of UNRRA might be hampered by such insidious and totally unfounded 'whisperings.'" He reminded Senator Connally that, for UNRRA to succeed, "it must have the full support and confidence of all people," and he warned that "if suspicions reflecting on its good faith are permitted to exist, UNRRA, no matter who heads it, will be foredoomed to failure and the suffering people of the world will be deprived of any chance for recovery." Lehman hoped that Connally would do everything in his power "to refute such suspicions" and that he would "always feel free" to contact Lehman directly with any questions or concerns about UNRRA.[20]

David Wyman, one of the leading scholars of America's response to the Holocaust, has charged that "Jews who were close to the President," including Herbert Lehman, "did very little to encourage rescue action" to save European Jews during the war. The vehemence of Lehman's response to Connally helps us understand why Lehman did not do more while at OFRRO and UNRRA to help his fellow Jews. As Richard Breitman and Alan Kraut have noted, "Jews in Congress as well as those who were close to the President walked a tightrope on issues of concern to Jews, lest they be vulnerable to the charge of using their positions to advance Jewish causes at the expense of the national interest." Not that Lehman needed one, but Connally's accusations served as a grim reminder that any actions Lehman took to help Jews could be misinterpreted and cause irreparable harm to UNRRA, so he bent over backward as Director General to ensure that there would be no truth to any such allegations.[21]

Herbert Lehman persisted in his work at UNRRA despite personal hardships and losses. In March 1944, Lehman left on a trip to meet with Allied officials in Cairo and London and to inspect facilities in the Middle East where UNRRA was about to absorb the operations of the British Middle East Relief and Rehabilitation Administration. However, Lehman slipped and fell while leaving a meeting in Algiers and suffered a serious knee injury, forcing him to stay in Algiers for more than a week until his leg was placed in a cast and he received medical permission to travel. The extra time in Algiers enabled Lehman to spend more time with his daughter Hilda Jane, who was serving there with the Women's Army Corps, but the problem with his leg forced him to change the plans for the rest of his trip. Lehman finally made it to Cairo after a painful eight-hour flight, but the doctors insisted that he cancel his stop in London, where he had expected to confer with British officials and see his son Peter, a pilot in the American Air Corps who was stationed in England. Upon his return to the United States, Lehman was taken off the plane on a stretcher and met by his wife and his daughter-in-law. As Lehman recorded in his diary of the trip, they "tried to give the impression that there was nothing wrong, but I could see from their faces that something had happened. They told me that they had received word that afternoon from the War Department of Peter's death." Peter Lehman, who had flown numerous missions over occupied Europe, had been killed when his plane crashed on a training flight over England, and Herbert Lehman's knee injury had prevented him from having one last visit with Peter before his death.[22]

President Roosevelt, whose sons were also serving in the armed forces, immediately extended to Lehman his "deep sense of personal sorrow of the bereavement which has fallen so heavily on you and Edith." The Lehmans "deeply appreciate[d] the message of sympathy" from President and Mrs. Roosevelt and drew comfort from knowing that Peter "willingly and courageously gave his life for his country and for a great cause." Lehman hoped that the President "will continue to get good reports from your boys and that they will all return safely to you and Mrs. Roosevelt."[23]

IV

Even before Congress had passed the UNRRA authorization bill, the State Department worried that federal "allocating and supply agencies" did not appreciate the importance of relief and rehabilitation activities and were not cooperating to ensure adequate supplies and transportation for UNRRA to carry out its mission. Undersecretary of State Edward Stettinius informed the President in mid-February 1944 that requests "for supplies and transportation facilities which will be necessary for carrying out relief and rehabilitation in areas liberated from enemy control . . . compete . . . with all other requirements, both domestic and for export," and that such requests were being treated as "secondary, to be filled only out of residues remaining after taking care of all other requirements." Stettinius pointed out the "great importance" of ensuring that the necessary supplies would be available "to prevent disease, chaos, and collapse" in "liberated areas," and he recommended that the President remind all the relevant agencies of "the importance of such relief and rehabilitation requirements." The President agreed, and on February 22, he so instructed the chairman of the War Production Board, the War Food Administrator, the Petroleum Administrator for War, and the War Shipping Administrator.[24]

Passage of the UNRRA authorization legislation in March 1944 did not actually provide Lehman and UNRRA with any funds; no money could go to UNRAA until Congress approved another bill appropriating the money. On May 5, 1944, the President formally asked Congress to appropriate $450,000,000 for U.S. participation in UNRRA and to authorize the transfer to UNRRA of an additional $350,000,000 in "supplies, services, and funds available under the Lend Lease Act." Roosevelt pointed out that it was impossible to predict exactly when "UNRRA relief operations in liberated areas will begin" because such activities depended on "military developments," but he estimated that the $450,000,000 would enable UNRRA "to finance advance purchases of supplies to provide for necessary services." He also thought it reasonable to assume that "the beginning of fuller relief operations by UNRRA may be accompanied by a decline in military and Lend-Lease requirements for operations in the European theatre, making surplus war material available," and he promised that "every effort" would be made "to utilize available stocks of goods held by any department or agency of the government."[25]

Lehman met with Roosevelt at the White House on May 31, 1944, to report to the President on his trip to the Middle East and discuss UNRRA problems in general. The Director General was still on crutches from his knee injury, but he was busy tending to UNRRA's needs, and he wanted Roosevelt's help in persuading Congress to appropriate the funds for UNRRA. Not coincidentally, a few days after Lehman's conference with the President, Ernest Lindley, a columnist who was known to be close to FDR, criticized Congress, especially the House Appropriations Committee and Representative John Taber (R-NY), its ranking Republican, for dragging their feet on the UNRRA appropriation bill. Lindley pointed out that "if the impending military operations on the Continent go well, UNRRA may find itself called upon to bring relief to large territories by the end of this year," and he noted that UNRRA "cannot prepare for these operations without knowing if and when the American contribution will be paid." He recalled Roosevelt's comments when the UNRRA agreement was signed at the White House, when the President had proclaimed that "this agreement shows that we mean business in this war in a political and humanitarian sense, just as surely as we mean business in a military sense." Lindley feared that the failure of the United States to appropriate funds for UNRRA made it appear that "all the other United Nations mean it—but not the United States," and he cautioned that such action—or inaction—"can serve only to create doubt about the good faith of the United States." He warned that "this is the sure way to fritter away American prestige and influence."[26]

On June 2, 1944—the same day that Lindley's column appeared—the House Appropriations Committee recommended favorably the UNRRA appropriation bill. But when the House considered the bill the next day, Representative Taber and the Republicans succeeded in having stricken from the measure the provision allowing the President to transfer $350,000,000 from Lend-Lease to UNRRA, criticizing such "juggling of funds" among various agencies and asserting that if UNRRA needed more funds, it could request them from Congress through the regular process. The Roosevelt administration was trying to persuade legislators to restore the funds when military developments in Europe came to UNRRA's rescue. The liberation of Rome on June 4, followed by the Allied landings in France two days later, made it clear that UNRRA would soon be needing to provide relief and rehabilitation to millions of people liberated from Axis rule. In this rapidly changing context, the Senate restored to the President the authority to transfer the money from Lend-Lease to UNRRA, provided that the Joint Chiefs of Staff agreed, and the House acquiesced in the Senate measure. On June 30, 1944, the President signed into law the bill appropriating all the funds he had requested for UNRRA.[27]

Immediately following the Allied landing in France, Lehman delivered a shortwave radio broadcast offering hope to the people of Western Europe. The Director General promised that "in the train of the United Nations armies will come the necessities of daily life," explaining that UNRRA was already working with the legitimate governments of Europe and military authorities "to see to it that urgently needed essential supplies are procured." He warned that "the task will not be easy," that "the world supply of food and clothing and seeds and tools and medicines and all the other needed things has been depleted by four years of war." Transportation was also in short supply. But Lehman pledged that "all the goods and services possible will be made available and fairly shared; that the free nations will act together in binding up the wounds of war as they are acting together in waging successful war."[28]

On July 6, 1944, President Roosevelt signed an executive order entitled "Participation by the United States in the Work of the United Nations Relief and Rehabilitation Administration." In anticipation of the enactment of the appropriations bill, UNRRA officials had been working on the directive with the Bureau of the Budget, the State Department, the FEA, and the Attorney General. In its final form, the order authorized the FEA Administrator "to exercise and perform, through any Executive department, independent establishment, or agency, all the functions and authority with respect to the expenditure of funds, and the provision of supplies and services related thereto, vested in the President" under the UNRRA Authorization and Appropriation Acts. The directive also recognized the primacy of the State Department, stipulating that "all activities of the United States government pertaining to its participation and membership in the United Nations Relief and Rehabilitation Administration shall be carried on in conformity with the foreign policy of the United States as defined by the Secretary of State."[29]

Roosevelt also sent FEA Administrator Crowley a detailed letter in which he explained how he expected his directive to be implemented. UNRRA officials had helped draft the letter, which was everything that Lehman could have hoped for. The President emphasized that "the success of UNRRA depends to a large extent upon the successful execution of the important functions of the Foreign Economic Administration . . . in assuring that UNRRA has available to it, when needed, the essential supplies, services, and funds." Therefore, he directed Crowley to "furnish every possible assistance to the Director General of UNRRA in the discharge of his duties," including "the determination of relief and rehabilitation needs, the preparation of requests for supplies, the distribution of supplies and services among liberated peoples, and accounting for the use of resources contributed by member nations." The President had "already stressed to the United States allocating agencies the importance of relief and rehabilitation programs," and he pointed out the "great importance . . . that there be available in all liberated areas those supplies that will be necessary for the health and welfare of peoples in those areas." Roosevelt knew that Crowley "will recognize in all your work relative to UNRRA the major significance of its needs and will press their importance throughout your Administration and with the allocating, procurement, and other agencies assisting in the work."[30]

Specifically, the President ordered Crowley to "provide at UNRRA's request supplies and services for the relief of victims of war . . . so long as such requests do not unduly dislocate the other supply programs with which the FEA is concerned." Since at least 10 percent of each country's contribution was to be in currency that could be spent outside of that nation, Roosevelt directed Crowley to "transfer up to $45,000,000 to the Director General at his request and up to $35,000,000 additional" if and when the funds appropriated to Lend-Lease were reassigned to UNRRA. Crowley was also to forward to UNRRA immediately $4,000,000 to cover the U.S. share of the agency's administrative expenses for 1944. Roosevelt explained that "all United States funds transferred to UNRRA will be expended at the discretion of the Director General in accordance with the broad policies determined by the Council or its Central Committee." The President was confident that he could depend on Crowley "to serve as guide, counsel, and friend to the United Nations Relief and Rehabilitation Administration."[31]

Herbert Lehman was ecstatic when he received a copy of the President's executive order and his letter to Crowley, making sure that UNRRA officials had copies of the documents and stressing their importance. Even after officials at UNRRA headquarters had sent copies of the letter to UNRRA's European Regional Office (ERO), Lehman and UNRRA staff in Washington worried that "recent reports from London indicate that the significance of the letter may not have been realized; and that many members of the ERO do not even know of its existence." As a result, UNRRA officials sent another copy of the letter to London and suggested that "it be circulated throughout the ERO," especially among "those staff members who have been decrying the absence of a statement by the President." Lehman and UNRRA General Counsel Abraham Feller emphasized that the letter was "very satisfactory," that it met "whatever need there may presently be for a statement by the President in support of UNRRA," and they recommended that the letter be made available to the press with an explanation of its significance. When an UNRRA administrator in London called "for some general statement or directive from the President and Prime Minister regarding the relationships" of the U.S. and British governments with UNRRA, Lehman replied that the President's letter to Crowley, along with Churchill's recent instructions that "British Departments give all possible assistance to UNRRA," constituted "a satisfactory basis upon which to build our relationships with the United States and United Kingdom Governments."[32]

In his position as Director General of UNRRA, Lehman had more success than he had had at OFRRO in bypassing the federal bureaucracy and bringing UNRRA's needs and problems directly to President Roosevelt's attention. UNRRA was now a higher priority as the liberation of Europe became a reality, and Lehman invoked his friendship with FDR on several occasions to break through various logjams. UNRRA often had problems recruiting high-quality personnel because it was not created until well into the war, at which point most of the best people were already working for agencies or departments directly involved in the war effort. In August 1944, Lehman informed Roosevelt that he had "met with serious difficulties" in his effort "to obtain the services of a suitable administrator for UNRRA to be responsible for field services involving the movement of UNRRA personnel to the devastated areas." Lehman wanted to hire Richard Brown, who headed the Division of Central Administrative Services in the Office for Emergency Management, but such a move required the President to release Brown from his present position. On August 29, 1944, Lehman wrote to Roosevelt, noting that "the rapid advance of the United Nations forces in the liberation of occupied territories accentuates the need for being fully prepared with suitable administrative personnel to handle the problems which face UNRRA" and requesting that the President "relinquish" Brown from his current duties, making him "available to UNRRA." Roosevelt immediately complied, and Brown went to work for UNRRA.[33]

Lehman met with President Roosevelt on September 8 to discuss the problems UNRRA was having "in planning and preparing for relief activities in Eastern Europe" and in acquiring and transporting supplies. As Lehman recorded in a memo for his files, he "outlined in some detail" UNRRA's "difficulties in obtaining information from the Soviets regarding their military plans for civilian relief and the difficulties of transport," noting that UNRRA was "eager to get supplies and personnel" into Poland and Czechoslovakia "just as rapidly as possible," but arrangements had to be made with Soviet authorities. In addition, Lehman "made it very clear" to Roosevelt that UNRRA "urgently needed his help" in instructing "the military and civilian agencies to render us every assistance," and that speed was of the essence. Much to Lehman's relief, the President assured him that UNRRA "would have this assistance." Roosevelt promised to instruct the civilian agencies to cooperate fully with UNRRA, and he even volunteered to contact General "Hap" Arnold, the head of the Army Air Force, to ensure that the armed forces assisted "in every way in furnishing planes if it did not interfere with military operations." FEA Administrator Leo Crowley briefly joined Lehman and Roosevelt and promised "his fullest cooperation and that of his organization," and later that day, Harry Hopkins, who had become the President's principal deputy in foreign affairs, assured Lehman that he understood "the importance of the situation" and would do everything he could to assist UNRRA.[34]

V

Congressional passage of the UNRRA appropriation in June and Roosevelt's executive order and letter to Leo Crowley in early July, along with the assurances Lehman received in early September from the President, Hopkins, and Crowley, signified the U.S. government's recognition of UNRRA's growing importance as the Allied armies advanced in Europe. Nonetheless, UNRRA seemed to be floundering when the UNRRA Council convened at Montreal on September 16, 1944. As the *New York Times* noted, "It was feared that UNRRA was on the verge of collapse because of its failure to get the consent of the Allied military authorities and of certain governments, notably Russia and France, to operate on liberated territory," and "because comparatively few supplies had been made available by the American-British-Canadian combined boards." People were losing patience with UNRRA, not realizing or caring that the UNRRA agreement and the resolutions adopted at Atlantic City the year before had made it clear that the military would be in charge for the first six months after a country was liberated. Most of UNRRA's attempts to stockpile supplies had been frustrated by shortages of both the needed commodities and shipping to transport the goods. Although everyone realized that shipping would be vital if UNRRA were to carry out its mission, UNRRA was not invited to participate in the Interallied Shipping Conference in London in July and August, and American and British officials engaged in the discussions did not even consult UNRRA until after they had finalized their agreement. Many people wondered why UNRRA was not providing aid to Italy, but UNRRA's charter allowed it to operate only in territories that had been liberated from enemy occupation, not nations like Italy that had been part of the Axis.[35]

Adding to the sense of malaise around UNRRA, columnist Drew Pearson warned in early September that no one should be "surprised if gnarled, wise old ex-Governor Herbert Lehman soon steps out as head of the United Nations Relief and Rehabilitation Administration." Pearson cited personal reasons for Lehman's likely departure, including Peter's death and Lehman's continuing physical problems from his fall in Algiers, as well as his desire "to campaign in New York State for President Roosevelt's re-election." But Pearson also claimed that "Lehman has been disappointed over the limited scope given to UNRRA," especially the agency's inability to undertake relief activities in Italy. Lehman added fuel to the speculation when he refused to comment on Pearson's story for ten days.[36]

Lehman finally responded to the rumors of his unhappiness at UNRRA during a press conference in Montreal, emphatically denying that he planned to resign as Director General or that he was in any way frustrated or dissatisfied with the scope and responsibilities of his position. He explained that any limitations on UNRRA had been self-imposed through the resolutions adopted by the Council at Atlantic City, and he pointed out that UNRRA was not very active in Western Europe because the liberated nations there had the financial reserves to purchase what they needed and the ability to distribute it without assistance from UNRRA. In the long run, Lehman emphasized, this would enable UNRRA "to extend greater aid to countries which do not have adequate financial resources." There is no evidence that FDR had followed up on Lehman's request that he intercede with Soviet authorities, but Lehman announced that the Soviet Union had invited UNRRA to send a mission to Moscow "to discuss the handling of UNRRA supplies for Eastern Europe."[37]

By the end of the UNRRA Council meeting in late September, the sense of doom and gloom surrounding UNRRA had been replaced with optimism. The Council sessions had featured give-and-take among various nations, with compromises resolving difficult issues such as an agreement to provide Italy with a "limited" program of $50,000,000 in relief. Military and supply authorities promised to cooperate with UNRRA, and the Council "warmly commended" Lehman's efforts, although it advised him "to decentralize the work to the regional offices and field missions for the sake of prompt action." UNRRA was now ready to utilize all the time and effort that had gone into the planning process and begin what the *New York Times* called "its real task, the actual provision of food, clothing, shelter and other relief to the liberated victims of the Axis."[38]

Despite all the promises and goodwill expressed at Montreal, Lehman and UNRRA continued to encounter difficulties. The Soviet Union had agreed in

Montreal that an UNRRA team could open discussions in Moscow, but the Soviet government kept postponing the mission. A few days after the Montreal conference adjourned, Lehman complained to Assistant Secretary of War John McCloy that UNRRA had been "confronted persistently by serious difficulties in obtaining overseas transportation for our staff." For UNRRA to meet its responsibilities, Lehman emphasized, he needed assurances of "the availability of expeditious transportation for the staff already accumulated and for the staff being recruited." Two weeks later, Drew Pearson reported that the State Department had rejected passport applications for two women that UNRRA wanted to hire to work overseas. Assistant Secretary of State Berle explained to Lehman that their applications had been denied because the Department believed that both women were Communists. But Lehman retorted that UNRRA was an international organization, not an American entity, that it had Russian Communists working for it, and that his own investigation had determined that the women were not Communists. As late as August 1945, the State Department was still refusing to issue passports for potential UNRRA employees whose loyalty it questioned.[39]

VI

Ever since 1928, Herbert Lehman had played a key role in Franklin Roosevelt's election campaigns, running alongside him on the Democratic ticket in 1928, 1930, 1932, and 1936, and vigorously supporting FDR's re-election in 1940. In 1944, however, Lehman declined all political appearances, explaining that his position as Director General of UNRRA required that he keep himself "entirely aloof from politics." When Benjamin Rabin, a Democratic candidate for Congress in New York City, asked Lehman for a letter of endorsement, Lehman replied that "as head of an international organization, the members of which must at all times keep themselves apart from political questions here and abroad," it would not be wise for him to "engage in any way in the coming campaign."[40]

With Herbert Lehman unable to play a major role in Roosevelt's re-election campaign, Edith Lehman stepped into the breach. Mrs. Lehman served as a sponsor of "Women Volunteers for Roosevelt," an "independent voters' committee" formed to rally support for the President, and on October 30, 1944, she made a statewide radio broadcast in which she advocated Roosevelt's re-election. Judge William Fitzsimmons, a New York Democratic stalwart and a member of the State Court of Claims, asserted that Mrs. Lehman's speech was "one of the finest and strongest political appeals yet delivered during this campaign," and he declared it "the finest I ever heard delivered by a woman at any time." Fitzsimmons poignantly noted in a letter to Herbert Lehman that "Mrs. Lehman's reference to those who have sons in the service displayed a marvelous control of personal feelings on her part in view of what you have both suffered as a result of this war." Herbert Lehman proudly sent a copy of Edith's remarks to Eleanor Roosevelt, pointing out that "from all reports it was very well received."[41]

Even though Lehman could not participate actively in Franklin Roosevelt's re-election campaign, he considered the 1944 presidential election crucial to the nation's future. He applied for an absentee ballot because he expected that his duties would keep him away from New York on Election Day, and he emphasized to a friend in Albany "how strongly" he felt about the election and "how deeply" he prayed "for President Roosevelt's re-election." He believed that "to make a change at this critical moment in the fight to win the war and the peace would be nothing short of a calamity," and he was confident that the American people would not make that mistake. When the President returned to Washington in triumph after the election, Lehman was among the guests who visited with him in his special rail car and welcomed him back to the nation's capital. Later that day, Lehman met with Roosevelt at the White House to discuss UNRRA's continuing difficulty in procuring supplies and shipping.[42]

VII

Allied troops advanced rapidly in Europe in the fall of 1944, mean-ing that UNRRA would soon be providing relief and assistance to liberated nations and refugees across the continent. Lehman planned to travel to Europe to inspect UNRRA facilities personally in mid-November 1944, but first he wanted to make sure that President Roosevelt was aware of "the supply and shipping problems" that UNRRA was experiencing at this crucial time when its operations were "imminent." The Director General met with Harry Hopkins at the White House on November 3, and Hopkins suggested that Lehman detail UNRRA's needs in a written memorandum that Hopkins would bring to the President with a favorable recommendation. Lehman followed Hopkins's advice, and in his memorandum he warned Roosevelt "that unless there is set aside for UNRRA some specified quantity of shipping, the current tremendous pressures on shipping" would make it impossible for UNRRA "to initiate even emergency relief operations." Accordingly, he asked the President to issue the necessary orders immediately to secure shipping for UNRRA "to carry 100,000 tons a month . . . for emergency operations in any of the following countries: Italy, Poland, Czechoslovakia, Yugoslavia, or Greece." Lehman emphasized that "considering the huge responsibilities that rest on UNRRA, shipping sufficient to carry 100,000 tons per month for emergency purposes is a very modest quantity," and he cautioned that if this amount did not prove to be adequate, he would return to ask for more. He assured the President, however, that he would not "ask for additional shipping unless it is absolutely necessary."[43]

In early November, George Summerlin, Chief of Protocol in the State Department, reminded White House aide Stephen Early that "the first anniversary of the signature of the UNRRA Agreement in the White House" was rapidly approaching, and he recommended that the President "send a brief message to Governor Lehman commending the accomplishments of the organization to date and reaffirming this government's interest in its success." The President did so, congratulating Lehman and the UNRRA staff on their "great progress . . . during this last year in preparing for the tremendous tasks ahead." Roosevelt was pleased at how far UNRRA had come, noting that "UNRRA men and women are actually engaged in bringing hard-won assistance to the gallant people of Greece." He acknowledged UNRRA's difficulties in trying to operate "in the face of the pressing and staggering demands which the fighting of a deadly war on many fronts has placed and will continue to place upon our resources of manpower, of supplies and of transportation." But Roosevelt was determined that "the liberated peoples . . . shall promptly receive the clothing, food, and other supplies which they need to start life over." The President was confident that Lehman's "inspiring leadership, together with the cooperation of the member governments, will result in making UNRRA an enduring example of international cooperation in action."[44]

Lehman traveled to Europe in mid-November to meet with UNRRA and military officials and inspect UNRRA facilities. As he explained in a letter to his wife a few days after his arrival in London, "supplies, shipping and inland transport are so short that there is much disappointment and complaint" with UNRRA. The Director General conceded that "part of the criticism is probably justified," but he also noted that "the military, the British government and other governments" were finding that "they cannot now carry out some of the responsibilities which they insisted on assuming and are anxious to place the onus on UNRRA." Lehman hoped to correct the record "in press conferences and otherwise" while he was in Europe. In one such meeting with reporters in London on November 16, Lehman emphasized that UNRRA was negotiating with the Soviet government about sending relief aid for Poland through Russia, that the military was still responsible for relief in Yugoslavia, and that UNRRA faced serious roadblocks in obtaining the necessary supplies and shipping. Lehman characterized his job as Director General of UNRRA as "the hardest job" he had "ever tackled, but the most worthwhile," and he warned that "UNRRA's problems are not over; they have just commenced."[45]

Herbert Lehman had always relied heavily upon his wife's counsel, and he regretted that Edith had not accompanied him to Europe. In France, Lehman met with U.S. military officials, including Eisenhower's Chief of Staff Walter Bedell Smith and General George Patton; signed "the agreement between the Military and UNRRA for work among displaced persons"; visited "the active combat area"; and inspected displaced persons' camps. In a letter to his wife, Lehman noted that there were "so many things I would like to discuss with you and get your advice. My men are fine but I think your judgment is usually better than any of ours. I feel very keenly my inability to consult with you on many matters."[46]

On December 5, while Lehman was still in Europe, President Roosevelt delivered to Congress "the first quarterly report on UNRRA expenditures and operations" as required by the UNRRA Authorization Act. The President highlighted the tremendous military progress that had been made in the war, listing the countries that had been liberated in whole or in part, and declared that United Nations forces "are now striking additional blows to complete the task of liberation and to achieve final victory over Germany and Japan." He emphasized that "UNRRA was established by the United Nations to help meet those essential needs of the people of the liberated areas which they cannot provide for themselves," and he proclaimed that the "colossal task of relieving the suffering of the victims of war is under way." According to the President, UNRRA was busy acquiring "necessary relief stocks" and recruiting needed personnel "to assure efficient and equitable administration of relief supplies and relief services," and he explained that "as rapidly as active military operations permit, UNRRA is undertaking operations in the field," noting that UNRRA officials were "already in or on the way to liberated areas of Europe and . . . preparing to go to the Pacific and the Far East." The President stressed that "the conditions which prevail in many liberated territories have proven unfortunately to be fully as desperate as earlier reports have indicated" because "the enemy has been ruthless beyond measure." The Nazis, Roosevelt charged, had "instituted a deliberate policy of starvation, persecution, and plunder which has stripped millions of people of everything which could be destroyed or taken away." He promised, however, that "the liberated peoples will be helped by UNRRA so that they can help themselves; they will be helped to gain the strength to repair the destruction and devastation of the war and to meet the tremendous task of reconstruction which lies ahead."[47]

Despite Roosevelt's assurances, UNRRA continued to be plagued by what Lehman described as "the inadequacy of the shipping available for essential civilian relief supplies." As Lehman explained in another letter to his wife, problems with "shipping supplies and inland transport" were "greatly affecting all civilian relief whether it be done by the military or by UNRRA." Even though he was still in Europe, Lehman decided that he had to bring the matter to the President's attention again, and on December 8, he sent a "personal message" to Roosevelt warning that unless the shipping logjam were broken, "the plight of the civilian population in areas liberated by our armies will be desperate." Lehman recalled that he had discussed with the President and with Harry Hopkins numerous times "the necessity of UNRRA being assured of adequate shipping to carry its supplies to different countries when required." Nonetheless, the Director General noted that "245,000 tons of cereals from the U.S. for civilian relief purposes" had been designated for shipment to Italy and the Mediterranean theater in December 1944, but that allotment had been "cut by 86,000 tons, due to the reduction of shipping allotted to the theatre." Moreover, similar cutbacks loomed for January and February. Lehman reminded Roosevelt that he and British Prime Minister Winston Churchill had specifically recommended that UNRRA become actively involved in Italy, but Lehman feared that "unless extra shipping is allotted," UNRRA would "not be able to undertake this programme of assistance to Italy." If that happened, Lehman warned, UNRRA would be "in the invidious position of not being able to proceed with an undertaking which was highly publicized at the time of the Montreal Conference and supported by all 44 nations." Lehman "respectfully but urgently" asked the President to "issue instructions allotting the additional tonnage which will be required for the movement of UNRRA supplies to Italy."[48]

Much to Lehman's relief, Roosevelt assured him that "the War Shipping Administration contemplates allocating shipping space directly to UNRRA in order to meet your January and February requirements for Italy." According to the President, the War Shipping Administration was "undertaking a broad review of the combined shipping position, during which it will consider UNRRA's requirements for subsequent months." This review would serve as the basis for a decision on "the shipping which can be provided from United States and British sources to cover the UNRRA program after February 1945." Although Lehman received no guarantees, he knew that the President had heard his desperate appeals, and as he noted in the diary that he kept of this trip, he was optimistic that UNRRA would be able to start its work in Italy "pretty promptly."[49]

British officials confirmed what Roosevelt had told Lehman about a review of "the shipping and supply situation," and Lehman believed that he was "at least in part responsible for this undertaking" since he had "continuously pounded on the subject, both in Washington and here in London and with the military." But the Director General worried that his absence from Washington would prevent him from ensuring that "UNRRA's needs will be included in any demand and in any plan that is adopted," and he instructed Deputy Director General Roy Hendrickson "to keep in very close touch" with the situation "and present UNRRA's needs to whatever group will be in charge of the survey." Lehman's concerns were exacerbated when he learned that Harry Hopkins had told Hendrickson that "it might be possible to obtain some shipping by obtaining 'broken storage,'" which Hendrickson interpreted to mean "bits and pieces," an option that Hendrickson thought "might help somewhat" but did not see as a real solution to UNRRA's problems.[50]

To ensure that UNRRA's "needs will not be overlooked," Lehman sent another cable to the President reiterating his complaints about "the inadequacy of the shipping available for essential civilian relief supplies." The Director General understood that "a resurvey will shortly be made in Washington of the shipping available for civilian supplies," and he wanted to make sure "that the present and prospective needs of UNRRA [would] be given adequate weight in the total picture." Lehman believed that with the "full and wholehearted cooperation of the contributing governments," adequate supplies could be made available to carry out UNRRA's mission, but he knew that such supplies "will be useless unless we have the shipping to carry them." He warned that "the success or failure of UNRRA will therefore depend almost wholly on its ability to secure adequate shipping to deliver supplies whether these be for Greece, Yugoslavia, Italy, Poland, Czechoslovakia, Albania, or other areas within its responsibility." Lehman emphasized that "UNRRA cannot do its work unless it has shipping and supplies."[51]

A clear sense of the difficulties UNRRA faced emerges from the records of conversations between American and British officials seeking to resolve the dilemma that had resulted from conflicting demands for shipping. When Secretary of State Stettinius and Harry Hopkins met with British Ambassador to the United States Lord Halifax and Richard Law of the British Foreign Office to discuss the shipping problem in mid-December, Hopkins warned that "'this thing would have to be handled in an extremely delicate way' because of military and other pressures." They agreed that "immediate relief for civilians to keep them happy and contented was a part of modern war," and they began work on a set of guidelines that could be approved by the President and the Prime Minister at their upcoming meeting at Malta in late January. James Reston of the *New York Times* neatly summarized UNRRA's predicament when he pointed out that "there are not enough ships in the world to carry the men and supplies necessary to win the war in the shortest possible time, to the various theatres of action, and at the same time to provide all the food and equipment that they would like to send the liberated areas."[52]

Upon his return to Washington, Lehman told a press conference in late December that there had been some progress in meeting UNRRA's shipping needs. Lehman reported that the Combined Shipping Board had assured him that UNRRA would receive "a moderate amount of tonnage to transport supplies" to Italy in January and February, as well as "a moderate amount of shipping space to carry relief supplies for Poland and Czechoslovakia" if arrangements could be made with Soviet officials to land and transport the material.[53]

As the date for Roosevelt's meeting with Churchill at Malta and the subsequent Big Three meeting with Stalin at Yalta rapidly approached, Hopkins, Law, and Assistant Secretary of State Dean Acheson finally agreed on a statement of principles to govern shipping to liberated countries for the first half of 1945. In a clear demonstration of how low UNRRA ranked in priority even for civilian relief, the agreement provided that a total of twenty-six ships were to be allocated for supplies going directly to France in the next three months, five ships were reserved for Belgium, and only two were assigned for UNRRA operations in Italy. These allocations were "not to be reduced except in the face of military necessity and not without prior discussion with Mr. Harry Hopkins." Although the Hopkins-Law-Acheson agreement represented an important step forward in recognizing civilian relief needs, it also showed that Western European nations such as France and Belgium were receiving preference over UNRRA in the allocation of scarce shipping resources.[54]

At Malta, the American Joint Chiefs of Staff objected strenuously even to the small diversion of shipping called for in the Hopkins-Law-Acheson memorandum, challenging the British assertion that some shipping could be diverted from military operations to civilian needs without adversely affecting military activities. Army Chief of Staff General George Marshall claimed that a shortage of forty ships had complicated planning in the Pacific and had been exacerbated when, "simultaneously, a demand for an additional forty ships to increase the bread ration in Italy had been put forward." In terms that would be difficult for the President to ignore, the Joint Chiefs cautioned against "the present determined effort to divert shipping to non-military uses, with the resulting effect on our military operations." They emphasized that "the decision lies between continuing unqualified priority to beating Germany and Japan or compromising this policy by diverting to non-military programs shipping essential to military operations." They warned that "any compromise almost certainly means prolongation of the war," and they explained that "the overriding objection from the military standpoint to these proposals which amount to slowing down our military effort is that the price is paid directly in the unnecessary loss of the lives of many American fighting men and also in expenditure of American resources."[55]

When Roosevelt and Churchill first discussed this issue at Malta, General Marshall reiterated his concern that "supplies for liberated areas, over and above those required for the prevention of disease and unrest," were being placed "in the same category as operational requirements." Marshall warned that "this would entail a change in the general priority at the expense of essential military requirements, which the United States Chiefs of Staff were disinclined to accept." At the first plenary meeting at Yalta two days later, Marshall emphasized that military "operations on the Western Front had been limited by the shortage of supplies due to inadequacy of shipping." After much jockeying back and forth, the American military got its way. In the "Basic Undertakings in Support of Overall Strategic Concept," the American and British Combined Chiefs of Staff agreed that they would "provide such supplies to the liberated areas as will effectively contribute to the war-making capacity of the United Nations against Germany and/or Japan," but this pledge was immediately undermined by the insertion of the words "within the limits of our available resources to assist other co-belligerents to the extent they are able to employ this assistance against the Enemy Powers in the present war." Efforts to provide civilian relief would be further limited by the need to "support the war-making capacity of our forces in all areas." As for shipping, General Marshall got his wish there as well, as the agreement stipulated that "shipping for other requirements will not be allocated without prior consultation with the appropriate Chiefs of Staff." Clearly, civilian relief and UNRRA remained at the bottom of the priority list.[56]

Besides the shipping problem, Lehman and UNRRA were also stymied by their inability to get permission from the Soviet Union for UNRRA to operate in Eastern Europe. Soviet officials had promised during the Montreal meeting of the UNRRA Council to cooperate with UNRRA's efforts to provide relief in Poland and Czechoslovakia, and Lehman had named an UNRRA team to travel to the area, but the Soviet government still had not issued the necessary visas or granted permission to land or transport supplies in Russian territory. Lehman again appealed to the President for help. Noting the rumors that the President would soon meet with Churchill and Stalin, Lehman asked him to discuss with Stalin "matters which affect some of the most important operations of UNRRA." The Director General explained that "UNRRA's plans for assistance in Poland and Czechoslovakia, an area always contemplated to be one of the most important in which UNRRA will serve, have been delayed and made difficult by our inability to obtain requisite information and permission from the Soviet Union for the transit of personnel and supplies through its territory to Poland and Czechoslovakia." Lehman was also concerned about reports that the Soviet Union opposed UNRRA's efforts to assist displaced persons in Rumania and Bulgaria, and he proposed an UNRRA mission to Moscow to improve relations with the Soviet Union. Lehman requested that the President "bring these matters to the attention of Marshal Stalin" because UNRRA urgently needed the Soviet Union's "full cooperation" in all of its work, especially in Poland, Czechoslovakia, Rumania, and Bulgaria.[57]

In the briefing book which the State Department prepared for the President for the Malta and Yalta conferences, the Department supported Lehman's recommendation that Roosevelt discuss UNRRA with Stalin. The Department agreed with Lehman that "it is important that UNRRA obtain the full cooperation of the Soviet government so that relief in Eastern Europe can go forward," but noted that "such cooperation has not been readily forthcoming."

The Department hoped that the recent opening of Black Sea ports to supplies for Eastern Europe "may indicate a complete reversal of the Soviet government's previous position with reference to UNRRA." But the Department pointed out that "there have been no developments as to the transit of UNRRA personnel through Soviet territory or as to the desired permission for Governor Lehman and his mission to visit Moscow." Although the Department placed some of the blame for these difficulties on UNRRA's "faulty handling of relations" with the Soviet Union, American officials speculated that the primary problem might be "the inability of the U.S.S.R. to make up its mind as to whether it desires to be a recipient of relief from UNRRA or to continue to receive supplies" elsewhere. The Department emphasized that it was "essential to the success of UNRRA that it receive the active cooperation of the Soviet government with respect to operations in Eastern Europe."[58]

Although Roosevelt, Churchill, and Stalin devoted considerable time and attention at Yalta to the problems posed by the liberated areas in Europe, there is no evidence to suggest that UNRRA was part of that discussion. The Yalta communiqué included a "Declaration on Liberated Europe" in which the U.S., the U.S.S.R., and Great Britain promised to work together to help people in the liberated nations "carry out emergency measures for the relief of distressed persons," but there were no details and no mention of UNRRA. Roosevelt followed much the same line in his report to Congress on the conference, focusing on the call for free elections in liberated nations without bringing up relief needs or UNRRA. Churchill, in his report to the House of Commons, noted that the lack of ships "lamentably hamper[s] our power to provide for the dire needs of liberated territories," and he vowed that Britain would do everything in its power "to help the liberated countries," as long as such action did not leave England dangerously short of essential commodities. But again, there was no specific reference to UNRRA, and the implication was that any goods that Britain supplied to liberated areas would be arranged on a country-to-country basis rather than through UNRRA.[59]

VIII

Roosevelt was concerned enough about the relief problem in Europe in late January 1945 that when he sent Special Counsel Samuel Rosenman to discuss with British authorities legal issues involved in prosecuting Nazi leaders after the war, he also instructed Rosenman to assess the flow of American civilian supplies to the continent. Lehman gave Rosenman, an old friend, a long memorandum in which he tried to convey some of the difficulties that UNRRA was facing. The Director General explained that even though "France, Belgium, the Netherlands, Luxembourg, and Norway" had not requested UNRRA's assistance, there had been "substantial public sentiment both in the U.K. and on the continent to the effect that UNRRA is not discharging its duty since there is acute suffering and need for relief in those countries about which UNRRA is doing nothing." Lehman noted that "this sentiment is also reflected in some official circles," and as a result, UNRRA was now considering whether it should provide "limited emergency welfare supplies" to countries in Western Europe that were able to pay and were supposedly making their "own arrangements for procurement and shipping of general civilian supplies." Lehman also pointed out the problems in dealing with the huge number of displaced persons all over Europe, as well as the continuing lack of clarity concerning the status of the Soviet Union, which had not requested UNRRA's assistance but had blocked UNRRA from aiding Poland and Czechoslovakia. Finally, he emphasized that UNRRA had been allocated only one ship for February and one for March to provide needed aid to Italy. But Rosenman's inspection trip was interrupted almost immediately after it began when Roosevelt summoned him to help work on the President's report to Congress on the Yalta conference.[60]

As the relief situation in Europe continued to deteriorate, UNRRA's Council for Europe proposed that UNRRA provide emergency assistance to the liberated people of Western Europe without waiting to work out all the financial arrangements. Sir Frederick Leith-Ross, who had been dealing with these issues since early in the war and who now headed UNRRA's European Regional Office, persuaded Lehman that UNRRA needed to take more aggressive steps to prevent death and disease from ravaging the continent, and UNRRA's Central Committee agreed in late February to offer immediate aid, even in countries that could pay for needed supplies. But despite this new authorization to act in Western Europe, Lehman warned that UNRRA would fail unless it received the "supplies, ships and inland transport" needed to get relief to the people in need. He stressed that "UNRRA is not a super-state"; it could not "commandeer shipping" or "demand supplies." To succeed, Lehman emphasized, UNRRA needed "the full cooperation of the governments concerned in the furnishing or distributing of supplies."[61]

Just as Lehman and UNRRA seemed to be making progress on the European front, their position with the American government bureaucracy deteriorated. Shortly after the President's return from Yalta, Lehman asked for an appointment with Roosevelt "at the earliest date possible" to discuss UNRRA's difficulties, and the two of them met for fifteen minutes on March 9. UNRRA's problems included a decision by the War Food Administration (WFA) to hold up requests for food for relief purposes until it was able to clarify "who we are trying to feed and how much." The WFA believed that UNRRA, the military, and nations that were able to pay were all seeking to feed the same people.[62]

To further complicate matters, James Byrnes, now the Director of War Mobilization and Reconversion, established a new "interagency committee to coordinate foreign shipments." Chaired by FEA Director Leo Crowley, the committee included high-level officials from the State, War, and Navy Departments, the War Shipping and War Food Administrations, and the War Production Board. Concerned about possible food and raw material shortages in the United States, Byrnes wanted the committee to "examine all of the related factors which pertain to the capabilities of the United States to export items for the support of the war, other than direct military lend-lease commitments," and specifically included within the committee's purview "all programs directed to relief, rehabilitation and industrial development." He emphasized that "military requirements must still have first priority, followed by the claims of the military agencies for relief supplies in the wake of battle," and he ordered that "all other requirements for relief, rehabilitation, and other export purposes must then be evaluated against our own minimum essential civilian economy."[63]

Lehman was "greatly disturbed" when he learned about the new committee and UNRRA's exclusion from it, which he believed "endangered UNRRA's position." He pointed out to his staff that the announcement of the new committee "contained no reference to UNRRA's responsibilities in this matter," and that "relief supplies other than those to be provided by the military authorities or by Lend-Lease were barely mentioned, and then only with the implication that they would receive the lowest priority." Lehman understood that "UNRRA as an international organization could formally have no seat upon a United States Government committee," but he believed that UNRRA "should be represented upon this committee and have an opportunity to present its case for relief supplies." The Director General knew that a committee "which set out to control the flow of United States supplies to liberated areas was of vital importance to UNRRA, which had in the past suffered from its inability to participate in discussions on main policy issues," and he thought it "reasonable that he serve on the committee to participate in discussions without vote." In this way, UNRRA would be able "to present its case at the time when decisions on the amounts of relief supplies to be provided by the military and by Lend-Lease were being made." He "felt very strongly that unless a vigorous protest was made at this stage, UNRRA would receive no consideration whatever from the supply authorities and its chances of getting supplies would remain as unsatisfactory as they had been in the past." After discussing the matter with his top aides, Lehman decided to send a letter to Byrnes reiterating "(a) UNRRA's responsibilities in the provision of relief supplies to liberated areas; (b) the United States government's responsibilities toward UNRRA; and (c) requesting the position of observer for UNRRA from the committee."[64]

Lehman met with Byrnes later that day and handed him the letter detailing his concerns about the new interagency committee and asking that UNRRA be allowed to participate as an observer in the committee's deliberations. Lehman noted that "the requirements for liberated areas have not received the orderly and urgent consideration which was obviously needed," so he was glad to see that "this matter, so important to the conduct of the war and the development of international peace and stability," would be coordinated at such a "high policy level." He worried, however, that "the already previously inadequate supplies for liberated areas may be further reduced in order to protect the present high consumption level in the United States." Lehman highlighted the American role in the establishment of UNRRA and "the obligation, expressed and implied, which the United States had undertaken to make adequate provision for relief and rehabilitation abroad." He pointed out that "the tragic consequences of failure to make such adequate provision have become abundantly clear in the territories already liberated." The Director General was confident that Byrnes would "agree that the time has come for vigorous and unrelenting efforts to reconsider the distribution of available resources in order to insure the bringing of adequate relief," and he stressed that "these efforts become all the more important now that the plans of the United States and the United Nations for the safeguarding of future peace and security must be brought to fruition."[65]

Byrnes rejected any kind of "continuing membership" for UNRRA on the interagency committee as "inappropriate," since "the committee was purely a United States body and would be considering a number of problems both domestic and international which were not relevant to UNRRA's operations." The only commitment Byrnes made was to promise to support "UNRRA's participation in any meeting should this be requested if UNRRA felt that its interests were being neglected or that decisions unfair to it were being taken." Byrnes expressed concern "over the future shipping and supply situation," but he assured Lehman that UNRRA's needs would "be as adequately met as the supply situation permitted." After further discussion with his advisors, Lehman issued a press statement restating many of the arguments set forth in his letter to Byrnes, attempting in this way to ensure "public awareness of UNRRA's concern in the decisions of the committee and the extent of the United States commitment towards UNRRA." The Director General emphasized that UNRRA's "operations will be profoundly affected" by the new committee's "deliberations and decisions," and he warned that further reductions in allocations of supplies and shipping for UNRRA would make it impossible for the agency to fulfill its mission.[66]

Lehman's dealings with the Combined Food Board and the Foreign Economic Administration in February and March 1945 illustrate many of the difficulties he faced as Director General of UNRRA. In a letter to Leo Crowley on March 14, Lehman noted that UNRRA had informed Crowley's staff and the Combined Food Board in mid-February how much food it hoped to ship from the United States in the second quarter of 1945, assuring Crowley that "in the light of the urgency of the need, the quantities that we asked for were meager indeed." Members of Lehman's and Crowley's staffs had worked together "to expedite their joint task of procuring and shipping these supplies," and Lehman emphasized to Crowley that he was "satisfied that everything possible was done by your staff to assist us in our efforts." Lehman noted, however, that "the allocations were not made" and their "joint efforts have so far met with little success with respect to sweetened condensed milk, evaporated milk, spray dried milk, roller dried milk, cheese, canned meat, canned mackerel, canned pilchard, oleomargarine, lard, salted pork bellies, rice, dry pinto beans, refined sugar, dried onions, dried prunes, and cod liver oil." Since the second quarter was only a little more than two weeks away, Lehman was writing again to War Food Administrator Marvin Jones and the Combined Food Board, "requesting that immediate action be taken," and Lehman begged Crowley "to do everything in your power to expedite the allocation and procurement of the food supplies needed by UNRRA immediately in order to load our boats during the three months beginning in April."[67]

In the accompanying letter to the Combined Food Board, UNRRA Acting Deputy Director David Weintraub detailed the box in which UNRRA was caught in its efforts to obtain American supplies and shipping. Weintraub noted that the War Food Administration needed at least "three weeks notice, after goods have been procured, . . . to deliver goods at shipside on time." UNRRA would have boats ready for loading on April 1, but the WFA and FEA could not move forward because the Combined Food Board had not approved any allocations for UNRRA. Weintraub urged that "immediate action be taken to complete at once the allocations" urgently requested a month ago and "to prevent a recurrence of the delays experienced to date."[68]

Part of the problem for Lehman and UNRRA was that many Americans, or at least their representatives in Congress, opposed shipping food abroad if it meant the continuation of wartime controls, shortages, and rationing. Senator James Eastland (D-MS) condemned the flow of American food overseas and threatened to introduce legislation if Crowley and the new interagency committee did not ensure adequate supplies for Americans. UNRRA was exploring the possibility of providing a small amount of assistance to Ethiopia when Eastland, a noted racist, demanded to know: "When did Ethiopia come into the war?" Forgetting or not caring that Ethiopia had been conquered by Italy in 1935, Eastland wondered why Americans should "go without adequate food to supply Ethiopia." Senators Styles Bridges (R-NH), Kenneth Wherry (R-NE), and Burnet Maybank (D-SC) echoed Eastland's concern over meat shortages in parts of the United States and praised the establishment of the Foreign Exports Committee as long overdue.[69]

President Roosevelt came to UNRRA's defense a few days later, stating at a press conference that "justice" and "decency" demanded that the United States continue providing food for civilian relief in Europe. The President denounced those who sought "to scare people to death about food shortages" in the United

States and minimized the inconveniences experienced by Americans during the war compared with the real risk of starvation overseas. Although he did not refer directly to UNRRA, Roosevelt made it clear that the Crowley committee was not intended to halt the shipment of American food overseas, and he expressed confidence that the American people would be willing to cut back domestic consumption if necessary "to help combat malnutrition abroad."[70]

The President and Mrs. Roosevelt also helped Lehman and UNRRA organize a collection of used clothing for UNRRA to distribute "to the peoples of war-devastated areas." In December 1944, UNRRA officials asked the President to appoint Henry Kaiser as national chairman of the United Nations Clothing Collection, which had the support of various religious groups and voluntary war relief agencies as well as UNRRA. Realizing that "as many war victims have died from exposure and lack of adequate clothing as have died from starvation," the President agreed "with Governor Lehman that this problem of securing clothing for war relief needs ranks high in urgency," and on January 22, 1945, he formally requested that Kaiser head this effort to collect "150,000,000 pounds of good used clothing." Mrs. Roosevelt helped persuade Kaiser to accept the position, which he did in late January, telling the President that he would be honored "to assist Director General Lehman in the service which you propose." Lehman, for his part, assured Kaiser that he could count on "the utmost support of every member of the staff of the United Nations Relief and Rehabilitation Administration" in "this great humanitarian enterprise."[71]

At Lehman's request, Mrs. Roosevelt hosted the first meeting of Kaiser's United National Clothing Collection at the White House on February 27, 1945. The Director General outlined the shortage of clothing and textiles, describing the available supplies as "pitifully small," and reported that the liberated countries considered clothing a higher priority than food. He emphasized that the clothing drive was the only way to secure the necessary supplies in a timely way. Mrs. Roosevelt lent her full support to the new effort, even suggesting a slogan for the committee to use: "What can you spare that they can wear?" The clothing drive was a big success, surpassing its goal and sending more than 150 million pounds of clothing overseas to help "the victims of the war to return to their factories, fields, and schools."[72]

UNRRA was still in crisis mode in March 1945 when vital decisions on supplies and shipping were pending. When two of his aides suggested that Lehman meet with various officials in London, the Director General explained that he was "loath to leave Washington" because the "critical nature of [the] supply and shipping situation at this time" might require his "personal intervention" in the "next several weeks." Lehman was somewhat mollified when Crowley promised that the interagency committee would keep Lehman informed when it considered "supply problems" in which Lehman was "vitally interested" and advise him of the committee's progress when "its evaluations may directly affect the UNRRA program." Crowley also noted that FEA representatives responsible for liberated areas would attend committee meetings "to ensure that the problems of these areas are given due attention." The FEA Director recalled that in the President's letter back in July, Roosevelt had directed him to "furnish every possible assistance to the Director General of UNRRA," and Crowley assured Lehman that he had done everything possible to carry out that responsibility. To illustrate the FEA's close cooperation with UNRRA, Crowley pointed out that the FEA had processed and "committed for procurement" $200,000,000 of the $260,000,000 in Requests to Supply that UNRRA had submitted, and he expected that "the remaining $60,000,000 in Requests, which have only recently been received," would be processed "within a week."[73]

Always concerned, and with good reason, that others were infringing on UNRRA's mission and scant resources, Lehman immediately contacted the

FIGURE 8.2. UNRRA Director General Herbert Lehman inspects aid bound for Poland and Czechoslovakia, March 22, 1945. Keystone-France/Gamma-Keystone via Getty Images.

President in late March when he "heard rumors that the Red Cross has asked for an appropriation in a very substantial amount to carry on medical, agricultural, and other relief in liberated areas." The Director General was not just being paranoid; FDR had discussed with Basil O'Connor, his former law partner who now headed the Red Cross, the possibility of federal funds going to the Red Cross for relief activities. Lehman emphasized to the President that UNRRA "has always been glad to cooperate in every possible way with the Red Cross and will, of course, continue to do so," but he warned that "if the Red Cross carried on work independently of UNRRA in those countries for which UNRRA has the responsibility, there not only would be duplication in expenditures and facilities, but the situation would probably become helplessly confused." Roosevelt referred Lehman's letter to Budget Director Harold Smith to prepare a response for his signature, but the President died before the letter had been drafted. Smith later informed President Harry Truman that Roosevelt had twice rejected the idea of a federal appropriation for the Red Cross, but had relented shortly before his death.[74]

Lehman also complained to the President on March 31 about "reports that the Army's claims for scarce food contain very large requirements on behalf of the civilian population of Germany." At a time when UNRRA was still having difficulty securing supplies and shipping, Lehman was outraged that "supplies for German civilians are to be delivered at the expense of the peoples of the liberated areas," and he warned that "the results are bound to be catastrophic politically and otherwise." Lehman understood that "under special circumstances the Army may be compelled to assume certain minimum responsibilities for the German civilian population," but he emphasized that "a higher responsibility rests on the United States to feed the Allied liberated areas first." He noted that "the supplies now being furnished or in immediate prospect for the Allied liberated areas are tragically below the level required to support even a minimum standard of living," especially "in the starved areas of Greece, Poland, and Yugoslavia" where "no meats and very little of dairy products are being allocated to UNRRA from the United States during April, May and June of this year." Speaking "on behalf of the liberated peoples affected," Lehman urged that "this matter [be] looked into in sufficient detail" to assess "the Army's total requirements and to establish a policy which will to the fullest extent protect the prior claim of the liberated areas to available supplies." As with Lehman's letter objecting to a possible appropriation for the Red Cross, Roosevelt referred the Director General's communiqué to the Director of the Budget to prepare a reply.[75]

Franklin Roosevelt never replied to these last two letters from Herbert Lehman. On April 12, 1945, the President suffered a cerebral hemorrhage and died at Warm Springs. Like the rest of the nation, Lehman was "shocked beyond measure by the President's untimely death," lamenting that "the world has lost one of its great leaders." Joining in the many public tributes to the President, Lehman asserted that Roosevelt had "sacrificed his life in the service of his fellow-men just as surely as if he had died on the battlefield." Lehman mourned "the loss of the greatest and bravest man" he had ever known, "a true friend" who had honored Lehman "with his friendship and trust for more than twenty-five years." Privately, Herbert and Edith Lehman conveyed their "heartfelt sympathy and love" to Mrs. Roosevelt, noting "how deeply" they grieved with her and her family in their "great sorrow." The Lehmans would miss "a beloved friend" whose friendship would "always remain an inspiration." In comforting the President's daughter, Anna Roosevelt Boettiger, the Lehmans emphasized that her father "was the greatest and most courageous man" they had ever known, and that "his untimely passing is an unmeasurable loss to free people everywhere." Herbert Lehman was among the mourners who attended the funeral service at the White House and the burial services at Hyde Park where the President was laid to his final rest.[76]

After all the ceremonies had concluded, Eleanor Roosevelt confided to Edith Lehman that "it was a comfort" to have Herbert along "on that trip to Hyde Park and here at the White House." She believed that "God in His infinite wisdom saw fit to take Franklin," and she knew that the Lehmans shared her relief that her husband had not suffered. The Lehmans were among the Roosevelts' "oldest and best friends," and Mrs. Roosevelt was confident that they would continue to work for her husband's ideals. In discussing the President's passing with many of his friends, Herbert Lehman emphasized that although "the world has suffered a grievous loss in President Roosevelt's death," Lehman hoped that the ideals for which Roosevelt "fought so long and for which he gave his life have become a potent force among people of this and other countries, and that they will become the cornerstone of a peace of security and justice."[77]

Roosevelt's death broke up "the Army Navy team," as FDR had described himself and Lehman back in 1928. The two had accomplished much together, first in Albany, then in Washington, and finally on the world stage. But UNRRA, their last joint activity, still had a way to go. At the time of Roosevelt's death, the war in Europe was almost over. In the Pacific, however, although the tide had turned, there was no end in sight in the war against Japan, meaning that the military would continue to commandeer American shipping and supplies that UNRRA needed to provide relief to the liberated people of Europe and Asia. Even though Roosevelt had been supportive of UNRRA and Lehman had frequently used his friendship with the President to bring UNRRA's problems to his attention, UNRRA still struggled to perform its mission. While the war was still going on, UNRRA would never be the President's or the nation's top priority. Roosevelt's second quarterly report to Congress on UNRRA, delivered on April 11, the day before he died, noted that "during the course of the war, UNRRA can help the liberated people only to the extent that military considerations of operations, supply, shipping, and distribution make it possible." The President explained that "the requirements of the armed forces for accelerated military operations have had the first call on our supplies, our shipping, and the unloading and transportation facilities in the liberated areas." Even with a friend in the White House, Herbert Lehman and UNRRA had not been able to loosen the military's grip on shipping and supplies. How would they fare under Roosevelt's successor, Harry Truman, who had no history with either Lehman or UNRRA?[78]

"UNRRA's Problem Is That It Is Trying to Cover a 6-Foot Man with a 2-Foot Blanket"

Herbert Lehman, Harry Truman, and UNRRA, 1945

The Director General received real support from President Truman, but, of course, the personal and intimate relationship which he had enjoyed with President Roosevelt no longer existed.[1]

In contrast to his close relationship with Franklin Roosevelt, Herbert Lehman barely knew FDR's successor, Harry Truman. As opposed to Lehman, who came from a wealthy family and enjoyed great success in business before seeking political office, Truman came from modest circumstances and suffered the failure of his haberdashery store before finding his true calling in politics. Like Al Smith in New York, Truman was the product of a political machine. The Pendergast machine that dominated Kansas City politics supported Truman for Jackson County Judge in the 1920s and then for U.S. Senator in 1934. Lehman first met Truman in December 1942 at a farewell dinner honoring Senator George Norris of Nebraska, a progressive icon who had just been defeated in his bid for re-election. Lehman respected Truman's work as head of the Senate Special Committee Investigating the National Defense Program, but other than a dinner given by the Women's National Democratic Club in February 1945, Truman's and Lehman's paths seldom crossed before Truman succeeded to the presidency in April 1945.[2]

Chapter title quotation: Leonard Lyons, *Washington Post*, November 10, 1945, p. 10.

I

In April 1945, during Truman's first week as President, Secretary of State Stettinius alerted him to "the critical character of the world food situation" and warned of "the disastrous political and economic results which may be expected if countries dependent on food imports, especially the liberated areas, have to go through another winter of want." Stettinius reported that the armed forces refused even to discuss their food requirements, and that "certain of the civilian agencies seem reluctant to carry out the 'tightening of the belt' anticipated by President Roosevelt." The Secretary urged the President to order the military to "cooperate fully" and "instruct the appropriate civilian agencies, particularly the War Food Administration, to explore all possible reductions in U.S. consumption which would not cut into the maintenance of our essential war economy." He also recommended that the President make Congress and the American people aware of "the facts of the food situation and this country's vital interests abroad," believing that "it is only against a background of enlightened public opinion that the necessary decisions can be made acceptable."[3]

Truman had some familiarity with UNRRA; as a Senator in 1944, he had voted to authorize and appropriate funds for the organization. His first dealings with UNRRA as President occurred on April 26, 1945, when Budget Director Harold Smith explained that President Roosevelt had asked him to draft a bill appropriating federal funds for the Red Cross for overseas relief activities. As Truman later recalled in his *Memoirs*, he realized that "appropriations of this nature would tend to undercut the UNRRA program," and he planned "to discuss the whole subject of foreign relief with Governor Lehman." When Smith brought the matter up again a week later, the President insisted that the Red Cross should continue to rely on private, voluntary contributions rather than federal funds.[4]

UNRRA confronted old and new problems during the first weeks of the Truman administration. Shortages of shipping and supplies, combined with a lack of cooperation from various governments and agencies, continued to plague UNRRA, while land mines, a lack of farm animals and machinery, and the German destruction of port facilities and railroad tracks increased the difficulty of providing relief and rehabilitation to starving people in Europe. Columnist Marquis Childs spoke for many Americans in late April 1945 when he voiced his outrage that "so little has been done to aid those who managed to survive the concentration camps and the torture pens," but he also noted UNRRA's difficulties in getting the "necessary cooperation from the military in Europe."[5]

The situation in Poland continued to vex Lehman and UNRRA and exemplified how difficult it was for the Director General and his organization to serve all their masters. Because the Soviet Union still had not allowed UNRRA personnel into Poland, Lehman appointed UNRRA Deputy Director Mikhail

Menshikov, a Soviet citizen, to head an UNRRA survey mission to Poland, hoping that Menshikov would have more success in obtaining Soviet coopera- tion. However, the anti-Communist Polish government-in-exile, headquartered in London, denounced UNRRA's plan to work with the Soviet-backed Pro- visional Polish government, and Averell Harriman, the American Ambassador to the Soviet Union, considered Menshikov's appointment a "very unfortunate development." Harriman warned the State Department that "UNRRA supplies would be used against our policies," and he urged that pressure be applied on the Soviet Union, including "taking a firm stand on the Polish issue." Despite Menshikov's appointment, the Soviet Union still refused to grant visas for an UNRRA team to enter Poland until July 1945.[6]

The Soviet government was not the only one impeding UNRRA's work. Lehman complained to Secretary of State Stettinius that the United States was not providing UNRRA with the support it needed "with respect to taxation and . . . censorship, courier and pouch facilities, code privileges, and travel regulations." The Director General charged that "in several instances, the effec- tive action taken by the United Kingdom and other governments to facilitate our operations has been nullified or rendered relatively useless" by the absence of "corresponding action" by the United States. According to Lehman, the matter had "now reached a point where the effect on our day-to-day opera- tions and on the morale of our officers, both in Washington and abroad, is so great as to hamper seriously the fulfillment of our primary responsibility to the governments and peoples of the United Nations." Other governments, he asserted, "are now tending to delay action requested by UNRRA because they are aware of the apparent indifference toward these matters on the part of the [U.S.] government."[7]

On April 30, President Truman released a summary of Samuel Rosenman's report on civilian supplies in Northern and Western Europe that had been commissioned by President Roosevelt. In words that presaged much of the thinking behind the Marshall Plan a few years later, Rosenman painted a bleak picture, noting that "the needs of northwest Europe's liberated areas are grave" and that "the future permanent peace of Europe depends largely upon restoration of the economy of these countries." He warned that "a chaotic and hungry Europe is not fertile ground in which stable, democratic and friendly governments can be reared," and he urged that the United States accept "the responsibility for providing a substantial share of most civilian supplies." Because "the available supply of many kinds of food is insufficient for minimum requirements," Rosenman called for "a re-examination of total requirements against our supplies," cautioned that "allocation of civilian supplies to liberated countries in all probability will cut into the ration of the American consumer," and recommended that "a widespread official and public campaign should be undertaken to inform the American people of the gravity of the needs of our

Allies in liberated Europe." As for UNRRA, Rosenman observed that "UNRRA's supply activities in northwest Europe are comparatively unimportant" except in dealing with the problem of displaced persons, and he suggested that in making arrangements for such people, "UNRRA should be encouraged to greater participation compatible with military necessities and the liberated countries' own decisions." Because UNRRA's activities with regard to displaced persons would be increasing, Rosenman advocated that it "be given appropriate consideration for supplies, transport and ocean shipping."[8]

In contrast to the summary, with its brief mention of UNRRA, Rosenman's full report, which remained classified for thirty-one years, contained a fifteen-page discussion of UNRRA and its role in northwestern Europe. Rosenman explained the various limitations and restrictions on UNRRA's activities, detailed some of the bureaucratic and administrative difficulties that the organization had encountered, and noted the widespread disappointment with UNRRA in northwestern Europe, where the agency was generally seen as "ineffective, over-cautious, uncertain and legalistic." He concluded that UNRRA's failures thus far stemmed from "a lack of really whole-hearted and effective backing by the U.S. and U.K.," and he called for stronger American support for UNRRA, "not only by laudatory speeches but by providing top personnel, shipping, and supplies."[9]

Herbert Lehman had his first meeting with President Truman on May 1, 1945. Lehman reiterated many of the complaints he had voiced a few weeks earlier in his letter to Stettinius and echoed Rosenman's conclusions about UNRRA's difficulties and its need for stronger support from the United States to accomplish its mission. The Director General stressed that "the devastation and needs of Europe are far greater than anticipated when UNRRA was formed," and he asserted that "UNRRA has regeared itself" to "meet the desperate relief and rehabilitation needs in liberated areas." But for UNRRA's reorganization "to be effective in operation," Lehman emphasized, it needed the U.S. government to give it "higher priority" for the "procurement of supplies, procurement of shipping space, [and] air travel," and it needed the Truman administration to send to Congress a "general immunity bill . . . granting certain privileges necessary for an international organization," a draft of which "has been under consideration in the State Department for more than a year." Lehman warned that "the success or failure of UNRRA, the first operating organization established by the United Nations, will be of great significance in the development of other international agencies such as those growing out of the San Francisco Conference."[10]

Germany surrendered on May 8, 1945, and while Herbert Lehman rejoiced with all Americans at the news, he understood that the end of the fighting in Europe meant increased pressure on UNRRA to provide relief for those in need on the continent. In a statement hailing the end of the war in Europe, Lehman emphasized that "the cessation of hostilities merely heightens the desperate plight of the many destitute millions," and he hoped that "the spirit which made it possible for us to share and pool the weapons of war will in turn . . . make it possible for us to share and pool the resources of peace."[11]

On May 20, 1945, New Yorkers celebrated I Am an American Day, and Herbert Lehman used the occasion to highlight UNRRA's activities in an address to an estimated 1,500,000 people gathered in Central Park. Lehman noted that "today UNRRA is hard at work," having "taken over relief responsibilities in Greece and Yugoslavia," and that it was "now sending supplies into Poland and Czechoslovakia." The Director General reported that UNRRA was "carrying on, at a cost of $50,000,000, a program of supplemental feeding for children, nursing and expectant mothers, medical work and care of displaced persons" in Italy; "caring for thousands of refugees" in Africa and the Middle East; and "assisting the military to care for and repatriate the great horde of displaced persons" in Germany. Although UNRRA was not expected to provide aid to "countries that had sufficient funds to pay for their own goods, such as France, Belgium, Norway, the Netherlands and the Soviet Union," UNRRA stood ready to assist those countries "because the problems of displaced persons and epidemic control transcend national boundaries." UNRRA's needs were "small in comparison with what is produced here at home," Lehman pointed out, but UNRRA had "not been able, unfortunately, to obtain even the limited supplies" it "so urgently" needed "to do a helpful job in the liberated countries." Lehman challenged his audience, emphasizing that "the American people must make a firm decision: Are we going to allow starvation in Europe or prevent it? If necessary, are we willing to make a small sacrifice at home in order that millions abroad can regain their health and dignity?" Lehman warned that "the eyes of devastated Europe and Asia were watching our actions," and he "had no doubt of what the response of the American people to this great issue would be."[12]

Having read Stettinius's memorandum and Rosenman's report, and having met with Lehman on May 1, Truman realized that more needed to be done to prevent widespread starvation in Europe. In a series of letters on May 21, the President alerted the War Department, the State Department, the Foreign Economic Administration, the War Food Administration, the War Production Board, the Solid Fuels Administration, the Foreign Shipments Committee, the War Shipping Administration, and the Office of War Mobilization and Reconversion to "the serious economic situation in the liberated countries" and emphasized "the need for action on the part of this government." Truman stressed that it was "the established policy of this government" to accept responsibility "as the principal source of civilian supplies" for "the liberated countries of northwest Europe," and he instructed each agency "to grant the priority necessary to meet the minimum civilian requirements of those of our allies who have been ravaged by the enemy to the fullest extent that the successful prosecution of military operations and the maintenance of our essential domestic economy permit." Disturbed by the "conflicting jurisdictions of the allocating authorities in Washington," the President asked Fred Vinson, Director of the Office of War Mobilization and Reconversion, to undertake "an immediate investigation of the supply machineries and procedures, including [the] role played by UNRRA, in so far as they affect the allocation of needed supplies," and to recommend specific steps to resolve the problem. Truman also ordered Elmer Davis, head of the War Information Office, to expand "our efforts to inform the American public as to the gravity of the needs of our Allies in liberated Europe," and to impart "to the people in these liberated areas an increased understanding of what this country has done and is continuing to do for them, including our own shortages and sacrifices."[13]

II

With the death of Franklin Roosevelt and the end of the war in Europe, former President Herbert Hoover hoped that his political exile and status as the Democrats' favorite whipping boy would end and that his experience and expertise in feeding the people of Europe after World War I would bring him back into public service. A longtime critic of Lehman and UNRRA, Hoover delivered a speech in New York in April 1945 in which he reportedly asserted that the amount of food that UNRRA planned to ship to Europe by the end of June was "not enough to feed Paris," dismissed UNRRA as "a political machine," and charged that "for the first time in warfare food was being used as a weapon." In another speech on V-E Day, Hoover warned that "it is now 11:59 on the clock of starvation," and he recommended that unless UNRRA could "start the flow of millions of tons of food monthly and begin within the next few days," the task should be turned over to the military. Perhaps realizing that his criticism of UNRRA in the previous speech had gone too far, this time Hoover tempered somewhat his comments about Lehman and UNRRA, noting that the Director General "has been hampered by power politics," and that "his organization has not had adequate transportation nor single-headed authority which these large scale operations urgently require." But no matter who was at fault, Hoover emphasized that "precious time has been lost." In a radio broadcast a week later, Hoover wrote UNRRA out of the picture completely, asserting that providing food to the starving people of Europe was "a job so long delayed that only the American Army can solve it."[14]

As Hoover and others sounded the alarm, ordinary Americans and Washington pundits joined in the criticism of Lehman and UNRRA and demanded Hoover's appointment as a food czar to undertake the job he had performed so well after World War I. Columnist Marquis Childs charged that Lehman and UNRRA, Leo Crowley and the FEA, and Marvin Jones and the War Food

Administration had "all failed to live up to the imperative demands of the food crisis," and Childs called for a "food boss" who would be armed "with a big enough club" to "straighten out some of the tangles" and obtain the food and the shipping necessary to help the people in desperate need in Europe. A "good Democrat" from New York asserted in a letter to President Truman that although Lehman "was such an able Governor," he had been "given a job about which he knew nothing" and recalled that after Lehman's appointment as the head of OFRRO, his "first act was to confer with Mr. Hoover." The writer believed that "Mr. Hoover should be given the job of feeding Europe" because "he is an expert." Similarly, a letter to the editor of the *Washington Post* suggested that "the man who should be appointed food administrator is the one who did such a splendid job after the first World War, Herbert Hoover. His ability in that line is unsurpassed."[15]

Harry Truman never considered Herbert Hoover the *bête noire* that Roosevelt and many other Democrats did, and Secretary of War Henry Stimson, who had served as Secretary of State under Hoover, urged the new President to meet with Hoover about the growing food crisis. Seeing the groundswell of public opinion for utilizing Hoover's expertise in dealing with the situation, and realizing the political benefits that would accrue from reaching out to the former President in a nonpartisan way, Truman invited Hoover to meet with him at the White House "to talk over the European food situation."[16]

Truman and Hoover met on May 28, at which time Hoover detailed his concern about the looming famine in Europe, explained how he had dealt with the situation after World War I, and stressed that help was needed in the next ninety days. During the meeting and in a subsequent memorandum he sent to the President, Hoover blamed "mismanagement" for many of the problems, declaring that UNRRA had been doomed "from the start," that "the dominance of power politics and the lack of authority made this organization incapable of administering the large economic problems of Europe." Even though Assistant Secretary of War John McCloy had previously explained to Hoover that the Army did not want the responsibility for feeding the people in liberated Europe, Hoover argued that the military alone was capable of providing the emergency assistance that was needed. The former President believed that America's efforts should focus on aiding the people of northwestern Europe and the Mediterranean, asserting that Soviet-occupied Eastern Europe was "entirely Russia's problem," and he recommended that the Secretary of Agriculture "should control or approve of all [food] purchases by the Army, Navy, Lend-Lease, UNRRA and any other government agency." After the meeting, the White House described the session as "very pleasant" and reported that Hoover had presented "some constructive ideas which the President was glad to receive."[17]

Writing in the *New York Times*, Arthur Krock pointed out all the differences between the situation in 1918–1919 and the present crisis, which made

Hoover's past experience less relevant, noting that "UNRRA and other existing jurisdictions would be in conflict" with Hoover or anyone else exercising such authority "unless they were abolished or submerged." Similarly, Drew Pearson reported a few weeks later that Hoover had "recommended that UNRRA be disbanded and the feeding job turned over to the Army in toto." According to Pearson, this suggestion reflected Hoover's dislike of "any form of international cooperation," but President Truman had rejected the proposal because "he believes in international cooperation."[18]

Despite some concern over Truman's meeting with Hoover, Lehman thought that "President Truman has taken hold very well indeed." The Director General confided to his son John that Truman, "of course, lacks Roosevelt's broad knowledge of foreign relations and his close association with Churchill, Stalin and the other leaders," but Lehman believed that the President "has shown firmness and power to make decisions" and was "gaining the confidence of the people." Based on what he had seen so far, Lehman predicted that Truman "will do well."[19]

III

Lehman and UNRRA faced more important problems in June 1945 than Hoover's re-emergence on the scene; there was mounting criticism that UNRRA was sending only a small quantity of supplies to Europe. The *New York Times* pointed out in early June why UNRRA was having such difficulty getting food to Europe: UNRRA was being "pushed around," it was "losing out in the struggle for shipping allocations," it was "beset by innumerable political considerations," and it was "generally out of the picture when viewed by combined boards concentrating on military strategy." The *Times* also noted that UNRRA's ability to carry out its plan for June "to ship as much as it has in the first five months of the year" depended in part "on our willingness to heed the late President Roosevelt's behest that to tighten our belt was the decent thing to do." Similarly, columnist Marquis Childs observed that "the weeks are passing, and yet nothing sufficiently positive or emphatic is being done about getting food to hungry Europe," and he deplored the severe cuts the United States government had made in UNRRA's requests for food to send to Greece, Yugoslavia, Poland, and Czechoslovakia.[20]

As he had done so many times during the Roosevelt years, Herbert Lehman complained directly to the President about the unfair treatment that UNRRA was receiving from the American bureaucracy. Lehman met with President Truman on June 13 and followed up with a series of letters detailing the problems confronting UNRRA. The Director General was "greatly worried about the prospects of suffering and actual starvation in certain areas in Europe in the months that lie ahead," pointing out that "of the 169,000 tons of food requested from the United States for loading in ships in July, the War Food Administration has promised us only 89,000 tons." Lehman explained to the President, "nothing short of a word from you will bring the food authorities of the United States to a realization of the necessity of meeting the urgent needs for food of the countries which UNRRA is charged with assisting." He expressed "great confidence" in Truman's "understanding of the needs of these countries" and his "conviction that UNRRA, as the first international organization growing out of this war, must not fail." Although Lehman was "aware, as everyone is, of the shortages which have developed in this country," he emphasized that "the amount we are asking for represents such a very small percentage of the food that is produced here" that he was "confident the people of the country will be willing to share it."[21]

Truman replied sympathetically to Lehman's concerns but made no commitment that anything would change. The President asserted that "the needs of UNRRA, and of the liberated peoples generally, are very close to my heart and to the heart of all Americans," but he knew that Lehman was aware of "the difficulties we face in meeting military and domestic needs." Truman noted, "We cannot always do as much as we would like for the liberated areas," although he agreed that "ways and means must be found to meet irreducible minimum needs and to prevent starvation." Accordingly, Truman asked the Office of War Mobilization and Reconversion and the War Food Administration to consider the issues Lehman had raised "with special care."[22]

Now that UNRRA was actually providing goods and services in Europe, it was rapidly running out of funds, and Lehman turned to the President for help in this area as well. Lehman and UNRRA officials alerted the FEA and the Bureau of the Budget in early June that the organization had exhausted the $450,000,000 that Congress had appropriated directly for UNRRA and that it now needed the additional $350,000,000 that had been given to Lend-Lease but could be transferred to the FEA for use by UNRRA. Lehman explained the situation to the President in their meeting on June 13 and in a follow-up memo, noting that for the transfer to occur, the Joint Chiefs of Staff had to "certify that the state of war permits the exercise of this authority." Lehman had informed FEA Director Crowley back in February that the original funds would likely be used up by the spring, and in late May Crowley had asked the Joint Chiefs to make the necessary certification, but as of June 18, Lehman reported, "this certification has not yet been issued." Without these funds, Lehman warned, "the UNRRA procurement program in the United States will come to a stop at the very time when our operations must be accelerated." He stressed that "UNRRA's situation becomes more difficult daily," and he asked the President "to expedite both the issuance of the certification by the Joint Chiefs of Staff and the transfer of the requisite funds." Truman asked Fred Vinson, head of the Office of War Mobilization and Reconversion, to "take care of it," and on June 27, Admiral William Leahy, on behalf of the Joint Chiefs of Staff, sent the required certification to the FEA, which subsequently made the funds available for UNRRA.[23]

Lehman also sought Truman's assistance in overcoming UNRRA's continuing difficulty in recruiting top people for high-level positions, but the President's reluctance to challenge the military meant that Lehman's efforts met with little success. When Lehman and the State Department agreed that Ferdinand Eberstadt of New York City was the best choice to head up UNRRA's crucial displaced persons operations, the President appealed to Eberstadt to accept the position. Truman also complied with a request that he ask the military to release Major General Donald Connolly to lead UNRRA's mission in Poland, and Colonel A. R. Guyler to direct UNRRA staff working "with displaced persons in the American occupation zone in Germany." But unbeknownst to Lehman or the President, Eberstadt was working for Secretary of the Navy James Forrestal on the possible consolidation of the nation's armed services, and Truman eventually acquiesced in Forrestal's wish to keep Eberstadt in the Navy Department. Similarly, the President deferred to Acting Secretary of War Robert Patterson's request that General Connolly remain in his post as Deputy Commissioner of the Army-Navy Liquidation Commission, leaving Colonel Guyler as the only one of the three men who actually went to work for UNRRA.[24]

On June 30, President Truman transmitted to Congress the third quarterly report on UNRRA's activities. The President reported that "millions of the liberated peoples are emaciated, hungry, and sick and they are without means of livelihood," and millions of others were "destitute, far from home and country, and without food and shelter." He noted that "UNRRA's shipments are now going forward in an increasing volume to Greece, Poland, Yugoslavia, Czechoslovakia and other nations to relieve the victims of war who have no other source of assistance," and that, with the end of the fighting in Europe "and the resulting decrease in European military demands for supplies and shipping, it is now possible for UNRRA to begin to accelerate the flow of needed supplies to liberated countries." But Truman warned that "this coming winter will be the period of greatest need" for food and medical supplies and for "agricultural, industrial and transportation equipment." Now was the time, he declared, for UNRRA and the world community to "keep faith with those who fought and died in order to bring freedom and relief from suffering to the liberated peoples and a secure peace to the world."[25]

While the President continued to support UNRRA, criticism of the organization continued to mount, especially from conservative members of Congress concerned about the cost and UNRRA's alleged ineffectiveness in responding to the crisis in Europe. Representative John Vorys (R-OH) tried unsuccessfully to prevent the transfer of Lend-Lease funds to UNRRA, and

Representative Everett Dirksen (R-IL) urged Congress "to take a good look at this agency" before appropriating any additional funds, asserting that "UNRRA has developed an odor and the time is at hand to carefully audit its personnel, its accounts and its activities." While not criticizing UNRRA directly, Democrats Harold Cooley of North Carolina, Harold Earthman of Tennessee, and George Grant of Alabama pointed out the deleterious effects of having UNRRA, the military, and the Board of Economic Warfare all competing for scarce food to prevent starvation in Europe. Upset that the United States was bearing most of the cost of UNRRA and that some nations had not met their expected contributions to the organization, Senator Harry Byrd (D-VA) planned to use the Joint Congressional Economy Committee, which he headed, to investigate UNRRA's expenditures. Lehman publicly defended UNRRA's "excellent work" as having "brought much relief to the people," asserting that the agency would "welcome a most careful study of its operations." But privately he conceded that "we still have great difficulties to overcome, many of which, unfortunately, are beyond our control."[26]

Before traveling to Europe in July to inspect UNRRA's operations on the continent, Lehman tried to generate as much favorable publicity for UNRRA as he could, making speeches and granting interviews in which he appealed to the member nations of UNRRA to make the sacrifices necessary to prevent widespread starvation and pestilence in the liberated countries. Although he understood that there were shortages of foodstuffs in supplying countries, the Director General feared that the cutbacks in allotments for UNRRA were having catastrophic effects. He pointed out, for example, that the United States had "promised 100,000,000 pounds of canned pork and 100,000,000 pounds of fat cuts in pork," but had delivered "less than 2,000,000 pounds of the former and 12,000,000 pounds of the latter," and had canceled the rest of the allotment. UNRRA had determined that 725,000,000 pounds of meat was "the minimum requirement," but the agency had only been able to obtain 44,000,000 pounds from the United States, Canada, and other donors. Lehman believed that small sacrifices would enable the members of UNRRA to meet Europe's needs, asserting that "if each of us would give one pint of milk a month, UNRRA could meet its schedules on milk." He noted that "in the great battles of the war," the United Nations "have been overwhelmingly victorious," but he warned that "the first great battle of the peace is yet to be won." That fight, he emphasized, was "against want, hunger and disease," which were "ravaging" most of Europe to an extent that people in the Western Hemisphere could "hardly grasp." Lehman stressed that "what we do, or fail to do, in the next critical six months will be the real test."[27]

Lehman left for Europe on July 5 to examine UNRRA facilities and meet with various officials. He arrived first in Rome to look at UNRRA activities in Italy, where UNRRA had shipped 50,000 tons of supplies and was caring for

300,000 people. Lehman had two audiences with Pope Pius XII, who praised UNRRA's work and hoped that its activities could be expanded through the "well-known generosity of the American people." Lehman went next to Greece, where the lack of trucks and the damage to railroad lines made it difficult to distribute the supplies that UNRRA was bringing in, problems that plagued Yugoslavia as well. In Belgrade, he met with Marshal Tito, who "thanked him for the help UNRRA had given," but Lehman suffered an attack of dysentery that prevented him from visiting the field operations he had hoped to see, and he flew to London in late July to await the upcoming third meeting of the UNRRA Council.[28]

While Lehman was on his trip, a report surfaced that he might resign when the UNRRA Council convened in London in August. According to a United Press story in the *Washington Post* on July 16, there was "an outside chance" that Lehman would leave UNRRA if he thought that "his departure would rally the public behind UNRRA's faltering efforts to obtain enough food and relief supplies for liberated Europe." A "close associate" of Lehman maintained that the Director General " 'wants intensely' to stay until the vast job of healing the wounds of war-torn Europe and the Far East is finished" but was "willing to sacrifice this personal desire if he can provoke public support for a greater flow of supplies from the uninvaded United Nations," especially the United States, Canada, and the countries of Latin America. The *Post's* editors questioned the wisdom of this strategy, not seeing how Lehman's resignation could possibly improve the situation, and urged him to "continue at his difficult post." At a press conference in Athens a few days later, Lehman denied that he had any intention of stepping down as Director General of UNRRA, asserting that he had "not given any consideration to resigning." He promised, "So long as I can be of assistance I shall continue to fight with the utmost spirit to obtain additional supplies for liberated Europe from supplying countries." What he had seen in Athens and elsewhere on his trip, Lehman declared, had reinforced his conviction of "the great need of the people and the necessity of bringing assistance to them." Nonetheless, rumors of Lehman's imminent departure from UNRRA persisted, especially after he was stricken with dysentery in Yugoslavia. Drew Pearson, who usually reflected Lehman's position sympathetically and accurately, reported on August 2 that Lehman, "tired of bucking red tape and Army brass hats, plans to resign as head of UNRRA at the coming London meeting."[29]

As the UNRRA Council prepared to convene in London in August 1945, the organization's finances became more and more of a concern. UNRRA had received the $350,000,000 originally appropriated to Lend-Lease, but it was rapidly running out of funds as it provided aid to starving people in Greece, Yugoslavia, Czechoslovakia, and Poland and prepared for operations in China and the Far East. American and British officials also wanted UNRRA to take over responsibility for relief activities in Italy, which would require additional funds. According to its own estimates, UNRRA would run out of money by the end of 1945 or early 1946 unless additional contributions were forthcoming.[30]

President Truman and administration officials realized the need to do something about UNRRA's precarious financial state, and on July 10, Assistant Secretaries of State Dean Acheson and Will Clayton discussed the problem with House Speaker Sam Rayburn, Majority Leader John McCormack, Minority Leader Joseph Martin, and members of the House Foreign Affairs and Appropriations Committees. Acheson explained the advantages of extending aid to Italy through UNRRA, where "the United States will bear two-thirds of the cost instead of 100 percent," and Foreign Affairs Committee Chairman Sol Bloom emphasized the need to provide assistance to Italy "so as not to allow communism to get a start." Clayton reported to the President that although the legislators had voiced "considerable criticism of UNRRA's management," they accepted "the necessity of doing something for Italy and the other countries," and he was confident "that it would be relatively easy to obtain the additional funds next fall if UNRRA has in the meantime reorganized and improved its administrative set-up." The President concurred, and the United States and Britain agreed to propose to the UNRRA Council that members make an additional contribution equal to 1 percent of their 1943 national income, which would raise another $1,800,000,000, $1,350,000,000 of it from the United States. As Acting Secretary of State Joseph Grew explained to U.S. diplomats, the United States "took this approach in place of [a] purely US program" because it wanted "to back [the] first United Nations organization which we had originally sponsored and to foster international rather than national considerations in handling relief and rehabilitation matters." Grew also pointed out that contributions from other members of UNRRA would reduce the cost to the United States of providing aid to Italy and other countries in need of assistance.[31]

As can be seen in Congressman Bloom's comments, the growing rift between the United States and the Soviet Union also affected UNRRA, as some American officials feared that the Russians were using UNRRA aid to maintain their domination in Poland, Czechoslovakia, and Yugoslavia. Worried that the Soviet Union was diverting to its own use UNRRA relief shipments to Eastern Europe, the State Department asked Ambassador Averell Harriman in Moscow to relay "any available information on amounts of food or other essential supplies being removed to Russia or consumed by Soviet forces in Poland and Czechoslovakia." American officials also inquired into reports from Yugoslavia that "UNRRA food and medical supplies" were being used to benefit the Communist Party rather than the civilian population. At the same time, American officials hoped that aid from UNRRA would help bolster the Italian government and make that nation less susceptible to the spread of communism.[32]

UNRRA's financial problems and its difficulty in navigating the split between the United States and the Soviet Union came together in July 1945 when the Soviet Union suddenly presented UNRRA with a request for $700,000,000 in relief and rehabilitation supplies. UNRRA immediately began examining the Soviet Union's ability to pay for supplies, and the Truman administration weighed the negative impact of the Soviet request on the possibility of obtaining additional funds from Congress for UNRRA. Believing that the Russian request had to be sidetracked or the "entire program" would "be jeopardized" in Congress, administration officials recommended that the Soviet Union seek financial assistance from the Export-Import Bank instead. Secretary of State James Byrnes suggested that perhaps "a much smaller sum, say fifty to one hundred million for emergency relief in Soviet territories" such as Ukraine and Byelorussia, could be managed within the additional UNRRA funds already contemplated.[33]

IV

After completing his inspection of UNRRA facilities in Italy, Greece, and Yugoslavia, and convalescing from his bout of dysentery, Director General Lehman opened the UNRRA Council meeting in London on August 7, 1945. In a brief welcome to the forty-four delegations, Lehman praised the wisdom and foresight of former British Prime Minister Winston Churchill, "whose government did so much to advance the work of UNRRA," and Franklin Roosevelt, "who launched this organization two years since and who gave its work indispensable support and encouragement." But in his formal report to the Council the following day, Lehman criticized UNRRA's member nations for not delivering the supplies they had promised, and he emphasized the organization's need for additional funds. Without those supplies and funds, he warned, UNRRA would be unable to meet its commitments and "the name of the United Nations will be a mockery in Europe this winter."[34]

With the fighting in Europe having ended in May, the U.S. Army-Navy Liquidation Commission announced on August 8 that the Foreign Economic Administration would have the top priority for purchasing overseas surplus goods either for its own purposes or for UNRRA. A week later, the UNRRA Council urged the military authorities of all supplying nations to turn over food, clothing, trucks, and any other material that could be used for relief and rehabilitation, and by mid-August, the American Army had turned over hundreds of trucks and other vehicles that UNRRA desperately needed to transport supplies to remote areas of Yugoslavia and Italy. The atomic bombing of Hiroshima and Nagasaki and the Soviet Union's declaration of war against Japan hastened the end of the war in Asia, meaning that China and other liberated countries in the Far East now needed UNRRA aid that had not been included in previous estimates of the organization's budget for 1946. The Allied victory in the Pacific led Lehman to increase his request for additional funding for UNRRA to more than $2,000,000,000.[35]

The tension of the UNRRA Council meetings and the difficulty in obtaining the needed money and supplies were affecting Lehman physically. At a dinner, one observer noted that the Director General, who may not have been completely recovered from his earlier siege of dysentery, "looked tired and had a nervous twitch in his face." Herbert Lehman took comfort from his wife's presence with him for this part of his long stay in Europe, a highlight of which came when they were received by the King and Queen of England on August 15. Their presence in London, however, caused the Lehmans to miss President Truman's invitation to attend a White House "service of thanksgiving and intercession to the Most High—thanksgiving for victory—supplication for guidance that the horrors of war may be followed by a peace of justice and righteousness."[36]

Although the President seemed understanding and sympathetic to UNRRA's needs, not everyone in his administration seemed to realize exactly how desperate the situation in Europe had become. In late May, Truman had reorganized his Cabinet, replacing many of the holdovers he had inherited from the Roosevelt administration. The President selected Representative Clinton Anderson (D-NM), a poker-playing buddy who had headed the House Special Committee to Investigate Food Shortages, as Secretary of Agriculture, and as Allen Matusow notes in his study of Truman's farm policies, "nothing cast greater suspicion on Truman's sincerity on the subject of relief than his appointment of Anderson, who was widely expected to put American consumers first in allocating scarce supplies." Anderson made it clear in various public statements that "America can't feed the world" and that "new food commitments to foreign nations will be reviewed very carefully" in order to "increase quantities of rationed commodities available for civilian use" in the United States. His solution to the problem of depleted stockpiles and potential shortages was to increase farm production through government subsidies and price supports. On the same day in mid-August when Truman asked the War Department to "determine immediately the extent to which and the time when surplus stocks may be made available" to UNRRA, Anderson declared that the end of the war meant the military's need for meat would be shrinking rapidly. Therefore, instead of urging Americans to tighten their belts to help relieve the suffering overseas, Anderson predicted that "we could easily be out of meat rationing in the fall season." The Secretary claimed that he had included in his calculations "not only present relief feeding but increased relief requirements" for the liberated countries to which the United States had already made commitments.[37]

With Lehman in London at the UNRRA Council meeting, it fell to UNRRA Deputy Director General Roy Hendrickson to respond to Anderson's remarks. Hendrickson seemed surprisingly unperturbed by Anderson's comments, noting that people in Southern and Eastern Europe did not eat much meat, and that what they really needed was "fat-back" from hogs, which supplied both protein and fat. The *Washington Post* expressed more concern over Anderson's statement than did Hendrickson, worrying that "efforts to alleviate the European food crisis would be seriously hampered by the diversion of anticipated surpluses from the export relief market into domestic distributive and consumer channels." Similarly, *The Nation* thought that "our authorities are misjudging the American people if they assume we are eager to return to bountiful living while Europe and the rest of the world starve." The editors wanted to "keep rationing strict if thereby Europe can get more meats and fats," and they advocated giving "UNRRA promptly the appropriation Mr. Lehman is asking for."[38]

By the end of the UNRRA Council meeting in London in late August, the organization had admitted Denmark and the Byelorussian and Ukrainian Soviet Socialist Republics to membership; asked member nations for supplies no longer needed by the military; deferred decision on what to do with displaced persons who did not wish to return to their native lands; authorized relief and rehabilitation aid to Italy, Austria, Korea, and Formosa; added Canada and France to the Central Committee; strengthened financial controls; requested member states to contribute an additional 1 percent of 1943 national income; and promised to complete its activities in Europe by the end of 1946 and in the Far East by March 31, 1947. The Soviet Union agreed to withdraw its request for $700,000,000 in UNRRA aid after Assistant Secretary of State Clayton warned that Congress would never approve additional funds for UNRRA if a substantial part of the money were promised to the Soviet Union, but Clayton assured the Soviets that the United States would support $250,000,000 in assistance to Byelorussia and the Ukraine.[39]

Lehman feared that the additional 1 percent contribution, which was expected to raise another $1,800,000,000, might not be enough to cope with the rapidly deteriorating situation in the liberated countries. In his closing remarks to the conference, he asserted that the end of the war should mean that the needs of the liberated countries would now have first claim on supplies and services, and that "UNRRA's policy need no longer be confined by considerations of military necessity." He noted that "now only military convenience is involved," and he hoped that "the services, supplies, organizational ability and personnel which the military machine possesses" would be made available to UNRRA.[40]

Herbert and Edith Lehman sailed for home on August 26 on the British liner *Queen Elizabeth*, along with fifteen thousand returning U.S. servicemen. Arriving in New York on August 31, Lehman emphasized UNRRA's need for "more money and more supplies," especially trucks, coal, food, and clothing, to help the people of Europe survive a "grim winter," and he announced that he planned to go to Washington as soon as possible to confer with President Truman. In a press conference in Washington a few days later, Lehman stressed the need for the United States to approve the $550,000,000 that had been authorized for UNRRA but not appropriated, as well as the additional $1,350,000,000 contribution just requested. Lehman expressed confidence that this "comparatively small amount," which paled beside the "hundreds of billions of dollars" spent fighting the war, would be made available "to help our friends back on the road of self-sufficiency." During the war, he noted, "we promised much to the occupied nations, while the Nazis still overran their lands," to encourage them to resist. Now, Lehman declared, "the time has come to redeem that promise."[41]

V

President Truman and the State Department worked closely with Lehman and UNRRA in the fall of 1945 to win congressional approval of the authorization and appropriation bills necessary to provide additional American funds for the organization. The Director General met briefly with Truman on September 6, the same day the President sent Congress a twenty-one-point program to help ease the economy back to a peacetime footing. Obviously, Lehman did not have a chance to influence Truman's message, but he had to be pleased when, near the end of the long list of proposals, the President urged Congress to "fulfill the commitment already made by appropriating the remaining $550,000,000 granted by the Congress for United States participation" in UNRRA and expressed confidence that the legislators would fully fund UNRRA's request for an additional $1,350,000,000 from the United States. Ten days later, Truman reiterated his support for UNRRA, reassuring the American people that "we have sufficient quantities of meat and dairy products to fulfill the requirements placed upon us by UNRRA and the paying governments for the last quarter of the year."[42]

As Truman prepared to call upon Congress to approve huge sums of money for UNRRA, the organization increasingly became a target for congressional brickbats. Representative Edith Nourse Rogers (R-MA), a senior member of the House Foreign Affairs Committee, opposed a huge outlay of funds for UNRRA, asserting that the United States should focus on its own postwar recovery instead. She denounced UNRRA as "a dire failure" that "should be liquidated," charged that UNRRA had "spent large sums and has nothing to show for it," and complained that "UNRRA representatives are going around Europe with uniforms but with no work to do." Representative J. Parnell Thomas (R-NJ) reportedly planned to ask the House Un-American Activities Committee to look into allegations that "UNRRA has been a vehicle for spreading Communistic propaganda in Europe," and Representative James Fulton (R-PA) described UNRRA as "the laughing stock" of Europe, "composed of impractical do-gooders and 'doodlers' who run around doing nothing" except complaining that "they don't like their uniforms." Representative Clarence Brown (R-OH), a newspaper publisher, wanted to be sure that other nations had contributed their fair shares to UNRRA before the United States approved any additional money, and he also proposed that UNRRA funds not be granted to any country lacking a free press that could independently investigate and report "the needs of the foreign countries and how UNRRA is functioning." As columnist Marquis Childs noted, much of this unease about UNRRA reflected "a growing distrust of the Soviets and their intentions in the world."[43]

An appearance before Senator Harry Byrd's Joint Committee on Reduction of Non-Essential Federal Expenditures in mid-September provided Herbert Lehman with the opportunity to refute much of the congressional criticism. Lehman rejected allegations that UNRRA was a "dire failure" that "was badly administered, paid excessive salaries, [and] tended to pure relief rather than to putting recipients back on their feet." He denied that he had ever "been on the point of resigning," although he admitted that "it has been an uphill fight," that he had, at times, "been disappointed because of difficulties in shipping, in getting supplies, in arrangements with the military." Despite "the greatest difficulties any organization in the world has had to face," Lehman claimed that "UNRRA is doing a good job." He reported that "every country of solid and substantial national income has made available or authorized its full 1 per cent of its national income" under UNRRA's original request, and when asked which countries had not yet paid their full commitment, he pointed out that the United States was the main nation in arrears. Lehman rejected suggestions that the U.S. General Accounting Office audit UNRRA's finances, asserting that it would not be proper or practical for UNRRA to have its finances examined by any national authority, but he explained that Assistant Secretary of State Clayton, as the U.S. representative to the UNRRA Council, enjoyed full access to UNRRA's financial information. He denied that Russia controlled UNRRA operations in Eastern Europe, insisting that UNRRA activities in Poland and Czechoslovakia were "under the supervision of UNRRA," and he revealed that the Soviet Union's request for $700,000,000 in aid from UNRRA had been scaled back to $250,000,000 for Byelorussia and the Ukraine. Finally, Lehman testified that UNRRA salaries averaged $2,800 annually, $3,800 for its employees in the United States, which was "slightly under the federal pay scale" and conformed to local pay rates elsewhere.[44]

In a letter to his son John on September 30, Herbert Lehman was more open and frank about UNRRA's problems. John Lehman was still on active military service in Germany, and he had passed on to his father concerns about what he had seen of UNRRA's work among the displaced persons there. Herbert Lehman did not dispute the accuracy of John's reports, conceding that some of UNRRA's operations had "suffered from lack of adequate supervision," but he hoped this situation "will be substantially improved" by the appointment of British General Sir Frederick Morgan, former Deputy Chief of Staff under General Eisenhower, to oversee the displaced persons' activities in Germany as a whole, and Colonel A. R. Guyler to head operations in the American zone. The Director General explained that UNRRA was "very rapidly developing a larger and better qualified corps of regional directors and supervisors" to enable the organization to "keep in touch with the camps more thoroughly." He observed that "some of the camps administered by UNRRA personnel are admirably conducted while others are poorly administered," illustrating the importance of "the personal equation." Lehman noted that his work continued to be "extremely hard" and his "worries and difficulties" had "not greatly decreased." He expected that the official request for more funds for UNRRA, which would be going to Congress soon, would "run into considerable difficulty."[45]

On October 4, 1945, President Truman formally asked Congress to appropriate the additional $550,000,000 already authorized for UNRRA, and a month later, he asked the legislators to authorize the additional $1,350,000,000 that UNRRA had requested. Accordingly, the Senate Foreign Relations Committee, the House Foreign Affairs Committee, and the Appropriations Committees in both chambers conducted extensive hearings on UNRRA, grilling Lehman and other officials. Lehman patiently and repeatedly defended UNRRA, explained how it worked and what it was doing in various countries, and emphasized the urgent need for additional funds for relief in Europe and the Far East. As Director General, Lehman was entitled to an annual salary of $15,000, but he revealed that he had "not accepted any compensation whatsoever, or reimbursement, save for transportation," and he vehemently denied "vicious articles" alleging that he had charged to UNRRA the cost of a reception he had hosted during the UNRRA Council meetings in London. He had personally "paid the bill," Lehman declared, for any and all entertaining he had done as Director General. Lehman remained confident that "the generous people of this country want to continue to give aid to the suffering people of the liberated countries," but as he confided to a friend, he could only "hope Congress will realize this and take proper action."[46]

Although Congress seemed likely to approve some money for UNRRA, the same coalition of conservative Republicans and Southern Democrats that had plagued President Roosevelt in the later years of the New Deal was in no hurry to enact expensive measures like the UNRRA appropriation, and Lehman and the Truman administration feared that Congress would attach conditions to the release of the funds. Members of the Appropriations Committees believed there was no need to act swiftly because UNRRA supplies already ordered would be distributed over the next few months. Returning from a two-month trip to Europe that had included meetings with Stalin and British Prime Minister Clement Attlee, Representative William Comer (D-MS) and six other members of the House Subcommittee on Postwar Economic Policy spoke for many of their colleagues when they demanded that relief in Eastern Europe be administered on "nonpolitical lines which do not permit Russia to siphon off supplies to the motherland, requiring replacements by UNRRA or the United States." Massachusetts Republican Christian Herter, one of the more thoughtful members of Congress, warned that the United States must stay involved in relief and rehabilitation efforts or "Western Europe will lapse into anarchy, with some kind of totalitarianism as the eventual outcome," and he recognized that UNRRA was "the only agency equipped to do the job." As columnist Marquis Childs noted, the main task for Lehman and the Truman administration was to assure responsible lawmakers such as Herter "that relief is not being used for political purposes and that the liberated nations are not simply lying down and waiting for Uncle Sam to come along with a handout."[47]

On October 30, the House Appropriations Committee reported to the floor a bill appropriating the $550,000,000 previously authorized for UNRRA. The committee's report detailed the contributions UNRRA had received from all nations, pointing out that "all of the larger contributors except the United States have already paid the full amount pledged," and it highlighted UNRRA's intention to utilize military surplus goods whenever possible. It did, however, criticize as "excessive" the number of employees in UNRRA's Washington headquarters, especially those in the higher pay scales. Two days later, the House approved the measure by a vote of 337 to 19, sending it on to the Senate.[48]

November 9, 1945, marked the second anniversary of the founding of UNRRA, and at a time when members of Congress were pillorying the organization daily, President Truman took advantage of the occasion to praise Lehman's and UNRRA's accomplishments and highlight UNRRA's role as a precursor to the United Nations Organization. In a letter to Lehman that was released to the press, Truman noted that "UNRRA has been and is today the proving ground for the capacity of the United Nations to work together to relieve suffering, prevent starvation, and restore hope to the people who have borne and resisted fascist invasion." The President took pride that "an American citizen is guiding this constructive international effort, the greatest and most difficult humanitarian effort ever undertaken," and he pledged that the United States government and the American people would continue to support Lehman and UNRAA as they worked to complete their task and build "a new and better world." Truman emphasized to Lehman, "our prayers and hopes go with you, as you guide UNRRA to the successful completion of its task."[49]

VI

While Congress was still working on the appropriation bill for the previously authorized $550,000,000 for UNRRA, the Truman administration began to focus on securing the second $1,350,000,000 contribution that the UNRRA Council had requested. In early November, Secretary of State Byrnes reminded the President that "UNRRA must have additional funds soon after the first of the year if the flow of relief supplies is not to be interrupted during the critical months ahead," and on November 13, President Truman formally asked Congress "to authorize a new appropriation of $1,350,000,000 for participation in the activities of UNRRA."[50]

The introduction of the authorization bill put Herbert Lehman in the awkward position of having to deal with different congressional committees simultaneously. The House Foreign Affairs Committee held hearings in mid-November on the new UNRRA authorization bill at the same time the Senate Appropriations Committee considered the appropriation bill for the $550,000,000 previously authorized by Congress. Lehman spent four long days testifying before the Foreign Affairs Committee, and he was scheduled to appear for a fifth day when Senator Kenneth McKellar (D-TN) scheduled the Appropriations Committee to meet at the same time. Lehman's protest that "it is hard to be in two places at one time" was of little avail, and rather than risk offending the key Senators on the Appropriations panel, Lehman juggled his session with the House and worked it in around his appearance before McKellar's group.[51]

At one point, Lehman became so exasperated by what he characterized as the "carping criticism and bitterness" of the Republicans on the House Foreign Affairs Committee that he exploded and gave an "impassioned" defense of UNRRA. With what the *New York Times* described as "his eyes flashing and his voice indignant," and speaking "with all the force" he could muster, Lehman readily admitted that "UNRRA has made mistakes." But he pointed out that the agency had "tackled a job of a nature and scope never attempted in the world before," beginning "its task while the war was still on and when it had to compete, usually with little success, with the armed forces for food and other supplies, for shipping with which to send them abroad and for personnel to handle the relief jobs." Lehman asserted that "UNRRA has nothing to apologize for" and wondered why, "in all this talk, practically nothing is said about the very great aid UNRRA already has rendered to the suffering people of Europe."[52]

At this crucial time when the UNRRA appropriation and authorization bills were pending in Congress, some well-known individuals and organizations stepped forward to defend Herbert Lehman and UNRRA and focus attention on the desolate and desperate conditions looming in Europe. In one of her "My Day" columns in mid-November, Eleanor Roosevelt noted that she had "never known a government agency—or, for that matter, a business agency—which did not suffer from some of the ills that have bedeviled the organizing period of UNRRA." She asserted that UNRRA's "main difficulties have been the troubles of a civilian organization functioning where, primarily, a war organization is in power," and she predicted that "as the armies retire, the civilian organization will improve." At a B'nai B'rith dinner, former Treasury Secretary Henry Morgenthau, Jr., described both the suffering of displaced people in Europe and UNRRA's efforts to deal with the situation. He praised Lehman's "magnificent leadership" of the organization and pointed out that it was easy to criticize UNRRA's shortcomings, but it was not a choice "between UNRRA and something better. Our choice is between UNRRA and nothing." The *New York Times* published a long article by C. L. Sulzberger warning that "Europe faces one of its bleakest, saddest winters since the chaos of the Thirty Years' War," and the paper's editors argued that UNRRA's help was "still desperately needed" to prevent starvation in Eastern and Southern Europe and in China. Marquis Childs explained in his column how the lack of funds threatened to cripple UNRRA's operations. He deplored "the dilatory indifference with which our lawmakers seem to face the crisis of our time," and he warned that "hunger will not wait forever." Gossip columnist Leonard Lyons quoted "a government observer" who summarized UNRRA's difficulties this way: "UNRRA's problem is that it is trying to cover a 6-foot man with a 2-foot blanket."[53]

General Dwight Eisenhower, Commander of U.S. Forces in Europe, provided the most important voice in support of UNRRA. Eisenhower was in Washington to testify before the House and Senate Military Affairs Committees on the unification of the armed forces and universal military training, and, at first, he declined Chairman Sol Bloom's invitation to discuss UNRRA with the House Foreign Affairs Committee, citing the brevity of his visit to Washington and previous commitments. But Bloom, Herbert Lehman, and others explained the importance of Eisenhower's appearance and persuaded the General to testify at an extraordinary session of the Foreign Affairs Committee on Thanksgiving morning. Mrs. Eisenhower had just been hospitalized with bronchial pneumonia, and, as Lehman later recalled, Eisenhower himself "had a terrific cold" and "never should have left his bed, but he came in to the Capitol and his testimony and his very strong endorsement of UNRRA was the thing that swung the tide."[54]

In his formal statement to the committee, Eisenhower pointed out that UNRRA had surmounted numerous difficulties, such as the military's "first call on resources of personnel, shipping, equipment and supplies of all kinds" during the war, but he believed that UNRRA was now "operating with steadily increasing effectiveness" in Germany. He noted that "UNRRA has been infused with new and vigorous leadership" in which he had "the fullest confidence" because UNRRA's new leaders in the field, such as General Sir Frederick Morgan, his former Deputy Chief of Staff, were "experienced administrators of unquestionable competence." Eisenhower believed that "the ravaged nations of the world are looking to UNRRA for their relief," and he warned that "if UNRRA were to fail them, they could not help but feel that not only had the United States failed them but that the hope of solution of world problems through United Nations action was an illusory one." Eisenhower concluded that UNRRA, "representing the United Nations, is already in position to meet the currently critical problem—the prevention of widespread suffering and starvation during the coming winter, of liberated peoples in Europe."[55]

Eisenhower's responses to questions posed by committee members proved to be even more illuminating than his prepared statement. When asked to comment on the idea that the Army should take over relief operations, Eisenhower replied that he "would object most seriously," emphasizing that "the Army is not a relief organization" and that providing such aid was a "civil job to be done by civil personnel and a civil organization." He believed that "this task requires trained social workers" rather than soldiers, recounting a recent visit to a "camp where they proudly showed me five infants born the day before," and observing that "the Army's experience is not quite up to taking care of babies." The General reiterated that no single nation, "no matter how opulent that nation might be," should be totally responsible for relief, which he insisted should be a cooperative and shared obligation among the nations of the world. Based on his experience commanding an Army composed of forces contributed by various countries, he asserted that it was "not only practical and realistic, but it is absolutely necessary" for "peoples of different nations to work together in a joint relief operation such as UNRRA." Eisenhower sympathized with UNRRA's difficulties in getting started while the war was still on, noting that "if anyone had given me the job of organizing UNRRA under the conditions that existed" at that time, "I think I would have thrown up my hands in helplessness," because the military had received everything it had asked for while UNRRA had to settle for the leftovers. He considered it "remarkable" that UNRRA "made any progress at all" under those conditions, and he "guarantee[d] that they are improving steadily."[56]

When Eisenhower had completed his testimony, Frank McNaughton of *Time* concluded that "there is no doubt that his argument today did a great deal to erase the opposition to extension of this relief program." McNaughton noted that "as a soldier," Eisenhower had "stressed primarily the importance and the meagerness of the relief program," and he believed that the General had "scored a ten-strike." According to McNaughton, Herbert Lehman, who had been seated "directly opposite Eisenhower, could scarcely conceal his pleased smiles." Lehman agreed with a friend that "Eisenhower's statement was . . . magnificent," and that the General had "made an excellent witness." Lehman understood that Eisenhower's "presence at the hearing and his fine and clearly expressed testimony" had "undoubtedly greatly strengthened our hands."[57]

After attending the Foreign Affairs Committee's session with General Eisenhower in the morning, Herbert Lehman delivered a radio address later in the day in which he contrasted the American people's enjoyment of Thanksgiving with the desperate need and struggle for food overseas that was exacerbated by Congress's failure to approve additional funds for UNRRA. UNRRA's operations, Lehman noted, were "grinding to a standstill" because the agency was running out of money, adding to "the suffering of innocent war victims in Europe and China." He emphasized that "the people of Europe and China are thankful that many years of death from the air—and slave labor—and concentration camps—are at an end," but he pointed out that "their danger has not abated," that "hunger and cold, disease and suffering stalk the streets and the by-ways." Lehman observed that those "who had to suffer the cruelties which we as a people were spared, have no turkey dinner for which to give thanks." Moreover, he asserted, "millions of them have not had even the assurance that they will have any food at all in the dreary winter months that lie ahead." "Tonight," Lehman declared, "in ruined Warsaw, nearly a million men, women and children are living in squalid holes and dugouts—without food, without fuel, or warm clothing, or sanitation." As Americans sat down to their Thanksgiving dinners, Lehman wanted them to remember that "millions of disease-carrying rats are feeding on corpses lying beneath the uncleared ruins of Warsaw." Lehman understood that these were not pleasant thoughts for Thanksgiving, or any other day, but he stressed that the scene he was describing was "tragically true," and it would get worse unless Congress appropriated the funds UNRRA needed to continue its activities.[58]

The day after Eisenhower's dramatic appearance before the House Foreign Affairs Committee, the Senate Appropriations Subcommittee unanimously recommended approval of the $550,000,000 originally authorized for UNRRA. The full Appropriations Committee followed suit a few days later. Faced with mounting pressure after Eisenhower's testimony, the committee, according to Senator McKellar, "just gave them all the money and told them to spend it as they liked." The Senate approved the measure on December 5, and after a conference committee reconciled the differences between the House and Senate bills, the final measure appropriating the $550,000,000 was approved on December 11, and President Truman quickly signed it into law.[59]

On the same day that the Senate Appropriations Committee sent the $550,000,000 appropriation for UNRRA to the Senate floor, the House Committee on Foreign Affairs recommended approval of the second $1,350,000,000 for UNRRA. The Foreign Affairs Committee explained that the new "contribution must be made before the end of December 1945 if there are to be uninterrupted relief shipments during this winter," warning that "every day's delay in making this contribution will, therefore, mean more disease, more starvation." The committee noted that it was "impressed with Governor Lehman's vigorous leadership, his thorough knowledge of the complex, world-wide relief problem and his successful efforts to improve the efficiency of his organization."[60]

With Congress scheduled to adjourn for its Christmas recess in a few weeks, time now became the crucial factor in the effort to win legislative approval for the UNRRA measures pending in Congress. On December 3, Truman met at the White House with Senate Majority Leader Alben Barkley of Kentucky, Senator McKellar, House Speaker Rayburn, and House Majority Leader McCormack, at which time he defined UNRRA funding as "must" legislation to be passed before lawmakers left town. The President urged the congressional leaders to make sure that the House Rules Committee reported the new UNRRA authorization bill to the floor for action, and that an identical authorization bill be introduced in the Senate where the Foreign Relations Committee would hold hearings on it immediately. Truman also wanted the leaders to see to it that hearings in the House on a new UNRRA appropriation commenced as soon as the authorization bill was approved, and he recommended that they consider working with the Republican leaders so that these actions would be "non-partisan in character."[61]

As the President had requested, the House Rules Committee forwarded the bill authorizing $1,350,000,000 for UNRRA to the floor, where Representative Bloom emphasized that "there is no alternative to UNRRA except starvation, epidemic and political chaos." The House approved the measure on December 6, 1945, by a vote of 327 to 39, sending it on to the Senate.[62]

By this time, congressional and public opinion had swung in favor of UNRRA. Herbert Lehman told his son John about Eisenhower's "splendid" testimony, and he noted that "the press, generally speaking, is behind us and is helping in every way possible." Numerous individuals and organizations had appeared before the House Foreign Affairs Committee in support of UNRRA, and several clergymen gave sermons advocating immediate action to help relieve the suffering in Europe. The *Washington Post* and *New York Times* continued to run stories detailing the horrible conditions in Europe, and editorials and letters urged full funding for UNRRA. Columnists Walter Lippmann and Marquis Childs deplored Congress's delay in acting on the UNRRA legislation, and Malvina Lindsay used her *Washington Post* column, "The Gentler Sex," to argue that American women were willing to accept less meat and other foodstuffs if it meant saving desperate people in Europe. By mid-December, Lehman recognized that "there has been a definite improvement in our public relations and in the appreciation of our work by the public and by Congress," and he thanked Arthur Hays Sulzberger, publisher of the *New York Times*, for the numerous articles and editorials that "greatly contributed to an understanding by the American people of the terrible situation abroad and of the urgent needs for relief." UNRRA Senior Deputy Director Robert G. A. Jackson later recalled that "voluntary organizations were of the greatest assistance" in building support among the American people for UNRRA during these crucial months, and he noted that "the American press in general and . . . the well-known columnists and commentators, threw their weight in as well."[63]

Herbert Lehman and the Truman administration quickly took advantage of the American public's new awareness of what UNRRA was accomplishing to move the remaining UNRRA legislation through Congress. On December 10, the President urged Senate Democratic leaders to begin hearings in the Foreign Relations Committee on the UNRRA authorization bill that had been passed by the House, and he formally asked Congress to appropriate the second $1,350,000,000 for UNRRA. The following day, Truman met with Lehman to discuss UNRRA's needs and the status of the UNRRA legislation. Senior Deputy Director Jackson later recalled that Lehman "fired every gun we possessed," and "the President responded well," but Senate leaders resented being pressured and gave Lehman and UNRRA officials "a very rough handling" when they testified before the Foreign Relations Committee on behalf of the second UNRRA authorization bill. Nonetheless, the Committee recommended approval of the authorization bill previously passed by the House, the Senate adopted the measure a few days later, and the President signed it into law on December 18, 1945.[64]

Even before Congress had concluded action on the UNRRA authorization bill, Senators suddenly decided to move ahead on the UNRRA appropriation as part of a much larger deficiency appropriation covering numerous agencies. Lehman and his aides had concluded that UNRRA could get by for a few months on $600,000,000 to $700,000,000, but the Senate Appropriations Committee recommended only $400,000,000 for UNRRA at this time. Although this would be enough money to see UNRRA through until Congress reconvened in January, Lehman feared that the legislators would be in no hurry to vote additional funds at that time, and he understood that UNRRA needed to capitalize on the momentum and public support that had been aroused. According to Senior Deputy Director Jackson, Lehman "decided to fight," going directly to the President, who "intervened most effectively," taking "a stronger line on this particular matter than on any other issue since his political honeymoon had ended." Swayed by pressure from the White House and public opinion, the Senate voted to include $750,000,000 for UNRRA as part of an overall $2,400,000,000 appropriation bill.[65]

As the House considered the $750,000,000 appropriation for UNRRA approved by the Senate, Representative Louis Ludlow (D-IN) read on the floor of the House a letter in which Lehman explained that UNRRA's funds, including the $550,000,000 just appropriated by Congress a few days earlier, would all be spent by the middle of February. The Director General emphasized that additional money was required immediately if UNRRA were to "ship food and clothing to Europe and China quickly enough to get the people through the winter" and "deliver enough seed, fertilizer and agricultural equipment in time for the spring planting." The House agreed to the $750,000,000 appropriation for UNRRA shortly before adjourning for Christmas, and the President added his signature a few days later. After stalling and taking no action on the UNRRA legislation for three months, Congress, in a two-week period, had passed the second UNRRA authorization bill and two appropriations bills contributing a total of $1,300,000,000 for UNRRA to continue its activities. And for good measure, the lawmakers finally passed legislation that Lehman had long sought allowing the President to extend certain privileges and immunities to UNRRA and other international organizations and their employees.[66]

Although Lehman and the Truman administration had hoped that Congress would fully fund the second $1,350,000,000 for UNRRA, they were satisfied that the $750,000,000 appropriation would see UNRRA and the people dependent upon it through the winter. Lehman hailed Congress's recent actions as "the most vital in UNRRA's history," believing that the $750,000,000 would give UNRRA "a breathing spell" to prepare its request to Congress "for the remaining $600,000,000." The UNRRA staff expressed its gratitude to Lehman for his "untiring and successful work" in getting "the President, the Congress, and the public in the United States" to recognize UNRRA's needs, and Lehman, "on behalf of the many millions who look to UNRRA for their daily bread and for help in restoring their economic strength," thanked President Truman for his "unfailing support of UNRRA." The Director General appreciated "the firm resolve of the American people to aid and succor the victims of war," and he assured the President that the new funds would enable UNRRA "to maintain the flow of supplies to the many countries dependent on UNRRA." The President pronounced himself "very happy at the final solution of the UNRRA problem," but he noted that "we are going to have difficulty with it every time it comes up."[67]

Herbert Lehman and President Truman had worked well together in the final months of 1945 to win congressional approval for continued funding of UNRRA. Senior Deputy Director Robert G. A. Jackson later described Lehman's efforts to win congressional approval of funding for UNRRA during this period "as the most important and critical" of all of UNRRA's activities, noting that Lehman had "worked tirelessly" and "demonstrated his political skill and ability, and combined with it courage and perseverance." Jackson also paid tribute to President Truman, recalling that Lehman "received definite assistance from the President and worked constantly with the leaders of the Democratic Party in Congress" on behalf of UNRRA. But sadly, this partnership between Lehman and Truman, which accomplished so much for UNRRA in 1945, quickly fell apart as the world grappled with the growing threat of famine and starvation in 1946.[68]

CHAPTER 10

"The Work of UNRRA . . . Will Ever Be Close to My Heart"

Lehman and Truman, 1946

Voluntary measures alone, no matter how energetically they are pursued, are not enough.[1]

The good will built up between Herbert Lehman and President Truman as they worked together to secure approval of the UNRRA legislation in the fall of 1945 soon dissipated as the world food situation deteriorated and they disagreed over what to do about it. The President had promised repeatedly that "the American people will not sit idly by with foodstuffs when other countries are starving," but he was reluctant to reimpose rationing, mandatory controls, or restrictions on domestic food consumption. While Secretary of Agriculture Clinton Anderson predicted that food would be plentiful in 1946, Lehman warned in an end-of-the-year radio broadcast that "the urgent needs of suffering people are far greater than our available resources." With the coming of "the grimmest winter in Europe since the Thirty Years War in the seventeenth century," Lehman emphasized that "we must husband our resources of food—and especially of wheat, which will be in short supply—so that we can help to keep that unhappy Continent alive during the critical months that lie ahead."[2]

Chapter title quotation: Herbert Lehman quoted in "Lehman Quits UNRRA because of Failing Health," *New York Times*, March 13, 1946, pp. 1, 17.

I

Herbert Lehman's relief at Congress's passage of the UNRRA legislation in December 1945 proved to be short-lived. It quickly became clear that the money appropriated by Congress would not allow UNRRA to meet everyone's needs as UNRRA continued to provide assistance in Albania, Czechoslovakia, Greece, Poland, and Yugoslavia; greatly expanded its operations in Italy and China; began its activities in Austria, Byelorussia, the Ukraine, Korea, and Formosa; and took on increased responsibility for displaced persons in Germany. The Director General realized that disappointingly small harvests in Europe were leading to increased demand for grain, a situation that was aggravated by difficulty in moving wheat in the United States from the growing regions to the coast for shipment overseas. At a press conference in late December, Lehman warned that "unless exceptional measures are taken by the supplying countries," UNRRA might not meet its planned January deliveries, and shipments in February and March might "fall considerably below" UNRAA's goals. This would result in a "reduction in the bread rations in some European countries" and a further deterioration in the "health and energy of millions of people." As Lehman confided to his former aide Charles Poletti, despite all the progress UNRRA had made in the last two months, "the urgent needs of the liberated countries loom up larger each day and, of course, are far beyond any resources that are at hand." Nonetheless, UNRRA would do everything it could because, "in many countries, UNRRA is now the only thing that stands between millions of people and starvation."[3]

As the food situation in Europe worsened, compounded by a severe rice shortage in Asia, British Prime Minister Clement Attlee appealed to President Truman for his "personal and active interest" and "the full co-operation" of American "agricultural, transport and shipping experts" to help "solve these problems." Conditions had deteriorated rapidly since Lehman had issued his dire report in late December, and Attlee warned the President that "unless the maximum quantities that can be spared are exported from all producing countries, there is a grave danger of wide famine in Europe and in Asia during the next few months." Attlee dispatched his Food Minister to Washington to discuss with Truman administration officials how they could close the "formidable" gap between the quantity of wheat requested and the amount available.[4]

Lehman met with the President at the White House on January 23, 1946, urging Truman to take strong and immediate action to deal with the wheat crisis. Lehman understood that supply shortages, transportation difficulties, inflation concerns, and the needs of other claimants meant that UNRRA's requests could not be met in full, but he stressed that even if UNRRA's efforts to increase its wheat allotments from Canada, Australia, and Argentina succeeded, UNRRA would still require 400,000 tons per month from the United States.

However, the U.S. Department of Agriculture had committed only "380,000 tons for January and 230,000 tons for February," and nothing for the months after that, leaving UNRRA 1,790,000 tons short of the 2,400,000 it needed for the first half of the year. The Director General emphasized that in trying to provide "a bare minimum bread ration" to people and countries in need, UNRRA faced "the gravest emergency" in its brief history, and he appealed directly to the President "for his personal assistance in meeting this desperate situation." Specifically, Lehman wanted the President to instruct the Department of Agriculture "irrevocably to commit to UNRRA for shipment" 190,000 metric tons of wheat in February to make up for the shortfall in allocations for January and February, and 400,000 tons per month in March, April, May, and June. Truman forwarded to Secretary Anderson the memorandum Lehman had left with him after their meeting, noting that he and Lehman had discussed "the extreme difficulty in which . . . UNRRA finds itself on account of the wheat situation," and he asked Anderson to meet with Lehman to see what the Secretary could do "to get this situation eased, if that is at all possible."[5]

When Undersecretary of State Dean Acheson echoed Lehman's concerns about "the amount of starvation that would take place in Europe this winter" at the Cabinet meeting on January 25, and Secretary Anderson described "the tight wheat situation," the President instructed Anderson, Acheson, and Secretary of Commerce Henry Wallace to devise a plan to meet this crisis. Anderson and the others consulted with Lehman, and by the end of January, the Truman administration had come up with a program to make more grain available for people overseas. The Secretary of Agriculture now conceded that "wheat needs in war ravaged countries in 1946 will be double those of the 1930s and will be the largest of any year on record." Concerned that many farmers were hoarding grain in anticipation of a price increase, Anderson urged farmers to market their crops, and the Commodity Credit Corporation moved up the expiration date on loans it had made, forcing farmers to sell their grain to pay back their loans. Lehman defended the President's commitment to solving this problem, assuring a group of New York ministers that Truman was "determined that this country will in every way that is possible assist in alleviating hunger, misery, and despair," and that the President had "wholeheartedly supported UNRRA in its work of bringing relief to suffering peoples abroad."[6]

On February 4, Prime Minister Attlee informed President Truman that Britain, recognizing that "heavy sacrifices must be made to help the less fortunate peoples of the world," was going to reduce its wheat imports even though such action would shrink British reserves "far below the safety level," increase its "extraction rate of flour from 80 per cent to 85 per cent and return to the darker bread which we accepted as a wartime necessity but hoped we had discarded with the end of hostilities," and reduce its fat ration to a level "which is lower than at any time during the war." The Prime Minister acknowledged that these measures would put "a severe strain on our people, who have been looking forward to some relaxation of the standards of austerity which they have cheerfully accepted throughout the war," but he believed that the British people would accept these hardships to prevent thousands of people from dying of starvation and many more thousands from going hungry. He asked for Truman's help in mitigating this looming disaster, urging the President to increase America's wheat exports, its flour extraction rate, and the amount of wheat and rice planted.[7]

Two days after receiving Attlee's message, President Truman announced his program to try to alleviate the grain shortage overseas. The President warned that "for the world as a whole, a food crisis has developed which may prove to be the worst in modern times," emphasizing that "more people face starvation and even actual death for want of food today than in any war year and perhaps more than in all the war years combined." Truman noted that while Americans consumed an average of 3,300 calories a day, "more than 125 million people in Europe will have to subsist on less than 2,000 calories a day; 28 million will get less than 1,500 calories a day and, in some parts of Europe, large groups will receive as little as 1,000 calories." The President stressed that "only through superhuman efforts can mass starvation be prevented," and he expressed confidence that "the conscience of the American people will not permit them to withhold or stint their cooperation while their fellow-men in other lands suffer and die."[8]

Truman outlined nine "emergency measures" the government was taking to help reduce America's grain consumption and make more wheat available for "the liberated people and to those who have fought beside us" in Europe and Asia. The President's program featured "a vigorous campaign to secure the full cooperation of all consumers in conserving food, particularly bread," and an increase in the wheat flour extraction rate to 80 percent (still less than the recently adopted rate of 85 percent in Britain, which the State Department had advocated for the United States). Distillers and brewers would not be allowed to use wheat in the production of beer or alcohol, and the use of other grains would be limited; grain shipments would receive priority on the railroads; and the Department of Agriculture would be given new power to control wheat and flour inventories and exports to divert grain from feeding animals to nourishing people. The President acknowledged that these measures "will no doubt cause some inconvenience to many of us," but he believed that "these inconveniences will be a small price to pay for saving lives, mitigating suffering in liberated countries, and helping to establish a firmer foundation for peace."[9]

Herbert Lehman appreciated the President's efforts "to increase the supplies of food for liberated areas," but he worried that they did not go far enough, that they relied too heavily on voluntary measures and would not conserve enough grain to make a difference. Lehman confided to a friend that although "the President and other high authorities here now are fully allied with our situation" and "are doing everything to alleviate it so far as possible," he feared that "there certainly will not be enough grain to go around," predicting "there will be much suffering until the new crop comes in." Lehman wondered whether "a direct appeal to the people to conserve wheat and other food stuffs would have any good results."[10]

The President focused on the food situation again at his news conference on February 7, explaining that "in most of the wheat-producing countries of the world, outside of the United States and Canada, there has been almost a total crop failure in wheat," and that a similar shortfall in rice production had occurred in the Far East. Truman emphasized that "the situation is so serious that we felt it was absolutely essential to take every measure possible to help keep the people in these countries from starving," asserting that it was "un-American . . . to let people starve." He also made it clear that UNRRA would "handle the equitable distribution of these food supplies in the various countries." But even with the newly adopted conservation measures, Truman conceded that the United States would be shipping less wheat than it had originally committed to send abroad. In response to a reporter's question, Truman expressed the hope that it would not be necessary to reimpose meat rationing, although he was willing to do whatever was necessary "to keep 10 or 15 million people from starving to death."[11]

Despite the President's tough talk, the world food situation continued to worsen as the United States failed to secure the quantity of wheat and other grains that UNRRA and the starving people in Europe and Asia needed. Prolonged droughts in other countries, the division of Europe into separate ideological camps with little movement of goods between them, transportation difficulties, strikes, hoarding, and black market activities exacerbated the problem, and Truman's program, relying for the most part on voluntary actions by Americans to reduce their bread and flour consumption, was inadequate. Barnet Nover pointed out in the *Washington Post* that "the food situation confronting vast populations in many parts of the world ranges from bad to catastrophic," but he noted that the President, his rhetoric notwithstanding, had not called upon the American people "to make a superhuman effort or anything like it." Flour millers belittled the higher extraction rate as "psychological diplomacy," a gesture that would save little wheat, and columnist Marquis Childs criticized the President and his advisors, especially those in the Department of Agriculture, for their failure to face facts that "have been fairly obvious for several months." Childs blamed the current crisis on "the way in which wartime controls were hastily removed after V-J Day" for political reasons, asserting that "the task of setting aside food for relief calls for extraordinary and courageous effort" overriding "the entrenched interests of those who are bent on normalcy at any cost." He denounced the Department of Agriculture for its earlier "Pollyanna approach" and condemned Secretary Anderson's "calm, casual" attitude at a time when U.S. grain elevators were full but the United States was falling further and further behind in meeting its grain commitments to UNRRA. But while the President and Secretary Anderson belatedly endorsed the retention of food subsidies and price controls, sought to increase wheat and rice production, and asked citizens to keep their victory gardens, they refused even to discuss rationing flour or wheat or other grains.[12]

Lehman met with Truman on February 20 to invite the President to address the upcoming session of the UNRRA Council, which was scheduled to convene in Atlantic City in mid-March. In a follow-up letter, Lehman pointed out that President Roosevelt, Canadian Prime Minister Mackenzie King, and British Foreign Minister Ernest Bevin of the host nations had greeted the delegates at the previous Council meetings, and he emphasized that Truman's "presence and remarks, would, of course, be of great assistance to UNRRA." Lehman believed that the upcoming meeting would be "the most important and critical in the history of UNRRA," noting that "many matters of importance, including food, displaced persons, etc., will be taken up, and the future of relief work in Europe and Asia will undoubtedly be discussed." The Director General hoped that Truman would be able to attend the opening session on March 15, but if that were not possible, the President would be welcome on any day that worked with his schedule.[13]

Much to Lehman's disappointment, the President declined the invitation to speak to the UNRRA Council. Truman claimed that the press of business made it difficult for him to leave the White House and that he could not "add to the commitments already made requiring his absence" from Washington. The President agreed that "the forthcoming meeting will be both important and critical," and he offered "to send a written message to the Council," asking Lehman to "submit a draft which would emphasize the pertinent problems with which the meeting will deal."[14]

On February 22, at a dinner sponsored by the Jewish War Veterans, Herbert Lehman accepted the New York State Conspicuous Service Cross awarded posthumously to his son Peter. Wiping away tears and speaking "in a voice choked with emotion," Lehman declared it " 'a great honor' to receive the medal 'on behalf of my boy.' " Speaking for the relatives of fifteen other posthumous honorees, Lehman emphasized that his son and the others "would not want to receive this medal merely because they were Jews." Although Peter "was proud to be a Jew," Lehman stressed, "my boy, if he could speak, and your boys, would want to have this medal as an American of Jewish faith, a tribute that is as proud as anyone could hope for." Herbert Lehman described the awards as especially appropriate "in times when some people would use prejudice and scapegoats by way of excuses, during times when some nations have risen to power through degrading practices of anti-Semitism."[15]

Lehman also used his remarks at the dinner to sound the alarm again on the world food situation, asserting that "if we are not careful we are going to lose the peace, the peace which our boys have fought for and made sacrifices." He stressed that "we are facing the most critical situation with respect to food that ever has faced anyone in the history of the world," and he argued that the United States and other nations had to make further sacrifices to deal with this crisis. He believed that such sacrifices "need not be so great that they will cause any great distress," and he cited as an example of needless waste his serving of four pieces of toast earlier in the day when he only wanted one. "Just a slight sacrifice," Lehman pointed out, would substantially increase the amount of food available for overseas relief, although he noted that "enough there will never be."[16]

The Director General also addressed the problem of Jews who did not want to remain in Germany and Austria, "the graveyard of all that was near and dear to them." Although he was not a "political Zionist," Lehman hoped that Palestine, "as the most available refuge for many years, will be given the right, the free right, the recognized right to admit vastly larger numbers of immigrants of the Jewish faith." Lehman called upon other nations to "open their doors more freely to the persecuted people of the world," but he emphasized that Palestine offered the best solution to this "complicated and difficult" situation. A few days later, Lehman was part of a delegation from the United Jewish Appeal that met with President Truman, who spoke sympathetically of the needs of the 1,500,000 European Jews who had survived the war but had been "left homeless, hungry, sick, and without assistance."[17]

II

By the end of February, the food situation had deteriorated considerably despite the Truman administration's efforts. In response to the worsening crisis, President Truman appointed a Famine Emergency Committee headed by Herbert Hoover to recommend measures to conserve food and grain. Hoover believed that the committee should focus on "a voluntary program" in which housewives, hotels, restaurants, bakers, packers, and millers would be encouraged to "eliminate waste, save unnecessary consumption and make use of substitutes," and the President agreed that voluntary steps were the way to go. In his announcement of the committee's formation, Truman reported that he had "directed the agencies of government to do everything possible" to "stop the spread of famine," but he emphasized that "government alone is not enough." Resolving this crisis would also require "an aggressive voluntary policy on the part of private citizens to reduce food consumption in this country." When the Famine Emergency Committee gathered at the White House for its first session, Truman called it "the most important meeting, I think, we have held in the White House since I have been the President." The committee quickly decided to concentrate on voluntary conservation efforts, calling upon Americans to reduce their consumption of wheat and wheat products by 25 percent and asserting that "Americans of good will can do more and do it faster than any system of government rationing orders."[18]

Herbert Lehman feared that the Truman administration and the Famine Emergency Committee's focus on voluntary measures would be insufficient to resolve the crisis, but when Lehman urged the committee to adopt rationing to free up the wheat and grain needed to prevent widespread starvation overseas, he found himself outnumbered by Hoover, Secretary Anderson, and others who argued that it would take too long to implement an effective rationing system. Hoover continued to insist that a voluntary program would be more effective than rationing, and at Truman's request, the former President agreed to undertake a trip to survey food conditions in Europe. Secretary Anderson, while conceding that U.S. food shipments were "likely to miss their goal by the greatest amount" yet, claimed that "a shortage of freight cars for wheat was the major difficulty in fulfilling American promises to help prevent starvation abroad," and he asserted that breaking "the transportation bottleneck" would accomplish more in getting American wheat overseas than "calling upon Americans to eat less." The administration increased grain prices, hoping that this would "accelerate the movement of wheat from farms and into export channels," but it rejected proposals to lower hog prices and other subsidies that made it more profitable to feed grain to animals rather than ship it overseas. The Department of Agriculture made it clear that it was not considering "the cutting down of food consumption by regulation," rejecting the idea of "wheatless" days as inefficient and "overrated as a conservation measure." Secretary Anderson won no friends when he compared the task of the Combined Food Board in allocating scarce food supplies to that of "a family of dog-lovers which has to decide which puppies to drown."[19]

Secretary of Commerce Henry Wallace, the most outspoken liberal remaining in Truman's Cabinet and an advocate of solving international problems through the United Nations rather than unilaterally, shared Lehman's frustration with the Hoover committee's emphasis on "approaching the food problem on a purely voluntary basis." Wallace feared that "there will be a lot of publicity," but that the result of the committee's efforts would be "business as usual, consumption as usual, and not much change in the amount of food available to Europe." He predicted that "the American people will get a nice glow out of pretending to do something for the starving but undoubtedly there will be several million people in the world who will starve to death in the next four months who could have been saved if we had used more vigorous methods."[20]

Despite his concern that the administration was not acting forcefully enough, Lehman realized that he could not openly criticize the President's policies at a time when UNRRA was completely dependent on the goodwill of Truman and the U.S. government to meet its commitments. Without mentioning any names, however, the *New York Times* noted that "other interested groups" had "expressed doubts" whether the Truman administration's "strictly voluntary program would achieve its objective." Conceding that "the reinstatement of rationing would be an extremely difficult administrative task," the *Times* reported that critics of the present policy believed that stronger action was needed.[21]

A friend's suggestion that "Hercules' work was child's play" compared to Lehman's, and that a photo of the Director General "as Atlas would be symbolic," seemed particularly apt in March 1946 as Lehman grew more and more frustrated, feeling the burdens of the world resting on his shoulders. Lehman and UNRRA were beset by criticism on all sides as the unavailability of grain forced the agency to curtail food shipments to all recipients. The leader of Poland protested directly to President Truman, while Italian Americans made their unhappiness known to Lehman and American officials. The Director General found the objections by Italian American organizations both "amusing and distressing" because Italy, a former member of the Axis, "has been reduced far less than any one of the other UNRRA countries," most of whom believed that Italy was receiving more than its fair share. Showing his growing weariness with the whole problem, Lehman confided to Charles Poletti that "it is pretty discouraging, in spite of everything we are doing to relieve the situation in the face of indescribable difficulties and frustrations and totally inadequate supplies, that we should nonetheless be subjected to criticism and expressions of dissatisfaction from the very people we are trying to assist." He "wish[ed] that Italy and all the other war-stricken countries needing food could receive what they so urgently need," but he realized that, "at least for the present, that is impossible."[22]

Lehman understood that although the Truman administration hoped to provide food to prevent widespread starvation overseas, its support for UNRRA was rapidly fading. The Director General realized that much of the idealism that had led to the formation of UNRRA and the United Nations had already dissipated by March 1946 as the United States and the Soviet Union entered the Cold War era and the United States responded to what it saw as Soviet intransigence and expansion in Europe and the Middle East. As Undersecretary of State Dean Acheson later observed, much of UNRRA's assistance, "largely supplied or paid for by the United States, went to Eastern Europe and was used by governments bitterly hostile to us to entrench themselves," and Secretary of State James Byrnes and Assistant Secretary Will Clayton came to believe that

American relief aid should be distributed directly by the United States as an instrument of American foreign policy rather than through an international agency such as UNRRA. In the summer of 1946, speaking of the upcoming demise of UNRRA, Clayton revealed his true feelings, and those of many Americans, when he remarked that "the gravy train is going around for the last time." As Amy Bentley points out in her study of food rationing during and immediately after World War II, "international relief under 'impartial' U.N. auspices . . . was among the first casualties of the cold war."[23]

Further evidence of the growing American disregard for UNRRA came when the State and War Departments began discussing closure of the displaced persons camps in Germany without giving the UNRRA Council the opportunity to review and recommend policies on this issue. Lehman pointed out that "the continuance of UNRRA's present responsibilities for displaced persons will be a major matter for consideration by the Council," and he emphasized to Secretary of State Byrnes and Secretary of War Robert Patterson that "it would be most unfortunate if any unilateral action should be taken by the United States government" prior to the UNRRA Council meeting. The Director General persuaded Byrnes not to proclaim a final determination but rather to announce shortly after the UNRRA Council meeting began that the State and War Departments were considering closing the camps in the American zone in the late summer and wanted to give UNRRA plenty of time to decide whether to accept responsibility for the displaced persons.[24]

President Truman's refusal to appear at the UNRRA Council meeting in Atlantic City added to Lehman's growing frustration with the President's attitude toward the organization and the world food crisis. On March 6, the Director General wrote to Truman again, acknowledging "the tremendous pressure" of the President's work and the need to "ration your time and strength" but emphasizing that "a personal greeting to the delegates is of such great importance" that he was "urgently renewing" his invitation. Lehman explained that Truman's "presence at one of the sessions, preferably on the opening day, March 15th, would give assurance to the delegates and their governments of the great interest which this country has in the relief and rehabilitation problems of the war-torn countries abroad." He pointed out that "because of the relatively small amount of wheat, fats, oils and other supplies which we can send to these countries because of the world shortage there is great disappointment in these countries and, in some of them, a feeling that that they have been let down," which "has resulted in much unfair criticism of the United States and of UNRRA." Lehman stressed that "nothing could more fully dissipate their fears or suspicions, or demonstrate the interest of this country and of UNRRA," than a personal appearance by Truman, and he hoped that the President would reconsider his decision and "attend the meeting of the Council."[25]

When Lehman failed to change the President's mind, he appealed to Secretary of State Byrnes "to attend the opening session and extend a welcome to the delegates on behalf of the United States." Lehman pointed out that there was an airfield in or near Atlantic City so the Secretary could make a quick trip from Washington to the UNRRA meeting, and he stressed that Byrnes's presence "will demonstrate the sincere interest of our government in the work and purposes of UNRRA" and would "be an encouragement to the delegates *as well as to me*" (emphasis added). But the Director General was no more successful with Byrnes than he had been with the President. Truman's and Byrnes's failure to address the UNRRA Council in person at a time when much of the world faced a famine of historic dimensions demonstrated clearly to Lehman, as well as to the foreign delegates, just where UNRRA now stood in the Truman administration's priorities.[26]

The final blow for Lehman came on March 11, 1946, when he met with Herbert Hoover, Secretary of Agriculture Anderson, and the Famine Emergency Committee. At a time when Lehman was warning that "the world food situation 'grows more critical each day,'" and stressing the need for the supplying governments "to make supreme efforts," similar to the actions they had taken during the war, "if widespread disaster is to be averted," the Hoover Committee agreed that "the world faces the gigantic emergency of famine among 500 million people due to war exhaustion of agriculture and the drouth." The group acknowledged that "a great human cry has come to us to save them over a terrible four months until their next harvest." But despite Lehman's pleas, the committee's action did not match its rhetoric, merely calling upon Americans voluntarily to reduce their wheat consumption by 40 percent and their fat usage by 20 percent by such tactics as eating open-face sandwiches and pies and thinner bread slices. Although the committee recognized "the crucial importance of adjustments that will limit consumption of feed grains by livestock" to free up wheat for shipment overseas, it made no specific suggestions on this point, waiting for a subcommittee to study the issue. The committee also asserted that the food crisis would be relatively brief and emphasized that it was asking Americans to make these sacrifices only for a period of 120 days.[27]

III

After a brief meeting with President Truman on March 12, 1946, Herbert Lehman announced that he was resigning as Director General of UNRRA as soon as a successor could be elected. According to Senior Deputy Director Robert Jackson, Edith Lehman had long worried that "the great and intense responsibilities which had been placed on the Governor during the last three

years had been such a burden that his health was in danger," and Herbert
Lehman now declared that he could no longer ignore "the advice of my physician, who, for many months" had urged him "to take a much-needed rest."
In his official letter to the UNRRA Central Committee, Lehman emphasized
that ever since Franklin Roosevelt had called him to service in Washington in
December 1942, he had devoted all of his time and energy to "the task of planning and organizing world-wide relief." He considered it a great honor as well as
a heavy responsibility to have been charged with "creating the first international
organization with great executive responsibilities," and though he regretted not
seeing the job through to completion, Lehman took solace in knowing that "in
the face of almost insuperable difficulties from the outset, a splendid international organization has been assembled which has labored loyally and selflessly
to carry out a great program of relief and rehabilitation in war-devastated areas
of the world." Lehman defended UNRRA's accomplishments, praised the agency
for carrying out "the greatest and most far-flung program of practical human
relief the world has ever known," and pointed out that UNRRA had saved
millions from starvation by sending "more than 6,000,000 tons of supplies to
the distressed people of the world." The Director General proclaimed that "the
work of UNRRA, which has been my life for the past several years, will ever
be close to my heart," and he promised to do anything he could as a private
citizen to help UNRRA "meet the difficulties confronting it."[28]

In most of his private correspondence with friends and colleagues, Herbert
Lehman continued to cite his health as the major reason for his resignation. But
while explaining to Carolin Flexner, his former assistant, that he was following
his doctor's advice, Lehman stressed that he was not seriously ill, implying that
he might have remained in his post under different circumstances. In a letter
to former Secretary of the Treasury Henry Morgenthau, Jr., who had quickly
fallen out of favor and been removed by President Truman, the Director General
let his guard down somewhat and allowed his anger and frustration to show.
Knowing that Morgenthau and his wife Elinor, who was Lehman's niece, were
"thoroughly familiar with the hard up-hill fight we have had in UNRRA,"
Lehman took "great satisfaction" in "the results that have already been achieved"
and "fervently hope[d] that the great program for relief and rehabilitation for the
suffering peoples of the world may continue without interruption." But Lehman
had reached the end of his rope, and he believed, in fairness to himself "as well
as to the work," he "should turn it over to someone else to carry on from this
point." Similarly, in a letter to former UNRRA official Fred Hoehler, Lehman
explained that he had "reached the end of my endurance."[29]

Previous reports that Lehman was about to resign as Director General had
cited his hope that such action would call attention to the lack of American support for UNRRA and somehow rally the public behind the organization and its
mission of feeding those in need. Not surprisingly, when Lehman stepped down
in 1946, some speculated that he had done so for this reason. The *New York*

Times applauded Lehman's service at UNRRA, but his resignation also led the paper's editors to question the Truman administration's attitude toward UNRRA. Recalling "the long record of slow progress and sometimes heart-breaking difficulty with which Mr. Lehman has striven" to carry out his responsibilities, the *Times* observed that Lehman had "never faltered" despite suffering "illness, accident and deep personal loss." The editors wondered, however, if Herbert Hoover's upcoming trip to Europe "might perhaps be the forerunner of a direct United States approach to the whole problem of world relief instead of continuing to pursue the international method," suggesting that Hoover's travel overseas to assess various countries' food needs, including nations that were part of UNRRA and whose needs UNRRA had presumably already evaluated, conveyed a lack of confidence in UNRRA and undermined its authority. Similarly, the *Washington Post* lamented that "our government for some inexplicable reason has hitherto treated UNRRA as a kind of stepchild." The *New Republic* blamed Lehman's resignation on his "disgust" with "the sham put up by the national administration in suddenly forming a Food Famine Committee and then sending Herbert Hoover to find out what everyone in UNRRA and in the Department of Agriculture has known for more than two years—that America, as the greatest food-supply source in the world, should have planned for the current food crisis, but instead fumbled it." The editors charged that "by abandoning rationing in the United States for reasons of political expediency, the rest of the world was left holding the bag—an empty one." They saw Lehman's resignation as "a gesture of protest against this kind of bumbling. It was as strong a protest as a man like Lehman, not given to dramatics, could make."[30]

At the opening of the UNRRA Council meeting in Atlantic City on March 15, Lehman read a message that he had drafted in which President Truman reaffirmed "the United States government's most earnest desire to support UNRRA in every way in the completion of its immense task." But the State Department's formal statement to the UNRRA Council revealed the Truman administration's real attitude toward UNRRA. The Department asserted that the United States remained "keenly sensitive to the needs of those millions suffering from the ravages of war and its aftermath." But the Department emphasized that "UNRRA was conceived and established to meet an emergency situation," that "it always has been intended that its primary relief activities should terminate as soon as possible," and that "no one has ever contended that UNRRA alone could solve all the economic ills of a post-war world or that large-scale programs of relief could be continued indefinitely." The Department stressed that the U.S. expected UNRRA to conclude its activities in Europe by the end of 1946 and in Asia by the end of the first quarter of 1947, after which time nations needed to develop their own resources to become self-sufficient or seek assistance from the International Monetary Fund or the World Bank.[31]

Although Lehman had cited his health in explaining his resignation, the real reason became clear over the next week as he began speaking out publicly against the Truman administration's failure to take stronger action to prevent widespread famine in Europe and Asia. In a speech in New York on March 17, Lehman declared that "a voluntary movement to conserve wheat . . . will not accomplish as much as must be done," emphasizing that "more official and formal steps will have to be taken to make food supplies available for distribution in greater quantities than are now in sight." On March 18, Lehman told the UNRRA Council that the "unjustified removal of food controls . . . had greatly contributed to the present tragic situation," and while Lehman mentioned no names, it was clear that he was criticizing the Truman administration because the United States was the only nation that had lifted food regulations. I. F. Stone pointed out in *The Nation* that Lehman's contention that national leaders, if they "are sufficiently courageous in their actions," needed to "take strong and maybe politically unpleasant measures," was clearly aimed at Truman and the United States, where food consumption was growing while the rest of the world was starving.[32]

Removing the gloves and any doubts as to how he felt about the President's policies, Lehman directly challenged the Truman administration when he argued in a special report to the UNRRA Council that "voluntary measures alone, no matter how energetically they are pursued, are not enough." Lehman believed that such steps "can be helpful," but he pointed out that "after food has moved into civilian channels, it is too late to recapture it for shipment abroad." In Lehman's view, rationing and set-asides were the only way that governments could "insure that the supplies needed will be on hand when they are needed," and he was confident that such steps "will be supported by consumers when they understand that it will provide food for people who fought the common enemy, and to help insure fair distribution in the supplying countries." He maintained that "far greater sacrifices can be made without injury from all exporting areas," and warned that "an enduring peace cannot be written in the midst of hunger and famine."[33]

The Truman administration quickly rejected Lehman's recommendation to reimpose rationing. Secretary of Agriculture Anderson asserted that by the time a rationing system could be reestablished, "the crisis would be largely over, since this is a 120-day sprint." The President was more diplomatic. At a press conference two days later, when a reporter asked how he felt "about Governor Lehman's suggestion that we return to wartime food rationing," Truman declared that "if it becomes absolutely necessary," he "wouldn't object to the return to wartime food rationing." But, the President emphasized, "that situation has not yet arrived," and he hoped it would "not be necessary." A week later, the Famine Emergency Committee again turned thumbs down on rationing, agreeing with Secretary Anderson that the crisis would be over before the rationing machinery could be up and running, and the President echoed that position at a news conference on March 28.[34]

Lehman disputed the Truman administration's contention that the food crisis would be relatively brief in duration. Based "on the evidence available to UNRRA on this subject," Lehman declared that Secretary Anderson and former President Hoover failed to "recognize the full scale of the emergency with which the United Nations are faced." Lehman welcomed the Department of Agriculture's prediction that "the crop outlook in the United States is very good," but he stressed the need for the U.S. government to "introduce measures which will ensure that the new crop is controlled in such a way that it is used to sustain the maximum number of human lives." As for Hoover's trip to assess other nations' food surpluses or deficits, Lehman agreed with Eleanor Roosevelt that Hoover "can do less good by taking a trip over there than he could by staying here" and "promoting the things which must be done in this country." Years later, Lehman still complained that Hoover's "mission was unnecessary, useless, and to some extent, harmful."[35]

IV

As the UNRRA Council concluded its meeting in late March 1946, it accepted "with profound regret" Herbert Lehman's resignation as Director General. Assistant Secretary of State Will Clayton read aloud for the delegates a letter in which President Truman praised Lehman for having "laid the foundation" for UNRRA and "prepared the structure of international cooperation which now is bringing effective aid to millions of our liberated allies." Now, "as supply ships carry to the devastated areas of Europe and Asia the relief goods which UNRRA has sought in every part of the world," Truman knew that "the people of the United Nations, no less than those receiving UNRRA aid," were grateful to Lehman for his role in "this collaboration in the interests of lasting peace." Foreign leaders joined in the tributes, thanking Lehman for his "inspiring leadership," which had made UNRRA "a symbol of hope and a source of life-sustaining aid to many millions of hungry people." In recognition of Lehman's "devoted and distinguished service," the UNRRA Council bestowed upon him the new title of "permanent Honorary Chairman of the Council" so that it might "have the benefit of his continued association" with the organization.[36]

Much to Lehman's dismay, President Truman chose former New York City Mayor Fiorello La Guardia to succeed Lehman as UNRRA's Director General. As columnist Doris Fleeson noted, the President hoped that La Guardia's "galvanic" leadership style would generate the public and congressional support for UNRRA that Lehman's quiet "integrity and heart" had failed to produce. Although Lehman and La Guardia both espoused liberal causes and had been close to Franklin Roosevelt, Lehman had often sparred with La Guardia in the past when the Mayor's brash and boisterous approach and penchant for publicity had clashed with Lehman's more sedate and quiet leadership. Lehman distrusted La Guardia from the time the newly elected Mayor had sought what the Governor considered to be dictatorial powers to deal with New York City's fiscal crisis in 1933, and Lehman never forgot that the Mayor had called him and his brother Irving "goniffs" during the 1941 mayoral campaign. Although Lehman knew that UNRRA would have to conclude its operations in the near future, he feared that La Guardia "would favor the liquidation of UNRRA at an earlier date." Nonetheless, Lehman extended to La Guardia his "hearty congratulations" and "best wishes for your complete success in this all important work." Although some British officials had complained privately that Lehman's lack of charisma had been part of UNRRA's problem, Eleanor Roosevelt pointed out in her newspaper column a few months later that the change in leadership at UNRRA did not make much difference, that La Guardia, "dynamic as he is, has not been able to get us really to face the problem." But Lehman later conceded that La Guardia had brought "a great deal of energy and purpose" to the position and had "probably made a very good Director General," and George Woodbridge, in the official history of UNRRA, asserted that La Guardia "used his flair for publicity to make people of all nations aware of the gravity of the emergency. Whereas Lehman's appeal had been directed to the intellect—for justice among the various claimants on world food stocks—La Guardia's was to the emotions—for food for 'millions of hungry, starving, dying people.' "[37]

Freed from his official UNRRA position, Lehman stepped up his attacks on President Truman's food policies. At a dinner sponsored by the National Citizens Political Action Committee marking the first anniversary of Franklin Roosevelt's death, Lehman denounced voluntary food conservation measures as "not a remedy but merely an insufficient palliative," asserting that "in every country, including the United States, there must be rigid control of food," including "rationing, more liberal set-asides, control of movement, limitation in the use of scarce commodities for all purposes other than for essential human consumption, increased extraction and greater efforts on the part of governments to capture the actual wheat at the source." He challenged the administration's contention that the food crisis would soon be over, warning that "the need during next winter will not be substantially less than that with which we are now faced." A few days later, addressing a mass meeting in Washington on the world food situation, Lehman condemned the Truman administration's "unrealistic program," which "fostered and drugged" Americans into complacency and resulted in "glutting ourselves in homes, hotels and restaurants." In mid-May, Lehman and a group of "one hundred prominent citizens" urged the President to use his "war powers" if necessary to "double our contribution to the fight against famine during the present crucial months," suggesting that rationing could be implemented quickly by using "the spare coupons in the sugar ration books now in the hands of most consumers."[38]

Publicly, President Truman accepted Lehman's resignation with equanimity and grace, declaring at a news conference on March 21 that he "was very sorry to see Governor Lehman quit," but noting that Lehman had "been in ill health" and had "wanted to quit immediately" when Truman had become President. Truman continued to take the high road amid Lehman's mounting criticism of the administration's response to the famine. Asked about Lehman again at another press conference in mid-April on the heels of Lehman's remarks at the mass meeting in Washington, Truman rejected as "very much mistaken" Lehman's claim that the administration had not done everything it could in response to the food crisis, but added: "Of course, Mr. Lehman's heart is in this thing," and Truman was glad it was "because we have got to make every effort possible to feed these people."[39]

Privately, however, Truman was furious at Lehman's continued attacks on the administration's food policies, and the President revealed his true feelings during a meeting with Budget Director Harold Smith on May 15. Smith recorded in his diary that they discussed the food problem, which had not subsided, and Smith criticized Secretary Anderson and the Agriculture Department's handling of the situation. When Truman asserted that "rationing would be a terrible headache," Smith disagreed, suggesting that "we should have started rationing in the beginning." Truman then made clear his anger at "Lehman's activities on the food front," claiming that Lehman, who "had bitched up UNRRA and who now was apparently running for the Senate from New York, was taking it out" on the President. Ignoring the failure of the United States to meet its commitments to UNRRA, the President charged that "Lehman had 'sat on his fanny' for several years, but now he is showing a great burst of activity over the international food situation about which he should have been doing something all along." A few weeks later, during a meeting with Smith and Basil O'Connor of the American Red Cross, Truman again showed his displeasure with Lehman, complaining that "Lehman had been released from UNRRA because of ill health, but had not been so ill that he could not turn around and spend a lot of time criticizing everyone connected with relief."[40]

Herbert Lehman never claimed to have all the answers, but he knew that the Truman administration's premature lifting of food controls in the United States and its reliance on voluntary conservation measures had exacerbated the threat of starvation, malnutrition, and disease facing millions of people in Europe and Asia in 1946. In April 1946, Pope Pius XII added his voice to those calling for stronger measures, asserting that "a small, scarcely noticeable rationing in the better supplied countries would result in such saving of food as would afford other peoples, harder hit by famine, a marked relief in their more urgent needs." As Bela Gold has shown, by May, "the tide of intensified

criticism" rose "to a thunderous crescendo," typified by Acting Secretary of State
Dean Acheson's acknowledgment that the United States was falling way short
of its commitments to UNRRA, and his demand that the United States adopt
"requisitioning of wheat for famine relief purposes." As Lizzie Collingham later
noted, "the world's hungry had to make do with less. They scraped along on
rations which, as 'one Italian worker said, were not enough to live on and not
enough to die on.'" Secretary of Agriculture Anderson later conceded that food
controls in the United States had been lifted in late 1945 "perhaps too hastily,"
and scholars have shown that it was only when the Truman administration
raised the price ceilings for corn and wheat in May that farmers made large
quantities of grain available for shipment overseas rather than hoarding it or
using it to fatten their animals. By the end of June, the Truman administration
finally obtained enough grain to meet Europe's minimum requirements and
the widespread starvation that Lehman and UNRRA had feared was avoided.[41]

Lehman later stated that "the most important part of my life was as
Director General of UNRRA." He recalled that "at the outset we had many
disappointments and heartaches and frustrations," but he believed that "we
did finally whip UNRRA into shape so that it served not only as the first
great international operating organization, but unquestionably saved the lives
of millions of people and placed scores of millions on the road to economic
and social recovery." Speaking at a meeting sponsored by the National Peace
Conference in June 1946, Lehman emphasized that "UNRRA has demonstrated that an executive international can operate successfully, . . . that a staff
of many nationalities can work together in harmony and with a true spirit of
international service," and that "the various peoples of the United Nations can
in fact work together for the common good of humanity." He took pride that
UNRRA had shipped "nearly twelve million tons of supplies," including "great
quantities of food, transportation equipment, raw materials, medical supplies,
[and] agricultural machinery," and that there was now every likelihood that
"widespread starvation will have been averted." In view of "the innumerable
difficulties of translating a war-time economy to the needs of peace, and the
sweeping changes in manpower and the difficulties of resettling labor," Lehman
considered it "wonderful that so much has in fact been achieved." Years later,
Lehman asserted that UNRRA "made more friends for the United States in
many parts of the world than any other activity that we carried on," and that
"UNRRA was the only thing that saved Italy and Greece from becoming Communist countries."[42]

Other observers celebrated how much Lehman and UNRRA had accomplished. Eleanor Roosevelt thought that UNRRA's success was "one of the great
achievements" of Lehman's life, noting that he had demonstrated "that he was
a good organizer and had the patience of Job" in getting the organization up
and running. The *New York Times* readily conceded that UNRRA had made

mistakes, that despite Lehman's best efforts UNRRA supplies had sometimes been used for political purposes, and that corruption and black market activities had occurred, but the *Times* emphasized that UNRRA had "meant life and hope to many millions of people," and that "the bulk of the goods, purchased at a total cost of more than $3,600,000,000, has gone or will go to those who need them." *New York Times* columnist Anne O'Hare McCormick reported that UNRRA, "despite a slow start, many mistakes, a top-heavy and often inefficient and injudicious personnel," had performed "a work of international salvage on a scale never attempted before and deserves the lion's share of credit for averting the worst consequences of the greatest catastrophe in history." Without UNRRA's help, she believed that "life could not have started again on any terms or at any level in the vast wastelands of Europe and Asia, filled with human debris more tragic and more dangerous than any material devastation." Writing in the *Washington Post*, former Undersecretary of State Sumner Welles lamented that Herbert Lehman's "great achievement . . . as administrator of UNRRA has not yet been sufficiently recognized here and in Europe." Welles praised Lehman for overcoming "almost insuperable handicaps and much unjustified criticism" to get UNRRA off the ground, stressing that the agency "has prevented social collapse in a large part of Europe." According to Welles, "had it not been for UNRRA, many millions in Italy, and an even greater proportion of the peoples of Austria and of central and eastern Europe, would have starved, and no military force could have prevented starving people from taking the law into their own hands."[43]

When Lehman's disagreement with the President over the food crisis and the future of UNRRA led Lehman to resign as Director General, Truman was glad to see him go. Although the President was sympathetic to the plight of the people overseas facing starvation, he was not willing to risk his political capital by forcing the American people to make the sacrifices needed to meet the crisis, and Lehman's repeated and public criticism clearly bothered him much more than he let on. The Truman administration never even acknowledged the letter from Lehman and "one hundred prominent citizens" urging stronger action to combat hunger overseas, ostensibly because it was released to the press before it was received at the White House. The relationship Lehman and Truman had forged in 1945 to win congressional support for UNRRA had dissolved in anger and bitterness, and it would take time for them to realize that they needed to work together to achieve the liberal goals that they shared, such as promoting and protecting the civil rights, constitutional liberties, and economic security of all Americans.[44]

CHAPTER II

"Fighting for the Cause of Progressive and Liberal Government"

Lehman and Truman, 1946–1948

I am very happy over the result of the election. It is a tribute not only to President Truman's great courage and fighting qualities, but I think also an endorsement by the American people of a liberal program for this country.[1]

On March 28, 1946, just a few days before his resignation as Director General of UNRRA took effect, Herbert Lehman celebrated his sixty-eighth birthday. But despite his age, Lehman had no intention of ending his public service, and his departure from UNRRA allowed him to devote more time and energy to his charitable and philanthropic efforts. Over the next few months, Lehman served as one of the honorary chairmen for the New York City United Jewish Appeal and resumed his active involvement as a vice chairman of the American Jewish Joint Distribution Committee. Enjoying his new freedom to speak out on public issues, Lehman congratulated President Truman on his "courageous and forthright veto" of a bill that would have stripped the Office of Price Administration of most of its power, opposed efforts by some in Congress to give the military control over America's atomic energy policy, and lent his name to a group of "130 leading citizens and experts in international law" who urged the U.S. government "to accept immediately . . . the compulsory jurisdiction of the new World Court." And of course he continued to warn

---

Chapter title quotation: Herbert Lehman to Henry and Elinor Morgenthau, November 8, 1946, Herbert Lehman Papers, Special Correspondence Files, Henry Morgenthau, Jr.

that UNRRA should not be disbanded until either its mission had been accomplished or the United Nations had established some other agency to take over its responsibilities for displaced persons and providing food relief to those in need. Lehman was disappointed but not surprised when the Truman administration proceeded with its plans to terminate UNRRA and distribute American relief aid unilaterally rather than through an international agency.[2]

I

Herbert Lehman had long aspired to serve in the U.S. Senate, and he hoped that 1946 might afford him the opportunity to realize that goal. Back in 1938, he had planned to run for the Senate rather than a fourth term as Governor, but Franklin Roosevelt and New York State Democratic leaders had persuaded him to run for Governor instead, emphasizing that he was the only Democrat who could defeat Thomas Dewey and protect the social and economic reforms that had been enacted in New York in the previous sixteen years. Upon leaving UNRRA in March 1946, Lehman again considered the possibility of running for the Senate. Most observers expected Democratic Senator James Mead to challenge Governor Dewey's bid for re-election rather than seeking another term in the Senate, and Herbert Lehman's name was prominent among those mentioned as possible successors to Mead in the Senate. On March 16, for example, gossip columnist Leonard Lyons wrote that "Herbert Lehman, free of his UNRRA cares, will be urged for the United States Senatorship from New York this fall," and two months later, the New York Times reported that Lehman viewed the Senate as an appropriate "forum for his abilities." Although Lehman would not actively seek the Senate nomination, the Times asserted that he would accept it if it were offered.[3]

At first, Lehman was ambivalent about running for the Senate in 1946, telling a friend that the situation did not "look too good . . . from a Democratic standpoint." By the summer, however, Lehman felt much more confident about the Democrats' chances in New York. He told friends and former UNRRA colleagues who were urging him to run that he was receiving "encouraging" reports from all over the state. Nonetheless, he noted that the political situation continued to be "quite unsettled," in large part because Senator Mead had not officially announced his candidacy for Governor, which meant that there was no opening yet for the Senate.[4]

New York Democrats consulted with President Truman and Democratic National Chairman Robert Hannegan about the potential ticket of Mead for Governor and Lehman for the Senate. As a former Senator, Truman appreciated the value of seniority in Congress and at first he was resistant to the plan for Mead to relinquish his Senate seat to run for Governor. The President met with Mead in mid-March, but Truman claimed that they did not discuss the political situation in New York, that he did not know whether Mead would run for Governor and Lehman for the Senate, and that he did not intend "to interfere in New York politics." Hannegan was one of the President's closest political advisors, having played a key role in Truman's re-election to the Senate in 1940 and his nomination for Vice President in 1944, and serving as Postmaster General in Truman's Cabinet. Shortly after Lehman left UNRRA in late March 1946, Hannegan reportedly "urged him to run for the United States Senate on a ticket headed by Senator James M. Mead as a New York gubernatorial candidate." Although New York Democratic leaders downplayed such reports, asserting that "no National Committee Chairman would think of injecting himself into a matter which is the concern of the State and not the national organization," those same party stalwarts "made no secret of their belief that Mr. Lehman would be a distinct asset to the New York ticket." A few days later, the President acquiesced in Mead's candidacy when Democratic State Chairman Paul Fitzpatrick and National Committee member Edward Flynn insisted that Mead was their strongest candidate to oppose Dewey, pointing out that defeating Dewey in New York in 1946 would remove him as a potential presidential rival in 1948.[5]

The administration's decision to back Mead for Governor opened the way for Lehman to run for the Senate, but Truman and Hannegan wavered over Lehman's candidacy for a while. Although the President never fired back publicly at Lehman's sharp criticism of his food policies and the decision to terminate UNRRA, Truman, as previously discussed, showed his anger at Lehman in private, complaining to Budget Director Harold Smith about Lehman's stewardship of UNRRA. One observer speculated that Truman and Hannegan "preferred headline-making Fiorello La Guardia for the Senate race" because neither Lehman nor Mead were "the most effective campaigners," and reports persisted that La Guardia was "the first choice of President Truman." But Fitzpatrick and Flynn met with Truman and Hannegan in Washington in mid-August, arguing that Mead and Lehman would be the strongest Democratic candidates in New York, and they persuaded the President and Hannegan to give the ticket their blessings. Truman and Hannegan realized that the Democrats' best strategy in 1946 was to tie the party's candidates to the legacy of Franklin Roosevelt, and Herbert Lehman's candidacy clearly embodied the FDR connection.[6]

The spirit of Franklin Roosevelt permeated the 1946 New York State Democratic Convention, with hardly a mention of President Truman. As was the case with Democrats all over the country, New York Democratic leaders stressed FDR's accomplishments and legacy in the campaign, inviting Eleanor Roosevelt to deliver the convention's keynote address, and Herbert Lehman and James Mead were seen as ideal candidates to run on FDR's record, as the *New*

York Times noted, "because of their close association with the late President." In her remarks to the delegates, Mrs. Roosevelt emphasized "the social and progressive legislation and administration" that Democratic Governors Al Smith, Franklin Roosevelt, and Herbert Lehman had provided New York for twenty years, and she recalled her husband's success in pulling the nation "out of a devastating domestic situation" in 1933 by restoring people's confidence and persuading them that there was "nothing to fear but fear itself." She also noted FDR's efforts to prepare the country for war in the days before Pearl Harbor, and his leadership of the country during World War II. In contrast to her frequent references to FDR and his policies, Mrs. Roosevelt never mentioned Truman by name. The closest she came was when she noted that "in Washington today the administration . . . has adhered to the progressive ideals of the Democratic Party," but had been stymied "in putting through many of the measures which represent the real spirit of the Democratic Party by a coalition of so-called conservative Democrats and reactionary Republicans." State Chairman Fitzpatrick was the only major speaker to mention Truman by name during the first day of the convention, praising the President for carrying out FDR's policies. Truman did receive some acclaim the following day when delegates adopted a platform endorsing his foreign policy and domestic agenda.[7]

On September 4, 1946, New York Democrats unanimously nominated Herbert Lehman and James Mead as their candidates for the U.S. Senate and Governor. In his acceptance speech, Lehman continued the trend of focusing on the Roosevelt legacy while virtually ignoring the present occupant of the White House. Lehman proudly recalled that Al Smith and Franklin Roosevelt had placed his name in nomination for Governor fourteen years earlier, and he asserted that "there is no more challenging, no more rewarding post than that of Senator from the great State of New York." He stressed that "in this shrinking world, foreign relations exert an ever-growing impact on domestic affairs," and he noted that as Director General of UNRRA, he had been "in close and constant touch with representatives of all the United Nations." His visits to "our gallant Allies" overseas had helped him "to understand how passionate was their devotion to the ideals for which we fought—how deep was their reverence for our greatly mourned leader—Franklin Delano Roosevelt." Lehman welcomed the opportunity once again to serve the people of the state and the nation, and he promised to "campaign in the spirit of that progressive and enlightened democracy" that he had "always espoused."[8]

To oppose Lehman, Republicans nominated New York State Assembly Majority Leader Irving Ives, a moderate from rural Chenango County who had recently been appointed as Dean of the newly established School of Industrial and Labor Relations at Cornell University. Ives was popular upstate and had a positive record of accomplishments in the Assembly, including his leadership in enacting a bill banning racial discrimination in employment. Based on his record, Ives was expected to make inroads among labor, African Americans, and other traditional Democratic constituencies.[9]

As Lehman began to plot his campaign strategy, Lithgow Osborne, who had served under Lehman as New York State Conservation Commissioner and in various positions in OFRRO and UNRRA, warned Lehman against associating himself too closely with President Truman, whose popularity was plummeting. Although Osborne realized that Lehman "must of course go along with the national administration on national issues," he urged Lehman to emphasize "New York's sovereignty within the limits of the Constitution and your determination to maintain it in essentials." Osborne advised Lehman to focus on "international affairs—where Ives is obviously weakest," suggesting that "in this field, the underlying theme song should be: 'Why send a boy to do a man's job?' "[10]

Before Lehman could even get his Senate candidacy off the ground, he became embroiled in a clash between President Truman and Secretary of Commerce Henry Wallace over American foreign policy toward the Soviet Union. On September 12, 1946, Wallace spoke at a campaign rally at Madison Square Garden sponsored by two left-wing organizations, the National Citizens Political Action Committee and the Independent Citizens Committee of the Arts, Sciences and Professions. Knowing that his remarks would be controversial, Wallace had shown them to President Truman, who had glanced through them quickly and given his approval, focusing on the speech as an effort to help Mead and Lehman and not paying very careful attention to the substance of Wallace's comments on foreign policy. Wallace began by warmly endorsing Mead and Lehman, emphasizing that "Herbert Lehman knows full well the problems and the opportunities facing the State of New York, the United States, and the United Nations," and asserting that Lehman's "great heart and great mind will be increasingly useful when he is a member of the United States Senate." After completing his political remarks, however, Wallace went on to discuss his vision of "The Way to Peace," rejecting a "get tough with Russia" policy and expressing a willingness to accept a Russian sphere of influence in Eastern Europe, which was seen as contradicting the hardline policy that Secretary of State James Byrnes had recently enunciated in Europe. The President, who had not realized the full import of Wallace's remarks, soon asked for and received Wallace's resignation from the Cabinet.[11]

Within a few days, according to the *New York Times*, "the Wallace case had become the prime issue in the New York State election" as the *Times* and Republican leaders demanded to know whether Lehman supported the program of President Truman and Secretary Byrnes or the policy of Henry Wallace. Republican National Chairman B. Carroll Reece urged voters to ask Lehman whether he "recognize[d] Mr. Wallace as a spokesman" on international affairs, and the *Times* believed that "the voters of the State are entitled to know which foreign policy each candidate favors." The *Times* assumed that Ives would fol-low the lead of Michigan Senator Arthur Vandenberg, the Republicans' leading voice in foreign affairs, and support Byrnes's hard line with the Russians, but the paper pointed out that Lehman's situation was more complicated because he was not just the candidate of the Democratic Party; he was also the nominee of the American Labor Party, which by this time was dominated by Communists who presumably agreed with Wallace's approach, and the Liberal Party, which had condemned Wallace's remarks. The *Times* stressed that there were "real and fundamental" differences between the policy advocated by the President and the Secretary of State on the one hand and the one championed by Wallace, and the editors argued that New Yorkers were entitled to "a forthright statement" from Lehman clarifying his position.[12]

Lehman tried to settle the issue in a statewide radio address on September 28, reiterating his "full support" for the State Democratic platform adopted just a few weeks earlier that praised the "forthright and vigorous foreign policy of the administration." He asserted that settling American-Soviet "differences in every area fairly and reasonably" was "the immediate, the challenging, task of statesmanship," that dealing with the Soviets required a mixture of "compro-mise and infinite patience" and "firmness," and that this was "the spirit which guides the foreign policy of our administration." Pointing out that "the attitude of the Soviet Union does not always seem calculated to make it easier," he complimented the Truman administration for countering such challenges "in a spirit of compromise, and with the display of patience and good will." Lehman sympathized with the burdens placed on the shoulders of the Secretary of State, who "must fashion the fateful decisions upon which the security and the welfare of the nation depend," stressing that "the nature of his critical assignment" should entitle him "to the support of a united people." That was the only way in which the Secretary could "find his way through the quicksands of diplomacy to the bright and tranquil future of our hopes."[13]

Much to Lehman's dismay, his speech failed to end the controversy as Republicans and neutral observers continued to question where he stood in the dispute between Wallace and the Truman administration. A Republican spokes-man denounced "Lehman's tragic failure in his speech tonight to express himself clearly on the basic question of the foreign policy of our country," alleging that Lehman had "declined to state whether he opposes or rejects the Wallace line of advocating a world that is half slave and half free." Ives claimed that rather than telling the American people whether he "follows his left wing" or "stand[s] forthrightly behind the American bipartisan foreign policy," Lehman had "issued a shadow doctrine, vague and insecure, which had something to please each of the political organizations and splinter parties he represents in this campaign." More significantly, and to Lehman's great disappointment, the editors of the *New York Times* wrote that they thought they knew, "from this speech, where

Mr. Lehman stands," but they complained that Lehman's response was not "explicit" enough because he had not mentioned either Wallace or Secretary of State Byrnes by name, and they called upon Lehman to "speak more plainly."[14]

When Ives continued to ask, "Where does Lehman stand on foreign policy?" Lehman realized he needed to speak to the issue again, which he did in another radio broadcast in late October. Lehman quoted from his earlier remarks and reiterated his unequivocal support for Truman and Byrnes and their foreign policy, explaining that he had not thought it necessary to mention the Secretary of State by name in his previous speech because he "assumed that everybody, including my opponent, knew that the foreign policy of the United States was that enunciated by our Secretary of State with the approval of the President, and that we had only one Secretary of State, and that his name was James F. Byrnes."[15]

The Republican attempt to associate Lehman with Henry Wallace's more conciliatory policy toward the Soviet Union reflected the GOP's overall strategy of charging that the Democrats were soft on Communism. As the Cold War between the United States and the Soviet Union intensified, the discovery of Communist spies in Canada fueled concern that Communists in the United States might similarly be aiding the enemy. Against this backdrop, Republican National Committee Chairman Reece claimed that Communists and their sympathizers had infiltrated the Democratic Party, which he asserted was now controlled by "Red-Fascists . . . beholden to the political ideology of Moscow." According to Reece, "the choice presented to the voters this year is Communism or Republicanism." Even after Truman had removed Wallace from the Cabinet, Reece charged that influential groups within the Democratic Party "accept every tune wafted from Moscow by way of the CIO-PAC" (the Congress of Industrial Organizations' Political Action Committee). Reece claimed that "the Democratic slate for November is a Democrat-PAC slate," and that in New York State, "it is likewise a Democratic-Communist slate." Two days before the election, Reece defined "Americanism or communism" as one of the crucial issues in the campaign.[16]

Actions by the American Labor Party, the American Communist Party, and Moscow radio seemed to support the Republican accusations that the Democrats were in league with the Communists. By 1946, Communists increasingly dominated the local units of the ALP, but not the statewide party committee, which endorsed the entire Democratic state ticket. After the ALP backed Lehman and Mead, the Communist Party in New York withdrew its candidates for Senate and Governor, not wanting to siphon off votes that Lehman and Mead would need to defeat "the reactionary Dewey slate." When a commentator on Moscow radio, speaking in English, urged listeners in the United States to vote for candidates endorsed by the CIO's Political Action Committee, which included Lehman and Mead, Republican leaders immediately accused the Soviet

Union of interfering in American elections and charged that the broadcast proved that a Democratic victory would serve the interests of the Soviet Union. Republicans reminded voters that Henry Wallace's controversial remarks had been uttered at a campaign rally for Lehman and Mead sponsored by left-wing organizations, and ALP State Chairman Hyman Blumberg did not help matters when he declared that his party was "in full agreement with Secretary Wallace" on foreign affairs. Such actions all provided credibility for Ives's and Dewey's efforts to link the Democrats with the Communists, such as when Ives criticized "the Democratic party and its fellow-travelers" for "their tendency to turn to government for the solution of everything." Analysts noted that "many old-line Democrats, particularly Catholics," resented the Democratic-ALP coalition and were offended by last-minute appearances by Wallace and Senator Claude Pepper (D-FL), described by the *New York Times* as leaders of "the far left wing," at rallies sponsored by radical groups supporting Mead and Lehman.[17]

Herbert Lehman and New York Democrats tried hard to rebut the Republican charges that they were soft on Communism. In a speech in Binghamton, Lehman emphasized "with all the force that lies in my being" that "I repudiate all Communist support, and I do not want any Communist votes." A week before the election, he promised to defend "the ideals and the principles of our democratic institutions . . . against fascism and communism alike," stressing that he neither sought nor wanted Communist support, declaring he "would rather go down to defeat than be beholden to them in the slightest measure." Lehman and Mead reiterated their opposition to Communism and Communists so often during the campaign that Robert Thompson, the Communist candidate for State Controller, warned that they were "jeopardizing the effectiveness of the anti-Dewey coalition and hurting their own chances of election by echoing Republican red-baiting." Nonetheless, despite Lehman's and Mead's best efforts, the Republicans succeeded in branding the Democratic candidates in New York with the "Communist taint."[18]

Besides the Communist issue, Ives and Republicans nationally also capitalized on the growing dissatisfaction with President Truman and his policies in 1946. The President's difficulties in handling the reconversion of the economy from wartime to peacetime, highlighted by growing labor unrest and meat shortages, resulted in Truman's approval ratings dropping from 82 percent in November 1945 to 32 percent in the fall of 1946. The *Chicago Tribune* observed that "the President has become a Democratic liability," with Democratic candidates "seldom, if ever, mentioning Mr. Truman," and the *New York Times* reported in early November 1946 that "the main issue in the election is the Truman administration and its handling of post-war economic problems." Republicans quipped, "To err is Truman," as they asked voters, "Had enough?" and GOP leaders claimed that record-setting registration figures in New York

City for a non–presidential election year augured a huge protest vote against "the jittery, bungling leadership in Washington." For days at a time, Ives ignored Lehman and focused his attacks on the President, charging that "the nation has had enough of the Truman administration's economy of scarcity, whether it is planned or the sorry result of unplanned ineptitude," and asserting that a Republican victory was needed to "throw off the choking regulations which are throttling agriculture, business and industry."[19]

Like most Democrats in 1946, Herbert Lehman emphasized his connections to Franklin Roosevelt rather than Harry Truman. Lehman linked his policies as Governor with those of Al Smith and Franklin Roosevelt, emphasized the links between his "little New Deal" in Albany and FDR's New Deal in Washington, and promised that as a Senator, he would "work for the attainment of the economic bill of rights proclaimed by Franklin D. Roosevelt." The Democratic National Committee distributed sound recordings with excerpts from some of FDR's more memorable speeches for its candidates to use, and Lehman welcomed the active involvement of the Roosevelt family in his campaign. Eleanor Roosevelt, described by *Washington Post* reporter Robert Albright as "New York's most poignant reminder that a dead President is being run in this race," noted in her newspaper column on Election Day her pleasure at delivering a final speech for Lehman "since he was one of my husband's friends and associates." Two of FDR's sons also campaigned for Lehman. Elliott Roosevelt recalled that his father "had always placed 'great trust' in former Governor Lehman" and called for his election so that the country would continue along the path that FDR had set: "government for all the people, not for the few." Franklin Roosevelt, Jr., emphasized the close ties between the Roosevelt and Lehman families, referring to Lehman as his "Uncle Herbert" and declaring: "I can think of no other man who can go forward along the liberal and progressive path of my father as well as Mr. Lehman can."[20]

But even while stressing his political roots as a friend and colleague of Franklin Roosevelt, Lehman refused to abandon Harry Truman, defending the President's efforts to guide the economy from war to peace and warning against the election of a Republican Congress. Although he had certainly had his differences with Truman over UNRRA and the world food shortage in the first half of 1946, Lehman blamed the country's problems on reactionaries in Congress, "Democratic as well as Republican," who had "sabotaged" the President's program, and he called for the election of liberal Democrats to Congress who would enact Truman's proposals to raise the minimum wage, end racial discrimination in employment, and solve the nation's housing crisis. Lehman emphasized that victories by Ives and Republican congressional candidates could lead to Republican majorities in Congress, meaning that "every committee of Congress would be under the control of the Republicans," empowering "such arch-reactionaries as Senator Robert Taft of Ohio," who "would become the Republican majority leader of the Senate," and Representative Joseph Martin of Massachusetts, who would become the Speaker of the House.[21]

In Lehman's view, the 1946 election was "one of the most crucial in modern American history" because it constituted "a fight between liberalism and reaction." He accused Ives and Dewey of "the purest hypocrisy" for "masquerading as liberals at election time," refuting their efforts to take credit for New York's "enlightened labor and social welfare code" that Lehman and his associates had enacted over "bitter and almost constant reactionary opposition." Lehman specifically recalled that Ives, when he was Speaker of the Assembly in 1936, had kept Lehman's social security program bottled up in the Rules Committee instead of allowing it to come to the floor for a vote, and the former Governor also detailed numerous instances when Ives had voted against "progressive and humane labor laws."[22]

Lehman's definition of the liberal agenda in 1946 went well beyond President Truman's, although Truman would later embrace many of the objectives Lehman espoused in 1946. Lehman advocated the adoption of "a national health program" and sought "to end discriminatory practices in elections, in employment, in education, or wherever and whenever they appear." He fully supported the President's proposal to make permanent the Fair Employment Practices Committee, but he believed that much more needed to be done to combat the "dark evil" of racism and racial discrimination. He emphasized that "the fight against racism is an American issue which reaches to the very roots of our democratic way of life," and that "racism must be rooted out, lock, stock and barrel, for the evil thing it is." Lehman pointed out that he had been on the NAACP's board of directors for many years, and, unlike the President, Lehman called for the enactment of anti-lynching legislation and outlawing the poll tax. Once elected, Lehman promised, he would do everything he could to exclude from the Senate Mississippi's Theodore Bilbo, an avowed racist and alleged member of the Ku Klux Klan, who had "urged that groups of American citizens be deprived of their civic and political rights" because of their "race, creed, color, or national origin."[23]

Lehman welcomed the support of Truman administration officials such as Averell Harriman, who had replaced Henry Wallace as Secretary of Commerce, and James Forrestal, Secretary of the Navy, both of whom hailed from New York and served among the honorary chairmen of the Independent Citizens Committee for Lehman. But confusion reigned over the President's role in the campaign. After DNC Chairman Hannegan met with the President in early October, the *New York Times* quoted Hannegan as saying that Truman "might make 'a number of speeches' and that he would also stump aggressively for Democratic candidates." Later in the same article, however, it was reported that Hannegan had said that "while it was possible that President Truman 'might' make some campaign speeches, he had no plans at this time, even tentative, for a speaking tour." White House Press Secretary Charlie Ross tried to clarify the situation the following day, telling reporters that the President had not made any plans to speak on behalf of Democratic candidates, although he left open the possibility that some appearances might still be scheduled. But as Truman's popularity continued to wane, it became clear that few Democrats wanted the President to campaign on their behalf, and that Truman had little inclination to make the effort and risk an unfriendly reception. The President did not partake in any political activities when he traveled to New York to address the United Nations in October, and when a group of Businessmen and Women for Mead and Lehman offered to sponsor a radio broadcast so Truman could "carry to the people the story of Republican obstructionism in the reconversion period," White House Secretary Matthew Connelly replied merely that the "President appreciates your interest but regrets [he] cannot comply with your suggestion."[24]

II

The issue of Palestine plagued President Truman throughout 1946 and had a major impact on Herbert Lehman's Senate candidacy. Like most of the descendants of German Jews who had immigrated to the United States in the mid-nineteenth century and found great success in this country, Lehman opposed Zionism and the creation of a Jewish state in Palestine. He believed that Palestine should be available as a haven to Jews facing persecution anywhere in the world, and that it should especially be open to Jews displaced by World War II, but he feared that the establishment of a Jewish state would raise questions concerning the loyalty of American Jews to the United States. President Truman agreed that Palestine should be opened to Jewish refugees from Europe after World War II, and he appealed to the British government to allow one hundred thousand displaced European Jews into Palestine. The British countered by suggesting an Anglo-American Committee of Inquiry, and much to the disappointment of American Jews, who had hoped for the immediate migration of the remnants of Eastern and Central European Jewry to Palestine, Truman accepted the British proposal. Lehman and many American Jews cheered in April 1946 when the Inquiry recommended that one hundred thousand European Jews should be admitted into Palestine, but the more ardent Zionists were disappointed at the committee's rejection of the idea of a Jewish state in Palestine.[25]

Herbert Lehman tried to impress upon the President the importance of the Palestine issue to American Jews. When the British continued to stall after receiving the Anglo-American Inquiry's report in late April, insisting that a committee of experts was needed to decide how to implement the Inquiry's recommendations, Lehman was one of seventy-five prominent Americans who took a large ad in the *Washington Post* on June 6, 1946, to urge "President Truman to stand firm" and force the British to carry out the Inquiry's recommendation that one hundred thousand Jews be allowed into Palestine immediately. The day after the ad appeared, Lehman requested a meeting with the President, but Truman, who by this time was exasperated with the seemingly unsolvable Palestine problem, refused to see him, suggesting that Lehman submit a memorandum instead. Two weeks later, Lehman wrote to the President, asserting that "the delay in admitting 100,000 Jews into Palestine as recommended by the Anglo-American Committee has brought disappointment and distress" to the American people, "gentile and Jew alike." Lehman emphasized that "Jewish refugees now in displaced persons camps in Europe . . . are in a most tragic plight and they are rapidly deteriorating," and he stressed that "their admission to Palestine is the one hope of saving them physically and spiritually." He urged Truman to "do everything possible to persuade and assist the British government in taking the necessary action immediately," warning that "delay will mean further great tragedy which cannot be explained to right thinking people of this and other countries."[26]

President Truman had agreed to the British request for a joint cabinet-level group to formulate plans to implement the Inquiry's recommendations, and the Morrison-Grady Committee, as the working group came to be known, finished its report in late July. The committee advocated partitioning Palestine into a small Jewish enclave and a much larger Arab territory, with the British retaining jurisdiction over the Negev region and the cities of Jerusalem and Bethlehem. The British would also control future immigration into the Jewish area, and the one hundred thousand Jewish immigrants from Europe would be admitted only if this plan were accepted in its entirety. American Jews were outraged at this retreat from the Inquiry's recommendations, and Herbert Lehman interrupted his vacation on Nantucket to cable the President, expressing his horror at "the gross injustices" of the Morrison-Grady report, asserting that its recommendations were "so at variance with American policy" that it was "inconceivable that our government could be a party to or accept this report." Lehman charged that the plan was "inhuman and immoral" because it made "the admission of one hundred thousand Jewish refugees into Palestine subject to the acceptance of a thoroughly unjust plan which strangles future development of the Jewish people of Palestine." In Lehman's view, this was tantamount to "making hostages of these helpless victims of Hitler's tyranny," and he warned that "when the implications of this latest British plan become fully evident, all right thinking Americans—Jew and gentile alike—will be deeply shocked." Lehman could not believe that Truman "will permit our government to approve of this plan," and he stressed that "it is not enough, Mr. President, to have asked for the immediate admission of one hundred thousand Jews into Palestine." The time for the enactment of the President's policy was "long overdue."[27]

Lehman hoped to discuss the American response to the Morrison-Grady report with Truman, but he had to settle for speaking with presidential secretary Matt Connelly instead. However, New York Senators Mead and Wagner, accompanied by James G. McDonald, a member of the Anglo-American Inquiry and the former League of Nations High Commissioner for Refugees, met with the President, who also met with the entire New York congressional delegation after first refusing to see them. Truman confided to McDonald that he had "about come to the conclusion that there is no solution," but he promised to "keep trying." Under pressure from Jewish groups and others, such as New York State Democratic Chairman Paul Fitzpatrick, who warned that if the President accepted the latest British plan for Palestine, "it would be useless for the Democrats to nominate a state ticket for the election this fall," Truman rejected the Morrison-Grady recommendations.[28]

New, more militant leadership of the Zionist movement in the United States intensified the threat the Palestine issue posed for Herbert Lehman and Democratic candidates in the 1946 elections. Rabbi Stephen Wise, a good friend of Lehman's who believed that the Democratic Party, with its progressive views on social issues, was the proper political home for American Jews, had been supplanted as the real leader of the American Zionist Emergency Council (AZEC) by Rabbi Abba Hillel Silver, a Republican from Cleveland who was close to Ohio Republican Senator Robert Taft. Silver believed that American Jews should use their political power to help their friends and punish their foes rather than always supporting the Democrats, and he urged Jewish voters to withhold their votes from Democratic candidates to demonstrate their displeasure with the Democrats' failure to live up to the 1944 platform plank, which had endorsed "the opening of Palestine to unrestricted Jewish immigration and colonization, and . . . the establishment there of a free and democratic Jewish commonwealth." As part of this strategy, the newly formed Greater New York Zionist Actions Committee published "An Open Letter" in the *New York Times* and other major New York newspapers deploring the Democrats' failure to "redeem" their frequent statements supporting a Jewish home and the admission of "100,000 homeless European Jews into Palestine." The new organization anticipated that Democratic candidates would again pledge their support for Jewish goals in Palestine, but it warned, "*We will not be content with these speeches. We do not seek new promises or new planks. The old ones are good enough. What we ask is that our Administration fulfill those old promises now.*" Even more ominously for Lehman and the Democrats, the Manhattan Zionist Region convention passed a resolution urging its members "to rebuke the Democratic Party for its faithlessness to the expressed will of the American people."[29]

Concerned that Jewish hostility over the continuing deadlock on Palestine would prove costly in the election, Herbert Lehman and Rabbi Wise met with President Truman on September 19, 1946, urging him to issue a strong statement on Palestine. By this time, Lehman and many other Jewish leaders had concluded that partition of Palestine into separate Jewish and Arab states was the only way to ensure that Palestine could serve as a refuge for displaced Jews in Europe and other Jews who might suffer persecution in the future. Lehman and Wise hoped that a presidential statement endorsing partition might win the support of moderate Zionists and facilitate talks with the British government to establish a viable Jewish state in Palestine. However, the State Department advised the President not to issue such a statement, warning that if the administration "yields to the pressure of highly organized Zionist groups just now and makes statements calculated to give support to their policies of the moment, we shall merely be encouraging them to make fresh demands and to apply pressure in the future whenever they conceive it to be in their interest for this government to make further statements on their behalf." Acting Secretary of State Will Clayton pointed out that supporting partition would antagonize the Arab world and would be "contrary to the recommendations both of the Anglo-American Committee of Inquiry and of the experts who drew up the Morrison-Grady scheme." The President assured Clayton that he was "very hesitant about saying anything on this subject" and hoped it would not be necessary for him to do so.[30]

Despite the State Department's opposition and his own reluctance to speak out, Truman decided to issue a statement on Palestine when he learned that New York Republican Governor Thomas Dewey was about to take a strong stand on Jewish immigration into Palestine. On October 4, the eve of Yom Kippur, the solemn Jewish Day of Atonement, the President released a statement in which he reviewed his efforts to secure the admission of one hundred thousand Jewish refugees into Palestine and declared that "substantial immigration into Palestine . . . should begin at once." Truman praised the Jewish Agency's proposal calling for "the creation of a viable Jewish state, in control of its own immigration and economic policies in an adequate area of Palestine instead of in the whole of Palestine," and he expressed his belief that "a solution along these lines would command the support of public opinion in the United States." The President hoped that a solution could be found to which "our government could give its support," and he promised that his "administration will continue to do everything it can to this end."[31]

New York Jews and Democratic political leaders welcomed Truman's comments. Herbert Lehman congratulated the President "heartily" on his "forthright statement regarding Palestine," and Brooklyn Congressman Emanuel Celler predicted that Truman's remarks would have a "very desirable political effect" upon the Democrats' prospects in New York. Rabbi Wise applauded Truman's decision to follow Lehman's and Wise's suggestion that he make clear to the American public that he was continuing his efforts to enable "at least 100,000 DPs . . . to leave the American Military Zone at once for Palestine" and to persuade the British to accept "the proposal of the Jewish Agency" for "a viable

Jewish State in an adequate area of Palestine." Since the President had stolen his thunder, Governor Dewey raised the ante in his speech to the United Palestine Appeal, demanding the "immigration not of 100,000, but of several hundreds of thousands" of Jews into Palestine. Rabbi Silver also objected to the President's statement, insisting that *all* of Palestine must become a Jewish state.[32]

As the election neared, Democrats' prospects seemed bleak as Herbert Lehman and Democrats all across the country faced a perfect storm gathered against them. Large groups of voters were angry over price controls, meat shortages, alleged Communist influence in the Democratic Party, labor disputes, Palestine, disarray in the Truman administration as typified by the Henry Wallace affair, and a myriad of other issues. With the President's approval rating down to 32 percent, many Democrats had adopted a defeatist attitude or were apathetic, while the Republicans had an attractive message in what Republican National Chairman B. Carroll Reece described as their campaign to "restore orderly, capable and honest government in Washington to replace controls, confusion, corruption and communism." Most observers predicted that the Republicans would capture the House of Representatives and might win the Senate as well.[33]

In New York, Dewey was expected to defeat Mead easily to win another term as Governor, but the Lehman-Ives race for the Senate was seen as a toss-up. Lehman was the only Democrat given a chance of winning statewide in New York in 1946, based on his personal popularity and his record as Governor, but he faced the same problems confronting Democrats nationwide, as well as a few that were unique to New York. Lehman had to contend with possible defections by Catholic voters alienated by Truman's failure to stop the spread of Communism in Europe and New York Democrats' alliance with the left-wing American Labor Party, Jewish voters upset that the President had not done more on Palestine, and left-wing voters angry over Truman's firing of Henry Wallace and Lehman's support for that action. Lehman was expected to run way ahead of the rest of the Democratic ticket, but his fate was thought to depend on whether Dewey rolled up a large enough majority to carry Ives in with him.[34]

Both nationally and in New York, the 1946 elections resulted in a landslide victory for the Republicans. Voters all across the nation registered their dissatisfaction with Truman and the Democrats, giving the Republicans a majority in both the Senate and the House of Representatives. In New York, the entire Democratic state ticket went down to defeat, with Dewey defeating Mead by 687,000 votes, the third largest margin in state history at that time. Unlike in 1938, when Herbert Lehman had defied the national trend in favor of the Republicans, the former Governor was not able to surmount the strong national sentiment favoring the Republicans this time. Lehman ran way ahead of his fellow Democratic candidates in New York, but he was not able to overcome Dewey's long coattails, losing to Ives by 250,000 votes. Analysts attributed Lehman's and the Democrats' defeat in New York to Dewey's popularity as

Governor; Truman's unpopularity as President; and many old-line Democrats' growing concern about their party's alliance with both the American Labor Party, which was dominated by Communists, and the CIO's Political Action Committee, which was also seen as under Communist control. Defections by Zionist Jews also took a toll on Lehman. As *New York Times* political writer Warren Moscow later noted, Lehman did not receive his usual solid backing from Jewish voters "because his record on the Palestine question was not then pleasing to the most ardent Zionists."[35]

Herbert Lehman gracefully accepted the first and only electoral defeat in his long political career. At 1:35 a.m., he sent Ives a telegram officially conceding the race, and a few minutes later, Lehman went on the radio to congratulate his opponent. Lehman noted that the people of New York had rendered their decision "after fair and open debate," and he called upon "all citizens to close ranks in a common effort to solve the problems which face the country in a troubled world," pledging his "full support" to such endeavors. Numerous friends and relatives wrote to console him, including Rabbi Wise, who asserted, "If there had not been such a heavy anti-administration tide, you would of course have been elected by a great vote." Lehman emphasized to Wise and others that he had "no regrets" about running for the Senate, that he was "fighting for the cause of progressive and liberal government," which he feared "will now be under serious threat." Lehman was "very deeply concerned at the implications of the Republican sweep," and although there were "not many of the old Roosevelt adherents left," he believed that they needed to "stand together and fight" as hard as they could to protect and expand FDR's New Deal. Personally, Lehman vowed "to continue to serve my community with all my strength."[36]

III

After his defeat in the Senate race, in which he had strongly supported the President's foreign and domestic policies, Lehman hoped that Truman would appoint him to a position that would make use of his knowledge and experience. There was some talk about Lehman as a candidate for the presidency of the World Bank, but the post he really wanted was succeeding John Winant as the U.S. Representative on the United Nations Economic and Social Council. When he heard about Winant's resignation in January 1947, Lehman immediately wired the President and the Secretary of State that he was "very much interested in being appointed" as Winant's replacement, and he embarked on an all-out campaign to secure the position. He enlisted Eleanor Roosevelt, Senator Wagner, labor leaders David Dubinsky of the ILGWU and William Green of the AFL, New York State Democratic Chairman Paul Fitzpatrick, and Democratic National Committee member Ed Flynn, among others, to contact the President on his behalf. Unbeknownst to Lehman, Truman had already offered the positon to his former Senate colleague Robert La Follette of Wisconsin, who had lost his bid for re-election to Joseph McCarthy, and when La Follette had turned it down for family reasons, the President had reached out to former Attorney General Francis Biddle. Thus, when Lehman met with the President on January 16, 1947, Truman explained that he had already "made a partial commitment" to someone else, but Lehman took solace in the President's assurance that had the position not already been promised to someone else, Truman "would have been glad to appoint" Lehman, who was "eminently well qualified for this work." In a letter to incoming Secretary of State George Marshall, Lehman emphasized that his "long service as Director General of UNRRA," as well as his "broad experience in social and economic problems" as Governor of New York and as a businessman, qualified him for this post if it became available in the future.[37]

Lehman accepted the President's explanation of a previous commitment at face value, but Truman's sincerity must be questioned. Even when Senate Republicans blocked Biddle's nomination, the President did not turn to Lehman. The Republicans rejected Biddle, according to Senator Arthur Vandenberg, because they saw him "as a veritable symbol of the 'New Deal,'" and Republicans believed they had "a mandate from last November's election *against* the perpetuation of these symbols." Truman may well have feared that Lehman would have encountered similar objections. With Biddle's nomination bottled up in the Senate, Lehman wrote to the President again in mid-June, reiterating his interest in the post, but Truman, looking to avoid another confirmation fight with the Republican-controlled Senate, nominated Assistant Secretary of State Willard Thorp instead. In letters to Mrs. Roosevelt, Ed Flynn, and others who had intervened on his behalf, Lehman described himself as "greatly surprised and much disappointed" at being passed over again. Looking back a decade later, Lehman recalled his disappointment at Truman's failure to appoint him to the Economic and Social Council, but he admitted that "Thorpe's selection was a good one," and Lehman realized in retrospect that he "would have been stymied and frustrated" in a position that "lacked authority" and offered little opportunity "for real usefulness."[38]

As the months went on, Lehman became more and more frustrated by Truman's failure to find an appropriate position for him. In November 1947, Ed Flynn conveyed Lehman's disappointment to the President and warned about the possible political repercussions in 1948 of slighting Lehman, whose "following not only in New York State but throughout the country is probably the greatest of any person of the Jewish faith in this country." The President replied that he had not forgotten about Lehman, but that "the proper nitch [*sic*] has not shown up." When Flynn wrote to Truman again a few weeks later, the President reiterated that he was still "trying to find the proper place" for Lehman. Flynn forwarded copies of his correspondence with the President to Lehman, who expressed his growing frustration and told Flynn to drop "the whole matter." He had originally contacted Truman about the UN position almost a year ago, Lehman noted, and he regretted that the President had "failed to recognize or utilize" his services. Lehman concluded that Truman believed that he was "looking for a 'job,'" not understanding that Lehman was quite busy and had "merely sought an opportunity" to serve his country again. Looking back ten years later, Carolin Flexner, Lehman's longtime aide, complained that Truman was "pretty nasty" to Lehman and failed to appreciate Lehman's "quality." Besides the UN appointment, "which would have been right in line with the UNRRA thing," she angrily recalled that Truman could have appointed Lehman "to any number of important and interesting places," but he never did.[39]

Lehman learned some of the harsh realities of politics and realized how little influence he now had when President Truman repeatedly passed over Lehman's recommendations of his good friend and former State Housing Commissioner Edward Weinfeld for a federal judgeship in 1946–1949. As seats on the bench opened up, Lehman recommended Weinfeld to the President numerous times, and he urged Senator Wagner, Ed Flynn, and Paul Fitzpatrick to do the same, but to no avail. Lehman was encouraged when Attorney General Tom Clark and Secretary to the President William Hassett promised that Weinfeld would receive "careful consideration," but Truman, who had come up through the Pendergast political machine in Kansas City, weighed political connections more heavily than other qualifications in making judicial appointments. Thus, the first vacancy for which Lehman suggested Weinfeld went to a candidate put forward by Flynn, and the second one was filled by an applicant favored by Tammany Hall. When four new judgeships were created in the Southern District of New York in 1949, Truman acknowledged Lehman's letter endorsing Weinfeld, but the President again appointed others instead. It was not until 1950 that Fitzpatrick and Tammany leader Carmine De Sapio agreed to support Weinfeld and Truman appointed him to the bench. Not coincidentally, by that time Lehman had been elected to the U.S. Senate and enjoyed a lot more clout than he had possessed in previous years when his recommendations of Weinfeld fell on deaf ears.[40]

Despite his disappointment at not securing the UN appointment or some other high-level position for himself or a judgeship for Weinfeld, Lehman strongly supported President Truman's major domestic and foreign policy initiatives in 1947–1948. Lehman urged the Senate to confirm Truman's nomination of David Lilienthal to head the Atomic Energy Commission, endorsed the Truman Doctrine providing military and economic assistance to Greece and Turkey, and joined with a group of other prominent citizens calling for the enactment of the administration's Universal Military Training Bill. He recommended that the President veto the anti-union Taft-Hartley bill and congratulated him when he did so, and Lehman testified on behalf of Truman's efforts to allow four hundred thousand displaced persons still in camps in Europe to come to the United States. Lehman was disappointed in the final version of the displaced persons bill approved by Congress, but he believed that a bad bill was better than no bill at all, and he applauded the President's "excellent and forceful statement" when Truman signed the "odious" measure into law. The Governor welcomed the report of the President's Committee on Civil Rights and hailed Truman's request that Congress enact anti-discrimination legislation based on that study as "an act of political courage and high statesmanship." On a more personal level, Lehman was happy to comply when the President asked him to represent the administration at the dedication of the Chapel of the Four Chaplains, commemorating the heroism of the four clergymen who had given their lifejackets to others when the USS *Dorchester* had been sunk during the war.[41]

Truman did appoint Lehman to some minor posts in this period. In September 1947, the President asked Lehman to serve on a new Citizens' Food Committee. A Cabinet Committee on World Food Programs had warned of "a grave food situation abroad," emphasizing that "adverse crop developments" in "recent weeks, both in North America and in Europe, make apparent a food shortage even worse than a year ago," and as he had done in 1946, Truman appointed a committee "to advise on ways and means of carrying out the necessary conservation effort." Chaired by Charles Luckman, the president of Lever Brothers, the group was to "develop plans for bringing the vital problem of food conservation to the attention of every American for action." Lehman, who had worked so hard as Director General of UNRRA to mitigate the food crisis in 1946, immediately accepted the President's request to serve on the committee. But as had been the case in 1946, Lehman wanted to go much further than the President and most of the members of the committee. Although he did not propose "a wheatless day," as erroneously reported in the *New York Times*, Lehman suggested to Luckman that "we try to be more specific in our recommendation for the saving of bread rather than merely make an appeal to save one slice a day." As he had in 1946, Lehman proposed a return to food rationing and price controls, and he called for the establishment of a permanent agency to encourage Americans to conserve food, but his ideas were rejected by the committee.[42]

Rising above his personal frustrations, Lehman worked tirelessly on behalf of the Truman administration's European Recovery Program, more commonly known as the Marshall Plan, which he saw as necessary to finish the job of rehabilitating Europe that UNRRA had begun. Lehman gave numerous speeches in favor of the massive aid program, and he served on the executive board of the Committee for the Marshall Plan to Aid European Recovery, a nonpartisan citizens group established to rally public support for the program. Lehman and other liberals in Americans for Democratic Action hailed the Marshall Plan as "the highest point United States foreign policy has reached since the death of Roosevelt," and, representing the American Jewish Committee at hearings conducted by the Senate Foreign Relations Committee, Lehman warned that "without adequate help from us," Western Europe would experience "political unrest" and "civil strife," in which "the human freedom to which we are dedicated" would be "trampled underfoot." The Communist coup in Czechoslovakia and the Berlin Blockade deepened Lehman's concern about the future of Europe, and in June 1948, he accepted an appointment from President Truman to serve on the Public Advisory Board that Congress had mandated to "advise and consult" with the Marshall Plan administrator on "general or basic policy matters."[43]

IV

Besides the Marshall Plan, Herbert Lehman's closest interactions with Harry Truman during this period involved Palestine, where Lehman played an important but often overlooked role in the President's decision to recognize the state of Israel. In November 1947, Lehman urged France, Haiti, and other nations to support a United Nations resolution partitioning Palestine into separate Jewish and Arab states. By this time, Lehman had concluded that the only way to ensure a haven for Jewish refugees from Europe was through partition and the establishment of a Jewish state in Palestine. After the UN resolution was approved and fighting broke out between Jews and Arabs in Palestine, Lehman objected to the U.S. government's embargo on arms shipments to both sides, arguing that the ban "works solely against the disciplined Jewish community of Palestine" because the Arabs were easily obtaining weapons elsewhere. In late March 1948, Lehman and many American Jews became alarmed when the Truman administration seemed ready to abandon partition in favor of some sort of trusteeship for Palestine. Lehman joined other leaders of the American Jewish Committee (AJC) in denouncing Arab violence in Palestine and urging the United Nations to enforce its partition plan and restore the peace. The AJC reviewed previous American support for partition and expressed "its keen regret at the modification of our government's position regarding Palestine."[44]

By this time, Truman was completely fed up with the Palestine issue. Caught between the conflicting demands of Arabs and Jews living in Palestine, Jewish American voters, American oil interests, political advisors focused on the 1948 election who favored partition, State Department officials who opposed partition as inimical to American foreign policy interests, and British intransigence, Truman complained to his old Kansas City friend Eddie Jacobson:

> The situation has been a headache to me for two and a half years.
> The Jews are so emotional, and the Arabs are so difficult to talk

with that it is almost impossible to get anything done. The British, of course, have been exceedingly noncooperative in arriving at a conclusion. The Zionists, of course, have expected a big stick approach on our part, and naturally have been disappointed when we can't do that.

Truman hoped that "it will work out all right," but he had "about come to the conclusion that the situation is not solvable as presently set up."[45]

On April 20, 1948, Herbert and Edith Lehman were on vacation in Arizona, but they were spending much of their time following "the world situation," especially developments in Palestine, on the radio. Not wanting to cut himself off from the decisions being made in Washington and elsewhere, the Governor instructed Carolin Flexner not to hesitate to give out his phone number if "any of the Palestine people" tried to reach him, although he did not see how he "could be of any particular assistance at this time" beyond what he had already done. Lehman soon got his chance to do more when President Truman asked him to "come down to Washington one day next week for a little visit," the first time since Lehman had resigned from UNRRA that Truman had invited him to the White House for a one-on-one meeting. The British mandate in Palestine was scheduled to end at midnight on May 14, and the President was in a quandary over what to do, receiving conflicting advice from his political aides and the State Department. He hoped that Lehman, who had never been associated with the Zionists or any of the more militant Jewish elements, could provide some insight into the thinking of moderate, traditional Jewish leaders and offer advice on how to proceed. As Lehman explained to Carolin Flexner, he was "in complete disagreement" with the President's "entire procedure on the Palestine tragedy," so he looked forward to the meeting as an opportunity to educate Truman and change his mind about how the United States should proceed in Palestine.[46]

Armed with the latest information from the Jewish Agency, Lehman discussed Palestine with the President at the White House on May 4. No record exists of their conversation, but both men seem to have been pleased with the meeting. A few days later, Lehman informed the President that he had been "so deeply interested in the subject which we discussed last Tuesday that I neglected to mention another matter which I had wished to bring to your attention" (a recommendation for a judicial appointment), and Truman added a handwritten message on the bottom of his response saying it had been "a pleasure to talk with you." When Lehman met with the press immediately after the meeting, he declined to reveal what the President had said, but he described Truman as "deeply interested and concerned about the situation" in Palestine. The Governor elaborated on his own views, which presumably he had just conveyed to the President. According to the *New York Times*, Lehman advocated "a trusteeship for the entire area of Jerusalem" and emphasized his support for "partition, with an international force to maintain peace." He also called for "the exclusion of all armed forces from Arab countries" and "a limited truce of three or four months under which there would be no final determination with regard to partition or trusteeship, but which would provide for substantial immigration and land purchase and free ingress and egress in all Palestine for peaceful people." Worried that he had not explained his position clearly and that early press reports had underplayed his support for partition, Lehman issued a clarification when he returned to New York, explaining that the proposed truce was designed to give the United Nations more time to arrive at a solution for Palestine. In the meantime, he declared, there should be "an acceptance of de facto occupation and administration by Jews of the Jewish part of Palestine."[47]

The President had told Lehman that if he "had any further thoughts on the Palestine question" to communicate them directly. Seizing the opportunity, Lehman submitted to Truman on May 5 a memorandum that he believed merited the President's "very serious consideration." Charles Fahy of the Jewish Agency had given the document to Undersecretary of State Robert Lovett the previous day, but Jewish leaders feared that the State Department might bury the message rather than showing it to the President, so they used Lehman as an alternative route to get it to the President. Fahy argued in the memorandum that "the United States should recognize the fact that the Jewish State will be proclaimed May 15th or 16th" and asserted that the American government should not take any action "between now and then which commits the United States to oppose such a State or which would encourage the Arab States to seek to overthrow it." The United States, Fahy warned, "must be very careful not to substitute ourselves for the British as opponents of Jewish aspirations for independence." Partition was about to become a reality, and Jewish success on the battlefield had "obviated the need for the U.N. to implement partition by force." Instead, Fahy insisted, "the U.N. needs to make clear to the Arab States that they must not use force against it." Truman "appreciated very much" Lehman's "sending me the views on Palestine in the memorandum of Mr. Fahy," and the President kept the document close at hand rather than dispatching it immediately to the files.[48]

As the date neared when the British mandate in Palestine would end, Lehman joined other prominent American Jews in asking the President to recognize the new Jewish state that would come into being. After speaking with Zionist leader Rabbi Abba Hillel Silver, Lehman wrote to the President on May 13, urging Truman to "recognize as promptly as possible the provisional government which will be proclaimed in Palestine on the termination of the mandate." Lehman recommended American recognition "as a matter of simple justice," but he also used the growing Cold War tensions with the Soviet Union to Israel's advantage, asserting that "it would be most unfortunate if other governments less sympathetic to our democratic way of life should give recognition before we did." Truman thanked Lehman for his letter, noting that "apparently our minds were running in the same channel." On May 14, as soon as the United States received official word that "a Jewish state has been proclaimed in Palestine and recognition has been requested by the provisional government thereof," the President announced that "the United States recognizes the provisional government as the de facto authority of the new State of Israel." Lehman immediately sent Truman his "sincerest congratulation and heartfelt thanks on your wise and just action in promptly recognizing the new State of Israel," assuring the President that "the great mass of American people regardless of religious faith will approve your course."[49]

Herbert Lehman was not the only Jewish leader in contact with Truman about Palestine in early May, and his influence with the President was certainly less than that of Truman's old friend and former business partner Eddie Jacobson and Zionist leader Chaim Weizmann. Nonetheless, it is noteworthy that Lehman was the only outsider invited to the White House to discuss the matter at this crucial time. Lehman's main contribution came in convincing the President that the vast majority of American Jews, including those who had never been associated with Zionism, now supported the establishment of the State of Israel.[50]

V

Political considerations obviously factored into Truman's decision to recognize Israel in 1948, a presidential election year, and Herbert Lehman enthusiastically and energetically supported Truman's re-election. The President faced a difficult contest against probable Republican candidate Thomas Dewey, and his troubles were compounded in December 1947 when Henry Wallace announced that he would run as a third-party candidate, appealing to liberals and progressives who sought a more conciliatory foreign policy toward the Soviet Union and a more active domestic program. Lehman forcefully denounced Wallace's candidacy, warning that it would result in "the election of reactionaries by dividing the liberal vote."[51]

Lehman stayed solidly in Truman's corner even when other Democrats urged that the President be replaced at the top of the ticket by General Eisenhower or some other candidate. As Lehman explained to Carolin Flexner in late April, except for Palestine, he believed that the President "has been unusually courageous in many ways and, on the whole," Lehman "agreed with most" of Truman's policies. When FDR's oldest son James Roosevelt, New York City

Mayor William O'Dwyer, Minneapolis Mayor Hubert Humphrey, and others sought to draft Eisenhower shortly before the Democratic National Convention, Lehman remained steadfast in supporting Truman.[52]

Herbert Lehman did join a different campaign led by Hubert Humphrey in 1948: the effort to include in the 1948 Democratic Party platform a strong plank endorsing the recommendations of President Truman's Committee on Civil Rights. As Humphrey explained in a letter to Lehman, southern Democrats' criticism of the report had dominated the public reaction, and he believed that "it was essential, both for the moral position of our party and for reasons of political realism," that northern and western Democrats make clear their support for specific action guaranteeing political, civil, and economic rights for all Americans. Lehman immediately added his name to the statement that Humphrey had drafted, and he looked forward to the Democratic National Convention and the debate over the controversial platform provision. However, the death of his sister, Hattie Goodhart, prevented Lehman from attending the convention where a strong civil rights plank was adopted over the protests of southern delegates, who walked out and subsequently nominated South Carolina Governor Strom Thurmond as the presidential candidate of the States' Rights Party.[53]

The combination of Dewey's proven popularity among New Yorkers and Wallace siphoning off left-wing votes made it unlikely that the President would carry the Empire State. State Democratic Chairman Paul Fitzpatrick insisted, however, that Truman had a chance in New York, that New Yorkers were not as fond of Dewey as it seemed, and that Wallace's campaign was losing ground as the election approached. The President accepted Fitzpatrick's advice that he make a quick trip across Upstate New York and a series of appearances in New York City near the end of the campaign, and on October 8, he traveled by train from Albany to Buffalo, stopping at numerous points along the way to attack "the 80th Republican 'do-nothing' Congress." The President belittled Dewey's claim to represent a new, more liberal brand of Republicanism, charging that the current Governor had been "forced to take a few steps along progressive lines, laid down by Alfred E. Smith, Herbert Lehman and Franklin D. Roosevelt." But he warned that "the Republican Party still stands for the old policies of taking care of the rich and letting the rest of us shift for ourselves."[54]

Herbert Lehman supported President Truman in 1948 in a number of ways. Lehman contributed generously to both the Democratic National Committee and the Democratic State Committee's fund-raising efforts, and he joined other New Dealers who had been closely associated with Franklin Roosevelt in trying to persuade voters to reject Henry Wallace's candidacy. In a statement released through Americans for Democratic Action, Lehman and others charged that Wallace's Progressive Party "represents a corruption of American liberalism" and "a betrayal of free people throughout the world." In the struggle "between those who believe in human freedom and those who do not," they declared, Wallace and his followers had "lined up unashamedly with the forces of Soviet totalitarianism." As for Wallace's domestic policies, Lehman and the others dismissed them as "merely an imitation of the Democratic Party program, touched up point by point in a demagogic attempt to outbid everybody for everything."[55]

In early October, Lehman wondered why he had not been asked to deliver any speeches on the President's behalf. Truman was in trouble with Jewish voters who were upset that the administration had apparently shifted its Palestine policy yet again, endorsing the Bernadotte plan that would strip Israel of two-thirds of its territory. The Truman campaign finally realized how crucial Lehman's help might be in winning back liberal Jewish voters who were leaning toward Wallace, or other Jews who were supporting Dewey because of their anger at the President's inconsistency on Palestine. In mid-October, the President and his advisors reached out to Lehman, inviting the Governor and Mrs. Lehman to a White House reception and enlisting Lehman to deliver three major speeches for Truman in the closing days of the campaign.[56]

As the campaign continued, Truman's problems with Jewish voters mounted. The President and his aides had agreed with Dewey and John Foster Dulles, Dewey's principal foreign policy advisor, that Israel was too important and too controversial an issue to allow it to become a political football to be kicked around, so neither side was speaking out on the subject. As a result, Truman ignored the advice of Chester Bowles, the Democratic candidate for Governor in Connecticut, who had counseled that a pro-Israeli statement or gesture at the time of the Jewish High Holidays in late September would "help as far as registration is concerned" among Jewish voters in his state and in New York. The President remained silent, and as Bowles had feared, the number of registrants in New York City, with its large Jewish population, dropped by 243,000 votes, while upstate, where the number of Jews was much smaller, registration increased by seventy-three thousand. The American Zionist Emergency Council, in a large ad in the *New York Times* on October 20, highlighted the contradiction between the Democratic Party platform's support for Israeli boundaries as outlined in the 1947 United Nations partition plan and the administration's acceptance of the Bernadotte plan, which significantly reduced Israeli territory. In big bold letters, the ad asked, "MR TRUMAN: Where Do *You* Stand on This Issue?" But the agreement between the parties prevented the President from responding.[57]

Lehman stepped into the breach at the very moment when Truman most needed help with Jewish voters, but he, too, was bound by the agreement not to make Israel a campaign issue. Therefore, Lehman did not mention Palestine or Israel during his first speech on Truman's behalf, a statewide radio broadcast on October 22. Instead, Lehman stressed domestic issues, emphasizing the gains farmers, workers, enlightened industrialists, legitimate investors, and small business owners had made in the last sixteen years under Democratic Presidents. Focusing on liberals who might be considering voting for Wallace or sitting out the election, Lehman insisted that "our best chance of maintaining and extending the principles of government for which liberal-minded Americans must constantly fight is under the leadership of the courageous Democratic President, Harry S. Truman, and a Democratic Congress."[58]

On the same day that Lehman made his speech defending the President, Dewey committed a major blunder when he released a letter asserting that "the Jewish people are entitled to a homeland in Palestine which would be politically and economically stable." Trying to capitalize on the disparity between the Democratic platform and the Truman administration's recent actions, Dewey emphasized his "whole-hearted support of the Republican platform," including "the Palestine plank." Presidential aide Clark Clifford immediately reported to Truman that Dewey had broken the agreement not to mention Palestine during the campaign. According to Clifford, this was "the best thing that has happened to us to date," because it meant that Truman and the Democrats were now free to defend the President's record on Palestine. Clifford explained to the State Department that Dewey had attacked the President's integrity by charging that Truman had "reneged on [the] Democratic Platform," and that the President had "to reaffirm his support of [the] Democratic Platform."[59]

Following Clifford's advice, Truman issued a lengthy statement on Israel two days later in which he declared that he stood "squarely on the provisions covering Israel in the Democratic platform," which endorsed "the claim of Israel to the boundaries set forth in the United Nations' resolution of Nov. 29" and "revision of the arms embargo" to allow Israel to defend itself. He criticized Dewey for injecting the Palestine issue into the campaign, reminded everyone that he had extended de facto recognition to the State of Israel, promised de jure recognition as soon as Israel had elected a permanent government, and pledged to expedite any loan requests made by the Israelis. The plan presently under consideration by the United Nations, Truman asserted, was intended only "as a basis of negotiation," and he emphasized that any modification of the borders put forth in 1947 "should be made only if fully acceptable to the State of Israel."[60]

As Democratic National Committee Publicity Director Jack Redding later recalled, Lehman's "voice was a potent one in Jewish circles in New York," so when Truman campaigned in New York City in late October, Democratic leaders sought to counter Jewish concern over the administration's Palestine policy by maximizing Lehman's involvement in the President's visit. Lehman agreed to be part of the committee greeting Truman upon his arrival at Grand Central Station and to serve as vice chairman of the Committee to Welcome President Truman at City Hall, but the funeral of Rabbi Judah Magnes, an old friend who had officiated at Herbert and Edith Lehman's wedding, prevented Lehman from carrying out these assignments. He did join Truman on the platform at a huge rally sponsored by the Liberal Party at Madison Square Garden on October 28, posing for pictures with the President and listening attentively as Truman restated his support for Israel and the borders recommended in 1947. Later that night, Truman asked Secretary Marshall to postpone any UN action on Israel until after the election.[61]

In his own remarks at the rally, Lehman delivered a ringing call for the President's re-election, reminding the audience that under the Republicans in 1932, workers could be fired for joining a union, employers were not required to negotiate with labor, and there was no Social Security or minimum wage. Lehman stressed that it was under Franklin Roosevelt's leadership in Washington and his own stewardship in Albany that effective labor legislation had been enacted on both the federal and state levels in the 1930s, and he resented Dewey's attempt "to claim credit for our enlightened labor program" that had been enacted "over ruthless Republican opposition during the previous twenty years." Lehman charged that "not only has Governor Dewey failed to extend the social gains won by Democratic Governors, . . . but he has been responsible for many pieces of affirmatively bad social legislation," such as "the raid on the unemployment insurance fund of nearly 300 million dollars for the benefit of favored business." Republican rhetoric, Lehman emphasized, had to be measured against "the record of Republican non-performance or mal-performance," and he warned that Republicans must not be allowed to enact other statutes like the Taft-Hartley Act that would take the country "back to the days before 1932."[62]

Although Dewey was still favored to win in New York, Democratic leaders felt momentum starting to shift in Truman's direction in the last days of the campaign. Wallace's support continued to fall as many liberals concluded that the Progressive Party was under Communist control and that a vote for Wallace would help elect Dewey. Trying to pull out all the stops, Democrats appealed to Eleanor Roosevelt to deliver a radio address for Truman from Paris, where she was attending the meetings of the United Nations. After some initial reluctance, Mrs. Roosevelt agreed to do the broadcast, and Democratic leaders quickly arranged for vice presidential candidate Alben Barkley to introduce Mrs. Roosevelt and Herbert Lehman to follow her remarks with some comments of his own. In her talk, Mrs. Roosevelt praised President Truman's courage and stressed that he "needs the people's mandate to help him if he's going to continue to be our President." Concluding the broadcast, Lehman expressed his confidence that "the majority of the American people know whom they can trust, and will vote on Tuesday for President Truman and Senator Barkley and a liberal-minded Congress." Lehman also included his name in a Liberal Party ad that appeared in the *New York Times* on November 1 that featured a letter from Mrs. Roosevelt supporting Truman's re-election and declared that "the entire New Deal political family of Franklin Delano Roosevelt and his closest co-workers whole-heartedly endorse the candidacy of Harry S. Truman for President."[63]

In one of the greatest upsets in American political history, Truman defeated Dewey and won another term as President in 1948. In New York, where Dewey's familiarity as Governor, Wallace's presence on the ballot, an increase in voter registration upstate, and a drop in New York City registration figures were expected to result in a 400,000 vote plurality for Dewey, the Republican Governor carried the state by only 61,000 votes. If not for the 510,000 votes for Henry Wallace, Truman would have easily defeated Dewey in New York too. Nationally, organized labor, liberals, African Americans, farmers, and other remnants of FDR's old coalition turned out for Truman in large enough numbers to offset left-wing votes lost to Henry Wallace and southern defections to Strom Thurmond, enabling the President to win re-election.[64]

Even though Truman failed to capture New York State, Democratic leaders appreciated all Herbert Lehman had done to help Truman close the gap in the Empire State. The day after Lehman's broadcast with Eleanor Roosevelt, Ed Flynn, remembering Lehman's disappointment at not being asked to participate until the final weeks of the campaign and his concern over the President's waffling on Palestine, thanked the Governor for making the speech and showing himself "to be the 'big man' " that Flynn always knew him to be. Flynn noted that there were "very few people who would have been as selfless" as Lehman had been in this campaign, asserting that it was men like Lehman "who make America great." Democratic State Chairman Paul Fitzpatrick emphasized that Lehman's "inspiring and statesmanlike speeches were a tremendous influence in the outcome of the election," and that "when the chips were down," Lehman "stood shoulder to shoulder with us in the fight for the Democratic Party." Commenting on Truman's "great victory," Lehman told Fitzpatrick how proud he was "to have had a part in it."[65]

Lehman and Truman gained new respect for each other from the 1948 election. Thrilled that Truman and the Democrats had carried the day, Lehman immediately cabled Truman "heartiest congratulations" on his "great victory" and gave the President "the highest credit" for his "courageous fight in the face of great odds." Lehman stressed to Ed Flynn how pleased he was "over the result of the election," which he believed was "a tribute not only to President Truman's great courage and fighting qualities, but . . . also an endorsement by the American people of a liberal program for this country." The President appreciated Lehman's efforts on his behalf, especially Lehman's remarks on the radio broadcast with Eleanor Roosevelt, thanking Lehman for the "great speech you made Sunday night before [the] election."[66]

CHAPTER 12

"If You Could See the Kind of People in New York City Making Up This Bloc That Is Voting for My Opponent"

Lehman and the Election of 1949

I know that Governor Lehman, when he comes to the Senate, will work for the liberal policies which mean greater progress and a better life for the people of New York and of the whole country.[1]

I

Herbert Lehman had never abandoned his dream of serving in the U.S. Senate, and another opportunity to realize that goal suddenly opened up in 1949. Senator Robert Wagner had been in ill health for more than two years, and on June 28, 1949, he resigned from the Senate. Governor Dewey promptly appointed John Foster Dulles, his longtime foreign policy advisor, to fill the vacancy, but Wagner had timed his resignation in such a way that state law required a special election in November to determine who would serve the final year of Wagner's Senate term.[2]

Democrats and Liberal Party leaders quickly coalesced around Herbert Lehman as their strongest candidate against Dulles, remembering, as the *New York Times* noted, that Lehman had "finished 400,000 votes ahead of the top

---

Chapter title quotation: John Foster Dulles quoted in "Czech Church Curb an Omen to Dulles," *New York Times*, October 6, 1949, p. 26.

of his ticket" when he had run for the Senate in 1946. On June 22, the Liberal Party policy committee unanimously declared that "Lehman was the logical choice" for Wagner's seat, and on June 29, newly elected Representative Franklin Roosevelt, Jr., removed himself from consideration, recommending instead that "the Democratic Party should follow the great tradition of Senator Wagner" by sending his " 'Uncle Herbert' Lehman to Congress." Labor leaders and Liberal Party stalwarts David Dubinsky and Alex Rose urged Lehman to accept the Senate nomination, as did Democratic State Chairman Paul Fitzpatrick, National Committee member and Bronx boss Ed Flynn, and New York City Mayor William O'Dwyer. Clark Eichelberger, executive director of the American Association for the United Nations, conceded that after the many years Lehman had devoted to public service, he was "entitled to a vacation from such duties," but he hoped that the Governor would take advantage of this "great opportunity . . . not only to stand for liberal domestic policies but for the United Nations." Lehman's old friend Lithgow Osborne spoke for many of the Governor's former associates and colleagues when he sent the following simple message: "Please run!"[3]

As Lehman confided to his old UNRRA associate Commander Robert G. A. Jackson, "the desire of so many people" that he run was "very gratifying." But when Democratic State Chairman Fitzpatrick and Ed Flynn met with Lehman on July 7 to report that "leaders of the Democratic Party throughout the state are in accord in urging that he be the Democratic candidate for United States Senator," Lehman surprised them by refusing to commit to the race, promising only to give them "an early answer." As Lehman explained to Jackson, "acceptance of the nomination would, in all probability, require making a hard campaign, the outcome of which, of course, would not be sure." Moreover, the Governor noted, he and Mrs. Lehman had come to value the "personal freedom" they had enjoyed in recent years to go where they wanted and do what they wanted, and they were not sure they were ready to give up that independence and flexibility.[4]

The complicated political situation in New York City contributed to Lehman's hesitancy, as he wanted to see how the Mayor's race, which was also on the ballot in 1949, shaped up before he committed to the Senate contest. President Truman, labor leaders, and others were pressing incumbent Mayor William O'Dwyer to reverse his earlier decision not to seek re-election, and Lehman hoped that O'Dwyer, by far the Democrats' strongest candidate, would run alongside him on the Democratic ticket. Lehman also thought that he might be able to persuade the Liberal Party to endorse O'Dwyer so that Lehman would not be placed in the awkward position of having different running mates on the Democratic and Liberal Party lines. But despite Lehman's efforts, the Liberals made it clear that they would not support O'Dwyer because of his ties to Tammany Hall.[5]

In his letter to Jackson, Lehman referred mysteriously to "some other matters which unfortunately have come up lately and which are very distasteful." He did not go into specifics, but the *New York Times* reported on July 11, 1949, that "some Catholic opposition to Mr. Lehman has developed because of his membership on a committee" that had opposed the banning of *The Nation* from New York City schools in 1948 when the magazine had published a series of allegedly anti-Catholic articles. Lehman's relations with Catholics had always been somewhat problematic, going back to his time as Governor when he had pushed for the adoption of the Child Labor amendment despite the Church's opposition, and had vetoed a bill to provide free transportation to private and parochial school children. During the controversy over *The Nation*, Francis Cardinal Spellman, head of New York's Catholic archdiocese, had taken Lehman to task, noting that the Church had "cooperated in having anti-Semitic publications banned from public institutions" and wondering why, therefore, Lehman's name was "linked to anti-Catholic groups." In response, Lehman had stressed his disappointment that the Cardinal had "interpret[ed] my protest against the banning of *The Nation* as linking me in any way with 'anti-Catholic groups.' " The Governor emphasized that he had always "opposed every attempt to throttle freedom of expression, even when such expressions were abhorrent" to him, and he asserted that to ban *The Nation* "without a public hearing, on the strength of one series of articles," was "undemocratic and dangerous in its implications." With Lehman emerging as the frontrunner for the Democratic nomination for the Senate in 1949, both State Democratic Chairman Paul Fitzpatrick and the *New York Times* received anonymous letters warning that many Catholics would not support Lehman if he were the Democratic candidate. According to the *Times*, Lehman's concern that "his candidacy might subject him to a 'whispering' campaign that he would not wish to go through . . . is believed to be a major factor in Mr. Lehman's reluctance to accept the senatorial nomination."[6]

The same day that the story appeared in the *New York Times* about Catholic opposition to Lehman's Senate candidacy, Eleanor Roosevelt warned Lehman that she had been told that Cardinal Spellman was "going to ask the Catholics of the State to oppose" Lehman because of his efforts "to prevent *The Nation* from being banned from public schools." Mrs. Roosevelt thought that this rumor "seems too stupid to be true," but she noted that "the Cardinal has been doing stupid things of late." Nonetheless, she could not take "this threat of Catholic opposition . . . very seriously" because Catholics knew from Lehman's years as Governor that "no one has ever been fairer to all races and creeds." Mrs. Roosevelt assured Lehman that if he ran for the Senate, "the State of New York should be deeply grateful" for his "willingness to serve," and she promised to do everything she could to help in his campaign. She believed that Catholics were "certainly heading into deep waters" if they were "going to oppose as a candidate a person as well fitted" as Herbert Lehman was for the Senate.[7]

Herbert and Edith Lehman appreciated Mrs. Roosevelt's "opinion and advice" as well as her support. The Governor confided that he was "very much troubled" by the Catholic situation. It was "almost inconceivable" to Lehman "that the very people who must know" that he had spent his "entire life" fighting "for religious and racial understanding" and had always "shown equal respect for all religions" would now be attacking him because he "dared to ask for a public hearing on the banning of a magazine that had had a creditable record of 85 years." Many people were urging Lehman to run for the Senate, but since the formal nominating convention would not occur until September, he planned "to look on for a time before coming to any final decision or making any formal announcement."[8]

A week later, when Cardinal Spellman broadened his fire and targeted Mrs. Roosevelt, Herbert Lehman rushed to her defense. The Cardinal claimed that Mrs. Roosevelt's recent newspaper columns criticizing his insistence that any federal funds going to the states for education should include parochial as well as public schools were merely the latest entry in her "record of anti-Catholicism." He accused her of "discrimination unworthy of an American mother" and charged that she "could have acted only from misinformation, ignorance or prejudice." As Edith Lehman later recalled, when Herbert Lehman "saw the Cardinal's statement," he told his wife: "I'm going to speak out . . . but we may as well kiss the senatorship goodbye." Ignoring the risk to his potential Senate candidacy, Lehman declared that he was "deeply shocked at the attack of Cardinal Spellman on Mrs. Roosevelt." Stressing his belief "that in our American democracy every responsible citizen is entitled to express his or her views without being subjected to the accusation of being against any religion or any race," Lehman emphasized that "the issue is not whether one agrees or disagrees with Mrs. Roosevelt on this or any other public question. The issue is whether Americans are entitled freely to express their views on public questions without being vilified or accused of religious bias." The Governor noted that "Mrs. Roosevelt has been a public figure for twenty-five years" and in all that time, he did "not know of a single act or word that would in the slightest degree indicate bias or prejudice against any religion or any race." In fact, Lehman asserted, "her whole life has been dedicated to a constant fight for tolerance and brotherhood of men as children of one God," and he was confident that Mrs. Roosevelt would "retain the trust and the affection of all peoples irrespective of creed or race."[9]

Looking back years later, Lehman categorized his defense of Mrs. Roosevelt as "the most courageous act" of his public life. He recalled that he had issued his statement supporting Mrs. Roosevelt "without consultation with any political figures and in simple justice to Mrs. Roosevelt." When asked at the time whether his disagreements with Cardinal Spellman would influence his possible Senate candidacy, Lehman declared that they would have no effect on his decision, asserting that there was "absolutely no relationship to it at all." Letters and telegrams poured in urging him to run despite the potential problem with Catholic voters. Freda Kirchwey, the editor of *The Nation*, expressed her regret that Lehman's courage in calling for a hearing before the magazine was banned had exposed him "to the attack of some of our Catholic friends," and she hoped that Lehman's "reluctance to run for the Senate was neither caused nor increased by Catholic criticism" of his defense of *The Nation*. She advised Lehman not to "give too much weight to the views of a few bigoted—and anonymous—opponents." Democratic Party stalwart Herbert Bayard Swope recommended that Lehman "accept the nomination for the Senate" despite "the threatened opposition of the Catholic Church," arguing that "the Church is making a dangerous error" and that it was Lehman's "duty to yourself, to the country and to the electorate to withstand dictatorial threats." Similarly, Algernon Black of the Society for Ethical Culture asserted that there was no one who stood "for the same principles" as Lehman "or who could bring the same years of experience and wise judgment to public affairs," and Black predicted, "It would give a tremendous new surge of strength and courage to those who have understood and tried to keep faith with the Roosevelt tradition" to have Lehman in a position where he "could help make policy in the crucial years that lie ahead."[10]

Lehman refused to be rushed into deciding whether to run for the Senate. As he told Freda Kirchwey, he knew that he "would enjoy being in the Senate" and believed that he "could make a useful contribution at this time," but there were "a number of considerations" besides potential Catholic opposition that he wanted to weigh. Even after Mayor O'Dwyer agreed to stand for re-election, strengthening the Democratic ticket, Lehman remained undecided about whether to run.[11]

Lehman's delay led some of his supporters to fear that Democratic Party leaders had cooled on his candidacy. On July 25, right after Lehman had defended Mrs. Roosevelt against Cardinal Spellman's attack, the *New York Post*, which had close ties to Eleanor Roosevelt and Americans for Democratic Action and a large readership among liberal, Jewish, working-class voters and intellectuals, asserted that Lehman's support for *The Nation* and Mrs. Roosevelt had turned the Democratic leaders' attitude toward his candidacy to "lukewarm." The *Post* cited as evidence the Democrats' failure to start a "Draft Lehman" committee to persuade him to run, and the silence of Ed Flynn, Mayor O'Dwyer, and Democratic State Chairman Fitzpatrick over the past few weeks "in the face of a whispering campaign started against the former Governor." All three leaders had originally urged Lehman to make the race, but the *Post* charged that they were backing away now because of Catholic opposition to Lehman. A few weeks later, a story in the *New York Daily News*, whose working-class readers tended to be more conservative Democrats, gave another reason why Democratic leaders might have lost some of their enthusiasm for a Lehman Senate candidacy: fear that Lehman running as the Democratic and Liberal candidate for the Senate might draw support to his running mates on the Liberal Party line, hurting the re-election chances of Mayor O'Dwyer, who was running only on the Democratic ticket. But Lehman emphasized years later that Flynn and Fitzpatrick never pressured him to withdraw his possible Senate candidacy because of his defense of Mrs. Roosevelt or his potential problem with Catholic voters.[12]

The *Post* article achieved the desired results; over the next few days, Democratic and Liberal Party leaders made it clear that they supported Lehman's candidacy despite the Catholic issue. The *New York Times* reported on July 28, 1949, that Flynn and Fitzpatrick still wanted Lehman as the Democratic candidate for the Senate. David Dubinsky, president of the International Ladies' Garment Workers' Union and a power in the Liberal Party, informed Lehman that local managers of the ILGWU "join with all liberal and progressive citizens in urging you to accept the nomination for United States Senator." A few days later, Adolf Berle, Jr., state chairman of the Liberal Party, renewed the group's formal invitation to Lehman to be its candidate for the Senate, pledging "the devoted support of all liberals," as well as Lehman's "many friends and admirers throughout the State."[13]

Perhaps the strongest argument for Lehman to run came from Jonathan Bingham, who was one of the leaders of the New York chapter of Americans for Democratic Action (ADA) and was married to Lehman's great-niece. Jonathan and June Bingham were both "very proud" of Lehman's "courageous statement on the Roosevelt-Spellman controversy," but Bingham emphasized to Lehman that "one of the consequences of the statement . . . is that it becomes terribly important for the future of the Democratic Party" that Lehman "run for the Senate." If Lehman were "not the Democratic candidate now," Bingham warned, "after what has happened, a great many liberals will become thoroughly disillusioned and disgusted with our party." As for the argument that Lehman "should stay out of the race in order to preserve party harmony," Bingham reported that from his vantage point, "few Catholics agree with Cardinal Spellman's tactics (even though they may agree with his stand on the issue)," so Lehman's "nomination would not cause the loss of any substantial Catholic support." Bingham asserted that "even if it did mean the loss of some support from that direction," it was "more important in the long run to preserve the party's standing with the independent liberal voters."[14]

Lehman worried that his candidacy might worsen the religious differences highlighted by the conflict between Mrs. Roosevelt and Cardinal Spellman, and that Catholic defections might cost him the election. But much to Lehman's relief, cooler heads prevailed upon Cardinal Spellman to make peace with Mrs. Roosevelt. Mayor O'Dwyer, a Catholic, recommended that "mutual friends . . . should bring about an understanding" between the Cardinal and the former First Lady, and Ed Flynn, who believed that this kind of religious division was very dangerous for the Democrats and for the nation, made a quick trip to Rome to meet with Pope Pius XII. Shortly thereafter, Flynn facilitated a phone conversation between Mrs. Roosevelt and Cardinal Spellman, during which they agreed to issue statements designed to defuse the conflict. The Cardinal explained that Catholics were asking for federal money only for auxiliary services such as transportation, and he declared: "I believe in and shall ever uphold the American right of free speech which not only permits but encourages differences of opinion." Mrs. Roosevelt stressed that the Cardinal had reached out to her, and that she considered his statement "clarifying and fair," and the Pope shared with a small group of American newspaper correspondents his satisfaction that the controversy had been resolved. As for Herbert Lehman, he was "very glad that a very regrettable incident has ended."[15]

Mrs. Roosevelt felt badly that she had exacerbated the tension between Lehman and the Catholic Church, and she did all she could to ensure that Lehman received strong support from Democratic leaders and that Cardinal Spellman would not work against Lehman's candidacy. When she was asked to serve as one of the honorary chairmen of Mayor O'Dwyer's re-election committee, Mrs. Roosevelt accepted only after she was assured that "Lehman would be nominated and would have the *full* support of the Democratic high command." When the Cardinal stopped by at Hyde Park for tea—the final step in their public reconciliation—Mrs. Roosevelt noted that there were rumors that the Cardinal was "opposed to Governor Lehman." Resorting to practical political arguments that she knew would be more effective with the Cardinal than appeals to morality or idealism, she warned that "if the figures show that the Catholic vote has gone appreciably against Lehman, it will make it impossible for any Catholic to get elected in this state for many years to come. Because a lot of liberals, Jews, and Protestants will be very resentful." The Cardinal quickly declared that he was "not opposed to Governor Lehman" and promised to "get in touch with Ed Flynn" as soon as possible to make his position clear.[16]

Resolution of the conflict between Cardinal Spellman and Mrs. Roosevelt intensified efforts to persuade Lehman to run for the Senate. The *New York Post* contrasted the "heavy pressure" Liberal Party leaders were exerting to persuade Lehman to run with the alleged inaction of Democratic leaders, who, according to the *Post*, had "not contacted him in nearly a month." Again, the *Post* story had the desired effect, leading Ed Flynn to declare: "I was for Lehman; I am for Lehman; I'll be for Lehman." Sporting goods retailer Henry Modell organized a committee to draft Lehman for the Senate and announced that both Flynn and State Democratic Chairman Fitzpatrick had assured him that Lehman's role in the controversy between Cardinal Spellman and Mrs. Roosevelt had not altered their support for his candidacy. Fitzpatrick and Mayor O'Dwyer spoke to Lehman on the phone, and Liberal Party leaders Alex Rose and David

Dubinsky lunched with him on August 11, all of them urging Lehman to run. Eleanor Roosevelt, used her "My Day" newspaper column on August 29, 1949, to extoll Lehman's virtues, emphasizing that "he has the heart and the experience to understand problems affecting human beings."[17]

The campaign to draft Lehman for the Senate soon reached President Truman. Henry Modell's Citizens Committee to Draft Lehman for the U.S. Senate wanted to enlist the President as one of its honorary chairmen, but White House aide Matthew Connelly explained that it would not be appropriate for the President to get involved in this kind of endeavor. Nonetheless, at his press conference on August 25, the President said that he "would be happy to see Governor Lehman in the Senate of the United States," although he claimed that he was "not in New York politics" and that this decision would be "up to the State of New York." Privately, however, the President told Lehman that he "hope[d] the New York Democrats have finally worked out a ticket that will win this fall and next year too," and he was "certainly glad to hear" that "you expect to be the next Senator from New York."[18]

On August 30, 1949, Herbert Lehman met with Alex Rose and David Dubinsky of the Liberal Party, and the following day he met with Henry Modell of the Draft Lehman Committee and then with Democratic Party leaders Paul Fitzpatrick and Ed Flynn. After his meeting with Fitzpatrick and Flynn, Lehman formally announced on August 31 that he had "informed the leaders of both the Democratic and Liberal Parties" that he had accepted the offer to be their candidate for United States Senator. Lehman asserted that "no post in the gift of the people offers a greater chance for public service . . . in view of the critical and challenging character of the issues which confront us in both the domestic and foreign fields," and he "welcome[d] the opportunity of participating in the solution of these issues." Lehman emphasized that "the warmth and insistence of the demand" that he run, which came "from so many quarters" and which he "deeply appreciate[d] as an expression of confidence," had played a major role in his final decision. Asked if he had "sought assurances from his political backers that prominent Roman Catholic laymen would serve on his campaign committee," Lehman declared that he had "no intention of forming a Catholic committee" any more than he had "of forming a Jewish committee." He was confident that "voters of the Catholic faith will approach their political duties in exactly the same spirit of good citizenship as those of the Protestant and Jewish faiths."[19]

II

Once Lehman announced his candidacy, President Truman quickly declared his support. When the President was asked about Lehman at a press conference on September 1, Truman made it clear that he was pleased with

Lehman's decision and revealed that he had written to Lehman a week ago "and told him I hoped he would run." Asked if he thought Lehman would win, the President proclaimed "Yes he will. Of course he will." The President's enthusiasm for Lehman reflected his gratitude for Lehman's support during the 1948 presidential election, as well as his antipathy toward John Foster Dulles, Lehman's likely rival. After one of their first meetings, when Dulles noted that the President had "made a 'pretty good' speech," Truman privately described the longtime lawyer and diplomat as "a stuffed shirt," and the President resented Dulles's actions in 1948 when, after negotiating with the Russians in Paris, Dulles traveled to Albany to brief Governor Dewey before reporting to the President or the Secretary of State. According to Truman's daughter Margaret, her father told Dulles that Lehman would win because Lehman "knew how to talk to the average man in New York," in contrast to Dulles, who had "been making millions for the big fellows so long" that he did not "know what people really think or what they're like."[20]

On September 7, 1949, when Dulles officially announced his candidacy to retain the Senate seat to which Governor Dewey had appointed him, he defined "statism" and the "welfare state" as the key issues in the election. Dulles warned, "in every country, including our own, powerful central governments" were "assuming an almost total responsibility for public welfare," and he asserted that this "trend to statism," whether one called it " 'dictatorship of the prole-tariat,' or the 'welfare state' or the 'fair deal,' . . . unless stopped, will be for everyone a bad deal."[21]

Dulles's candidacy and his attack on the Fair Deal as "statism" came up at the President's news conference on September 8. Asked what he thought about "Dulles getting bitten by the political bug," Truman refused to comment except to say that "any man has a right to run for office if he wants to." When a reporter asked if the President could define "statism," Truman replied, "I don't think I can, because the dictionaries are in disagreement as to what it means. I don't think anybody knows what it means. It simply is a scare word." Asked if he expected "to make a political speech in New York before November," the President said he probably would do so if it would be helpful.[22]

In his speech formally accepting the Democratic nomination for the Senate in mid-September, Herbert Lehman vigorously endorsed the Fair Deal policies of President Truman and tried to make the fight for civil rights the key issue in the campaign. Stressing that "the eradication of social injustice and the creation of equal opportunity for all must be the constant aim of progressive government," Lehman praised "the present fight for civil rights which President Truman is now waging" as "an act of great political courage." He called upon "progressive Republican voters . . . to express themselves on these measures," and he urged "fair-minded Democrats, both south and north of the Mason-Dixon Line, to insist that the Democratic Party stand squarely behind the

President's recommendations." Referring to recent incidents in Peekskill, New York, where veterans' groups and others had protested African American singer Paul Robeson's appearances because of his pro-Communist politics and attacked concert-goers, Lehman denounced "lynching and mob violence, whether it be in Peekskill or Mississippi," as "inexcusably vicious and indescribably sinister." Such actions, he warned, "create disunity at home . . . weaken our prestige internationally and make us vulnerable to the world-wide offensive being waged by communism against American democracy." Lehman emphasized that now was the time to "fight for equality of opportunity in employment, in education, . . . [and] to fight for equality of all our citizens," and he pledged to "make that fight with all the strength" at his command.[23]

Lehman moved quickly to mollify Catholic voters who might have resented his support of *The Nation* and his defense of Mrs. Roosevelt in her recent clash with Cardinal Spellman. He endorsed "federal aid to education, which is sorely needed if we are to advance our standards of education," and he claimed that he had always believed that state and federal aid for parochial schools was appropriate as long as it was confined to auxiliary services such as transportation and health services. Therefore, he opposed the Braden bill pending in the House of Representatives that would have prohibited federal aid from going to parochial schools for any purpose. Governor Dewey and other Republican leaders immediately charged that Lehman had switched his position for political reasons, but Lehman explained that his support for Mrs. Roosevelt had always been based on her right as an individual to speak out on public issues and to defend her against charges that she was anti-Catholic, rather than her position on the Braden bill or any other particular legislative proposal.[24]

In accepting the Republican nomination for the Senate, John Foster Dulles elaborated on his earlier theme that Truman and the Democrats were taking the country down "the road to statism." He claimed that "the present administration in Washington seeks more and more power over the lives of more and more people," warning that "the accumulation of federal power is already near the peril point, . . . the point of no return." According to Dulles, "If the Congress were now to grant the new powers which the President has already asked for, the result would be a government so powerful that there could be no turning back. We would then be, not a self-reliant people, but a dependent people—on leash from birth to death to a federal bureaucracy." If the President got his way, Dulles asserted, "socialized medicine would provide doctor, nurse and hospital" when a baby was born; federal aid to education would dictate that the youngster receive "the kind of schooling which the politicians in Washington decree for him"; public housing would limit his residential options; the Brannan Plan would manage agriculture and the nation's food supply; jobs in the private sector would become fewer and fewer as government payrolls continued to grow; and taxes would rise higher and higher.[25]

Lehman did not back down from Dulles's charge that he supported the President's program and "a welfare state"; in fact, Lehman embraced the term and denounced the Republican scare tactics. Lehman emphasized that during his years as Governor, the Republicans had charged repeatedly that the Democrats, by proposing a state minimum wage law for women and children, setting the work week at forty hours, and other such measures, had been leading the State "straight to socialism." The Governor took pride in having been "the head of a welfare State, a State that serves the welfare of all its people," and he promised that if he were elected to the Senate, he would "work for a welfare state, not only for the people of New York but all the people of this great nation."[26]

Lehman's endorsement of Truman's Fair Deal and the welfare state initially included the President's proposed compulsory national health insurance to be financed and administered on the model of Social Security. Republicans had immediately denounced Truman's plan as "socialistic," and the American Medical Association had mobilized its considerable resources to prevent the enactment of "socialized medicine" in the United States. Dulles and Dewey condemned Lehman "as an apostle of socialized medicine," which, according to Dewey, Lenin had once described as "the keystone in the arch of the socialized state." Medical practitioners organized a massive public relations campaign against the health insurance plan, including a "Doctors for Dulles Committee" that emphasized in a mailing to all doctors and dentists in New York that "a vote for Dulles is a vote against political medicine and against compulsory health insurance." The committee urged doctors to use their influence "in every possible way to win votes for Senator Dulles," and their efforts generated 2.4 million letters or post cards in which medical professionals exhorted their patients to vote for Dulles.[27]

Worried about the possible impact of the doctors' efforts on Dulles's behalf, Lehman backed away from his previous support for the President's plan for compulsory national health insurance. In a radio broadcast in mid-October, Lehman emphasized that he opposed socialized medicine and endorsed a government partnership with voluntary health insurance programs to cover more people and provide them with greater protection. But Lehman's advisors feared that the Governor's statement had created confusion among his supporters without gaining any votes from "those who are against health insurance." Trying to clarify Lehman's position, his campaign sent a letter "to every doctor and dentist in the state" in which the Governor reiterated, "I do not favor socialized medicine" and emphasized that he opposed "governmental controls of medicine." He insisted, however, "that every man, woman, and child in the nation, regardless of economic status, is entitled to full access to adequate medical services."[28]

Like President Truman in 1948, Lehman enjoyed strong support from organized labor during his run for the Senate in 1949. Lehman had compiled an outstanding record on labor issues during his ten years as Governor, and he had enjoyed widespread union support in his previous campaigns. In announcing that he would run for the Senate on August 31, Lehman made it clear that he supported repeal of the Taft-Hartley Act, and he delivered his first major campaign address at the New York State CIO convention in mid-September. Recognizing the importance of Lehman's election to the issues they considered dear, and the national implications of the contest in New York, the State AFL and CIO temporarily put aside their usual suspicion and hostility toward each other and worked together on Lehman's campaign, the first time they joined forces in a political contest. As Louis Hollander of the Amalgamated Clothing Workers and the CIO explained, workers were "not going to be frightened by the words 'statism' and 'welfare state.'" They were "much more concerned with the problems that face so many of us—the possibilities of unemployment, the threat of insecurity in old age, the lack of decent housing, the task of meeting medical bills, the run-down schools and crowded classrooms our children are forced to attend." Hollander emphasized that "if unemployment insurance, old age pensions, social security, public housing, shorter hours and decent minimum wages are what Dulles means when he talks of the 'welfare state,' then let's have bigger and better welfare states." George Meany of the AFL, who had worked closely with Lehman in the 1930s when Lehman was Governor and Meany was president of the New York State Federation of Labor, declared that "a more sincere and devoted friend of the working people than Mr. Lehman has never been produced in New York or any other State." Meany noted that it was during Lehman's years as Governor that New York had adopted unemployment insurance, the forty-hour work week, improvements in the state's workmen's compensation system, and maximum hours and minimum wages for women. Labor's efforts on Lehman's behalf in 1949 culminated in a massive rally at Madison Square Garden sponsored by the AFL, the CIO, and the Railroad Brotherhoods, at which speaker after speaker voiced support for Lehman, the New Deal, and President Truman's Fair Deal.[29]

III

Many observers hailed the Lehman-Dulles race as one that would clarify national issues and be conducted in a dignified manner befitting the quality of the two men. *New York Times* columnist Arthur Krock rejoiced that "for the first time in many years," the voters "will be able to make their choices on clear-cut national issues." Krock expected that Lehman, with his strong support "for President Truman's 'welfare state' program," and Dulles, who had "attacked the concept of the 'welfare state' as destructive of the American character," will "present a very definite choice in November." But hopes for a high-level discussion of the issues quickly faded. Although the welfare state continued to be a major topic in the campaign, discussion of its merits was often drowned in a sea of red-baiting and charges of bigotry and anti-Semitism. Remembering that Lehman and the Democrats had been vulnerable to charges that they were soft on Communism in 1946, when they had been endorsed by the American Labor Party, Dulles hoped the ploy would work again this time even though the Democrats had severed all ties with the ALP, which was now completely under Communist control. Dulles began the red-baiting in his acceptance speech, asserting that the ALP's decision not to nominate a Senate candidate was really an attempt to aid Lehman and the Democrats. He claimed that "the half million Communists and fellow travelers who last year voted for Henry Wallace" would cast their votes for Lehman this time. In a speech in Binghamton a few days later, Dulles charged that when Lehman was Director General of UNRRA "he was surrounded by Communists. He was passing out American food and supplies to them and seeing them use it to get political control of the countries where it was distributed." Despite this first-hand exposure to "the evils of communism," Dulles maintained, Lehman had failed to sound the necessary alarms, demonstrating that Lehman's anti-communism appeared only "during political campaigns" when the former Governor "said his daily dozen of anti-Communist words." Dulles conceded that Lehman was "no Communist," but alleged that it was not a coincidence that "the Communists are in his corner." In another speech a few days later, Dulles accused Lehman of engaging in "the old New Deal game of spanking the 'Commies' and their fellow-travelers in public and coddling them in private."[30]

In a letter to a supporter, Lehman lamented that the campaign was not being conducted on the level that he had hoped for, blaming it on Dulles's use of tactics that Lehman "would never go in for." In a statewide radio address on September 23, the former Governor tried to answer his opponent's red-baiting and focus the campaign back on the New Deal and the Fair Deal. Lehman regretted having to address the "phantom issue" that Dulles had raised, emphasizing that Communist support was something that he had "never in all my career wanted, never invited, and never been willing to accept." He asserted that "the prime objective of the American Communists in recent years has been to defeat liberal candidates and to elect reactionaries" because they "see in reactionary Republicanism the one best hope of creating that demoralization at home that might destroy all our efforts to hold communism in check abroad." Lehman defined the campaign as a conflict between "the fighting liberalism of Al Smith, Bob Wagner, Franklin Delano Roosevelt and Harry Truman," and "reaction stark and naked—the philosophy which has dominated the thinking of Republican leaders from before the days of Herbert Hoover until now." Liberals, he declared, believe "that in a modern industrial society, government must assume a greater degree of responsibility for the general welfare than was the case in an earlier day," while the "reactionary leaders of the Republican stamp contend that government should leave hands off and entrust the general welfare of the community solely to the free play of economic forces and to the arbitrary decisions of powerful business and industrial leaders." When his opponent "conjures up the terrifying vision of statism and the welfare state," Lehman stressed, "he is merely returning to the same old refrain and the same old tactics that Republican leaders have used in opposing every single piece of progressive legislation for the past thirty years." But liberals were determined, Lehman maintained, "to preserve the United States as the land of freedom and opportunity" not "for the privileged few," but "for every American citizen as a matter of right."[31]

Believing that Dewey's decision to run a moderate, statesmanlike campaign against Truman had backfired in 1948, Dulles, with the help of Dewey and his political advisors, ran an aggressive, hard-hitting campaign that sought to rally the small town and rural base of the Republican Party in Upstate New York to offset the large majority Lehman would receive in New York City. In the process of appealing to these voters, however, Dewey and Dulles starting using various code words that could easily be interpreted as anti-Semitic, such as when Dewey, speaking in Utica in early October, called for "Democrats and Republicans alike" to join in a "holy crusade" to elect Dulles to the Senate. The Lehman campaign believed that Dewey's use of the phrase "holy crusade" represented a specific appeal to nominally Democratic Catholic voters whose support for Lehman was questionable after his conflict with Cardinal Spellman during the summer. Lehman campaign manager Edward Maguire immediately charged that "the term 'holy crusade' for hundreds of years has had a specific connotation," and Lehman complained that Dewey's "use of the term 'holy crusade' was a thinly disguised call to all the latent forces of bigotry and prejudices in American life." A few days later, Dulles added fuel to the fire when he addressed a rally at Geneseo and asserted that Communists in New York City were supporting Lehman. Hoping to increase upstate voter turnout, Dulles declared: "If you could see the kind of people in New York City making up this bloc that is voting for my opponent, if you could see it with your own eyes, I know that you would be out, every last man and woman of you, on election day."[32]

Lehman quickly seized the opportunity presented by Dulles's comment to energize a campaign which up until then had been somewhat lacking in vigor and enthusiasm. The former Governor declared that "the implication of this insulting statement which reflects on all of the citizens of the City of New York is crystal clear," signifying that Dulles "regards many of our New York people with scorn and regards them as second-class citizens." Mindful of the large concentration of Jewish voters in New York City, Lehman accused Dulles of trying "to array class against class and to appraise people by their race or color or national origin." Although Dulles always claimed that the "bloc" he was referring to was Communists and American Labor Party voters in New York City who would turn out in great number for his opponent, Lehman rejected that explanation as "pure hypocrisy," pointing out that even Dulles knew that "you cannot recognize a Communist by his looks."[33]

The two candidates went back and forth, Dulles trying to minimize the damage while the Lehman campaign played up Dulles's remarks to maximize the vote in New York City. Dulles alleged that it was Lehman who "has injected religious and racial issues into this campaign" by "using charges of bigotry as a defense against legitimate criticism," and influential Jews such as Bernard Baruch attested publicly that Dulles was not a bigot. Lehman disclaimed any knowledge of whether Dulles was "a bigot in [his] daily life," but he insisted that Dulles had "played the part of a bigot in this campaign." A group of black leaders in New York City denounced Dulles's "inflammatory statements," and the *Baltimore Afro-American* pointed out that "the only persons who could be readily identified by a look at them are colored people." Lehman's campaign used sound trucks in New York City quoting Dulles's comments, urging voters to "look around at your neighbor" and "look at yourself in the mirror tonight. You are the people John Dulles was talking about. A more open appeal to bigotry, prejudice, and un-Americanism is hard to imagine. Vote against bigotry, prejudice and reaction. Vote against John Dulles."[34]

As the candidates exchanged barbs and accusations of "liar" and "bigot," and the campaign grew more and more bitter, Dulles suddenly challenged Lehman to "meet face to face" in a debate. In that forum, Dulles suggested, they could discuss whether Lehman had accepted Communist support in previous elections, Dulles's record of fighting bigotry, whether Lehman favored the Truman administration's plan for "socializing medicine," and numerous other issues on which the two candidates disagreed. As Lehman later recalled, he was content to run on his record, and he realized if he "tried to debate with a man who was as experienced as a lawyer as Dulles was, as facile a speaker as Dulles," Lehman "would be at a disadvantage." Accordingly, Lehman rejected Dulles's debate proposal, dismissing it as a "press agent stunt" that would "make a circus out of what should be a serious presentation to the public of public issues." Lehman noted that Dulles's letter had been released to the press before he had even received it, and he condemned "the antics, misrepresentations and distortions" that were part of Dulles's "futile efforts to submerge the vital issues of the campaign." Trying to capitalize on Lehman's refusal to debate, Dulles's campaign events began to feature an empty chair bearing the sign: "Reserved for Mr. Lehman."[35]

With good reason, the Lehman campaign continued to worry about possible defections by Catholic voters. In mid-September, the Reverend Francis Burns emphasized to eight thousand pilgrims at the Shrine of North American Martyrs in upstate Auriesville that Catholics should vote for candidates who had demonstrated that "they would give to the Catholic child the educational advantages he is entitled to under the Constitution." Reverend Burns made it clear that he was referring "especially to the coming election to the exalted office of United States Senator," and he urged Catholics not to allow "the red herring of church and state to be drawn across the real issue—namely, that Catholic children as Americans are entitled to certain educational benefits such as free bus transportation, free lunches, free health welfare and free-non-religious textbooks." A month later, the *New York Times* reported that upstate Democratic leaders feared "the prospect of defections in the Senate race by voters of Irish extraction," who believed that "Lehman had no business picking a fight with the Cardinal."[36]

A group called Protestants and Catholics United Against the Election of Herbert H. Lehman distributed a leaflet entitled "Do You Believe in God?" that aired the litany of Catholic grievances against Lehman. The leaflet charged that Lehman "has a long record of opposition to anything Christian" and claimed that he was "pledged to wipe the name of God from all textbooks and even from classroom discussion in the public school system." It alleged that Lehman had "viciously attacked the Superintendent of New York City's Schools . . . for banning a small magazine, *The Nation*, which preaches hate against Catholics, from public school libraries," and it reminded voters that "Lehman rushed to the aid of Mrs. Roosevelt, when that lady was exposed by Cardinal Spellman as an anti-Catholic bigot." The leaflet also accused Lehman of being "one of the nation's leading pro-Communist apologists," asserting that "he opposes the independence of the United States" and that "he admits he is fighting for a World Government in which the Soviet Union would take a leading part." Purportedly quoting the *Daily Worker*, the leaflet observed that "the American Labor Party and the Communist Party will back Herbert H. Lehman this November," and it urged "parents and enlightened public spirited citizens . . . to see that the minds of American youth are not perverted by false doctrines." It warned that "Lehman is a leader of that false liberal school that holds that it is alright to teach Marx or Freud's ideas but not those of Jesus Christ," and that people like Lehman want to "open our schools to Communists but bar active Christians." The leaflet cited Reverend Burns's recommendation that "all Christians" should vote only for candidates who support federal aid to parochial schools. Realizing, perhaps, that its case against Lehman focused almost exclusively on Catholic concerns, the group tried to broaden its appeal, predicting that "in view of the Communist strategy throughout the world, mass attacks against Protestants soon will follow anti-Catholic maneuvers" because "Communists hate all religion." The leaflet concluded by exhorting people to "Vote to defeat Herbert H. Lehman! Elect John Foster Dulles to the United States Senate!"[37]

The Lehman campaign hoped that a radio speech on his behalf from former Postmaster General James Farley and the endorsement of former Senator Wagner, both Catholics, might limit the losses among Catholic voters. Farley agreed to make the broadcast, and in his address he asserted that Lehman's "many qualities of head and heart" and his "much broader and sustained experience" as Governor of New York and Director General of UNRRA made him "ideally suited" for the Senate. Similarly, Wagner emphasized in a written statement that "a vote for Herbert Lehman is a vote of confidence not only in his long record of outstanding service but for the principles that guided me throughout my whole career."[38]

Much to Lehman's regret, the editors of the *New York Times* also urged voters to support Dulles's Senate candidacy. Publisher Arthur Hays Sulzberger, an old friend who had worked with Lehman on many charitable and philanthropic endeavors, informed him in mid-October that the *Times* would be endorsing Dulles, noting that "this is the first time in your long political life that we have not supported you, and I hope that you will know that the decision has not been an easy one." In an editorial on October 18, the *Times* extolled the virtues of both candidates, describing them as "two men of unimpeachable integrity, high principles, broad outlook and deep devotion to the public interest, each eminently qualified to represent New York at Washington." But the editors emphasized Dulles's "direct participation in the making of a foreign policy which has become the first line of Western defense against Soviet aggression," as well as his key role in leading "the Republican Party away from its pre-war isolationism" and making "the present bipartisan policy of the United States a reality." Dulles's election, the *Times* concluded, "would greatly strengthen the power of the 'internationalist' group of Republicans in Congress."[39]

IV

President Truman took considerable interest in the New York Senate election, which was generally seen as a referendum on his Fair Deal and a harbinger of the 1950 congressional elections. The President had stated earlier that he would be glad to speak in New York if it would be helpful to Lehman, but State Democratic Chairman Paul Fitzpatrick, after meeting with Truman in mid-September to discuss the campaign, declared that a presidential appearance would not be necessary, that Lehman would win by three hundred thousand votes. Truman explained to former Secretary of Agriculture Clinton Anderson, now a Senator from New Mexico, that "the campaign in New York between Dulles and Governor Lehman is a crucial one," and the President approved plans for Attorney General J. Howard McGrath and Secretary of Labor Maurice Tobin, both of whom were Catholic, to campaign for Lehman in New York to try to limit defections by Catholic voters.[40]

Eleanor Roosevelt informed the President in early October that she was "getting rather anxious about the way the campaign is going here for both

Governor Lehman and Mayor O'Dwyer." She noted that "the Catholic Church is showing no great backing for Governor Lehman" and that she felt "a little responsible for the situation here because undoubtedly Governor Lehman's statement against the Cardinal's letter" to her was "one of the things influencing the Catholic hierarchy." Mrs. Roosevelt reported that "Upstate the Republicans are making a vigorous senatorial fight," employing "their 'holy crusade' against the communists" to make "a direct appeal for the Catholic vote," and she worried that "like so many campaign tricks it may succeed in swinging the votes." She emphasized that her "chief concern is the good of the party in the future," warning that "if in this state it is evident that there has been defection in the Catholic vote where Governor Lehman is concerned," the result would be "a great desertion from the Democratic Party by a great many of the Jews, some Protestants and some liberals—all of whom will join the Liberal Party which will weaken the Democratic Party." She wondered if "it would be very advisable" for the President to come to New York for the big labor-sponsored rally at Madison Square Garden for Lehman and O'Dwyer. Doing everything she could to help the Lehman campaign, Mrs. Roosevelt served as one of the honorary chairmen of the Independent Citizens' Committee for Lehman's election, delivered a radio address on Lehman's behalf, and praised him frequently in her "My Day" columns.[41]

Truman appreciated Mrs. Roosevelt's views on the situation in New York and replied that he wanted to do everything he could to help, "particularly in supporting the candidacy of Governor Lehman." The President explained that Paul Fitzpatrick had advised him not to come to New York because such a visit would make it look like Lehman "was in distress and needed help." Truman made it clear that if the Democratic leaders in New York determined that his presence would be "helpful," he was "standing by to aid in any manner that can be of real help," but he needed to "avoid under all circumstances . . . any act or gesture which could be construed as unwarranted interference by an outsider." He "certainly want[ed] to see Governor Lehman win," the President emphasized, and he was "ready and anxious to make whatever contribution" he could "to achieve that happy result."[42]

Although the President refrained from becoming too involved personally in the Lehman campaign, other administration officials faced no such constraints. At a luncheon for Democratic leaders from across New York State, Democratic National Chairman William Boyle proclaimed the administration's support for Lehman's election, and Vice President Alben Barkley, Secretary of Labor Tobin, Attorney General McGrath, and Federal Security Administrator Oscar Ewing actively campaigned on Lehman's behalf. Tobin delivered a rousing radio address in which he urged New Yorkers to send Herbert Lehman to the Senate to "preserve our social gains," emphasizing that the "statism" and "welfare state," which Dulles complained about so often, included federal guarantees for bank deposits, old-age insurance, and the right of workers to bargain collectively. Similarly, Ewing denounced Dulles as an "arch apostle of reaction on all matters which concern the plain folk," a man who was "seeking vainly to bring back all the conditions that caused the debacle of 1929, rather than to enlarge and improve the measures that rescued us."[43]

In mid-October, the Lehman campaign decided that it wanted more direct help from the President after all. State Chairman Fitzpatrick informed National Chairman Boyle and White House aide Matthew Connelly that Lehman would "be deeply indebted for a strong personal note of endorsement from President Truman." According to Fitzpatrick, Lehman now believed that a strong statement from the President "would be one of the most effective factors in his election," that it would be used "on flyers, in advertisements, and pamphlets, etc." Fitzpatrick also reported that the Lehman campaign "would very much like to feature a talk of several minutes by President Truman" as the highlight of "a state-wide broadcast" planned for the Saturday night before the election. In Fitzpatrick's opinion, "a word of support from the President would be most appropriate and will successfully climax our campaign in New York State to elect Governor Lehman."[44]

The President quickly sent Lehman a strong letter endorsing his candidacy. Truman emphasized that Lehman enjoyed his "warmest support" and expressed his "complete faith" in Lehman's "wisdom and deep understanding of the needs of the people." Lehman's "long and fruitful experience in both domestic and international affairs" would be "of inestimable value," and the President "look[ed] forward with pleasure" to welcoming Lehman in January "as a Democratic member of the United States Senate." The President noted that "the New York senatorial race is being watched attentively from coast to coast," and that "the same reactionary forces which have been so determined to make the government the servant of the selfish interests rather than the servant of all the people" were "making a desperate fight" against Lehman. "They must be stopped in New York State on November eighth," the President declared, assuring Lehman that he had not "the slightest doubt of the outcome."[45]

Lehman appreciated Truman's "splendid letter" and was "very grateful" for the President's "faith and confidence in me." When Lehman traveled to Washington a few days later to speak at a ceremony at which former Senator Wagner's papers were presented to Georgetown University, Truman sought to give Lehman's campaign a further boost by meeting with him at Blair House, the President's temporary residence while repairs were being made at the White House. After their meeting, Truman escorted Lehman to the porch where photographers took pictures of the two of them. Lehman told reporters that the President had offered to come to New York to campaign for him, but they had agreed that such action was not necessary. Lehman declared: "I expect to win and the President is also very confident of my victory."[46]

FIGURE 12.1. President Truman extends his best wishes to Senate candidate Herbert Lehman after their meeting at Blair House, October 23, 1949. AP Images.

Mainly because of logistics and travel schedules, Truman initially respond-ed less than enthusiastically to the Lehman campaign's request that he partici-pate in a radio broadcast for Lehman, asking aide Matthew Connelly, "Will we be back from Missouri?" and concluding that "I guess we'll have to do it." The news that the President was going to deliver a radio address on Lehman's behalf led Democrats and Republicans to argue over the significance of Truman's growing involvement in the campaign. Lehman's advisors stressed that they were still very optimistic about his prospects, but wanted to put the full weight of the presidency behind him because of "the national character the election has assumed," while New York State Republican Chairman William Pfeiffer charged that this action "emphasizes the desperation of the Lehman management."[47]

On Saturday, November 5, President Truman spoke for five minutes dur-ing the Lehman campaign's half-hour, statewide, radio broadcast. "As a Demo-crat," Truman proclaimed, he welcomed this election in which "the voters have a clear-cut issue before them," namely, "whether or not they will have a United States Senator who will work to promote the general welfare of the people." The President reminded voters that this election was to fill the seat previously held by Senator Wagner, who was "known throughout our country for his great achievements in labor and welfare legislation—in housing, in health and in social security—achievements which have helped to make this country the most progressive and powerful democratic nation of all time." And Governor Lehman, Truman emphasized, "will carry on that tradition of working for the welfare of all the people." New Yorkers knew Lehman's "record as a just, humane and liberal Chief Executive" who had fought as Governor "for the same policies that Franklin D. Roosevelt fought for as President," and Truman was confident that, as a Senator, Lehman "will work for the liberal policies which mean greater progress and a better life for the people of New York and of the whole country." The President asserted that "the office of Senator from New York . . . should be filled by a man who believes in the progressive measures that brought New York to the forefront among our states in promoting the people's welfare," not someone "who would put a stop to the great advances in social legislation that have been pioneered by his own state." In addition to bringing "to the Senate a constructive and progressive approach to domestic affairs," Truman stressed, Lehman would also bring "wide personal experience and mature wisdom in the handling of our foreign relations." Ignoring his own dissatisfaction with Lehman's leadership of UNRRA, which the President now hailed as "the greatest world-wide relief and rehabilitation effort in history," Truman argued that Lehman had "proved himself an outstanding example of the best kind of international statesman and public servant" and "won universal respect and gratitude for his deep understanding of the problems that grew out of the war." Truman was certain that "as a United States Senator, Herbert Lehman will strengthen our efforts to bring peace and prosperity to all mankind," and he urged New Yorkers to "vote for Herbert Lehman, William O'Dwyer, and the whole Democratic ticket."[48]

Most observers saw the Lehman-Dulles race, in which the main issue was so clearly defined by Dulles's attacks on "statism" and Lehman's defense of "the welfare state," as a referendum on the Truman administration and the Fair Deal and a precursor to the 1950 congressional elections and the 1952 presidential campaign. Arthur Krock noted in the *New York Times* that Truman had "become unusually active," on Lehman's behalf, "going beyond the act of endorsing a Democratic nominee which is customary in such circumstances," largely because "Dulles has made Mr. Truman's domestic program a direct issue between himself and Governor Lehman." Krock asserted that a Dulles victory would embolden "opposition to that program in Congress by Republicans and a number of fence-sitting Democrats." Frank Kent of the *Wall Street Journal* called the New York senatorial election "the most significant political event of the year," declaring that a Dulles victory "would encourage the Republicans and depress the Democrats about 1950 and 1952—particularly as the line on national issues is drawn more sharply than in any by-election for a long time." Columnist Mark Sullivan emphasized that a victory for Lehman, so clearly identified as a supporter of Roosevelt and Truman and the New and Fair Deals, would encourage the President "to press his legislative program upon the present Congress . . . with renewed vigor." A Lehman defeat, however, "would be a serious setback to President Truman." It would "give elation, hope and determination to the Republicans," who "would be strongly encouraged to continue resistance to Mr. Truman's legislative program in Congress," and it would enable the GOP to look "forward to the 1952 presidential election with confidence, determination and high morale."[49]

With the nation's eyes fixed on the Lehman-Dulles contest, New Yorkers went to the polls on November 8, 1949, and elected Herbert Lehman to the United States Senate by a margin of two hundred thousand votes. Lehman carried New York City by eight hundred thousand votes, negating Dulles's six hundred thousand plurality Upstate. Some New York City Catholics did abandon Lehman, voting for O'Dwyer but not Lehman, but their defections were more than offset by the strong support Lehman received from organized labor and the four hundred thousand votes he received on the Liberal Party line. Lehman's triumph was the first for a Democrat in a statewide election in New York since FDR had carried the state in 1944, and the first in a nonpresidential year since Lehman and his running mates had won in 1938. Dulles conceded at 10:45 p.m., after which Lehman issued a formal statement thanking New Yorkers for "the great new opportunity of public service" and pledging to devote "to your service all the strength of mind and body and heart that lies in me."[50]

Recalling the President's prediction of the election's outcome, Dulles also wired the President that evening, simply stating, "You win." Truman was attending a dinner hosted by the Women's National Democratic Club in Washington when he received the first reports indicating a Lehman victory, and according to the *Washington Post*, "between the entrée and the salad," the President "jubilantly" informed his fellow diners that Lehman was leading in New York. The *Post* also reported that "after dessert, when guests at the head table were being introduced," Truman announced that "the *New York Times* and the *New York Daily News*, both of which supported Dulles, both concede to Lehman and O'Dwyer." The President declared that Lehman's victory in New York added to the Democrats' responsibility to carry out the promises in their 1948 platform to secure and protect "the welfare and the prosperity of the United States of America, and the welfare and the prosperity of the world as a whole," and he predicted that Lehman's triumph "will have a very decided effect on the elections of 1950."[51]

Truman and Lehman exchanged warm messages after the election, reflecting the close political ties that had developed between them over the past two years. The President congratulated Lehman "upon the further confidence which the people of the Empire State have registered in your leadership," emphasizing that "we need in the national legislature the counsel which you can give out of your wisdom and long experience." Lehman thanked Truman for his good wishes, proclaiming that "the vote clearly indicated approval by the people of New York State of the great cause which you are so ably leading" and in which Lehman was "proud to have a part."[52]

Liberals and labor leaders who had played key roles in Lehman's triumph agreed with State Chairman Paul Fitzpatrick that "the election of Senator Lehman is of state, nation-wide and international significance." Eleanor Roosevelt exclaimed that Lehman's election "gives us a man of heart and character and experience in many fields to represent us in the Senate," Senator Hubert Humphrey rejoiced that New Yorkers had affirmed Lehman's "principle that government must have a heart as well as a brain," and historian Arthur Schlesinger, Jr., hailed Lehman's victory as "a historic vindication of the principles of liberal government in this country." David Dubinsky of the ILGWU and the Liberal Party called Lehman's triumph a "decisive blow to reactionary forces in our state" delivered by "progressives, liberals, and trade unionists . . . who have demonstrated they mean to go forward and not backward in the progress made under Roosevelt and Truman." Similarly, Michael Quill and Matthew Guinan of the Transport Workers Union asserted that Lehman's victory "constitutes unequivocal endorsement of President Truman's fair deal [sic] program and repudiation of the Dewey-Dulles-GOP reaction and foreshadows the defeat of Taft-Hartley, Condon-Wadlin proponents in 1950." Sir Frederick Leith-Ross, a British official with whom Lehman had worked closely during the war, noted that his old friend's election provided "reassurance to the world that the progressive tide of the New Deal is still running strong."[53]

Shortly after the election, Herbert Lehman described the campaign as "a bitter and hard-fought battle" that seemed "interminable," but, like many others, he saw his victory as an endorsement of the liberal principles of the New Deal and the Fair Deal. As he told Vice President Alben Barkley, Lehman believed that "the vote clearly indicated that the people of New York approve the cause of liberal government for which we have been working for so many years under the inspired leadership of President Roosevelt and President Truman." He explained to Mary McLeod Bethune, the renowned black educator, that he took special pleasure in his victory because he knew "of no election in recent years when the issue of liberalism versus reaction was so clearly defined or so important." Lehman predicted that his victory would have "a great effect on the elections of 1950," and he emphasized to Connecticut Governor Chester Bowles that Dulles's election "would have given reactionaries all of [sic] the country a tremendous boost, and they would have redoubled their efforts in 1950 and 1952."[54]

Herbert Lehman's election to the Senate in 1949 marked the realization of a goal that he had held for more than a decade. He had rejected Tammany leaders' attempt to nominate him for the Senate rather than Governor in 1932, but by 1938, Lehman had looked longingly at the opportunity to serve in the Senate. However, he had let party leaders persuade him to run for Governor one last time to prevent Thomas Dewey and the Republicans from capturing the statehouse in Albany. Then in 1946, Lehman had fallen victim to the Republican landslide and Irving Ives had defeated him in the Senate race. Lehman had long coveted a place in the Senate not because he wanted the prestige and stature that went with such a position, but, as he explained in an interview a few days after his victory in 1949, because he believed that being a Senator would enable him to continue working for "the general welfare of all the people." The Senator-elect saw his triumph as a strong endorsement of "the liberal and enlightened policies of President Truman," and he promised to "fight vigorously" for Truman's civil rights program. He also pledged to work "for repeal of the Taft-Hartley Act," and for "federal aid to education, increased medical care for all the people and expansion of social security."[55]

CHAPTER 13

"I Will Not Compromise with My Conscience"

Lehman and McCarthyism, 1950–1952

Sometimes a man can be proud of the enemies he makes.[1]

Herbert Lehman was seventy-one years old when he proudly took the oath of office as New York's junior Senator in January 1950, telling a reporter he experienced "a very real thrill" when he took his seat in the Senate. Realizing his lack of seniority and status in the Senate, Lehman planned to remain in the background as he learned its culture and mores, hoping "to make a little news, but as little noise as possible." But as Republicans and conservative Democrats stepped up their attacks on the Truman administration's Far Eastern policy, and Senator Joseph McCarthy (R-WI) began his reign of terror, Herbert Lehman could not remain silent.[2]

I

What Secretary of State Dean Acheson later described as "the attack of the primitives" began in 1949 and accelerated rapidly in 1950. In a speech to a Democratic dinner in mid-February 1950, President Truman noted that the victory in the 1949 New York Senate race by "my good friend Governor Lehman" had clearly demonstrated that the American people rejected Republicans' denunciations of the New Deal and the Fair Deal as "statism" aimed at

---

Chapter title quotation: Herbert Lehman in 96 *Congressional Record* 14627 (September 12, 1950).

establishing "the welfare state." But while Americans may have embraced the domestic programs of Franklin Roosevelt and Harry Truman, they were less certain about their foreign policies, especially in the Far East. With bipartisan support in Congress, the President had implemented the Truman Doctrine, the Marshall Plan, and NATO to contain Communism in Europe, but billions of dollars in U.S. aid had not prevented a Communist victory over Chiang Kai-shek and the Chinese Nationalists, who were driven off the mainland and took refuge on the island of Formosa in 1949. John Foster Dulles's emphasis on his role as one of the architects of the bipartisan foreign policy had prevented him from exploiting the growing concern over the administration's policy toward China during his campaign against Lehman, but other Republicans and a few conservative Democrats had spent much of 1949 blaming the Truman administration for the "loss" of China.[3]

Ignoring the advice of former President Herbert Hoover, Senator Robert Taft (R-OH), and other "Asia Firsters," Truman announced in January 1950 that the United States would not use military force to defend Chiang Kai-shek and the Chinese Nationalists on Formosa. Republicans responded by intensifying their criticism of the President and Secretary of State Acheson. Senator William Knowland (R-CA), one of the leaders of the China Lobby, charged the President with "appeasement of aggression . . . surrender on the installment plan," and Nebraska Senator Kenneth Wherry, the Republican floor leader, denounced the administration's decision as a "complete, abject surrender to the Red Communists in the Far East." Even Senator Arthur Vandenberg (R-MI), the main Republican pillar supporting bipartisanship in foreign policy, regretted that the President had proclaimed such a policy without consulting Congress.[4]

Senator Lehman grew more and more concerned as Secretary of State Acheson's efforts to defend the administration's decisions on China and Formosa merely encouraged Republicans to step up their attacks on the policy and on him personally. Acheson did not suffer fools gladly, and his aristocratic manner and condescending tone alienated many in Congress, as did his assertion that all the United States could do now in China was stand by and wait and hope that the Chinese people realized that aligning with the Soviet Union was not in China's national interest. Nor did the Secretary's contention that Formosa and Korea lay beyond America's defense perimeter in Asia win him any friends among the Asia Firsters. In a letter to Acheson in mid-January 1950, Lehman condemned the "the clamor of those who would serve selfish political ends by irresponsible denunciations and attacks" and denounced "the people who would have us occupy Formosa, or send the navy to 'protect' it, or establish a condominion [sic] over it." Lehman did "not know what can be done of a positive nature in the present situation," but he was certain that "clinging to the dead hand of a regime which has completely lost the confidence of the Chinese people and in defense of which that people raises not a finger, could be a fatal error." The Senator wanted to be helpful to the administration on this matter, and he suggested making his letter public along with whatever response Acheson might offer to enlighten public opinion.[5]

In the Senate, Lehman took a leading role in defending Acheson and the Truman administration against the constant attacks now emanating from Senator Knowland and others. When the Secretary of State replied to Lehman's letter in early February, Lehman inserted the exchange in the *Congressional Record* and used it as the basis for a speech on the Senate floor. Far from abandoning Chiang Kai-shek, Lehman pointed out, the United States had provided the Chinese Nationalists with more than $3.5 billion in assistance. Lehman agreed with Acheson that any move to occupy or defend Formosa, as suggested by Herbert Hoover and other prominent Republicans, contradicted America's longtime policy of respecting the territorial integrity of China and would be counterproductive in trying to win the confidence and support of the Chinese people away from the new Communist regime. When Senator Knowland questioned Lehman's commitment to the fight against Communism, Lehman stressed that he had "fought communism for more than 15 years," and he noted that he had also "fought fascism and nazism," which he believed "have been and may again be a very grave threat to the peace and security of this country and of the world." As for the criticism that Acheson had practically invited the Communists to attack Formosa, Korea, and other areas on the mainland of Asia by defining them as beyond the American defense perimeter, Lehman emphasized that the fight against Communism in Asia would be won not by setting "an imaginary line or a strategic line," but by gaining "the confidence and respect of all the peace-loving and freedom-loving people of the world," by "making them believe and know that when we talk about democracy, we mean democracy; that when we talk about human rights and the dignity of the individual, whether in China or in the United States, we mean just that, and we are willing to make sacrifices for just that."[6]

II

Republican accusations that the Truman administration's policies in Asia had been mistaken or ill-conceived soon gave way to charges that the Communists had succeeded in China and elsewhere because the State Department was riddled with Communists. The President had tried to put to rest the issue of Communist subversives within the U.S. government by issuing an executive order in March 1947 establishing the Federal Employee Loyalty Program, but highly publicized investigations by the House Committee on Un-American Activities (HUAC), the Communist victory in China, and the Soviet Union's detonation of an atomic device had kept the subject in the headlines. And then there was the Alger Hiss case. Hiss was a former high-ranking State Department official, and his conviction in January 1950 on perjury charges for denying under oath that he had passed secret documents to Soviet agents convinced many Americans that there were Communist spies working in the American government. President Truman's original dismissal of the Hiss case as "a red herring" and Secretary of State Acheson's invocation of a biblical passage to explain why he refused to turn his back on Hiss, an acquaintance of long standing, even after Hiss had been found guilty, led many Americans to believe that not only were there spies within the American government, but that the Truman administration was protecting and covering up for them rather than trying to root them out. As Herbert Lehman later recalled, the Hiss case gave Senator Joseph McCarthy and others "a weapon to beat, flog, and attack the liberals with," making it a "very great blow to liberalism."[7]

In the immediate aftermath of Hiss's conviction, at a time when many Americans were so frightened of the Communist threat that they were willing to curb people's rights and liberties, Senator Lehman spoke out loudly and clearly against the growing hysteria. Addressing the Washington chapter of Americans for Democratic Action on January 27, 1950, Lehman took issue with Representative Richard Nixon (R-CA) and others who asserted that the Hiss case proved that the President's loyalty program was too lenient. Lehman derided such complaints, noting that "some reactionaries would be satisfied only if there were public executions, at dawn and at dusk, of every government employee caught in the act of having a liberal thought." The Senator warned that those who "insist that we must suppress free inquiry in order to preserve our institutions and our way of life" were guilty of "heresy of the worst kind," and he emphasized that America had to defend itself against Communism "without at the same time sacrificing some of our democratic principles." Lehman believed that no one should be branded as disloyal "except after a judicial proceeding, with all the safeguards for the accused which Anglo-Saxon and American law provides."[8]

Just a few weeks after Hiss was found guilty, and a few days after physicist Klaus Fuchs was arrested by British authorities and charged with passing secret information about the atomic bomb to the Soviet Union, Senator Joseph McCarthy burst into the news with his wild charges that the United States was losing the Cold War because the Truman administration and the Democrats were infested with Communists. In a speech in Wheeling, West Virginia, on February 9, 1950, the Wisconsin Republican claimed, "I have in my hand a list of 205—a list of names that were made known to the Secretary of State as being members of the Communist Party and who nevertheless are still working and shaping policy in the State Department." McCarthy reiterated his sensational allegations in subsequent speeches over the next few days, reducing the exact number of "card-carrying Communists" in the State Department to fifty-seven, with the others described now as security risks. The numbers changed again on February 20, as did the status of the alleged perpetrators, when McCarthy repeated his accusations on the Senate floor. This time he asserted that there were eighty-one known Communists or *Communist sympathizers* who had worked at the State Department "*at one time or another*" (emphasis added).[9]

Herbert Lehman immediately joined Senate Democratic Leader Scott Lucas of Illinois and a few others in challenging McCarthy's incredible accusations. Lehman ridiculed McCarthy's contention that individuals could be identified as Communists because "they walked like Communists, looked like Communists, and talked like Communists," and he rejected McCarthy's use of "guilt by association"—condemning people as Communists because some of their friends or acquaintances might have some connection to Communism or to alleged Communist-front organizations. Lehman appreciated McCarthy's refusal to make public "the names of men accused on somewhat unsubstantiated charges," but he chided McCarthy for his "unwillingness to submit the names to the responsible official, the head of the State Department," so that they could be removed from their posts without delay.[10]

Over the next few weeks, as a subcommittee of the Senate Foreign Relations Committee began investigating McCarthy's charges that the State Department was riddled with Communists, Herbert Lehman tangled with some of the more reactionary members of the Senate over a proposal to liberalize the Displaced Persons Act of 1948. Lehman had first dealt with the DP issue at UNRRA, and he continued to feel deeply that the United States had a humanitarian obligation to help these people whose lives had been torn asunder by the war. He disliked the current law, which he considered "cruel and deceptive," and he strongly supported efforts to ease its restrictions. But rather than loosening the rules, Senator Pat McCarran (D-NV) and the Judiciary Committee drafted a bill that would make it more difficult for DPs to find refuge in America, clearly reflecting McCarran's anti-Semitic tendencies and his desire to limit the number of Jews who might enter the United States. Lehman understood that there was "a large and bitter opposition to any liberalization of the DP bill except in such a subtly negative form as McCarran has proposed." Nonetheless, he denounced the Judiciary Committee's proposal, asserting that it "shuts the door to the displaced persons still further, until only a tiny crack would remain," and he joined a bipartisan group of eighteen Senators who offered a substitute bill to remove some of the more objectionable provisions of the existing statute.[11]

During the debate over the DP bill, Herbert Lehman listened in amazement as Senator James Eastland (D-MS), a senior member of the Judiciary Committee, asserted that any weakening of the DP law threatened America's national security, that the Displaced Persons Commission's administration of the present law had been "shocking," and that members of the Commission were "guilty of moral treason." Eastland claimed that an Army colonel had told the Judiciary Committee that he had "caught officers of the Russian secret police trying to filter into the United States" as displaced persons. Trying to refute the allegations by Eastland and fellow Judiciary Committee member William Jenner (R-IN) that the DP program was a sieve through which Communists and criminals were coming to America, Lehman detailed the thirty steps through which DPs had to pass, including clearances from the FBI, Army Counter-intelligence, the Displaced Persons Commission, the State Department, and the Immigration and Naturalization Service. Lehman complained that in the remarks of those who wanted to limit the DP program, he had "heard more misstatements, more inaccuracies," than he "ever thought possible on the floor of the United States Senate." When Jenner claimed that an unnamed Displaced Persons Commission employee had testified that thirty thousand of the DPs admitted so far were "poor security risks," Lehman noted that of the 134,000 people who had come to the United States under this program, only three had later been subjected to deportation proceedings.[12]

Lehman's disagreement with Eastland and Jenner quickly escalated into an ugly incident in the Senate during which Lehman stood up to some of the Senate's nastiest bullies. Eastland had not been present for the first part of Lehman's remarks, but he had returned in time to challenge Lehman's description of the screening process. A few days later, Eastland charged on the floor of the Senate that Lehman had employed "deliberate untruths" and engaged in "unethical conduct" with his allegations of "misstatements" and "inaccuracies." Senator Matthew Neely (D-WV), who agreed with Lehman that the DP law needed to be liberalized, immediately rose to Lehman's defense, asserting that Eastland had violated Senate rules by "calling the junior Senator from New York a liar" and asking that Eastland be required to take his seat because he had accused a colleague of conduct "unworthy or unbecoming a Senator." Senator John Sparkman (D-AL), who was presiding over the Senate at the time, ordered Eastland to be seated, but a majority of Senators promptly voted to allow Eastland to proceed, whereupon he resumed his attack on Lehman, and the whole process was repeated, with McCarran and Jenner joining in the assault against Lehman. Lehman had originally planned to insert in the *Congressional Record* but not read on the Senate floor a statement detailing what he characterized as twelve serious misstatements contained in Eastland's previous remarks on the DP bill, but he now insisted on delivering his speech before the Senate. He carefully refrained from accusing Eastland of "deliberate misstatements," asserting instead that the Mississippian, "in the heat of his enthusiasm," had made "overstatements . . . which could only be called misstatements of fact." Eastland replied by again accusing Lehman of deliberately presenting "a tissue of falsehoods." Taking solace from the bitter exchange with Eastland and Jenner, two of the most vicious members of the Senate, and McCarran, one of the most powerful and vindictive Senators, Lehman later told reporters: "Sometimes a man can be proud of the enemies he makes."[13]

Despite his status as a newcomer in the Senate, Lehman continued to play a leading role in resisting Senator McCarthy's efforts to exacerbate the growing anti-Communist hysteria in Congress and the nation. The day after Eastland verbally attacked Lehman in the Senate, Senator Millard Tydings (D-MD) and a subcommittee of the Senate Foreign Relations Committee began investigating McCarthy's allegations that "at least fifty-seven" Communists were either still working or had recently been employed at the State Department. McCarthy claimed that New York City attorney Dorothy Kenyon, who had previously been part of the U.S. Mission to the United Nations, had been associated with more than twenty Communist-front organizations in the past, and he accused Ambassador-at-Large Philip Jessup of having "an unusual affinity for Communist causes." Herbert Lehman had known both Kenyon and Jessup for many years, having worked with Kenyon in Americans for Democratic Action and other liberal causes, and having brought Jessup with him to Washington in 1943 to help set up OFRRO and then UNRRA. Lehman realized that if Kenyon and Jessup could be targeted by McCarthy for such bogus attacks, other innocent people were also at risk. When Kenyon testified before the Tydings committee to clear her name, Lehman congratulated her on "how completely" she "answered the charges" against her, and he inserted her opening statement in the *Congressional Record* to make her rebuttal to McCarthy more readily available. Lehman also sought to place in the *Record* a letter to the *New York Times* in which Henry Stimson, who had served as Secretary of State under Herbert Hoover and Secretary of War under Franklin Roosevelt, declared that McCarthy, with his "indiscriminate accusations, . . . directly and dangerously impedes the conduct of the foreign affairs of our government."[14]

As McCarthy quickly identified new targets and stepped up his attacks, Herbert Lehman remained one of the few Senators willing to go toe-to-toe with him. McCarthy now charged that Professor Owen Lattimore of Johns Hopkins University, who had worked for the Office of War Information during World War II and later served as an occasional consultant for the State Department on Far Eastern affairs, was "the top Russian espionage agent" in the United States. Ignoring his earlier allegations that there were 205, or eighty-one, or even fifty-seven Communists in the State Department, McCarthy pronounced himself "willing to stand or fall on this one," asserting that any substantiation of his allegations against Lattimore should be taken as validation of all his accusations. On March 30, 1950, McCarthy read to the Senate excerpts from a classified letter that, McCarthy claimed, showed that Lattimore had advanced the Communist cause in the Far East in 1943. When Lehman asked if the letter had been turned over to the Tydings committee and McCarthy conceded it had not, Lehman complained that McCarthy, by quoting selectively from documents that he refused to submit to the proper investigating authorities, was making "a spectacle and a sensation for the press and the galleries" in such a way that "an accused man has no chance to answer." McCarthy then offered, if Lehman would "step over here," to "show him part of a document which will make it very clear to him why it would be completely unfair" to release the full text. Lehman advanced toward McCarthy, asking to see the letter, but when he insisted on seeing the whole letter so he could "read it in my own way," McCarthy refused, insisting that the Senator from New York return to his seat. Columnist Stewart Alsop, who was in the press gallery that day, later wrote that McCarthy had contemptuously dismissed Lehman, snarling, "Go back to your seat, old man." According to Alsop, "Lehman looked all around the chamber, appealing for support," but when none came, he reluctantly returned to his seat. For Alsop, the failure of any of Lehman's more senior colleagues to support him in his confrontation with McCarthy "seemed to symbolize the final defeat of decency and the triumph of the yahoos."[15]

When other Republicans joined McCarthy in launching a concerted attack against Dean Acheson and the Truman administration's Far Eastern policy, Senator Lehman stood out again as one of the few Democrats willing to defend the embattled Secretary of State. Senior Democrats remained silent when Senator Wherry charged that Acheson was "a bad security risk" who was "the idol of left-wing, appease Russia agitators," but Lehman rose to Acheson's defense, praising the Secretary as "a public servant of vision, profound intelligence, courage, resourcefulness, and high patriotism—qualities without which we would have no hope today of winning in the great struggle for peace in which we are engaged." A few days later, after Senator Styles Bridges (R-NH) told reporters that "a whole group of Republicans" were about to "go after" Acheson and the Truman administration's policies in Asia, Lehman objected that a "politically inspired" attack against the Secretary "undermines confidence at home or abroad in the integrity and continuity of American foreign policy [and] weakens the structure of the free world." Acheson greatly appreciated Lehman's vigorous "defense of me and of the State Department," noting that "at a time when the attack was bitterest," Lehman was "among the very first in the Senate" to speak on Acheson's behalf.[16]

Desperate to restore some sense of order and bipartisanship in American foreign policy, the Truman administration responded enthusiastically when Senator Vandenberg, the Republican leader in foreign affairs, called for a return to an "unpartisan" foreign policy in late March 1950. On March 28, 1950, the State Department announced the appointment of former Republican Senator John Sherman Cooper of Kentucky to serve as a special advisor to the Secretary of State, hoping that this would satisfy the Republicans, but Vandenberg insisted that the President also name John Foster Dulles to a high-level foreign policy position. Many moderate Republicans blamed the breakdown in bipartisanship on what Senator Irving Ives described as New York Democrats' "deliberate partisan effort" in the 1949 Senate race "to injure Mr. Dulles' reputation and to belittle his contribution to bipartisan foreign policy," so Republicans now argued that Dulles's return to the State Department was necessary to heal the breach between the parties.[17]

In discussing Dulles's possible appointment, Secretary of State Acheson realized it might affect Herbert Lehman's re-election in 1950. Truman, Acheson, and Dulles agreed that the appointment should not look like a deal in which Dulles had promised not to run for the Senate that fall, so no such commitment was sought or offered. But Dulles told Acheson confidentially that he had "no love for politics" and "really disliked the thought of being in the Senate for six years where he would have to spend 90% of his time on matters in which he has little interest." Dulles assured Acheson that if he was "doing really interesting work and serving a useful purpose in the Department," he would not be a candidate in 1950.[18]

Acheson discussed the matter with Senator Lehman before officially announcing Dulles's appointment. Like many Democrats, Lehman still resented Dulles's harsh attacks on him and on the Truman administration's domestic policies during the 1949 campaign, and he worried that the appointment would bolster Dulles's stature as a candidate if he ran again in 1950. The Secretary explained that the President did not want to do anything "which would in any way injure or prejudice Senator Lehman's political standing in New York," and without revealing the assurances he had received from Dulles, Acheson confidently predicted that Dulles "will certainly not run for the Senate" if he were "given responsible work" in the State Department. Acheson also stressed that Senator Vandenberg "thought Dulles' appointment would help greatly in the overall situation." Lehman listened skeptically to the Secretary's assurance that "the President had the political welfare of the Senator very much in mind in suggesting this appointment," but Lehman realized that it was a done deal and this was just a courtesy call. Lehman promised not to "object or obstruct" any action that "the President and the Secretary of State thought was necessary for the implementation of bipartisan foreign policy."[19]

When the State Department announced Dulles's appointment on April 6, Lehman released a statement saying only that he would not object if the President and the Secretary of State believed it would be helpful "to enlist the services of Mr. Dulles." Not being privy to Acheson's conversations with Dulles, Lehman still expected Dulles to run against him again in 1950, and as he told New York State Democratic Chairman Paul Fitzpatrick, he "was not at all pleased with the Dulles appointment," which "would make the campaign next fall much more difficult." When Dulles was asked by reporters whether his new position ruled out another run for the Senate, he emphasized that "no commitment on this point had been sought or given," but the *New York Times* reported that "it was obvious he felt that if the new post worked out, he would remain in it, and out of the Senate race."[20]

In late spring and early summer, Lehman welcomed the entrance of other, more senior Senators into the fight against Senator McCarthy. On May 3, 1950, Lehman was part of a group of eight Democratic Senators who confronted McCarthy over his original allegation in Wheeling that there were 205 known Communists still working in the State Department. Even after the Democrats used local newspaper accounts and affidavits from people who were present that evening to show that he had used the number 205, McCarthy refused to confirm or deny that he had done so. The Democrats tried to attack McCarthy's credibility by demonstrating that he had derived the number 205 from information contained in a letter written by Secretary of State Byrnes in 1946, which obviously could not address how many Communists were employed in the State Department in 1950. A month later, Herbert Lehman was among the first to congratulate Senator Margaret Chase Smith (R-ME) when she made her famous "Declaration of Conscience." Smith criticized those in the Senate who engaged in "hate and character assassination sheltered by the shield of congressional immunity," denouncing those in her party who hoped to ride "to victory through the selfish political exploitation of fear, bigotry, ignorance, and intolerance." Lehman welcomed Smith's "condemnation of the current smear campaign" and praised her for bringing "home to the American people both the evil and the danger of trial by accusation, not trial based on evidence or on proof, but merely on accusation, innuendo, and smear."[21]

Lehman's active opposition to McCarthy and McCarthyism did not go unnoticed by the demagogue's supporters, some of whom also injected anti-Semitism into the mix. On May 29, 1950, the *Chicago Tribune* published an anti-Semitic diatribe written by Walter Trohan, head of its Washington bureau, which charged that Lehman, Supreme Court Justice Felix Frankfurter, and former Secretary of the Treasury Henry Morgenthau, Jr., constituted "the secret government of the United States." Allegedly, "a person with highest State Department connections" had identified Frankfurter "as the most powerful man in the government," Lehman "as a powerful Wall Street force," and Morgenthau "as the spokesman of the powerful Zionist group." Although Trohan conceded in the article that "none of the three has been named as a fellow traveler or has ever fallen under any suspicion of taint of Communism," he accused all three men of being "woven into the case of Alger Hiss, convicted perjurer-spy." He pointed out that "Lehman's niece, Mrs. Helen Lehman Buttenwieser . . . is a firm supporter of Hiss" and that the Hisses had lived in her home for several months after his trial. Trohan also noted that Lehman "played a major role in opposing Senator McCarthy in the latter's efforts to expose Communism in the government, particularly in the State Department," and that "Lehman has defended the State Department thruout [*sic*] the investigation." When Morgenthau raised the possibility of filing a law suit, Lehman doubted "the wisdom of anyone answering this libelous article," and he stressed that he was "far too busy to engage in a controversy regarding a story which is palpably untrue and biased."[22]

III

The outbreak of the Korean War and the arrests of Julius and Ethel Rosenberg and others on charges that they had conspired to pass atomic secrets to the Soviet Union intensified the anti-Communist hysteria in the United States in the summer of 1950. These events overshadowed the Tydings committee's majority report dismissing Senator McCarthy's allegations about Communists in the State Department as "a fraud and a hoax . . . perhaps the most nefarious campaign of half-truths and untruth in the history of this republic." Moreover, the refusal of the committee's two Republicans to sign the committee's report undermined its credibility, leading many people to agree with Senator McCarthy that the report was further evidence of a Democratic cover-up and constituted "a green light to the Red fifth column in the United States." It was in this context that the U.S. Senate considered the Internal Security Act of 1950, and Herbert Lehman had to decide how far he would go in standing up for his beliefs and principles. He understood that in the midst of the Red Scare then occurring, any position or vote that could be seen as "soft on Communism" would be a serious liability and might jeopardize his bid for re-election that fall.[23]

The Internal Security Act originated in various proposals that Republican Representatives Karl Mundt of South Dakota and Richard Nixon of California, Senator Homer Ferguson of Michigan, and others had introduced in previous years to require members of the Communist Party and Communist-front organizations to register with the United States government. The Mundt-Nixon bill had passed the House in 1948, but it never reached the floor in the Senate. In the summer of 1950, however, with American boys fighting against Communism in Korea and Soviet spies being arrested in America, anti-Communist legislation took on new urgency.[24]

Herbert Lehman had long considered anti-Communist legislation an unconstitutional violation of the American people's most basic rights and liberties. As Governor in 1938, he vetoed a bill that would have prohibited Communists from teaching or holding civil service positions in New York State, asserting that such legislation would "abridge freedom of speech, freedom of thought, freedom of the press, and freedom of assembly." A decade later, Lehman worried that his brother-in-law Frank Altschul and many of Lehman's "other liberal friends, in their zeal to curb Communism," were supporting legislation that Lehman believed was "a threat to the maintenance of our democratic principles." In

1950, Lehman confided to Altschul that Senator Mundt's proposal was "so bad that from the very start" Lehman "had no doubt" as to where he "would stand if it came to a vote," but he knew that his position would "be unpopular in many quarters, particularly at this time."[25]

Realizing that anti-Communist legislation enjoyed widespread support in 1950, Lehman hoped that the Democratic Policy Committee would prevent such bills from reaching the Senate floor where, as one of Lehman's aides conceded, "the pressures on the Senators once it comes up may be too powerful to overcome." However, Mundt and others refused to let the matter languish. Mundt emphasized that "American boys are dying in Korea in bloody fighting against Communism," and he asserted that Congress needed to pass his bill and stop "coddling Communists at home who lie in ambush ready to sabotage our heroic efforts abroad." Senate Majority Leader Scott Lucas of Illinois was locked in a tight battle for re-election in 1950, and his opponent was citing Lucas's refusal to bring the anti-Communist bill to the floor as evidence that Lucas was soft on Communism. Giving in to the mounting pressure, Lucas agreed to put the Mundt-Ferguson bill on the Senate agenda.[26]

Herbert Lehman tried to avoid taking a definitive stand on the Mundt-Ferguson bill for as long as he could. When the New York City CIO Council urged him in March 1950 to oppose such legislation because it "would endanger civil rights and union rights under the guide [sic] of fighting subversive activities," Lehman noted that he was still studying the proposed legislation and he qualified his promise to fight the bill by basing it on the union's interpretation of the measure. As late as August 3, 1950, Lehman told an American Legion representative that he was still "studying this legislation" and was "in the process of determining" his position on the bill. He pledged to support "such legislation as may be found necessary to punish espionage, sabotage, or attempts to subvert our form of government by intrigue, force, or violence." However, he also stressed the need "to safeguard our precious rights and freedoms which constitute the heart of our way of life." Lehman explained that the problem was reconciling the peoples' "constitutional rights with the necessity of preventing some few individuals from using those rights for destructive and subversive purposes."[27]

Recognizing the growing strength behind the Mundt-Ferguson bill and, as one presidential aide noted, the difficulty of "beat[ing] something with nothing," the Truman administration and its allies in the Senate sought to sidetrack the measure by proposing a less stringent bill that would tighten existing espionage laws and require increased supervision of aliens. In a special message to Congress on August 8, 1950, the President reminded everyone that the leaders of the Communist Party of the United States had already been convicted of violating the Smith Act of 1940, which made it a crime "to advocate or teach the overthrow of the United States Government . . . by force or violence . . . or to be a member of such a group, knowing its purpose." Without mentioning the Mundt-Ferguson bill by name, Truman asserted that the measure now pending in Congress was "unnecessary, ineffective, and dangerous" because it "would spread a legal dragnet sufficiently broad to permit the prosecution of people who are entirely innocent or merely misguided," while "the real conspirators against our institutions" would be driven "further underground, . . . making it more difficult to reach them." Truman understood that "extreme proposals of this type reflect the widespread public concern about communism which most of our people feel today," but he warned that "we must not be swept away by a wave of hysteria." He emphasized that "the principal protection of a free society against subversion is an alert and responsible citizenry dedicated to the advancement of freedom through democratic means."[28]

Senators immediately offered their own interpretations of the President's message. Senator Mundt claimed that Truman "endorses completely all the major provisions and purposes" of his bill and suggested that the measure should now be approved by unanimous consent, but Majority Leader Lucas asserted that further study was required to compare the President's proposal with the Mundt-Ferguson bill, and he recommended that the President's message and the pending bills all be referred to the Judiciary Committee. While Lucas refused to challenge directly Mundt's contention that Truman now supported his bill, Senator Lehman denied emphatically that the President's remarks could be construed that way, arguing that the President's message constituted "almost a complete rejection of the principles of the Mundt-Ferguson bill," which "would actually place in jeopardy the liberties of the people of our country." When the presiding officer asked formally if there were any objections to considering the Mundt-Ferguson bill, Lehman objected, and the matter was referred back to the Judiciary Committee.[29]

Two days later, Senator McCarran, the conservative Democratic chairman of the Judiciary Committee and a longtime advocate of anti-Communist legislation, suddenly introduced a broad anti-Communist bill of his own. McCarran wanted to make sure that any such measure bore his name, and his proposal contained all the features of the Mundt-Ferguson bill to which Truman had objected, as well as new provisions which Herbert Lehman and liberal Democrats found even more unpalatable. A week later, Lehman and nine other Senators introduced a bill along the lines President Truman had recommended, but McCarran dismissed their proposal as "milk and water" that "would not satisfy the people." Ignoring the administration-backed measure, the Judiciary Committee reported to the floor McCarran's proposal, which required all Communist and Communist-front organizations and their members to register with the Attorney General, created a five-member Subversive Activities Control Board to determine which organizations had to register, prohibited individuals from becoming or remaining members of any such organizations,

and barred members of these organizations from working for the government
or in defense plants or applying for passports. The bill also made it illegal "for
any person knowingly to combine, conspire, or agree with any other person
to perform any act which would substantially contribute to the establishment
within the United States of a totalitarian dictatorship, the direction and control
of which is to be vested in, or exercised by or under the dominion or control
of, any foreign government, foreign organization, or foreign individual." In
addition, the bill tightened immigration restrictions, strengthened espionage and
deportation laws, extended the statute of limitations for espionage and other
crimes, and imposed fines of up to $10,000 and imprisonment for up to ten
years for any violations of its provisions. This was a perfect example of what
Harry Truman had in mind a few years later when he wrote that McCarran's
"record for obstruction and bad legislation is matched by that of only a very
few reactionaries."[30]

After McCarran began the formal Senate debate on his bill on September
5, 1950, with a two-hour, section-by-section analysis of the measure, Herbert
Lehman replied for the opposition with a thirty-three-page speech in which he
charged that the McCarran bill represented "the most dangerous and violent
curtailment of our civil liberties of any legislation that has ever been proposed in the American Congress." Rather than focusing on subversive actions,
Lehman complained, the bill would "outlaw views and penalize persons for
their thoughts and beliefs" and establish "guilt by association and inference,"
violating "the First, Fifth, and Eighth Amendments to the Constitution." The
bill's criteria for defining Communist and Communist-front organizations were
"so dangerously vague," Lehman cautioned, that action could be taken "against
almost any organization which at any time has taken a stand for public housing, for fair employment practices, for the Brannan plan [federal subsidies for
farmers], for rent control, for health insurance, against the Taft-Hartley Act,
or against aid to Franco" because the Communist Party had taken the same
position. Instead of bringing Communists out in the open or providing a basis
for prosecuting them, Lehman asserted that this bill "will drive Communists
completely underground." After all, "what dyed-in-the-wool Communist will
run to the nearest registration office to list himself as such and expose himself
to the penalties" of this bill? "Real professional spies and saboteurs," Lehman
maintained, were "far too clever to be caught in this net" because "they are
not members of the Communist Party and they keep away from it." When the
United States had enacted "the notorious Alien and Sedition laws" in 1798,
Lehman emphasized, they had not been employed against French agents and
provocateurs, as originally intended, but against newspaper editors and critics
of the Adams administration. Similarly, Lehman warned that the McCarran
bill would not "catch only those whose views you hate. All of us," he feared,
"may become victims of the gallows we erect for the enemies of freedom."[31]

Lehman's opposition to the McCarran bill led the Nevada Democrat and other proponents of such legislation to attack Lehman bitterly for allegedly protecting Communists. McCarran had taken an instant disliking to Lehman because Lehman was Jewish; because Lehman was a symbol of New Deal liberalism and international cooperation, causes which McCarran equated with Communism; and because Lehman failed to show the proper deference to senior Senate colleagues like McCarran. After Lehman finished detailing his objections to the proposed legislation, McCarran demanded to know: "Is the Senator from New York trying to defend Communist front organizations?" The following day, Senator Mundt joined in, challenging Lehman's competence and intelligence, accusing him of "deliberately perverting" the bill's contents and asserting that Lehman had repeated "the outright Communist arguments appearing in the Communist press." McCarran resumed the attack a few days later, declaring that "the Senator from New York is more to be pitied than blamed" for his unfamiliarity with the text of the various bills and existing statutes such as the Smith Act. Although Lehman had emphasized that he was not a lawyer, McCarran noted, that had not prevented Lehman from voicing various legal opinions on the proposed legislation and its likely effects. According to McCarran, however, "it should not take a lawyer, nor even a law student, to see the absurdity" of Lehman's statements.[32]

In an election year, and at a time when American soldiers were fighting and dying to prevent the spread of Communism in Korea, the McCarran bill presented Herbert Lehman and liberal Democrats with a dilemma. Even though Lehman and the others believed the bill violated Americans' freedom of speech, freedom of assembly, and freedom from self-incrimination, they knew it would be risky to vote against a measure that most of the public saw as a necessary weapon in the fight against Communism. They had already seen Senator Frank Graham defeated in a Democratic primary in North Carolina in part because his opponent had been able to brand Graham as soft on Communism. Wanting to vote for some sort of anti-communist bill to appease the voters, Lehman and his liberal colleagues had introduced the administration-backed proposal, hoping that it might provide such a vehicle, but the House's rejection of a similar measure in late August made it clear that their bill stood no chance of being adopted.[33]

Desperate for an alternative to the McCarran bill, Lehman, Harley Kilgore (D-WV), Paul Douglas (D-IL), Hubert Humphrey (D-MN), Estes Kefauver (D-TN), and Frank Graham drafted a proposal that they hoped to substitute for the McCarran text. Under this bill, the President would be authorized to proclaim an "internal security emergency" if there were an invasion, an insurrection, a declaration of war, or a congressional resolution authorizing him to do so. In such emergencies, when there were "reasonable grounds" to believe that an individual might "engage in or may conspire with others to engage in acts of espionage or sabotage," such a person could be detained in an internment camp, similar to what had been done with Japanese Americans during World War II. Reasonable grounds for internment would include membership in the Communist Party after January 1, 1949. Detainees would be entitled to a preliminary hearing and an appeal, and all such actions would be subject to further review by the courts. As Julius Edelstein, Senator Lehman's chief assistant, noted, "The operational weaknesses of this amendment are many and its constitutional weaknesses" were "profound." Nonetheless, Edelstein thought that this measure would "certainly impress the public" that Lehman was "determined to act against Communists." From Edelstein's point of view, "the only real dangers" in the proposal were that it would pass and that the Republicans would use it to claim that Lehman was "more of a Fascist" than Dewey. On the whole, Edelstein believed that "this is a pretty bad bill," but it was better than McCarran's version. The measure would likely "come under very heavy attack from some of the liberal organizations," but Edelstein advised that "the political logic of the situation" required that Lehman "go along" with it.[34]

On September 6, 1950, Lehman, Kilgore, and the other sponsors of the amendment met with President Truman, seeking his support for their proposal. The session was supposed to be off the record, but the *New York Times* and the *Washington Post* reported the next day that the Senators had advised the President that the "political temperament" of the nation demanded a strong anti-Communist measure and that the McCarran bill would "scoot to passage unless a tough substitute" were devised. Truman reiterated his opposition to McCarran's bill on constitutional grounds, but much to the Senators' disappointment, he refused to endorse their internment camp proposal. At a press conference the next day, Truman explained that although he considered the liberals' bill "an improvement" over McCarran's text, he would not commit to signing any bill until he saw the final product that emerged from Congress.[35]

Lehman and the others hoped to substitute their proposal for the McCarran bill, but the Senate, by a vote of 45 to 29, rejected their attempt to replace the McCarran text with their own version of the bill. Much to the liberals' dismay, the Senate then added their amendment and its internment camp provision to the McCarran text, making what they considered to be a bad bill even worse. At this point, however, Lehman and the other liberals had run out of options; they had to vote for or against the McCarran bill as amended, and few of them were willing to risk their political futures by voting against a measure that seemed certain to pass anyhow. As Paul Douglas later recalled, once the attempt to substitute their amendment for the McCarran bill had failed, "The administration forces decided to give in and accept the revised bill. They would thus escape being branded as pro-Communists and opponents of internal security. To oppose the bill would mean being labeled pro-Communist. It was with heavy hearts that Humphrey and I conferred together just before the roll call and decided that as a practical matter we would vote for the bill."[36]

But Herbert Lehman chose a different path. Ignoring pleas from New York State Democratic Chairman Paul Fitzpatrick and Tammany Hall leader Carmine De Sapio, who warned that voting against the bill might imperil his re-election that fall, Lehman denounced the proposed legislation as "unwise, unworkable, and indefensible." He insisted that the McCarran bill "will not prevent subversive activities by Communists, but will, instead, increase the strength of the underground Communist movement." Lehman understood that many New Yorkers and many Americans believed, erroneously, "that the McCarran bill is an anti-Communist bill. Because of this misunderstanding," he noted, "some of my colleagues, whom I highly respect, will vote for the McCarran bill," an action which he predicted they would soon regret. As for himself, Lehman declared,

> I will not compromise with my conscience. I will not betray the people of my state in order to cater to the mistaken impression which some of them hold. I shall try to clarify the issue and not to confuse it. I am going to vote against this tragic, this unfortunate, this ill-conceived legislation. My conscience will be easier, though I realize my political prospects may be more difficult. I shall cast my vote to protect the liberties of our people.[37]

Only seven Senators voted against the McCarran bill on the final tally: Senators Graham, Kefauver, Theodore Francis Green (D-RI), Edward Leahy (D-RI), James Murray (D-MT), Glen Taylor (D-ID), and Herbert Lehman. As numerous commentators pointed out, Lehman was the only one of the seven who had to face the voters that November. William Benton (D-CT), who joined Douglas and Humphrey in voting for the measure reluctantly, recognized that Lehman had cast "a very dangerous vote politically," and he told Lehman that "I never admired you more than yesterday in the vote on the McCarran Act." An article in the *Buffalo Evening News* praised all seven Senators who had voted against the McCarran bill, but it singled out Lehman for "special mention since he is the only Senator up for re-election in November who voted against the measure." The article noted that Lehman's "courageous stand dramatizes the meaning of what happened in the Senate—by its very rarity." Similarly, columnist Drew Pearson noted on his radio program that Lehman "may have sacrificed his chance of re-election," and theologian Reinhold Niebuhr recommended in a letter to the *New York Times* that "a special accolade should be awarded to Senator Lehman" who was "the only Senator facing a fall re-election" who "dared to brave the dangerous hysteria which is arising in this country." *The Nation* believed that in his opposition to the McCarran Act, Lehman had emerged from his previous role as "a good, reliable second baseman" and "develop[ed] into another Joe DiMaggio."[38]

After a conference committee reconciled the differences between the House and Senate versions of the Internal Security Act, both chambers approved the bill by veto-proof margins on September 20, 1950. This put the issue before President Truman, who had suggested earlier that he would not sign the McCarran bill, but he had reserved his final decision until he saw the exact text adopted by Congress. Democratic Majority Leader Scott Lucas and the party's congressional leadership urged the President to sign the bill, pointing out that its lopsided support made its final passage inevitable and asserting that the President's approval of the measure would minimize the Republicans' use of anti-Communism as a campaign issue against the Democrats. But Herbert Lehman, Estes Kefauver, and James Murray advised the President to veto the measure with "a message of such force and clarity" that it "would arouse the nation to a realization of the dangers we confront, and would bring our people, who are ordinarily so vigilant and so jealous of our heritage of freedom, to a prompt understanding of the hazards of this legislation." Although they recognized that "the preponderant vote in both Houses in favor of this omnibus measure" would make it difficult to prevent it from being enacted into law, Lehman and the others promised to do all they could to sustain the President's veto in the Senate.[39]

Truman appreciated the Senators' "thoughtful insight and true wisdom concerning the Internal Security Act," and he agreed with his aides that "the signing of the bill would represent an action of moral appeasement on a matter of highest principle." Accordingly, even though he knew Congress would likely override his action, the President vetoed the McCarran bill, charging that "instead of striking blows at communism," this legislation "would strike blows at our own liberties." He asserted that "requiring Communist organizations to divulge information about themselves" would be about as effective "as requiring thieves to register with the Sheriff," and he argued that the adoption of this measure "would delight the Communists, for it would make a mockery of the Bill of Rights and of our claims to stand for freedom in the world." The enactment of this legislation, Truman warned, would "destroy all that we seek to preserve" by sacrificing "the liberties of our citizens in a misguided attempt to achieve national security." The President sent every member of Congress a copy of his veto message, urging them "to read and consider this message very carefully" before they voted on overriding his veto.[40]

Herbert Lehman welcomed the President's "stirring and thought-provoking" veto message, asserting on the floor of the Senate that Truman had "aligned himself with all the great defenders of liberty in this country and in others, not only of this time but of all time." He praised the President for standing firm "in the face of political pressures which were tremendous," predicting that the President's veto of this bill assured him "the precious accolade of history." Privately, Lehman described the President's veto message as "one of the great state documents of our time." He asked White House aide Matthew Connelly if the President could "inscribe a copy of the message to me," a request with which Truman gladly complied, sending Lehman a copy of the veto message on which he wrote: "To Senator Herbert H. Lehman with thanks for his support." Eight years later, Lehman still considered the President's message "one of the finest veto documents I have ever seen."[41]

As Truman and Lehman feared, the House and the Senate quickly overrode the President's veto by substantial margins. The House voted less than an hour after receipt of the President's veto message, clearly ignoring Truman's request that legislators read and think about his views before acting. In the Senate, however, Lehman and a small group of liberals, including Kefauver, Humphrey, Douglas, Murray, and Graham, aided by maverick Republican William Langer of North Dakota, engaged in an extended discussion of the bill, hoping that the additional time would allow the President's veto message to rouse the public enough to change the outcome in the Senate. Lehman's earlier prediction that some of his liberal colleagues would regret their original votes in favor of the McCarran Act quickly came to pass as Senators Douglas, Humphrey, Kilgore, and Dennis Chavez (D-NM), all of whom had voted for the bill originally, now voted to uphold the President's veto; Langer would have done the same if he had not collapsed on the Senate floor after speaking for five hours during the all-night debate on the bill. But after more than twenty hours of continuous debate, twenty-six Democrats, including Majority Leader Lucas, joined thirty-one Republicans to override the President's veto by a vote of 57 to 10. Despite all of Herbert Lehman's efforts, the McCarran Internal Security Act had been enacted into law.[42]

Lehman tried unsuccessfully to change or repeal the McCarran Internal Security Act in subsequent years, but history eventually upheld his view that this was "one of the worst pieces of legislation ever placed on the statute books." As Lehman had predicted, the Communist Party refused to register under the Act, leading to years of litigation that culminated in 1965 when the Supreme Court ruled unanimously that compelling such registration violated the Fifth Amendment's protection against self-incrimination. Ironically, even though Richard Nixon had been one of the original proponents of the Internal Security Act, he later presided over and assisted in its demise. The Nixon administration, seeking to dispel rumors that it planned to utilize the internment camp provisions of the measure to hold black militants and antiwar protestors, called for the repeal of the relevant sections of the McCarran Act in 1969, and Congress finally did so in 1971. And after an abortive attempt to resuscitate the Subversive Activities Control Board by executive order in 1971, President Nixon acceded to congressional demands to eliminate the agency in 1973 by ending its funding.[43]

IV

Herbert Lehman planned to run for a full term in the Senate in 1950, and his prospects for winning re-election seemed excellent. The only way that Lehman could be defeated, many observers believed, was if Governor Dewey ran against him, or if Dewey sought a third term in Albany, which would result in a huge turnout of GOP voters. But Dewey announced in mid-June that he would not be a candidate in 1950, and John Foster Dulles removed himself from consideration in mid-August when he announced that he would continue to serve as a consultant in the State Department, leaving the Republicans without a strong challenger to oppose Lehman.[44]

Despite strong support from Democrats, organized labor, and the Liberal Party, Lehman hesitated about running again in 1950. In mid-May, he confided to a friend, "I have not yet decided whether I wish to be a candidate again this fall." He found the work in the Senate "strenuous but very interesting indeed," but he was "to some extent disillusioned." Although Congress had "enact[ed] part of the progressive program announced by Presidents Roosevelt and Truman," Lehman lamented, "we have been beaten on a great many important issues." While he had "been frequently on the losing side," he remained confident that he had been "on the right side of most of the issues," and he "believe[d] that in time they will prevail." However, especially at the age of seventy-two, Lehman noted that "a six year term is a pretty long commitment."[45]

Before committing to run for re-election, Lehman stressed to Democratic National Committee member Ed Flynn and Democratic State Chairman Paul Fitzpatrick the importance of the Democrats nominating for Governor in 1950 "a strong campaigner" who would attract support from "all factions of the party" and win approval from the Liberal Party. The Senator wanted to avoid a repeat of what had happened in 1949 when he had been burdened with different running mates on the Democratic and Liberal Party lines. In mid-August, before the Democratic leaders settled on their choice for Governor, Flynn orchestrated what he and most observers thought was a major coup that would guarantee victory for Lehman and the Democrats' entire statewide ticket when he persuaded President Truman to nominate New York City Mayor William O'Dwyer to be U.S. Ambassador to Mexico. O'Dwyer's resignation as Mayor would add that office to the ballot in November, ensuring a large turnout in overwhelmingly Democratic New York City, which would, presumably, propel the Democratic state candidates to victory.[46]

Democrats and Liberals quickly coalesced around Lehman as their candidate for Senator and State Supreme Court Justice Ferdinand Pecora for Mayor. Pecora had won widespread acclaim in 1933 when he led the Senate's investigation into corruption in the banking and securities industries, and his selection left only the gubernatorial nominee in question. With the Republicans expected to nominate Lieutenant Governor Joe Hanley to succeed Dewey, Democratic leaders passed over prominent New Dealers and Fair Dealers such as Franklin Roosevelt, Jr., Averell Harriman, and Manhattan Borough President Robert Wagner, Jr. Seeing Hanley as a weak candidate who could be defeated by virtually any Democrat, especially with the mayoral contest bringing out large numbers of Democratic voters in New York City, Democratic leaders chose as their gubernatorial candidate Judge Albert Conway of the State Court of Appeals. With Conway, an Irish Catholic from Brooklyn, running alongside Pecora, a Protestant of Italian heritage, and Lehman, a Jew, the Democratic ticket was designed to appeal to the Democrats' main voting constituencies.[47]

However, organized labor and liberals within the Democratic Party objected to Conway as the party's gubernatorial nominee. Louis Hollander, chairman of the CIO Political Action Committee, expressed his group's disappointment at the Democratic leaders' "failure to agree on a gubernatorial candidate of the caliber we recommended," and he charged that Judge Conway's record on the Court of Appeals showed him to be "anti-labor" and "anti-Negro." Similarly, Bryn Hovde of Americans for Democratic Action cautioned that ADA and its supporters would not "work and vote for a gubernatorial candidate whose support of the liberal position has been or ever can be questioned." Hovde hoped "that the New York voters will be given the chance to vote for a Governor in the tradition of our four great exponents of liberalism, Smith, Roosevelt, Wagner, and Lehman."[48]

Compounding the problem for Democratic Party leaders, Herbert Lehman threatened not to run on a ticket including Judge Conway. In a telephone conversation with State Democratic Chairman Fitzpatrick on September 1, Lehman reported that "he had received from many quarters, labor, liberal, and Negro, strongest representations against Conway and indications that many groups would either actively oppose or, at best, merely be passive" in the campaign. "If such a situation developed," Lehman warned, "the ticket would be sure to go down to defeat." Lehman "was completely disaffected by the entire situation" and "did not wish . . . to get in the middle between his labor and liberal friends and the Party." Moreover, recalling his past problems with Catholics, the Senator wanted to avoid being put in the position of opposing a Catholic candidate "when that opposition might be interpreted as bias against" the Catholic faith. Accordingly, Lehman informed Fitzpatrick that he "thought his only course lay in withdrawing from the situation entirely and declining to run." Fitzpatrick assured Lehman that he had spoken to Hollander and others and was well aware of the growing opposition to Conway's nomination. The chairman "understood the necessity of having a strong and united ticket," and "he was confident that the situation would be adjusted" to Lehman's satisfaction in the next few days. In the meantime, he asked the Senator "to refrain from making any statements to the press" until everything was resolved. Sure enough, the Democratic leaders persuaded Judge Conway to remove his name from consideration for the governorship, clearing the way for Lehman to accept the Democratic and Liberal Parties' nominations for Senator.[49]

The Republican Party in New York also seemed to be in disarray for a while before emerging with a familiar figure at its head. Governor Dewey had removed himself from consideration for a third term back in June, clearing the way for seventy-four-year-old Lieutenant Governor Joe Hanley to run to succeed him. By late August, however, many Republican leaders, including Roy Howard, head of the Scripps-Howard newspaper chain and publisher of the *New York World-Telegram and Sun*, and many of the party's major financial backers were pressuring Hanley to step aside so they could renominate Dewey, citing the war in Korea and the need for experienced leadership in times of crisis. Republican leaders believed that with the New York City mayoralty race now on the ballot too, only Dewey, with his proven vote-getting ability state-wide, could prevent a Democratic victory. At first, Hanley resisted all efforts to push him aside, but Dewey's supporters finally convinced Hanley to remove himself from consideration, and on September 2, Hanley joined the chorus of Republican leaders asking Dewey to run again. Dewey agreed, and, in turn, he asked his fellow Republicans to nominate Hanley for the U.S. Senate seat held by Herbert Lehman, a request that the GOP State Convention enthusiastically granted. Republicans hoped that a huge vote for Dewey might sweep Hanley into the Senate on Dewey's coattails.[50]

Rejecting stronger candidates such as Franklin Roosevelt, Jr., who was seen as too closely associated with the CIO Political Action Committee, Democratic leaders finally united behind Representative Walter Lynch, an Irish Catholic from the Bronx, to oppose Dewey. Lynch was acceptable to all the party's major constituencies, but he was relatively unknown, especially upstate, he was likely to be denounced by Republicans as the candidate of "Boss Flynn," and he was thought to have little chance against Dewey. In their conversation on September 1, Fitzpatrick told Lehman that Lynch was emerging as the likely replacement for Conway on the Democratic ticket and "asked whether Lynch would be acceptable to the Senator." Lehman replied that "as far as he knew, Lynch was a fine man with a liberal record," but he advised that a thorough investigation be conducted to ensure that Lynch or any candidate "could command united support and was invulnerable to major attack." Once the leaders settled on Lynch, Lehman briefly left Washington, where the Senate was debating the McCarran Internal Security bill, to attend the Democratic State Convention. Lehman warmly and enthusiastically endorsed his "old and good friend, Judge Walter Lynch," praising him as "a man of selfless devotion to the public inter-est, . . . a leader in the fight for liberal tax and social security legislation, . . . a good Democrat and a great liberal."[51]

The Lehman-Hanley race began while the Senate was considering Senator McCarran's proposed Internal Security Act, and Lehman made no effort to downplay his opposition to the bill, explaining that the McCarran bill "would not harm Communists at all, because they could and would evade it," but it would "endanger ordinary patriotic citizens and legitimate patriotic organizations, such as labor unions and even church groups which take an active interest in social questions." Lehman actually brought up his opposition to the Internal Security Act more frequently than Hanley, who merely noted that most of Lehman's fellow Democrats in Congress voted to enact the bill over the President's veto.[52]

The suggestion that Lehman was soft on Communism reared its head in another form, however, when Republicans tried to link Lehman with Alger Hiss. The Senator's niece, Helen Lehman Buttenwieser, was part of the team of lawyers working on Hiss's appeal of his perjury conviction, and she accompanied Hiss to court for a hearing on his appeal in mid-October. In case her name was not enough for people to make the familial connection, the *New York Times* specifically identified her as the Senator's niece in the second paragraph of a front-page article. More damningly, on October 19, 1950, Roy Howard's *New York World-Telegram and Sun*, which was supporting Dewey and Hanley, published a letter that Lehman had written to Hiss on August 6, 1948, immediately after Hiss had first testified before the House Un-American Activities Committee and denied Whittaker Chambers's allegations that Hiss had been part of a secret Communist cell in Washington in the 1930s. In the letter, Lehman had expressed his "complete confidence" in Hiss's loyalty and stressed that, "in common with your many other friends, I know that under no conceivable circumstances could you fail to safeguard the interests of your country." Lehman had congratulated Hiss on his "forthright and complete" statement before the committee, and he hoped that Hiss's "denial will catch up with the unfair accusations that have been made."[53]

Victor Lasky, a writer for the *World-Telegram and Sun* who had covered the Hiss trial, had obtained a copy of Lehman's letter to Hiss while doing research for a book on the case, and in April 1950, he had written to Lehman to verify the letter's authenticity and to ask if the Senator had "changed your views concerning Alger Hiss." In a follow-up note two weeks later, Lasky informed the Senator that "the purported Lehman-to-Hiss message was circulated by Mr. Hiss' friends in what apparently was a money-raising drive." Lehman immediately contacted his niece, who reported that Hiss's supporters were "wracking our brains" to figure out how Lasky had obtained the letter. She explained that Hiss's supporters had not used Lehman's letter to raise funds for his appeal, and while there might be people raising money who were "not under our control, none of these people would have access to the letters." She noted that copies of the letter had been shared with board members of the Carnegie Endowment, Hiss's former employer, and she speculated that William Bullitt, an Endowment trustee who had been the first U.S. Ambassador to the Soviet Union and "has been quite active against Alger," might have given the letter to Lasky.[54]

Lehman had replied to Lasky in early May, acknowledging "having written Alger Hiss a friendly letter of confidence in 1948," but emphasizing that if his letter "was circulated in a money-raising drive," it was without his "knowledge or authorization." The Senator ignored Lasky's query about his current opinion about Hiss, and there the matter rested until the *World-Telegram and Sun* printed the letter in the middle of Lehman's re-election campaign in October 1950. In addition to publishing the letter, the paper asked if Lehman would "write the same letter today," if he "support[ed] the activities of your niece, Mrs. Helen Buttenwieser, in behalf of Alger Hiss," and whether Lehman had "seen Alger Hiss recently." A few days later, the *World-Telegram and Sun* added a few more questions, wanting to know if Lehman "contribute[d] money to Alger Hiss' defense," and whether he "help[ed] pay for printing of the trial record."[55]

Lehman responded immediately to the *World-Telegram and Sun*'s publication of the Hiss letter. In a formal statement released that same day, Lehman declared that he had "no apology to make," emphasizing that he had written the letter to Hiss on August 6, 1948, "long before his indictment, trial, and subsequent conviction." The Senator noted that Hiss was then serving as the president of the Carnegie Endowment for International Peace, a position to which he had been appointed on the recommendation of John Foster Dulles and other distinguished citizens. Hiss had impressed Lehman and gained his confidence when they had worked together on the Citizens Committee for the Marshall Plan, and thus, when Hiss had "categorically denied the charges made against him in the course of his appearance before the House Committee on Un-American Activities," Lehman had "assumed that he was telling the truth" and had done what he "felt was the human thing to do." Because Lehman "attach[ed] great importance to that basic rule of conduct which so long governed the Anglo-Saxon world—to consider a man innocent until he has been found guilty"—he had sent Hiss "a line to express my sympathy in the difficult position in which he found himself." And, the Senator stressed, "that's all there is to the story." When asked a few days later for a further comment, Lehman insisted, "I have nothing to add to the statement I made."[56]

Although the *World-Telegram and Sun* and a few others tried to keep the issue alive, neither Governor Dewey nor Joe Hanley raised it on the stump. Perhaps because of Dulles's vulnerability for having hired Hiss at the Carnegie Endowment, Dewey, when asked "What about Lehman and the Communists— the letter he wrote to traitor Alger Hiss?" took the high road, noting that the letter "was written two years ago, . . . before Hiss was indicted and convicted." Dewey emphasized, "I have known Governor Lehman for a great many years.

Everybody knows he's no Communist. No one should ever suspect him of it, or draw the inference that he is. I would hope that he would say today that he did not have the same views he had then." Lehman did say exactly that in early November when the Commander of New York Department of the Catholic War Veterans wanted to know why Lehman had not made "a full repudiation" of his letter to Hiss. The Senator replied, "Obviously, in the light of what has happened since August 1948, I would not write the same letter today." Recalling the whole controversy years later, Lehman maintained, "under the same circumstances I would write exactly the same letter to a man in whom I had full confidence." But, he added, "politics has taught a whole lot of people that it's a dangerous thing to write letters!"[57]

Lieutenant Governor Hanley learned a similar lesson that fall about the perils of letter writing. On September 5, three days after Hanley dropped his candidacy for Governor, he wrote a letter to Suffolk County Republican Chairman W. Kingsland Macy, who, along with Rochester newspaper publisher Frank Gannett, had been among his strongest supporters for the governorship. Hanley was under considerable stress at the time: he was blind in one eye and in danger of losing his sight in the other, he was supposedly in debt because of a failed investment by one of his parents, he had borrowed $30,000 from Macy and Gannett to pay off this obligation and finance his campaign for Governor, and he was under pressure from Republican leaders to withdraw in favor of Dewey. In the letter to Macy, Hanley reported that he had just met with Governor Dewey, from whom he had received "certain unalterable and unquestionably definite propositions" promising that if Hanley would run for the Senate, he was "definitely assured of being able to clean up" his "financial obligations within ninety days" so that he "could be clear for the first time in twenty years." Among those obligations was the loan from Macy and Gannett, which Hanley promised would be repaid in full "within a short time." Hanley noted that he would be "assured of an adequate living compensation if elected, in a perfectly legal and unquestionable way," and, if he were defeated, he had "an iron-clad unbreakable arrangement" that he would be given a state job "at sufficient compensation" to increase his "net income." Hanley explained that this agreement "removes all the gamble from the picture" and enabled him "to face the future with confidence and the knowledge" that even if he lost his eyesight, he "would still have a comfortable living" and be able to meet his responsibilities. Hanley apologized for disappointing Macy and described himself as "humiliated, disappointed, and heartsick" over the whole situation.[58]

Ignoring suggestions from Dewey that he burn the letter in the name of party unity, Macy sought to use the missive to his advantage. He hoped to use the letter to embarrass Dewey by showing that the Governor had been directly involved in the effort to push Hanley aside, thus putting the lie to Dewey's attempt to portray himself as a reluctant candidate. Macy also thought that he could use the letter to further his own ambitions for the Senate nomination and to wrest control of the state Republican Party away from Dewey and his allies. Accordingly, Macy made numerous copies of the letter that he shared with other Republican leaders. One copy soon fell into the hands of the Democrats, who apparently planned to release it shortly before the election, when it would do the most damage. The Democrats believed that the letter would doom Hanley's candidacy and tarnish Dewey's reputation for incorruptibility by revealing that the Governor had promised Hanley a state job for clearing Dewey's path to renomination.[59]

To forestall the Democrats' plan and to get out ahead of the story, Hanley released the letter on October 16, charging the Democrats with waging a "whispering campaign" against him and denying that Dewey had promised him anything. Hanley explained that cashing in a life insurance policy would enable him to pay off his debts, and the realization that he could receive his state pension while serving in the U.S. Senate, as Lehman was doing, had eased his concerns about the cost of living in Washington. He claimed that Dewey had merely expressed a desire not to lose Hanley's twenty-four years of experience and knowledge about New York State if he were unsuccessful in his race for the Senate. In a statewide radio broadcast the following night that was in some ways a precursor to Richard Nixon's famous "Checkers" speech two years later, Hanley again denied any wrongdoing, discussing his financial circumstances and citing his indebtedness after twenty-four years in public service as proof of his honesty and evidence that he faced the same financial burdens as most Americans. A few days later, Hanley expanded on this theme of the Republicans as the party of average Americans rather than plutocrats, contrasting his financial plight with Lehman's wealth. Hanley asserted that a man like himself who had "no portfolio of stocks and bonds in a Wall Street bank, . . . no safety box full of securities" earning "thousands a year," better understood "the millions of little guys in this state" and would do a better job of representing them in the Senate "than a fellow who is so well off that he says, 'I don't need a job.' "[60]

Democratic gubernatorial candidate Walter Lynch had a field day with the Hanley letter, charging Dewey with "criminal disregard of the laws of the State and the mandates of decency and morals" and making the alleged quid pro quo one of the central issues of his campaign. Herbert Lehman, however, refrained for the most part from exploiting Hanley's blunder. Although the New York Times proclaimed on the front page on October 23 that "Lehman Says Hanley Letter Startling," the Senator's first direct public comment on the letter was much milder than the headline suggested. After Lynch had quoted extensively from the letter, Lehman merely stated that Lynch's "illuminating, accurate and startling description" of the letter's contents had "covered that field, at least for this meeting, as well as any one man can do it. It is a startling situation." The Senator then went on to deliver a prepared speech on a bill he had introduced that sought to increase the number of medical practitioners in rural areas. Lehman's reluctance to capitalize on the Hanley letter probably stemmed from his own problems with the Hiss letter, which the *World-Telegram and Sun* published three days after the Hanley letter hit the newspapers, as well as Lehman's long-established preference for campaigning on his record and on the issues rather than personalities. As the *New York Times* noted in late October, leaders of both parties agreed that Lehman's "adherence to issues and his avoidance of mudslinging have increased his stature." When the campaign was over, Lehman observed that he was "much less exhausted than on previous occasions" because this race "lacked the disagreeable personality problems of past campaigns," and Hanley made a point of praising Lehman for the "clean manner" in which the Senator had conducted his campaign.[61]

Even if the Hanley letter did not prove the corrupt bargain that Democrats claimed, it raised serious questions about Hanley's health and his judgment, and most observers believed that it pretty much clinched Lehman's re-election. However, as Lehman confided to Senator Elbert Thomas (D-UT), "a split in New York City" greatly complicated the political situation for Lehman and the Democrats. Ed Flynn's brilliant stratagem of creating a vacancy in City Hall blew up in his face when City Council President Vincent Impellitteri, who had become Acting Mayor, refused to abdicate when Democratic and Liberal Party leaders chose Pecora as their standard-bearer. Rejecting an offer of a state Supreme Court judgeship, Impellitteri ran for Mayor as an independent, denouncing the party bosses who had rejected his candidacy. Most experts believed that Impellitteri had no chance of winning, but, as the *New York Times* noted, his candidacy threatened Lehman and other Democratic candidates because "those who cast their votes for Impellitteri, down near the bottom of the voting machine in column 6, might not bother to return to the Democratic line to vote for Lynch for Governor [and] Lehman for Senator." Impellitteri tried to quiet such fears, declaring on numerous occasions, "I stand 100 per cent behind the candidacy of Senator Lehman," and asserting that his own candidacy would actually help Lehman because it would bring a huge turnout in New York City that would benefit the state ticket, but Liberal Party Vice Chairman Alex Rose and others feared that Democrats voting only for Impellitteri "may make the difference between election and defeat for Lehman and Lynch." Rose warned that "Lehman's defeat would be a great blow to the labor, liberal, and progressive forces of our country." Lehman had "become a great symbol of American liberalism for our whole nation and for the world," which was "why he is the central target of all reactionaries."[62]

When New Yorkers went to the polls on November 7, 1950, many voters demonstrated that party loyalty had been replaced by a new spirit of independence and assessing each candidate on his merits rather than hewing to a straight party line. Herbert Lehman was the only Democrat to win statewide, defeating Hanley by 264,780 votes. In the race for Governor, Dewey trounced Lynch by more than 570,000 votes, and the Republican candidates for Lieutenant Governor, Attorney General, and Controller were also victorious. In New York City, despite running as an independent candidate, Impellitteri rolled to victory over Pecora by 220,000 votes. As Dewey had promised, he made sure that Joe Hanley was taken care of after the election, helping him secure appointment as "special counsel to the State Division of Veterans Affairs at an annual salary of $16,000," a sinecure that included an additional $6,000 for travel and office expenses, and also allowed Hanley to draw his $4,000 a year pension and establish a private law practice in Albany. As for Herbert Lehman, as he told one of his nieces, he now "look[ed] forward to a six year term with no campaigns in view."[63]

Democratic candidates in other states did not fare as well as Lehman, and the defeats suffered by such prominent Democrats as Senate Majority Leader Scott Lucas in Illinois, Senate Majority Whip Francis Myers in Pennsylvania, and Senator Millard Tydings in Maryland overshadowed Lehman's victory in New York. Although the Democrats retained nominal control of Congress, and their losses of five Senate seats and twenty-eight House seats were smaller than in the previous three midterm elections, their continued majority depended on conservative Southerners who were opposed to much of the President's Fair Deal. Even more ominously, Senator McCarthy, who had been actively involved in the Maryland and Illinois races, received much of the credit for Tydings's and Lucas's defeats. Richard Nixon's victory in California over Helen Gahagan Douglas was also seen as a victory for red-baiting and McCarthyism. Harold Ickes, who had served as FDR's Secretary of the Interior, attributed the Republican successes "to the widespread hysteria that prevails in the United States," and columnist Marquis Childs wrote that "in every contest where it was a major factor, McCarthyism won." President Truman interpreted the results very differently, observing that "Senator Lehman and Senator Benton, who stood squarely for Democratic principles and fought for them, won in spite of adverse conditions," while Lucas and others "who tried a policy of appeasement were overwhelmingly defeated." Similarly, *The Nation* rejected the conventional wisdom, asserting that Tydings had been defeated not because of McCarthy, but because "his record as an arch-conservative" had dissuaded labor and blacks from rallying to his defense. But as Lehman confided to his great-niece June Bingham and her husband, his pleasure at being re-elected was "materially marred by disappointments in the State and the loss of many friends in the United States Senate." With good reason, Lehman feared that "the next session of Congress will be difficult and frustrating."[64]

V

Much to Herbert Lehman's dismay, most of his next six years in the Senate proved to be as "difficult and frustrating" as he had feared. First and foremost, the problem of McCarthyism continued to vex the Senate and the nation, and as Lehman recalled in 1954, "for a long time," his "was a 'lone voice in the wilderness'" in standing up to Senator McCarthy. As David Caute graphically observed in *The Great Fear*, with the defeats of Senators Tydings and Lucas in 1950, "Lehman now became McCarthy's most vigorous critic in a Senate where few dared to burn their political fingers by flushing fire from his nostrils." Mrs. Lehman lamented the toll that the "emotionally difficult and exhausting" battles with McCarthy inflicted on her husband's health and well-being, but Herbert Lehman always took great pride that he was among "the very first to fight McCarthyism."[65]

Lehman continued to challenge Senator McCarthy and McCarthyism in all its forms. In December 1950, Lehman forcefully defended Anna M. Rosenberg when McCarthy and a cabal of right-wingers and anti-Semites tried to block her appointment as Assistant Secretary of Defense. Conservative radio broadcaster Fulton Lewis, Jr., anti-Semitic white supremacist Gerald L. K. Smith, and others charged that Rosenberg, who had previously served as a regional director for the National Recovery Administration, the Social Security Administration, and the War Manpower Commission, had been a member of Communist front organizations and had associated with numerous fellow travelers. Lehman declared publicly that Rosenberg was "one of the most capable women I have ever met," and that he had "always found her completely loyal and deeply devoted to the interests of our country." Moreover, as Rosenberg later recalled, Lehman refused to let the matter rest with a mere statement on her behalf. When the Senate Armed Services Committee held hearings on her nomination, Lehman exercised his privilege as a Senator and attended "every single hearing" even though he was not a member of the committee, and when a witness erroneously identified Rosenberg as a Communist sympathizer he had met years ago, Lehman "was so shocked" that she "saw the tears rolling down his face." Although the man's testimony was quickly discredited and Rosenberg was confirmed, she never forgot Lehman's "magnificent" response to the "histrionics and hysteria" that characterized this period.[66]

While most Senators cowered, concerned that their scalps might join Tydings's and Lucas's in McCarthy's trophy case, Herbert Lehman helped William Benton challenge McCarthy and Senate Republicans on the Senate floor on February 1, 1951. By prearrangement, Lehman was presiding over the Senate when Benton criticized McCarthy's appointment to the Senate Appropriations subcommittee that had jurisdiction over the State Department's funding.

Benton questioned the wisdom of giving "the potential power of life or death over any government department—the power to grant or withhold funds, or to allot them in detail—to any Senator who had proved himself an implacable and . . . irresponsible enemy of the Department." A seat on this subcommittee, Benton charged, would enable McCarthy to carry out his policy of "if you can't make one libel stick, try another, and then try another." When McCarthy ally Herman Welker (R-ID) protested that Benton was out of order, that he had violated the rules of the Senate by inferring "malicious and bad conduct" to McCarthy and "imputing to him conduct and motives unworthy of a Senator," Lehman, as the presiding officer, ruled that Benton's remarks did not violate the rules of the Senate, and a motion by Majority Leader Ernest McFarland (D-AZ) that Benton be "be permitted to proceed in order" was approved. A few days later, Benton thanked Lehman "for missing your lunch and taking the chair when I gave my talk about Senator McCarthy." Realizing that his ignorance of the Senate's rules had gotten him into difficulty, Benton was grateful that Lehman had rescued him from unforeseen troubles. Years later, Benton recalled that when he first spoke out against McCarthy, "only Herbert, among the liberal senators, came forward publicly in support," most of the other liberals believing that "the timing was wrong." According to Benton, "with Herbert, the right time for espousing the right cause was always *now*. . . . There was never any question where Herbert Lehman stood!"[67]

On February 12, 1951, Democratic Senators Harley Kilgore, Herbert Lehman, Olin Johnston (SC), and Hubert Humphrey noted that it had been one year since Senator McCarthy's original speech in Wheeling, West Virginia, and they pointed out that McCarthy had never come forward with his list of 205 "card-carrying Communists" allegedly working in the State Department. Kilgore claimed that because of McCarthy's wild charges, "a fog of confusion has risen and spread across the land," and he demanded that McCarthy "come to bat with his proof and not merely with allegations." Lehman complained that McCarthy, "without one shred of evidence, purely on the basis of irresponsible and vicious statements," had sought "to blacken the names of great Americans, patriotic and loyal Americans, who have served their country with distinction and devotion," including such men as Secretary of State Acheson, Ambassador-at-Large Philip Jessup, Secretary of Defense George Marshall, and former Secretary of State Cordell Hull. Lehman praised Senator Benton's earlier remarks objecting to McCarthy's appointment to the Appropriations subcommittee that oversaw the State Department's funding, but he questioned why "very few newspapers in this country made any substantial mention of the speech, or of the issue involved," and why "the newspapers simply permitted the issue to die without any substantial reference to it." This lack of coverage of Benton's speech and the issue he had raised, Lehman believed, demonstrated that "there is hysteria, that there is panic, that there is fear on the part of people that if they raise their voices in any way in defense of those who may be accused irresponsibly, they will be accused of being 'soft' toward Communism." Supporting Lehman's point about the press treating McCarthy with kid gloves, Drew Pearson noted that the day after the Democrats' February 12 attacks on McCarthy, "not one word of this criticism against McCarthy appeared in the *New York Times* or the *New York Herald Tribune* or the *Washington Post*."[68]

In one of his most controversial acts as President, on April 11, 1951, Harry Truman fired General Douglas MacArthur from his command of United States and United Nations forces in the Far East after the General publicly challenged the President's policy of keeping the war in Korea limited to that peninsula. MacArthur's dismissal triggered a partisan debate over America's Far Eastern policy, with Senators McCarthy and Jenner calling for the President's impeachment, and Richard Nixon advocating that Truman be censured and MacArthur reinstated. Democrats sprang to the President's defense, with Lehman and Senator Robert Kerr (D-OK) warning that MacArthur's recommendation to utilize Chiang Kai-shek's Chinese Nationalist forces against Communist China would widen the war in Asia. Senator Taft and Senator Homer Capehart (R-IN) noted in response that the United States was already fighting a war against Red China on the Asian mainland. Lehman and Capehart engaged in an especially nasty exchange when Lehman charged that Capehart had answered affirmatively a few months earlier when asked if he favored "the United States engaging in an all-out war with Red China." Capehart emphasized that he "would send American soldiers to kill those who were killing American soldiers, regardless of where they were," and Lehman asserted that Capehart's "very frank statements . . . show that he and his associates desire to embroil the United States and the United Nations in an all-out land war in Red China."[69]

The disagreement among Senators over Far Eastern policy boiled over ten days later when Herbert Lehman, Hubert Humphrey, Robert Taft, and Homer Capehart taped an episode of the radio program *Meet Your Congress*. Lehman claimed that Capehart's support for using Chinese Nationalist troops in Korea showed that he was "for a declaration of war on China, which would mean all-out world war," while Capehart denied the allegation and retorted that Lehman and Humphrey seemed to be "sympathetic with Communist China." When Humphrey protested that Capehart's remark was an "absolute vilification," Capehart charged that the two Democrats were "not fundamentally opposed to the Communist government in China." Humphrey replied that Capehart was "a prevaricator" who was "deliberately indulging in falsehood and character assassination," while Lehman emphasized that he had "fought more strenuously against Communism" than Capehart ever had, and he asserted that Capehart's remark constituted "a libelous statement." Capehart denied that his words were libelous and challenged Lehman and Humphrey: "If you want to do something about it, it is perfectly agreeable to me."[70]

In a scene out of the Worldwide Wrestling Federation playbook, the Senators continued their verbal fireworks on their way out of the studio, and the conflict quickly escalated into a pushing and shoving match. As the *New York Times* described it, thirty-nine-year-old "Hubert H. (The Lip) Humphrey," five feet eleven inches tall and weighing 160 pounds, followed fifty-three-year-old "Homer E. (Slugger) Capehart," also five feet eleven inches tall but weighing 220 pounds, to the studio door, where, according to Capehart, Humphrey called him "an S.O.B. without the initials." Humphrey denied using any profanity, not even "gosh darn," claiming that he merely told Capehart that he "deeply resent[ed] this type of vilification, character assassination, and malicious unfounded statements" and wanted "no more of it." At that point, Capehart admitted, he grabbed hold of Humphrey "by the lapel of his coat and pushed him out of the studio." The seventy-three-year-old Lehman, five feet seven inches tall and weighing 165 pounds, tried to intervene on Humphrey's behalf, tapping Capehart on the shoulder and swinging him around, at which point Capehart, who asserted that Lehman attacked him "from the rear," shoved Lehman back into the studio. Although the *New York Times* treated the skirmish in a jocular way, giving a "round by round" account as if it were a boxing match, the *Washington Post* stressed in an editorial that it was "especially disgusting to see Senators resorting to these tactics when they should be setting an example to other citizens" about the need "for cool heads and deliberate decisions—not hot words, emotional outbursts or the use of physical force to end an argument."[71]

Refraining from further fisticuffs, Herbert Lehman used a major Senate speech on April 24 to respond to Capehart and others who had denounced the President's Far Eastern policy and his firing of MacArthur. Lehman believed that Truman "had no alternative" but to remove MacArthur, emphasizing that under the American system of civilian rule, "no military commander has the right to try to secure, by public appeals, approval of his own policies as against the declared policies of his government." American intervention in Korea, Lehman proclaimed, was "designed to prevent world war rather than to precipitate it," but he feared that MacArthur's policies "would involve us in a big war in order to bring a speedy end to a small one." The Senator pointed to the present involvement in Korea to refute the allegations that the Truman administration "is appeasing Communism in Asia while opposing Communism in Europe," but he emphasized that "Europe is the only continent besides our own which possesses any considerable economic power," and he cautioned that Europe was "the prize Stalin is after." When Senator Wherry tried to rebut Lehman's argument, asserting that the large volume of mail Senators were receiving and the vast throngs turning out for parades showed that the American people agreed with General MacArthur's recommendations, Lehman conceded, "the majority of the letters, telegrams, and postal cards" he was receiving "favored the

MacArthur position," but he emphasized, "I act on the basis of my conscience, not on the basis of the volume of my mail."[72]

After a brief interlude of relative quiet, the McCarthy front erupted again in August 1951 when the Senate Rules Committee's Subcommittee on Privileges and Elections issued a scathing report denouncing McCarthy's role in the 1950 Maryland Senate race in which Millard Tydings had been defeated. Trying to ensure that the subcommittee's report received sufficient attention, Senator William Benton introduced a resolution three days later asking the Rules Committee to determine whether McCarthy's actions warranted his expulsion from the Senate. As was his normal operating procedure, rather than answering the charges raised by the report, McCarthy leveled new accusations, attacking by name twenty-six alleged current or former State Department employees who were purportedly being investigated as possible security risks. McCarthy's targets again included Ambassador-at-Large Jessup, who, according to McCarthy, had vouched for Alger Hiss's loyalty, echoed the Communist line as set forth in *The Daily Worker*, and "was affiliated with not one, not two, not three, not four, but with five organizations officially named as fronts for and doing the work of the Communist Party."[73]

Herbert Lehman and Senate Majority Leader Ernest McFarland responded immediately to McCarthy's attack on Jessup, denouncing what McFarland described as McCarthy's use of "innuendo and insinuation" to "charge a high official of this government, a man who had served his country for a lifetime with distinction and honor, with being a traitor or a near traitor." McFarland condemned the use of "smear" tactics and lamented, "when the name of any member of the Senate becomes an adjective for mud slinging, we have come a far way from the tradition of those great men who preceded us here; we have torn down the dignity and standing and respect that this body should enjoy." Lehman deplored "the process of making charges in public against the loyalty of certain persons under the protection of congressional immunity" as "a form of character assassination which all of us must abhor and condemn," and he defended Jessup against McCarthy's "shabby and dastardly treatment." When Senator Wherry protested that Lehman had violated the Senate's rules, Lehman agreed to change the word "dastardly" to "cowardly," and he emphasized that "the time is long overdue when we should have rebuked the authors of antics reflecting on men without supporting the charges with any real evidence."[74]

In mid-September 1951, Lehman crossed swords again with Senator McCarran, who had appointed himself as chairman of the Judiciary Committee's newly created Internal Security Subcommittee. The subcommittee was hearing testimony from former Communist Louis Budenz, who asserted that the Communist victory in China had been the result of a plot by various Communist sympathizers inside the U.S. government. According to Budenz, the plotters included then Vice President Henry Wallace, who had traveled to Russia and China in 1944; State Department official John Carter Vincent; and Professor Owen Lattimore, who had been targeted by Senator McCarthy in 1950. Syndicated columnist Joseph Alsop wrote a series of columns in which he accused Budenz of lying to the subcommittee, pointing out numerous inconsistencies between Budenz's current testimony and his previous statements. In a brief speech on September 14, Herbert Lehman asked for an investigation into Alsop's allegations "that some of the key testimony given before the subcommittee was demonstrably false." He described Alsop's "grave, published charges" as a "stain upon the Senate," and he hoped that an immediate inquiry would quickly resolve the matter. Lehman also sought to insert Alsop's columns into the *Congressional Record*, normally a routine request, so that all of his colleagues would "know the kind of accusation that has been leveled against a committee of the Senate." When Senator Owen Brewster (R-ME) threatened to block the unanimous consent required to place the articles in the *Record*, arguing that McCarran should first be given an opportunity to respond to the articles, Lehman agreed to withdraw his request temporarily.[75]

Later that day, Lehman renewed his attempt to place the Alsop articles in the *Record*, pointing out how unusual it was for Senators to object to such a request. This time, McCarran responded with both barrels blazing, asserting that Lehman, by offering "an unsworn, unsupported statement which accuses me of suborning perjury, . . . has overstepped every bound I have ever known of in the Senate." Lehman protested that he had not accused the Nevada Senator of anything; he had merely called for an investigation into Alsop's charges. But McCarran ally Senator Herman Welker objected to Lehman's request, which again prevented the insertion of the Alsop columns into the *Congressional Record*.[76]

Lehman finally succeeded in getting the Alsop articles into the *Congressional Record* ten days later. This time, instead of asking unanimous consent to insert the columns into the *Record*, Lehman planned to read them on the floor of the Senate. Senator Brewster objected again, asserting that if Lehman included the columns in his remarks, he would be violating the rules of the Senate because "the articles certainly do impute unworthy motives and unworthy conduct" to another Senator. But even when Senators Welker, Walter George (D-GA), Leverett Saltonstall (R-MA), and George Malone (R-NV) joined in the effort to prevent Lehman from reading the columns into the *Record*, Lehman refused to yield, and Senator Kenneth McKellar (D-TN), who was presiding, ruled that Lehman could proceed since he had not yet made any statements to which anyone could object. Once Lehman began reading the columns aloud, the opposition melted away, and he proceeded to read the Alsop columns, with their criticism of the McCarran subcommittee, into the *Record*.[77]

Like most Democrats, Herbert Lehman hoped that Wisconsin voters would rid the Senate of McCarthy in the 1952 elections, but, in the meantime, Lehman and William Benton continued to challenge McCarthy at every opportunity. When Benton waived his congressional immunity while asserting that McCarthy was guilty of "fraud and deceit" and "hit and run" tactics that reminded people in Europe of Hitler, Lehman immediately praised Benton for performing "a great service to our country." When McCarthy followed through on his threat to sue Benton for libel and slander, Lehman was the only Senator to come to Benton's defense, pledging "to support Senator Benton in his proper efforts to require decency, integrity, and responsibility in persons who hold the high office of United States Senator." Two years later, McCarthy quietly dropped his law suit.[78]

VI

One of Herbert Lehman's biggest disappointments in the Senate came in 1952 when he, Hubert Humphrey, and other liberals failed to prevent the adoption of the McCarran-Walter Immigration Act, a measure that Senator Wayne Morse (R-OR) later denounced as "an act of desecration to the Statue of Liberty." This new proposal by McCarran increased the total number of immigrants allowed to enter the United States by only a few hundred, and it retained the quota system based on the 1920 census, which resulted in large, unused allocations for England, Germany, and other countries in Northern and Western Europe, while much smaller quotas for Italy, Poland, and other nations in Southern and Eastern Europe were oversubscribed. The bill prohibited any transfer of unused slots from one country to another, and rather than counting immigrants from colonies in the Western Hemisphere as part of the mother country's quota, as had previously been the case, it imposed quotas of one hundred on Jamaica and other such dependencies, effectively slowing to a trickle the number of immigrants who could enter the United States from the Caribbean. McCarran's proposal also made it easier to deport aliens, and it created what the *New York Times* called "a special kind of second-class citizenship" for naturalized citizens, who could lose their citizenship and be expelled for minor offenses or past or future membership in the Communist Party or any organization designated as a Communist front. The only redeeming features of the bill were that it lifted the barrier to Asians becoming American citizens, established quotas of one hundred for Japan and other Asian nations whose citizens had previously been barred from coming to the United States, and prohibited discrimination based on gender.[79]

Herbert Lehman condemned McCarran's immigration bill, charging that it reflected a "xenophobic" and "racist" attitude "of fear, suspicion, and distrust of the foreigners outside our country, and of the aliens within our country." Lehman asserted that the proposal was premised "on the assumption that America is under the constant threat of losing her Anglo-Saxon character because of immigration, and that the so-called blood-stock of America, described as Anglo-Saxon and Nordic, is the basis of America and must be preserved from contamination by foreign immigrants." As Lehman noted, however, "This racist philosophy based on belief in blood-stocks and the superiority of the Nordic strain" was "strikingly similar to the basic racial philosophy officially espoused so unfortunately and with such tragic consequences in Nazi Germany." According to Lehman, McCarran and the bill's supporters failed to realize that "America was settled and peopled entirely by immigrants from many lands and many continents," and that "what makes America is not the racial or national ancestry of our inhabitants, but the very mixture and melding of many cultures and blood strains, and the fusing of those streams, in a climate of freedom and opportunity into a mighty river of energy, industry, and individual dignity." The McCarran bill, Lehman warned, "would choke and cut off immigration, erect new barriers, and establish new tests and devices whose only purpose can be, not to halt the admission of subversives and undesirables—we all agree on and favor restrictions to that end—but to curtail, impede, strangle, and eliminate all but a trickle of immigration."[80]

Trying to avoid some of the mistakes they had made in their belated and futile opposition to the Internal Security Act two years earlier, and hoping to slow down the momentum building behind McCarran's proposal so that various religious groups could organize a public education campaign on the issue, Lehman and a group of liberal Senators drafted an alternative immigration bill. The Lehman-Humphrey bill, as it came to be known, did not go as far as Lehman would have liked, but it would have brought about what the Senator described as "a more liberal immigration policy within a framework of greater security for the United States." The Lehman-Humphrey bill based all quotas on the 1950 census, increased the actual number of immigrants entering the United States by permitting unused slots to be shifted from one country to another, eliminated racial barriers and gender distinctions, and made it easier for political and religious refugees to enter the United States.[81]

During Senate consideration of the immigration bill, Senator McCarran treated Lehman and the liberals with his usual disdain and contempt. The Lehman-Humphrey bill was referred to the Judiciary Committee, but McCarran refused to convene a hearing on the measure, claiming that the committee had already considered all the relevant issues and that it was "an insult to the integrity of the Senate and committee" to suggest otherwise. McCarran belittled Lehman and the other liberals, noting that "every Senator who voted against the Internal Security Act and who is still a member of the Senate is listed as a sponsor of the so-called Humphrey-Lehman substitute bill." He asserted that opposition to his bill was limited to "small isolated 'radical' groups" and "a gang of cloak and suiters from New York," and he equated Lehman's position to that being taken by Communists and their supporters who "are bent upon the destruction of our protective immigration and naturalization system." McCarran refused to yield to Lehman for questions, although he allowed Senator Mundt and other supporters of the bill to interrupt him frequently. When McCarran finally finished his remarks, rather than listening to Lehman's response and engaging in a real dialogue over the bill, he left the Senate chamber and virtually all the measure's supporters went with him, leaving Lehman to address a mostly empty hall. As Lehman's aide Julius Edelstein later recalled:

> Lehman considered Senate debate as a great thing, where truth was thrashed out and logical decisions arrived at. . . . But McCarran did him the utter discourtesy of absenting himself from the floor, and not only him but everybody who was on the opposite side of this particular question. They declined to listen to him. They gave him the total absent treatment. . . . Of course, to Lehman it seemed a travesty of the senatorial process.[82]

Believing that enactment of the McCarran bill would be worse than leaving the current immigration law intact, Lehman and his liberal colleagues hoped to take advantage of the Senate's desire to adjourn soon for the summer's presidential nominating conventions and the fall campaign. Lehman and his allies proposed more than one hundred amendments to the 302-page bill to ensure "sufficient debate to acquaint the Senate with both sides of this question." When McCarran accused Lehman and Humphrey of engaging in a "filibuster-by-amendment" against the bill, they denied any such plan, emphasizing that they "do not believe in filibusters" and merely desired to "debate this issue on the merits of the case." While Lehman, Benton, Humphrey, Paul Douglas, Brien McMahon (D-CT), and John Pastore (D-RI) continued to make the case against the bill, McCarran remained silent, knowing that he had the votes. On May 19, the Senate rejected a motion to send the matter back to the Judiciary Committee, and two days later, it defeated an attempt to substitute the Lehman-Humphrey bill for the McCarran text. As the Senate quickly rejected the liberals' amendments, Lehman and his colleagues concluded that their best chance of blocking the McCarran bill was to round up enough votes to sustain a presidential veto of the measure, so they did not object on May 22 when the Senate approved the McCarran bill by a voice vote.[83]

While Senate and House conferees reconciled some technical differences between their versions of the immigration bill, Lehman and his allies worked feverishly to persuade President Truman to veto the measure. Lehman confided to Eleanor Roosevelt that he was "very hopeful that the President will veto the bill and that we will be able to muster enough votes to sustain it," but he also noted that "it would be very helpful" if she "could urge the President to veto the bill." He even enclosed a draft letter she could send to the President. Lehman, Humphrey, Benton, and Senator Blair Moody (D-MI) met with Truman on June 5 to deliver the same message in person, and, along with Senator Warren Magnuson (D-WA) and Lehman aide Julius Edelstein, they conferred with the President again on June 9 to report that they had enough votes to sustain a veto. Truman did not need much persuading, and on June 25, he vetoed the measure on the grounds that it "would perpetuate injustices of long standing against many other nations of the world . . . and intensify the repressive and inhumane aspects of our immigration procedures." Lehman, Humphrey, and the others immediately congratulated the President on his "courageous decision" to veto the McCarran bill and pledged to do their "utmost" to uphold his veto and continue the "fight for sound, humane, and forward-looking immigration legislation." At the same time, Senator McCarran denounced the President's veto as "one of the most un-American acts" he had seen during all his years in the Senate, and he charged that Truman had "adopted the doctrine that is promulgated by *The Daily Worker*."[84]

    Once again, however, Senator McCarran prevailed as the Senate voted 57 to 26 to override the President's veto. As Lehman explained to John Slawson of the American Jewish Committee, the bill's opponents lost once again partly because they were poorly organized. According to Lehman, "many of our people were absent . . . and we had no time to get them back" when the Senate refused to postpone the vote until the following week. In addition, McCarran undermined the opposition to the measure when he revealed that the State Department had urged the President to sign the bill, although he neglected to explain that this recommendation reflected the State Department's fear that if it did not do so, McCarran would use his authority as chairman of the Appropriations Subcommittee to hold the State Department's budget hostage. The State Department's position, which emphasized that Japan and other Asian countries supported the bill because it would allow a small number of their citizens to enter the United States, shocked and embarrassed Lehman and the bill's opponents, and Senator Benton complained to Department officials that it "had cost them the two votes necessary to sustain the veto." Even after Congress adopted the McCarran-Walter Act, which Lehman later characterized as "a bill of abominations," Lehman continued his efforts to liberalize the nation's immigration laws. He understood that the fight "for effective changes in the McCarran-Walter Act" would need to "go on for a long time." Significant reforms along the lines Lehman envisioned were not enacted until 1965.[85]

CHAPTER 14

"A Poison Has Begun Spreading Throughout Our Land"

Lehman and McCarthyism, 1953–1954

His record against McCarthy will stand to his everlasting credit.[1]

Republican victories in the 1952 elections enhanced Senator McCarthy's power and influence. The Wisconsin Republican won his own battle for re-election, and his campaign forays into Connecticut were seen as contributing to the defeat of William Benton, one of McCarthy's chief critics in the Senate. As William S. White pointed out in the *New York Times* in early 1953, all Senators were aware that McCarthy had helped defeat Millard Tydings in 1950, and they believed that his intervention in 1952 had helped bring down Benton, Democratic leader Ernest McFarland in Arizona, Joseph O'Mahoney in Wyoming, and others. Although Benton's defeat had more to do with the Eisenhower landslide, which Herbert Lehman described as "the irresistible tide which no one could stem," most Democrats agreed with *New York Times* reporter Cabell Phillips that McCarthy's "pike is already decorated with the heads of half a dozen former Senators who were so injudicious as to tangle with him," and Benton's "head is now one of the prize trophies on the aforementioned McCarthy pike."[2]

I

Benton's defeat left Herbert Lehman as one of the few Senators ready and willing to stand up to McCarthy. With Republican Dwight Eisenhower

---

Chapter title quotation: Herbert Lehman in 99 *Congressional Record* 2299 (March 25, 1953).

in the White House and the Republicans in the majority in the Senate, new Senate Minority Leader Lyndon Johnson and most of the Democrats adopted the position that McCarthy was now "a Republican problem" to be handled by the Eisenhower administration and Republican Senators. According to LBJ aide Bobby Baker, Johnson believed that "you don't get in a pissin' contest with a polecat," and he decided to treat McCarthy "like he was a rattlesnake . . . to keep a great distance but to realize that he had a lethal capacity." Lehman, on the other hand, thought that a bully like McCarthy had to be challenged and confronted at every opportunity, and since the Democratic leadership would not do so, Lehman took the task upon himself. When John Oakes wrote in the *New York Times Magazine* in April 1953 that "no member of Congress— Democratic or Republican—cares personally to tangle with McCarthy," a letter to the editor immediately pointed out that "Senator Lehman of New York has courageously spoken up on the floor of the Senate and off it in regard to his low opinion of Senator McCarthy and his sordid tactics." The *Times* itself observed a few months later that Lehman was one of the "few Senators in recent months [who] have had the stomach directly to criticize Mr. McCarthy's activities on the Senate floor."[3]

Unlike President Dwight Eisenhower, who informed his aides that he would not "get into the gutter" to fight against McCarthy and McCarthyism, Herbert Lehman was prepared to do whatever was necessary to stop what he called "the forces of ignorance and inquisition." In late March, for example, when the Senate debated the nomination of career diplomat Charles (Chip) Bohlen to be Ambassador to the Soviet Union, McCarthy condemned Bohlen's "complete, wholehearted 100 percent cooperation with the Acheson-Hiss-Truman regime," wanting "no part of a man who was part of the Acheson betrayal team" and a " 'chip' off the old block of Yalta." In the process of making his case against Bohlen, McCarthy also smeared Averell Harriman, charging that the former Ambassador to the Soviet Union, under whom Bohlen had served in Moscow, had "a consistent record as a guy who hits only to left field," and that Harriman's "admiration for everything Russian is unrivaled outside the confines of the Communist Party."[4]

While most of the Democrats sat on the sidelines and took pleasure in McCarthy's attacks on Secretary of State John Foster Dulles and Acting Senate Majority Leader William Knowland, Herbert Lehman's rage and indignation boiled over. Although Lehman had not planned to speak, he felt compelled to act because he believed that "from the halls of Congress, a poison has been spreading throughout our land," allowing innocent victims to be slandered with no chance to defend themselves. Lehman pointed out that in all the years of Bohlen's long government service, "there has never been a blemish on his record, there has never been any reflection on his loyalty, his integrity, or his character; and yet, on the basis of flimsy rumor, this fine public servant has in recent days been pilloried and assaulted; his character has been placed under suspicion, and his usefulness in the service of his country, of course, has been tremendously lessened." Lehman also objected to McCarthy's "unfounded accusations" against Harriman, emphasizing that he knew of "no man who is more loyal or more devoted, or who has been more eager to serve his country, or who has been more effective in the service of his country than Averell Harriman." Lehman quoted from James Forrestal's recently published diary to show that Harriman had been among the first in the American government to warn about the dangers the Soviet Union would pose in the postwar world.[5]

As he watched McCarthy's Permanent Subcommittee on Investigations, Senator William Jenner's Internal Security Subcommittee, and Representative Harold Velde's (R-IL) House Un-American Activities Committee investigate and harass civil servants, teachers, librarians, labor leaders, newspaper editors, churchmen, entertainers, and others, Lehman grew more and more appalled at this spread of McCarthyism to virtually all aspects of American life. In a speech to the annual dinner of the New York State Democratic Committee on April 29, 1953, Lehman noted that much had been said in recent campaigns about the threat of "Creeping Socialism," but he stressed that the real danger to the country was " 'Creeping McCarthyism,' a subtle poison which has already eaten deep into the muscles and sinews of our body politic, . . . sapped the courage of millions of our fellow citizens, . . . gnawed at the roots of our civil liberty, [and] . . . weakened the fabric of our faith in democracy itself." Lehman worried that "the presumption of guilt now surrounds anyone accused by McCarthy, Jenner, Velde, and their ilk," pointing out that these "investigators, who might better be called inquisitors, have taken office, self-nominated and self-elected, as the anointed guardians of our national security, the high prosecutors of the disloyal, and the supreme judges of the loyalty and morality of everyone." For Lehman, it was paramount "that the time-tested institutions of America which are synonymous with freedom and for whose protection the Bill of Rights was written into the Constitution—the press, the stage, our colleges and universities, and our churches—all these must be completely free from intimidation or coercion by the would-be thought police of congressional investigating committees." Lehman realized that "a frontal attack on McCarthyism" might not be "the way to political victory," but he warned that "we cannot compromise with this evil thing." It was necessary to confront this deadly disease to "keep faith with freedom."[6]

Recognizing that Lehman had become his most vocal, if not necessarily his most powerful, adversary, Joe McCarthy struck back at him on the floor of the Senate in mid-June 1953, asserting that Lehman had committed "a rather gross abuse of the franking privilege" in trying to send out "100,000 copies" of his speech on "Creeping McCarthyism." McCarthy charged that Lehman, as "one of the wealthiest members of the Senate," should pay for the folding, stuffing, and mailing of such materials, and he demanded an immediate response from Lehman. But other than assuring McCarthy that the number of copies "was less than one-tenth of 100,000," Lehman refused to be rushed or bullied, insisting that he would "reply in my own time."[7]

Lehman took the floor later that day to respond to McCarthy's allegations. He noted that McCarthy's accusations "are made in exactly the pattern that has been followed by the Senator from Wisconsin for a very long time," attempting "to intimidate, to frighten, to put on the defensive all those who are in disagreement with him . . . by making statements unsupported by facts, in the hope that he can entangle his critics in irrelevant discussion with him and in endless denials of his charges and finally thus to silence these critics." Lehman emphasized that he was "not easily intimidated," and that he had

> no apology to make for pointing out to the people of the country the great threat to their freedoms which has come through the efforts, and I am sorry to say the partially successful efforts, of certain persons in this country—including the Senator from Wisconsin—to silence those who would oppose the effort to impose complete conformity and complete orthodoxy on every thought and every action of the people of this country.

Lehman promised to "continue to speak out on any subject" that he thought was "right and just and in the interest of the people of the United States," and he vowed to continue to make his views known to "as wide a constituency" as possible.[8]

In an exchange that provided a textbook example of McCarthy's tactics, the Senator from Wisconsin continued his verbal assault, badgering Lehman for the exact number of franked envelopes sent to the folding room. But instead of responding directly to McCarthy's accusations, Lehman went on the offensive, offering "to submit to the appropriate committee of the Senate a complete statement of the number of franked envelopes he has used in the four years during which he has been a member of the Senate, if the Senator from Wisconsin will do the same." When Lehman pledged to continue "to fight McCarthyism so long as I have strength," McCarthy responded in his typical fashion, ignoring Lehman's proposal and promising to continue his fight against Communism no matter "how many Lehmans, how many Tydings, how many *Daily Workers* make attacks on McCarthy." In the wake of McCarthy's verbal assault, only Wayne Morse rose to Lehman's defense, denying "any insinuation, innuendo, or criticism of the Senator from New York as being a 'pinko,' a fellow traveler, or a Communist," and paying tribute to Lehman as "not only a conscientious, patriotic, anti-Communist liberal, but, in my judgment, the greatest liberal in American public life today."[9]

Later that day, after he had an opportunity to ascertain all the facts, Lehman issued a press release summarizing the matter. He pointed out that the only reason the issue had arisen was because he had not inserted his speech into the *Congressional Record*; had he done so, the cost of copying, folding, stuffing, and mailing copies of his remarks would have been borne by the taxpayers. Instead, Lehman had paid to have the speech copied by a printing company, and then copies had been "routinely delivered to the Senate folding room," which informed Lehman's office that it "would not fold the speeches and insert them in envelopes because it was not a congressional reprint." The Senator's staff immediately arranged to have the folding and stuffing done "outside the Capitol," with Lehman paying for the work. "At no time was any question raised concerning my right to send these speeches out under my frank," Lehman emphasized, and he reported that eighteen thousand copies of the speech had been prepared for mailing, not the one hundred thousand that McCarthy had alleged. Lehman considered McCarthy's accusations "especially audacious because only last year the Post Office Department was trying to collect from Senator McCarthy a sum of money for mailing, under his franking privilege, a considerable number of commercial advertisements for a book he wrote," and because McCarthy "sends out a weekly newspaper column under his frank." But Lehman understood that his use of the frank was not "the real issue." What was really at stake, he maintained, was "whether Senator McCarthy can browbeat those who dare to criticize his methods, who do not agree with his shocking procedures."[10]

Realizing that Lehman had not been intimidated or silenced, McCarthy continued firing smears and innuendos at him. Supposedly acting in his capacity as chairman of the Appropriations Subcommittee on Treasury and Post Office, McCarthy informed Lehman on June 30 that he had received "a number of your franked envelopes, some containing a copy of your speech, 'Creeping McCarthyism,' and others urging the recipient to purchase an article entitled 'McCarthy's Finances,' put out by the leftwing and, as you know, to a great extent Communist-influenced ADA" (Americans for Democratic Action). McCarthy wanted to know if Lehman thought this was "the proper use of the frank," and he also sought "an estimate of the number of pieces of this material you mailed out under the frank."[11]

Lehman responded a week later, reiterating that his "use of the frank" was "both legal and proper" because "all congressional mail involving public business may be sent under frank." It was "perfectly obvious," Lehman asserted, that McCarthy's "interest is not in my use of the frank," but rather "my efforts to arouse the country to the danger of the creeping paralysis of our freedom in thought and action" resulting from McCarthy's activities. The letters referring people to the ADA article on "McCarthy's Finances," Lehman explained, were replies to constituents asking for the Senate Subcommittee on Elections and

Privileges' official report on McCarthy, "only a handful of copies of which were printed." Lehman was pleased to inform McCarthy that his recent attacks had piqued public interest in Lehman's "Creeping McCarthyism" speech, exhausting his supply and requiring the printing of additional copies to meet the demand, and Lehman was "encouraged, indeed, that so many Americans are interested in what is now going on in Washington, and are rousing themselves to demand leadership in the fight to defend their freedoms and liberties."[12]

Lehman's battles with McCarthy brought him both commendations and scorn. He reported to a Georgetown University professor that he had "received a tremendous amount of mail, more than 90% of which strongly supports my position," and he told Averell Harriman that he had received "a bushel basket" of "letters from newspaper editors enclosing . . . franked shipments of Jumping Joe's column," as well as "stamps, dollar bills, and checks in great profusion from people who want us to continue to mail our speeches out but who were, of course, confused by McCarthy's fallacious and misleading charges." Arthur Schlesinger, Jr., of Harvard University and ADA, praised Lehman's "dignified, brave, and uncompromising" response to McCarthy's assault on the Senate floor, but he wished that more of Lehman's colleagues "had spoken up after McCarthy's disgraceful attack." In Schlesinger's opinion, "almost the worst thing McCarthy has done is to make cowards of so many decent men." John Slawson of the American Jewish Committee thought that Lehman's "stand on the McCarthy intimidation (as you rightly called it) attempt is magnificent," and "a source of courage and inspiration to countless numbers who feel as you do but still remain inarticulate." He believed that Lehman's "type of leadership is essential at this time in the effort to preserve our basic liberties." In contrast, conservative author Victor Lasky wanted to know if Lehman had given permission for "the Communist monthly, *Jewish Life*," to print the full text of Lehman's "Creeping McCarthyism" speech in a forthcoming issue, and a letter to the *New York Times* asserted that Lehman "has always seemed to favor a velvet glove policy—the soft, gentle treatment—in anything having to do with subversion and communism." *Human Rights*, a right-wing publication, called attention to *The Daily Worker*'s "prominent coverage" of Lehman's attacks on Senator McCarthy and charged that "Senator Lehman, however innocently, now seems particularly close to the Communist line in his extravagant attacks on what he calls 'McCarthyism.' In fact, some remark that it is not 'McCarthyism' which is the real danger today—it is 'Lehmanism.'"[13]

In the middle of the franking controversy, Lehman carried the fight to McCarthy's home state, speaking about "The Straitjacket of Fear" at a Jefferson-Jackson dinner in Milwaukee on June 20, 1953. Lehman asserted that while "the forces of reaction and repression" sought to dismantle the New Deal and the progress the nation had made in the last twenty years, public attention was diverted and focused almost "exclusively upon the possible plots and conspiracies of home-grown Communists and former Communists and of fellow travelers and former fellow travelers." This fear of domestic Communists, Lehman charged, was stoked by "unscrupulous forces" who were "quite ready to adopt the evil means of Communist strategy in order to gain for themselves the privilege of power." McCarthy was "the leader and frontrunner" of these forces, but Lehman emphasized that "the devil in this case is not a single individual, but the entire spirit of evil which broods over our land." Lehman maintained that McCarthyism "threatens the rights, the dignity, and the security of those individuals singled out for inquisition, smear, and attacks; it threatens the entire structure of our civil liberties; it threatens the orderly processes of government by paralyzing the executive branch, and by turning the legislative branch into a series of star chambers with unchecked power of destruction over the lives and reputations of countless individuals." As long as he had "breath and energy," Lehman vowed, he would "continue to fight . . . against all the evils of McCarthyism, and against the spirit of fear" that McCarthy and his allies personified.[14]

II

In his remarks on "Creeping McCarthyism," Lehman had expressed concern over the recent European tour of the State Department's overseas libraries by McCarthy staffers Roy Cohn and G. David Schine, characterizing them as "two brash and brazen youths who, under the aegis of the McCarthy committee, turned all our embassies and foreign missions upside down." A few weeks later, Senator Mike Monroney (D-OK) joined Lehman in waging what the *New York Times* described as an "all-out and head-on" attack against McCarthy, delivering a blistering speech in the Senate in which he echoed Lehman's denunciation of "the keystone cop chase of Messrs. Cohn and Schine across all Europe." Appearing on NBC's *Meet the Press* a few days later, McCarthy rose to Cohn's and Schine's defense, labeling Monroney's criticism of his two aides as "a flagrant example of anti-Semitism." This was too much for Herbert Lehman to swallow. In the Senate the next day, Lehman asserted that allegations of anti-Semitism against Monroney and others who dared to criticize Cohn's and Schine's behavior were "wholly false and ridiculous." Lehman noted that he himself, and "many individuals of Jewish faith, as well as of Christian denominations," had "repeatedly criticized and repudiated the antics of these two brash young men" who "have been doing our country and the cause of anticommunism great harm both here and abroad." Lehman was "certain that most members of my religious faith, not as Jews, but as Americans, are anything but proud of these two young men," and he complained that "to brand criticism of them as 'anti-Semitism' is pure and arrant demagoguery, raising an ugly symbol in defense of indefensible conduct."[15]

As was usually the case with McCarthy, the exchange over Cohn and Schine quickly escalated the following day into what the *Washington Post* described as "some of the bitterest name-calling heard on the Senate floor in years." McCarthy defended Cohn's "outstanding work in exposing and securing the conviction of Communists," but rather than just focusing on Cohn's impressive record in helping prosecute the leaders of the Communist Party and the Rosenbergs, McCarthy, as was his wont, attacked Monroney and Lehman. He charged that Monroney "led off" the attempted "smear" and "character assassination," but "when he was caught, he did not answer. Apparently he did not have the guts to do it," so he "called upon the junior Senator from New York" for help. Turning his attention to Lehman, McCarthy read into the *Congressional Record* the letter that Lehman had written to Alger Hiss in 1948. Rushing to the floor to reply to McCarthy's verbal assault, Lehman claimed that McCarthy's "tactics of fear and smear demonstrated here today . . . are a rebuke, not to me, although my name was mentioned, but to all of us who tolerate such tactics." He pointed out that he had written the letter to Hiss long "before there was any real evidence against him," that the letter had been "trotted out in the political campaign of 1950" by his opponents to no avail, and that the voters of New York had again expressed their confidence in him at the polls. Turning the tables on McCarthy, Lehman demanded to know why McCarthy refused to "explain why he accepted the support of the Communist Party when he was a candidate for the Republican nomination for the Senate in 1946." More significantly, Lehman highlighted one of the key issues that would eventually lead to McCarthy's downfall the following year, asserting that the Senator from Wisconsin had "many questions to answer—questions raised in an official report of a Senate committee which he has refused to answer, thereby showing his complete contempt for the Senate and for the public." Instead of answering those questions, Lehman declared, McCarthy "makes charges and pretends to expose Communists and charges his fellow Senators with religious bias and high crimes." Lehman emphasized that it was time that "the Senate as a whole assume some responsibility in this matter," rather than allowing Senators "to be vilified and misrepresented and blackened" by "a man who has himself been charged with misdemeanors, but who has not even had the guts to answer to the Senate and to the American people."[16]

Like heavyweight fighters, Lehman and McCarthy kept going at each other, looking for a weak spot to deliver a knockout blow. Sounding almost like McCarthy, Lehman kept hammering away, asking whether McCarthy had "at any time, in 1946 or prior to that time, ever repudiated the support of the Communist Party." McCarthy parried the blow, asserting that no such action had been necessary "because the Communists did not support me." Counterpunching, McCarthy charged that Lehman, as Director General of UNRRA, had employed three men who later refused to answer when asked if they were

Communists, and he demanded to know whether Lehman had "examine[d] the FBI reports which showed they were Communists at the time he gave them places under him in UNRRA." But Lehman refused to play by McCarthy's rules. Instead of debating what these three individuals might have said, done, thought, or believed at some point in their lives, Lehman took full credit for UNRRA's accomplishments, calmly reminding McCarthy that UNRRA had employed "20,000 people scattered all over the world, doing God's work in bringing food, clothing, shelter, sustenance, and hope to starving people abroad." Lehman noted that he had been "elected Director General of UNRRA by the vote of fifty [*sic*] nations," and he boasted that "nothing in my whole life, including . . . my membership in the United States Senate . . . has ever given me the satisfaction of soul and heart that my service in UNRRA did because UNRRA saved the lives of hundreds of millions of people." "Of course there were Communists in UNRRA," Lehman snorted. "It was an international organization, whose membership included many Communist countries." If McCarthy thought that Lehman would "apologize for anything I did in UNRRA, he has a second, a third, a fourth, and a tenth guess coming to him, because my association with UNRRA is one thing, beyond anything else I have ever done in my life, that brings me satisfaction." When McCarthy could "show that he saved the lives of 1,000 people," as compared to the 100 million people who Lehman claimed were saved by UNRRA under his leadership, then McCarthy "would have a right to exult."[17]

Neither Lehman nor McCarthy wanted to let the other get the last word. McCarthy insisted that he was not accusing Lehman "of being a Communist or of being a Communist sympathizer," and Lehman thanked him for such "a very generous concession," but McCarthy asserted that Lehman's "record of hiring Communists and of writing letters of condolence to men accused of being espionage agents" meant that people should disregard Lehman's "bitter attacks upon men like Roy Cohn, who, during his short span, has been convicting the Communists the junior Senator from New York has been trying to defend." Lehman did get in the final blow, emphasizing that he was "spending so much time in fighting 'mc carthyism,'" which he deliberately spelled with a lowercase "m," because he believed in justice, in the Bill of Rights, and in the U.S. Constitution.[18]

Lehman's denial that the criticism of Cohn and Schine reflected anti-Semitism brought him plaudits from major Jewish groups and leaders and condemnations from McCarthy's supporters. Joseph Proskauer, a longtime leader of the American Jewish Committee, heartily congratulated Lehman for rebuking McCarthy, noting that "it had to be said" and Lehman was "the man to say it," and David Petegorsky of the American Jewish Congress believed that Lehman's "forthright challenge to Senator McCarthy's irresponsible attempt to inject religious considerations in areas where they have utterly no relevance was another example" of Lehman's "courage and leadership." Not everyone was pleased however. Judge Albert Cohn, Roy Cohn's father, had been appointed to the Appellate Division of the New York State courts by Herbert Lehman in 1937, but he was "shocked" at what he considered to be Lehman's unwarranted attack on his son, wanting to know the basis for Lehman's assertion that most American Jews were embarrassed by Roy Cohn's behavior. Similarly, Victor Lasky questioned Lehman's presumption "to speak in the name of American Jews," charging that "lehmanism," which he refused to capitalize, was "a menace to America [and] to American Jews," and he urged Lehman to "keep your trap shut," warning that " 'brash and senile old men' can often be as disturbing as 'brash young men.' "[19]

III

Herbert Lehman faced a dilemma in early February 1954 when the Senate considered a $214,000 appropriation for McCarthy's Subcommittee on Investigations. Lehman surprised many of his supporters by voting for the funds, which were approved overwhelmingly, but he quickly regretted his action, apologizing to Senator J. William Fulbright (D-AR), the only Senator who voted against the appropriation. In response to the many queries he received about his vote, Lehman explained that he did not want his opposition to McCarthy's methods and procedures to be confused with his support for "the general investigatory powers of congressional committees." He noted that the subcommittee's Democrats had recently wrung "some important concessions in regard to committee procedure" from McCarthy, and he stressed that "nothing would more conveniently play into the hands" of Senator McCarthy than cutting off the subcommittee's funding, allowing McCarthy to claim that his investigation had been "sabotaged."[20]

In clarifying his vote on the appropriation, Lehman also promised to work "for a fair set of rules and procedures which will prevent the perversion of congressional investigation into congressional inquisition." With McCarthy's recent browbeating of Brigadier General Ralph Zwicker in mind, Lehman joined Wayne Morse in sponsoring legislation to establish "a mandatory code of procedure" that would enable Senate committees "to carry on in a legitimate fashion the investigations which are within the power and the right of the Senate, but which would protect witnesses and protect innocent persons who appear before Senate committees or whose name had been brought into the hearings." Lehman's proposal, along with similar resolutions introduced by Senator Prescott Bush (R-CT) and others, were referred to the Senate Rules Committee, from which they never returned. Rules Committee Chairman and McCarthy ally William Jenner denounced all such measures as the product of "Communists, pinkos, and eggheads" who wanted to change the rules to "hamstring and destroy Senate committees."[21]

In a letter to his former Senate colleague William Benton, who had been one of the few Senators willing to challenge McCarthy, Lehman lamented that "the number of members of Congress who are willing to raise their voices has not subsequently grown." That began to change, however, in March 1954, when Senator Ralph Flanders (R-VT) denounced McCarthyism on the floor of the Senate. Claiming that McCarthy was "doing his best to shatter" the Republican Party, Flanders asserted that McCarthy belonged to "a one-man party, and that its name is 'McCarthyism.'" Pointing out that McCarthy had actually uncovered only one Communist, an army dentist whose refusal to sign the required loyalty oath had gone unnoticed, Flanders charged that McCarthy "dons his war paint. He goes into his war dance. He emits his war whoops. He goes forth to battle and proudly returns with the scalp of a pink army dentist." Flanders believed that McCarthy's meager results illustrated "the depth and seriousness of Communist penetration in this country at this time," emphasizing that the real danger the nation faced came from Communist expansion overseas. As soon as Flanders finished his speech, Herbert Lehman welcomed him to the cause, congratulating him on "his very fine statement" and concurring "wholeheartedly" with Flanders's remarks. At a press conference the following day, President Eisenhower praised Flanders's "service" in warning that "internecine warfare" imperiled the Republican program. Lehman was "greatly heartened" by these developments and, as he told Benton, he believed that "more and more people are becoming alerted to the dangers of mccarthyism and the threat which it poses to us." There was still "a long way to go," but Lehman was "hopeful that we are now on our way."[22]

Shortly after Flanders's speech, the Senate decided to investigate the Army's complaint that McCarthy and Roy Cohn had sought special treatment for former committee consultant G. David Schine, who had been drafted, and McCarthy's countercharge that the Army was holding Schine as a "hostage" to stop the Senator from probing Communist infiltration in the Army. Herbert Lehman hoped that the investigation would be conducted by the Senate Armed Services Committee rather than McCarthy's Permanent Subcommittee on Investigations, but when the members of the Armed Services Committee refused to get involved, the matter remained under the subcommittee's auspices. Even with Senator Karl Mundt temporarily replacing McCarthy as chairman, Lehman had "grave doubts" that the panel would be able to "get at the true facts behind this controversy" and make "an honest and objective appraisal of what happened."[23]

During the subcommittee's televised hearings, McCarthy escalated his attacks on the Eisenhower administration, becoming an embarrassment and a liability to the Republicans. As a result, Lehman vigorously opposed any attempt to end the hearings prematurely or move them behind closed doors. He realized that the American people were now seeing for themselves that McCarthy was a liar and a bully with no real evidence to back up his accusations. Terminating or closing the proceedings before discovering who was responsible for the "faked photograph" and "the phony FBI letter" McCarthy and his aides had introduced into evidence, Lehman warned, would be a "whitewash," would vindicate "the practice of slipping Senator McCarthy secret security reports," and would "mean that the infamous practice of violating the security of governmental files will spread like a plague through the government." Lehman defended President Eisenhower's invocation of executive privilege to prevent members of the executive branch from testifying about the content of their discussions, and he welcomed the Eisenhower administration's belated rejection of "the anarchist thesis that Senator McCarthy, or anyone else who undertakes to carry on investigations, has the right to violate the law or to induce others to violate the law." But Lehman chided the administration for not moving more quickly against McCarthyism and, even now, for opposing McCarthyism only on narrow, institutional grounds, urging Eisenhower "to defend not only the powers of his office but also the liberties of the American people now so sorely threatened by the philosophy of McCarthyism." After the hearings concluded, Lehman wrote to John McClellan (AR), Stuart Symington (MO), and Henry Jackson (WA), the three Democrats on the subcommittee, emphasizing that the Senate and the American people owed them "a debt of gratitude" for bringing out "many of the facts which McCarthy sought to hide."[24]

As the Army-McCarthy hearings neared their end, Senator Flanders became more and more outraged by McCarthy's behavior, and on June 11, 1954, Flanders formally proposed that Senator McCarthy be stripped of his committee chairmanships because of his refusal to cooperate with the Senate Subcommittee on Privileges and Elections that had investigated Senator Benton's charges against McCarthy in 1952. The Republican leadership greeted Flanders's resolution, which would highlight the split within the party over McCarthy, with a distinct lack of enthusiasm, as did Southern Democrats, who feared any precedent departing from the seniority system and deposing committee chairmen. Flanders's resolution was referred to the Senate Rules Committee, but the Vermont Republican warned that if the committee tried to bury the measure, he would use a discharge petition to force it out of the committee, or submit a new proposal over which he could retain control.[25]

Herbert Lehman had never accepted Democratic Leader Lyndon Johnson's view that one could not move against McCarthy until the Wisconsin Republican had offended the Senate's conservatives, the "institutional" Senators who wielded the real authority in the chamber. Even though it often seemed like he was playing a solo, Lehman had kept up the drumbeat against McCarthyism, believing that McCarthy and McCarthyism had to be denounced at every opportunity because they endangered the rights and liberties of the American people. In Lehman's opinion, the Flanders resolution was a start, but he believed that the measure was too narrowly drawn, focusing as it did only on McCarthy's contemptuous behavior toward a Senate committee. Lehman emphasized that one had to consider "the whole range of harmful activities, practices, means, methods, assumptions, usurpations, violations, and abuses" that McCarthy had committed, as well as their impact on "the prestige of the Congress and on the fundamental institutions of law and government which characterize our country." Lehman also feared that Flanders's proposal would never emerge from the Rules Committee, so on June 17, 1954, he introduced a resolution of his own to revoke McCarthy's chairmanships, charging that McCarthy had interfered in the administrative and law enforcement functions of the executive branch; encouraged individuals to send him classified information; attempted "to intimidate and harass" government officials, including Army officers, and the press; and violated "the civil liberties, privileges, rights, and immunities of United States citizens guaranteed under the Bill of Rights." Knowing that it was "highly unlikely" that the Rules Committee would "act on or even consider" his resolution or Flanders's, Lehman tried to prevent his proposal from being sent to committee. But Vice President Nixon, who was presiding, ruled that unanimous consent was required to allow Lehman's resolution to lie on the table, from where it could be brought up for action at any time, and Senate Republican Leader Knowland immediately objected, meaning that Lehman's proposal now joined Flanders's in the black hole of the Rules Committee from which neither of them ever returned.[26]

It soon became apparent that Lehman and Flanders lacked the votes to oust McCarthy from his chairmanships, so with advice and assistance from Lehman's chief aide Julius Edelstein and others, Flanders changed his tack on July 20, serving notice that he would introduce a new resolution—a resolution condemning McCarthy because his conduct "is unbecoming a member of the United States Senate, is contrary to senatorial traditions, and tends to bring the Senate into disrepute." When Flanders finished his statement, Herbert Lehman immediately complimented him on his "eloquent and convincing remarks" and promised his "wholehearted support" for Flanders's resolution to censure McCarthy. While less enthusiastic than Lehman, Lyndon Johnson and Democratic leaders were willing to consider Flanders's new motion, which did not threaten the seniority system or committee chairmanships.[27]

On July 28, Lehman formally urged his colleagues to vote for the resolution condemning Senator McCarthy, arguing that the measure's approval was necessary "to restore the prestige of the United States Senate which has been so seriously injured by the junior Senator from Wisconsin, Joseph McCarthy." Lehman emphasized that Article I of the Constitution explicitly gave each House of Congress "the right and responsibility to punish its members for disorderly behavior," and he asserted that the Senate could no longer evade its responsibility to decide whether McCarthy had "so conducted himself as to merit punishment." In Lehman's opinion, censure was "a mild remedy for such a dread and contagious disease as McCarthyism . . . a mild punishment for acts which have worked incalculable damage on the Senate and on the country." Lehman understood that the Senate had a long tradition as "a gentlemen's club," but he argued that McCarthy had "placed himself beyond the protective pale of personal camaraderie in the Senate," citing McCarthy's "unconscionable attacks" over the years on numerous Senators, including Herbert Lehman. Denying the argument advanced by some that McCarthy had performed an important service in alerting people to "the danger of Communist infiltration and subversion," Lehman charged that McCarthy had "made a mockery of the congressional investigating process" and "ridden roughshod over the rights of scores of American citizens, using his position in the Senate to smear, denounce, and ruin individuals," slandering "some of the noblest public servants this country has ever had," imputing to Franklin Roosevelt, Harry Truman, General George Marshall, and many others "the high crime of treason." Although Lehman would have preferred a stronger punishment, he understood that one could only "meet the challenge of McCarthyism with the weapons that have been given to us as United States Senators," and he called for an early vote in which the Senate could register its disapproval of Senator McCarthy.[28]

Lyndon Johnson and the Senate Democratic Policy Committee invited Lehman and a few other critics of McCarthy to a meeting on July 29 to discuss whether Senate Democrats should take a formal party position on the censure resolution. Lehman welcomed the opportunity to speak with the Democratic leaders, emphasizing that he had "never subscribed to the thesis" that McCarthy was "a Republican responsibility." He believed that "every man in the Senate has a responsibility" to act in this matter, and he warned that "the Democratic Party will suffer if it does not take a stand." When some Senators questioned the wisdom of the party taking an official position, fearing that such action might lead the Republicans to close ranks around McCarthy, Lehman retreated, explaining that he did not mean that the party should take an official stand on the resolution, but that "it would be very helpful" if "some of our leaders would announce their support" for the censure resolution. Stuart Symington and Henry Jackson, who had been part of the subcommittee that had conducted the Army-McCarthy hearings, suggested that the censure be put off until the report on those hearings had been completed, but Lehman disagreed, stressing that "McCarthyism is above and beyond the scope of these hearings." Lehman feared that any postponement or delay on the censure resolution "would give us a terrible black eye." As Johnson had planned all along, the Policy Committee decided not to take a party position on the censure, declaring it "a matter of conscience upon which each individual Senator should vote his convictions without regard to party affiliations."[29]

As the Senate neared a vote on the censure resolution, Lehman challenged his fellow Senators not to "sit idly by and divest ourselves of any responsibility" for McCarthy's actions, not to "make pious protests in private while maintaining silence in public," not to "content ourselves by saying that, while we disapprove of the methods of the junior Senator from Wisconsin, it is up to the voters of Wisconsin, or to the Republican Party, or to President Eisenhower, to discipline this reckless colleague of ours." According to the Constitution, Lehman declared, "it is our individual responsibility as Senators. It is no one else's." Why then, Lehman wanted to know, did the Senate "hesitate to take such action as is merited?" Did Senators "fear the political repercussions of a vote to censure the junior Senator from Wisconsin?" Was that the real reason for "the timidity, the apprehensions, and the doubts which have characterized the position of so many of us in regard to the Flanders resolution?" Lehman emphasized that such fear was "a measure of the danger represented" by McCarthy, who "has spread fear, intimidation, suspicion, and reprisal throughout the length and breadth of this great land of ours." Lehman called upon his colleagues to "face this danger," to "put aside this fear." He asserted that "whatever the political repercussions, history will honor us for a vote of censure," and he believed that their constituents would do so as well. Therefore, he urged Senators to "vote overwhelmingly, without regard to partisan considerations," to approve the censure resolution.[30]

Lehman worried, with good reason, that Majority Leader Knowland and Minority Leader Johnson would sidetrack the censure resolution rather than allowing it to come to a vote. Many Senators feared that taking a stand one way or the other on McCarthy would cost them votes, and many of them agreed with Johnson that "you should have an indictment and specific allegations and proof before you render the execution." Senator McClellan, who had tangled with McCarthy during the Army-McCarthy hearings and was well respected by his colleagues, thought that the matter should be referred to a special committee, telling the Democratic Policy Committee that the problem with the Flanders resolution was that "it says a man is guilty of misconduct but doesn't specify what the misconduct is." McClellan thought "it would be setting a bad precedent . . . to censure a man without committee hearings." Lyndon Johnson feared that the Flanders resolution would be defeated if it came to an immediate vote, "making McCarthy a hero in the eyes of the public," but he believed that working through a select committee would generate additional votes against McCarthy.[31]

On August 2, Senator Knowland formally proposed the creation of a special committee composed of three Democrats and three Republicans to consider the proposed censure of Senator McCarthy and report back to the Senate "expeditiously." When Lehman and others protested that the Majority Leader's motion would allow the matter to be postponed indefinitely, Senator Ives offered an amendment requiring the committee to report back before the Senate adjourned for the year. With this proviso added, Lyndon Johnson, John

McClellan, and Walter George (D-GA), the senior Democrat in the Senate, endorsed the measure, which practically guaranteed its passage. Despite the objections of Lehman, Flanders, and a few others who urged the Senate to consider the censure resolution without further delay, Senators voted 75 to 12 to refer the censure resolution to a special committee. With great difficulty, Lehman tried to find a bright side in this setback, admitting in a letter to his nephew Arthur Goodhart that the results so far in the fight he and his associates were waging against McCarthy and McCarthyism were "somewhat disappointing," but taking solace in the knowledge that they were doing all they could "to alert the American people and to protect their interests."[32]

IV

In August 1954, while the special committee considered whether to recommend McCarthy's censure, Senator John Marshall Butler (R-MD) and the Senate Judiciary Committee reported a bill that would allow the Attorney General and the Subversive Activities Control Board to strip labor unions that were infiltrated with Communists of their rights to organize and bargain collectively under the Wagner Act. Herbert Lehman conceded that Communist influence in a few unions was a serious problem, but he pointed out that the CIO had already expelled nine unions because of Communist influence, and he warned that "the ill-chosen, hastily contrived, blunderbuss bill before us" would take the initiative for fighting Communism "away from the responsible leadership of the labor movement—away from the Walter Reuthers and George Meanys, away from the host of anti-Communist officers and members of the CIO and AFL—and would repose it in the hands of the government." Lehman feared that "this bill would place in the hands of an Attorney General who might be antagonistic to labor, a powerful weapon to cripple labor, [and] to break strikes," and that it could be used "as a means of impeding and paralyzing union organization efforts in parts of the country now unorganized, where local management will readily swear and affirm that any union is, per se, communistic." Instead of enacting this "highly dangerous piece of legislation," Lehman urged his colleagues to follow the lead of the House Judiciary Committee, which had suggested "the establishment of a bipartisan study commission to investigate this serious matter." But most Senators, eager to record their opposition to Communism in an election year, rejected the commission plan that would have delayed any action until 1955 at the earliest.[33]

At one point during the discussion of the Butler bill, Lehman complained that "there is no measure before us to outlaw or liquidate the Communist Party. . . . Instead, the administration recommends a measure to liquidate labor unions." Seeking to fill that gap and protect organized labor, Hubert Humphrey sought to substitute for the Butler bill a measure to criminalize membership in the Communist Party. Humphrey was up for re-election in 1954, and he saw his bill to ban the Communist Party as an opportunity for liberal Democrats to help their labor friends and burnish their own anti-Communist credentials. Humphrey later claimed that another benefit of banning the Communist Party would be that it would shift proceedings against alleged Communists from congressional hearing rooms to the courts, where the accused would enjoy the constitutional rights and protections that had been trampled upon by congressional investigating committees.[34]

Herbert Lehman considered the Humphrey bill "an honest, sincere, and undisguised frontal attack on the Communist conspiracy, led by the Communist party, in this country," and he quickly joined as a cosponsor of the substitute measure. But as Julius Edelstein acknowledged, Humphrey's plan "was much too clever," and in a replay of the events leading to the passage of the McCarran Internal Security Act in 1950, Humphrey's substitute was added to Butler's proposal rather than substituted for it. Herbert Lehman cast the only vote against this arrangement, objecting to the anti-union provisions that remained in the bill.[35]

Lehman had strong reservations about the new combined measure and he "deplore[d] the haste" with which Congress was proceeding on this bill without any committee hearings or reports. But given the strength of the anti-Communist climate that still prevailed in 1954, even Herbert Lehman found it difficult to oppose a bill that was intended, as Lehman put it, "to meet the criminal Communist conspiracy." Lehman voiced no complaints or concerns at the time against those sections of the bill that curtailed the rights and liberties of members of the Communist Party, focusing his criticism only on the harmful effects the legislation would have on labor unions. Skeptical that the measure would accomplish anything, Lehman hoped that the next Congress would revise the law to make it "more meaningful" while removing its more "dangerous" provisions. Nonetheless, after much soul-searching, Lehman succumbed to the pleadings of Hubert Humphrey, Wayne Morse, and aide Julius Edelstein, announcing that despite his "misgivings" and "with considerable reluctance," he would vote for the final bill. Lehman regretted his decision almost immediately, confessing in a lecture at Columbia University a few years later that he had "always been sorry" that he did not join Senator Estes Kefauver in voting against the bill.[36]

Lehman's vote in favor of the Communist Control Act marked a departure from his usual opposition to such measures. As Julius Edelstein, Lehman's chief advisor, noted at the time, Lehman's was often "the only voice raised in opposition" to congressional actions infringing on the rights and liberties of the American people. For example, at virtually the same time that Congress was adopting the Communist Control Act, the Senate moved to cite prominent left-wing author and educator Corliss Lamont; New York City attorney Abraham Unger, who had represented the leaders of the Communist Party when they were accused of violating the Smith Act; and engineer Albert Shadowitz for contempt for their refusal to answer questions put to them by Senator McCarthy. Unlike most unfriendly witnesses summoned to appear before McCarthy, however, none of the three had invoked their right against self-incrimination under the Fifth Amendment. Instead, they had asserted that questions about their political beliefs violated their rights under the First Amendment. Lamont and the others also claimed that McCarthy's investigation of possible subversion exceeded the parent Committee on Government Operation's legitimate areas of inquiry, which were supposed to be government waste and inefficiency. When the Senate considered whether to cite the three men for contempt, Lehman noted that Lamont had specifically denied under oath that he had ever been a member of the Communist Party, and Lehman argued that the Senate needed to examine the serious issues that Lamont and the others had raised rather than merely rubber-stamping McCarthy's request to charge them with contempt. Accordingly, Lehman objected to pursuing legal action against Lamont and the others, but only two Senators joined him in voting not to cite Lamont for contempt, and Lehman stood alone against charging Shadowitz and Unger. Lehman's concerns were later validated when the courts dismissed the contempt charges against Lamont and the others, ruling that McCarthy's subcommittee had no authority to investigate Communist subversion among private citizens.[37]

V

During the debate over establishing the special committee to consider the charges against Senator McCarthy, the Wisconsin Republican, as usual, tried to turn the tables and intimidate Lehman, Flanders, and his other main antagonists. McCarthy asserted that if he were given the right to cross-examine his accusers, they would "either indict themselves for perjury, or they will prove what consummate liars they are, by showing the difference between their statements on the floor of the Senate and their testimony in the hearing." Lehman promptly assured McCarthy, "if I am requested to appear by the committee to support any charges I have made against the junior Senator from Wisconsin, I shall be very glad, indeed, to do so, and I shall be glad to testify under oath with all that that implies." When McCarthy tried to press Lehman on whether he would allow McCarthy to cross-examine him, Lehman made it clear that he would do so "if the committee so decides," emphasizing that the ultimate decision as to the committee's procedures rested with the committee, not McCarthy.[38]

Lehman had planned to go abroad after the Senate recessed in August, but the possibility that he might be called to appear before the committee considering the censure resolution prevented him from going too far. While the Senator and his wife vacationed in Sun Valley, Idaho, Lehman's staff kept busy preparing for his possible testimony, organizing material to substantiate "every charge and accusation" Lehman had ever made against McCarthy. Expecting McCarthy to go on the attack, Lehman's aides researched the records of former UNRRA staffers who had gone to work for the United Nations and run afoul of the Senate Internal Security Subcommittee or some loyalty board. They also looked into the records of other former UNRRA officials. As Julius Edelstein pointed out, even if Lehman were not called to appear before the committee, all this material would come in handy during the floor debate on McCarthy's censure to prevent the distortion of "McCarthy's wrongdoings . . . into a question of whether or not he violated certain technical requirements as to appearance before Committees, etc.," in which case the public would "lose sight of his really vicious practices and achievements."[39]

The special committee included Republicans Arthur Watkins of Utah as chairman, Frank Carlson of Kansas, and Francis Case of South Dakota, and Democrats Edwin Johnson of Colorado, John Stennis of Mississippi, and Sam Ervin of North Carolina. Ideologically, they ranged from moderate to conservative, with nary a liberal in the bunch, and none of them had spoken out previously about McCarthy. Except for Case, all were highly respected by their colleagues and were members of the Senate "club," insiders concerned about the reputation of the Senate. As the committee began its work, Edith Lehman worried that "the complexion of the committee is surely not strong and neither is it anti-McCarthy," and she feared that McCarthy would "run the proceedings in his usual way and . . . it will develop into his trying some Senators instead of the reverse." But her concerns proved to be unwarranted. Watkins presided over the committee with a firm hand, the group completed its work expeditiously, and in late September, it recommended unanimously that McCarthy be censured because of his "contemptuous, contumacious, and denunciatory" behavior toward the Subcommittee on Privileges and Elections in 1952 and his "reprehensible" treatment of General Zwicker while investigating Communists in the Army. The committee also criticized McCarthy's conduct in a number of other instances, but it did not believe they warranted censure. As Lehman had feared, however, the Republican leadership put off consideration of the committee's recommendation until November 8, six days *after* the midterm elections, so that Senators running for re-election would not have to worry about antagonizing voters by supporting or condemning Senator McCarthy. Publicly, Lehman hailed the committee's report, asserting that "it is now clear that Senator McCarthy should not only be censured but should be removed immediately from his chairmanship of senatorial committees," but privately Lehman complained that the committee's "findings were not as strong" as he would have liked. Nonetheless, he thought that the committee "on the whole did a good job," expected that its findings "will be sustained," and believed that no matter the outcome in the full Senate, "McCarthy has been seriously weakened."[40]

Lehman and the others who had "been holding the banner up for years" against McCarthy would have preferred a much stronger censure resolution and a more active role in the final consideration of the measure, but, as Julius Edelstein noted, they were reluctantly "staying in the background" and letting "the very conservative members of the Watkins Committee" drive the measure through the Senate. Edelstein hoped that Lehman, "at an appropriate time," would be able to discuss "the larger effects of McCarthy and mccarthyism," including "the terrible way in which he has perverted the whole congressional process," the damage he had caused to American prestige abroad, and "the way he has undermined the relationship between the legislative and the executive branches of government." But Edelstein reported, "Lyndon Johnson and others are literally demanding that we refrain from rocking the boat," forcing Lehman to "keep all these thoughts and feelings in check for the moment in order to give right of way to the censure resolution which is based upon a very narrow foundation." Edelstein "hate[d] to see the entire issue decided on as narrow a basis as the Watkins report establishes," but he was "pretty well convinced that the size of the vote is more important than the arguments that are made."[41]

Herbert Lehman worried that the Senate would further "emasculate what is already a very much watered-down resolution." Senator Case had already backtracked from the committee's recommendation, suggesting that the whole matter could be settled if McCarthy would just apologize. But as Edelstein noted, "McCarthy himself was "resisting as strongly as possible being taken off the hook." Even before the debate began, McCarthy predicted that he would be censured, insulting many of his colleagues when he claimed that his critics now included not only Flanders and Lehman and other Senators "who fight those who fight Communism," as well as "self-styled liberals on the Republican side," but also the Lyndon "Johnson group, who dislike McCarthy" because he "pinned the Communist label on Democrats," and "the Watkins type, who are afraid of what the newspapers might say about them if they don't oppose McCarthy." Rather than apologizing for any of his past deeds, McCarthy launched a bitter attack on the Watkins committee, charging that "the Communist Party . . . has now extended its tentacles to that most respected of American bodies, the United States Senate," and "has made a committee of the Senate its unwitting handmaiden." McCarthy's abusive language and contemptuous behavior toward the Watkins committee soon became additional grounds for his censure.[42]

When McCarthy entered Bethesda Naval Hospital on November 17 for treatment of an elbow injury, the Senate voted 76 to 2 to recess until November 29. Lehman argued for a shorter delay, but he and Senator Fulbright were the only ones to oppose the twelve-day postponement. When the Senate resumed consideration of the censure resolution on November 29, Fulbright read into the *Congressional Record* some of the mail he had received in the interim, letters filled with "unadulterated hate, vituperation, and abuse." Many of the correspondents directed their venom not only at Fulbright, but also at Herbert Lehman, bitterly denouncing him in virulently anti-Semitic terms. One particularly vicious letter asserted that when Fulbright "joined the only Jew to vote against 76 Senators, that proved you were the henchmen for the Jew Deal," and recommended that "H.H. Lehman should be deported out of this nation to Russia, or let Germany take that 'bird' in and give him the gas like Hitler did." An "ex-marine who fought in the South Pacific" warned against opening "the gates of this nation for the commy Jews that Hitler did not kill," charging that Fulbright was "one of the phony pinko punks connected with Lehman, Morse, Flanders, and Bennett." A Pennsylvania man condemned Lehman as "an old hand at subtley [*sic*] pushing for expansion of Communist influence" and sarcastically advised "Senator Halfbright," as McCarthy often called Fulbright, to "just keep working with Lehman and you surely will become a great Senator, working toward the loss of all of our franchised rights." One writer noted that the only Senators to vote against allowing "McCarthy time off to recover from his illness" were "Red-loving Fulbright and the rotten Jew, Herbert Lehman, the pal of Hiss," while another correspondent suggested that Fulbright "tie hyena Morse and jackal Lehman around your foul coyote neck and jump into the Potomac."[43]

As the vote on the censure resolution neared, McCarthy backpedaled from some of his more outrageous comments, conceding, for example, that he was guilty of "an unfortunate choice of words" when he had described Senator Robert Hendrickson (R-NJ) as "a living miracle, a man without brains and without guts." But McCarthy demonstrated his lack of contrition when he acknowledged that he should not have "referred to the Watkins committee as the 'handmaidens of the Communist Party,' because a handmaiden is a female servant, and certainly the members of the committee are not female servants." When McCarthy offered to strike out any words he had used that had offended his colleagues, Lehman emphasized that "the question now before the Senate goes far beyond the use of words or of language or a belated apology for their use," stressing that McCarthy had attacked "the integrity, the good faith, the character, and the loyalty of the entire Senate." Incredibly, Lehman's assertion that McCarthy had used "insulting language," which the *Washington Post* described as "one of the milder comments of the acrimonious debate," was found to be a violation of the Senate rules when McCarthy ally Everett Dirksen (R-IL) complained that Lehman had impugned the motives or integrity of another Senator. This was just one example of what *New York Times* reporter William S. White later described as Lehman being held "by niggling and almost brutal Senate action to the most literal inhibitions of the least important of all the rules," while other Senators, who were members of what White called "the Senate club," were afforded much more leeway. The following day, for example, when Senator Flanders inserted into the *Congressional Record* a Thanksgiving message of friendship to the Soviet people, Senator Jenner demanded to know "by what reasoning, by what process of mind, by what course of twisted thinking," Flanders had referred to "these tyrants, these murderers, as 'my friends, my Soviet brothers.'" Flanders, in response, charged that Jenner "has taken leave of his intelligence" to interpret Flanders's letter in that way. But despite the ferocity of their remarks, which went much further than anything Lehman had said the previous day, neither Jenner nor Flanders was accused of violating Senate rules.[44]

Herbert Lehman tried to comply with Lyndon Johnson's request that he and the others who had carried the fight against McCarthy from the beginning remain in the background and let the Watkins committee members make the case for censure, but in the final days before the vote, Lehman felt compelled to speak out. Believing that the Watkins committee's resolution was too narrowly focused on McCarthy's disrespect for Senators, Senate committees, and the Senate as an institution, worried that it ignored the damage McCarthy had inflicted on the national fabric and individual citizens, and fearing that the measure would be watered down even further, Lehman asserted in a speech to the Senate on November 30 that Senators needed to look beyond McCarthy's specific acts and see the "whole pattern of conduct, unchanging in its nature down to this very day," to get "an authentic picture of McCarthy and McCarthyism—that dangerous phenomenon which has damaged the morale of the government service, spread fear and distrust throughout the land, and impaired the prestige of the United States among free people everywhere." Lehman stressed that it was not McCarthy but the Senate that was "on trial at the bar of public opinion in our own country, and at the bar of world public opinion, too," warning that any weakening of the censure resolution "would serve notice upon the nation that the Senate is unable to control the fair administration of its own processes; and that the Senate can be successfully paralyzed and frustrated by one of its members—all without discipline by the Senate itself." Adoption of the Watkins resolution, he emphasized, was necessary "to restore the prestige and dignity of the Senate, and to repair the injury done it and the nation by a long succession of improprieties by Senator McCarthy."[45]

Before voting on the censure resolution, the Senate adopted an amendment proposed by Republican Senator Wallace Bennett of Utah deleting the charge concerning McCarthy's mistreatment of General Zwicker but adding a new section condemning McCarthy's conduct toward the Watkins committee. Although Lehman agreed that McCarthy's response to the Watkins committee provided additional grounds for censure, he opposed eliminating the abuse of General Zwicker, pointing out that these changes meant that the censure resolution was based solely on McCarthy's behavior toward Senators and Senate committees and said nothing about McCarthy's actions against government employees and private citizens. Lehman believed that Senators should defend not only "the dignity and the reputation" of the Senate but also "the rights provided under our Constitution and our Bill of Rights to every man and woman in this country." But a majority of Senators agreed with Bennett that McCarthy's actions toward General Zwicker did not warrant censure, so that charge was replaced in the resolution by a provision condemning McCarthy's actions concerning the Watkins committee. With that change, the Senate voted 67 to 22 to censure McCarthy, with the Democrats voting unanimously for the measure, and the Republicans splitting right down the middle.[46]

Herbert Lehman considered the Senate's action against McCarthy "highly satisfactory," but he noted in a letter to an old friend that he did "not believe that the war against mccarthyism is as yet won," stressing that "we must continue to be very alert and to fight against all evidence of totalitarian hate and fear." In accepting the Franklin D. Roosevelt Four Freedoms Award in mid-December, Lehman observed that in censuring McCarthy, "the Senate voted against the man," but had "yet to confront the 'ism,'" explaining that the censure vote represented "a clear condemnation of Senator McCarthy for which the nation should be very grateful," but emphasizing that "it was by no means a clear repudiation of mccarthyism" because it was neither "a repudiation of the evil and dangerous forces behind the man," nor "a repudiation of the evil and dangerous assaults he and his partisans have directed against the body of our liberties, our traditions, and our way of life." Lehman emphasized that McCarthy's censure had not removed the threat coming from "the forces of fear," including "the reactionary right" and "the anti-Communist vigilantes of the present day," the "Johnny-come-latelys in the struggle against Communism" who had "discovered the Communist threat only three or four years ago, and immediately staked a claim to it, as their own private preserve, for full political exploitation." For Lehman, "Senator McCarthy, the man, was never the main issue. He was and is but a symbol." In Lehman's view, "the issue was, *and is*, freedom, our civil liberties, and the principles of justice, of decency and morality," and he stressed that "on these grounds, the struggle must go forward, unceasingly and untiringly, until victory is won."[47]

Herbert Lehman deserves considerable credit for the Senate's condemnation of McCarthy. As the *Washington Post* observed in an editorial, "the American people owe a special debt of gratitude for this accomplishment to Senators Flanders, Lehman and Fulbright, who brought the original censure charges." Lehman found it somewhat ironic that Flanders and Fulbright received so much acclaim for their role in the fight against McCarthyism, noting that in contrast to himself, neither of them "got into the fight until nearly two years after it started." Lehman proudly recalled that his active involvement in the fight against McCarthy went back long before the censure resolutions of 1954; he had battled with McCarthy since February 1950 when he had challenged

McCarthy's original accusation that the State Department was riddled with Communists. Even in the dark days of 1953, when the Eisenhower administration and Senate leaders had remained silent as McCarthy and Roy Cohn and congressional inquisitors rode roughshod over the Constitution, Lehman had spoken out repeatedly, emphasizing that McCarthy's unsubstantiated charges and allegations represented an attack on the rights and liberties of all Americans. Lehman's efforts had finally borne fruit when the Army-McCarthy hearings made McCarthy an embarrassment to the Republicans and to the Senate establishment, resulting in McCarthy's formal chastisement. Others who wielded more power and influence finally responded to the alarm bells that Lehman had been ringing throughout McCarthy's reign of terror.[48]

CHAPTER 15

"The First Duty of Liberals Is Not to Exercise Power, but to Uphold Principle"

Herbert Lehman and Lyndon Johnson, 1950–1954

You'll suffer the fate of those crazies, those bomb-thrower types like Paul Douglas, Wayne Morse, Herbert Lehman. You'll be ignored, and get nothing accomplished you want.[1]

I

In a lecture at Columbia University in 1958, Herbert Lehman looked back upon his time in the Senate from 1950 to 1956. After his election in 1949, Lehman recalled, he arrived in Washington committed to advancing the liberal program of economic and social reforms on which he had campaigned: "to broaden and increase social security coverage and benefits, more aid for the needy, the helpless, and the handicapped, to provide more public housing and better schools," and "to fight for civil rights legislation." But Lehman did not realize until he got to Washington "how small—and how frustrated" the liberal group was with which he was aligned. According to Lehman, his fellow liberals felt "isolated from the mainstream of the Senate," like "they were aliens in an alien land and needed to accommodate themselves to the conservative majority." They believed "that the course of wisdom was to hold back and let conservatives take the lead, in the hope that the conservatives might agree to

---

Chapter title quotation: Herbert Lehman, "Travail of Liberalism, 1945–," Second Speranza Lecture, Columbia University, April 16, 1958, Herbert Lehman Papers, Speech File.

383

some mild advances if liberals would agree to follow but not try to lead." As Lehman related, "The paradox was that the Democratic Party was supposed to be the liberal party; yet in a Congress with a Democratic majority, the conservatives were overwhelmingly dominant."[2]

Lehman's idealism and his refusal to compromise his liberal principles frequently brought him into sharp conflict with Lyndon Johnson and the Democratic Senate leadership. One would be hard-pressed to think of two Senators more different than Herbert Lehman and Lyndon Johnson. Lehman was born into a wealthy New York City family in 1878, while Johnson was born into a poor family in the hill country west of Austin, Texas, thirty years later. Lehman's father made a fortune in investment banking, while Johnson's father struggled to make a living in farming, ranching, real estate, and politics. Lehman attended Dr. Julius Sachs's School for Boys and graduated from Williams College, while Johnson's education included a one-room schoolhouse and a degree from Southwest Texas State Teachers College. Lehman entered politics at the advanced age of fifty, while Johnson lived and breathed politics from a young age. Lehman was small and unremarkable in appearance, while Johnson was big and physically imposing. Elected to the Senate in 1949, Lehman saw the Senate as the culmination of his years in public service, while Johnson, elected one year earlier, hoped to use the Senate as a springboard to the presidency. Lehman hoped to persuade people by the force of his arguments, while Johnson sought to dominate them by the force of his personality. About the only attributes Herbert Lehman and Lyndon Johnson shared were their strong support for Franklin Roosevelt and the New Deal in the 1930s and their belief that the power of the federal government should be used to improve the lives of the American people, whether that meant bringing electricity to farmers in Texas or relief to the unemployed in New York City.[3]

Lyndon Johnson and Herbert Lehman entered a Senate in which a conservative coalition of Republicans and Southern Democrats had maintained effective control since the late 1930s. Johnson quickly found his path to power in this body, attaching himself to Richard Russell (D-GA) and becoming a member of the Senate "club," the insiders who exercised real power and influence in the chamber. Russell and the Southerners facilitated Johnson's quick ascension to the Democratic leadership, and Johnson's dependence on their support and on right-wing Texas oil and gas men for financing his campaigns led him to downplay his liberal tendencies and generally adhere to the conservative position on most issues during his first term in the Senate. After his elevation to Senate Democratic leader in 1953, Johnson enhanced his power by mastering and ruthlessly employing the Senate's arcane rules to his advantage. Lehman, on the other hand, as he explained to his good friend and fellow liberal Paul Douglas (D-IL), rejected the contention of William S. White of the *New York Times* and others that "the mark of a good Senator is accommodation and a willingness to bow to the will of the inner club." Lehman never sought acceptance into the Senate establishment, which had little use for liberal agitators who refused to compromise and insisted on speaking out, even if theirs were the only voices being raised. He did not fit well in a body where getting ahead usually meant going along, and Senate Democratic Leader Scott Lucas later reported that Lehman's Southern and Western colleagues "loathe[d] him." Lehman and his fellow liberals never matched Johnson or Russell or Pat McCarran in their expertise in the Senate's rules and traditions, and thus Lehman, Douglas, and other liberals frequently found themselves being ruled out of order and their proposals shunted off to unfriendly committees from which they never returned. While Lyndon Johnson accumulated more and more power in the Senate, Herbert Lehman grew more and more frustrated as most of his colleagues remained silent for so long about the evils of McCarthyism and passed such hateful measures as the Internal Security Act of 1950 and the McCarran-Walter Immigration and Naturalization Act of 1952.[4]

Both Lehman and Johnson liked to employ the "half-a-loaf" maxim to explain their actions as Senators, and their use of this analogy illuminates the differences between their political philosophies and beliefs. Shortly after leaving the Senate, Lehman recalled that as a Senator, his "fellow-liberals" confronted him "with the loaf-of-bread challenge." Did he "want to insist on the whole loaf and get nothing," or, by keeping quiet and going along, "perhaps succeed in getting a slice!" Most of his fellow liberals, Lehman recounted, favored the "one-slice solution," but he "decided to go for the loaf." He believed that "the function of the liberal is to uphold and project liberal principles and programs," and while he was "willing to compromise for half, if necessary," he would only do so "after the case for the whole had been made." In his opinion, "the first duty of liberals is not to exercise power, but to uphold principle," even if that meant "sacrificing the opportunity to hold power." Lyndon Johnson, who was seldom described as a liberal in the 1950s, bristled at the common perception that as Senate leader he compromised too easily. However, he accurately noted the difference between his approach and Lehman's in a letter in 1956 in which he lamented the Senate's failure to revise the nation's immigration laws. Johnson believed "that the way to handle this issue is to begin nibbling at it. If we nibble long enough, we will break its back." Johnson understood that Lehman did not "believe in this approach as much as" Johnson did, but he thought they agreed "fundamentally" on what they were "trying to accomplish." In a speech in May 1963, Johnson, now Vice President, maintained, "frequently in life I have had to settle for progress short of perfection. I have done so because—despite cynics—I believe that half a loaf is better than none. But my acceptance has always been conditioned upon the premise that the half-loaf is a step towards the full loaf—and that if I go on working, the day of the full loaf will come." In other words, while Lehman saw his role as making the liberal case in the strongest terms possible and resisting efforts to water down needed reforms, Johnson, at least until he became President, thought that change would come only in small increments.[5]

II

Herbert Lehman's support for civil rights for all Americans originated long before he came to the U.S. Senate. Reminiscing in 1957, Lehman noted that his wife had recently "found a box of compositions" that he had written for a college course almost sixty years ago. One of the essays had been "on some phase of civil rights and discrimination," and Lehman discovered that his "views were not very different today from what they had been at that time." Lehman's good friend and mentor Lillian Wald had been one of the founders of the National Association for the Advancement of Colored People in 1909, and she had served on its board and taken an active role in the organization's activities until 1918. Lehman himself was elected to the NAACP's board of directors in November 1929, and he remained a staunch champion of the association for the rest of his life, often referring to it as "our organization" in his correspondence with NAACP Secretary Walter White. In March of 1930, when philanthropist William Rosenwald offered to donate $1,000 a year for three years if the NAACP could obtain similar pledges from four other benefactors, Lehman immediately stepped forward with such a contribution. The NAACP's finances remained precarious, however, and starting in 1933 and continuing through the 1940s, Lehman made similar challenge grants to help the organization's fund-raising efforts. The Governor allowed the NAACP to use his name when it approached potential donors, and on more than one occasion in the 1950s, he contributed $5,000 to the organization. When the NAACP organized its Legal Defense and Education Fund in 1940, Lehman became one of its original incorporators, and, despite his reluctance to take on any additional obligations, he agreed to serve on the Fund's board of directors. Even though contributions to the Fund were tax deductible and donations to the NAACP itself were not, Lehman continued to earmark most of his contributions to the parent organization, forsaking any tax benefit.[6]

As Governor, Lehman compiled an admirable record in the area of civil rights. The *New York Amsterdam News* reported in 1938 that Lehman had "appointed more colored citizens to New York State jobs" than all his predecessors combined. He named the NAACP's Walter White to the board of visitors for the New York State Training School for Boys, and when he received complaints of segregation and discrimination against African American inmates at the New York State Training School for Girls, he immediately appointed a committee including White to investigate. Lehman endorsed the commission's conclusion that placing African American girls in separate cottages from white girls "cannot be justified and should not be tolerated." Lehman selected Colonel Benjamin O. Davis, the highest ranking African American in the regular Army, as the first African American to command Harlem's famed 369th Infantry Regiment of the New York National Guard, and when Davis was recalled to active service in 1940, Lehman chose Lieutenant Colonel Chauncey Hooper, another African American, to succeed him. Lehman signed into law numerous bills to outlaw discrimination in various aspects of life in New York State, including measures prohibiting public utilities or projects supported by public funds from discriminating in hiring; barring educational institutions that received state money from rejecting applicants based on their race, creed, or color; making it illegal for insurance companies to refuse to issue policies because of race; punishing lynching and mob violence against persons accused or suspected of committing a crime; banning discrimination in the state civil service; and prohibiting retail stores, movie theaters, and other establishments open to the public from discriminating based on race or color. After the Harlem riots in March 1935, Lehman forwarded to the State Legislature a package of reforms designed to relieve the "disgraceful" housing conditions in Harlem, and two years later he signed a bill creating a committee to study "the economic, cultural, health, and living conditions among Negroes" in New York. Many African American workers benefited directly from Lehman's "Little New Deal" measures, including black New York laundry workers who enjoyed both a significant reduction in their hours and a substantial increase in their pay when New York enacted a minimum wage law for women. Lehman's work on behalf of New York's African Americans led a biographer of Adam Clayton Powell, Jr., to conclude that Lehman was "the first Governor (Roosevelt included) to pay genuine attention to the black community of Harlem."[7]

On the national level, Lehman's efforts to advance the cause of civil rights met with mixed results. When Walter White appealed to him for help when the Wagner-Costigan anti-lynching bill was stalled in Congress in 1934, Lehman issued a strong public statement condemning lynching, and in 1935 Lehman joined a group of governors, mayors, bishops, and editors asking President Roosevelt to include the anti-lynching bill among his legislative priorities. But Roosevelt refused to risk antagonizing Southern Democrats by endorsing the measure. Lehman had more success in challenging the Civilian Conservation Corps in 1937 when it refused to enroll any more African Americans in New York State. Lehman immediately denounced such discrimination, declaring that "we in this State have always taken the position that it is wholly unjustified to make any difference in the handling of relief or other social activities between our white and colored population," and his efforts resulted in the CCC establishing two new companies in New York to accommodate African Americans who had sought to enlist.[8]

Governor Lehman tried to ensure that African Americans in New York State shared in the economic opportunities that opened up during World War II. In a message to the State Legislature on January 14, 1941, Lehman reported that "some of our largest concerns in and about New York City have closed their doors to Negroes," and he urged the lawmakers "to eliminate the vicious practice of discrimination in all businesses affected with a public interest." Three months later, Lehman proudly signed into law a measure prohibiting companies engaged in defense work from refusing "to employ any person in any capacity on account of race, creed, or color." In 1942, he approved bills making it a crime for defense industries "to refuse employment to any person, otherwise qualified, because of national origin or the race, color, or creed of such person," and authorizing the State Industrial Commissioner to investigate "charges of discrimination by public utilities, labor organizations, or war and defense industries."[9]

Lehman's strong support for civil rights helped him win the backing of most African Americans in his campaigns for public office. Although the *New York Amsterdam News* supported the Republican ticket in 1928 and 1930, the *Baltimore Afro-American* reminded its New York readers in 1930 that Lehman was a member of the NAACP's board of directors, and the NAACP's Walter White, in a letter that was published in the *Amsterdam News*, urged blacks to vote for Lehman, "a loyal, uncompromising, and generous friend of the Negro." When Lehman ran for Governor in 1932, White emphasized publicly Lehman's financial support for the NAACP and Lehman's "courage" in standing up to "those who would keep the Negro in a position of inferiority." Lehman carried the Assembly Districts located in Harlem by a plurality of ten thousand votes in 1932, and by thirteen thousand in 1934. By 1936, as more and more African Americans were deserting the Republican Party, now symbolized by Herbert Hoover rather than Abraham Lincoln, and replacing Lincoln's portrait over the fireplace with FDR's, the *Amsterdam News* finally saw the light, endorsing Lehman and Roosevelt for re-election. African American voters showed their enthusiasm for Lehman in torchlight parades and mass rallies in Harlem, and by giving him a majority of thirty thousand votes in the Harlem Assembly Districts. Two years later, the *Amsterdam News* asserted that "the colored citizens of this State have benefited more through the social legislation sponsored by Governor Lehman . . . than any other group in the State," and proclaimed: "the Negro must cast his vote for the re-election of Governor Lehman." Not surprisingly, Lehman again carried the Harlem Assembly Districts, this time by a margin of twenty-six thousand votes. The editors of the *Baltimore Afro-American* held Lehman in such esteem that they believed that he deserved "consideration for the Democratic nomination for the presidency" in 1940, declaring: "No other Democrat is more able, progressive, cultured, or qualified by experience and achievement to lead the party than he." Lehman's popularity among African

Americans enabled him to carry the Harlem Assembly Districts by thirty-two thousand votes when he ran for the Senate against Irving Ives in 1946, and by forty-five thousand over John Foster Dulles in 1949, when African American voters were angered by Dulles's comment that upstate voters would be sure to go to the polls if they "could see the kind of people in New York City" who were supporting Lehman.[10]

III

While Herbert Lehman had been in the forefront of the fight to ensure that African Americans enjoyed their full rights as American citizens, Lyndon Johnson had resisted federal efforts to address the race issue in the South. Although Johnson may have been personally sympathetic to the plight of African Americans and other minority groups, he subordinated such compassion to his political ambitions. As Robert Caro has written, Johnson served in the House of Representatives from 1937 to 1948, and during those years "he had a 100 percent record against not only legislation aimed at ending the poll tax and segregation in the armed forces but even against legislation aimed at ending lynching." When Johnson kicked off his campaign for the Senate in 1948, he denounced President Truman's civil rights proposals as "a farce and a sham—an effort to set up a police state in the guise of liberty." Johnson emphasized that he had "voted AGAINST the so-called poll tax repeal bill," asserting that the matter should be left to the individual states to decide, and he had "voted AGAINST the so-called anti-lunching bill," claiming that each "state can, and DOES, enforce the law against murder." As for a Fair Employment Practices Committee, Johnson bragged that he had "voted AGAINST the FEPC" because "if a man can tell you whom you must hire, he can tell you whom you can't hire."[11]

After his election to the Senate in 1948 by a mere eighty-seven votes, Johnson quickly aligned himself with Senator Richard Russell and the Southerners who controlled the chamber. Johnson demonstrated his fealty to Russell and the Southern bloc when he delivered his maiden speech on the Senate floor on March 9, 1949, as part of a Southern filibuster intended to prevent the Senate from changing Rule XXII, the cloture rule. Rule XXII allowed the Senate to limit debate on bills themselves but not on motions to make such measures the pending business, enabling Southerners to engage in endless debate whenever a motion was made to take up a civil rights bill. As opposed to some of the Southern firebrands like James Eastland of Mississippi, who made little attempt to conceal their disdain and disgust for African Americans and other minorities, Johnson claimed to be defending free speech and states' rights and to have the best interests of African Americans at heart. Speaking for an hour and a half, Johnson argued that "the freedom to speak" was "more precious" than "the freedom to enact laws hastily," warned that there was "no such thing as a 'reasonable limit' on free speech," and asserted that "good intentions, gentle reforms, and reasonable limits have destroyed more freedoms than evil forces could ever do." When the South opposed civil rights measures such as those proposed by President Truman, Johnson maintained, it was "not attempting to keep alive the old flames of hate and bigotry"; rather, it was "trying to tell the rest of the nation that this is not the way to accomplish what so many want to do for the Negro."[12]

Southern Senators welcomed Johnson to their fight against civil rights legislation. Senator Russell praised Johnson's speech as "one of the ablest I have ever heard on the subject," and despite Johnson's later denials, Caro demonstrates convincingly that Johnson attended meetings of the Southern caucus. Commenting on Johnson during his Senate years, Senator Clinton Anderson (D-NM) later described him as being "as Southern as hominy grits." Johnson became one of Russell's sentries, deputized to make sure that civil rights measures were not slipped onto the Senate calendar when no one was looking, and the Southerners prevented any of President Truman's civil rights bills from reaching the Senate floor in 1949. A few days after Johnson's speech, the Senate did modify Rule XXII, allowing cloture to be used to end filibusters on procedural motions, but in return, Russell, Johnson, and the Southerners, with the help of Republican conservatives led by Senator Kenneth Wherry of Nebraska, won the adoption of the so-called Wherry rule, which raised the requirement for cloture from a two-thirds vote of Senators present to a two-thirds vote of the Senate, and prohibited cloture completely on any future attempts to change the Senate rules on filibusters. In other words, no matter how many Senators were present, sixty-four votes would now be required to end a filibuster, and any subsequent efforts to amend Rule XXII could be subjected to endless debate.[13]

When Herbert Lehman was asked years later if he was sorry he had not stuck to his guns and demanded the Democratic senatorial nomination in 1938, he replied that he regretted it only because if he had been elected to the Senate in 1938 and re-elected in 1944, by 1950 he "would have been one of the senior Senators, and of course probably the chairman of some important committees." Lehman realized that men like Richard Russell and Pat McCarran exercised such vast influence in the Senate in part because of their seniority and their control of the major committees. Southern Democrats, who did not have to worry about Republican challengers in those days, tended to amass the greatest seniority, and thus either they or their conservative allies like McCarran were firmly ensconced as the chairmen and senior members of all the important committees. Northern liberals, on the other hand, had difficulty building up their seniority because they often had to engage in competitive races against Republican challengers, and they were usually consigned to the less important committees. Typically, Lehman's first committee assignments in 1950 included the Labor and Public Welfare Committee, which dealt with issues that were important to Lehman but was already stacked with liberals, and the Interior and Insular Affairs Committee, which held little interest for a New Yorker.[14]

As a Senator, Herbert Lehman tried in numerous ways to advance the cause of civil rights. He appointed Frances Williams, an African American, as one of his legislative assistants, making her the first African American to hold such a position. In his first meeting with the press after being sworn in as a Senator in January 1950, Lehman emphasized his determination to support civil rights legislation "with all the vigor" at his command, and the next day he applauded the President's State of the Union address, which included a call for a floor vote on Truman's civil rights proposals, still languishing in Congress. At his first meeting of the Senate Democratic Conference in early January, Lehman served notice that he would not be silent on civil rights issues to maintain party unity or facilitate the flow of legislation. When Senate Majority Leader Scott Lucas, Richard Russell, and others proposed that all Democrats oppose as non-germane any civil rights amendments to pending legislation, Lehman, along with Paul Douglas and Hubert Humphrey, pointed out the difficulty they would have in voting against any civil rights amendments and refused to make any promises or commitments to oppose such measures. Lehman did, however, agree with his fellow Democrats that "during the present session of Congress, amendments which are not germane be not offered to pending legislation."[15]

Civil rights groups and labor organizations decided to make the enactment of the President's proposed bill to establish a Fair Employment Practices Commission (FEPC) their top legislative priority in 1950. Such measures had been introduced in Congress since 1944, they had been the subject of extensive hearings, they had been reported favorably to the full Senate three times, and both political parties had promised in their 1948 platforms to support such legislation. Lehman assured Roy Wilkins of the NAACP and the National Council for a Permanent Fair Employment Practices Committee that he was "completely committed . . . to the enactment of a suitable and equitable Federal Employment Practices Act" and would "oppose any attempt to defeat FEPC by filibuster." But even though civil rights groups ascertained that a majority of Senators supported an FEPC bill, prospects for approval or even floor action on the measure seemed slim because the bill's proponents lacked the sixty-four votes needed to end a Southern filibuster. At a meeting of the Senate Democratic Conference in late February, Senator Lucas promised that "at a proper time in the not too far distant future the F.E.P.C. legislation would be called up." Lehman stressed his desire "to cooperate with the leadership," but he made it clear that on this issue, he "reserve[d] freedom of action on his own part for the future."[16]

After postponing consideration of the Fair Employment Practices bill in favor of Marshall Plan appropriations and other legislation, Senator Lucas finally tried to bring the FEPC measure before the Senate in early May 1950, only to be met by a Southern filibuster designed to prevent any action on the bill. In an address on the floor of the Senate on May 10, Herbert Lehman called for a Senate vote on the FEPC bill, asserting that "the simple concept that no man has a right to deny his fellow man the opportunity to earn a living for reasons of race, color, creed, or national origin is so elementary in a free democratic society that millions of people both here and abroad must wonder what has prevented us from enacting this legislation long ago." When a coalition of Republicans and Southern Democrats tried to sidetrack debate on the FEPC bill, Lehman proposed that the Senate remain in session well into the evening, but his motion was ruled out of order, and the Senate proceeded on the FEPC bill at a leisurely pace.[17]

On May 16, Lehman joined a group of thirty-six Senators who signed a formal petition to invoke cloture to end the filibuster and make the FEPC bill the pending business of the Senate. Tempers flared as the vote on the cloture resolution neared. Utilizing the same smear and "guilt by association" tactics that Senator Joseph McCarthy and the Republicans were using so effectively, Senator Walter George (D-GA) and other Southern Democrats claimed that the idea of an FEPC bill had originated with the Communist Party. When Hubert Humphrey denounced such allegations as "blasphemy," he was promptly ruled out of order for defaming his Southern colleagues. Herbert Lehman quickly came to Humphrey's defense, asserting that "the Senator from Minnesota is entirely correct and within his rights and is justified in doing so when he brings to light the accusation by innuendo, by implication, which has been made, namely that those who favor the FEPC bill are Communists or Communist sympathizers." But despite Lehman's and Humphrey's best efforts, the cloture motion received only fifty-two votes, twelve short of the sixty-four required to end the filibuster. While Democrats and Republicans argued over which party was to blame, Lehman lamented the Senate's action, calling it "a tragic defeat for a rightful cause, the cause of equal rights and freedom for all our people." He promised Roy Wilkins of the NAACP that he would "continue to fight for this legislation in every way and at every level which promises any hope of success . . . until victory is won."[18]

In contrast to Lehman's active role in the fight over the FEPC bill, Lyndon Johnson sat on the sidelines during the debate, declining to speak in defense of the filibuster as he had in 1949. This time, Johnson contented himself with voting against cloture and introducing into the Appendix of the *Congressional Record* an editorial from the *El Paso Herald-Post* applauding the Southerners for their use of the filibuster against "this odious bill" whose support came "from the Communists, the leftists, the practical politicians, and those who live by promoting 'causes.'" Johnson had clearly established his credentials with Senator Russell and the other Southern leaders in 1949, and there was no need for him to take an active part in the battle in 1950.[19]

Twelve Senators had been absent from the cloture vote on May 19, so Majority Leader Lucas scheduled another cloture vote for July 12, 1950, giving everyone a month's notice this time and telling Democratic Senators that "only illness or more serious misfortune should excuse from voting a Senator who is favorable to cloture on the motion to take up FEPC." Trying to answer Southern charges that FEPC legislation was Communist inspired, Lehman placed in the Appendix to the *Congressional Record* a copy of the NAACP's 1919 action plan, which included among the organization's objectives for that year "an equal chance for a livelihood in public and private employment." Ignoring the fact that Southerners like James Eastland saw little difference between civil rights groups like the NAACP and the Communist Party, Lehman emphasized that this goal enunciated by the NAACP in 1919 "is precisely the principle underlying FEPC legislation," which meant that "FEPC legislation antedated even the birth of the Communist Party in America." Lehman also tried to connect the battle for FEPC with the war in Korea that had broken out a few weeks earlier, warning the Senate that the failure to enact FEPC legislation would tell African Americans and other minorities fighting in Korea, "You are good enough to fight for your country, you are good enough to risk your lives; you are good enough to die, but if by good fortune you come back safely, you are going to be second class citizens again, without the rights which other American citizens possess." Sensing the defeat that followed, Lehman vowed that "this fight for equality in employment, education, civil and political activities must go on." But as would so often be the case in the Senate, Lehman's fine words failed to sway any votes, and the cloture resolution failed again, this time falling nine votes short of the required sixty-four.[20]

Not wanting to abandon the goal of prohibiting discrimination in employment, Lehman urged President Truman in October 1950 to follow Franklin Roosevelt's example from 1941 and issue an executive order requiring that "all defense contracts must contain a clause barring discrimination in employment under such contracts." Lehman knew that such action would not take the place of needed legislation in this area, but he believed that the United States, if it were "to be a leader among the free nations in the cause of democracy—must certainly eliminate discriminations based on race, creed, or color from any activities over which the federal government has any control." Under pressure from Lehman and civil rights leaders, Truman finally issued Executive Order 10210 in February 1951, banning discrimination by companies working on defense contracts, but as William Berman has noted, "Executive Order 10210 was essentially meaningless because it lacked an enforcement clause."[21]

The success of the Southerners and their allies in preventing the Senate from even considering the FEPC bill convinced Herbert Lehman that "under the present cloture rule, it is impossible to bring civil rights legislation to a vote." Lehman complained that "the requirement that sixty-four affirmative votes must be cast in order to bring up a measure for debate is undemocratic and un-American," charging that it represented "legislative self-paralysis" because it "fastens the will of the minority upon the majority and makes it impossible to break that stranglehold." Consequently, on August 24, 1950, Lehman introduced a resolution to change Senate Rule XXII so that cloture could be invoked by a two-thirds vote of Senators present after two days of debate, or by a simple majority of Senators present after fifteen days of deliberations. Lehman emphasized that FEPC "is not the issue here"; the problem was that under Rule XXII, "a small handful of Senators could make it impossible for the Senate even to take up" legislation that was vital to the nation's security. Even though nine other liberal Democrats joined in cosponsoring Lehman's motion, he had no illusions that his proposal would be adopted any time soon. He realized that Rule XXII, which guaranteed the right of unlimited debate on any attempt to modify the current procedure, doomed any such effort to failure. But Lehman hoped that "the day will not be far distant when this proposal will be adopted," which "will be a great day for democracy, for civil rights legislation, and for orderly procedure in this great body."[22]

Despite losing the fight for the FEPC bill, Lehman continued to work in other ways for civil rights in 1950. In June, he helped defeat Senator Russell's attempt to include in the extension of the Selective Service Act a provision to allow draftees to choose whether to serve in integrated or segregated units. When William Hastie's nomination to be the first African American to serve on a federal appeals court bogged down in the Senate Judiciary Committee in midsummer, Lehman "respectfully" urged Senator McCarran to use his "influence to bring Judge Hastie's nomination to a vote as soon as possible," emphasizing that Hastie was "eminently qualified" for this appointment. And two months after the outbreak of the Korean War, Lehman publicly praised the record of African American troops in Korea, citing various newspaper articles to show that "these Negro Americans are worthy of the highest acclaim as soldiers of the United States and fighters for freedom." Lehman hoped that "the reports of Negro heroism from Korea" would "speed up the Army's program of abolishing segregated units."[23]

When Herbert Lehman ran for re-election to the Senate in 1950, he enjoyed solid support from African Americans despite the presence of noted black activist W. E. B. Du Bois on the ballot as the candidate of the American Labor Party. Harlem Assemblyman Hulan Jack seconded Lehman's nomination at the Democratic State Convention, longtime YMCA leader and civil rights activist Channing Tobias served as one of the honorary chairmen of Lehman's campaign committee, and famed African American educator Mary McLeod Bethune delivered a major radio address highlighting Lehman's efforts in the Senate "to remind his colleagues that the shame and blot of discrimination furnished ammunition to our enemies more deadly than bullets and shells." Congressman Adam Clayton Powell, Jr., made radio broadcasts on Lehman's behalf, stressing the Senator's long record of supporting FEPC measures both in Albany and in Washington, and invited him to speak at the Abyssinian Baptist Church on the Sunday before the election, and A. Philip Randolph of the Brotherhood of Sleeping Car Porters helped rally Harlem voters in support of Lehman, emphasizing the Senator's "exceptional civil rights and pro-labor record." Campaigning in Harlem, Lehman promised to work for "strong and sound" rent control legislation and vowed to continue his efforts to enact civil rights legislation by removing "that major obstacle, the filibuster." Because of Lehman's long record advocating for civil rights and his strong support from African American leaders, Lehman received 64,154 votes in Harlem's four Assembly Districts, compared to 19,495 for Republican candidate Joe Hanley and 13,920 for Du Bois.[24]

IV

In January 1951, Senate Democrats had to replace Majority Leader Scott Lucas of Illinois and Assistant Majority Leader Francis Myers of Pennsylvania, both of whom had been defeated in the November elections. For Majority Leader, Lehman and Democratic liberals coalesced around Joseph O'Mahoney of Wyoming, but Senate Democrats, by a vote of 30 to 19, chose instead Ernest McFarland, "a middle-of-the roader" from Arizona who enjoyed strong support from Southern Democrats because he had always opposed cloture and civil rights legislation. Lyndon Johnson was the only Senator interested in the Assistant Majority Leader or Whip position, and with Richard Russell's blessing, Johnson was elected Assistant Democratic Leader without opposition. McFarland's and Johnson's ascension demonstrated the South's stranglehold on the Democratic caucus and signaled that President Truman's civil rights program had no chance of reaching the Senate floor for debate, much less being enacted.[25]

Understanding the importance of committee assignments, Herbert Lehman, Paul Douglas, and Hubert Humphrey urged the newly elected Democratic leaders to appoint liberals to the Democratic Steering Committee, which determined which Senators sat on which committees, and the Democratic Policy Committee, which controlled the flow of bills to the Senate floor. They also requested that "there be adequate additional **liberal** representation on the Finance, Commerce, Judiciary, Appropriations, and Foreign Relations Committees" (emphasis in the original). Lehman and the others warned that whether the Democratic Senate majority worked cooperatively in the 82nd Congress "depends upon fair representation of all elements in [the] organization of the Senate," and they emphasized that "the country's as well as the party's interest requires the most serious considerations of these requests." However, McFarland and Johnson saw little reason to grant the liberals' demands, especially since Lehman and the others had opposed McFarland for Leader. Consequently, liberals received scant representation on the Steering and Policy Committees. McFarland claimed that all the appointments to the Steering Committee went by seniority, except for that of Allen Frear, a moderate from Delaware, who was supposedly added "to assure geographic balance," but this explanation made little sense since it left Brien McMahon of Connecticut as the only Senator on the Steering Committee from the Northeast or the industrial Midwest. The situation was not much better on the Policy Committee, where Theodore Francis Green of Rhode Island joined McMahon as the only members from Northern states. As for the Senate's standing committees, Frear received a seat on the Finance Committee, Willis Smith of North Carolina went on the Judiciary Committee, and Guy Gillette of Iowa and John Sparkman of Alabama joined the Foreign Relations Committee, while Lehman and his fellow liberals remained consigned to lesser committees. Lehman hosted a meeting at his apartment at which thirteen Democratic Senators who believed that their party could succeed only by espousing liberal positions on civil rights and other issues discussed how to strengthen their position within the party and the Senate, but they undercut their own strategy when, according to the *New York Times*, they rejected any intention to "organize as a separate bloc" and promised to "operate through the party's duly elected leadership in the Senate even though that leadership did not reflect 'the liberal viewpoint' on many domestic issues."[26]

Lehman's discouragement mounted a few months later when Kentucky Senator Virgil Chapman's death created a vacancy on the Democratic Policy Committee. Liberals supported either Lehman or Paul Douglas as Chapman's successor, and the *New York Times* reported that "Lehman is Senator McFarland's choice" for the position. But either the *Times* report was in error, or Lyndon Johnson persuaded McFarland to change his mind, because Earle Clements of Kentucky received the coveted slot instead of Lehman. As Clements later explained, he was "a very junior member of the Senate" at the time, and he had not done anything to distinguish himself, but he had developed a good relationship with Lyndon Johnson when they had served together in the House of Representatives. According to Clements, he was appointed to the Policy Committee because Johnson and the powers that be did not want the seat to go to Lehman or Douglas, and they could justify Clements's selection by explaining that "he just took the place of another Kentuckian."[27]

Despite the unpromising political climate in Congress, Herbert Lehman continued to battle for civil rights in 1951–1952. In late February 1951, when the Senate considered the Universal Military Training bill that had been drafted by Lyndon Johnson's Armed Services subcommittee, Lehman proposed an amendment "to protect members of the Armed Forces against individual or mob violence" by "making it a federal offense to kill or assault members of the armed services" performing their official duties. As Lehman's legislative assistant Julius Edelstein later noted, however, Lehman "was not good at the quick thrust, the repartee, which . . . marks the skillful debater," and he floundered badly as the Senate considered his amendment, insisting at one point that Senator Robert Kerr "cannot put words into my mouth . . . I myself will put words in my mouth." Despite strong support from Douglas and Humphrey, Lehman's proposal suffered what the NAACP's Walter White characterized as a "coalition lynching" at the hands of the "Dixiecrats and Republicans," who rejected Lehman's attempt to protect those who were being asked "to offer up their lives if need be, to save the nation and the free world."[28]

With war raging in Korea, Lehman had more success in pushing the Defense Department to accelerate the armed forces' compliance with President Truman's 1948 executive order calling for "equality of treatment and opportunity" in the military services "as rapidly as possible." In March 1951, Lehman led a group of six Senators who met with his old friend Anna Rosenberg, now serving as Assistant Secretary of Defense, to express their dissatisfaction with the Army's dawdling on implementing the President's directive. Lehman and Humphrey later wrote to Secretary of Defense George Marshall, acknowledging "the progress that has been made" but asserting that the Army could be doing more "to reduce rapidly, and soon to eliminate, the indignity of segregation from the armed forces of the United States," and wanting to know "what further steps are contemplated toward the achievement of the desired goals and some idea as to the rate of progress which might be expected." Marshall delayed responding to Lehman and Humphrey for almost a month so that he could provide them a detailed account of the Army's "plans for the integration of Negro personnel" in the Far East, including the Defense Department's plans "to inactivate the Negro 24th Infantry Regiment," the Army's last remaining African American regiment, and to "replace it with an integrated infantry regiment." After the military announced the plan on July 27, Lehman publicly congratulated the Army and the Defense Department. He pointed out, however, that "there now remains the task of ending segregation in other units of the Army," and Lehman vowed that he and other Senators would continue working "until every segment of segregation within the armed forces is eliminated here and abroad."[29]

Lehman also condemned discrimination against African American civilians. When a mob in the all-white Chicago suburb of Cicero rioted to prevent a black family from renting an apartment there in July 1951, Herbert Lehman was the only member of Congress to speak out in the Senate or the House chamber in the next two months against this expression "of hate and prejudice." Lehman noted that events in Cicero demonstrated that "the ugly blight of prejudice is not the peculiar property of any region of the country, but is found, lamentably, north of the Mason and Dixon's line as well as south." He hoped that the day would soon come when "hate and prejudice based on race, creed, or color have been banished forever from our land and that equality before the law and in the enjoyment of their human rights is accorded to all Americans."[30]

In June of 1951, Lehman joined with Senators Humphrey, Douglas, and others in sponsoring a series of bills to end discrimination in employment, make lynching a federal crime, and outlaw the use of the poll tax in federal elections, but they had no illusions that such measures would make it to the floor of the Senate, much less be enacted into law. Lehman and the others recognized that the main obstacle remained Senate Rule XXII, which made it almost impossible to invoke cloture to break a Southern filibuster against civil rights bills. A few months earlier, Lehman had reintroduced his amendment to the Senate rules to make it easier to cut off debate, reiterating his "hope that this rule may be adopted so that civil rights legislation may be brought to a vote in the Senate," but his proposal had been referred to the Rules Committee from which it was not expected to emerge.[31]

But with one eye on the elections of 1952, when African American voters might determine the outcome of the presidential and numerous senatorial races, a subcommittee of the Senate Rules Committee met in October 1951 to consider Lehman's resolution to change Senate Rule XXII, along with similar measures submitted by other Senators. Lehman urged the panel to recommend to the full Senate his proposal to allow a two-thirds majority of Senators present to force a vote after forty-eight hours of debate, or a simple majority of Senators to close off debate after two weeks of deliberations. He condemned the current rule as "a plain prescription for potential legislative paralysis" that "may well threaten all legislation, and our very form of government in a future crisis." While Lehman believed that "the minority must be protected in its precious right to offer its views in the marketplace of ideas, and to seek majority status through argument and persuasion," he knew "of no principle of democracy which would permit a minority permanently to block the majority in its will for action and decision. That is not debate," he declared; "that is deadlock." Lehman was not optimistic, but he hoped that "the aroused sentiment of the American people can and will force this undemocratic provision from our rule books."[32]

Lehman questioned the constitutionality of Senate Rule XXII, but he offered no practical suggestions as to how to overcome this seemingly insurmountable obstacle. However, Walter Reuther, the head of the United Auto Workers (UAW) and a member of the Leadership Conference on Civil Rights, proposed a possible solution during his testimony before the Rules subcommittee. As Kevin Boyle has pointed out in his study of Reuther and the UAW's liberalism, the union's leadership had concluded that the filibuster "was the linchpin of the conservative coalition's power to define the national agenda," with "the Dixiecrats trading their votes against economic reforms in exchange for the Republicans' refusal to vote cloture on civil rights bills." Having identified the problem, the UAW enlisted noted liberal lawyer and ADA cofounder Joseph Rauh to find a solution, which Rauh and UAW Washington representative Paul Sifton promptly did. Working from a brief prepared by Rauh and

Sifton, Reuther told the subcommittee that the Senate could "get out of this dead-end filibuster alley that we are in" by recognizing that the Senate was not a continuing body and that rules adopted by one Senate were not binding on its successors. This would mean that the next Senate could adopt a new set of rules by majority vote when it convened in January 1953. In the meantime, Reuther warned that "majority rule in the Senate of the United States is now and will be the No. 1 civil rights issue in the 1952 campaign and elections."[33]

On January 29, 1952, the Senate Rules Committee proposed a small change in Rule XXII to allow two-thirds of Senators present and voting, rather than two-thirds of the Senate, to invoke cloture. In recommending this minor alteration to the present rule, the committee rejected Lehman's and other proposals to make more significant modifications in the current practice and left untouched that part of the rule prohibiting cloture on any attempt to change the Senate's rules. This meant that Senators would still be able to use the filibuster to block any meaningful changes in Rule XXII. Lehman considered the committee's resolution "very unsatisfactory," explaining to Senator Estes Kefauver that the proposal recommended by the Rules Committee "would still leave the rules indefensibly protective of the right to filibuster and not at all protective of the right to act," which Lehman considered "fully as precious as the right to debate." A few weeks later, Lehman told the Leadership Conference on Civil Rights that the Rules Committee proposal was the product of "cynical men" in both political parties who wanted to prevent civil rights legislation from reaching the Senate floor.[34]

Herbert Lehman and advocates of civil rights legislation continued to find themselves stymied. Despite Lehman's urging, President Truman refused to issue an executive order creating an FEPC with "effective enforcement provisions," fearing that to do so would jeopardize legislative approval of his defense program. Senate Majority Leader McFarland made it clear in January 1952 that he hoped for a short session that would allow Congress to adjourn before the political campaigns started in earnest, meaning that he would not press for civil rights measures or changes in the filibuster rule that would lead to lengthy debates. Consequently, despite pressure from labor and civil rights groups, the Democratic Policy Committee refused to call up for floor action the Rules Committee's mild modification in the filibuster rule. In June, Lehman moved on behalf of himself and twelve other liberal Democrats to substitute his original proposal to change the filibuster rule for the version recommended by the Rules Committee, but Lehman had "little hope that we can get action on this measure this year." Nonetheless, he believed that eventually, "the people of this country are going to insist on action."[35]

As the congressional session drew to a close, Lehman and other liberals wanted to ensure that civil rights remained on the nation's agenda even though they knew there was no chance of such legislation being adopted. On June 20,

1952, Lehman was part of a bipartisan group of sixteen Senators who introduced a new FEPC bill, which the Senate Labor and Public Welfare Committee reported out favorably four days later. Even though Senators Humphrey and Ives, its chief sponsors, had weakened the bill considerably, ceding priority to state and local commissions and emphasizing "conciliation, mediation, conference, and persuasion" rather than prosecution, there was still no possibility of the measure being acted upon before Congress adjourned. Humphrey explained that the goal in reporting the bill at this time was "educational," and there was some talk that the measure might serve as a model for the platforms that would be adopted at the upcoming presidential nominating conventions. On July 4, Lehman celebrated the holiday by introducing for himself and twelve colleagues a revised version of his bill to make it a federal crime to attack members of the armed forces who were in uniform and carrying out their assigned duties. Lehman had no illusions that any of these measures would be passed before Congress adjourned, but he wanted them to remain in the public eye and "be available for consideration by the public and by the Congress should it be recalled into special session."[36]

V

The reluctance of Senator McFarland and Democratic leaders to move forward on civil rights issues in 1952 reflected their desire to prevent what Robert Albright of the *Washington Post* described as "a bitter filibuster at the start of a presidential election year [that] could split the Democratic Party beyond hope of repair before the November balloting." McFarland, who had always opposed cloture in the past, was loath to push rules or legislation that threatened to tear the Democrats apart, especially since any attempt to change the current rules could easily be blocked by a Southern filibuster. Thus, the real battle for civil rights in 1952 was fought not in Congress, but rather in Chicago at the Democratic National Convention.[37]

The adoption of a strong civil rights plank explicitly endorsing President Truman's civil rights program had precipitated a walkout by Southern delegates at the Democratic National Convention in 1948, and Democratic National Chairman Frank McKinney's top priority in 1952 was "to reunite the party and remove the disunity that existed in 1948." McKinney took very seriously the threats by Southern Democrats that they might bolt the party again in 1952, especially after South Carolina Governor James Byrnes warned that "the electoral votes of the Southern states can no longer be taken for granted by any party or candidate." But party leaders also had to contend with liberals like Herbert Lehman, who emphasized in a speech to New York Democrats in June that "we must not retreat one inch" on civil rights, which had "become the symbol of

Democratic Party determination to achieve justice for all men regardless of race, color, or creed." Lehman insisted that the Democratic platform should advocate a change in the filibuster rule "so that civil rights legislation can be brought to a vote," and he asserted that the Democrats should "support all those practical rights measures which were recommended by President Truman's historical Civil Rights Commission, including an F.E.P.C. with enforcement powers." The Senator stressed that "if we seek to buy victory at the price of principle, if we betray the faith of those minority groups who until now have reposed their confidence in us, we will not only lose the election, but we will lose our integrity." Hoping somehow to bridge these competing interests within the Democratic Party, McKinney and party leaders appointed a platform committee including all elements of the party, with Herbert Lehman as a representative of the party's liberal wing.[38]

Unlike McKinney, Lehman believed that adopting a platform with a strong civil rights plank, including a call for revision in the filibuster rule, should be a higher priority than a harmonious convention, and the Senator intended to use his position on the platform committee to ensure that the Democrats produced such a document. When President Truman, in a speech at Howard University in June 1952, highlighted all the progress that had been made in civil rights under his leadership in the last seven years, Lehman immediately praised the President's "statesman-like pronouncement" and promised that during the platform committee's deliberations, he would "cite this speech and fight for strong, specific, platform planks for an FEPC law with teeth in it." A few weeks before the convention, Lehman confided to his good friend and Senate colleague William Benton that "we are probably going to have the same kind of fight over the Civil Rights section of the Platform as we had in 1948—perhaps even sharper and more critical." Lehman noted that reiterating the 1948 platform "would not be at all satisfactory to the minority groups" who know that "we cannot get the Civil Rights program through Congress without cloture," and he emphasized that "we will need to fight for cloture and win on cloture."[39]

As the *New York Times* reported on the eve of the platform committee's hearings, "Democrats seeking a strong civil rights plank in their party platform for 1952" looked to Lehman "to lead an attack against civil rights legislation's greatest obstacle, the Senate filibuster." As Arkansas Democratic Congressman Brooks Hays later wrote, Southerners, for good reason, regarded the "unyielding" Lehman as their "biggest problem." At a press conference shortly after his arrival in Chicago, Lehman stressed his determination "to fight for a strong and forward-looking platform which will be outspoken and unequivocal on the great issues of our time, including but not confined to civil rights." The Senator hoped this would not lead Southern delegates to bolt from the convention and the party, but he was willing to run that risk. Fighting for the whole loaf,

Lehman warned at the platform committee's first hearings that although he would prefer not to, he was prepared to take the civil rights issue to the floor of the convention if necessary to win approval for a document that supported federal civil rights legislation and curbs on filibusters.[40]

When the platform committee concluded its hearings and began to compile its report, Lehman insisted on a strong civil rights plank that included federal guarantees of equal employment opportunities for everyone without distinction as to race, creed, color, or national origin. Concerned, however, that such language might lead Southern delegates to walk out, party leaders, including President Truman, House Speaker Sam Rayburn, and House Majority Leader and Platform Committee Chairman John McCormack of Massachusetts, preferred a more conciliatory provision along the lines of the Humphrey-Ives bill that had recently been reported by the Senate Labor and Public Welfare Committee. That measure stressed mediation and persuasion rather than legal proceedings and gave the states more leeway to implement their own anti-discrimination laws. Hubert Humphrey, who had led the fight for the strong civil rights plank that had triggered the Southern walkout in 1948, favored appeasing the South this time in the name of party unity. But in a clear indication of Lehman's stature in the liberal wing of the party, Humphrey warned that if "the general"—meaning Lehman—insisted on stronger language, then Humphrey would have to serve as one of his "lieutenants" in the floor fight that might follow. Lehman was adamant that the platform should endorse legislation creating a federal Fair Employment Practices Commission empowered to prevent or punish discrimination, and he held firmly to his belief that the Democrats should advocate changing the filibuster rule so that civil rights legislation could actually reach the Senate floor for action.[41]

After much haggling, the Democrats began to coalesce around a compromise civil rights plank that was modeled on the 1948 platform except that it omitted any reference to President Truman, who was not a candidate this time. As had been the case four years earlier, the proposed platform did not specifically recommend a federal FEPC; instead, it called for federal legislation to secure for all Americans "(1) the right to equal opportunity for employment; (2) the right to security of persons; (3) the right to full and equal participation in the nation's political life, free from arbitrary restraints." In a victory for Lehman and the liberals, a new section entitled "Improving Congressional Procedures" was added to deal with the stumbling blocks of the filibuster in the Senate and the Rules Committee in the House. In this provision, the Democrats declared: "In order that the will of the American people may be expressed upon all legislative proposals, we urge that action be taken at the beginning of the 83rd Congress to improve congressional procedures so that majority rule prevails and decisions can be made after reasonable debate without being blocked by a minority in either House."[42]

Lehman had wanted the Democrats to endorse explicitly the establishment of an effective FEPC and a change in the filibuster rule, but as the
platform committee neared the end of its task, he realized that he stood alone
in insisting on such language. After much discussion and deliberation, Congressman William Dawson of Illinois, an African American, persuaded Lehman to
accept the more moderate civil rights plank "in the interest of party 'unity,' " and
not to file a minority report that would lead to a divisive floor fight. Dawson
assured Lehman that the civil rights "plank was all right and that in his opinion
it would prove satisfactory to colored people." Lehman reluctantly agreed to go
along, but he warned Senator Spessard Holland of Florida that "if the South
made any protest from the floor" or tried "to modify the plank any further,"
Lehman would "introduce my strong plank from the floor." As Lehman had
feared, a few Southern diehards did try to change the document from the floor,
but House Speaker Sam Rayburn, who was presiding, ruled that the platform
had already been adopted before any amendments could be proposed.[43]

Herbert Lehman would have preferred that the civil rights sections be "still
stronger," but he believed that "the end result is a better, more liberal platform
than what we had in 1948," and he hailed the Democrats' pledge "to remove
from the legislative roadway the barrier of the filibuster" when the new Congress
convened in January. Lehman's enthusiasm for the platform grew in subsequent
weeks as he boasted to Hubert Humphrey in early September that their efforts
had resulted in "excellent platform declarations on matters with which we were
particularly concerned." Walter White agreed with Lehman's assessment of the
Democratic platform, reporting to the NAACP board that Lehman had "waged
an uncompromising fight" within the platform committee, blocking Southern
efforts "to evade the issue" of the filibuster and federal FEPC legislation. White
credited Lehman for the Democrats' adoption of a civil rights plank that was
"stronger than any ever taken by a political party."[44]

VI

Besides agreeing on the civil rights plank in the platform, the Democrats
also had to nominate presidential and vice presidential candidates and resolve
a contentious dispute over whether to require Southern delegates to promise
to support the party's nominee. Like many Democrats, Lehman had followed
the career of Governor Adlai Stevenson of Illinois and hoped that Stevenson
would be the party's candidate in 1952. Stevenson's efforts to enact an FEPC
law in Illinois and his decisive action during the Cicero riot, when he sent in
the National Guard to protect the African American family trying to move into
the neighborhood, had impressed Lehman and party liberals, while Stevenson's
preference for state action on civil rights rather than federal legislation made him

acceptable to Southern and conservative Democrats. He had also earned liberals' plaudits for resisting the national anticommunist hysteria and refusing to retract his statement vouching for Alger Hiss's character even after Hiss's conviction. When President Truman cleared the way with his announcement on March 29, 1952, that he would not seek another term, Lehman and leading liberals met with Stevenson the following day, urging him to run. According to Stevenson aide and biographer John Bartlow Martin, Lehman and the others argued that "Stevenson represented the Democrats' only hope of winning," and Stevenson seemed willing, agreeing that he should let people know shortly that he would "accept the nomination if offered it." But despite Truman's entreaties and most Democrats' importuning, Stevenson threw the Democratic race into turmoil on April 16 when he declared that he was a candidate for re-election as Governor of Illinois and "could not accept the nomination for any other office."[45]

With Stevenson seemingly out of the race, Lehman and the New York delegation, along with many liberals in other states, rallied around veteran businessman and diplomat Averell Harriman as their candidate for the presidential nomination. New York State Democratic Chairman Paul Fitzpatrick first floated the possibility of Lehman as the state's "favorite son" candidate to hold the delegation together, but Lehman, citing his age, stepped aside in favor of Harriman, whose vast international experience and strong support for Truman's Fair Deal policies, including civil rights, made him an attractive candidate. Lehman and other liberals sought to ensure that the party's nominee would continue the domestic and foreign policies of Franklin Roosevelt and Harry Truman, and although Harriman had never run for public office, he seemed to be the candidate best suited to assume that mantle. Lehman agreed to serve with Franklin Roosevelt, Jr., as honorary chairmen of Harriman's campaign and worked to round up support for Harriman's candidacy. Despite Lehman's efforts, however, Harriman's candidacy, like those of Vice President Alben Barkley and Senators Estes Kefauver of Tennessee, Richard Russell of Georgia, and Robert Kerr of Oklahoma, failed to generate sufficient excitement and support among fellow Democrats to capture the nomination.[46]

Harriman's and Kefauver's best hopes for victory lay in demanding that all delegates pledge to support the party's nominee, which might lead to a Southern walkout, leaving Northern liberals in control of the convention. But President Truman, Speaker Rayburn, and Adlai Stevenson's supporters sought to prevent such a bolt, and they eventually brokered a compromise that led to the seating of all the "regular" Southern delegations. Party leaders and convention delegates concluded that Stevenson was the Democrats' only viable candidate against the popular Republican nominee, General Dwight Eisenhower, and the reluctant Stevenson finally consented to run if nominated. After the second ballot, Harriman withdrew in favor of Stevenson, and the Illinois Governor won the nomination on the third ballot.[47]

Recalling his initial enthusiasm about Stevenson, Herbert Lehman hailed the Illinois Governor's selection as a victory for the liberal wing of the Democratic Party, asserting that Stevenson was "a liberal candidate" with a liberal record, who would be running on a liberal platform that included calls for "broad-scale social welfare programs, revision of our immigration laws, and all-out support of the administration's foreign policy." Lehman reminded everyone of the Democrats' "strong and unequivocal civil rights plank" and claimed that "even our Southern brothers and sisters are coming to understand the necessity of a forthright stand on civil rights." A few weeks after the convention, Lehman emphasized to State Democratic Party Chairman Fitzpatrick that he was "very much pleased with the nomination of Adlai Stevenson" and he believed Stevenson "should make a strong candidate and an excellent president."[48]

Lehman and New York Democrats hoped that their switch to Stevenson would give them some influence over his choice of a running mate, and they argued that putting a liberal like Harriman, Kefauver, or Franklin Roosevelt, Jr., on the ticket would improve the party's chances in key Northern states such as New York. But President Truman, DNC Chairman McKinney, Sam Rayburn, and other party leaders urged that a Southerner be chosen to prevent Eisenhower and the Republicans from making inroads in that region. Their first choice, reportedly, was Senator Russell, but, as expected, Russell preferred to remain in the Senate where he wielded considerable authority and did not have to support someone else's policies. Russell had allegedly promised to support Lyndon Johnson for the vice presidency if Russell failed to win the presidential nomination, but recognizing that Johnson would never be accepted by the Northern liberals, Russell recommended instead Senator John Sparkman of Alabama, who had helped craft the compromise civil rights plank in the platform and, as the *New York Times* noted, was more "acceptable to the Old Guard in the South and the Young Turks of the North." Presumably, Lehman, at age seventy-four, was one of the "Young Turks of the North."[49]

Comparing Sparkman's record in the Senate with Lyndon Johnson's shows why Lehman and Northern liberals preferred Sparkman. Although both Southerners had opposed any and all civil rights measures in Congress, Sparkman had achieved an almost perfect liberal rating from Americans for Democratic Action in the 82nd Congress, and the CIO gave him a similarly high score for his votes on issues of interest to labor. Lyndon Johnson, however, worried about shoring up his strength among conservatives in Texas, and he had voted against the liberal position on half of the key votes tabulated by ADA in 1952.[50]

Sparkman's selection as Stevenson's running mate stirred up considerable concern among liberals and African Americans because of Sparkman's opposition to federal action on civil rights. Outspoken Harlem Congressman Adam Clayton Powell, Jr., denounced Sparkman's selection as one of the "great tragedies of our time," asserting that Sparkman's dismal record on civil rights offset all his positive votes on other issues. Powell condemned the Democrats for combining "a weak civil rights platform" with a presidential candidate in Stevenson who was "totally uncommitted" on civil rights, and a Southerner for Vice President, and declared that he would not campaign for the national ticket. The NAACP's Walter White disagreed with Powell's interpretation of the Democratic platform, but he shared the Congressman's concerns about Sparkman, explaining that "it will be difficult, if not impossible, for the Democratic Party to sell to Negro voters, as well as to many other civil rights advocates, any nominee whose voting record has been one of consistent opposition to the civil rights objectives of the Democratic Party as stated in the 1948 platform and reaffirmed and extended in the platform adopted here only two days ago." Herbert Lehman saw the platform as the key to Sparkman winning over African American and liberal supporters, describing the vice presidential candidate as "a real fighting liberal" on every issue except civil rights. For Sparkman "to win the support of New York and of liberals generally in this election," Lehman declared, "he must accept, without reservation, the fine civil rights plank in our platform. He must not only accept that plank but advocate its effectuation as the policy of the Democratic Party."[51]

Herbert Lehman worried that the Republicans would exploit African Americans' lack of enthusiasm for the Democratic ticket, and his fears were realized in early August when sixteen liberal Republicans tried to appeal to African American voters by asserting that an effective federal FEPC law would be enacted more quickly under Republican leadership. Lehman responded immediately, charging that it was "an insult to the public intelligence" for the GOP to claim that its platform was stronger than the Democrats' "historic advance" in this area. He noted that Eisenhower was "on record that he does not believe that civil rights should be made 'a federal compulsory thing,'" and he pointed out that while the Republican platform called for "enacting federal legislation to further just and equitable treatment in the area of discriminatory employment practices," it also opposed "federal 'duplication' of state efforts to end discrimination in employment, and ominously warns against the dangers of federal 'bureaucracy' to deal with employment discrimination. If this doesn't mean that the Republican Party is publicly committed against FEPC," Lehman declared, "I am not familiar with the English language." The Senator emphasized that the 1952 Democratic platform marked the first time either of the major parties had taken "a definite and clear position against the fundamental barrier which has up to now blocked all civil rights legislation—the filibuster," while the Republican platform "pretends it never heard of the filibuster or of amending the rules of the Senate and the House." Lehman stressed that if Stevenson and Sparkman "accept the full letter and spirit of our civil rights plank," then "the Democratic Party will continue to be, as it has been for the past twenty years, the civil rights party, and the party that will lead the way to a solution of this heavy problem, and the eradication of the shameful blot of discrimination from our national life."[52]

Despite his ringing defense of the Democratic platform, Lehman believed that Stevenson needed to take a stronger position on civil rights. Two days after the Republican appeal to African American voters, Lehman wrote to Stevenson about the "considerable concentration of public attention on the subject of civil rights, and on your attitude, and our Party's attitude toward this subject." Lehman explained that his interest in civil rights stemmed from his "deep moral conviction on this whole subject," and from his role "as a public official and as a Democrat, for the effect which our Party's position on this subject will have on the outcome of the election." Stevenson's stance on this issue, Lehman stressed, would also have a major impact "on the prospects for constructive civil rights legislation in the Congress in 1953."[53]

In his acceptance speech at the Democratic convention, Stevenson promised to "talk sense to the American people," and he tried to live up to that pledge when he came to New York in late August to address what he described privately as "the all-out civil rights people." In his remarks to the Democratic and Liberal Party Conventions, Stevenson lamented the absence of Herbert Lehman, who was vacationing in Europe. In contrast to Eisenhower, who had disavowed much of the Republican platform, Stevenson praised the Democratic Party platform, declaring, "I stand on that platform." Stevenson defined civil rights as "the right to be treated equally before the law . . . the right to equal opportunity for education, employment, and decent living conditions," and the guarantee that "none of these rights shall be denied because of race, color, or creed." He asserted that state and local governments should take the lead in developing their own "positive employment practices program—a program adapted to local conditions, emphasizing education and conciliation, and providing for judicial enforcement." But he acknowledged that the Democratic platform "also favors federal legislation . . . when states fail to act and inequalities of treatment persist." Stevenson voiced his support for an FEPC along the lines of the Humphrey-Ives proposal, an FEPC that would "stay out of any state with an effective state commission," and he called for "a nonpartisan and nation-wide educational program, to proceed by persuasion as far as possible." Any complaints or violations should trigger "very careful deliberation and full and fair hearings," and "enforcement would be by order of a court, not an administrative body." As for the filibuster, Stevenson believed in "the principle that majority rule shall prevail after reasonable debate." Stevenson's strong words in favor of civil rights, reiterated at a meeting with African American leaders the following day, satisfied liberals and civil rights leaders, including Representative Adam Clayton Powell, Jr., who now gave the Democratic nominee his blessing.[54]

Herbert Lehman returned from his vacation in mid-September, and a few days later he met with Stevenson to discuss the campaign. Lehman readily agreed to campaign actively for Stevenson's election, throwing himself "unreservedly into the campaign," appearing "in a number of states" with both President Truman and Stevenson. The Senator spoke in African American neighborhoods, where he emphasized the differences between the Democrats and the Republicans on civil rights, and before Jewish groups and labor rallies, where he promised that Stevenson would work to eliminate "discrimination based on race, creed, color, or national origin" and eradicate "those frightful concepts of racism, bigotry, and prejudice which were revalidated only this year in the incredible and intolerable McCarran immigration law." Reprising a line from his own speech against the McCarran Internal Security Act, Lehman expressed certainty that if Stevenson were elected, "the next President of the United States will never compromise with his conscience." As the campaign progressed and the Northeast came to be seen as "the decisive battleground," the *New York Times* listed Lehman behind only President Truman and Vice President Barkley as a surrogate campaigner "who might be able to influence the outcome" of the election in Stevenson's favor. Lehman's enthusiastic support of the Democratic ticket contrasted sharply with what historian Herbert Parmet later described as Lyndon Johnson's " 'perfunctory,' 'halfhearted,' or 'virtually non-existent' " efforts on behalf of the party's presidential nominee.[55]

Two days before the election, Lehman described the 1952 campaign as "a very difficult and bitter one." As he confided to his former UNRRA deputy Robert Jackson afterward, Lehman "never was very confident of victory," but he "did not foresee the tremendous vote by which Eisenhower was swept into office," or the Republican majorities in Congress. Lehman agreed with his Democratic Senate colleague Mike Monroney that there was nothing the Democrats could have done to reverse the outcome because the American people "were bent on electing a national hero," and Lehman believed that "Eisenhower's victory . . . was due more to his personal popularity than to acceptance of the views and policies of the Republican Party."[56]

VII

Shortly before Congress had adjourned in July 1952, Herbert Lehman had gone out of his way to praise Majority Leader Ernest McFarland and Democratic Whip Lyndon Johnson "for the spirit of unity which, under their leadership, has been achieved in this body during the last few days." Lehman asserted that the Democrats were "leaving Washington with as great a degree of good will among ourselves as any that has been achieved in any year within the memory of the members of the Senate." The motive behind Lehman's kind words became clear a few weeks later when, after the death of Senator Brien McMahon, Lehman asked McFarland "whether you intend to appoint anyone to the Senatorial positions which were held by Brien McMahon." If so, Lehman wished "to be considered for appointment to the Foreign Relations Committee" in view of his "long and intimate knowledge of foreign affairs." But since the Senate had already adjourned for the year, McFarland left the position vacant.[57]

Like Scott Lucas before him, McFarland's tenure as Majority Leader proved to be short-lived when the Arizona Democrat went down to defeat in the Eisenhower landslide in 1952. McFarland's defeat meant that the Democrats had to choose a new leader again, and Lyndon Johnson, the Assistant Democratic Leader, moved quickly to assume the top spot, although the Republican victories in 1952 meant that the Democrats would now be the minority party in the Senate. Johnson gained the endorsement of Richard Russell, who made sure that everyone knew he supported Johnson's candidacy, but Johnson did not want to be perceived merely as the Southerners' candidate, so he set out to win support from Northern liberals too. However, Herbert Lehman and a few other liberals believed that Johnson was too closely connected with the Southerners and the conservatives in the party, and they backed liberal James Murray of Montana instead. But Lehman and the others quickly realized that Murray's candidacy was doomed because Johnson had already secured enough votes to be assured of victory. Consequently, a liberal delegation consisting of Lehman, Hubert Humphrey, Paul Douglas, and Lester Hunt of Wyoming met with Johnson, offering to support him, as Humphrey later recalled, in return for "better committee assignments, [and] more power for liberals on the Steering and Policy Committees of the Senate Democratic caucus." According to Humphrey's account of the meeting, Johnson "listened to us briefly, then politely but curtly dismissed us by telling us that he had the votes he needed and that he wasn't in the mood to make concessions." When the final vote occurred in the Democratic caucus a few days later, Murray received only five votes, Lehman's and Humphrey's among them, and Humphrey quickly moved to make the vote for Johnson unanimous. But Lyndon Johnson never forgot that Herbert Lehman had been part of the small group that had opposed his elevation to Democratic leader.[58]

Herbert Lehman hoped to improve his committee assignments when the 83rd Congress convened in January 1953. Immediately after Lyndon Johnson's elevation to Democratic leader, Lehman reiterated his desire to serve on the Foreign Relations Committee. He realized "that there is little likelihood of this preference being satisfied at the present time," but Lehman wanted his request to "continue as a matter of record." The Senator was willing to settle for a lesser position, and he asked for a "transfer from the Interior and Insular Affairs Committee" to either the Armed Services or Banking and Currency Committees. Johnson was busy rearranging the Democratic members on Senate committees to serve both his own political future and what he saw as the party's interests, and according to the new "Johnson Rule," each Democratic Senator was to have a place on a major committee before anyone had a second such assignment. That meant giving liberals substantive assignments, including Hubert Humphrey and Mike Mansfield going on the Foreign Relations Committee and former Secretary of the Air Force Stuart Symington of Missouri getting the seat Lehman sought on the Armed Services Committee. Johnson granted Lehman his next choice, moving him from the Interior Committee to the Banking and Currency Committee, which, as Lehman explained to his nephew Arthur Goodhart, included within its jurisdiction "legislation affecting most of the economic problems including all forms of price, wage, and rent controls," and "supervision over the Federal Reserve System, the RFC [Reconstruction Finance Corporation], and other economic agencies." Johnson had not acted out of any solicitude for Lehman, however; as Senator Clinton Anderson later noted, Johnson used committee assignments, "as he used most of his authority in the Senate, to serve his own ambitions." Shifting Lehman off the Interior Committee opened a place there for Price Daniel, Johnson's fellow Texan, who used the seat to push Texas's claim to offshore oil rights, helping to secure Johnson's home base for his re-election in 1954.[59]

By the beginning of 1953, Herbert Lehman had concluded that the only way to enact civil rights legislation was to change the Senate's filibuster rule, but he knew that the main obstacle blocking such action was Rule XXII itself, which allowed unlimited debate on any attempt to change the rules. Picking up on Walter Reuther's earlier suggestion that Rule XXII could be modified at the beginning of a new Congress, Lehman and his liberal colleagues planned, when the Senate convened for the first time in the 83rd Congress, to offer a motion that the Senate adopt all of its previous rules except Rule XXII. Such a motion would immediately be challenged, and no matter whether Vice President Barkley ruled it in or out of order, his decision would be appealed to the entire Senate. Debate on such rulings was limited, and the final verdict would be rendered by a majority vote of Senators. This strategy was controversial because it challenged the long-held belief that the Senate was a continuing body whose rules remained in effect from one Congress to the next, but Lehman and his supporters saw it as their best, if not their only, way around the current filibuster rule.[60]

As Julius Edelstein later noted, when it came to "the fight to change Rule XXII," Senator Lehman "was always in the lead." Shortly before the new Congress convened, Lehman, Paul Douglas, Hubert Humphrey, and Irving Ives invited about thirty of their colleagues who were known to favor modification of the filibuster rule to a meeting in Lehman's office to discuss how to proceed when the new Senate assembled for the first time. Only about half of the invitees attended or sent representatives, but Lehman was "encouraged" by their response to his argument that the Senate was not "a continuing body." He asserted that the expiration of any pending treaties, bills, or nominations when Congress adjourned *sine die* proved that the Senate was not a continuing body, and that there was "no justification for the contention that the rules of the preceding Senate are continuing when no other work of the preceding Senate extends over to the new Congress." He noted that it was "a basic congressional axiom that no Congress can bind a succeeding Congress," so why, he asked, "should it be considered that rules adopted, by majority vote, in the first session of the Senate in 1789, are binding and in effect in the Senate of 1953, without affirmative, majority action on the part of the Senate of 1953?" Lehman also emphasized that more than civil rights legislation was at stake, warning that delaying tactics could endanger "our national welfare, safety, and security." The group agreed to meet again later in the week, giving them more time to refine their plan, devise specific language for their motion, and rally additional support.[61]

With the Republicans holding a narrow majority in the new Senate, Lehman and his allies knew that the GOP would play a major role in determining the success or failure of their attempt to change the filibuster rule. Recalling that Eisenhower had said at one point during the campaign that he was "very strongly in favor of curbing the filibuster," Lehman and his supporters hoped that a significant number of Republicans would join them. In the interests of bipartisanship, Lehman had enlisted Senator Ives as one of the sponsors of the original meeting, and Ives reported that a least six Republicans would support the challenge to the current rule. But Senator Robert Taft, the incoming Majority Leader, wielded considerable influence among his Republican colleagues, and his opinion would go a long way in determining how they voted. Moreover, as Majority Leader, Taft would play a key role in the parliamentary maneuvering over any motion that the Senate adopt new rules. Taft's record on civil rights was somewhat mixed; he had supported anti-lynching legislation and measures to end the poll tax, and although he had consistently opposed a meaningful FEPC, he had twice voted for cloture in 1950 to allow an FEPC bill to reach the floor of the Senate. Taft worried now about maintaining party unity, especially since the Republicans had only a one vote majority in the Senate, and he wanted to avoid a lengthy debate over the filibuster rule that would delay the reorganization of the Senate. Seeking to consult with the President-elect, Taft hurried to New York to confer with Eisenhower, who refused to get involved in the controversy, insisting that Senators resolve the issue on their own. When queried by the press, Taft refused to state his position on the matter until meeting with his Republican colleagues, but Lehman and the liberals feared the worst when Taft went on to say that "he had always thought of the Senate as 'a continuing body.' "[62]

Prospects for success in changing the filibuster rule plummeted further when Senator Richard Russell, the leader of the Southern Democrats, met with Senator Taft to discuss the effort to modify Rule XXII. Although Taft remained publicly noncommittal, his meeting with Russell suggested that the coalition between Southern Democrats and conservative Republicans that had long dominated Congress would continue. Russell asserted that a long line of precedents clearly established that the Senate was "a continuing body" whose rules remained in effect unless amended in the standard way, and he warned that there would be "chaos" if the Senate determined that its rules had to be adopted anew every two years because "anyone having a majority of one could put through any rule he wanted." Since Republican control of the Senate depended on the unreliable vote of Wayne Morse of Oregon, who had originally been elected as a Republican but had now declared himself an Independent, Taft was more than willing to cooperate with Russell and the Southern Democrats on this issue in anticipation of their support on other matters.[63]

The death knell for Lehman's efforts came at the caucus of Republican Senators on January 2, 1953. According to Senator Eugene Millikin of Colorado, after a two-hour discussion during which Senator Taft had asserted that the Senate was a continuing body and Senator Ives had argued that it was not, Republican Senators had agreed with the Majority Leader that "the Senate is a continuing body, and that the existing rules should continue until they are amended in the regular way." Millikin emphasized that the vote had been "overwhelmingly in favor" of the idea that the Senate was a continuing body, and that the opposition had been "barely discernible."[64]

Even though they understood that the Republican caucus' opposition meant that their attempt to modify the filibuster rule was doomed to failure, Herbert Lehman and the proponents of changing Rule XXII vowed to move forward with their efforts when the Senate convened the next day. As Senator Ives conceded after the Republican meeting, the situation was "not too rosy," but "we feel it is something we must do." Publicly, Lehman claimed to be "considerably more optimistic," noting that even after the Republican meeting, fifteen Senators, including four Republicans, had met in his office to discuss strategy, and he predicted that he would have twenty co-sponsors for his motion, as well as additional supporters. Writing to his nephew, however, Lehman admitted that "the outlook of success is not too encouraging." Nonetheless, he believed that "the fight is very worthwhile and even if we should be beaten, it will serve the purpose of bringing the whole subject pretty clearly before the American people."[65]

To maximize their slim hopes for victory, Lehman and his allies decided that the motion that the new Senate formally take up consideration of its rules would receive wider support if it were offered by Senator Clinton Anderson, a moderate Democrat from New Mexico who had never been in the forefront of the fight for civil rights, rather than Lehman or one of the more outspoken liberals. As Anderson later explained, "coming from a state in which there were few Negroes," he had "never quite acquired a passionate feeling about racial injustice." He had grown increasingly frustrated, however, "against a set of rules which permitted a small body of men to obstruct the business of the Senate," and he "took it as a personal challenge to break the power of the filibuster over rational Senate procedures." If Anderson's motion succeeded, Senator Ives would then demonstrate Republican support for the effort by proposing a new rule that would allow forty-nine Senators, a majority of the body, to invoke cloture after fourteen days. Lehman hoped in this way to rally additional support for their effort from moderate Republicans and Democrats.[66]

When the new Senate convened for the first time on Saturday, January 3, 1953, Senator Anderson, on behalf of himself and Democratic Senators Lehman, Douglas, Green, Humphrey, Hunt, Jackson, Kennedy, Kilgore, Magnuson, Mansfield, Murray, Neely, and Pastore, and Republican Senators Ives, Duff, Hendrickson, and Tobey, and Independent Wayne Morse, moved that, "[i]n accordance with Article I, section 5, of the Constitution, which declares that 'Each House may determine the rules of its proceedings,'" the Senate "take up for immediate consideration the adoption of rules for the Senate of the Eighty-third Congress." All sides then accepted Senator Taft's suggestion to defer debate on Anderson's motion until the following Tuesday. Over the next few days, Taft's plan became clear: he had dissuaded Senator Russell and the Southerners from asserting that Anderson's motion was out of order, which would have triggered a ruling from Vice President Barkley that would have led to an appeal to the body and a vote. Instead, Taft intended to let the debate proceed for a day or two, after which he would move to table the proposal, an action which would terminate all discussion and require an immediate vote. The Majority Leader was confident that in this way, Anderson's motion could be disposed of with minimal interference to the Senate's proceedings.[67]

Taft opened the debate on January 6 by emphasizing that "a very large majority" of the Republican caucus believed that the Senate was "a continuing body, with continuing rules," and that he had "failed to find a single precedent holding the other way." While he believed that Rule XXII should be "changed and liberalized somewhat," he insisted that any such change should be enacted through the regular process for amending the Senate rules, and he asserted that if a sufficient majority in the Senate desired to pass civil rights legislation, it could do so under the current rules. Signaling Southern Democrats' support for Taft's position, Senator Russell immediately voiced his agreement with the Majority Leader's contention that the Senate was a continuing body because two-thirds of its membership always remained intact. Seeking to appeal to anti-union Republicans, Russell also alleged that the UAW's Walter Reuther, a *bête noire* to most conservatives for his union-organizing activities and liberal agenda, had engaged in "'goon squad' tactics" in suggesting that the Senate's rules could be changed at the beginning of a new Congress.[68]

As the primary sponsor of the motion that the Senate reconsider its rules, Senator Anderson led off in presenting the case for its adoption, but Herbert

Lehman could not sit by quietly and he quickly joined the fray. In response to Taft's assertion that the Senate could modify the filibuster rule through the regular procedure, Lehman pointed out that under Rule XXII, "debate on a change in the rule cannot be limited," meaning that "if one or two or three Senators wish to carry on a filibuster," they could prevent the Senate from acting. When Lehman asked if the Senate had ever voted "on the question of whether the Senate has the right to adopt its own rules," Taft conceded that the issue had never been raised until 1917, when Senator Thomas Walsh (D-MT) had brought it up in the aftermath of the filibuster by what Woodrow Wilson had denounced as "a little group of willful men" who had prevented the Senate from voting on the President's proposal to arm American merchant ships. At that time, Taft acknowledged, "the Senate bypassed the question" by adopting, for the first time in its history, a cloture rule that could be used to end debate. In response to Senator Russell's complaint that those arguing that the Senate could adopt new rules with each new Congress were "relying on the inherent rights of the Senate" rather than the written rules, Lehman replied that the reality was exactly the opposite. "For 168 years," he asserted, "we have acquiesced—supinely, if you will—in the continuation of rules adopted back in 1789" rather than following the written law of the Constitution, which "distinctly states that each House shall have authority to adopt its own rules." And when Russell continued to insist that the Senate was a continuing body, Lehman questioned why, if that were the case, the Senate had to begin anew its consideration of any bills, treaties, and nominations that might have been pending when the previous Senate adjourned. If, as Russell alleged, such procedures were necessary to afford new Senators an opportunity to participate in the business of the Senate, Lehman wondered why that same principle should not apply to the Senate's rules, providing new Senators with the chance to be involved in adopting those rules?[69]

After Taft and Anderson had concluded their remarks, Herbert Lehman began his formal presentation on the motion. Despite frequent interruptions by Senator John Marshall Butler (R-MD), Lehman managed to make his case that "the majority of the Senate—of this Senate—and the Senate of each new Congress has the right to adopt its own rules at the beginning of the session." He stressed that this was "a constitutional right, clearly expressed in our basic law," as well as "the inherent right of any democratic representative body." Denying each new Senate "the right to adopt its own rules," he claimed, violated "basic principles of representative government" because it gave "the past an unearned veto power over the actions of the present." Rule XXII as amended in 1949 should not be allowed to "paralyze the right of the majority to modify the rules of the Senate to meet the needs of changing times and conditions." Using the Cold War to buttress his case, Lehman asserted that "a small minority of the Senate should not be able to set up procedural roadblocks, as the Soviet

Union has so successfully done in the Security Council of the United Nations." Although some had argued that "the right of so-called unlimited debate is necessary to protect the rights of the minority in the Senate," Lehman explained that "in practice, the filibuster has been used by the minority to oppress the majority, to frustrate it and to deny it the right to act." In his opinion, "the time has come to protect the majority in its right to act, and thus to protect the country." But "to do this, the majority must exercise its right to adopt rules to safeguard majority rule in the Senate and in the nation."[70]

Having already delivered his major address on the issue, Lehman played a lesser role when the Senate resumed its consideration of the Anderson motion the following day. He inserted in the *Congressional Record* a brief prepared by the Leadership Conference on Civil Rights "in support of the proposition that the majority of the Senate of each new Congress has the constitutional right to adopt rules of proceedings for the Senate of that Congress unfettered by the actions or rules of the Senate of any preceding Congress," as well as a memorandum drafted by the same organization responding to the Republican Policy Committee's study asserting that the Senate was a continuing body. Liberal Democrats James Murray, Paul Douglas, Hubert Humphrey, and Matthew Neely of West Virginia joined Republicans Robert Hendrickson of New Jersey and Irving Ives, and Independent Wayne Morse, in restating the arguments in favor of the proposal. Republicans Leverett Saltonstall of Massachusetts, H. Alexander Smith of New Jersey, and Homer Ferguson of Michigan sided with Southern Democrats John Stennis of Mississippi, Spessard Holland of Florida, and Burnet Maybank of South Carolina in opposing it. The debate covered no new ground, and Lehman contented himself with asking the motion's supporters friendly questions while directing more pointed queries to its opponents. In the late afternoon, after everyone who wished to speak had been heard, Senator Taft formally moved to table the Anderson motion, and the Senate immediately voted 70 to 21 to do so, as forty-one Republicans and twenty-nine Southern or conservative Democrats chose to kill the proposal.[71]

Herbert Lehman was disappointed but not surprised at the failure of the effort to persuade the Senate to adopt new rules at the start of the 83rd Congress. He confided to his nephew that he had "expected that we would get about 21 or 22 votes, which is exactly what we did," but as he explained to Francis Biddle of Americans for Democratic Action, he was "not too greatly discouraged" because he "believe[d] that we have brought to at least part of the American people a realization of the evils of endless filibusters which prevent majority action by the Senate." Lehman knew that there was no chance now of the Senate passing civil rights legislation in the next two years, but, as he told his colleagues, while he and his supporters may have "lost the first round," they were determined that "this is only the beginning of a long and historic fight to establish majority rule in the United States Senate."[72]

Lyndon Johnson, the newly elected Democratic leader in the Senate, never spoke publicly during the debate over the Anderson motion, but he was active behind the scenes. As the *New York Times* noted, Johnson stood "with the rest of the Southerners in fundamental opposition, not only to a rules change but also to the civil rights bills themselves." Johnson wanted to highlight Democratic unity in the Senate, not seeing any value "in calling up bills so that Jim Eastland and Herbert Lehman can insult each other," and he was furious that Lehman and the liberals had brought up as the Senate's first order of business a motion that emphasized the divisions within the Democratic Party. Johnson not only voted with the majority to table the proposal, but according to Senator Anderson, Johnson was "calling the tune for most of the Democrats" and coordinating strategy with Senator Taft to limit Democratic support for the motion.[73]

Lehman again joined with Hubert Humphrey, Irving Ives, and others in cosponsoring the same civil rights bills they had introduced in the previous Congress, but with the filibuster rule still intact there was little chance of any such measures being adopted. As the *New York Times* noted, "with the debate rules unchanged, the Southern bloc still will be in a position to talk down bills it considers unfavorable to the South," and "no civil rights bill was at all likely to be enacted by this Congress short of a contest of physical endurance ending in the collapse of the Southern and allied opposition through fatigue," a possibility that seemed as remote as ever. The only real progress in civil rights in 1953–1954 came with the Supreme Court's historic *Brown v. Board of Education* decision in May 1954, declaring laws that required separate schools for African American children to be unconstitutional. Lehman had long supported the elimination of segregation in public schools; as Governor in 1938, he had worked with the State Legislature to remove from the State Education Law a provision allowing local school districts in New York to separate school children by race. Now, Lehman cheered the Supreme Court's unanimous decision "outlawing the evil and degrading practice of segregation in our schools," praising the justices for finding "the meaning of our Constitution to be identical with the meaning of moral law," and predicting that the decision would be of "transcendental significance for the future of our country."[74]

VIII

On issues other than civil rights, Herbert Lehman often contributed to the Democratic unity that Lyndon Johnson craved in the 83rd Congress, recognizing Johnson's skill and leadership in highlighting those areas where Democrats agreed rather than those where they differed. For example, Lehman and Johnson and the vast majority of Democrats supported Eisenhower's nomination of career diplomat Charles Bohlen to be Ambassador to the Soviet Union, and Lehman agreed with all his Senate Democratic colleagues that Social Security should be expanded and extended beyond President Eisenhower's request. To protect New York's dairy farmers, Lehman joined Johnson, James Eastland, and most Democrats in opposing the administration's plan to reduce farm parity payments by switching from fixed to flexible price supports. In 1954, when Eisenhower asked Congress for a three-year extension of his authority to negotiate reciprocal trade agreements lowering tariff barriers, Lehman and most of the Democrats supported the President's request, in contrast to Republicans, who insisted that the program only be allowed to continue for a year at a time. And in what Johnson described as a stunning show of "responsible solidarity," even though Senate Democrats differed over whether to strengthen or weaken the Taft-Hartley Act's restrictions on labor unions, they unanimously opposed the Eisenhower administration's proposed changes in the law after the Republican majority in the Senate refused to consider Democrats' amendments that went beyond the scope of the administration's proposals. Similarly, when Eisenhower and the Republicans proposed statehood for Hawaii but not Alaska, all but two of the Senate's Democrats demanded statehood for both. Lehman and liberal Democrats thought that both territories deserved statehood, while Southerners, who opposed the addition of any new states because it would dilute their influence in the Senate, believed, correctly, that linking Alaska and Hawaii would mean statehood for neither.[75]

But there were, of course, numerous issues on which Herbert Lehman and Lyndon Johnson parted ways. As opposed to Johnson, who had to balance his responsibilities as Democratic leader, his obligations to Richard Russell and his fellow Southerners, his connections to wealthy Texas oil and gas men, his need to win re-election in Texas in 1954, and his higher political ambitions, Lehman's status as an elder statesman and his lack of any personal ambition left him free to follow his principles and vote his conscience. Hubert Humphrey later recalled that he envied Lehman's standing as "an emancipated man" whose "every bit of energy . . . could be directed right towards the legislative or the social objective that he was seeking" because he did not have to be "at all concerned about momentary political currents." According to Humphrey, Lehman's freedom from having to weigh the impact of his actions on his political future "gave him extra strength" and "extra courage," and young liberal Senators regarded Lehman "as a real stalwart, and a man of great integrity and tremendous personal conviction. A very moral man." One did not hear words like these used to describe Lyndon Johnson in the 1950s, when Johnson supported and Lehman opposed legislation vesting ownership of offshore oil and mineral rights in Texas and other coastal states rather than the nation as a whole, and the Dixon-Yates bill to facilitate private rather than public development of atomic power to generate electricity.[76]

The controversy over the Bricker Amendment in 1953–1954 illustrates the differences between how Lehman and Johnson performed their roles in the Senate. Senator John Bricker's (R-OH) proposal to amend the Constitution to limit the effects within the United States of treaties and executive agreements enjoyed widespread support in the Senate, but Lehman believed that it was "one of the most dangerous proposals ever made in the Senate," the product of "the ostrich isolationist element in our country" that wanted to "get the United States of America out of the U.N." and "get the U.N. out of the United States of America." Lehman made it clear that he would vote against "any constitutional amendment curtailing the powers of the President to make treaties and executive agreements" because he believed such limitations "would seriously hamper our relations with foreign countries and our relations with other free nations with which we must cooperate if we are not willing to accept a position of isolation." Lyndon Johnson agreed that the Bricker Amendment would be a dangerous intrusion on the powers of the President and the federal government in foreign affairs, but he needed to tread softly because of the measure's popularity in Texas. Claiming to support the goals of the Bricker Amendment, Johnson voted for a milder version of the measure while working behind the scenes to scuttle it.[77]

Herbert Lehman considered the McCarran-Walter Immigration and Naturalization Act that had been adopted in 1952 "one of the most unfortunate statutes, . . . one of the most indefensible laws ever to be on the statute books of the United States," and the Senator and his staff worked with "legal scholars and experts in the field" to revise it. Lehman welcomed "the humanitarian purposes" behind an emergency immigration bill proposed by the Eisenhower administration in April 1953, but when Senator McCarran and Congressman Walter inserted in the bill what Lehman denounced as "onerous" administrative restrictions and definitions based on "ethnic origin," Lehman had "strong doubts" that anywhere near the two hundred thousand immigrants authorized under this Refugee Relief Act would be admitted to the United States. Lehman also worried about reports that in return for allowing the measure to pass, McCarran and other immigration opponents had extracted a promise from congressional leaders not to seek major changes in the McCarran-Walter Act in 1954. Since the Refugee Relief Act did nothing to correct what Lehman believed to be "the dangers and evils of the McCarran-Walter Act," Lehman introduced on August 3, 1953, a comprehensive immigration reform measure to abolish the current "National Origins Quota System which fixes an indefensible concept of racism into our laws" and replace it with a "Unified Quota System" that would not discriminate based on country of origin. Even though Congress was about to adjourn for the year, Lehman introduced the bill at this time so that it would be available for "public comment and discussion" now and for hearings and committee action when Congress returned in 1954. The

New York Times hailed Lehman's proposal as "a monumental measure . . . that should serve as the basis in the next few months for intelligent discussion of this problem that means so much to the welfare of the United States and to our position of leadership in the free world."[78]

On August 13, 1953, Lehman wrote to the President, citing Eisenhower's previous criticism of the McCarran-Walter Act and inviting him to join in the effort to eliminate "racism, discrimination, and injustice from our immigration laws." Lehman asked the President to consider supporting part or all of his bill, or to offer "constructive suggestions" for new provisions that could be "substituted for the restrictive, unfair, and discriminatory laws which are now on our statute books." Hoping that maximum publicity for his letter would put pressure on the President to respond, Lehman's staff distributed a press release and copies of the letter "to the full press list, to the upstate dailies, to the messenger list, the columnists, the Jewish press, the labor press," and others. "Because of the August doldrums," the Senator's aides were instructed to "call the reporters of the main press outlets—the *New York Times*, the *Herald Tribune*, the AP, UP, and INS, the *Washington Post* and the *Star*—and tell them that such a release is being issued." And Chief of Staff Julius Edelstein ordered that the release be sent "to the Catholic Press Service and, if there is such a thing, to the Protestant Press service. Also to the JTA."[79]

Lehman failed to enlist Eisenhower or any Republicans or any of the powers that be in Congress in his quest for immigration reform. A presidential aide's promise that the Senator's "suggestions will be thoroughly studied" constituted the administration's only response to Lehman's letter, and Representative Jacob Javits (R-NY) rebuffed numerous requests from Lehman that they work together on a bipartisan immigration bill. Arthur Watkins, the Republican leader in the Senate on such matters, urged the President to reject Lehman's proposal, dismissing it as a "largely political" attempt "to offset, if possible, the advantage the Republicans have gained during the present session on this subject" by passing the Refugee Relief Act, and Watkins's opposition meant that the Senate would not even hold hearings on Lehman's bill in 1954. Lehman was no more successful in rousing interest among his Democratic colleagues. Lyndon Johnson demonstrated his opposition to any meaningful reforms in this area in 1953–1954 when he explained to a constituent that he had voted for the Refugee Relief Act "only after receiving assurances that every possible safeguard would be established to prevent an influx of communist agents and undesirables."[80]

Seeing the opposition in Congress to any meaningful immigration reform, Lehman focused on gathering support outside the Legislature, convening a meeting at his home in early November 1953 of representatives of liberal, labor, and religious groups. Hoping to educate "the public in regard to some of the objectionable features of the McCarran-Walter Act" and the need for "liberal, humane, and workable immigration and citizenship legislation," Lehman sought to establish "a nation-wide Citizens Committee to conduct a campaign of education looking toward the revision of our immigration and citizenship laws." Creating such an organization turned out to be a much more arduous task than Lehman or aide Julius Edelstein had expected, however, and the National Committee on Immigration and Citizenship was not up and running until 1956.[81]

By the end of the 83rd Congress in December 1954, Herbert Lehman and Lyndon Johnson had established their basic roles in the Senate. Lehman remained an uncompromising liberal, fighting for civil rights, immigration reform, and other liberal causes, opposing special privileges for the power companies and the oil and gas industries, but lacking any real power to achieve the objectives for which he fought so valiantly. Lyndon Johnson's stock, however, was rising. Democratic victories in the 1954 congressional elections, including Johnson's own re-election, his continued support from Richard Russell and the Southern bloc, his success in manipulating his colleagues and minimizing intraparty quarrels, and his triumph in uniting Senate Democrats behind the resolution to censure Joe McCarthy added significantly to his stature. As Robert Caro has observed, Lehman and Johnson inhabited two different worlds: Lehman's was a world "in which principles mattered" more than power and could not be compromised; Johnson's "was a world in which deals could always be made, bargains could always be arranged, in which men were reasonable in compromising their principles, except for a few crazies like Lehman and Douglas, who had so little power that they could safely be ignored." When the new Senate convened in January 1955, Johnson would wield even more power as the Majority Leader, a change that did not bode well for Herbert Lehman and the liberal principles and goals that were so dear to his heart.[82]

CHAPTER 16

"An Inveterate Crusader"

Lehman and Johnson, 1955–1956

We Democrats from the Northern states were at the bottom of the totem pole of prestige. Of all these, Douglas, Humphrey, and Lehman were at first the very lowest. It was suspected that we not only advocated liberal causes, but also actually believed in them.[1]

Herbert Lehman rejoiced in the re-election of liberal colleagues Paul Douglas, Hubert Humphrey, and others in 1954, and with the support of Independent Wayne Morse, Democrats recaptured control of the Senate. But instead of improving Lehman's status in the Senate, the Democrats' return to the majority increased his frustration as bills that were important to him never reached the floor for debate or were quickly tabled, and he suffered outrageous slings and arrows directed at him by the new Majority Leader, Lyndon Johnson. Southern Democrats still controlled the levers of power, and Democrats unanimously chose Johnson to serve as Majority Leader, rewarding what Walter George characterized as Johnson's "demonstrated capacity for bringing unity to our party." Johnson ruthlessly consolidated his authority as Majority Leader and sought to avoid divisive issues like civil rights that would highlight discord within the Democratic ranks, and he could usually persuade recalcitrant colleagues to his point of view by the "treatment," in which he engulfed a colleague in his huge physical presence and kept at him until the wavering

---

Chapter title quotation: Senator Earle Clements describing Herbert Lehman, 102 *Congressional Record* 15100 (July 27, 1956).

legislator capitulated. As Paul Douglas later described it, "to Johnson, the Senate was a circus and he was the ringmaster, putting the animals through their paces by the lure of the carrot and the sharp crack of the whip." But unlike Hubert Humphrey and some of the other Senate liberals, Lehman would not play the game according to Johnson's rules, emphasizing to aide Julius Edelstein, "I do not wish to put myself under obligations to Lyndon." Realizing that there was little he could do to make Lehman a loyal member of his team, Johnson isolated Lehman and treated him with contempt, making his life in the Senate miserable in ways both large and small.[2]

I

Although Johnson aide Bobby Baker exaggerated when he later claimed that Lehman "became very bitter" and "really despised, loathed, and hated Lyndon Johnson" because of the way in which Johnson repeatedly bypassed Lehman's requests for better committee assignments, Lehman certainly resented the new Majority Leader's mistreatment. Lehman contacted Johnson immediately after the Democratic victory in 1954 became apparent, requesting to move from the Banking and Currency Committee to the Foreign Relations Committee, emphasizing that he was personally acquainted with many foreign leaders from his days at UNRRA. Johnson acknowledged Lehman's "splendid qualifications" to serve on the Foreign Relations Committee, but he warned that "there are always many applicants for the Senate Foreign Relations Committee and there are many considerations that must be taken into account" when the Democratic Steering Committee made the assignments in January.[3]

Reading between the lines, Lehman realized that he had little chance of being appointed to the Foreign Relations Committee, so he set his sights instead on transferring to the Judiciary Committee, which had jurisdiction over immigration matters and civil rights. Lehman had been frustrated in 1953 and 1954 when his efforts to reform the McCarran-Walter Act had come to naught, and he hoped that a seat on the Judiciary Committee might enable him to help fulfill the Democratic Party's pledge in 1952 to revise the nation's immigration statute. Although he understood that Senators who were lawyers usually received preference for the Judiciary Committee, Lehman pointed out that there were precedents for non-lawyers to serve on the committee, and he noted that his appointment would remedy the absence of any Democrats from the Northeast on the committee. He did not mention it in his letter to Johnson, but Lehman's interest in civil rights legislation, most of which would need to pass through the Judiciary Committee, also contributed to his desire to serve there.[4]

Although Johnson promised that Lehman's "qualifications will be presented forcefully" when the Democratic Steering Committee made its assignments, the Majority Leader had no intention of putting Lehman on the Judiciary Committee. As Johnson aide George Reedy later recalled, "That committee was very rough and tumble, not the place for Herbert Lehman, who was a very nice fellow." Although Reedy recognized that Lehman "was very kind-hearted, very tender, very gentle," he also noted dismissively that Lehman "at times reminded me of Little Lord Fauntleroy." More importantly, Johnson had little respect or use for Lehman, who refused to compromise in the interests of party unity and kept pushing civil rights bills, immigration reform, and other controversial legislation that tended to fracture the precarious harmony Johnson was trying to build among Democratic Senators. The Judiciary Committee was almost equally split between liberals and conservatives, and Johnson planned to restore the liberal but more malleable Joseph O'Mahoney of Wyoming, who had been re-elected to the Senate after a two-year absence, to his former seat on the Judiciary Committee. That left one seat open on the committee, and Lehman's appointment would tip the balance in favor of the liberals, which would not sit well with Richard Russell and Johnson's Southern patrons. Columnist Drew Pearson reported on January 2, 1955, that Johnson wanted the last seat on the Judiciary Committee to go to Price Daniel, his conservative colleague from Texas, whom Pearson described as "more representative of the Texas oil lobby than the lobby itself."[5]

The Supreme Court's decision in *Brown v. Board of Education* the previous spring, which had enraged much of the South and most of its Senators, also factored into Johnson's bypassing of Lehman for the seat on the Judiciary Committee. Lehman's repeated efforts to change the Senate's cloture rule to make it possible to enact civil rights measures led most of the Southerners to agree with Johnson aide George Reedy that Lehman and Julius Edelstein, his chief assistant, were "obsessed with the civil-rights issue." According to Bobby Baker, Johnson felt the need, in the wake of the *Brown* decision, to "protect his ass, . . . to do something positive to keep the respect of Senator (Richard) Russell and the Southern contingency," and putting Lehman on the Judiciary Committee would have had the opposite effect, infuriating Russell and the Southern bloc. In Baker's words, the decision to put Daniel on the committee instead of Lehman was a "brilliant tactical move to protect Lyndon Johnson's Southern flank."[6]

When the Democratic committee assignments were announced in early January 1955, and Lehman discovered he had been passed over for the seats he had sought on either the Foreign Relations or Judiciary Committees, he vented his frustration in an angry letter to Johnson. Lehman questioned the wisdom of Johnson's previously stated criteria that committee assignments would either be based on seniority or the need to give every new Democratic Senator a significant committee position, asserting that "ideological and geographic factors should also be given due weight." Moreover, Lehman charged that in some of the actual committee assignments, especially Senator Daniel's selection for the Judiciary Committee, Johnson had violated his own guidelines, since Lehman outranked Daniel in seniority and Daniel was not a new Senator. Lehman also noted that with Daniel's appointment, the Judiciary Committee lacked any members from "the great industrial states of the East, the West, or the Middle West," and that the Democratic Policy Committee similarly did not include any representatives from New York and the other large, industrial states of the Northeast and the Midwest. As a result, "the problems and viewpoints of these states, which contain so large a share of the population—and the voters," were not being heard by the Democratic Party's leadership in the Senate. Lehman did not expect there to be any changes in the decisions that had already been made, but he wanted to state "for the record" his opinion that "overlooking the political and legislative importance of the representation of New York State, and of the other similar states, in committee assignments and in policy considerations is unwise, unfortunate, and seriously harmful to the Party."[7]

Johnson took umbrage at Lehman's complaints. After explaining the impossibility of giving "every Senator the committee assignment that he seeks or that he is entitled to on the basis of experience and ability," and the inevitability that some Senators would be disappointed, Johnson recalled that Lehman had already been moved to the Banking and Currency Committee. Minimizing his control over the Steering Committee, Johnson claimed that the group had voted unanimously to place Daniel on the Judiciary Committee because Steering Committee members believed "that the Judiciary Committee should be composed of lawyers." As for the Policy Committee, Johnson pointed out that most of its members predated his tenure as Democratic leader. He took responsibility only for Senator Murray, who had been recommended by Lehman and the liberals in 1953, and Carl Hayden of Arizona, the second most senior member of the Senate. Changing his tone and trying to assuage Lehman's feelings somewhat, Johnson emphasized that he held Lehman "in very high esteem as a man who has spent many years in the service of the people," and he promised to look for opportunities "not to enhance your position, because it does not need to be enhanced, but to give you greater opportunities for the service of which you are capable."[8]

Despite his kind words, Johnson never made any effort to find Lehman a position commensurate with his experience. Johnson could not have been pleased when columnist Drew Pearson revealed that Lehman had "sent a bitter letter" to Johnson complaining that the Majority Leader had "violated Lehman's seniority privileges and cheated him out of committee assignments he deserved," and that Johnson's "I did the best I can" response "only enraged the New Yorker more." Pearson noted that "the suave Texan seems to be able to butter up every Democratic Senator except the man who's been Governor of New York more terms than anyone in history." In May 1956, when Senator Barkley's death opened up a seat on the Foreign Relations Committee, Lehman wrote immediately to Johnson to renew his request for a seat on that body, reminding the Majority Leader that "on at least three occasions," Lehman had been passed over for the Foreign Relations Committee in favor of men with less seniority. Johnson never responded in writing to Lehman's application, but a few weeks later he announced that Russell Long of Louisiana, who outranked Lehman in seniority by one year and played by Lyndon Johnson's rules, would fill the vacancy on the Foreign Relations Committee. Lehman could take some solace, however, in knowing that his close friend and fellow liberal stalwart Paul Douglas was succeeding Barkley on the Finance Committee.[9]

II

As the opening of the 84th Congress in January 1955 drew near, the Leadership Conference on Civil Rights urged Herbert Lehman and the others who had led the fight for the Senate to adopt new rules in 1953 to renew their efforts. John Gunther, the legislative representative of Americans for Democratic Action, recognized that such an attempt was unlikely to succeed, but he believed that "since the fight was made at the beginning of the Republican 83rd Congress, it would be a serious political error for the Democratic 84th Congress to pass it up," especially since "the 1952 Democratic Party Platform included a promise to do something about this rules matter." James Carey of the CIO agreed that "this matter should be brought up at the beginning of each new Congress until the inevitable victory is won," and Roy Wilkins and the NAACP requested that the new Senate, when it convened for the first time, adopt new rules to make it possible to end the filibusters that blocked civil rights legislation.[10]

As Paul Douglas and other civil rights advocates both in and out of the Senate recognized, Herbert Lehman was "the driving force in this fight" to change the Senate rules, and Lehman was willing to lead the charge once again if he had any troops ready to follow him. But Lehman aide Julius Edelstein worried that few if any of the Senators who had participated in the struggle in 1953 were willing to do so again, and he cautioned Gunther that "without an Army, we can't very well have a battle." Lehman and Edelstein wanted "some assurance that we are not going to be alone in the fight, nor be asked to lead a lone charge." Unless they had "a solid corps of fighters," Edelstein thought, "the best we can do is to make a record."[11]

Lyndon Johnson did not want his ascension to Majority Leader to be marred by a divisive debate highlighting differences among the Democrats over changing the Senate's filibuster rule. Alerted by Max Kampelman of Hubert Humphrey's office that Walter Reuther and "some of the liberals" were considering renewing their efforts to change the cloture rule "by claiming that the Senate is not a continuing body and is entitled to write new rules at the beginning of every session," Johnson agreed with aide George Reedy that "many Southerners feel overwhelmed by the Supreme Court segregation decision and this is certainly no time to be pouring oil on fires." Johnson let it be known that he would not look kindly on an opening session disrupted by a fight over the Senate's rules, which would contradict his emphasis on Democratic Party unity. Hubert Humphrey, who had become Johnson's chief intermediary with the Senate liberals, publicly signaled his willingness to go along with Johnson when he announced in late December that he would reintroduce most of the civil rights bills he had sponsored in previous Congresses but had no intention of pushing for a vote on them. Retreating from his previous all-out advocacy of civil rights legislation, and echoing Lyndon Johnson's philosophy, Humphrey explained that the Democrats would "try to find as many things as we can agree on and go forward in that area, rather than accent our disagreements."[12]

Despite Lyndon Johnson's opposition, Herbert Lehman still wanted to challenge the Senate's rules at the opening session of the new Congress, and he hosted a meeting in his office on January 4, 1955, to ascertain how much support he had for such a fight. A group of liberal Democratic Senators or their representatives listened while Lehman argued for renewing the attack on the filibuster rule. However, as Paul Douglas later recounted, Hubert Humphrey "sealed his alliance with Johnson" by emphasizing the need for "party unity" and urging that the new Majority Leader be given an opportunity to bring the Southerners around to changing the rule through the regular Senate procedures. Humphrey asserted that the liberals needed to learn from the repeated failures of "the 'devil' theory of politics" and their lack of success in confronting the Southerners head-on. A challenge on the floor, he feared, would reveal that they had lost votes since 1953, representing a serious and perhaps fatal setback in their long-term efforts to change the rules. Wayne Morse and Paul Douglas agreed with Humphrey, which left Lehman virtually alone in warning his colleagues that they were "making a very serious mistake" in "trying to postpone something which cannot be postponed." Convinced that Johnson had shown his true colors two years earlier when he had supported Taft's strategy to table the Anderson motion, Lehman had no faith or trust that the Majority Leader would be more amenable to their cause later in the session. But Lehman's pleas fell on deaf ears, and, much to his disappointment, he was not able to rouse sufficient support among his colleagues for another attempt to change the Senate's rules. When Roy Wilkins learned what had transpired at the meeting, he assured Lehman that the other Senators' reluctance to join him in this effort merely "highlights, in our opinion, the sterling, courageous and consistent service" Lehman had "given throughout the years to liberal causes." Wilkins predicted that time would vindicate Lehman's position on this issue as well as his courage and his "devotion to principle."[13]

As was usually the case, Lyndon Johnson easily outmaneuvered Lehman and his erstwhile allies. Paul Douglas later noted that while Johnson had been planning his strategy for weeks, the liberals, typically, were slow to organize, "hastily convened on the night before we were to vote." Moreover, besides using Humphrey as his agent within the liberal camp, Johnson controlled the Democratic Steering Committee, which formally determined the committee assignments that would be announced a few days *after* the opening session. The NAACP's Walter White complained that some Senators "selected expediency over principle," and that "some shrewd horse trading over committee member-ships went on behind the scenes which caused abandonment of the proposed change of Senate rules by the former liberals." Hubert Humphrey tried to mollify White, asserting that "the liberal position on the committees this year is far better than it has been in recent years," but Humphrey admitted a few years later that "a number of Senators were being given committee assignments, and those members did not wish to jeopardize those committee assignments by getting involved in the rules fight." New Mexico's Clinton Anderson, who had made the motion in 1953 that the Senate adopt new rules, was silent on the issue in 1955 when he became chairman of the Joint Committee on Atomic Energy, which oversaw numerous facilities in his home state, and Wayne Morse, whose vote gave the Democrats control of the Senate, received a coveted seat on the Foreign Relations Committee. Herbert Lehman was the rare Senator who could not be swayed by Johnson's control over committee assignments and other favors that the Majority Leader dispensed to members of his team, and Johnson made sure that Lehman remained stuck on the Banking and Currency Committee and his legislative initiatives rarely saw the light of day.[14]

Bereft of allies to make a formal challenge to the rules when the new Senate convened on January 5, 1955, Lehman nonetheless believed that it was important to keep the issue alive, so he delivered a speech for the record on January 6 in which he asserted that the absence of a motion for the Senate to adopt new rules did not mean that he and his colleagues had "abandoned the position we took two years ago." On the contrary, he emphasized, "we maintain that position. We subscribe to it." Lehman denounced "the presently ineffective and self-perpetuating cloture rule," especially the section "which forbids cloture on any proposal to change any rule," as "the most undemocratic—indeed the most antidemocratic—provision in any rule, regulation, or statute to be found in the United States." He vowed "to do everything" he could "to see that Rule XXII is modified at the earliest possible date, thus freeing the Senate from the straitjacket of paralysis in which it has been confined by Rule XXII in its present form." Senator Humphrey, who two days earlier at the meeting in

Lehman's office had argued against contesting the Senate's rules, now sought to preserve his liberal credentials, agreeing with Lehman that "our convictions remain unchanged" that each new Senate "has the right and should exercise the right to establish its own rules." But Humphrey made it clear that rather than raising the issue at the opening session, he would "move in an orderly manner to change those rules," and he hoped that the Rules Committee would give his subsequent proposal "fair and favorable consideration."[15]

Paul Douglas and the other liberals quickly realized that they had made a horrible mistake in succumbing to Johnson's and Humphrey's entreaties rather than heeding Lehman's warning. Even though Lehman promised to do all he could to fight for what he described as "reasonable and equitable civil rights legislation—meaningful legislation, legislation that will mark real progress on the civil rights front," it quickly became clear, as a *New York Times* headline reported, that "Civil Rights Bills [Were] Doomed in Capital." As Douglas later noted, "There was no change in Johnson's opposition to civil rights and not the slightest softening in the attitude of the South." According to one count, "Liberals introduced forty-four separate civil rights bills in the first half of 1955, but Johnson . . . made sure that none reached the floor."[16]

III

In an interview in 1957, Wayne Morse characterized Herbert Lehman's opposition to President Eisenhower's Formosa Resolution in 1955 as "the greatest exhibition of courage among the many courageous acts which Herbert Lehman committed when he was in the Senate." Chiang Kai-shek's Chinese Nationalists had taken refuge on the island of Formosa (Taiwan) after being driven off the mainland in 1949, and Chiang's forces had also retained control of a number of islands just off the mainland, including Quemoy and Matsu, which were one hundred miles from Formosa. In September 1954, the Chinese Communists began shelling these coastal islands. The Eisenhower administration, fearing that the bombardment of Quemoy and Matsu was a prelude to an attack against Formosa, sought to reassure the Chinese Nationalists and their American supporters by negotiating a mutual defense treaty with Chiang's regime in which the United States promised to defend Formosa and the nearby Pescadores. The President submitted the treaty to the Senate for its approval on January 6, 1955, and the Foreign Relations Committee was preparing to hold hearings on the agreement when the Chinese Communists stepped up their attacks against the offshore islands in mid-January.[17]

Eisenhower realized that the crisis in the Formosa Straits had the potential to escalate into war at a moment's notice. If that happened, he believed that he probably had the legal authority under the Constitution to use American armed forces to protect Formosa and the Pescadores even though the treaty had not yet been approved, but he understood that the situation was not so clear when it came to the offshore islands like Quemoy and Matsu. Accordingly, the President consulted with the legislative leaders about the possibility of a congressional resolution authorizing him to use the armed forces to protect Formosa and the surrounding islands against armed attack. Eisenhower emphasized that it would be "foolish to try to strain to the limit my constitutional power" when a congressional resolution would "serve notice on the Communists" that the United States was united in its determination to defend Chiang Kai-shek. As for the offshore islands, Eisenhower and Dulles wanted the resolution to be vague so the President would retain the utmost freedom of action to deal with events as they developed. Hence, on January 24, 1955, Eisenhower asked Congress for the authority

> to employ the Armed Forces of the United States as he deems necessary for the specific purpose of securing and protecting Formosa and the Pescadores against armed attack, this authority to include the securing and protection of such related positions and territories of that area now in friendly hands and the taking of such other measures as he judges to be required or appropriate in assuring the defense of Formosa and the Pescadores.[18]

Several aspects of the Formosa Resolution troubled Herbert Lehman. Early in 1950, he had warned against a continuing American commitment to defend Chiang Kai-shek's corrupt and discredited regime, now removed to Formosa. But the Korean War had changed the context of events in Asia, and McCarthyism had altered the political environment in Washington, leading President Truman and then President Eisenhower to pledge to protect Formosa. Recognizing that the situation had changed considerably in five years, Lehman explained to his colleagues in 1955 that while he strongly favored "a resolution that affirms congressional support for the defense of Formosa and the Pescadores," he would not endorse "the policy of defending the Quemoy Island group and the Matsu Island group and the Tachen Island group, right off the mainland of China." Although none of these territories was mentioned by name in the proposed resolution, Lehman noted that the measure would authorize the President to use the armed forces to secure and protect "such related positions and territories of that area now in friendly hands," which could easily be construed to include the offshore islands. Lehman feared that Chiang Kai-shek and elements within the Eisenhower administration and the right wing of the Republican Party would use the resolution to involve the United States in a war over Quemoy and Matsu and other islands that might be important in terms of Chinese Nationalist morale, but were of little military significance.[19]

Lehman also worried that the proposed resolution gave "the President unlimited powers." Going back to his years as Governor, Lehman had always been concerned about unchecked executive power. In 1934, he had rejected Mayor La Guardia's bid for what Lehman considered to be "dictatorial powers" to deal with New York City's budget crisis, and in 1937 Lehman had opposed Franklin Roosevelt's attempt to pack the Supreme Court, fearing that it would undermine the separation of powers that was such an essential component of the United States constitutional system of government. And now in 1955, Lehman feared that the provision of the Formosa Resolution authorizing the President to take "such other measures as he judges to be required or appropriate in assuring the defense of Formosa and the Pescadores" would be giving the President "a blank check of dangerous authority" that could be used "to involve us in a war which we do not want and which the free world does not want."[20]

Most legislators agreed with Walter George, the senior Democrat in the Senate and chairman of the Senate Foreign Relations Committee, who "commend[ed] the President for coming to Congress with this request" and urged his colleagues to back Eisenhower's efforts to block this latest Communist threat. Reluctant to oppose outright the President's appeal for congressional support, Lehman and a few others sought to amend the proposed resolution to remove what they considered to be its most objectionable provisions. Lehman and Hubert Humphrey offered an amendment to limit the resolution to the defense of Formosa and the Pescadores by removing any mention of "related positions and territories of that area now in friendly hands," and Lehman and Wayne Morse co-sponsored Estes Kefauver's substitute proposal, which would have limited American involvement to the defense of Formosa and the Pescadores and given the United Nations a greater role in settling the dispute in the Formosa Straits. But most Senators succumbed to the pressure to pass the resolution quickly and in exactly the same form that it had already passed the House of Representatives, rejecting any and all amendments.[21]

On January 28, 1955, the Senate voted 85 to 3 to approve the Formosa Resolution. Only William Langer, an isolationist Republican from North Dakota who opposed all overseas commitments, including American membership in the United Nations; Wayne Morse, who denounced the resolution as "a blanket grant of preventive war power to the President of the United States" that would allow him to order "a military strike against any point on the mainland of China if he judges such action is required to defend the areas named in this resolution"; and Herbert Lehman voted against the measure. Just before the final vote, Lehman reiterated his concern that the resolution constituted "a pre-dated blank check of authority" giving "permission for the President to send our forces into the Quemoy and Matsu and Tachen Island groups." He emphasized that the United States, as "the leading power of the free world," had "a responsibility to all the American people . . . to all our allies . . . [and] to mankind" not to risk going to war over these territories that "may be important to Chiang Kai-shek, but . . . are not essential to the security of the United States or of the free world."[22]

Wayne Morse later recalled that opposing the Formosa Resolution was more dangerous than he and Lehman had realized at the time. According to Morse, some of their colleagues in the Senate were "sitting by, listening to every word we said, for the purpose of seeing if we didn't say something that would permit the filing of a resolution of censure against each one of us, on the ground that we were violating some secrecy of committee confidence." The debate over the Formosa Resolution occurred less than two months after the Senate had voted to censure Joe McCarthy, and certainly some of McCarthy's right-wing compatriots would have loved to turn the tables and censure Herbert Lehman, who had fought so long and hard against McCarthy and McCarthyism.[23]

Lyndon Johnson played only a minor role in the debate over the Formosa Resolution in 1955. Worsening pain from a kidney stone compelled the Majority Leader to seek treatment at the Mayo Clinic, so he was not in Washington to help the administration and Senator George guide the measure through the Senate. Despite his absence from the Capitol, Johnson and his staff made sure that he was recorded in opposition to all the proposed amendments and in favor of the final resolution. Johnson expressed his satisfaction with the result, explaining to Senator Styles Bridges (R-NH) that even though he "had to follow the progress of the Formosa resolution at a great distance and through meager newspaper accounts, . . . it sounds as though everything came out all right in the end." Johnson considered the vote on the measure "a tough one," and he was "glad that the final vote went as high as it did." The Formosa Resolution later served as the model for Johnson's Gulf of Tonkin Resolution, approved by Congress in August 1964.[24]

Herbert Lehman never regretted his vote against the Formosa Resolution. As he told Wayne Morse when another crisis erupted over Quemoy and Matsu in 1958, Lehman believed that "developments have tragically demonstrated the accuracy of our predictions made in 1955," and even though Lehman was no longer in Congress, he promised to continue to raise his voice "regarding this highly dangerous situation" into which the United States had allowed itself to be maneuvered by Chiang Kai-shek. Keeping that pledge, Lehman wrote a letter to the editor that was published in the *New York Times* in which he recalled his warning that the Formosa Resolution "was a blank check." Lehman asserted that the "check has now been filled out by the administration, at the instance of the Formosa government, to read 'Quemoy and Matsu.'" He again cautioned against confusing Formosa's defense with that of Quemoy and Matsu, charging that the Eisenhower administration's claim that the Formosa Resolution constituted a commitment to defend these offshore islands "threatens to destroy both the unity of the free world nations and the peace of the world."

Lehman emphasized that "not a single American life, not to speak of the peace of the world, should be sacrificed for the defense of Quemoy and Matsu."[25]

IV

Herbert Lehman hoped that the Democratic victories in the 1954 congressional elections, the death of Senator McCarran, and what he believed was growing public dissatisfaction with the McCarran-Walter Act would facilitate revision of the nation's immigration laws in the 84th Congress. As he prepared to reintroduce his bill amending the 1952 McCarran-Walter Act, Lehman reported to the measure's previous co-sponsors that he had "received favorable comments on this bill and indications of widespread support from civic, religious, labor, education, and business groups," and that "every day brings new incidents which serve to illustrate the inequities which arise under present immigration and naturalization law." On February 25, 1955, Lehman introduced his bill "to overhaul, revise, and replace the discriminatory, oppressive, and inhospitable immigration and citizenship laws now on our statute books." In a press release, Lehman and his twelve co-sponsors denounced the current McCarran-Walter Act, with its "many booby traps for citizens, for resident and immigrant aliens, and for visitors," as "a mess which must be cleaned up without delay," and they stressed that "in the present state of world affairs," it was "intolerable that we should continue to maintain our own Iron Curtain against visitors and alien immigrants alike, while criticizing the Iron Curtain abroad." Lehman and the others reassured their colleagues that their bill "provides full and comprehensive security against the admission of subversive and undesirable aliens into the United States" and "tightens existing loopholes which now permit millions—yes, millions—of unscreened aliens to flood across our Northern and Southern land borders." It would also, they explained, "remove the intolerable barriers which now keep renowned scientists, scholars, and men of letters from coming to our shores as visitors, . . . eliminate racism and national discrimination from our immigration laws, . . . [and] eradicate the status of second-class American citizenship which now is fastened on millions of naturalized Americans." According to Lehman and the bill's supporters, their proposal "would limit immigration, but not stifle it," restoring America to its traditional role "as the hope of the oppressed and the persecuted everywhere, an asylum for the brave, the venturesome, and the freedom-seeking abroad—within the limits of our conservative capacity for assimilation."[26]

Two months later, Lehman introduced for himself and Senators Humphrey and Douglas a bill to amend the Refugee Relief Act, which had authorized the admission of 209,000 immigrants to the United States, only a mere trickle of whom had actually entered the country. Lehman faulted both the statute itself and the way in which the Eisenhower administration had administered it for the resulting "paralysis of the refugee program," complaining that "technical amendments adopted in committee—booby-traps—had robbed the act of its truly humanitarian aspects," leaving "a bureaucratic nightmare full of hair-splitting interpretations of law, frustrations, disappointments, and heartbreak for refugees and escapees from behind the Iron Curtain and for their friends and relatives in the United States." He regretted that his prediction "that only a small percentage of the refugees and escapees whom we undertook to assist by means of that legislation would ever actually be assisted" had "sadly come true," pointing out that in the almost two years that the law had been in effect, "considerably less than 1,000 actual refugees and escapees have been admitted into the United States." Lehman's amendments were intended to increase the number of refugees allowed into the United States to 224,000 and to ensure that they actually arrived by permitting visas to be transferred between categories, extending the cut-off date, allowing voluntary agencies as well as individuals to sponsor refugees by providing the necessary guarantees for their housing and employment, and removing some of the "unworkable" security requirements. His proposal would leave intact the severe restrictions of the McCarran-Walter Act, but it would take the administration of the law away from the State Department's Bureau of Security and Consular Affairs and vest it instead "in a full-time administrator who would operate in the Department of State" but "would not be subject to the bureaucratic control of any division chief."[27]

For a brief time, it appeared that Lehman and the Eisenhower administration might be able to work together to liberalize the Refugee Relief Act. At a news conference just a few days after Lehman introduced his amendments to the measure, the President expressed his dissatisfaction with the way the refugee program was operating and called for revising the law, in response to which Lehman promptly praised the President's belated "cognizance of the crippling defects in the Refugee Act." A month later, Eisenhower sent to Congress ten specific recommendations for amendments to the Refugee Relief Act, a number of which echoed the changes Lehman had previously proposed, such as letting voluntary agencies sponsor refugees, repealing the requirement that refugees document their whereabouts and activities during the previous two years, and loosening the definition of escapee or refugee. But Eisenhower's revisions left the administration of the program under the State Department's Bureau of Security and Consular Affairs, headed by McCarthy ally Scott McLeod; retained the cut-off date of December 31, 1956; and maintained, for the most part, the quotas limiting the number of people of specific nationalities who could enter the United States under the statute. Despite these deficiencies, Lehman hailed the President's proposals as a "sound" beginning.[28]

But even the President's more limited proposals to ease the path for refugees ran into difficulty in Congress. Fourteen Republican Senators quickly endorsed the administration's amendments, which Senator Watkins introduced in the Senate. But Senator Jenner spoke for many of the restrictionists when he expressed concern about any loosening of the security requirements, and Senator Eastland and the Judiciary Committee's Internal Security Subcommittee raised similar concerns when they heard testimony from a retired military officer who claimed that "all responsible American officials in Europe recommend that no relaxation of screening or other preparations be made" because any such modifications would open the door for "Communist agents disguised as 'refugees' whose entry 'might constitute a considerable danger to United States security.'" Moreover, Congressman Walter remained the chairman of the House Immigration Subcommittee, and he continued to oppose any loosening of the restrictions written into the Refugee Relief Act. Prospects for action brightened briefly when a Senate Judiciary Subcommittee on refugees held hearings on the various proposals in mid-June, giving Lehman and others an opportunity to reiterate all the reasons why the Refugee Relief Act needed to be amended. But the full Judiciary Committee found itself deadlocked over the measure, and Congress adjourned for the year in early August, with Senator Harley Kilgore, the chairman of the Judiciary Committee and its Subcommittee on Immigration, charging that the administration had paid only lip service to its own proposal, failing to testify in support of the measure and contenting itself with criticizing the Democratic-led Congress's failure to adopt the changes rather than working for their approval.[29]

V

On the surface, Herbert Lehman and Lyndon Johnson maintained cordial relations in the Senate despite their differences on specific issues. On March 28, 1955, Johnson used the occasion of Lehman's seventy-seventh birthday to pay tribute to him on the floor of the Senate, proclaiming that "few men in our history had had such a distinguished and brilliant career," and praising Lehman for having "devoted his entire adult life to the service of the American people." Johnson emphasized that "those of us who know the junior Senator from New York know equally well that he is only standing on the threshold of achievement," noting that Lehman was "a man with a deep sense of duty who will never give up his struggle for the things he believes are good and right . . . a man who has never made an error of the heart." Acknowledging that he and Lehman had "differed on many occasions," Johnson claimed that he had "never lost the feeling of friendship and respect" for Lehman, and he inserted in the *Congressional Record* an editorial from the *New York Times* summarizing Lehman's achievements. Senators Kefauver, Green, Fulbright, Humphrey, Barkley, Chavez, Neuberger, Mansfield, Monroney, Sparkman, and Martin (R-PA) echoed the Majority Leader's sentiments. Lehman was in New York for a brief birthday celebration when all these kind words were uttered, but when he returned to Washington the following day, he immediately told Johnson how "deeply grateful" he was "for your very generous comments and for your expressions of friendship, which I shall always greatly treasure."[30]

Beneath the veneer of congeniality, however, Johnson often behaved contemptuously toward Herbert Lehman. Besides denying Lehman the committee assignments he sought, Johnson, as Robert Caro notes, upon seeing a message that "Senator Lehman called—please call him back," would often toss the message in the trash. According to Lehman aide Julius Edelstein, there were times when Johnson "wouldn't return Lehman's phone calls for days," if he returned them at all. Similarly, Johnson made it a point to isolate and exclude Lehman from conversations in the cloakroom and often left the Senate chamber when Lehman began speaking. As Johnson aide Harry McPherson later recalled, Johnson voted against Lehman "frequently, and moved to table his amendments swiftly when there was more likely bigger game afoot." McPherson conceded that to Lehman, Johnson "must have appeared the embodiment of heedless power, running roughshod over good." Trying with little success to soften the blow, McPherson maintained that "just as often, however, Johnson was solicitous" of Lehman and "liked to be on Lehman's side when he could." While Johnson did occasionally vote with Lehman, such instances were usually designed to help Johnson burnish his liberal credentials in pursuit of his political ambitions. More significantly, Johnson made sure that the civil rights bills and proposals to change the Senate rules that were of the utmost importance to Herbert Lehman never saw the light of day in the Senate.[31]

According to former LBJ aide Booth Mooney, Johnson envied the favorable treatment Lehman often received in the newspapers, in contrast to what LBJ considered to be the negative stories about himself. When informed by press aide George Reedy that reporters and columnists often wrote about Lehman because of his sincerity, Johnson instructed Reedy that he "would like to become known as 'Mr. Sincerity' of the Senate." Having read somewhere about the power of subliminal messages, Johnson started working the word "sincere" into his conversations with the press, but to no avail. The Majority Leader failed to appreciate that Lehman had earned his reputation for sincerity by demonstrating his honesty and integrity from the time he first sought elective office in 1928. As Julius Edelstein later recalled, if Lehman "simply read off the names in a telephone directory and nothing else, people would comment on how sincere he was in his reading." Johnson had many positive qualities that made him an effective Majority Leader, but sincerity was not one of them.[32]

Despite all the slights and insults inflicted by Lyndon Johnson, Herbert Lehman demonstrated his great compassion and decency when Johnson suffered a serious heart attack on July 2, 1955. As soon as Lehman heard about

Johnson's illness, he sent a telegram to Johnson at Bethesda Naval Hospital, expressing his concern and distress and praying for Johnson's "early and complete recovery." When the Senate next met on July 5, Acting Majority Leader Earle Clements updated his colleagues on Johnson's condition and inserted into the *Congressional Record* a number of newspaper articles and editorials praising Johnson's accomplishments as Senate Democratic leader. At that point, Clements yielded the floor to Herbert Lehman, who moved "That the Senate stand in silent prayer to the Almighty for the early and complete recovery of the majority leader, the beloved senior Senator from Texas." Lehman's resolution was immediately approved without objection, and as the *Washington Post and Times-Herald* reported, "the legislators stood in silence, with heads bowed, for 1 minute and 15 seconds." Reporter James Lee called it "one of the most poignant occasions in congressional history."[33]

Lyndon and Lady Bird Johnson greatly appreciated Lehman's thoughtfulness. Lady Bird, who stayed at her husband's side for the duration of his hospitalization, thanked Lehman for his "good wishes and prayers . . . during the critical hours of Lyndon's illness," adding that she would always remember Lehman's "resolution for silent prayer in the Senate" as "one of the most touching things that has happened to us in our twenty-odd years here." A week later, she again thanked Lehman for his prayer resolution, which she described as "not only a generous act," but "the act which meant the most to Lyndon at that time." She "believe[d] that it was the prayers of Lyndon's friends and colleagues that pulled him through the dark and troubled hours." Lyndon Johnson shared his wife's sentiments. A few months later, when he was recovering at the Johnson ranch in Texas, Johnson told Lehman, "One of the most important things that ever happened to me in my life was that minute of silent prayer you led in the Senate." Johnson emphasized, "It came at a time when both Lady Bird and I felt that no other source of strength was adequate," and he believed "it was the faith and the prayers" of his "friends and well-wishers" that had pulled him through. Johnson promised never to forget Lehman's "warm, human gesture which was prompted by your generous heart."[34]

Besides prayers and get-well wishes, Lehman also sent Johnson a more tangible gift, a small transistor radio that he could listen to in his hospital room. Lady Bird wondered how Lehman had chosen "something that would delight Lyndon so much and bring him so much pleasure," stressing that " 'the little radio is really darling and such a wonderful thing for someone who is in bed." She reported that "Lyndon is enjoying it many hours of the day and shows it to all the doctors and nurses who come in." A few years later, Hubert Humphrey recalled that during Johnson's hospitalization, Lehman had given him a "little transistor radio, which meant so much to Lyndon" that Humphrey had heard him "speak of it a hundred times." According to Humphrey, regardless of Lehman's political differences with Johnson, "when Lyndon was stricken you could see the pain of it right in Lehman's face, and he responded as you would expect he would."[35]

VI

After Congress adjourned for the year in early August 1955, Lehman and his fellow liberal Democrats changed their strategy in their quest for immigration reform. Rather than pursuing the stopgap solution of amending the Refugee Relief Act, Lehman and his allies shifted their focus to revising the McCarran-Walter Act itself. Senator Kilgore wanted to hold hearings on the effectiveness of the nation's overall immigration policy under the McCarran-Walter Act, but he had been unable to do so, he charged, because the Eisenhower administration had "ducked every invitation to testify" before his subcommittee, and because the President and his advisors had "failed to come to grips with this vital issue and formulate policy." When Kilgore announced in mid-September that hearings would be held in November, Lehman explained that what was needed was "a most comprehensive set of hearings on basic immigration law reform—hearings in which those who are interested in such reform can sketch out their demands." He emphasized the "need to draw the big picture so that when the President and the administration finally submit their recommendations, they will be seen in perspective . . . as the fringe proposals they are certain to be," and he stressed the need "to make a clear presentation of the changes which most of the great sectarian and non-sectarian organizations in America desire—the abolition of the National Origins Quota System and the abolition of the distinction between naturalized and native-born citizens." Lehman believed that amending the McCarran-Walter Act would "take a great deal of public education to accomplish," and he hoped that the hearings would "be a factor in impressing upon the public mind the severe discriminations and inequities contained in this law."[36]

When the Senate Judiciary Subcommittee on Immigration and Naturalization held four days of hearings in late November and early December 1955 on his proposal to revise the McCarran-Walter Act, Lehman condemned the current law as "a pyramid of unfounded fears—fear of foreigners, fear of criminals, fear of Communists and anarchists, and fear even of naturalized American citizens," and he called for "a strong and consistent bipartisan effort to erase from our statute books the shame of the McCarran-Walter Act." But even though Senators John Kennedy (D-MA) and Clifford Case (R-NJ) and spokesmen for numerous labor and religious groups echoed Lehman's plea for reform, the Eisenhower administration did not send anyone to testify at the hearings, claiming that the matter was still under review. The administration's silence led Lehman to conclude that there was little likelihood that meaningful changes would be enacted. Nonetheless, he believed that the hearings, at which every speaker except the representative from the American Legion urged that the McCarran-Walter Act be revised, constituted significant progress.[37]

Herbert Lehman needed Lyndon Johnson's help when Senator Kilgore and Senator Hennings both failed to show up on the second day of the hearings, leaving Republican Senator Arthur Watkins to preside. Lehman begged Johnson to ensure that Hennings was present to conduct the remaining sessions, warning that "we could not turn over the hearings to people who were antagonistic to any substantial revision of the McCarran-Walter Act." The matter was not only important to him personally, Lehman emphasized, but "it was of far greater importance to the Democratic Party" because Hennings's absence would have "a disastrous affect [sic] on the Party in states like New York, New Jersey, Pennsylvania, Michigan, Massachusetts, and others." Johnson promised Lehman that he would "do what he could to get Hennings to conduct the hearing," and Hennings was in the chair when the committee held its final hearings on the matter.[38]

Up to this point, Lyndon Johnson had not participated in the debate over changing the nation's immigration policies. He had voted for the McCarran-Walter Act in 1952, but his re-election in 1954 allowed Johnson to take a more favorable view of revising the immigration laws, and in November 1955, Johnson endorsed immigration reform as part of his "program with a heart." In his first major speech after his heart attack, Johnson sought to demonstrate his physical recovery, answer liberal criticism that the Democrats' congressional leaders focused on "party unity" at the expense of liberal objectives, and attract support for a spot on the national ticket in 1956. Johnson's platform included numerous objectives on which he and Herbert Lehman agreed, such as expanding Social Security coverage; reducing taxes for low-wage earners; providing federal aid for school, hospital, and highway construction; amending the Constitution to eliminate the poll tax; and revising "the immigration and naturalization laws to insure that they are fair and just." Johnson aide Bobby Baker sent a copy of the speech to all Democratic Senators, explaining that this was the program that Johnson "believes should be considered at the second session of the 84th Congress."[39]

The commitment of Lyndon Johnson and the Senate Democratic leadership to immigration reform, the Eisenhower administration's embarrassment at not testifying at the Senate hearings, and the fact that 1956 was an election year forced the President and his aides to shake off their lethargy on this issue and recommend specific changes in the McCarran-Walter Act. Four days after the Judiciary Subcommittee concluded its hearings in December 1955, Attorney General Herbert Brownell announced that the administration would propose in January a "drastic revision" to "humanize" and eliminate the "great inequalities" in the nation's immigration laws. In his State of the Union address in January, the President specified the changes he wanted to see enacted, asserting that the number of people of each nationality group admitted to the United States should be based on the 1950 census rather than data from 1920, and recommending that some pooling of unused quotas be allowed. Eisenhower reported "substantial progress in the flow of immigrants under the Refugee Relief Act of 1953," but he renewed his call for the amendments to that law that he had proposed in 1955, and he suggested more flexibility in allowing refugees in Greece and Italy and "escapees from behind the Iron Curtain" to fill unused slots originally intended for Germany and Austria. Herbert Lehman characterized the administration's proposals as "promising," but he noted that they "do nothing about the real evils" in the McCarran-Walter Act, retaining a system that was based on a potential immigrant's nationality, and making "no mention whatever of the degrading status of second-class citizenship impressed on our naturalized citizens by that shameful law." The *Washington Post and Times-Herald* agreed with Lehman that the President's proposals fell far short of the "drastic revision" that Brownell had indicated would be coming, and far short of the "fundamental overhauling of the national origins quota system" that was needed. But "inadequate as such changes may be," the *Post* emphasized that they were "urgently needed and will be welcome" and pointed out that the real test of the administration's intentions would be how much leadership the President exerted on behalf of these proposals.[40]

This time, the President did follow through, sending a special message to Congress on February 8, 1956, in which he called for major revisions in the immigration laws. Among other changes, Eisenhower recommended increasing the number of immigrants to be admitted from 154,657 to 220,000, with the additional slots to be allocated based on actual immigration to the United States since 1924, which meant that the additional sixty-five thousand openings would go to countries in Southern Europe. The President also urged that unused quota numbers be pooled, making spaces available for potential immigrants from other countries. The President's proposals were "better and more comprehensive" than Lehman had expected, and the Senator was pleased that Eisenhower "has come a considerable way down the road I and others have been pointing out for the last few years." Lehman complained, however, that the President's plan still lacked many of the important elements of his own bill, such as "eliminating the national origins quota system, wiping out the distinctions between native-born and naturalized citizens . . . and establishing standards of justice and equity for the treatment of all aliens—those seeking admission here, and those already resident here." Nonetheless, Lehman hoped that the President's proposals would result in some congressional action in 1956.[41]

Some Senators and Congressmen remained adamantly opposed to any significant changes in the current immigration laws. Senator Watkins argued that many of the criticisms of the present law were "obviously overstated and exaggerated," and he emphasized that Senators should not "open wide our doors to accommodate the countless numbers of Asians and Europeans who would come to our shores." Even more ominously, Congressman Walter remained, in the words of the *New York Times*, "a power in Congress on immigration affairs," and he charged that "the President's proposals cast a threatening shadow over the basic immigration policies established by the McCarran-Walter Act." Walter warned that pooling unused quota slots would attract "minority pressures, with political gain rather than national welfare the basic consideration," and he claimed that "if, indeed, there are reasons for amending the immigration laws, they do not appear in the President's proposals, nor in the parade of politically inspired measures which have preceded them." Watkins's lukewarm support and Walter's determined opposition led the *New York Times* to observe that "a determined effort by the administration and the Democratic leadership" would be needed to push any changes in the immigration laws through Congress.[42]

Efforts to revise the McCarran-Walter Act suffered a major setback when Senator Kilgore, the chairman of the Judiciary Committee and its Subcommittee on Immigration and Naturalization, and a strong supporter of immigration reform, died from a cerebral hemorrhage on February 28, 1956. Under the Senate's tradition of seniority, James Eastland of Mississippi, the senior Democrat on the Judiciary Committee, would succeed Kilgore as its chairman, and Eastland had warned on numerous occasions that loosening the restrictions imposed by the McCarran-Walter Act would enable the nation's enemies to "flood the United States with criminals and Communist agents." William S. White of the *New York Times* once described Eastland as "a bitter and vehement racist," and the Senator often bragged to the people back home how he had used his power as chairman of the Judiciary Committee's Subcommittee on Civil Rights to ensure that no civil rights measures advanced to the full committee. With Eastland as chairman of the Judiciary Committee, not only would civil rights measures be doomed, but immigration reform, too, would be dead. The NAACP's Clarence Mitchell warned Democrats that Eastland would be "a stinking albatross" around their necks, but despite urgent appeals from the NAACP, ADA, and others that the post not be given to Eastland, Lyndon Johnson and the Democratic Steering Committee recommended unanimously that Eastland be elevated to the chairmanship of the Judiciary Committee. Johnson and the Steering Committee also ignored Hubert Humphrey's suggestion that the "trouble brewing in liberal ranks" over Eastland's promotion could be mollified by naming Lehman to fill Kilgore's seat on the Judiciary Committee, selecting instead the liberal but more pliable Matt Neely to replace his fellow West Virginian.[43]

Only Herbert Lehman and Wayne Morse objected when Eastland's appointment as chairman of the Judiciary Committee came before the full Senate. Eastland later recalled that he had enjoyed Lyndon Johnson's "support all the way," and the Majority Leader had "worked it out so that these two fellows would make speeches against me but would not ask for a role [*sic*] call vote," which would highlight the division among Senate Democrats and force Senators to be recorded on a controversial issue in an election year. After Morse detailed the three previous instances in which the Senate had ignored seniority in choosing a committee chairman and his reasons for opposing Eastland, Lehman tried to demonstrate Eastland's unfitness for this position by quoting some of the Mississippian's more outrageous statements, including his vow to "protect and maintain white supremacy throughout eternity," his claim that "the Negro race is an inferior race," his contention that "New York, for all practical purposes, is a Communist state," and his assertion that the Supreme Court was "indoctrinated and brainwashed by leftwing pressure groups," leading to its "corrupt decisions" and "monstrous crime[s]." Lehman also cited Eastland's active role in establishing white citizens' councils to show that Eastland was "a symbol of racism in America, . . . a symbol of defiance to the Constitution of the United States as interpreted by the Supreme Court," which should "completely disqualify him from presiding as chairman of the Judiciary Committee." Lehman believed that "a great many" of his colleagues felt the same way he did, but few of them shared his willingness to challenge Eastland, Lyndon Johnson, or the seniority system. According to the *New York Times*, when a voice vote was taken on Eastland's appointment, "the voices of Senators Morse and Lehman could be heard loudly calling 'no,'" but from the press gallery, it appeared that only "one or two other voices also had been in the negative."[44]

VII

Lyndon Johnson sought to move the Senate forward on immigration reform in 1956, but, as Lehman had feared, the Majority Leader ran into a roadblock in Eastland. As one advocate of immigration revision noted, Eastland's record was "no better on immigration than it is on civil rights," and Eastland not only headed the full Judiciary Committee, but he also made himself the chairman of the subcommittee through which any immigration bill would have to pass. Gerald Siegel of the Democratic Policy Committee staff reminded Johnson that he had included immigration reform in his "program with a heart," and Siegel emphasized that "Senate Democrats need to regain the leadership in this field, which—in the minds of many foreign-born Americans, their children, relatives, and friends—has been seized by President Eisenhower and the Republican Party." But at a hearing with Attorney General Herbert Brownell on the President's proposed modifications in the McCarran-Walter Act, Eastland made very clear his opposition to any change in the national origins quota system or any other major aspects of the nation's immigration policy.[45]

Determined to get something through the Senate in 1956, Johnson instructed the Democratic Policy Committee staff to draft a bill that would be acceptable to all factions within the Democratic Party, including Senator Eastland and Congressman Walter, who opposed any major changes in the current statute, and Herbert Lehman, who wanted significant modifications in the nation's immigration laws. Siegel and the Policy Committee staff used Lehman's bill to amend the Refugee Relief Act as their starting point, retaining most of its "liberalizing features," but deleting "a few controversial provisions." Siegel hoped that leaving the refugee program under Scott McLeod and the Bureau of Security and Consular Affairs rather than creating a new administrator for it, and extending the law for one year rather than four, would result in a bill "capable of being reported by the Judiciary Committee expeditiously" and winning Senate approval. He reported that Congressman Walter was willing to go along with "a substantial modification of the immigration laws" if he could be assured that "no personal attacks [will] be made on him." Trying to demonstrate that "immigration is not 'alien' to humor," one Lehman staffer pointed out that some of the Senator's allies would probably oppose "this method of Waltering down the immigration bill," but Lehman at this point was willing to accept almost anything. Johnson's plan foundered, however, when Eastland and the Judiciary Committee reported to the floor only a measure to allow 350 sheepherders and their families into the country on an emergency, non-quota basis.[46]

The Judiciary Committee's failure to recommend anything more than relief for Western sheep ranchers dismayed Lehman and others who supported meaningful changes in the immigration laws. Senator Watkins emphasized that the sheepherders' bill "constitutes in no way an immigration program for this year," and he solicited a letter from the President in which Eisenhower reiterated his support for revision of the nation's immigration laws. Lehman wondered why Congress was asked every two years "to admit more sheepherders above quota limits," but never got "an opportunity to vote on basic legislation to revise our quota system so that these special sheepherder bills will not be necessary." The time had come, he stressed, "for Congress to face the issue frankly and to admit that the McCarran-Walter Act is a cruel, unreasonable, and repressive law, and that action must be taken to change it substantially." Lehman hoped that the Judiciary Committee would "show as much consideration for human beings as it has shown for sheep," and he vowed to continue to fight for "a reasonable, fair, humane, and workable immigration law."[47]

By early June of 1956, a disappointed Herbert Lehman confided to Chester Bowles that "while there is a growing realization of the need of drastic revision of our immigration and naturalization laws in Congress and in the country generally," he feared that "under the present circumstances we are not going to get anything of substantial importance at this session" of Congress. The *New York Times* agreed, reporting that the outlook for amending the Refugee

Relief Act was "doubtful at best," and that prospects were "considered extremely bleak" for amending the McCarran-Walter Act. But Lehman, Lyndon Johnson, and other supporters of immigration reform realized that they could use the Judiciary Committee's sheepherder bill as the vehicle for wider revisions to the immigration laws by amending the bill on the floor of the Senate, bypassing the roadblock of the Judiciary Committee. Moreover, the Judiciary Committee's bill set a precedent by removing the quota deductions that had been required in the previous sheepherder bills, opening the door for Lehman and others to advocate similar quota forgiveness for national groups that had oversubscribed their quotas and borrowed against future years under the Displaced Persons Act. And since the House had already approved the measure, it would go to a Senate-House Conference Committee rather than having to go through the whole time-consuming legislative process in the House at a time when Congress was preparing to adjourn.[48]

As the 84th Congress wound toward its close in late July 1956, Lyndon Johnson redoubled his efforts to forge a compromise immigration bill that could be passed as an amendment to the sheepherder bill. But a single objection could prevent the Senate from taking up the sheepherder bill, and each time the measure was called on the Senate calendar, an objection was heard. So Johnson continued to negotiate with Senator Eastland, Republican Leader Knowland, Senator Watkins, Senator Everett Dirksen (R-IL), and Congressman Walter, among others, to find a compromise acceptable to all sides. Most everyone involved in the talks agreed to eliminate the fingerprinting requirements, increase the age and number of refugee orphans who could be admitted, allow the entry of people convicted of "petty offenses" before coming to the United States, assist family members in joining relatives already residing in the United States, and make it more difficult to deport refugees who had lied "to avoid repatriation to Communist-controlled countries." But disagreement remained over proposals to restore the quota slots that had been mortgaged under the Displaced Persons Act, reallocate unfilled quota slots annually to those countries having smaller allotments, and allow the fifty thousand openings still available under the Refugee Relief Act to be filled by "escapees" from Communist countries even after that statute expired. On July 26, Johnson finally secured the approval of all the key players for a bill including all these provisions, and he offered a unanimous consent agreement to make the sheepherders' bill the pending business in the Senate. When no one objected, it appeared that Johnson had once again done the impossible, persuading, cajoling, pressuring his colleagues—whatever it took—to bring an immigration bill to the floor where Senators would have an opportunity to amend it and then adopt this part of his "program with a heart." Murrey Marder of the *Washington Post and Times-Herald* speculated that Johnson had accomplished this miracle—persuading Southern Senators to allow the immigration measure to come to the floor—by promising not to allow any action in the Senate on the civil rights bill that had been passed by the House.[49]

On July 27, the last day of the 84th Congress, when the Senate finally considered immigration reform, Herbert Lehman formally offered as amendments to the sheepherder measure his comprehensive bills to revise the McCarran-Walter Act and the Refugee Relief Act. Lehman conceded that such wide-ranging measures as he was proposing "should have had the benefits of the detailed judgment of the Judiciary Committee," but he noted that the committee had "refused to give the necessary study and attention" to his proposal and had similarly "overlooked the analogous proposals made by other members of the Senate and the recommendations of the President of the United States." Thus, he explained, an amendment to the pending sheepherder bill was "the only way . . . to bring this proposed legislation before the Senate for its consideration." Lehman pledged his support for the more limited amendments that would subsequently be presented by others, welcoming "any progress that can be made on this front, even inches of progress." But he insisted that the Senate should also have the opportunity to vote "for the major changes that everyone knows are needed," including replacing "the iniquitous and discriminatory national origins quota system" with "a unified quota system which retains a fixed ceiling on total immigration into the United States." As Lehman had anticipated, his amendment to revise the McCarran-Walter Act was easily defeated on a voice vote, and he subsequently withdrew his proposed amendment to the Refugee Relief Act since most of its provisions had been incorporated into the leadership's amendment that was to follow.[50]

After the rejection of Lehman's amendment, Senator Dirksen introduced the compromise amendment on which Lyndon Johnson and the leadership of both parties had been working. Dirksen explained the provisions of the bill, the most controversial of which was the redistribution of approximately 18,500 quota slots annually from England and other nations that did not use all of their huge allocations, to Italy and Greece and other countries that completely filled their much smaller quotas. Calling himself a "realist" who understood that there were "certain things the House of Representatives will not accept," Dirksen warned his colleagues against, "in our efforts to get a whole loaf, finally rejecting any bread if we can get it." Lyndon Johnson, who seldom spoke on the floor, described the difficulties he and the Policy Committee staff had encountered in trying to craft a bill that was acceptable to Senators Lehman, Watkins, and Eastland, among others. The Majority Leader knew that the substitute was weaker than Lehman might have liked, and that it went further than Eastland would have preferred, but he believed "it represents the best compromise which can be reached," and he urged his colleagues to "go along with this very modest, moderate approach which is made in this proposal."[51]

Senator Eastland had agreed to the unanimous consent agreement to allow the bill to come to the floor, but he now objected to the proposed amendment. Complaining that there had not even been time to print the last-minute measure that was available only "in mimeographed form," Eastland claimed that he had "never agreed to this proposal," nor had he "been consulted about the wisdom of it." Clearly speaking for the record and his constituents back home, Eastland charged that two days earlier, he and Senator Jenner "were called in and shown, for the first time, this substitute, and we were informed that it would be offered as an amendment to the sheepherders' bill. We were not asked what our opinion was. There was no negotiation. We were simply called in and notified of what was to be done." Eastland argued that reallocating unused quota slots would "change the cultural pattern of our immigration system from Northern and Western Europeans to Southern and Eastern Europeans," and that "quota numbers normally available only to countries of the free world would be allocated to many countries under Communist domination," making Communist nations "the greatest beneficiaries" of such changes. He emphasized that this issue "goes to the heart of our Republic and our basic Christian ideals," asserting that the substitute "would emasculate the McCarran-Walter Act." Senator Jenner agreed with Eastland that the proposed substitute would "strike at the heart of our entire immigration policy which is built upon the national origins quota formula." But despite Eastland's and Jenner's protestations and the opposition of a few others, the Senate approved the substitute by a voice vote. Majority Leader Lyndon Johnson had succeeded in getting the Senate to pass an immigration reform bill, which would certainly enhance his credentials at the upcoming Democratic National Convention.[52]

After the Senate completed action on the immigration bill, Assistant Majority Leader Earle Clements paid special tribute to Herbert Lehman for his leadership of the "forces fighting for immigration reform." Clements noted that changing the country's immigration laws had been one of Lehman's "chief crusades" ever since he had entered the Senate, and all Senators recognized what "an inveterate crusader" Lehman was "for the causes in which he believes." In Clements's judgment, the Senate bill was a reflection of Lehman's "tireless activities on this front," his unstinting efforts "not only in the Senate, but in the country at large." Despite Lehman's disappointment that the bill did not go further, Clements concluded, Lehman nonetheless "supported and voted for it" because he recognized it as "a step forward" and "helped make possible today's action."[53]

The Senate had passed the immigration reform bill, but the measure still needed the approval of the House of Representatives before it could become law. Gerald Siegel and the Senate Democratic Policy Committee staff had worked with Congressman Walter during the negotiations leading up to the Senate's adoption of the bill, and they thought Walter was on board. The Senate debate had not included any personal attacks on either McCarran or Walter, and there was nothing significant in the final Senate bill that had not been there all along during the discussions. Nevertheless, an alarm should have gone off on July 26 when Walter warned his House colleagues that despite "substantial and persistent unemployment or underemployment" in certain parts of the United States, including Walter's own Pennsylvania, the Senate was attempting "to increase at this time the number of immigrants that this country admits annually under regular immigration quotas." Although Walter hoped that the sheepherder bill under consideration in the Senate would be adopted with "certain desirable amendments," he feared that other provisions might be added that "attempt to wreck our quota system."[54]

The following day, when the Senate bill reached the House, Walter made sure it never got to the floor for a vote. Senator Eastland and Richard Arens, a McCarran protégé who was serving both as Eastland's chief aide on the Senate Immigration Subcommittee and as staff director of the House Committee on Un-American Activities, now chaired by Walter, persuaded the Congressman that reallocating unused immigration quotas breached the McCarran-Walter Act and would lead, inevitably, to other breaks in the immigration wall erected by that statute. Lyndon Johnson and others tried to convince Walter that the number of immigrants admitted in this way would be small, but their efforts came to naught as Walter claimed that the Senate provision "permitting the redistribution of immigration quotas represents a most drastic departure from the principles of our immigration laws." He asserted that the McCarran-Walter Act "has worked very well and to the benefit of the United States in the four years that passed since it was placed on our statute books," and he called for congressional hearings in 1957 "to ascertain how much of the propaganda leveled against the Immigration and Nationality Act is prompted by purely political considerations, how much of it stems from those who would sacrifice the security, the welfare, and the economy of this country on the altar of foreign interests, and how much of it is based on humanitarian and justifiable legal grounds." Without action by the House, immigration reform was dead for 1956.[55]

Lehman aide Julius Edelstein and Lyndon Johnson drew different lessons from Congress's failure to pass the immigration bill. Edelstein believed that it had been a mistake to "retreat to a position of favoring the pooling of quotas" rather than insisting on their repeal, arguing that advocates of reform should have realized that "the opponents of immigration reform will fight just as hard against quota pooling . . . as against the outright abolition of the National Origins Quota." He cited Congressman Walter's comments and actions as proof that the strategy of moderation had failed, complaining that Walter had blocked the immigration bill in the House because it "casts a faint and almost indiscernible shadow upon the sacrosanct National Origins Quota System." Lyndon Johnson disagreed, confiding to Herbert Lehman that he was "particularly disheartened" by their "failure on the Immigration Bill" because he had his "heart set on that one." But Johnson defended his view that "the way to handle this issue is to begin nibbling at it," asserting that "if we nibble long enough, we will break its back." In this instance, Johnson's nibbling strategy had succeeded in the Senate, where he wielded considerable influence over his colleagues, but not in the House, where he held little sway.[56]

VIII

Lyndon Johnson had included significant reform of the nation's immigration laws in his "program with a heart," but the only civil rights measure on Johnson's agenda had been a constitutional amendment to outlaw the poll tax, a change that would take years to enact. The Majority Leader saw civil rights as an issue that highlighted the differences among Democrats, and thus he used his considerable skills and powers to prevent civil rights legislation from reaching the Senate floor in 1956.[57]

Herbert Lehman, on the other hand, considered the enactment of meaningful civil rights legislation a moral imperative. In December 1955, he told a New York City rally sponsored by the Leadership Conference on Civil Rights that "the whole struggle for civil rights—for equal treatment under law and equal opportunity for every man, woman, and child, regardless of race, creed, or national origin—must be carried forward relentlessly and tirelessly until victory is won," emphasizing that "there must be no delay in this struggle for reasons of political expediency—or any other." Lehman was not optimistic about "the prospects of major legislative action on civil rights in the coming session of Congress," but he stressed the "need to offer full-scale battle in this cause, no matter how great the odds, nor how bleak the prospect," because "we know we are on the side of right, we know that we are animated by high moral purpose, we know that much of the world watches what we do, and measures our country by the dedication we show in this cause. Let us not flag nor fail," he concluded.[58]

In his remarks to the gathering in New York City, Lehman also promised to offer an anti-segregation amendment to a bill providing federal funds for school construction. Popularly known as the Powell Amendment after its chief proponent, Harlem Congressman Adam Clayton Powell, Jr., and strongly supported by the NAACP, this amendment and others like it were designed to deprive Southern states of federal funding for various programs if they maintained segregated facilities, a strategy later incorporated in Title VI of the Civil Rights Act of 1964. Clarence Mitchell, the head of the NAACP's Washington

office, considered Lehman "Powell's counterpart in faithfully offering the provision in the upper chamber," but unlike Powell, Lehman refused to let the
amendment torpedo essential legislation. In 1955, when President Eisenhower
sought to create a military reserve of 2.9 million men, Powell tied the House of
Representatives and the Eisenhower administration in knots for six weeks over
an amendment prohibiting the assignment of any men to segregated National
Guard units. The House finally resolved the issue by approving a bill without
any reference to the National Guard, and the Senate followed suit, most legislators agreeing with the President that Powell's amendment was "extraneous"
and should not be attached to such a vital piece of legislation. Lyndon Johnson
believed that since "the issue . . . has been settled in a number of different
forms by the courts and by the executive agencies," Congress was no longer
the proper "forum for such debate." Herbert Lehman voted for the reserves
bill "with misgivings and heartaches," believing that the measure perpetuated
segregation in the National Guard by its silence on the issue, but accepting the
arguments of the President and others that the expansion of the reserves was
"absolutely necessary" for the nation's security.[59]

As illustrated by the controversy over the reserves bill, the Powell Amendment presented liberal legislators like Lehman with a dilemma: any bill that
included such a provision would likely be defeated in the House or filibustered
to death in the Senate, meaning that the overall goal of the bill, such as providing badly needed reserve forces, would not be realized. Lehman fully recognized
that this quandary applied to the school construction bill as well, and, as usual,
he dealt with it head on. As he explained at the rally in New York, he did not
believe that federal funds should go to school districts and states that were "trying to avoid, evade, and defy the Supreme Court decree" on school integration,
so he planned to propose an amendment to the federal school construction
bill that would deny funds to such localities. Even if Lehman was the only
Senator to support such an amendment, he pledged to "fight for it, with all
the strength" he could muster. But belying his reputation as an extremist who
refused to compromise or accept half a loaf, Lehman emphasized that because
he believed "with equal fervor in the cause of federal aid to education," he
would "vote for and support a federal aid to education bill" even if, despite
his best efforts, "the anti-segregation amendment is defeated." NAACP leader
Roy Wilkins later recalled a meeting at which he tried to persuade Lehman
to oppose any bill that lacked an anti-segregation amendment. Lehman agreed
that "the federal government ought not to subsidize segregation," but he also
noted that "we need more schools. We need classrooms. Children are made
to suffer deprivation in public education when the federal government could
do something about it." Lehman was "torn between these two loyalties," and
Wilkins understood that Lehman, "who had fought too many losing, unpopular
battles for the sake of principle . . . was being precisely honest." The Senator

and his staff drafted an amendment to hold in escrow the money that would otherwise go to those school districts that were defying the Supreme Court's school desegregation decision, with the money to be released when those districts demonstrated their "good faith" in complying with the *Brown* decision. But Lehman never got the chance to introduce the amendment in the Senate because the House, after approving the Powell Amendment, rejected the whole school construction bill, and Alabama Democrat Lister Hill, who was running for re-election in 1956, kept the Senate version of the measure bottled up in the Labor and Public Welfare Committee that he chaired.[60]

On March 12, 1956, Walter George read aloud on the floor of the Senate a "Declaration of Constitutional Principles" in which nineteen Southern Senators and seventy-seven Southern members of the House of Representatives denounced "the unwarranted decision of the Supreme Court in the public school cases . . . as a clear abuse of judicial power." The "Southern Manifesto," as it came to be known, claimed that the Supreme Court Justices had "substituted their personal political and social ideas for the established law of the land," thereby "destroying the amicable relations between the white and Negro races." It praised those states that had promised "to resist forced integration by any lawful means," and its signers pledged "to use all lawful means to bring about a reversal of this decision which is contrary to the Constitution and to prevent the use of force in its implementation." Even before George had finished his presentation, Herbert Lehman was on his feet, asking to be recognized when George concluded his remarks. Senator Strom Thurmond obtained the floor first, but the South Carolina Democrat yielded to Lehman, who became the first Senator to object to the Manifesto. Lehman wanted to make sure that no one mistook the lack of a formal response to the Southern statement as acceptance of the views expressed therein, declaring that he was "wholly in disagreement" with those who opposed the Supreme Court's decision, and that he expected to speak more on the subject in the near future.[61]

Lyndon Johnson did not sign the Southern Manifesto, explaining that as Majority Leader, he had to work with all factions within the Democratic Party, and thus his Southern colleagues neither showed him the document nor asked for his assent. Senator Richard Neuberger (D-OR) described Johnson's decision not to sign the declaration as "one of the most courageous acts of political valor I have seen take place in my adult life," but Robert Caro and others have shown that Richard Russell and other Southern leaders had made a calculated decision not to involve Johnson with the Manifesto. They did not want to do anything that might harm Johnson's chances for national office, and signing the declaration would have marked him as a Southern candidate, dooming any likelihood of his achieving higher office. Moreover, school desegregation was not as divisive an issue in Texas as it was in the deep South, and Johnson had little to fear from political repercussions back home if he did not sign the

Manifesto. Nonetheless, Johnson reassured his constituents and his colleagues that he agreed with their opposition to the Supreme Court's decisions, asserting that the federal government should not be involved in what he characterized as an issue of state sovereignty, and that racial matters should be left to state and local officials to resolve.[62]

To Herbert Lehman, civil rights and compliance with decisions of the United States Supreme Court certainly were federal issues, and, as promised, he responded to the Southern Manifesto before the week was out. In one of his more eloquent speeches, Lehman emphasized that the current crisis was not just the South's problem but "America's problem," that both the North and the South bore responsibility for the denial "to a major share of the population the basic human rights we pretend, in our Constitution, to assure to all, without distinction on the basis of race, creed, color, or previous condition of servitude." But Lehman believed that the Manifesto, in which members of Congress pledged to try "to overturn the Supreme Court decision in the school segregation cases, . . . cannot go unchallenged . . . cannot go unanswered in full measure," because "its effect was surely to support the doctrine of nullification," directly challenging the supremacy of the federal judiciary. In his opinion, efforts to defy the Supreme Court's decisions were an attack upon "the very bedrock of our nation, and of our particular form of government," which relied upon every individual abiding by the judgments of the Supreme Court. If each person decided which decisions to accept, the result would be "chaos and disorder."[63]

Lehman explained that his passion on this issue, which he felt "more keenly than any other issue," stemmed from his belief that "the massive injustice of discrimination and repression against these of our fellow Americans who happen to have a skin color of a different shade" was "absolutely unjustifiable" and "absolutely intolerable." He identified "with anybody and everybody who is suffering from discrimination," declaring that "while they are suffering and are being denied their basic rights, I am not without pain, and I do not feel my rights to be secure." The Senator also deplored President Eisenhower's call for moderation on this issue and his warning against extremists on both sides, accusing the President of falsely equating "those who go about obeying the law, in an orderly and practical manner," with "those who defy and resist the law." He urged the President to carry out his "responsibility to see that the laws are faithfully executed . . . and to defend the Constitution, as interpreted by the Supreme Court."[64]

IX

With Senator Eastland firmly entrenched as the chairman of the Senate Judiciary Committee, there seemed little likelihood of civil rights legislation reaching the Senate floor in 1956. The Eisenhower administration's slowness to act in this area, reflecting both the President's reluctance to increase federal involvement on this issue and the division among his advisors over whether to appeal to African American voters in the North or build on the gains the Republicans had made with whites in the South, also reduced the chances of meaningful civil rights action in 1956. But in mid-April, hoping to highlight the split among the Democrats on this issue in an election year, Attorney General Brownell proposed elevating the civil rights section in the Justice Department into a separate division headed by a new Assistant Attorney General and creating a bipartisan commission to determine whether African Americans were being denied the right to vote and the equal protection of the law commanded by the Constitution. Liberal Democrats complained about the modesty of the administration's proposal, its transmission to Congress coming so late in the President's term and the legislative session, and Brownell's repeated failures to endorse or even comment on civil rights measures sponsored by Senator Lehman and others that had been pending for months. At the same time, Richard Russell and Southern lawmakers denounced the administration for political pandering to minorities in an election year.[65]

The House Judiciary Committee strengthened the administration's civil rights proposal, adding to the bill provisions to allow the Justice Department to initiate school desegregation suits, bring civil suits against individuals who tried to prevent people from voting, and seek federal injunctions when people's civil rights were threatened. Southern opponents managed to drag out consideration of the measure, but the House finally approved it on July 23, less than a week before Congress was scheduled to adjourn. The bill's chances in the Senate had never been bright, but the slowdown in the House made Senate action at such a late date nearly impossible. As Murrey Marder noted in the *Washington Post and Times-Herald*, the House's passage of the bill merely sent it to the Senate for what was expected to be a quick burial, and it would take "a legislative miracle to bring it out of committee and pass it before this rapidly-closing session of Congress ends."[66]

Meanwhile, Herbert Lehman and other supporters of civil rights legislation grew increasingly frustrated as Senator Eastland kept all such measures bottled up in the Senate Judiciary Committee. Thomas Hennings's Subcommittee on Constitutional Rights approved a number of civil rights measures, but Eastland dragged his feet on holding hearings of the full committee. On June 8, the NAACP's Roy Wilkins complained that Eastland was conducting "a filibuster which transfers delaying action from the Senate floor to the committee room," and a month later, Herbert Lehman reported to the Senate that he had been scheduled to testify before the Judiciary Committee on pending civil rights legislation on numerous occasions during the last three weeks, only to have all of his appearances "postponed for one reason or another." When

Lehman offered to submit a written statement in lieu of a personal appearance to expedite the committee's work, Eastland insisted that the committee wanted Lehman to testify in person, but Lehman noted that the latest hearing, scheduled for that afternoon, had been cancelled when a Senator had objected to the committee meeting while the Senate was in session. Without making any direct accusations, Lehman noted that a number of his constituents believed that "the Judiciary Committee is itself conducting a filibuster in order to avoid acting on civil rights legislation and reporting it to the Senate." Lehman hoped that the Judiciary Committee "would belie this complaint and act promptly," and he emphasized his willingness to support virtually any civil rights measures, whether it be his own bills or the Eisenhower administration's, "that do the job, that protect the unprotected in the enjoyment of their constitutional rights . . . that protect the physical security and the political equality of our citizens, and which improve the machinery of government established to help achieve these purposes."[67]

Lyndon Johnson did not share Eastland's extreme racist views, but the Senate Majority Leader supported the Mississippian's efforts to prevent any civil rights legislation from reaching the Senate floor in 1956. As Emmett Till's murder in Mississippi, the bus boycott in Montgomery, and the continuing controversy over the implementation of the Supreme Court's decision in *Brown v. Board of Education* raised the nation's awareness of the plight of African Americans in the South, Johnson wanted to avoid a futile debate over a civil rights bill that Richard Russell and his Southern colleagues would filibuster to death. The Majority Leader realized that such a divisive debate, highlighting the differences among the Democrats, would only harm both his personal political ambitions and the party's chances in the 1956 elections.[68]

A frightening incident occurred in Washington, D.C., in mid-July, which showed how dangerous it could be to lead the fight for equality for all Americans, not just in Mississippi, but even in the nation's capital. On the night of July 13, crosses were burned in front of the Sheraton-Park Hotel, where Herbert Lehman and Earl Warren, the Chief Justice of the Supreme Court, both resided; outside the homes of Supreme Court Justice Felix Frankfurter and a local leader of the NAACP; and at the apartment of Solicitor General Simon Sobeloff, who had argued on behalf of the Justice Department in the implementation phase of the *Brown* case. Next to the burning cross at the hotel, police found paper signs indicating that the crosses were aimed at Lehman and Warren, and expressing anger at the Supreme Court's decision in *Brown*. The police quickly arrested an Arlington, Virginia, man, who explained that he "wanted to influence the greater populace of the wrongness of the Supreme Court decision," and authorities charged him with "kindling a bonfire between sundown and sunrise." Since Lehman had played no direct role in the events culminating in the *Brown* decision, his inclusion among the targets that night, along with Frankfurter and Sobeloff, showed a dangerous tendency among some of the more extreme critics of the decision to mix racism with anti-Semitism.[69]

As the end of the congressional session drew near, Herbert Lehman, Paul Douglas, and a few others belatedly developed a strategy to force action on civil rights legislation. Douglas invited Lehman, Thomas Hennings, and Hubert Humphrey for a "confidential" lunch in Douglas's office on July 13, warning that unless they took "some concerted action," they were "likely to wind up empty-handed and discredited" in their constituencies. Knowing that the civil rights bills pending in the Senate would never escape from Eastland's Judiciary Committee, Lehman, Douglas, and Hennings sought to save from a similar fate the Eisenhower administration's civil rights measure that the House was about to approve. They understood that their only chance would come when the House-passed bill was initially presented to the Senate, when they could object to sending it to committee, placing it instead directly on the Senate calendar, from where they could move for its immediate consideration. Such a plan would not lead to the bill's approval, but they hoped a floor debate over the measure would educate the American people about the need for such legislation and the need to change the Senate's rules so that such measures could be debated and adopted. They decided that Douglas would proceed to the House chamber when the bill was about to be passed, wait while it went to be printed, and, after it was signed at the House dais, accompany the clerk carrying the bill to the Senate. This way, when the bill was read in the Senate and the usual motion was offered to refer it to the appropriate committee, Douglas, Lehman, or Hennings could object.[70]

As usual, Lyndon Johnson was way ahead of Lehman and those who wanted the civil rights bill discussed on the floor of the Senate. Probably through Hubert Humphrey, Johnson learned about the liberals' plan, and he and House Speaker Sam Rayburn made sure that the House bill was printed in record time and rushed to the Senate without ever coming back to the House chamber, where Douglas was waiting. Unbeknownst to Douglas, he probably passed the House aide carrying the bill to the Senate while he rushed to the House. When Douglas arrived at the House of Representatives, he later recalled, "the clerk feigned ignorance" as to the bill's whereabouts. Douglas soon realized what had happened, but when he hurried back to the Senate, it was too late. Eastland had called a rare meeting of the Judiciary Committee to make sure that Hennings was not in the Senate chamber, leaving Lehman to guard the Senate floor and make sure that the bill did not slip through. But according to Johnson biographer Merle Miller, the "unsuspecting Senator Lehman, knowing his friend could not walk *that* fast, allowed himself to be briefly decoyed off the floor." Johnson had designated Alabama Democrat Lister Hill, later described by Robert Caro as "the Southerners' fastest talker," to preside over the Senate that day, and as soon as Lehman left the Senate chamber, the House bill was delivered to the Senate and Hill quickly referred it to the Judiciary Committee without objection. Writing about the incident years later, Douglas generously noted that Lehman "was overworked and ill" at the time and blamed himself for "trying to cover too many bases" without enough assistance. He lamented that he had as allies upon whom he could depend only Lehman and "one man whose attendance was extremely irregular," meaning Hennings.[71]

Johnson then used his power as Majority Leader and the arcane rules of the Senate to ensure that the civil rights bill did not rear its head again in the last days of the congressional session, and to teach Douglas, Lehman, and Hennings a lesson about who was the boss in the Senate. Licking their wounds, Lehman, Douglas, and Hennings planned to move the next day, during what was called "the morning hour," to bring the bill back from the Judiciary Committee. However, instead of the Senate adjourning at the end of the day, Johnson moved that the Senate recess until the next morning, which meant that it would remain the same legislative day when the Senate reconvened, and thus there would be no "morning hour"—there would be no opportunity to try to retrieve the civil rights bill from the Judiciary Committee. Douglas tried to object when Johnson called for the recess, but the Majority Leader coldly reminded him that a motion to recess was not subject to objections, but was "a question for a majority vote." On the ensuing voice vote, the Senate approved the Majority Leader's motion to recess rather than adjourn, and Lehman, Douglas, and Hennings were powerless to prevent it.[72]

When the Senate reconvened the next morning, Johnson and his Southern compatriots continued to teach Lehman and Douglas and their small band about the workings of the Senate. Hennings immediately questioned the absence of the usual "morning hour" when committee reports and various motions were in order, only to be told by presiding officer Walter George of Georgia that because "the Senate recessed yesterday, morning business is not in order except by unanimous consent." When Hennings then requested unanimous consent to discharge the House-passed civil rights bill from the Judiciary Committee, Senator Russell promptly objected. Seeking to clarify the situation, Lehman asked whether that same process could be continued each day until the close of this session of Congress, eliminating the morning hour and preventing him or any other Senator from moving "to discharge a committee from further consideration of a bill" except by unanimous consent. Johnson replied that Lehman's interpretation was correct, that "new material cannot be introduced unless there is either a morning hour or unless unanimous consent is given." In response to a question from Douglas, Johnson made clear his intention to have the Senate recess at the end of the day, so the whole process would be repeated, as Johnson icily explained, "to prevent the introduction of bills at the last minute without following the regular procedure of the Senate." When Lehman asked Johnson "whether he recalls any time during his entire career in the Senate when there was not a morning hour because of an objection," Johnson claimed not to have "done any research on the question," but he stressed that it was not his practice "to program proposed legislation which has not been reported by a committee." Without mentioning any names, Johnson complained about "some Senators who would, without consulting the Majority Leader, have their own programs," who wanted "to discharge committees and consider measures hurriedly on the floor of the Senate." Johnson vowed not to let those Senators endanger important legislation that had been cleared by committees and reported to the floor, including the Mutual Security appropriation bill, the federal pay raise bill, and the farm bill, and he warned specifically that he "was not going to take the responsibility for and have the blood" on his hands "from the killing of the Social Security bill."[73]

Lehman and Douglas refused to concede defeat. Despite knowing, as Lehman put it, that they had "just a long-shot chance of succeeding" in their "emergency effort" to bring the civil rights bill before the Senate, they turned to "extraordinary parliamentary maneuvers" to accomplish their goal. As Douglas explained, they believed that if Senator Russell could object to their motions to free the civil rights bill from the Judiciary Committee, and if "resort is to be made to every technicality so as to prevent the Senate from registering its opinion in this matter," then "two can play at that game as well as one." Accordingly, Douglas or Lehman began objecting when Senators sought unanimous consent for routine business that was usually transacted during the morning hour, such as introducing bills or amendments, trying to insert material into the *Congressional Record*, or delivering committee reports. Lehman and Douglas were not optimistic, realizing that "the Senate leadership of both parties" opposed their efforts, the rules of the Senate worked against them, and they were "getting very little help from the rest of the Senate—either Democratic or Republican." Lyndon Johnson grew more and more angry as he watched Douglas and Lehman try to grind the Senate to a halt, and he sarcastically congratulated Senator Neuberger on his "breakthrough" in placing a statement in the *Record*, leading Lehman to concede that "he was asleep at the switch when he permitted the particular insertions referred to to be made."[74]

Not content with having blocked Lehman's and Douglas's efforts to bring the civil rights bill before the Senate, Johnson sought to humiliate them by demonstrating just how little support they had among their colleagues. When Douglas moved that the Senate adjourn for five minutes to bring about a morning hour, his motion was ruled out of order, since the Senate had already agreed to recess at the end of the day. However, Johnson intervened to ask that Douglas's motion be put to a vote to show how the rest of the Senate felt about such obstructionist tactics. Minority Leader Knowland immediately supported Johnson, characterizing the issue as "a vote of confidence in the leadership of the Senate—not only the majority leadership, but the minority leadership as well," and urging his colleagues to uphold "orderly procedure in the Senate" by rejecting Douglas's motion to adjourn. The presiding officer was about to conduct a voice vote, which would have quickly and easily disposed of Douglas's motion with a minimum of fuss, but Johnson wanted a roll call vote, which would embarrass and punish Douglas and Lehman for their temerity. At Johnson's request, Karl Mundt asked for the yeas and nays, and the Senate overwhelmingly rejected Douglas's motion to adjourn, 76 to 6, with Lehman, Hennings, Langer, Ives, and George Bender (R-OH) being the only Senators to side with Douglas. Lehman and Douglas were abandoned by most of their erstwhile allies, including Hubert Humphrey, who once again aligned himself with Lyndon Johnson, and Wayne Morse, who was absent for the vote but at least was paired in favor of Douglas's motion.[75]

For Douglas, Lehman's steadfast support represented the only positive aspect of the fight to bring the civil rights bill to the floor. After returning to his office, the highly decorated World War II veteran later recalled, he "shed tears for the first time in years," despairing over the prospects of ever enacting civil rights legislation. Venting some of his feelings in a letter to Lehman, Douglas explained that what "seemed to be a purely procedural matter and will be represented by some as a cranky move . . . was really the only way even to be allowed to present a motion to discharge the standing committee and to give the Senate at least a chance to vote either for civil rights or the cloture, which would have been the same thing." Douglas resented Johnson's effort "to humiliate" him, and thus he was especially grateful for Lehman's support, "both for the principle of the thing, which is the most important matter," and for Lehman's help "when the going was rough [and] when most of those" Douglas had regarded as "friends" had deserted him and "deserted the principle." Douglas was "proud to have been associated" with Lehman in this struggle for civil rights, a sentiment that Lehman reciprocated.[76]

Bloodied and beaten but not bowed, Lehman and Douglas returned to the fray the next day. When the Senate reconvened on July 25, Lehman immediately asked whether the Senate was "now in the morning hour," only to be informed by Vice President Nixon, who was presiding, that there was no morning hour because the Senate had recessed rather than adjourned, and thus bills and motions could only be introduced by unanimous consent. Lehman expressed concern that some future Senate leader, "of lesser stature and of lesser integrity than the leadership of today . . . could recess the Senate at the close of business on the very first day of the session, and if he had sufficient votes behind him, he could continue to recess the Senate every day until the end of the session," resulting "in legislation exclusively by unanimous consent, and not in an orderly way of a democratic legislative body." Lyndon Johnson conceded that Lehman's interpretation of the rules was correct, but he emphasized that "the majority of the members of the Senate would have to be corrupt as well as the leadership to bring about such a situation," because such action would depend on the consent of a majority of the Senate. Lehman conceded that "until three days ago," he had not known nor even "suspected that there was not a morning hour each day, regardless of whether it was a legislative or a calendar day," but he could "not recollect a single instance" in his seven years in the Senate when there had not been a morning hour. Fed up with Lehman's intransigence, Lyndon Johnson insisted that "there will not be an adjournment based on what one Senator says or on what two Senators say, when important legislation must be acted on by the Senate," and he reminded Lehman that "the question of an adjournment was submitted to the Senate last night," and "the Senate determined whether it wanted to adjourn." Johnson warned that he would "not be threatened, bludgeoned, intimidated, or forced to move an adjournment at a specific time or on a specific day by any Senator," although he expected that "the Senate will adjourn sometime between now and the sine die adjournment," after it had acted on various measures already on the calendar.[77]

Having demonstrated to one and all who controlled the Senate, Lyndon Johnson finally called for the Senate to adjourn rather than recess on July 26, the penultimate day of the 84th Congress. Thus, a morning hour finally occurred on July 27, enabling Senator Douglas, on behalf of himself and Senators Lehman and Hennings, to file what he described as his "legislative waif," his motion to discharge the Judiciary Committee from any further consideration of the civil rights bill. Since such measures could not be acted upon for twenty-four hours, filing the motion was a futile gesture, but Douglas believed it to be a necessary one. Lamenting the fate of civil rights legislation in the Senate, Douglas plaintively suggested that the appropriate inscription for such bills coming to the Senate should be taken from Dante's account of the engraving on the gates of hell: "Abandon hope all ye who enter here." Douglas wondered how much longer the Senate and the nation would "permit man-made rules to prevent us from even considering measures which the vast majority of the people desire?" Realizing that the civil rights bill was dead for this Congress, Lehman allowed Douglas to carry on alone this time, focusing instead on the effort to amend the nation's immigration and naturalization laws. As for civil rights, Lehman knew that the battle would soon resume at the Democratic National Convention, set to open the following week in Chicago.[78]

CHAPTER 17

"A Symbol of Courage and Conscience in Public Affairs".

Herbert Lehman and the Election of 1956

My voice in behalf of men of courage fighting for high principles, for equal justice and dignity for all, and for a world at peace, will never be silenced.[1]

I

Despite Adlai Stevenson's crushing defeat in the presidential election of 1952, Herbert Lehman, like many other liberals, believed that Stevenson had "emerged from the campaign an even bigger man than when he entered," and Lehman looked forward to Stevenson's "continuing leadership of the Democratic Party." The Senator told Stevenson that "in spite of the vote," he had won "the respect and admiration of all of the people of this country," and Lehman hoped that Stevenson would "not close the door to future political activities." Emphasizing that the Democratic Party had "far too few men of stout hearts, wise heads, and high ideals," Lehman urged Stevenson to "remain the titular head of the Democratic Party which tremendously needs your leadership."[2]

Lehman's respect and admiration for Stevenson grew over the next few years as Stevenson articulated a liberal alternative to what he decried as the Eisenhower administration's "government by business men" and "dollar diplomacy." In February 1953, for example, Stevenson told Democrats gathered at their annual Jefferson-Jackson Day dinner in New York that their party, now

---

Chapter title quotation: "To Herbert Lehman," Editorial, *New York Post*, August 22, 1956, p. 47.

the opposition for the first time in twenty years, "must contribute much more than epithets and smears and witch hunts to the solution of our problems," emphasizing that "only a government which fights for civil liberties and equal rights for its own people can stand for freedom in the rest of the world." Taking advantage of the opportunity to acknowledge Stevenson as the Democrats' leader, Lehman followed him to the microphone and praised Stevenson for having "achieved the distinction, unprecedented in this century, of becoming, in defeat, the unchallenged symbol and hope of his party." According to Lehman, Stevenson had "become the ideal not only of the 27 million Americans who voted for him in the recent election, but of uncounted millions more at home and abroad—of all who cherish the virtues of consistency, intelligence, understanding, and honesty." The Democrats, Lehman proclaimed, were marching forward "under a leader with supreme and demonstrated talents for clear thinking, plain talking, and forward looking."[3]

In 1952, when Stevenson had first declined to seek the Democratic presidential nomination, Herbert Lehman had supported Averell Harriman. Two years later, Lehman helped Harriman win the Democratic nomination for Governor of New York and campaigned enthusiastically on his behalf, but the Senator remained steadfastly committed to Stevenson. After Harriman's victory in 1954, when Tammany Hall leader and Democratic National Committee member Carmine De Sapio and New York State Democratic Chairman Richard Balch suggested that Harriman might be the Democratic presidential candidate in 1956, Lehman agreed that Harriman was "a distinguished American, an old friend, and an outstanding public figure" who would add "luster to the high traditions of the Democratic Governors of New York." But Lehman made it clear that when it came to the party's presidential candidate in 1956, he preferred "that great and eloquent apostle and leader of liberal democracy, Adlai Stevenson." Asked in May 1955 about a possible Harriman candidacy, the Senator reiterated that Harriman was a "fine man, fine man," but Lehman was still supporting Stevenson.[4]

Herbert Lehman found himself in a key position in the second half of 1955 as Stevenson and Harriman maneuvered for the Democratic presidential nomination. De Sapio and Michael Prendergast, the new State Democratic Chairman, continued to assert that Harriman should be the party's presidential nominee in 1956, but when Harriman and Lehman met in early August 1955, they both publicly confirmed their support for Stevenson. Harriman and Stevenson met a few days later, at which time Stevenson made clear his intention to run again if he was "wanted" and if the party thought he would be the "strongest" candidate, but Stevenson concluded that Harriman had not been dissuaded from seeking the nomination. Despite Harriman's pronouncements of fealty, Stevenson believed that Harriman "has the inclination and has seen some lush green valleys from Tammany's heights." Stevenson was eager to meet with Lehman, believing that he would be "most effective in avoiding any misunderstanding" with Harriman, but the Senator and his wife had just left on a European vacation.[5]

In the early fall of 1955, momentum seemed to be shifting away from Stevenson and in favor of Harriman, who became more circumspect about his intentions. Prendergast, described by the *New York Times* as Harriman's "chief political lieutenant," declared in mid-September that Harriman was prepared to challenge Stevenson at the convention for the Democratic nomination, and Harriman refused to disavow the state chairman's statement. President Eisenhower's heart attack in late September, which threated to remove him as a candidate for re-election in 1956, heightened interest in the Democratic nomination since the party was now seen as having a much better chance of winning the election. Harry Truman visited Albany, where he praised Harriman as a "genius" who had "all the qualifications for the presidency." The former President refused to endorse any candidate for 1956, but he noted, "if I were a citizen of New York, I know who I'd be for." When Harriman was asked the next day on *Face the Nation* whether he still supported Stevenson, the Governor replied that he had "no obligation to Mr. Stevenson whatsoever," that he was "not at all morally bound" by his previous statements supporting Stevenson because he "never said" he would support Stevenson "at the convention."[6]

Stevenson had wanted for some time to confer with Herbert Lehman, and Arthur Schlesinger, Jr., advised that with Truman's support elevating Harriman into a real threat for the nomination, Stevenson should contact Lehman as soon as possible to request his endorsement. Schlesinger believed that it was crucial to block Harriman in his home state, and former Secretary of the Air Force Thomas Finletter, author and longtime Lehman friend Barbara Ward Jackson, and other Stevenson supporters in New York immediately stepped up their efforts, actively wooing Herbert Lehman and Eleanor Roosevelt. Schlesinger also recommended that Stevenson urge Lehman to run for re-election to the Senate in 1956, asserting that Lehman's presence on the ticket would boost the Democrats' chances of carrying New York. Lehman returned from Europe in mid-October, and a week later, Stevenson called on the Senator at his New York apartment. Stevenson did most of the talking at the meeting, later apologizing for having treated Lehman "like a very patient father confessor—or a psychiatrist," and for "unloading such a squalid mass of feeling at your feet." He emphasized that "whoever the presidential candidate and whatever the circumstances next fall," Lehman's candidacy for re-election to the Senate "would help the ticket here in New York, . . . the presidential candidate included." Stevenson understood that one could not ignore the Senator's and Mrs. Lehman's age, but he hoped that Lehman would, once again, serve "the public interest," stressing that "this is one case at least where the *public* and the *party* interest have happily coalesced." Stevenson realized that Lehman was "struggling with the decision" about whether to cross the party leaders in New York by publicly reaffirming his support for Stevenson at this time, and Stevenson was "quite content to await it in your good time—whatever it is."[7]

According to Lehman's chief of staff Julius Edelstein, all of the Senator's principal advisors, including Edelstein, "urged him not to make a statement for Stevenson" at such an early point in the campaign because doing so would antagonize De Sapio and state party leaders who wanted New York's delegation to the 1956 Democratic National Convention to be fully committed to Harriman. But Harriman's decision to renege on his promise to support Stevenson offended Lehman, whose affection and esteem for Stevenson had only intensified since 1952. As Edelstein later explained, Lehman "felt so strongly that this was the right thing to do and the decent thing to do" that, after conferring with De Sapio and New York City Mayor Robert Wagner, Jr., and meeting with Harriman to inform him of the decision, Lehman reiterated his support for Stevenson in a public statement on October 20, 1955. Lehman emphasized that he had "campaigned vigorously with Adlai Stevenson in 1952" and had "frequently discussed public questions with him" in subsequent years. During that time, Lehman had "formed a high admiration" for Stevenson's "character, for his ability, and for his broad and liberal views, both in domestic and international affairs." Lehman recalled, "Many months ago I stated publicly that of the many well-qualified Democrats available for nomination, my preference was Adlai Stevenson and that I expected to support him," and the Senator saw "no reason" to change that opinion.[8]

Lehman's endorsement represented a major boost for Stevenson's campaign at a time when it appeared to be foundering, and it also marked the beginning of a rift between Lehman and the party bosses in New York. Stevenson valued Lehman's support more "than almost anyone" he could think of, and he issued a statement welcoming "this expression of support from so distinguished an American" as his "old friend Herbert Lehman." The *Chicago Tribune* pointed out that "Lehman was the first major Democrat in New York to pledge support to Stevenson," and the *New York Times* called Lehman's decision a "blow to Harriman" that signaled Lehman's "disapproval of the campaign of Mr. De Sapio and other New York Democrats to win the presidential nomination for Governor Harriman." When Stevenson formally announced his candidacy for the presidency on November 15, the *Times* noted that Stevenson's declaration highlighted "the division between Senator Herbert H. Lehman and other New York Democratic leaders." Lehman reaffirmed his support for Stevenson, predicting, "He will make a strong candidate and, I am convinced, an outstanding President." The Senator also emphasized his determination to attend the Democratic National Convention as a Stevenson delegate, warning that he would run in the primary if the State Committee did not name him as a delegate-at-large. Although De Sapio eventually included Lehman in the state delegation, the Tammany boss never forgot nor forgave Lehman's heresy, and he exacted his revenge in various ways, including banishing Lehman to the last row of the delegation at the 1956 National Convention.[9]

II

In endorsing Stevenson for the Democratic nomination, Lehman put aside any concerns about Stevenson's commitment to civil rights. Lehman assumed that Stevenson shared his unshakable devotion to the cause, but Stevenson's more restrained position on the issue resurfaced in February 1956. The civil rights issue was exploding at the time, as the Montgomery Bus Boycott continued under the leadership of Martin Luther King, Jr.; Emmett Till's killers bragged about their deed in an article in *Look* magazine; and a mob prevented Autherine Lucy, an African American, from attending the University of Alabama despite a federal court order for her admittance. But despite the growing turmoil, Adlai Stevenson, as columnist Robert Spivack noted, often seemed tardy and reluctant when addressing civil rights. According to Stevenson biographer John Bartlow Martin, most of Stevenson's liberal friends like Herbert Lehman, and probably Stevenson himself, failed to realize that Stevenson "lacked a strong emotional commitment to the civil rights cause," which often became apparent in his "cool, rather legalistic and pre-eminently rational approach to segregation." In early February, for example, the day after the University of Alabama caved in to violent demonstrators by suspending Autherine Lucy, Stevenson was asked by an African American minister in Los Angeles whether the time had come for the federal government to use troops to enforce its school desegregation decisions. Stevenson replied that such action "would be a great mistake. It would be a revival of the Civil War." He emphasized that "it's the spirit of men that will change these things for the better; it will not be troops or bayonets." Stevenson insisted that "the answer to elimination of all prejudice is time," asserting that "we must proceed gradually, not upsetting habits or traditions that are older than the Republic," and that it might take until the hundredth anniversary of the Emancipation Proclamation in 1963 before "the spirit of that declaration will be enforced." When asked whether he supported the denial of federal funds to states whose school systems remained segregated, Stevenson stressed that education was the key to "improving race relations" and that "phenomenal" progress had been made in this area. Instead of cutting off federal aid, he called for strengthening educational facilities in all the states, cautioning that "you should not cut off your nose to spite your face."[10]

African Americans in the audience were not the only ones disturbed by Stevenson's remarks; his liberal supporters were aghast, none more so than Herbert Lehman, who now realized that Stevenson lacked Lehman's sensitivity, passion, and conviction on civil rights. Stevenson had urged Lehman to offer "advice and counsel," and Lehman did so now, albeit "with great hesitation." Lehman knew that Stevenson "must have received many communications and importunings on this subject," and he understood "the problem that it must present to you, both in a political and in a moral sense." He realized that Stevenson's recent remarks in California were "not lightly said, nor, in any sense, insincere," but Lehman could not refrain from expressing his deep concern over Stevenson's position on this issue, based on the way that his comments had been reported in the press.[11]

Stevenson's emphasis on " 'gradualism' and 'education' as the way to make progress on the human rights front" greatly troubled Lehman, who wondered whether Stevenson appreciated what these words "mean to Negroes and to White people who are deeply concerned with the civil rights issue." He pointed out that these words had "been used by apologists for discrimination and injustice for many years . . . as an excuse for inaction and for denial of equal rights to a great share of our population." As a result, "to advocates of civil rights," these were "words of frustration and denial." In Lehman's opinion, it was "difficult to speak of the enlightening effects of 'education' in a situation such as we have in some places, chiefly some parts of the South, where all the *active* education is in the direction of prejudice and discrimination." He explained that "people who go to segregated schools learn, among other things, discrimination, and are conditioned not only to the separation of the races, but to the existence of distinctions on the basis of race." Lehman asserted that "the most powerful and effective forces at work in these areas are those bent on maintaining the status quo and defending the vested interests of segregation and discrimination," and he believed that "these institutions rarely disintegrate from within." They did, however, "succumb to attacks from without," and he observed that real progress against segregation had been made only since 1933, when "the 'threat' of FEPC developed." According to Lehman, "Integration in the Armed Services, abolition of discrimination in interstate travel, and all the rest of the progress that has been recorded, resulted from administrative, legislative, or judicial fiat, and not from 'education.' "[12]

Lehman emphasized that "the question of segregation in the public schools is only one of the critical fighting civil rights issues today," along with "the denial of voting rights to an overwhelming majority of Negroes in certain states, the question of physical violence and security, and many others." He asserted that "the denial of the protection of the Bill of Rights and of the Fifteenth Amendment to many people in the South" had "become too glaring to be overlooked," and that "they must be confronted in one way or another." The Senator realized "how deeply ingrained is the feeling of prejudice in certain parts of our country," and he understood "the fighting attachment of those people to their prejudices and their so-called local customs," but he stressed that "these prejudices cannot be justified in moral terms," which was why, "when a breach is made in them by fiat and by legislation enforcing moral law, they dissipate much more quickly than one might consider logically possible." Lehman acknowledged that "it will take time to accomplish the full range of our objectives on the civil rights front," but he believed that "the date we set for making a good-faith start toward achieving each of our objectives must be now, in order that our goals may be achieved in measurable time." Setting "a distant target date," he warned, "merely postpones for that length of time coming to real grips with the problem."[13]

The Senator understood the "difficulties" Stevenson faced, "both intellectual and political," but Lehman believed that he owed Stevenson a clear statement of his own views on the subject as well as a "frank" response to what Stevenson had said in Los Angeles. Lehman knew that Stevenson was "well accustomed, and well equipped, to resist" the "many pressures" he would "be subjected to," and Lehman assured him that this was "not an attempt to apply pressure"; this was merely Lehman's effort to set forth his "feelings" and his "reactions" to Stevenson's comments, and Lehman hoped Stevenson would "accept them as such." If and when Stevenson had the time, Lehman "would be pleased" to explore the subject further with him.[14]

Stevenson's return from his West Coast swing coincided with Herbert Lehman's visit to Chicago to accept an award from the Decalogue Society of Lawyers, and Herbert and Edith Lehman lunched with Stevenson on February 19, at which time they discussed Stevenson's position on civil rights. Stevenson disagreed with much of what Lehman had said in his letter, underlining and writing the word "No!" in the margin of the letter where Lehman had asserted that the education system in much of the South reinforced prejudice and discrimination, scribbling another "No!" where Lehman had questioned the setting of 1963 as a target date, and adding a final "No!" where Lehman had referred to the "many pressures" to which Stevenson was being subjected. In a letter to a friend the day after the meeting with the Lehmans, Stevenson described the Senator as "more pained than indignant, and of course anxious to be helpful." Lehman had restated the concerns he had raised in his letter, and Stevenson had given him a copy of a formal statement that he had released on the topic a few days earlier in which he had reiterated his fear that "punitive action by the federal government may actually delay the process of integration in education," called for school desegregation to proceed "with all reasonable speed," and urged that the issue of civil rights be removed from the political arena and the presidential campaign. By this time, Stevenson had concluded that his problem was "largely one of attitude," and although he recognized "the necessity for mingling more passion" with his "reason," he continued to believe "that the ultimate sanction, force, will solve nothing." Stevenson thanked Lehman for his "all too brief visit," and for his "patience and understanding" of Stevenson's "attitude about the civil rights matter," and welcomed Lehman to "come again, stay longer, and bring Edith!"[15]

As Lehman and other campaign advisors suggested, Stevenson started to take a firmer stand on civil rights, demonstrating more of what Arthur Schlesinger, Jr., called "a convincing emotional concern" on this issue. Speaking in Hartford, Connecticut, in late February, Stevenson made what the *New York Times* described as "his most forthright declaration thus far on the civil rights issue," asserting that "the most crucial issue within this beloved land of ours today [is] equal rights for all—regardless of race and color." Similarly, in a speech at the University of Minnesota a week later, Stevenson declared that it was

> clearly a matter of grave national concern when a girl in Alabama is denied her constitutional rights by mob violence or by subterfuge, or when murder goes unpunished in Mississippi, or when American citizens are denied peaceful occupancy of their homes in my own state of Illinois, or when citizens are denied, whether by physical or economic coercion, their right—and duty—to vote.

Stressing the national scope of the racial problem in America, Stevenson emphasized that "before we cast a stone at Alabama," people should remember that "racial discrimination in some degree is still a fact of life for the great majority of our Negro citizens who live outside the South," and that such treatment "consigns them to segregated neighborhoods" and "denies them full employment opportunity." According to Stevenson, "the full accommodation of our Negro citizens in this society of ours is in truth an American dilemma, which demands the best that is in us." Stevenson's remarks in Minnesota so impressed Herbert Lehman that he inserted the speech in the *Congressional Record* and used the occasion to reiterate his support for Stevenson, his "announced choice for the Democratic nomination for the presidency."[16]

Lehman remained steadfast in his support for Stevenson even when the campaign faltered. The Senator readily agreed when Thomas Finletter and the New York Stevenson for President Committee asked him to speak at a $100-a-plate dinner on April 25, and his check for $1,000 to reserve a full table was especially appreciated in the aftermath of Estes Kefauver's victories over Stevenson in the New Hampshire and Minnesota primaries. After Stevenson delivered a major speech before the American Society of Newspaper Editors on April 21 in which he called for a suspension of American testing of nuclear weapons, he had dinner the next night at Herbert and Edith Lehman's Washington apartment. Lehman told the press that the meeting was "purely social," and Stevenson emphasized to the Lehmans how much he appreciated the night off from his "endless 'primary' journey." He thanked the Lehmans for providing "a good time—a comforting time and a relaxing time," all of which were in short supply during the campaign. A few days later, when Lehman introduced Stevenson at the fund-raising dinner in New York, the Senator insisted that Stevenson was "the best equipped man to serve this nation and the cause of freedom throughout the world in the exalted office of the presidency." Asked by the press about Harriman's and De Sapio's absence from the dinner, Stevenson emphasized instead that he had been "delighted with the appearance of Senator Lehman, Mayor Wagner, and others." Finletter told Lehman "how much everyone enjoyed your remarks the other evening at the dinner," and he could not think of "anyone [who] has been more help to Adlai than you."[17]

In early summer 1956, Carmine De Sapio tried to spring a trap on Lehman that would help Harriman secure the Democratic presidential nomination. At Lehman's request, De Sapio came down to Washington in mid-June and confirmed that Lehman would be a New York delegate-at-large at the Democratic National Convention despite his support for Stevenson. But De Sapio also asked Lehman to represent New York on the platform committee, as he had in 1952. Harriman's main chance for the nomination at this point was a split over civil rights that resulted in Southern delegates bolting from

Figure 17.1. Herbert Lehman, Eleanor Roosevelt, and Adlai Stevenson at the "Tribute to Stevenson" dinner in New York City, April 25, 1956. AP Images.

the convention, as had happened in 1948, and De Sapio knew that Lehman, notwithstanding his enthusiasm for Stevenson, would fight for a strong civil rights plank rather than the milder provision that Stevenson favored. Lehman refused to fall for De Sapio's ploy. Describing his previous service on the platform committee as "extremely burdensome," Lehman informed De Sapio and the press that he would not serve in that capacity in 1956 because he wanted "to be free to make very active efforts at the convention in behalf of Adlai Stevenson's nomination as the presidential candidate."[18]

Even though Lehman declined to serve on the Democratic Party platform committee in 1956, Lyndon Johnson's success in preventing the Senate from taking up the House-passed civil rights bill and his heavy-handed treatment of Lehman and Douglas convinced Lehman that the Democrats, and the nation, needed a strong civil rights plank in 1956. When Stevenson briefly took a tougher stance on civil rights on August 8, enunciating his "feeling that the platform should express unequivocal approval" of the Supreme Court's decisions on school desegregation, Lehman welcomed Stevenson's new position, noting it was "in full agreement" with his own, and Lehman promised to push for a sound

FIGURE 17.2. Senator Lehman and Tammany Hall leader Carmine De Sapio confer at the Democratic National Convention in Chicago, August 15, 1956. AP Images.

civil rights plank when he testified before the platform committee. Although Stevenson's managers quickly backtracked from the candidate's more vigorous advocacy of civil rights, fearing that a fight over civil rights would weaken his candidacy, Herbert Lehman told the platform committee on August 10 that "the successful fight that was waged in 1948 at the Democratic Convention for a more adequate civil rights plank" had demonstrated the party's "courage and honesty," and he urged the Democrats to be forthright once again and explicitly endorse the Supreme Court's "moral and righteous decision" against segregation in public schools.[19]

With reports circulating in the press that the platform committee was about to adopt a civil rights plank that simply promised that the Democratic Party would "continue its efforts to eliminate illegal discriminations" and made no mention of the Supreme Court's school desegregation decisions, Lehman continued to fight for a stronger statement that specifically endorsed the Court's ruling in *Brown v. Board of Education*. Lehman, Roy Wilkins of the NAACP, and Walter Reuther of the United Auto Workers met on August 12 with a large group of liberal delegates to plan their strategy for a fight on civil rights on the floor of the convention, but Lehman and his cohort faced a difficult task. The platform accurately reflected Stevenson's views and was a statement that most of the delegates, North and South, could live with. Moreover, former President Harry Truman and liberal stalwarts Hubert Humphrey and Eleanor Roosevelt accepted the platform as the best that could be obtained from the convention. But for Herbert Lehman, battling for a stronger civil rights plank was a matter of principle and conscience, and as Mrs. Roosevelt later recalled, Lehman was doing "the only thing that he could do, because he had been in this fight for so long."[20]

Lehman did not want to do anything that would hurt Stevenson's chances of winning the nomination and the fall election, but he could not accept a platform that merely noted that "recent decisions of the Supreme Court of the United States relating to segregation in publicly supported schools and elsewhere have brought consequences of vast importance to our nation as a whole and especially to communities directly affected." Nor was he satisfied with echoing a civics textbook by recognizing that the Supreme Court was "one of the three constitutional and coordinate branches of the federal government, superior to and separate from any political party, the decisions of which are part of the law of the land." While Lehman and his followers scrambled to gather the eleven signatures needed from members of the platform committee to bring a minority report to the floor, they also met with party leaders behind the rostrum, trying to reach agreement on compromise language to avoid a floor fight. When the negotiators failed to agree on wording they could all accept, platform committee chairman John McCormack of Massachusetts reported the committee's draft on civil rights, and Robert Short of Minnesota formally offered the minority plank calling for FEPC legislation and explicitly pledging to carry out the Supreme Court's school desegregation decisions. Senator Paul Douglas, Governor G. Mennen Williams of Michigan, Walter Reuther of the UAW, Joseph Rauh of ADA, and a few others criticized the majority plank and helped rally the troops, but as the *New York Times* reported, it was Senator Lehman who "took the lead in supporting the minority's proposed 'hard' plank. Mr. Lehman, his voice shaking, cried out against 'the massive injustice' of racial discrimination." Given only two minutes to address the convention, Lehman declared that civil rights "is America's problem," and he condemned "discrimination against fellow Americans who happen to have a different shade of skin than ours. If we are a law-abiding people," he asked, "what excuse can there be for not pledging to carry out the decisions of the Supreme Court?" But any chance that Lehman and his supporters might have had for victory slipped away when Harry Truman, stressing his accomplishments in this area, pronounced the civil rights plank "the best one this convention has ever had put before it." Speaker Sam Rayburn quickly conducted a voice vote on the dueling civil rights planks and ruled that the platform committee's version was adopted. When Lehman tried to protest and demand a roll call vote, he found that the New York microphone had mysteriously gone dead or never been turned on, and Rayburn promptly adjourned the convention.[21]

III

With the platform settled, Democrats now focused on choosing their candidate. Estes Kefauver had bowed out of the race in late July, leaving Stevenson as the frontrunner and Harriman as his main challenger. Lehman and Eleanor Roosevelt continued to support Stevenson, providing him with a strong counter to Harriman's claims that he was the only candidate who would wage a "vigorous" fight for the progressive ideals of the New Deal and the Fair Deal. Columnist Steward Alsop pointed out that the influence of Herbert Lehman, Hubert Humphrey, and Eleanor Roosevelt in the Stevenson campaign made it hard to portray him as a reactionary on racial matters. When Harriman insisted that he stood "for the only principles which will win in this campaign . . . the principles of Franklin D. Roosevelt and Harry S. Truman," Stevenson emphasized that Harriman could not claim "any exclusive rights to those principles," suggesting that any doubts about his commitment to liberal Democratic ideals could be resolved by checking "with Mrs. Roosevelt and Senator Lehman," each of whom, the *New York Times* noted, was solidly in Stevenson's corner and had long been considered "a champion of Democratic liberalism."[22]

Despite Stevenson's waffling on civil rights, Lehman continued to work for Stevenson's nomination at the convention. After Lehman's presentation before the platform committee, he discussed the campaign with Stevenson that evening, and he met with Harry Truman the next day, trying to dissuade the former President from endorsing Harriman. When Truman went ahead and bestowed his blessing on Harriman anyway, citing the former diplomat's long experience in foreign policy and his dedication "to the principles of our party—the New Deal and the Fair Deal," Lehman was one of seven prominent Democrats who sought to prevent Truman's remarks from having a bandwagon effect. Lehman and the others went on TV immediately to voice their continuing support for Stevenson. The Senator also helped persuade Michigan Governor G. Mennen Williams that his state's delegates should support Stevenson, assuring Williams that Stevenson would pursue an active civil rights program if elected.[23]

In addition to Stevenson and Harriman, Lyndon Johnson hoped to win the Democratic presidential nomination in 1956. Johnson's heart attack in 1955 had seemed at first to disqualify him, but President Eisenhower's recovery from his own heart attack in 1955, followed by his ileitis surgery in June 1956, showed that a serious illness was not a fatal impediment to seeking or occupying the White House. Johnson realized that his success in preventing civil rights legislation from reaching the floor of the Senate and his protection of oil and gas interests guaranteed that an active candidacy on his part would spur liberal opposition, so he contented himself publicly with leading the Texas delegation as a "favorite son." But supporters such as Virginia Senators Harry Byrd and A. Willis Robertson praised Johnson's record as Majority Leader, asserting that it demonstrated Johnson's "presidential stature," and predicting "that when his name is offered to the Chicago convention as the favorite son of Texas, he will draw support not only from the South but from other areas of the nation."[24]

Believing that Stevenson had the nomination wrapped up, Johnson had not pressed his candidacy. However, when Truman's endorsement of Harriman threatened to block Stevenson and open up new possibilities, Johnson declared that he was now a "serious candidate" for the nomination. At the very least, commentators like William S. White of the New York Times predicted that Johnson would play a key role in determining the party's nominee. But Johnson soon discovered that he had much less influence at the convention than he expected. Truman's actions actually benefited Stevenson, as liberals like Lehman, worried that Johnson might emerge as the nominee, stepped up their efforts on Stevenson's behalf, while conservatives, fearing that Harriman might somehow win the nomination, remained committed to Stevenson as the more moderate of the two. As a result, Johnson's candidacy failed to rouse much support from anyone other than his fellow Texans and his Senate colleagues, few of whom had much influence in their state's delegation. Rather than contenting himself with the role of king-maker by endorsing Stevenson, Johnson insisted on remaining an active candidate, forfeiting any chance he might have had to win concessions or wield influence with Stevenson.[25]

The Stevenson forces assembled what one analyst termed "a carefully balanced group" to nominate him at the convention, including Herbert Lehman to represent the liberal wing of the party. Stevenson's speech writers Arthur Schlesinger, Jr., and John Bartlow Martin wrote all the nominating and seconding remarks, and Lehman's, naturally, sought to reassure the delegates about Stevenson's liberalism and his commitment to civil rights. Lehman emphasized that Stevenson possessed a "truly liberal spirit," that he understood "the duties and the responsibilities of government towards the people—all the people," and that he supported "exact justice to all of our people regardless of race, color, or creed, regardless of economic or social status." The Senator took great pleasure in offering the convention "a great Democrat, a great liberal, an eloquent and inspiring leader, the most creative figure in our day—Adlai Stevenson."[26]

After the convention nominated Stevenson for President and Tennessee Senator Estes Kefauver for Vice President, Herbert Lehman pronounced himself satisfied with the results. As he told his longtime assistant Carolin Flexner, he believed that "the team of Stevenson and Kefauver should make an exceedingly strong ticket," and he was "hopeful that we may win in November," although he realized that "at the present moment the Republicans still seem to have the edge." Despite their failure to obtain a stronger platform on civil rights, Lehman explained to Mrs. Roy Wilkins that "the fight which we made was very worthwhile and will be of much use in the future." He predicted that "within a reasonably short time the whole country will recognize that every man, woman and child, regardless of race, color, or religion, must receive all their rights guaranteed by our Constitution and by our statutes."[27]

IV

Almost as soon as Herbert Lehman won re-election to the Senate in 1950, questions arose because of his age as to whether he would serve his full term and seek another in 1956, when he would be seventy-eight years old. Lehman wrestled with the decision and tried to keep his options open as long as he could. At a Stevenson campaign rally in Brooklyn in 1952, Lehman told the audience that he probably would not run again. But a year later, when rumors began circulating that he planned to retire, the Senator tried to put such reports to rest, emphasizing to a group of Jewish educators that he intended to stay in the Senate as long as he was "physically able" and felt "needed" and "useful." When Harlem Congressman Adam Clayton Powell, Jr., claimed a few days later that Lehman had decided to retire from public office, the Senator told Powell that press reports predicting his retirement "were entirely inaccurate and unauthorized." As Lehman's chief aide Julius Edelstein explained in January 1954, the Senator had no plans to resign and had made no decision yet on 1956.

Edelstein did not know what Lehman would do in 1956, and he did not think Lehman knew either, but if Lehman remained "in his present state of health and if there is a big demand that he run again," Edelstein expected he would do so. Regardless, Edelstein pointed out that it would "lessen his influence" if Lehman were seen as a lame duck with three years to go in his Senate term.[28]

In 1955, Lehman's friends and political associates began urging him to run again. In January, prominent New York attorney C. C. Burlingham warned Lehman that New York City Mayor Robert F. Wagner, Jr., "has his eye on your seat" and hoped Lehman "will sit him out." Lehman replied that he had not yet "given any serious thought" to whether he would run again in 1956, and probably would not decide "until late next year." A few months later, Lehman's former counsel and Lieutenant Governor Charles Poletti and his family sent birthday wishes that included the following verse:

> Now '56 looms up ahead;
> We are short of fearless men.
> For our state and for our nation—
> H.H.L. *must* run again.

Governor Averell Harriman told upstate Democrats in April that "there is no question that Senator Lehman is going to run again," calling him "one of the great Senators in our nation," and asserting that "there is no doubt in my mind that he will be re-elected." Similarly, Tammany Hall leader Carmine De Sapio described Lehman as "physically hale and hearty" and "on the job," noting that he was "a young man compared to some of his colleagues in the Senate." De Sapio pointed out that "Lehman's presence on the ticket is always an asset" and he predicted that Lehman's candidacy would help the Democrats carry New York in the 1956 presidential election. When asked about Harriman's and De Sapio's statements, Lehman emphasized that he had not made any decision yet on 1956.[29]

By late summer 1955, Lehman was leaning against running for re-election, but a report in the Hearst-owned, rabidly anti-Communist *New York Daily Mirror* almost made him change his mind. Notorious gossip and crime writer Lee Mortimer alleged in his column on August 24, 1955, that former McCarthy aide Roy Cohn was "Carmen Di [*sic*] Sapio's secret 'dark horse' for Lehman's Senate seat in '56 after Wagner and Harriman knock themselves out fighting for it." Lehman's brother-in-law Frank Altschul sent a copy of the article to the Senator, joking that "it is nice to know that you are apt to have such a worthy successor," and observing that "if nothing else could determine you to run again, I should think that this might!" Lehman noted that Mortimer was "the author of one of the most vicious and lying books that has ever been circulated in Washington," and he assured Altschul, "if the report were true—and

I am sure that it is not—it certainly would make me sit up and take notice and possibly even change my present plans, which however, as you know, are not irrevocably fixed."[30]

Mayor Wagner was a much more plausible successor than Roy Cohn if Lehman decided not to seek re-election. Despite the public support Lehman was receiving from De Sapio and Harriman, there was speculation that party leaders, angered by Lehman's preference for Adlai Stevenson over Harriman for the Democratic presidential nomination in 1956, wanted the Senator to move aside. Conservative columnist George Sokolsky wrote in late October 1955 that Lehman's support for Stevenson rather than Harriman was inconsequential because "Lehman, while respected in the Senate, does not cut much political ice." According to Sokolsky, "Lehman knows that the professionals in his party want him to retire to make room for Mayor Robert F. Wagner of New York, who would like to have his late father's seat in the United States Senate." Perhaps hoping to give Lehman a not-so-subtle shove, Sokolsky asserted that "Lehman will not quit even if he lives to be 120 years old and therefore the professionals regard him as an obstacle," and Sokolsky claimed that party leaders would be pleased if Lehman "were put into the Cabinet or sent out as an ambassador, anything to remove him as a political bottleneck in New York State." Although De Sapio and the political leaders in New York resented Lehman's endorsement of Stevenson, they also realized that the Senator was one of their best vote-getters, and that any move to push him out in 1956 would alienate large numbers of Jewish and liberal voters and endanger the entire Democratic ticket. Thus, De Sapio, who had helped elect Wagner as Mayor in 1953 and Harriman as Governor in 1954 and now controlled the New York State Democratic Party organization, continued to support Lehman publicly. Wagner, who was grateful for Lehman's help in winning the mayoralty in 1953, insisted that his focus was on running for another term as Mayor in 1957, and he predicted that Lehman would be re-elected to another term in the Senate.[31]

Republicans also began to look covetously at Lehman's Senate seat in late 1955, hoping that the Senator might retire, or that he might prove vulnerable because of his age and his liberal record. The New York Times reported in November 1955 that Republican National Chairman Leonard Hall had listed Lehman as one of three Democratic Senators "marked by Republican Party leaders for political oblivion after the 1956 election." With the Democrats currently enjoying a slim 49 to 47 majority in the Senate, every seat was critical; a net gain for the Republicans of one seat in 1956, if accompanied by Eisenhower's re-election, would give the Republicans control of the Senate. Each party would have forty-eight Senators, but Vice President Nixon would cast the tie-breaking vote. Although reluctant to challenge Lehman, with whom he agreed on most issues, New York State Attorney General Jacob Javits seemed more than willing to run for the Senate in 1956 if he could secure the Republican nomination. Javits had already demonstrated his statewide appeal by his victory over Franklin Roosevelt, Jr., in the race for Attorney General in 1954, when he had been the only member of the Republican state ticket to win, and Javits would make a formidable candidate against Lehman or any other Democrat in 1956. Being Jewish would help Javits cut into Lehman's usual huge majority among his fellow Jews, and Javits's liberal stance on civil rights might enable him to make significant inroads among black voters who, although they still held Lehman in high esteem, were becoming disillusioned with the Democrats as they saw Lyndon Johnson and James Eastland prevent civil rights legislation from reaching the floor in the Senate. However, there was some question whether the liberal Javits could secure the Republican nomination because, as political commentator Robert Spivack explained, conservative, "old-line Republicans don't consider Javits a 'Republican.'"[32]

Despite being asked numerous times, Lehman refused to declare his intentions, leading political pundits to try to read between the lines in the Senator's every word. When Lehman was honored by Americans for Democratic Action in early February 1956, some thought that he might use the opportunity to reveal his plans, but he told reporters he still had not made up his mind. Attempting to read the tea leaves, the *New York Times* reported in May that at a major fundraiser for Bronx Democrats, Lehman had gone out of his way "to reaffirm his friendship for Governor Harriman," and "some construed this as an indication" that Lehman "planned to run for re-election this fall."[33]

Lehman's private correspondence with close friends at this time makes it clear that he really was still undecided about seeking another term in the Senate, and that Mrs. Lehman would play a key role in his final decision. In March, he told Arthur Corscadden, a former aide during Lehman's years as Governor who had offered political advice and analysis over the years, that he had "not yet decided" whether to run for re-election, explaining that there were "a lot of factors" that he and Mrs. Lehman "must take into consideration" before they reached a decision. Lehman emphasized that he would "do nothing unless" Mrs. Lehman was "entirely in agreement." He did not see any need to make a quick decision since the nominating convention was still six months away, and he appreciated that most of his friends were "willing to await" his decision. As late as May 30, 1956, Lehman confided to Charles Poletti, "I have not yet made up my mind what I want to do about running next November."[34]

A clearer indication of Lehman's thinking came on June 22, during his remarks in the Senate on the McCarran-Walter Immigration Act. After calling for an end to the present "national origins quota system" and its replacement with "a reasonable, fair, humane, and workable immigration law," Lehman pledged to continue fighting with all his strength for such a law while he was "in the Senate, or outside the Senate" if he chose not to return for another term. Such a statement on the floor of the Senate showed that Lehman was seriously contemplating retirement at the end of his term.[35]

Speculation and evidence that Lehman was leaning against running again continued to mount. When he declined to serve on the platform committee at the Democratic National Convention on the grounds that such duty would be "extremely burdensome," a front-page story in the *New York Times* asserted that Lehman's action "raises a serious doubt . . . as to his availability for renomination this fall." Like many observers, the *Times* had assumed up to this point that Lehman's indecision about running was merely the Senator "following the normal political ritual" that "calls for a 'draft' of a popular candidate whose term is expiring." According to the *Times*, however, party leaders now worried that "if a two-week service on the platform committee would overtax the Senator's strength, would he be able to withstand the rigors of an intensive campaign that would keep him continuously on the go for at least six weeks this fall?" Although Lehman was tired from a grueling session of Congress and knew that the closing weeks would include nasty confrontations on immigration and civil rights, the *Times* failed to realize that Lehman had refused to serve on the platform committee so as to evade De Sapio's attempt to embarrass the Senator and Adlai Stevenson by highlighting the conflict between their positions on civil rights.[36]

In a phone interview with the *Times* in early July, Lehman lent more credibility to the speculation that he would not run again. Lehman voiced "real doubt as to his willingness to undertake another statewide political campaign this fall," but denied that such concerns had any "connection with his desire to escape service on the platform committee." He emphasized that he was in good health, but he explained that before deciding whether to seek re-election, there were "a lot of things he would like to talk over with Mrs. Lehman." Sounding like he was leaning against running, Lehman also mentioned his "desire to see a lot more" of his family and "to do a great many things" he had "always wanted to do" but had "not had the time for," such as "more traveling, some writing, and lecturing."[37]

As the press continued to speculate on Lehman's future plans, with the *New York Times* reporting that many Democrats were pressuring Lehman to run again because his "bona fides as a civil rights champion . . . would subtly help many Democrats in many states," the Senator met with Adlai Stevenson in Washington on July 19 to notify him of what Lehman described in a subsequent letter as "my very strong personal inclination not to seek re-election." Stevenson appreciated the advance notice, and certainly understood Lehman's desire for "the tranquility and peace you want and have so richly earned." Stevenson understood that "on any basis—my self-interest, yours, your family, the party, the State of New York, the nation"—Lehman deserved "a fuller measure of serenity and repose" than he was "likely to get, not to mention a deeper gratitude." But "as a possible candidate for President," Stevenson knew full well that Lehman's "value to the ticket in the most important state is irreplaceable." Although he did not want "to dissuade" Lehman from the course the Senator "and Edith deem wise," Stevenson noted that "some people are sentenced to perpetual servitude," and he wondered if Lehman was "one of those" so afflicted. So as not to lessen Lehman's influence at the Democratic National Convention, Stevenson hoped that Lehman would wait until after the gathering in Chicago to make a final decision, and if Lehman did leave the Senate, Stevenson prayed that "in retirement from public life," Lehman would "find the solace and quiet years" he sought and so richly deserved. Lehman agreed that any public announcement of his decision should come after the Democratic convention, and as late as August 20, Leonard Lyons reported that "Sen. Herbert Lehman will be a candidate for re-election if Stevenson asks him to run."[38]

While in Chicago for the Democratic National Convention, Lehman confided to a few people that he was leaning against running again. However, by the last day of the meeting, rumors started spreading that Lehman had decided to seek another term, perhaps reflecting an attempt to change his mind by those he had informed of his probable decision. The Senator met with the press on August 17 to deny such reports. When asked whether the crisis in the Middle East, where Egyptian leader Gamal Nasser had seized the Suez Canal, would influence his decision whether to stay in the Senate, Lehman emphasized that although he was "deeply interested in the Middle East, . . . in civil rights, in housing, and in a great many other things," his decision whether to run again would "be based entirely on personal considerations." Asked what some of those personal considerations might be, Lehman refused to elaborate, although he noted that Mrs. Lehman and other family members wanted him to retire, believing that "they are entitled to more of my time than I have been able to give them in a great many years." Lehman gave no other hints as to which way he was leaning, promising only that he would make his final decision before the Democratic State Convention convened on September 10.[39]

On August 21, 1956, Herbert Lehman formally announced that he would not be a candidate for re-election. With his wife Edith at his side, Lehman recalled that "public service" had been his "life for nearly thirty years," and despite some "frustrations and disappointments," he had "found it a deeply rewarding experience," and he hoped that he had made "some contribution" to his state "and to the nation." Lehman explained that his work as Lieutenant Governor, Governor, Director General of UNRRA, and Senator had afforded him "unbounded satisfaction" despite "the inevitable personal sacrifices." He noted, however, that "the family of a man in public life makes the greatest sacrifice," and his was "no exception." Lehman emphasized that his wife and children had "always stood wholeheartedly" behind him, and "had it not been for their unfailing support and encouragement," he would "have hesitated to continue so long in the field of work" he loved. Lehman also acknowledged his "loyal and devoted staff, whose untiring labors" had facilitated his efforts. However, "after serious and soul-searching consideration, and with a very heavy heart," and "after much inner conflict and with a deep sense of sadness," he had decided not to seek another term in the Senate. He wished that his term was not expiring, because his health was fine and his vigor and strength had not greatly diminished over the years, and he would have relished remaining in the Senate for a few more years. But having run for office nine times, Lehman knew "full well the stress and the strains of a state-wide campaign," the "weeks of strenuous schedules, long hours, trying decisions, with inevitable strain on one's physical resources." Lehman promised that even after his Senate term ended, his "voice in behalf of men of courage fighting for high principles, for equal justice and dignity for all, and for a world at peace, will never be silenced." He would continue to battle for the issues and the causes he believed in. He also pledged to take an active role in the campaign to elect Adlai Stevenson because he believed that Stevenson, if elected, "will make a very great President of the United States." He had made his decision, Lehman noted, despite pleas from Stevenson and Governor Harriman that he run again, and he recommended that Democrats nominate Mayor Wagner to succeed him in the Senate.[40]

Tammany chief Carmine De Sapio, Liberal Party strategist Alex Rose, and labor leaders David Dubinsky of the ILGWU and Jacob Potofsky of the Amalgamated Clothing Workers all tried to change Lehman's mind. Similarly, the editors of the *New York Post* refused to accept Lehman's decision "without striving to communicate to him our hope that he may yet be persuaded to make this one final fight." They wanted to make sure that Lehman did not "underestimate the intensity and depth of popular feeling about his place in our political life." The *Post* argued that Lehman was "a symbol of courage and conscience in public affairs," and asserted that "his re-election would be one of the great and meaningful moral victories of an age so often marked by flabby complacency and cynicism in high places." The Senator appreciated all this support, but he made it clear that his decision was "irrevocable." After meeting with Lehman, Alex Rose lamented, "We are reluctantly reconciled to the inevitable"—"the Senator's decision must be accepted as final."[41]

As usual, Edith Lehman played a key role in her husband's decision. She was always his closest advisor, and he had tremendous respect for her political acumen. Mrs. Lehman confided to her brother Frank Altschul that both she and her husband felt "sad and glad," but she was "relieved that the decision has finally been made." In interviews conducted in 1957, Hubert Humphrey emphasized that Edith Lehman was concerned about her husband's health, "justly concerned that he was overdoing," and Brooklyn Congressman Emanuel Celler agreed that "Mrs. Lehman's influence was largely the determining factor" in the Senator's decision not to run again. Publicly, however, Mrs. Lehman minimized her role, saying merely that she was "very satisfied" with the Senator's decision and "glad that he is going to have more time for his family and personal activities." She was gratified that her husband was leaving office "with the affection he has," but she also confessed to feeling some "sadness" that "some ties are being broken."[42]

Herbert Lehman's growing frustration in the Senate and his demeaning treatment by Lyndon Johnson also factored into his decision to retire. Lehman felt trapped forever on the Banking Committee and the Labor Committee, and although their portfolios were important, Lehman longed for a seat on the Foreign Relations or Judiciary Committees, which he knew would never be forthcoming as long as Johnson controlled the committee assignments. Lehman had also been disappointed that, at Johnson's behest, Hubert Humphrey and other presumed liberals had deserted him in the fight to change the filibuster rule and the effort to bring meaningful civil rights legislation to the floor of the Senate. Lehman could never accept Johnson's blocking of civil rights legislation nor his belief that the best way to deal with issues like immigration reform was "to begin nibbling at it." As Lehman looked into the future, neither the prospect of a Senate continuing under the grip of Lyndon Johnson nor one where the Republicans held sway promised much success for the principles and programs in which he believed. Lehman thought that leaving the Senate and freeing himself from the yoke and tether of Johnson and the Southern Democrats might even give him more freedom to speak out on important issues. As he explained to his old friend and former FDR speechwriter Samuel Rosenman, he planned to "continue to fight outside the Halls of Congress for those causes and issues" that had been "so dear" to his heart over the years, and he hoped that his "voice as a private citizen without any political axe to grind may still be effective."[43]

Although Julius Edelstein later recalled that Lehman came to regret his decision to retire, the Senator was content with it, at least at first. On the day of the announcement, he confided to longtime aide Carolin Flexner that he was "relieved that [the] decision has been made," but he had very mixed emotions, both "sad and happy." In numerous letters over the next few weeks to colleagues such as Wayne Morse and Paul Douglas, and old friends like Arthur Corscadden, Lehman explained that he had reached his decision not to run again only after he and Edith "had given long and prayerful consideration" to his retirement. He was confident he had made the right decision, although he knew "full well" that he would miss the work, his friends in Washington, and "the great privilege" he had enjoyed of "serving the people . . . for so long." Even though he would "no longer have a public forum in the Senate," he vowed to make his "voice heard on those issues" for which he had fought for so many years. He expected to play an active role in the Stevenson campaign and the New York Senate race, and he was considering "having a biography written" if he could "find the right man to do so."[44]

Tributes poured in after Herbert Lehman announced that he was not seeking re-election to the Senate. The *New York Times* cited "his leadership in humanizing the immigration laws, in reducing the barriers of discrimination, in championing civil liberties, in promoting public housing and slum clearance" and noted that "it is not without reason that in these and other matters he has been called the 'conscience of the Senate.'" The *Washington Post and Times-Herald* described him as "a front-line, never-lagging fighter for the rights of minorities and for the eradication from American life of all discrimination based upon race, religion, or ancestry" and agreed that Lehman "has been justly characterized as 'the Senate's conscience.'" Adlai Stevenson was "proud that this fine American" was his friend, and Estes Kefauver remembered how Lehman had "always fought conscientiously for progressive, liberal causes even when the going was rough." Eleanor Roosevelt hated "to see the conscience of the Senate leave that chamber," and she hoped Lehman would "continue to give us the benefit of his wisdom and leadership as a citizen during the years to come." Samuel Rosenman, who had been with Lehman during his first run for office in 1928, told him that "nobody can look with equanimity upon your leaving the Senate," emphasizing that "yours has been at times the only voice raised in defense of human rights and human decency when they are attacked by McCarthyism and similar sinister influences." Former Senator Frank Graham from North Carolina, with whom Lehman had served briefly in 1950, called Lehman's decision "a national calamity," describing him as a "fighting champion of labor and humane causes for working people, farmers, little business people, minority groups, disinherited people and all sorts of people, big and little, known and unknown, in America and in the world." Asserting that "the country will suffer a real loss as a result of your decision," North Dakota Republican Senator William Langer joked that the real reason for Lehman's retirement was that the Senate had "raised the retirement so that you can live on the $2500 or so that you will receive from the government!" Lehman confessed that "the very generous editorials and other comments" touched him "very deeply," and even though he was "not deserving of even a small part of the fine things that have been said," he was "human enough to have greatly enjoyed reading them."[45]

V

Even though Lehman had cited the physical demands of a statewide campaign as the main reason for not seeking re-election, columnist Marquis Childs noted in late October 1956 that Lehman was "working like a Trojan for the Democratic cause," and Democratic vice presidential candidate Estes Kefauver later observed that Lehman campaigned "harder for the election of the national ticket than he would have worked for himself." New York Republican State Chairman L. Judson Morhouse was confident that Lehman's retirement would result in the election of a "Republican Senator to give full support to President Eisenhower's policies and programs," and Lehman agreed with Democratic leaders that the best way to remedy the potential weakness of the Democratic ticket without Lehman was to nominate Robert F. Wagner, Jr., to run for his father's old Senate seat. Wagner already enjoyed high name recognition with the voters, and he had proven himself a strong candidate in winning the New York City mayoral election in 1953. Lehman joined forces with Carmine De Sapio and others to persuade Wagner to make the race, boosting Wagner's candidacy at the New York State CIO convention, inviting the Mayor to a private meeting at the Senator's home, and formally nominating and hailing Wagner as "my political heir" at the State Democratic Convention. The Senator spoke at numerous campaign events across the city and state on behalf of the Democratic ticket and made generous financial contributions to the Stevenson and Wagner campaigns. Anna Rosenberg, co-chair of the Stevenson campaign in New York, found it "rather amusing" that Lehman had refused to run "because he could not go through another strenuous campaign," but he "campaigned just as strenuously for Stevenson as he did for himself." Lehman agreed that he had "worked as hard" as he "ever did as a candidate," but despite Lehman's efforts, Stevenson again lost to an Eisenhower landslide, and Republican Jacob Javits defeated Wagner and captured Lehman's Senate seat.[46]

Lyndon Johnson had chimed in with fulsome praise upon hearing the news of Lehman's retirement. Lehman's departure, Johnson declared, would leave his fellow Senators "with a sense of loss, but also with a prayerful hope" that Lehman would "now have the well-deserved rest" he had earned by his "illustrious career." Lehman's name, Johnson proclaimed, was "the symbol of integrity and conscience and as long as such values are cherished by Americans," Lehman would be "an effective force on the national scene." Responding in kind, Lehman told Johnson how much he appreciated Johnson's "generous comments" and how much their friendship had meant to him. Lehman considered it "a great privilege" to have served with Johnson, and although the two men had "not always seen eye to eye" on everything, Lehman assured Johnson of his "great admiration and affection." Lehman hoped that their "friendship will not diminish in the coming years," and that he would "still have an opportunity of working with" Johnson to achieve some of their common objectives.[47]

Once the pleasantries were out of the way, Lehman revealed what he really thought of Johnson and his leadership in January 1957, in a speech to the Lexington Democratic Club in Manhattan. Lehman asserted that the 1956 presidential election was lost when "the Democrats in Congress failed to make the issues" after they won majorities in both the House and the Senate in the

1954 elections. Instead, Lehman charged, "almost everything the leadership did during that time was designed to prevent any controversial issue from being seriously joined or vigorously debated." He acknowledged that "the Democratic-controlled Eighty-fourth Congress did pass some fairly good legislation in fields like Social Security and health research," but he noted that "this legislation was passed by maneuver rather than by debate." Without mentioning any names, Lehman noted, "We were constantly urged by the leadership to speak briefly and softly lest we wake sleeping dogs." As a result, he charged, "on the two main issues of our times—civil rights and foreign policy—there was a virtual blackout. The civil rights issue was buried alive." After the Democrats won control of Congress in 1954, he recalled, "the Democratic watchwords of the day, in January 1955, were 'party unity' and 'don't rock the boat.'" And "since civil rights legislation obviously disturbed party unity and rocked the boat, it was kept out of sight to the fullest extent possible." Lehman remembered that "even most of our liberal friends in Congress went along with this 'line,'" that he "was practically alone in pressing for action on an anti-filibuster rule at the opening of the Eighty-fourth Congress," that "there were only two of us to oppose the election of Senator Eastland to the chairmanship of the Senate Judiciary Committee," and that "there were only a baker's half-dozen who fought unsuccessfully to salvage some civil rights legislation out of the chaos of the closing days of that Congress."[48]

Calling for liberal leadership of the Democratic Party, Lehman argued that for Democrats to succeed in the future, they "must put principle above party unity," ensure that "the majority philosophy in the party must prevail," and guarantee that "the liberal philosophy of our party must be reflected in the programs the party advocates." Specifically, Lehman stressed that Democrats "must never again turn a deaf ear to the pleas for a strong civil rights platform . . . just to keep the Southerners satisfied," emphasizing that "on the issue of civil rights, human rights, and human decency, it is no longer possible for the Democratic Party to temporize or compromise." And, in a direct rebuke to Lyndon Johnson and House Speaker Sam Rayburn, Lehman complained that Democrats had not been served wisely or well by the insistence of "the Democratic leaders in the House and Senate" that "they are the ones who speak for the party." Lehman recommended instead that an annual party convention be convened "to define party policy by drawing up a platform or a set of principles, just as the present national conventions do."[49]

Lehman continued his attack on Johnson's leadership in a speech to the National Democratic Club in March 1958. Naming names this time, he charged that Johnson and Rayburn, listening "to the voters of Texas rather than to the voters of the nation as a whole," had failed to define the issues on which the Democrats could have won the 1956 presidential election. Lehman emphasized that the times are too serious and crucial and the issues of the day too momentous to permit the leadership of the party out of power to rest exclusively in the hands of individuals who happen to be the party leaders in Congress, no matter how able and far-sighted they may be as individuals, and no matter how well they may represent their own states or congressional districts.[50]

Despite his frustration with Johnson's leadership, the seniority system, the filibuster rule, and other customs of the Senate, Herbert Lehman believed that he had played an important role in the Senate. As Julius Edelstein explained to Carey McWilliams of *The Nation*, Lehman had become "the spokesman and Senate bellwether of liberals throughout the nation." His voice, according to Edelstein, was "regarded as the unadulterated voice of liberalism in the Senate and is listened to respectfully not only by Senate liberals, but by conservatives as well, even though they may not agree with him." Edelstein argued that even though Lehman's name may not be "attached to any major law or program now on the statute books," he "had a powerful impact on all kinds of legislation, representing always the viewpoint of labor, minorities, the underprivileged, and the otherwise voiceless," because "on most legislation of social import, Senator Lehman establishes the upper asking price from which the ultimate compromise figure is ultimately reached." Lehman agreed that his contribution should not be measured by the number of bills that carried his name. He thought that "the greatest service" he "could render on issues (even on apparently forlorn hopes) was to arouse the consciousness of people"—both Senators and the public—"to fight against injustices and evil." Lehman believed that he had accomplished this goal in his "continuous fight against mccarthyism [*sic*], against the unfair and unreasonable security investigations, against the unfair immigration laws, against the giveaway program of turning over our public resources for private exploitation, and many others." Lehman emphasized that without his early and constant opposition to McCarthyism, "the public consciousness would not have been aroused," and he also thought that his opposition to the Formosa Resolution and possible American involvement in Quemoy and Matsu had helped avert "an all-out war."[51]

Lehman and Edelstein overestimated Lehman's importance in the Senate. Although Lehman played a significant role as one of the first Senators to stand up to McCarthy, it was only when the Senate establishment and the Eisenhower administration decided that the Senator from Wisconsin had become an embarrassment and a liability that the Senate took action against him. And despite Lehman's efforts, the Internal Security Act of 1950 and the McCarran-Walter Immigration Act were adopted and remained on the statute books, and civil rights legislation still could not reach the floor of the Senate. Standing up for his principles and refusing to compromise with his conscience, Lehman became a liberal icon during his years in the Senate, the leader of a small band of liberals who spoke out loudly and clearly on civil rights, immigration reform, and other issues. However, other than making a public record of his views, Lehman's accomplishments were limited in a Senate dominated by Lyndon Johnson. Contrary to Edelstein's account, Johnson, Pat McCarran, and other lawmakers sometimes left the Senate chamber when Lehman began to speak, ignoring him rather than listening to him and engaging in respectful debate. But Lehman did manage to keep civil rights, immigration reform, and other long-cherished liberal goals in the forefront of the nation's consciousness in the 1950s, laying the groundwork for their later enactment into law in 1964 and 1965 as part of President Lyndon Johnson's Great Society—the same Lyndon Johnson who had repeatedly blocked Herbert Lehman's efforts on these matters in the Senate from 1950 to 1956.[52]

CHAPTER 18

"A Little Less Profile and a Little More Courage"

Herbert Lehman and John Kennedy, 1950–1959

[Herbert Lehman's] clear and courageous voice has been a force for reason in our public life for three decades. His enduring vitality, undiminished concern for human needs, and broad vision, are as evident today as they were during his years in the Senate and in other public positions.[1]

When seventy-one-year-old Herbert Lehman took his seat in the Senate in January 1950, thirty-two-year-old John Kennedy was already in the middle of his second term in the House of Representatives, and the contrasts between the two men extended beyond the difference in their ages. Kennedy, tall and lean, possessed tremendous charisma, almost like a movie star, and his youth and good looks attracted women voters in particular. Lehman, short and bald, lacked Kennedy's physical attributes, but he made up in sincerity and earnestness what he was missing in magnetism and star appeal. Lehman's Judaism helped him with New York voters, enabling him to reach the U.S. Senate, the pinnacle of his political ambitions, but while Kennedy's Catholicism contributed to his political appeal in Massachusetts, it posed a seemingly insurmountable obstacle to the national ambitions he harbored. Lehman was very conscientious in performing his Senate duties, participating in more than 99 percent of the roll call votes in 1950, while Kennedy was often absent from the House. Lehman embraced his role as a liberal icon, passionate in his devotion to civil rights, civil liberties, and other liberal causes, while Kennedy

---

Chapter title quotation: Eleanor Roosevelt on John Kennedy, quoted in Mike Wallace, *Between You and Me*, p. 42.

minimized his commitment to liberal principles, explaining that he represented "the poorest district in Massachusetts" and the needs of his constituents forced him "to take the liberal line." Kennedy told a reporter for the *Saturday Evening Post* that when people complained that he was not a "true liberal," he wanted "to tell them I'm not a liberal at all."[2]

I

In contrast to Herbert Lehman, who came to public service later in life out of a desire to improve economic and social conditions in the United States in the 1920s, John Kennedy decided in 1946, while still in his late twenties, that a seat in Congress would allow him to pursue his interest in foreign affairs. Capitalizing on his youth, his war record, and his father's wealth and determination to see one of his sons achieve high political office, Kennedy easily defeated ten rivals for the Democratic nomination in Massachusetts's 11th Congressional District and then cruised to victory in the general election. As a member of the House of Representatives, Kennedy compiled a liberal record reflecting the economic interests of his mostly working-class, Irish and Italian American district, pushing for improvements in housing, wages, and Social Security, and opposing the anti-union Taft-Hartley Act.[3]

Lehman and Kennedy both supported the Marshall Plan and American aid to rebuild Western Europe in the late 1940s, but they differed sharply on Far Eastern policy. In January 1949, after Mao Tse-tung and the Chinese Communists defeated Chiang Kai-shek's Chinese Nationalists, Kennedy charged in a series of speeches that "the vital interest of the United States in the independent integrity of China was sacrificed" at Yalta by "a sick Roosevelt, with the advice of General Marshall and other Chiefs of Staff." Kennedy accused the Truman administration of sending aid that "was too little and too late" and asserted that American diplomats and China experts, including Owen Lattimore, had been "so concerned . . . with the imperfection of the democratic system in China after twenty years of war and the tales of corruption in high places that they lost sight of our tremendous stake in a non-Communist China." After recounting "the tragic story of China, whose freedom we once fought to preserve," Kennedy claimed that "what our young men had saved, our diplomats and our President have frittered away." Herbert Lehman, on the other hand, believed that Chiang Kai-shek was responsible for his own downfall, and he devoted one of his first speeches in the Senate in 1950 to defending the Truman administration's Far Eastern policies.[4]

Kennedy and Lehman also disagreed about how to deal with Senator Joe McCarthy and the threat of Communist subversion within the United States. As previously discussed, Herbert Lehman was one of the first Senators to challenge McCarthy's wild charges and accusations, and he was one of the few members of Congress to oppose the Internal Security Act in 1950. As a member of the House of Representatives, Kennedy did not have to deal directly with McCarthy at this time, but he did tell a seminar of Harvard students and faculty in November 1950 that he "knew Joe pretty well, and he may have something." Like most members of Congress, Kennedy voted for the Internal Security Act, explaining to the group at Harvard that the country needed to do more about the problem of Communists in the United States.[5]

Herbert Lehman consistently compiled a more liberal record in Congress than John Kennedy. Americans for Democratic Action gave Lehman a perfect score for his votes in 1950, 1951, and 1952, while Kennedy went against the ADA position by supporting the McCarran Internal Security Act in 1950 and voting for cuts in foreign aid to America's allies in 1951. Unlike Lehman, who was present for all but one of the roll calls tabulated by ADA, Kennedy missed numerous votes each year, especially in 1952 when he was busy campaigning in Massachusetts for the Senate. Like many Massachusetts politicians in the 1950s, Kennedy tried to distance himself from ADA, realizing that the liberal organization served as a convenient whipping boy for conservatives.[6]

Although Lehman and Kennedy differed on the Internal Security Act in 1950, they agreed in 1952 that the McCarran-Walter Immigration bill moved America's immigration policies in the wrong direction. As the House considered the bill in April 1952, Kennedy objected that the measure "restricts rather than liberalizes our immigration system" because it still "bases its quota allotments on 1920 census data," continues to discriminate against potential immigrants from Southern and Eastern Europe, and severely limits immigration from the Caribbean. Kennedy hoped that the House would recommit the bill to the Judiciary Committee and adopt instead something along the lines of what Herbert Lehman had proposed in the Senate. Lehman congratulated Kennedy on his exposition of "the dangers inherent in the Walter-McCarran Bill," and he welcomed the Congressman's "support of a liberal approach to our immigration problems." But despite Kennedy's and Lehman's objections, Congress adopted the restrictive McCarran-Walter Immigration and Naturalization Act into law in June 1952.[7]

John Kennedy set his sights on winning a seat in the Senate in 1952, and the Kennedy campaign sought to curry favor among Jewish voters in what figured to be a very close contest against incumbent Republican Senator Henry Cabot Lodge, Jr. Jewish voters had reservations about Kennedy because of the reputed anti-Semitism of his father, Joseph Kennedy, and the senior Kennedy's support of Senator McCarthy. In addition, Jewish voters worried about the Congressman's introduction of an amendment to the Foreign Aid bill in 1951 that would have cut $35,000,000 intended for countries in the Middle East, including Israel, and his apparent indifference to civil liberties as reflected in his vote for the McCarran Internal Security Act and his refusal to criticize Senator McCarthy. To counter such concerns, Kennedy spoke before numerous Jewish groups and emphasized his strong support for Israel, and he made sure to highlight his opposition to the McCarran-Walter Act, which Rabbi Judah Nadich of the Jewish Community of Greater Boston had denounced as a "codification of xenophobia" and "a national disgrace." When Kennedy's aides asked Senator Lehman's office for "some material on immigration," Julius Edelstein gladly forwarded copies of Lehman's speeches on the issue and some additional information, although he wondered "just what use Congressman Kennedy is making of this and how much impact it is having."[8]

Edelstein soon got his answer when Kennedy delivered a major speech in Cambridge focusing on the McCarran-Walter Act. At a time when Lodge was trying to call attention to Kennedy's frequent absences in the House, Kennedy stressed that "three additional votes in the United States Senate would have killed the discriminatory, unfair, and un-democratic immigration bill, the McCarran-Walter Act, which is now law." Kennedy pointed out that religious leaders of all major faiths "had spoken with one voice against this law," which "had been described 'as worse than the infamous Alien Act of 1798,'" but according to Kennedy, while Herbert Lehman and others had fought to sustain the President's veto of this bill, "Mr. Lodge was absent."[9]

Realizing that they needed to do more than just exploit Lodge's absence from the final vote on the McCarran-Walter Act if they hoped to carry the Jewish vote, Kennedy and his advisors sought to associate the Congressman with Jewish members of Congress, including, of course, Herbert Lehman. To "counterbalance" Lodge's history of support for Israel and Jewish causes, Kennedy's staff suggested, among other steps, securing "endorsements by fellow members of Congress who are Jews," including possibly "pix of Lehman and Kennedy or at least a statement to run with pix of Lehman." The Kennedy camp drafted letters endorsing Kennedy to be signed by Jewish Congressmen Abraham Ribicoff of Connecticut, Adolf Sabath of Illinois, Sidney Fine of New York, and others, but rather than asking Lehman for an explicit endorsement, the Kennedy campaign utilized Lehman's April letter praising Kennedy's opposition to the McCarran-Walter bill. Lehman's letter was featured prominently in a series of ads praising Kennedy as a "CHAMPION OF HUMAN RIGHTS" that ran in the Jewish press all across Massachusetts, including both English- and Yiddish-language papers. Kennedy's pursuit of Jewish voters paid off handsomely in November when he captured 60 percent of the vote in Jewish neighborhoods, a huge increase over the 33 percent won by Lodge's opponent in 1946.[10]

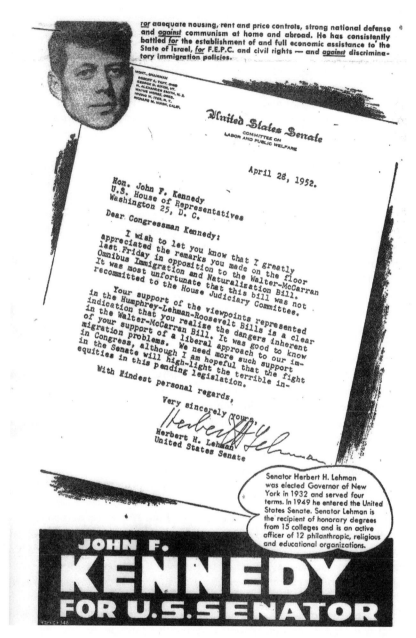

FIGURE 18.1. Herbert Lehman letter used in an advertisement for Senate candidate John F. Kennedy, October 23, 1952. Courtesy of *The Jewish Advocate*.

II

Kennedy's election to the Senate provided Lehman and liberal Democrats with another vote on most issues. Even before Kennedy was officially sworn in as a Senator, he participated in the January 2, 1953, meeting in Lehman's office in which Lehman and his allies plotted their strategy for amending the Senate's filibuster rule. Kennedy co-sponsored the motion affirming the new Senate's right to determine its own rules, and even though he took no part in the debate on the floor, he voted with Lehman and the others in their unsuccessful effort to make it easier for the Senate to cut off debate on contentious matters such as civil rights legislation.[11]

Lehman and Kennedy saw their roles as Senators very differently, as illustrated by their actions during the debate over the Bricker Amendment in 1953–1954. Both men joined with other liberal Democrats to help the Eisenhower administration beat back the Bicker Amendment and the various substitutes intended to limit the effects of treaties and executive agreements within the United States. But Lehman believed that his responsibility as a Senator included educating and arousing both his colleagues and the American people "against injustices and evil," and he spoke out eight times during the month-long debate on the Bricker Amendment, which he described as "one of the most dangerous proposals ever made in the Senate." Kennedy took a more limited view of his duties as a Senator, however, and he played only a minor role in the Senate's consideration of the measure. He inserted a press release into the *Congressional Record* explaining why he opposed "any constitutional amendment containing restrictions on our treatymaking power" or any proposal that would "unduly restrict the President's authority in world affairs," but he only spoke once during the floor debate on the measure. Despite the difference in their level of activism on the issue, Kennedy and Lehman both voted against Senator George's substitute proposal, which fell one vote short of the two-thirds majority required to approve the amendment and send it on to the House of Representatives.[12]

In January 1954, John Kennedy served as one of the sponsors when Herbert Lehman addressed the Massachusetts chapter of Americans for Democratic Action at its annual Roosevelt Day dinner. Lehman publicly acknowledged Kennedy's presence at the dinner, characterizing his colleague as "a courageous, patriotic Senator" as exemplified by his recent vote for the St. Lawrence Seaway, which most people in Massachusetts saw as a threat to the port of Boston. In contrast to Kennedy, who, as usual, sought to distance himself from ADA, Lehman defended the organization as a positive force in American politics. When a constituent objected to Kennedy's involvement with the dinner, Kennedy quickly explained that he was not a sponsor of ADA, but only of the dinner honoring Franklin Roosevelt and featuring Herbert Lehman.[13]

The issue that dominated the Senate in the early 1950s and most clearly illustrated the differences between Herbert Lehman and John Kennedy was Senator Joe McCarthy. While Lehman was one of the first Senators to stand up to McCarthy, Kennedy showed none of Lehman's moral outrage at McCarthy and his methods. When questioned about McCarthy at the Harvard seminar in 1950, Kennedy responded with what one of the students present later described as "nonchalance and minimal concern." Worried about Massachusetts's 750,000 Irish Catholics, who were among McCarthy's strongest supporters, Kennedy mostly avoided any direct mention of McCarthy during the 1952 Senate election while brandishing his own anti-Communist credentials. When one of his advisors suggested that Kennedy approve a newspaper ad attacking both Communism and Senator McCarthy, Kennedy's father vetoed the idea, and when Adlai Stevenson campaigned with Kennedy in Massachusetts in 1952, he followed the recommendation of Kennedy aide and future Kennedy brother-in-law Sargent Shriver that he emphasize Kennedy's role in exposing Communists.[14]

In 1953 and the first half of 1954, McCarthy used his power as chairman of the Senate Committee on Government Operations and its Permanent Subcommittee on Investigations to look for Communists in the State Department's Voice of America and Overseas Information Libraries, and in the U.S. Army. While Herbert Lehman continued to speak out loudly and clearly against McCarthyism, Kennedy, as biographer James MacGregor Burns later wrote, "straddled the fence" on the issue, muting any concern that McCarthy was abusing witnesses hauled before the committee. When Lehman, Wayne Morse, Estes Kefauver, and Paul Douglas asked Kennedy to join them in 1954 in sponsoring a measure to curb some of McCarthy's excesses by imposing a "Code of Fair Procedure" on congressional committees, Kennedy declined, later explaining, "I had never known the sort of people who were called before the McCarthy committee. . . . I did not identify with them, and so I didn't get as worked up as other liberals did."[15]

During the summer of 1954, as the Senate finally began to move against Senator McCarthy, Herbert Lehman remained in the forefront of McCarthy's critics while John Kennedy, like many of his colleagues, stayed silent. When Senator Flanders introduced his resolution to censure McCarthy for conduct unbecoming a Senator, Lehman immediately pledged his full support for Flanders's efforts, while Kennedy remained quiet. Columnist Drew Pearson listed Kennedy among the Senators who were "either planning to vote for McCarthy or are leaning toward him," while the anti-McCarthy National Committee for an Effective Congress considered Kennedy "non-committal." Lehman hosted a meeting of liberal Senators, many of whom, including Kennedy, had not yet tipped their hands, and according to Kennedy aide and biographer Theodore Sorensen, Kennedy and the others agreed at this meeting to support McCarthy's censure if a bill of particulars were drawn up specifying the actions for which

McCarthy was to be admonished. Sorensen even prepared a speech for Kennedy supporting the censure resolution on the narrow grounds that McCarthy had not properly controlled committee staffers Roy Cohn and G. David Schine. But much to Kennedy's relief, he never had to deliver the speech because the Senate, instead of voting immediately on the censure resolution, sent the matter to a special committee. In contrast to Lehman, who asserted that there was more than enough information to act on the censure resolution, Kennedy followed the lead of Democratic leader Lyndon Johnson and Arkansas Democrat John McClellan, voting with most of the Senate to send the matter to the committee. While Lehman, Flanders, and a few others who had been the most vocal supporters of censure resisted the referral of the resolution to the special committee, fearing that it would never again see the light of day, Kennedy assured the press that the delay was only temporary, that the subject would return to the Senate floor where everyone would "have a chance to vote on this matter."[16]

As Kennedy had predicted, the Watkins committee reported back to the full Senate a few months later, recommending that McCarthy's actions be condemned as injurious to the Senate. But while Herbert Lehman and the rest of the Senate were debating the fate of Senator McCarthy, John Kennedy was in a hospital in New York, recuperating from back surgery that nearly proved fatal when infection and complications set in. Kennedy could have instructed aide Theodore Sorensen to arrange a pair for him on the vote, as fellow Democrats Albert Gore and George Smathers did, to show how he would have voted had he been present, but Kennedy made no such request. Kennedy and Sorensen later explained that they did not believe Kennedy should vote because he had been too ill to follow the full debate, comparing his situation to that of a juror who should not render a verdict without hearing all the evidence. This argument is not persuasive, however, because Kennedy had been prepared to vote for censure back in August, and if anything, McCarthy's contemptuous behavior toward the Watkins committee had strengthened the case against him. More revealing is Kennedy's comment when a reporter asked in 1956 why the Senator had not spoken out publicly against McCarthy. Noting McCarthy's great popularity among Massachusetts's Irish Catholic voters, Kennedy asked, "What was I supposed to do—commit hari-kari?" There is no evidence that Kennedy planned his back surgery to coincide with the debate on McCarthy; he scheduled the procedure while the Senate was in recess, and had things gone smoothly, he would have been back in Washington in time for the censure vote. However, his absence and his failure to issue any statement on the matter at the time left him as the only Democrat not recorded in favor of McCarthy's censure, a status that would haunt him, especially with Democratic liberals like Herbert Lehman and Eleanor Roosevelt, for the next six years.[17]

Kennedy used much of the time while he was recuperating from his back surgery to write, with considerable assistance from aide Theodore Sorensen and others, the Pulitzer Prize–winning *Profiles in Courage*, an account of how eight Senators ranging from John Quincy Adams to Robert Taft had risked their political futures by voting their consciences or taking unpopular stands. The contrast between the courageous acts described in the book and Kennedy's failure to condemn Joe McCarthy led Eleanor Roosevelt and others to quip in subsequent years that Kennedy needed to "show a little less profile and a little more courage." Kennedy sent inscribed copies of the book to his Senate colleagues, writing in Herbert Lehman's copy: "Senator Lehman, a Senator of courage and integrity." Thanking Kennedy for the book "and particularly for your very friendly inscription," Lehman looked "forward to reading it at the first opportunity," confident that he would "greatly enjoy it."[18]

Lehman's enjoyment was probably short-lived, however. In the book, Kennedy praised Senator Taft's courage in complaining that Nazi leaders convicted at Nuremberg in 1946 were prosecuted under ex post facto laws. Kennedy also noted that "the Democratic nominee for United States Senator in New York" that year, reflecting common opinion, had "expressed his deep shock at the Taft statement and his certainty that it would be repudiated by 'right-thinking and fair minded Americans.'" Kennedy did not name that Democratic nominee for the Senate in New York in 1946, but knowledgeable people knew, and the book's index made it clear, that Kennedy was talking about Herbert Lehman. Obviously, Kennedy could not include in the book every Senator who had jeopardized his career by standing on principle, and there was no reason to expect that he would have cited Lehman's courage when he was the only Senator running for re-election who had voted against the Internal Security Act of 1950. However, Lehman could not have been pleased that rather than being listed among those who had demonstrated great political courage, he was included among those taking the popular rather than the principled position on the Nuremberg trials.[19]

Like Kennedy, Lehman believed that courage was "one of the greatest of political virtues." In December 1956, as Lehman's tenure in the Senate was coming to an end, Clayton Knowles of the *New York Times* asked him to name some of the great men he had known in his many years of public service. Lehman noted that courage was a requisite for greatness, and he praised Franklin Roosevelt as "a man of great vision and courage who saw the need of fighting with all his strength to gird this country against the rising tide of dictatorship." Lehman also commended Theodore Roosevelt for having had "the courage to stop raids on the nation's resources," Harry Truman for having "the courage of his convictions on domestic and world issues" and being "particularly great in his vetoes," and Woodrow Wilson for his "courageous pioneering in the area of international cooperation and government responsible to the people." Knowles pointed out that Lehman's admiration for such men had not resulted in his following them blindly, recalling specifically Lehman's opposition to FDR's court-packing bill in 1937. He also noted Lehman's courage in agreeing to run against Thomas Dewey for Governor in 1938 and challenging Senators McCarthy and McCarran during his first year in the Senate.[20]

III

Herbert Lehman continued to take more liberal positions and play a more active role in the Senate than John Kennedy in 1955–1956. ADA gave Lehman perfect ratings in both years, while Kennedy went against the ADA position in 1955 when he supported higher tariffs and the nomination of former investment banker Harold Patterson to a seat on the Securities and Exchange Commission, and in 1956 when he voted for the Eisenhower administration's flexible farm parity program and against a constitutional amendment for the direct election of the President. While Lehman co-sponsored Hubert Humphrey's full package of civil rights legislation, Kennedy only signed on to Humphrey's bill to prohibit discrimination in employment. Kennedy did co-sponsor Lehman's proposal to protect African American members of the military by making it a federal crime to attack uniformed members of the armed forces who were on active duty, but in contrast to Lehman, who advocated for these bills and tried to testify on them before the Judiciary Committee before finally submitting a written statement, Kennedy remained silent. When Lehman and Paul Douglas tried to force action on civil rights at the end of the 84th Congress, they received no help from Kennedy, who did not want to alienate the South on the eve of the Democratic National Convention at which he hoped to be nominated for the vice presidency.[21]

One area where Lehman and Kennedy did work together was in their efforts to revise the McCarran-Walter Immigration Act that had been passed over their objections in 1952. In 1953 and again in 1955, Kennedy co-sponsored Lehman's bills to remove what Lehman denounced as the "racial and national bias" that characterized the nation's immigration laws. When a Senate Judiciary Subcommittee finally held hearings in June 1955 on Lehman's proposals, Lehman was the leadoff witness and Kennedy submitted a letter supporting the changes that Lehman advocated. In November 1955, when another subcommittee held further hearings on the matter, Lehman again testified in person, and Kennedy again sent a written statement urging the committee to adopt the comprehensive immigration bill that he and Lehman and other Senators had introduced. With Lyndon Johnson's help, Lehman's and Kennedy's efforts finally bore fruit in the last days of the 84th Congress when the Senate passed a measure redistributing some of the unused immigration quota slots from countries in Northern and Western Europe to Southern and Eastern European nations. However, the bill died in the House of Representatives when Congressman Walter's objections prevented it from coming to a vote.[22]

The cooperation between Lehman and Kennedy to secure enactment of a federal flood insurance program in 1955–1956 also strengthened the personal ties between the two men. Lehman had never forgotten the extensive flood damage he had seen in New York's Southern Tier while Governor in the 1930s, and the torrential rains associated with Hurricane Diane in August 1955 and the resulting floods that devastated much of New England sounded the alarm for Kennedy. In the aftermath of Diane, the Eisenhower administration offered federal disaster loans and encouraged people to contribute generously to the Red Cross, but Lehman and Kennedy believed that the federal government should enable people to purchase insurance against the loss of their homes, businesses, and personal property in such calamities. Lehman promised that when Congress reconvened in January, he would introduce a bill creating a program under which people could purchase insurance against both natural disasters like floods and man-made calamities such as atomic warfare. When Kennedy and Leverett Saltonstall, his Republican colleague from Massachusetts, circulated a proposal to establish a narrower program that would provide only flood insurance, Lehman assistant Julius Edelstein suggested that Lehman and Kennedy work together on this issue.[23]

The Senate Banking and Currency Committee exercised jurisdiction over insurance matters, and in late September 1955, Chairman J. William Fulbright asked Senator Lehman to hold hearings on behalf of the committee on the feasibility of establishing a federal disaster insurance program. Between October 31 and December 19, Lehman conducted eight hearings in the "areas ravaged by hurricane-fed floods," including sessions in Washington, D.C.; Upstate New York; New England; and the Carolinas. At the request of Senators Kennedy and Saltonstall, Lehman scheduled one of the hearings in Boston, where he welcomed Kennedy as the leadoff witness, thanked him for his "very clear statement," and asked him to sit at the committee table when he had finished his presentation. While Lehman was in Boston for the hearing, Kennedy hosted a reception in Lehman's honor at the Harvard Club, which Lehman very much appreciated. The reception signified both the growing friendship between the two men and Kennedy's courting of party elders in advance of the 1956 Democratic National Convention.[24]

When Congress met in January 1956, prospects appeared bright for passage of flood insurance. Lyndon Johnson had included "disaster insurance to protect our people from the ravages of nature" in his "Program with a Heart," and President Eisenhower declared in his State of the Union message that "an experimental program of flood-damage indemnities should be undertaken." Kennedy and Saltonstall introduced their flood insurance bill; Senator

"Tell Us More About This"

Figure 18.2. "Tell Us More about This," November 3, 1955. A 1955 Herblock Cartoon, © The Herb Block Foundation.

Prescott Bush (R-CT) submitted the administration's proposal to create a five-year, $3,000,000,000 "experimental" flood insurance program; and Senator Lehman, on behalf of himself, Senator Kennedy, and eight other Democrats, introduced a revised proposal under which a flood insurance program would begin immediately and further study would determine whether other disasters should be included in the program in the future. Lehman went out of his way to recognize Senator Kennedy's contribution, emphasizing that his "new bill was drafted in consultation with Senator Kennedy" and consistently referring to it as the "Lehman-Kennedy bill."[25]

     Herbert Lehman demonstrated his growing skill as a legislator as he worked to win Senate approval of a flood insurance bill despite the opposition of the U.S. Chamber of Commerce, the *Wall Street Journal*, the *Los Angeles Times*, and most of the insurance industry. As chairman of the Banking Committee's

Subcommittee on Securities, to which the various flood insurance measures were referred, Lehman conducted additional hearings on the bills, and he negotiated at length with Senator Bush and other members of the subcommittee and then the full committee to win their approval of a bill the committee could report to the floor. When the committee unanimously recommended the bill to the full Senate, Senator Kennedy praised Lehman for all "the work he has done" in getting the bill this far. After adopting an amendment requiring states to pay part of the subsidies needed to make the insurance affordable, the Senate approved the flood insurance bill 61 to 7, leading Kennedy to congratulate Lehman "on the effective way" he had "handled this bill."[26]

Senate approval did not complete the legislative process, however. After the Senate passed its bill, the House Banking and Currency Committee reported a flood insurance bill to the floor in mid-July 1956, but with the end of the congressional session rapidly approaching, Lehman advised Governor Luther Hodges of North Carolina and other supporters of flood insurance to urge the House leadership of both parties and the Rules Committee to move the bill forward quickly. On July 25, the House passed its flood insurance bill by a voice vote, and a few days later, a conference committee reconciled the differences between the Senate and House measures. As Congress prepared to adjourn, the Senate and the House approved the bill on July 27, and President Eisenhower signed it into law on August 7.[27]

Herbert Lehman disliked some of the provisions of the final flood insurance bill, especially the requirement that states participate in the subsidies, but this time he settled for half a loaf, recognizing that a flawed flood insurance program was better than no program at all. As he told his colleagues, he was pleased that Congress, for the first time, had enacted "an experimental program of flood insurance that should go far toward relieving the anguish of those affected by floodwaters," one that would "accomplish a humanitarian and practical method of helping flood victims to help themselves through a program of insurance." Most observers rightly credited Lehman for the bill's enactment. New York Governor Averell Harriman applauded Lehman's leadership on this issue, noting that "nothing would have been passed had it not been" for Lehman's efforts, and Governor Hodges congratulated Lehman on "the dedicated work" he had done in connection with this "fine piece of legislation." Unfortunately, all of Lehman's efforts went for naught in 1957 when the House of Representatives, hell-bent on reducing federal spending, refused to appropriate the funds necessary to administer the flood insurance program. Not until 1968 did Congress finally create and fund the Federal Flood Insurance Program, which remains in effect today under the auspices of the Federal Emergency Management Agency (FEMA).[28]

Despite Herbert Lehman's growing respect and affection for John Kennedy, he did not think that the thirty-nine-year-old Senator from Massachusetts

was ready for a place on the national ticket in 1956. When presidential nominee Adlai Stevenson left the choice of his running mate up to the Democratic
National Convention, Lehman, like the rest of the New York delegation, supported New York City Mayor Robert Wagner, Jr., on the first ballot. But on
the second ballot, after Wagner withdrew, and with the voting expected to be
close, Tammany boss Carmine De Sapio and other party leaders cast ninety-
six and a half of New York's ninety-eight votes for Kennedy, believing that the
Democrats needed a Catholic on the ticket to have any hope of carrying New
York. Rejecting De Sapio's attempt to dictate to the delegates which candidate
to support, Lehman joined Lester Martin, a textile manufacturer from Brooklyn
who had been a strong supporter of Estes Kefauver's presidential bid, in casting their one and a half votes for Kefauver. As Lehman explained a few days
later, he believed that Kennedy was "a fine and most intelligent young man"
who "will go far," but he voted for Kefauver instead because he thought that
Kennedy was "young and more or less inexperienced."[29]

IV

Herbert Lehman was leaving the Senate at the end of 1956, but he
made it clear in a "farewell" letter to his many friends and followers, or, as
he called them, his "mailing list family," that although he was "relinquishing
public office," he was "not retiring from public affairs and will not so long
as God gives me strength." Lehman kept a small apartment and an office
in Washington, headed by his chief aide Julius Edelstein, and he assured his
supporters that he planned to "remain active in the causes" to which he had
"devoted so many years."[30]

In a letter to John Kennedy and fifty other Senators or Senators-elect
on December 27, 1956, Herbert Lehman stressed the need to remove "the
filibuster roadblock to civil rights legislation," and he noted that the first issue
that would confront the new Senate when it convened in January would be "a
motion to adopt rules for the Senate, including a new anti-filibuster rule (Rule
22)." Asserting that "each new Senate, at the opening of a new Congress," had
the right to determine its own rules and procedures, Lehman urged Senators to
support this effort to ensure "the right of each Senator to have an equal voice
in regard to the rules under which the Senate operates." Lehman recalled that a
similar proposal had been tabled at the request of Senator Taft in 1953, and he
argued that liberals had made "a fundamental error" when they had disregarded
his advice to renew the battle in 1955. "It would be an even worse mistake"
he warned, "to fail to push this with all possible vigor in 1957." "If there were
one last fight" in which he "would like to be able to participate before retiring
from the Senate," Lehman declared, "this would be it," and he emphasized that

a victory on this motion would clear the way for civil rights legislation to be considered on its merits on the floor of the Senate.[31]

Roy Wilkins invited Lehman to attend the Leadership Conference on Civil Rights' dinner on January 2 for "final consultation on [the] anti-filibuster campaign . . . prior to [the] motion to be made January 3rd at [the] opening session of [the] Senate." The civil rights leader appreciated Lehman's "letter to Senators on this matter" but declared that "most of all we treasure your long fight for civil rights and your clear perception of the evil functioning of Rule 22." Lehman gladly participated in the strategy session for the attack on the filibuster rule, agreeing to contribute a formal message to his former colleagues that Senator Douglas would read during the debate.[32]

By Senate tradition, former Senators are allowed access to the Senate floor, and Herbert Lehman availed himself of that privilege to attend the opening sessions of the Senate in the 85th Congress to witness the attempt to change the Senate's rules. As he had in 1953, Senator Clinton Anderson of New Mexico proposed that the Senate use its authority under Article I, Section 5, of the Constitution to determine its rules, and Majority Leader Lyndon Johnson, much like Senator Taft had done in 1953, immediately moved to table Anderson's motion. A motion to table is not debatable; thus Johnson's motion could have led to a quick and unceremonious burial for Anderson's proposal. However, Johnson also presented a previously arranged unanimous consent agreement under which the Senate would spend six hours the following day debating Anderson's motion before voting whether to table it. During the debate that ensued on January 4, Hubert Humphrey quoted from Herbert Lehman's remarks during the 1953 debate and Wayne Morse paid tribute to "the leadership and inspiration given by the giant of American liberalism—Herbert Lehman of New York," predicting that "when eventually this fight is won," Lehman's "pioneering and steadfast championship of human freedom will be credited with pointing the way and marking the path." Similarly, Paul Douglas emphasized that "we who support the adoption of legislation for equality of opportunity have been greatly heartened throughout the years by the steadfast, courageous, and indomitable devotion to civil rights of that outstanding pioneer and champion in the cause, Herbert H. Lehman." Allowing former Senators access to the Senate floor had its risks, however, as Lehman, out of habit, raised his hand when the presiding officer called for the yeas and nays on a motion.[33]

During his remarks on the Senate rules, Douglas noted that Lehman's "voluntary retirement from the Senate has deprived us of his vote and his eloquent voice on the floor today," but as had been previously agreed, Lehman sent a message that Douglas presented to the Senate. In his missive, Lehman asserted that "the issue of rule 22, and of the right of the Senate to adopt new rules at the opening of Congress, is inseparable from the issue of civil rights," declaring that "the pending vote is truly the key vote on civil rights for this

Congress." But he also argued that more than civil rights was at stake, that this was also "a key vote on the fair and democratic procedures, and on the broad principle of justice." Lehman stressed that "civil rights legislation must be passed to achieve justice in our land," and that "the Anderson motion must be approved to achieve justice in the United States Senate." For those who supported this motion, Lehman prayed for "satisfaction in the rightness of their efforts—and success."[34]

Despite Lehman's prayers and good wishes, supporters of the Anderson motion failed to change the Senate's rules. They gained newfound support from Vice President Richard Nixon and moderate Republicans seeking to expand upon the inroads Eisenhower and the GOP had made in the black vote in 1956, but Richard Russell and Southern Democrats remained steadfastly opposed to any change in the filibuster rule, threatening to bog the Senate down in debate over every rule if the Anderson motion passed. As was often the case, Lyndon Johnson proved to be the key figure in determining the outcome. Johnson had decided that the Senate had to pass some sort of civil rights bill to burnish his credentials as a national rather than a Southern leader and to ensure that the Republicans could not continue to blame Senate Democrats for preventing any action in this area, but first he needed to reassure Russell and the Southerners of his loyalty by protecting the filibuster rule. Thus, Johnson worked tirelessly to block the liberals' efforts. He had declared his opposition to any attempt to change the Senate rules back in November, and George Reedy and Gerald Siegel of his staff had prepared memoranda defending the present cloture rule and advising him to follow the same tabling procedure Taft had employed in 1953 to defeat Anderson's motion. Johnson delayed the meeting of the Democratic Steering Committee at which committee assignments would be determined to maximize his influence and make sure that he had the votes to table Anderson's motion, even going so far as threatening to withhold from eighty-nine-year-old Theodore Francis Green his long-held dream of ascending to the chairmanship of the Foreign Relations Committee unless Green voted with Johnson on this matter. Johnson's motion to table Anderson's proposal passed by a vote of 55 to 38, but as Thomas Hennings noted in a letter to Herbert Lehman, the thirty-eight votes against tabling the Anderson motion were a substantial increase from the twenty-one votes they had received in 1953. Hennings saw this as a clear "indication that the issue is becoming better understood and that in the end we shall succeed."[35]

John Kennedy retreated considerably in 1957 from his support for the effort to revise the Senate rules in 1953. Kennedy voted with most Northern Democrats against tabling the Anderson motion in 1957, but as Nick Bryant noted in his book on Kennedy and civil rights, this time Kennedy "took a position but not a stand." In 1953, Kennedy had co-sponsored the Anderson motion and had participated in the strategy sessions in Lehman's office, but this time Kennedy had no involvement other than his vote. Kennedy's vote allowed him to tell a Massachusetts NAACP leader a few days later that "my own vote was cast in support of Senator Anderson's motion," and a summary of his civil rights record prepared by his office later claimed that he "was one of the few Senators who fought twice (1953 and 1957) to change Senate Rule 22 in order to end filibusters." But Kennedy's almost complete absence from the fight for the Anderson motion in 1957 stemmed from his political ambitions and from what both Theodore Sorensen and Arthur Schlesinger, Jr., have described as his lack of a strong emotional commitment to civil rights at this time in his career. Kennedy had received strong support from the South in his bid for the vice presidency in 1956, which he hoped to retain in his quest for the presidency in 1960, and he was reluctant to take any steps that would jeopardize his Southern backing. And even though Kennedy could not afford to alienate liberals and his Massachusetts constituents by voting to table the Anderson motion, his failure to co-sponsor it in 1957 made it clear to Lyndon Johnson, Richard Russell, and the Southerners that he was not rabid on this issue like Lehman, Douglas, and a few others.[36]

Kennedy's realization that Lyndon Johnson had the power to bestow upon him the seat he coveted on the Foreign Relations Committee, which would enhance his stature as a serious contender for the presidency in 1960, also factored into his actions at this time. Thus, Kennedy proclaimed his support for Johnson's continued leadership of the Senate, praising the Texan's "progressive record" and "uniquely effective leadership," and calling for Democrats to maintain "party unity." A few days after the vote on the Anderson motion, Johnson and the Democratic Steering Committee rewarded Kennedy by appointing him to the Foreign Relations Committee. Based on seniority, that slot should have gone to Estes Kefauver, but unlike Kennedy, Kefauver not only voted for the Anderson motion, he spoke out on the matter, arguing that the measure should be passed in accordance with the promise in the Democratic platform "to improve congressional procedures so that majority rule prevails and decisions can be made after reasonable debate." While Kennedy's vote for the Anderson motion could be understood and forgiven as necessitated by his Massachusetts constituency, Lyndon Johnson considered Kefauver's actions heresy not required by the voters of Tennessee and proof of Kefauver's unreliability. Thus, the seat on the Foreign Relations Committee went to Kennedy rather than Kefauver.[37]

A few days later, Kennedy again demonstrated his loyalty to Lyndon Johnson and his indifference to civil rights when he co-sponsored a resolution to loosen the current filibuster rule by allowing two-thirds of Senators present and voting, rather than two-thirds of the total Senate membership, to close off debate. Introduced by Republican leader William Knowland and supported by Lyndon Johnson, the proposal seemed like a step forward in loosening the filibuster rule, but it also included a provision declaring that the Senate rules remained in effect from one Congress to the next unless changed in accordance with Senate rules, which would make it impossible for the Senate to adopt new rules by majority vote at the beginning of a new Congress. This stipulation made the resolution unacceptable to most Senators who had supported the Anderson motion, but not to Kennedy, who sided with Johnson and Knowland. Once again, Kennedy could tell his constituents that he supported changing the filibuster rule, but the specific change he endorsed was the version that was least objectionable to the South. Kennedy's lip service to the anti-filibuster cause served its purpose, as the *Boston Chronicle*, which served the black community in Boston, cheered in an editorial that Kennedy had "voted with the liberal wing of the Democratic Party in an attempt to change the filibuster rules," and that Kennedy "thus demonstrates by his deeds that he believes in the passage of civil rights legislation and the rule of the majority as contrasted with the rule of the minority."[38]

V

Although the Anderson motion to change the filibuster rule enjoyed only lukewarm support from Senator Kennedy, the proposal won a strong endorsement from the newly formed Democratic Advisory Committee (DAC). Established by Democratic National Chairman Paul Butler and the Democratic National Committee's Executive Committee in late 1956, the DAC represented an attempt by party liberals to counter the Democrats' conservative leadership in Congress by advocating a program that would "advance the well-being of all citizens through liberal and enlightened social progress." The committee included former President Harry Truman, two-time presidential candidate Adlai Stevenson, and, in an advisory role, Eleanor Roosevelt. But congressional leaders Sam Rayburn and Lyndon Johnson recognized that the DAC constituted a challenge to their authority, so they declined to serve and discouraged other members of Congress from doing so. As a result, liberals dominated the DAC, and at its first meeting on January 4, 1957, the group approved the effort in the Senate to adopt "a new realistic rule to limit unreasonable debate," emphasizing that such action kept "faith with the position taken in the 1956 Democratic platform."[39]

Herbert Lehman was not an original member of the DAC, but he agreed completely that the Democrats needed to present a liberal alternative to the American people rather than speaking through their more conservative congressional leadership. Believing that neither the Democratic National Committee nor "the Democratic contingent in Congress" could "speak for the party as a whole between quadrennial conventions," Lehman proposed that the Democrats, and all parties, "hold annual conferences or conventions of duly selected delegates to determine the policy and program of the party in question for the ensuing year," and he suggested that this whole matter be studied by the new Democratic Advisory Committee.[40]

Democratic leaders realized that the DAC would benefit from Herbert Lehman's involvement, and they asked Lehman to attend the National Democratic Conference in San Francisco in February 1957 and "to chair the section on Human Resources, including civil rights, education, health, etc." At the San Francisco meeting, the Democratic National Committee gave its official blessing to the formation of the DAC, and the DAC voted unanimously to add Herbert Lehman as an at-large member of the group. Lehman hoped that the DAC, by generating and advocating liberal alternatives, might remedy the political apathy that seemed to grip the Democratic Party and the nation, and he quickly became one of the DAC's chief financial backers.[41]

According to James Sundquist, Lehman quickly became the "goad and conscience" of the Democratic Advisory Council "on the most divisive issue of the day—civil rights," and Herbert Parmet later wrote that Lehman, "single-mindedly" and almost single-handedly, fought to ensure that the DAC opposed "gradualism" and appeasing the South. At the Democratic meetings in San Francisco, Lehman lived up to the *Chicago Tribune*'s depiction of him as "one of the nation's most vociferous advocates of a liberal policy on the party's touchiest issue," arguing that the DAC needed to adopt a strong statement on civil rights to fulfill its role as a proponent of liberal causes. He complained that Eisenhower and the Republicans had failed to carry out the Supreme Court's decision to desegregate public schools in the South, and that the Democrats, out of deference to their Southern wing, had not taken a clear and forthright stand on civil rights. Rather than being "a Negro issue," Lehman stressed, civil rights was "an American issue" and one on which "we can't afford to pussyfoot any longer." At the end of the meetings, the DAC accepted the recommendation of Lehman's Human Rights panel and condemned the Eisenhower administration's "woeful lack of concern" on civil rights. Conveniently ignoring the role played by Southern Democrats in the Senate, the DAC claimed that the civil rights measures introduced by Democrats in Congress had been "consistently sabotaged by the Republican leadership" and urged Congress to enact the "pending legislation introduced by Democratic members in their unflagging efforts to eliminate discrimination."[42]

In contrast to Herbert Lehman, who embraced his role with the Democratic Advisory Council, John Kennedy kept his distance from the group. Kennedy was among the six Senators originally named to the DAC, but for two months he neither accepted nor declined the invitation. The only Senators who defied Lyndon Johnson and accepted seats on the Council were Estes Kefauver, who was appointed a member at-large because he had been the party's vice presidential candidate in 1956, and Hubert Humphrey, who was trying to refurbish his liberal credentials after his failure to win the vice presidential nomination in 1956. Although Humphrey continued to support Johnson for Senate Majority Leader, his call for Democrats to pursue a more liberal agenda in 1957 and his presence on the DAC caused a serious chill in his relations with Johnson. Wanting to avoid a similar fate, Kennedy eventually notified DNC Chairman Butler in early February 1957 that his race for re-election to the Senate in 1958 would not leave him sufficient time to serve on the DAC. Kennedy belatedly agreed to join the DAC in November 1959, hoping it would boost his support among liberals in his campaign for the Democratic presidential nomination in 1960.[43]

VI

Herbert Lehman hoped that Congress would enact "sound civil rights legislation" in 1957, but as he told Senator Hennings, he worried that the lawmakers would "accept compromises which would emasculate this legislation." The climate for passing civil rights legislation appeared more favorable than in the past as the Republicans sought to expand on the inroads they had made among African Americans in the 1956 election, and the Democrats wanted to retain their support among black voters. Moreover, Lyndon Johnson had concluded that the Senate needed to pass a civil rights bill, not only to protect the Democrats' political fortunes but also to transform Johnson from a Southern politician into a national statesman and a viable contender for the presidency in 1960. With the liberals' package of civil rights bills languishing once again in committee, Paul Douglas and most Senate liberals joined forces with Republican leader William Knowland and most of the GOP to employ the same strategy Douglas and Lehman had tried in 1956. Once the Eisenhower administration's civil rights bill passed in the House of Representatives, Douglas and the others planned to place it directly on the Senate calendar rather than sending it to its death in Senator Eastland's Judiciary Committee. Although Lyndon Johnson voted with Richard Russell and the Southerners to refer the bill to the committee, he allowed Douglas and his allies to win this round, part of Johnson's grand scheme for maneuvering a mild civil rights bill through the Senate in 1957.[44]

The Lehmans vacationed in Europe during the summer of 1957, but the former Senator closely followed the progress of the civil rights bill. As he told Tom Hennings, Lehman knew that his "decision not to run again last November was both wise and necessary," but the debate over the civil rights bill left him "itching to be in the fight" with his "liberal friends" in support of what he knew was "a just cause." Lehman was "greatly disturbed and distressed" that what he considered to be a weak bill to begin with was further damaged when the Senate added a provision granting jury trials to those accused of criminal contempt for defying a court order and preventing someone from voting. The Senate also struck from the bill the section authorizing the Attorney General to seek injunctions in school desegregation cases and other civil rights offenses other than interfering with the right to vote. While the bill still called for establishing a Civil Rights Commission with subpoena power, creating a Civil Rights Division within the Department of Justice, and permitting the Justice Department to intervene in voting rights suits, Lehman declared that the measure, "in its present form, is merely a gesture." As he told Wayne Morse, after the "emasculating amendments were adopted," had he still been in the Senate, Lehman was sure that he "would have voted against it." Lehman believed that the changes the Senate had made to the bill were "a clear notification that within the foreseeable future there will be no civil rights reform legislation save that affecting voting rights," and he predicted that "the jury trial amendment will cause endless confusion and trouble." In his opinion, "the Democratic Party and the liberal cause has suffered a great setback, which will be demonstrated in coming elections."[45]

Not only was Lehman disappointed in the final version of the Civil Rights Act of 1957, but as he told Tom Hennings, he could not "understand how some of our former liberals lined up with the other side." Hennings reported that the liberals "had the rug jerked out from under us by Mr. Eisenhower," who had admitted at a press conference that he really did not fully understand various provisions of the bill, resulting in those sections quickly being dropped from the measure. Paul Douglas, however, pointed to the key role played by Lyndon Johnson, explaining that "Johnson was most adroit and by complicated and subtle moves induced most of the Northern and Western Democrats away from us." As Robert Caro and others have shown, Johnson masterfully peeled off liberals like Frank Church of Idaho, winning their support for amendments weakening the civil rights bill in return for Southern votes for the Hells Canyon dam in the Northwest and promising favorable committee assignments. Johnson knew that amendments reducing the impact of the bill would diminish Southern opposition and allow him to bring the measure to a vote.[46]

John Kennedy was among the liberals whose votes on the civil rights bill disappointed Lehman. Seeking to secure Southern support for the presidency in 1960, Kennedy tried to hedge his bets on the civil rights bill, sometimes siding with the liberals to appease the NAACP and liberal groups in Massachusetts, but voting with Lyndon Johnson and the Southerners at crucial moments. Although Kennedy claimed that he was "participating in conferences with Senators Douglas, Humphrey, and others on the present debate," Douglas later wrote, "Kennedy kept aloof from the caucuses of the Northern and Western liberals" that Douglas organized. Instead of voting to place the House-passed civil rights bill directly on the Senate calendar, Kennedy supported the motion to refer it to

Senator Eastland's Judiciary Committee, from which it was unlikely ever to return. Kennedy tried to minimize the significance of this action, explaining to critics that his vote on this "procedural issue . . . in no way indicates any lessening of effort on my part to bring about the best civil rights bill possible without crippling amendments." He pointed out that "Senators Morse, Anderson, Mansfield, Murray, Magnuson, and others who have, and always will have, '100% records' on this issue" had also voted to follow the regular procedure of sending the bill to committee from where it could, theoretically, be recalled by a discharge petition if necessary.[47]

Kennedy emphasized to his constituents that he would "not vote for any ruinous amendments either with respect to the question of the right to vote or any other civil right sought to be protected by the bill," and he joined with most of the liberals in their unsuccessful effort to retain the section allowing the Justice Department to intervene in school desegregation and other civil rights cases as well as voting rights disputes. But as Nick Bryant has shown, Southerners did not need Kennedy's vote on this section of the bill after Eisenhower had abandoned it. For most liberals, the "crippling" and "ruinous" jury trial amendment was the key to the bill, weakening it beyond repair. But after assuring the NAACP's Clarence Mitchell, "You don't have to worry about me on that. I'm all right," Kennedy voted with Lyndon Johnson and the Southerners in favor of the amendment, asserting that adding it to the bill was necessary to avoid a filibuster and secure the measure's enactment. Kennedy also claimed that legal authorities had advised him that the jury trial amendment would have minimal effect. But Kennedy clearly understood the impact that the jury trial amendment would have, stressing to a Southern correspondent that this "moderate" civil rights bill "will be effected by *Southern* courts, and juries considering civil rights cases will be *Southern* juries." Kennedy's equivocation on the civil rights bill helped him maintain Southern support for his presidential bid in 1960, but it hardened the belief among liberals like Lehman and Eleanor Roosevelt, who were already skeptical about Kennedy because of his failure to condemn McCarthyism, that they needed to look elsewhere for a candidate in 1960.[48]

The Lehmans were still in Europe in September 1957 when Arkansas Governor Orval Faubus defied a court order and used the Arkansas National Guard to prevent nine black children from entering Little Rock's all-white Central High School. Already "disturbed and discouraged" at the weakness of the recently passed Civil Rights Act of 1957, Herbert Lehman was "distressed beyond measure" at what was happening in Arkansas, telling William Benton that "we are in a sorry way when the Governor of a State can defy the power of the federal government in enforcing the provisions of the Constitution." This was "about as near to nullification as anything" Lehman had seen in his lifetime. He "hope[d] that in this instance the President will exert real leadership," but he was not optimistic given Eisenhower's tepid response so far to implementing the Supreme Court's decision in *Brown v. Board of Education*. As Lehman feared, Eisenhower temporized in the first weeks of the Little Rock crisis, advising "patience" rather than taking decisive action. Lehman agreed with many of his fellow Democrats who condemned Faubus for using the National Guard "to bar the Negro students" and complained that Eisenhower's failure to insist that states and localities obey "the Constitution and laws of the United States has been substantially responsible for the trouble at Little Rock."[49]

Typically, John Kennedy remained silent during the worst of the Little Rock confrontation, not wanting to antagonize his Southern or Northern supporters. He finally spoke out in early October, after President Eisenhower's federalization of the Arkansas National Guard and dispatch of federal troops had secured the students' admission to the school. Kennedy declared that "neither mob violence nor the defiance of lawful court order can ever be justified or condoned," emphasized that "the Supreme Court's ruling on desegregation of schools is the law of the land," and stressed that the President "alone has the responsibility for deciding what steps are necessary to see that the law is faithfully executed." Basically, Kennedy finessed the underlying issue of school integration, focusing instead on the President's authority to maintain law and order. A week later, when Kennedy was addressing the Young Democrats of Mississippi, the state's Republican chairman challenged him to state where he stood on the events in Little Rock. Kennedy had hoped to avoid discussing racial issues, but now he had no choice. Acknowledging to his audience that "we do not see eye to eye on all national issues," Kennedy gave what he described as the same answer he had given in Boston, that he "accepted the Supreme Court's decision on desegregation as the law of the land." Even though people might disagree about that ruling, Kennedy hoped that "most of us do agree on the necessity to uphold law and order in every part of the land." The Senator then transformed what had loomed as a divisive sectional issue into a partisan dispute in which he and his audience of Young Democrats could unite by asking whether Mississippi Republicans agreed with President Eisenhower and Vice President Nixon on this matter. After a momentary silence, the audience of Young Democrats of Mississippi gave Kennedy a loud and long ovation. The headline in the African American newspaper the *Atlanta Daily World* demonstrated the success of Kennedy's gambit to appeal to both the North and the South: "Sen. Kennedy Courts Southern and Northern-Liberal Support." Further evidence of Kennedy's accomplishment came from the *Boston Globe*, which made the exaggerated claim that "Sen. Kennedy came out solidly, in Mississippi, for public school integration," and from *Washington Post and Times-Herald* columnist Carroll Kilpatrick, who praised "Kennedy, the Moderate," as the man "who can bridge the chasm between the North and South in the Democratic Party."[50]

In contrast to Kennedy, Herbert Lehman believed that "the fight for full civil rights must be a continuing one and carried on as vigorously as possible." Knowing that discrimination and prejudice were not limited to the Jim Crow laws and practices in the South, Lehman spoke out frequently against the de facto segregation that was common in the North, especially in housing. In June 1956, when Lehman was honored by the National Urban League as "the conscience of the Senate and the nation in the fight for full equality of opportunity for all Americans," he cited Harlem as "both illustration and proof that the acute manifestations" of the race problem were not limited to the South. He noted that "Harlem is a community rich in tradition and culture," but he also depicted Harlem, with its "poverty, congestion, substandard housing and substandard schooling," and with its "high incidence of crime and juvenile delinquency," as "a rebuke to us of the North, and a challenge to clean up our own backyard even as we press forward with our efforts to bring justice and equality to the Negroes and other oppressed minorities in the South." Lehman emphasized that "we need residential integration in New York City," asserting that "housing segregation is responsible for the high incidence of school segregation in our metropolis," and he condemned current slum clearance and public housing practices that perpetuated "a pattern of segregation." In a letter to Mayor Wagner, Lehman regretted that his speech had been interpreted by some as an attack upon the Mayor and his housing policies, but Lehman also stressed that the city "shouldn't be moving 'with all deliberate speed' to remedy the housing segregation in New York City." Lehman believed that "we have all been short-sighted in the way that we have located some of our housing projects, in a manner to intensify the pattern of segregation and at the same time to intensify the housing crisis." In October 1957, Lehman told the New York State Committee on Discrimination in Housing that such discrimination was the most pressing civil rights issue in the North, and he urged Mayor Wagner to support pending legislation to prohibit discrimination in housing in New York City.[51]

On March 3, 1958, Herbert Lehman received an honorary degree from Howard University, and he used the occasion to deliver a major address that, as he told Wayne Morse a few days later, "expresses more clearly and more fully my stand on civil rights than any of my many other speeches on the same subject." At a time when Sputnik had demonstrated the need for America to improve the education of all children, Lehman condemned as "outrageous" and bordering on "treasonable" the South's insistence on maintaining segregated schools or, in some locales, shutting down the public schools. He denounced "so-called gradualists" who "wring their hands" and ask for "patience," pointing out that "the memory of every American Negro encompasses more than 100 years of slavery before the Declaration of Independence, 77 more years of slavery in this land of liberty after 1776, and 90 years of segregation after the Emancipation Proclamation." Almost four more years had passed since the Supreme Court's decision in *Brown v. Board of Education*, and Lehman wondered, "What does patience mean against this background of 300 years of waiting?" He praised the heroism of "those patient men and women of the Negro race who have so long endured the degradation of segregation and still work with restraint and reason to achieve their goal of simple equality of treatment as American citizens." In his opinion, however, "the greatest heroes of all" were "those little schoolchildren in Little Rock and in many, many other places less renowned, who have walked the gantlet of hate and prejudice to break the trail for the onward march of brotherhood." Their example, their courage, and their patience, he asserted, "should put to shame those timid men who say that we are moving too fast and have too little patience." Lehman rejected the contention of President Eisenhower and others that the school desegregation conflict had been caused by extremists on both sides. He could not be neutral in this battle between the forces of oppression and those seeking to uphold the Constitution, Lehman declared, and he emphasized that "the entire civil rights struggle, in all its phases, is everybody's job." All Americans needed to do whatever they could to "ease the tension between the races" and "help quiet fears and eradicate prejudices among whites and Negroes alike." People in the North, he noted, had "our own special responsibilities—to rid our own house of unofficial but effective segregation and discrimination."[52]

In closing, Lehman quoted a letter a Vietnamese teenager had written to the editors of the *Washington Post and Times-Herald* in which she had asked: "Why are there still a lot of white Americans [who] do not get along with black Americans? Do they still have the impression that black Americans are their slaves? I think America is a democratic and free country, so such a colored separation must be ended. The trouble at Little Rock. Do you think that was a big shame hung over America?" Lehman hoped that one day soon Americans would "be able to tell this girl and others that the evil conditions referred to no longer exist," and he emphasized that Americans could hasten that day "if we dedicate to it all our efforts and energies, and if all men of good will, under inspired leadership, will lend themselves to this great task." He stressed that "freedom, justice, equality, and brotherhood are the brightest banners we have" to meet the challenge posed by "the forces of totalitarianism," and he urged that America raise those banners "for the whole world to see" and "march forward under them, with unflinching hearts, to attack the forces of darkness, hate, prejudice, and fears, wherever they may be—at home and abroad."[53]

Lehman's speech won the plaudits of liberals and civil rights advocates. Hubert Humphrey inserted Lehman's remarks into the *Congressional Record* and praised the speech as "one of the greatest addresses on the subject of civil rights" that he had ever heard, and NAACP leader Roy Wilkins applauded this latest "reiteration of the well-known Lehman stand on justice and equality," especially "the paragraphs on the children of Little Rock and elsewhere who have met persecution with dignity and courage." Americans were "fortunate, indeed," Wilkins concluded, to have Lehman "still giving inspired leadership to the forces which seek the moral salvation of our nation."[54]

VII

In August 1958, Quemoy and Matsu became front-page news again as Communist China resumed shelling the off-shore islands after a three-year hiatus. Chiang Kai-shek had spent much of that time reinforcing his positions on the islands, stationing one-third of his total army there despite American admonitions and threatening to invade the mainland. The Eisenhower administration failed to appreciate how provocative Chiang's actions seemed to the Chinese Communists, who were also upset that direct talks with the United States had broken off a few months earlier, that U.S. weapons continued to flow to Chiang, and that the hated idea of "two Chinas" seemed on its way to becoming a reality. The President and his advisors feared that the renewed shelling of Quemoy and Matsu would soon be followed by a Communist invasion of the islands, and they worried that the loss of Quemoy and Matsu would trigger a domino-like reaction, toppling Chiang in Formosa and other friendly regimes in East Asia. Eisenhower also believed that the United States had to show its friends and its foes alike that it would stand by its ally. But rather than stating clearly what the United States would do if the Communists attacked Quemoy or Matsu, the President preferred, as he explained in his memoirs, to "keep the Communists guessing." Thus, while he urged that the crisis be settled by negotiations, his inflammatory references to Munich and the failure of "appeasement" to prevent World War II alarmed many Americans, including Herbert Lehman, who worried that the United States might go to war over Quemoy and Matsu.[55]

In early September, when President Eisenhower asserted that the Formosa Resolution gave him unilateral authority "to employ the armed force of the United States for the defense not only of Formosa but of related positions such as Quemoy and Matsu" if he "believed their defense to be appropriate in assuring the defense of Formosa," Julius Edelstein urged Lehman to speak out immediately on the issue. He pointed out that the reluctance of most Democrats other than Wayne Morse to "rock [the] boat" meant that a statement from Lehman "might get some attention." At a meeting of the national board of Americans for Democratic Action on September 19, Lehman went public with his concerns over American policy in the Formosa crisis, emphasizing that "not a single American life, not to speak of the peace of the world, should be sacrificed for the defense of Quemoy and Matsu." He asserted that

America's vital interests were not at stake in the offshore islands, and that the United States had no moral or legal justification for getting involved in their defense. Instead of risking a war with Communist China, Lehman urged that a cease-fire be negotiated to allow Chiang Kai-shek to remove his forces from the islands, and he recommended that the question of proper ownership of the islands be turned over to the United Nations or the International Court of Justice. Lehman lamented that, as he had feared, the Formosa Resolution had turned out to be "a blank check for this country to defend the offshore islands," a check that "has now been filled out by the administration, at the insistence of the Formosan government, to read 'Quemoy and Matsu,'" and he warned that "this commitment threatens to destroy both the unity of the free nations and the peace of the world." A few days later, the *New York Times* and the *New York Herald Tribune* both published the complete text of Lehman's statement to ADA as a letter to the editor, enabling him to reach a much wider audience for his criticism of the administration's Far Eastern policy.[56]

John Kennedy congratulated Lehman on his "very fine statement . . . regarding the situation in the Formosa Strait." The Senator remembered well Lehman's leadership in 1955 "in the effort to exclude explicitly Quemoy and Matsu from the intent of the Formosa resolution," and he recalled that even though he had been absent from Washington at the time because of his back surgery, he had made sure he was paired in favor of Lehman's amendment. Kennedy observed that "subsequent events have more than vindicated" Lehman's "clear exposition and prophecies," and Kennedy reported that he had "attempted in recent days to develop a point of view similar to the one" that Lehman had expressed back in 1955. Lehman appreciated Kennedy's kind words and stressed "how deeply concerned" he was over the deteriorating world situation. He prayed that "some way will be found to avoid a conflict in the Far East," but he feared that "we are in so deep, due to the fact that we permitted ourselves to be maneuvered into a dangerous position by Chiang Kai-shek, it is hard to see in what manner we can extricate ourselves."[57]

Senator Kennedy continued to associate himself with Herbert Lehman on this issue, reporting that his "mail continues to indicate a very broad agreement" with Lehman's position. When a correspondent questioned why Kennedy had not voted against the Formosa Resolution in 1955 and why he was not listed among the Senators who had supported Lehman's amendment explicitly excluding the offshore islands from the resolution's purview, Kennedy aide Myer Feldman assured the letter writer that Kennedy was in fact "paired in favor of the Lehman amendment in 1955," failing to mention that Kennedy had also been announced as favoring the final resolution. Thanking Professor George McT. Kahin of the Department of Far Eastern Studies at Cornell University for his "thoughtful letter" on the Formosa situation, Kennedy emphasized that he and his Democratic colleagues on the Senate Foreign Relations Committee had "been helped by the advice and influence of university experts and men such as Mr. Acheson and Senator Lehman."[58]

The Formosa crisis ended in the fall of 1958 when the Chinese National-ists were able to send supplies to Quemoy and Matsu despite the Communist shelling, and the United States and Communist China resumed their talks in Warsaw. Herbert Lehman hoped that the United States would "use the addi-tional time that has been granted to us by the 'cease fire' order to make all efforts to extricate ourselves from our vulnerable and highly dangerous position in Quemoy and Matsu," but Chiang made no move to give up his hold on the islands. Quemoy and Matsu remained a pressure point where Mao Tse-tung and the Chinese Communists could create a crisis at any time, and the islands would again become a focus of contention during the Kennedy-Nixon presidential race in 1960.[59]

VIII

In opposing the liberals' effort to change the Senate's filibuster rule in January 1957, Majority Leader Lyndon Johnson and Republican leader Wil-liam Knowland had argued that the Senate could change its rules at any time through the standard procedures, and they had proposed a resolution lowering the number of votes required to invoke cloture from two-thirds of the entire Senate to two-thirds of Senators present and voting. Senator Douglas and a group of liberals had introduced their own resolution allowing a majority of the Senate to cut off debate, which was approved by the Senate Rules Com-mittee in the spring of 1958. But since the current Rule 22 allowed unlimited debate on any attempt to change the rules, Southern objections prevented the Senate from acting upon the Rules Committee's recommendation. Nonethe-less, Senator Hennings, the chairman of the Rules Committee, explained to Herbert Lehman that the committee's action was "of considerable importance" and "should help us in the coming fight in the 86th Congress." John Ken-nedy regretted the Senate's failure to act on the filibuster rule, asserting that "there is no reason why, after sufficient debate and education, a small minority of Senators should be able to block needed legislation through an outmoded, undemocratic, and unjust procedural device." Without specifying exactly what change he supported, Kennedy called for a renewed effort to change the cloture rule in the next Congress.[60]

Democrats looked forward to the 1958 congressional elections with great optimism. President Eisenhower remained personally popular, but people were questioning his seeming lack of leadership in foreign and domestic affairs. The Soviet Union's launching of the Sputnik satellite suggested that the administra-tion's emphasis on balancing the budget had allowed the United States to fall behind the Soviets scientifically and militarily, and presidential aide Sherman Adams had been forced to resign for accepting gifts from a friend and then intervening on the friend's behalf with the Federal Trade Commission. The United States was in the throes of a severe recession, and people were concerned about pocketbook issues, including unemployment and increases in the cost of living. Labor disliked the new restrictions imposed by the Landrum-Griffin Act, and farmers wanted higher prices for their crops. In addition, the party occupying the White House traditionally lost seats in midterm elections, and the large number of Republican Senators who had been carried into office in the Republican sweeps of 1946 and 1952 were running this time without the benefit of anger at the Truman administration or the reassuring presence of Eisenhower at the top of the GOP ticket.[61]

Herbert Lehman played an active role in the 1958 elections. Besides campaigning in New York for the re-election of Governor Harriman and the election of Democratic Senate candidate Frank Hogan, Lehman contributed generously to the campaign coffers of numerous liberal Democrats who were running for the Senate, including Ernest Gruening in Alaska, Harrison Williams in New Jersey, William Proxmire in Wisconsin, Philip Hart in Michigan, Gale McGhee in Wyoming, Howard Cannon in Nevada, Claire Engle in California, Eugene McCarthy in Minnesota, John Pastore in Rhode Island, and Albert Gore in Tennessee. Lehman based his contributions on whether the candidate was a liberal, his chances of winning, whether he had been a Senate colleague, and how much he needed the money. Despite their having served together in the Senate for four years, Lehman did not contribute any money to John Kennedy's re-election campaign against a weak opponent. Kennedy had access to plenty of money and did not need Lehman's help, and Kennedy's vote on the jury trial amendment in 1957 had reinforced the doubts that Lehman and other liberals had about Kennedy.[62]

Business leaders and Republicans in a number of states placed on the ballot in 1958 "right-to-work" initiatives designed to ban union shops and labor contracts that required workers to join unions to keep their jobs. The measures' proponents hoped to increase turnout by conservative, anti-union voters, weaken organized labor, and attract new businesses to their states. However, as the *Washington Post and Times-Herald* noted, this strategy had a "boomerang" effect, energizing union workers and their supporters, including Herbert Lehman and Eleanor Roosevelt, who agreed to serve as co-chairs of the National Council for Industrial Peace that was formed to oppose the right-to-work initiatives. In a speech a few weeks before the election, Lehman proclaimed that labor unions were "the greatest single safeguard of the right of workers to be employed and to be treated fairly on the job," and he warned that "the so-called right-to-work law . . . is aimed at crippling and destroying the power of the union to safeguard these rights." Lehman's efforts helped defeat right-to-work initiatives in Ohio, California, Washington, Colorado, and Idaho; only in Kansas did the voters approve such a measure. Moreover, most of the voters who went to the polls to vote against the right-to-work proposals also voted for Democratic candidates, bringing down such Republican stalwarts as Senator John Bricker in Ohio. AFL-CIO president George Meany commended Lehman for his "untiring and splendid efforts . . . in combating the notorious anti-labor legislation which parades under the misnomer of 'right-to-work,'" and Walter Reuther of the United Auto Workers thanked Lehman for his help in developing "a better public understanding of the issues involved in the so-called right-to-work campaign." Reuther believed that without the efforts of Lehman and Mrs. Roosevelt and their committee, "the results of the election in this important area might have been quite different."[63]

Much to Herbert Lehman's delight, Democrats picked up thirteen seats in the Senate in the 1958 elections, and two more a few weeks later when Alaska elected its first two Senators, giving the Democrats a 62 to 34 majority in the new Senate that would convene in January 1959. Moreover, many of the new Democrats were liberals who hailed from Northern and Western states, threatening Southern and conservative control of the Senate. Lehman knew "nearly all of the men who were elected to the Senate," and he considered "most of them able and real liberals." He believed that "the influence of the liberal group will be much enhanced and the power of the conservative leadership proportionately reduced." Allen Drury of the *New York Times* observed that "numerically the new Democratic majority is, in the main, a liberal majority" and he predicted that the new Senate would certainly change the filibuster rule, although he cautioned that the revision might not be "the all-out banishment of extended debate that some liberals have long demanded." The *Washington Post and Times-Herald* agreed that "it already was a foregone conclusion that the new Senate, as one of its very first acts, would move to liberalize the Senate's so-called filibuster rule." The only question was whether the new Senate would adopt a rule allowing two-thirds of those present and voting or a majority of the Senate to cut off debate. Buoyed by the liberal Democrats' new strength, Paul Douglas expected "a speedy end to Rule 22, the Senate debate-foreclosing stricture that has kept civil rights and other progressive legislation from passing." Confident that almost all of the new Senators would support a motion for the Senate to adopt new rules, Douglas promised that abolishing the filibuster rule would be "the first order of business before Congress next session."[64]

Herbert Lehman worked closely with liberal Senators who wanted to change the Senate's filibuster rule when the 86th Congress convened in January 1959. Realizing that Lyndon Johnson had outmaneuvered them in previous years when they had been slow to organize, liberals began to plan much earlier this time for the fight on Rule 22. In late September 1958, Douglas and Hubert Humphrey wrote to all Democratic Senate candidates, and Republican Senators

Clifford Case of New Jersey and Jacob Javits of New York did the same for Republican candidates. The four Senators denounced the filibuster rule as the "silent executioner" that had weakened the Eisenhower administration's civil rights bill in 1957 and explained that "the same fate awaits similar legislation at the next session" unless the Senate exercised its power under the Constitution to "determine the Rules of its proceedings" when the new Congress met in January. Lehman was "delighted to know" that Douglas and the others "again intend to proceed vigorously in this fight," and he was "sure that most of the new Democrats elected" would support Douglas's "fight to change Rule XXII" and to enact "liberal legislation."[65]

A few weeks after the election, columnist William S. White argued in the *Washington Evening Star* against any major changes in the filibuster rule, criticizing liberals who sought such revisions. White, who Paul Douglas later described as "the journalistic hatchet man for Lyndon Johnson," asserted that a fight over the filibuster rule would benefit Richard Nixon and the Republicans at the expense of the Democrats and to the detriment of any future "economic, racial, religious, or sectional" minority. He charged that "a fraction [*sic*] of advanced liberals," led by Douglas, Humphrey, Case, and Javits, was "advancing an alteration so extreme that its adoption would end the Senate as a unique deliberative body" by permitting "the barest Senate majority, or 49 members, to put on cloture after 15 days," a change that "would make the Senate only a somewhat slower House of Representatives." According to White, "the filibuster in Senate history has been more often a liberal than a conservative implement," citing Wayne Morse's twenty-two-and-a-half-hour diatribe against the tidelands oil bill as an example. He noted that the last Congress had enacted a civil rights bill despite the filibuster rule, but that had not "satisfied the liberals, who think it did not go far enough," and he maintained that the real impediment to civil rights legislation was that "far more rank and file Senators have had it on their lips than in their hearts." Rather than the radical change in the rules proposed by Douglas and the others, White believed that most Senators would support allowing two-thirds of the Senators present and voting to invoke cloture instead of the current requirement of two-thirds of the entire Senate.[66]

Herbert Lehman had never been a big fan of White, and Lehman seized the opportunity to contribute to the fight against the filibuster by rebutting White's article. In a long reply published in the *Washington Evening Star*, Lehman claimed that White's column, instead of being "an impartial commentary . . . was too much slanted in a Southerly direction." He challenged White's thesis "that the Senate's present filibuster rule is a safeguard for liberal causes and principles," noting that in his seven years in the Senate, he "always found the filibuster rule (Rule XXII) working against those causes and principles rather than for them." According to Lehman, "the present form of Rule XXII as adopted in 1949 was drafted with only one purpose in mind: to perpetuate the power of Southern Senators to block civil rights legislation, even if such legislation was desired by a substantial majority of the Senate and of the country." Lehman asserted that Wayne Morse's "marathon speech" against the "tidelands oil give-away," had been an attempt to delay a vote so that public opinion could be mobilized, not "a true filibuster" intended "to prevent a proposal from coming to a vote."[67]

In Lehman's opinion, White's description of the Douglas, Humphrey, Case, and Javits proposal as "extreme" and a threat to the Senate's status "as a unique deliberative body" was "very misleading and untrue." Lehman maintained that the measure was "actually a very moderate one, which carefully preserves the role of the Senate as a deliberate forum for extended debate and appeal to the public conscience and opinion." In response to White's concern that matters could be rushed through the Senate under this proposal, Lehman explained that if this change in the rules were adopted, "three periods of extended debate" could still occur: debate would be unlimited until a cloture resolution was filed, fifteen days of debate would follow the submission of a cloture resolution, and if a majority of the Senate then voted for cloture, each Senator would still have one hour to speak on the matter. Moreover, Lehman pointed out, this process would first occur on the motion to consider a bill, which meant that "there could be a practical minimum of one month of debate on just a preliminary procedural motion." Then the whole process would be repeated on the measure itself, consuming another month. "Can a proposed rule which would permit a practical minimum of two months of debate before a piece of legislation could be forced to [a] vote be properly described as 'extreme' or dangerous to the status of the Senate as a 'deliberative' body?" Lehman asked.[68]

As to the modest change in the rule that White preferred, namely, Lyndon Johnson's proposal to reduce the requirement for cloture from two-thirds of the Senate to two-thirds of those present and voting, Lehman denounced this as "a mere shadow proposal without substance." He reported that "a study of the cloture votes of the past forty years shows that not a single motion on a civil rights bill would have prevailed" if Johnson's proposal had been in effect, proving that "this change in the filibuster rule would be virtually meaningless." Lehman stressed that it was the current rule, not the Douglas proposal, that "threatens not only the status of the Senate, but the most vital interest of our country." He charged that the filibuster rule, "by preventing the Congress from dealing constructively with the subject of civil rights—which Congress should have done years ago," had "helped to bring about the present civil rights crisis." It was "already very late on the clock of history," Lehman noted, but he believed that "it may still not be too late" if "the new Senate, with a fresh mandate given by the people on November 4, moves promptly to rectify past errors."[69]

Lehman hoped that his response to White would make a real difference. He "personally sent copies of White's column" and his response to many of his "friends in the Senate," including John Kennedy, and he received many favorable replies. William Proxmire (D-WI) believed that Lehman, by explaining that there would still be "a minimum period of two months" for debate under the Douglas-Humphrey-Javits-Case proposal, had provided "a mighty devastating argument to those who say that this would chop off debate and end freedom of speech in any sense in the Senate." Clair Engle (D-CA) congratulated Lehman on his "most compelling" answer to White and promised "to support and fight for the Humphrey-Douglas proposal to change Senate Rule 22," while Harrison Williams (D-NJ) shared Lehman's "sincere desire to see Rule 22 modified along the lines now being proposed by Senator Douglas and others." Williams agreed that each new Senate had the right "to adopt its own rules," and he pledged to "bring whatever weight a freshman Senator can toward tipping the scales in the direction of a more democratic Rule 22." Senator Douglas "had several thousand copies" of Lehman's article reprinted for distribution "all over the country," and he believed "it is helping a lot."[70]

But ambivalent or negative responses from Senators who had voted for the Anderson motion in 1957 suggested that Douglas's proposal for majority cloture might not be as popular as Lehman and its supporters thought it was. Dennis Chavez (D-NM) told Lehman he was "amenable to reason" and promised that his "mind will not be made up either one way or the other" until he heard "all sides" and completed his "own research and investigation," but he thought "the country and the Senate have done pretty well under the [current] rule." Gordon Allott (R-CO) explained that he planned "to support a modification of Rule 22," but he emphasized that he would oppose any measure allowing a majority of the Senate to end debate. He asserted that "Senator Douglas and some others are entirely wrong" on this issue, claiming that their proposal "would not only break down the tradition of the Senate, it breaks down the fundamental principle upon which the House and Senate were established and have conducted their business." Frank Lausche (D-OH) agreed that "Rule 22 should be modified so as to insure adequate debate for the presentation of minority views, while at the same time bringing to an end the practices which the Senate has been compelled to suffer through the use of the filibuster." However, Lausche did not specify whether he supported majority cloture or allowing a two-thirds majority of those voting to close debate. Henry Jackson, a liberal Democrat from Washington, complimented Lehman on his "excellent presentation" of the issues in his letter to the *Washington Evening Star*, but while Jackson agreed "that there should be a substantial change in the present Rule" and recalled that he had "supported the changes made during the previous years," he was "going to withhold judgment as to the specific change" until he returned to Washington and took "a good look at the various proposals." Joseph O'Mahoney of Wyoming, another liberal Democrat, had read Lehman's response to White's column, but he still found it "difficult to believe that it would be a step forward to give a mere majority of the Senate the power to shut off debate." In his many years in the Senate, O'Mahoney could not "think of a measure that was ever killed by filibuster which the Senate really wanted to pass," and he reminded Lehman that FDR's court-packing plan "would have been passed by a majority if it had not been that the Senate Judiciary Committee was free to hold lengthy hearings and the members of the Senate were free to debate the issue." These possible defections from the ranks of those who had supported changing the filibuster rule in the past signaled that the Douglas proposal was in more trouble than Lehman and its supporters seemed to realize.[71]

As the 86th Congress prepared to convene on January 7, 1959, Herbert Lehman and his allies remained confident of victory. Although he feared "crippling amendments," Lehman was "hopeful that Rule 22 can be changed at the opening of Congress, along the lines for which we have been fighting for so many years." Clinton Anderson, who once again would be sponsoring the motion for the Senate to adopt new rules, expressed confidence that the Senate would "assert its right to adopt the rules under which it operates, unfettered by the dead hand of the past," and Hubert Humphrey was "sure that the victory will be ours." Appearing on *Meet the Press* on January 4, Paul Douglas predicted that the liberals would win the fight over whether the Senate could establish new rules by majority vote at the beginning of a new Congress, but he was less certain whether the Senate would adopt majority cloture. He noted that about one-third of the Senators were uncommitted and their votes would be decisive. But after meeting with fifteen liberal Democrats and three Senators' aides on January 6, Douglas was more confident. Jacob Javits added to the optimism, announcing that at least fifteen of the Senate's thirty-four Republicans would vote for the Anderson motion. Douglas, Javits, and liberal leaders in both parties met to plan their strategy, and Douglas welcomed the "happy degree of cooperation" as a demonstration that the liberals could work together across party lines as effectively as conservatives had done for so many years. The NAACP's Roy Wilkins declared that "a revision of Senate Rule 22 to make it possible to stop a filibuster by majority vote also seems probable" in 1959, and Marjorie Lawson of the National Council of Negro Women reported to Senator Kennedy that civil rights leaders counted at least thirty-three sponsors for the Anderson motion. According to Lawson, "The NAACP has been estimating the number of favorable votes on the motion at 51 since last week." Excited by the prospect of victory on this issue for which he had fought for so long, Herbert Lehman went to Washington to watch the proceedings on January 7, confiding to Richard Neuberger, "It would, of course, be a tremendous satisfaction to me to see the Rule finally changed."[72]

As usual, Senate Majority Leader Lyndon Johnson posed the main threat to the liberals' attempt to change the Senate's rules and adopt majority cloture. Lehman predicted that Johnson would make "every effort" to water down their proposal, as Johnson was trying to forge a solution that would modify the cloture rule without provoking a Southern filibuster. A minor change, of course, would not satisfy the liberals, but Johnson was less worried about them. Marjorie Lawson noted in her memo to Kennedy that "Johnson's careful work of the last four or five days" seemed to be paying off, as could be seen in the "long but shallow editorial" in the *Washington Post and Times-Herald* on January 5, one day after Johnson had lunched with a member of the paper's editorial staff. Ignoring the damage to minority children of continued segregation in Southern schools, the editorial expressed concern over the "psychological impact" that majority cloture might have on the South, warning that "too drastic a change might, instead of paving the way for constructive national legislation, promote new neuroses and resistance against what would be considered a rule of force." Instead of the liberals' proposal for majority cloture, the editors endorsed the Johnson-Knowland plan to require a two-thirds vote of Senators present and voting to end a filibuster. Lawson worried that the editorial "is the tip-off, and there are other straws in the wind which indicate that the liberals have lost some ground they shouldn't have lost," and she cautioned that "the *Post* editorial is certain to influence moderate opinion, both on the Hill and in organizations." When liberal leaders met with Johnson on the eve of the Senate's opening, the Majority Leader emphasized his belief that they were wrong to call for majority cloture, and he informed them that he might preempt their move with his own resolution when the Senate convened the next day.[73]

Herbert Lehman watched from the floor with great anticipation as the new Senate held its first meeting on January 7, 1959. Lehman enjoyed mingling with his old friends and colleagues, but his joy quickly turned to despair when Lyndon Johnson used his power as Senate Majority Leader to gain recognition before Senator Anderson could move that the Senate adopt new rules. Johnson introduced Senate Resolution 5, co-sponsored by most of the Senate leaders from both parties, to lower the requirement for cutting off debate from two-thirds of the Senate to two-thirds of Senators present and voting. The proposal would also make changes in the rules subject to the same cloture provisions as all other matters, and it stipulated that "the rules of the Senate shall continue from one Congress to the next Congress unless they are changed as provided in these rules." By offering a specific proposal to change Rule 22, Johnson hoped to satisfy those who wanted to modify the filibuster rule, demonstrating that there was no need to adopt the liberals' position that the Senate could adopt new rules every two years.[74]

Douglas and his allies had amassed thirty-three sponsors for the Anderson motion to have the Senate consider its rules for the 86th Congress, but when Vice President Nixon, who was presiding, recognized Anderson to offer his motion, Johnson noted that he still had the floor. Realizing that the Anderson motion would supersede his own as the pending business, Johnson promptly moved that the Senate adjourn, a motion that is not debatable. Douglas, Javits, and several others, wanting Senator Anderson to have the opportunity to offer his motion, then made the fatal error of demanding a roll call vote on Johnson's adjournment motion, only to see it pass easily by a vote of 73 to 23, with even some liberals like Hubert Humphrey voting to adjourn. Because the issues and the parliamentary situation were confused, and many Senators were eager to adjourn because they had special celebrations planned to mark the opening of the new Congress, Douglas complained that "Johnson pulled a fast one," and Senator Case charged that the Majority Leader had acted "in a rough, high-handed manner." But the press the next day highlighted the overwhelming margin by which the Senate had approved Johnson's motion to adjourn, reporting that this was a huge victory for Johnson over the liberals. The headline in the *Washington Post and Times-Herald*, for example, declared: "Liberals Lose Round in Senate," and the article emphasized that "a resurgent band of bipartisan liberals, intent on reforming the Senate's old filibuster rules, took a licking in the opening round." Similarly, the *New York Times* explained that Johnson had "seized and held the initiative on the floor . . . and mustered a crushing 73-to-23 vote to keep control of the parliamentary situation," leaving "the bipartisan anti-filibuster bloc badly off balance." Even Herbert Lehman admitted that after Johnson's dominance that first day, he feared that the Majority Leader "would wholly prevail."[75]

The Johnson resolution would make it a little easier to end a filibuster, since absent Senators would no longer count against the two-thirds majority required to invoke cloture, and it would make it possible, at least in theory, to end a filibuster against a change in the rules. However, liberals pointed out numerous times over the next few days that these changes amounted to less than they seemed. They argued that the change from two-thirds of the Senate to two-thirds of those present and voting would not make much difference since most Senators were present for cloture votes. Moreover, the liberals knew that the proviso in the Johnson resolution about the rules remaining in effect from one Congress to the next would eliminate their opportunity to revise the rules by majority vote at the opening of a new Congress, making it almost impossible for them to alter the filibuster rule. Paul Douglas claimed that Johnson was merely "offering us, in effect, the old rule, with a blue ribbon tied around its chin. It is the old rule. It is the old straitjacket," and Herbert Lehman warned that Johnson's proposal "accomplishes little or nothing, but is so cleverly worded that it will undoubtedly deceive a great many people."[76]

Lyndon Johnson allowed Senator Anderson to offer his motion when the Senate reconvened on January 8, with the understanding that after sufficient debate, Johnson would move to table the proposal. Even though Herbert Lehman had been out of the Senate for two years, he still figured prominently in the debate and the effort to modify the filibuster rule. Attempting to appeal to liberals who were on the fence, Douglas paid tribute to "the beloved former Senator from New York, Herbert Lehman, who led the struggle for many years," and he inserted into the *Congressional Record* Lehman's response to William White in which Lehman had pointed out that even under majority cloture, there would still be eight to ten weeks of full discussion before a Senate vote. When Spessard Holland (D-FL) quoted a new column in which White denounced the "indefensible extremism" of Douglas, Javits, and the other "advanced liberals in both parties" who wanted to change the filibuster rule to allow "a bare majority or a margin of one vote" to halt a filibuster, Douglas reiterated how Lehman had "so thoroughly demolished" White's earlier column. Showing his frustration with the whole process, Douglas tried to rub some salt in old Southern wounds, asserting that Lehman's "demolition of Mr. White's argument was almost equivalent to the demolition by some of the armies in 1865." Senator Joseph Clark (D-PA) "would not go quite that far," but he agreed that, "to the objective and modern observer, Senator Lehman had substantially the better of the argument." Edward Hollander, ADA's national director, believed that the liberals were "still receiving the dividends" of Lehman's "unrelenting efforts" on this issue when he was in the Senate, and Hollander was confident that "there are further dividends to come in the future."[77]

The liberals may have had the better of the arguments, but, as usual, Lyndon Johnson had the votes. When the vote came on January 9, the Senate once again tabled the Anderson motion, this time by a count of 60 to 36. Despite the influx of liberals elected in 1958, the Anderson motion actually fared worse in 1959 than it had in 1957, when it had lost 55 to 38. Douglas, Javits, and their supporters were no more successful three days later, when the Senate voted 67 to 28 against the Douglas amendment for majority cloture, 58 to 36 against a proposal by Thruston Morton (R-KY) to lower the requirement for cloture to three-fifths of those present and voting, and then 72 to 22 in favor of Lyndon Johnson's resolution to allow two-thirds of the Senators voting to cut off debate. Liberals split on the final vote, with Hubert Humphrey deciding that some change was better than none, while Wayne Morse warned "the half-a-loafers" that "they will not even get a slice of legislative bread out of the Johnson proposal; all they will get will be the political wrapper, and that is not edible." Morse, Paul Douglas, Jacob Javits, and a few other liberal diehards joined Southern reactionaries in voting against the Johnson resolution, an unusual grouping to say the least. Press accounts noted that Johnson had won the votes of many of the new Democrats by campaigning for them in 1958 and by delaying committee assignments until after the votes on the filibuster issue had been completed.[78]

Herbert Lehman was very disheartened at the results. Before any of the votes had occurred, he told a former colleague that he hoped that "very substantial changes will be made so that after full debate any bill can be brought

before the Senate for a vote." After all the votes had been taken and the magnitude of the liberals' defeat became clear, Lehman admitted he was "greatly
disappointed at the outcome," especially the willingness of "some of our new
liberal Senators" to abandon the cause. Lehman had placed "great confidence"
in some of these men and had even contributed to their campaigns, but he
surmised that "the lure of committee assignments and possible appropriations
proved too much for some of them." Lehman confided to Clinton Anderson
that the votes "of some of our newly elected liberals" suggested that Lehman had
"overestimated their intestinal fortitude." He did not mention any names, but
he had contributed to the successful campaigns of Howard Cannon in Nevada,
Ernest Gruening in Alaska, Gale McGee in Wyoming, and Robert Byrd and
Jennings Randolph in West Virginia, all of whom sided with Lyndon Johnson
on the important votes. Senate newcomers Vance Hartke of Indiana and E. L.
Bartlett of Alaska also voted consistently with Johnson, while Thomas Dodd
of Connecticut voted against the Anderson motion but for Senator Douglas's
proposal. According to columnist Drew Pearson, these men had all promised
at one time or another to support the Anderson motion, and Cannon was
even one of its co-sponsors, but they all reversed themselves under pressure
from Lyndon Johnson and the enticement of favorable committee assignments.
Lehman could take some solace from the votes of newcomers Clair Engle of
California, Philip Hart of Michigan, Eugene McCarthy of Minnesota, Edmund
Muskie of Maine, Frank Moss of Utah, and Harrison Williams of New Jersey,
all of whom defied Lyndon Johnson's threats and blandishments and voted
with the liberals throughout. Hart in particular acknowledged and especially
appreciated Lehman's "encouragement in the attempt to modify Rule XXII."[79]

John Kennedy had told his constituents, "I fully intend to support efforts
to revise Senate Rule XXII, with respect to the filibuster," but behind the scenes,
he hoped that a compromise would emerge that he could vote for without losing support in the black community or in the South. Marjorie Lawson of the
National Council of Negro Women, who was aiding Kennedy's efforts to line
up support from African Americans for the Democratic presidential nomination
in 1960, kept him fully briefed on "the positions of various Negro organizations on an acceptable revision of the filibuster rule." Lawson reported in early
December that "the NAACP is making it quite plain that Senator Johnson's
compromise is unacceptable and the Negro press supports this point of view,"
and she advised Kennedy not "to make a statement about which form of revision
you favor, unless you are going along with Senator Douglas." She warned Kennedy "to avoid falling into any NAACP mousetraps," explaining that "despite
the oratory, civil rights leadership is looking for an acceptable compromise."
Wanting to avoid taking a definite position on the issue until he absolutely had
to, Kennedy never replied to Lehman's letter sharing his response to William
White's column.[80]

By the time the Senate convened in January, Kennedy had decided to co-sponsor the Anderson motion for the Senate to adopt new rules, as he had in 1953 but not in 1957. Realizing that he needed to stand with the party liberals on this issue if he hoped to capture the presidential nomination in 1960, Kennedy agreed with the secretary of the Liberal Citizens of Massachusetts that "this procedural question is basic to the whole fabric of our civil rights . . . and the enlargement of civil rights opportunities for all Americans." Having been informed by Lawson that the NAACP was "standing pat on the Douglas proposal," and not wanting to jeopardize his recent rapprochement with Roy Wilkins, who had been angered by Kennedy's vote for the jury trial amendment and his apparent courting of the South, Kennedy came out in favor of majority cloture rather than Johnson's "two-thirds of those present and voting" formula. As Kennedy had hoped, his "sponsorship of the Anderson motion and support of the Douglas revision" were received by civil rights leaders "with great warmth and approval." After the Senate tabled the Anderson motion, Kennedy continued to support the Douglas proposal for majority cloture, but when both that measure and Senator Morton's three-fifths compromise were defeated, Kennedy voted for the Johnson resolution on the grounds that some revision in the filibuster rule was better than nothing. Kennedy's support for the Anderson motion and the Douglas proposal helped him build support in the liberal community, as can be seen in the letter Kennedy received from ADA national director Edward Hollander expressing his "sincere admiration and gratitude for the firm stand you took on majority rule." Hollander understood "the very great pressures working against the liberalization of the rules," and thus Kennedy's "votes on the principle" were "all the more appreciated." Even while supporting the Northern liberal position on the filibuster in 1959, however, Kennedy was careful not to burn his bridges with the South. Although he co-sponsored the Anderson motion and voted for the Douglas proposal, he never spoke on their behalf.[81]

IX

Herbert Lehman and John Kennedy differed over how forcefully to pursue civil rights for African Americans, but they agreed, as Lehman put it, that America's immigration and naturalization laws were "a national and world scandal." Even after leaving the Senate, Lehman remained committed to immigration reform, working with Julius Edelstein and former Truman administration Solicitor General Philip Perlman to raise money for the citizens' group they had formed to educate the public and build support for changing the immigration laws. Interviewed in 1957, Julius Edelstein lamented that "no one Senator has really taken over immigration, with the personal enthusiasm and interest" of

Senator Lehman, but he did note that "Kennedy put in a bill with some of the things" that had been in Lehman's comprehensive immigration and naturalization reform bill. Ralph Dungan, Kennedy's legislative assistant on this issue, later explained that Kennedy's interest in immigration reform was "almost wholly political," reflecting the strong feelings of Portuguese, Italian, and Jewish immigrants in Massachusetts and their descendants on the issue. Dungan also noted that "it was always good" to be "identified with Lehman and all those great Eastern liberals." Whatever his motives, Kennedy, like Lehman, had opposed the McCarran-Walter Act in 1952, and he supported Lehman's subsequent efforts to liberalize the nation's immigration and naturalization policies.[82]

In 1957, Kennedy took the lead among Senate Democrats in pushing for "humanitarian" changes in the immigration and naturalization statutes. Kennedy would have preferred major revisions in the McCarran-Walter Act, but he knew that such alterations were unlikely with James Eastland ensconced as the head of the Senate Judiciary Committee and its Immigration Subcommittee, and Francis Walter, often referred to in Congress as "Mr. Immigration," still heading the House Judiciary Subcommittee on Immigration. Walter made it clear that he would not accept any major changes in the immigration law that bore his name, using his position as chairman of the House Committee on Un-American Activities (HUAC) to charge that "the spearhead of the over-all drive for mutilation" of the McCarran-Walter Act "is the Communist Party and its affiliates." Kennedy pared down his bill to obtain Walter's blessing, dropping from the bill various provisions that would have reallocated thirty thousand unused visas from Northern and Western European countries to Southern and Eastern European nations that had small quotas and long waiting lists. As finally enacted, S. 2792 authorized the admission into the United States of spouses, parents, and children of people who had already come to America, orphans adopted by American citizens, Hungarian and other refugees fleeing Communism in Eastern Europe and turmoil in the Middle East, and certain skilled professionals such as doctors and scientists. It also restored quota slots that had been used by displaced persons entering the United States under previous legislation, forgave immigrants who had lied about their country of origin to avoid repatriation to the Soviet Union, and allowed the Attorney General to waive the requirement that foreign visitors to the United States be fingerprinted. Kennedy recognized that the final bill "does not go as far as many of us would have liked," but he pledged to continue his efforts to attain "more far-reaching adjustments in our immigration policy in future years." Herbert Lehman was "greatly disturbed and distressed" that Congress had made only minimal changes in the immigration laws, and he agreed with Kennedy that the fight "for effective changes in the McCarran-Walter Act will go on for a long time."[83]

As promised, Kennedy continued to push for further revisions in the immigration laws, but Congressman Walter and Senator Eastland still blocked the path to significant modifications. Consequently, Kennedy turned to a literary effort to try to rouse support for immigration reform. In 1958, the Anti-Defamation League of B'nai B'rith commissioned Kennedy to write a pamphlet entitled "Immigrants All" as part of its One Nation Library. The booklet was to be "geared primarily for high school use . . . and written in as popular a style as possible." Eager to burnish his credentials as an author and an intellectual, Kennedy, with the help of Theodore Sorensen and Ralph Dungan of his staff, produced a short book, *A Nation of Immigrants*, which Herbert Parmet has described as "a gracefully written, somewhat filiopietistic summary of Atlantic migration to America designed to convince readers about the inherent bias of the quota system." In the book, Kennedy paid homage to "Senator Lehman and others" for sponsoring "the most liberal bill offered in recent years," which would have increased the number of immigrants admitted annually from 154,000 to 250,000. In addition, Kennedy noted, "instead of using the test of where the immigrant was born, the Lehman bill would have made the applicant's individual training and qualifications the test for admission." Kennedy stressed that "neither Senator Lehman nor anyone else sought the enactment of legislation which would make over the face of America."[84]

As the 86th Congress prepared to convene in January 1959, Representative Walter tried to expand the jurisdiction of the House Committee on Un-American Activities to include immigration and passport matters. In June of 1957, the U.S. Supreme Court had invalidated John Watkins's conviction for contempt of Congress for refusing to name former members of the Communist Party at a HUAC hearing, ruling that Watkins's rights under the First Amendment trumped the committee's authority to investigate because the committee's proceedings did not serve a legitimate legislative purpose. The Court's decision threatened to put an end to HUAC's circus-like proceedings where witnesses invoked their constitutional rights not to answer questions about their political beliefs and associations. To counter the decision's possibly fatal impact on HUAC, Walter sought to create a new Committee on Internal Security that would encompass all of HUAC's previous functions and add immigration and passport issues to its jurisdiction, giving the committee a valid legislative mandate. Walter explained that "because much that happens in the immigration field is related to our security, it just seems natural that both should be together." He expressed confidence that the Democratic leadership in the House of Representatives supported his plan, and that the only opposition would come from "long time antagonists of the committee who fear it would be even more difficult to put out of business if its jurisdiction is broadened."[85]

Herbert Lehman certainly qualified as a "long time antagonist" who would have liked to put HUAC out of business, and he adamantly rejected Walter's assertion that immigration was primarily a security matter. At a press conference on January 2, 1959, Lehman complained that putting immigration matters under a Committee on Internal Security "would be an unbearable affront to millions of Americans of foreign birth and descent," and he warned that "its effect would be to give our enemies abroad a new propaganda whip with which to beat us." Lehman charged that Walter's plan was "designed to serve only two purposes: to enlarge the authority of Mr. Walter, and to breathe permanent life into the moribund Un-American Activities Committee," and Lehman expressed his astonishment at reports indicating that this change had "the support of the House leadership on both sides of the aisle." Continuing his attack two days later, Lehman stressed that putting immigration matters under HUAC "would immediately label every alien as a suspect or a potential enemy of this country," which "would be morally, politically, internationally, and nationally wrong."[86]

Lehman reiterated his opposition to Walter's "audacious" and "deeply frightening and disturbing" initiative in an article in the *Washington Post and Times-Herald* on January 6, 1959. He warned against giving Walter and HUAC "a lease of new authority at the expense of two very vital areas of our civil liberties, and indeed, at the expense of our national dignity and prestige," asserting that Walter "already exercises far too much power in this field." Lehman argued that giving Walter and HUAC staff director Richard Arens the authority "to summon for questioning any individual who had ever obtained a United States passport" would be "deliberately putting the fox in charge of the hen house." He hoped that the leadership in the House of Representatives would come to its senses and "have second thoughts about this move," especially in view of "the liberal mandate given by the people" in the 1958 congressional elections.[87]

Not content with speaking out at press conferences and submitting material to newspapers, Herbert Lehman also worked behind the scenes to scuttle Walter's power grab. On December 30, 1958, Lehman telephoned Harry Truman to enlist the former President's help in blocking Walter's plan. Truman was unaware of Walter's scheme and, according to a memo Lehman wrote for his files immediately after the conversation, "seemed very much outraged" when Lehman told him about it. Lehman emphasized his concern "that the plan had the tentative approval of the House leadership," and he warned that "the plan, if carried out, would be both morally indefensible and politically wrong, as it would immediately declare to the people of this country and to free people all over the world that aliens were considered by us as suspects and potential enemies." He stressed that the transfer of authority over immigration matters to HUAC "would give offense and great concern to the foreign-born groups who would . . . very naturally and very properly feel that they had been betrayed by the Democratic Party." Lehman and Truman reminisced about Truman's veto of the Internal Security Act in 1950, with Lehman describing Truman's veto message as "one of the finest veto documents I have ever seen" and remembering that he had been one of the few Senators who had fought to sustain the veto. As for the present situation, Truman offered to discuss the matter with

Speaker of the House Sam Rayburn when they had dinner together in Washington on January 9, but Lehman feared "that this might be too late as there was a great possibility that a resolution would be brought up on the opening day of the session, January 7," and he urged Truman to contact Rayburn "as soon as possible." Truman replied that he would be in Washington on January 5, and to Lehman's great relief, he promised that "he would try to get in touch with Rayburn even before that." Lehman described the former President as "most cordial in his attitude, and . . . convinced that any such course was [*sic*] proposed by Congressman Walter would be most harmful and the wrong thing to do."[88]

Lehman and Truman were not the only ones to take up the cudgels against Walter's effort to extend HUAC's reach. The *Washington Post and Times-Herald* denounced Walter's attempt "to build a wall of legislative restrictions around and across the United States" and urged that HUAC "be abolished, not reorganized and expanded." According to the *Post and Times-Herald*, "the worst part of Mr. Walter's plan to consolidate his suzerainty is the suggestion implicit in his proposal that immigration and passport matters are primarily security questions." Brooklyn Democrat Emanuel Celler, who headed the House Judiciary Committee that currently exercised jurisdiction over immigration matters, had worked with Lehman for years to try to liberalize the McCarran-Walter Act. Celler now warned that "lumping immigration with un-American activities . . . would 'stigmatize' immigration by leaving an implication that there was something 'sinister' about it." Eleanor Roosevelt, Reinhold Niebuhr, and others took out a half-page ad in the *Washington Post and Times-Herald* calling on the House of Representatives "to eliminate the House Committee on Un-American Activities as a Standing Committee," and *Washington Post and Times-Herald* cartoonist Herblock joined in the effort to derail Walter's plan. Herbert Lehman hailed Herblock's cartoon, published on January 5, 1959, as "one of the most effective and best cartoons" Herblock had ever done.[89]

Herbert Lehman's determined opposition to Congressman Walter's plan paid off on January 5, 1959, when Speaker Rayburn announced his opposition to Walter's attempt to bring immigration and passport matters under the jurisdiction of a reorganized HUAC. Asked about Walter's initiative at a press conference, the Speaker replied: "We're not going to do that," effectively killing the proposal to give HUAC authority over immigration and passport issues. Lehman considered the defeat of Walter's proposal "a very substantial victory," and he believed that his publicizing the scheme had been instrumental in its defeat. As he told Senator Richard Neuberger, "until two or three weeks ago nobody knew of this proposal," which had "the approval of the Majority and Minority leadership in the House." But Lehman had "alerted many organizations and influential individuals," and their involvement, he believed, had led to Rayburn's announcement that the proposal was dead. Lehman especially

"The Idea Is To Set It Up In A Quick Change, See?"

FIGURE 18.3. "The Idea Is to Set It Up in a Quick Change, See?" January 5, 1959. A 1959 Herblock Cartoon, © The Herb Block Foundation.

thanked former President Truman for his help in blocking Walter's "ill-advised proposal," noting that Truman's "cooperation was of inestimable value and most influential in persuading the House Democratic Leadership not to give approval to the scheme."[90]

By 1959, Herbert Lehman and John Kennedy had gained new respect for each other, often sharing the dais or serving together among the honorary chairmen at various testimonial dinners. On the occasion of Lehman's eightieth birthday in March 1958, Kennedy hailed his former colleague, whose "clear and courageous voice has been a force for reason in our public life for three decades," and he inserted into the *Congressional Record* a *New York Times* editorial commending "Mr. Lehman's 80 Good Years." Kennedy observed that Lehman's "enduring vitality, undiminished concern for human needs, and broad vision are as evident today as they were during his years in the Senate and in other public positions." In sending Lehman the relevant page of the *Congressional Record*, Kennedy noted that Lehman had "no idea how much all of us here miss you," knowing "there are many good battles ahead of us today where we are going to miss you even more." Later that year, Lehman welcomed Kennedy as a fellow honorary degree recipient from Brandeis University, and Kennedy agreed to be an honorary sponsor of an Israel Bonds testimonial dinner for Lehman and to be the featured speaker at a dinner inaugurating the Herbert H. Lehman Institute of Ethics at the Jewish Theological Seminary of America.[91]

In his remarks at the Herbert Lehman Institute dinner in November 1958, Kennedy claimed that "no assignment" could have given him "more pleasure than to join in paying tribute to one of the world's great citizens, one of the most eminent Americans living today, and certainly one of the most able and distinguished men ever to serve in the United States Senate." He asserted that Lehman's "leadership, the ardor of his ideals, and the vast dimensions of his wisdom and interests have all made him one of the great public servants of our time," and he predicted that the impact of Lehman's "statesmanship will not be lost upon this nation for generations to come." Although Lehman had "left several offices," he had "never retired," for he had "never been satisfied with the accomplishments of the past or underestimated the possibilities of the future." According to Kennedy, "those of us who sat with him in the back row of the Senate" knew that Lehman had lived up to the Talmudic precept to "be bold as a leopard, light as an eagle, fleet as a hart, and strong as a lion." Kennedy hoped that those who came to study in the Herbert Lehman Institute would "take inspiration" from Lehman's "example and strive to live up to his mark."[92]

Upon John Kennedy's re-election to the Senate in 1958, Herbert Lehman immediately wired his "heartiest congratulations" on Kennedy's "magnificent victory." Kennedy responded with a friendly note thanking Lehman for his "most heartening" message and hoping that his "future record" would warrant Lehman's continued confidence. Neither man mentioned 1960, but the key question looming over their future relationship was whether Lehman considered Kennedy a strong, experienced, and consistent enough liberal to support him for the Democratic presidential nomination in 1960. Kennedy's fulsome praise of Lehman in the late 1950s clearly was intended, at least in part, to win the liberal icon's backing in 1960. But while Lehman and many like-minded liberals agreed that Kennedy certainly had the charm and good looks—the profile—to run for President, they wondered whether he had the courage to provide the leadership the nation needed on civil rights and other issues confronting the American people.[93]

CHAPTER 19

"You Weren't Double-Crossed, I Was"

Herbert Lehman, John Kennedy, and the Bosses, 1958–1960

[De Sapio's] final act of folly was the attempt to exclude Herbert Lehman—the most respected and distinguished Jewish political figure in New York—from the 1960 Democratic delegation.[1]

I

Before Herbert Lehman could begin to focus on the 1960 presidential election, he had to deal with the situation in New York City and in the New York State Democratic Party. Lehman's relations with Tammany Hall had fluctuated over the years, ranging from close cooperation during Al Smith's campaigns in the 1920s to overcoming Tammany chieftain John Curry's opposition when Lehman sought the governorship in 1932. Lehman had minimized any identification with the party bosses during his years in Albany and in Washington, relying on citizens committees and individuals he trusted rather than the party organization to run his campaigns. He joined Tammany leader Carmine De Sapio in supporting Robert F. Wagner, Jr., for Mayor of New York City in 1953 and 1957, and Averell Harriman for Governor in 1954, regarding De Sapio as "a great improvement over his predecessors." But Lehman believed that political organizations like Tammany Hall had "progressively become less powerful" because government assistance programs had reduced the need for

---

Chapter title quotation: John Kennedy to Herbert Lehman, November 5, 1960, quoted in Moscow, *The Last of the Big-Time Bosses*, p. 168.

their "charitable and relief" services—the "bucket of coal," basket of food, or money for the rent. In an interview in 1957, Lehman noted that "the voters have already demonstrated that they are increasingly selective in casting their votes. And they don't listen, the way they used to listen, to the advice of their election leader." Like many New York liberals, Lehman was disappointed in Tammany's less than enthusiastic support for Adlai Stevenson in 1952 and 1956, and events at the New York State Democratic Convention in Buffalo in 1958 created a rift between Lehman and De Sapio that erupted into a very public fight between party regulars, commanded by De Sapio, and insurgent reformers led by Herbert Lehman and Eleanor Roosevelt.[2]

At an eightieth birthday tribute luncheon attended by 1,200 people in March 1958, Herbert Lehman urged New York Democratic leaders to nominate a candidate with a "liberal philosophy" for the Senate seat currently held by Republican Irving Ives, asserting that "we need men of wide knowledge and high vision in government." Warning that "it is not enough to elect men who know or claim to know the problems of their state or congressional district or local constituency," Lehman emphasized that "we need men who know the world in which we live." Although Lehman did not mention any potential candidates by name, it was widely assumed that his remarks signaled his support for former Secretary of the Air Force Thomas Finletter, with whom Lehman had worked on Stevenson's campaigns and the Democratic Advisory Council. In an interview a few weeks later, Lehman praised Finletter's "great experience in both national and international affairs," calling him "the best Senator we could send to Washington." However, De Sapio and Democratic leaders did not share Lehman's enthusiasm for Finletter as a possible Senate candidate, preferring an Irish Catholic who would bring ethnic balance to the ticket. In addition, although Governor Harriman had forgiven Finletter for supporting Stevenson rather than Harriman for the Democratic presidential nomination in 1956, De Sapio and New York Democratic Party leaders had neither forgotten nor forgiven Finletter's apostasy.[3]

When Finletter formally announced his candidacy for the Democratic Senate nomination on July 23, 1958, Herbert Lehman, who was vacationing in Europe, immediately cabled his support, asserting that "Tom Finletter would be much the best man we can send to Washington" because Finletter's "experience and . . . knowledge of foreign affairs . . . would be a great asset at this time." However, as Lehman confided to a friend, "knowing the factors that frequently enter into the selection of a candidate," he was "not too hopeful" that Finletter would be nominated. As Lehman's chief aide Julius Edelstein had reminded him a few months earlier, although Lehman still wielded some influence with his fellow Democrats, the nomination would be controlled by the state Democratic "organization in which De Sapio and Harriman are greater powers."[4]

As Lehman feared, the New York State Democratic Convention rejected Finletter and nominated longtime Manhattan District Attorney Frank Hogan instead. Lehman was still in Europe at the time of the State Convention in Buffalo, but Edelstein was in close touch with Democratic and Liberal Party leaders, conveying Lehman's wishes and reporting back to him. Lehman did what he could for Finletter, but despite his efforts, Harriman's indecisiveness and De Sapio's control of the convention ensured that the nomination went to Hogan, De Sapio's handpicked candidate. Adding insult to injury, De Sapio then rewarded Erie County Democratic leader Peter Crotty with the nomination for Attorney General in return for Crotty's support of Hogan. Even though Lehman did not attend the Buffalo convention, De Sapio's and the bosses' naked display of their power left Lehman and liberal Democrats with a bitter taste that would not soon be forgotten. The problem, Julius Edelstein emphasized in a long memorandum to Lehman, was not Hogan, who "made an excellent acceptance speech" and "heavily emphasized his liberal inclinations." The problem was "what to do about De Sapio," who had defied both Governor Harriman and Mayor Wagner, as well as Lehman, in securing Hogan's and Crotty's nominations.[5]

"Deeply disappointed that Finletter was not nominated," and "shocked and deeply distressed" at what had occurred in Buffalo," Lehman feared that the Democrats had managed to transform "the easy victory which we foresaw a few months ago" into a "tough and hard" fight. In Lehman's opinion, what had transpired at the convention "has done grievous harm to the Democratic Party not only in the coming November election, but possibly for a long time." But realizing the need to keep the Democrats in the majority in the U.S. Senate, Lehman did everything he could to salvage Hogan's campaign. The Liberal Party had nominated Finletter as its Senate candidate, hoping that the Democrats would follow suit, but now, in the aftermath of the Democratic convention, Finletter's presence on the ballot would take votes away from Hogan and increase the possibility of Republican candidate Kenneth Keating winning the election. Finletter, therefore, declined the Liberal Party's nomination, urging the Liberals to back Hogan instead, but they were loath to accept the District Attorney because of the way in which his nomination had been arranged by De Sapio and the Democratic Party bosses. Herbert Lehman reached out from Switzerland to Liberal Party leaders Alex Rose and David Dubinsky, urging them to accede to Hogan's candidacy. Emphasizing the need for Democrats and Liberals to unite behind Hogan to prevent a Republican victory, Lehman stressed that Hogan "had a long and excellent record as [a] public official" and "has always been completely fair to labor and a strong supporter of civil rights." Lehman expressed confidence that Hogan would "carry forward the policies we have long espoused for the security and welfare of all the people of [the] state and nation," and he persuaded a reluctant Liberal Party to accept Hogan as its Senate candidate. Recognizing how crucial Lehman's "timely and essential intercession with the Liberal Party" had been, Hogan conveyed his appreciation to Lehman and his hope that his "efforts in the future" would continue to merit Lehman's "confidence and trust."[6]

Although 1958 promised to be a Democratic year across the nation, Herbert Lehman worried that the fiasco in Buffalo had handed New York Republicans "a tremendously valuable issue of 'boss control,'" and he was sure "they will use it to the utmost." Sure enough, Congressman Keating and Republican gubernatorial candidate Nelson Rockefeller immediately made De Sapio and "bossism" the major theme in their campaigns. Lehman did what he could to help Hogan and Governor Harriman, serving as one of the honorary chairmen of their Independent Citizens' Committee, but a painful sciatic condition limited Lehman's personal appearances with the candidates, forcing him to rely on letters to the editor and radio and television speeches. When the Rockefeller-Keating campaign quoted Lehman's negative comments about the Democratic convention in an ad, charging that De Sapio and the bosses controlled Harriman and the Democratic Party in New York, Lehman objected to the Republicans' use of his name and his words. Standing beside Harriman at a rally in the Garment District a few weeks later, Lehman asserted that despite the liberal policies that Rockefeller was espousing in the campaign, Harriman was the only "heir to the liberal tradition of Al Smith, Franklin Roosevelt, and myself." Lehman also tried to rally support for Hogan, emphasizing that the District Attorney was an "able, sincere, and dedicated man" who stood "for the same liberal principles which Bob Wagner and I fought for in the United States Senate through the years."[7]

Despite Lehman's efforts and the national trends in favor of the Democrats in 1958, Rockefeller's relative youth (he was fifty years old; Harriman was sixty-seven) and energy and his vigorous campaigning all across the state propelled him to a huge victory over the remote and somewhat plodding Harriman, and Rockefeller's coattails helped Keating defeat Hogan as well. As the *New York Times* noted, the "bossism" issue played a major role in the election results; because of De Sapio's heavy-handedness, "defeat was snatched out of the jaws of victory." Hogan never shook free from suspicions concerning De Sapio's motives for wanting to move him from the District Attorney's office to the Senate, and Harriman never recovered from the public humiliation of his own party ignoring his wishes. Trying to find a bright spot in the Democrats' dismal showing in New York, Lehman hoped that "the result of the election will lead to a reorganization of our party and its leadership in the State, which is obviously greatly needed."[8]

II

Herbert Lehman's disenchantment with De Sapio and the Democratic Party bosses stemmed not just from their ignoring his choice for the 1958 Senate race. According to De Sapio biographer and former *New York Times* reporter Warren Moscow, Lehman resented the way in which De Sapio and the others had humiliated Harriman and "demeaned the office of Governor," which "reflected on all who had held it, including himself." Lehman could not recall a time when "a Governor of the State or a Mayor of New York City" had been "so disregarded and repudiated by the [party] organization" as had happened at the Buffalo convention, and he also believed that the way in which De Sapio and the bosses controlled the party organization discouraged young idealists from getting involved in party affairs. Lehman resisted any effort to dislodge De Sapio until after the election was over, but once Harriman and Hogan had been defeated and the magnitude of the Democrats' disaster in New York in 1958 became apparent, Lehman prepared to move against De Sapio and the party bosses. Eleanor Roosevelt quickly joined her old friend in his efforts against De Sapio. In addition to wanting to see the Democratic Party in New York become more liberal and democratic, she had never forgiven De Sapio for denying her son, Franklin Roosevelt, Jr., the gubernatorial nomination in 1954.[9]

Shortly after the 1958 election, Lehman became actively involved in efforts to free the Democratic Party in New York from the taint of bossism. On November 13, Lehman aide Julius Edelstein and Governor Harriman's "close personal advisor" George Backer attended a meeting of Young Democrats who were calling for De Sapio's ouster, and on November 14, Lehman met with Harriman, Mayor Wagner, and New York State Democratic Chairman Michael Prendergast, a De Sapio ally, to discuss the future of the Democratic Party in New York. Harriman wanted to create a state group modeled on the national Democratic Advisory Council to formulate a Democratic alternative to the Republican program in Albany, but Lehman refused to join such a body "unless it was made perfectly clear that this Council would have no connection whatsoever with the State Committee or with the New York political leaders." Believing "very strongly that the issue lies much more deeply than merely being a matter of legislative policy, and that it was important to remove the image of 'bossism' in the State," Lehman was relieved when Harriman dropped the idea, emphasizing to the Governor in late December that "a real effort must be made to revitalize the Democratic Party in this State and to erase the image of 'bossism'; otherwise, it would be very doubtful within any measurable time that the Democratic Party could regain the confidence of the people." Moreover, Lehman stressed that his "usefulness would be very much impaired if there was any false suspicion whatsoever" that he "would have any dealings with the political leaders who brought on the mess in Buffalo."[10]

Putting Lehman's thoughts into action, on January 22, 1959, Lehman, Eleanor Roosevelt, and Thomas Finletter announced the formation of the New York Committee for Democratic Voters (CDV) to promote reform within the New York Democratic Party. Lehman and the others asserted that "the wide-spread feeling of protest among many voters against 'boss rule' in our party" explained the Democrats' dismal showing in the recent state elections at a time when Democrats elsewhere were winning victory after victory. They charged that the problem in New York was that "the machinery of party affairs remains largely in the hands of old-style professionals" who "feel that they and the Democratic Party are one and the same," who believe that "the Democratic voters and elected Democratic public officials are not much more than auxiliaries to be tolerated and to be consulted pro forma, but not to have a voice in the basic decisions." Lehman, Finletter, and Mrs. Roosevelt argued that the party's greatest need in New York was "to involve in its affairs the many enrolled Democrats, who for one reason or another have not participated in or been represented in party affairs," and they warned that "the election of a Democratic President in 1960 may well turn on the condition of the New York State Democratic Party." They called upon all Democrats "to advocate and advance the principles of democracy within all the reaches of the Democratic Party organization of New York," so that it could "advance the party's political programs in State and nation, rather than to serve the urge for personal power by political professionals."[11]

Although the CDV's official statement never mentioned De Sapio by name, the group's announcement was widely seen as a declaration of war against the Tammany leader. Lehman and the others had agreed not to personalize their efforts by attacking De Sapio directly, but Lehman made it clear in responding to questions that the group was committed to ousting De Sapio. For the Democrats to rebound, Lehman emphasized, they had to destroy the image of bossism, which meant removing De Sapio.[12]

The CDV's prospects for replacing De Sapio looked slim, however. The New York Young Democrats cheered the CDV's statement, asserting that "the party has grown stale and tired under the present management and that the time is long overdue for new, younger, more vigorous leadership," but most observers agreed with Otsego County Democratic Chairman Alexander Carson when he dismissed the new group and its leaders, proclaiming that "Mrs. Roosevelt and Mr. Lehman have had their day." The *New York Times* reported that most Democratic leaders considered Lehman, Finletter, and Mrs. Roosevelt " 'old Turks' who lack the organizational strength to unseat De Sapio in the tightly knit city organization which he firmly controls." Tom O'Hara of the *New York Herald Tribune* described the effort as the "egg-head rebellion," and the editors of the conservative *Chicago Tribune* characterized Lehman, Finletter, and Mrs. Roosevelt as "a left-'liberal' cabal." More importantly, Harriman refused to join the new group, Mayor Wagner first declared his neutrality and then his support for De Sapio, and State Controller Arthur Levitt, the only Democratic survivor of the 1958 statewide election debacle, refused to get involved in the intraparty strife. As Lehman confided to Paul Douglas, he understood that his "efforts here to revitalize the Democratic Party and destroy the image of 'bossism' will be a hard, and possibly a long fight," but he thought he had "a good chance of succeeding." Even if the attempt failed, Lehman believed it would "nonetheless have a salutary effect on the party."[13]

Lehman left most of the logistics and details of organizing the Committee for Democratic Voters to Julius Edelstein, George Backer, and Thomas Finletter, but after returning from a month in California, where he worked with Columbia University professor Allan Nevins on his biography, Lehman devoted considerable time, energy, and money to the battle to reform New York Democrats. Recognizing that "it will require considerable money and a host of vigorous, dedicated people who wish to reclaim the party for its members" for the CDV to achieve its goals, Lehman hosted a meeting of "50 or 60 members of insurgent groups, mainly young people," on February 21. A few days later, Herbert and Edith Lehman each contributed $2,500 to the CDV, and Lehman addressed a fund-raising dinner for the organization on March 5. Recalling how he had overcome "the strongest kind of opposition by almost all the organization leaders of the state" to his nomination for Governor in 1932, and how he, Al Smith, and Franklin Roosevelt had battled "against the machine's worst instincts," Lehman told the potential donors that it was necessary now "to reform the organization and return its control to the voters themselves . . . for the sake of the Democratic Party state-wide and nationally, and for the sake of good government in our city, state, and country." Trying to keep attention focused on the CDV's efforts, Lehman granted television interviews and discussed the effort to reform New York's Democratic Party when he addressed the Women's National Democratic Club in Washington, D.C., in mid-March. Later that month, Lehman "got out of a sick bed" to speak to the FDR–Woodrow Wilson Independent Democrats, who were challenging Tammany leadership in their district on the West Side of Manhattan. He hosted another fund-raising dinner on April 1 and met with reform leaders Edward Costikyan and Jean McCabe of the New Democratic Club on Manhattan's East Side on April 2. Before leaving for Europe on April 8, Lehman explained to reporters that the CDV "would not attempt to pick candidates for district leaderships," but "would give financial aid and advice to insurgent candidates it decided to help." People were starting to pay attention to the reform movement, as could be seen when the New York press corps, at its annual dinner in March 1959, lampooned Lehman, Finletter, and Mrs. Roosevelt for their battle against De Sapio and bossism with the following ditty:

> Rub-a-dub, dub
> Just three in a tub.
> Politically they are at sea.
> They'd put all the rap
> On poor old De Sap
> How ungrateful can liberals be?[14]

After returning from Europe in early June, Lehman spent much of the summer working on behalf of reformers who were challenging incumbent party leaders. On June 11, Lehman and Mrs. Roosevelt headlined a fund-raising dinner for Charles McGuiness and the Village Independent Democrats, who were challenging De Sapio's position as district leader, and in an interview a week later, Lehman, for the first time, explicitly called for the removal of State Democratic Chairman Prendergast. In a speech to the insurgent Lenox Hill Club in late June that had to be delivered by Julius Edelstein because Lehman's sciatica was acting up again, Lehman charged that most of the Tammany clubs were "just gin rummy, poker, and marching clubs, in which political activity is confined to . . . the district boss and his immediate henchmen." Most of these groups, Lehman complained, were "closed corporations which regard with cruel suspicion young people more interested in the burning public issues than in the soothing question of patronage," discouraging involvement by any but "the least sensitive and least capable."[15]

As the September 15, 1959, primary approached, Lehman intensified his efforts on behalf of insurgent candidates. He spoke at a motorcade rally in the 6th Assembly District, addressed a gathering sponsored by the Riverside Democratic Club to support the re-election of reform leader William Fitts Ryan in the 7th Assembly District, and donated $500 to the campaign of Irving Wolfson and Catherine Hemenway for district leaders in the 5th Assembly District North, to which the CDV contributed another $1,000. Urging voters to support Wolfson and Hemenway over the organization's candidates, Lehman returned to the theme that the party organization had prevented new and younger leaders from emerging, claiming that Tammany "had reduced district political clubs to political 'soup kitchens' where 'the party faithful are supposed to stand in line and wait for their turn to be served.'" Similarly, Lehman warned a group convened by the Village Independent Democrats that "boss domination has deprived our party of the confidence of a very great number of voters," making it impossible for the Democrats to "become the chosen instrument of the people's will until the stigma of bossism is substantially eradicated."[16]

Herbert Lehman and the Committee for Democratic Voters fell short in their attempt to unseat De Sapio in the 1959 Democratic primary elections, but the narrow margin by which De Sapio survived showed that the CDV's message resonated with many Democratic voters and set the stage for the group's future success. De Sapio won re-election as district leader in Greenwich Village, but only by six hundred votes out of more than nine thousand cast; three of his allies were defeated by candidates backed by the CDV; three other De Sapio henchmen were defeated in Harlem by candidates loyal to Congressman Adam Clayton Powell; and four incumbent district leaders supported by the CDV were re-elected. Lehman hailed Charles McGuinness's strong showing against De Sapio in Greenwich Village as "an amazing showing," and George Backer cheered that the reform movement's "victories and near victories mean that in its next contest there should be and will be a complete triumph for those young men and women who wish to see the Democratic Party once again the vehicle for their aspirations for progressive government and a political party that is responsive to the people."[17]

Although De Sapio had retained his position, most observers agreed with the *New York Times* that he had suffered "a bloody nose" and that "De Sapio's days as a powerful boss [were] numbered." Lehman explained to his old UNRRA colleague Robert G. A. Jackson that "the reform movement made almost spectacular gains in ten or twelve contested Assembly Districts and undoubtedly De Sapio's prestige has been badly damaged." Lehman was confident that "if the young people can keep up the fight and we oldsters can help them a bit, as we have, bossism in this state is on the way out." The surprisingly strong showing of the reformers in 1959 marked the beginning of the transfer of power in the Democratic Party in New York City from the old party chieftains, who had long controlled the party's machinery, to a new generation of leaders, younger, more educated, and more idealistic than their predecessors, men and women who had been inspired by Adlai Stevenson and Herbert Lehman and who sought to forge a party more committed to liberal principles than patronage.[18]

Herbert Lehman hosted a victory party at his home in late September for eighty leaders of the recent battle against De Sapio and bossism. Lehman proclaimed that the primary results had been "a great victory," but he stressed that the fight had just begun. De Sapio had narrowly survived, but the voters had given him "an overwhelming vote of 'no confidence,'" after which he could "no longer act or pretend to speak as the unchallenged chief of the Democratic Party organization of this city and state." Looking to the future, Lehman asserted that a reformed Democratic Party should "rouse the people from their apathy, their cynicism, and their resignation" to lead the fight "against the tremendous problems which now beset our city—racial tensions and hostilities, spreading slums, and the pollution of the very air we breathe." Lehman was "willing to continue to give advice and counsel to those engaged in carrying on this movement," but he emphasized that younger people "must furnish the driving power—the man and woman power—to carry this movement on to its inevitable triumph."[19]

After many meetings and discussions throughout the fall of 1959, the Committee for Democratic Voters announced in December "the broadening of its structure and the reconstitution of its Executive Committee" to advance "the goals and purposes of the reform movement." Lehman, Finletter, Mrs. Roosevelt, former New York City Police Commissioner Francis Adams, and noted attorney Lloyd Garrison would "serve as a Board of Advisors," but the CDV's day-to-day operations would now be directed by an expanded Executive

Committee chaired by Irving Engel, a well-known New York attorney who had frequently worked with Herbert Lehman on Jewish and liberal causes in the past. Longtime Lehman aide Julius Edelstein, who had played a major role in the reorganization, was also a member of the Executive Committee, and he could be counted on to ensure that the wishes of Herbert Lehman and the other members of the advisory board were made known to the group. Engel vowed that the committee would continue the fight to democratize the New York Democratic Party and replace "boss control" with "a leadership based on the will of the voters," but with 1960 being a presidential election year, the CDV seemed likely to focus on more than just local intraparty affairs. As the *New York Times* noted, it was "expected that the reorganized group will move quickly to influence the choice of delegates to next year's Democratic National Convention in favor of a liberal presidential nominee and platform."[20]

III

The Committee for Democratic Voters' challenge to De Sapio and the party leaders had important ramifications in the race for the Democratic presidential nomination in 1960. Herbert Lehman warned that unless the present image of the New York Democratic Party as an organization controlled by political bosses was erased, New York's influence at the Democratic convention in 1960 would be greatly diminished, and the Republicans would have a good chance of carrying the state. The CDV believed that "the 1960 presidential election is of the utmost importance," and asserted that "delegates to the 1960 Democratic convention should be selected by the Democratic voters on the local level and not be picked by a few leaders."[21]

Herbert Lehman knew that the CDV would be fatally weakened if it were seen as promoting or opposing a particular candidate for the presidency in 1960, so he worked assiduously to maintain both his own and the organization's impartiality among the potential nominees. In March 1959, when Lehman's brother-in-law Frank Altschul expressed interest in Hubert Humphrey as a presidential candidate, Lehman noted his "admiration and affection for Hubert," but he stressed that he had "not in the slightest degree" made up his mind yet as to who he would support in 1960. Similarly, Lehman told Senator Richard Neuberger a few months later, "There are a number of men in our party," any one of whom "would be a good candidate and a great President," but he pointed out that the Democratic Convention was "still fifteen months off" and Lehman was in no hurry to endorse anyone. Because Lehman, Finletter, and Mrs. Roosevelt had all been active in Adlai Stevenson's campaigns, and Mrs. Roosevelt had frequently voiced her reservations concerning John Kennedy, the leaders of the CDV had to deny repeatedly what Lehman described as "malicious" rumors that their group opposed Kennedy's nomination in 1960. Lehman understood that such allegations were designed to weaken the CDV with Catholic voters who strongly supported Kennedy's candidacy and looked askance at the CDV's liberal leadership. In an attempt to put such charges to rest, the CDV emphasized in its July 1959 statement of principles that "the Committee does not intend to take a position for or against any candidate for the Democratic nomination." When a reporter asked Lehman in August "if he thought a Roman Catholic, such as Senator John F. Kennedy of Massachusetts, could win," Lehman replied: "I certainly do," explaining that "religious prejudice is much less than in the days of Al Smith."[22]

Carmine De Sapio expected to be a major power broker at the Democratic National Convention in 1960, controlling New York State's 114 votes, but the insurgents' success in 1959 threatened that dream. The Tammany leader had hoped to lead a bloc of uncommitted delegates that he could deliver to a candidate at a strategic moment, but with his image now tarnished by the bossism charge, De Sapio's endorsement might be seen as a liability rather than an asset. After the September 1959 primary, columnist Roscoe Drummond asserted, "The sharp setback handed to Tammany leader Carmine De Sapio . . . strengthens the liberal forces in New York State, led by former Sen. Herbert Lehman, Eleanor Roosevelt, and Thomas Finletter," whose "support will more likely go to Adlai Stevenson or Hubert Humphrey than to Senator Kennedy."[23]

In pursuing the Democratic presidential nomination, John Kennedy tried to straddle the line between the party bosses and the reformers in New York, much as he was trying to appeal simultaneously to whites in the South and blacks in the North. Early in 1959, Kennedy accepted an invitation from Peter Crotty, the Democratic leader in Buffalo, the state's second largest city, to serve as the featured speaker at the Erie County Democrats' annual Grover Cleveland dinner, and Kennedy responded enthusiastically when Crotty, who was closely aligned with De Sapio, offered to host a private breakfast for Kennedy with fifty-five upstate Democratic county chairmen. As the *New York Times* noted of the Buffalo gathering, it was not a coincidence that "the party leadership in this predominantly Roman Catholic industrial community" spoke "glowingly" of Kennedy's "possible presidential candidacy." The following month, however, Arthur Schlesinger, Jr., arranged for Kennedy to reach out to the reformers when he hosted a dinner at which Kennedy met with Thomas Finletter. But still wooing the bosses, the Kennedy campaign decided in October 1959 to send Rhode Island Governor Dennis Roberts to New York to meet with Crotty, State Chairman Mike Prendergast, and Albany boss Dan O'Connell in pursuit of delegates.[24]

Nothing better illustrated Kennedy's difficulty in trying to appeal to both the bosses and the reformers than his indecision about whether to speak to the Lexington Democratic Club (LDC), one of the city's first insurgent groups and one whose roster included Herbert Lehman among its honorary members and Thomas Finletter on its advisory council. In June 1959, Schlesinger urged Kennedy to accept an invitation to address the group, which he described as "an important liberal sounding-board." Similarly, Mary Bancroft, an old friend who was on a first name basis with Kennedy and was now a member of the club's executive committee, advised that "talking to the LDC will have a good effect—for 1960." But John Stillman, chairman of the Orange County Democratic Committee, while agreeing that it was a good idea to have Kennedy "identified with the new and younger, Liberal and Democratic element in the party," questioned "whether an appearance at the Lexington Club is the best way to go about it," and he hoped "this invitation will not be accepted until all its implications have been fully considered." After initially agreeing to address the group, Kennedy backed out in late October, explaining to Finletter, "in view of the fact I shall not come into New York again to speak for many months, it would not be wise for me to come only to this occasion, particularly as I am going to be engaged after the first of the year in other areas of the country." Finletter lamented Kennedy's change of mind, explaining that because of his "high regard" for Kennedy, he wanted him to "meet and speak to groups like this in New York so they would get to know" Kennedy, while another Kennedy supporter regretted the Senator's "cancelling for the simple reason that just the mere sight of you would have thrown the reform group into such confusion that Eleanor R. would have found herself without an army." Much to the consternation of the Kennedy camp, the liberal *New York Post* learned about Kennedy's reversal and, correctly, attributed it to pressure from Bronx boss Charles Buckley, who did not want Kennedy cozying up to the reformers of the Lexington Club.[25]

Worried that Kennedy was losing ground with New York liberals because of his decision not to speak to the Lexington Democratic Club, Arthur Schlesinger, Jr., suggested that Kennedy might be able "to repair the damage" by attending the December 7 dinner of the Democratic Advisory Council at which Mrs. Roosevelt would be honored. Trying to burnish his credentials with liberals, Kennedy had finally, in November 1959, joined the DAC, which, as the *New York Times* noted, was widely perceived as "dominated by 'liberal' elements in the party." With all the potential Democratic presidential candidates except Lyndon Johnson planning to attend the dinner, Kennedy hoped that his participation in the DAC event would help mend fences and broaden his appeal among party liberals.[26]

Herbert Lehman played a prominent role in the Democratic Advisory Council meetings leading up to the dinner for Mrs. Roosevelt. At the DAC session on December 5, Lehman formally proposed adoption of the Council's Science and Technology Committee's proposal to create a "National Peace Agency" that would redirect America's scientific and technical knowledge from weapons to peaceful purposes, such as inspection systems that would allow the verification of disarmament agreements. Two days later, Lehman and former Governor Averell Harriman sponsored the DAC's concluding luncheon at the Hotel Pierre, at which time Lehman emphasized that "the Democrats had to pick a bold liberal candidate to win" in 1960. Lehman also showed where his heart really lay for 1960, predicting that regardless of whether Adlai Stevenson was the Democratic candidate, Stevenson "would be an 'important factor' at the 1960 convention."[27]

On December 28, 1959, Senator John Kennedy informed Herbert Lehman and many others that he would be announcing his formal candidacy for the presidency on January 2. Kennedy sent out a copy of the statement he planned to make, explaining that he "would be very grateful" for Lehman's support. There is no evidence that Lehman, who was very conscientious about acknowledging communications, responded to Kennedy's letter or the Senator's official declaration of his candidacy a few days later.[28]

Lehman's lack of enthusiasm about Kennedy's announcement stemmed from his preference for other candidates. Conservative columnist George Sokolsky misrepresented the purpose of the Committee for Democratic Voters when he wrote in early January 1960 that "the reform Democrats in New York, led by Eleanor Roosevelt and Herbert Lehman, are seeking control of the New York State delegation to the Democratic Convention in the interest of Adlai Stevenson," but Sokolsky's comments accurately reflected the high regard that Lehman and Mrs. Roosevelt still held for Stevenson. But with Stevenson denying any interest in the nomination, Lehman had to look elsewhere, and Hubert Humphrey's liberal record on most issues certainly corresponded more closely to Lehman's positions on civil rights and other matters than did Kennedy's more circumspect views. While Lehman "discount[ed] many of the flattering things" Humphrey had said about him over the years, the two men and their wives had developed a close friendship during their years together in Washington. Lehman had great "admiration and affection" for Humphrey, and Humphrey considered Lehman "a real friend," describing their relationship as "one of the real compensations for all the grief and hardship involved in public life." When Humphrey and his wife came to New York for the DAC meetings and the dinner for Mrs. Roosevelt, Humphrey wanted "very much" to meet with Lehman, and the Humphreys had breakfast at the Lehmans' home, at which time they presumably discussed Humphrey's plans to announce his candidacy for the presidency in a few weeks. Like Kennedy, Humphrey included Lehman among those who received advance notice of the formal declaration of his candidacy, and on the bottom of the form letter, Humphrey thanked Lehman for his "encouragement and friendship." Lehman had not even acknowledged Kennedy's candidacy, but he quickly welcomed Humphrey's, telling the Minnesotan how much he and Edith liked Humphrey's statement. Lehman characterized Humphrey's declaration as "a dignified document" that clearly expressed Humphrey's political philosophy, and Humphrey looked forward to receiving Lehman's "advice and counsel" in the months ahead, noting that Lehman's "mature wisdom" would "always be a source of strength." Mrs. Lehman was an early and generous donor to the Humphrey for President Committee, telling a friend that Humphrey "is a wonderful speaker and, more important, knows what he is talking about."[29]

IV

Herbert Lehman had attended every Democratic National Convention since 1928 except for 1944, when he was Director General of UNRRA, and he looked forward to attending the 1960 convention in Los Angeles in July. State Democratic Chairman Prendergast declared in November 1959 that he would be "delighted" if Lehman were part of the New York delegation once again in 1960, but Lehman's continued fight against the party bosses endangered his selection as a delegate to the party gathering. As Lehman explained to Mrs. Roosevelt, he believed that "democratizing the Democratic Party" should include "the election in many of the districts of liberal delegates to the national convention who will be independent of boss control." When the Democratic National Committee allotted additional votes and delegates to New York in January 1960, Lehman, Mrs. Roosevelt, and the Committee for Democratic Voters' Advisory Committee strongly suggested in a letter to Prendergast and in a press release that these additional delegates "should be selected directly by the Democratic voters" in each congressional district, warning that any other manner of selecting these additional delegates "could only lead to the conclusion that a small group of party 'bosses' were trying to grab power, rather than welcoming an opportunity for a wider representation based on democratic procedures." If the State Committee were "to arrogate to itself . . . the right to name the additional delegates," Lehman cautioned, such action "will be rightfully resented by Democrats" and "the result would be harmful to the prestige of our party and to its cause."[30]

Prendergast claimed he was "pleased to receive" Lehman's recommendation, which he characterized as "the first *constructive* suggestion" he had ever received from Lehman's group. The state chairman hoped that "this represents a change in policy" and that intraparty disputes would now be settled privately, thereby avoiding "the constant 'bickering'" in the press that, he charged, was "undermining our position in the battle to defeat Republicanism in this state and nation." Prendergast asserted that "unless we 'bury our differences' for the time being, we will be aiding the cause of Nixonism, perhaps even placing in jeopardy the electoral votes of New York State . . . which could even mean the difference between national victory and defeat in 1960." He urged Lehman and

Mrs. Roosevelt to reconsider their decision not to attend the State Committee dinner on February 13, where they would be among "our Dais Guests," and to "place the principles of our great party and the many good causes we champion in common, above everything else, until such time as we are able to restore the government of the United States to the responsible hands of the people, where it belongs." Prendergast was not asking Lehman to abandon the "fight to unseat Mr. De Sapio or myself," he explained, "but merely to put the interests of party unity ahead of personalities until after Election Day." Despite Prendergast's call for the Democrats to settle their differences quietly, Prendergast, like Lehman, released his letter to the press.[31]

As this dispute with Prendergast illustrated, Lehman, despite his desire to pass the torch to younger men and women, remained the leader of the reform movement, and he replied to Prendergast that he was "glad to know that the State Committee is giving careful consideration" to the CDV's recommendation that "the additional delegates to the Convention . . . be elected directly by the Democratic voters in each congressional district and not selected by the State Committee." But Lehman loudly rejected Prendergast's call to postpone the fight for party reform in the name of party unity. In a letter to Prendergast that was also released to the press, Lehman noted that he would be out of town at the time of the State Committee dinner, but he made it clear that even if he were available, he "would not attend the dinner" because his presence at that event "would inevitably be taken by the public as an endorsement of the present political leadership of the Democratic Party and would give people the impression" that Lehman and his associates were "shadow-boxing," which was "very far from the truth." Echoing the position he had so often taken as a Senator, Lehman explained that the reformers were "unwilling to sacrifice" their "principles merely for the sake of party unity"; they welcomed "party unity, but not at the expense of principle." He warned that "unless the Democratic Party rids itself of the stigma of 'bossism' and takes vigorous steps to improve the political climate of the party, the Democrats of New York State will have little influence either at the convention in Los Angeles or in the election."[32]

On February 4, 1960, after consulting with most of the state's Democratic county chairmen, Prendergast announced that the State Committee would appoint New York's additional delegates to the Democratic National Convention. Lehman immediately denounced the plan as "contrary to what we conceive to be democratic practice," pointing out that it would allow the party leaders to pick twenty-seven of New York's 114 delegates to the convention, almost one-quarter of the state's total. But despite Lehman's opposition, the Democratic State Committee overwhelmingly adopted Prendergast's proposal when it met ten days later.[33]

Looking to attract a large crowd and reduce the state party's substantial debt, De Sapio and Prendergast invited Senator Kennedy to be the main speaker at the State Committee's $100-a-plate dinner on February 13. The dinner allowed Kennedy to see firsthand the bitter struggle going on between Lehman and the party bosses. Without mentioning Lehman or any of the reformers by name, Prendergast castigated them in his remarks at the dinner, noting that "some guests may be missing by their own well-publicized choice, but the party goes on." Ignoring Lehman's and Mrs. Roosevelt's decades of service to the Democratic Party, Prendergast denounced "those nominal Democrats who would utilize headlines to establish themselves as the sole judges of the destinies of the Democratic Party." Fending off the charges of "bossism," Prendergast pledged that New York's actions at the convention would reflect the views of the entire delegation rather than the opinions "of any one individual party leader, special group, or self-appointed spokesman."[34]

Despite his fondness for Hubert Humphrey, Herbert Lehman remained uncommitted among the candidates seeking the 1960 Democratic presidential nomination. Despite Adlai Stevenson's refusal to declare himself a candidate, Lehman predicted in a letter to Allan Nevins that Stevenson would be "receptive" to overtures and "would be very much of a factor at the convention in Los Angeles." But Lehman stressed, "I have reached no decision as yet as to whom I will support," wanting "to watch developments in the next few months." Lehman believed the race had "now narrowed down to Kennedy, Hubert Humphrey, Adlai Stevenson, Johnson, and Symington," but he did not think that any of them had yet garnered "anything approaching a majority of the delegates." Lehman was "concerned that as of the moment no one of our candidates has sufficient strength to win against Nixon," complaining that "we constantly hear more of the weaknesses of our candidates than of their strength."[35]

As the race for the Democratic presidential nomination heated up in the spring of 1960, Herbert Lehman urged his fellow Democrats to select Adlai Stevenson for President and John Kennedy for Vice President. Lehman was impressed by Kennedy's victories in a string of Democratic primaries, but in a television appearance and an interview in mid-April, he predicted that the Democratic convention would be deadlocked, which would make Stevenson a serious possibility once again, and Lehman believed that a ticket with Stevenson at the top and Kennedy as the vice presidential candidate "could develop and would be excellent." Lehman did not expect that religion would "play as important a part in the election as some people think," and he anticipated that "the prejudice, hatred, and suspicion" would be much less than when the Democrats had nominated Al Smith in 1928. In a letter to Nevins in late April, Lehman emphasized, "I have not either declared or decided who I would support at the convention if I am a delegate," but he noted that he had stated publicly "on a number of occasions" his belief that "a ticket of Stevenson for President and Kennedy for Vice President would be the strongest that we Democrats could nominate."[36]

A few weeks later, after Kennedy's victory over Hubert Humphrey in the West Virginia primary demonstrated the Massachusetts Senator's ability to win in a heavily Protestant state, Lehman declared, "On the basis of his conduct in the primaries, and of the positions he has taken on various public issues, I have now decided that I personally want to see Jack Kennedy on the national ticket." But Lehman emphasized that he thought Kennedy's proper place was as Stevenson's running mate, not at the top of the Democratic ticket. As he explained to Wayne Morse, in the aftermath of the Soviet Union's shooting down of an American U-2 spy plane and the capture of its pilot, and the resulting collapse of the Paris summit talks between President Eisenhower and Soviet Premier Nikita Khrushchev, Lehman believed that "in this most crucial period of the nation's existence, we need a man of long experience, training, and mature judgment at the head of the government." In Lehman's opinion, the young Senator from Massachusetts had yet to demonstrate these qualities, while Stevenson possessed them in abundance.[37]

While Lehman called publicly for a Stevenson-Kennedy ticket, John Kennedy and his campaign team worked to solidify Kennedy's support in New York for the top spot on the Democratic slate. Kennedy and his operatives ignored both the reformers and De Sapio and Prendergast, working instead through local leaders, including County Chairmen Charles Buckley in the Bronx, Joseph Sharkey in Brooklyn, Peter Crotty in Buffalo, and John Stillman in Orange County. As Anthony Akers, who headed up the Citizens' Committee for Kennedy that was established in New York after the convention, later recalled, De Sapio and Prendergast thought that "the religion factor" would prevent Kennedy from winning the nomination and the presidency, and thus they remained "lukewarm all the way through" about Kennedy, trying to spark "boomlets for Stuart Symington and for Lyndon Johnson" instead. Akers noted, however, that "most of the Democratic county chairmen across New York State were Irish Catholics at the time and had an emotional commitment to JFK as the pre-eminent leader in that community nationally, and they wanted him for their candidate." Sharkey reported in late April that Kennedy's support in Brooklyn was growing rapidly, and he warned, "If we're not for Kennedy, the Kennedy crowd will run over us." On the eve of the Bronx County Democrats' fund-raising dinner in May, at which Kennedy was the featured speaker, Buckley urged New York Democrats to join the Kennedy bandwagon, emphasizing that Kennedy's presence at the top of the Democratic ticket would provide the greatest boost for local candidates in November. Kennedy's cultivation of the county leaders and local bosses did not endear him to Lehman and the reformers, many of whom still had their doubts about Kennedy dating back to his failure to speak out against Joe McCarthy.[38]

As the New York Democratic primary on June 7 approached, Lehman and his fellow reformers continued their fight against De Sapio and the party bosses over the makeup of the New York delegation to the national convention. The Committee for Democratic Voters reiterated that it was not backing any particular candidate for the presidency, emphasizing that it was "supporting reform candidates for delegate to the Democratic National Convention, regardless of whether they are pledged to Senator Kennedy, Governor Stevenson, Senator Humphrey, or any other aspirant." Their focus, the insurgents stressed, was "to fight for an unbossed delegation" in which delegates would "reflect the views of their electorates—and their own consciences—rather than the dictates of the political bosses." Reform leaders in the 17th Congressional District reached an agreement with the De Sapio forces that they would split the district's delegates to the convention and that the State Committee would appoint Lehman and Mrs. Roosevelt as delegates to the convention if they wished to attend.[39]

Herbert Lehman worked tirelessly on behalf of reform candidates running in the primary for district leader, the State Legislature, and seats in Congress. Mrs. Roosevelt told her daughter in mid-April that "yesterday, at least 40 reform N.Y. City candidates were photographed here with Sen. Lehman & me," and a few days later the executive director of the CDV reported that "the sound truck tapes recorded by Senator Lehman and Mrs. Roosevelt were also available for endorsed candidates." Lehman appeared at meetings and rallies for reform candidates all over the city, boosting William Fitts Ryan, who was challenging incumbent Congressman Ludwig Teller on Manhattan's West Side, and Herbert Rubin, who was seeking the Democratic nomination for Congress in a district in Queens. Of the $6,841.93 raised by Ryan's campaign, the CDV donated $3,150 and Herbert Lehman personally contributed an additional $1,200. Speaking on behalf of reform candidates in the Bronx, Lehman claimed that he was personally fond of Bronx County Chairman Charles Buckley, but he denounced Buckley as "one of the most absolute bosses in the boss-ridden party organization of the city and state." Lehman warned that unless Democrats installed "a new and responsive leadership in our party organization and begin to change the fetid political atmosphere which surrounds New York City . . . the voters will react with increasing vigor against our party in the presidential election and in the mayoral election next year."[40]

The June primary elections resulted in what the *New York Times* described as a "smashing" victory for Herbert Lehman and the reformers over De Sapio and the party organization. The *New York Herald Tribune* neatly summarized the situation in its headline, declaring "De Sapio Candidates Routed in Key Manhattan Districts," and the *Washington Post and Times-Herald* concurred that De Sapio had "suffered one of the worst setbacks of his political career." Insurgent William Fitts Ryan defeated Congressman Teller on Manhattan's West Side, where a reform candidate also triumphed over a sitting State Senator, while two CDV-backed candidates on the East Side defeated the organization's choices in two State Assembly contests. As the *Herald Tribune* noted, "Worst of all for Mr.

De Sapio was a humiliating defeat within his Greenwich Village home area," where two candidates backed by Lehman defeated De Sapio's choices for spots on the State Committee. The *Herald Tribune* noted that the eighty-two-year-old Lehman had "raised the issue of 'bossism' last year and maintained the cry against Mr. De Sapio at any and every opportunity since that time," visiting "every rally and meeting, however small, that he could to call on the average voters to turn Mr. De Sapio out." One Ryan supporter reflected after the election that he did not think Ryan "would have won unless we had Lehman's backing in the campaign," emphasizing that they had succeeded because they had "turned the fight into a Lehman versus De Sapio fight instead of a Ryan versus Teller fight." Similarly, political scientist James Q. Wilson, in assessing Ryan's victory over Teller, wrote that while "it appeared as if an Irishman [Ryan] had beaten a Jew [Teller] in a Jewish district, in fact, a Jewish elder statesman [Lehman] had beaten an Italian boss [De Sapio]." The *New York Times* wondered if De Sapio's "days as the top Democratic leader in New York may be numbered," and Lehman believed that the election results showed that De Sapio "cannot influence the voters of New York City, not even those in his own district."[41]

In the aftermath of the reformers' victories over De Sapio and the party organization in the primaries, an article in the *Christian Science Monitor* asked: "Has the hold of the Tammany chieftain on the delegation to the Democratic National Convention, beginning July 11, been weakened?" The answer was not long in coming. Nine days after the primary, De Sapio and Prendergast demonstrated their complete control over the state's delegation to the convention. In what presidential election chronicler Theodore White characterized as "a day of long knives and dirty politics in New York, the De Sapio-Prendergast machine vented its spite on the reformers" and "excluded former Governor Lehman, one of New York's most revered Democrats, from the convention delegation." In a statement released just before the State Committee met to name the rest of the delegation, Prendergast and De Sapio recalled Lehman's sharp criticism of the State Committee's decision to appoint the additional at-large delegates, and they claimed that "neither Senator Lehman nor Mrs. Roosevelt has affirmatively indicated any desire to us to be elected as a delegate-at-large from the State of New York." The State Committee loyally backed De Sapio and Prendergast, voting 284 to 14 to reject a proposal to substitute Lehman for another delegate. Not content with the rebuke to Lehman, De Sapio and Prendergast also reneged on a previous agreement to include four reform leaders among the delegates from Manhattan congressional districts. In what was widely construed as "an open declaration of war against the reform movement," Prendergast bitterly denounced the insurgents as "a destructive force masquerading as a reform movement," and he vowed that he was "not going to stand idly by any longer and see good, able, decent people forced into undeserved defeats in primaries on election day because the electorate was confused, misguided, and lied to, and our people slandered." The state chairman angrily urged Democratic leaders to "fight fire with fire—propaganda with facts—slander with truth and if necessary, revert to the philosophy of our ancestors of an eye for an eye and a tooth for a tooth."[42]

As Lehman and others quickly pointed out, Prendergast's and De Sapio's action seemed to confirm everything that Lehman and the reformers had been saying about the bosses controlling the Democratic Party in New York. Responding publicly with what he described to his brother-in-law as "a short and restrained statement," Lehman asserted that the State Committee's action was "just another reflection of the shortsightedness of the bosses" who did not want Lehman "to have any voice in the decisions of the New York delegation and of the national convention." Speaking more frankly to columnist Doris Fleeson, Lehman described the incident as "a dramatic example of both the stupidity and the ruthlessness of De Sapio, Prendergast, and their associates," which "has already caused great resentment among Democrats and Independents." Similarly, Irving Engel of the CDV argued that "if anyone has had any doubts with regard to the boss-ridden character of the present leadership of the Democratic Party in New York, those doubts will have been resolved by the autocratic rejection by the State Committee of Herbert H. Lehman as a delegate-at-large to the national convention." The editors of the *New York Herald Tribune* agreed that De Sapio and Prendergast had provided Lehman with "ammunition" and "the best proof that his protestations are valid," and the *New York Times* observed that "the little men" controlling the New York Democratic Party had acted "with a pettiness that dishonors them and the party" in dropping Lehman, "the Elder Statesman of the party, the pilot of many victories, the wise counselor of old, the conscience of the party's better days."[43]

Prendergast and De Sapio's heavy-handed treatment of Lehman quickly backfired, as prominent Democrats rallied around Lehman. Mayor Wagner, who had come under criticism from Lehman and the reformers at times, immediately distanced himself from De Sapio and the party leaders, telling reporters that he had recommended that the State Committee "consider the names of Mrs. Roosevelt and Senator Lehman as delegates" and had suggested that the committee should ask Lehman and Roosevelt if they wished to be included in the delegation. William vanden Heuvel, a reformer who was the Democratic candidate for Congress in Manhattan's 17th Congressional District, criticized the party leaders in a letter to the *New York Times*, condemning their attempt "to weaken and humiliate the man who symbolizes the greatest achievements of the Democratic Party." Vanden Heuvel predicted that such "shortsightedness" and "myopia can only lead to defeat for that leadership," and he urged the New York delegation "to reconstitute itself" to include Herbert Lehman, "the 'conscience' of our party." Lehman's longtime friend Anna Rosenberg urged Prendergast "to reconsider this unfortunate decision" to exclude Lehman and

Mrs. Roosevelt from the New York delegation, emphasizing that "there are no two Americans in the Democratic Party with a more distinguished record of service to humanity, to the Democratic Party, and to the entire free world." Former President Truman described Lehman's exclusion as "the darndest foolishness I've ever heard of," and former Harriman aide Daniel Patrick Moynihan, writing in *Commentary* a year later, described the "attempt to exclude Herbert Lehman—the most respected and distinguished Jewish political figure in New York—from the 1960 Democratic delegation" as De Sapio's "final act of folly."[44]

While De Sapio and Prendergast defended the State Committee's exclusion of Lehman from the convention delegation, Mayor Wagner and others sought to overturn the party leaders' action. Prendergast emphasized that Lehman's rejection was not "the decision of a few leaders, but the overwhelming opinion of the members of the State Committee," and he maintained that it "reflected the reaction of members of the party who have worked tirelessly for the Senator in his campaigns and who resented his recent attacks upon those duly constituted leaders elected by the enrolled voters of our party under legal democratic procedures." Despite Prendergast's hardline position, Wagner "was very much distressed at what had happened at the meeting of the State Committee" and he promised to work to reverse Lehman's exclusion. Franklin Roosevelt, Jr., volunteered to give up his seat as a delegate in favor of Lehman, and State Controller Arthur Levitt made the same offer. Brooklyn leader Joseph Sharkey later blamed "Manhattan"—meaning De Sapio, the party leader in Manhattan—for the decision to exclude Lehman. Sharkey had gone along with the original decision to omit Lehman from the delegation, but he quickly realized that the Democrats had jeopardized their standing in Brooklyn's large Jewish community by treating Lehman with such disdain. New York City Council President Abe Stark, a Sharkey protégé who had risen through the ranks of the Brooklyn Democratic organization, publicly characterized Lehman's exclusion as "an injustice," emphasizing that "an unfortunate mistake has been made by doing this to a man who was a four-term Governor and a former Senator and a former head of the United Nations Relief and Rehabilitation Agency." Even though Sharkey resented what he considered to be Lehman's holier than thou attitude, he put aside his personal feelings and, along with Bronx boss Charles Buckley, he set out to undo the State Committee's decision.[45]

Under pressure from Wagner, Sharkey, and many others, and realizing they had committed a horrible public relations blunder, Prendergast and De Sapio tried to mitigate the damage when the New York delegation met in Albany on June 23. Prendergast announced that he would relinquish his seat in the delegation to Lehman if the former Governor wished to be a delegate, a move that won unanimous approval. Lehman had told Mayor Wagner that he was not inclined, at this late date, to accept an invitation to be part of the New York delegation should one be forthcoming; however, after reading press reports of Prendergast's action and the delegation's unanimous request that he be made part of the delegation, Lehman stated that he would accept if he were now asked to be a delegate, but only "on the understanding that I will be completely free to cast my vote and to raise my voice as my conscience dictates." As Eleanor Roosevelt remarked, it was "the rare delegate who, like Senator Lehman," could insist upon the freedom to vote his conscience, but Prendergast understood that he had no choice but to comply with Lehman's demand. Trying to make the best of the situation, Prendergast asserted that New York delegates had always enjoyed "complete freedom" in casting their votes at party conventions. Writing to friends, Lehman noted that the bosses' efforts to "punish" those who opposed them had sparked "strong and spontaneous resentment on the part of the public," demonstrating "the power of informed and aroused public opinion." According to Douglas Dales of the *New York Times*, De Sapio's and Prendergast's "backtracking" and having to eat "a large portion of crow . . . gave a public demonstration of the weakness of their leadership and cast the gravest doubts on whether they still possessed the political shrewdness attributed to them in the past." Similarly, Murray Kempton of the *New York Post* wondered whether Prendergast, in yielding his seat to Lehman, was "on the road either to Damascus or Waterloo."[46]

The infighting among New York Democrats placed John Kennedy in an awkward position because Kennedy knew that if he won the presidential nomination, he would need Lehman's help to carry New York in the November election. Seeking to consolidate his support among New Yorkers, Kennedy attended a Gracie Mansion reception in his honor hosted by Mayor Wagner on June 16, the same day the Democratic State Committee voted to exclude Lehman from the convention delegation. In the aftermath of having been left off the delegation, Lehman did not appear at the event, and Kennedy clearly would have preferred to skip it as well. According to Theodore White, Kennedy "had been angered by the machine's affront to Lehman, whose support he felt essential to carrying New York" in the general election, and the Senator from Massachusetts "sat there on the lawn, . . . distant and frothy," shaking hands with party brass but displaying no warmth or affection. The next day, Kennedy conferred with party leaders and spoke at a luncheon at De Sapio's National Democratic Club. When asked to comment on the State Committee's exclusion of Lehman from the convention delegation, Kennedy dodged the question, saying he never got involved in the specifics of delegate selection other than in his own Massachusetts. But he let some of his pique with party leaders show, declaring that he had "a great and high regard" for Lehman, his former Senate colleague, and considered him an outstanding Democrat. Kennedy expected that Lehman's "influence will be an important factor in the convention," and he predicted that the former Senator "will be an important factor in the Democratic Party in the fall."[47]

As the pre-convention maneuvering continued, Kennedy's courtship of the New York delegation began to bear fruit without his incurring any obligation to either De Sapio or the reformers. While De Sapio and Prendergast maintained their neutrality, Bronx leader Charles Buckley, an old friend of Kennedy's father and one of Kennedy's earliest and most vociferous supporters in New York, announced on June 19 that he would press the New York delegation to endorse Kennedy at its meeting later that week. Warning that "this is no time for cute politics," Buckley asserted that "the sentiment is all for Kennedy" and that "it's time we stopped pussy-footing and gave the people what they want." He also argued that "Kennedy is the only candidate who can help us elect our local ticket." The following day, in a concerted effort by the Kennedy campaign to keep the bandwagon rolling, Mayor Wagner declared that he, too, was supporting Kennedy for the nomination and would urge the rest of the New York delegation to do the same. When the New York delegation met on June 23, De Sapio and Prendergast finally gave their blessing to Kennedy, and a straw poll of the New York delegation revealed that most of the delegates were ready to vote for him. But De Sapio and Prendergast had waited so long that they were now chasing the Kennedy bandwagon rather than leading it in New York. And at the convention, they showed their readiness to jump off the Kennedy express at the first opportunity. According to Robert Kennedy, De Sapio tried to make a deal that would have allowed New York to cast thirty votes for Lyndon Johnson on the first ballot, with the promise that Kennedy would get them back on the second round. Robert Kennedy rejected the proposal, emphasizing that the Kennedy campaign expected to win on the first ballot.[48]

V

Herbert Lehman valued his independence as a delegate because while most of the New York delegation was now supporting John Kennedy, Lehman was engaged in a last-ditch effort to make Adlai Stevenson the Democratic presidential nominee, believing that the nation needed an experienced hand at the helm at a time when relations with the Soviet Union were deteriorating. Lehman had been calling for a Democratic ticket of Stevenson for President and Kennedy for Vice President, and Eleanor Roosevelt came to the same conclusion in June 1960. As she later explained, she "was stirred by reading a statement by two of our leading historians, Henry Commager and Arthur Schlesinger, Jr., who declared that while Adlai Stevenson was undoubtedly the best candidate for the presidency," they accepted at face value his protestations that he was not seeking the nomination, and thus they were supporting John Kennedy. In Mrs. Roosevelt's opinion, "It seemed absurd to accept anyone as second best until you had done all you could to get the best," so she set out "to clarify" whether Stevenson would become a candidate or accept a draft for the nomination. Stevenson repeated his previous statements that he was not pursuing the nomination, but he left the door open a crack when he told Mrs. Roosevelt that he would, as always, "serve my country and my party whenever called upon." That was enough for Mrs. Roosevelt, Herbert Lehman, and others who ignored Stevenson's insistence that he was not a candidate and set to work on his behalf, trying to create the "groundswell" they knew would be necessary to nominate him. Lehman contributed $1,000 to the Stevenson cause, and the *Los Angeles Times* reported that Lehman and Senator Mike Monroney of Oklahoma were writing to convention delegates, urging them to vote for Stevenson. On June 23, former Wisconsin Democratic Chairman James Doyle announced that at the request of Mrs. Roosevelt, Herbert Lehman, and others, he would be coordinating the different volunteer organizations being mobilized for Stevenson, and by June 26, the New York Stevenson for President Committee had gathered more than three hundred thousand signatures on petitions calling for Stevenson's nomination. Lehman looked forward to the convention at which he would be among the leaders in the effort to nominate Adlai Stevenson one more time.[49]

As the Democratic National Convention approached, Herbert Lehman redoubled his efforts to build support for Adlai Stevenson, and the pro-Stevenson drive seemed to be making real progress. Just before leaving for the convention in Los Angeles, Lehman corrected what he charged was the "misleading" impression State Chairman Prendergast had left with the New York State delegates when they had caucused in Albany in late June. Prendergast had reported that a recent poll he had commissioned showed that Kennedy would be the party's strongest candidate in New York in November, capturing 58 percent of the vote against Vice President Richard Nixon, the likely Republican nominee. But Lehman pointed out that Prendergast had cherry-picked the results of the poll to present Kennedy in the most favorable light, suppressing the same poll's finding that New York Democrats preferred Stevenson over Kennedy for the presidential nomination by 44 percent to 38 percent. Democratic National Chairman Paul Butler had initially turned down requests by Stevenson's supporters for space in the headquarters hotel because Stevenson was not an avowed candidate, but when Lehman, Mrs. Roosevelt, and Oklahoma Senators Mike Monroney and John Carroll appealed to Butler to reconsider his decision, they managed to secure two small rooms for the Stevenson forces in the convention headquarters hotel. The Associated Stevenson for President Committees of California included Lehman among those calling for Stevenson's nomination in its large ad in the *Los Angeles Times*, asserting that "America wants Adlai," and urging Californians to "tell your delegates you want Adlai Stevenson." Stevenson promised not to object if his name were placed in nomination, and he assured his supporters and those who doubted his willingness to run a spirited campaign that, "if selected by the convention," he would, "of course, accept the draft and campaign with vigor and a sense of real purpose." Pennsylvania Governor David Lawrence, while not endorsing Stevenson, pronounced him "the best qualified man in either party to be President," and a letter to the editor of the *New York Post* endorsed Lehman's call for "a ticket of Adlai Stevenson for President and Sen. John F. Kennedy for Vice President." Lehman noted that he had suggested such a pairing "many weeks ago," and he still believed that such a ticket "would be of benefit not only to the Democratic Party, but to all the people of the country, regardless of political affiliation."[50]

Upon his arrival in Los Angeles, Lehman quickly got to work trying to persuade delegates to support Stevenson's nomination. What the *Los Angeles Times* described as "a small but jubilant band of Stevenson partisans, sensing growing support for their man," welcomed Lehman at Union Station "with chants of 'Let's swing to Stevenson,'" and Lehman reiterated his view that a Stevenson-Kennedy ticket would be the Democrats' best bet in November. Appearing on the CBS broadcast *Face the Nation*, Lehman predicted that Kennedy's support would start to slip away on the second ballot, opening the way for Stevenson. He explained to a gathering of fifty to sixty Stevenson delegates from across the country that Kennedy's strength in the New York delegation did not represent the "down-to-earth" thinking of most New York Democrats, and that after Kennedy fell short on the first few ballots, his "strength will decline and Mr. Stevenson's will rise until he wins the nomination." Lehman also tried to help Stevenson with African American voters, reassuring a rally organized by the NAACP that Stevenson "fundamentally feels on civil rights the same way I do."[51]

At the convention, Lehman maintained his distance from the rest of the New York State delegation, partly by choice and partly because De Sapio and Prendergast tried to exclude him as much as possible. On the eve of the convention, Lehman quipped to a reporter, "I'm not exactly the most popular member of the delegation, you know," which the Associated Press ranked as "one of the greatest understatements" of the convention. The New York delegation was housed in the Ambassador Hotel, but all the rooms there were booked by the time Lehman was belatedly named a delegate, and he had to stay a few miles away at the Beverly Wilshire. Perhaps because he was staying at a different location from the rest of the delegation, or, more likely because De Sapio and Prendergast did not want him to be there, Lehman did not know until he learned from a reporter that the New York delegation's initial caucus in Los Angeles was scheduled for Monday, July 11.[52]

When the New York delegation caucused on July 11, Lehman tried to rally the latent support for Stevenson that he believed existed in the New York delegation. Speaking on Stevenson's behalf, Lehman emphasized that the world situation, which he described as "the most serious threat to the nation and the world, not in my lifetime but in the annals of the history of the United States," required a man of Stevenson's experience to respond to "difficulties no man can foresee." Along with Eleanor Roosevelt, Lehman was certain that the influence of De Sapio and Prendergast prevented New York delegates from voting their conscience, a view that was confirmed in his mind when Stevenson received only three and a half votes at the caucus. The following night, Lehman's assessment was substantiated when what Theodore White characterized as "a rump faction in New York State's delegation" met "to reconsider Stevenson's chances," and Lehman led twenty members of the Empire State delegation to a meeting in Stevenson's hotel suite. The *New York Times* agreed with Lehman and Mrs. Roosevelt that "with every New York City leader from Mayor Wagner down committed to Mr. Kennedy, and the State Chairman as well, it has been politically impossible for many of the delegates to get out of line. It was generally conceded that except for political considerations, the strength of both Mr. Stevenson and Senator Johnson would have been considerably greater." Edwin Weisl, Jr., who headed Lyndon Johnson's forces in New York in 1960, later recalled that "there was real sympathy" for Johnson and Stevenson among the New York delegates, who resented "being steam-rollered by the leaders of the State delegation." Weisl claimed that "the majority of the New York delegation would have voted for Stevenson and Johnson combined, and that Kennedy would have gotten a minority in an actual free ballot," except for the "irresistible" pressure that was exerted on the delegates by the party leaders. According to Weisl, "in those days there still was an organization in the New York Democratic Party, and it was able to assert control over the delegates."[53]

Lehman's efforts on Stevenson's behalf extended well beyond the New York delegation. In fact, Mrs. Lehman later complained that her husband "was fighting for Stevenson at a time when Stevenson was not fighting for himself." The *New York Post*, which was supporting Stevenson, reported that "the opening day of the convention found Eleanor Roosevelt, Herbert Lehman, the leaders of the California state delegation, and thousands of volunteers all chanting, in their separate ways: 'We Want Adlai' and 'All The Way With Adlai.'" In his account of the convention, Theodore White wrote about "Eleanor Roosevelt and Herbert Lehman, so vividly and evocatively pleading the cause of Stevenson" to the Minnesota delegates, and Minnesota Governor and Kennedy supporter Orville Freeman blamed "some very skillful emotional work by Herbert Lehman" for the failure of Hubert Humphrey and the Minnesota delegation to support Kennedy after Humphrey released his delegates. According to Freeman, Lehman spoke at a Minnesota caucus and "got very emotional about Humphrey and what Humphrey had done and about the primary campaign and all the rest." By the time Lehman finished, Freeman later recalled, "he had that Minnesota delegation completely upset and had projected, in effect, that a vote for Kennedy rather than for Stevenson was disloyal to Humphrey." Lehman "had done it in a fashion that made Humphrey feel good, made everyone feel sorry for him, and made it difficult for him to be for Kennedy." It was, in Freeman's opinion, a "very skillful piece of operation."[54]

While not directly involved in the platform fight in 1960, Lehman hailed the Democrats' 1960 manifesto, which included what the *New York Times* described as "the strongest civil rights plank in party history." With both parties competing for black votes in New York and other key states, the Democratic platform emphasized "The Rights of Man" as its theme and promised to use the power of the federal government to end discrimination in voting, education, and employment. The Democrats pledged action on many of the issues that Lehman had fought for in the Senate, and Lehman praised the platform as "a historic document in furthering the cause of human rights—civil rights—and bringing about a just and humane immigration policy." Lehman noted that it was "a unique experience" for him "to be able to support a civil rights plank," recalling that at previous conventions, he had "always had to fight for a minority report." Congressman Adam Clayton Powell, Jr., who had deserted the Democrats and supported Eisenhower's re-election in 1956, joined Lehman in saluting the 1960 platform, calling it "the best platform either party has written in the history of politics." Powell proclaimed that "the civil rights plank is totally acceptable to my group. It is perfect."[55]

On the third day of the convention, Herbert Lehman and the other delegates got down to the business of nominating a presidential candidate, and Lehman and Eleanor Roosevelt both delivered speeches seconding Stevenson's nomination. Lehman had persuaded his fellow Stevenson supporters that the two-time candidate "should be nominated at the time the other nominations are made," rather than waiting until the convention was deadlocked to offer Stevenson as a candidate. It was "essential" that Stevenson "make a reasonable showing" on the early ballots, Lehman emphasized, which could only happen if his name were formally offered in nomination. After Senator Eugene McCarthy of Minnesota nominated Stevenson, imploring the delegates not to "reject this man who made us all proud to be Democrats," and pleading with them not "to leave this prophet without honor in his own party," Mrs. Roosevelt beseeched her fellow Democrats to nominate Stevenson, declaring, "We want the best." Herbert Lehman asserted that New Yorkers "overwhelmingly" preferred Stevenson, but referring to the party bosses' control of the New York delegation, Lehman lamented that "a situation that prevails" in the Empire State prevented the delegates from voting for the candidate of their choice.[56]

Lehman's political differences with the state party leaders almost resulted in fisticuffs on the convention floor. Lehman had arranged with Mayor Wagner, the New York delegation's titular head, to carry the New York State banner during the long and loud demonstration that accompanied Stevenson's nomination, but Wagner was nowhere to be found when Lehman went to pick up the banner. According to the *New York Post*, when Lehman reached for the standard, "two Tammany bruisers, . . . cigars clenched in their mouths, held it fast. Lehman began to tug. The two began shoving Lehman." As District Attorney Hogan and others moved to assist Lehman, Wagner finally became aware of what was happening and intervened on Lehman's behalf, shouting that he had "told Lehman he could have the standard" and ordering the men to "give it to him. Now!" The eighty-two-year-old Lehman decided that at his age it might be best not to risk being jostled in the boisterous demonstration, so he passed the banner to fellow Stevenson supporter Stanley Lowell of Manhattan, who marched with it through the aisles.[57]

Adlai Stevenson enjoyed the support of Herbert Lehman, Eleanor Roosevelt, and the gallery at the convention, but John Kennedy had the votes of the delegates who determined the party's nominee. Eleanor Roosevelt noted in her column that while Stevenson had received the loudest demonstration and cheers at the convention, "the votes of the delegates—or rather the votes of their leaders—were, however, for Sen. John F. Kennedy," who won the nomination on the first ballot. Lehman reported to Robert Jackson that "there was tremendous sentiment at the convention for Adlai, but, unfortunately, the greater number of the delegates had committed themselves, either personally or through their leaders," to Kennedy. As Connecticut boss and Kennedy lieutenant John Bailey later recalled, Mrs. Roosevelt "and Lehman, both, were supporting Stevenson, but the delegates weren't, and this was true in the great demonstration that they put on at the convention—they had the demonstrators but no delegates were marching in the procession." Arthur Schlesinger, Jr., observed that it had been the Stevenson supporters such as Herbert Lehman and Eleanor Roosevelt who "had kept the liberal spirit of the [Democratic] party alive in the dark years," but he asserted that "the Stevenson movement was not tough enough or serious enough or professional enough. It lacked the basic instinct for power necessary for success in a hard world." After Kennedy won the nomination, Lehman quickly cabled his "heartiest congratulations and all good wishes."[58]

After Kennedy's nomination as the Democratic presidential candidate, attention focused on Kennedy's running mate. Kennedy shocked most observers by offering the vice presidency to Lyndon Johnson, and Johnson surprised and dismayed most of his friends, most of Kennedy's advisors, and most liberals by accepting. As he had with Kennedy, Lehman immediately wired Johnson his "heartiest congratulations and all good wishes," but like most liberals, labor leaders, and civil rights groups, Lehman was less than thrilled by Kennedy's decision, telling reporters that he did not think that Johnson's selection would help the Democrats carry New York. Lehman promised to "work for the ticket and vote for it," but according to the *New York Post*, Lehman showed "no perceptible enthusiasm" when he discussed the Democrats' prospects in New York. When Kennedy and Lehman met privately after the convention and Kennedy asked Lehman's opinion of Johnson's nomination, Lehman reminded Kennedy that he "had served with and under Senator Johnson for more than seven years" and he "considered Senator Johnson a man of ability." Although Lehman "had not agreed" with Johnson "on a number of issues," he believed that Johnson "had made an effective leader of the Senate Majority." Lehman thought that Johnson's selection as Kennedy's running mate "was in all probability good strategy on a national basis since it would please the South, who probably are unhappy about the platform and their sense of isolation." Lehman also believed it would lessen Southern opposition to Kennedy based on his religion, but he feared that "in a number of localities, notably in New York and California, it might weaken the ticket to some extent."[59]

VI

John Kennedy understood that to carry New York's forty-five electoral votes in November, he needed to overcome the split between the reformers and the party bosses. Even before the convention, James Landis, the former dean of Harvard Law School who was an old friend and colleague of Joseph Kennedy and was now practicing law in New York City, had warned Robert Kennedy that the "rift between important liberal elements in the Democratic Party and the professional organization" could jeopardize John Kennedy's chances in the state. Although the liberals were not about to vote for Richard Nixon, Landis worried that if the party bosses controlled the campaign in New York, "the spur necessary to get vigor and activity out of this liberal element, and hence to get out their votes, will be missing." He recommended that "some kind of a citizens committee covering the entire state should be organized as soon as possible," but that this needed to be done without "antagonizing the professional politicians" who "more or less sat on their hands and did very little" in the Stevenson campaigns in 1952 and 1956. Landis volunteered to arrange a meeting for Robert Kennedy next time he was in New York "with a group of individuals who are familiar with and understand this problem, who have declined to participate actively in the Lehman-Roosevelt revolt, but who can give you a good sense as to how these forces can be harnessed in behalf of Jack."[60]

At first, the Kennedy campaign underestimated the difficulty in working around the dispute between the Lehman group and the bosses. Robert Kennedy told Landis that "regarding possible liberal support for Jack in New York," he thought that "as long as we can dovetail the operations with the regular Democratic organization so that they are not concerned that we are trying to take them over," then everything could be worked out "satisfactorily." On the last day of the Democratic convention in Los Angeles, John Kennedy promised De Sapio and Prendergast that unlike Stevenson in 1952 and 1956, he would not allow any entity other than the regular party organization to run his campaign in New York, and Mayor Wagner, who was thought to be "on relatively good terms with the leaders of both groups," agreed to try to broker a truce between the insurgents and the party regulars.[61]

After meeting with De Sapio, Prendergast, and Wagner on July 14, John Kennedy met with Herbert Lehman on July 15, and he quickly learned how difficult it would be to get the reformers and the party bosses to work together in his campaign. According to Lehman's account of their meeting, a Kennedy aide phoned that morning to say that the nominee wanted to call on Lehman, who readily agreed. When Kennedy arrived almost two hours late, accompanied by "a very considerable number of newspaper men and photographers," Lehman congratulated Kennedy on his nomination, Kennedy replied that Lehman's and Mrs. Roosevelt's support would be "greatly important in bringing victory to the ticket," and Lehman noted that he "had stated on a number of occasions" that he "would support the nominee of the Democratic convention." Lehman emphasized that the reformers "wanted to support the ticket," but he warned that "they would do so only if an arrangement could be worked out under which we would neither be asked or expected to work through the Tammany machine." The former Senator expressed concern about reports that Kennedy "had reached an agreement with Prendergast and De Sapio and that the regular organization (Tammany) would handle the campaign in New York State," making it "very clear" to Kennedy "that if this was the case," he "did not believe that the independents, liberals, and reform groups," which he thought were "essential to success," would "carry on a vigorous and militant campaign." Kennedy assured Lehman that although "he had had talks with some of the New York political leaders," he "had made no agreement whatsoever." Kennedy stressed "how much he wanted, and felt he needed, the support that would come to him from the independent, liberal, and reform groups."[62]

The two men "then discussed the possibility of creating a Citizens Committee or a separate committee for the reform groups and their friends." When Kennedy asked for recommendations on "who could head such a committee," Lehman said he "was not ready to make any suggestions at this time." Asked whether he "thought that Bob Wagner could take the lead in creating or heading the independent committee or committees," Lehman replied "very frankly" that while he "liked Bob Wagner" and had hoped that Wagner would succeed him in the Senate, he "was quite convinced that under present circumstances, the reform and other independent groups would not accept" Wagner's leadership. Kennedy knew that "Prendergast, De Sapio, and the other leaders would not favor giving a strong position to the independent groups," but "he thought it would be advantageous to do so," giving Lehman "the very definite impression" that Kennedy intended to "encourage or create such an independent committee or committees and work closely with them." Lehman reiterated "the urgent necessity of enlisting the full support of the independents and liberals who could be of the utmost help in bringing out registration and personally contacting people, in making house-to-house canvases and in developing voting interest and support within their districts." When the reporters and photographers were brought in at the end of the meeting, Lehman "repeated almost exactly" what he had said to Kennedy about the need in New York for "an entity independent of the regular organization" and emphasized that it was his understanding that the Kennedy campaign "would seek to bring about such an arrangement."[63]

In the immediate aftermath of the convention, Kennedy encountered great difficulty in squaring the circle that was the New York Democratic Party. One day after promising De Sapio and Prendergast that the regular organization, rather than an independent group, would run the campaign in New York, Kennedy had assured Lehman that a citizens committee or some such unit would be established on his behalf in New York. A few days later, the *New York Times* reported that Senator Kennedy had approved the idea of an independent committee to work in concert with the regular Democratic organization, and Robert Kennedy told the press that "he would like to see former Senator Herbert H. Lehman take the lead in the formation of such a group and also head it." As the *Times* noted, after all his years in public service, Lehman had "a considerable party and independent following," and his active involvement in the campaign "undoubtedly would produce votes from Jewish, Negro, and other groups for Senator Kennedy." As might have been expected, however, Kennedy's courtship of Lehman and the reformers angered Prendergast and the party bosses. As Lehman and the insurgents seemed to be gaining prominence in the upcoming campaign at the party leaders' expense, Prendergast went public with his unhappiness at recent developments, emphasizing that he intended "to exercise the authority invested in me as state chairman at all times." Prendergast reiterated that he "had opposed the formation of a Citizens for Kennedy committee here, believed he had an 'arrangement' with Senator Kennedy that none would be set up, and knew 'only what I read in the papers' about the plans for one." He conceded that Lehman's participation might be "very helpful in the campaign," but he argued that "forming a citizens' committee is another thing." Trying to pacify Prendergast after the latter's outburst, Senator Kennedy declared that he planned to work "very closely" with Prendergast in New York because "he is the leader."[64]

In an effort to resolve the intraparty warfare that threatened John Kennedy's chances to carry New York in November, campaign manager Robert Kennedy came to Manhattan in late July to cut through the Gordian knot presented by New York Democrats. During two days of meetings with leaders of all the different factions, including a number of sessions with reform leaders at the Lehmans' Park Avenue apartment, Kennedy "emphasized that individual differences must be submerged and forgotten at least until after Election Day if the Democratic national ticket was to win the state." Exasperated by the internecine conflict, Kennedy finally exploded at one session with Lehman and the insurgents, exclaiming: "Gentlemen, I don't give a damn if the state and county organizations survive after November, and I don't give a damn if you survive. I want to elect John F. Kennedy." Eventually, Kennedy persuaded Prendergast and De Sapio to accept a citizens committee that would "supplement the work of the regular organization but not work under it," but Prendergast and De Sapio extracted a promise from Kennedy in return that someone other than Herbert Lehman would be the head of such a group. A few days later, Robert Kennedy announced that Anthony Akers, a longtime friend of John Kennedy, would head the Citizens for Kennedy Committee in New York. Akers had been the Democrats' sacrificial lamb in the last three elections in the heavily Republican 17th Congressional District, and while he had "many friends in the reform Democratic groups," he had "not been identified with it," making him acceptable to both party regulars and the insurgents. Kennedy also announced that William Walton, an artist from Washington, D.C., was being brought in to serve as JFK's "personal representative in the city to handle liaison."[65]

The Kennedy campaign wanted Herbert Lehman and Eleanor Roosevelt to serve as honorary chairmen of the Citizens for Kennedy Committee, but despite all of Robert Kennedy's efforts, Lehman and Mrs. Roosevelt held back from accepting until they received certain assurances. As Anthony Akers later recalled, Robert Kennedy's outburst had "antagonized Governor Lehman and some of the others," who "wanted their terms of reference spelled out; they wanted to know that the presidential candidate was going to appear before their group during the campaign at a reasonable number of events and under appropriate auspices and so on." Lehman and Mrs. Roosevelt also wanted to make sure that Adlai Stevenson would be given a significant role in the Kennedy campaign. Senator Kennedy called Lehman in early August to discuss the situation, and a Kennedy aide quoted Lehman as saying he was "very satisfied with the way things are going in New York." But Lehman immediately protested in a telegram to Kennedy that the campaign aide had misrepresented what he had said. Lehman explained that carrying New York was a "most difficult enterprise requiring maximum mobilization of all non-organization and independent voters of diverse affiliations and interests," and he stressed that he was "not yet satisfied" that the "proposed campaign structure will be adequate to this need." He hoped that everyone understood that "much remains to be done to achieve [the] structure and representation" that he believed was "essential adequately to tackle the job." Much to Akers's dismay, it took a few more weeks to satisfy the concerns of Lehman, Eleanor Roosevelt, and the reform leaders on these matters, which delayed the formal announcement of the Citizens for Kennedy group until August 17. At that time, the Kennedy campaign formally opened the headquarters of the New York City Citizens for Kennedy Committee and announced that Herbert Lehman and Eleanor Roosevelt would serve as the group's honorary co-chairs.[66]

While Lehman was trying to decide how active to be in the Kennedy campaign, he received a letter from Francis Sayre, who had worked with Lehman in the State Department and UNRRA. Sayre reported that he and his wife had heard from Republican friends "disparaging remarks about Mr. Kennedy's private life in Washington and his relationship with women." Sayre was married to Woodrow Wilson's daughter, and they remembered the "unpardonable and utterly untrue slurs cast by Republican politicians some forty-five years ago about Woodrow Wilson's private life—slurs which were utterly without foundation," and Sayre hoped that the rumors he had heard about Kennedy were "similarly utterly untrue." He wanted to know if "such whispered reports" had "any slightest foundation," and, if not, whether there was "any practical and feasible way of answering them." Herbert Lehman, who was completely devoted to his wife of fifty years, naively assured Sayre that during his time in Washington, he had "never heard any reports from reliable sources that would in any way bear out the rumors which you and Mrs. Sayre have heard." Lehman noted that "in Washington, there are always unsubstantiated rumors regarding prominent men and women," and that personally, he "paid and will pay very little attention to them."[67]

Having committed himself fully to the Kennedy campaign by mid-August, Herbert Lehman tried to persuade a reluctant Americans for Democratic Action to support Kennedy as well. When the ADA national board met on August 27 to consider whether to back the Kennedy-Johnson ticket, many in the group were unenthusiastic about the candidates and preferred to make no endorsement. Others who supported the ticket did so halfheartedly and mainly because of their opposition to Republican candidate Richard Nixon. Arthur Schlesinger, Jr., reported to Kennedy that one speaker neatly summarized the sentiments of many in the meeting when he proclaimed: "We don't trust Kennedy and we don't like Johnson; but Nixon is so terrible that we have to endorse the Democrats." At that point in the meeting, Julius Edelstein read what Schlesinger described as "a splendid letter from Herbert Lehman" in which Lehman argued that "Senator Kennedy must be elected not only because the alternative would be tragic for America, but also because his election would place in the White House a man clearly and unequivocally committed to the most liberal program that has ever been presented to the American public in a major party platform within my memory." After several hours of often contentious debate, Lehman's position narrowly prevailed, and the ADA board endorsed Kennedy and the Democratic ticket, but only after removing any mention of Lyndon Johnson's name.[68]

VII

John Kennedy and his advisors realized how important Herbert Lehman's active involvement in the campaign could be. Arthur Schlesinger, Jr., warned in late August that the Kennedy campaign had failed so far "to elicit the all-out support of the kind of people who have traditionally provided the spark in Democratic campaigns," namely, "the liberals, the reformers, the intellectuals—in general, people who have entered politics, not because it is their livelihood, but because they care deeply about issues and principles." Schlesinger feared that putting Lyndon Johnson on the ticket to appeal to Southern voters had hurt Kennedy's candidacy among Northern liberals, and he stressed that it was not worth gaining "some votes in Virginia at the price of losing New York." He advised Kennedy to "take a strong liberal line from now on," emphasizing that "Herbert Lehman and Tom Finletter will bring you many more votes than [Senator] Harry Byrd and [Representative] Howard Smith" of Virginia. Schlesinger also recommended "well-publicized consultations" with Lehman "and the other leaders who have the confidence of the issue-minded people." Events at the ADA board meeting had confirmed Schlesinger's belief that Kennedy needed to do more to win over liberal leaders like Lehman, and he warned that the Republicans' strongest issue in New York was their "opposition to Carmine and the Democratic bosses." If the party regulars were "allowed to dominate" Kennedy's campaign in New York, Schlesinger warned, Kennedy would be "playing into" the Republicans' hands.[69]

Worried about whether Jewish voters would support a Catholic candidate for the presidency, the Kennedy campaign knew it needed Herbert Lehman's active assistance with his fellow Jews. In early September, John Kennedy complained to his brother Robert that the campaign was not utilizing Connecticut's Jewish Governor Abe Ribicoff enough with voters in New York City, asserting that "Prendergast should arrange to have him speak at least two or three times a week in New York—the Bronx, Brooklyn, or perhaps Westchester." Kennedy also noted that "we should try to get Herbert Lehman to do the same," and he suggested that they "should plan at the appropriate time to have an ad run in the *NEW YORK TIMES* and the *NEW YORK POST* signed by Herbert Lehman and Mrs. Roosevelt." An analysis of the campaign in New York State prepared by pollster Louis Harris in mid-September showed that New York contained "the largest number of undecided voters encountered anywhere in the nation," especially among Jewish voters, and advised that "campaigning by Governor Stevenson and Mrs. Roosevelt, but most of all by Senator Lehman, can be effective here." As Mayor Wagner's son later recalled, Lehman was "practically God" in New York's liberal Jewish community, and his active involvement on Kennedy's behalf was seen as crucial in persuading Jewish voters to support Kennedy.[70]

Having spent most of August vacationing in Lake Placid, Herbert Lehman returned to New York City in early September, ready to campaign vigorously on Kennedy's behalf. As Kennedy's New York City campaign coordinator William Walton later recalled, once Lehman and Mrs. Roosevelt committed to the campaign, they were willing to do anything and go anywhere Walton asked, even speaking from the back of flatbed trucks on street corners. Robert Kennedy complained in mid-September that preliminary registration figures in New York were down eight hundred thousand from 1958, and he called upon Lehman to "re-emphasize [the] gravity of [the] situation" to his organization. On September 14, New York Citizens for Kennedy and Johnson took out a full-page ad in the *New York Times* welcoming John Kennedy to New York and urging people to register to vote. The ad featured Adlai Stevenson, Eleanor Roosevelt, and Herbert Lehman, with Lehman urging "all Americans to support and vote for Senator Kennedy, a man of ideas and action, under whose leadership our country will move forward as it must in both domestic and world affairs." That afternoon, Lehman introduced Kennedy at a "Workers' Rally for Senator John F. Kennedy," which was intended "to further registration and to bring out the voters on Election Day." Later that day, Lehman spoke briefly at a dinner at which Kennedy accepted the Liberal Party's nomination for the presidency, telling the crowd that Kennedy "clearly understands the need of these times." A week later, Lehman reported that Kennedy had "made considerable gains within the past two or three weeks and that things are going reasonably well, although there is still lots to be done." In mid-October, Robert Kennedy thanked Lehman for his "invaluable assistance" in "making this registration drive the greatest in history."[71]

Lehman also tried to help Kennedy deal with the religious issue during the campaign. In mid-September, the *New York Times* found, surprisingly, that many New York Catholics were voting for Nixon for President, and Louis Harris reported to the Kennedy campaign that 20 percent of Catholic voters in New York State were still undecided, and only 65 percent of Catholics who had made up their minds planned to vote for Kennedy. After the influential Reverend Dr. Norman Vincent Peale and a group of Protestant ministers asserted that the injection of religion into the campaign was "not the fault of any candidate" but resulted from "the nature of the Roman Catholic Church, which is, in a very real sense, both a church and also a temporal state," Kennedy confronted the issue head-on when he addressed a large gathering of Protestant ministers in Houston on September 12. Emphasizing that he was the Democratic Party candidate for President, not the Catholic candidate, Kennedy reaffirmed his belief "in an America where the separation of church and state is absolute— where no Catholic prelate would tell the President (should he be a Catholic) how to act, and no Protestant minister would tell his parishioners for whom to vote." Kennedy refused to accept the insidious idea that "40,000,000 Americans lost their chance of being President on the day they were baptized," and he promised that "if the time should ever come . . . when my office would require me to either violate my conscience, or violate the national interest, then I would resign the office." At a rally in New York a few days later, Lehman urged the two thousand people in the audience to reject the growing specter of "religious bigotry" in the campaign. A few weeks later, Lehman publicly attributed Kennedy's improving chances in New York to a backlash against the "vicious religious issue raised by certain clerics and laymen," and later that month, Lehman warned that Republican assertions that "all Catholics are going to vote for Senator Kennedy . . . amounted to 'a subtle appeal to prejudice.' " Lehman did not expect that all Catholics would support the Democratic ticket, and he hoped and expected that "the American people will repudiate religious bigotry with such a landslide of votes that it will never again raise its ugly shape on the national scene."[72]

Putting aside his previous differences with Lyndon Johnson, Lehman eventually embraced the Democratic vice presidential candidate. Lehman updated Johnson on the situation in New York in a phone call in mid-September, and two weeks later, he reported to Johnson his "feeling that our ticket is gaining, at least in New York." In early October, Johnson attended a coffee hosted by the Citizens Committee for Kennedy and Johnson at which Lehman introduced him. Ignoring their many clashes in the Senate, Lehman stressed that "when it came to housing, when it came to medical care, when it came to all questions effecting [sic] the social welfare of the people," he and Johnson "were on the same side." Johnson thanked Lehman for the kind remarks and claimed that he might not even be alive in 1960 if it were not for Lehman's thoughtfulness, relating how Lehman had offered the resolution for a moment of silent prayer in the Senate after Johnson had suffered his heart attack in 1955, at a time when Johnson was "just about to throw in the towel." Johnson hailed Lehman as "one of the greatest humanitarians" he had "ever known."[73]

As John Kennedy noted when he accepted the Liberal Party's nomination for the presidency, Herbert Lehman, by his very presence, served "as a reminder that the fight for full constitutional rights for all Americans is a fight that must be carried on in 1961," and the Kennedy campaign utilized Lehman effectively in its efforts to win support from African American voters. Dwight Eisenhower had captured 39 percent of the black vote in 1956, and both parties realized four years later that African American votes could tip the balance in several key states, including New York. The Kennedy campaign organized a Conference on Constitutional Rights in New York in mid-October to show its commitment to civil rights and develop concrete plans to carry out the Democratic Party platform's liberal plank on civil rights. Herbert Lehman chaired one of the panels at the conference, and he used the opportunity to assail the Eisenhower admin-

FIGURE 19.1. Herbert Lehman discusses the campaign with Democratic vice presidential candidate Lyndon Johnson at a coffee sponsored by the Citizens Committee for Kennedy and Johnson, October 6, 1960. Courtesy of the Lyndon Baines Johnson Presidential Library.

istration's inaction on civil rights. He pointed out that Senator Kennedy had called for "executive action to end discrimination in federal housing programs," in contrast to President Eisenhower, who had done little on this issue. Lehman was prominently featured when Kennedy addressed the conference on October 12, as he was when Kennedy addressed a rally at the Hotel Theresa in Harlem later that day. Kennedy appreciated Lehman's participation in the symposium, telling Lehman that "the conference and your part in it were important additions to the campaign." On October 17, the Democratic National Committee made available to campaign officials in all states a "1-minute film of Governor Lehman talking about the rights of man and social welfare problems," another "1-minute film of Governor Lehman talking about civil rights," and a third film in which "Mrs. Roosevelt and Governor Lehman discuss Sen. Kennedy's record and both of them tell why they support Sen. Kennedy." The DNC emphasized that "all spots with Mrs. Roosevelt, Governor Stevenson, and Governor Lehman are particularly good for California, New York, Northwest, Pittsburgh, Chicago, etc." A few days before the election, the *Los Angeles Sentinel*, an African

American paper, carried an ad from the Los Angeles chapter of the International Ladies' Garment Workers' Union urging readers to "Tune In to the 'Fight For Civil Rights,'" a radio broadcast featuring Herbert Lehman and other leading Democrats arguing that Kennedy was the real advocate of civil rights in the 1960 election.[74]

Pollster Louis Harris warned the Kennedy campaign in October that "the Jewish vote had not firmed up" yet in New York, emphasizing that "the undecided among this group are still the highest in the country," and he recommended that Kennedy "should plan on a strong statement on the Israel question in New York City." Following Harris's advice, Kennedy utilized a letter to Herbert Lehman to reaffirm his "stand on the principle of free passage through the Suez Canal," charging that "there has been too much rhetoric and too little leadership in this area," and asserting that "the influence of the United States and other maritime powers must be brought to bear on a just solution that removes all discrimination from the Suez Canal." Kennedy also argued that "the opportunity for peace is jeopardized by the arms race in the Middle East," and he called for "an international effort . . . to prevent this dangerous race." If the arms race could not be stopped, he stressed that the United States "should not

FIGURE 19.2. Herbert Lehman and Mayor Robert Wagner campaign with Democratic presidential candidate John Kennedy, October 12, 1960, © Burton Berinsky.

condone any imbalance between the powers" that could lead to war. As had obviously been pre-arranged, Lehman immediately released Kennedy's letter to the press to demonstrate the candidate's commitment to Israel.[75]

John Kennedy valued Herbert Lehman's experience in international affairs and Lehman came to appreciate Kennedy's views on American foreign relations. In mid-September 1960, speaking at the Democratic Women's Luncheon in New York City, Kennedy called for "a bipartisan effort . . . to use the national assets that we now have . . . in the fight for peace," and he listed among those assets Presidents Truman and Eisenhower, Adlai Stevenson, Eleanor Roosevelt, and Herbert Lehman. A few weeks later, when the issue of whether the United States was or should be committed to the defense of Quemoy and Matsu reared its head again, Kennedy recalled that "in 1955, an amendment to the Formosa Resolution that would have drawn our lines clearly and thus prevented this buildup, was introduced by a great United States Senator, Senator Herbert Lehman of New York." Kennedy stressed that he had supported Lehman's amendment then and wished it had been added to the resolution at that time. Many of the questions in the Kennedy-Nixon debates that year concerned American policy on Quemoy and Matsu, and one can assume that the offshore islands were among the topics discussed when Kennedy met with Lehman immediately after the third debate.[76]

Besides praising and defending John Kennedy, Lehman eagerly joined in the Democratic attacks on Republican presidential candidate Richard Nixon. At a rally in the Bronx in mid-October, Lehman condemned Nixon as "a political chameleon," emphasizing that the Vice President had first come to prominence in the late 1940s "as an arch-conservative" but had since "been all over the lot, changing back and forth with the political winds as he sensed them." In a statewide television broadcast ten days later, Lehman described Nixon as "a threat to civil liberties," pointing out that the Internal Security Act of 1950 had originated as the Mundt-Nixon bill. Lehman denounced that measure as "probably the most useless and costly piece of legislation passed in many years," complaining that "even today, ten years after that legislative brain-child of Mr. Nixon, after thousands of hearings and endless court proceedings, the first penalties of that blunderbuss law have yet to be applied to the first Communists." In late October, speaking at a ceremony marking the seventy-fourth anniversary of the dedication of the Statue of Liberty, Lehman hailed Kennedy's commitment to "the complete overhaul of the McCarran-Walter Act," including "the abolition of the National Origins Quota System and the elimination of second class citizenship for naturalized citizens." In contrast to Kennedy's consistent efforts over the years to amend this law, Lehman noted that Nixon had supported the bill in 1952 and only recently had called for some modest changes in the statute. Lehman charged that this was just one of many examples where Nixon had "voted one way and now talks another." Lehman also cited Nixon's recent assertion that "the prestige of the United States was never higher than it is today," which Lehman claimed "could be explained in only one of two ways: as a demonstration either of colossal ignorance, or of contempt for the intelligence of his listeners." Either way, Lehman emphasized, Nixon had shown that he "is disqualified for the presidency."[77]

VIII

For most of the campaign, Lehman's reformers and the regular Democratic Party organization papered over their differences as they worked separately for a Kennedy victory, but hostility and distrust remained on both sides. For Lehman and the reformers, their truce with the party regulars was a temporary expedient. As Lehman explained to his brother-in-law in late August, the insurgents had agreed, "for the duration of the campaign," to "lay aside any attempt to gain advantage for the reform movement," but they had "made it perfectly clear that as soon as the election was over," they would resume their "activities working towards reform of the Democratic Party and a change in the leadership." As a result of the continuing conflict, when John Kennedy visited New York, he had to balance his campaign appearances between events sponsored by the two factions, with De Sapio and Prendergast appearing alongside the candidate at some stops, while Lehman and Mrs. Roosevelt were featured at others. Reformers believed that De Sapio and the bosses, not overscheduling and bad weather, caused Kennedy to arrive more than five hours late for a West Side rally at which Herbert Lehman waited in the rain to introduce Kennedy to the crowd.[78]

Prendergast and De Sapio intensified their petty and heavy-handed treatment of Herbert Lehman and Eleanor Roosevelt in the closing days of the campaign, sealing their fate with the Kennedys. The state party organization arranged for Kennedy's last New York appearance to be a televised address from the New York Coliseum on November 5, and in a rare display of Democratic unity, reformers and regulars agreed to appear together on the same platform for the only time during the campaign. Lehman and Mrs. Roosevelt accepted on the assumption that, as usual, and like the other dignitaries and party notables present, they would be allowed to speak briefly to the crowd, but when they learned they were not going to be permitted to speak, they threatened to skip the event. Understanding the importance of these two liberal icons in mobilizing former Stevenson supporters and other voters, Robert Kennedy immediately ordered Carmine De Sapio to allow Lehman and Mrs. Roosevelt to speak, but De Sapio insisted on hearing directly from John Kennedy that these were his wishes. JFK promptly contacted De Sapio and told him in no uncertain terms that "he wanted Mrs. Roosevelt and Governor Lehman to be there and to speak and that he assumed that this had all now been done since he sent word." De Sapio agreed, but he asked Kennedy to speak to Prendergast as well. Kennedy did so, but much to his surprise, he had to plead with the state chairman to allow Lehman and Mrs. Roosevelt to speak. Kennedy arrived at the rally just in time to deliver his address, well after the preliminary speakers had made their remarks, and he had no idea there had been any problems until, on his way out of the arena, an angry Herbert Lehman complained that he had been "double-crossed," that he had not been allowed to speak. Kennedy replied, "You weren't double-crossed, I was," and he vowed to "get the dirty son of a bitch bastard who did it if it's the last thing I do."[79]

The Kennedy campaign gratefully acknowledged all that Herbert Lehman had done for the candidate. On the eve of the election, Anthony Akers, the head of the Citizens Committee for Kennedy and Johnson, told Lehman that "not in this life" would he "lose the memory of seeing you and Mrs. Lehman waiting hours in a cold rain for a presidential caravan which finally had to be postponed until 10:30 P.M. because of the television schedule. All of us felt there was something of the greatness that is America waiting there with you." Akers emphasized that "Senator Kennedy and all of us who have worked in this campaign will always be grateful for the guidance and strength of leadership" that Lehman had given "so selflessly" and without which New York "might not now be reflecting such odds-on strength for the Democratic ticket." Noting the mistreatment to which Lehman had been subjected by the party bosses, Akers struggled to come up with the right words to express his anger at "those who reneged on the speaking schedule which was to precede the televised program last night." Lehman expressed his "very great satisfaction to have had a part in organizing the Citizens Committee for Kennedy and Johnson and to work under its banner." In contrast to his fears when the citizens committee was first organized in the late summer, Lehman, too, was confident that Kennedy would "carry New York State by a very sizable margin."[80]

When New Yorkers went to the polls on November 8, 1960, they voted overwhelmingly for John F. Kennedy, who carried the state by almost four hundred thousand votes. Lehman immediately extended to the President-elect his "heartiest congratulations" and "warmest good wishes for your success and happiness in your tremendous task," and he sent a similar message to Vice President–elect Lyndon Johnson. Lehman considered the election results "a great victory for both Jack Kennedy and for the nation." Discarding his earlier misgivings stemming from Kennedy's youth and inexperience, Lehman now asserted that Kennedy's "record in the Congress and his campaign indicated that he has the makings of a great leader." Lehman's only regret was that Kennedy had not won by a large enough margin to claim "a very definite mandate" for his policies, but he thought that Kennedy would, "nevertheless, be able to get through the major part of his program."[81]

CHAPTER 20

"To Free This City . . . from the Shackles of the Boss System"

Herbert Lehman and the Bosses, 1961–1963

I think the reform fight which we waged in New York was one of the most important phases of my political career, and I shall always be glad that I had the opportunity of so actively participating in it.[1]

I

Even while basking in the glow of John Kennedy's victory, Herbert Lehman and the reformers immediately resumed their fight against bossism in the New York Democratic Party. Speaking at a Victory Dinner celebration sponsored by the Citizens for Kennedy and Johnson Committee, Lehman announced that the cease-fire between his group and the party regulars had expired now that the presidential election was over. Emphasizing that the reformers had "worked as hard as any people possibly could to bring out the registration and the vote and to bring the issues home to the people," Lehman promised to continue the "fight for reform in the Democratic Party and to democratize the Democratic Party and make it responsive to the voters." Irving Engel, the chairman of the Committee for Democratic Voters (CDV), confirmed that the "truce is over," warning that the Democratic Party in New York "will not be able to give

---

Chapter title quotation: Press Release, "Statement of Hon. Herbert H. Lehman at Press Conference, 820 Park Avenue, New York City, Sunday, July 9, 1961," Herbert Lehman Papers, Special Subject Files, New York City Reform Politics, July 1961.

President Kennedy the support he requires to put over his program unless and until it has been cleansed of the present leadership."[2]

Carmine De Sapio responded the next day with what the *New York Times* described as "bitter language which suggested that he had been having difficulty for some time in restraining himself in his dealings with both Mr. Lehman and Mrs. Roosevelt." The Tammany leader denounced "the selfish divisive activities of a small group of self-proclaimed prophets who, themselves, want nothing less than to be bosses," complaining that "these self-styled Democratic leaders were preaching disunity and disruption." Claiming that Lehman and the other "so-called insurgents" were guilty of "hypocrisy" in their professed concern over Kennedy's program, De Sapio recalled that "Senator Lehman was probably the most active and impassioned man at the convention in Los Angeles in opposition to the nomination of Senator Kennedy." According to De Sapio, the Democratic Party organization and "thousands of loyal party workers" who "toiled day and night" deserved the credit for Kennedy's victory in New York, and he believed that "the time has come to stop coddling those who, resting on past laurels, resort to deceit and demagoguery as they permit themselves to be used by opportunists who desire to ruin the Democratic Party." He promised that "if it's a 'war' they want, they shall have it."[3]

Lehman quickly replied to what he characterized as De Sapio's "intemperate and utterly misleading statement." He emphasized that the reformers had "joined in giving Senator Kennedy our most enthusiastic and vigorous support," but they had made it clear "that once the presidential campaign was over, we would again resume the attack on Mr. De Sapio's leadership." The insurgents' continued backing of Kennedy, Lehman stressed, would not be affected by their "determination to carry on the struggle for the revitalization of the Democratic Party in this city and for the elimination of that boss rule of which Mr. De Sapio is the outstanding personification." Backing his words with actions, Lehman hosted a series of meetings in November and December 1960 at which Manhattan insurgent leaders planned their campaign to remove De Sapio and reform the New York County Democratic organization, and the former Governor told biographer Allan Nevins in mid-December that he was "giving as much time to the effort to improve the political climate of the party in New York" as he possibly could. Lehman believed it was "only a question of a relatively short time before De Sapio, and possibly Prendergast, too, will be replaced by better men."[4]

The Kennedys gratefully remembered Herbert Lehman's enthusiastic support during the election, with Robert Kennedy telling Lehman "what a major difference" Lehman and his "associates made in the campaign. You were a tremendous help." At the same time, Robert and John Kennedy never forgot Prendergast's and De Sapio's insubordination at the Coliseum rally, and thus they joined Lehman and the reformers' efforts to oust the two party leaders.

Press reports a few days after the election indicated that the President-elect was "really furious" at Prendergast and was considering possible replacements for the state chairman. Kennedy aides complained publicly that the party leaders had "pulled some terrible fast ones" and "were high-handed with President Kennedy himself," citing in particular the organization's defiance of Kennedy's "direct orders" that Herbert Lehman and Eleanor Roosevelt be allowed to speak at the Coliseum gathering. William Walton, Kennedy's campaign coordinator in New York, contrasted the reformers' donation of $77,000 raised at a breakfast a few days before the election with the $23,000 collected by the State Committee at a similar event, "most of which went for the costs of the meal itself." Based on such experiences during the presidential election, the Kennedys concluded that Prendergast and De Sapio could not unite the Democratic Party in New York to retain control of City Hall in 1961 and defeat Governor Rockefeller in 1962, which would eliminate Rockefeller as a potential threat to JFK's re-election in 1964. They sought, therefore, to oust Prendergast as state chairman, knowing that such action would also reduce De Sapio's power and prestige. The *New York Times* reported in mid-November that the Kennedy administration planned to bypass Prendergast and De Sapio in dispensing federal patronage in New York, and, as the *Times* noted, depriving the leaders of the lifeblood of patronage would be "a first step toward forcing them out."[5]

John Kennedy went out of his way to demonstrate his friendship with Herbert Lehman and his disdain for Prendergast and De Sapio. When the President-elect came to New York on January 8, he met with Lehman at the latter's Park Avenue apartment for thirty-five minutes, explaining to reporters afterward that he had come "to pay my respects to an old friend." Kennedy denied that they had discussed local politics, but Lehman admitted that they had, "just a little." During the pre-inaugural period, Kennedy also found time to confer with Mrs. Roosevelt, Mayor Wagner, and many others, but he purposely ignored Prendergast and De Sapio.[6]

The Lehmans looked forward to attending John Kennedy's inauguration and the surrounding festivities. As Herbert Lehman explained to the President-elect, he and Mrs. Lehman "could not deprive" themselves "of the pleasure of being in on the beginning" of what they were sure would be "an historic administration." The Lehmans and Eleanor Roosevelt were scheduled to be honored at a dinner and reception that Kennedy planned to attend the night before the inauguration, and Lehman expected to "proceed to the platform with the members of the Senate" at the inauguration itself. However, Lehman fell ill a few days before the inauguration and his doctors prohibited him from traveling to Washington, worrying that "the strain of the many affairs" to which Lehman had been invited "might be harmful." Nonetheless, Lehman insisted that Mrs. Lehman go to Washington for the festivities, many of which were canceled because a major snowstorm crippled Washington the day before the inauguration. When Lehman realized he would not be able to attend the inauguration ceremonies, he immediately cabled Kennedy to convey his "warmest good wishes" and his "prayers for [a] full measure of success and happiness" in Kennedy's "incomparably difficult and important task," and he expressed confidence that Kennedy would "make a great President." Lehman watched the inaugural proceedings on television, and as he told Robert Kennedy a few days later, he was very impressed with the President's "magnificent" inaugural address and he believed that the new administration was "certainly off to a splendid start."[7]

After the inauguration, President Kennedy continued to snub De Sapio and Prendergast. When John Bailey was installed as the new head of the Democratic National Committee, Kennedy greeted many of the political leaders gathered in Washington for the occasion, but not De Sapio and Prendergast. The Kennedy administration refused to funnel patronage through De Sapio and Prendergast, and in late January Kennedy publicly demonstrated his antipathy to De Sapio and Prendergast when he named Thomas Finletter, a co-founder of the Committee for Democratic Voters, as U.S. Ambassador to NATO, and Jonathan Bingham, who was married to Lehman's great-niece, to represent the United States on the United Nations Trusteeship Council. As the *New York Times* noted, these appointments emphasized Kennedy's "apparent policy of deliberately cold-shouldering New York's two top Democratic Party officials" and "suggest that the President or his staff consulted former Senator Herbert H. Lehman before making them." A few months later, Kennedy nominated Herbert Lehman's great-nephew Robert Morgenthau to be U.S. Attorney for the Southern District of New York. Morgenthau had headed the Bronx Citizens Committee for Kennedy and Johnson, and, like Bingham and other politically active members of Lehman's extended family who lived in the Riverdale section of the Bronx, he had maintained friendly relations with Bronx boss Charles Buckley. But even though the Bronx leader pronounced Morgenthau's appointment as "entirely satisfactory," it was widely known that Morgenthau had not been among the candidates that Buckley had recommended for the position. In July 1961, Robert Kennedy complained to DNC Chairman John Bailey that he had heard that "the recommendations of Mike Prendergast in New York are being accepted." This was "most inadvisable if true," and Kennedy demanded a report.[8]

As opposed to Lehman and the insurgents, who wanted to reform the whole system to diminish the power of the party leaders such as De Sapio and Prendergast, the Kennedy administration's enmity toward Prendergast and De Sapio was personal rather than a rejection of bossism in general. This difference became apparent when the President and his advisors sought to replace Prendergast with Erie County Democratic Chairman Peter Crotty, one of JFK's earliest supporters in New York. Bronx chief Charles Buckley and Brooklyn leader

Joseph Sharkey had reportedly consented to Crotty as Prendergast's successor, and in contrast to his public shunning of Prendergast, President Kennedy very publicly hosted Crotty and his wife at the White House in mid-March, which, the *New York Times* noted, was "tantamount to White House endorsement" of Crotty as Prendergast's replacement. However, the editors of the *New York Post* spoke for many of the reformers when they voiced their disappointment with the Kennedy administration's apparent backing of Crotty, warning that the Erie County boss's "appointment is unlikely to convince any independent liberal voters that a new day is at hand, or to stir the enthusiasm of young people who respond to the vision of the New Frontier."[9]

The President's support for Crotty as Prendergast's replacement created a dilemma for Herbert Lehman and the reformers, who bitterly recalled that Crotty had backed De Sapio's choice of Frank Hogan for the Senate in 1958 in return for Crotty's own nomination for Attorney General. When Crotty's name had first surfaced in December 1960 as the Kennedy administration's choice to succeed Prendergast, the *New York Times* noted that "Crotty is facing opposition from the insurgent wing of the state Democratic Party headed by former Senator Herbert H. Lehman and Mrs. Franklin D. Roosevelt," and Lehman reportedly advised the President early in 1961 that the reformers objected to Crotty, seeing him as little improvement over Prendergast. In mid-March, when Kennedy entertained the Crottys at the White House, Lehman was in Florida recovering from a bout of bronchial pneumonia and spending time with his grandchildren, but the *New York Post* reported that Lehman had "not changed his opinion since January, when he told President Kennedy that Crotty would 'not be well received as state chairman by the Democratic reform movement.'" Some reformers wanted to defy the President by trying to block Crotty's selection, asserting that Crotty succeeding Prendergast would constitute "only a change of face," not the fundamental changes they wanted. But Lehman and others realized it would be counterproductive to fight with the Kennedy administration on this matter. According to the *New York Times*, thirteen reform district leaders, "all connected with the Lehman wing of the party," met right after Kennedy had hosted Crotty at the White House and "decided to abstain from public criticism of Mr. Crotty," realizing that "if he was elected, we 'will have to work with him.'" Four of the reform leaders delivered the same message to DNC Chairman Bailey in Washington a few days later, reportedly promising that "the full, 13-member [reform] caucus would stand aside from maneuvering over a State Chairman," and pledging that "if Crotty were picked," they would "judge him by his performance." When the CDV's General Committee met on March 29 to consider whether to oppose Crotty's selection as state chairman, Lehman argued by telephone and telegram from Florida that in view of the Kennedy administration's support for Crotty, such opposition would be "most foolish" and "an exercise in political futility," and he asked that the CDV not take any formal action until he returned to New York on April 8. Much to Lehman's dismay, the CDV General Committee ignored his request for a delay and adopted a resolution opposing Crotty's possible selection as state chairman on the grounds that Crotty had been "one of the principal architects of the 1958 Democratic debacle."[10]

The CDV's failure to honor Lehman's plea to defer action on Crotty highlighted a growing tension between Lehman and some in the reform movement who were beginning to resent his leadership, or any leadership at all. Lehman told Oliver Pilat of the *New York Post* that he "was surprised and not at all pleased . . . at the arbitrary action by the General Committee" on his "request that the matter be delayed," and Julius Edelstein reported to Lehman that the refusal to postpone formal consideration of the resolution opposing Crotty, despite previous promises to do so, reflected increased "hostility" toward Lehman and the other advisors who had founded the CDV and contributed their time, their energy, their prestige, and, in Lehman's case, their financial support to the reform movement. Edelstein believed that the problem stemmed partly from structural weaknesses in the CDV and the reform movement, but also from the "ambition of certain individuals" who sought to stake their claims to leadership roles by taking more radical positions. Newspaper reports echoed Edelstein's view. Tom O'Hara noted in the *New York Herald Tribune* that "hotheads in the movement" had "snubbed the sage advice of Herbert H. Lehman," and Oliver Pilat observed in the *New York Post* that "control of the Democratic reform movement" had apparently "shifted to a younger, more militant faction." Pilat and O'Hara both pointed out that after James Lanigan had proposed and secured passage of the resolution against Crotty, later that same night he had been chosen by the Village Independent Democrats (VID) to oppose De Sapio for district leader. According to Pilat, "Several speakers in the VID leadership cited Lanigan's stand against Crotty" in arguing for Lanigan, with one Lanigan supporter shouting: "Something historic took place tonight. . . . Lanigan revolutionized the reform movement. He showed it will not back down even though our elders, who should know better, tell us otherwise." In a not-so-subtle shot at Lehman, the *New York Post* asserted that "New York Democrats need an authentic new leadership drawn not from the backrooms but from the new political generation of which Mr. Kennedy has become a leader and symbol."[11]

II

Although structural deficiencies in the CDV and personal ambitions contributed to the conflict, the biggest issue separating Lehman from the more militant reformers in 1961 was whether to support Mayor Robert F. Wagner for a third term. De Sapio had played the key role in selecting Wagner as the

Democratic Party candidate for Mayor in 1953 and had directed his re-election in 1957, but Wagner had also maintained good relations with Herbert Lehman and Eleanor Roosevelt, both of whom had worked closely with and fondly remembered the Mayor's father. Recognizing that a divided party imperiled his chances of winning re-election in 1961, Wagner had tried, unsuccessfully, to unite the warring factions within the Democratic Party. In March 1960, Irving Engel, chairman of the renamed New York Committee for Democratic Voters (NYCDV), warned Herbert Lehman that "there is increasing pressure to have the NYCDV attack the Wagner administration" based on "the revelations of corruption and inefficiency . . . which have caused a great drop in Bob Wagner's standing with the voters." As Lehman and the reformers resumed their battle against the party bosses in the fall of 1960, Lehman confided to a friend that he did "not know just what attitude the Mayor is going to take, and it is quite possible that the reform fight may extend into the mayoralty campaign next year."[12]

Lehman met and discussed "the leadership question" frequently with Wagner in the fall of 1960, and by early December, the Mayor reportedly "had concluded that he must accept the replacement of Mr. De Sapio if the factional fighting within the New York County Democratic organization was to be ended." Mrs. Roosevelt was glad to know that Wagner was talking with Lehman and, apparently, had "finally decided he must take some action and make some decisions." The Mayor made his first break from De Sapio in late December when he called for "an outstanding independent Democrat," rather than a De Sapio–backed organization candidate, to replace Manhattan Borough President Hulan Jack, who had been convicted of accepting favors from a real estate developer and then trying to cover it up. After a two-hour meeting with Lehman in early January, Wagner told the press that they had discussed "a substitute" for De Sapio, and he hinted that he and Lehman would have an official announcement "on that in the near future."[13]

Some of the more militant reform leaders feared that Lehman was preparing to endorse Wagner for re-election if the Mayor broke with De Sapio, and they wanted to make sure that Lehman and Wagner realized that Lehman could not speak for all elements in the reform movement on this matter. As much as they wanted to get rid of De Sapio, some of the insurgents were not willing to commit to Wagner to accomplish that objective. On January 3, 1961, the executive committee of the Village Independent Democrats, which had taken the lead in the effort to oust De Sapio as district leader, passed a resolution condemning the Wagner administration for "laxity and ineffectiveness," denouncing Wagner and his aides for their "close association" with De Sapio and Tammany Hall, and questioning whether a third term for the Mayor would "differ materially from its predecessors." One of the leaders of the anti-Wagner group explained to the *Village Voice* that the resolution reflected concern that "Senator Lehman might be making arrangements in his talks with Wagner that we may not agree with." A few weeks later, the *New York Times* reported that some of the reform leaders were "becoming increasingly disturbed" about Lehman's conversations and possible commitment to the Mayor. According to the *Times*, a substantial minority of the reform group did "not want to become committed to support-ing the Mayor in a primary fight for renomination if the regular organizations in the five boroughs decide to oppose him," and they preferred "to support an independent if the Mayor becomes the organization candidate."[14]

Aware of the opposition to Wagner by some in the reform movement, Lehman continued to speak very highly of the Mayor, but he insisted that he had not made any promises or commitments. Lehman told the *Village Voice* that he had heard the criticism of the Mayor, some of which he thought was "justified, and some not," but he emphasized that "in our talks with Mayor Wagner and other possible candidates, we have made no commitments." On February 3, when Wagner finally called publicly for De Sapio's resignation as county leader, Lehman quickly praised the Mayor for taking an action that Lehman had advocated "for a long, long time." Expanding on his views a few days later in a television interview, Lehman hailed Wagner's support "for many of the things the reform movement stands for," asserting that it took great cour-age for the Mayor "to declare himself, to break his alliances, to burn his bridges to a very considerable extent." But Lehman stressed that "there have been no commitments made by our group to the Mayor, nor has the Mayor asked for any commitments." A few weeks later, while vacationing in California, Lehman issued a statement reiterating that he did not "have any ties, commitments, or understandings with Mayor Wagner or with any other person concerning the coming mayoralty election." Emphasizing that he was speaking only for him-self "and not for the reform movement," Lehman also declared that he would "oppose as strongly" as he could "any candidate for Mayor who runs as Mr. De Sapio's candidate or in support or defense of the system of bossism which Mr. De Sapio represents or upholds."[15]

Herbert Lehman and the reformers remained split over whether to sup-port Mayor Wagner's re-election and over Lehman's role in the movement. In early March, after Wagner strongly hinted at the annual City Hall corre-spondents' dinner that he would run again, Francis Adams, one of Lehman's fellow CDV advisors, strongly endorsed the Mayor. However, State Senator and West Side reform leader Manfred Ohrenstein and Greenwich Village insur-gents James Lanigan and John Westergaard, who were both seeking to unseat De Sapio as district leader, all declared their opposition to a third term for the Mayor, and Congressman William Fitts Ryan, who had been elected with the help of Lehman and the CDV, called upon Wagner to "commit himself wholeheartedly to the anti-De Sapio movement" if he wanted the reformers to back his candidacy. Keeping its options open, the CDV created a Committee on City-Wide Elections to interview possible candidates for Mayor and other offices. CDV leaders conferred with Mrs. Roosevelt in early April over the "sharp division within the group on whether Mayor Wagner should be considered for renomination," and on April 10, two days after his return to New York, Herbert Lehman met with the executive committee of the CDV in the morning and with district leaders associated with the reform movement in the afternoon so that he could be brought up to date on the political situation. Lehman announced that evening that the reformers "had adopted a 'wait and see' attitude for the present toward this year's city campaign," emphasizing that there was no commitment to support the Mayor or any other candidate, and that the reform group's final decision "will be influenced by what takes place in City Hall." But as the CDV General Committee's passage of the resolution opposing Crotty ten days earlier had demonstrated, not all of the reformers were willing to follow Lehman's leadership on the mayoral race and other matters. While City Councilman Louis Okin cautioned that "if we ask Governor Lehman to win elections for us, we ought to listen to him between times," Timothy Taylor, who hoped to replace Okin on the Council, emphasized that he "did not believe in boss dictation by Senator Lehman or anyone else."[16]

The CDV's decision to oppose Crotty despite Lehman's request for a delay, reform opposition to Mayor Wagner, and the increasingly public challenge to Lehman's leadership led the former Governor to reassess his role in the CDV. Seeking to clear the air at a CDV meeting on April 20, 1961, Lehman emphasized that he had "spent a third of a century building up a public and personal reputation—building people's confidence in both the soundness and the independence" of his judgments. He stressed that his reputation was his "greatest offering to the reform movement" and the CDV because there were "quite a few thousands of people in New York City and throughout the State" who listened to his "opinions and judgments with some respect and who sometimes follow them." While Lehman was "quite willing to share . . . whatever prestige" he had "for the purpose of advancing the goals of the reform movement," he was not willing to allow the CDV General Committee to use his reputation "as a rubber stamp to be affixed to motions passed in bursts of passion or emotion or considerations of self-interest rather than on the basis of sober, sound political judgments." Lehman did "not want to be a boss," describing the idea as "ridiculous" and asking "a boss of what?" But neither did he want "to be a stooge for the General Committee or for any committee or organization." He had "never been willing to subordinate [his] conscience or [his] judgment in such a manner," and he was "not going to start" doing so "here and now, at the age of 83."[17]

At the conclusion of the meeting, Herbert Lehman's future role in the CDV was still up in the air. State Assemblyman Mark Lane gratefully acknowledged Lehman's contributions to the reform movement, asserting that "no reform candidate could have won without the support of Senator Lehman and Mrs. Roosevelt." Lehman agreed to meet with Lane and other members of the General Committee to consider various changes in the group's structure that would make it more difficult for the CDV to ignore his recommendations, but the upcoming mayoral race still loomed as an issue on which Lehman and many of the reform leaders differed. According to the *New York Times*, many of the reformers left the CDV meeting that night fearing that Lehman and Mrs. Roosevelt "might abandon the movement if, as some of its members have been urging, it decides to oppose Mr. Wagner's renomination this September."[18]

The question of whether to support Mayor Wagner for another term in City Hall delayed a reconciliation between Lehman and the CDV. Julius Edelstein noted that the CDV "is 'our s-o-b.' We gave it birth and life." But Edelstein feared that "our creature has grown, if not into a Frankenstein's Monster, at least into an entity with glaring defects and deficiencies." Many of the problems with the organization, Edelstein observed, were "illustrated most strikingly in the vehement anti-Wagner consensus" within the group. "The activist constituency of the NYCDV," he asserted, "is more united against Wagner than on any other single 'issue,' principle, or purpose." In Edelstein's opinion,

> the chief dream-fantasy of the club activists is one of running their local candidates in the primaries on a "pure" reform ticket, headed by a "pure" reform candidate for mayor, running against Wagner. . . . They don't think, at this point, that their mayoralty candidate would necessarily win; but with such a set-up they are sure that their local candidates would win—especially if Mrs. Roosevelt and Senator Lehman supported them.[19]

Although some of the more militant reformers still wanted to ignore Lehman's advice and replace Wagner with a candidate who, in the *New York Post*'s words, "approaches the office with passion, freshness, and energy," most of the insurgents realized that they needed to follow Lehman's recommendation to be more "realistic" if they hoped to achieve any of their goals. An agreement was reached that strengthened Lehman's authority in the CDV, and the group went along with his advice to proceed more slowly on the mayoral issue. Emphasizing that the electoral "situation is a peculiarly and unusually fluid one, with many factors to be determined by forces beyond our control," including "the candidacy or non-candidacy of Mayor Wagner for re-election," Lehman persuaded the CDV City-Wide Elections Committee to work with him and consult "representatives of labor, minority groups, independent organizations, the Liberal Party, Mayor Wagner, and other declared and possible candidates for all city-wide offices" before taking any formal action. Lehman convinced the CDV's General Committee in early June to withhold any statement of endorsement or opposition to any particular candidate, warning that premature action against Wagner would isolate and "destroy the reform movement."[20]

With the CDV and most of the reform groups falling into line behind him, Lehman began to move closer to an endorsement of Mayor Wagner. In a television appearance on May 14, Lehman insisted that he had not made up his mind yet whether to support the Mayor, and he emphasized that he did not have the authority to speak for the reform group as a whole. But Lehman predicted that if Wagner sought re-election, he would enjoy the support of most of the reform Democrats if he made it clear "that he is going to continue his efforts to reform the Democratic Party, to improve the climate of the Democratic Party, and to change the leadership." In a radio interview a week later, Lehman acknowledged that he had, in the past, criticized the Mayor's difficulty in making decisions and asserting himself on important issues, but Lehman claimed that there had been a "marked change" in the Mayor in recent months, that Wagner's "courageous break" from De Sapio and other decisive acts "overbalanced" his earlier concerns about the Mayor.[21]

On June 19, Lehman vehemently denied a story in the *New York Herald Tribune* that claimed that he had told Bronx boss Charlie Buckley during the 1960 Democratic National Convention that the "nomination of John F. Kennedy was the greatest calamity the Democratic Party" had suffered in his lifetime. Lehman did "not recall" any conversation with Buckley "on any subject at the Convention," and he cited as proof of his high regard for Kennedy his advocacy before the convention of a Stevenson-Kennedy ticket. He had met with Kennedy the day after the convention, Lehman recalled, and had "immediately assured" Kennedy of his "wholehearted support," which he had given "in very full measure throughout the campaign." It seems likely that Buckley or one of his henchmen made up the alleged incident to cause trouble between Lehman's reformers and Catholic Democrats in the battle between the insurgents and the party bosses.[22]

III

After consulting with Herbert Lehman, President Kennedy, and many others, Mayor Wagner announced on June 22 that he would seek a third term in City Hall. Wagner made it clear that he was running as a reform Democrat rather than an organization candidate by declaring that he would run on a ticket that included Deputy Mayor Paul Screvane for City Council President and current City Council President Abe Stark for Controller, thus demoting Stark and dropping current Controller Lawrence Gerosa completely. When Stark refused to run with Wagner, he was replaced on the ticket by City Budget Director Abe Beame who, like Stark, provided ethnic and geographic balance to the ticket because he was Jewish and he hailed from Brooklyn. While Lehman insisted that "the reform group" had not tried "to dictate the choice of running mates," wanting "the Mayor to be independent," Lehman and the reformers had objected to the generally conservative Gerosa and did not think that Stark, as Council President, was suitable to succeed the Mayor if Wagner left to take a position in Washington or for any other reason. Tammany leader Carmine De Sapio, Bronx boss Charles Buckley, and Brooklyn chief Joseph Sharkey quickly rejected the Mayor's slate, with Buckley complaining that Wagner had been "listening to people he shouldn't be listening to," but Herbert Lehman declared that it was "a refreshing turn in the political history of our city to have the public leader of the Democrats of the city provide the leadership rather than the bosses." Lehman asserted that Wagner had "shown strong leadership in putting a slate together which commends itself to me." Speaking only for himself, Lehman thought he could "wholeheartedly support the ticket as proposed by the Mayor."[23]

A few weeks after Wagner's announcement, De Sapio, Buckley, Sharkey, and the other Democratic Party leaders in New York City endorsed State Controller Arthur Levitt for Mayor, setting up a primary battle between Levitt and Wagner. Herbert Lehman was on vacation in Lake Placid when the news broke about Levitt's candidacy on July 7, but he immediately issued a statement in which he charged that "it is perfectly clear . . . that Levitt is a candidate of the bosses against Mayor Wagner, who is pledged to good government and whose nomination and election will mean the end of the machine as it now exists." The eighty-three-year-old Lehman promised to use all the strength he could command to "fight against boss candidate Levitt and for Mayor Wagner."[24]

Herbert Lehman saw the mayoral election as the crucial battle in the fight against De Sapio and the party bosses. Demonstrating the depth of his commitment to Wagner's candidacy, Lehman rushed back to New York City to address the media on July 9. Emphasizing that he was speaking personally, not for the CDV, Lehman characterized the upcoming primary and general election as a rare opportunity for New Yorkers "to free this city with one blow from the shackles of the boss system, and to open the doors to the prospect of a new day and a new deal for the Democratic Party of New York, and above all, for the people of the City of New York." Although Lehman realized that there had been "shortcomings" in Wagner's two terms as Mayor, he blamed most of them on "the boss system," claiming that "the political climate of this city has long been poisoned by boss rule." But now, he insisted, "we have a chance, under Mayor Wagner's leadership, to achieve almost the total goals of reform not only in Manhattan, but throughout the City." Lehman dismissed Levitt as "an amiable gentleman" whose "candidacy for Mayor is as transparent as a Fifth Avenue show-window," asserting that "right behind Mr. Levitt stand Messrs. De Sapio, Buckley, Sharkey, Prendergast, and their allies," seeking "to re-establish their complete control of the Democratic Party organization, and of the city government of New York." "Make no mistake about it," Lehman warned, Levitt's nomination "would unquestionably put Carmine De Sapio back in the rider's seat as the Number One boss of New York City and State politics." Ignoring the irony that he was speaking about the man who had been Mayor for the last eight years, Lehman stressed that only "Mayor Wagner's renomination and re-election can turn a clean, fresh page in the history of New York City," and Lehman pledged to do everything he could to help Wagner's campaign.[25]

The Mayor's re-election prospects received a big boost in late July when the CDV formally endorsed him. By this time, with the Mayor clearly positioned as the anti-boss candidate, the editors of the *New York Post*, the Village Independent Democrats, and numerous reform clubs that had originally been skeptical or hostile to the Mayor's candidacy had come around to Herbert Lehman's point of view and saw the Mayor as their best opportunity to defeat De Sapio and the bosses. State Chairman Michael Prendergast assisted the reform cause when he returned to the fray, bitterly denouncing the insurgents as "the sinister forces of splinterism" and urging Democrats to vote for Levitt to repudiate "the self-ordained, self-proclaimed, power-hungry, political calendar liberals who don and discard the liberal cloak whenever it suits their own personal convenience and political ambitions." Wagner also facilitated the CDV's support by coming out in favor of a six-point program to reform the Democratic Party, thus aligning himself with the insurgents' efforts to liberalize the party rules and organization. On July 25, the CDV Governing Committee voted 84 to 1, with three abstentions, to endorse the Mayor, giving him the experienced foot soldiers and political operatives he needed to circulate petitions, coordinate campaign activities, and compete with the party organization.[26]

The September 7 primary election caused Herbert Lehman to cut short his summer vacation in Lake Placid, but even when he was supposed to be relaxing in the Adirondacks, Lehman "was on the telephone discussing the . . . political situation far more" than he would have liked. As he explained to friends, Lehman believed that Wagner and the reformers had "an uphill fight, since the political machines in the five counties are well organized, and many of the voters have been in the habit of following De Sapio and the other county political leaders," but he hoped "to show . . . how great a calamity would come to New York if control of the city were turned over to De Sapio and his associates." Lehman conceded that "Wagner has undoubtedly made mistakes during the years he has been in office," but he emphasized that "in the last year" the Mayor had "shown great courage by repudiating the political machine and the bosses." When the Wagner campaign filed the petitions needed to get on the Democratic Party primary ballot, Lehman congratulated the Mayor and promised that as soon as he returned to New York City in a few days, he would "be at your disposal until Primary Day," and he pledged "to plunge into the campaign with all the strength and vigor" he could muster.[27]

The *New York Times* noted that Herbert Lehman was "in a position to be of considerable help" to Wagner in both the primary and the general election because Lehman had "a large following, particularly among voters with liberal leanings," and he was "influential with the rank and file of Democrats, who will decide the outcome of the primary." Louis Harris, Wagner's pollster, pointed out that "the most popular Jew in New York is Herbert Lehman," and he advised the Mayor that Jewish voters "will respond best of all to the bossism issue." As Chris McNickle later noted in his history of New York City mayoral elections, "in the battle to win Jewish voters, Herbert Lehman was an unmatchable weapon." Wagner's campaign literature featured Lehman prominently, often in juxtaposition to De Sapio and the bosses, and Lehman appeared with Wagner in a televised broadcast, emphasizing that he was at the Mayor's side "in this all-out fight, fight to the finish struggle against the evil political machine led by Carmine De Sapio and his fellow bosses." Julius Edelstein reminded the Wagner campaign that Lehman was available "to accompany Mayor Wagner on tours of appropriate areas in which the Mayor might benefit from identification with Senator Lehman," such as Harlem and Coney Island. Edelstein stressed that although Lehman "has nothing to gain from such appearances except exhaustion," the Senator "wants more than anything else to see Wagner win and is willing to make whatever expenditures of energy that he can properly afford to achieve this result." Lehman later estimated that he "made somewhere between thirty and forty appearances" at campaign rallies and events throughout the city, and Mrs. Lehman recalled that she "couldn't control" her husband during the 1961 election, when he would ignore the risks and " 'take the most awful chances' in climbing ladders to impromptu platforms" despite his age and his history of "leg and hip fractures." At Lehman's joint appearances with the Mayor, the *New York Times* reported, "Mayor Wagner rarely missed a chance to evoke memories of the former Governor's eminence during the Rooseveltian New Deal," while Lehman, "in turn, referred repeatedly to 'the late, great Senator Wagner,' father of the Mayor." The *Times* also noted that "to those of middle age and beyond, Mr. Lehman was the greater attraction." On September 3, in what the *New York Times* described as "an arduous afternoon that would have exhausted a man half his age," Lehman spent six hours in the hot sun campaigning with the Mayor on the beaches of Brooklyn. The *New York Post* observed that the "one image of human gallantry [that] will endure regardless of the outcome" of the primary election was "the unforgettable portrait of an 83-year-old man named Herbert Lehman trudging through the sun-scorched streets from one end of the city to the other with his earnest pleas for support of the Wagner ticket." The *Post* noted that Lehman had no personal stake in the outcome; thus, his active involvement reflected "the sense of dignity and well-being that comes from doing what he deeply believes to be right. Perhaps that is why, even under the broiling sun, he seems to be having the time of his long and distinguished life."[28]

Wagner and Lehman succeeded in making De Sapio and bossism the major issue in the primary, with Lehman repeatedly asserting that Levitt "*is the* Bosses' candidate. He *is* the defender of the Boss system." Levitt and the bosses tried to attack Lehman's role in the Mayor's campaign, but their efforts fell on deaf ears. In the closing days of the campaign, anonymous leaflets, which the Wagner campaign attributed to De Sapio and Bronx boss Charles Buckley's operatives, were distributed to Irish voters in the Bronx depicting the Mayor as a puppet controlled by Lehman, Mrs. Roosevelt, Alex Rose of the Liberal Party, and Michael Quill of the Transport Workers Union. Another flyer tried to tar Wagner and Lehman with Senator McCarthy's old tactic of guilt by association, reprinting a *New York Daily News* story charging that Lehman's niece, Helen Buttenwieser, had provided $100,000 in bail so that convicted Soviet spy Dr. Robert Soblen could be released from jail pending his appeal.[29]

Lehman's prominence in Wagner's campaign immunized the Mayor against charges of anti-Semitism. In criticizing the Mayor's original plan to demote City Council President Stark to Controller, Brooklyn boss Joseph Sharkey had suggested that such a move would offend "the Jewish people in this town [who] might feel that they were trying to get rid of him and make it impossible for a Jew to become Mayor," a charge that Bronx leader Charles Buckley quickly echoed. Shortly before the primary, Levitt charged that pro-Wagner sanitation men in Queens had distributed anti-Semitic campaign literature that urged "Irish American Democrats" to "Vote for Wagner for Mayor . . . or else you will have a Levitt or Lefkowitz as Mayor." (Republican mayoral candidate Louis Lefkowitz, like Levitt, was Jewish.) Herbert Lehman was "so outraged by the Levitt charges that he did not trust himself to make immediate comment." When he did respond twenty-four hours later, Lehman condemned Levitt's "scandalous statement" as "a transparent, despicable foul blow, . . . the most malicious tactic of any campaign I recall in my sixty years of politics." He denounced Levitt for "raising the dangerous spectre of anti-Semitism solely to serve the cross [*sic*] purposes of political expediency," and he defended the Mayor as "one of the finest liberals" he had ever known, a man "without a shred of religious bigotry" who "has done more to cement relations between religious and ethnic groups in this city than any Mayor." Lehman had "made as much of an investigation into Mr. Levitt's charges as was possible after reading his statement," and he had found that there was "not the shadow of substance to those charges. . . . If there were the slightest breath of truth to these accusations," Lehman declared, he "would not be campaigning day after day, and night after night, for Mayor Wagner's renomination and election."[30]

Besides boosting Wagner, Lehman also devoted considerable time and effort in 1961 to helping local reform candidates, especially James Lanigan, who was challenging De Sapio for district leader in Greenwich Village. Lehman, Mrs. Roosevelt, and Adlai Stevenson recruited Lanigan to run against De Sapio, and Lehman personally guaranteed that sufficient funds would be available for the effort. Lehman made his first major speech of the campaign at a $100-a-plate dinner sponsored by the CDV to raise money for reform candidates for City Council and district leader, and he endorsed such local candidates as Theodore Weiss for City Council and Irving Wolfson and Catherine Hemenway for district leaders in the 5th Assembly District North, hailing them as "staunch fighters against De Sapio and for the reform of the Democratic Party." On primary day, even before the polls had opened, Lanigan thanked Lehman for his "generous contribution" and for his "magnificent speech last night at our rally," emphasizing that Lehman's "great and stout heart" had given the reform movement the courage it needed to succeed.[31]

Much to Lehman's delight, Wagner and the insurgents won a huge victory in the primary elections on September 7, 1961. With a record number of Democratic voters going to the polls, Wagner defeated Levitt by almost 160,000 votes to capture the Democratic nomination for Mayor, Lanigan defeated De Sapio for district leader in lower Manhattan, making De Sapio ineligible to continue as New York County Democratic leader, and reform candidates won fourteen out of sixteen races for district leaders. In contrast to his actions in the Senate, where Lehman had so often refused to compromise on his principles, he had advised the reformers to be practical and realistic; rather than rejecting Wagner, Lehman had counseled that the insurgents could use the Mayor as their vehicle to defeat the bosses. This strategy paid off at the polls, enabling the reformers to inflict a crushing defeat on De Sapio and the regular party organization. Lehman cheered the results as "a real victory for all the people of the City of New York," and he was hopeful that the Mayor "will rise to his responsibilities" and "we will have an honest, decent, experienced and unbossed administration."[32]

Observers rightfully credited Herbert Lehman with playing the key role in Wagner's victory. The *New York Times* noted that Wagner had consulted with both Lehman and former Democratic National Committee Chairman James Farley daily, and that Lehman's influence with the Bronx's "predominantly Jewish population" had been a crucial factor in Wagner carrying every Assembly district in the Bronx. Lloyd Garrison, who served alongside Lehman as one of the CDV's advisors, asserted that Lehman, "more than anyone else," had "helped to bring about" this "triumph of morality and courage and leadership," and Eleanor Roosevelt used her "My Day" column to "congratulate the Mayor, Mr. Screvane, and Mr. Beame, and above all Senator Lehman, whose stout campaigning helped immeasurably to win the primary." An editorial in *The Day-*

Jewish Journal attributed Wagner's victory to "the tireless work of the great Jewish leader, Herbert Lehman," and Anthony Akers, who had been appointed U.S. Ambassador to New Zealand as a reward for chairing the Citizens Committee for Kennedy and Johnson, informed Lehman that Tammany's defeat had even made the newspapers in New Zealand. Akers stressed, "this victory would not have taken place without the wonderful guidance, counsel, constant and most helpful support and assistance" that Lehman had "so generously . . . given to the 'reform' movement in New York." Hubert Humphrey congratulated Lehman "on a tremendous victory," which he saw as "another great success" in Lehman's "remarkable record of public service," and "a victory for better government and for the Democratic Party." Humphrey believed that Lehman had again "demonstrated that courage, persistence, determination, and conviction win out," and he emphasized that Lehman's "example is a wonderful inspiration to all of us." William Shannon, on leave from his job as a columnist at the *New York Post*, saw Wagner's victory as "an encouraging omen of the future of politics in New York," and "a richly deserved tribute" to Lehman for his many "years of unselfish leadership in the cause of clean politics." Since 1928, Shannon declared, Lehman had "done more than any other public figure to provide an example of integrity in public life." Julius Edelstein neatly summarized Lehman's role in Wagner's victory when he observed that Lehman, all by himself, "as a symbol of all that is good and pure in politics, swayed thousands and thousands of votes . . . and gave Wagner a sort of *Good Housekeeping* stamp of approval, which was incontrovertible."[33]

IV

Exhausted by his active campaigning for Wagner, Lehman took a brief vacation in Atlantic City before returning to New York in late September for the opening of the new Children's Zoo in Central Park, which the Lehmans had made possible. In June of 1960, Herbert and Edith Lehman, following up a suggestion from longtime New York City Parks Commissioner Robert Moses, celebrated their fiftieth wedding anniversary by donating $500,000 to build a Children's Zoo in Central Park. As Herbert Lehman explained, "Many New York children have never seen a goose or a chicken or a pig or a rabbit," and he and Mrs. Lehman "thought it would be both educational and enjoyable for them to get to know these animals, to feed them, and to learn to love them." The announcement of the Lehmans' gift came right after Prendergast and De Sapio had excluded Lehman from the New York delegation to the 1960 Democratic National Convention, leading the *Chicago Tribune* to observe that the new zoo might include "rabbits, ducks, geese, lambs, doves, kittens, piglets, and a talking crow . . . but it is a cinch that there will be no striped

Tammany tigers among the inmates to be admired." Work began on the zoo in late 1960, but a difficult winter, followed by strikes in the asphalt and concrete industries, delayed its formal opening until September 1961. Besides the animals, the zoo featured "a child's-size Noah's Ark," "a plastic blue whale with a mouth that is wider than a Volkswagen and higher than a telephone booth," "the white rabbit from Alice in Wonderland," and other attractions that were "built around stories familiar to children." The Lehmans were "delighted" with the final product, and Herbert Lehman took great pride that the zoo attracted over one hundred thousand visitors in its first three weeks, and over a million guests in its first year of operation. Mrs. Lehman was especially pleased when Parks Commissioner Newbold Morris informed her in February 1963 that "Mrs. Kennedy, accompanied by Caroline and surrounded by five Secret Service men," had toured the zoo. Eleanor Roosevelt congratulated the Lehmans on the zoo, emphasizing that "it is so like you both to give pleasure to children," and one young mother, reading the plaque acknowledging that the zoo was a gift from "Governor and Mrs. Herbert H. Lehman," expressed her surprise that "you could do that on a Governor's salary." The Lehmans were very proud of their role in creating the Children's Zoo, and when Lehman believed that his biographer was giving too much credit for the zoo to Robert Moses, Lehman immediately corrected him, emphasizing that "Moses had nothing to do with the construction of the zoo. His sole contribution was in suggesting the project in the first place."[34]

V

Herbert Lehman continued to play a key role as Mayor Wagner's staunchest advocate and defender in the general election campaign. In mid-October, Lehman lamented that "there was a considerable let-up after the primaries and it is hard to rekindle the very great interest that was developed among the voters of the city during the primary." He expected "that Wagner will win out, but it will not be a push-over and there will have to be very active and vigorous campaigning between now and November 7th." When the *New York Times* endorsed Republican Louis Lefkowitz instead of Wagner, citing primarily "the inadequacies of administration and the woeful defects in Wagner's leadership," Lehman immediately responded with a letter to the editor in which he charged that the *Times* had overlooked "the fact that Mayor Wagner has made himself the active leader of the forces of political and governmental reform." In so doing, Lehman asserted, Wagner "has shown political and moral courage to an unusual degree" and "has shown every disposition to realize the great potential of an administration free of all boss or machine influence." According to Lehman, "New Yorkers have an opportunity which will not come again in our lifetime—that of electing a Mayor pledged to use the power of his position to reform and revitalize the majority political party and, at the same time, to tackle, on the basis of unquestioned experience and competence, the problems of housing, crime, education, air pollution, and group tensions, to name only a few." As opposed to Wagner, who was now clearly identified "with the cause of political reform," Lehman argued that "Mr. Lefkowitz is thoroughly identified as a G.O.P. regular, . . . a member of the inner hierarchy of the G.O.P. machine." A few days later, Lehman reported that he was "going around with Mayor Wagner to a great many places," and Lehman was optimistic based on "the size and enthusiasm of the crowds."[35]

In the last two weeks before the election, Lehman campaigned all across the city at the Mayor's side, attacking Lefkowitz at every opportunity. At a press conference in Manhattan, Lehman charged that Lefkowitz was "the candidate of political reaction," and he asserted that the Republican Party "draws its main support from the special interests which have always sought, as far back as" he could remember, "to stop all social progress." Campaigning with the Mayor in Queens a few days later, Lehman denounced the Republicans as "reactionaries opposed to 'every forward-looking program' from factory inspection in Gov. Alfred E. Smith's day to minimum wages, unemployment insurance, and Social Security in the Thirties, and rent control today." At a rally sponsored by the Liberal Party and the ILGWU, Lehman challenged Lefkowitz's attempt to portray himself as "a La Guardia type of Republican," pointing out that when Lefkowitz had run for Congress in 1940, he had run "as the anti-New Deal candidate; he attacked both the New Deal and Franklin D. Roosevelt. So Mayor La Guardia supported the other fellow." According to Lehman, Lefkowitz was "a dyed-in-the-wool party machine man, who is not just the hand-picked candidate of the bosses, but is indeed one of the bosses," and newspaper ads for Wagner featured Lehman's so-called exposé of Lefkowitz's record. Lehman's barrage was having its desired effect, leading Lefkowitz to respond in the campaign's closing days by accusing Wagner of using Lehman as his "hatchet man."[36]

On November 7, 1961, Wagner was re-elected Mayor of New York City by a margin of almost four hundred thousand votes. Wagner's triumph was seen as a personal victory for the Mayor and a tribute to Herbert Lehman. In celebrating with his supporters that evening, Wagner thanked first and foremost "that great stalwart fighter for democracy here and all over our nation, a man who went out with us all summer in the hot sun, climbed the ladders up on the spots to speak to the people of this city, and has done it even all through this election campaign, one of the greatest Americans of our time, former Senator Herbert H. Lehman." The Mayor also thanked Mrs. Lehman for allowing her husband to take on such a strenuous schedule of appearances. Eleanor Roosevelt noted in her newspaper column a few days later that "former Senator Herbert H. Lehman contributed greatly to Mayor Wagner's success," and Abe Beame, who had been elected City Controller on Wagner's ticket, expressed his "deepest appreciation for the tremendous support" Lehman "gave to our ticket," asserting that Lehman "was responsible to a major degree for the kind of victory we won." He stressed that Lehman's "vigorous campaigning was an inspiration to all of us," and he was "grateful for the spark and prestige" Lehman "gave to our cause." Former Democratic National Chairman Paul Butler credited Lehman for "the results of yesterday's election," attributing Wagner's triumph "to the magnificent part" that Lehman had "played, not only in the current reform movement, but also in the modern political history of your city and state and the nation." Butler observed that "the energy and strength" that Lehman "put into the primary and general election campaigns amazed many people, but not those of us who know of your deep devotion to the highest ideals and standards in public life." He believed that Lehman had "performed a great service for your city and state and for the Democratic Party." Former State Democratic Chairman Paul Fitzpatrick told Lehman that in voting for Wagner, "the people of the greatest city in the world have again expressed their confidence in you."[37]

Lehman appreciated all the accolades for his role in Wagner's re-election. He admitted that he had "worked very hard on behalf of Mayor Wagner's ticket and the reform movement," but he believed that "the splendid results more than compensated for the many hours of hard work and worry." Lehman considered his efforts "well worthwhile" because he was "convinced that the Mayor is determined to go through with the program he so often announced during the campaign," and he was confident that Wagner would "give the city a clean, honest, humane, progressive, and unbossed administration for the next four years."[38]

VI

After Wagner's victory, Herbert Lehman, now eighty-three years old and exhausted by months of strenuous political battles, headed to Florida to rest and consider his future involvement in the reform movement. Lehman and Julius Edelstein had been thinking about Lehman's formal role in the movement ever since the spring when the CDV had ignored Lehman's advice and opposed President Kennedy's choice of Peter Crotty for state chairman, and Edelstein had warned after Wagner's primary victory that Lehman had to be careful to avoid getting entangled in the reformers' personal ambitions and internal conflicts. As he looked around the political landscape in mid-November 1961, Lehman saw that the reform movement had been "victorious" beyond his "fondest hopes." De Sapio had been toppled, Buckley and the other bosses had been weakened, and Democrats in New York were amending their rules to make the party more open and democratic. Lehman proudly noted that having elected county committee members in all five boroughs, State Committeemen, State Assemblymen, State Senators, City Councilmen, and a member of Congress, the reform movement was "now city-wide in scope." Prendergast still chaired the State Committee, but he had no influence with the Kennedy administration in Washington or Mayor Wagner in New York. Patronage appointments were being channeled through the Mayor, and the reform movement could rightly claim credit for "providing the ideological springboard" for Wagner's "renomination and re-election . . . over the opposition of the total leadership and almost all the elements of the party machine and of course of the Republican Party too." Lehman stressed that "the major elements of political power have been shifted from the party organization to the elected officials who are responsible to the people—to the Mayor and his fellow office holders."[39]

Herbert Lehman had devoted his time and energy over the last three years "almost exclusively to the reform movement," putting aside many other interests that he had "long cherished and felt deeply about" because he "believed that the advancement of the purposes of the reform movement were of paramount importance" for his "party, city, state, and nation." But Lehman thought that it was time now for the CDV to reassess "its future scope, structure, and purposes," and he insisted that this task should be undertaken by new leaders. Given all that had been accomplished, Lehman saw a need for "fresh and yet mature leadership," explaining that the time had come "when, in good conscience," he could "lay down the organizational burdens" he had carried. Therefore, he informed the CDV's General Committee in late November that he was "resigning my position as Advisor to the NYCDV." Lehman would still use his "strength and energy . . . to support the principles and purposes for which the NYCDV was founded," he would continue to work for "good government for the people of the city and State," and he would retain his "interest in the continuing efforts to reform the procedures, the leadership, and the structure of the party organization." But he would do so "from a position outside of any formal organizational affiliation."[40]

Lehman's resignation did not mean that he was riding off into the sunset; he meant it when he said he was going to remain involved in the reform effort. As a number of observers noted, Lehman had included a warning to Mayor Wagner in his statement resigning from the CDV, hoping that "there will be no future cause for disillusionment which would be politically disastrous for Mayor Wagner as well as for the public interest." Implicit in these remarks was the threat that if the Mayor strayed from the reform agenda, Lehman would call him on it. As the *Christian Science Monitor* noted, "Mayor Wagner will be acting with Lehman eyes peering over his shoulder," watching to see "how closely will the Wagner domination of the Democratic Party conform with the reform ideals cherished by Mr. Lehman and his followers." Acknowledging his

great debt to Lehman and cementing the Senator's influence in his administration, Wagner named longtime Lehman aide Julius Edelstein to be his new
executive assistant.[41]

Lehman remained especially interested in the naming of De Sapio's replacement as New York County Democratic leader. The reformers had endorsed John
Harrington, an Eastside reform leader, for the post, while party regulars and
African Americans supported J. Raymond Jones, a longtime district leader in
Harlem who had been the only "old-line" leader to support Wagner's renomination. The Mayor had the power to break the deadlock between Harrington
and Jones, but, typically, Wagner tried to avoid making a choice. He feared
that endorsing Harrington would associate him too closely with the reformers
and alienate African American voters, who had been his strongest supporters
during the primary and general elections. At the same time, Wagner knew
that he couldn't afford to turn his back on Lehman and the reformers either.
So Wagner did what he usually did when faced with such a predicament: he
stalled and delayed and hoped that somehow the situation would resolve itself.
The Kennedy administration tried to help Wagner by appointing Jones's wife,
a longtime federal official, as Director of Customs for the Virgin Islands, but
her husband maintained his residence in New York and refused to withdraw
his candidacy for county leader. Jones also rejected Wagner's proposal to create
a new position of New York City Democratic Coordinator for him, realizing
that the Mayor was offering an empty title with no real authority.[42]

Upon his return to New York in early December, Herbert Lehman
promptly joined the battle over De Sapio's successor. Lehman explained to
Manhattan Borough President Edward Dudley, an African American, that "he
had a high regard for Mr. Jones but could not support him because he was a
'regular' rather than a 'reform' district leader." In a television interview a few
days later, Lehman emphasized that he had urged the Mayor "not to appoint
any one of the old-line Tammany leaders, but rather to appoint a leader from
one of the reform clubs." He stressed that he had made this recommendation
in spite of his "high regard for Raymond Jones," because he believed that the
selection of Jones or anyone associated with the old party organization "would
come as a great disappointment and disillusionment to many of the people of
the city who have been led to believe that everything would be done by the
Mayor to bring about real reform." Lehman met with Jones the following day,
and even though Jones detailed his record of opposing De Sapio on numerous
occasions, Lehman continued to insist that the new leader should be someone
from one of the reform clubs.[43]

Much to Lehman's dismay, some observers saw the leadership contest
as a racial issue. The *New York Times* asserted that Wagner was resistant to
Jones's candidacy because, with Edward Dudley re-elected as Manhattan Borough President, Jones's "selection would give Negroes two top Democratic posts

in Manhattan." The editors of the *Amsterdam News* and the *Washington Afro American* quickly picked up on this theme, charging that Lehman was blocking Jones's candidacy to become the first African American leader of Tammany Hall solely because of his race. They also suggested that Lehman was acting like no less of a boss than the man he had deposed. Harlem Congressman Adam Clayton Powell, Jr., quickly jumped into the fray, asserting that the reformers' objections to Jones amounted to "a lynching, Northern style," and "a form of bossism that is worse than Carmine De Sapio ever dared to try." Powell erroneously claimed that Lehman, in all his years as Governor, had only named one African American to public office. Former baseball great Jackie Robinson, a strong supporter of Republicans Richard Nixon and Nelson Rockefeller, also chimed in, asking whether liberal opposition to Jones, "led by the respected Senator Lehman," reflected the desire of "leading people of both parties . . . to hold the Negro down?"[44]

Lehman took offense when Dr. Kenneth Clark, the noted black psychologist, and other African American leaders complained that Lehman was ignoring Jones's many demonstrations of independence from and opposition to De Sapio and overlooking Jones's "identification with and acceptance of the basic principles of the reform movement." Lehman replied that he admired and respected Jones but could not support him for county leader because many people considered Jones to be a "representative of the regular political leaders." Jones's selection, Lehman argued, would "be considered by many a retreat, if not a surrender by the Mayor, and would subject him and his administration to charges of bad faith." Lehman greatly regretted that "in certain quarters" his opposition to Jones "has been attributed to racial discrimination." He had hoped that his "long and active participation in the fight for civil rights and equal opportunity for all" for "more than sixty years—would be sufficient to refute this charge," but he now realized that this wish, "regrettably was [in] vain." Clark and the others, who were also "disturbed at the unwarranted introduction of the issue of racial discrimination into the discussion of this problem," agreed with Lehman that "there is absolutely no basis by which any reasonable person could charge" him "directly or indirectly with racial discrimination on this or any other issue," and they volunteered "to state this publicly" at any time if Lehman wished them to do so. Lehman met with Clark and the others in mid-January, but they made no progress in resolving their differences over whether Jones should become the leader of Tammany Hall. Years later, Jones emphasized to his biographer that "the objection to me was *not* based on race, as some have argued, but rather on the conflicting ideologies of the Regulars and the Reformers."[45]

Lehman sought to minimize any damage caused by his opposition to Jones's candidacy to head the New York County Democratic Committee. Although he had "made it a hard and fast rule not to insert any paid advertisements" bearing his name "in any publication, including souvenir journals," Lehman purchased a $100 "Gold Page" in the Carver Democratic Club's souvenir journal honoring Jones in mid-January 1962. To prevent being besieged with similar requests, however, Lehman asked that his "message be signed: 'From a friend.'" That summer, Lehman sent a congratulatory telegram when Jones was honored at a testimonial dinner for his "distinguished service in the field of government and human relations," and in 1963, Lehman agreed "to serve as an Honorary Chairman of the Citizens Committee for the election of J. Raymond Jones to the City Council" and contributed $250 to Jones's campaign fund. As Jones later explained, getting Lehman's public support was intended to ensure support from the reform elements in the party to offset any loss of votes resulting "from the likely bad behavior of [Congressman Adam Clayton] Powell."[46]

Reluctant to make enemies by choosing between Jones and Harrington, between the regulars and the reformers, between the African American community and the liberals, Wagner kept postponing the meeting to choose a new Tammany leader. It was widely understood that a majority of the district leaders would follow Wagner's recommendation, but delay followed delay as the Mayor tried to avoid offending anyone and hoped that a consensus would develop. Finally, in early March 1962, the Mayor extended what the *New York Times* described as his "tacit support" to Edward Costikyan, whose name had been circulating for months as a possible compromise choice. Costikyan was a reformer and an early supporter of Wagner's re-election, but many of the insurgents viewed him with suspicion because he and his New Democratic Club had never joined the CDV. At the meeting of the New York County Democratic Executive Committee on March 2, 1962, Costikyan, now backed by the Mayor and the regulars, received nine and two-thirds votes, defeating Harrington, who received six and one-third votes from the reform bloc. Many of the reformers felt frustrated at this turn of events, angered at the lack of clear signals that the Mayor supported Costikyan, and the rejection of the reform alternatives they had suggested if Harrington was unacceptable. Reached by telephone in California where he was vacationing, Herbert Lehman praised Costikyan as "a young man of ability and vigor," and, getting to the crux of the matter, Lehman noted that Costikyan "was the Mayor's choice."[47]

Costikyan's selection as De Sapio's successor marked the culmination of a busy week in which Mayor Wagner also secured the ouster of Michael Prendergast as state chairman. Prendergast's days had been numbered for a long time, but he had speeded up his demise by endorsing independent candidate Lawrence Gerosa over Wagner in the mayoral election. Now, in late February and early March 1962, the combined strength of Wagner and the Kennedy administration in Washington persuaded a majority of the State Committee to abandon Prendergast and replace him with William McKeon, an attorney from upstate Cayuga County. At a meeting at Gracie Mansion, Wagner secured the agreement of a majority of the State Committee to amend the rules to allow the dismissal of officers by a majority vote. The Mayor reported that Herbert Lehman, who had long sought Prendergast's ouster, agreed that McKeon "would make a good state chairman." Lehman immediately cabled McKeon his congratulations, offering to assist the new leader in any way that he could.[48]

While generally supportive of reform candidates, Lehman made an exception in the 1962 Democratic primary contest in the 1st Assembly District, which encompassed the Greenwich Village and Murray Hill neighborhoods in Manhattan. The Village Independent Democrats (VID) had proved to be one of the most militant of the reform clubs, reluctant to follow the recommendations of Lehman and the other CDV advisors in the 1961 mayoral race and other matters. Relations between Lehman and the VID further deteriorated in 1962 when the group rejected Lehman's request that it nominate former Democratic National Chairman James Farley as a delegate to that fall's Democratic State Convention in recognition of Farley's long service to the party and his strong support of Mayor Wagner in the primary election. When Ed Koch, a young attorney who was one of the leaders of the VID, challenged incumbent State Assemblyman William Passannante, a party regular who had supported De Sapio, Lehman surprisingly endorsed Passannante, who had compiled a liberal record in Albany. In a telegram to Passannante declaring his support, Lehman emphasized that he was still committed to the reform cause "with all my heart," but he explained that "one of the main purposes of political reform . . . is to select and elect the best men to public office." Lehman asserted that "this purpose would be traduced and denied by the nomination of an untested and inexperienced person" instead of Passannante, and Lehman expressed confidence that Passannante would "continue to work and fight for good government and a democratic Democratic Party too." In a letter to Allan Nevins, Lehman stressed that between Passannante and Koch, he "felt strongly that Passannante was infinitely the better man and had made a fine record in the New York State Legislature during the eight years he served in the Assembly." There were, however, additional reasons for Lehman's decision. The *New York Times* reported that Lehman opposed Koch's candidacy partly because the former Governor "had become concerned about the activities of extreme elements in the reform group," and later accounts noted that Lehman hoped that supporting Passannante over Koch would counter the prevailing notion that the reform movement sought to promote Jewish candidates at the expense of Italian Americans.[49]

Koch did not take the rejection well, declaring that "the reform movement is bigger than Senator Lehman." He charged that Lehman's support of Passannante reflected Lehman's view "that the reform movement should have ended" with the ouster of De Sapio as Tammany leader. He also criticized Lehman for abandoning the CDV; being willing to accept President Kennedy's effort to install Peter Crotty, "the Buffalo boss," as Democratic state chairman; and trying to foist Farley's election as a delegate to the State Convention on the reformers of the district. The following day, after Mayor Wagner, too, endorsed Passannante, Koch claimed that Lehman was seeking to establish "a new boss system" in the Democratic Party and had employed "boss" tactics such as "the threat of withholding funds" to force the reform movement to support Wagner's re-election in 1961. Koch characterized himself as one of the "true reformers," in contrast with the "lukewarm reform position of the Mayor and Senator Lehman." After he was trounced by Passannante in the primary, a disconsolate Koch complained to Mrs. Roosevelt, who had been the only major reform leader to support him, that what should have been a victory for himself and the VID had been "savagely wrested" away "by forces which included Carmine De Sapio, Mayor Wagner, and Senator Herbert H. Lehman." In his concession speech, Koch complained that "politics is a dirty business," and, much like Richard Nixon later in the year, he promised, "I will never run again."[50]

VII

As the 1962 New York gubernatorial election approached, Herbert Lehman and New York Democrats hoped that with the party rid of De Sapio and Prendergast, they would be able to regain the governorship. They believed that Governor Nelson Rockefeller was vulnerable because of his recent divorce, increases in state taxes, the formation of the New York State Conservative Party that objected to Rockefeller's liberal brand of Republicanism, and Rockefeller's clear intent to run for President in 1964. The Kennedy administration in Washington also wanted to see Rockefeller defeated, which would remove him as a potential opponent in 1964. However, after Mayor Wagner made it absolutely clear that he would not seek the governorship after having just been re-elected to another term in City Hall, the Democrats lacked a strong candidate to oppose Rockefeller. As Herbert Lehman explained to his old friend Sir Robert Jackson, he thought "Rockefeller can be beaten by the right man," but he conceded that the Democrats "have not as yet been able to unearth a strong candidate."[51]

With Wagner out of the picture, and Lehman and New York Democrats foundering in their search for a gubernatorial candidate "of high moral character and ability" who "can cut down Rockefeller's majority and even have an outside chance of beating him," the Kennedy administration proposed Robert Morgenthau, U.S. Attorney for the Southern District of New York, as a possible nominee. Underwhelmed by the current crop of potential candidates, which included Appellate Court Judge Bernard Botein, Queens District Attorney Frank O'Connor, upstate Congressman Samuel Stratton, and businessman Howard Samuels, the President and his advisors maintained a public stance of neutrality, but they worked behind the scenes for Morgenthau's nomination. As the son of Henry Morgenthau, Jr., Franklin Roosevelt's Secretary of the Treasury, Robert Morgenthau enjoyed a high level of name recognition. In addition, he had served ably in his year as U.S. Attorney, he had friends in both the reform and regular wings of the Democratic Party, and he fulfilled the perceived need to nominate a Jewish candidate. The fact that Morgenthau was Herbert Lehman's great-nephew did not hurt either at a time when New York Democrats were looking for "another Herbert Lehman." Lehman had to tread carefully, however, to make sure that he could not be accused of "bossism" or nepotism in securing Morgenthau's nomination; therefore, he remained in the background until just a few days before the party convention, when he announced that he planned to vote for Morgenthau. Lehman expressed his confidence that "Morgenthau, in character and ideals, in achievement, in integrity, and in service to his country will, if nominated, be a very strong candidate, and if elected, will make an outstanding Governor."[52]

Even though De Sapio had been removed from the scene, the charge of "bossism" still reverberated during the State Democratic Convention in 1962. Herbert Lehman was not pleased when *New York Times* publisher Arthur Hayes Sulzberger wondered: "Haven't we still got bosses, but isn't the difference that these bosses (Mrs. Roosevelt, Herbert Lehman, etc.) are ones whom we trust?" Congressman Stratton vowed to make a floor fight at the convention on the issue of "bossism," and though he spared Lehman, he charged that Mayor Wagner was trying to "stampede" the convention into supporting Morgenthau. Bronx boss Charles Buckley, who was close to the Kennedy administration and had, with the President's help, just survived a primary challenge for his congressional seat, gave credence to Stratton's complaints when he delivered to Morgenthau the almost unanimous backing of the Bronx delegation. Lehman put a positive spin on the convention, however, telling Mrs. Roosevelt that "the Convention was about as rough and rowdy as any" he had "ever attended," but asserting that the tumult and turmoil proved that the convention "was completely open and demonstrated that the day of the boss is pretty well gone, at least for the time being."[53]

Herbert Lehman did what he could to help Morgenthau, contributing generously to his campaign fund. Lehman was realistic enough to understand that Morgenthau had "an uphill fight," but he thought that "Rockefeller has lost ground," and he expected that "the newly formed Conservative Party will take a considerable bloc of votes away from him." Campaigning with Morgenthau, Lehman promised at a Coney Island street rally that Morgenthau "will be a full-time Governor, not one like Mr. Rockefeller, who is more interested in getting into the White House than serving in Albany," and he asserted in the Bronx that Morgenthau would "return good government to Albany by being a full-time Governor." Although Morgenthau later remembered an appearance in Brighton Beach when Lehman "climbed up the lifeguard tower to campaign for me," such actions were rare in 1962. As Lehman confided to Allan Nevins, this time he was "not be able to repeat my performance of two years ago, when I tramped the streets of New York, climbed on ladders and spoke on street corners." The eighty-four-year-old Lehman had to admit, "I just do not have the strength to do it, even if my doctors permitted me to do so."[54]

With the campaign limited to seven weeks because the Republican-controlled State Legislature had scheduled the primary in mid-September, Morgenthau never stood a chance against Rockefeller, and circumstances conspired to eliminate any possibility that Morgenthau might upset the incumbent. As Chris McNickle later noted, Morgenthau was "a highly competent and decent man," but he "turned out to be a miserable campaigner." Herbert Lehman conceded that Morgenthau "is no orator," but he asserted that the candidate "has improved in speaking" and "has been able to project on television and radio his sincerity, integrity, and intelligence." Morgenthau's campaign strategy relied heavily on associating himself with the Kennedy administration; in his acceptance speech at the convention, for example, Morgenthau emphasized that he was part of the new "generation that has been called to leadership in Washington," and he stressed that he was "proud to have worked side by side with our great Democratic President, John F. Kennedy." The Kennedy administration, eager to derail Rockefeller's White House ambitions by defeating him in New York, planned to aid Morgenthau in every way that it could. The President attended a fund-raising breakfast for Morgenthau and campaigned with him on Columbus Day. But Kennedy had to cancel a second planned appearance on Morgenthau's behalf when the Cuban Missile Crisis erupted, diverting the President's attention, as well as the attention of the American people, away from the campaign. Vice President Johnson, Attorney General Robert Kennedy, and other federal officials abandoned plans to campaign with Morgenthau because of the administration's decision to forego partisan activity during this perilous time, and the Morgenthau campaign scrapped television ads that it had taped featuring the candidate and the President. Herbert Lehman believed that Morgenthau was "conducting a good campaign" and "making a great many friends," but he emphasized that Morgenthau, "like other Democratic candidates in many other states, is greatly handicapped by the fact that the President and his main advisers are unable to take any part in the campaign." Lehman agreed that "the President's decision to have his administration stay out of campaigning during the critical situation confronting us was . . . a wise and proper one," but he feared that "it will hurt the Democratic candidates in many states—particularly Illinois, California, and New York."[55]

Pre-election estimates suggested that Governor Rockefeller would easily surpass his 1958 plurality of 573,000 votes, with some supporters predicting that his victory margin might reach as high as one million votes, which would clearly propel him to the forefront in the race for the Republican presidential nomination in 1964. But when the votes were cast on November 6, 1962, Rockefeller won the expected victory, but only by half a million votes, and he ran well behind Senator Jacob Javits and Attorney General Louis Lefkowitz, his running mates on the Republican ticket. Rockefeller's victory margin actually dropped slightly from 1958 to 1962, weakening his prospects for 1964. But Rockefeller's fall-off resulted mainly from the loss of 140,000 votes to Conservative Party candidate David Jaquith and a Democratic gain of one hundred thousand votes in Buffalo and Erie County. Despite, or perhaps in part because of, the Democrats' desperate search for "another Herbert Lehman," and despite Lehman's efforts on Morgenthau's behalf, Rockefeller actually did better among Jewish voters in 1962 than he had in 1958. Some Jewish voters were clearly offended by all the talk about the "Jewish vote" and the assumption that they would vote for a candidate based solely on his religion. Looking at the election results, some Democrats lamented their party's failure to nominate a stronger candidate who might have been able to defeat Rockefeller. Other than Mayor Wagner, however, it remained a mystery who that mythical candidate might have been. It was not easy to find "another Herbert Lehman." In fact, liberal Republican Senator Jacob Javits, who won re-election in 1962 by almost a million votes, probably came the closest of any New Yorker to fitting that bill in 1962.[56]

Morgenthau greatly appreciated Lehman's "tremendous help . . . before, during, and after the convention," fondly recalling Lehman's efforts on his behalf, especially "the day we spent together campaigning in Coney Island and Brighton Beach." He knew that Lehman had done everything he could to help during the campaign, and that Lehman deserved much of the credit for "whatever success" Morgenthau's candidacy had achieved. Lehman called the results "a moral victory," and he praised Morgenthau for running "a vigorous, clean, and constructive campaign," especially given "the strong handicaps of time, money, and personnel with which you were confronted." Lehman pointed out that the campaign had brought Morgenthau's "name and your personality to the attention of the people," and he was certain that they had "gained a good impression of you." Lehman emphasized that the forty-three-year-old Morgenthau still had "plenty of time" for public service, pointing out that he himself was fifty when he was first elected Lieutenant Governor in 1928 and seventy-one when he was elected to the Senate in 1949. Lehman's prediction quickly came true; a few weeks after the election, President Kennedy reappointed Morgenthau as U.S. Attorney for the Southern District of New York, and Morgenthau went on to win election as Manhattan District Attorney nine times, beginning in 1974.[57]

In 1963, Ed Koch abandoned his pledge to be done with politics and was elected president of the Village Independent Democrats. He then ran for district leader against Carmine De Sapio, who was trying to regain his old position. As Jack Newfield and Wayne Barrett explain in their unauthorized biography of

Koch, the future Mayor had learned from his defeat the previous year that he needed Herbert Lehman's help "to reassure the older generation of mostly Jewish voters who lived in the apartment buildings along lower Fifth Avenue that Koch was not a radical." Koch swallowed his pride and apologized to Lehman, stating on WNBC-TV's *Searchlight* program that having called Lehman a boss was "an error on my part and I regret having said it." Lehman had hoped that the VID would "nominate candidates of such stature and caliber that they will commend themselves strongly to the voters of the district," and in his opinion, Koch was not a candidate of such stature, but Lehman realized that once the VID put Koch forward as its candidate, endorsing a different candidate would split the reform vote and result in a De Sapio victory. In one of his last political acts, Lehman announced in mid-August 1963 that he was supporting Koch for district leader, and that he had agreed to serve as honorary chairman of a special committee organized on Koch's behalf. Nonetheless, it was telling that Lehman's public statements during the campaign focused on the danger of allowing De Sapio, "who for many years has been a handicap to the entire Democratic Party," to recapture his position, rather than espousing the virtues of Ed Koch. On primary night, Koch edged De Sapio by forty-one votes out of the more than nine thousand that were cast. With Lehman's help, Koch and the reform movement had narrowly fended off De Sapio's comeback attempt.[58]

CHAPTER 21

"To Inspire Men and Women
of All Generations"

Herbert Lehman and President Kennedy, 1961–1963

Senator Lehman has served our nation well for many decades. The scope
of his interests and the degree of his devotion to his ideal[s] provide an
example to all Americans.[1]

I

Herbert Lehman had high hopes for John Kennedy's presidency, predicting that Kennedy would "make a fine President," but as a former chief executive
himself, albeit on the state level, Lehman realized that Kennedy needed to surround himself with talented associates to succeed. Like many liberals, Lehman
would have preferred to see Adlai Stevenson as Secretary of State rather than
Ambassador to the United Nations, but he was relieved when Kennedy named
Dean Rusk as Secretary of State rather than Senator J. William Fulbright, believing that the Arkansas Democrat's opposition to civil rights and labor legislation
and his hostility to Israel rendered him unsuitable for that post. Lehman also
welcomed the appointment of his former Senate colleague Chester Bowles as
Undersecretary of State, confident that Bowles would, "as always, do a great

---

Chapter title quotation: John Kennedy to Herbert Lehman, March 27, 1963, Herbert Lehman
Papers, Special Correspondence Files. John Kennedy.

603

job." Lehman was "simply delighted" that Stevenson had "accepted the greatly important position of Ambassador to the United Nations," and in late December 1960, with most of the new administration in place, Lehman observed that Kennedy's "appointments thus far, on the whole have been good—many of them outstanding." A few weeks later, Lehman hailed the selection of Arthur Schlesinger, Jr., as a Special Assistant to the President as "another indication of the fine men with whom" Kennedy "has surrounded himself." After Kennedy had been in office for a few months, Lehman reported to Robert G. A. Jackson that "Kennedy is off to a very good start. With very few exceptions, I think his appointments have been excellent, and he has undoubtedly given a new spirit to the people of this country. I only hope that we will not expect too much from him in too short a time."[2]

Lehman did not enjoy much success in recommending people for positions in the Kennedy administration. Besieged with requests from job candidates seeking his endorsement, Lehman made it a policy not to suggest individuals unless he "was personally acquainted with him or her" and the applicant had specifically asked Lehman for a recommendation. When Lehman met with the President-elect on January 8, 1961, Kennedy encouraged Lehman to submit names of people who Lehman thought "would render valuable service," so Lehman sent him five names of men who were "successful in business or in the professions" and for whose "high character" he could vouch: Anthony Akers, who had chaired the Citizens Committee for Kennedy and Johnson; R. Peter Straus, the head of Straus Broadcasting in New York City; Irving Engel, former president of the American Jewish Committee and chairman of the Committee for Democratic Voters; Frank Altschul, Lehman's brother-in-law, who was a retired investment banker, secretary of the Council on Foreign Relations, and a former director of Radio Free Europe; and Harold Linder, an investment banker and former Assistant Secretary of State for Economic Affairs. Linder was also a longtime friend and colleague of Lehman on the Joint Distribution Committee and a generous contributor to Lehman's Senate campaigns. A few weeks later, Lehman recommended former New York City Police Commissioner and fellow CDV advisor Francis Adams to Robert Kennedy for a "responsible position" in the Justice Department, and later that year, when Lehman heard that George Backer, who had helped start the CDV, was being considered to be Ambassador to Poland, Lehman sent the President a strong letter supporting Backer's appointment. The President appreciated Lehman's "wise counsel," but only Akers and Linder received presidential appointments, and Akers's nomination as U.S. Ambassador to New Zealand owed more to his long relationship with Kennedy and his service in the Kennedy campaign in 1960 than to Lehman's endorsement. Linder, however, believed that Lehman's "great help and intercession" on his behalf was a key factor in his appointment as head of the Export-Import Bank. Julius Edelstein, Lehman's longtime aide, failed to obtain the position he sought on Kennedy's staff, but Lehman was pleased when Kennedy appointed CDV co-founder Tom Finletter as U.S. Ambassador to NATO, Lehman's great-nephew by marriage Jonathan Bingham as U.S. Representative to the UN Trusteeship Council, and great-nephew Robert Morgenthau as U.S. Attorney for the Southern District of New York.[3]

Based on his experience in the Senate, Lehman worried that President Kennedy would "encounter many difficulties in Congress with his program." He correctly predicted in mid-March 1961 that some of Kennedy's "legislation, notably his aid to education bill, will run into real difficulties . . . if the parochial school issue is pushed," and he joined a group of "prominent Protestant and Jewish clergymen and laymen" who tried to rally support for Kennedy's $5,000,000,000 aid to education bill, which excluded parochial schools. Lehman agreed with Kennedy's emphasis on "pushing legislation to remedy some of the weaknesses which he outlined in his campaign and at other times," but Lehman thought that "so much legislation has been introduced that . . . the public just can't grasp it all and therefore will not bring pressure on Congress to enact it." He believed that it had been "much easier for F.D.R." to get legislation passed quickly in the New Deal "because so many people were the victims of the depression of the early 30's and truly suffered from its effects." But the situation in 1961 was very different, "since a much smaller number of people have been affected by the recession, and in most cases even they not as severely as in 1933." Nonetheless, Lehman hoped that "much important legislation will get through Congress before the end of the session." Two years later, in January 1963, Lehman believed that Kennedy was "doing a fine job and has the confidence of the great majority of our people," but he still feared that in Congress, "J.F.K. will be defeated on some of his important measures."[4]

Herbert Lehman and John Kennedy remained in touch throughout Kennedy's presidency. In January 1962, when Lehman was honored by the America-Israel Cultural Foundation, the President sent his greetings, emphasizing that "Senator Lehman has served our nation well for many decades," and pointing out that "the scope of his interests and the degree of his devotion to his ideal[s] provide an example to all Americans." Herbert and Edith Lehman were among the guests at the White House for a luncheon honoring the Prime Minister of Norway in May 1962, and Lehman served as one of the honorary chairmen and contributed $5,000 to a fund-raising birthday salute to the President at Madison Square Garden later that month. Eye surgery prevented Lehman from attending the event, and, quickly following up on the suggestion of United Artists president and celebration co-chair Arthur Krim, Kennedy thanked Lehman for his efforts in organizing the event and added his "good wishes to those of all your friends for a very speedy recovery." Lehman was "delighted" later that year when Kennedy nominated Secretary of Labor Arthur Goldberg to a seat on the Supreme Court, and even while he was on vacation in the Adirondacks that summer, Lehman stressed to people he encountered that Kennedy was "doing a fine job." After attending a breakfast meeting with the President on October 12, 1962, Lehman reported to Attorney General Robert Kennedy how pleased he was to see the President "looking so well despite his almost unbearable burdens."[5]

The only sour note in Lehman's relations with the Kennedys in this period involved an attempt to solicit Lehman's support for Ted Kennedy, the President's youngest brother, who was seeking the Democratic nomination for the U.S. Senate in Massachusetts in 1962. Lehman rejected Arthur Krim's request that he meet with Ted Kennedy before Labor Day, arguing that it would be inappropriate "to inject myself in any way into the primary of another state." After Kennedy won the nomination, Krim urged Lehman to endorse him, but Lehman explained that, with the exception of one "old and very close friend" who was "an experienced legislator," he had adopted a policy of not endorsing Senate candidates outside of New York, and he did not "believe that Ted Kennedy has the experience or the qualifications which would justify . . . making an exception in his case."[6]

II

Herbert Lehman and John Kennedy had tried as Senators to reform American immigration and naturalization laws that imposed quotas based on national origins and limited the rights of naturalized citizens. But most of their efforts had been blocked by Congressman Walter and other defenders of the McCarran-Walter Act. During the presidential election campaign in 1960, Kennedy pledged that a Democratic administration would give "high priority" to implementing the party platform's call for "amendments to the immigration and naturalization laws to ban discrimination based on national origin." In campaigning for Kennedy in the Bronx, Lehman contrasted Kennedy's vote to uphold President Truman's veto of the McCarran-Walter Act with Nixon's support of that legislation, and in a speech commemorating the seventy-fourth anniversary of the dedication of the Statue of Liberty, Lehman argued that Kennedy, like the Statue of Liberty, stood "for a liberal, humane, and just immigration policy."[7]

On February 5, 1961, Lehman addressed the annual meeting of United HIAS Services, which had been founded in the 1880s as the Hebrew Immigrant Aid Society and had been assisting Jewish immigrants ever since. After detailing his unsuccessful efforts to revise the McCarran-Walter Act, Lehman asserted that the situation in 1961 was "radically different" from previous years because "we now have a new President and a new spirit in the White House and in Washington." Lehman emphasized that Kennedy "has been an advocate of immigration reform throughout his political career" and expressed confidence that the President was "wholly committed to the proposition that the discrimination and bigotry must be taken out of our immigration and naturalization laws." But Lehman cautioned that the President was "above all, a practical-minded man" who "knows the legislative process and the compromises which are entailed," and he expected that Kennedy would retain his Senate habit of "making detours, wherever possible, from legislative roads which have been too much traveled in emotional controversy." Lehman was "ready to accept and embrace any hope for substantial progress on this front, and to acclaim any real progress which is actually made," but he warned that "it would be foolish . . . for us to depart from our principles and offer compromises to the opponents of immigration reform before the legislative battle has even been joined." He stressed that "it is still up to us who want immigration reform to supply the pressure from below which will facilitate, encourage, and support bold leadership in this matter from above." By helping to enact such reforms, Lehman concluded, "we will make the name of America ring out again throughout the world as the synonym of freedom, hospitality, and opportunity."[8]

Julius Edelstein sent a copy of Lehman's speech to White House aide Myer Feldman, lamenting that Lehman's televised comments that same day on the political battle with De Sapio had "blanked out his speech on immigration," but Edelstein optimistically predicted that Lehman's remarks would "have an impact on immigration-minded people" and would receive "extensive circulation in the 'trade.'" But Edelstein grossly overstated Lehman's influence, and despite the Democratic Party platform and Kennedy's advocacy during the campaign for major changes in the nation's immigration laws, the President did not push for significant reforms in this area in 1961 and 1962. Kennedy's experience as a Senator trying to revise the immigration laws had taught him that no such measure could pass the House of Representatives without the blessing of Congressman Francis Walter, who still chaired the House Judiciary Subcommittee on Immigration. Thus, when questioned in August 1961 about the administration's intentions on this issue, the President reported that "we have consulted with Congressman Walter and others as to what we can do to improve our immigration laws and we are going to continue to do so." On its own initiative, Congress made some minor changes in the immigration and naturalization laws in 1961 and 1962, but the discriminatory quotas based on national origins remained in effect, and the Kennedy administration remained on the sidelines during this process, not pushing for the more sweeping changes proposed by Senators Philip Hart (D-MI), Jacob Javits, and others. In the meantime, Walter's subcommittee began a lengthy study of the current law "to guide Congress in the consideration of any revision of our immigration policy," which critics of the McCarran-Walter Act correctly saw as a delaying tactic to prevent any significant revisions in the statute in the 87th Congress.[9]

In July 1963, President Kennedy finally sent a special message to Congress proposing major revisions in the nation's immigration laws, including the gradual abolition of the national origins quotas. Senator Hart introduced the administration's bill in the Senate, and Brooklyn Democrat Emanuel Celler, Lehman's old friend and comrade in arms in the fight for immigration reform, took the lead in the House. Under Kennedy's proposal, the national origins quotas would be phased out over five years, replaced by a system that gave preference to those with special skills, education, or training, followed by those whose admission would reunify families. Lehman liked the administration's bill, and he praised the efforts of Senator Hart and "other liberal Senators . . . to secure the passage of the President's proposal for liberalized immigration and naturalization laws." Senator Hart replied that "President Kennedy's recommendations to completely abandon the national origins quota system" reflected Lehman's "great leadership . . . in this effort for so many years." Hart reported that Congress was currently preoccupied with the President's proposed civil rights legislation, which he considered "another long overdue reform for human rights," but he hoped that hearings on the immigration bill would begin in the fall. However, even with the recent death of Representative Walter, the immigration bill's prospects in the House seemed slim because of what the *New York Times* described as the House's traditional reluctance "to increase immigration, particularly in times of widespread unemployment," or to "increase the proportion of immigrants from the 'non-Nordic' countries."[10]

President Kennedy planned to push strongly for his immigration bill in 1964. He was working on a revised version of his little book, *A Nation of Immigrants*, which was released after his death with a new introduction by Robert Kennedy, with excerpts published in the *Saturday Evening Post* in October 1964. After Lehman's death in December 1963, the editors of the *Washington Post and Times-Herald* suggested that the enactment of the pending immigration reform measure, which closely resembled the comprehensive bill Lehman had long championed, "would be Herbert Lehman's best monument." In much the same way that President Johnson called for the approval of President Kennedy's civil rights bill "as the martyred leader's most fitting memorial," Robert Segal, writing in the Cincinnati-based *American Israelite*, asserted that "the passage of remedial legislation cutting the nationals [*sic*] origins quota principle out of our Immigration and Naturalization Law would be a fine memorial" to Herbert Lehman, and Robert Kennedy, in his 1964 campaign for a Senate seat from New York, predicted that "when the time finally comes that we reform our immigration laws," Herbert Lehman "will be remembered as the first to point the way." Lyndon Johnson had supported immigration reform since 1956, and he endorsed the immigration bill in his State of the Union address in 1964. The following year, the liberal 89th Congress passed the Immigration and Nationality Act Amendments of 1965, based in large part on Lehman's old omnibus reform bill and Kennedy's more recent proposal. Even though Herbert Lehman and John Kennedy did not live to see it happen, their efforts helped pave the way for the United States, finally, to abolish the national origins quotas that had discriminated against potential immigrants based on their country of birth since the 1920s.[11]

III

As always, the issue of civil rights for all Americans remained very close to Herbert Lehman's heart, and, perhaps remembering Kennedy's ambivalence on this matter as a Senator, Lehman used the occasion of presenting the ADA's Distinguished Service Award to Martin Luther King, Jr., in late January 1961 to urge the new President to move forward in this area. Eleanor Roosevelt observed how appropriate it was that Lehman, "who has so vigorously championed civil rights and civil liberties" for so many years, was making this presentation to Dr. King. Lehman noted the "exciting spirit" of a new generation in Washington, a generation that knew "that a fresh and vigorous start must be made on what President Kennedy has called the unfinished business of this generation," and he hoped that the President concurred that the main piece of unfinished business was "the matter of human rights." Declaring that "we have far to go to complete this unfinished business," Lehman emphasized that "the steadfast courage of the federal courts must be matched henceforth by the executive and legislative branches acting now in concert," that "many difficult programs of action will be required of the executive departments," and that "new legislative authority and supporting appropriations will be needed from Congress." He asserted "that under the national leadership of President Kennedy, we are going to move ahead speedily on all these fronts," but he warned that "we must not rely solely on what comes down from above," calling upon liberals in ADA and African Americans under King's leadership "to push harder than ever from below, in order to encourage and to support leadership from above."[12]

Lehman cheered Kennedy's appointment of Robert Weaver, an African American and the chairman of the board of the NAACP, as Federal Housing Administrator. Weaver had been part of UNRRA's mission in the Ukraine and Governor Harriman's administration in Albany, and Lehman predicted that Weaver would bring "vigor, understanding, and sympathy" to his new post in the Kennedy administration. Kennedy's nomination of Thurgood Marshall, the head of the NAACP's Legal Defense Fund, to the federal Circuit Court of Appeals in September 1961 also pleased Lehman, who had been one of the original incorporators of the Legal Defense Fund in 1940. He regretted that Marshall would "be leaving the arena" where he had "fought so faithfully and so effectively for many years," but he believed that Kennedy's selection of

Marshall "was timely, wise, and appropriate." Lehman was outraged that Senator Eastland held up Marshall's confirmation for almost a year, denouncing the delay as "completely unjustified and inexcusable," and another example of "the almost unlimited power that, under our congressional system, is given to the chairman of a committee."[13]

Like many of his fellow liberals and civil rights supporters, Lehman disapproved of Kennedy's appointment of Southern racists to important federal positions. For example, Lehman was unhappy when the President nominated, and the Senate approved, Charles Meriwether to be a director of the Export-Import Bank. As opposed to Lehman's friend Harold Linder, whom Kennedy had tapped to head the Export-Import Bank based in part on his extensive experience in international trade and finance, Meriwether had no familiarity with the issues under the bank's jurisdiction, but he had managed John Patterson's successful gubernatorial campaign in Alabama, leading Patterson to appoint him as Alabama's State Finance Director. Meriwether had previously run the unsuccessful campaign of a white supremacist candidate for the U.S. Senate in 1950, defended school segregation, and accepted support from the Ku Klux Klan for Patterson's campaign in 1958. But Patterson had been the first Governor to endorse John Kennedy for President, and Meriwether's nomination to the Export-Import Bank represented a payment on the political debt that Kennedy owed the Alabama Governor. Understanding the political realities behind the President's appointment of Meriwether, Lehman was nonetheless "very much distressed" by the Senate's approval of Meriwether, telling Wayne Morse that the number of votes for Meriwether, especially from "some of our liberal friends . . . came as a considerable shock to me."[14]

The NAACP continued to be the focus of most of Herbert Lehman's civil rights activities. Lehman had first been elected to the NAACP's board of directors in 1930, and he continued to serve in that capacity until his death. As NAACP Executive Secretary Roy Wilkins noted in June 1961, Lehman's importance to the organization extended beyond his annual "exceptionally generous financial contribution," which was "in itself a rarity" since such donations were not tax-deductible because of the NAACP's lobbying on legislation. Although they had to share Herbert Lehman "with a host of others who labor for the righting of great wrongs," the NAACP considered him "a sturdy and unshakable ally in all good causes." But most of all, Wilkins emphasized, because Lehman's "passion and enthusiasm never seems to waver," the NAACP found him to be "a source of renewed spirit whenever there is a temptation to yield, even briefly, to weariness or discouragement in the face of the mammoth obstacles." During the Freedom Rides across the South in the spring and summer of 1961, Lehman quickly complied with the NAACP's appeal to its board members to write to the Interstate Commerce Commission "urging prompt movement" on Attorney General Robert Kennedy's call for desegregation of interstate bus terminals. Wilkins explained that the ICC's reputation for acting slowly on such matters had triggered the request, and he believed that Lehman's "letter has had maximum effect, not only because of your signature, but because of your insistence on the right thing being done, consistent with the law."[15]

Despite the Attorney General's appeal to the Interstate Commerce Commission, Lehman, like many liberals and civil rights activists, was disappointed at the Kennedy administration's slowness to act on civil rights. In a heartfelt letter to the President on October 24, 1961, Lehman reminded the President that during the campaign, Kennedy had stated that "discrimination in all housing activities aided in any way by the federal government" could be ended "with a stroke of the pen" by issuing an executive order banning such practices. Lehman recalled chairing "the panel on executive action" at Kennedy's "Civil Rights Conference in New York City" last October and hearing testimony demonstrating that, "over the past quarter of a century, the federal government has been, in effect, subsidizing, aiding, and spreading residential discrimination and segregation through its housing programs." Lehman appreciated the steps the Kennedy administration had taken in the area of civil rights, including the President's "Executive Order on employment; the ICC's action with regard to transportation; [and] the Department of Justice's activities with regard to voting, transportation, and education." But Lehman emphasized that "the one great remaining area for action is that of housing," noting that "the surroundings in which our children grow up deeply influence their full development and aspirations." Lehman was "continually dismayed by the eroding effects of housing segregation on the minds and personalities of our young people," and he stressed that "our nation simply cannot afford this waste of human resources." In Lehman's opinion, the federal government could not "afford to delay any longer meeting its moral and constitutional obligations." Lehman urged the President "to issue immediately a sweeping Executive Order . . . barring discrimination in all housing which is aided in any manner whatsoever by activities of the federal government."[16]

The President "was delighted to hear from" Lehman and thanked him for sharing his views on "the housing matter," which Kennedy characterized as "a far reaching decision and one we have been considering carefully." Kennedy emphasized that "we are working hard on many fronts in the Civil Rights field and we want to progress steadily with a large national commitment behind it," and he attached a "Summary of Civil Rights Progress in the Last Nine Months" that the administration had been sending to those who criticized it for not doing enough in this area. The four-page summary greatly exaggerated the administration's accomplishments, highlighting, for example, the eventual use of federal marshals to protect the Freedom Riders while ignoring the administration's initial reluctance to intervene on their behalf. But based on Kennedy's response, Lehman realized that there was little he could do at this point to push the President further on this issue.[17]

Lehman once again showed his personal commitment to equal rights for all Americans when the *New York Amsterdam News* reported in October 1961 that Lehman, Governor Rockefeller, and many other prominent New Yorkers belonged to the "lily-white, Jim Crow" Metropolitan Club in Washington, D.C. The club's exclusionary policies had come to light earlier in the year when Robert Kennedy had urged the group to change its practice of barring blacks, including African diplomats, from membership, and discouraging its members from entertaining black guests. In contrast to Rockefeller, who vowed to remain a member, Lehman resigned immediately after the newspaper article appeared, explaining that he had not used the facility for many years and had forgotten that he was a member. Lehman emphasized that he would never "knowingly belong to an organization that practices discrimination on the basis of race, creed, or color," a stance that won him plaudits from James Hicks, the editor of the *Amsterdam News*. Hicks praised Lehman for this demonstration of his "compassion for the feeling of minorities," especially since Lehman was "at a point in his career where from a standpoint of political or financial support, he actually doesn't need the support of minority groups or anyone else."[18]

As he demonstrated in his letter urging the President to ban segregation in federally assisted housing, Herbert Lehman preferred to work behind the scenes to prod the Kennedy administration into taking stronger action to end segregation in the United States. Not everyone agreed with working quietly. Martin Luther King, Jr., and other civil rights activists believed that direct action challenging the status quo was needed to bring about change, and by 1962, King was publicly criticizing the lack of progress in civil rights under President Kennedy. In addition to leading marches and demonstrations in Southern cities, King and the Southern Christian Leadership Conference (SCLC) asked Herbert Lehman in May of 1962 to be one of the "initiators" of a petition calling upon President Kennedy "to issue an executive order on the basis of the Fourteenth Amendment of the Constitution outlawing all forms of segregation throughout the fifty states of our great nation." The petition noted that Abraham Lincoln's Emancipation Proclamation, which had been issued as an executive order ninety-nine years earlier, had "only freed the Negro *physically*," while the years since 1863 "have been a bitter catalogue of wasted human potential and uncalculated frustration imposed by the *psychological* slavery of segregation and discrimination." Improving race relations in the United States, the petition emphasized, was necessary to preserve America's "moral integrity," and with the filibuster preventing Congress from acting, King and the SCLC wanted Kennedy to issue a second Emancipation Proclamation in 1963. The petition urging the President to do so would be presented to him on May 17, 1962, the eighth anniversary of the Supreme Court's decision in *Brown v. Board of Education*, and it would then be circulated nationally with the goal of attracting five million signatures.[19]

After some deliberation, Lehman declined to lend his name to the SCLC's petition. He explained that he had "for many years made it a hard and fast rule not to sign group petitions, advertisements, or other statements" because he found "it more effective to act as an individual" in his "personal capacity." Lehman emphasized that he had "during the past several months" frequently made his "views known to the President on a number of facets of civil rights, notably the issuance of an Executive Order on discrimination in housing and the elimination of discrimination in all bus, rail, and air terminals." He believed that his "views have received careful consideration" and that "action has been taken regarding some of them," and he thought he could "be of more assistance to the cause of civil rights by continuing" his "long established policy" rather than signing the SCLC's petition.[20]

On May 5, 1962, Attorney General Robert Kennedy addressed the annual dinner of the American Jewish Congress. Herbert Lehman had extended the invitation on behalf of the group, and introduced Thurgood Marshall, who was receiving the organization's American Liberties Medallion, an award that Lehman had received in 1956. Much to Lehman's delight, Robert Kennedy used the dinner to make a major speech on civil rights, calling for greater efforts to "achieve a full measure of freedom and social progress for all Americans." The Attorney General condemned literacy tests that were used unfairly "to deny a substantial number of Americans the right to vote because of their color," citing the case of a "Negro who has a National Science Foundation grant for research who was declared illiterate and therefore denied the right to vote." In Kennedy's opinion, the voting problem and the misuse of literacy tests were "so deep-rooted and so manifestly unfair" that federal legislation was needed as "a major step in remedying this situation." Just a few days later, however, a Southern filibuster blocked Senate action on the administration's bill to prevent the use of literacy tests in federal elections. Lehman wrote to Kennedy a few weeks later, telling the Attorney General how much he "appreciated your splendid address," and how much he regretted "the Senate's failure to approve legislation banning the unfair use of literacy tests." He was confident, however, that the Kennedy "administration will continue to press for this and other civil rights reforms through legislative, as well as through executive and judicial means," and he thanked the Attorney General again for his "leadership in advancing human rights." Kennedy found Lehman's "comments about our work in civil rights . . . particularly gratifying" and assured him that the administration "will continue to make a major effort to end discrimination wherever we find it."[21]

The Kennedys did not have to look very hard to find further evidence of segregation and discrimination. In July 1962, Martin Luther King and the leaders of the SCLC were arrested for marching and demonstrating against segregation in Albany, Georgia, and in September, a mob tried to prevent James Meredith, an African American, from registering at the University of

Mississippi. When the President sent federal troops to protect Meredith and enforce court orders calling for his admittance, Lehman offered his "heartiest congratulations" on Kennedy's "admirable handling of the Mississippi situation," praising the President for having sustained the rule of law—"a principle of government from which we can never dare to retreat." Lehman confided to a friend that he felt "shamed and humiliated" by events in Mississippi and was "unable to explain it to some of my friends abroad." He described the situation in Mississippi as "one of the worst that I have known in recent years," but he thought "the President and the Attorney General had handled it well," using "force only as a last resort."[22]

Even though many of the high points of the civil rights movement still lay ahead, a nasty dispute in 1962 between the NAACP and the International Ladies' Garment Workers' Union (ILGWU) put Herbert Lehman in the middle between his longtime associates in both organizations and foreshadowed some of the divisions that later shattered the civil rights coalition of blacks, Jews, and organized labor that Lehman personified. The NAACP was disappointed in the AFL-CIO's tolerance of segregation and discrimination in its affiliated unions, and in August 1962, NAACP labor secretary Herbert Hill asserted before a House subcommittee that the ILGWU was guilty of "de facto racial segregation" against black and Puerto Rican workers. Hill charged that blacks and Puerto Ricans in the ILGWU were "discriminated against and relegated to second-class membership" by confining them to lower-paying jobs and excluding them from leadership positions. A. Philip Randolph, the head of the Brotherhood of Sleeping Car Porters and the highest ranking African American in the AFL-CIO hierarchy, defended the union, and ILGWU President David Dubinsky denounced all such charges against his union as "untruthful, irresponsible, a gross exaggeration, unfair, imaginative, and done in a spirit of revenge." Dubinsky pointed out that House Education and Labor Committee Chairman Adam Clayton Powell and Subcommittee Chairman Herbert Zelenko (D-NY), who was conducting the hearings, were both being challenged for re-election by candidates endorsed by the Liberal Party, of which Dubinsky was a longtime vice president, and he claimed that the hearings constituted a blatant case of Powell and Zelenko retaliating against their political opponents.[23]

In mid-October, the NAACP Board of Directors passed a resolution defending Hill's allegations against the ILGWU and urging the congressional subcommittee "to pursue a vigorous and thoroughgoing investigation of racial discrimination within the International Ladies' Garment Workers' Union." An outraged David Dubinsky, who had always considered himself and his union to be in the forefront of the fight against religious and racial intolerance, responded by appealing to his old friend Herbert Lehman, who had mediated numerous disputes in the garment industry, lent the union money to keep it afloat during the Great Depression, and served on the NAACP's board of directors. Having been away from New York City, Lehman "knew nothing about the situation" until Dubinsky's daughter told him about it at a dinner they both attended, and she reported to her father that Lehman had "expressed astonishment at the entire proceeding" and had made it clear that he "would not have participated in any condemnation of the ILGWU." Dubinsky filled Lehman in on the political context of the hearings, but in addition to expressing his anger at Powell and Zelenko, he bitterly condemned the NAACP's endorsement of Hill's charges of racism and discrimination in the ILGWU. Dubinsky, who had fought against Communists in the ILGWU and had helped found the Liberal Party because of Communist influence in the American Labor Party, engaged in some red-baiting of his own, denouncing the "Trotskyite tactics" the resolution's supporters had allegedly employed in waiting to bring up the measure until most of the NAACP board members had left the meeting. Dubinsky regretted burdening Lehman with all this, but in view of Lehman's interest in the union over the years, he hoped Lehman would acquaint himself "with the facts."[24]

Lehman accepted as truth Dubinsky's version of events and immediately complained to NAACP Executive Secretary Roy Wilkins that he was "shocked and saddened to learn of the resolution adopted by the Directors of the NAACP accusing the International Ladies' Garment Workers' Union of discrimination against Negroes and Puerto Ricans." He reminded Wilkins that he had "been associated with the cause of civil rights and equal opportunity" for almost his entire life, had been a member of the NAACP Board of Directors "for upwards of thirty years," and had been "one of the incorporators of the Legal Defense Fund of the NAACP" and a strong supporter of its work. Lehman was "proud of the great contributions which the NAACP and its Legal Defense Fund have made to the cause of freedom, equality, and the protection of the civil rights of all persons," and he had "also been proud of the fact that the NAACP and the ILGWU," with which he had been "closely associated for nearly half a century, were working side by side in our common great cause." He emphasized that "the ILGWU, like the NAACP, has been a tower of strength in defense of minority groups, and militant in seeking to advance the cause of racial equality and of equal opportunity for all," and he stressed that the ILGWU "has been and is one of our truly great democratic labor organizations and has raised the standard of living and the dignity of hundreds of thousands of working men and women, including large numbers of Negroes and Puerto Ricans." He had not been present at the meeting on October 8 when the resolution on the ILGWU had been adopted, Lehman explained, partly because "no prior notice had been given that this very important resolution would be presented." He then repeated, in less incendiary terms, Dubinsky's assertion that the resolution had been adopted near the end of the meeting after most of the directors had left. Lehman wanted to "disassociate" himself "completely from this resolution," which he considered "unfortunate and unjust," and which he believed had been "hurtful to the NAACP and to the cause of democracy, civil rights, and equal opportunity for all people, regardless of race, creed, color, or national origin," and he informed Wilkins that he was sending Dubinsky a copy of his letter.[25]

Wilkins quickly refuted Dubinsky's allegations about how the NAACP had handled the resolution. He had not been present at the October 8 meeting either, Wilkins explained, but he reported that the minutes showed that "the ILGWU resolution was taken up as the first order of business" and "thus had the consideration of the entire attendance of the Board of Directors." Moreover, Wilkins pointed out that this was the second time the board had considered the matter, "the first having occurred at the policy meeting of September 10." According to Wilkins, "although the Board's support of the substance of the resolution seemed evident" at the September meeting, it had been decided "to reconsider the resolution at the October 8 meeting." Wilkins emphasized that in its "various statements on the ILGWU over the past years," the NAACP had "always acknowledged that the ILGWU has been a 'liberal' trade union and . . . noted many of the fine attributes in its outstanding history." However, he stressed, the NAACP had been "disturbed, increasingly in recent years, over the ILGWU policies which have restricted—in a discriminatory fashion—the opportunities open to its Negro and Puerto Rican membership (which is now 25% of the whole and some 50% of the New York City membership)," and he believed that such policies "do not measure up to the liberal political philosophy on which the ILGWU's reputation is based."[26]

Letting loose now with both barrels, Wilkins disparaged what he considered to be the ILGWU's lackluster record in the fight for civil rights, asserting that "while there has been no doubt as to its philosophical stand, it has never matched certain other unions (some of which are much poorer) in both the manpower and the funds devoted to the civil rights struggle on the practical—not the philosophical—level." In contrast to the Steelworkers, the United Automobile Workers, the International Union of Electrical Workers, and the Packinghouse Workers, Wilkins complained, the ILGWU "has not participated consistently, under its own name, in the long struggle for enactment of FEPC [Fair Employment Practices Commission] legislation, nor has it notably aided in the efforts of the past ten or twelve years to persuade the Congress to enact civil rights legislation." Although the leaders of the ILGWU may have verbally supported civil rights "in ways which may have seemed best to them, and through channels they deemed serviceable," Wilkins observed that they had "seldom done so through the established Leadership Conference on Civil Rights." Softening his tone, Wilkins recognized that Lehman had, "for so many years . . . been a source of inspiration and strength to the cause of civil rights, through the NAACP as well as through other organizations," and he regretted very much that the NAACP had done anything that had disturbed Lehman, "much less saddened and shocked" him. Lehman was "too much the great inspiration to liberals in our time to have such a matter intrude upon" him like this, and Wilkins promised to bring Lehman's letter to the board's attention at its November meeting.[27]

Herbert Lehman had no answer for the growing antagonism between the ILGWU and the NAACP, and he forwarded a copy of Wilkins's letter to Dubinsky without comment. Meanwhile, tempers flared and rhetoric escalated on both sides. Gus Tyler of the ILGWU blamed Hill for the "widening rift between the NAACP and the progressive labor movement," and AFL-CIO President George Meany denounced Hill as "the chief prosecution 'expert' . . . in a political attack on the I.L.G.W.U., a union whose record shines like a beacon in the history of human progress." But Hill stuck to his guns, claiming that "no statement or explanation by officials of the ILGWU or their apologists" refuted his allegations, and Wilkins complained that "the record of the AFL-CIO is much talk and few deeds on civil rights." By late 1962, however, both sides realized they needed to bury the hatchet. Wilkins met with Dubinsky three times in late 1962, and the NAACP leader sent Meany a conciliatory note in which he commended the AFL-CIO for its support of civil rights. The ILGWU and other unions, particularly Walter Reuther's United Auto Workers, participated prominently in the March on Washington the following August, and in 1965, Wilkins accepted Dubinsky's invitation to address the ILGWU's convention. In his remarks, Wilkins praised the labor movement for its commitment to social justice, but he noted that some "deeply ingrained patterns of racial discrimination" had not been eliminated, especially in the building and construction unions. He acknowledged that the NAACP and the ILGWU had not always seen eye to eye, but he reported that he and Dubinsky, after detailed discussions and extensive examination of documentary evidence, had "discovered that neither (the union nor the N.A.A.C.P.) was as bad as had been pictured." But despite the peaceful resolution and papering over of their differences, the disagreement between the NAACP and the ILGWU portended some of the bitter divisions between white liberals and black activists, between Jews and African Americans, and between labor union members and affirmative action proponents that later plagued the civil rights movement.[28]

Although Herbert Lehman refused to join in the NAACP's attack on the ILGWU, the lack of progress on civil rights continued to bother him. He correctly predicted to Hubert Humphrey in January 1963 that the Senate "debate over Rule 22 will soon come to an end with the usual result." Lehman believed, however, "that the fight is just as worthwhile today as it was ten or twelve years ago" when he "had the privilege of being an active participant" with Humphrey "in the battle." In mid-May, Lehman confided to a friend that he was "very much disturbed and concerned over the Birmingham situation," where peaceful civil rights marchers had been met with police dogs and fire hoses. Lehman feared that events in Birmingham had "done us more harm in

Africa, Europe, and Asia than we can undo in five years of effort and generous aid." He noted that "it has had a devastating effect in this country too and has seriously impaired the acceptance by many people of the concept that there must be law and order and exact justice, legal and moral, for all of our citizens."[29]

Lehman sympathized with President Kennedy's dilemma in dealing with the situation in Birmingham, telling a friend that "the President is handling the situation as well as it can be handled," and supporting Kennedy's determination to protect "the fundamental right of all citizens to be accorded equal treatment and opportunity." Lehman was glad that Kennedy was "not allowing himself to be stampeded into taking ill-considered and irresponsible action," especially since "the pressure on him must be very great," and was coming "from both the South and the North." A few weeks later, just before Kennedy's televised appeal defining civil rights as "a moral issue" and calling for the enactment of meaningful civil rights legislation, Lehman assured Kennedy of his "continued and utmost cooperation," along with that of the American Jewish Committee, for the President's "valiant and unending struggle to erase social injustice and lift the barriers of prejudice and discrimination." Lehman applauded Kennedy's efforts to "establish the firm foundation of freedom and justice without which there can be no abiding peace."[30]

Not surprisingly, Herbert Lehman preferred to work with Roy Wilkins and the NAACP, with which he had been connected for more than thirty years, rather than Martin Luther King and the SCLC, as can be seen in Lehman's response to the March on Washington for Jobs and Freedom in August 1963. Wilkins and King and other African American leaders worked together on the event, which sought to rally support for the civil rights bill that Kennedy had finally sent to Congress in the aftermath of the demonstrations in Birmingham, but it was Wilkins whom Lehman applauded afterward, congratulating him and his "associates on a wonderful demonstration." Lehman's only regret was that "convalescence from a broken hip made it impossible" for him "to participate physically in the march," but he reported that he watched "it all day on television with a feeling of great admiration, renewal, and hope." Lehman observed that the event "was obviously very carefully and wisely planned and executed," and he believed that "the nation must have been deeply impressed by the earnestness, dignity, and dedication of the marchers and onlookers." Wilkins replied that he and the other organizers "were gratified that the long hours of planning and teamwork required to implement the March achieved such favorable results," describing it as "a most moving experience." In contrast to Lehman's warm note to Wilkins, there is no indication that Lehman contacted King, whose "I Have a Dream" speech marked the high point of the day's events.[31]

Later that year, Lehman contributed $1,000 to help support the Prince Edward Free School Association that was formed to educate African American children in that Virginia county that had closed its public schools four years earlier rather than integrate them. The Justice Department, under Special Assistant to the Attorney General William vanden Heuvel, had organized the association and helped raise the private funds to operate the schools, and Robert Kennedy gratefully acknowledged Lehman's "personal efforts . . . which were instrumental in opening the schools on schedule." Kennedy wanted Lehman to know that his assistance was "greatly appreciated by all of us who share your concern for the welfare of these children." Vanden Heuvel recalled many years later that "the project had broad support from the liberal philanthropic community of New York," and "a $1,000 contribution was important, especially from Senator Lehman."[32]

Besides his interest in civil rights, Herbert Lehman had long been concerned about the rights of poor people accused of a crime. When he read in the *Christian Science Monitor* in early January 1963 that Attorney General Robert Kennedy was about to propose "a new, nationwide system of 'public defenders' for federal courts," Lehman immediately congratulated Kennedy on his leadership on this issue. Lehman noted that he had "long advocated the creation of 'public defenders' both in the federal courts and in the state courts," having observed as Governor "the well-nigh complete helplessness of impoverished defendants in presenting their cases to the courts." Lehman hoped very much that Kennedy's efforts would succeed, "and that many of the states" would "follow suit," and he offered to do anything he could to help in New York. The Attorney General very much appreciated Lehman's "kind offer of support" and informed Lehman that after two years of studying the problem, the administration was on the verge of submitting legislation to Congress. Kennedy suggested that anything Lehman could do to bring about the "active endorsement by leading members of the bar and judiciary, as well as by bar groups, will do much to stimulate favorable action in Congress," and he also believed that "a favorable reception and active support by the New York congressional delegation would be of invaluable assistance." Specifically, Kennedy noted that "the American Bar Association will consider this legislation in February," and that "prior endorsement by the bar associations in the State of New York, particularly the Bar Association of the City of New York and the New York County Lawyers Association, would be most helpful to the ABA in its consideration of this subject."[33]

Lehman appreciated the opportunity to be helpful on this important issue. He advised Kennedy that whatever legislation was proposed should "provide for sufficient funds for defendants and their counsel to investigate cases thoroughly and to secure the appearance of witnesses who may reside at considerable distance but whose testimony, in many cases, may be vital." He believed that the inability to have their cases researched and presented adequately was "the greatest handicap imposed on impoverished defendants or those with very limited means." As Kennedy had suggested, Lehman wrote "to the Bar Association of the City of New York, and the New York County Lawyers Association, as well as to Congressman Emanuel Celler, [the] senior member of the New York delegation in the House," urging them to support the administration's initiative in this matter. The Attorney General gratefully acknowledged Lehman's "valuable endorsement" of the administration's efforts, and in March, he sent Lehman copies of the proposed legislation as well as his letter to the President and the President's letter transmitting the bill to Congress. Lehman was glad to receive the documents and hoped that the President's proposal, "or similar legislation, will be enacted at an early date," which it was as part of the Criminal Justice Act of 1964.[34]

IV

Herbert Lehman maintained his strong interest in foreign affairs after leaving the Senate, and he generally supported Kennedy's actions in that area, hoping that the young President would learn from mistakes such as the Bay of Pigs fiasco in Cuba, where most of the invading force was quickly captured by Castro's forces. When President Kennedy asked Eleanor Roosevelt, Walter Reuther, and Milton Eisenhower to raise funds to purchase tractors that would then be sent to Cuba in exchange for the prisoners, Lehman contributed $1,000 to the Tractors for Freedom Committee that was organized. Eleanor Roosevelt appreciated knowing that she had Lehman's "support in this venture," because she always believed that she was on the right side of an issue when Herbert Lehman agreed with her position. Lehman hoped that the failure in Cuba, "while greatly costly, may in the future save us from at least some mistakes in our relationship with Africa, Asia, and Latin America." When Kennedy addressed the nation after his trip to Europe and the failed Vienna Summit meeting with Soviet Premier Nikita Khrushchev, Lehman applauded "the frankness and honesty" of the President's remarks, and when Kennedy reported to the nation on the Berlin crisis in late July, Lehman assured him that "the whole nation will stand behind you." Kennedy appreciated Lehman's "personal pledge of support" and knew that he could count on Lehman to help meet the "great continuing need to enhance public understanding of our problems abroad and our need for increasing vigor as a society here at home." When Kennedy addressed the United Nations in September, Lehman thought that the President's "magnificent" speech "should be convincing to all the free and the uncommitted peoples." In March 1962, Lehman told his former UNRRA associate Robert G. A. Jackson that although the President had "made some mistakes," Lehman thought that "on the whole," Kennedy "has shown courage, imagination, industry, and high principles, both in domestic and foreign affairs." During the Cuban Missile Crisis that fall, Lehman asserted that President Kennedy "handled the Cuban

situation magnificently," and he praised Adlai Stevenson's "wonderful" presentation of the American case at the United Nations.[35]

Besides cheering the President's remarks, Lehman also helped rally the
public behind some of Kennedy's foreign policy initiatives. Lehman served on
the Citizens Committee for International Development, which was formed in
the summer of 1961 to build public and congressional support for the administration's foreign aid bill. According to presidential aide Ralph Dungan, "the
President followed the work of the committee closely" and asked Dungan to
thank Lehman and the other members for their help in winning congressional
approval of the foreign aid legislation. At Hubert Humphrey's request, Lehman
submitted a letter supporting the Kennedy administration's bill to establish a
United States Disarmament Agency within the State Department, and Lehman
made clear his willingness to testify in favor of the measure. In October 1961,
George McGovern, the director of Kennedy's Food for Peace program, relayed
to Lehman the President's request that Lehman "serve on the Board of Trustees
of the U.S. Freedom From Hunger Foundation," which was being established
"to generate enlightened and decisive support" for the UN Food and Agriculture
Organization's "five-year Freedom From Hunger Campaign." McGovern stressed
that Lehman's "membership on the Board will help to highlight the interest
of this country in utilizing our knowledge and resources in a broad attack on
human hunger and misery." Lehman, who had been involved with such issues
since his days at the Joint Distribution Committee and then at UNRRA, replied
that he would "be very glad indeed to serve on the Board," whose members
were announced by the President just before Thanksgiving.[36]

When the Kennedy administration negotiated a limited nuclear test ban
treaty with the Soviet Union in 1963, Lehman congratulated the President
and asserted that Kennedy's speech to the nation on the treaty "was one of the
most important" of Kennedy's career, giving "both hope and a warning to the
people of this country and of the world." Lehman confided to a friend that
he hoped the treaty, which banned atmospheric testing of nuclear weapons,
"will be confirmed by the Senate by a very large margin," but he feared that
"it will run into some difficulties," observing that "there is always a substantial
number of members of the Senate who are 'agin' everything, and will want to
extend needlessly the debate on the Test Ban Treaty." He would "breathe easier"
when he knew "that it has received the required two-thirds vote." The President
appreciated Lehman's "generous expression of support for the nuclear test ban
treaty," explaining that even though the agreement "does not resolve all of the
issues and conflicts that separate the nations of the world," he believed it represented "a beginning in the long and tortuous road toward peace." He noted
that now it would be up to the Senate and, "in the larger sense, the people of
the United States," to "decide whether the treaty should be ratified," and he
emphasized that the assistance of Lehman and others like him would "make

the process of ratification more expeditious." Trying to do what he could to help ease the treaty's path in the Senate, Lehman joined the Citizens Committee for a Nuclear Test Ban, which was formed "for the purpose of supporting ratification of the nuclear test ban treaty." Much to Lehman's relief, the Senate moved quickly and approved the limited nuclear test ban agreement by a wide margin in September 1963.[37]

V

Israel remained one of Herbert Lehman's primary concerns. Lehman often stressed that he was not a Zionist, but he had urged President Truman to recognize Israel in 1948 and had become a strong supporter of the Jewish state from that point on. Herbert and Edith Lehman visited Israel in 1949 and were "tremendously impressed by the achievements which are almost miraculous," but Lehman also realized "the tremendous number of problems and difficulties that lie ahead," which he thought could be solved, but only with "a great deal of help from the outside." Elihu Elath, the Israeli Ambassador to the United States, believed that Lehman's trip to Israel had been helpful in "the strengthening of relations between Israel and the United States," and Lehman continued to advocate on Israel's behalf and contributed generously to the United Jewish Appeal and other fund-raising efforts to help Israel absorb the refugees who were pouring in from Europe and from Arab countries. When the Lehmans toured Israel again in 1959, a water desalinization laboratory in Beersheba and a village in Northern Galilee were named after Lehman, who was "deeply impressed by the almost incredible progress and growth that has come to our little sister Republic since our last visit ten years ago." Lehman congratulated Israeli Prime Minister David Ben Gurion, noting that "the desert has really been made to bloom and some of your institutions are as fine as any I have seen in the older countries."[38]

Despite his growing attachment to the state of Israel, Lehman resented the World Zionist Organization's assertion in 1961 that it had the right to tell American Jews what their attitudes and opinions should be on the Jewish state. When Dr. Nahum Goldmann, the Zionist group's president, claimed that his organization could define the proper relationship between American Jews and Israel, the American Jewish Committee (AJC), which Lehman had been associated with for decades, promptly challenged Goldmann's assertion. The AJC had always been sensitive to the issue of "dual loyalty"—the charge that American Jews' interest in Israel compromised their loyalty to the United States—and Lehman now joined in a statement issued by the AJC denying that the World Zionist Organization, or anyone else, had the authority to act as a spokesman for American Jews. The AJC emphasized that "Jews of the United States are not a monolithic entity within American society," and that for American Jews, "their outlook toward Israel, like their attitudes toward all other interests—religious, social, civic, or cultural—are determined by each person for himself and find expression in a variety of organizations." The statement stressed that even the AJC "does not presume to speak for the Jews of America," but its leaders believed that "many American Jews share our view which repudiates the assumption of central authority by any organization, whether Zionist or otherwise."[39]

The discriminatory treatment against American Jews by Saudi Arabia and other Arab countries had bothered Lehman for many years. Saudi Arabia did not allow Jews into its territory, whether as tourists, employees of the Arabian-American Oil Company, or even American servicemen, and most of the Arab states refused to do business with American companies that traded with Israel or had Jews among their executives. Lehman believed that it was shameful for the United States to acquiesce in such despicable practices, and in June 1956, he had introduced a sense of the Senate Resolution "opposing discriminatory action against United States citizens because of religious faith or affiliations." Senator John Kennedy had co-sponsored Lehman's resolution, which was modified by the Foreign Relations Committee and then passed unanimously by the Senate. Four years later, the Democratic Party platform of 1960 promised that a Democratic President would seek "an end to boycotts and blockades" and declared that "protection of rights of American citizens to travel, to pursue lawful trade, and to engage in other lawful activities abroad without distinction as to race or religion is a cardinal function of the national sovereignty." After winning the Democratic nomination, John Kennedy specifically endorsed these positions, telling Rabbi Israel Goldstein of Congregation B'nai Jeshurun in New York that "the persistence of the Arab states in maintaining a 'state of war' against Israel is clearly the root cause of the discriminations" against American Jews, and pledging that a Democratic administration would "take immediate steps to eliminate discrimination on the grounds of race, religion, or color practiced against Americans abroad."[40]

When discrimination against American Jews by Saudi Arabia and other Arab nations continued despite the inclusion of language in the 1960 Mutual Security Act and the 1961 Foreign Assistance Act declaring that such practices were "repugnant" to American principles and traditions, Herbert Lehman and the leaders of the American Jewish Committee asked to meet with President Kennedy in early 1962 to discuss the "infringement of rights of American citizens arising from the Arab boycott." The AJC emphasized in its request for the meeting that "Senator Lehman is particularly anxious to be present," but scheduling issues delayed the meeting until April 30, 1962, by which time Representatives James Roosevelt (D-CA) and Seymour Halpern (R-NY) had each introduced bills in Congress cutting off American aid to countries that discriminated against American citizens based on their religion, race, or color.

Halpern complained that he had been "unable to secure a visa to visit American aid projects in Saudi Arabia because he is Jewish," and he asserted that "the time is long past due that this government demand that these Arab states cease this insulting practice against Americans in which they demand 'security clearance' on their religious conviction in order to visit or deal with these countries."[41]

Lehman and representatives of the AJC met with the President on April 30, 1962, emphasizing that they "were not at the White House on problems pertaining to Israel at this time." Rather, they stressed, they were there to discuss the "steady erosion of the rights of certain American citizens" over the last fourteen years "without adequate action on the part of our government in defense of those rights." The AJC explained that some Arab nations would not grant a visa to a holder of an American passport unless he submitted "a Baptismal certificate or other satisfactory evidence that he is not of the Jewish faith," and as a Jewish Congressman had recently experienced, airports in certain Arab nations insisted that Jewish passengers remain on the plane while other passengers were allowed to disembark and use the airport's facilities. Moreover, American companies wanting to trade with Arab nations were "required to reveal whether they have Jews among their stockholders, directors, managerial staff, or employees," and Jewish soldiers in the American armed forces were not allowed to serve in Saudi Arabia, which also barred "Jewish civilians even as employees of Aramco, which holds the oil concession from Saudi Arabia." Such practices were not new; they had gone on for fourteen years, and while Democratic and Republican administrations had "expressed regret" and "deplored the discriminatory practices," there had "been no vigorous, effective action" by the American government. The AJC pointed out that historically the United States had "firmly resisted any effort by foreign countries to discriminate among American citizens on the basis of race or religion," and it reported that Holland, England, and other countries had "resisted Arab pressures with no untoward results." Herbert Lehman "reminded the President of the resolutions with reference to Arab country discrimination of American Jews" that he and Kennedy had sponsored when they were in the Senate together, and Lehman and the others stressed that "a positive declaration by the President would be extremely helpful."[42]

Scholars Steven Spiegel and Warren Bass have shown that the Middle East was a "low priority" for John Kennedy, whose "Arab-Israeli diplomacy was largely based on Cold War strategy rather than ethnic politics." In other words, maintaining good relations with Saudi Arabia and preventing Communist expansion in the Middle East were more important to Kennedy than placating American Jewish leaders, although there was nothing to stop him from trying to do both. The President explained to Lehman and the AJC leaders that he understood the "seriousness and importance" of the problem they had described, but he emphasized that the power of the United States was not "what we think it is in certain areas of the world, such as the Middle East." He noted that Jordan had recently agreed to remove the question about religion from its visa application, and he reported that he had spoken to King Ibn Saud of Saudi Arabia about this issue during the King's recent visit, pointing out to the King that Saudi Arabia "took an even severer position in the matter of practicing discrimination against American Jews than did Nasser." The President discussed the situation in each of the Arab states, observing that "the United States had very little influence in Iraq," but he hoped that "something could be done in Jordan as has already been demonstrated, and perhaps in some other Arab League states." Kennedy promised to have Myer Feldman, one of his aides who handled Jewish matters, including Israel, check to see if there had been any change in Saudi policy since his conversation with the King. He would also make sure the State Department was aware of his interest in the matter, and he suggested that the situation should be reviewed again in July, asking that the AJC contact him at that time. Demonstrating his concern for the larger, Cold War issues, Kennedy rejected the possibility of conditioning foreign aid on the recipients' ending all discriminatory practices, as some in Congress had suggested. While he agreed that "the matter should always be in the minds of our negotiators," he asserted that "it would not be practical to adopt as an operating procedure the withholding of foreign aid from the offending country," warning that to do so might help drive such countries into "the Communist orbit." In thanking the President a few days later for meeting with the delegation, Lehman noted that Kennedy's "knowledge and understanding of this problem and the actions already taken and those contemplated by you" encouraged the AJC to believe that Kennedy would "succeed in enlightening responsible Arab officials," and that the State Department would follow through on the President's policy.[43]

As Kennedy promised, Myer Feldman checked with the State Department to ascertain whether any progress had been made with the Saudis and other Arab states on this matter. In response to Feldman's prodding, the State Department reported on June 30 that some progress had been made in persuading Syria and Jordan to loosen their restrictions, but Saudi Arabia had not modified its exclusionary policies. President Kennedy continued to pursue the subject, bringing it up again when he met with Saudi Crown Prince Faysal in October 1962. Faysal "promised to take up the matter immediately upon his return with the King and the Saudi government with a view to seeing what could be done about it," but he cautioned "that any fruitful results were not likely to emerge quickly."[44]

The issue of Arab nations discriminating against Jewish Americans came to a head in June 1963 when the *New York Times* reported that "United States servicemen of the Jewish faith have been serving in Saudi Arabia for several weeks, despite strong objections in the past by the Saudi Government to their presence there." The report, triggered by Congressman Emanuel Celler's comments during a radio interview, embarrassed the Saudi government, especially Faysal, who was now the King. Faysal complained to U.S. Ambassador Parker Hart that Kennedy "had asked him to do something about Jews in transit through the kingdom and he had done so," arranging "that no queries be put to transients regarding their religion." Faysal now called upon the U.S. government to "publicly denounce Congressman Celler's statement regarding the sending of Jewish servicemen to Saudi Arabia," threatening "not to let any U.S. servicemen enter the Kingdom until he received a U.S. response to this demand." But the Kennedy administration was not about to alienate Celler, the chairman of the House Judiciary Committee and a staunch supporter of Kennedy's domestic and foreign policies. Nor did the President want to be seen as condoning discrimination against Jewish Americans abroad at the same time that he was calling for an end to segregation and discrimination against African Americans here at home. With the two countries at an impasse, the United States postponed the deployment of an American air unit that had been ready to conduct a training operation with Saudi forces. After two weeks of posturing, the operation proceeded, with the Saudis maintaining that they had not changed their visa policy barring Jews, and the United States insisting that its "policy of non-discrimination among American citizens on grounds of race, creed, or color is firmly established." As Warren Bass has noted, the solution constituted an early version of "Don't ask, don't tell," with the Saudis agreeing not to ask about the religion of American troops and the United States not volunteering that information.[45]

Lehman and the American Jewish Committee remained concerned about Kennedy's policy in the Middle East, especially the President's efforts to woo Egypt's Gamal Nasser, described by one Kennedy administration official as "the Mister Big of the Arab World." In acknowledging and sending greetings to the annual meeting of the American Jewish Committee in May 1963, President Kennedy singled out for special praise his "good friend and colleague, Governor Herbert H. Lehman, who only recently celebrated his eighty-fifth birthday." Lehman appreciated the President's kind words, but in his response, he asserted that "current disturbing developments in the Middle East and the rising tensions in the area" required "additional affirmative action by the United States . . . to help stabilize the situation there while there is still time," and he attached a "Statement on the Middle East" that the AJC had recently adopted. The AJC worried about the recent federation established among Egypt, Syria, and Iraq, which "incorporates for the first time in a constitutional document the 'liberation of Palestine' as a basic objective," and the American decision to grant official recognition to "the Nasser-backed rebel regime in Yemen—whose power is maintained only through the continued presence of one-third of Egypt's regular army." Ignoring the Kennedy administration's agreement to sell Hawk anti-aircraft missiles to Israel to offset the "ultra-modern" planes Egypt had received from the Soviet bloc, the AJC called upon the Kennedy administration to "take immediate and sustained action to maintain the balance of arms between the Arab countries and Israel." The AJC also recommended that the United States "provide a formal guarantee, upon request, of the independence and integrity of any state in the region," and it wanted the United States to "vigorously discourage the violent hate campaign against Israel conducted by the Arab states." Finally, the AJC asked the Kennedy administration to "re-evaluate the present U.S. policy of impartiality toward peaceful nations and those nations pursuing belligerent policies inimical to the peace and stability of the Middle East."[46]

Kennedy often used Deputy Special Counsel Myer Feldman as his buffer to deliver bad news to the Jewish community, and the President, not wanting to get trapped into a stronger commitment or guarantee to Israel, had Feldman respond to Lehman on his behalf. Feldman emphasized that the administration shared Lehman's "concern over developments in the Middle East that might disturb the existing uneasy peace," as well as Lehman's "hope that a permanent peace will ultimately be achieved," and he assured Lehman that the AJC's statement and recommendations "will be considered." Recalling Lehman's meeting with the President the previous year about Arab countries' discriminatory practices against American Jews, Feldman reported that "we have made considerable progress in the area of relationships between American Jews and Arab States," and he promised that the administration would "continue to work in this direction." Lehman complained to Kennedy's brother-in-law Steve Smith that Feldman had replied to his letter rather than Kennedy, but a presidential response was not forthcoming.[47]

VI

During his lifetime, Herbert Lehman received numerous medals and awards from various nations and humanitarian organizations, but Mrs. Lehman always felt that her husband's work at UNRRA had not been fully appreciated and recognized. In 1947, Abe Feller, who had served as UNRRA's General Counsel, had urged that Herbert Lehman "should be the recipient of the Nobel Peace Prize," and Professor Philip Jessup of Columbia University, who had worked with Lehman at UNRRA, and Lithgow Osborne, Lehman's Conservation Commissioner in New York and then a Deputy Director General of UNRRA, had taken the lead in putting Lehman forward as a candidate for the Nobel Prize. But despite the energetic efforts of Lehman's former UNRRA associates, the Nobel Peace Prize for 1947 had been awarded to the Quakers, the Society of Friends, in the United States and Great Britain, in recognition of their many years of "great humanitarian work."[48]

In 1961, Edith Lehman learned that a new prize for "peace, humanity, and brotherhood among peoples" had been established in memory of Eugenio Balzan, an Italian newspaperman who had left Italy in protest against Mussolini's fascist regime and become a wealthy financier in Switzerland. Alberto Tarchiani, Italy's Ambassador to the United States in 1946, had presented Herbert Lehman with the Great Cross of the Order of the Crown of Italy in 1946 as "tangible proof" of Italy's gratitude for UNRRA's assistance, and Mrs. Lehman now asked the Italian diplomat if her husband's work as Director General of UNRRA would qualify him for this new honor. The prizes were to be awarded by a foundation presided over by the Presidents of Italy and Switzerland, and if Tarchiani agreed that Herbert Lehman would be a worthy candidate, Mrs. Lehman would appreciate it if the Ambassador would "place his name for consideration before the proper authorities." After making various inquiries, Tarchiani reported that the process for the new award had not yet been settled, but he had "very warmly recommended" to the President of the Italian Senate and to the Swiss committee "the candidacy of Governor Lehman for his wonderful work at the UNRRA from 1943 to 1946, and for many other merits as a political leader and a humanitarian." A few days later, however, Tarchiani informed Mrs. Lehman that the initial Balzan Prize for 1962 would be going to the Nobel Institution, and that an international commission would be established to receive nominations in subsequent years.[49]

David Morse, the Director General of the International Labor Organization, took the lead in organizing a campaign in 1962 to nominate Herbert Lehman for the 1963 Balzan Prize. Morse's wife was an old family friend of the Lehmans, and Lehman had tried to recruit Morse for UNRRA in 1945, only to lose out because Morse had already accepted the position of General Counsel to the National Labor Relations Board. Eleanor Roosevelt allowed Morse to use her name in soliciting distinguished Americans for a committee to sponsor Herbert Lehman's nomination for the award, and Adlai Stevenson, Arthur Goldberg, George Meany, Roy Wilkins, Ralph Bunche, and Lyndon Johnson all agreed to serve on the committee. Stevenson could "think of no more deserving recipient, nor a more fitting tribute," to Lehman's "dedicated, selfless service to all mankind over many years," and Bunche agreed that there was no one "more deserving of the recognition which would accompany the Balzan award." But despite the committee's efforts, Lehman lost out again, this time to Pope John XXIII. Lehman greatly appreciated Morse's work and that of Mrs. Roosevelt and the rest of the committee and emphasized that he "was in no way disappointed" because he "never felt there was a possibility of . . . being a recipient of the prize so many years after the work of UNRRA was completed."[50]

Herbert Lehman and John Kennedy were both saddened by the death of Eleanor Roosevelt in November 1962. The President hailed Mrs. Roosevelt as "one of the great ladies in the history of this country" whose "loss will be deeply felt by all those who admired her tireless idealism or benefitted from her good works and wise counsel." Her "memory and spirit," Kennedy declared, "will long endure among those who labor for great causes around the world." Herbert Lehman mourned the passing of this "great lady" who had been at his side in so many battles for human rights and dignity, telling Franklin Roosevelt, Jr., "how deeply grieved" he and Edith were at the passing of this beloved woman who enjoyed "the deepest affection of the entire world." Similarly, the Lehmans consoled Mrs. Roosevelt's daughter, Anna Halsted, recalling that her mother's "sympathies knew no bounds of race, color, creed, or national origin," and that "no effort was too much in her fight against injustice or to better the lot of the underprivileged throughout the world." In his public response to Mrs. Roosevelt's death, Lehman stressed that "her place can never be filled in the hearts of countless people whom she has befriended and helped over a life of unfailing service and selfless devotion," and he noted that "the world is much poorer for her going." The Kennedys and the Lehmans attended her funeral at Hyde Park a few days later, along with Presidents Truman and Eisenhower, and numerous former New Deal officials. During the service, former Roosevelt advisor Tom Corcoran whispered to Arthur Schlesinger, Jr., that "there will never again be an occasion on which all these people will gather together," and Adolf Berle, part of FDR's original Brain Trust and a longtime leader of the Liberal Party in New York, observed that "this funeral was distinctly the end of an era," that Herbert Lehman and the other "great and lesser great figures of the New Deal, now old and white-haired," who had gathered for the sad occasion, were "visibly going over the horizon line which divided politics and history."[51]

March 28, 1963, marked Herbert Lehman's eighty-fifth birthday, and Kennedy advisor Arthur Schlesinger, Jr., suggested that "this would seem a good occasion for a presidential tribute." Mrs. Lehman planned a gala dinner-dance to celebrate the event, and Herbert Lehman insisted that she not make any changes in party after he fell and broke his hip, meaning he would have to attend in a wheelchair. Immediately upon hearing of Lehman's injury, the President, "having had a little familiarity with the problems of convalescence myself," wished Lehman a "swift and complete" recovery. Kennedy sent warm birthday greetings to Lehman that were read aloud at the party by Hubert Humphrey. Regretting that he and Jackie were not able to "join you personally in this observance," the President noted that although Lehman had "not been in active political service" in recent years, "you have pursued with undiminished vigor and integrity the many endeavors with which your career has been so long identified," and he declared that Lehman's "voice and your influence have continued to inspire men and women of all generations."[52]

The President was not the only one to cheer Lehman on the occasion of his eighty-fifth birthday. Mayor Wagner proclaimed March 28th as "Herbert

Lehman Day," recalling the former Governor and Senator's many years of service in Albany and Washington, including his tenure as the head of UNRRA, and praising Lehman as "a glowing example of both personal and public integrity and nobility." The *New York Times* described Lehman as "one of the best loved citizens of New York" and thanked him "for the many useful and enlightened services he has performed for the people of this city and this state." Lehman's long career as a "liberal and humanitarian," the *Times* observed, "has been marked consistently by courage and a generous interest in the well-being of his fellow men. To have him still with us, always ready to speak up for what he thinks is right and never reluctant to come down hard on what he thinks is wrong," the *Times* concluded, "is something to celebrate, and be grateful for."[53]

Herbert Lehman reciprocated John Kennedy's birthday wishes, serving as one of the honorary chairmen of the President's Club of New York, which sponsored a gala dinner celebration at the Waldorf-Astoria Hotel a few days before the President's forty-sixth birthday in May. Like the other six hundred guests at the affair, Lehman had contributed at least $1,000 to the Democratic National Committee to become a member of the President's Club. Lehman also sent "happiest birthday congratulations and warmest good wishes" on the President's actual birthday. On a more serious note, when the Kennedys' newborn son died of lung problems just thirty-nine hours after his premature birth, the Lehmans extended their "deepest sympathy" to the President and Mrs. Kennedy "in your great sorrow," and the President thanked the Lehmans for "thinking of us at this very difficult time," describing their note as "a comfort to me and my family" for which they were "very grateful."[54]

President Kennedy believed that "a nation reveals itself not only by the men it produces but also by the men it honors," and in 1963, he revived the Presidential Medal of Freedom and established a process for awarding this distinction to individuals "who have made exceptionally meritorious contributions to the security or national interest of the United States, to world peace, or to cultural or other significant public or private endeavors." Undeterred by past disappointments when the Nobel and Balzan Prizes had been awarded to others, Herbert Lehman's family let it be known that "the Governor would regard most highly some official public recognition by the U.S. government of his services to the nation as Director General of OFFRA [*sic*] and UNRRA during the war." Lehman's wife Edith and his son John thought that the new Presidential Medal of Freedom was exactly the kind of tribute that Herbert Lehman deserved, especially since Lehman had "received honors from some foreign governments for this service . . . but never from his own." Unbeknownst to Herbert Lehman, John Lehman discussed the idea with Stanley Karson, who had worked on Lehman's Senate staff before moving on to the Institute of Life Insurance, and Karson forwarded the suggestion to Senator Hubert Humphrey and to presidential advisor Arthur Schlesinger, Jr., asserting that Lehman's work at OFRRO and UNRRA certainly met the criteria for the new award. Karson urged Senator Humphrey to discuss the matter during an upcoming visit to the White House.[55]

Senator Humphrey followed through on the idea, and he made sure that Herbert Lehman was among those considered by the committee tasked with recommending possible recipients of the new award. The group, which included Attorney General Robert Kennedy, Supreme Court Justice Arthur Goldberg, and Undersecretary of State George Ball, among others, met a number of times in the spring of 1963, and it winnowed an original list of 149 potential nominees down to thirty-seven. Herbert Lehman was among those who survived the cut, the committee recommending that Lehman be honored for his "political service to the people of America and humanitarian activities at home and abroad." The President made some changes to the committee's list, and on July 1, 1963, Kennedy informed Herbert Lehman that he would be among the thirty-one recipients of the new Presidential Medal of Freedom to be announced on July 4. Kennedy stressed that "this is the highest civil honor conferred by the President of the United States for service in peacetime," congratulating Lehman and extending his "warm best wishes."[56]

Herbert Lehman was thrilled to learn that he would receive the Presidential Medal of Freedom. As he explained to his nephew Arthur Goodhart, and to his many friends and relatives who congratulated him, Lehman had not realized that he "was being considered and the news therefore came . . . as a complete surprise." Lehman was "delighted and honored to be included in the list of very distinguished men and women to receive the award." Having learned of Hubert Humphrey's role in putting his name forward, Lehman thanked him profusely for his part in making it possible for Lehman to receive this award, which he considered "one of the greatest honors of my long public life."[57]

The original plan was for the awards to be presented in September, but because of delays in striking the new medals, the ceremony was postponed until November. In November, it was pushed back again, this time until December 6. However, on November 22, 1963, two weeks before the scheduled presentation, President Kennedy was assassinated while riding in a motorcade in Dallas, Texas. In a telegram to Jacqueline Kennedy, Herbert and Edith Lehman noted, "Words cannot express the shock and grief which we feel at the terrible loss that you and the people of the world have sustained in the tragic death of your wonderful husband and our great President and friend," conveying their "deepest sympathy from the bottom of our hearts." Similarly, the Lehmans sent their "heartfelt sympathy" to Robert Kennedy, lamenting "the great loss which has come to you, to us and to all the world in the tragic death of a great President who had won the confidence and affection of people everywhere." The *New York Times* reported that Herbert Lehman, a "strong supporter of the President's policies, was too shocked to frame a formal statement" but had condemned the President's murder as "the greatest catastrophe that our nation has suffered since the assassination of President Lincoln." A few days later, Lehman forwarded to Robert Kennedy a column by Max Freedman published in the *Los Angeles Times* that Lehman believed "shows unusual perception of the great qualities possessed by your brother, whose tragic and untimely death has saddened almost everybody in this country and the Free World." In this column, Freedman emphasized that John Kennedy, in contrast to "so many others [who] were content merely to curse the darkness," had lit "a fire to inspire us with new purpose," asserting that "Kennedy's achievement in destroying religious prejudice as a test of political office will endure." Expressing views that Lehman clearly shared, Freedman predicted that Kennedy would "be remembered as the man who broke the furrows and walked always to the horizon," and that "the ultimate tragedy is that his capacity for growth as a national and world leader has ended."[58]

CHAPTER 22

"We Mourn That He Is Gone but Glad That He Had Lived"

Herbert Lehman and President Johnson, 1963–1964

Herbert H. Lehman: Citizen and statesman, he has used wisdom and compassion as the tools of government and has made politics the highest form of public service.[1]

I

John Kennedy's death suddenly elevated Vice President Lyndon Johnson, Herbert Lehman's former Senate colleague, to the presidency. As discussed earlier, Lehman and Johnson's relationship in the Senate had often been contentious, with Lehman blaming Johnson for blocking meaningful civil rights legislation and other reforms dear to Lehman's heart, and Johnson dismissing Lehman as one of the liberal "crazies" who stubbornly refused to compromise. Johnson never forgot, however, that Lehman had requested a moment of silent prayer on the floor of the Senate when the Majority Leader had suffered his heart attack in 1955. Herbert Lehman had campaigned enthusiastically for the Kennedy-Johnson ticket in 1960, and he had maintained sporadic contact with the Vice President during John Kennedy's presidency.[2]

Chapter title quotation: Lyndon Johnson to Edith Lehman, December 18, 1963, Herbert Lehman Papers, Special Correspondence Files, Johnson.

633

On November 23, 1963, in the immediate aftermath of John Kennedy's assassination, the Lehmans extended to the new President their "deepest sympathy in the great loss that has come to all of us in the tragic death of your associate and our great President." Herbert and Edith Lehman were "confident" that Johnson "will carry on the traditions and principles of our country with great dedication and skill," and they wanted Johnson to know that he had their "fullest support" and "warmest good wishes in the tremendous duty" he had assumed. After Johnson addressed a Joint Session of Congress on November 27, delivering a moving tribute to Kennedy and calling upon Congress to enact the stalled civil rights bill as a memorial to the slain leader, Lehman congratulated the President on his "magnificent address," emphasizing that "we are all very proud of you." Johnson was deeply touched by Lehman's message. Noting that Lehman had spent his "life in a magnificent battle for the integrity and the dignity of all human beings," Johnson prayed that he could "somehow find the strength and the ingenuity to translate into a reality the goals" that Lehman had always championed.[3]

Herbert Lehman had maintained his political and philanthropic activities in 1961–1963 despite a series of ailments. In the spring of 1961, he contracted bronchial pneumonia, and in 1962 he was stricken with gout. As Lehman explained to William Benton, he was "very much humiliated" at the latter diagnosis because he "had always understood that gout came from high living and hard drinking," neither of which were charges to which Lehman could "plead guilty." Later that spring, Lehman underwent successful cataract surgery, but while in France that summer, he suffered through a bout of bronchitis. Lehman's most serious physical problem occurred when he fell and broke his hip while vacationing in Palm Springs in mid-February 1963. As Mrs. Lehman reported to friends and family, her husband was "in great pain" for a few days until the doctors were able to operate and insert a pin, "which greatly lessened the pain." At the Lehmans' insistence, Herbert Lehman's eighty-fifth birthday celebration went on as planned on March 27, 1963, despite the guest of honor being in a wheelchair. Lehman's hip still bothered him that summer and fall, and he experienced anxiety and chest pains the night after President Kennedy's assassination, but his physician monitored him closely, noting that "the chest pain never returned and his EKG remained normal." Thus, Herbert Lehman appeared to be in reasonably good health for a man his age when he prepared to travel to Washington in early December 1963 to receive the Presidential Medal of Freedom.[4]

Upon assuming the presidency, Lyndon Johnson stressed the need for stability and continuity, insisting that events such as the presentation of the Presidential Medals of Freedom on December 6 should proceed on schedule. Herbert Lehman looked forward to receiving the award and seeing old friends in Washington, and he planned to travel on Thursday, December 5, to make sure that nothing interfered with his presence at the ceremony. But after he awoke, dressed, talked on the phone, and had breakfast that morning, Herbert Lehman suddenly suffered a fatal heart attack and died in his bedroom at nine that morning. Lehman's former Senate colleague William Benton noted that it seemed "particularly touching that Herbert was stricken as he was about to go to Washington to receive the Presidential Medal of Freedom!" and President Johnson wired his condolences to Mrs. Lehman, stressing, "Lady Bird and I are grieved to learn of the death of Governor Lehman." Johnson emphasized that Lehman's "spirit, his dedication to the public interest, his compassion and understanding of the problems of people will always serve as a high example to those in public life." In his public statement on Lehman's death, the President praised the former Governor and Senator as a "distinguished leader who ably served his state and nation," and he quoted the citation on the Medal of Honor that Lehman had been scheduled to receive the next day: "Citizen and statesman, he has used wisdom and compassion as the tools of government and has made politics the highest form of public service."[5]

Government officials, political and religious leaders, newspaper editors, and many others joined President Johnson in paying tribute to Herbert Lehman. Hubert Humphrey remembered that despite Lehman's age, he was "the youngest at heart" of the liberal group in the Senate, a man dedicated "to progressive principles and to liberal thought." Mayor Wagner described him as "a father to our whole city and state," declaring that he had "never known a better man, a kindlier man, or a more courageous man," and lamenting that "the people have lost a dedicated and brilliant champion, a spokesman for all that is best in our nation." Adlai Stevenson characterized Herbert Lehman as "the conscience of political liberalism in America," emphasizing that Lehman "was a true elder statesman, but neither years nor custom ever stalled the vigor of his ideas or his ideals," and Roy Wilkins of the NAACP bemoaned the loss of this "beloved comrade in the fight for racial justice." The *New York Times* mourned the passing of this "great man of private heart and public courage" who had "battled relentlessly against the troops of evil" on "matters close to his heart—immigration to continue the American dream and civil rights to uphold the American Constitution." New York City Human Rights Commission Chairman Stanley Lowell captured the sentiments of many people when he noted that "the passing of Herbert H. Lehman, like the death of John F. Kennedy, has taken from each of us a bit of our collective conscience. Equality for all, regardless of race, color, or religion, was Herbert Lehman's lifelong passion." The *Chicago Defender*, one of the nation's leading African American newspapers, praised the "broad social vision" of this "undaunted crusader for justice and human equality," observing that "while Governor Lehman's body returns to dust; his spirit lives on." In the days following Lehman's death, similar tributes from organizations and individuals with whom he had been closely associated for decades filled the columns of the *New York Times*, with the International Ladies' Garment Workers' Union, the American Jewish Committee, Hadassah, the NAACP, the Henry Street Settlement, Mount Sinai Hospital, the Committee for Democratic Voters, the Eleanor Roosevelt Memorial Foundation, his neighbors at 820 Park Avenue, and many others paying their respects to "this fearless champion of freedom, equality, and human dignity."[6]

II

Lyndon Johnson and his advisors saw Herbert Lehman's death as a political opportunity that the President could use to his advantage. New York State Democratic Chairman William McKeon called the White House to report that Lehman's funeral was scheduled for Sunday, December 8, at one o'clock at Temple Emanu-El in New York City, and, looking ahead to the 1964 election, he suggested that Johnson's "attendance at this service would be most helpful with the liberal faction in New York." Not content merely to send flowers and condolences, the President realized that paying his respects to this great liberal icon in person might help him win the support of liberals nationwide who had never liked or trusted him. At the very least, using Air Force One to bring a liberal contingent from Washington to the funeral would generate favorable publicity and give the President the chance to persuade his passengers of his genuine support for civil rights and other liberal causes, as well as putting them in his debt for facilitating their travel to the funeral. Presidential assistant Arthur Schlesinger, Jr., noted that the President could "go with one or two people, call on Mrs. Lehman, give her the Medal of Freedom which her husband was to receive today, and go on to the funeral," or he could take a larger contingent with him to New York, including "people (a) who had a genuine connection with Herbert Lehman and (b) who will do the President some political good." Expecting that Johnson would choose the second option, Schlesinger immediately began compiling a list of Supreme Court Justices, Cabinet officers, Senators and Representatives, and other Washington notables who might be invited to accompany the President to New York for the funeral. Schlesinger's list included Supreme Court Justice Arthur Goldberg; Senators Hubert Humphrey, Paul Douglas, Joe Clark, Wayne Morse, Jacob Javits, and Kenneth Keating; Representatives James Roosevelt and William Fitts Ryan; Attorney General Robert Kennedy; Secretary of Labor Willard Wirtz; labor leaders George Meany and Walter Reuther; NAACP Washington Bureau Director Clarence Mitchell; Averell Harriman; and Franklin D. Roosevelt, Jr. The final list for Air Force One grew considerably from Schlesinger's initial recommendations, as most of the Supreme Court Justices, Senators Mike Mansfield, Lister Hill, J. William Fulbright, Maurine Neuberger, Ralph Yarborough, and others "accepted the

President's invitation to fly up to and return from New York," as did Mrs. Hubert Humphrey and Mrs. Paul Douglas. A number of New York Congressmen met the presidential party at Idlewild (now Kennedy) Airport, and others joined them at the Temple.[7]

Schlesinger's explanations for including and excluding various individuals showed some sensitivity to the Lehman family, but they also highlighted the political aspects of the President's trip to New York for Lehman's funeral. Schlesinger pointed out that bringing Congressman and Bronx boss Charles "Buckley or old-line Democrats would cause an adverse reaction." On the other hand, even though liberal activist Joseph Rauh "has been very critical of the President in the past," he had "put out a statement the other day on behalf of the District Democratic Committee pledging full support to the President" and was "exceedingly influential in labor and liberal circles." Schlesinger emphasized that Rauh "was very close to Herbert Lehman," and Schlesinger thought "it would be a great thing, and impressive in New York, if the President were to invite him to come." Rauh later recalled people's surprise at seeing him with the President given their previous disagreements, but Johnson skillfully used the trip to New York to discuss the blocked civil rights bill with Rauh and the Vietnam situation with Senator Mansfield. Writing in the *New York Post*, liberal columnist James Wechsler described Johnson's invitation to Rauh to accompany him to the funeral as "perhaps the most extraordinary move Mr. Johnson has made toward reunion with the liberal bloc," and he noted that "Mr. Lehman would have been pleased to realize that his death had provided the inspiration for this quiet drama."[8]

Observers recognized that Johnson was taking advantage of the political opportunity presented by Lehman's funeral. Chalmers Roberts of the *Washington Post and Times-Herald* noted that when Lehman and Johnson had served together in the Senate, "Lehman often found Mr. Johnson too conservative," and he pointed out that many in the "large party of liberal Democratic members of Congress and party officials" who went to New York with the President "were far more friendly to the late Senator" than they were to Johnson. Bernard Nossiter, Roberts's colleague at the *Post*, reported that "despite the solemnity of the day, the President's visit had some political undertones," noting that Johnson "appeared determined to impress New Yorkers and liberals." Columnist Doris Fleeson wrote that "Johnson sought to identify with a liberal Democratic Party by paying homage to the departed statesman, Herbert Lehman, who was loved and honored above most men," and Walter Trohan, the conservative *Chicago Tribune*'s Washington Bureau Chief, feared that Johnson's presence at the funeral had succeeded in its goal of winning favor with "the nation's Jewish and liberal communities." Senator Paul Douglas, one of Lehman's few allies in the Senate in the fight for civil rights and other liberal causes, battles in which Lyndon Johnson often led the opposition, pointed out the irony that "having attacked Lehman in life," Johnson "paid him full homage in death."[9]

Mrs. Lehman tried to dissuade the President from attending her husband's funeral, realizing that Johnson's presence would inevitably shift the spotlight away from Herbert Lehman and onto the President. She phoned the White House and spoke to Johnson on Friday afternoon, December 6, couching her suggestion that he not attend in terms of concern for his safety and security. Knowing "how terribly busy" the President was, Mrs. Lehman apologized for bothering him and told him how much she appreciated his telegram and his letter expressing his condolences. She wished that "Herb could know" that the President was planning to come to the funeral because "it would have meant a great deal to him." But emphasizing Johnson's great importance to the nation in the aftermath of President Kennedy's death, Mrs. Lehman wondered whether it was "wise" for the President to "take that risk" of traveling to New York. Johnson brushed aside her concerns, declaring, "I'm going to be there, period." He was certain that Herbert Lehman was "looking down on us and getting things ready for us" and knew that Johnson was coming to the funeral. The President recalled that when he had suffered his heart attack, Herbert Lehman "got up and for the first time in the history of the Republic, since the Senate was organized, he had them stand and pray for me, and I don't believe I'd have made it except for that." Johnson wished he could "assuage your grief and make you stronger," and he assured Mrs. Lehman that "the good Lord will help you through the trying days that are going to be ahead." He also reported that he was inviting many of Lehman's "friends in Washington to come up with me, like Abe Fortas and some of the men up in the Senate—Senator Douglas and Senator Clark and some of the better people that he knew." Realizing that nothing she could say would change the President's mind, Mrs. Lehman gave in and thanked the President for his thoughtfulness. Herbert Lehman's son John also called the White House and informed the President's aides that the Lehman family preferred not to have the Medal of Freedom presented to the family on the day of the funeral, fearing that it would disrupt the flow of the service or create an awkward situation on the sidewalk afterward.[10]

Lehman's body lay in state on Friday and Saturday, December 6 and 7, at the Universal Chapel in Manhattan to allow dignitaries and common people alike to pay their respects to the beloved statesman and console his family. Friends and political foes came to offer their condolences, including Cardinal Spellman, Mayor Wagner, State Attorney General Louis Lefkowitz, Manhattan District Attorney Frank Hogan, ILGWU President David Dubinsky, Lehman's former Lieutenant Governor Charles Poletti, and many others. Men in "shabby jackets" mingled with women in "rich furs." An elderly African American man explained that he "had to come" because Lehman "was so good to me, so good to my people," while others broke down, overcome with emotion at the loss of their longtime leader.[11]

III

Herbert Lehman's funeral on Sunday, December 8, 1963, occurred just two weeks after John Kennedy had been assassinated in Dallas, so security was heavy for Johnson's trip to New York, his first excursion outside of Washington since succeeding to the presidency. Johnson landed at Idlewild Airport shortly after noon, from where he proceeded directly to Temple Emanu-El along an unpublicized route, guarded by heavily armed Secret Servicemen and two thousand New York City policemen. "Full security" was in effect, with "no stops for lights, etc." on the way to the Temple. When the President and Mrs. Johnson arrived at the Temple a few minutes before the service was scheduled to begin, the sanctuary's 2,200 seats were already filled with 1,500 invited guests and seven hundred members of the public who wished to pay their respects, while an additional 1,500 people listened to the service over a loudspeaker set up in another room. The President and his party immediately took their seats in the front row on the right, and Mrs. Lehman and the family entered shortly thereafter and sat in the front row on the left.[12]

Dr. Julius Mark, Senior Rabbi of Temple Emanu-El, presided over the funeral service. He began his tribute to Herbert Lehman by reciting Psalm 15, which asks: "O Lord, who shall sojourn in Thy holy tabernacle? Who shall dwell upon Thy holy mountain?" The answer, composed thousands of years earlier, sounded like it was written with Herbert Lehman in mind:

> He that walketh uprightly, and worketh righteousness,
> And speaketh truth in his heart;
> He that hath no slander upon his tongue,
> Nor doeth evil to his fellow,
> Nor taketh up a reproach against his neighbor; . . .
> He that doest these things shall never, never be moved.

The Rabbi then read Lehman's favorite prayer, a prayer for peace, God's "most precious gift."[13]

To demonstrate "the undying love for America, the profound respect for religious convictions of all men and the staunch loyalty to his own faith which dwelled in the great heart of Herbert H. Lehman," Rabbi Mark quoted from a letter Lehman had written three years ago to a young Jewish boy who had asked whether being Jewish had assisted or handicapped Lehman in his political career. Lehman did not believe "that being a Jew" had "either helped or harmed" him, asserting that "generally speaking, the American people choose their public officials by their impression of the man or woman." He conceded that "bias and prejudice still exist to some degree in this country," but in his opinion, "it is far less than it was 30 or 40 years ago." To his "fellow Jews who may want some day to become publicly known and feel that Judaism may hold them back because of either discrimination or prejudice," Lehman stressed that "any man who is seeking public office and allows his ambition to affect his religious affiliation is not worthy of the confidence of his fellow citizens." Lehman's final advice to the boy encapsulated the principles that Lehman had tried to follow in his public life: "Never be ashamed of being a Jew. Never try to hide it. Never try to compromise with your convictions because they may not agree with those of the group in which you find yourself."[14]

Mrs. Lehman had asked her husband's good friend Judge Edward Weinfeld to deliver the eulogy at the funeral. Lehman had appointed Weinfeld as New York State Commissioner of Housing in 1939, and had recommended him for a federal judgeship many times before President Truman finally appointed Weinfeld to the federal bench in 1950. As Weinfeld's biographer notes, Lehman had been "a surrogate father" to Weinfeld, who was twenty-three years younger than Lehman. The two spoke on the phone frequently, including a half-hour conversation the morning of Lehman's death. Weinfeld "was deeply touched that Mrs. Lehman asked" him "to deliver the eulogy, but greatly concerned whether" he "would measure up and say in a simple way what we all felt about this warm and gentle friend of impeccable integrity."[15]

Weinfeld emphasized in his eulogy that "Herbert Lehman had no doubt of the answer to the taunting biblical inquiry: Am I my brother's keeper?" Lehman's life, Weinfeld asserted, "was a decisive and an affirmative response" that "man does have a responsibility to his fellow man." For Lehman, "the cause of social justice and the betterment of all mankind was without limit," and Lehman's actions, Weinfeld stressed, "were deeply rooted in his belief in the worth of each individual. He knew no distinction of race, color, or creed." Lehman's career, Weinfeld pointed out, was one of "service to the city, the state, the nation, and the world" that was "without parallel in our times for its duration, its dedication, and devotion, and for its impact upon millions of people here and throughout the entire world." Weinfeld recounted how Lehman, as Director General of UNRRA, had saved hundreds of thousands of lives "under conditions that would have discouraged and defeated a lesser man, a less determined fighter, a man less concerned with human life." He was "a man of peace, yet he met every assault on democracy with an iron will and an inner fire that carried the day," a man whose "capacity for righteous indignation was never dulled by the years. This was a man of matchless courage and rare integrity . . . who left the world a better place than when he entered it."[16]

Capturing Lehman's essence, Weinfeld noted that Lehman "brooked no compromise with principles," that "he deeply felt the responsibility for our freedom," and that he understood that "whenever those freedoms are threatened, they can be preserved only by forthright and vigorous action, no matter what the personal and political consequences." Recalling Senator McCarthy's reign of terror, Weinfeld remembered that "in the dark suspicious days of our nation . . . when fear seemed to have paralyzed most of our leadership, Herbert Lehman dared to stand alone fighting those who would have destroyed the meaning of our democratic way of life." Fortunately, Lehman's "courage inspired courage in others, and gradually and happily, America came back to her senses." Weinfeld emphasized that "in those years, it was not easy to be a lonely fighter, yet this kind and gentle man was fearless in meeting head-on the forces of hatred and bigotry."[17]

Speaking on a more personal level, Weinfeld noted that "Lehman's great public career was equaled by his devotion to family and friends," and he highlighted "the great love and constant devotion of Herbert and Edith Lehman over a period of more than fifty-four years." Weinfeld recalled the many occasions when Lehman was "about to address a vast assembly when he would search for his companion and upon sighting her somewhere in the audience, exchange with her their familiar wave of affection before commencing his address." Herbert Lehman's many battles, Weinfeld observed, "were made more bearable because of Edith's encouragement and support." Weinfeld explained that "to have enjoyed the warmth and the friendship of the Governor and his beloved Edith . . . was to have experienced one of life's richest blessings." Lehman "never forgot the personal, intimate items which mean so much in terms of human relationships," never being too busy "to call on a birthday, an anniversary or other happy event to share the joy or, if the occasion required, to express the sorrow and sympathy of a friend." Weinfeld recalled Lehman's "abiding love of children" and thought that it was entirely appropriate that as the funeral service was proceeding at Temple Emanu-El, children were paying their own tribute to Lehman "just across the street, by enjoying the Children's Zoo that he and Edith so wonderfully provided for them."[18]

Weinfeld hailed the citation accompanying the Presidential Medal of Freedom, which Lehman had been preparing to travel to Washington to receive, as "a touching tribute," but he emphasized that "no citation, no award, is needed to remind us of the outstanding services" Lehman had "rendered to all mankind." Lehman's "works and his deeds, the love and affection of a grateful people, remain his lasting tribute." Because of Herbert Lehman and his accomplishments, Weinfeld concluded, "the world is a better place in which to live. This shall be a comfort to his family and friends. Herbert Lehman is forever enshrined in our hearts."[19]

After Weinfeld had finished, Rabbi Mark offered his own tribute to Herbert Lehman, thanking God "for this warm, modest, courteous, gallant public servant and humanitarian, whose wise and understanding heart was literally on fire with a passion for human dignity and human freedom, whose soul revolted against every form of prejudice and injustice, regardless of who the victim might be." While Lehman's "death grieves us," the Rabbi proclaimed, his "life blessed us," and his "memory will forever be an inspiration to all who would build a better world of justice, freedom, and peace." Rabbi Mark noted that "truth, indeed, reigned supreme in the inmost parts of this wonderful human being, called the conscience of the Senate," asserting that Lehman "was the conscience of America and the Free World, whose profile was edged in rugged courage, impeccable integrity, and innate love for all human beings, particularly little children." It was "not likely that we shall ever see his like again," the Rabbi lamented, "for of Herbert Lehman, it may be truthfully said that he never caused a tear to flow save only when he died." He urged Lehman's friends and family to "try to think of him as not having died but as having lived beautifully, selflessly, blessedly." The Rabbi closed the service with the following lines from Shakespeare's *Hamlet*:

> Now cracks a noble heart.
> Good night, sweet prince,
> And flights of angels
> Sing thee to thy rest.[20]

When the service ended, Rabbi Mark led the Recessional, followed by the Honorary Ushers, the casket, the Lehman family, and then the President. Mrs. Lehman stopped on the sidewalk outside the Temple, and as had been previously arranged, President and Mrs. Johnson embraced her and offered their condolences. Mrs. Lehman thought the ceremony had been perfect, later telling Rabbi Mark, "how deeply moving your services were at Herbert's funeral; it was exactly the kind of service that he would have liked—simple, dignified, and full of sentiment." Back in Washington that evening, Lyndon Johnson thanked Arthur Schlesinger, Jr., for compiling the list so quickly of those who had accompanied the President to the funeral. Johnson also observed that "the services were unusual"—reflecting perhaps his unfamiliarity with a typical Jewish funeral service—but he quickly added that he had "heard many favorable comments."[21]

As Mrs. Lehman had feared, Johnson's presence at the funeral dominated the news stories the next day, but as she wrote to the President, she appreciated "the touching tribute you and Mrs. Johnson paid to Herbert by coming here from Washington to attend his funeral." Mrs. Lehman was relieved to know that the President "had arrived back in Washington without incident." Johnson graciously replied a few days later, thanking Mrs. Lehman "for your kindnesses and your warm friendship over the years." The President asserted that Herbert Lehman's "passing was a great personal loss to me," but he acknowledged that it was "an even greater—more terrible loss to you, your family, and to the Nation." Johnson noted that "we all took comfort in the eloquent and beautiful eulogy," and stressed that "we mourn that he is gone but glad that he had lived." He assured Mrs. Lehman she could just call if there was anything that he or Lady Bird could do for her.[22]

The only sour note at this time was an obituary entitled "The Highest Form" that appeared in the December 13, 1963, issue of *Time* magazine. Although the article was generally favorable, it seemed at times to belittle Lehman and minimize his accomplishments. The Lehman family, highly protective of Herbert Lehman's legacy, protested that "some of the descriptive phraseology employed is in very poor taste as well as highly inaccurate." As Lehman's brother-in-law Frank Altschul informed Time, Inc., president James Linen, he thought the description of Lehman "as a 'do-gooder' hardly seems fairly descriptive of a man who for more than half a century fought for the highest principles in governmental and human relations." Altschul also objected to the article's assertion that Lehman "became best known for his passionate but somehow hapless tirades against the evils of Joe McCarthy," pointing out that "well before the unlamented McCarthy era, Herbert Lehman was internationally known as the Director General of UNRRA and nationally known as the four-time Governor of the State of New York." Altschul agreed that Lehman's fight, "at first almost alone—against the evils of McCarthyism added to his stature," but he complained that to describe Lehman's speeches on the issue as "somehow hapless tirades" diminished the importance of Lehman's role in the battle against McCarthyism. *Time* neither printed Altschul's letter nor offered a correction or apology.[23]

IV

The presentation of the Presidential Medals of Freedom had proceeded as scheduled on December 6, 1963, despite the death of Herbert Lehman. When Undersecretary of State George Ball read the list of honorees, he stopped when he reached Herbert Lehman's name, noting that "we were all deeply saddened to here [*sic*] yesterday of the death of this great citizen," and the President read the citation that accompanied Lehman's medal. Lehman's was not the only posthumous award, as President Johnson had added the recently deceased President Kennedy and Pope John XXIII to the list of recipients.[24]

President Johnson delivered his first State of the Union address on January 8, 1964, announcing that he had reduced the federal budget below the previous year's spending total, declaring "unconditional war on poverty in America," and urging Congress to pass the tax cuts that had been proposed by President Kennedy. Picking up on causes that had been dear to Herbert Lehman, Johnson called civil rights "a moral issue" and appealed for the abolition of "not some, but all, racial discrimination" through the passage of the pending civil rights bill, and he advocated reform of the nation's immigration laws to do away with quotas based on national origins. Johnson also proposed increased federal funding "for education, for health, for retraining the unemployed, and for helping the economically and the physically handicapped," all of which, and more, would be enacted into law in 1964–1965 as part of Johnson's Great Society. In foreign affairs, Johnson pledged to maintain America's "military safety and superiority" while working for "a world that is free from hate; a world of peace and justice and freedom and abundance for our time and for all time to come." Mrs. Lehman congratulated the President on his address, emphasizing "how happy Herbert would have been with" Johnson's "direct, courageous, and comprehensive speech to the nation" in which he "touched on all the subjects that had been closest" to Lehman's heart and "which he had fought for over the years." She predicted that "the nation will respond enthusiastically," and assured the President that "the confidence of our friends all over the world will have been immensely fortified."[25]

The Lehman family had requested that the presentation of the Presidential Medal of Freedom not be squeezed into President Johnson's trip to Lehman's funeral. In early January, Herbert Lehman's son John contacted Edwin Weisl, who was widely known as "President Johnson's personal 'eyes and ears' in New York," to tell him that Mrs. Lehman would be "leaving the city" in early February "for a much needed rest," and that "it would be very much appreciated by the Lehman family if she could come to Washington and receive" the medal from the President prior to her departure. In relaying the message to the President, Weisl emphasized that Herbert Lehman "was probably the most beloved and influential liberal in the State of New York" and noted that "the entire Lehman family is among the most charitable, civic minded, and highly respected families." Weisl also pointed out that Herbert Lehman's cousin Robert (Bobby) Lehman was "a leading banker and businessman," and "a Johnson man 'from way back when.'" Weisl was aware of the many demands that were made upon Johnson, but he thought that the President "would want to know about" this one.[26]

The President was eager to comply with the request, and White House aide Bill Moyers told Weisl that "the President will be pleased to see Mrs. Lehman on either the 28th or the 29th of this month," whichever date Mrs. Lehman preferred. Mrs. Lehman chose January 28, and the President's staff arranged for the ceremony to occur in the Cabinet Room at 11:00 a.m. on that date. The White House team went all out to make the event a momentous one, inviting Edith Lehman, John Lehman, and Mrs. Lehman's sister, Hilda Altschul Master; the Lehmans' close friends Hubert and Muriel Humphrey and Paul and Emily Douglas; Lehman's former Senate colleagues Wayne Morse, Clinton Anderson, J. William Fulbright, and Lister Hill; New York Senators Jacob Javits and Kenneth Keating; New York Congressmen William Fitts Ryan and Emanuel Celler; Supreme Court Justice Arthur Goldberg; Attorney General Robert Kennedy; Mrs. James Roosevelt; Averell Harriman; Arthur Schlesinger, Jr.; Julius Edelstein; and Judge Edward Weinfeld, among others. When the guests were all assembled, the President entered the Cabinet Room and strode to the podium, at which point Undersecretary of State George Ball, who had presided over the ceremony for the other recipients, announced the President, who addressed the group and formally presented the medal to Mrs. Lehman.[27]

In his remarks at the presentation, Johnson recalled that one of his "first—and most rewarding acts" as President "was to confer the Presidential Medal of Freedom for distinguished achievements on thirty-three individuals." But he noted that "the brilliance of that occasion was marred by the absence of two men: John Kennedy, who conceived and planned these new civil honors, and Herbert Lehman, whose death in New York occurred just minutes before his departure to Washington to receive this award from a grateful nation." Johnson declared that it was "altogether fitting that in special ceremony we present Herbert Lehman's Medal of Freedom to the one person who shared his life and

FIGURE 22.1. President Johnson presenting Herbert Lehman's Presidential Medal of Freedom to Mrs. Lehman, January 28, 1964. Courtesy of the Lyndon Baines Johnson Presidential Library.

his hopes, his triumphs and his disappointments, who was always with him in sunshine and in sorrow." As "the friends of Herbert Lehman who are gathered here today" well knew, "Edith Lehman was the indispensable companion" who "was always there." Senator Lehman, Johnson observed, "was an unusual man who "believed in the worth of the human being, . . . the goodness and the rightness of the individual citizen." The President then read the citation that accompanied Lehman's Medal: "Herbert H. Lehman, citizen and statesman. He has used wisdom and compassion as the tools of government and he has made politics the highest form of public service."[28]

Mrs. Lehman thanked the President and all those in attendance for honoring her husband in this way. She pointed out that "the knowledge that this medal was coming to him added a great deal to his last hours of life." She also praised Johnson for his actions since becoming President, noting that Herbert Lehman had been "very thrilled and very encouraged and very happy" with Johnson's speech to the Joint Session of Congress in late November calling for the passage of civil rights legislation. The President closed the ceremony by emphasizing again what an "unusual man and a most thoughtful person" Herbert Lehman was. Johnson remembered that when he "was hovering between life and death" after his heart attack in 1955, Lehman had "offered a Senate resolution that the Senate pray for my recovery." Lehman's resolution had come "just at the time when I needed every prayer I could get," Johnson recalled, "and his prayer was answered." Johnson believed that Lehman had "made it possible for me to be here today."[29]

The next day, Mrs. Lehman wrote to the President to thank him again. Recalling Johnson's earlier comment that Herbert knew that the President was coming to his funeral, Mrs. Lehman noted that "the same thought went through my mind yesterday as I attended the moving ceremony at the White House." Johnson's "beautiful eulogy of Herbert touched" her "deeply," and she appreciated Johnson's "thoughtfulness and generosity," which had made it possible for so many of her husband's "friends and former colleagues" to gather "to pay him honor." She could not "put into words" her gratitude or express adequately how much "the warmth and sincerity of the ceremony" meant to her, and she would always "cherish" the memory of this "deeply moving occasion." She informed the President that "the medal will be displayed in a spot of Herbert's own choosing, commanding the most prominent place in a cabinet alongside his Distinguished Service Medal from World War I, which was his proudest possession," and "the citation will hang on the wall nearby where family and friends can read and enjoy the simple and perfectly-chosen words." A few years later, when the Herbert Lehman Suite (now the Herbert Lehman Center for American History) containing Lehman's papers opened at Columbia University, the citation from Lehman's Presidential Medal of Freedom was inscribed on the wall outside the facility, and the medal itself was prominently displayed.[30]

V

Lyndon Johnson looked forward to the 1964 Democratic National Convention in Atlantic City as a coronation, a celebration that would bestow the party's blessing on his presidency and wipe away any thought that his occupancy of the White House was somehow tainted because he had succeeded to the presidency upon John Kennedy's assassination. The President wanted a convention that would display to the nation the unity of the Democrats behind his candidacy, and he sought to control every detail of the convention to achieve this result. As Theodore White later reported, Johnson was the "stage manager of his own Convention. . . . Seats and schedules and decorations and arrangements and cameras had danced at his command," and delegates to the convention "danced on the strings that ran from the White House to the Pageant Motel, where his personal staff edited, approved, disapproved, arranged matters to suit his fancy." Historian Eric Goldman, who was serving at the time as a special consultant to the President, later compared Johnson's influence on the convention to that of "the mother of the bride, considering, controlling, fussing over every detail. This was to be *his* convention, leading to *his* triumph." Hubert Humphrey agreed that "the convention, for all practical purposes," had been the President's show. Johnson "wrote the music, choreographed the action, chose the stars, and virtually wrote their lines. What Lyndon wanted, Lyndon got. He accepted every cheer as adulation, and when it reached a crescendo, it seemed to erase the ghost of John Kennedy's presidency from his mind."[31]

As the convention approached, Johnson was obsessed about two potential threats to the harmonious image that he wanted the Democrats to present. The President worried that Robert Kennedy would somehow steamroll the gathering into nominating him for the vice presidency, weakening Johnson's authority by showing that the President could not even control his own party. To lessen Kennedy's influence at the convention, Johnson delayed the filmed tribute to John Kennedy, to be introduced by Robert Kennedy, until the last night of the convention, after the vice presidential candidate had already been chosen. The President also feared that the demand of the Mississippi Freedom Democrats (MFD) that they be seated as the legitimate delegation from their state would split the party: if the convention upheld the MFD's objection to the regular, segregated, Mississippi delegation, Southern delegations might walk out, but if the convention rejected the challenge, African Americans and Northern liberals would be angered. Johnson assigned vice presidential aspirant Hubert Humphrey to mediate the dispute and devise a compromise that all sides could live with, suggesting that Humphrey's selection as the vice presidential candidate might depend on his success in this delicate mission. Humphrey, UAW President Walter Reuther, and Joseph Rauh, the lawyer representing the MFD, eventually worked out an agreement under which two members of the MFD would be seated as delegates at-large, with the rest invited to attend the convention as guests, and promised that changes in the party rules would ensure that Mississippi sent an integrated delegation to the 1968 convention. But the MFD rejected the offer as tokenism, insisting that they be recognized as representing Mississippi, "not a place named 'at-large.'"[32]

While Johnson focused on Bobby Kennedy's alleged plot to steal the vice presidential nomination and the situation with the Mississippi Freedom Democrats, another problem suddenly intruded: which Democratic dignitaries who had passed away since the last national convention would be recognized at the 1964 convention? Preliminary plans called for paying tribute to President Kennedy, Eleanor Roosevelt, longtime Speaker of the House Sam Rayburn, and former DNC Chairman Paul Butler. Some White House aides wondered whether Butler was worthy of inclusion with the others, and there were also questions about who should offer the tributes. Johnson's original plan was for "Adlai Stevenson to do Mrs. Roosevelt, President Truman to do Sam Rayburn, and the President himself to do John F. Kennedy," but as one Johnson advisor noted, "the trouble with all this is that no one has told Adlai; President Truman has announced that he is not going to the convention; [and] if the President appears for the memorial before accepting the nomination it will make his speech 'one hell of an anti-climax.'"[33]

But Lyndon Johnson and the convention organizers had not reckoned with Edith Lehman, who zealously guarded her late husband's memory and reputation. Mrs. Lehman had been very supportive of the President, sending a lovely floral bouquet to welcome Johnson when he delivered a speech in New York, and contributing at least $1,000 to become a member of the President's Club for his re-election campaign. But when Mrs. Lehman discovered in late July that Herbert Lehman was not among those who would be honored posthumously at the Democratic National Convention, she immediately tried to make her displeasure known to President Johnson through intermediaries. Realizing that Johnson was making all the important decisions about the convention but not wanting to disturb him during the Tonkin Gulf crisis, Mrs. Lehman "tried to get the message" to the President "through others." She "talked this all over with Hubert Humphrey," who promised that he would inform the President about her belief that her husband was being slighted. She also prevailed upon Mayor Wagner and others to write to the President, urging that an additional name be added to the list of those to be honored at the Democratic National Convention, a name "which is honored by millions throughout America," including Johnson himself: "the late, beloved Herbert H. Lehman. Would it not be a fine and fitting thing to pay tribute to this great American, too?" Wagner asked the President. After all, Lehman had been "an active and dedicated Democrat for well over 60 years and earned a place among the great men of this country." Wagner hoped that the President would forward this suggestion "with your endorsement to the officials in charge of the programming of the national convention."[34]

When Edith Lehman realized that her indirect pleas were having no effect, she took matters into her own hands. On August 20, just a few days before the convention was to open, she telephoned President Johnson directly to complain about the plan to honor four people in a memorial service at the Democratic National Convention. She apologized for bothering the President, but she feared her attempts to convey her concern to the President "didn't get to you." Johnson disingenuously claimed that this was the first he was hearing about the matter, so Mrs. Lehman explained that she "was very disturbed" when she read in the paper a few weeks ago that the convention was going to pay tribute to President Kennedy, Mrs. Roosevelt, Sam Rayburn, and Paul Butler. She felt that there was "a terrific omission" that "will not only be resented by me but a great many other people if that happens." Playing dumb, Johnson asked, "What omission?" to which Mrs. Lehman curtly replied: "Do I have to tell you that my husband would be an omission?" She asserted that "there has been nobody over the years who has played a more important part in the Democratic Party or rendered greater service to the party or been more helpful than he." And she claimed that the President had shown by his words and his deeds that he felt that way about Herbert Lehman too.[35]

Not wanting to offend Mrs. Lehman, liberal Democrats, and Jewish voters, all of whom revered the memory of Herbert Lehman, Johnson continued to maintain his ignorance of the whole situation, asserting that Democratic National Committee Chairman John Bailey "has not discussed it with me," that Hubert Humphrey "has not mentioned it to me," and that this was the first he was hearing of it. The President claimed that the only memorial he was aware of was a film honoring President Kennedy, and maybe a tribute to Sam Rayburn "because he had been the permanent chairman for many conventions." He "wouldn't have any objection" to something honoring Mrs. Roosevelt, but he knew nothing about any plan to do so, and he insisted that there were no "plans to honor the Congressmen or the Senators or the Governors throughout the United States individually at the convention in a memorial service," and that no remembrance of Paul Butler was scheduled. Johnson emphasized that he had "certainly paid all the respect and memorial to Senator Lehman," and he did not know what more he could do. He did not want anyone to "interpret anything that I've done as a slight to Senator Lehman," and he wanted to give Lehman "any honor that we can," but he did not "know where we would start though and stop if we started with Paul Butler and went all over the United States." Trying to end the conversation, Johnson noted all "the problems that I'm carrying here," and he promised that even though he had nothing to do with the arrangements for the convention, he would "ask those who are doing it to do their very best and see that" Herbert Lehman received "all the honor that we can give him every way we can."[36]

Mrs. Lehman refused to take the hint and did not allow the conversation to end. She insisted she did not "want anything special," she just felt that if Sam Rayburn and Paul Butler were going to be honored, if "they're going into the people in the Democratic Party whom they feel have been lost in the last year," she believed "it would be a great slight if under those circumstances" her husband were omitted. Exasperated, Johnson asked Mrs. Lehman, "What would you like to be done for your husband? Tell me and we'll try to work it out." But Mrs. Lehman replied that she "wouldn't dream of telling" the President what to do. She did ask him, however, to "talk it over with Hubert Humphrey," and Johnson agreed to do so, suggesting that he might ask Humphrey "to make a speech at some time at the convention." But the President again pointed out the impossibility of recognizing "each Chairman that has passed away or each Congressman or each Senator." Not surprisingly, Mrs. Lehman took umbrage at this grouping of her husband with "every Governor and every Senator," emphasizing that she did not put other Democrats in the same class as her husband. Johnson quickly agreed that Herbert Lehman belonged in a higher category than most politicians, but he also observed that "other women would put their husbands in that class" too. Mrs. Lehman insisted, however, that other wives "wouldn't have the right to, really," elevate their husbands to the same stature as Herbert Lehman, and she emphasized that she wasn't saying that "just because I'm his wife." Desperate now to get off the line, Johnson asked, "Would it be alright if I just turned this over to Hubert and asked him to handle it?" Mrs. Lehman thought that "would be fine" and apologized again for disturbing Johnson. She explained that she "just had to get it off my chest," and that "somebody said to me the only person who has the right to say yes or no on this is the President."[37]

A furious Lyndon Johnson kept his word and contacted Hubert Humphrey almost immediately after hanging up the phone with Mrs. Lehman. In between talking about Bobby Kennedy's alleged plans to disrupt the convention and other matters, Johnson filled Humphrey in on his conversation with Mrs. Lehman. The President complained, "Miz Lehman calls me up crying," and, exaggerating the length of the seven-and-a-half-minute conversation, asserted that she had kept him on the line "for 20–30 minutes." Johnson grumbled with some justification that he "couldn't get rid of her" and regretted that he had taken her call. The President accused Humphrey of acceding to Mrs. Lehman's contention that "it was an outrage they weren't honoring her husband." Because Humphrey had promised to discuss the matter with the President, Mrs. Lehman was now disappointed that Johnson had not rectified the situation. Humphrey explained that Mrs. Lehman and several others had written to him about the matter, and that she had called him about it a few weeks ago. Humphrey had spoken to DNC Chairman Bailey, and he had also talked to Cliff Carter, Johnson's chief lieutenant at the DNC. He had followed up with a letter to Bailey suggesting that any memorials include Herbert Lehman. Johnson admitted to Humphrey what he had denied to Mrs. Lehman—that he had been involved in discussions of this matter, but he emphasized that the problem was that "if you honor Lehman, then you—where do you go with [the late Oklahoma Senator Robert] Kerr, where do you go with [the late New Mexico Senator Dennis] Chavez, and where do you go with each Governor and Senator?" Johnson stressed that he was too busy with "all the troubles in the world without chickenshit things coming up like a woman like that crying over the phone and getting every Jew in America mad" at him. The President wanted Humphrey to call Mrs. Lehman "and tell her that we're not gonna honor Paul Butler. Just the President [Kennedy] and the President's wife [Mrs. Roosevelt]. Truman was gonna say something about Mr. Rayburn but Truman's not coming. And that you'll see that they do have a resolution for her husband and that you'll praise him and try to get her satisfied" with a "proper memorial so the President doesn't have to worry." Humphrey, who was still waiting to see if Johnson would choose him as his running mate, agreed that the President "ought not to be bothered about it at all" and promised to "take care of it."[38]

It had already been decided that the final night of the convention would include Bobby Kennedy introducing the film tribute to his late brother, Adlai Stevenson remembering Eleanor Roosevelt, and former DNC Chairman James Farley honoring Sam Rayburn, to be followed by the candidates' acceptance speeches. President Johnson had discussed with Mrs. Lehman the possibility of Hubert Humphrey recognizing her husband's contributions to the party and the nation, but with Humphrey emerging as Johnson's choice for the vice presidential nomination and needing to deliver his acceptance speech, it fell to New York City Mayor Robert Wagner to honor the memory of Herbert Lehman and other Democratic officials who had passed away since the last convention. After the tributes to President Kennedy, Mrs. Roosevelt, and Sam Rayburn, Wagner was scheduled to offer a formal resolution expressing the Democrats' "deep and sincere tribute" to those "former members and officers of our party" who had "contributed greatly to the success of our country, its people, and the Democratic Party during their lifetime" but had passed away since the 1960 Democratic convention.[39]

In remarks probably prepared by Julius Edelstein, Lehman's former chief of staff who was now an aide to the Mayor, Wagner was planning to mention briefly other Senators who had passed away in the last few years, but the Mayor intended to focus most of his comments on a glowing tribute to Herbert Lehman, "a man unique both in stature and in the values he represented for millions of his fellow Americans." However, Wagner never got a chance to deliver his speech. The tumultuous welcome for Robert Kennedy when he came to the podium to introduce the film tribute to his late brother, Adlai Stevenson's eloquent remembrance of Eleanor Roosevelt, and James Farley's reminiscence about Sam Rayburn put the convention behind schedule, and Wagner had to discard his prepared remarks and settle instead for asking the convention "to please rise and join with me in a moment of silence to honor the distinguished and great Democratic Senators who have died since 1961: Herbert H. Lehman of New York, Estes Kefauver of Tennessee, Dennis Chavez of New Mexico, Robert Kerr of Oklahoma, and Clair Engle of California." Eliminating Wagner's tribute to Lehman ensured that Hubert Humphrey and Lyndon Johnson delivered their acceptance speeches in prime time, when the television audience was greatest. Once again, as had happened so often in the Senate, Lyndon Johnson's political needs prevented Herbert Lehman from receiving the acclaim he was due.[40]

"Consistently Liberal"

Herbert Lehman and Liberalism

To have been, as you have, consistently liberal throughout your life is, I think, a wonderful example to your fellow citizens. Your career is the best rebuttal I know of the cynical definition that a liberal "is a man with both feet firmly planted in mid-air and supported by the Ford Foundation."[1]

In an article in the liberal journal *The Nation* in the fall of 1950, Hartley Howe cheered that Senator Herbert Lehman, a former banker, had grown and developed from "a good, reliable second baseman . . . into another Joe DiMaggio." Howe was pleasantly surprised at Lehman's commitment to the liberal agenda, especially his politically risky vote against the McCarran Internal Security Act. Interviewed in 1957, Eleanor Roosevelt agreed with the suggestion that Herbert Lehman had "grown much more liberal" over time. Mrs. Roosevelt believed that Lehman had always been a "humanitarian," which she attributed "to his close association with Lillian Wald when he was young," but she asserted that Lehman's "broad liberalism, the liberalism of feeling what government should do, not purely as a charity and an interest in human beings but as a government policy—that has grown tremendously over the years." James Wechsler of the liberal *New York Post* shared this view that Lehman had become more liberal over time, describing Lehman in 1961 as a "refutation of the ancient theory that men's convictions must grow flabbier with age." Accord-

---

Chapter title quotation: Bartley Crum to Herbert Lehman, April 14, 1958, Herbert Lehman Papers, Special Correspondence Files, Crum.

ing to Wechsler, Lehman was "a competent, enlightened Governor of New York, but his fighting liberal spirit is primarily a manifestation of his later years, and it grows rather than diminishes."[2]

But while Herbert Lehman appreciated his prominent place in the liberal pantheon in the 1950s and '60s, he objected to the suggestion that he had become more liberal over time. In Lehman's opinion, he had been fighting for liberal causes his entire life. In his Oral History interviews in 1957 and in his Speranza lectures at Columbia the following year, Lehman talked about recently finding "a box of compositions" that he had written in college, including "one on immigration and one on some phases of civil rights and discrimination." Upon rereading these essays that he had written sixty years earlier, Lehman discovered that his "views were not very different today from what they had been at that time." Lehman insisted that he had always subscribed to the liberal philosophy, which he defined as a commitment to "(1) the freedom and dignity of every individual; (2) the economic welfare of and security of every individual; (3) the achievement of social justice—for minorities as well as majorities, and for other nations as well as our own; and (4) the attainment of world peace and security in ways of cooperation and brotherhood." Lehman went on to describe his shock and horror at seeing the tenements and slums in New York City in the late 1800s, and he credited Lillian Wald with inspiring his devotion to helping his fellow human beings. But Lehman had realized that voluntary and philanthropic efforts alone could not handle the problems confronting the nation in the early 1900s; government involvement was needed "to limit the growth of monster corporations," improve working conditions in the nation's factories, and make the political process more responsive to the will and needs of the people. These beliefs led him to support Woodrow Wilson, Al Smith, and Franklin Roosevelt, as he realized the importance of strong and enlightened leadership to accomplish this liberal agenda.[3]

Herbert Lehman enthusiastically supported Franklin Roosevelt's New Deal and instituted his own "Little New Deal" in New York to provide unemployment insurance, social security, and other programs to help New Yorkers survive the Great Depression and lessen the likelihood of another massive economic breakdown in the future. But in contrast to some of Roosevelt's advisors, who saw the Depression as an opportunity to transform the United States into a nation with a planned, centralized economy, Leman accepted the American capitalist, democratic system as long as safeguards were built in to protect the American people from the unfettered greed of big business. He was slower than Roosevelt or Al Smith to decide on a course of action, and he lacked Roosevelt's oratorical skills to persuade with soaring rhetoric. Lehman continued wrestling with problems even after he made up his mind, and this seeming indecision led some to question his commitment to liberal principles. For Harold Ickes and others, Lehman's opposition to FDR's court-packing plan and his reluctance to proclaim his wholehearted support for every aspect of the New Deal when he was running for re-election in 1938 proved that Lehman was still a conservative banker at heart. How else could one explain Lehman's resistance to removing the roadblock the Supreme Court had erected against so many liberal reforms and Lehman's hesitancy to endorse the entirety of the New Deal? Roosevelt and his aides failed to appreciate Lehman's agony in deciding how to proceed on the court-packing plan and to accept at face value his explanation that his opposition was based on his overriding concern for the separation of powers among the different branches of the government. Nor did Roosevelt's advisors understand Lehman's belief that voters should focus on state issues and Lehman's record in Albany rather than events in Washington in deciding whether to re-elect him as Governor in 1938.[4]

While Herbert Lehman remained steadfast in his support of liberalism as he defined it, other liberals abandoned their more radical notions and moved closer to Lehman's definition after World War II. As Alan Brinkley, Jennifer Delton, and others have shown, by the 1950s, liberalism meant, in Delton's words, a belief in "government as a positive force in society, one that could promote economic growth and social harmony at home and contain Communism abroad." According to David Plotke, liberals rejected the old doctrine of laissez-faire and Herbert Hoover's American Individualism, advocating instead "government action to achieve economic stability, enhance social security, and expand political representation." Herbert Lehman demonstrated his commitment to this liberal program when he explicitly endorsed the "welfare state" during his race for the Senate in 1949, and in his strong support for civil rights before, during, and after his years in the Senate.[5]

Herbert Lehman refused to compromise his liberal beliefs, asserting that "the first duty of liberals is not to exercise power, but to uphold principle," and complaining that too many of his liberal colleagues sacrificed their liberal principles for personal ambition, settling too often for one slice of bread rather than fighting for the whole loaf. Lehman believed that pushing for the extreme liberal position would move the debate and the final compromise solution closer to what the liberals were seeking, giving them half a loaf rather than a single slice. He thought that "a fight is worthwhile even if you know you're going to lose it. . . . It's the only way to crystalize attitudes, educate people. And in the end," he emphasized, "I've seen many hopeless causes win out." Hubert Humphrey envied Lehman's status as "an emancipated man" who had "already lived a full life" and had enjoyed political success before coming to the Senate. Humphrey believed that Lehman, as opposed to most politicians, did not have to worry about the next election, and that this freedom allowed him to vote his conscience. On those rare occasions when Lehman, after wrestling with his conscience, chose the prudent option rather than the principled path, such as when he joined Humphrey and other Senate liberals in proposing the internment camp alternative to McCarran's Internal Security bill in 1950, and when he voted in 1954 to continue funding for Joseph McCarthy's Subcommittee on Investigations and to adopt Humphrey's Communist Control Act, Lehman immediately regretted his decisions.[6]

Herbert Lehman had great faith in the American people. As Governor of New York, when his social security bill or some other liberal reform was being stymied by the Republicans in the State Legislature, Lehman would threaten to appeal directly to the people, a threat that usually won the desired cooperation. But if not, Lehman would take to the radio to explain the issue to the people of the state, confident that they would put pressure on their representatives to go along with his proposals. And although Lehman often found his later efforts in the U.S. Senate frustrated by Lyndon Johnson and others, he took great solace in knowing that he was sowing seeds for the future; he remained confident that an aroused nation would eventually surmount the arcane rules of the Senate and enact the liberal reforms that were needed to ensure freedom, dignity, justice, and economic security for every American.

When Herbert Lehman died in December 1963 at the age of eighty-five, most of the liberal reform agenda he had advocated was still bogged down in Congress. But just seven months later, President Lyndon Johnson signed into law the Civil Rights Act of 1964, a measure based in part on the civil rights bills for which Herbert Lehman had fought so hard for so many years. The Voting Rights Act of 1965 soon followed, as did the Immigration and Nationality Act of 1965, which finally removed from the nation's immigration laws the quotas based on national origins that Lehman had so despised. President Johnson's success in 1964–1965 in winning approval for civil rights legislation, immigration reform, Medicare and Medicaid, and the rest of his Great Society highlighted what scholars G. Calvin Mackenzie and Robert Weisbrot have christened "the liberal hour."[7]

But Herbert Lehman, too, deserves credit for what Julian Zelizer has called "the liberal ascendancy" of the mid-1960s. In his thirty-five years as Lieutenant Governor and Governor of New York, Director General of UNRRA, U.S. Senator, and elder statesman, Herbert Lehman fought the Republicans in the State Legislature in Albany to provide economic security for New Yorkers; battled the bureaucracies in the Roosevelt and Truman administrations and UNRRA to feed the starving people in Europe and Asia; challenged the McCarrans, the McCarthys, and the Lyndon Johnsons in the U.S. Senate to protect the civil rights and civil liberties of all Americans; and toppled De Sapio and the bosses in New York to make the Democratic Party more democratic and responsive to the will of the people. Herbert Lehman showed in New York that a government following liberal principles could make a difference. As a Senator, few measures enacted into law bore his name, but as Arthur Schlesinger, Jr., noted, it had been Herbert Lehman and a few others who "had kept the liberal spirit of the [Democratic] Party alive in the dark years," ensuring that the need for federal civil rights legislation, immigration reform, and other liberal goals remained in the public's consciousness until Congress, and the nation, were ready to enact them into law.[8]

Notes

Preface

1. J. R. Moehringer, author of *Sutton*, a biography of bank robber Willie Sutton, quoted in *Westchester Journal News*, September 30, 2012, 3B.

2. Eleanor Roosevelt to Herbert Lehman, January 16, 1962, Lehman Papers, Special Files, Eleanor Roosevelt, Rare Books and Manuscripts, Columbia University Libraries.

3. Nevins, *Herbert Lehman and His Era*.

4. Carolin Flexner to Jacob Marcus, June 19, 1944, Herbert Lehman Papers, Personal Correspondence and General File of the Director General of UNRRA, "M," C47–67; and William Shannon to Herbert Lehman, May 19, 1955, Lehman Papers, Special Files, Shannon. On Nevins's search for anecdotes, see J. W. Fulbright to Allan Nevins, April 30, 1962, Lehman Papers, Special Files, Fulbright; Chester Bowles to Nevins, May 16, 1962, Lehman Papers, Special Files, Bowles; Nevins to Mrs. Lehman, August 9, 1962, and Nevins to Herbert Lehman, August 14, 1962, both in Lehman Papers, Special Files, Nevins.

Chapter 1. "A Dearly Beloved Friend": Herbert Lehman and Lillian Wald

1. Herbert Lehman to Katherine Faville, March 18, 1940, Herbert Lehman Papers, General Correspondence, 1933–1940, Folder 27 (9), Henry Street-Visiting Nurse Service, Columbia University Library.

2. Herbert Lehman Oral History Transcript (hereinafter HHLOH), Columbia University Oral History Collection (hereinafter CUOHC), pp. 9–10, 34, 148–150; Eleanor Roosevelt Oral History Transcript, Herbert Lehman Project (hereinafter HHLP), CUOHC, p. 6; Babette Newgass Lehman to the President and Directors of the Mount Sinai Hospital, January 1912; and Secretary, Mount Sinai Hospital, to Mrs. Mayer Lehman, January 15, 1912, both in Herbert Lehman Papers, Special Correspondence Files, Babette Newgass Lehman; "For Lehman Politics Is Business Plus," *New York Times* (hereinafter *NYT*), June 14, 1931, SM-6; Stephen S. Wise to Herbert Lehman,

November 9, 1932, in Voss, ed., *Stephen S. Wise*, p. 175. After most of the research for this book had been concluded, the Special Correspondence Files of the Herbert Lehman Papers (hereinafter LP, SF) were digitalized and made available online at http://lehman. cul.columbia.edu/. Since the Special Correspondence Files are arranged by correspondent and date and easy to use, digital document numbers will be included only for those documents in the Special Correspondence File that might otherwise be difficult to find. On the history of the Lehman family, see Nevins, *Herbert H. Lehman and His Era*, pp. 3–26; Flade, *The Lehmans*; and Libo, ed., *Lots of Lehmans*, pp. 3–47.

3. "Lillian Wald Dies; Friend of the Poor," *NYT*, September 2, 1940, p. 15; HHLOH, p. 148; "To Further Interests of Humanity," *NYT*, February 12, 1895, p. 13; "Women in Many Fields," *NYT*, December 8, 1897, p. 5; "Charity Gives Way to Welfare Work," *NYT*, May 17, 1926, p. 20. The literature on Lillian Wald is vast. See, for example, her two autobiographies, *The House on Henry Street* and *Windows on Henry Street*; Duffus, *Lillian Wald*; Daniels, *Always a Sister*; and Feld, *Lillian Wald*.

4. HHLOH, pp. 34, 148–149.

5. HHLOH, pp. 57–61, 187–190; Memorandum, Herbert Lehman to Allan Nevins, January 4, 1962, p. 8, LP, SF, Nevins.

6. Morrie Golden to Herbert Lehman, March 29, 1938, and attached "Extracts from Letters by Some of Your Patriot Boys"; and Carolin Flexner to Basil O'Connor, January 20, 1956, all in LP, SF, Herbert H. Lehman, documents 0530_0289, 0530_0290, and 0530_0375; "Herbert L. Abrons, 92, Lawyer, Businessman and Philanthropist," *NYT*, January 22, 2005, B-6.

7. Wald, *The House on Henry Street*, pp. 164–166; "Inquiry into Child Labor," *NYT*, June 7, 1903, p. 8; Wald, "New Children's Bureau," Letter to the Editor, *NYT*, February 1, 1912, p. 12; Herbert Lehman to Lillian Wald, December 24, 1910, LP, SF, Lillian Wald; Felt, *Hostages of Fortune*, p. 44; Davis, *Spearheads for Reform*, pp. 131–134; Trattner, *Crusade for the Children*, pp. 56–57, 95–96, 98, 119; Daniels, *Always a Sister*, p. 48.

8. Wald, *Windows on Henry Street*, pp. 49–50, 26–31, 333–334; "Negro Committee to Meet," *NYT*, May 9, 1910, p. 3; Wald, *The House on Henry Street*, pp. 161–163; Davis, *Spearheads for Reform*, pp. 95, 101–102; Daniels, *Always a Sister*, pp. 49–50; Kellogg, *NAACP*, pp. 12–17, 56, 114, 179, 250, 297–300, 305–306; Roy Wilkins Oral History Transcript, HHLP, CUOHC, pp. 1–3, 10–11; Carolin Flexner to Basil O'Connor, January 20, 1956, and "Partial List of the Activities of Former Governor Lehman Since His Retirement from the U.S. Senate," August 1, 1963, both in LP, SF, Herbert H. Lehman, documents 0530_0375 and 0530_0441. See chapter 15 for more on Lehman, the NAACP, and civil rights.

9. "Pacifists Gratified," *NYT*, January 24, 1916, p. 4; "Settlement Work Real Preparedness," *NYT*, May 24, 1916, p. 8; "Pacifists Approve President's Action," *NYT*, February 27, 1917, p. 2; Wald, *Windows on Henry Street*, pp. 285–312; Duffus, *Lillian Wald*, pp. 145–188; Feld, *Lillian Wald*, pp. 107–113; HHLOH, pp. 104, 117–124; Lehman to Francis Sayre, February 28, 1917; Lehman to Henry Morgenthau, March 23, 1917; and Lehman to George Creel, April 18, 1917, all in LP, Colonel Herbert H. Lehman's Armed Forces Record, 1917–1963, Oversize Folio.

10. Lehman to General Wood, April 19, 1917; Lehman to Charles Eiseman, May 9, 1917; Secretary of the Navy Josephus Daniels to Lehman, May 16, 1917; all

in LP, Colonel Herbert H. Lehman's Armed Forces Record, 1917–1963, Oversize Folio; "Textile Expert for Navy," *NYT*, May 19, 1917, p. 3; HHLOH, 100, 112, 701; "Colonel Lehman's War Record," n.d., LP, SF, Herbert H. Lehman, document 0530_0281; Herbert Lehman's Distinguished Service Medal Citation, LP, General Correspondence, 1913–1926, War Department, 1920–1922, C19–23; "Lehman a Success in Many Activities," *NYT*, November 9, 1932, p. 10; Memorandum, Herbert Lehman to Allan Nevins, January 4, 1962, p. 6, LP, SF, Nevins.

    11. HHLOH, pp. 146–147, 152–156; Carolin Flexner Oral History Transcript, HHLP, CUOHC, pp. 2–8, 11–12; Handlin, *A Continuing Task*, pp. 19–47; and Bauer, *My Brother's Keeper*, pp. 17, 23.

    12. Wald to Lehman, December 26, 1916, and Lehman to Wald, April 21, 1917, both in LP, SF, Lillian Wald; "$1,000,000 Obtained for Henry St. Work," *NYT*, November 13, 1916, p. 13.

    13. Wald to Lehman, October 19, 1917; Lehman to Viola Conklin, June 2, 1919; Lehman to Conklin, July 19, 1920; Lehman to Elsa Herrmann, January 23, 1924; and Lehman to Wald, November 30, 1926, all in LP, SF, Lillian Wald; HHLOH, p. 190; Lehman to Henry Weil, August 11, 1934, September 1, 1934, and July 27, 1938; Lehman to Carolin Flexner, September 1, 1934; Flexner to Lehman, July 13, 1936; and Lehman to Sylvia Friedland, July 25, 1938, all in LP, General Correspondence, 1933–1940, 27 (8), Henry Street Settlement; Wald, "Country Air for City Children," Letter to the Editor, *NYT*, August 1, 1925, p. 10; Lehman to John Schiff, June 5, 1939, LP, General Correspondence, 1933–1940, 27 (9), Henry Street-Visiting Nurse Service.

    14. Lillian Wald, "For Colonel Lehman," Letter to the Editor, *NYT*, October 22, 1928, p. 22.

    15. "Outside toilets" quoted in Duffus, *Lillian Wald*, p. 277.

    16. Wald, *Windows on Henry Street*, pp. 38–39; "First Model Homes to Rise on East Side," *NYT*, April 3, 1929, p. 26; "Title Taken to Site for Model Homes," *NYT*, May 2, 1929, p. 53; Lehman to Carolin Flexner, April 25, 1929, LP, SF, Aaron Rabinowitz; Aaron Rabinowitz, "Part of the Speech Delivered by Mr. Aaron Rabinowitz, Member of the State Housing Board of New York, at the Housing Conference, April 29, 1931, in Boston, MA," LP, Special Subject File 2, Amalgamated Housing Project; Duffus, *Lillian Wald*, p. 278; "In Grand Street Stands a Cooperative Apartment Building Which Combines Architectural Beauty with Modern Facilities and Affords a Striking Contrast to the Near-by Tenements, Dingy and Sunless," *NYT*, October 26, 1930, XX-4; Arthur H. Sulzberger to Lehman, November 10, 1930, and Lehman to Sulzberger, November 14, 1930, LP, SF, Arthur H. Sulzberger; "Hall of Fame Lobbying Pays Off," *NYT*, November 8, 1970, p. 47; "Aaron Rabinowitz Is Dead at 89; Pioneer in Housing Development," *NYT*, April 4, 1973, p. 46.

    17. Wald to Lehman, October 8, 1930, LP, SF, Lillian Wald; Roosevelt-Lehman Citizens' Committee, "Social Workers Endorse Franklin D. Roosevelt and Herbert H. Lehman for Re-Election," n.d., Franklin Roosevelt Papers, Vertical File, Campaign Literature, 1930, Roosevelt-Lehman Citizens' Committee, Franklin D. Roosevelt Library (hereinafter FDRL).

    18. "Not allowing my name" quoted in Duffus, *Lillian Wald*, p. 295; HHLOH, pp. 306–307; Daniels, *Always a Sister*, pp. 58–59; John Elliott, Mary Simkhovitch, and Lillian Wald, "An Outstanding Candidate," Letter to the Editor, *NYT*, September 30,

1932, p. 18; "Choice of Lehman Urged in Messages," *NYT*, October 3, 1932, p. 3; "100 Women Enroll to Aid Democrats," *NYT*, October 25, 1932, p. 10. On Smith's and Roosevelt's efforts to secure the gubernatorial nomination for Lehman in 1932, see chapters 2 and 3.

19. Wald, *Windows on Henry Street*, p. 44; Lehman to Wald, December 19, 1934, and Wald to Lehman, May 13, 1935, LP, SF, Lillian Wald; Duffus, *Lillian Wald*, p. 315; Daniels, *Always a Sister*, p. 60.

20. HHLOH, p. 151; "'Staggering' Margin Is Seen for Lehman," *NYT*, October 26, 1934, p. 8; Wald to Lehman, May 26, 1936, LP, SF, Lillian Wald; "Seeks Aid of Convention in 'Draft-Lehman' Move," *NYT*, June 22, 1936, p. 1; "Social Workers Unite for Lehman," *NYT*, October 29, 1936, p. 14; "Democrats Form Campaign Machine," *NYT*, March 20, 1938, p. 17; Daniels, *Always a Sister*, p. 153. On Helen Hall succeeding Wald at Henry Street, see Felix Warburg to Lehman, May 9, 1933, LP, SF, Warburg; and Hall, *Unfinished Business in Neighborhood and Nation*.

21. HHLOH, p. 151; "Henry Street 'Alumni' Mark Anniversary," *NYT*, April 30, 1933, p. 30; "Roosevelt Aids Henry St. Service," *NYT*, November 14, 1934, p. 21; Lehman to Carolin Flexner, May 13, 1939, LP, General Correspondence, 1933–1940, 27 (9), Henry Street-Visiting Nurse Service; Daniels, *Always a Sister*, p. 153.

22. "Meeting of Visiting Nurse Service Staff of Henry Street Settlement," March 9, 1940, in *Public Papers of Herbert H. Lehman: Forty-Ninth Governor of the State of New York, 4th Term, 1940*, pp. 669–671; "Lehman Praises Lillian D. Wald, 73," *NYT*, March 10, 1940, p. 19; Katherine Faville, Director of Nursing Services, to Lehman, March 16, 1940, LP, General Correspondence, 1933–1940, 27 (9), Henry Street-Visiting Nurse Service.

23. "Rites Tomorrow for Lillian Wald," *NYT*, September 3, 1940, p. 17.

24. "Settlement Will Gain," *NYT*, March 11, 1943, p. 24; Lehman to Harry Rubenoff, December 10, 1943, LP, UNRRA, Personal Correspondence and General Files, "R," II, 48–82; "50 Years of Service Marked by Henry St.," *NYT*, December 13, 1943, p. 26.

25. "Lieut. Peter Gerald Lehman Killed in Plane Crash at Base in England," *NYT*, April 12, 1944, p. 3; Leonard Lyons, "Loose-Leaf Notebook," *Washington Post* (hereinafter *WP*), May 14, 1946, p. 4; "Henry St. Acquires New Welfare Unit," *NYT*, November 15, 1948, p. 28; Hall, *Unfinished Business*, pp. 64, 73, 89, 227; "Lehmans Dedicate a Youth Center as Memorial to Son Killed in War," *NYT*, November 29, 1948, p. 25; "The Lehman Gift," Editorial, *NYT*, November 18, 1948, p. 26.

26. Herbert Lehman, Nicholas Kelley, Winslow Carlton, and Helen Hall to Mrs. Franklin Roosevelt, February 11, 1958, Eleanor Roosevelt Papers, 1957–1962, Lehman, FDRL; "Delinquency Test Opens on Eastside," *NYT*, February 3, 1959, p. 26; "Henry St. Fund Sought," *NYT*, March 19, 1959, p. 29; "$500,000 Donation Given Settlement," *NYT*, November 10, 1961, p. 36; "Group She Helped Found in '17 Keeps Mrs. Lehman's Days Full," *NYT*, April 25, 1965, p. 80.

27. HHLOH, p. 190; "Lehman Outlines His Social Philosophy," *NYT*, August 9, 1936, SM-5; Lehman to Leo Arnstein, November 29, 1940, LP, SF, Lillian Wald; "President Honors Miss Wald's Work," *NYT*, December 2, 1940, p. 23; Frances Perkins Oral History Transcript, CUOHC, III: 61–62.

Chapter 2. "On a Chinese Laundry Ticket":
Herbert Lehman and Al Smith

1. "Lehman's Speech of Acceptance," *NYT*, October 5, 1932, p. 16.

2. On Herbert Lehman's background, education, and business experience, see Nevins, *Herbert Lehman and His Era*, pp. 3–54. The most recent biographies of Smith are Slayton, *Empire Statesman*, and Finan, *Alfred E. Smith*. See also Smith's autobiography, *Up to Now*; Handlin, *Al Smith and His America*; Josephson and Josephson, *Al Smith*; O'Connor, *The First Hurrah*; and "Alfred E. Smith Dies Here at 70; 4 Times Governor," *NYT*, October 4, 1944, pp. 1, 19.

3. HHLOH, pp. 13–15, 53; Nevins, *Herbert H. Lehman and His Era*, pp. 13, 20.

4. HHLOH, p. 55; Herbert Lehman, "The Triumph of Liberalism," First Speranza Lecture, Columbia University, April 9, 1958, LP, Speech Files. In the Speranza lecture, Lehman stated that Theodore Roosevelt was the only Republican candidate for President he ever voted for, but in his Oral History, Lehman noted his decision not to support Bryan in 1908.

5. HHLOH, pp. 95–96. Werner, *Tammany Hall*, pp. 482–564, presents a highly critical view of Murphy, but Connable and Silberfarb, *Tigers of Tammany*, pp. 231–268, and Weiss, *Charles Francis Murphy, 1858–1924*, portray Murphy much more favorably.

6. Werner, *Tammany Hall*, pp. 529–531; Wesser, "The Impeachment of a Governor," pp. 407–412; Friedman, *The Impeachment of Governor William Sulzer*, pp. 15–37; Weiss, *Charles Francis Murphy*, pp. 49–50; Freidel, *Franklin D. Roosevelt: The Apprenticeship*, pp. 97–116; and LaCerra, *Franklin Delano Roosevelt and Tammany Hall of New York*, pp. 43–54.

7. Lehman to Sulzer, June 24, 1912, and Sulzer to Lehman, July 4, 1912, both in State of New York, Proceedings of the Court for the Trial of Impeachments, II: 1116–1117, 1405; Friedman, The Impeachment of Governor William Sulzer, pp. 24, 27, 200–201.

8. "Sulzer Invites Murphy to Fight For Leadership," *NYT*, January 3, 1913, p. 1; "Roosevelt to Speak for Sulzer Primary," *NYT*, May 9, 1913, p. 2; "$45,000 Verbeck Deal Attacked," *NYT*, January 9, 1913, pp. 1, 2; "Find Sulzer Spent $7,000 Beyond Law," *NYT*, September 5, 1913, p. 8; Francis Willard, Secretary, Direct Primary Campaign Committee, to Lehman, August 20, 1913, and August 26, 1913; and Fred Hinrichs to Lehman, October 25, 1913, and October 28, 1913, all in LP, General Correspondence, 1913–1926, Direct Primary Campaign (1), 19 (7); Friedman, *The Impeachment of Governor William Sulzer*, pp. 32–116.

9. "To Investigate Acts of Sulzer," *NYT*, June 12, 1913, pp. 1, 2; Sulzer to Lehman, June 30, 1913; and Joint Investigating Committee of the Legislature of the State of New York, Subpoena Issued to Herbert Lehman, Esq., August 26, 1913, both in LP, SF, Sulzer; "Move to Impeach or Indict Sulzer," *NYT*, August 8, 1913, p. 1; "Find Sulzer Spent $7,000 Beyond Law," *NYT*, September 5, 1913, p. 18; Friedman, *The Impeachment of Governor William Sulzer*, pp. 117–147; Weiss, *Charles Francis Murphy*, pp. 55–58; Slayton, *Empire Statesman*, pp. 103–104; Finan, *Alfred E. Smith*, pp. 92–94.

10. State of New York, *Proceedings of the Court for the Trial of Impeachments*, II: 1121–1122, 1127; "Sulzer, Allan Ryan Says, Tried to Get Him to Call Off

Murphy; . . . Lehman's a Free Gift," *NYT*, October 8, 1913, pp. 1, 2; "Quotes Mrs. Sulzer, Said Stock Was Hers, Josephthal Testifies—Other Witnesses for Defense," *NYT*, October 8, 1913, p. 2; Wesser, "The Impeachment of a Governor," pp. 432–438; Friedman, *The Impeachment of Governor William Sulzer*, pp. 148–240; Lifflander, *The Impeachment of Governor Sulzer*, pp. 294–295.

11. HHLOH, pp. 90–91, 151–152, 193, 701; "Democrats Name Smith as Head of State Ticket," *NYT*, July 25, 1918, pp. 1, 6; "Memorandum, Herbert Lehman to Allan Nevins," January 4, 1963, p. 9, LP, SF, Nevins; Eleanor Roosevelt Oral History Transcript, HHLP, CUOHC, p. 1; James Farley Oral History Transcript, HHLP, CUOHC, pp. 25–26; Perry, *Belle Moskowitz*, pp. xiii, 98–107; Proskauer, *A Segment of My Time*, pp. 40–52, 102–105; Hacker and Hirsch, *Proskauer*, pp. 24, 53–58; Finan, *Alfred E. Smith*, pp. 100–103, 120–128, 140–151, 154–155; Slayton, *Empire Statesman*, pp. 128–133, 135–139, 148–149.

12. HHLOH, pp. 193–194; Slayton, *Empire Statesman*, 203–204, 208, 211–216; Finan, *Alfred E. Smith*, pp. 175–182; Burner, *The Politics of Provincialism*, pp. 74–92, 117–118.

13. HHLOH, p. 194; Lehman to George Van Namee, April 24, 1924, and Van Namee to Lehman, April 26, 1924, both in Franklin Roosevelt Papers, Campaign of 1924, Box 3, Committee for the Nomination of Smith for President, Correspondence, New York City, "L," FDRL; Lehman to Franklin Roosevelt, May 2, 1924; Lehman to Roosevelt, May 8, 1924; Roosevelt to Lehman, May 10, 1924; and Lehman to Roosevelt, May 22, 1924, all in Franklin Roosevelt Papers, Campaign of 1924, Box 11, General Correspondence, "L," FDRL; "250 on Committee to Work for Smith," *NYT*, May 5, 1924, p. 2; Slayton, *Empire Statesman*, pp. 205–207.

14. HHLOH, pp. 152, 194–196; "Smith Names Board in Garment Dispute," *NYT*, June 17, 1924, p. 40; "Cloak Firms Yield as Strike Is Called," *NYT*, July 8, 1924, p. 34; "Smith Peace Plan for Garment Trade," *NYT*, July 14, 1924, p. 15; Perry, *Belle Moskowitz*, pp. 174–175; Dubinsky and Raskin, *David Dubinsky*, pp. 63–64. The commission was headed by lawyer George Gordon Battle and included New York State Industrial Commissioner Bernard Sheintag, Columbia University professor Lindsay Rogers, banker Arthur Wolf, and Herbert Lehman.

15. "Cloak Firms Yield as Strike Is Called," *NYT*, July 8, 1924, p. 34; "Smith Peace Plan for Garment Trade," *NYT*, July 14, 1924, p. 15; HHLOH, p. 196; Lehman to Hubert Humphrey, March 11, 1958, LP, SF, Hubert Humphrey; "Lehman, Uviller Named Mediators in Dress Walkout," *NYT*, March 8, 1958, pp. 1, 18; "End of a Strike," Editorial, *NYT*, March 12, 1958, p. 30; Dubinsky and Raskin, *David Dubinsky*, p. 143.

16. HHLOH, pp. 198, 313–314; Lehman to Roosevelt, July 10, 1924, Franklin Roosevelt Papers, Campaign of 1924, Box 11, General Correspondence, "L," FDRL; Murray, *The 103rd Ballot*. Lehman is listed as 1st Vice-President of the National Democratic Club on the letterhead on Thomas Rush, President, National Democratic Magazine, Inc., to Dear Sir, n.d., Franklin Roosevelt Papers, Campaign of 1924, Box 7, Democratic National Convention, Montana-New York, FDRL.

17. "Leaders Endorse Smith as Labor Aid," *NYT*, October 20, 1924, p. 3; Rabbi Wise Praises Governor's Record; . . . Lehman also Is for Him," *NYT*, October 23, 1924, p. 6; "Smith's Campaign Cost Him Nothing," *NYT*, November 25, 1924, p. 5; "Spent $45,103 in State," *NYT*, November 27, 1924, p. 21; "Smith Plurality Now Put at

112,179," *NYT*, November 7, 1924, p. 3; Slayton, *Empire Statesman*, pp. 218–220. William Marcy in 1836 had been the last Governor to win a third term.

18. HHLOH, pp. 210–213, 215; "Smith and Wagner to Stump Together; . . . Col. Lehman to Aid Smith," *NYT*, October 1, 1926, p. 2; "Denies State Debt Is What Mills Says; . . . Lehman Quotes Controller for Total Funded Indebtedness—Explains Bigger Sum," *NYT*, October 15, 1926, p. 7; "Gov. Smith Asserts Water Power Policy Is the Real Issue," *NYT*, October 19, 1926, pp. 1, 17; "Mills Scents Spoils in Smith Power Plan; Hits Brooklyn Milk," *NYT*, October 20, 1926, pp. 1, 6; "Straus Says Smith Gave City Pure Milk," *NYT*, October 21, 1926, p. 5; "Smith Wins by 260,000, Wagner 125,000; Race Hot Up-State," *NYT*, November 3, 1926, p. 1; Slayton, *Empire Statesman*, p. 231.

19. HHLOH, pp. 210–211; "Col. Lehman Proposed for State Chairman," *NYT*, December 24, 1926, p. 20; "Lehman to Direct Smith's 1928 Boom," *NYT*, March 19, 1927, p. 3; "Choice of Lehman Disturbs Tammany," *NYT*, March 24, 1927, p. 27.

20. HHLOH, pp. 211–212; "No Active Campaign for Smith in View," *NYT*, April 4, 1927, p. 25; "Corning to Remain Democratic Head," *NYT*, June 1, 1927, p. 29; Elisabeth Marbury to Norman Mack, January 18, 1927, quoted in Perry, *Belle Moskowitz*, p. 256, n. 30; Eleanor Roosevelt to Elinor Morgenthau, quoted in Lash, *Love, Eleanor*, pp. 105–106.

21. "Smith Offered to Nation as Presidential Candidate at Democratic Rally Here," *NYT*, January 7, 1927, pp. 1, 3; "N. D. Baker Evasive on Smith Candidacy," *NYT*, March 25, 1927, p. 14; "Smith Cause Aided by Jackson Dinner, Leaders Here Say," *NYT*, January 14, 1928, pp. 1, 2; HHLOH, pp. 217–218; Perry, *Belle Moskowitz*, pp. 189–191; Slayton, *Empire Statesman*, pp. 242–243, 268. On Smith's inner circle, see also "Second Place Choice to Await Smith's Nomination," *NYT*, June 26, 1928, p. 3; "Governor Smith's 'Kitchen Cabinet,'" *New York Times Sunday Magazine*, September 23, 1928, pp. 6, 7, 20.

22. Herbert Lehman to Frank Leo Murray, September 1, 1956, LP, SF, Alfred E. Smith; HHLOH, p. 771; Marshall, "An Open Letter to the Honorable Alfred E. Smith," *The Atlantic Monthly* 139 (April 1927): 540–549; Smith, "Catholic and Patriot: Governor Smith Replies," *The Atlantic Monthly*, 139 (May 1927): 721–728; Proskauer, *A Segment of My Times*, pp. 54–61; Hacker and Hirsch, *Proskauer*, pp. 88–92; and Perry, *Belle Moskowitz*, p. 188.

23. Herbert Lehman to Dr. Peter Sarup, August 7, 1954, LP, SF, Arthur L. Goodhart; "Van Namee Lists Contributions by New Yorkers and Expenditures to Aid Gov. Smith in Campaign," *NYT*, May 11, 1928, p. 2; "Democrats Wipe Out Deficit from 1924," *NYT*, March 8, 1928, pp. 1, 8; "Smith's Friends Ready to Give All for Governor; . . . Todd, Lehman and Riordan, Relating Their Contributions, Promise to Give More," *NYT*, May 17, 1928, pp. 1, 2; "Al Smith's Friends," Editorial, *New York World*, May 18, 1928, copy in LP, SF, Alfred E. Smith; HHLOH, pp. 234, 237–238.

24. Lehman to Franklin Roosevelt, July 5, 1928, and Roosevelt to Lehman, July 20, 1928, both in Franklin Roosevelt Papers, Campaign of 1928, Box 8, General Correspondence, New York City, "L," FDRL; Freidel, *Franklin D. Roosevelt: The Ordeal*, pp. 241–242.

25. HHLOH, pp. 227–229; Eleanor Roosevelt to Elinor Morgenthau, quoted in Lash, *Love, Eleanor*, p. 108; "Democrats Select Fund Drive Chiefs," *NYT*, June 30,

1928, p. 2; "Gov. Smith Enjoins Aides to 'Get Busy,'" *NYT*, July 13, 1928, pp. 1, 3; "$60,703 Contributed to Democratic Fund," *NYT*, August 2, 1928, pp. 1, 2; "Democratic Gifts in August $455,797, 4 of $50,000 Each," *NYT*, September 8, 1928, pp. 1, 2; "Democratic Fund Up $876,420 in Month," *NYT*, October 6, 1928, pp. 1, 3; "Campaign Funds Exceed $9,000,000," *NYT*, November 3, 1928, p. 5; "Democrats List Funds at Albany," *NYT*, November 27, 1928, p. 26; Overacker, *Money in Elections*, pp. 153–161. On Raskob, see also "Raskob Elected Chairman, Stresses Dry Law Change as Big Democratic Issue," *NYT*, July 12, 1928, pp. 1, 2; HHLOH, pp. 236–238; and Slayton, *Empire Statesman*, pp. 259–263; on Baruch, see Baruch, *The Public Years*, p. 210; and Schwarz, *The Speculator*, pp. 191–193.

26. HHLOH, pp. 235, 238. On the 1928 election, see also Lichtman, *Prejudice and the Old Politics*.

27. HHLOH, p. 231; "Al Smith Denounces Intolerance," *Chicago Tribune*, September 21, 1928, pp. 1, 8.

28. HHLOH, pp. 230–238; Perry, *Belle Moskowitz*, p. 204; "Smith Assails Intolerance, Answers Foes on Record, Oklahoma Crowd Cheers," *NYT*, September 21, 1928, pp. 1, 2; "Al Smith Denounces Intolerance," *Chicago Tribune*, September 21, 1928, pp. 1, 8; Proskauer, *A Segment of My Times*, pp. 61–62; Hacker and Hirsch, *Proskauer*, pp. 95–96; Slayton, *Empire Statesman*, ix–xv, 299–317; Finan, *Alfred E. Smith*, pp. 215–219.

29. "Smith Wants Young to Run for Governor," *NYT*, July 16, 1928, pp. 1, 5; "Owen D. Young Refuses to Run for Governor," *NYT*, July 19, 1928, p. 1; Farley, *Behind the Ballots*, pp. 52, 79–80; James Farley Memo, 1928, Farley Papers, Box 37, Private File, 1918–1930, Library of Congress (hereinafter LC); Lehman to Julius Henry Cohen, February 5, 1947, LP, SF, Franklin Roosevelt; Lehman to Peter Sarup, August 7, 1954, LP, SF, Arthur L. Goodhart; HHLOH, pp. 241–250; Paul Block, "This Year the Democrats Should Nominate a Protestant for Governor of New York," Editorial, *Brooklyn Standard Union*, reprinted in *NYT*, September 27, 1928, p. 19; "Lehman Not Seeking Place on the Ticket," *NYT*, September 30, 1928, p. 8; "Smith to Pick State Ticket at Rochester Conference Today, May Draft Wagner," *NYT*, October 1, 1928, p. 1; "F. D. Roosevelt Drafted by Democrats; . . . Lehman Receives a Place," *NYT*, October 2, 1928, pp. 1, 13; "Roosevelt Yields to Smith and Heads State Ticket; . . . Lehman as Running Mate," *NYT*, October 3, 1928, pp. 1, 12; "Choice of Roosevelt Elates Gov. Smith," *NYT*, October 3, 1928, pp. 1, 12; "Roosevelt Held Out to the Last Minute," *NYT*, October 3, 1928, p. 12; Slayton, *Empire Statesman*, pp. 349–356; Finan, *Alfred E. Smith*, pp. 236–240; Franklin Roosevelt to Herbert Lehman, October 3, 1928, LP, SF, Franklin Roosevelt. For more on the effort to persuade Roosevelt to accept the nomination, see chapter 3. On Owen Young, see Case and Case, *Owen D. Young and American Enterprise*, pp. 270, 417, 419, 423, 553–559. On Albert Ottinger, see Bellush, *Franklin D. Roosevelt as Governor of New York*, pp. 14–16.

30. "Brother May Back Lehman," *NYT*, October 3, 1928, p. 2; HHLOH, 235–236, 253–254; Rosenman quoted in "Herbert H. Lehman: The Making of a Leader," WABC-TV, March 28, 1965, p. 20, copy in LP. On Arthur Lehman, see Libo, ed., *Lots of Lehmans*, pp. 137–158.

31. HHLOH, pp. 235–236. On the Ku Klux Klan in upstate New York, see "Roosevelt Assails Campaign Bigotry," *NYT*, October 18, 1928, p. 3; Jackson, *The Ku Klux Klan in the City*, p. 173; Lay, *Hooded Knights on the Niagara*.

32. "Untermyer Assails Ottinger on Power," *NYT*, October 24, 1928, p. 18; Wise to Lehman, October 4, 1928, LP, SF, Stephen S. Wise; Breitman and Lichtman, *FDR and the Jews*, pp. 31–34.

33. HHLOH, pp. 229, 256; "Hoover Wins 407 to 69; . . . Hoover Carries New York by 125,000," *NYT*, November 7, 1928, pp. 1, 2; "Latest Tabulation of the Election Returns in the City, State and Nation," *NYT*, November 8, 1928, p. 13.

34. HHLOH, pp. 251–253; "Roosevelt Is Victor by Slim Plurality; . . . Lehman, Conway and Tremaine Leading," *NYT*, November 7, 1928, pp. 1, 2; "State Ticket Leads Smith in City Vote; . . . Lehman, Conway and Crouch Far Ahead," *NYT*, November 8, 1928, p. 18; "Roosevelt Wins by 23,616; Ottinger Doubts Figures and Starts Inquiry Here," *NYT*, November 9, 1928, p. 1; "Roosevelt Margin Is Placed at 23,000; Farley of Democratic Committee Says Lehman Has 13,800 and Tremaine 11,000," *NYT*, November 17, 1928, p. 8; Bellush, *Franklin D. Roosevelt as Governor of New York*, p. 27. On Charles Lockwood, see "Gilchrist Heads New Transit Board," *NYT*, April 21, 1926, pp. 1, 2; "State Republicans Name Ottinger and Houghton," *NYT*, September 30, 1928, pp. 1, 5.

35. "Sees Democrats Gaining," *NYT*, November 23, 1928, p. 18; HHLOH, pp. 238–239; John Cogley Oral History Transcript, p. 24, John F. Kennedy Library (hereinafter JFKL).

36. "Smith Is Cheered as He Pledges Life to State's Welfare," *NYT*, December 30, 1928, pp. 1, 15; HHLOH, pp. 258–259; Franklin Roosevelt, "Written for the Record," April 6, 1938, in Elliott Roosevelt, ed., *F.D.R.*, II: 771–773; Flynn, *You're the Boss*, pp. 74–76; Freidel, *Franklin D. Roosevelt: The Triumph*, pp. 16–22; Perry, *Belle Moskowitz*, 205–207; Slayton, *Empire Statesman*, pp. 357–360; Finan, *Alfred E. Smith*, pp. 242–243; Caro, *The Power Broker*, pp. 294–298.

37. HHLOH, pp. 230, 299–300, 305–307; "Roosevelt Will Make Fight for Lehman; Battle on at Albany," *NYT*, October 2, 1932, pp. 1, 3; "City Leaders Leave for Party Sessions," *NYT*, October 2, 1932, p. 3; Flynn, *You're the Boss*, pp. 105–110; Farley, *Behind the Ballots*, pp. 172–174; LaCerra, *Franklin Delano Roosevelt and Tammany Hall of New York*, pp. 70–75; Huthmacher, *Senator Robert F. Wagner and the Rise of Urban Liberalism*, pp. 102–104. On Curry, see also HHLOH, p. 221; "John Curry Dies; Headed Tammany," *NYT*, April 26, 1957, p. 25; and Connable and Silberfarb, *Tigers of Tammany*, pp. 277–287.

38. "Flying in the face of Providence" quoted in "Smith Leads Fight to Block Walker; Back in Fighting Mood," *NYT*, October 6, 1932, pp. 1, 13; "Chinese laundry ticket" quoted in Josephson and Josephson, *Al Smith*, p. 442; Handlin, *Al Smith and His America*, pp. 168–169; and Moscow, *Politics in the Empire State*, p. 21. See also "Roosevelt and Lehman Insist on Lehman as Curry Holds Out on Convention Eve; . . . Smith Urges Curry to Support Lehman," *NYT*, October 3, 1932, pp. 1, 3; "Lehman's Nomination Appears Certain as Roosevelt and Smith Warn Curry," *NYT*, October 4, 1932, pp. 1, 17; James Farley Oral History Transcript, HHLP, CUOHC, p. 8; James Farley Memo, Democratic State Convention, Albany, 1932, in Farley Papers, Box 37, Private File, 1932, LC; Farley, *Behind the Ballots*, pp. 172–174; Flynn, *You're the Boss*, pp. 106–110; Lewis, *Man of the World*, pp. 199–204; Davis, *FDR: The New York Years*, p. 373. On Roosevelt's efforts to secure the gubernatorial nomination for Lehman, see chapter 3.

39. HHLOH, pp. 263–264, 299–304; James Farley Memo, Democratic State Convention, Albany, 1932, Farley Papers, Box 37, Private File, 1932, LC; Farley, *Behind the Ballots*, pp. 174–176; "Col. Lehman Nominated for Governor; . . . Lehman Sticks to Guns; Backed by Roosevelt and Smith, He Refuses to Bow to Curry," *NYT*, October 5, 1932, pp. 1, 16; "Curry Defeat Complete," *NYT*, October 5, 1932, pp. 1, 16.

40. Lehman to Allan Nevins, February 29, 1960, LP, SF, Nevins; HHLOH, p. 225; "M'Cooey Lets Tide Turn; Holds Aloof as Brooklyn Delegates Swing to Victory Vote for Lehman," *NYT*, October 4, 1932, pp. 1, 17; "McCooey Is Forced to Yield on Lehman," *NYT*, October 5, 1932, p. 16.

41. Memorandum, Herbert Lehman to Allan Nevins, January 4, 1962, p. 4, LP, SF, Nevins; Benjamin Buttenwieser Oral History Transcript, CUOHC, pp. 757–758.

42. HHLOH, p. 303.

43. "Ex-Gov. Smith's Nomination of Lehman," *NYT*, October 5, 1932, p. 17. On Smith's reconciliation with Roosevelt, see "Convention Cheers as Smith and Roosevelt Meet and Clasp Hands on Platform, Smiling Broadly," *NYT*, October 5, 1932; Farley, *Behind the Ballots*, pp. 176–177; Freidel, *Franklin D. Roosevelt: The Triumph*, p. 337; Slayton, *Empire Statesman*, pp. 373–374.

44. "Lehman's Speech of Acceptance," *NYT*, October 5, 1932, p. 16.

45. "Smith to Aid Ticket in Tour of 5 States," *NYT*, October 8, 1932, pp. 1, 3; "O'Brien Set to Wage Militant Campaign; . . . Knifing of Lehman Denied," *NYT*, October 9, 1932, p. 27; "Text of Former Governor Smith's Address in Tammany Hall Last Night," *NYT*, October 20, 1932, p. 16; "Former Governor Smith's Speech Assailing Record of Republicans," *NYT*, November 5, 1932, p. 11.

46. HHLOH, pp. 310–312; "Col. Lehman and Col. Donovan: The Two Nominees Contrasted," *NYT*, October 9, 1932, XX-4; "Lehman Attacks Donovan on Dry Act," *NYT*, October 20, 1932, p. 16; "Lehman Opens Fire in Up-State Fight," *NYT*, October 21, 1932, p. 16; "Lehman Declares Donovan 'Semi-Dry,'" *NYT*, October 23, 1932, p. 25; "Lehman Pledges Aid to Seaway Project," *NYT*, October 26, 1932, pp. 1, 8; "Lehman Outlines His Labor Program," *NYT*, October 29, 1932, p. 4; "Low Utility Rates Pledged by Lehman," *NYT*, November 5, 1932, p. 10; "Lehman Foresees Victory for People," *NYT*, November 6, 1932, p. 33. On Donovan, see Waller, *Wild Bill Donovan*, pp. 42–44.

47. "State Victory Solid; Lehman Gets Record Party Plurality of 887,000," *NYT*, November 9, 1932, pp. 1, 16; "Democratic Sweep Is Record for City," *NYT*, November 9, 1932, p. 5; "Governor Lehman," Editorial, *NYT*, November 9, 1932, p. 18; "Lehman Vote Leads State Party Sweep," *NYT*, November 10, 1932, p. 15.

48. On Smith's opposition to the New Deal, see "Smith Heads Group Calling on Democrats to Repudiate Roosevelt and the New Deal; Smith Warns of a Bolt," *NYT*, June 22, 1936, pp. 1, 2; "Ex-Gov. Smith Declares for Landon; 'Remedy for All Our Ills,'" *NYT*, October 2, 1936, pp. 1, 5; "Smith Links Reds with Roosevelt," *NYT*, November 1, 1936, pp. 1, 42; "Smith Says Roosevelt Aroused Spirit of Class Hatred in Nation," *NYT*, October 24, 1940, pp. 1, 8; "A. E. Smith Calls Third Term a Peril," *NYT*, October 27, 1940, p. 39; "New Deal Imperils Party, Says Smith," *NYT*, September 27, 1940, p. 14; Finan, *Alfred E. Smith*, pp. 300–327; Slayton, *Empire Statesman*, pp. 378–389.

Chapter 3. "That Splendid Right Hand of Mine":
Lieutenant Governor Herbert Lehman
and Governor Franklin Roosevelt

1. HHLOH, p. 258.

2. "Lehman, 80, Sets Same Brisk Pace," *NYT*, March 28, 1958, p. 17; "Governor Roosevelt's Address," *NYT*, October 5, 1932, p. 17.

3. On Lehman and Sulzer, see chapter 2. On FDR and Sulzer, see their correspondence in Franklin Roosevelt Papers as New York State Senator, File 328, William Sulzer, January 1911–June 1913; and Franklin Roosevelt Papers as Assistant Secretary of the Navy, Box 60, Correspondence, William Sulzer, FDRL; and Freidel, *Franklin D. Roosevelt: The Apprenticeship*, p. 178. On the Seabury campaign, see William Barber to Franklin Roosevelt, October 17, 1916, Franklin Roosevelt Papers as Assistant Secretary of the Navy, 1913–1920, Box 40, Personal Files, Subject File, Political, (2), on which Lehman and Roosevelt are both listed among the members of the Seabury Campaign Committee. On FDR and Wilson, see Freidel, *Franklin D. Roosevelt: The Apprenticeship*, pp. 134–156, 174–182, 190–191. On Lehman and Wilson, see HHLOH, pp. 99, 199–200.

4. HHLOH, pp. 100–113; Henry Morgenthau, Jr., Oral History Transcript, HHLP, CUOHC, p. 2; "Colonel Lehman's War Record," n.d., LP, SF, Herbert H. Lehman, document 0530_0281; "Textile Expert for Navy," *NYT*, May 19, 1917, p. 3; "Lehman a Success in Many Activities," *NYT*, November 9 1932, p. 10.

5. Lehman to Franklin Roosevelt, July 3, 1928, Roosevelt to Lehman, July 20, 1928, and Lehman to Roosevelt, July 25, 1928, all in Franklin Roosevelt Papers, Campaign of 1928, General Correspondence, New York City, "L," FDRL. On Lehman and Smith, see chapter 2. On FDR and Smith during this period, see Freidel, *Franklin D. Roosevelt: The Ordeal*, pp. 63–64, 116–119, 160–178, 199–200, 217–221, 227–244; Ward, *A First-Class Temperament*, pp. 497–499, 508–510, 641–644, 690–699, 778–780, 784–787; Finan, *Alfred E. Smith*, pp. 178–181, 237–240; and Slayton, *Empire Statesman*, pp. 146–148, 205–211, 254–255.

6. HHLOH, pp. 241–244, 250; "Smith Wants Young to Run for Governor," *NYT*, July 16, 1928, pp. 1, 5; "Smith in Jurist Role Traps a Fugitive," *NYT*, July 17, 1928, pp. 1, 8; "Owen D. Young Refuses to Run for Governor," *NYT*, July 19, 1928, p. 1; Farley, *Behind the Ballots*, pp. 52, 79–80; James Farley Memo, 1928, Farley Papers, Box 37, Private File, 1918–1930, LC; Lehman to Julius Henry Cohen, February 5, 1947, LP, SF, Franklin Roosevelt; Davis, *FDR: The Beckoning of Destiny*, pp. 843–844; Flynn, *You're the Boss*, p. 68; Bellush, *Franklin D. Roosevelt as Governor of New York*, pp. 8–10; "Democrats Press Roosevelt to Run," *NYT*, September 27, 1928, p. 2; "Roosevelt Held Out to the Last Minute," *NYT*, October 3, 1928, p. 12; Freidel, *Franklin D. Roosevelt: The Ordeal*, pp. 249–253.

7. HHLOH, pp. 245–247; Lehman to Julius Henry Cohen, February 5, 1947, and Franklin Roosevelt to Herbert Lehman, October 3, 1928, both in LP, SF, Franklin Roosevelt; Davis, *FDR: The Beckoning of Destiny*, pp. 844–853; Flynn, *You're the Boss*, p. 69; Bellush, *Franklin D. Roosevelt as Governor of New York*, pp. 8–10; "Democrats Press Roosevelt to Run," *NYT*, September 27, 1928, p. 2; "F. D. Roosevelt Drafted by

Democrats," *NYT*, October 2, 1928, pp. 1, 13; "Roosevelt Yields to Smith and Heads State Ticket," *NYT*, October 3, 1928, pp. 1, 12; "Roosevelt Held Out to the Last Minute," *NYT*, October 3, 1928, p. 12; Franklin Roosevelt, "Written for the Record," April 6, 1938, in Elliott Roosevelt, ed., *F.D.R*, II: 771–773; Freidel, *Franklin D. Roosevelt: The Ordeal*, pp. 252–256.

8. "Roosevelt Held Out to the Last Minute," *NYT*, October 3, 1928, p. 12; "Roosevelt and Lehman," Editorial, *NYT*, October 18, 1928, p. 28; Roosevelt to Lehman, October 3, 1928, LP, SF, Franklin Roosevelt; "Roosevelt Opposes any Move to Revive New York Dry Law," *NYT*, October 9, 1928, p. 1; Eleanor Roosevelt Oral History Transcript, HHLP, CUOHC, pp. 2–3.

9. HHLOC, pp. 241–242, 247–248; "Democrats Await Rival's State Slate," *NYT*, September 4, 1928, p. 3; "Democrats Press Roosevelt to Run," *NYT*, September 27, 1928, p. 2; "Doubt Roosevelt Will Be Candidate," *NYT*, September 28, 1928, p. 6; "Lehman Not Seeking Place on the Ticket," *NYT*, September 30, 1928, p. 8.

10. HHLOH, pp. 239–240, 248–250, 253; "Roosevelt to Make Wide Tour of State," *NYT*, October 13, 1928, p. 3; "Lehman Derides 'Prosperity' Issue," *NYT*, October 13, 1928, p. 4; "Roosevelt Denies Tariff Is an Issue," *NYT*, October 17, 1928, p. 19; "Roosevelt Assails Campaign Bigotry," *NYT*, October 18, 1928, p. 3; "Roosevelt Assails State Republicans," *NYT*, November 4, 1928, p. 3; Bellush, *Franklin D. Roosevelt as Governor of New York*, pp. 10–28. See also chapter 2 on Lehman's activities during the 1928 election.

11. Roosevelt to Lehman, November 4, 1928, and Lehman to Roosevelt, November 6, 1928, both in FDR Papers, Campaign of 1928, General Correspondence, New York City, "L"; HHLOH, p. 250; "Roosevelt Is Victor by Slim Plurality," *NYT*, November 7, 1928, pp. 1, 2; "Latest Tabulation of the Election Returns in the City, State and Nation," *NYT*, November 8, 1928, p. 13; Bellush, *Franklin D. Roosevelt as Governor of New York*, p. 27; Breitman and Lichtman, *FDR and the Jews*, pp. 34–35.

12. HHLOH, pp. 265–266, 776; Irving Lehman to Franklin Roosevelt, December 28, 1928, FDR Papers as Governor of New York, Box 48, Irving Lehman, FDRL; "Roosevelt Takes the Oath as Governor," *NYT*, January 1, 1929, pp. 1, 2; "benefit of Colonel Lehman's great ability" quoted in Jewel Bellush, "Roosevelt's Good Right Arm," 425; "Roosevelt Cabinet Drops Formality," *NYT*, January 11, 1929, p. 25; Lehman to Roosevelt, July 27, 1931, and Roosevelt to Lehman, July 29, 1931, both in FDR Papers as Governor of New York, Box 48, Herbert Lehman; Roosevelt to Lehman, July 30, 1931, LP, SF, Franklin Roosevelt; Inscription on *Public Papers of Franklin Delano Roosevelt, 1929*, recorded in William Liebmann, comp., "Tributes to Herbert H. Lehman: Selected from Autograph Inscriptions in Presentation Copies of Their Books," p. 6, LP, SF, Herbert H. Lehman, document 0530_0444, p. 6. On Roosevelt's Cabinet and "Turkey Cabinet," see Henry Morgenthau, Jr., Oral History Transcript, HHLP, CUOHC, pp. 6–7; Freidel, *Franklin D. Roosevelt: The Triumph*, pp. 26–27, 121–123. On FDR's visits to Warm Springs during this period, see Eleanor Roosevelt Oral History Transcript, HHLP, CUOHC, p. 2; and Lippman, *The Squire of Warm Springs*, p. 60. On Irving Lehman, see Libo, ed., *Lots of Lehmans*, pp. 185–205.

13. HHLOH, pp. 257–258; Eleanor Roosevelt Oral History Transcript, HHLP, CUOHC, pp. 3–5; Eleanor Roosevelt, *This I Remember*, p. 68; Schlesinger, *The Age of Roosevelt: Vol. 1: The Crisis of the Old Order, 1919–1933*, p. 406.

14. "Col. Herbert H. Lehman Long Active in Politics; Once a Banker, Ran for

Office First in 1928," *NYT*, October 5, 1932, p. 17; Roosevelt to Lehman, April 11, 1929, in Elliott Roosevelt, ed., *F.D.R.*, I: 47–48; Jewel Bellush, "Roosevelt's Good Right Arm," pp. 426–427; Tugwell, *The Democratic Roosevelt*, pp. 180–181.

15. HHLOH, pp. 434–435; "Lehman Will Tour the State Hospitals," *NYT*, April 23, 1929, p. 17. On FDR using his wife to inspect state facilities, see Lash, *Eleanor and Franklin*, pp. 331–332. On other matters keeping Lehman busy, see Lehman to Roosevelt, April 30, 1929, FDR Papers as Governor of New York, Box 48, Herbert Lehman. The Superintendent of Public Works' August 15, 1929, report can be found in *Public Papers of Franklin D. Roosevelt, Forty-eighth Governor of the State of New York, 1929*, pp. 590–608.

16. HHLOH, pp. 435–438; "For Action on Hospitals," *NYT*, May 14, 1929, p. 2; "Finds Fire Hazard in State Hospital," *NYT*, May 11, 1929, p. 4; "Lehman Denounces Hospital Crowding," *NYT*, May 23, 1929, p. 24; "Ward's Island Evils Shock to Lehman," *NYT*, May 28, 1929, pp. 1, 14; "Lehman Answers Hospital Critics," *NYT*, June 3, 1929, pp. 1, 6; "Lehman Tells Need for Hospital Fund," *NYT*, June 16, 1929, N-2; "State Bond Issue Wins by Huge Vote," *NYT*, November 5, 1930, p. 3; "Agree to Rush Work by State to Aid Idle," *NYT*, November 26, 1930, pp. 1, 4; Lehman to Roosevelt, November 26, 1930, FDR Papers as Governor of New York, Box 48, Herbert Lehman; "Lehman Gratified by Hospital Tour," *NYT*, August 12, 1932, p. 11.

17. Lehman to Roosevelt, April 30, 1929, and Roosevelt to Lehman, May 3, 1929, both in FDR Papers as Governor of New York, Box 48, Herbert Lehman; "Lehman Picks Moses for Banking Inquiry in City Trust Crash," *NYT*, April 26, 1929, pp. 1, 10; "Fight to Save Banks Reviewed by Lehman," *NYT*, November 4, 1932, pp. 1, 14; "Commends Lehman for Aid to City Trust," *NYT*, November 6, 1932, p. 33; Bellush, *Franklin D. Roosevelt as Governor of New York*, pp. 103–113; Freidel, *Franklin D. Roosevelt: The Triumph*, pp. 92–94; Davis, *FDR: The New York Years*, pp. 127–129; Jewel Bellush, "Roosevelt's Good Right Arm," pp. 429–433. On the ill will between Roosevelt and Moses, see Caro, *The Power Broker*, pp. 283–298. For the full text of Moses's report, see Report of Commissioner Moses, *Public Papers of Franklin D. Roosevelt, 1929*, pp. 367–398.

18. HHLOH, pp. 296–297, 481–484; "Broderick Praised by Smith in Court," *NYT*, May 19, 1932, p. 17; "Trial of Broderick Reveals Tense Drama of Bank Failure," *NYT*, June 5, 1932, XX-3; "Fight to Save Banks Reviewed by Lehman," *NYT*, November 4, 1932, pp. 1, 14; Bellush, *Franklin D. Roosevelt as Governor of New York*, pp. 113–123; Freidel, *Franklin D. Roosevelt: The Triumph*, pp. 186–192; Jewel Bellush, "Roosevelt's Good Right Arm," pp. 433–434; Lehman to Allan Nevins, March 16, 1961, pp. 8–10, LP, SF, Nevins.

19. HHLOH, 372–382; "8 Convicts Killed in New Auburn Riot; . . . Hold Warden Hostage," *NYT*, December 12, 1929, pp. 1, 2; " 'No Compromise' Was Lehman Order," *NYT*, December 12, 1929, p. 2; "Seven at Auburn Face Murder Charge; Roosevelt to Call Court," *NYT*, December 13, 1929, pp. 1, 2; Lehman to Allan Nevins, March 16, 1961, p. 7, and Memorandum, Lehman to Nevins, January 4, 1962, p. 11, both in LP, SF, Nevins.

20. Bellush, *Franklin D. Roosevelt as Governor of New York*, pp. 58–75, quote is from p. 68; "Prison Experts Urge 1,500 as Housing Limit," *NYT*, September 13, 1929, p. 25; Lehman to Adolph Lewisohn, September 26, 1929, LP, SF, Lewisohn; "Roosevelt to Urge Wide Prison Reform," *NYT*, December 30, 1929, p. 3; "Many Prison Riots in

Last Six Months," *NYT*, December 12, 1929, p. 3; "Overcrowding Blamed for Prison Outbreaks," *NYT*, July 28, 1929, XX-7; "Ascribes Outbreak to Long Sentences," *NYT*, December 12, 1929, pp. 1, 3; "Kieb Plans to Spend $10,000,000 in 1930," *NYT*, December 14, 1929, p. 10; "Legislature Passes Roosevelt's Bill for Prison Relief," *NYT*, January 7, 1930, pp. 1, 4; "State Bond Issue Wins by Huge Vote," *NYT*, November 5, 1930, p. 3. On Lehman's and Roosevelt's study of the issue, see Adolph Lewisohn to Lehman, September 13, 1929, and attached article, September 11, 1929; Lewisohn to Lehman, October 17, 1929, and attached letter, n.d.; and Lehman to Lewisohn, October 23, 1929, all in LP, SF, Lewisohn.

21. "Cloak Strike Hangs on Parley Today," *NYT*, July 10, 1929, p. 16; "Peace Basis Fixed at Cloak Parley," *NYT*, July 11, 1929, p. 16; "Aids War on Sweatshops," *NYT*, July 23, 1929, p. 49; Dubinsky and Raskin, *David Dubinsky*, pp. 78–79; Lehman to Hubert Humphrey, March 11, 1958, LP, SF, Humphrey. On the Advisory Commission in the cloak and suit industry, see the voluminous correspondence in LP, SF, George Gordon Battle, and LP, SF, Raymond Ingersoll. On Lehman's loan to the ILGWU, see Morris Sigman to Lehman, June 12, 1928, LP, SF, Sigman; HHLOH, pp. 197–198; Dubinsky and Raskin, *David Dubinsky*, p. 75; "Fete for Lehman Aids Candidates," *NYT*, September 22, 1956, p. 12; Bellush, *Franklin D. Roosevelt as Governor of New York*, pp. 198–199; Bernstein, *The Lean Years*, p. 85. Julius Rosenwald and Felix Warburg also made large loans to help keep the ILGWU afloat. Jewel Bellush notes that Lehman lent the union another $25,000 in $5,000 installments in 1929–1930. See Jewel Bellush, "Roosevelt's Good Right Arm," p. 443, n. 36.

22. J. D. Posner to Franklin Roosevelt, November 30, 1929, and Herbert Lehman to Roosevelt, December 17, 1929, both in LP, SF, Franklin Roosevelt; "Dress Peace Signed After 8-Day Strike," *NYT*, February 13, 1930, pp. 1, 12; "Lehman Settles New Dress Dispute," *NYT*, February 23, 1930, p. 24; "unlimited patience" quoted in Jewel Bellush, "Roosevelt's Good Right Arm," p. 439; "Topics of the Times: On Public Business," *NYT*, February 15, 1930, p. 16.

23. Bellush, *Franklin D. Roosevelt as Governor of New York*, p. 198.

24. "Calls Hat Industry to Albany Parley," *NYT*, October 5, 1931, p. 39; Zaritsky to Lehman, May 13, 1932, LP, SF, Zaritsky; Bellush, *Franklin D. Roosevelt as Governor of New York*, p. 206; "Strike Vote Brings Garment Peace Step," *NYT*, July 15, 1932, p. 17; "Lehman Wins Delay in Garment Strike," *NYT*, July 19, 1932, p. 19; "Lehman Brings Peace in the Garment Trades; Averts Strike of 27,000 in Contract Dispute," *NYT*, July 24, 1932, pp. 1, 19; "Garment Contract to Be Signed Today," *NYT*, July 29, 1932, p. 36; "Lehman Advocates Labor Arbitration," *NYT*, August 24, 1932, p. 6; Robert Parmet, *Master of Seventh Avenue*, p. 84.

25. *New York World*, May 6, 1930, quoted in Jewel Bellush, "Roosevelt's Good Right Arm," p. 441; "Lehman Has Appendicitis," *NYT*, April 15, 1930, p. 29; Roosevelt to Lehman, April 23, 1930, LP, SF, Franklin Roosevelt; Lehman to Roosevelt, May 5, 1930, FDR Papers as Governor of New York, Box 48, Herbert Lehman; Roosevelt to Lehman, May 14, 1930, in Elliott Roosevelt, ed., *F.D.R.*, I: 120–121. On the deaths of Bloch and Hamill, see "Maurice Bloch Dies After an Operation," *NYT*, December 6, 1929, p. 26; and "Associates Laud Hamill's Career," *NYT*, January 14, 1930, p. 3.

26. Roosevelt to Lehman, July 29, 1930, and Lehman to Roosevelt, August 1, 1930, both in FDR Papers as Governor of New York, Box 48, Herbert Lehman; "Gave $211,488 to Aid Roosevelt Campaign," *NYT*, November 22, 1930, p. 2; "Talkie Tour Starts Roosevelt Campaign," *NYT*, October 2, 1930, pp. 1, 2; Freidel, *Franklin D. Roosevelt: The Triumph*, pp. 158–159.

27. "Ward Is Criticized by Roosevelt Here," *NYT*, October 4, 1930, p. 4; "Gov. Roosevelt's Radio Speech," *NYT*, October 10, 1930, p. 17; "Governor Stresses Equity of Regime," *NYT*, November 2, 1930, p. 20. See also Roosevelt-Lehman Citizen's [*sic*] Committee, "Re-Elect Lieutenant Governor Herbert H. Lehman: Keep Progressive Government," and campaign flier, "The Best Ever," both in Vertical File, Campaign Literature, 1930, Roosevelt-Lehman Citizens' Committee, FDRL.

28. "Tuttle Nominated on Wet Platform; Makes Tammany Defiance the Issue; . . . Cheer Tuttle 18 Minutes," *NYT*, September 27, 1930, pp. 1, 2; "Baumes a Teacher in Early Career," *NYT*, September 27, 1930, p. 4; "Lehman Demands Baumes's Dry View," *NYT*, October 15, 1930, p. 4; "Lehman Disputes Claims of Tuttle," *NYT*, October 18, 1930, p. 10; "Roosevelt Asserts Republicans Block Progress of State," *NYT*, October 19, 1930, pp. 1, 28; "Governor, Accepting, Calls Tuttle Both Wet and Dry; Charges Hoover Influence," *NYT*, October 4, 1930, pp. 1, 4; "Talkie Tour Starts Roosevelt Campaign," *NYT*, October 2, 1930, pp. 1, 2; "Roosevelt Opens Fight Over Radio," *NYT*, October 10, 1930, pp. 1, 17; "Governor on Screen Here," *NYT*, October 23, 1930, p. 29; "Democratic Landslide Sweeps Country . . . Roosevelt Winner by More Than 700,000; . . . Tuttle Is Swamped," *NYT*, November 5, 1930, pp. 1, 3; "Governor," *NYT*, November 6, 1930, p. 14; "Lieutenant Governor," *NYT*, November 6, 1930, p. 14; Bellush, *Franklin D. Roosevelt as Governor of New York*, pp. 150–174; Freidel, *Franklin D. Roosevelt: The Triumph*, pp. 147–166; Davis, *FDR: The New York Years*, pp. 166–189.

29. HHLOH, p. 282–283; Roosevelt to Lehman, November 17, 1930, LP, SF, Franklin Roosevelt; "Lehman Plans Jobs on State Buildings," *NYT*, November 21, 1930, p. 5; "Agree to Rush Work by State to Aid Idle," *NYT*, November 26, 1930, pp. 1, 4.

30. "Lehman Declares Tax Rise Must End," *NYT*, June 12, 1931, p. 44; HHLOH, p. 283–285; "Governor Considers $25,000,000 Relief for Unemployment," *NYT*, August 25, 1931, pp. 1, 8; "Roosevelt Asks $20,000,000 for Jobless, Raising Fund by a 50% Income Tax Rise; Would Provide Work with 5-Day Week," *NYT*, August 29, 1931, pp. 1, 2; "Text of Gov. Roosevelt's Message on Unemployment Relief," *NYT*, August 29, 1931, p. 2; "Republican Fight Wanes," *NYT*, September 10, 1931, pp. 1, 2; "Relief Compromise Reached at Albany After Conference Lasting till 2 A.M.," *NYT*, September 19, 1931, pp. 1, 2; "State Relief Plan Is First in Nation," *NYT*, September 27, 1931, p. 6; Bellush, *Franklin D. Roosevelt as Governor of New York*, pp. 126–149; Freidel, *Franklin D. Roosevelt: The Triumph*, pp. 217–227.

31. Farley, *Behind the Ballots*, p. 72; Flynn, *You're the Boss*, pp. 84–85; Lehman to Roosevelt, April 2, 1932, and Roosevelt to Lehman, May 11, 1932, both in Franklin Roosevelt Papers as Governor of New York, Box 48, Herbert Lehman; "New York Backs Two-Thirds Rule," *NYT*, June 27, 1932, p. 10; "Walker Vote Stirs Weary Delegates," *NYT*, July 2, 1932, p. 4; "Lehman Predicts Roosevelt Landslide," *NYT*, July 29, 1932, p. 4.

32. "Lehman Is Slated to Win Nomination," *NYT*, July 25, 1932, p. 3; "Move by Roosevelt to Support Lehman for Governor Likely," *NYT*, July 15, 1932, pp. 1, 5; "Fit to Be Governor," Editorial, *NYT*, July 16, 1932, p. 10; "Smith Is Expected to Endorse Lehman," *NYT*, July 17, 1932, p. 2; "Lehman Off Today on His State Tour," *NYT*, July 27, 1932, p. 3; "Word from Lehman Expected Today," *NYT*, August 4, 1932, p. 4.

33. "Lehman Comes Out for Governorship," *NYT*, August 5, 1932, pp. 1, 3.

34. HHLOH, pp. 263–264, 299, 305–307; "Curry and McCooey to Support Ticket," *NYT*, July 3, 1932, p. 10; "Move by Roosevelt to Support Lehman for Governor Likely," *NYT*, July 15, 1932, pp. 1, 5; "Reports Thacher Support," *NYT*, July 16, 1932, p. 3; "Smith Is Expected to Endorse Lehman," *NYT*, July 17, 1932, p. 2; "Walker, if Removed, to Run for Governor," *NYT*, August 1, 1932, pp. 1, 6; "Tammany Is Bitter against Governor," *NYT*, September 2, 1932, pp. 1, 6; "Roosevelt Chances Hurt," *NYT*, September 3, 1932, pp. 1, 3; Roosevelt to Adolph Ochs, September 5, 1932, in Elliott Roosevelt, ed., *F.D.R.*, I: 298; Farley, *Beyond the Ballots*, p. 172. On Roosevelt and the ongoing scandals with Tammany Hall and Mayor Walker, see Davis, *FDR: The New York Years*, pp. 227–236, 253–254, 300–305, 353–355.

35. Henry Morgenthau, Jr., to Lehman, September 8, 1932, LP, SF, Morgenthau; "State Committee Backs Roosevelt on Curry's Orders," *NYT*, September 10, 1932, pp. 1, 2; Roosevelt to Felix Frankfurter, September 14, 1932, in Elliott Roosevelt, ed., *F.D.R.*, I: 300–301; "Tammany Is Seen Turning to Lehman." *NYT*, September 25, 1932, p. 31. On the Morgenthaus, Roosevelts, and Lehmans, see Morgenthau, *Mostly Morgenthaus*, pp. 243–265.

36. "Tammany, in a Deal, Flouts Roosevelt, . . . Governor's Man Ignored," *NYT*, September 30, 1932, pp. 1, 3; "Berry Strips M'Kee of Budget Powers; Roosevelt Asks M'Cooey to Aid Lehman," *NYT*, October 1, 1932, pp. 1, 2; Rosenman, *Working with Roosevelt*, pp. 59–60, 83–84. Lehman reappointed Rosenman to the State Supreme Court in 1933. See "Rosenman Named to Supreme Court, *NYT*, July 20, 1933, p. 21.

37. "Roosevelt Set on N.Y. Fight Over Lehman," *New York Herald Tribune*, October 2, 1932, clipping in Democratic Party National Committee Papers, Library and Research Bureau Papers, 1932–1933, Lehman Press Clippings, FDRL; "Governor Is Ready for Lehman Contest," *NYT*, October 2, 1932, p. 1; "Roosevelt and Smith Insist on Lehman as Curry Holds Out on Convention Eve; . . . Ultimatum by Governor," *NYT*, October 3, 1932, pp. 1, 3.

38. HHLOH, 300–304; "Col. Lehman Nominated for Governor; . . . Lehman Sticks to Guns," *NYT*, October 5, 1932, pp. 1, 16; Farley, *Behind the Ballots*, pp. 172–176; Flynn, *You're the Boss*, pp. 105–109. A more detailed account of this confrontation in Curry's hotel room and Al Smith's role in helping Lehman win the nomination can be found in chapter 2.

39. "Governor Roosevelt's Address," *NYT*, October 5, 1932, p. 17; "Col. Lehman Nominated for Governor; . . . Lehman Sticks to Guns," *NYT*, October 5, 1932, pp. 1, 16; "Smith Leads Fight to Block Walker; . . . Back in Fighting Mood," *NYT*, October 6, 1932, pp. 1, 13.

40. "Lehman's Speech of Acceptance," *NYT*, October 5, 1932, p. 16.

41. "Roosevelt Opens Lehman Campaign," *NYT*, October 9, 1932, pp. 1, 27; "Roosevelt Calls Donovan Utility Ally in Two Speeches for the State Ticket; . . . Governor Starts His Tour," *NYT*, October 19, 1932, pp. 1, 14; "Governor Roosevelt's Speech

at Rochester Urging Colonel Lehman's Election," *NYT*, October 19, 1932, p. 14; "Speech Made by Governor Roosevelt at Buffalo Last Night," *NYT*, October 19, 1932, p. 15.

42. "Text of Governor Roosevelt's Address at Brooklyn Rally," *NYT*, November 5, 1932, p. 10; "Lehman Foresees Victory for People," *NYT*, November 6, 1932, p. 33.

43. "Roosevelt Winner in Landslide! Sweep Is National," *NYT*, November 9, 1932, pp. 1, 2; "Lehman Governor, O'Brien Mayor; State Victory Solid," *NYT*, November 9, 1932, pp. 1, 16; "Roosevelt Pledges Recovery Fight; Hoover Gets Six States," *NYT*, November 10, 1932, pp. 1, 2; "Lehman Vote Leads State Party Sweep," *NYT*, November 10, 1932, p. 15; "Roosevelt Margin in State, 593,938," *NYT*, November 11, 1932, p. 8; "Governor Lehman," Editorial, *NYT*, November 9, 1932, p. 18.

Chapter 4. "The New Deal in Washington Is Being Duplicated by the 'Little' New Deal at Albany": Governor Lehman and President Roosevelt, 1933–1936

1. Samuel Rosenman Oral History Transcript, HHLP, CUOHC, pp. 20–21.

2. Roosevelt, *The Autobiography of Eleanor Roosevelt*, p. 163; "To Retain Present Cabinet," *NYT*, December 31, 1932, p. 2; "Lehman Is Faced by Hard Problems," *NYT*, January 1, 1933, p. 2; Summary of Interview with Henry Morgenthau, Jr., HHLP, CUOHC, p. 2; "Senate Approves 'Cabinet,' " *NYT*, January 5, 1933, p. 13; Hopkins to Lehman, December 27, 1932, and Lehman to Hopkins, December 29, 1932, LP, SF, Hopkins; "Roosevelt Car Loses No. 1," *NYT*, December 28, 1932, p. 19; "Roosevelt Bids Albany Farewell," *NYT*, January 1, 1933, p. 3. Morgenthau went to Washington to head up the new Farm Credit Administration, and in 1934 he became Secretary of the Treasury. See Morgenthau, *Mostly Morgenthaus*, pp. 267, 272–273.

3. "Lehman Gratified at Record 'Tribute,' " *NYT*, November 10, 1932, p. 5; "Lehman Takes Oath Privately Tonight in Ceremony Here," *NYT*, December 31, 1932, pp. 1, 2; "Lehman Takes Oath Here as Governor in Brief Ceremony," *NYT*, January 1, 1933, pp. 1, 3; "Lehman in Capital for Inauguration as Governor Today," *NYT*, January 2, 1933, pp. 1, 20; "Inaugural Is Widely Broadcast," *NYT*, January 3, 1933, p. 12. On Clara Lehman Limburg, see Libo, ed., *Lots of Lehmans*, pp. 115–129.

4. Samuel Rosenman Oral History Transcript, HHLP, CUOHC, pp. 4–5; James Farley Oral History Transcript, HHLP, CUOHC, pp. 6–7; Charles Poletti Oral History Transcript (1957), HHLP, CUOHC, pp. 7, 10; Mrs. Herbert H. Lehman, "Executive Mansion Tells Own Romantic Story in Autobiography Penned by Mrs. Lehman," *New York World-Telegram*, April 2, 1940, and Herbert Lehman to Edith Lehman, August 25, 1937, both in LP, SF, Edith Altschul Lehman; Herbert Lehman to Irving Lehman, December 10, 1938, LP, SF, Irving Lehman; HHLOH, pp. 139–141, 387–391.

5. "Col. Lehman to Name J. J. Canavan His Aide," *NYT*, December 18, 1928, p. 20; "Canavan Is Named to Parole Board," *NYT*, November 10, 1934, p. 4; HHLOH, pp. 384–385; "News Writer Named Lehman's Secretary," *NYT*, March 7, 1935, p. 3; Frankfurter to Lehman, December 7, 1932, and Lehman to Frankfurter, December 13, 1932, LP, SF, Frankfurter; "Mrs. Lehman Shares Political Burdens," *Christian Science Monitor*, January 2, 1937, copy in LP, SF, Edith Altschul Lehman; "Lehman Is Running at Urging of His Wife, First Time She Has Backed Re-Election Drive," *NYT*, November

4, 1950, p. 8; Charles Poletti Oral History Transcript (1957), HHLP, CUOHC, pp. 6–9; Anna Rosenberg Oral History Transcript, HHLP, CUOHC, p. 14; Benjamin Buttenwieser Oral History Transcript, CUOHC, p. 756; HHLOH, pp. 492–494; Samuel Rosenman Oral History Transcript, HHLP, CUOHC, pp. 1–2; Nevins, *Herbert H. Lehman and His Era*, pp. 107, 152–160.

6. HHLOH, pp. 226, 264–266, 332–336, 718–719; Charles Poletti Oral History Transcript (1957), HHLP, CUOHC, p. 19; Frances Perkins Oral History Transcript, CUOHC, III: 514–515; 624–626; Flynn, *You're the Boss*, p. 125.

7. "Lehman Urges Beer Law, Relief, Labor Legislation; . . . Message Is Non-Partisan," *NYT*, January 5, 1933, pp. 1, 12; "Text of Governor Lehman's First Address to Legislature, Delivered in Person," *NYT*, January 5, 1933, p. 12. For Lehman's views on Prohibition, see Memorandum, Lehman to Allan Nevins, January 4, 1962, p. 13, LP, SF, Nevins.

8. Joseph Broderick to Herbert Lehman, December 14, 1935, and enclosed Memorandum, "Bank Holiday," LP, Special Subject File 7a, Bank Holiday, 1933, Broderick; Henry Bruère to Lehman, October 15, 1935, and enclosed Memorandum, "The Bank Holiday," LP, Special Subject File 7b, Bank Holiday, 1933, Bruère; Joseph Canavan to Carolyn [*sic*] Flexner, March 27, 1933, Lehman Papers, Special Subject File 7c, Bank Holiday, 1933, Canavan; HHLOH, pp. 480–483, 489–491; "Two-Day Holiday for Banks Here, Lehman's Order; . . . Governor Acts After an All-Night Conference with Banking Heads," *NYT*, March 4, 1933, pp. 1, 23; Lehman to Allan Nevins, February 29, 1960, LP, SF, Nevins.

9. "Roosevelt Inaugurated, Acts to End the National Banking Crisis Quickly; Plan to Use Scrip Here," *NYT*, March 5, 1933, pp. 1, 25; "Lehman Awaiting White House Views," *NYT*, March 5, 1933, p. 25; "Roosevelt Orders 4-Day Bank Holiday, . . . Use of Scrip Authorized," *NYT*, March 6, 1933, pp. 1, 2; "Bank Bill Is Enacted," *NYT*, March 10, 1933, pp. 1, 2; "Roosevelt in Swift Pace Revitalizes Government," *NYT*, March 12, 1933, E-1; "Many Banks in the City and Nation Reopen Today for Normal Operations, . . . Roosevelt Appeals on the Radio for Full Confidence; Sound Banks Classified," *NYT*, March 13, 1933, pp. 1, 3; "135 Banks Reopen Here," *NYT* March 14, 1933, pp. 1, 2; Lehman to Roosevelt, March 16, 1933, Roosevelt Papers, PPF 93, Lehman, 1933–1935, FDRL.

10. Frances Perkins Oral History Transcript, CUOHC, III: 507–509, 514–515, 624–626; IV: 62–63; Perkins to Lehman, March 4, 1933, LP, SF, Perkins; "Miss Perkins Ready for Cabinet Duties," *NYT*, February 24, 1933, p. 2; "Roosevelt Names Last of Cabinet," *NYT*, March 1, 1933, pp. 1, 2; "Cabinet Sworn in at White House," *NYT*, March 5, 1933, F-2; Martin, *Madam Secretary*, pp. 233–242.

11. "Conferees Agree on States' Aid Bill," *NYT*, May 6, 1933, p. 6; Lehman to Roosevelt, May 19, 1933, and Roosevelt to Lehman, May 19, 1933, both in Franklin Roosevelt Papers, OF 444, Box 1, FERA, April–July 1933, FDRL. On Hopkins's life and career, see McJimsey, *Harry Hopkins*.

12. Lehman to Roosevelt, May 19, 1933, Roosevelt Papers, OF 444, Box 1, FERA, April–July 1933; "Federal Aid Post Given to Hopkins," *NYT*, May 20, 1933, p. 5; "Lehman Obtains Federal Aid Data," *NYT*, May 28, 1933, p. 10.

13. "Minimum Wage Law Asked by Lehman for Women, Minors," *NYT*, February 28, 1933, pp. 1, 12; Roosevelt to Lehman, April 11, 1933, LP, SF, Franklin Roosevelt;

Stephen Early, "The President has sent the following telegram . . . ," April 12, 1933, Roosevelt Papers, PPF 93, Lehman, 1933–1935; "President Seeks Minimum Pay Acts," *NYT*, April 13, 1933, p. 1; Frankfurter to Roosevelt, April 14, 1933, in Freedman, ed., *Roosevelt and Frankfurter*, pp. 125–126; Ingalls, *Herbert H. Lehman and New York's Little New Deal*, pp. 106–108.

14. "254,000 to March Under NRA Today," *NYT*, September 13, 1933, p. 3; "1,500,000 Cheer Vast NRA Parade; . . . Fervor Sweeps Throngs," *NYT*, September 14, 1933, pp. 1, 3; "Johnson Pledges Credit; . . . Lehman Hails Progress," *NYT*, September 14, 1933, pp. 1, 2.

15. Ingalls, *Herbert H. Lehman and New York's Little New Deal*; Lehman to Roosevelt, December 23, 1933, Roosevelt Papers, PPF 93, Lehman, 1933–1935.

16. Lehman to Roosevelt, June 2, 1933, and Roosevelt to Lehman, November 26, 1933, both in LP, SF, Franklin Roosevelt; "Governor Lehman Improves, Sees a Few Callers; President Phones and Many Send Messages," *NYT*, September 30, 1933, p. 3; "Lehman Still Gains; Has Restful Day," *NYT*, October 2, 1933, p. 21; "Lehman Undergoes an Operation Here," *NYT*, October 22, 1933, pp. 1, 3; "Lehman Improves but Has Pleurisy," *NYT*, October 31, 1933, p. 23; "Lehman Improves; Has 'Restful' Day," *NYT*, November 8, 1933, p. 23; "Gov. Lehman Rests at Atlantic City," *NYT*, November 27, 1933, p. 19; "Lehman Back at Work After Long Illness," *NYT*, December 15, 1933, p. 4; Lehman to Roosevelt, December 23, 1933, Roosevelt Papers, PPF 93, Lehman, 1933–1935; "Dinner Guests at the White House, Thursday Evening, May 17," Franklin Roosevelt Papers, Social Entertainments, Office of the Chief of Records, Box 14, Dinner for Governor Lehman, May 17, 1934, FDRL; "Lehmans Honored in the White House," *NYT*, May 18, 1934, p. 20.

17. HHLOH, pp. 286–288; Lehman to the President, January 17, 1934, in "Lehman Appeals for More CWA Aid," *NYT*, January 23, 1934, p. 2; Lehman to Hopkins, January 17, 1934, David Niles Papers, Box 21, WPA Administration: Political Affairs, 1933–1934, Harry S. Truman Library (hereinafter HSTL); "Roosevelt to Ask $1,166,000,000 Aid; Stands Pat on CWA," *NYT*, January 23, 1934, p. 1.

18. Early to Rosenman, January 29, 1934; Rosenman to Early, February 1, 1934; D. J. to Steve, n.d.; and Early to Rosenman, February 5, 1934, all in Roosevelt Papers, OF 91, Lehman. Roosevelt's objections to letters to him being released to the press before he received them dated back to his days as Governor. See "Governor Roosevelt Announces Policy Regarding Communications Given to Public Press before Receipt by Him," November 15, 1929, *Public Papers of Franklin D. Roosevelt, 1929*, p. 634.

19. Lehman to Elinor Morgenthau, March 20, 1934, LP, SF, Henry and Elinor Morgenthau; "Roosevelt Warns Foes of City Bill," *NYT*, March 17, 1934, pp. 1, 3.

20. "Wife of the Candidate," *New York World-Telegram*, November 1, 1934, copy in LP, SF, Edith Altschul Lehman; Lehman to Roosevelt, May 12, 1934, LP, SF, Franklin Roosevelt.

21. "Lehmans Honored in the White House," *NYT*, May 18, 1934, p. 20; "Kenneally Makes Peace Overtures," *NYT*, May 20, 1934, p. 17; James Farley Memo, June 15, 1934, Farley Papers, Box 37, Private File, May–September 1934, LC; Lehman to Roosevelt, August 7, 1934, and Roosevelt to Lehman, August 8, 1934, both in LP, SF, Franklin Roosevelt; "Gov. Lehman to Run Again," *NYT*, August 8, 1934, pp. 1, 7; "Roosevelt Hails Lehman Decision," *NYT*, August 10, 1934, p. 4.

22. "The State Campaign Opens," *NYT*, October 7, 1934, XX-3; "Nation Watching Election In State as New Deal Test," *NYT*, November 4, 1934, N-1; "Republicans Name Moses for Governor on 3D Ballot," *NYT*, September 29, 1934, pp. 1, 7; "Moses Sees Need for a New Party," *NYT*, November 6, 1934, p. 21; "Moses Declares Alger Report Aims to Shield Lehman," *NYT*, October 9, 1934, pp. 1,12; "Moses Says Rival Is Tammany Ally," *NYT*, October 10, 1934, p. 2; "Moses Ridicules Rival on Utilities," *NYT*, October 16, 1934, 4; "Moses Charges Lehman 'Lied' on Milk Problem," *NYT*, October 24, 1934, pp. 1, 9; "Sales Tax Vital, Moses Declares," *NYT*, October 30, 1934, p. 15; "Moses Links Rival to Utility Finance," *NYT*, November 2, 1934, pp. 1, 12; Caro, *The Power Broker*, pp. 360–362, 402–425.

23. HHLOH, 564; Carolin Flexner Oral History Transcript, HHLP, CUOHC, p. 58b; "Democrats Block Moses Park Post," *NYT*, January 5, 1934, p. 2; "Gov. Lehman Again Rejects LaGuardia 'Dictator' Plan; . . . Mayor Ready for Parley," *NYT*, January 9, 1934, pp. 1, 2; "City Economy Bill Slated for Action," *NYT*, January 15, 1934, p. 2; "Text of Gov. Lehman's Speech Accepting Nomination," *NYT*, October 16, 1934, p. 2; "Roosevelt Ready to Give His Backing to Lehman Drive," *NYT*, October 17, 1934, pp. 1, 16; "Lehman, Angered, Replies to 'Lie,' " *NYT*, October 25, 1934, pp. 1, 9. On the relationship between Lehman and Moses over the years, see Duane Tananbaum, "Allies and Adversaries: Herbert Lehman and Robert Moses," unpublished paper presented at conference on "Robert Moses: New Perspectives on the Master Builder," Columbia University, March 2007.

24. James Farley Memo, September 27, 1934, Farley Papers, Box 37, Private File, May–September 1934; Farley Memos, October 18, 1934, October 25, 1934, and "Friday before Election 1934," all in Farley Papers, Box 37, Private File, October–December 1934; "Roosevelt Backs Lehman; . . . President Hails Friend," *NYT*, November 3, 1934, pp. 1, 4. On Roosevelt's longstanding distaste for Moses, see Caro, *The Power Broker*, pp. 283–298.

25. "New Deal Scores Nation-Wide Victory; Lehman Wins, . . . State Ticket Wins," *NYT*, November 7, 1934, pp. 1, 3; "Moses Is Defeated in His Own District," *NYT*, November 7, 1934, p. 3; "President Phones Lehman," *NYT*, November 8, 1934, p. 3; Roosevelt to Harold Content, November 9, 1934, Roosevelt Papers, PPF 1926, Harold Content; "Farley Acclaims Victory for Party," *NYT*, November 7, 1934, pp. 1, 4; Farley Memo, October 25, 1934, Farley Papers, Box 37, Private File, October–December 1934; "Moses Is Reappointed to State Park Job; Senate Confirms Nomination by Lehman," *NYT*, March 5, 1936, p. 23; "Lehman Renames Moses to Long Island Park Post," *NYT*, May 13, 1942, p. 20; Moses to Lehman, May 16, 1942, LP, SF, Robert Moses; HHLOH, pp. 566–567; Lehman to Allan Nevins, February 29, 1960, LP, SF, Nevins; Charles Poletti Oral History Transcript (1978), pp. 198–199, CUOHC.

26. Lehman to Roosevelt, December 5, 1934; Roosevelt to Lehman, December 14, 1934; Lehman to Roosevelt, December 18, 1934; and Roosevelt to Lehman, January 1, 1935; all in Roosevelt Papers, PPF 93, Lehman, 1933–1935; "Gov. Lehman Warns at Inaugural Fete of State Aid Trend," *NYT*, January 2, 1935, pp. 1, 2.

27. "Gov. Lehman Urges Job Insurance Law," *NYT*, January 3, 1935, pp. 1, 13; "Text of Gov. Lehman's Message to the Legislature on the State's Chief Problems," *NYT*, January 3, 1935, p. 14; "State's New Social Program Covers an Extensive Field," *NYT*, January 6, 1935, XX-3; HHLOH, pp. 357–364, 444–445, 518, "Bill Signed to

End Compensation Evil," *NYT*, March 29, 1935, p. 12; "Lehman Signs Bill Raising School Age," *NYT*, April 25, 1935, p. 23; "Job Insurance Bill Signed; . . . Lehman Hails Measure," *NYT*, April 26, 1935, pp. 1, 15; "Lehman Acclaims Year's Legislation," *NYT*, May 6, 1935, pp. 1, 8; Frances Perkins to Lehman, April 19, 1935, LP, SF, Perkins; Frankfurter to Lehman, April 29, 1935, LP, SF, Frankfurter; George Meany Oral History Transcript, HHLP, CUOHC, pp. 2–5; Goulden, *Meany*, pp. 38–47, 337; Ingalls, *Herbert H. Lehman and New York's Little New Deal*, pp. 79–83, 134–136; Lehman to Allan Nevins, December 23, 1961, and Memorandum, January 4, 1962, pp. 14–15, both in LP, SF, Nevins.

28. "Lehman Acclaims Year's Legislation," *NYT*, May 6, 1935, pp. 1, 8; HHLOH, p. 291; Lehman to Harry Hopkins, September 11, 1935, attached to Lehman to Roosevelt, September 11, 1935, Roosevelt Papers, OF 91, Lehman; "President Talks Relief to Lehman," *NYT*, September 10, 1935, p. 7; "New WPA Delays Seen at Hyde Park," *NYT*, September 18, 1935, p. 16; Poletti to Hopkins, September 18, 1935, and Suggested Letter, David Niles Papers, Box 21, WPA Administration: Political Affairs, 1935–1936, HSTL; Hopkins to Lehman, September 19, 1935, LP, SF, Hopkins; "Lehman Accepts Plans for State to Assume 'Dole,'" *NYT*, November 7, 1935, pp. 1, 12; Aubrey Williams to President Roosevelt, November 11, 1935, Roosevelt Papers, OF 91, Lehman; "Lehman Visits Roosevelt; Governor and President Discuss State Relief," *NYT*, November 12, 1935, p. 7; "Roosevelt Weighs Relief Plea by Lehman to Save State Outlay of $4,000,000 a Month," *NYT*, November 13, 1935, p. 4; Roosevelt to Lehman, November 27, 1935, Roosevelt Papers, PPF 93, Lehman, 1933–1935.

29. "All State Forces Battle the Flood," *NYT*, July 10, 1935, p. 2; "Lehman Appeals for Roosevelt Aid in Flood Relief," *NYT*, July 14, 1935, pp. 1, 8; "Asks Roosevelt for CCC Flood Aid," *NYT*, July 30, 1935, p. 9; "2,500 Will Clear State Flood Area," *NYT*, August 2, 1935, p. 15; "CCC Starts Today on Up-State Farms," *NYT*, August 10, 1935, p. 3.

30. Stephen Early to Lehman, August 8, 1936; Walter Brown to Early, August 10, 1936; Early to Lehman care of Brown, August 10, 1936; and James Mahoney, Memorandum for the Governor, August 11, 1936, all in LP, SF, Franklin Roosevelt; "Great Crowds Acclaim Roosevelt on Inspection Tour in Pennsylvania," *NYT*, August 16, 1936, pp. 1, 26; "Flood Control 'Nearing,'" *NYT*, August 16, 1936, p. 28.

31. HHLOH, p. 146; Roosevelt to Lehman, December 14, 1934, Roosevelt Papers, PPF 93, Lehman, 1933–1935; "New York County Will Lose Heavily in Redistricting," *NYT*, November 18, 1934, pp. 1, 13; "Tammany Is Firm, Dooling Declares," *NYT*, March 27, 1935, p. 10; "Governor Appeals to Public to Force Reapportionment," *NYT*, April 8, 1935, pp. 1, 15; "Redistricting Foes Assail Gov. Lehman," *NYT*, April 9, 1935, p. 12; "Tammany Blocks Districting Again," *NYT*, April 12, 1935, p. 10; "Redistricting Bill Passed by Senate," *NYT*, April 13, 1935, pp. 1, 2; "Liberal Assembly Asked by Lehman in Plea for Party," *NYT*, October 29, 1935, pp. 1, 9; "Eaton Sees Party Gains as Farley Accepts Vote as Test of the New Deal," *NYT*, November 4, 1935, pp. 1, 3; "Republicans Win Majority of 14 in State Assembly; . . . Decisive Gains in State," *NYT*, November 6, 1935, pp. 1, 20; "Lehman Discounts Loss of Assembly," *NYT*, November 6, 1935, p. 20; "Roosevelt Finds Vote Satisfying," *NYT*, November 7, 1935, p. 3; Arthur Krock, "New York Result Blow to New Deal," *NYT*, November 6, 1935, pp. 1, 20; "Farley and Eaton Continue to Clash," *NYT*, November 7, 1935, p. 14.

32. "Lehman Decides to Retire in 1936; Candidate Hunted," *NYT*, May 20, 1935, pp. 1, 2; "Lehman Undecided on 1936 Candidacy," *NYT*, May 24, 1935, p. 9; "Eight Mentioned for Post," *NYT*, May 24, 1935, p. 9; "National Chiefs for Lehman Race," *NYT*, May 25, 1935, p. 6; "Two Parties Stirred over Governorship," *NYT*, May 26, 1935, E-11; Missy LeHand to James Butler, June 11, 1935, Roosevelt Papers, PPF 93, Lehman, 1933–1935; "Roosevelt Victory Sure, Says Farley," *NYT*, September 5, 1935, p. 8.

33. "Lehman Will Dine with the President," *NYT*, March 6, 1936, p. 4; "Lehman at White House," *NYT*, March 7, 1936, p. 13; "Lehman Candidacy Will Aid Roosevelt," *NYT*, March 17, 1936, p. 7; Lehman to Roosevelt, March 17, 1936, LP, SF, Franklin Roosevelt.

34. Roosevelt to Henry Morgenthau, Jr., March 19, 1936, in Elliott Roosevelt, ed., *F.D.R.*, I: 572; "Roosevelt, Here, Defends Cost of 'Rebuilding' Nation; Urges Lehman Re-Election," *NYT*, April 26, 1936, pp. 1, 32; "The President's Address Outlining His Social and Political Philosophy," *NYT*, April 26, 1936, p. 32.

35. HHLOH, pp. 445–448, 459–471; "Gov. Lehman Asks Rise in Liquor Tax for Social Costs," *NYT*, March 3, 1936, pp. 1, 10; "G.O.P. Will Fight Lehman 'New Deal,'" *NYT*, March 8, 1936, E-6; Russell Owen, "The Man Behind the 'Little New Deal,'" *New York Times Magazine*, March 15, 1936, pp. 4, 21; "Partisan Row Marks End of Legislature," *NYT*, May 10, 1936, E-7; "Relief Bills Voted by Albany Senate; Assembly Chided," *NYT*, May 1, 1936, pp. 1, 4; "Gov. Lehman Moves to Break Deadlock on Social Security," *NYT*, May 5, 1936, pp. 1, 14; "Assembly Rejects New Lehman Plea on Social Security," *NYT*, May 6, 1936, pp. 1, 4; "Lehman to Appeal to People for Aid on Social Security," *NYT*, May 7, 1936, pp. 1, 4; Lehman Appeals for Security Bills," *NYT*, May 8, 1936, pp. 1, 17; "Security a Myth, Wadsworth Says," *NYT*, May 9, 1936, pp. 1, 6; "Text of Wadsworth's Talk on Social Security," *NYT*, May 9, 1936, p. 6; "Lehman Assails Foe's View," *NYT*, May 9, 1936, p. 6; "Lehman in Person Urges Social Bill," *NYT*, May 12, 1936, pp. 1, 16; "Legislature Kills State Social Aid; All-Night Session," *NYT*, May 14, 1936, pp. 1, 4; Ingalls, *Herbert H. Lehman and New York's Little New Deal*, pp. 88–92.

36. James Farley Memo, May 22, 1936, Farley Papers, Box 39, Private File, May 1936; Lehman to Roosevelt, May 20, 1936, LP, SF, Franklin Roosevelt; "Arthur Lehman, Banker, Is Dead," *NYT*, May 16, 1936, p. 15. On Arthur Lehman, see Libo, ed., *Lots of Lehmans*, pp. 137–158.

37. HHLOH, pp. 595–596; "Lehman Not to Run Again," *NYT*, May 21, 1936, pp. 1, 16; "The Governor's Statement," *NYT*, May 21, 1936, p. 1; "Mrs. Fatman Dies; Governor's Sister," *NYT*, February 20, 1936, p. 19; "Lehman Stands on Statement," *NYT*, May 23, 1936, p. 2; "Lehman Outlines His Social Philosophy," *New York Times Magazine*, August 9, 1936, pp. 5, 23. On Settie Lehman Fatman, see Libo, ed., *Lots of Lehmans*, pp. 89–104.

38. James Farley Memo, May 18, 1936, Farley Papers, Box 39, Private File, May 1936; "Lehman Not to Run Again," *NYT*, May 21, 1936, pp. 1, 16; "Drive Begun Here to 'Draft Lehman,'" *NYT*, May 21, 1936, pp. 1, 16.

39. "Governor Lehman's Decision Makes a Stir in the Nation's Capital," *NYT*, May 21, 1936, p. 16; "Drive Begun Here to 'Draft Lehman,'" *NYT*, May 21, 1936, pp. 1, 16; "Lehman Is Deluged by Messages Demanding That He Run Again," *NYT*,

May 22, 1936, pp. 1, 2; "Roosevelt Again 'Hopes' for Lehman," *NYT*, May 23, 1936, p. 2; Eleanor Roosevelt to Lehman, May 23, 1936, Eleanor Roosevelt Papers, Box 636, Personal Letters, 1936, Lehman, FDRL; Maurice Davidson to President Roosevelt, May 28, 1936, and Roosevelt to Davidson, June 2, 1936, Roosevelt Papers, PPF 3249, Davidson; "Party Sees Chance to Draft Lehman," *NYT*, June 1, 1936, p. 2; HHLOH, pp. 592–594. On Davidson's role in La Guardia's election, see Garrett, *The La Guardia Years*, pp. 96–97, 100, 107; and Mann, *La Guardia Comes to Power*, pp. 19, 68, 79–88.

40. Arthur Krock, "In Washington: Lehman's Action May Affect National Political Scene," *NYT*, May 21, 1936, p. 22; Krock, "Sifting the Candidates, Nation Surveys Future," *NYT*, May 24, 1936, E-3; "All Eyes on New York," Editorial, *NYT*, May 27, 1936, p. 22; "9 Doubtful States to Decide Election," *NYT*, May 31, 1936, E-6; "Up-State Republicans in Race for Governor," *NYT*, June 7, 1936, p. 65; HHLOH, pp. 592–594; Eleanor Roosevelt Oral History Transcript, HHLP, CUOHC, p. 7; Samuel Rosenman Oral History Transcript, HHLP, CUOHC, pp. 5–7; Charles Poletti Oral History Transcript (1957), HHLP, CUOHC, pp. 10–11.

41. Lehman to Mrs. Roosevelt, May 27, 1936, Franklin Roosevelt Papers, PPF 93, Lehman, 1936–1939; "Unique Drive for Lehman," *NYT*, June 23, 1936, pp. 1, 14.

42. Wise to Lehman, June 11, 1936, LP, SF, Stephen S. Wise; "Mack Spurs Drive to Draft Lehman," *NYT*, June 17, 1936, p. 2; "Seeks Aid of Convention In 'Draft-Lehman' Move," *NYT*, June 22, 1936, p. 1; Maurice Davidson to Franklin Roosevelt, May 28, 1936, and June 4, 1936, both in Roosevelt Papers, PPF 3249, Davidson; "Lehman Urged to Run," *NYT*, June 19, 1936, p. 8; Edward Gluck, Secretary, New York Young Democratic Club, to Governor Lehman, June 20, 1936, LP, SF, Franklin Roosevelt; "Democrats Elect Sheridan Leader," *NYT*, June 21, 1936, p. 3; "Join Draft Lehman Move," *NYT*, June 21, 1936, p. 2; "Westchester Drive Is On," *NYT*, June 24, 1936, p. 14; "Lehman May Be Seconder," *NYT*, June 22, 1936, p. 4.

43. "Loyalty to President Intensified by Revolts; . . . Convention Opens Today," *NYT*, June 23, 1936, pp. 1, 12; "Unique Drive for Lehman," *NYT*, June 23, 1936, pp. 1, 14; "Delegates from All Over Nation Signing Petition to Gov. Lehman to Run Again," *NYT*, June 25, 1936, p. 17; "Drive by Lehman Men Becomes Convention Issue," *NYT*, June 26, 1936, p. 15; Edward Gluck to the President, June 25, 1936, Roosevelt Papers, OF 300, Box 25, New York, 1933–1945, "L"; HHLOH, pp. 593–594.

44. "Lehman May Be Seconder," *NYT*, June 22, 1936, p. 4; "Delegates from All Over Nation Signing Petition to Gov. Lehman to Run Again," *NYT*, June 25, 1936, p. 17; Turner Catledge, "Roosevelt Nominated by Acclamation; Demonstrations for Him and Lehman; Drama in Night Session," *NYT*, June 27, 1936, pp. 1, 9; "Enthusiasm Runs High," *NYT*, June 27, 1936, pp. 1, 8; James Farley Memo, n.d., but probably June 26, 1936, Farley Papers, Box 39, Private File, June 1936; "President Thanks Lehman, Hails Tribute to Him," *NYT*, June 27, 1936, p. 1; HHLOH, pp. 592–596; James Farley Oral History Transcript, HHLP, CUOHC, p. 14.

45. "Roosevelt Nominated by Acclamation; Demonstrations for Him and Lehman; Drama in Night Session," *NYT*, June 27, 1936, pp. 1, 9; "Lehman Gets New Plea," *NYT*, pp. 1, 27; "Mrs. Lehman Reconciled to Governor's Course," *NYT*, July 1, 1936, p. 16; HHLOH, p. 596.

46. Roosevelt on Way to Hyde Park Home," *NYT*, June 28, 1936, p. 24; "Encouraged by Hyde Park Trip," *NYT*, June 28, 1936, p. 27; "Lehman Silent on Race after

Visit to Roosevelt," *NYT,* June 29, 1936, pp. 1, 8; Lehman to Eleanor Roosevelt, May 27, 1936, Franklin Roosevelt Papers, PPF 93, Lehman, 1936–1939; "Roosevelt Expected to Draft Lehman After Convention; A 'Keynote' by Robinson," *NYT,* June 25, 1936, pp. 1, 12; Franklin Roosevelt to Lehman, June 29, 1936, in Elliott Roosevelt, ed., *F.D.R.,* I: 597; Ickes, *The Secret Diaries of Harold L. Ickes, Vol. II,* pp. 167–168; James Farley Personal Memoranda, June 29 and June 30, 1936, Farley Papers, Box 39, Private File, June 1936.

47. Roosevelt to Lehman, June 29, 1936, in Elliott Roosevelt, ed., *F.D.R.,* I: 596–597. The original handwritten letter is document 0784_0136 in LP, SF, Franklin Roosevelt.

48. "Roosevelt 'Happy' over Lehman Move," *NYT,* July 1, 1936, pp. 1, 16.

49. "Lehman Yields to Pressure, Will Run for Third Term," *NYT,* July 1, 1936, pp. 1, 16; Lehman to Arthur Goodhart, July 22, 1936, LP, SF, Arthur Goodhart.

50. James Farley Personal Memo, June 30, 1936, Farley Papers, Box 39, Private File, June 1936; "Roosevelt 'Happy' over Lehman Move," *NYT,* July 1, 1936, pp. 1, 16; "Lehman Yields to Pressure, Will Run for Third Term," *NYT,* July 1, 1936, pp. 1, 16; "Farley Praises Lehman for Candidacy; Predicts a Double Victory in November," *NYT,* July 1, 1936, p. 16; Frankfurter to Roosevelt, July 11, 1936, in Freedman, ed., *Roosevelt and Frankfurter,* pp. 345–346.

51. "Decision of Lehman Is Assailed by Eaton," *NYT,* July 1, 1936, p. 16; "Lehman Yields to Pressure, Will Run for Third Term," *NYT,* July 1, 1936, pp. 1, 16.

52. Arthur Krock, "In the Nation: How the Lehman Candidacy Affects the President," *NYT,* July 1, 1936, p. 24; James Hagerty, "Lehman's Aid in State a Boon to Roosevelt," *NYT,* July 5, 1936, E-7.

53. Frances Perkins Oral History Transcript, CUOHC, II: 511; "New Labor Party Formed in State to Back Roosevelt," *NYT,* July 17, 1936, pp. 1, 7; "Lehman Welcomes Labor Party's Aid," *NYT,* August 14, 1936, p. 9; "Mayor Will Speak for Labor Party," *NYT,* October 11, 1936, p. 40; "Huge Labor Rally Warned by Lehman of 'Sinister' Foes," *NYT,* October 28, 1936, pp. 1, 21; "Parties of the Left," *NYT,* November 8, 1936, E-2; Moscow, *Politics in the Empire State,* pp. 102–107; Kessner, *Fiorello H. La Guardia and the Making of Modern New York,* pp. 408–410; Fraser, *Labor Will Rule,* pp. 363, 371.

54. "State Labor Backs Roosevelt and Lehman for Re-Election," *NYT,* August 26, 1936, pp. 1, 10.

55. Democratic State Committee, Press Release No. 33, for September 17th [1936], James Farley Papers, Box 39, Private File, September 16–30, 1936.

56. "State Republicans Score New Deal; Republican Talks Sharp," *NYT,* September 29, 1936, pp. 1, 18; "Bleakley Calls Lehman a 'Robot,'" *NYT,* October 10, 1936, p. 9.

57. "War on Privilege Vital, Lehman Says," *NYT,* September 20, 1936, pp. 1, 31; "Lehman's Address at Dinner of Young Democrats Here," *NYT,* September 20, 1936, p. 31.

58. "Lehman Pledges to Serve Out Term," *NYT,* September 30, 1936, pp. 1, 16; "Harmony Marks Democratic Convention as Entire Ticket Is Swiftly Approved," *NYT,* September 30, 1936, p. 16.

59. James Farley Memoranda, September 24, 1936, and September 29, 1936, Farley Papers, Box 39, Private File, September 16–30, 1936; "State Democrats Gather

in Harmony," *NYT*, September 27, 1936, pp. 1, 3; "Roosevelt Sets Course," *NYT*, September 28, 1936, pp. 1, 7; "Roosevelt Is Set for Drive on Foes," *NYT*, September 29, 1936, pp. 1, 23; "Roosevelt Hits 'False Issue' of Communism; . . . The President Opens Fire," *NYT*, September 30, 1936, pp. 1, 17; "Roosevelt's Address to the State Democrats," *NYT*, September 30, 1936, p. 17.

60. HHLOH, p. 473; "Lehman Says Rival Is Foe of Security," *NYT*, October 14, 1936, pp. 1, 12; "Lehman Denounces Drive on Security," *NYT*, October 31, 1936, pp. 1, 6; "Roosevelt Ends 5,000 Mile Tour," *NYT*, October 18, 1936, pp. 1, 32; "Informal Extemporaneous Remarks at Albany, N.Y., October 17, 1936," in Samuel Rosenman, comp., *The Public Papers and Addresses of Franklin D. Roosevelt; Vol. 5: The Public Approves, 1936*, pp. 515–516.

61. W. A. Warn, "The Nation's Eyes Are on New York," *NYT*, November 1, 1936, E-4.

62. Lehman to Arthur Goodhart, November 12, 1936, LP, SF, Arthur Goodhart; "Victorious Chiefs Jubilant over Decisive Endorsement of the New Deal," *NYT*, November 4, 1936, p. 11; "Roosevelt's Plurality Is 11,000,000; . . . History's Largest Poll," *NYT*, November 5, 1936, pp. 1, 2; "Roosevelt Swept the State by 1,114,972; Lehman Plurality over Bleakley 528,858," *NYT*, November 15, 1936, p. 5.

63. "Lehman Vote Cut," *NYT*, November 4, 1936, pp. 1, 5; "Roosevelt Swept the State by 1,114,972; Lehman Plurality over Bleakley 528,858," *NYT*, November 15, 1936, p. 5; HHLOH, pp. 597–599; "Smith Threatens a Revolt on Roosevelt Leadership; Calls New Deal Socialism," *NYT*, January 26, 1936, pp. 1, 36; "Text of Address of Alfred E. Smith at Anti-New Deal Dinner in Washington," *NYT*, January 26, 1936, p. 36; "Smith Will Attack Gov. Lehman Next, Backing Bleakley," *NYT*, October 10, 1936, pp. 1, 9; "Lehman Says Rival Is Foe of Security," *NYT*, October 14, 1936, pp. 1, 12; "Cheers, Boos Meet Smith at Chicago," *NYT*, October 23, 1936, p. 19; "Smith to Stay Silent on State Campaign," *NYT*, October 30, 1936, p. 15; "Smith Links Reds with Roosevelt," *NYT*, November 1, 1936, pp. 1, 42; Carolin Flexner Oral History Transcript, HHLP, CUOHC, pp. 52–53; "Coughlin Assails Lehman and Mead," *NYT*, July 26, 1936, p. 3; "Friend of Farley Bolts the Party," *NYT*, September 27, 1936, p. 29; Moscow, *Politics in the Empire State*, pp. 120–121; Bayor, *Neighbors in Conflict*, pp. 46–48.

64. Russell Owen, "The Man Behind the 'Little New Deal,'" *New York Times Magazine*, March 15, 1936, pp. 4, 21; S. J. Woolf, "Lehman or Bleakley: Two Men, Two Views," *New York Times Magazine*, October 11, 1936, pp. 4, 5, 10.

Chapter 5. "The End of a Beautiful Friendship"?
Lehman and Roosevelt, 1937–1939

1. Arthur Krock, "In the Nation: Possible Effects of Governor Lehman's Letter," *NYT*, July 20, 1937, p. 22.

2. Lehman to Roosevelt, December 3, 1936, LP, SF, Franklin Roosevelt; and Roosevelt to Marvin McIntyre, n.d.; McIntyre, Memo, December 5, 1936; Roosevelt to Lehman, December 9, 1936; and Lehman to Roosevelt, December 15, 1936; all in Franklin Roosevelt Papers, PPF 93, Lehman, 1936–1939.

3. Lehman to the President, December 28, 1936; Roosevelt to Lehman, December 28, 1936; Lehman to the President, December 29, 1936; all in Roosevelt Papers,

PPF 93, Lehman, 1936–1939; "Lehman Again Inaugurated; Pledges Fight for Ideals," *NYT*, January 2, 1937, pp. 1, 5; "Roosevelt in Telegram Congratulates Lehman," *NYT*, January 2, 1937, p. 5.

4. HHLOH, p. 446, 473; "Lehman Stresses Social Security; Asks State Relief," *NYT*, January 7, 1937, pp. 1, 15; "Text of Governor Lehman's Message Read by Him before the Legislature," *NYT*, January 7, 1937, p. 14; "Many Reform Acts Urged by Lehman," *NYT*, January 7, 1937, p. 15; "Lehman Bills Favored by Legislature's Mood," *NYT*, January 10, 1937, p. 70; "Security Bill Wins in Albany Senate; New Wage Law Up," *NYT*, January 14, 1937, pp. 1, 4; "State G.O. P. Has Eyes on 1940," *NYT*, January 31, 1937, p. 68; "Lehman Bill Wins on Social Security," *NYT*, February 11, 1937, pp. 1, 6; "Security Measure Signed by Lehman," *NYT*, February 16, 1937, p. 8.

5. "Child Labor Curb Offered by Smith," *NYT*, March 6, 1934, p. 6; Lehman to Lillian Wald, December 19, 1934, LP, SF, Wald; "Jewish Governor" quoted in Trattner, *Crusade for the Children*, p. 197. See also "Text of Gov. Smith's Annual Message to Legislature Detailing His Policies; 48-Hour Week for Women, Income Tax Cut, and Law Enforcement Advocated," *NYT*, January 8, 1925, pp. 20–22; "Farmers Fight Vote on Child Labor Law," *NYT*, January 22, 1925, p. 21; "Charge Reds Back Child Labor Ban," *NYT*, February 25, 1925, p. 2; "Smith, 60, Intends to Work until 90," *NYT*, December 31, 1933, pp. 1, 3; "Senate Committee Kills the Ratification of Child Labor Amendment by the State," *NYT*, April 19, 1934, p. 1; "Mayor Sees Lehman Lax on Child Labor," *NYT*, April 5, 1935, pp. 1, 3; "Lehman to Appeal His Case to People," *NYT*, April 7, 1935, E-7; Felt, *Hostages of Fortune*, pp. 195–216; HHLOH, pp. 477, 702–703; Finan, *Alfred E. Smith*, pp. 301–302; and Ingalls, *Herbert H. Lehman and New York's Little New Deal*, pp. 115–119.

6. "Roosevelt Pleads on Child Labor Act," *NYT*, January 9, 1937, p. 5; Lehman to Roosevelt, January 8, 1937, LP, SF, Franklin Roosevelt; Lehman Affirms Child Labor View," *NYT*, February 2, 1937, p. 3; "Ban on Child Labor Approved, 38 to 12, by Albany Senate," *NYT*, February 3, 1937, pp. 1, 10; "Roosevelt Spurs Child Labor Foes," *NYT*, February 5, 1937, p. 12; "Child Labor Ban Gains Momentum; . . . A 'Surprise' at Albany," *NYT*, February 7, 1937, p. 68; Felt, *Hostages of Fortune*, pp. 213–214.

7. "Assembly Delays Child Labor Curb," *NYT*, February 4, 1937, p. 14; Lehman to Perkins, February 5, 1937, LP, SF, Perkins; "Child Labor Leaders Converge on Albany for Test of the Bill," *NYT*, February 21, 1937, p. 76; "Roosevelt Makes Child Labor Plea to the Assembly," *NYT*, February 23, 1937, pp. 1, 6; "Child Labor Bill Menaced by Shift in the Assembly," *NYT*, February 24, 1937, pp. 1, 16; "Lehman Presses Child Labor Fight in Appeal by Radio," *NYT*, March 6, 1937, pp. 1, 4; "Text of Gov. Lehman's Appeal for Child Labor Amendment," *NYT*, March 6, 1937, p. 4; "Child Labor Bill Dies in Assembly; Vote Is 102 to 42," *NYT*, March 10, 1937, pp. 1, 20; Leo Lehmann, "The Catholic Church in Politics": IV: "The Church and Social Legislation," *New Republic*, December 7, 1938, pp. 122–123; HHLOH, pp. 477, 702–703; Felt, *Hostages of Fortune*, p. 214.

8. "Lehman Promises Wage Law Fight," *NYT*, October 13, 1936, p. 12; "Lehman Stresses Social Security; Asks State Relief," *NYT*, January 7, 1937, pp. 1, 15; "Text of Governor Lehman's Message Read by Him before the Legislature," *NYT*, January 7, 1937, p. 14; "Many Reform Acts Urged by Lehman," *NYT*, January 7, 1937, p. 15; "'Sound' Wage Law Urged by Lehman," *NYT*, January 13, 1937, p. 6; "State to

Re-enact Minimum Wages," *NYT*, March 30, 1937, pp. 1, 15; "Lehman Plans Wage Talks; Albany Undecided," *NYT*, March 31, 1937, pp. 1, 10; "President Revives Wage Law Plans," *NYT*, March 31, 1937, pp. 1, 10; "8 States to Meet on New Wage Law," *NYT*, April 1, 1937, p. 13; Lehman Submits Minimum Pay Plan to Legislature," *NYT*, April 6, 1937, pp. 1, 18; "Minimum Pay Bill Signed by Lehman," *NYT*, April 28, 1937, p. 9; HHLOH, p. 474; Charles Poletti Oral History Transcript (1957), HHLP, CUOHC, p. 6. In *Morehead v. New York ex rel Tipaldo*, 298 U.S. 587 (1936), the U.S. Supreme Court ruled 5 to 4 that New York State's 1933 minimum wage law for women and minors employed in industry violated the individual worker's freedom of contract. But in March 1937, the Court upheld a similar Washington State law in *West Coast Hotel v. Parrish*, 300 U.S. 379 (1937). See Leuchtenburg, "The Case of the Wenatchee Chambermaid," in Leuchtenburg, *The Supreme Court Reborn*, pp. 163–179. In *Muller v. Oregon*, 208 U.S. 412 (1908), the U.S. Supreme Court had upheld an Oregon law setting maximum hours for women in factories and laundries, ruling that women's special status entitled them to such protection.

9. "Lehman Promises Wage Law Fight," *NYT*, October 13, 1936, p. 12; "Text of Governor Lehman's Message Read by Him before the Legislature," *NYT*, January 7, 1937, p. 14; "Roosevelt Calls on Courts to Help Adapt Constitution to Our Needs; . . . Basic Law Upheld," *NYT*, January 7, 1937, pp. 1, 4; "Text of President Roosevelt's Message Read in Person before Congress," January 7, 1937, p. 2; Leuchtenburg, "The Origins of Franklin D. Roosevelt's 'Court-packing' Plan," in Leuchtenburg, *The Supreme Court Reborn*, pp. 108–110.

10. "Roosevelt Asks Power to Reform Courts . . . ; Surprise Message," *NYT*, February 6, 1937, pp. 1, 8; "Bill Is Introduced," *NYT*, February 6, 1937, pp. 1, 9; "Six on High Bench Eligible to Retire," *NYT*, February 6, 1937, pp. 1, 10; Leuchtenburg, "FDR's 'Court-packing' Plan," in Leuchtenburg, *The Supreme Court Reborn*, pp. 132–162.

11. HHLOH, pp. 605–607, 614, 621; Lehman to Wald, January 11, 1934, LP, SF, Wald; Lehman to La Guardia, January 5, 1934, LP, SF, La Guardia; Samuel Rosenman Oral History Transcript, HHLP, CUOHC, pp. 9–10; 101 *Congressional Record* 992 (1955). On Lehman and the Formosa Resolution, see chapter 16.

12. HHLOH, pp. 605–606; Lehman to Roosevelt, February 26, 1937, LP, SF, Franklin Roosevelt; "Heck Assails Plan 'to Control Courts'; . . . Lehman Is Silent," *NYT*, February 6, 1937, p. 11.

13. "New Act Opens in Court Bill's Stormy Drama," *NYT*, July 18, 1937, E-3; Samuel Rosenman Oral History Transcript, HHLP, CUOHC, pp. 11–12; Leuchtenburg, "FDR's 'Court-packing' Plan," in Leuchtenburg, *The Supreme Court Reborn*, pp. 132–162.

14. HHLOH, pp. 605–607; Charles Poletti Oral History Transcript (1957), HHLP, CUOHC, pp. 12–14.

15. "Lehman Calls Court Plan Dangerous and Asks Wagner to Vote Against It," "Gov. Lehman's Letter," and "Letter Is Surprise," all in *NYT*, July 20, 1937, pp. 1–3. On Wagner, see Wagner to Lehman, July 21, 1937, LP, SF, Wagner; "Wagner Reserves Opinion on Court," *NYT*, July 22, 1937, pp. 1, 2; and Huthmacher, *Senator Robert F. Wagner and the Rise of Urban Liberalism*, pp. 221–223.

16. *NYT*, July 20, 1937, pp. 1–3, 22; "Lehman Calls Court Plan Dangerous and Asks Wagner to Vote Against It; . . . Letter Is Surprise," *NYT*, July 20, 1937, pp. 1, 3;

"Lehman Long Ally of the President," *NYT*, July 20, 1937, p. 3; "Court Bill's Foes Hail Lehman Aid," *NYT*, July 20, 1937, p. 3; "The Governor's Letter," Editorial, *NYT*, July 20, 1937, p. 22; "Court Change to Be Shelved for Present, . . . to End Long Fight," *NYT*, July 21, 1937, pp. 1, 2; "Court Bill Is Killed, 70 to 20, . . . a Full Surrender," *NYT*, July 23, 1937, pp. 1, 2; Turner Catledge, "Combination of Forces Defeated the Court Bill," *NYT*, July 25, 1937, p. 49; Baker, *Back to Back*, pp. 258–259; Shesol, *Supreme Power*, pp. 496–500. Lehman's letter was important, but Max Freedman over-states its significance when he describes it as "a letter which changed American history." There was already considerable opposition to the President's proposal before Lehman's letter. On the other hand, Burt Solomon never even mentions Lehman's letter, completely overlooking its significance. See Freedman, ed., *Roosevelt and Frankfurter*, p. 403; Solo-mon, *FDR v. the Constitution*; James Farley Oral History Transcript, HHLP, CUOHC, pp. 1–2. Walter Trohan, the longtime Washington correspondent of the conservative *Chicago Tribune*, later claimed that when Roosevelt learned about Lehman's letter, he commented off the record to the reporters gathered around him at Hyde Park, "What else could you expect from a Jew?" However, the accuracy of Trohan's account, which is not supported by any other sources, seems highly questionable. The President was in Washington, not Hyde Park, when the Lehman letter hit the papers. Moreover, as discussed in chapter 13, Trohan was not above writing anti-Semitic diatribes for the *Tribune*. See Trohan, *Political Animals*, pp. 5–6, 99; and Walter Trohan Oral History Transcript, HSTL, pp. 51–53.

17. James Farley, Personal Memorandum, July 21, 1937, Farley Papers, Box 41, Private File, July 1937; Farley, *Jim Farley's Story*, p. 94; Scroop, *Mr. Democrat*, p. 158; Roosevelt to Frankfurter, July 20, 1937, and July 22, 1937, in Freedman, ed., *Roosevelt and Frankfurter*, pp. 403–404; "Roosevelt Is Firm," *NYT*, July 20, 1937, pp. 1, 2; "Court Change to be Shelved for Present, Capital Hears After White House Parleys; . . . to End Long Fight," *NYT*, July 21, 1937, pp. 1, 2; Ickes, *Secret Diaries*, II: 171.

18. Ickes, *Secret Diaries*, II: 166–168.

19. Herbert Lehman to Franklin Roosevelt, January 22, 1937, and Edith Lehman to Marguerite LeHand, January 26, 1937, both in Franklin Roosevelt Papers, PPF 93, Lehman, 1936–1939; Certificate signed by Harry Doherty appointing Herbert Lehman Honorary Chairman for New York for the Birthday Ball for the President, January 1937, LP, SF, Franklin Roosevelt; Eleanor Roosevelt to Edith Lehman, January 25, 1937, Elea-nor Roosevelt Papers, Box 655, White House Correspondence, Personal Letters, 1937, LE; Herbert Lehman to Franklin Roosevelt, February 26, 1937, and Herbert Lehman to President and Mrs. Roosevelt, June 30, 1937, both in LP, SF, Franklin Roosevelt; "Lehman Acclaims a 'Vitalized' Era," *NYT*, March 5, 1937, p. 15; Charles Poletti Oral History Transcript (1957), HHLP, CUOHC, pp. 13–14.

20. Edith Lehman to Wagner, February 25, 1937, LP, SF, Robert F. Wagner, Sr.; Charles Poletti Oral History Transcript, 1957, HHLP, CUOHC, pp. 12–14; Ickes, *Secret Diaries*, II: 232–233. On Mrs. Lehman's role in general, see "Mrs. Lehman Shares Politi-cal Burdens," *Christian Science Monitor*, January 2, 1937, LP, SF, Edith Altschul Lehman.

21. Herbert Lehman to John Lehman, September 30, 1945, LP, UNRRA, Personal Correspondence and General Files, John Lehman; HHLOH, p. 98; Herbert Lehman to Irving Lehman, July 19, 1937; Irving Lehman to Herbert Lehman, July 20, 1937;

and Irving Lehman to Herbert Lehman, July 24, 1937; all in LP, SF, Irving Lehman; Samuel Rosenman Oral History Transcript, HHLP, CUOHC, pp. 9–10; Moscow, *Politics in the Empire State*, p. 20; McKenna, *Franklin Roosevelt and the Great Constitutional War*, pp. 514–515.

22. Arthur Krock, "In the Nation: Possible Effects of Governor Lehman's Letter," *NYT*, July 20, 1937, p. 22; HHLOH, p. 607; Samuel Rosenman Oral History Transcript, HHLP, CUOHC, p. 10; "Roosevelt's Views of Aides Disclosed," *NYT*, June 20, 1947, p. 14; Eleanor Roosevelt Oral History Transcript, HHLP, CUOHC, pp. 7–8; "Lehman to Attend Fete," *NYT*, August 30, 1938, p. 19; "Governors Predict Roosevelt Tax Aid," *NYT*, September 17, 1937, pp. 1, 26.

23. Ickes, *Secret Diaries*, II: 282; "Labor Party Turns Fire upon Lehman," *NYT*, July 20, 1937, p. 3; "The Shape of Things," *The Nation*, July 24, 1937, p. 85; "The Week," *New Republic*, July 28, 1937, pp. 317–318.

24. Steve to Mr. President, August 26, 1937; Roosevelt to Stephen Gibbons, August 29, 1937; Joseph Biben to Franklin Roosevelt, March 2, 1938; S.T.E. to Missy, March 3, 1938; F.D.R., Memorandum for S.T.E., March 4, 1938; and Roosevelt to Lehman, March 28, 1938; all in Roosevelt Papers, PPF 93, Lehman, 1936–1939; Farley, *Jim Farley's Story*, p. 125.

25. "Lehman Is Urged for Wagner Seat." *NYT*, March 7, 1938, p. 7; "State Democrats to 'Draft' Wagner," *NYT*, April 12, 1938, pp. 1, 14; "State Candidates Discussed," *NYT*, June 5, 1938, p. 74; Lehman to Lillian Wald, July 1, 1938, LP, SF, Lillian Wald; HHLOH, pp. 500, 670.

26. Ickes, *Secret Diaries*, II: 282; "The Shape of Things," *The Nation*, January 8, 1938, p. 31; "Fall Plans Upset by Copeland's Death," *NYT*, June 18, 1938, p. 3; "Death of Copeland Shifts Poll Line-Up," *NYT*, June 19, 1938, pp. 1, 28.

27. James Hagerty, "Death of Copeland Shifts Poll Line-Up," *NYT*, June 19, 1938, pp. 1, 28; Hagerty, "Foes of Lehman's Candidacy Ask President to Back Mayor Instead," *NYT*, June 22, 1938, pp. 1, 6; Warren Moscow, "Lehman to Run for Senate; . . . Governor in Lead," *NYT*, June 22, 1938, pp. 1, 6; "Await Roosevelt View," *NYT*, June 22, 1938, p. 6.

28. Farley, *Jim Farley's Story*, pp. 139–140.

29. Editorial, "Candidate for Senator," *NYT*, June 22, 1938, p. 22; "Foes of Lehman's Candidacy Ask President to Back Mayor Instead," *NYT*, June 22, 1938, pp. 1, 6; "Labor Party Threatens 3-Cornered State Race Unless Terms Are Met," *NYT*, June 23, 1938, pp. 1, 6.

30. "Foes of Lehman's Candidacy Ask President to Back Mayor Instead," *NYT*, June 22, 1938, pp. 1, 6; "Lehman Declines to Name Senator," *NYT*, June 23, 1938, pp. 1, 6; "President Urges Fund to Fight Spies," *NYT*, June 25, 1938, pp. 1, 4; "Roosevelt Ready to Accept Lehman," *NYT*, June 25, 1938, pp. 1, 2.

31. "La Guardia Will Not Run for U.S. Senate This Year; 1940 Candidacy Possible," *NYT*, June 26, 1938, pp. 1, 3.

32. "Washington Notes: Labor's Army Makes Contact," *New Republic*, July 20, 1938, p. 306; "Labor Names M'Goldrick with Hillman and Wagner for Independent Ticket," *NYT*, July 2, 1938, pp. 1, 2; "The Shape of Things," *The Nation*, July 9, 1938, p. 29; "Washington Notes: The ALP Breaks Loose," *New Republic*, August 10, 1938,

p. 16; "Dubinsky Assails Failure of Labor to Name Lehman," *NYT*, July 3, 1938, pp. 1, 4; "Antonini Rejects Boom for Hillman," *NYT*, July 6, 1938, p. 10; Fraser, *Labor Will Rule*, pp. 437–438.

33. "High Court Chance Seen for Wagner," *NYT*, July 11, 1938, pp. 1, 2; "Balanced Budget and Cash Surplus Shown for State," *NYT*, July 6, 1938, pp. 1, 4; "Roosevelt Aids Campaigns of Barkley and Bulkley; Explains New York Deficit; 'Not Interfering,'" *NYT*, July 9, 1938, pp. 1, 3; "President Roosevelt's Speeches for Ohio and Kentucky Senators," *NYT*, July 9, 1938, p. 2; "President Stirs Albany Issue by State Deficit Statement," *NYT*, July 10, 1938, pp. 1, 2; "Desmond Sees Rift Widened," *NYT*, July 10, 1938, p. 2.

34. Roosevelt to Lehman, June 13, 1938, and Lehman to Roosevelt, August 30, 1938, LP, SF, Franklin Roosevelt. There are no letters from FDR inviting Lehman to Hyde Park during this period in either the Lehman Papers or the FDR Library.

35. Lehman to Roosevelt, August 30, 1938, LP, SF, Franklin Roosevelt.

36. "Race for Governor Impends," *NYT*, January 16, 1938, p. 67; "Lehman to Attend Fete," *NYT*, August 30, 1938, p. 19; Roosevelt to Lehman, September 7, 1938, and Lehman to Roosevelt, September 9, 1938, both in Roosevelt Papers, PSF Subject File, Box 141, Lehman; "Roosevelt Likens '38 Fear-Mongers to Those of 1788," *NYT*, September 18, 1938, pp. 1, 43; "Lehman Asks Vigilance," *NYT*, September 18, 1938, p. 43; Arthur Krock, "In the Nation: On the 'Redrafting' of Governor Lehman," *NYT*, September 9, 1938, p. 20; "Lehman Is Drafted for Fourth Term," *NYT*, October 1, 1938, pp. 1, 6.

37. Farley, *Jim Farley's Story*, pp. 109–113, 117, 136, 142–143; La Guardia to Roosevelt, February 1, 1938, Roosevelt Papers, PSF Subject File, Box 141, La Guardia; Jackson, *That Man*, pp. 31–38; Herbert Bayard Swope to Roosevelt, May 25, 1937, Roosevelt Papers, PPF 331, Swope; "Jackson Willing to Be Nominee, He Says at Party Peace Council," *NYT*, January 9, 1938, pp. 1, 5; "Boom for Jackson to Be Revived Here," *NYT*, February 14, 1938, p. 34; "Wagner Bars Race for Governorship," *NYT*, September 26, 1938, pp. 1, 9; Flynn, *You're the Boss*, p. 152.

38. "'Draft' of Lehman Put to Roosevelt as Party's Tactic," *NYT*, September 8, 1938, pp. 1, 7; Arthur Krock, "In the Nation: On the 'Redrafting' of Governor Lehman," *NYT*, September 9, 1938, p. 20; "Policy and Politics," *The Nation*, September 10, 1938, pp. 236–237; "Democrats Plan to Draft Lehman," *NYT*, September 27, 1938, p. 4; Poletti to Lehman, n.d., but probably May or June 1938, document 0737_0042, LP, SF, Charles Poletti; HHLOH, pp. 262–263, 651–652, 670–671; Flynn, *You're the Boss*, p. 152; Farley, *Jim Farley's Story*, pp. 125, 147; Moscow, *Politics in the Empire State*, pp. 87–88. On Dewey's ambitions, see also Felix Frankfurter to Lehman, October 4, 1938, LP, SF, Frankfurter.

39. James Farley, Personal Memorandum, September 26, 1938, Farley Papers, Box 43, Private File, September 1938; HHLOH, pp. 671–672; "Draft of Lehman Near, Farley Says," *NYT*, September 29, 1938, p. 21. Farley's memorandum is dated September 26, but it was clearly written after the convention had concluded on September 30.

40. "Draft of Lehman Near, Farley Says," *NYT*, September 29, 1938, p. 21; "Democrats Await Lehman's Reply," *NYT*, September 30, 1938, pp. 1, 17; James Farley, Personal Memorandum, September 26, 1938, Farley Papers, Box 43, Private File, September 1938; HHLOH, p. 262.

41. James Farley, Personal Memorandum, September 26, 1938, Farley Papers, Box 43, Private File, September 1938. In January 1939, FDR nominated Felix Frankfurter to fill this vacancy on the Supreme Court. The fifty-six-year-old Frankfurter was younger than Irving Lehman, but he was from Massachusetts, hardly a Western state. See "Frankfurter Is Nominated as Supreme Court Justice," *NYT*, January 6, 1939, pp. 1, 11; "Frankfurter Akin to Holmes, Cardozo," *NYT*, January 6, 1939, p. 11.

42. James Farley, Personal Memorandum, September 26, 1938, Farley Papers, Box 43, Private File, September 1938; "Democrats Await Lehman's Reply," *NYT*, September 30, 1938, pp. 1, 17; "Lehman Is Drafted for Fourth Term; He Attacks Dewey," *NYT*, October 1, 1938, pp. 1, 6; "Mrs. Lehman Is 'Reconciled' to the Governor's Decision to Stand for Re-Election," *NYT*, October 1, 1938, p. 7; HHLOH, pp. 262–268, 652–653, 671–673; Charles Poletti Oral History Transcript (1957), HHLP, CUOHC, pp. 19, 21–22; Carolin Flexner Oral History Transcript, HHLP, CUOHC, p. 58.

43. "Mrs. Lehman Is 'Reconciled' to the Governor's Decision to Stand for Re-Election," *NYT*, October 1, 1938, p. 7.

44. HHLOH, pp. 637–644, 650, 652–654, 672; Charles Poletti Oral History Transcript (1957), HHLP, CUOHC, pp. 16–17; James Farley, Personal Memorandum, September 26, 1938, Farley Papers, Box 43, Private File, September 1938; "Dewey Nominated by Republicans; Attacks Tammany," *NYT*, September 30, 1938, pp. 1, 15; "Address of Thomas E. Dewey Accepting Nomination," *NYT*, September 30, 1938, p. 14; "Lehman Is Drafted for Fourth Term; He Attacks Dewey," *NYT*, October 1, 1938, pp. 1, 6; "Governor's Acceptance," *NYT*, October 1, 1938, p. 7; "Lehman's Decision Filled with Drama," *NYT*, October 1, 1938, p. 7; "The News of the Week in Review: New York, Lehman vs. Dewey," *NYT*, October 2, 1938, E-2; "Governor Lehman Here, Plans Campaign," *New York Journal and American*, October 1, 1938, pp. 1, 4. On Dewey, see also Moscow, *Politics in the Empire State*, pp. 29–31. On Lehman's appointment of Dewey in 1935, see Smith, *Thomas E. Dewey and His Times*, pp. 147–152; "Dewey Chosen by Lehman to Head Racket Inquiry; Acceptance Held Certain," *NYT*, June 30, 1935, pp. 1, 3; "Lehman Appeals to 'Racket Ridden' for Aid in Inquiry," *NYT*, July 6, 1935, pp. 1, 28; Memorandum, Lehman to Allan Nevins, January 4, 1962, p. 15, LP, SF, Nevins. On Lehman's efforts as Governor to combat organized crime, graft, malfeasance, and corruption, see Nevins, *Herbert H. Lehman and His Era*, pp. 177–187; and Tananbaum, *Drawn to Public Service*, pp. 19, 38–45.

45. James Farley, Personal Memorandum, September 26, 1938, Farley Papers, Box 43, Private File, September 1938; Roosevelt to John Boyd Thacher, September 30, 1938, Roosevelt Papers, PSF Subject File, Box 141, Lehman; "Roosevelt 'Happy' Lehman Will Run," *NYT*, October 1, 1938, p. 8; Raymond Clapper, "Noble Experiment," clipping from *Washington Daily News*, October 1, 1938, and Early to Clapper, October 1, 1938, both in Roosevelt Papers, PPF 93, Lehman, 1936–1939.

46. Jackson to Rosenman, October 3, 1938, Rosenman Papers, Box 2, General Correspondence, Jackson, FDRL.

47. "Antonini Rejects Boom for Hillman," *NYT*, July 6, 1938, p. 10; "Laborites Name Lehman, Wagner; Adopt Platform," *NYT*, October 4, 1938, pp. 1, 17; "Close Finish Is Likely in the State Campaign," *NYT*, October 9, 1938, p. 80.

48. "The Labor Party Shows Its Colors," *New Republic*, October 12, 1938, p. 254; "Washington Notes: The ALP Cashes In," *New Republic*, October 19, 1938, p. 304;

"Lehman Should Win," *The Nation*, October 8, 1938, p. 342; "Next Week's Elections," *The Nation*, November 5, 1938, p. 469; "The Shape of Things," *The Nation*, November 19, 1938, p. 521.

49. "Roosevelt Awaits Pennsylvania Plea," *NYT*, October 6, 1938, p. 2; "President Plans to See Lehman," *NYT*, October 5, 1938, p. 2. On FDR's attempted purge of conservative Democrats in the primaries, see Farley, *Jim Farley's Story*, pp. 120–150; Dunn, *Roosevelt's Purge*; Wolf, "The 1938 Purge: A Re-Examination," in Wolf, Pederson, and Daynes, eds., *Franklin D. Roosevelt and Congress*, II: 108–121; Allswang, *The New Deal and American Politics*, pp. 121–126; Polenberg, "Franklin Roosevelt and the Purge of John O'Connor"; Patterson, *Congressional Conservatism and the New Deal*, pp. 270–287; and Scroop, *Mr. Democrat*, pp. 165–173.

50. Roosevelt, Memorandum to Herbert H. Lehman, October 10, 1938, in Elliott Roosevelt, ed., *F.D.R.*, II: 815; John Godfrey Saxe to Roosevelt, October 7, 1938, and Roosevelt to Saxe, October 11, 1938, Roosevelt Papers, PPF 1763, Saxe.

51. Bill to the President, October 14, 1938, Roosevelt Papers, PSF, Box 141, Lehman. Even with the help of the staff at the Franklin Roosevelt Library, I have not been able to identify the writer of this memo, signed only "Bill," with the notation at the bottom: "Head of the King Syndicate." The higher the Crossley rating, the more listeners a radio program had.

52. James Farley, Personal Memorandum, October 14, 1938, Farley Papers, Box 43, Private File, October 1938; "President to Speak on State Race; Radio Talk Will 'Interest Nation,'" *NYT*, October 15, 1938, pp. 1, 6; "Roosevelt Speaks for Lehman Nov. 4," *NYT*, October 16, 1938, p. 14.

53. "Lehman Silent on the New Deal After His Talk with Roosevelt," *NYT*, October 19, 1938, pp. 1, 6; Arthur Krock, "In the Nation: Quiz Not Based on Lehman's Chief Problem," *NYT*, October 20, 1938, p. 22; Krock, "In the Nation: Trials of a Good Samaritan in Politics," *NYT*, October 25, 1938, p. 22.

54. "An Independent Governor," Editorial, *NYT*, October 26, 1938, p. 22; "Lehman Silent on the New Deal After His Talk with Roosevelt," *NYT*, October 19, 1938, pp. 1, 6; "Lehman Refuses to O.K. New Deal at F.D.R. Parley," *New York Daily News*, October 19, 1938; "Wagner Advocates New Deal Avowal," *NYT*, October 23, 1938, pp. 1, 34.

55. "Mayor Is Neutral in Governor Race," *NYT*, October 1, 1938, p. 8; "La Guardia Aid Claimed for Dewey," *New York Journal and American*, October 4, 1938, p. 5; "Republicans See Mayor for Dewey," *NYT*, October 4, 1938, pp. 1, 26; James Farley, Personal Memorandum, October 14, 1938, Farley Papers, Box 43, Private File, October 1938; "La Guardia Insists Lehman Proclaim He Is for New Deal," *NYT*, October 22, 1938, pp. 1, 2; Arthur Krock, "In the Nation: The Mayor Grasps the Horn of a Dilemma," *NYT*, November 4, 1938, p. 22; Williams, *City of Ambition*, pp. 272–274.

56. M. A. LeHand to Mrs. E. L. Masters, October 21, 1938, Roosevelt Papers, PPF 93, Lehman, 1936–1939; "Gov. Lehman Urges Aid for President in Humane Aims," *NYT*, October 23, 1938, pp. 1, 34.

57. Arthur Krock, "In the Nation: Quiz Not Based on Lehman's Chief Problem," *NYT*, October 20, 1938, p. 22; "Dewey's Address at Republican Rally in Utica," *NYT*, October 21, 1938, p. 14; "Six Picked for Hines Jury as He Stands Trial Alone; Dewey Names Politicians," *NYT*, August 16, 1938, pp. 1, 12; "Geoghan to Be Superseded in

Brooklyn Graft Cases; Lehman Plans Full Inquiry," *NYT*, October 14, 1938, pp. 1, 3; "Dewey Denounces Party 'Monopoly,'" *NYT*, October 21, 1938, pp. 1, 4; "Dewey Declares Governor Fought Drive for Clean Government Here; . . . Assails Race Issue," *NYT*, November 4, 1938, pp. 1, 4; "State Campaign Issues Are Defined," *NYT*, October 23, 1938, p. 73; "Lehman Promises to Serve Full Four Years in Office; . . . Replies to Rumor," *NYT*, October 15, 1938, pp. 1, 5; James Farley, Personal Memoranda, October 3, 1938, October 4, 1938, October 7, 1938, October 19, 1938, October 30, 1938, and October 31, 1938, all in Farley Papers, Box 43, Personal File, October 1938; Farley, *Jim Farley's Story*, p. 148. While Lehman was concerned about Catholic defections, there is no basis whatsoever for Ronald Bayor's assertion that Lehman's opposition to Roosevelt's court-packing plan was part of an effort by the Governor to win back Catholic voters. See Bayor, *Neighbors in Conflict*, p. 48. On Dewey's campaign and the Hines trial, see also Smith, *Thomas E. Dewey and His Times*, pp. 252–274.

58. "Lehman Promises to Serve Full Four Years in Office; He and Poletti Spurn Reds; Replies to Rumor," *NYT*, October 15, 1938, pp. 1, 5; "Addresses of Lehman and Poletti," *NYT*, October 15, 1938, p. 5; "Lehman Charges Falsity and Vilification to Rival; . . . Governor Hits Out," *NYT*, October 25, 1938, pp. 1, 10; "Bray Is Pledged to Lehman Ticket," *NYT*, October 24, 1938, pp. 1, 3; "Bray Introduces Lehman at Utica," *NYT*, October 26, 1938, pp. 1, 5; HHLOH, pp. 267–268; "Priest Won Over to Poletti Cause," *NYT*, October 19, 1938, pp. 1, 4; "Geoghan to Be Superseded in Brooklyn Graft Cases; Lehman Plans Full Inquiry," *NYT*, October 14, 1938, pp. 1, 3; "Amen Is Appointed in Geoghan's Place For Graft Inquiry," *NYT*, October 18, 1938, pp. 1, 27; "Lehman, Up-State, Cites His Record; Challenges Rival," *NYT*, October 21, 1938, pp. 1, 12; "Dewey's Address at Republican Rally in Utica," *NYT*, October 21, 1938, p. 14; "Lehman Accepts 'Bookkeeper' Title," *NYT*, October 22, 1938, pp. 1, 3; Charles Poletti Oral History Transcript (1957), HHLP, CUOHC, p. 19; Bayor, *Neighbors in Conflict*, pp. 48–50.

59. "National Issues Enter the New York Campaign," *NYT*, October 30, 1938, p. 73; Arthur Krock, "In Washington: The Coming Sources of Post-Election Behavior," *NYT*, November 1, 1938, p. 22; "Lehman and Rival Are Even in Survey," *NYT*, October 24, 1938, p. 3; "Dewey and Lehman Found Even in Race," *NYT*, November 3, 1938, p. 5; "Up-State Figured 450,000 for Dewey," *NYT*, October 31, 1938, p. 7; "Wallace Praises Lehman Policies," *NYT*, November 4, 1938, p. 19.

60. Berle and Jacobs, eds., *Navigating the Rapids, 1918–1971*, p. 190; "La Guardia Will Support Governor; . . . Decision by Mayor," *NYT*, November 3, 1938, pp. 1, 3; "Mayor Calls Lehman 'Our Great Governor,'" *NYT*, November 5, 1938, p. 4; "'A Progressive Governor' Wins a Word from Mayor," *NYT*, November 6, 1938, p. 36; "Forum Scores Bias," *NYT*, November 7, 1938, pp. 1, 5; Arthur Krock, "In the Nation: The Mayor Grasps the Horn of a Dilemma," *NYT*, November 4, 1938, p. 22; HHLOH, p. 612; Kessner, *Fiorello H. La Guardia and the Making of Modern New York*, pp. 463–464; Williams, *City of Ambition*, p. 274.

61. "Roosevelt Appeals for Gov. Lehman, Wagner, Mead, Murphy of Michigan; . . . Presses New Deal," *NYT*, November 5, 1938, pp. 1, 5; "Text of President's Address from Hyde Park on Issues in the Coming Election," *NYT*, November 5, 1938, p. 5; "Roosevelt Talk Termed 'Magnificent' by Lehman," *NYT*, November 5, 1938, p. 5; James Farley, Personal Memorandum, November 4, 1940 [*sic*], Farley Papers, Box

43, Private File, November 1938; "Both Parties See Victory in State," *NYT*, November 6, 1938, p. 39; "State for Willkie, Survey Indicates," *NYT*, October 29, 1940, p. 21.

62. "Dewey Declares Governor Fought Drive for Clean Government Here; . . . Assails Race Issue," *NYT*, November 4, 1938, pp. 1, 13; "Anti-Semitism Seen in Republican Drive," *NYT*, November 4, 1938, p. 19; Moscow, *Politics in the Empire State*, p. 22; Smith, *Thomas E. Dewey and His Times*, p. 272.

63. "Roosevelt Is Back at Hyde Park Home," *NYT*, November 3, 1938, p. 3; "Roosevelt Appeals for Gov. Lehman, Wagner, Mead, Murphy of Michigan; . . . Presses New Deal," *NYT*, November 5, 1938, pp. 1, 5; "Text of President's Address from Hyde Park on Issues in the Coming Election," *NYT*, November 5, 1938, p. 5; "Lehman Says Foes Raise Race Issue; Lehman Fears Isms," *NYT*, November 6, 1938, pp. 1, 34; "The Text of Governor Lehman's Address Winding Up His Campaign Here," *NYT*, November 6, 1938, p. 34; HHLOH, p. 774.

64. "Gov. Lehman and His Slate Elected; Big Republican Gains in the Nation; . . . State Vote Close," *NYT*, November 9, 1938, pp. 1, 2; "G.O.P. Groundswell," *NYT*, November 13, 1938, E-1; "Governors Elected," *NYT*, November 10, 1938, p. 24; "Lehman Is Victor by 67,506 Margin," *NYT*, November 10, 1938, p. 13; "Governor Lehman's Vote," Editorial, *NYT*, November 11, 1938, p. 24; "Governor Lehman Re-Elected," Editorial, *NYT*, November 9, 1938, p. 22; HHLOH, pp. 650–651; Plesur, "The Republican Congressional Comeback of 1938." Official vote tallies are from Hutchins, ed., *The New York Red Book, 1940*, p. 453. The City Hall estimate of two hundred thousand votes influenced by La Guardia is from "Mayor Denounces Conditions in Kings," *NYT*, November 4, 1938, pp. 1, 16.

65. Arthur Krock, "Big Republican Gains in the Nation; . . . Win Back 10 States," *NYT*, November 9, 1938, pp. 1, 4; "Roosevelt 'Grins' Over State Results," *NYT*, November 9, 1938, p. 5; "Gov. Lehman and His Slate Elected; Big Republican Gains in the Nation; . . . State Vote Close," *NYT*, November 9, 1938, pp. 1, 2; "Vote Splits State Control," *NYT*, November 13, 1938, p. 77; Ickes, *Secret Diaries*, II: 499; "Ickes Says Roosevelt Won in Vote; Wallace Calls It a New Deal Defeat," *NYT*, November 11, 1938, pp. 1, 20; "Roosevelt Holds Coalition Threat to 'Liberalism' Dim," *NYT*, November 12, 1938, pp. 1, 9; "G.O.P. Groundswell," *NYT*, November 13, 1938, E-1; Patterson, *Congressional Conservatism and the New Deal*, pp. 288–337. The unsuccessful Republican Senate candidates in New York in 1938 were John Lord O'Brian, who lost to Senator Wagner, and Edward Corsi, who lost to Representative James Mead.

66. "President Opens Fair as a Symbol of Peace; . . . Roosevelt Speaks," *NYT*, May 1, 1939, pp. 1, 4; "President Is Host to 24 Governors," *NYT*, June 29, 1939, p. 25; "King Tries Hot Dog and Asks for More," *NYT*, June 12, 1939, pp. 1, 5; Roosevelt to Lehman May 19, 1939, and Lehman to Roosevelt, May 22, 1939, LP, SF, Franklin Roosevelt; "Signs Roosevelt Library Bill," *NYT*, May 24, 1939, p. 29.

67. "Lehman Protests Slash in WPA Fund," *NYT*, January 19, 1939, p. 8; Patterson, *Congressional Conservatism and the New Deal*, pp. 294–324; Divine, *The Illusion of Neutrality*, pp. 229–285.

68. "State Senate Shift," *NYT*, November 10, 1938, pp. 1, 13; "Legislature Votes Republican Budget, Slashing Lehman's," *NYT*, April 29, 1939, pp. 1, 4; "$64,000,000 in New Taxes Asked in Lehman's Budget; Year's Outlay $411,682,122; Largest in History," *NYT*, January 31, 1939, pp. 1, 15; "G.O.P. at Albany Sees Gain for '40," *NYT*,

May 22, 1939, p. 2; "$150,000,000 Housing Voted as Legislature Adjourns; Budget Reduced $25,000,000," *NYT*, May 21, 1939, pp. 1, 37; "Lehman's and Moffat's Views on Republican Budget Plan," *NYT*, April 28, 1939, p. 18; "Lehman Calls Legislature as Court Upsets Budget; Education Cuts Held Legal; Lump Sum Banned," *NYT*, June 22, 1939, pp. 1, 4; "Republicans Split Anew with Lehman on Eve of Session," *NYT*, June 23, 1939, pp. 1, 2; "School Pay Cuts Defeated as Legislature Adjourns," *NYT*, July 11, 1939, pp. 1, 35.

Chapter 6. "Fighting for Freedom, for Security, and for the Dignity of Man": Lehman and Roosevelt, 1933–1942

1. HHLOH, pp. 546.

2. HHLOH, p. 538; Irving Lehman to President Roosevelt, September 21, 1933, copy attached to Irving Lehman to Henry Morgenthau, Jr., October 5, 1933, Henry Morgenthau, Jr. Papers, Box 185, Correspondence, Judge Irving Lehman, FDRL; Breitman and Kraut, *American Refugee Policy and European Jewry, 1933–1945*, pp. 7–8, 11–12; Breitman and Lichtman, *FDR and the Jews*, pp. 67–71.

3. Transcript of Phone Conversation between Lehman and Wise, LP, SF, Stephen S. Wise, document 0974_0051. There is no date on this document, although "Feb?" and "1933?" were both added at some later date. The conversation was probably on March 21, 1933. The document is misidentified as a speech on April 24, 1933, in the digital version of the Lehman Papers Special Files. See also Wise to Louis Brandeis, March 23, 1933, in Voss, ed., *Stephen S. Wise*, pp. 180–181; "250,000 Jews Here to Protest Today," *NYT*, March 27, 1933, p. 4; "Lehman Appeals to German People," *NYT*, March 28, 1933, p. 12; Flade, *The Lehmans*, pp. 90–91; Wise, *Challenging Years*, pp. 240–245; Breitman and Lichtman, *FDR and the Jews*, pp. 52–54.

4. Jay Pierrepont Moffat to George Gordon, April 4, 1933, Moffat Papers, Am 1407, vol. 3, Houghton Library, Harvard University; Freidel, *Franklin D. Roosevelt: Launching the New Deal*, pp. 390–398; Roosevelt to Irving Lehman, May 18, 1933, Roosevelt Papers, PPF 436, Irving Lehman; "Drive to Aid Jews Opened by Lehman," *NYT*, June 15, 1933, p. 9; Irving Lehman to President Roosevelt, September 21, 1933, and Irving Lehman to Secretary Hull, September 27, 1933, both attached to Irving Lehman to Henry Morgenthau, Jr., October 5, 1933, Henry Morgenthau, Jr. Papers, Box 185, Correspondence, Judge Irving Lehman; Breitman and Lichtman, *FDR and the Jews*, pp. 60–63, 67–72; Shogan, *Prelude to Catastrophe*, p. 115.

5. McDonald to Warburg, October 10, 1935, in Breitman, Stewart, and Hochberg, eds., *Refugees and Rescue*, pp. 44–45; McDonald to Warburg, October 29, 1935, and Lehman to Roosevelt, November 15, 1935, both in LP, SF, Franklin Roosevelt; Lehman to Roosevelt, November 1, 1935, in Nixon, ed., *Franklin D. Roosevelt and Foreign Affairs*, III: 50–51. On the passage of the Nuremberg laws, see "Reich Adopts Swastika as Nation's Official Flag; . . . Anti-Jewish Laws Passed," *NYT*, September 16, 1935, pp. 1, 11; "Hope of Reich Jews Is Dimmed by Events," *NYT*, September 22, 1935, E-6. On McDonald, see "M'Donald Named as Refugee Chief," *NYT*, October 27, 1933, p. 10; "League Aid Asked by M'Donald to End Nazi Persecution," *NYT*, December 30, 1935, pp. 1, 12; "Reich Law Defined as Officials' Whim," *NYT*, December

30, 1935, p. 12; "Text of Resignation of League Commissioner for German Refugees," *NYT*, December 30, 1935, p. 12; and Breitman, Stewart, and Hochberg, eds., *Advocate for the Doomed*. On Warburg, see "F. M. Warburg Dies at 66 in Home Here," *NYT*, October 21, 1937, pp. 1, 18; and Chernow, *The Warburgs*.

6. Roosevelt to Lehman, November 13, 1935, in Nixon, ed., *Franklin D. Roosevelt and Foreign Affairs*, III: 64–66.

7. Lehman to Roosevelt, June 15, 1936, in Nixon, ed., *Franklin D. Roosevelt and Foreign Affairs*, III: 323; Warburg to Lehman, June 5, 1936; and Herbert Samuel to Warburg, May 27, 1936, both in LP, SF, Franklin Roosevelt; Lehman to Warburg, June 15, 1936, LP, SF, Warburg.

8. Roosevelt to Lehman, July 2, 1936, in Nixon, ed., *Franklin D. Roosevelt and Foreign Affairs*, III: 341–343; Breitman and Kraut, *American Refugee Policy and European Jewry, 1933–1945*, p. 38.

9. Lehman to Warburg, July 14, 1936, and Warburg to Lehman, July 17, 1936, both in LP, SF, Felix Warburg; Breitman and Kraut, *American Refugee Policy and European Jewry, 1933–1945*, pp. 48–50.

10. "U.S. Asks Powers to Help Refugees Flee from Nazis," *NYT*, March 25, 1938, pp. 1, 8; "Roosevelt Holds Out Haven to Oppressed of All Lands within Quota Provisions; Hull Plan Upheld," *NYT*, March 26, 1938, pp. 1, 4.

11. Lehman to Roosevelt, March 31, 1938, and Roosevelt to Lehman, April 4, 1938, both in LP, SF, Franklin Roosevelt. On the Evian Conference, see Feingold, *The Politics of Rescue*, pp. 22–33; and Breitman and Lichtman, *FDR and the Jews*, pp. 102–110.

12. Lehman to Roosevelt, October 10, 1938, LP, SF, Franklin Roosevelt. On Lehman's attitude toward Palestine "as a homeland" and "a real haven for many thousands of our oppressed co-religionists in Germany," see Lehman to Stephen S. Wise, May 14, 1937, LP, SF, Wise.

13. Roosevelt to Lehman, October 13, 1938, LP, SF, Franklin Roosevelt; "British Issue Plan to Make Palestine Independent by '49," *NYT*, May 18, 1939, pp. 1, 5; "Washington Silent on the White Paper," *NYT*, May 18, 1939, p. 3; "Hull States View on Palestine Issue," *NYT*, May 30, 1939, p. 11; Breitman and Lichtman, *FDR and the Jews*, pp. 119, 238–241.

14. HHLOH, pp. 541–542, 546–547; Eleanor Roosevelt Oral History Transcript, HHLP, CUOHC, p. 10; "22,000 in Army Fete Parade in 5th Ave.," *NYT*, April 9, 1939, pp. 1, 28; "The President of the United States Opens the World's Greatest World's Fair," *NYT*, May 1, 1939, p. 5.

15. "White Organizes Aid to the Allies," *NYT*, May 20, 1940, p. 11; "Planes For Allies," *NYT*, June 7, 1940, pp. 1, 14; "Our Help Pledged," *NYT*, June 11, 1940, pp. 1, 6; Committee to Defend America by Aiding the Allies, "Between Us and Hitler Stands the *British* Fleet," *NYT*, July 30, 1940, p. 13; "Pershing Would Let Britain Have 50 Old U.S. Destroyers to Guard Our Own Liberty," *NYT*, August 5, 1940, pp. 1, 3; "Destroyer Aid for Britain Seen as Vital to Her and Our Defense," *NYT*, August 5, 1940, p. 3; "Urges Trade By U.S. for British Ships," *NYT*, August 6, 1940, p. 3; Charles Burlingham, Thomas Thacher, George Rublee, and Dean Acheson, "No Legal Bar Seen to Transfer of Destroyers," Letter to the Editor, *NYT*, August 11, 1940, E-8–9; Edith Lehman to Roosevelt, August 6, 1940, LP, SF, Franklin Roosevelt. On the

Destroyers-Bases Agreement, see the book by Herbert Lehman's great-nephew, Philip Goodhart, *Fifty Ships That Saved the World*.

16. "Roosevelt Favors Draft; . . . Need of Men Vital," *NYT*, August 3, 1940, pp. 1, 6; "Man-Power Appeal Voiced by Lehman," *NYT*, August 18, 1940, p. 2; "Army Is Inspected by the President," *NYT*, August 18, 1940, p. 3.

17. "Landon Suggests Lehman for 1940," *NYT*, November 24, 1938, p. 31; "Garner and Hull Leading in Survey," *NYT*, December 2, 1938, p. 15; "Garner 1940 Lead Doubled in Survey," *NYT*, March 26, 1939, p. 60; "Garner Stronger in Survey of 1940," *NYT*, May 21, 1939, p. 4; "Farley Gain Found among Democrats," *NYT*, June 14, 1939, p. 8; HHLOH, pp. 771–772; Carolin Flexner Oral History Transcript, HHLP, CUOHC, pp. 61–62.

18. HHLOH, p. 687; "Asks Lehman to Back Farley as Candidate," *NYT*, March 8, 1940, p. 8; "Roosevelt to Lehman, March 26, 1940, in Elliott Roosevelt, ed., *F.D.R.*, II: 1009; James Farley Oral History Transcript, HHLP, CUOHC, pp. 19–20; Farley, *Jim Farley's Story*, p. 230; Donahoe, *Private Plans and Public Dangers*, pp. 141–142; Scroop, *Mr. Democrat*, pp. 181–183.

19. Arthur Krock, "In the Nation: Mr. Dewey Goes to the Head of the Class," *NYT*, April 4, 1940, p. 20; Lehman to Roosevelt, March 29, 1940, Roosevelt to Lehman, April 3, 1940, and Lehman to Roosevelt, April 4, 1940, all in LP, SF, Franklin Roosevelt; "Roosevelt Receives Lehman at Hyde Park," *NYT*, April 9, 1940, p. 20; "Lehman Charges Dewey Backers Blocked Progressive State Bills," *NYT*, April 19, 1940, pp. 1, 16; "Action on Cabinet Attacked by Dewey," *NYT*, June 21, 1940, p. 4; "Field Is Still Led by Dewey, Willkie," *NYT*, June 21, 1940, p. 17. On Dewey and wiretaps, see Smith, *Thomas E. Dewey and His Times*, pp. 253–254; on Dewey's campaign for the 1940 Republican nomination, see ibid., pp. 285–314.

20. HHLOH, pp. 689–693; "Lehman for Third Term," *NYT*, July 12, 1940, p. 16; "Lehman, Seconding, Extols Roosevelt," *NYT*, July 18, 1940, p. 7; Donahoe, *Private Plans and Public Dangers*, p. 177.

21. "Platform Trouble," *NYT*, July 16, 1940, pp. 1, 5; "Lehman Is Urgent on Foreign Policy," *NYT*, July 17, 1940, p. 6; "Platform Is Ready," *NYT*, July 17, 1940, pp. 1, 3; "Roosevelt Renominated on First Ballot; . . . 'Stay Out' Plank," *NYT*, July 18, 1940, pp. 1, 6; "Text of the Declaration of Principles as Adopted by the Democratic Convention," *NYT*, July 18, 1940, p. 4; "Text of President's Speech Accepting 3d Nomination," *NYT*, July 19, 1940, p. 2; "Roosevelt, Accepting, Feels He Must Serve with Others in Crisis; . . . President on Radio," *NYT*, July 19, 1940, pp. 1, 3.

22. "Roosevelt, Accepting, Feels He Must Serve with Others in Crisis; . . . President on Radio," *NYT*, July 19, 1940, pp. 1, 3; "Lehman to Stump State in Campaign," *NYT*, August 4, 1940, p. 2; "Flynn to Confer with Roosevelt," *NYT*, September 4, 1940, p. 22; "New York State's Vote Held Vital to Willkie," *NYT*, October 13, 1940, p. 74. On Willkie's and Roosevelt's campaigns, see Parmet and Hecht, *Never Again*.

23. "Gov. Lehman Asks 3D Term as Blow to the Dictators," *NYT*, October 1, 1940, pp. 1, 19; "Text of Gov. Lehman's Address to the State Democratic Convention," *NYT*, October 1, 1940, p. 18.

24. "Gov. Lehman Asks 3D Term as Blow to the Dictators," *NYT*, October 1, 1940, pp. 1, 19; "Text of Gov. Lehman's Address to the State Democratic Convention," *NYT*, October 1, 1940, p. 18; "Wallace Demands Barring of Hitler," *NYT*, August 30,

1940, p. 1; Memorandum, Lehman to Allan Nevins, January 4, 1962, p. 17, LP, SF, Nevins.

25. "Willkie Retorts to Lehman's 'Innuendo': Repeats His Opposition to the Dictators," *NYT*, October 2, 1940, p. 15.

26. "Lehman Answers Willkie's Charge," *NYT*, October 3, 1940, p. 19.

27. Editorial, "Hitler as the Issue," *NYT*, October 1, 1940, p. 21; Arthur Krock, "In the Nation: The Last Time Lehman's Argument Was Used," *NYT*, October 3, 1940, p. 24; Krock, "In the Nation: Some Drops from What Seems a Witch's Brew," *NYT*, October 30, 1940, p. 22.

28. "Lehman Held 'Blind' to 3D Term Danger," *NYT*, October 3, 1940, p. 20; "Proskauer Attacks Lehman on Dictators," *NYT*, October 5, 1940, p. 13; "They Don't Like Roosevelt," *New Republic*, October 14, 1940, p. 508; "Governor Lehman's Speech," Letters to the Times, *NYT*, October 3, 1940, p. 24; "The Lehman Statement," Letters to the Editor, *NYT*, October 6, 1940, E-9.

29. "Hitler and Mussolini Meet Today; Dictators on Way," *NYT*, October 4, 1940, p. 1; "President Amused by Axis Opposition," *NYT*, October 5, 1940, p. 3; "Hitler as the Issue," Editorial, *NYT*, October 5, 1940, p. 14; Arthur Krock, "Wishes of Dictators Made Campaign Issue," *NYT*, October 6, 1940, E-3.

30. "New York State's Vote Held Vital to Willkie," *NYT*, October 13, 1940, E-8; "Two Vote Studies Give Willkie Victory," *NYT*, October 24, 1940, p. 17; "State for Willkie, Survey Indicates," *NYT*, October 29, 1940, p. 21; Parmet and Hecht, *Never Again*, pp. 244, 259–261; "Roosevelt to Make Political Tour, with 5 Major Speeches, One Here," *NYT*, October 18, 1940, pp. 1, 15; "Roosevelt Is Seen by 2,000,000 in City," *NYT*, October 29, 1940, p. 14; "Roosevelt Says Opposition Hindered Defense; Sabotage Charged," *NYT*, October 29, 1940, pp. 1, 12; "Speeches of Lehman, Mead and Wagner at Meeting in Garden," *NYT*, October 29, 1940, p. 19; "Texts of President Roosevelt's Speeches at the Garden Rally and during His City Tour," *NYT*, October 29, 1940, p. 17; "Roosevelt to Tour 5 Boroughs Today, Making 6 Speeches," *NYT*, October 28, 1940, pp. 1, 8; "President Breaks Ground for Tunnel," *NYT*, October 29, 1940, p. 15; "Need for Guidance of Youth Stressed," *NYT*, October 29, 1940, p. 13; "President Reviews R.O.T.C. at Fordham," *NYT*, October 29, 1940, p. 19. Roosevelt directed much of his criticism at House Republican Leader Joseph Martin of Massachusetts, and New York Republicans Bruce Barton and Hamilton Fish.

31. "New York Vote Is Key in Election Today," *New York Herald Tribune*, November 5, 1940, p. 1; "State Race Looms as Closest Known," *NYT*, November 3, 1940, p. 50; "Result in Balance in Gallup Survey," *NYT*, November 4, 1940, p. 11; "Governor Attacks Willkie's Record," *NYT*, October 31, 1940, p. 26; Wallace Charges Nazi Pressure Here; Labor Rally Held," *NYT*, November 1, 1940, pp. 1, 17; "Job Gains Cited by Wallace Here," *NYT*, November 1, 1940, p. 15; "Lehman in Harlem Urges Third Term," *NYT*, November 3, 1940, p. 51; "Governor Praises Roosevelt Policy," *NYT*, November 5, 1940, p. 17.

32. "Dr. Wise Assails Campaign Use of Race Issues," *New York Herald Tribune*, October 28, 1940, p. 6; "Asks Gratitude for Vote," *NYT*, October 28, 1940, p. 12; Lehman to Benjamin Buttenwieser, November 1, 1940, and November 5, 1940, both in LP, SF, Franklin Roosevelt; "Radio Plea to Jews Withheld by Lewis," *NYT*, November

1, 1940, p. 20; Wise, *As I See It*, pp. 259–264; Wise, *Challenging Years*, pp. 229–230.

33. Lehman to Buttenwieser, November 1, 1940, LP, SF, Franklin Roosevelt; "Survey Shows Jewish Leaders Backing Willkie," *New York Herald Tribune*, October 28, 1940, p. 6.

34. Buttenwieser to Lehman, November 4, 1940, LP, SF, Franklin Roosevelt.

35. Lehman to Buttenwieser, November 5, 1940, LP, SF, Franklin Roosevelt.

36. "Roosevelt Margin Narrow in State," *NYT*, November 7, 1940, p. 20; "Labor Party Holds It Swung New York," *NYT*, November 7, 1940, p. 21; "States' Electors Vote Roosevelt In," *NYT*, December 17, 1940, p. 31; "Salaries Donated at Albany," *NYT*, December 17, 1940, p. 31.

37. "Remarks of Governor Lehman Over the Radio at 1:00 A.M.–November 6, 1940," and Lehman to Roosevelt, November 7, 1940, both in LP, SF, Franklin Roosevelt; "Text of the Willkie Address Urging 'Loyal Opposition,'" *NYT*, November 12, 1940, p. 12; "Willkie Endorses 'All-Out' Aid Bill with Time Limit on President's Power; Will Fly to Britain to Make a Survey; Full Debate Urged," *NYT*, January 13, 1941, pp. 1, 4; "Roosevelt Has a Talk with Willkie and Gives Him Letter to Churchill; . . . President Cordial," *NYT*, January 20, 1941, pp. 1, 6; Peters, *Five Days in Philadelphia*, pp. 184–185.

38. "Legislature Set for Defense Task," *NYT*, January 6, 1941, p. 7; "Lehman Demands Fullest State Aid in 'Total Defense,'" *NYT*, January 9, 1941, pp. 1, 15; "Governor Lehman's Message to the Legislature Dealing Solely with Defense Problems in State," *NYT*, January 9, 1941, p. 14; "Defense Bill Is Signed," *NYT*, February 21, 1941, p. 7; "Lehman's Budget Slashed $1,586,789," *NYT*, March 6, 1941, pp. 1, 14; "Highlights of the Session," *NYT*, April 4, 1941, p. 37; "1,106 Bills Piled Up for Lehman Action," *NYT*, April 5, 1941, p. 32. On the New York State Council of Defense, see Hartzell, *The Empire State at War*.

39. "Roosevelt Asks All-Out Aid to Democracies; . . . Will Lend Arms," *NYT*, January 7, 1941, pp. 1, 3; "Lehman for Speed in Helping Britain," *NYT*, January 26, 1941, p. 16; "Lehman Sees War if Dictators Win," *NYT*, February 9, 1941, p. 19.

40. Telegram, Hull to Lehman, n.d.; Telegram, Lehman to Hull, December 11, 1940; Lehman to Hull, January 27, 1941; Hull to Lehman, February 11, 1942; and Lehman to Hull, February 13, 1942, all in LP, SF, Hull; Lehman to Roosevelt, May 15, 1941; Flexner to Marie Ginsberg, July 24, 1941; Edward Anderson to Lehman, December 1, 1941; and Acting Secretary Welles to Lehman, March 23, 1942, all in LP, Flexner Files, Aid Requests, Duschnitz Family, C17-148; Roosevelt to Lehman, May 20, 1941; Roosevelt to Lehman, June 3, 1941; and Lehman to Roosevelt, June 6, 1941, all in LP, SF, Franklin Roosevelt; Lehman to Morris Troper, July 18, 1941, and Lehman to James Rosenberg, August 21, 1941, both in LP, General Correspondence, 1941–1942, Duschnitz Family, C40-62; Lilli [Duschnitz] to Edith and Herbert, August 22, 1942, Edith Lehman Papers, Lilli Duschnitz, C189-37. On the Mayer Lehman Charity Fund, see Lehman to Elinor Morgenthau, May 19, 1939, and June 21, 1939; Elinor Morgenthau to Lehman, July 15, 1939; Lehman to Elinor Morgenthau, September 9, 1939; Elinor Morgenthau to Lehman, September 17, 1939; and Lehman to Elinor Morgenthau, September 26, 1939, all in LP, SF, Henry and Elinor Morgenthau, Jr.; and Flade, *The Lehmans*, pp. 95–97.

41. "Albany Dogs' Party Aids British Relief," *NYT*, July 17, 1941, p. 22.

42. "Unity Is Keynote of Columbus Day," *NYT*, October 13, 1941, p. 20; "Lehman Demands Free Sea at Once," *NYT*, October 26, 1941, p. 25. On the 1941 revisions to the Neutrality Acts, see Reynolds, *From Munich to Pearl Harbor*, pp. 155–156.

43. "O'Dwyer Backed by Gov. Lehman; City Race Mixed," *NYT*, October 22, 1941, pp. 1, 17; "Lehman Praises O'Dwyer Career," *NYT*, October 28, 1941, p. 20; "Text of Governor Lehman's Speech in the Bronx," *NYT*, October 28, 1941, p. 20.

44. "Roosevelt Backs Mayor on Record of Honest Rule; Tammany Is Bitter," *NYT*, October 25, 1941, pp. 1, 10; "Lehman Praises O'Dwyer Career," *NYT*, October 28, 1941, p. 20; "Text of Governor Lehman's Speech in the Bronx," *NYT*, October 28, 1941, p. 20.

45. HHLOH, pp. 610–611; "Controller Vote in State Barred by Appeal Court," *NYT*, October 28, 1941, pp. 1, 21; "Mayor 'Abusive,' Lehman Asserts; 'Cad,' Says Farley," *NYT*, October 29, 1941, pp. 1, 16; "Lehman Charges Mayor's 'Insults' Prove Him Unfit," *NYT*, November 1, 1941, pp. 1, 13; "Denies He Abused Lehman," *NYT*, November 2, 1941, p. 45.

46. HHLOH, pp. 610–612; "Mayor 'Abusive,' Lehman Asserts; 'Cad,' Says Farley," *NYT*, October 29, 1941, pp. 1, 16; "Lehman Charges Mayor's 'Insults' Prove Him Unfit," *NYT*, November 1, 1941, pp. 1, 13.

47. HHLOH, pp. 610–612; "'Abusive' Mayor Again Attacked by Tammany Men," *NYT*, October 30, 1941, pp. 1, 16; "'Slurs' by Mayor Stressed by Foes," *NYT*, October 31, 1941, p. 46; "Denies He Abused Lehman," *NYT*, November 2, 1941, p. 45; "La Guardia Lead Seen Shortened," *NYT*, November 3, 1941, pp. 1, 13; "La Guardia Wins a Third Term by 133,841; O'Dwyer Vote High," *NYT*, November 5, 1941, pp. 1, 14; "Reform Has a Close Call," Editorial, *NYT*, November 5, 1941, p. 22; McGoldrick interview cited in Garrett, *The La Guardia Years*, p. 273; Lehman to La Guardia, November 5, 1941, LP, SF, La Guardia; Kessner, *Fiorello La Guardia and the Making of Modern New York*, pp. 497–499. Historian Ronald Bayor has shown that La Guardia actually received a higher percentage of the Jewish vote in 1941 than he had in 1937, and that it was Irish, Italian, and German voters who deserted the Mayor this time, mainly over his support of the President's foreign policy of aiding England. But there is no way of telling how much higher La Guardia's total among Jewish voters might have been if not for his attack on Lehman. See Bayor, *Neighbors in Conflict*, pp. 137, 142–145.

48. "Lehman Orders Caution," *NYT*, December 8, 1941, p. 4; "Lehman Puts State on Wartime Basis," *NYT*, December 9, 1941, p. 42; "Lehman Attacks Rumors of Raids," *NYT*, December 11, 1941, p. 21; "7-Day Production Is Roosevelt Aim," *NYT*, December 10, 1941, p. 19; "Lift State Laws for 7-Day Week," *NYT*, December 13, 1941, p. 21; "One Plate for New York Autos in 1942, the Other to Be Kept for Use in 1943," *NYT*, December 14, 1941, pp. 1, 40; "Committee to Set War Work Hours," *NYT*, December 16, 1941, p. 39; "7-Day Week for Women Workers Is Asked by 12 Defense Plants," *NYT*, December 17, 1941, p. 36; "Knox Hails State for 7-Day Week Plan," *NYT*, December 19, 1941, p. 3; "Lehman Sets Up Rubber Rationing," *NYT*, December 24, 1941, p. 12; "Lehman Proposes New OCD Authority," *NYT*, January 16, 1942, pp. 1, 16; "Gov. Lehman's Message to Legislature on Civilian Defense," *NYT*, January 16, 1942, p. 16; "Big State Outlays Barred by Budget," *NYT*, January 27, 1942, p. 17;

"Defense Labor Bill Approved by Lehman," *NYT*, January 30, 1942, p. 14; "Forty-Mile Speed Now Law in State," *NYT*, April 23, 1942, p. 1; "Lehman Ends Tennis; Shoes to Rubber Pile," *NYT*, July 2, 1942, p. 1; "Lehman Summons 'Fighting Dollars,'" *NYT*, May 2, 1942, p. 15; "Lehman Buys Bonds on Salary," *NYT*, January 14, 1942, p. 42.

49. "Lehman Calls on Roosevelt," *NYT*, April 8, 1942, p. 13; "President to Call Lehman to Capital for War Service," *NYT*, April 12, 1942, pp. 1, 4; "Lehman Is Silent on War Job Story," *NYT*, April 13, 1942, p. 17; "Lehman Report Is Denied," *NYT*, April 15, 1942, p. 15.

50. "Lehman Calls on Roosevelt," *NYT*, April 8, 1942, p. 13; James Farley Oral History Transcript, HHLP, CUOHC, p. 38; Farley, *Jim Farley's Story*, pp. 347; HHLOH, pp. 721–722; "State Slates Weighed," *NYT*, January 26, 1942, p. 17, 27; "President to Call Lehman to Capital for War Service," *NYT*, April 12, 1942, pp. 1, 4; Moscow, *Politics in the Empire State*, pp. 86–92; Scroop, *Mr. Democrat*, pp. 205–212; Syrett, "Roosevelt vs. Farley."

51. Berle and Jacobs, eds., *Navigating the Rapids*, p. 412; "To Aid Spanish Fascists," *NYT*, December 1, 1936, p. 15; "Bennett Assailed at Red Convention," *NYT*, August 30, 1942, p. 37; "The Shape of Things," *New Republic*, July 2, 1938, p. 3; HHLOH, p. 713, 716, 718–720; "Talk of Mead for Albany," *NYT*, November 20, 1941, p. 35; "Mead Considering Race for Governor," *NYT*, February 21, 1942, p. 32; "Aide Denies Mead Seeks State Post," *NYT*, March 5, 1942, p. 18; "President to Call Lehman to Capital for War Service," *NYT*, April 12, 1942, pp. 1, 4; "Lehman Is Silent on War Job Story," *NYT*, April 13, 1942, p. 17; "Silent on Governorship," *NYT*, April 14, 1942, p. 23; "Criticism of War Spurs Republicans," *NYT*, March 2, 1942, p. 21; James Farley Oral History Transcript, HHLP, CUOHC, p. 38; Charles Poletti Oral History Transcript (1957), HHLP, CUOHC, pp. 24–25.

52. "Movement Looms to 'Draft Lehman,'" *NYT*, May 4, 1942, pp. 1, 9.

53. "Lehman Declares He Won't Run Again for Governorship," *NYT*, May 8, 1942, pp. 1, 22; Lehman to Roosevelt, May 7, 1942, LP, SF, Franklin Roosevelt; HHLOH, pp. 710–711, 717–718; Poletti Oral History Transcript (1957), HHLP, CUOHC, p. 27; Moscow, *Politics in the Empire State*, p. 86.

54. Warren Moscow, "Lehman Declares He Won't Run Again for Governorship," *NYT*, May 8, 1942, pp. 1, 22; HHLOH, pp. 710–712, 717–718.

55. Roosevelt to Lehman, May 11, 1942, and Lehman to Roosevelt, May 15, 1942, both in LP, SF, Franklin Roosevelt; "Lehman Sees President; Silent on Federal Post," *NYT*, May 21, 1942, p. 4; "Lehman Call to War Post Expected within a Month," *NYT*, May 22, 1942, pp. 1, 22; "Lehman Will Stay at Post Full Term Despite U.S. Pleas," *NYT*, May 26, 1942, pp. 1, 15.

56. "Democrats Split on Governorship," *NYT*, May 8, 1942, p. 22; "Bennett Is Willing to Run for Governor," *NYT*, May 9, 1942, p. 18; "Mead 'Determined' Not to Run," *NYT*, May 8, 1942, p. 22; "Parties Lining Up on Governorship," *NYT*, May 17, 1942, E-5; Farley, *Jim Farley's Story*, pp. 351–352; "Governorship Pact Is Hinted as Farley Visits White House," *NYT*, June 7, 1942, pp. 1, 37; James A. Hagerty, "Bennett Backers See His Nomination," *NYT*, June 8, 1942, p. 17.

57. "Party Strategy May Drop Poletti," *NYT*, June 9, 1942, p. 25; "Choice of Bennett Virtually Certain as Kelly Backs Him," *NYT*, June 10, 1942, pp. 1, 16; "Lehman Champions Poletti as Successor; Declares President Is Uncommitted on Race," *NYT*,

June 12, 1942, p. 38. Previous accounts have all missed Lehman's crucial role in reversing Roosevelt's decision not to oppose Bennett's candidacy, reporting instead that Lehman merely followed Roosevelt's lead. See especially Arthur Krock, "Bennett's Nomination a Victory for Farley," *NYT*, August 23, 1942, E-3; Farley, *Jim Farley's Story*, pp. 347–358; Moscow, *Politics in the Empire State*, pp. 86–92; Syrett, "Roosevelt vs. Farley: The New York Gubernatorial Election of 1942"; and Scroop, *Mr. Democrat*, pp. 205–214.

58. "He Has Endorsed No One, the President Declares," *NYT*, June 13, 1942, p. 17; "Bennett Rejected by All A.L.P. Heads," *NYT*, June 13, 1942, p. 17; "Choice of Bennett Virtually Certain as Kelly Backs Him," *NYT*, June 10, 1942, pp. 1, 16; "Labor Left Wing Assails Bennett," *NYT*, June 12, 1942, p. 38; "Holds President Shuns State Race," *NYT*, June 18, 1942, p. 42; "Mead Again Denies State Aspirations," *NYT*, June 20, 1942, p. 11.

59. "Roosevelt Dodges Query about Mead," *NYT*, July 18, 1942, p. 15; "Poletti Is Boomed by the State C.I.O.," *NYT*, June 20, 1942, p. 11; "CIO Blacklists Dewey, Bennett; State Convention Acts After Lehman Urges Both Parties to Name 'True Liberals,'" *NYT*, June 21, 1942, pp. 1, 33; Lehman to Roosevelt, June 27, 1942, LP, SF, Franklin Roosevelt.

60. Berle and Jacobs, eds., *Navigating the Rapids*, pp. 416–417; "New Dealers Open Drive to Give Mead State Nomination," *NYT*, July 22, 1942, pp. 1, 22; "Text of Letters Sent to Mead Urging Him to Run," *NYT*, July 22, 1942, p. 22; "Mead, Backed by President, Enters Race for Governor; . . . 'Yields' to Pleas," *NYT*, July 23, 1942, pp. 1, 7.

61. HHLOH, p. 711; "Farley Statement Terms Mead Unfit for Governor," *NYT*, July 23, 1942, pp. 1, 6; "Mead-Bennett Acrimony Is Seen as Paving Way for a Dark Horse," *NYT*, July 24, 1942, pp. 1, 34; "Lehman Throws Support to Mead, Dropping Poletti, His First Choice," *NYT*, July 27, 1942, pp. 1, 10; "A.L.P. Right Wing Is Out for Mead; 3D Party Shelved," *NYT*, July 28, 1942, pp. 1, 18.

62. "Farley Summons Leaders to Parley Tomorrow Night," *NYT*, August 17, 1942, pp. 1, 8; Hassett, *Off the Record with F.D.R., 1942–1945*, pp. 104–106; Roosevelt to Lehman, August 18, 1942, LP, SF, Franklin Roosevelt; "Roosevelt's Plea for Harmony Fails on Convention Eve," *NYT*, August 19, 1942, pp. 1, 17; "Floor Fight Today to Decide Nominee in State Contest," *NYT*, August 20, 1942, pp. 1, 14; Farley, *Jim Farley's Story*, p. 354; HHLOH, p. 722; James Farley Oral History Transcript, HHLP, CUOHC, pp. 39–40.

63. "Lehman Stresses Social Gains Here," *NYT*, August 20, 1942, p. 15; "Text of Governor Lehman's Keynote Address at Democratic Convention," *NYT*, August 20, 1942, p. 15; "New Dealers Open Drive to Give Mead State Nomination," *NYT*, July 22, 1942, pp. 1, 22; "Bennett Wins Nomination on First Ballot, 623–393; Poletti, O'Leary Renamed," *NYT*, August 21, 1942, pp. 1, 10; "Political Drama Enacted in Open," *NYT*, August 21, 1942, p. 12; "Bennett's Nomination a Victory for Farley," *NYT*, August 23, 1942, E-3; Will Chasan, "Farley Picks a Loser," *The Nation*, August 29, 1942, p. 166; Farley, *Jim Farley's Story*, p. 357; HHLOH, p. 714, 720, 722–724.

64. "Bennett Wins Nomination on First Ballot, 623–393; Poletti, O'Leary Renamed," *NYT*, August 21, 1942, pp. 1, 10; HHLOH, p. 714; Charles Poletti Oral History Transcript (1957), HHLP, CUOHC, pp. 25–26.

65. "Bennett Wins Nomination on First Ballot, 623–393; Poletti, O'Leary Renamed," *NYT*, August 21, 1942, pp. 1, 10; "Political Drama Enacted in Open," *NYT*, August 21, 1942, p. 12; "Alfange Is Named by A.L.P. to Run for Governorship," *NYT*, August 23, 1942, pp. 1, 36; "Alfange's Defeat Won A.L.P. Prestige," *NYT*, August 23, 1942, p. 36; "Lehman Pledges Help to Bennett," *NYT*, August 28, 1942, pp. 1, 38; "State Slate Aided by Mrs. Roosevelt," *NYT*, September 25, 1942, p. 15; "Roosevelt Backs Bennett in Race as Best Qualified," *NYT*, October 5, 1942, pp. 1, 36; "Roosevelt's Endorsement Helps Bennett's Cause," *NYT*, October 11, 1942, E-10; "Mead Joins Tour to Help Bennett," *NYT*, October 14, 1942, p. 17.

66. "President Urges Bennett Election; Hits 'Protest' Vote," *NYT*, October 24, 1942, p. 1; "President Is Emphatic," *NYT*, October 24, 1942, pp. 1, 13; "Lehman Assails Dewey on Record," *NYT*, October 24, 1942, p. 13; "Bennett Men Hail Roosevelt Stand," *NYT*, October 24, 1942, p. 13; "Bennett Gets More Roosevelt Aid," *NYT*, October 25, 1942, E-10; "Bennett Campaign Reaches a Climax," *NYT*, October 31, 1942, pp. 1, 13; "New York's Vote Seen as Augury of '44 Race," *NYT*, November 1, 1942, E-3; "Dewey Elected Governor in State Sweep; . . . 20-Year Rule Ends," *NYT*, November 4, 1942, pp. 1, 4; "Gallop Poll Accuracy Shown in Election; Off by One-Half of 1% in Dewey Race," *NYT*, November 5, 1942, p. 30; "Alfange Rejoices Over A.L.P. Voting," *NYT*, November 4, 1942, p. 3; "Republicans Imperil Control of Congress; Margin Is Narrow," *NYT*, November 5, 1942, pp. 1, 30; "Poletti Defeated," *NYT*, November 5, 1942, pp. 1, 20; "Midterm Verdict," *NYT*, November 8, 1942, E-1; "Dewey's Plurality Officially 647,628," *NYT*, December 15, 1942, p. 30; Untitled AP article, "Thomas E. Dewey polled more votes . . . ," *NYT*, December 15, 1942, p. 30; HHLOH, p. 727; Scroop, *Mr. Democrat*, p. 212; Moscow, *Politics in the Empire State*, pp. 91–92.

67. "War Work Parley Called by Lehman," *NYT*, May 29, 1942, p. 15; Summary of Joint Telegram from Lehman and La Guardia to the President and the President's subsequent action, June 2, 1942, Roosevelt Papers, OF 91, Lehman; "More War Orders Sought for City," *NYT*, June 3, 1942, p. 25; "Lehman to Join Parley," *NYT*, June 13, 1942, p. 13; "Move to Get Jobs for New York Idle," *NYT*, June 20, 1942, p. 8; "New York Gains in War Contracts," *NYT*, November 18, 1942, p. 19; "200,000 Cut Listed in City's Jobless," *NYT*, November 10, 1942, p. 29; Williams, *City of Ambition*, pp. 332–336.

68. Wise to Lehman, July 13, 1942; Lehman to Wise, July 15, 1942; Wise to Lehman, July 17, 1942; and Wise to Lehman, July 24, 1942; all in LP, SF, Wise; "Nazi Punishment Seen by Roosevelt," *NYT*, July 22, 1942, pp. 1, 4.

69. Lehman's remarks are reported in "Nazi Punishment Seen by Roosevelt," *NYT*, July 22, 1942, pp. 1, 4.

70. "Nazi Punishment Seen by Roosevelt," *NYT*, July 22, 1942, pp. 1, 4; Wyman, *The Abandonment of the Jews*, pp. 24–25; Breitman and Lichtman, *FDR and the Jews*, p. 198.

71. "Lehman Commends State's War Work," *NYT*, September 28, 1942, p. 23; Hartzell, *The Empire State at War: World War II*.

72. "Lehman Call to War Post Expected within a Month," *NYT*, May 22, 1942, pp. 1, 22; "Roosevelt Weighs Appointing Lehman Arbiter of Wages," *NYT*, June 27, 1942, pp. 1, 10; "President Starts Wage Curbs Study," *NYT*, July 28, 1942, p. 10; "New Board Mapped to Fight Inflation," *NYT*, August 20, 1942, p. 40; "President Works on

Message," *NYT*, September 5, 1942, p. 7; "Roosevelt Order Monday Expected to Fix Pay Scales and to Limit Farm Prices," *NYT*, September 5, 1942, pp. 1, 7; Herbert Lehman to Irving Lehman, August 28, 1942, LP, SF, Irving Lehman; Farley, *James Farley's Story*, p. 352; "Roosevelt Freezes Wages, Rents, Farm Prices; Names Justice Byrnes Economic Director; . . . New Era Ordered," *NYT*, October 4, 1942, pp. 1, 44; "Byrnes Steered New Deal Bills," *NYT*, October 4, 1942, p. 44; "The President and His Critics," *New Republic*, October 12, 1942, p. 464.

73. "Roosevelt to Byrnes, October 22, 1942, in Elliott Roosevelt, ed., *F.D.R.*, II: 1357; Summary of Memorandum, Byrnes to Roosevelt, November 2, 1942, Roosevelt Papers, OF 5175, Lehman, Director UNRRA; "Lehman to Direct Relief of Peoples Freed from Axis," *NYT*, November 21, 1942, pp. 1, 6.

Chapter 7. "Governor Lehman . . . Doesn't Know the Way Things Are Done in Washington": Lehman, Roosevelt, and OFRRO, 1942–1943

1. Franklin Roosevelt to A. I. Parsky, Herbert H. Lehman Dinner Committee, January 31, 1943, Roosevelt Papers, PPF 93, Lehman, 1940–1945.

2. Edwin (Pa) Watson to Lehman, November 5, 1942; Watson to Lehman, November 9, 1942; Lehman to Watson, November 11, 1942; and Lehman to Roosevelt, November 12, 1942; all in LP, SF, Franklin Roosevelt; "Lehman Visits Roosevelt in Washington, Reviving Talk of a War Job for Governor," *NYT*, November 12, 1942, p. 16; Franklin Roosevelt to James Byrnes, October 22, 1942, in Elliott Roosevelt, ed., *F.D.R.*, II: 1357–1358; Summary of Memorandum, Byrnes to the President, November 2, 1942, Franklin Roosevelt Papers, OF 5175, Lehman, Director UNRRA; Blum, ed., *The Price of Vision*, p. 130; HHLOH, pp. 741, 749–750; "Lehman Forecasts Years of Service in War-Torn Lands," *NYT*, November 22, 1942, pp. 1, 47.

3. "Lehman Forecasts Years of Service in War-Torn Lands," *NYT*, November 22, 1942, pp. 1, 47; "Announced by White House," *NYT*, November 22, 1942, p. 47. Even though the United Nations itself was not established formally until 1945, the nations fighting against the Axis powers began calling themselves the United Nations in January 1942. See "26 Nations Pledge All Resources for Victory; . . . War Pact Is Signed," *NYT*, January 4, 1942, pp. 1, 4.

4. "Lehman to Direct Relief of Peoples Freed from Axis," *NYT*, November 21, 1942, pp. 1, 6; "Lehman Forecasts Years of Service in War-Torn Lands," *NYT*, November 22, 1942, pp. 1, 47; Acheson, *Present at the Creation*, pp. 42–43, 64–67; "Negotiations for the Establishment of a United Nations Relief and Rehabilitation Administration," U.S. Department of State, *Foreign Relations of the United States, 1942, Volume I: General, The British Commonwealth, The Far East* (hereinafter *FRUS* with Year and Volume), pp. 89–149; Memorandum of Conversation by the Secretary of State, December 24, 1942, *FRUS, 1942*, I: 158–159; Hull to Roosevelt May 5, 1942, and attached telegram to the American Embassy in London, April 29, 1942, Franklin Roosevelt Papers, OF 4966, UNRRA, 1942; HHLOH, pp. 732–733, 741–746, 750; Lehman to Arthur Hays Sulzberger, December 9, 1942, LP, SF, Sulzberger; "Allies to Confer on Rehabilitation," *NYT*, December 10, 1942, p. 12.

5. Rosenman, *Working with Roosevelt*, p. 399; Nicholas, ed., *Washington Despatches, 1941–1945*, p. 123; Eleanor Roosevelt Oral History Transcript, HHLP, CUOHC, p. 11; Perlzweig quoted in Breitman and Lichtman, *FDR and the Jews*, p. 225. Because of an error in transcription, the Eleanor Roosevelt Oral History Transcript mistakenly says "journeys," with a question mark added by the transcriber, when the word should be "Germans." Fighting anti-Semitism and helping Jews were never among Roosevelt's higher priorities. See Breitman and Lichtman, *FDR and the Jews*.

6. Eleanor Roosevelt to Lehman, November 26, 1942, Eleanor Roosevelt Papers, Box 767, Personal Letters, 1942, Lehman; "Mr. Lehman's New Post," Editorial, *NYT*, November 23, 1942, p. 22; Perkins to Lehman, December 5, 1942, LP, SF, Perkins; Proskauer to Lehman, November 23, 1942, LP, SF, Proskauer; Edith Lehman to Frank Altschul, November 24, 1942, LP, SF, Frank Altschul; Carolin Flexner Oral History Transcript, HHLP, CUOHC, p. 12.

7. "Lehman Arranges to Begin New Task," *NYT*, November 26, 1942, p. 37; "Lehman Bids State Guard Social Gains," *NYT*, December 2, 1942, pp. 1, 29; "Lehman's Valedictory to the State," *NYT*, December 2, 1942, p. 29; HHLOH, p. 747; Carolin Flexner Oral History Transcript, HHLP, CUOHC, p. 39. Lehman's resignation elevated Lieutenant Governor Charles Poletti to the governorship until Dewey was inaugurated on January 1, 1943.

8. Hoover quoted in Best, *Herbert Hoover*, I: 218; Hoover to Lehman, November 24, 1942; Hoover to Lehman, November 25, 1942; Hull to Hoover, June 28, 1941; Hoover to Hull, June 3, 1941; Hull to Hoover, May 10, 1941; Hoover to Hull, April 24, 1941; and Lehman to Hoover, November 28, 1942, all in LP, SF, Hoover; "Lehman, Hoover Confer on Relief," *NYT*, December 4, 1942, p. 17; Smith, *An Uncommon Man*, pp. 318–320.

9. "Food for Children of Belgium Urged," *NYT*, February 19, 1943, p. 9; "Feed-Europe Plan Revised by Hoover," *NYT*, February 21, 1943, p. 23; "Hoover Urges Aid to Hungry Europe," *NYT*, November 5, 1943, p. 5; Reynolds to Lehman, February 20, 1943, LP, SF, Hoover; Franklin Roosevelt, "Very Confidential Memorandum for Hon. Herbert H. Lehman," March 8, 1943, Roosevelt Papers, PPF 820, Hoover; R. W. Hadden to Representative John McCormack, February 17, 1943; McCormack to McIntyre, March 1, 1943; McIntyre, Memorandum for the President, March 3, 1943; and Lehman to McIntyre, March 16, 1943, all in Franklin Roosevelt Papers, President's Secretary's File, Box 7, Confidential File, "H"–General; Lehman to Roosevelt, June 3, 1943, Roosevelt to Lehman, June 11, 1943, and Lehman to Roosevelt, August 6, 1943, all in LP, SF, Franklin Roosevelt; Smith, *An Uncommon Man*, pp. 309, 319–321. On Edith Cavell, see Souhami, *Edith Cavell*.

10. "Lehman Sworn in as Relief Director," *NYT*, December 5, 1942, p. 17; Hull to Lehman, December 4, 1942, LP, SF, Hull.

11. Arthur Krock, "In the Nation: Sometimes 'Easy Does It,' but Not in War-time," *NYT*, July 13, 1943, p. 20; Wallace to Hull, June 17, 1942; Wallace to Roosevelt, June 17, 1942; and Roosevelt to Hull, June 24, 1942, all in Franklin Roosevelt Papers, OF 4966 UNRRA, 1942; and Blum, ed., *The Price of Vision*, p. 114. On the problems among the Board of Economic Warfare, the State Department, and Jesse Jones, see Acheson, *Present at the Creation*, pp. 39–42, 45; Blum, ed., *The Price of Vision*, pp. 53–229; "Statement by Vice President Wallace, Chairman of the Board of Economic Warfare,"

June 29, 1943, in Blum, ed., *The Price of Vision*, pp. 641–659; and Byrnes, *All in One Lifetime*, pp. 192–193. Krock did not name Flynn in the original article as the source of the quotation about Roosevelt's management style, attributing it to "another political manager of the President's affairs," but later, in his memoirs, Krock credited Flynn for the remark. See Krock, *Memoirs*, p. 202. On Jesse Jones, see Fenberg, *Unprecedented Power*, pp. 328–329, 334–336, 357–360. The War Refugee Board was another example of Roosevelt creating an agency whose place in the bureaucracy was not clear. See Matz, "Sweden, the United States, and Raoul Wallenberg's Mission to Hungary in 1944," p. 140. On the tangled lines of responsibility in FDR's wartime administration, see also Moreira, *The Jew Who Defeated Hitler*.

12. "'British Lehman' Is Urged," *NYT*, December 10, 1942, p. 12; Acheson, *Present at the Creation*, p. 42; HHLOH, pp. 732–734, 741, 749–750; "Sets Up Foreign Branch," *NYT*, December 3, 1942, p. 4; "Wickard Named Food Administrator," *NYT*, December 7, 1942, pp. 1, 18; "Will Work with Lehman," *NYT*, December 7, 1942, p. 18.

13. Roosevelt, Memorandum for Secretary Hull, December 11, 1942, LP, SF, Franklin Roosevelt; HHLOH, pp. 741–743, 749–750.

14. Lehman to Frank Altschul, December 16, 1942, LP, SF, Altschul; "Lehman Receives Albany's Tributes," *NYT*, December 22, 1942, p. 14; Herbert Lehman to Irving Lehman, December 28, 1942, LP, SF, Irving Lehman; Lehman to Altschul, January 6, 1943, Frank Altschul Papers, Catalogued Correspondence 128b, Lehman, Columbia University Library.

15. Rudolph Forster, Memorandum for Honorable James H. Rowe, Jr., December 24, 1942, and attached Draft Executive Orders; and Roosevelt, Memorandum for the Director of the Budget, December 28, 1942; both in Roosevelt Papers, OF 5175, Lehman, Director of UNRRA.

16. Nicholas, ed., *Washington Despatches*, pp. 136; Acheson, *Present at the Creation*, p. 43.

17. Hull to Smith, February 2, 1943; "Executive Order," February 1943; Smith to the Attorney General, February 4, 1943; Smith, Memoranda for the President, February 6, 1943; Biddle, Memorandum for the President, February 11, 1943; all in Roosevelt Papers, OF 5175, Lehman, Director of UNRRA.

18. G. G. T. [White House Secretary Grace Tully], Memorandum for R. F. [Executive Clerk Rudolph Forster], February 16, 1943; Smith, Memorandum for the President, February 24, 1943; Smith, Memorandum for the President, March 3, 1943; all in Roosevelt Papers, OF 5175.

19. Roosevelt, Memorandum for Harry Hopkins and James Byrnes, February 16, 1943; Byrnes, Memorandum for the President, March 9, 1943; both in Roosevelt Papers, OF 5175. On Byrnes as the "assistant president," see Byrnes, *All in One Lifetime*, pp. 155, 161–215.

20. Carolin Flexner Oral History Transcript, HHLP, CUOHC, pp. 42–43; Lehman to Roosevelt, March 13, 1943, LP, SF, Franklin Roosevelt.

21. Roosevelt, Memorandum for James Byrnes, March 15, 1943; and Byrnes, Memorandum for the President, March 17, 1943; both in Roosevelt Papers, OF 5175.

22. Rosenman, Memorandum for the President, March 18, 1943, Roosevelt Papers, OF 5175. On Rosenman's role in drafting executive orders, see Rosenman, *Working with Roosevelt*, pp. 276–277.

23. Roosevelt to Lehman, March 19, 1943, *Department of State Bulletin*, March 27, 1943, p. 256.

24. See the various drafts in Roosevelt Papers, OF 5175. To compare the original State Department proposal with the President's letter, see "Executive Order," February 1943, attached to Attorney General Biddle, Memorandum for the President, February 11, 1943, Roosevelt Papers, OF 5175, and Roosevelt to Lehman, March 19, 1943, *Department of State Bulletin*, March 27, 1943, p. 256.

25. Edith Lehman to Frank Altschul, March 29, 1943, LP, SF, Altschul; Lehman to Hugh Jackson, February 9, 1960, LP, SF, Hugh Jackson.

26. Memorandum of Conversation, by the Secretary of State, December 24, 1942, *FRUS, 1942*, I: 158; "Allies Ask Lehman to Hasten His Trip," *NYT*, March 20, 1943, p. 6; Lehman to Roosevelt, March 13, 1943, LP, SF, Franklin Roosevelt; "Visit of Herbert H. Lehman to London," *Department of State Bulletin*, April 3, 1943, p. 279; "Lehman to Visit London for Data; Plans No Negotiations on Relief," *NYT*, April 4, 1943, p. 1; "Lehman in London to Survey Relief Needs of Countries to Be Liberated from Axis Grip," *NYT*, April 9, 1943, p. 4; "Former Governor in London for Relief Survey," *NYT*, April 10, 1943, p. 3; "Lehman Guest of King," *NYT*, April 17, 1943, p. 14; "Wilhelmina Warns Netherland Traitors in 'Flaming Protest' on Easter Broadcast," *NYT*, April 25, 1943, p. 16; "Lehman Sees Haakon," *NYT*, April 16, 1943, p. 7; "Lehman Describes Allied Relief Plan," *NYT*, May 9, 1943, p. 19; "Peter Lehman Transfers," *NYT*, March 31, 1943, p. 2; "Lehmans Meet in Britain," *NYT*, April 25, 1943, p. 25; "Lehman and His Son Heard Here on Radio," *NYT*, April 29, 1943, p. 23; "Lehman Impressed with Relief Work," *NYT*, April 22, 1943, p. 12; Winant to the Secretary of State, April 26, 1943, LP, Personal Correspondence and General File of the Director General of UNRRA, London, Official Letters, April 1943, 47–63; HHLOH, p. 753.

27. Lehman, "Statement of Policy for Relief and Rehabilitation in Future Liberated Areas," May 8, 1943, Roosevelt Papers, OF 20, Box 11, Department of State, 1943.

28. Ibid.

29. I. F. Stone, "Crumbs for Small Business," *The Nation*, February 20, 1943, p. 260; Jerry Kluttz, "The Federal Diary," *Washington Post* (hereinafter *WP*), May 13, 1943, B-1; Mr. Reynolds, Memorandum to Governor Lehman, "Coordination of postwar relief operations," May 13, 1943, LP, Personal Correspondence and General File of the Director General of UNRRA, Clippings, 46–13.

30. Roosevelt to Hull, May 8, 1943, LP, SF, Franklin Roosevelt; Smith, Memorandum for the President, June 3, 1943, Roosevelt Papers, OF 4966, UNRRA, 1943.

31. Smith, Memorandum for the President, June 3, 1943, Roosevelt Papers, OF 4966, UNRRA, 1943; "The Day in Washington," *NYT*, May 19, 1943, p. 15; Roosevelt, Memorandum for the Director of the Budget, May 21, 1943, Roosevelt Papers, OF 20, Box 11, Department of State, 1943.

32. Roosevelt, Memorandum for the Secretary of State, May 11, 1943; EMW, Memorandum for the President, May 17, 1943; Hull, Memorandum for the President, May 18, 1943; Memorandum with Respect to the Letter of the President of May 8, 1943 to the Secretary of State Referring to Operations in New Areas," May 18, 1943; all in Roosevelt Papers, OF 20, Box 11, State Department, 1943.

33. Roosevelt to Hull, Roosevelt to Stimson, Roosevelt to Knox, Roosevelt to Morgenthau, Roosevelt to Stettinius, Roosevelt to Lehman, and Roosevelt to Wallace, all June 3, 1943, all in Roosevelt Papers, OF 20, Box 11, State Department, 1943.

34. "Coordination of Economic Operations of Civilian Agencies in Liberated Areas: Letter of the President to the Secretary of State, June 3, 1943, and 'Plan for Coordinating the Economic Activities of U.S. Civilian Agencies in Liberated Areas,'" *Department of State Bulletin*, June 26, 1943, pp. 575–579.

35. I. F. Stone, "Hull Wins Power Over Foreign Relief from Lehman," *PM*, June 8, 1943, clipping in Roosevelt Papers, OF 5175, Lehman, Director of UNRRA; Lehman to Roosevelt, June 5, 1943, LP, SF, Franklin Roosevelt; Lehman to Hull, June 17, 1943, UNRRA Papers, Microfilm Reel DG/12, Letters from Lehman to State Department, 1943, LP.

36. Smith, Memorandum for the President, June 7, 1943, and Roosevelt, Memorandum for James Byrnes, July 13, 1943, both in Roosevelt Papers, OF 20, Box 11, State Department, 1943; Acheson, *Present at the Creation*, p. 44–46; Carolin Flexner Oral History Transcript, HHLP, CUOHC, pp. 40–42.

37. Acheson, *Present at the Creation*, pp. 68–71; Hull to Roosevelt, May 25, 1943, and Hull to Roosevelt, June 7, 1943, both in Roosevelt Papers, OF 4966, UNRRA, 1943; "U.S. Offers Plan for World Relief," *NYT*, June 11, 1943, pp. 1, 9. For the details of the negotiations on the UNRRA agreement, see *FRUS, 1943*, I: 851–910. For the text of the draft agreement, see "Draft Agreement for United Nations Relief and Rehabilitation Administration," *Department of State Bulletin*, June 12, 1943, pp. 523–527.

38. Hull to Roosevelt, June 7, 1943, and F.D.R., Memorandum for General Watson, June 8, 1943, both in Roosevelt Papers, OF 4966, UNRRA, 1943; "President to Seek Food Relief Set-Up," *NYT*, June 10, 1943, p. 28; Acheson, *Present at the Creation*, p. 71; Divine, *Second Chance*, p. 117.

39. Acheson, *Present at the Creation*, pp. 71–72; Vandenberg, ed., *The Private Papers of Senator Vandenberg*, pp. 66–74; "Urges Hull Modify World Relief Pact," *NYT*, July 9, 1943, p. 15; Hull, Memorandum for the President, August 10, 1943, Roosevelt Papers, OF 4966, UNRRA, 1943; "Senators May Vote Pacts by Majority Along with House," *NYT*, August 18, 1943, pp. 1, 11; "Plan for Majority on Pacts Limited," *NYT*, August 19, 1943, p. 15; Divine, *Second Chance*, pp. 117–118.

40. "WFA Denies Food to Lehman Agency," *NYT*, August 15, 1943, pp. 1, 40.

41. Lehman to Roosevelt, August 30, 1943, LP, SF, Franklin Roosevelt.

42. Ibid.

43. Ibid.

44. Ibid.

45. Ibid.

46. Lehman to Hull, August 30, 1943, and Hull to Lehman, September 4, 1943, both in LP, SF, Hull.

47. Hull, Memorandum for the President, September 4, 1943, Roosevelt Papers, OF 20, Box 11, State Department, 1943.

48. Department of State, Memorandum for the President, September 4, 1943, LP, SF, Hull.

49. Ibid.

50. Ibid.

51. See marginal comments on Department of State, Memorandum for the President, September 4, 1943, LP, SF, Hull.

52. "Hull to Take Reins Over All Agencies in Economic Field," *NYT*, September 3, 1943, pp. 1, 7; C. B. Baldwin Heads Relief for Italy," *NYT*, September 5, 1943, p. 5; Blum, ed., *The Price of Vision*, p. 251.

53. "Conflicts Impair State Department, President Is Told," *NYT*, August 4, 1943, pp. 1, 4; Arthur Krock, "In the Nation: The Situation in the State Department," *NYT*, August 6, 1943, p. 14; "Welles Is Reported Taking Diplomatic Post," *NYT*, August 11, 1943, pp. 1, 6; "Stettinius Named for Welles Post; Crowley Shifted," *NYT*, September 26, 1943, pp. 1, 14; Eleanor Roosevelt Oral History Transcript, HHLP, CUOHC, pp. 11–12; Krock, *Memoirs*, pp. 205–207; Gellman, *Secret Affairs*; Welles, *Sumner Welles*. On Hopkins's diplomatic missions, see Roll, *The Hopkins Touch*; and O'Sullivan, *Harry Hopkins*.

54. Byrnes, *All in One Lifetime*, p. 197; "Stettinius Named for Welles Post; Crowley Shifted," *NYT*, September 26, 1943, pp. 1, 14; "Foreign Economic Administration and Foreign Relief: Appointment of Leo T. Crowley as Foreign Economic Administrator and Appointment of Herbert H. Lehman as Special Assistant to the President," White House Press Release, September 25, 1943, in *Department of State Bulletin*, September 25, 1943, pp. 205–206; "The President Does Some Juggling," *New Republic*, October 4, 1943, p. 441; Acheson, *Present at the Creation*, pp. 46–47.

55. Byrnes, *All in One Lifetime*, p. 198.

56. White House Press Release, September 25, 1943, Roosevelt Papers, OF 91, Lehman; Roosevelt to Lehman, September 25, 1943, LP, SF, Franklin Roosevelt; "Stettinius Named for Welles Post; Crowley Shifted," *NYT*, September 26, 1943, pp. 1, 14.

57. "Continuation of Foreign Relief and Rehabilitation Operations," *Department of State Bulletin*, October 2, 1943, pp. 223–224; Lehman to Crowley, October 4, 1943, and Crowley to Lehman, October 8, 1943, UNRRA Papers, Microfilm Reel DG/8, Foreign Economic Administration, Crowley, LP.

58. Lehman, Memorandum to the President, n.d., attached to S. I. R. [Samuel Rosenman], Memorandum for the President, October 1, 1943, Rosenman Papers, Box 17, Subject File, UNRRA, FDRL.

59. Roosevelt, Memorandum for S. I. R., September 6, 1943, Roosevelt Papers, OF 20, Box 11, Department of State, 1943; and Lehman, Memorandum to the President, n.d.; Memorandum by the President, S. I. R. Draft, October 1, 1943; S. I. R., Memorandum for the President, October 1, 1943; and Acheson to Rosenman, October 21, 1943; all in Rosenman Papers, Box 17, Subject Files, UNRRA. On Rosenman's appointment as the President's Special Counsel, see "President Names Rosenman as Aide to Advise on Draft and Court-Martials," *NYT*, September 15, 1943, p. 30; Lehman to Rosenman, September 16, 1943, LP, SF, Rosenman; Rosenman, *Working with Roosevelt*, p. 379.

60. S. I. R., Memorandum for the President, October 19, 1943; and Memorandum by the President, "Organization of United Nations Relief and Rehabilitation Administration," October 19, 1943; both in Roosevelt Papers, OF 4966, UNRRA, 1943.

61. Mrs. J. M. Helm, Secretary to Mrs. Roosevelt, to Lehman, October 19, 1943, and Lehman to Mrs. Roosevelt, November 1, 1943, both in LP, SF, Eleanor Roosevelt; Lash, *A World of Love*, pp. 85–86. Francis Sayre quickly followed Lehman to UNRRA, where he served as Diplomatic Advisor.

62. Hull to the President, August 31, 1943; Roosevelt, Memorandum for the Secretary of State, September 6, 1943; and Lehman to Dr. Kelchner, October 27, 1943; all in Roosevelt Papers, OF 4966, UNRRA, 1943; The Secretary of State to Certain Diplomatic Representatives, September 21, 1943, in *FRUS, 1943*, I: 994–996; "'Big Four' Approve a New Relief Plan for the Liberated," *NYT*, September 24, 1943, pp. 1, 13; "Proposed Relief Plan of the United Nations," *NYT*, September 24, 1943, p. 12.

63. On Hull's popularity and prestige, see Nichols, ed., *Washington Despatches*, pp. 62, 135, 272, 345, 432, 466; Divine, *Second Chance*, pp. 154–155; Krock, *The Consent of the Governed*, pp. 108–109; Gellman, *Secret Affairs*, pp. 153–154, 337–338.

Chapter 8. "Freedom from Want": Lehman, Roosevelt, and UNRRA, 1943–1945

1. HHLOH, p. 739.

2. "44 Nations Sign Relief Pact; President Hails World Aid," *NYT*, November 10, 1943, pp. 1, 3; "President's Address to the Relief Conferees," *NYT*, November 10, 1943, p. 4; "Signers of Relief Pact at White House; Envoys of 44 Nations at the Ceremony," *NYT*, November 10, 1943, p. 4; Eleanor Roosevelt, *This I Remember*, p. 314; S. I. R. [Samuel Rosenman], Memorandum for Grace Tully, November 5, 1943, and "UNRRA Speech–11/9/43," both in Rosenman Papers, Box 24, Material for FDR Speeches and Messages, Establishment of UNRRA, November 9, 1943; Rosenman, *Working with Roosevelt*, pp. 399–400; Acheson, *Present at the Creation*, pp. 76–77. For a full history of UNRRA's administrative structure, its personnel, and its accomplishments, see Woodbridge, ed., *UNRRA*.

3. "44 Nations Meet to Arrange Relief," *NYT*, November 11, 1943, p. 5; "War Relief Body Headed by Lehman; Aid Pledged to All," *NYT*, November 12, 1943, pp. 1, 13.

4. "Text of Lehman's Address in Accepting Directorship of United Nations Relief," *NYT*, November 12, 1943, p. 13.

5. "First Aid to the Liberated," Editorial, *NYT*, November 16, 1943, p. 22; "UNRRA Is Praised by Jan Masaryk," *NYT*, December 13, 1943, p. 6.

6. "Roosevelt Seeks Congress Action on UNRRA Funds," *NYT*, November 16, 1943, p. 1; "The President on Relief," *NYT*, November 16, 1943, p. 12; "President Asks Aid of U.S. in Rehabilitation," *WP*, November 16, 1943, p. 1; H.J. Res. 192, 78th Cong., 1st sess., November 15, 1943; Bloom, *The Autobiography of Sol Bloom*, p. 267.

7. Hull to Lehman, November 16, 1943, LP, SF, Hull; Crowley to Lehman, November 16, 1943, LP, Personal Correspondence and General File of the Director General of UNRRA, "C," C46-11; Memorandum, The Combined Production and Resources Board, the Combined Raw Materials Board, the Combined Food Board, and the Combined Shipping Adjustment Board to Lehman, November 25, 1943, UNRRA Papers, Microfilm Reel DG/9, Lehman, January–July 1945 [*sic*], LP; "UNRRA Recognizes India's Food Crisis," *NYT*, December 2, 1943, p. 16; Lehman to Fred Hoehler, November 29, 1943, LP, UNRRA, "H," C46-7.

8. Lehman to Crowley, October 4, 1943, and Crowley to Lehman, October 8, 1943, both in UNRRA Papers, Microfilm Reel DG/8, Foreign Economic Administra-

tion, Crowley; Arthur Krock, "In the Nation: Loose Cogs in Foreign Economic Policy Machine," *NYT*, November 19, 1943, p. 18.

9. On Krock's connections with Hull and the State Department, see Krock, *Memoirs*, pp. 81, 160–161, 202–211; Blum, ed., *The Price of Vision*, pp. 144, n. 3, and 312; Nicholas, ed., *Washington Despatches*, pp. 154, 231–232.

10. John L. Loeb to Lehman, December 4, 1943, LP, Personal Correspondence and General File of the Director General of UNRRA, "L," C47-46; Note by Sayre on Lehman Memorandum forwarding Acheson's letter of January 19, 1944, LP, Personal Correspondence and General File of the Director General of UNRRA, Lehman, Herbert, Memos, August 1943–March 1944, C47-52.

11. Burns, *Roosevelt*, pp. 513–514; HHLOH, p. 739.

12. Letter of the Secretary of State to the Chairman of the House Foreign Affairs Committee, December 7, 1943, in *Department of State Bulletin*, December 11, 1943, p. 416; "Hearings Begin on UNRRA Funds," *NYT*, December 8, 1943, p. 12; U.S. Congress, House, *To Enable the United States to Participate in the Work of the United Nations Relief and Rehabilitation Administration; Hearings*, House Committee on Foreign Affairs, 78th Cong., 1st and 2nd sess., 1943–1944, pp. 5–6, 21, 105–118, 217–229 (hereinafter *UNRRA Authorization Hearings, House, 1943*); "Possible Political Use of UNRRA Funds Admitted by Acheson," *WP*, December 8, 1943, p. 7; "Our Relief Grant to Be Spent Here," *NYT*, December 8, 1943, p. 15; "Says We Can Spare UNRRA Supplies," *NYT*, December 10, 1943, p. 21.

13. Nicholas, ed., *Washington Despatches*, pp. 289–290.

14. Nicholas, ed., *Washington Despatches*, p. 290; "Lehman Links War to UNRRA Success," *NYT*, December 11, 1943, p. 7; *UNRRA Authorization Hearings, House, 1943*, pp. 119–154; Bloom, *The Autobiography of Sol Bloom*, pp. 267–268.

15. "President's Message on National Budget as Complicated by the War and Coming Victory," *NYT*, January 14, 1944, pp. 10–11.

16. "House Group Backs Funds for UNRRA," *NYT*, January 13, 1944, p. 7; *Authorizing the United States to Participate in the Work of the United Nations Relief and Rehabilitation Administration*, H. Rept. 994, 78th Cong., 2d sess., January 17, 1944; "UNRRA," Editorial, *WP*, January 24, 1944, p. 6.

17. "Bloc Moves to Cut UNRRA Donation," *WP*, January 21, 1944, p. 3; "Republicans Split on UNRRA in House," *NYT*, January 21, 1944, p. 10.

18. Herbert Lehman, "Half a Billion Hungry People," *New York Times Magazine*, January 30, 1944, SM3, 30–31. See also "The State Department Speaks," *Department of State Bulletin*, January 22, 1944, pp. 100–103.

19. "1,350,000,000 Fund Is Voted for UNRRA," *NYT*, January 26, 1944, p. 11; Campbell and Herring, eds., *The Diaries of Edward R. Stettinius, Jr.*, p. 17; Bloom, *The Autobiography of Sol Bloom*, p. 268; "Senate Unit Told Italy Pays for Aid," *WP*, February 11, 1944, p. 5; U.S. Cong., Senate, *United Nations Relief and Rehabilitation Organization; Hearings*, Senate Committee on Foreign Relations, 78th Cong., 2d sess., 1944; "Senate Group Authorizes UNRRA Funds," *WP*, February 15, 1944, pp. 1, 3; "Senate Approval of Bill Providing $1,350,000,000 for UNRRA Expected Today," *WP*, February 17, 1944, p. 5; "UNRRA Bill Voted in Full by Senate," *NYT*, February 18, 1944, p. 8; "UNRRA Fund Vote," Editorial, *WP*, February 20, 1944, B-4; "Agree on UNRRA Terms," *NYT*, March 15, 1944, p. 3; "UNRRA Compromise Adopted by Senate," *NYT*,

March 22, 1944, p. 21; "House Votes Right to Give UNRRA Fund," *NYT*, March 23, 1944, p. 8; "Bill to Join UNRRA Signed," *NYT*, March 29, 1944, p. 16. For the text of the final bill, see Public Law 267, 78th Cong., 2d sess., 58 Stat. 122-128 (1944).

20. Lehman to Connally, February 29, 1944, LP, SF, Connally.

21. Wyman, *The Abandonment of the Jews*, pp. 315–316; Breitman and Kraut, *American Refugee Policy and European Jewry, 1933–1945*, p. 87. Similarly, Congressman Sol Bloom worried that any actions he took to help his fellow Jews would be seen as "discrimination in favor of my people." See Bloom, *The Autobiography of Sol Bloom*, pp. 272–274. On the difficult position of Jews who were close to Roosevelt, see also Shogan, *Prelude to Catastrophe*; and Moreira, *The Jew Who Defeated Hitler*.

22. "Lehman Will Visit Britain, Middle East," *NYT*, March 8, 1944, p. 3; Herbert Lehman to Edith Lehman, March 17, March 22, March 27, and March 30, 1944, all in LP, SF, Edith Lehman; "Former Governor Injured in Fall," *NYT*, March 19, 1944, p. 21; "UNRRA to Take Over Balkan Relief May 1," *NYT*, April 7, 1944, p. 3; Cairo Diary, March 12–April 10, 1944, p. 75, LP, Personal Correspondence and General File of the Director General of UNRRA, C46-12; "Lieut. Peter Gerald Lehman Killed in Plane Crash at Base in England," *NYT*, April 12, 1944, p. 3; "Lieut. Lehman Honored," *NYT*, October 15, 1944, p. 4.

23. Franklin Roosevelt to Herbert Lehman, April 11, 1944, and Lehman to Roosevelt, April 28, 1944, both in LP, SF, Franklin Roosevelt.

24. Stettinius to the President, February 19, 1944; Roosevelt to Donald Nelson, February 22, 1944; Roosevelt to Marvin Jones, February 22, 1944; Roosevelt to Harold Ickes, February 22, 1944; and Roosevelt to Emory Land, February 22, 1944; all in Roosevelt Papers, OF 4966, UNRRA, 1944.

25. "$450,000,000 Fund for UNRRA Asked," *NYT*, May 5, 1944, p. 5.

26. "Lehman Reports to the President," *NYT*, June 1, 1944, p. 5; Ernest Lindley, "UNRRA Agreement," *WP*, June 2, 1944, p. 5. On Lindley's close ties with Roosevelt, see Nicholas, ed., *Washington Despatches*, pp. 90, n. 2, and 172.

27. Foreign Economic Administration Appropriation Bill, 1945–Including Defense Aid (Lend-Lease) and Participation by the United States in the United Nations Relief and Rehabilitation Administration, H. Rept. 1591, 78th Cong., 2d sess., June 2, 1944; "House Committee Approves 4 ½-Million [*sic*] UNRRA Fund," *WP*, June 3, 1944, pp. 1, 3; "Lend-Lease Funds Approved by House," *NYT*, June 4, 1944, pp. 1, 26; "Rome Captured Intact by the 5TH Army After Fierce Battle Through Suburbs; . . . Americans in First," *NYT*, June 5, 1944, pp. 1, 3; "Landings Find UNRRA Short of Funds," *WP*, June 9, 1944, p. 12; "UNRRA," Editorial, *WP*, June 15, 1944, p. 6; "UNRRA Fund Voted in Debate on Peace," *NYT*, June 14, 1944, pp. 1, 12; "Congress Rushing to Quit This Week," *NYT*, June 19, 1944, p. 21; "UNRRA from Lehman," Drafted by Schachter, June 28, 1944, UNRRA Papers, Microfilm Reel GC/3, Chronological Memos, Schachter, June 1, 1944–December 31, 1944, LP; "Bill Aiding Allies Signed," *NYT*, July 1, 1944, p. 6. For the text of the bill, see H. R. 4937, 78th Cong., 2d sess., Public Law 382, 58 Stat. 627-631 (1944).

28. "Lehman Tells People of Occupied Europe Aid from UNRRA to Follow Invading Armies," *NYT*, June 8, 1944, p. 6.

29. Oscar Schachter, Memorandum to Edward Miller, June 15, 1944; Schachter, Memorandum to Karl Borders, July 1, 1944; and Schachter, Memorandum to A. H.

Feller, July 4, 1944, all in UNRRA Papers, Microfilm Reel GC/3, Chronological Memos, June 1–December 31, 1944, LP; Attorney General Biddle to the President, July 6, 1944, and Paul Appleby, Memorandum for the President, July 4, 1944, both in Roosevelt Papers, OF 4966, UNRRA, 1944; Executive Order 9453, "Participation by the United States in the Work of the United Nations Relief and Rehabilitation Administration," 9 *Fed. Reg.* 7637, July 11, 1944.

30. Roosevelt to Crowley, July 6, 1944, in Rosenman, comp., *The Public Papers and Addresses of Franklin D. Roosevelt, 1944–45: Victory and the Threshold of Peace*, pp. 417–418; A. H. Feller to George Mooney, August 23, 1944, UNRRA Papers, Microfilm Reel GC/3, Chronological Memos, Schachter, June 1–December 31, 1944, LP.

31. Roosevelt to Crowley, July 6, 1944, in Rosenman, comp., *The Public Papers and Addresses of Franklin D. Roosevelt, 1944–45: Victory and the Threshold of Peace*, pp. 417–418.

32. Roosevelt to Lehman, July 6, 1944, Roosevelt Papers, OF 4966, UNRRA, 1944; A. H. Feller to George Mooney, August 23, 1944, UNRRA Papers, Microfilm Reel GC/3, Chronological Memos, Schachter, June 1–December 31, 1944, LP; Lehman to Fred Hoehler, September 4, 1944, UNRRA Papers, Microfilm Reel DG/2, Correspondence, Reading File, Chronological, August–September, 1944, LP.

33. Lehman to Roosevelt, August 29, 1944, LP, SF, Franklin Roosevelt; "Head of OEM Division Resigns," *NYT*, September 15, 1944, p. 16; HHLOH, p. 735. The International Committee of the Red Cross experienced similar difficulty in recruiting "capable and suitable persons." See Matz, "Sweden, the United States, and Raoul Wallenberg's Mission to Hungary in 1944," p. 142, n. 183.

34. Lehman, Memo for Files, September 11, 1944, LP, SF, Franklin Roosevelt.

35. "Speed for UNRRA Urged By Lehman," *NYT*, September 27, 1944, p. 13; "UNRRA Organizes for Speedy Action," *NYT*, September 17, 1944, p. 23; "UNRRA Supplies Short," *NYT*, September 19, 1944, p. 6; "Interallied Shipping Conference," *FRUS, 1944, II:* 639–737, esp. pp. 680, 690, 699–702; Edward G. Miller, Jr., "The Second Session of the Council of UNRRA," *Department of State Bulletin*, October 29, 1944, pp. 501–502; "The Shape of Things," *The Nation*, September 30, 1944, pp. 366–367.

36. Drew Pearson, "The Washington Merry-Go-Round," *WP*, September 6, 1944, p. 10; "UNRRA Cut Itself, Lehman Declares," *NYT*, September 18, 1944, p. 5.

37. "UNRRA Cut Itself, Lehman Declares," *NYT*, September 18, 1944, p. 5.

38. "Army to Let UNRRA Run Europe Relief," *NYT*, September 20, 1944, p. 10; "UNRRA Ready To Enter Upon Its Actual Task," *NYT*, September 24, 1944, E-6; "UNRRA Job To Take Lehman to Moscow," *NYT*, September 26, 1944, p. 7; "Speed for UNRRA Urged by Lehman," *NYT*, September 27, 1944, p. 13; Miller, "The Second Session of the Council of UNRRA," *Department of State Bulletin*, October 29, 1944, pp. 501–508, 524; "UNRRA for Italy," *New Republic*, October 9, 1944, pp. 445–446.

39. "Lehman's UNRRA Mission to Russia Is Postponed," *WP*, October 22, 1944, M-8; Lehman to John McCloy, UNRRA Papers, Microfilm Reel BA/1, Side 2, Director General, LP; Drew Pearson, "The Washington Merry-Go-Round," *WP*, October 18, 1944, p. 11; H. E. Caustin, Notes of Meeting with the Director General on the Issue of Passports to UNRRA Personnel and Travel Facilities for the Families of UNRRA Personnel, February 23, 1945, UNRRA Papers, Microfilm Reel DG/10, Meetings—Notes of

Meetings, LP; Lawrence Duggan, Acting Diplomatic Adviser, Memorandum, "Issuance of Passports," August 6, 1945, UNRRA Papers, Microfilm Reel DA/4, Country File, United States, LP.

40. Lehman to Helen Leighton, April 22, 1944, LP, Personal Correspondence and General File of the Director General of UNRRA, Political, C47–77; Lehman to Benjamin Rabin, August 28, 1944, LP, Personal Correspondence and General File of the Director General of UNRRA, "R" (I), C48-81.

41. "Women to Aid Roosevelt," NYT, October 5, 1944, p. 11; "Mrs. Lehman for Roosevelt," NYT, November 1, 1944, p. 17; Judge William Fitzsimmons to Herbert Lehman, LP, Personal Correspondence and General File of the Director General of UNRRA, "F," C46-23; Lehman to Mrs. Roosevelt, November 3, 1944, LP, SF, Eleanor Roosevelt.

42. "Lehman Asks Absentee Ballot," NYT, September 30, 1944, p. 5; Lehman to David Walsh, Jr., November 7, 1944, LP, Personal Correspondence and General File of the Director General of UNRRA, "W," C49-118; "200,000 Welcome Roosevelt in Rain to Capital 'Home,'" NYT, November 11, 1944, pp. 1, 8; "Roosevelt Guess on Majority Low," NYT, November 11, 1944, p. 8.

43. "Lehman Going Soon Abroad for UNRRA," NYT, November 10, 1944, p. 5; Lehman to Hopkins, November 6, 1944, and Lehman to the President, November 6, 1944, both in LP, SF, Hopkins.

44. George Summerlin, Memorandum for Mr. Early, November 3, 1944, Roosevelt Papers, OF 4966, UNRRA, 1944; Roosevelt to Lehman, November 9, 1944, in Rosenman, comp., The Public Papers and Addresses of Franklin D. Roosevelt, 1944–45: Victory and the Threshold of Peace, p. 416; "Lehman Going Soon Abroad for UNRRA," NYT, November 10, 1944, p. 5.

45. "Lehman in London to Speed Aid," NYT, November 14, 1944, p. 20; Herbert Lehman to Edith Lehman, November 14, 1944, and November 16, 1944, LP, SF, Legal Size, Box 3, UNRRA, Herbert Lehman-Edith Lehman Correspondence; "Russia to Examine UNRRA's Polish Aid," NYT, November 17, 1944, p. 8.

46. Herbert Lehman to Edith Lehman, November 26, 1944, and December 5, 1944, LP, SF, Legal Size, Box 3, UNRRA, Herbert Lehman-Edith Lehman Correspondence.

47. Oscar Cox, Memorandum for Mr. Stephen Early, November 15, 1944, Roosevelt Papers, OF 4966, UNRRA, 1944; "The President Transmits to the Congress UNRRA's First Quarterly Report on Expenditures and Operations," December 5, 1944, in Rosenman, comp., The Public Papers and Addresses of Franklin D. Roosevelt, 1944–45: Victory and the Threshold of Peace, pp. 434–435; "Says Europe's Need for Relief Is Great," NYT, December 6, 1944, p. 5.

48. Lehman to the American Embassy to Transmit to President Roosevelt, December 8, 1944, LP, SF, Franklin Roosevelt; Herbert Lehman to Edith Lehman, December 9, 1944, LP, SF, Legal Size, Box 3, UNRRA, Herbert Lehman-Edith Lehman Correspondence; Roy Hendrickson, Memorandum on Telephone Conversation with the Director General, December 8, 1944, UNRRA Papers, Microfilm Reel DG/10, Meetings, Director General, LP.

49. London and Paris Diary, November 11, 1944–December 26, 1944, p. 95, LP, Personal Correspondence and General File of the Director General of UNRRA, C47-65;

Stettinius, for Governor Lehman from President Roosevelt, December 17, 1944, LP, SF, Franklin Roosevelt.

50. London and Paris Diary, November 11, 1944–December 26, 1944, pp. 105–106, LP, Personal Correspondence and General File of the Director General of UNRRA, C47-65; John Corson to Lehman, December 15, 1944, UNRRA Papers, Microfilm Reel DG/2, Caustin File, cont., LP.

51. London and Paris Diary, November 11, 1944–December 26, 1944, pp. 106–107, LP, Personal Correspondence and General File of the Director General of UNRRA, C47-65; Lehman to the American Embassy to Transmit to President Roosevelt, December 15, 1944, LP, SF, Franklin Roosevelt.

52. "The Stettinius Record," Week of 17–23 December 1944, *FRUS: Conferences at Malta and Yalta, 1945*, p. 437; James Reston, "U.S. and Britain to Confer on Dire Needs of Europe," *NYT*, December 15, 1944, pp. 1, 6.

53. "Lehman Gets a Few Relief Ships; Russia Silent on UNRRA in Poland," *NYT*, December 30, 1944, pp. 1, 4; "Text of Lehman's Report of Tour," *NYT*, December 30, 1944, p. 4.

54. "Memorandum of Agreement between the United States and the United Kingdom Concerning the Shipment of Supplies to Liberated European Countries During the First Six Months of 1945," January 14, 1945, *FRUS: Malta and Yalta, 1945*, pp. 420–422.

55. Meeting of the Combined Chiefs of Staff, February 2, 1945, ibid., p. 534; The Joint Chiefs of Staff to the President, January 30, 1945, ibid., pp. 534–536.

56. Meeting of the Combined Chiefs of Staff with Roosevelt and Churchill, February 2, 1945, 6 p.m., on Board the U.S.S. *Quincy* in Grand Harbor, ibid., p. 541; First Plenary Meeting, February 4, 1945, 5 p.m., Livadia Palace, ibid., p. 576; Report of the Combined Chiefs of Staff to President Roosevelt and Prime Minister Churchill, February 9, 1945, ibid., pp. 827–831.

57. Lehman to the President, January 19, 1945, ibid., pp. 108–109.

58. Stettinius, Memorandum for the President, January 18, 1945, ibid., pp. 42–43; Briefing Book Paper, "Relations between UNRRA and the Soviet Government," ibid., pp. 109–110.

59. "The Yalta Conference," ibid., pp. 547–996; "Text of the Big Three Announcement on the Crimea Conference," *NYT*, February 13, 1945, p. 4; "Report of President Roosevelt in Person to the Congress on the Crimea Conference," *NYT*, March 2, 1945, p. 12; "The Text of Churchill's Report to the House of Commons on the Allies' Decisions at Yalta," *NYT*, February 28, 1945, p. 14.

60. "Rosenman Mission to Study Supplies," *NYT*, January 23, 1945, p. 13; Rosenman, *Working with Roosevelt*, p. 518–520; Lehman to Rosenman and attached Memorandum on UNRRA Policies and Present Activities for Judge Samuel I. Rosenman, February 8, 1945, Rosenman Papers, Box 17, Subject Files, UNRRA; "Rosenman in London; Goods Sped to France," *NYT*, March 7, 1945, p. 5.

61. Leith–Ross to Lehman, February 3, 1945, LP, SF, Leith-Ross; "UNRRA Help for Western Europe Sought," *WP*, February 18, 1945, M-5; "UNRRA Widens Program to Help End Suffering in Western Europe," *NYT*, February 27, 1945, p. 8; "Rehabilitation: A Road to Peace," Address by Herbert H. Lehman," February 24, 1945, Roosevelt Papers, OF 4966, UNRRA, Misc.; "UNRRA Held Basis of Lasting Peace,"

NYT, February 25, 1945, p. 30; "Calls for Relief Growing Louder in Europe," *NYT*, March 11, 1945, E-5.

62. Memorandum for Mr. Hassett, March 5, 1945, Roosevelt Papers, OF 4966, UNRRA, 1945; Hassett, *Off the Record*, p. 322; "WFA Balks at Draining U.S. of Food for Relief Abroad," *WP*, March 11, 1945, M-1.

63. "Text of Byrnes' Order Creating Stiffer Control of War Exports," *WP*, March 12, 1945, p. 2; "Export Gate Established to Protect U.S. Supply," *WP*, March 12, 1945, pp. 1, 2.

64. H. E. Caustin, Notes of Meeting with the Director General on the Establishment of United States Inter-Agency Committee to Coordinate Foreign Shipments, March 12, 1945, 9:45 a.m., UNRRA Papers, Microfilm Reel DG/10, Meetings, Director General, LP.

65. Lehman to Byrnes, March 12, 1945, UNRRA Papers, Microfilm Reel DG/2, Correspondence, March 1945, LP.

66. Second Meeting on this Subject," March 12, 1945, 4:00 p.m., UNRRA Papers, Microfilm Reel DG/10, Meetings, Director General, LP; "Lehman Sees Export Curb as Peril to UNRRA," *WP*, March 13, 1945, pp. 1, 2.

67. Lehman to Crowley, March 14, 1945, UNRRA Papers, Microfilm Reel DG/2, Correspondence, March 1945; Lehman to Marvin Jones, March 14, 1945, UNRRA Papers, Microfilm Reel DG/2, Correspondence, March 9–March 20, 1945; both in LP.

68. Weintraub to the Combined Food Board, March 14, 1945, UNRRA Papers, Microfilm Reel DG/2, Correspondence, March 9–March 20, 1945, LP.

69. "Lehman Jab at Export Curbs Stirs Senate Ire," *WP*, March 14, 1945, p. 1; "UNRRA Help for Western Europe Sought," *WP*, February 18, 1945, M-5; Woodbridge, *UNRRA*, II: 334–336. On Eastland, see Asch, *The Senator and the Sharecropper*.

70. "Roosevelt Asks Belt Tightening," *NYT*, March 17, 1945, pp. 1, 18; "Decency Forces Food-Sharing with Europe, Roosevelt Says; President Expresses Doubt Home Front Has Suffered Much," *WP*, March 17, 1945, pp. 1, 2; "U.S. Exports of Food Will Not Decline and May Even Increase, WFA and President Indicate," *Wall Street Journal*, March 17, 1945, p. 3.

71. Acting Director General Roy Hendrickson to the President, December 23, 1944, UNRRA Papers, Microfilm Reel DG/2, Correspondence Reading File, Chronological, December 17–December 30, 1944, LP; "Big Clothing Drive for Europe Is Set," *NYT*, January 28, 1945, p. 16; Lehman to Mrs. Roosevelt, February 1, 1945, and February 6, 1945, and Lehman to Kaiser, February 6, 1945, all in UNRRA Papers, Microfilm Reel DG/2, Correspondence, February 1–February 8, 1945, LP.

72. Lehman to Mrs. Roosevelt, February 6, 1945, UNRRA Papers, Microfilm Reel DG/2, Correspondence, February 1–February 8, 1945; Lehman to Mrs. Helm, Secretary to Mrs. Roosevelt, February 13, 1945, UNRRA Papers, Microfilm Reel DG/2, Correspondence, February 9–February 14, 1945; both in LP; "Lehman Asks for Used Clothing for Liberated People of Europe," *NYT*, February 28, 1945, p. 13; "Clothing Drive Goes Over the Top," *NYT*, July 5, 1945, p. 8.

73. UNRRA from Lehman, drafted by Caustin, March 19, 1945, UNRRA Papers, Microfilm Reel DG/4, Chronological Reading File Correspondence, January–April 1945; Crowley to Lehman, March 20, 1945, UNRRA Papers, Microfilm Reel GC/3, Committee: Food; both in LP.

74. Lehman to Roosevelt, March 24, 1945, UNRRA Papers, Microfilm Reel DG/2, Correspondence, March 21–March 31, 1945, LP; Dulles, *The American Red Cross*, pp. 366, 516; FDR, Memorandum for the Director of the Budget, March 25, 1945, Roosevelt Papers, OF 4966, UNRRA, 1945; Truman, *Memoirs*, I: 97, 226.

75. Lehman to Roosevelt, March 31, 1945, UNRRA Papers, Microfilm Reel DG/18, Side 2, United States Government–UNRRA Relations, LP; FDR, Memorandum for the Director of the Budget, April 2, 1945, Roosevelt Papers, OF 4966, UNRRA, 1945. The March 31, 1945, letter from Lehman to Roosevelt is misfiled chronologically in the middle of March 1946 documents.

76. "President Roosevelt Is Dead; . . . End Comes Suddenly at Warm Springs," *NYT*, April 13, 1945, pp. 1, 3; Statement by Herbert H. Lehman on the Death of President Roosevelt, April 12, 1945, LP, SF, Franklin Roosevelt; Edith and Herbert Lehman to Mrs. Roosevelt, April 13, 1945, LP, SF, Eleanor Roosevelt; Edith and Herbert Lehman to Mrs. John Boettiger, LP, SF, Anna Roosevelt Halsted; "Roosevelt Is Buried with Solemn Rites, . . . Grave Is in Garden," *NYT*, April 16, 1945, pp. 1, 3.

77. Eleanor Roosevelt to Edith Lehman, April 19, 1945, LP, SF, Eleanor Roosevelt; Herbert Lehman to Rudolf Bicanic, April 19, 1945, LP, Personal Correspondence and General File of the Director General of UNRRA, Franklin Roosevelt.

78. Roosevelt to Lehman, October 3, 1928, LP, SF, Franklin Roosevelt; "UNRRA to Provide Relief of 2 Billion," *NYT*, April 12, 1945, p. 12.

Chapter 9. "UNRRA's Problem Is That It Is Trying to Cover a 6-Foot Man with a 2-Foot Blanket": Herbert Lehman, Harry Truman, and UNRRA, 1945

1. Robert G. A. Jackson, untitled manuscript, August 1954, p. 19, LP, SF, Jackson, document 0442_0136.

2. HHLOH, p. 133; "Norris Predicts Bitter Contest in U.S.," *WP*, December 11, 1942, p. 19; "Trumans Guests at Club Dinner," *WP*, February 16, 1945, p. 10. On Truman's background and career before the presidency, see Hamby, *Man of the People*.

3. Memorandum by the Secretary of State to President Truman, April 16, 1945, in *FRUS, 1945*, II: 1085–1086; Truman, *Memoirs*, I: 45.

4. Truman, *Memoirs*, I: 97, 226.

5. "UNRRA Rushing Aid in Liberated Zone," *NYT*, April 27, 1945, p. 27; "Forty UNRRA Teams Kept from Germany as Equipment Is Held Up on Dock in Britain," *NYT*, April 28, 1945, p. 8; "Lack of Transport Slows Grain Export," *NYT*, April 29, 1945, S-4; "Famine Treads Heels of Peace in Europe," *WP*, May 6, 1945, M-4; "No Further Food Reductions Seen by Government Experts," *WP*, May 9, 1945, pp. 1, 2; Marquis Childs, "Washington Calling: Victims of Nazism," *WP*, April 27, 1945, p. 6.

6. "UNRRA Unit Chief Quits; Russian Heads Temporary Group," *WP*, March 24, 1945, p. 6; "UNRRA Is Attacked as Backing Lublin," *NYT*, April 5, 1945, p. 14; Memorandum by Mr. Charles Bohlen, Assistant to the Secretary of State for White House Liaison, to the Secretary of State, April 19, 1945, and Minutes of the Secretary of State's Staff Committee, April 21, 1945, both in *FRUS, 1945*, V: 832, 836–837; 842–844; "Leave Soon for Warsaw," *NYT*, July 7, 1945, p. 10.

7. Lehman to Stettinius, April 13, 1945, UNRRA Papers, Microfilm Reel DG/2, Correspondence, April 1945, LP.

8. Rosenman, *Working with Roosevelt*, pp. 518, 545; "Rosenman Tells Truman U.S. Help Must Save Europe from New War," *NYT*, May 1, 1945, p. 15; "Text of Judge Rosenman's Report on Europe," *NYT*, May 1, 1945, p. 15; Truman, *Memoirs*, I: 308.

9. Rosenman Mission, "UNRRA in North West Europe," April 15, 1945, Truman Papers, White House Central Files, Confidential Files, Box 31, Rosenman Report (4), HSTL.

10. "The President's Day," May 1, 1945, Truman Papers, Daily Presidential Appointments, HSTL; Lehman, Memorandum for the President, May 1, 1945, UNRRA Papers, Microfilm Reel BA/3, Side 1, The President, LP.

11. "Tools to Aid Europe Are Asked by Lehman," *NYT*, May 9, 1945, p. 15.

12. "Vast Crowd Hears 'Feed-Europe' Plea," *NYT*, May 21, 1945, pp. 1, 11.

13. Memorandum by the Secretary of State to President Truman, April 16, 1945, and President Truman to the Secretary of War, May 21, 1945, in *FRUS, 1945*, II: 1085–1086, 1096–1097; Rosenman Mission, "UNRRA In North West Europe," April 15, 1945, Truman Papers, White House Central Files, Confidential Files, Box 31, Rosenman Report (4), HSTL; Lehman, Memorandum for the President, May 1, 1945, UNRRA Papers, Microfilm Reel BA/3, Side 1, The President, LP; Summary Sheet re: Memo from Judge Samuel Rosenman, May 21, 1945, Truman Papers, OF 423, UNRRA, 1945; "President Orders Relief for Europe," *NYT*, May 23, 1945, p. 9.

14. "Hoover Assails UNRRA on Food; Sees Tragedy for Cities of Europe," *NYT*, April 8, 1945, p. 20; "Feed Victims Now, Hoover Appeals," *NYT*, May 9, 1945, p. 16; "Bread for Europe Asked by Hoover," *NYT*, May 17, 1945, p. 4; Smith, *An Uncommon Man*, pp. 343–346. There is some question as to the accuracy of the *New York Times* report on Hoover's April 8 speech. A friend of both Lehman and Hoover who was present for the speech told Lehman a few days later that "the reported transcription of Mr. Hoover's remarks was inaccurate; that some of the statements accredited to him were made by other speakers, some were not made at all, and that Mr. Hoover voiced *no* criticism of you." See H. E. Caustin Memorandum to Kathleen Louchheim, "*New York Times* article on Hoover Speech," April 16, 1945, UNRRA Papers, Microfilm Reel DG/4, Chronological Reading File, Correspondence, January–April, 1945, LP.

15. Marquis Childs, "Washington Calling: Food and the Peace," *WP*, May 23, 1945, p. 9; George Behr to President Truman, May 16, 1945, Truman Papers, OF 423-A, Endorsements, Hoover; Albert S. Brown and E. T. P., "Paging Herbert Hoover," Letters to the Editor, *WP*, May 21, 1945, p. 6; Marquis Childs, "Washington Calling: Hoover and the Food Crisis," *NYT*, April 13, 1945, p. 8; Childs, "Food for Europe: Comparing 1918–1945," *WP*, April 24, 1945, p. 6; "Food in Europe," Editorial, *NYT*, May 11, 1945, p. 18.

16. Stimson Diary, May 2, 1945; Edgar Rickard Diary, May 30, 1945; and Truman to Hoover, May 24, 1945; documents 4, 15, and 10 in "Hoover and Truman: A Presidential Friendship," Part I: "The End of Exile," online: http://www.trumanlibrary.org/hoover/exile.htm; "Mr. Truman Calls Mr. Hoover," Editorial, *NYT*, May 28, 1945, p. 18; Smith, *An Uncommon Man*, pp. 341–346; Bentley, *Eating for Victory*, pp. 146–147.

17. Personal Memo of Herbert Hoover, May 28, 1945; Hoover, Memorandum on the Organization of Foreign Relief and Rehabilitation, May 30, 1945; and Hoover, Memo-

randum on Reorganization of the War Food Agencies," May 30, 1945; documents 14, 16a, and 16b in "Hoover and Truman: A Presidential Friendship," Part I: "The End of Exile"; Smith, *An Uncommon Man*, pp. 346–348; Truman, *Memoirs*, I: 309–310, 465; "Truman Hears Hoover on Food; Invites Landon, Dewey for Talks," *NYT*, May 29, 1945, pp. 1, 7; "Marquis Childs, "Washington Calling: Feeding Europe," *WP*, June 13, 1945, p. 8.

18. Arthur Krock, "Hoover and Food Job," *NYT*, May 30, 1945, p. 20; Drew Pearson, "The Washington Merry-Go-Round," *WP*, June 22, 1945, p. 9.

19. Herbert Lehman to John Lehman, June 2, 1945, LP, Personal Correspondence and General File of the Director General of UNRRA, John Lehman, 47–58.

20. "Europe Looks to U.S. for the Food It Needs," *NYT*, June 3, 1945, E-7; Marquis Childs, "Washington Calling: Feeding Europe," *WP*, June 13, 1945, p. 8.

21. "The President's Day," June 13, 1945, Truman Papers; Lehman to Truman, June 15, 1945, Truman Papers, OF 423, UNRRA, 1945.

22. Truman to Lehman, June 23, 1945, and Truman, Memorandum for the War Food Administrator, June 23, 1945, both in Truman Papers, OF 423, UNRRA, 1945.

23. Oscar Schachter to Sherman Sheppard, June 6, 1945, UNRRA Papers, Microfilm Reel GC/3, Chronological Memos, Schachter, January 1–December 13, 1945; Lehman to the President, June 18, 1945, UNRRA Papers, Microfilm Reel DG/3, Correspondence, June 1945; both in LP; M. C. Latta, Memorandum for Judge Vinson, June 19, 1945, Truman Papers, OF 423, UNRRA, 1945; U.S., Cong., House, *Fourth Report to Congress on United States Participation in Operations of UNRRA*, H. Doc. 309, 79th Cong., 1st sess., October 11, 1945, pp. 4, 29.

24. Lehman to the President, June 23, 1945; Acting Secretary of State Grew, Memorandum for the President, "UNRRA Request for Mr. Ferdinand Eberstadt," June 26, 1945; Truman to Eberstadt, June 29, 1945; Eberstadt to the President, July 6, 1945; James Byrnes, Memorandum for the President, July 29, 1945; Truman to Forrestal, August 1, 1945; Forrestal to the President, August 9, 1945; James Vardaman, Jr., Memorandum for the Secretary of the Navy, August 14, 1945; Received Over Direct London Circuit, "Please Pass to President Truman from Governor Lehman," August 7, 1945; Byrnes, Memorandum for the President, August 17, 1945; Truman to the Secretary of War, August 17, 1945; Patterson to the President, August 24, 1945; Truman to Patterson, August 25, 1945; all in Truman Papers, OF 423, UNRRA, 1945; Lehman to Acheson and Clayton, June 23, 1945, and attached draft, President to Eberstadt, n.d., and Hendrickson to Clayton, July 7, 1945, all in UNRRA Papers, Microfilm Reel DG/3, Correspondence, 1945, LP. On UNRRA's difficulty in obtaining high-quality staff, see Robert G. A. Jackson, untitled manuscript, August 1954, pp. 3–16, LP, SF, Jackson, document 0442_0136. On Eberstadt and Forrestal, see Millis, ed., *The Forrestal Diaries*, pp. 63, 87–89, 114, 162, 165, 200–203; Dorwart, *Eberstadt and Forrestal*, pp. 89–107; Donovan, *Conflict and Crisis*, pp. 139–140.

25. "Operations of UNRRA: Third Quarterly Report," *Department of State Bulletin*, July 8, 1945, pp. 52–53; "Truman Says UNRRA Is Ready for the Big Job," *NYT*, July 1, 1945, p. 19. For the full text of the report see U.S., Cong., House, *Third Report to Congress on United States Participation in Operations of UNRRA*, H. Doc. 251, 79th Cong., 1st sess., June 30, 1945.

26. "House Rejects Bar to Food for Europe," *NYT*, June 28, 1945, p. 5; "Asks Inquiry into UNRRA," *NYT*, July 1, 1945, p. 12; "House Report Charges Chaos in

Relief Task," *WP*, July 11, 1945, p. 9; "U.S. Paying 72 Per Cent of UNRRA's Cost," *WP*, July 20, 1945, p. 7; "Byrd Committee to Probe UNRRA," *WP*, July 20, 1945, p. 11; "House Group to See Working of UNRRA," *NYT*, July 20, 1945, p. 10; "Lehman Says UNRRA 'Welcomes' Inquiry," *NYT*, July 21, 1945, p. 6; Lehman to Harry Hopkins, July 4, 1945, LP, SF, Hopkins.

27. "Urges Sacrifices So Europe May Eat," *NYT*, July 4, 1945, p. 6; "Millions to Be Hungry in Europe This Winter," *NYT*, July 22, 1945, p. 67. See also John Corson, "Can UNRRA Stop Famine?" *The Nation*, July 21, 1945, pp. 57–59.

28. "Lehman Flies to Europe," *NYT*, July 6, 1945, p. 24; "Lehman Arrives in Rome," *NYT*, July 8, 1945, p. 14; "Pope Sees Lehman Again," *NYT*, July 10, 1945, p. 7; "UNRRA Aids Five Countries, Lehman Says," *NYT*, July 11, 1945, p. 3; "Lehman Arrives in Athens," *NYT*, July 14, 1945, p. 13; "Transport Dearth Hindering Greece," *NYT*, July 19, 1945, p. 12; "Lehman in Belgrade for Yugoslav Survey," *NYT*, July 23, 1945, p. 12; "Tito Thanks Lehman," *NYT*, July 26, 1945, p. 7; "Lehman, Ill, Gives Up Trip," *NYT*, July 25, 1945, p. 7; "Lehman Arrives in London," *NYT*, July 29, 1945, p. 14. On UNRRA's difficulty in obtaining trucks, see Drew Pearson, "The Washington Merry-Go-Round," *WP*, July 6, 1945, p. 10.

29. "Lehman Held Ready to Quit to Aid UNRRA," *WP*, July 16, 1945, p. 3; "UNRRA's Needs," Editorial, *WP*, July 17, 1945, p. 6; "Lehman to Keep Post," *NYT*, July 20, 1945, p. 6; Drew Pearson, "The Washington Merry-Go-Round," *WP*, August 2, 1945, p. 12. For additional reports that Lehman was about to resign, see Leonard Lyons, "Loose-Leaf Notebook," *WP*, August 2, 1945, p. 7; and Jerry Kluttz, "The Federal Diary," *WP*, August 7, 1945, p. 3.

30. The Acting Secretary of State to the Ambassador in the United Kingdom (Winant), June 11, 1945, *FRUS, 1945*, II: 1099–1102.

31. Clayton to the Secretary, July 30, 1945, and attached Memorandum for the President, "UNRRA," Truman Papers, OF 423, UNRRA, 1945; "Extension of UNRRA Relief for Italy," Executive Session of the House Committee on Foreign Affairs, July 10, 1945, in U.S., Cong., House, Committee on International Relations, Selected Executive Session Hearings of the Committee, 1943–1950, *Problems of World War II and Its Aftermath, Part 1: Postwar International Organization, Relations with Italy*, Historical Series, 1976, I: 104, 113; The Acting Secretary of State to the Ambassador in Italy (Kirk), July 17, 1945, *FRUS, 1945*, II: 993–994.

32. The British Embassy to the Department of State, May 15, 1945; The Acting Secretary of State to the Ambassador in the United Kingdom (Winant), June 11, 1945; The Acting Secretary of State to the Ambassador in the Soviet Union (Harriman), May 30, 1945; The Acting Secretary of State to the Ambassador in the United Kingdom (Winant), July 30, 1945 all in *FRUS, 1945*, II: 1091–1095, 1099–1102, 983–984, 999–1000.

33. See the correspondence between the State Department and Assistant Secretary of State Clayton, in London for the UNRRA Council meeting, in *FRUS, 1945*, II: 1001–1011, 1017–1019.

34. Address by Herbert H. Lehman, "Third Council Session of UNRRA," August 7, 1945, *Department of State Bulletin*, August 12, 1945, p. 215; "Bevin Ties Britain to Role in UNRRA," *NYT*, August 8, 1945, p. 16; "UNRRA in '46 Needs $1,516,905,150

More," *NYT*, August 9, 1945, p. 19; "UNRRA Asks More Money during 1946," *WP*, August 9, 1945, p. 5.

35. "Priorities Issued on Surplus Abroad," *NYT*, August 9, 1945, p. 29; "UNRRA Seeks Lien on War Surpluses," *NYT*, August 17, 1945, p. 8; "Italy to Get 22,000 Trucks," *NYT*, August 17, 1945, p. 8; "Yugoslavs Get U.S. Trucks," *NYT*, August 19, 1945, p. 20; "UNRRA Puts Focus on Far East Needs," *NYT*, August 10, 1945, p. 13; "Lehman Requests $500,000,000 More," *NYT*, August 12, 1945, p. 25; "New Burden Laid on UNRRA by End of War in Pacific," *NYT*, August 19, 1945, E-10.

36. Katherine Fite to Mr. and Mrs. Emerson Fite, August 12, 1945, Katherine Fite Lincoln Papers, Box 1, War Crimes, HSTL; "Royal Couple Receive Lehmans," *NYT*, August 16, 1945, p. 5; Matthew Connelly to Lehman, August 15, 1945, and Lehman to Connelly, September 4, 1945, both in LP, SF, Truman.

37. "Truman Changes Cabinet, Biddle, Perkins, Wickard Out; Jones Quits the Food Post," *NYT*, May 24, 1945, pp. 1, 20; Matusow, *Farm Policies and Politics in the Truman Years*, pp. 9–10; "Can't Feed World, Anderson Asserts," *NYT*, July 12, 1945, p. 9; "Anderson Moves to Release Meat," *NYT*, July 15, 1945, p. 41; Acting Secretary of War Robert Patterson to the President, August 24, 1945, Truman Papers, OF 423, UNRRA, 1945; "Meat Rationing May Stop in Fall, Anderson Declares," *NYT*, August 18, 1945, pp. 1, 24; Truman, *Memoirs*, I: 326; Anderson, *Outsider in the Senate*, pp. 52, 55–57; Collingham, *The Taste of War*, pp. 477–478.

38. "Meat Rationing May Stop in Fall, Anderson Declares," *NYT*, August 18, 1945, pp. 1, 24; "Food Sharing," Editorial, *WP*, August 20, 1945, p. 6; "The Shape of Things," *The Nation*, September 15, 1945, p. 242. On Hendrickson's apparent indifference or incompetence, see also the comments by Henry Wallace in Blum, *The Price of Vision*, p. 544.

39. For the resolutions passed by the UNRRA Council at the London meeting, see Woodbridge, *UNRRA*, III: 138–148. On the Soviet request for aid and the American response, see the Ambassador in the United Kingdom (Winant) to the Secretary of State, August 22, 1945; the Secretary of State to the Ambassador in the United Kingdom (Winant), August 23, 1945; the Ambassador in the United Kingdom(Winant) to the Secretary of State, September 5, 1945; and the Acting Secretary of State to the Ambassador in the Soviet Union (Harriman), September 8, 1945; all in *FRUS, 1945*, II: 1017–1019, 1021, 1024–1027.

40. "New Funds Sought by UNRRA Council," *NYT*, August 25, 1945, p. 9.

41. "*Queen Elizabeth* on Way," *NYT*, August 27, 1945, p. 7; "5 Transports Due with 17,000 Today," *NYT*, August 31, 1945, p. 7; "Lehman, Arriving, Sees 'Grim Winter,'" *NYT*, September 1, 1945, p. 6; "Lehman Calls Aid to Allies Our Duty," *NYT*, September 6, 1945, p. 11.

42. "The President's Day," September 6, 1945, Truman Papers, Daily Presidential Appointments; "Large Problems of Post-War America Are Laid Before Congress by President in Message," *NYT*, September 7, 1945, pp. 16–18; "UNRRA Speeds Aid, Needs More Funds," *NYT*, September 9, 1945, pp. 1, 17; "Truman Reaffirms Relief for Freed Peoples of Europe," *NYT*, September 18, 1945, pp. 1, 13; "Truman Statement on Aid to Europe," *NYT*, September 18, 1945, p. 13. Ben Shephard asserts that UNRRA "received only token support from the Truman administration" in seeking money from

Congress during the fall of 1945, a position with which I strongly disagree. The Truman administration staunchly supported Herbert Lehman and UNRRA during 1945. It was not until 1946 that the Truman administration abandoned Lehman and UNRRA. See Shephard, *The Long Road Home*.

43. "UNRRA Request Opposed," *NYT*, August 13, 1945, p. 17; "UNRRA Called a Failure," *NYT*, August 24, 1945, p. 9; "Called 'Dire Failure,'" *WP*, August 24, 1945, p. 4; "'Laughing Stock' of Europe," *NYT*, September 13, 1945, p. 7; "Urges a Free Press under UNRRA Funds," *NYT*, August 27, 1945, p. 32; "Aid for Nations Curbing Press Hit by Brown," *WP*, August 27, 1945, p. 7; Marquis Childs, "Washington Calling: Aiding Europe Boldly," *WP*, October 4, 1945, p. 6.

44. "Lehman Hits Back at UNRRA Critics," *NYT*, September 21, 1945, p. 7.

45. Herbert Lehman to John Lehman, September 30, 1945, LP, Personal Correspondence and General File of the Director General of UNRRA, John Lehman, 47–58. On UNRRA's activities and difficulties in Europe at this time, see Shepard, *The Long Road Home*, pp. 138–164; and Gibson, *Jacko, Where Are You Now?*, pp. 67–74.

46. U.S., Cong., House, Estimate of Appropriation for the United Nations Relief and Rehabilitation Administration, Communication from the President of the United States, House Doc. 305, 79th Cong., 1st sess., October 4, 1945; "Truman Requests UNRRA Fund Speed," *NYT*, October 9, 1945, p. 2; "$1,350,000,000 Asked for UNRRA by Truman," *NYT*, November 14, 1945, pp. 1, 10; "Text of Truman UNRRA Message," *NYT*, November 14, 1945, p. 10; U.S., Congress, House, Committee on Appropriations, *United Nations Relief and Rehabilitation Administration, 1946; Hearings*, before the Subcommittee of the Committee on Appropriations, 79th Cong., 1st sess., 1945, p. 33; U.S., Cong., House, Committee on Foreign Affairs, *Further Participation in Work of UNRRA; Hearings*, before the Committee on Foreign Affairs, 79th Cong., 1st sess., 1945, pp. 65–66, 92–93; Lehman to Mrs. Charles Heming, November 19, 1945, LP, Personal Correspondence and General File of the Director General of UNRRA, "H," 46–29; "UNRRA 'Progress' Is Told by Lehman," *NYT*, September 13, 1945, p. 7; "UNRRA Fund Speed Urged On Congress," *NYT*, October 12, 1945, p. 21; "Aid Abroad Is Put on Practical Basis," *NYT*, November 17, 1945, p. 5; "Lehman Rebukes Critics of UNRRA," *NYT*, November 20, 1945, p. 11; "Acheson Says UNRRA Is Important in Getting New League Functioning," *NYT*, November 21, 1945, p. 8; U.S., Cong., Senate, Committee on Appropriations, *United Nations Relief and Rehabilitation Administration, 1946; Hearings*, before the Subcommittee of the Committee on Appropriations, 79th Cong., 1st sess., 1945; Acheson, *Present at the Creation*, p. 132.

47. Frank McNaughton to David Hulburd, "UNRRA Appropriations," October 12, 1945, McNaughton Papers, Box 10, McNaughton Reports File, October 1–18, 1945, HSTL; "House Globe-Trotters Home, Urge 'Give-Take' Policy on U.S.," *WP*, October 11, 1945, pp. 1, 2; "Congress Is Kept Busy by Truman's Proposals," *NYT*, October 14, 1945, E-10; Marquis Childs, "Washington Calling: Spotlight Turned on UNRRA," *WP*, October 12, 1945, p. 8; "Shows Displaced Are Now Well Fed," *NYT*, October 11, 1945, p. 8. Herter went on to serve as Secretary of State in the last years of the Eisenhower administration. See Noble, *Christian A. Herter*.

48. U.S., Cong., House, Committee on Appropriations, *Additional Appropriation, Fiscal Year 1946, for United Nations Relief and Rehabilitation Administration*, House Rept. 1166, 79th Cong., 1st sess., October 30, 1945; Letter from the Secretary of State, n.d.,

U.S., Cong., House, Committee on Appropriations, *United Nations Relief and Rehabilitation Administration, 1946; Hearings*, before the Subcommittee of the Committee on Appropriations, 79th Cong., 1st sess., 1945, pp. 269–270; "$550,000,000 More Backed for UNRRA," *NYT*, October 31, 1945, p. 5; "UNRRA Fund Voted, with Cut-Off Date," *WP*, October 31, 1945, pp. 1, 2; "Free-Press Rider Put on UNRRA Aid," *NYT*, November 2, 1945, p. 4.

49. Truman to Lehman, November 8, 1945, LP, SF, Truman; "World Chiefs Hail UNRRA," *NYT*, November 11, 1945, p. 26.

50. Byrnes, Memorandum for the President, November 7, 1945, Truman Papers, OF 423, UNRRA, 1945; "$1,350,000,000 Asked for UNRRA by Truman," *NYT*, November 14, 1945, pp. 1, 10; "Text of Truman UNRRA Message," *NYT*, November 14, 1945, p. 10.

51. "House Fight Begins on New UNRRA Fund," *NYT*, November 13, 1945, p. 11; "Aid Abroad Is Put on Practical Basis," *NYT*, November 17, 1945, p. 5; "Lehman Rebukes Critics of UNRRA," *NYT*, November 20, 1945, p. 11; "Acheson Says UNRRA Is Important in Getting New League Functioning," *NYT*, November 21, 1945, p. 8; U.S., Cong., Senate, Committee on Appropriations, *United Nations Relief and Rehabilitation Administration, 1946; Hearings*, before the Subcommittee of the Committee on Appropriations, 79th Cong., 1st sess., 1945, p. 73; U.S., Cong., House, Committee on Foreign Affairs, *Further Participation in Work of UNRRA; Hearings*, before the Committee on Foreign Affairs, 79th Cong., 1st sess., 1945, pp. 191, 202, 240.

52. "Lehman Rebukes Critics of UNRRA," *NYT*, November 20, 1945, p. 11; U.S., Cong., House, Committee on Foreign Affairs, *Further Participation in Work of UNRRA; Hearings*, before the Committee on Foreign Affairs, 79th Cong., 1st sess., 1945, pp. 134–135, 155–157.

53. Eleanor Roosevelt, "My Day," November 17, 1945, online: http://www.gwu.edu/~erpapers/myday/displaydoc.cfm?_y=1945&_f=md000185; "Text of Address by Henry Morgenthau, Jr. at Testimonial Dinner Given in His Honor by B'nai B'rith," November 7, 1945, copy in LP, SF, Morgenthau; C. L. Sulzberger, "Europe Faces Dread Winter; Food, Fuel and Hope Scarce," *NYT*, November 13, 1945, pp. 1, 12, 13; "UNRRA Must Be Sustained," Editorial, *NYT*, November 15, 1945, p. 18; Lehman to Arthur Hays Sulzberger, November 16, 1945, UNRRA Papers, Microfilm Reel DG/3, Correspondence, November 1945, LP; Marquis Childs, "Washington Calling: Hunger Won't Wait," *WP*, November 14, 1945, p. 6; Leonard Lyons, *WP*, November 10, 1945, p. 10.

54. "Ask Eisenhower for UNRRA Advice," *NYT*, November 15, 1945, p. 5; Eisenhower to Sol Bloom, November 15, 1945, and accompanying fn. 1, in Chandler and Galambos, eds., *The Papers of Dwight David Eisenhower*, VI: 536–537; Eisenhower to Lehman, November 15, 1945, LP, SF, Eisenhower; Frank McNaughton to David Hulburd, November 16, 1945, and November 22, 1945, McNaughton Papers, Box 10, McNaughton Reports File, November 16–30, 1945, HSTL; "Gen. Eisenhower's Wife Stricken at Iowa Reunion; Fear Pneumonia," *NYT*, November 18, 1945, pp. 1, 35; "Eisenhower, Ill, Enters Hospital," *NYT*, November 24, 1945, p. 21; HHLOH, pp. 738–739; Bloom, *The Autobiography of Sol Bloom*, p. 324.

55. "Must Help Europe, Eisenhower Says," *NYT*, November 23, 1945, pp. 1, 3; "Eisenhower Plea for UNRRA Aid to Europe," *NYT*, November 23, 1945, p. 3; U.S.,

Cong., House, Committee on Foreign Affairs, *Further Participation in Work of UNRRA; Hearings*, before the Committee on Foreign Affairs, 79th Cong., 1st sess., 1945, pp. 281–284. Morgan's appointment turned out to be a disaster for UNRRA when he asserted in early 1946 that Europe's Jews were "growing into a world force," that Jews arriving in Germany from Poland were "well dressed, well fed, rosy cheeked and have plenty of money," and that their movement was part of a "well-organized, positive plan to get out of Europe" and emigrate to Palestine. Morgan's remarks were seen by many as anti-Semitic and called into question his suitability to oversee UNRRA's displaced persons activities in Germany. Morgan was first dismissed and then, after a personal appeal heard by Lehman, reinstated, but the whole incident brought tremendous embarrassment to Lehman and UNRRA. See "UNRRA Aide Scents Jews' Exodus Plot," *NYT*, January 1, 1946, pp. 1, 3; "Morgan's Charges Stir Jewish Ire," *NYT*, January 3, 1946, p. 3; First draft, Aide-Memoire, "Lt. Gen. Sir F. E. Morgan's statements concerning the Jewish displaced persons problem and the events leading to his resignation," n.d., UNRRA Papers, Microfilm Reel DG/4, Chronological Reading File, Correspondence, January–March, 1946, LP; "Morgan Restored by UNRRA Director," January 30, 1946, pp. 1, 7; Robert G. A. Jackson, untitled manuscript, August 1954, pp. 29–34, LP, SF, document 0442_0136; Nevins, *Herbert H. Lehman and His Era*, pp. 292–295; Gibson, *Jacko: Where Are You Now?*, pp. 76–79; Shephard, *The Long Road Home*, pp. 151–153, 157–164.

56. U.S., Cong., House, Committee on Foreign Affairs, *Further Participation in Work of UNRRA; Hearings*, before the Committee on Foreign Affairs, 79th Cong., 1st sess., 1945, pp. 284–290; Frank McNaughton to David Hulburd, November 22, 1945, McNaughton Papers, Box 10, McNaughton Reports File, November 16–30, 1945, HSTL; "Eisenhower Advocates UNRRA Fund," *WP*, November 23, 1945, pp. 1, 5.

57. Frank McNaughton to David Hulburd, November 22, 1945, McNaughton Papers, Box 10, McNaughton Reports File, November 16–30, 1945; Lehman to Dr. Harvey Greenstein, LP, Personal Correspondence and General File of the Director General of UNRRA, "G," 46–27.

58. Lehman's remarks quoted in "Must Help Europe, Eisenhower Says," *NYT*, November 23, 1945, pp. 1, 3.

59. " 'Free Press' Rider on UNRRA Is Upset," *NYT*, November 24, 1945, p. 4; "Relief Fund Voted, Minus Press Rider," *WP*, November 24, 1945, pp. 1, 2; U.S., Cong., Senate, Committee on Appropriations, *United Nations Relief and Rehabilitation Administration, 1946; Hearings*, before the Subcommittee of the Committee on Appropriations, 79th Cong., 1st sess., 1945, pp. 85–93; "Senate Committee Approves $550,000,000 for UNRRA," *WP*, November 27, 1945, p. 1; "$1,900,000,000 Bills for UNRRA Favored," *NYT*, November 27, 1945, pp. 1, 6; U.S., Cong., Senate, Committee on Appropriations, *United Nations Relief and Rehabilitation Administration Participation Act, 1946*, S. Rept. 798, 79th Cong., 1st sess., November 26, 1945; "Senate Passes Bill for Fast UNRRA Aid," *NYT*, December 6, 1945, p. 28; "Senate Votes Funds for UNRRA Minus Free Press Provision," *WP*, December 6, 1945, p. 1; "House Votes 2d Fund for Foreign Relief," *WP*, December 7, 1945, p. 3; U.S., Cong., House, *United Nations Relief and Rehabilitation Administration Participation Bill, 1946; Conference Report*, House Report 1355, 79th Cong., 1st sess., December 10, 1945; "Congress Puts Approval on UNRRA Funds," *WP*, December 12, 1945, p. 8; "$550,000,000 Fund to UNRRA Approved,"

NYT, December 12, 1945, p. 9; H.J. Res. 266, 79th Cong., 1st sess., 1945; P.L. 79–259, 59 *Stat.* 609–610 (1945).

60. "$1,900,000,000 Bills for UNRRA Favored," *NYT*, November 27, 1945, pp. 1, 6; U.S., Cong., House, Committee on Foreign Affairs, *Further Participation in Work of UNRRA*, House Report 1311, 79th Cong., 1st sess., November 27, 1945.

61. "The President's Appointments," December 3, 1945, and attached Acheson, Memorandum to the President, "Funds for UNRRA," Truman Papers, PSF, Box 68, President's Appointments File Daily Sheets, December 1945; "Lehman Says UNRRA Faces a Breakdown," *NYT*, December 4, 1945, p. 4.

62. U.S., Cong., House, Committee on Rules, *Consideration of H.R. 4649*, House Report 1332, 79th Cong., 1st sess., December 4, 1945; 'Senate Passes Bill for Fast UNRRA Aid," *NYT*, December 6, 1945, p. 28; "Senate Votes Funds for UNRRA Minus Free Press Provision," *WP*, December 6, 1945, p. 1; "New UNRRA Fund Approved by House," *NYT*, December 7, 1945, p. 5; "House Votes 2d Fund for Foreign Relief," *WP*, December 7, 1945, p. 3; "UNRRA Settlement," Editorial, *WP*, December 8, 1945, p. 6.

63. Herbert Lehman to John Lehman, December 7, 1945, LP, Personal Correspondence and General File of the Director General of UNRRA, John Lehman, 47–58; U.S., Cong., House, Committee on Foreign Affairs, *Further Participation in Work of UNRRA*, House Rept. 1311, 79th Cong., 1st sess., November 27, 1945, p. 7; "Sermons Urge U.S. to Relieve World Hunger," *WP*, November 26, 1945, p. 7; "Speed for UNRRA," Editorial, *WP*, November 30, 1945, p. 6; "No Time for Politics," Editorial, *WP*, December 5, 1945, p. 6; "Funds for UNRRA: Letters Decry Congress' Stalling," *WP*, November 30, 1945, p. 5; Barnet Nover, "Facing Winter: UNRRA and the Four Horsemen," *WP*, December 13, 1945, p. 6; "Italian Need of UNRRA Aid Seen Desperate," *WP*, December 13, 1945, p. 9; "For a World-Wide Christmas," Editorial, *NYT*, December 15, 1945, p. 15; "Survey Shows UNRRA Vital to the Distressed of Europe," *NYT*, December 17, 1945, pp. 1, 4, 5; "Next Year's Relief Needs in Italy Dwarf Assistance Given in 1945," *NYT*, December 17, 1945, p. 4; "Poland Hopes to Speed Recovery With Stimulant of Outside Help," *NYT*, December 17, 1945, p. 4; "Dollars for Peace," Editorial, *NYT*, December 18, 1945, p. 26; Walter Lippmann, "Today and Tomorrow: Plausible Nonsense," *WP*, December 6, 1945, p. 10; Marquis Childs, "Washington Calling: Delay in Voting UNRRA Funds," *WP*, December 10, 1945, p. 6; Malvina Lindsay, "The Gentler Sex: Let Them Know We Care," *WP*, December 1, 1945, p. 10; Lehman to Corrington Gill, December 18, 1945, LP, Personal Correspondence and General File of the Director General of UNRRA, "G," 46–27; Jackson, untitled manuscript, August 1954, p. 24, LP, SF, Jackson, document 0442_0136.

64. Jackson, untitled manuscript, August 1954, pp. 24–27, LP, SF, Jackson, document 0442_0136; "The President's Day," December 11, 1945, Truman Papers, Daily Presidential Appointments; "The Day in Washington," *NYT*, December 12, 1945, p. 11; U.S., Cong., House, *Estimate of Appropriation for the United Nations Relief and Rehabilitation Administration, Communication from the President of the United States*, House Doc. 384, 79th Cong. 1st sess., December 11, 1945; U.S., Cong., Senate, Committee on Foreign Relations, *Enabling the United States to Further Participation in the Work of the United Nations Relief and Rehabilitation Administration*, Senate Rept. 856, 79th Cong., 1st sess., December 13, 1945; "Senators Speed Funds for UNRRA," *NYT*, December 14, 1945, p. 12; "Senate Bill for $1,350,000,000 to UNRRA Sent to White House,"

NYT, December 18, 1945, pp. 1, 14; "Truman Signs Bill to Swell UNRRA Funds," *WP*, December 19, 1945, p. 5; H.R. 4649, 79th Cong., 1st sess., 1945; P.L. 79–262, 59 *Stat.* 612–613 (1945).

65. Jackson, untitled manuscript, August 1954, pp. 25–27, LP, SF, Jackson, document 0442_0136; Frank McNaughton to Robert Low, December 14, 1945, McNaughton Papers, Box 10, McNaughton Reports File, December 1945, HSTL; The Acting Secretary of State to Certain Diplomatic and Consular Officers, December 15, 1945, *FRUS, 1945*, II: 1055–1056; "UNRRA $750,000,000 Passed by Senate," *NYT*, December 16, 1945, p. 21; "UNRRA Worried over Funds," *NYT*, December 16, 1945, E-10.

66. "$750,000,000 Fund Voted for UNRRA," *NYT*, December 20, 1945, p. 2; "House, Senate Rush Pellmell into Holidays," *WP*, December 21, 1945, pp. 1, 2; H.R. 4805, 79th Cong., 1st sess., 1945; P.L. 79–269, 59 *Stat.* 632–634 (1945); H.R. 4489, 79th Cong., 1st sess., 1945; P.L. 79–291, 59 *Stat.* 669–673 (1945).

67. "Text of Lehman Statement on UNRRA Outlook for 1946," *NYT*, December 23, 1945, p. 4; Lehman to Corrington Gill, December 18, 1945, LP, Personal Correspondence and General File of the Director General of UNRRA, "G," 46–27; Burton Palmer to Lehman, UNRRA Papers, Microfilm Reel BA/1, Side 2, Director General–Memos, LP; Lehman to Truman, December 21, 1945, Truman Papers, PSF, Box 129, Subject File, Agencies, UNRRA; Truman to Congressman A. Willis Robertson, December 14, 1945, Truman Papers, OF 423, UNRRA, 1945; Truman to Henry Morgenthau, Jr., December 21, 1945, Truman Papers, OF 423 UNRRA, 1945, Misc.

68. Jackson, untitled manuscript, August 1954, pp. 23, 27, LP, SF, Jackson, document 0442_0136.

Chapter 10. "The Work of UNRRA . . . Will Ever Be Close to My Heart": Lehman and Truman, 1946

1. "Lehman Asks Food Rations in U.S. to Combat Famine," *NYT*, March 20, 1946, pp. 1, 12.

2. "Truman Pledges Food to Starving," *NYT*, November 28, 1945, p. 17; "Food Aplenty in '46 Seen by Anderson," *NYT*, December 7, 1945, p. 18; "Lehman Stresses Misery in Europe," *NYT*, December 31, 1945, p. 16. On Anderson's mishandling and misunderstanding of the food situation in this period, see Matusow, *Farm Policies and Politics in the Truman Years*, pp. 8–19; Bernstein, "The Postwar Famine and Price Control, 1946," pp. 235–237; Gold, *Wartime Economic Planning in Agriculture*, pp. 454–455; Collingham, *The Taste of War*, pp. 478–480; Bentley, *Eating for Victory*, pp. 151–155.

3. "2 Soviet Republics to Get UNRRA Help," *NYT*, December 23, 1945, pp. 1, 5; "Text of Lehman Statement on UNRRA Outlook for 1946," *NYT*, December 23, 1945, p. 5; Lehman to Poletti, December 28, 1945, LP, SF, Poletti.

4. Attlee to Truman, January 3, 1946, in Williams, *A Prime Minister Remembers*, pp. 135–138; Truman, *Memoirs*, I: 467–468; "Britain Cuts Wheat Call," *NYT*, January 12, 1946, p. 5.

5. "The President's Day," January 23, 1946, Truman Papers, Daily Presidential Appointments; "Text of Memorandum Left with President Truman by the Director Gen-

eral, 23 January 1946," LP, SF, Truman; Truman, Memorandum for Clinton Anderson, January 24, 1946, Truman Papers, OF 307-A, Wheat.

6. Blum, *The Price of Vision*, pp. 543–544; "What's News," *Wall Street Journal*, January 31, 1946, p. 1; "Loans to Farmers on Wheat Called," *NYT*, February 1, 1946, p. 36; "Review and Outlook: Progress of the Week—An Editorial Appraisal," *Wall Street Journal*, February 2, 1946, p. 1; Lehman to Dr. Frank Laubach, January 31, 1946, LP, Personal Correspondence and General File of the Director General of UNRRA, "L," C47–46; Lehman to Oscar Cox, February 6, 1946, LP, SF, Cox.

7. Williams, *A Prime Minister Remembers*, pp. 139–142; Truman, *Memoirs*, I: 469–471.

8. "Truman Call for Food to Europe," *NYT*, February 7, 1946, p. 15.

9. "Truman Call for Food to Europe," *NYT*, February 7, 1946, p. 15; Truman, *Memoirs*, I: 468–469; "Washington Wire," *Wall Street Journal*, February 15, 1946, p. 1.

10. Lehman to the President, February 6, 1946, Truman Papers, OF 423, UNRRA, January–May 1946; Lehman to Lithgow Osborne, February 14, 1946, LP, SF, Osborne; Lehman to Oscar Cox, February 18, 1946, LP, SF, Cox.

11. President's News Conference, February 7, 1946, in *Public Papers: Truman, 1946*, pp. 109–111; "Truman Promises Rationing of Meat if Needed to Save Lives of Hungry Millions; Asks We Eat Less," *NYT*, February 8, 1946, pp. 1, 8.

12. "What's News," *Wall Street Journal*, February 6, 1946, p. 1; "Reason Moot, but Fact Is: People Are Hungry," *WP*, February 10, 1946, B-1; Barnet Nover, "A Hungry World: We Cannot Let Them Starve," *WP*, February 9, 1946, p. 7; "Washington Wire," *Wall Street Journal*, February 15, 1946, p. 1; Marquis Childs, "Washington Calling: U.S. Controls and Food for Europe," *WP*, February 11, 1946, p. 7; Marquis Childs, "Washington Calling: Getting Our Wheat Abroad," *WP*, February 28, 1946, p. 7; "Anderson Mapping Higher Food Goals," *NYT*, February 16, 1946, p. 26; "Government Asks Big Crop Expansion," *NYT*, February 22, 1946, p. 22; "Wheat Export to Miss Goal, Anderson Says," *WP*, February 22, 1946, p. 3; Bernstein, "The Postwar Famine and Price Control, 1946," p. 238; Matusow, *Farm Policies and Politics in the Truman Years*, pp. 20–22.

13. "The President's Day," February 20, 1946, Truman Papers, Daily Presidential Appointments; Lehman to the President, February 21, 1946, Truman Papers, OF 423, UNRRA, January–May 1946.

14. Matthew Connelly to Lehman, February 27, 1946, Truman Papers, Of 423, UNRRA, January–May 1946.

15. "Lehman Demands Food for World," *NYT*, February 23, 1946, p. 6.

16. "Lehman Demands Food for World," *NYT*, February 23, 1946, p. 6.

17. "Lehman Demands Food for World," *NYT*, February 23, 1946, p. 6; "The President's Day," February 25, 1946, Truman Papers, Daily Presidential Appointments; "Truman Pledges Justice for Jews," *NYT*, February 26, 1946, p. 8.

18. Hoover to Anderson, February 26, 1946, Document 27, "Hoover and Truman: A Presidential Friendship," online: http://www.trumanlibrary.org/hoover/world.htm; "Truman Summons Hoover and Others on Food Aid Abroad," *NYT*, February 28, 1946, pp. 1, 14; "New 'Famine' Board Asks U.S. Cut Wheat Use by 25%," *NYT*, March 2, 1946, pp. 1, 14; Truman, *Memoirs*, I: 472–473; Hoover, *An American Epic*,

IV: 115; Best, *Herbert Hoover*, II: 286–287; Smith, *An Uncommon Man*, p. 352; Kennedy, "Herbert Hoover and the Two Great Food Crusades of the 1940s," in Nash, ed., *Understanding Herbert Hoover*, p. 97.

19. Lehman to Harry Greenstein, February 28, 1946, LP, Personal Correspondence and General File of the Director General of UNRRA, "G," 46–27; Hoover, *An American Epic*, IV: 115; "Hoover Maps Plan to Feed Europe," *NYT*, March 1, 1946, p. 8; "New and Larger Committee Formed to Act in World's Food Crisis; Hoover to Direct the Program," *Wall Street Journal*, March 2, 1946, p. 2; "Grain Prices Go Up in Move to Draw Wheat off Farms," *NYT*, March 3, 1946, pp. 1, 40; "Anderson to Avoid Forced Food Cuts," *NYT*, March 3, 1046, p. 40; "Pooling of Boxcars Expected to Speed U.S. Grain to Ports," *WP*, March 3, 1946, M-1; "Hoover to Examine Food Needs Abroad," *NYT*, March 6, 1946, pp. 1, 19; Blum, *The Price of Vision*, pp. 554–555; Bernstein, "The Postwar Famine and Price Control, 1946," pp. 238–239.

20. Blum, *The Price of Vision*, pp. 37–49, 554–555.

21. "Anderson to Avoid Forced Food Cuts," *NYT*, March 3, 1946, p. 40.

22. Benno Stoneham to Herbert Lehman, January 27, 1946, LP, Personal Correspondence and General File of the Director General of UNRRA, "Si–Sz," 48–92; Lehman to the President, and attached "Draft of Proposed Reply," February 28, 1946, UNRRA Papers, Microfilm Reel DG/3, Correspondence, January and February 1946, LP; "Exchange of Messages with President Bierut of Poland Concerning Grain Shipments by UNRRA," March 18, 1946, *Public Papers of the Presidents: Truman, 1946*, pp. 161–162; Lehman to Poletti, March 6, 1946, LP, SF, Poletti. On UNRRA's efforts in specific countries, see Woodbridge, *UNRRA*, II; and the essays in "Relief in the Aftermath of War," Special Issue, *Journal of Contemporary History*, 43: 3 (July 2008).

23. Acheson, *Present at the Creation*, p. 201; "End of UNRRA Is Sought by Agency's Big Backers," *NYT*, July 27, 1946, pp. 1, 4; "Clayton Replies to 'Gravy Train,'" Communication, *WP*, August 19, 1946, p. 7; Byrnes, *Speaking Frankly*, p. 146; Byrnes to Lehman, March 22, 1946, LP, SF, Byrnes; Robert G. A. Jackson, untitled manuscript, August 1954, p. 21, LP, SF, Jackson, document 0442_0136; C. Tyler Wood Oral History Transcript, pp. 24–25, and Nathan Becker Oral History Transcript, pp. 35, 46–47, both in HSTL; Bentley, *Eating for Victory*, p. 168; Hirschmann, *The Embers Still Burn*; Pemberton, *Harry S. Truman*, p. 84.

24. Lehman to the Secretary of State, February 28, 1946, LP, SF, Byrnes; Lehman to the Secretary of War, February 28, 1946, LP, Personal Correspondence and General File of the Director General of UNRRA, Displaced Persons Reports, C46-21; "U.S. Studies Closing DP Camps in Europe; Byrnes to Bar Enforced Repatriation," *NYT*, March 16, 1946, p. 8.

25. Lehman to the President, March 6, 1946, Truman Papers, OF 423, UNRRA, January–May 1946.

26. Lehman to the Secretary of State, March 6, 1946, UNRRA Papers, Microfilm Reel DG/3, Correspondence, March 1946, LP; Robert G. A. Jackson, untitled manuscript, August 1954, p. 37, LP, SF, Jackson, document 0442_0136; "UNRRA's Relief Aid Hailed by Truman," *NYT*, March 16, 1946, p. 8.

27. Attendees at March 11, 1946, Meeting of the Famine Emergency Committee, attached to "Secretary Anderson's Appointments," March 11, 1946, Clinton Anderson Papers, Box 14, Appointments File, HSTL; "Food Crisis Worse Each Day, Lehman

Announcement Warns," *WP*, March 11, 1946, pp. 1, 2; "Nation Asked to Sacrifice Wheat, Fats for 120 Days," *WP*, March 12, 1946, pp. 1, 2; "Americans Are Asked to Cut Wheat Use 40%, Fats 20%," *NYT*, March 12, 1946, pp. 1, 6; Drew Pearson, "The Washington Merry-Go-Round," *WP*, March 26, 1946, p. 14; Gold, *Wartime Economic Planning in Agriculture*, pp. 466–467.

28. "The President's Day," March 12, 1946, Truman Papers, Daily Presidential Appointments; "Lehman Quits UNRRA Post Because of Failing Health," *NYT*, March 13, 1946, pp. 1, 17; Robert G. A. Jackson, untitled manuscript, August 1954, pp. 37, 39, LP, SF, Jackson, document 0442_0136.

29. Lehman to Francis Sayre, March 12, 1946, LP, SF, Sayre; Lehman to Abe Feller, March 21, 1946, LP, SF, Feller; Carolin Flexner to Lehman, March 13, 1946, LP, Personal Correspondence and General File of the Director General of UNRRA, Resignation, Messages of Regret, 47–54; Henry Morgenthau, Jr., to Lehman, March 15, 1946, and Lehman to Morgenthau, March 25, 1946, both in LP, SF, Morgenthau; Lehman to Fred Hoehler, March 26, 1946, Lehman Papers, Personal Correspondence and General File of the Director General of UNRRA, Resignation Replies, 47–55. On Morgenthau and Truman, see Blum, *From the Morgenthau Diaries*, III: 421–473; and Truman, *Memoirs*, I: 327.

30. "Mr. Lehman Resigns," Editorial, *NYT*, March 13, 1946, p. 28; "American Slated for Lehman Post," *NYT*, March 15, 1946, p. 8; "UNRRA's Problems," *NYT*, March 17, 1946, E-1; "Mr. Lehman Resigns," Editorial, *WP*, March 14, 1946, p. 8; "Lehman Resigns in Disgust," *New Republic*, March 25, 1946, p. 398. For similar sentiments that the premature ending of rationing had caused much of the problem, see Chester Bowles, Director of the Office of Economic Stabilization, to Lehman, March 20, 1946, LP, SF, Bowles; and Bowles, *Promises to Keep*, pp. 131–132.

31. Lehman to Matthew Connelly, March 13, 1946, Truman Papers, OF 423 UNRRA, January–May 1946; Connelly to Lehman, March 14, 1946, LP, SF, Truman; "UNRRA's Relief Aid Hailed by Truman," *NYT*, March 16, 1946, p. 6; "Text of Truman's Letter," *NYT*, March 16, 1946, p. 8; "Fourth Council Session of UNRRA: Statement by the Representative of the United States," March 17, 1946, *Department of State Bulletin*, March 31, 1946, pp. 527–528; "Broaden Agencies, Big Powers Urged," *WP*, March 19, 1946, p. 2; "Clayton Replies to 'Gravy Train,'" Communication, *WP*, August 19, 1946, p. 7; Robert G. A. Jackson, untitled manuscript, August 1954, p. 21, LP, SF, Jackson, document 0442_0136.

32. "Truman Program Held Inadequate," *NYT*, March 18, 1946, p. 11; "One World Board to Combat Famine Urged by Lehman," *NYT*, March 19, 1946, pp. 1, 12; "Broaden Agencies, Big Powers Urged," *WP*, March 19, 1946, p. 2; I. F. Stone, "Fumbling with Famine," *The Nation*, March 23, 1946, pp. 335–336.

33. "Lehman Asks Food Rations in U.S. to Combat Famine," *NYT*, March 20, 1946, pp. 1, 12; "Lehman Calls for Return to Rationing," *WP*, March 20, 1946, pp. 1, 2. Amy Bentley argues that rationing would have worked because it would have discouraged farmers from feeding grain to livestock or hoarding grain in hopes of higher prices. She also cites public opinion surveys to show that the American people would have supported rationing to prevent starvation overseas. See Bentley, *Eating for Victory*, pp. 142–170.

34. "Anderson Opposes Plan for Return of Rationing," *NYT*, March 20, 1946, p. 12; "President's News Conference," March 21, 1946, *Public Papers: Truman, 1946*, p.

164; "Truman Food Group Opposes Rationing," *NYT*, March 27, 1946, p. 1; "President's News Conference," March 28, 1946, *Public Papers: Truman, 1946*, p. 173. But see Bentley, *Eating for Victory*, pp. 152–153.

35. "Worse 1947 Famine Facing Europeans, Lehman Forecasts," *NYT*, March 23, 1946, pp. 1, 4; Eleanor Roosevelt, "My Day," March 15, 1946, online: http://www.gwu.edu/~erpapers/myday/displaydoc.cfm?_y=1946&_f=md000287; Lehman to Allan Nevins, July 24, 1962, LP, SF, Nevins.

36. "UNRRA Ends Clash on Refugee Care," *NYT*, March 29, 1946, pp. 1, 4; "President Lauds Lehman Relief Aid," *NYT*, March 26, 1946, p. 17; United Nations Relief and Rehabilitation Administration, "Consideration of the Resignation of the Director General," Sixteenth Plenary Meeting of Council, March 28, 1946; and *Letters of Tribute to Herbert H. Lehman* (Stamford: Overlook Press, n.d.), both in Herbert Lehman Materials, Special Collections, Leonard Lief Library, Lehman College.

37. "La Guardia Is Nominated to Be New UNRRA Head," *NYT*, March 22, 1946, pp. 1, 4; Doris Fleeson, "LaGuardia [*sic*] Given Lehman's Job," *Boston Globe*, March 22, 1946, p. 20; Lehman to La Guardia, March 22, 1946, UNRRA Papers, Microfilm Reel DG/4, Chronological Reading File, Correspondence, January–March 1946, LP; HHLOH, pp. 759, 762; Eleanor Roosevelt, "My Day," May 8, 1946, online: http://www.gwu.edu/~erpapers/myday/displaydoc.cfm?_y=1946&_f=md000333; Robert G. A. Jackson, untitled manuscript, August 1954, pp. 39–40, LP, SF, Jackson, document 0442_0136; Woodbridge, *UNRRA*, I: 420; Hirschmann, *The Embers Still Burn*, pp. 3–7; Kessner, *Fiorello La Guardia and the Making of Modern New York*, pp. 579–580; Shephard, *The Long Road Home*, pp. 57, 230–232; Williams, *City of Ambition*, pp. 398–399.

38. "Heed Roosevelt's Legacy, Wallace Cautions Nation," *NYT*, April 13, 1946, pp. 1, 4; "Davis Says Crisis in Food Gets Progressively Worse," *NYT*, April 17, 1946, pp. 1, 16; "Committee of 100 Asks Famine Help," *NYT*, May 12, 1946, pp. 1, 30; William Hassett, Memorandum for Chester Davis, May 14, 1946, and attached Lehman et al. to the President, May 11, 1946, Truman Papers, OF 426, Misc., 1945–1946. The "one hundred prominent citizens" also included, among many others, Clarence Pickett of the American Friends Service Committee, Walter White of the NAACP, Walter Reuther of the CIO, Alf Landon, George Shuster of Hunter College, Charles Seymour of Yale University, Rabbi Stephen S. Wise, Reverend Harry Emerson Fosdick, and Reinhold Niebuhr.

39. "President's News Conference," March 21, 1946, *Public Papers: Truman, 1946*, p. 164; "President Lauds Lehman Relief Aid," *NYT*, March 26, 1946, p. 17; "President's News Conference," April 17, 1946, *Public Papers: Truman, 1946*, p. 203.

40. Harold Smith, Conference with the President, May 15, 1946, Harold Smith Papers, Box 1, Diary File, 1946, May; Smith, Conference with the President, June 11, 1946, Smith Papers, Box 1, Diary File, 1946, June; both in HSTL. On Lehman's continued criticism of the Truman administration's food policies, see "Lehman Calls World Food Crisis Worse; Reiterates Plea for Return of Rationing," *NYT*, May 11, 1946, p. 3; "Committee of 100 Asks Famine Help," *NYT*, May 12, 1946, pp. 1, 30; "Strict Rationing Urged by Lehman," *NYT*, May 17, 1946, p. 10.

41. "Pope Bids World Prevent Famine; Fears for Peace," *NYT*, April 5, 1946, pp. 1, 8; Gold, *Wartime Economic Planning in Agriculture*, p. 475; "Acheson Assails Three-Fifths Lag in May Food Relief," *NYT*, May 8, 1946, pp. 1, 17; Collingham, *The*

Taste of War, p. 481; "Jumps Grain Prices and Cattle Feeds," *NYT*, May 9, 1946, p. 24; "6-Month Goal Met in Famine Relief, President Reports," *NYT*, June 28, 1946, pp. 1, 4; "Government Statements on World Food," *NYT*, June 28, 1946, p. 4; Anderson, *Outsider in the Senate*, p. 71; Bernstein, "The Postwar Famine and Price Control, 1946," pp. 239–240; Matusow, *Farm Policies and Politics in the Truman Years*, pp. 29–37.

42. Lehman to Philip Jessup, January 14, 1957, LP, SF, Jessup; "Address of Herbert H. Lehman at Meeting of National Peace Conference at National Board of YWCA," June 18, 1946, LP, Speech File; Lehman to Francis Sayre, May 31, 1957, LP, SF, Sayre; HHLOH, pp. 758–761, 771; Lehman to Mrs. Paul Douglas, January 25, 1958, LP, SF, Paul Douglas and Emily Taft Douglas. See Woodbridge, *UNRRA*, for a final statistical accounting of UNRRA's activities.

43. Eleanor Roosevelt Oral History Transcript, HHLP, CUOHC, p. 14; Roosevelt, *This I Remember*, p. 314; "UNRRA Nears the End," Editorial, *NYT*, July 28, 1946, E-8; Anne O'Hare McCormick, "The World Meets Again in Geneva with UNRRA," *NYT*, August 5, 1946, p. 20; Sumner Welles, "Need for Relief," *WP*, August 14, 1946, p. 7.

44. William Hassett, Memorandum for Chester Davis, May 14, 1946, and attached Lehman et al. to the President, May 11, 1946, Truman Papers, OF 426, Misc., 1945–1946.

Chapter 11. "Fighting for the Cause of Progressive and Liberal Government": Lehman and Truman, 1946–1948

1. Herbert Lehman to Edward Flynn, November 4, 1948, Flynn Papers, Box 15, Lehman, FDRL

2. Lehman to Edward Warburg, April 5, 1946; Warburg to Lehman, August 15, 1946; and Lehman to Warburg, August 19, 1946; all in LP, SF, Edward Warburg; "Four Accept Fund Posts," *NYT*, April 29, 1946, p. 11; Lehman to the President, June 30, 1946, Truman Papers, OF 28–Misc. (June–August 1946); "Group Forms for Civilian Atom Control," *WP*, March 28, 1946, pp. 1, 4; "U.S. Urged to Join World Court Now," *NYT*, May 29, 1946, p. 15; "Lehman Urges U.N. to Fill UNRRA Role," *NYT*, August 4, 1946, pp. 1, 27; "90 Urge a New UNRRA," *NYT*, December 4, 1946, p. 24; "La Guardia Urges UNRRA's End Oct. 1," *NYT*, August 8, 1946, pp. 1, 6; "Clayton Replies to 'Gravy Train,'" Communication, *WP*, August 19, 1946, p. 7; "U.S. Opposes Role in Joint Relief Aid," *NYT*, November 29, 1946, p. 8.

3. "State Chairmen Back Mead for Governor," *NYT*, December 15, 1945, p. 12; "Up-State Leaders Favorable to Mead," *NYT*, January 28, 1946, p. 14; "ALP Backs Mead for Governorship; His Chance Seen Greatly Advanced," *NYT*, March 23, 1946, p. 14; Leonard Lyons, "Broadway Bulletin," *WP*, March 16, 1946, p. 10; "Lehman Sentiment for Senate Grows," *NYT*, May 21, 1946, p. 21.

4. Lehman to Lithgow Osborne, February 14, 1946; Osborne to Lehman, July 31, 1946; and Lehman to Osborne, August 8, 1946; all in LP, SF, Osborne; Lehman to Hugh Jackson, August 16, 1946, LP, SF, Jackson.

5. "The President's News Conference," March 14, 1946, and March 28, 1946, *Public Papers: Truman, 1946*, pp. 158, 172–173; "Lehman Rumor Doubted," *NYT*, March 24, 1946, p. 20. On Hannegan and Truman, see Truman, *Memoirs*: I: 160–162,

324; Blum, *The Price of Vision*, pp. 364–375, 402–403; Thomas Eagleton and Diane Duffin, "Bob Hannegan and Harry Truman's Vice Presidential Nomination," *Missouri Historical Review*, 90: 3 (1996): 265–283.

6. Harold Smith, Conference with the President, May 15, 1946, Harold Smith Papers, Box 1, Diary File, 1946, May, HSTL; Smith, Conference with the President, June 11, 1946, Smith Papers, Box 1, Diary File, 1946, June; Marquis Childs, "Washington Calling: Hannegan's Strategy," *WP*, August 21, 1946, p. 8; "All New York Parties Open Election Battle," *NYT*, August 25, 1946, p. 84; "Truman Reported Favoring Ticket of Mead-Lehman," *WP*, August 17, 1946, p. 7; "Convention Issue Set by Democrats," *NYT*, August 28, 1946, p. 18.

7. "Convention Issue Set by Democrats," *NYT*, August 28, 1946, p. 18; "Text of Democratic Keynote Speech by Mrs. Eleanor Roosevelt at Albany," *NYT*, September 4, 1946, p. 12; "Democrats Stress Roosevelt Record; Fight Dewey in '48," *NYT*, September 4, 1946, pp. 1, 3; "Dewey 'Ambitions' Hit by Democrats," *NYT*, September 5, 1946, p. 12; "Text of Platform Adopted by Democratic Convention at Albany," *NYT*, September 5, 1946, p. 12. On FDR's legacy and the Democrats in 1946, see also Alonzo Hamby, "The Liberals, Truman, and FDR as Symbol and Myth," *Journal of American History*, 56: 4 (March 1970): 859–867; and Leuchtenburg, *In the Shadow of FDR*, pp. 1–40.

8. "Democrats Select Mead and Lehman; Dewey Is Assailed," *NYT*, September 5, 1946, pp. 1, 14; "Acceptance Speech of Former Governor Lehman," *NYT*, September 5, 1946, p. 14.

9. "Republicans Name Dewey and Ives; Albany Team Kept," *NYT*, September 5, 1946, pp. 1, 16; "Ives Led Anti-Bias Fight," *NYT*, September 5, 1946, p. 17; "The State Tickets," Editorial, *NYT*, September 5, 1946, p. 19; Moscow, *Politics in the Empire State*, pp. 83–85; Chen, "'The Hitlerian Rule of Quotas.'"

10. Memorandum, L. O. to H.H.L., "Up-State Senatorial Campaign," attached to Osborne to Lehman, September 7, 1946, LP, SF, Osborne.

11. "Wallace Warns on 'Tough' Policy toward Russia," *NYT*, September 13, 1946, pp. 1, 4; "Text of Wallace's Speech Describing the Way to Obtain Peace," *NYT*, September 13, 1946, p. 7; "Wallace Speech Is Seen Embarrassing to Byrnes," *NYT*, September 13, 1946, p. 4; Marquis Childs, "Washington Calling: Truman's Blunder," *WP*, September 17, 1946, p. 6; "Wallace Ousted, Starts a 'Fight for Peace'; . . . The President Acts," *NYT*, September 21, 1946, pp. 1, 2; "PAC Calls Action a Blow to Peace," *NYT*, September 21, 1946, p. 3; Blum, *The Price of Vision*, pp. 612–632; Truman, *Memoirs*, I: 557–560; Byrnes, *All in One Lifetime*, pp. 371–376; Hamby, *Beyond the New Deal*, pp. 34–36, 127–136; Donovan, *Conflict and Crisis*, pp. 219–228; Schapsmeier and Schapsmeier, *Prophet in Politics*, pp. 152–160; Markowitz, *The Rise and Fall of the People's Century*, pp. 181–193.

12. "The Wallace Case," *NYT*, September 22, 1946, E-1; "Party Campaign Ban Shaped for Both Wallace, Pepper," *NYT*, September 21, 1946, pp. 1, 3; "Time for Plain Speaking," Editorial, *NYT*, September 20, 1946, p. 28; "Truman, Wallace Assailed by Ives," *NYT*, September 22, 1946, p. 3. Labor leaders David Dubinsky, Alex Rose, and others had withdrawn from the American Labor Party in 1944 in response to the growing Communist influence in the organization and had formed the Liberal Party as the new vehicle to achieve their political objectives. On the Communists' capture of the ALP and the formation of the Liberal Party, see Moscow, *Politics in the Empire State*, pp. 102–119; "Communists Take Full ALP Control," *NYT*, January 8, 1948, pp. 1, 14.

13. "Policy of Truman Backed by Lehman," *NYT*, September 29, 1946, pp. 1, 51; "Lehman Gives Views on Our Foreign Policy," *NYT*, September 29, 1946, p. 51.

14. "Attack on Ives Decried," *NYT*, September 29, 1946, p. 51; "Lehman 'Straddle' Charged by Ives," *NYT*, October 2, 1946, pp. 1, 8; "Mr. Lehman's Foreign Policy," Editorial, *NYT*, September 30, 1946, p. 21.

15. "Ives Asks Lehman for Foreign Views," *NYT*, October 23, 1946, p. 20; "Lehman Supports Policies of Byrnes," *NYT*, October 27, 1946, p. 43.

16. Bowen, "Communism vs. Republicanism"; " 'Economic Cannibalism' Charged to the Administration of Truman," *NYT*, July 17, 1946, p. 15; "Reece Denounces Truman's Tactics," *NYT*, September 27, 1946, p. 16; "Election Test," *NYT*, November 3, 1946, p. 91; Donovan, *Conflict and Crisis*, pp. 231–234; Donaldson, *Truman Defeats Dewey*, pp. 7–8. On Communist spies in Canada, see "Canada Seizes 22 as Spies; Atom Secrets Believed Aim," *NYT*, February 16, 1946, pp. 1, 6; and Knight, *How the Cold War Began*. On concern about Soviet spies in the United States during this time, see "Rankin Trails 'Ring,' " *NYT*, February 17, 1946, p. 19; "FBI Seizes Russian as Spy While Taking Ship for Home," *NYT*, March 27, 1946, pp. 1, 12; "House Report Hits Red-Front Group," *NYT*, June 8, 1946, p. 2; "Espionage in Canada," Editorial, *NYT*, July 17, 1946, p. 22; "Budenz Names the 'Secret Head' of Communists in United States," *NYT*, October 18, 1946, pp. 1, 4; Morgan, *Reds*.

17. "Democratic Deal Irks Labor Party," *NYT*, September 4, 1946, p. 15; "Head of ALP Backs Wallace on Policy," *NYT*, October 4, 1946, p. 12; "N.Y. Communists Withdraw Slate in Fight on Dewey," *WP*, September 10, 1946, p. 5; "Soviet Radio Urges Backing PAC to Prevent 'Reactionary' Congress," *NYT*, October 21, 1946, pp. 1, 2; "Chapman Charges Soviet Meddling," *NYT*, October 22, 1946, p. 21; "GOP Calls Moscow's 'Vote PAC' Proof the Soviets Back Democrats," *NYT*, October 22, 1946, p. 21; "Chapman Repeats Charge of 'Leftists,' " *NYT*, October 31, 1946, p. 16; "Ives' Speech Declaring Isolationism Is Dead," *NYT*, September 5, 1946, p. 17; "Dewey Accuses Foe of 'Buying' ALP Aid by Naming Epstein," *NYT*, September 6, 1946, pp. 1, 5; "State Campaign Draws to Close," *NYT*, October 27, 1946, E-7; " 'Overwhelming' Victory Predicted for the Republican State Ticket," *NYT*, November 3, 1946, pp. 1, 24; "Party Campaign Ban Shaped for Both Wallace, Pepper," *NYT*, September 21, 1946, pp. 1, 3; "Left Wing Is Active in Campaign Finale; Last Talks Tonight," *NYT*, November 4, 1946, pp. 1, 3; "Wallace Wavers on Mead Defeat," *NYT*, November 4, 1946, p. 3; "3 Big State Factors," *NYT*, November 7, 1946, pp. 1, 13; "Democrats Shy at Leftists but Won't Go Conservative," *NYT*, November 7, 1946, pp. 1, 13. On the role of the minor parties in New York, see Moscow, *Politics in the Empire State*, pp. 102–119. On Catholics' antipathy toward Communism and the ALP, see Zeitz, *White Ethnic New York*, pp. 93–97, 114–140.

18. "Lehman Bars Communist Aid and Criticizes All Extremes," *NYT*, October 19, 1946, pp. 1, 10; "Mead, Lehman Hit Dewey 'Liberalism,' " *NYT*, October 31, 1946, pp. 1, 18; "Chides Mead, Lehman," *NYT*, October 23, 1946, p. 16; "Democrats Shy at Leftists but Won't Go Conservative," *NYT*, November 7, 1946, pp. 1, 13.

19. Gallup, *The Gallup Poll*, I: 537, 604; "3 Weeks to Go, No Meat, New Deal in Panic," *Chicago Tribune*, October 14, 1946, pp. 1, 10; "State Candidates, Issues, Forecasts," *NYT*, November 3, 1946, E-6; "Huge Registration Viewed as Augury of Dewey Triumph," *NYT*, October 14, 1946, pp. 1, 11; "Ives Says Truman Distrusts People," *NYT*, October 14, 1946, pp. 1, 14; "Ives Says Political Expediency Caused

Lifting of Meat Controls," *NYT*, October 16, 1946, p. 31; Donovan, *Conflict and Crisis*, pp. 229–238; Hartmann, *Truman and the 80th Congress*, pp. 3–10; Leuchtenburg, "New Faces of 1946"; Bernstein, "Clash of Interests."

20. "Stable Peace Tops Lehman's Program," *NYT*, October 31, 1946, p. 17; "Text of Lehman Talk to PAC Women," *NYT*, September 25, 1946, p. 14; "Lehman Assails Dewey on Housing in State," *NYT*, November 3, 1946, p. 25; "President Now Has No Plans to Make Campaign Speeches," *WP*, October 29, 1946, pp. 1, 4; "Election Test," *NYT*, November 3, 1946, E-1; Robert Albright, "N.Y. Democrats Link Victory Possibility to Big Registration," *WP*, October 5, 1946, pp. 1, 4; "Lehman Endorsed by Mrs. Roosevelt," *NYT*, October 22, 1946, p. 19; Eleanor Roosevelt, "My Day," November 5, 1946, online: http://www.gwu.edu/~erpapers/myday/displaydoc.cfm?_y=1946&_f=md000487; "Elliott Roosevelt Backs Mead, Lehman," *NYT*, October 18, 1946, p. 13; "Mead Says Rival Fails the Veteran, Is Threat to Labor," *NYT*, November 1, 1946, pp. 1, 3; "Lehman Assails Rivals on Trade," *NYT*, October 30, 1946, pp. 1, 20.

21. "Text of Lehman Talk to PAC Women," *NYT*, September 25, 1946, p. 14; "Lehman Says Dewey Poses," *NYT*, October 11, 1946, p. 12; "Stable Peace Tops Lehman's Program," *NYT*, October 31, 1946, p. 17; "Mead and Lehman Stroll at Coney," *NYT*, November 4, 1946, p. 3.

22. "City Registration Heavy on First Day," *NYT*, October 8, 1946, pp. 1, 16; "Mead and Lehman Stroll at Coney," *NYT*, November 4, 1946, p. 3; "Text of Lehman's Talk to PAC Women," *NYT*, September 25, 1946, p. 14; "Lehman Assails Record of Dewey," *NYT*, October 15, 1946, p. 8; "Ives Reactionary, Lehman Charges," *NYT*, November 1, 1946, p. 3.

23. "Text of Lehman's Talk to PAC Women," *NYT*, September 25, 1946, p. 14; "Stable Peace Tops Lehman's Program," *NYT*, October 31, 1946, p. 17; "Lehman Promises Move to Bar Bilbo," *NYT*, October 20, 1946, p. 13; "Liquidation of Klan Is Pledged by Mead," *NYT*, October 12, 1946, p. 21. Jonathan Bell stresses Lehman's support in 1946 for an "ambitious progressive political program" and "an expansive vision of social democracy." See Bell, *The Liberal State on Trial*, pp. 18–20. On Truman's less than stalwart support for civil rights legislation during the first years of his presidency, see Hamby, *Beyond the New Deal*, p. 65.

24. Millis, ed., *The Forrestal Diaries*, p. 213; "To Campaign for Lehman," *NYT*, October 23, 1946, p. 16; "Truman Considers Campaign Details," *NYT*, October 2, 1946, p. 6; "What's News—World-Wide," *Wall Street Journal*, October 3, 1946, p. 1; "Mead Hopes Dimmed by Dewey Power," *WP*, October 6, 1946, M-1, 2; "The President's News Conference," October 24, 1946, *Public Papers: Truman, 1946*, pp. 463–465; "Truman Reserves Opinion on Vote," *NYT*, October 25, 1946, p. 14; Emmet McCormack, Chairman, Businessmen and Women for Mead and Lehman, to the President, October 25, 1946, and Matthew Connelly to McCormack, October 28, 1946, both in Truman Papers, OF 136-A, June 1946–June 1947. On the President's schedule for his visit to New York to address the United Nations, see "Ticker-Tape War Tests U.N. Today," *NYT*, October 23, 1946, p. 2.

25. HHLOH, pp. 165–168; "Joint Palestine Body Bars a Jewish State, but Urges Entry of 100,000 Refugees," *NYT*, May 1, 1946, pp. 1, 14. This paragraph and the following ones on Palestine are based in part on the following accounts: Ganin, *Truman, American Jewry, and Israel*; Urofsky, *We Are One!*; Cohen, *American Jews and the Zionist Idea*; and Dinnerstein, *America and the Survivors of the Holocaust*.

26. "There Is a Limit to What Even Jews Can Endure," *WP*, June 6, 1946, p. 10; Record of Telephone Call from Governor Lehman, June 7, 1946; Matthew Connelly to Lehman, June 7, 1946; and Lehman to President Truman, June 7, 1946; all in Truman Papers, PPF 2513, Lehman; Lehman to the President, June 20, 1946, Truman Papers, OF 204-Misc (June 1946).

27. "Divided Palestine Is Urged by Anglo-U.S. Cabinet Body, Delaying Entry of 100,000," *NYT*, July 26, 1946, pp. 1, 4; Lehman to Truman, July 30, 1946, Truman Papers, OF 204-C, Cabinet Committee on Palestine and Related Problems.

28. Lehman to Truman, July 30, 1946, and Roberta Barrows, Memorandum for David Niles, July 31, 1946, both in Truman Papers, OF 204-C, Cabinet Committee on Palestine and Related Problems; RB to Mrs. Klar, June 21, 1946, and Emanuel Celler to Matt Connelly, June 25, 1946, both in Truman Papers, OF 204-Misc (June 1946); McDonald to the President, July 29, 1946; Celler to the President, July 31, 1946; and Truman to McDonald, July 31, 1946, all in Truman Papers, OF 204-Misc (July 1946); Fitzpatrick to Truman, August 2, 1946, Truman Papers, OF 204–Misc., August–September 1946; "Byrnes Seen Urging Truman to Accept Divided Palestine," *NYT*, July 30, 1946, pp. 1, 4; "Truman Recalls Palestine Group," *NYT*, August 1, 1946, pp. 1, 10; Ganin, *Truman, American Jewry, and Israel*, pp. 80–93.

29. "Text of Platform Adopted by the Democrats," *NYT*, July 21, 1944, p. 12; "An Open Letter," *NYT*, September 30, 1946, p. 18; "Democrats Scorned by Local Zionists," *NYT*, September 30, 1946, p. 8; Ganin, *Truman, American Jewry, and Israel*, pp. 34–48, 99–103; Urofsky, *We Are One!* pp. 84–93.

30. "The President's Day," September 19, 1946, Truman Papers, Daily Presidential Appointments; Wise to the President, October 7, 1946; Clayton, Memorandum for the President, September 12, 1946; and Truman, Memorandum for Clayton, September 14, 1946; all in Truman Papers, White House Confidential File, Box 43, State Department, Palestine (2); "Haven for Jews Urged by Lehman," *NYT*, September 30, 1946, pp. 1, 9. On the growing support of non-Zionist Jews for partition, see Hacker and Hirsch, *Proskauer*, pp. 145–147.

31. "President's Statement on Palestine," *NYT*, October 5, 1946, p. 2; "Truman's Palestine Plea Flouted Foreign Advisers," *NYT*, October 7, 1946, p. 4; Drew Pearson, "Washington Merry-Go-Round," *WP*, October 11, 1946, p. 12; Ganin, *Truman, American Jewry, and Israel*, pp. 104–105.

32. Lehman to the President, October 7, 1946, and Celler to the President, October 7, 1946, both in Truman Papers, OF 204-Misc (October 1946); Wise to the President, October 7, 1946, Truman Papers, White House Confidential File, Box 43, State Department, Palestine (2); "Dewey Bids Britain Open Up Palestine to Immigrants Now," *NYT*, October 7, 1946, pp. 1, 5; "Silver Demands All of Palestine," *NYT*, October 27, 1946, p. 20.

33. "Election Test," *NYT*, November 3, 1946, E-1; Gallup, *The Gallup Poll*, I: 604; "Prediction Gives Republicans a Chance for Both Houses," *NYT*, November 3, 1946, pp. 1, 5.

34. "'Overwhelming' Victory Predicted for the Republican State Ticket," *NYT*, November 3, 1946, pp. 1, 24; "Left-Wing Is Active in Campaign Finale; Last Talks Tonight," *NYT*, November 4, 1946, pp. 1, 3; Parmet, *The Democrats*, pp. 57–58.

35. "Republicans Control Congress with 51 in Senate, 249 in House; . . . Landslide Result," *NYT*, November 7, 1946, pp. 1, 3; "Dewey and Ives Win in a State

Sweep; . . . State Lead 650,000," *NYT*, November 6, 1946, pp. 1, 3; "Democratic-ALP Break Likely; 3 Big State Factors," *NYT*, November 7, 1946, pp. 1, 13; "Record for Dewey in Official Count," *NYT*, December 14, 1946, p. 10; Charlton Ogburn to Lehman, November 12, 1946, LP, SF, Frank Altschul, document 0015_0257; Moscow, *Politics in the Empire State*, pp. 44–46; Parmet, *The Democrats*, pp. 64–65; Zeitz, *White Ethnic New York*, pp. 93–98, 126–129, 133–135.

36. " 'Verdict of People' Accepted by Lehman," *NYT*, November 6, 1946, p. 4; Wise to Lehman, November 7, 1946, and Lehman to Wise, November 9, 1946, both in LP, SF, Stephen Wise; Lehman to Henry and Elinor Morgenthau, November 8, 1946, LP, SF, Henry Morgenthau, Jr.

37. "Lehman Mentioned to Succeed Meyer," *NYT*, December 6, 1946, p. 34; "Winant, Forrestal, and Lehman Mentioned for World Bank President," *Wall Street Journal*, December 16, 1946, p. 3; "Winant Quits Post in U.N. Body," *NYT*, January 3, 1947, p. 10; Lehman to the President, [January 3, 1947], LP, SF, Truman, document 0906_0043 (misdated as June 6, 1947, in the list of the digital documents in the Lehman Papers); Lehman to Secretary Byrnes, [January 3, 1947], LP, SF, Byrnes, document 0125_0013 (misdated as March 22, 1946, in the list of digital documents in the Lehman Papers); Lehman to Senator Wagner, n.d., LP, SF, Wagner, document 0928_0065 (misdated March 22, 1944, in the list of digital documents in the Lehman Papers); and Eleanor Roosevelt to Truman, January 8, 1947; Dubinsky to the President, January 3, 1947; Green to the President, January 13, 1947; Fitzpatrick to the President, January 2, 1947; Byrnes, Memorandum for the President, "Appointment of Senator La Follette," January 9, 1947; and Truman to Eleanor Roosevelt, January 13, 1947; all in Truman Papers, OF 85-Q, Endorsements; Lehman, Request to See the President, January 13, 1947, and Telegram, Connelly to Lehman, January 14, 1947, both in Truman Papers, OF 1082; "The President's Day," January 16, 1947, Truman Papers, Daily Presidential Appointments; "Lehman Confers with Truman," *NYT*, January 17, 1947, p. 18; Lehman to George Marshall, January 24, 1947, LP, SF, Marshall; Lehman to Eleanor Roosevelt, July 14, 1947, LP, SF, Eleanor Roosevelt; "Biddle to Succeed Winant in U.N.," *NYT*, January 28, 1947, p. 13; Eleanor Roosevelt Oral History Transcript, HHLP, CUOHC, pp. 14–15.

38. Vandenberg to the President, March 12, 1947, and attached Vandenberg to Clayton, March 5, 1947; and George Marshall, Memorandum for the President, July 10, 1947; all in Truman Papers, OF 85-Q, UN Economic and Social Council (2); "Nomination of Biddle Pigeonholed," *WP*, March 17, 1947, p. 3; Lehman to the President, June 16, 1947, and Truman to Lehman, June 18, 1947, both in LP, SF, Truman; "Biddle Nomination to U.N. Withdrawn," *NYT*, July 13, 1947, pp. 1, 15; Lehman to Mrs. Roosevelt, July 14, 1947, LP, SF, Eleanor Roosevelt; Lehman to Edward Flynn, July 17, 1947, LP, SF, Flynn; Lehman to Julius Edelstein, September 8, 1957, LP, SF, Allan Nevins, document 0679_003.

39. Flynn to the President, November 7, 1947, Truman Papers, OF 1082; Truman to Flynn, November 12, 1947, LP, SF, Truman; and Flynn to the President, December 3, 1947; Truman to Flynn, December 9, 1947; and Lehman to Flynn, December 20, 1947; all in LP, SF, Flynn; Stewart Alsop, "Truman Needs a Repair Kit, Too," *WP*, September 7, 1947, B-5; Carolin Flexner Oral History Transcript, HHLP, CUOHC, p. 61.

40. Weinfeld to Lehman, November 27, 1946; Lehman to Weinfeld, December 1, 1946; Lehman to Truman, December 2, 1946; Lehman to Clark, December 2, 1946; Hassett to Lehman, December 11, 1946; Clark to Lehman, December 17, 1946; Lehman to Weinfeld, December 23, 1946; all in LP, SF, Weinfeld; Lehman to Wagner, February 20, 1947, LP, SF, Wagner; Lehman to Truman, April 7, 1948, and Truman to Lehman, April 14, 1948, both in LP, SF, Truman; Fitzpatrick to Lehman, April 14, 1948, LP, SF, Fitzpatrick; Lehman to Weinfeld, April 19, 1948; LP, SF, Weinfeld; Flynn to Lehman, April 20, 1948, LP, SF, Flynn; Lehman to Truman, May 7, 1948, LP, SF, Truman; Lehman to Flynn, January 5, 1949, LP, SF, Flynn; Lehman to Truman, August 24, 1949, and Truman to Lehman, August 27, 1949, both in LP, SF, Truman; Lehman to William Boyle, n.d., LP, SF, Weinfeld, document 0947_0115, given the date of March 1, 1950, in the list of digital documents in the Lehman Papers; Lehman to Truman, April 1, 1950; Boyle to Lehman, April 3, 1950; Matthew Connelly to Lehman, April 6, 1950; Fitzpatrick to Lehman, May 26, 1950; Lehman to Boyle, June 1, 1950; Boyle to Lehman, June 6, 1950; Weinfeld to Lehman, June 10, 1950; and Lehman to Senator McCarran, July 14, 1950, all in LP, SF, Weinfeld; "Weinfeld Likely to Succeed Rifkind," *NYT*, May 25, 1950, p. 26; "Weinfeld Named to Federal Bench Here; Bar, Party Leaders Hail Truman's Choice," *NYT*, July 11, 1950, p. 21. On Truman and the Pendergast Machine, see Hamby, *Man of the People*.

41. "Senators Predict Lilienthal Choice," *NYT*, February 23, 1947, p. 42; "Lehman Supports U.S. Aid to Greece," *NYT*, April 10, 1947, p. 6; "Military Training Sped in Congress," *NYT*, June 27, 1947, p. 5; Lehman to the President, June 6, 1947, LP, SF, Truman; Lehman to the President, June 22, 1947, Truman Papers, OF 407, Taft-Hartley Veto, Pro, A-Z; "Lehman Supports 400,000 DP Influx," *NYT*, July 3, 1947, p. 7; "Hope of Europe's DP's Rests with Congress," *NYT*, July 20, 1947, E-7; "DP Compromise Denounced," *NYT*, June 19, 1948, p. 13; Lehman to the President, July 1, 1948, LP, SF, Truman; Dinnerstein, *America and the Survivors of the Holocaust*, pp. 137–182; "ERP Defense Pacts Urged by Lehman," *NYT*, April 3, 1948, p. 4; Truman to Lehman, November 22, 1947, and Lehman to Matthew Connelly, November 28, 1947, both in LP, SF, Truman; Daniel Poling to Lehman, November 26, 1947, and Philadelphia Interfaith Sponsoring Committee, Invitation, December 15, 1947, both in LP, SF, Poling.

42. "The President's News Conference," September 25, 1947, in *Public Papers: Truman, 1947*, pp. 436–438; Truman to Lehman, September 25, 1947, and Lehman to the President, September 26, 1947, both in Truman Papers, OF 174-F, Citizens for Food Committee (1); "Truman Asks Food Saving to Help Hungry Abroad; . . . Crisis Is Worse Than Year Ago Because of World Crop Shortages," *WP*, September 26, 1947, pp. 1, 2; "Wheatless Day Opposed," *NYT*, October 23, 1947, p. 12; Lehman to Luckman, October 23, 1947, LP, SF, Luckman; "Permanent Board on Food Proposed," *NYT*, November 15, 1947, p. 4; "Text of Truman and Luckman Letters," *NYT*, November 21, 1947, p. 19; "Luckman Leaving, States Food Needs," *NYT*, December 4, 1947, p. 21.

43. Lehman to the President, July 1, 1947, and attached Press Release, June 30, 1947, LP, SF, Truman; "Lehman Supports Marshall's Plan," *NYT*, July 1, 1947, p. 5; "Lehman in Plea for Food Warns on Chaos in Europe," *NYT*, October 12, 1947, pp. 1, 12; "Non-Partisan Unit Headed by Stimson to Back Europe Aid," *NYT*, November

16, 1947, pp. 1, 3; "Unofficial Statesmen," Editorial, *WP*, November 18, 1947, p. 10; Committee for the Marshall Plan to Aid European Recovery to Friend, February 19, 1948, Truman Papers, OF 426-L (1945–May 1948); "Speed Requested on Marshall Plan," *NYT*, December 10, 1947, p. 2; John Slawson to Lehman, January 24, 1948, LP, SF, Slawson; "Barkley Attacks Hoover's Aid View," *NYT*, January 25, 1948, pp. 1, 18; "Lehman Warns of Dangers Facing U.S. if Adequate Fund for ERP Is Delayed," *NYT*, February 20, 1948, p. 9; Lehman to the President, May 5, 1948, LP, SF, Truman; "12 Named to ECA Board," *WP*, June 20, 1948, M-4; "The President's Day," July 16, 1948, Truman Papers, Daily Presidential Appointments; Paul Hoffman to Lehman, August 5, 1948, LP, SF, Hoffman. On the Marshall Plan as a successor in some ways to UNRRA, see Acheson, *Present at the Creation*, p. 726; Donovan, *Conflict and Crisis*, p. 280; Douglas, *A Full Life*, p. 265; Eleanor Roosevelt, "My Day," July 3, 1947, online: http://www.gwu.edu/~erpapers/myday/displaydoc.cfm?_y=1947&_f=md000695.

    44. Lehman to Henri Bonnet, November 26, 1947, LP, SF, Bonnet; "Partition Vote of Haiti Explained," *Baltimore Afro-American*, December 13, 1947, p. 18; Lehman to Rabbi Wise and enclosed Address for Delivery at the Zionist Organization of America Dinner Commemorating the Thirtieth Anniversary of the Balfour Declaration, November 3, 1947, LP, SF, Stephen Wise; "Immediate Action to Save DP's Urged," *NYT*, November 4, 1947, p. 16; "Lehman Asks End of Arms Embargo," *NYT*, February 19, 1948, p. 6; Abba Hillel Silver to Lehman, March 20, 1948, LP, SF, Silver; "Jewish Group Here Urges U.N. Action," *NYT*, March 29, 1948, p. 2; Cohen, *Truman and Israel*, pp. 149–198.

    45. Truman to Jacobson, February 27, 1948, Truman Papers, OF 204-Misc., February 1948 (2).

    46. Connelly to Lehman, April 20, 1948, and Lehman to Connelly, April 22, 1948, both in LP, SF, Truman; Lehman to Flexner, April 20, 1948, and April 26, 1948, LP, SF, Carolin Flexner.

    47. "The President's Day," May 4, 1948, Truman Papers, Daily Presidential Appointments; Carolin Flexner to Lehman, April 22, 1948, LP, SF, Flexner; Lehman to the President, May 7, 1948, Truman to Lehman, May 10, 1948, and Lehman, Memorandum, May 7, 1948, all in LP, SF, Truman; "Lehman Advocates Holy City Trustee," *NYT*, May 5, 1948, p. 14.

    48. Lehman to the President, May 5, 1948; Memorandum Submitted by Mr. Fahy to Mr. Lovett, May 4, 1948; and Truman to Lehman, May 10, 1948; all in LP, SF, Truman; handwritten notation, "The Pres. Kept the memo," at the bottom of Lehman to the President, May 5, 1948, Truman Papers, OF 204-Misc., May 1948; Ganin, *Truman, American Jewry, and Israel*, p. 182.

    49. Lehman to Silver, May 14, 1948, LP, SF, Silver; Lehman to the President, May 13, 1948; Truman to Lehman, May 15, 1948; and Lehman to Truman, May 15, 1948; all in LP, SF, Truman; "Zionists Proclaim New State of Israel; Truman Recognizes It and Hopes for Peace; . . . U.S. Moves Quickly," *NYT*, May 15, 1948, pp. 1, 3.

    50. Jacobson to Matt Connelly, February 18, 1948, Truman Papers, OF 204-Misc., February 1948 (2); Weizmann to the President, April 9, 1948, Truman Papers, OF 204-Misc., April 1948; Weizmann to the President, May 13, 1948, David Niles Papers, Box 33, General File, Israeli Affairs, 1948, HSTL; Beschloss, *Presidential Courage*, pp. 196–234.

51. "Wallace to Run; Pledges 3D Party to Bar War Policy; Democrats Scored," *NYT*, December 30, 1947, pp. 1, 15; "Lehman Assails Wallace Tactics," *NYT*, March 27, 1948, p. 8; Schmidt, *Henry A. Wallace*; Donaldson, *Truman Defeats Dewey*, pp. 57–60.

52. Americans for Democratic Action, New York State, "Political Action Policy," April 3, 1948, LP, SF, Americans for Democratic Action; "Democrats Urged to Run Eisenhower," *NYT*, April 4, 1948, p. 45; "State Democrats Hedge on Truman," *NYT*, April 17, 1948,. p. 9; Lehman to Flexner, April 26, 1948, LP, SF, Flexner; "19 Party Leaders Make Caucus Call to Block Truman," *NYT*, July 4, 1948, pp. 1, 14; "50 Top Democrats Back Rights Plank," *NYT*, July 5, 1948, p. 26; Donaldson, *Truman Defeats Dewey*, pp. 136–144.

53. Humphrey to Lehman, June 10, 1948, and Lehman to Humphrey, June 15, 1948, both in LP, SF, Humphrey; "50 Top Democrats Back Rights Plank," *NYT*, July 5, 1948, p. 26; Lehman to Carolin Flexner, April 26, 1948, LP, SF, Flexner; "Mrs. Goodhart, Sister of Ex-Gov. Lehman, 88," *NYT*, July 14, 1948, p. 23; Paul Fitzpatrick to Lehman, July 16, 1948, LP, SF, Fitzpatrick; "Truman, Barkley Named by Democrats; South Loses on Civil Rights, 35 Walk Out; South Beaten on Race Issue as Rights Plank Is Widened," *NYT*, July 15, 1948, pp. 1, 8; "Truman Is Shunned in Votes of South," *NYT*, July 15, 1948, pp. 1, 9; "Southerners Name Thurmond to Lead Anti-Truman Fight," *NYT*, July 18, 1948, pp. 1, 3; Donaldson, *Truman Defeats Dewey*, pp. 157–166, 184; Gardner, *Harry Truman and Civil Rights*, pp. 87–104; Cohodas, *Strom Thurmond and the Politics of Southern Change*, pp. 154–193; Crespino, *Strom Thurmond's America*, pp. 61–84. On Hattie Lehman Goodhart, see Libo, ed., *Lots of Lehmans*, pp. 69–82.

54. "Southern Revolt, Gaining Strength, Aids Republicans; . . . Wallace Deepens Split," *NYT*, September 13, 1948, pp. 1, 8; "2 Truman Swings in New York Urged," *NYT*, September 15, 1948, p. 24; "Truman Says GOP Perils Prosperity," *NYT*, October 9, 1948, pp. 1, 8; "Rear Platform and Other Informal Remarks in New York," October 8, 1948, *Public Papers: Truman, 1948*, pp. 699, 714.

55. Lehman to William Neale Roach, June 10, 1948, LP, SF, Democratic National Committee; Louis Johnson to Lehman, September 15, 1948, and Lehman to Johnson, September 29, 1948, both in LP, SF, Johnson; Lehman to Paul Fitzpatrick, September 29, 1948, LP, SF, Fitzpatrick; Truman to Lehman, October 16, 1948, LP, SF, Truman; "$1,503,709 Paid Out, Democrats in Red," *NYT*, October 26, 1948, pp. 1, 4; "Group of High Roosevelt Officials Denounce Wallace's Candidacy," *NYT*, October 23, 1946, p. 6.

56. Leonard Lyons, *WP*, October 7, 1948, B-14; American Zionist Emergency Council, Advertisement, "Another Reversal, Another Betrayal," *NYT*, September 30, 1948, p. 23; Redding, *Inside the Democratic Party*, p. 229; Lehman to the White House Social Secretary, October 14, 1948, LP, SF, Truman; "Lehman to Speak for Truman," *NYT*, October 21, 1948, p. 20. On the importance of Lehman's endorsement for Democratic candidates, see also Isaacs, *Jews and American Politics*, p. 142. On Jewish discontent over the President's Palestine policy, see Cohen, *Truman and Israel*, pp. 243–249; and Snetsinger, *Truman, the Jewish Vote, and the Creation of Israel*, pp. 124–128.

57. Bowles quoted in Cohen, *Truman and Israel*, p. 244; "Dewey Aides Sure of State as GOP Registration Rises," *NYT*, October 20, 1948, pp. 1, 23; American Zionist Emergency Council, Advertisement, "MR. TRUMAN: Where Do *You* Stand on This Issue?" *NYT*, October 20, 1948, p. 33. On the agreement to keep Israel out of the

campaign, see Clark Clifford to the President, October 23, 1948, Clifford Papers, Box 13, Subject File, Palestine—Misc. Memos (3), HSTL; and Snetsinger, *Truman, the Jewish Vote, and the Creation of Israel*, pp. 127–128.

58. "Lehman Praises Democrats' Record," *NYT*, October 23, 1948, p. 6.

59. "Dewey Warns GOP to Shun Any Abuse," *NYT*, October 23, 1948, pp. 1, 7; Clifford to the President, October 23, 1948, Clifford Papers, Box 13, Subject File, Palestine—Misc. Memos (3); Cohen, *Truman and Israel*, p. 252.

60. "Truman Reaffirms His Israel Stand in Reply to Dewey," *NYT*, October 25, 1948, pp. 1, 2; "Truman on Palestine," *NYT*, October 25, 1948, p. 2.

61. Redding, *Inside the Democratic Party*, p. 229; Lehman to Paul Fitzpatrick, October 26, 1948, LP, SF, Fitzpatrick; Mayor William O'Dwyer to Lehman, October 25, 1948, and Lehman to O'Dwyer, October 26, 1948, both in LP, SF, Truman; "Final Tribute Paid Dr. Judah Magnes," *NYT*, October 29, 1948, p. 26; Nevins, *Herbert H. Lehman and His Era*, p. 52; "Truman in Strongest Plea for Israel Backs Boundaries in First U.N. Plan; . . . Stresses Security," *NYT*, October 29, 1948, pp. 1, 3; "The Text of Truman's Address at Madison Square Garden," *NYT*, October 29, 1948, p. 4; "U.S. Switches on Palestine, Won't Consider Sanctions; Change Is Laid to Truman," *NYT*, October 30, 1948, pp. 1, 2; Cohen, *Truman and Israel*, pp. 254–255.

62. "Lehman Condemns Record of Dewey," *NYT*, October 29, 1948, p. 3.

63. Redding, *Inside the Democratic Party*, pp. 226–232; "Mrs. Roosevelt Backs Truman and Party; Barkley, Lehman Join Her in Radio Appeal," *NYT*, November 1, 1948, p. 17; Advertisement, "A Message from Mrs. Eleanor Roosevelt," *NYT*, November 1, 1948, p. 48.

64. "Dewey State Edge Is Put at 400,000," *NYT*, October 31, 1948, p. 64; "The Political Picture in the 48 States: A Pre-Election Survey," *NYT*, October 31, 1948, E-4; "Tabulation of How States Cast Votes in Election," *NYT*, December 11, 1948, p. 10; Donaldson, *Truman Defeats Dewey*, pp. 184–220.

65. Flynn to Lehman, November 1, 1948, LP, SF, Flynn; Fitzpatrick to Lehman, November 12, 1948, and Lehman to Fitzpatrick, November 16, 1948, both in LP, SF, Fitzpatrick.

66. Lehman to Truman, November 3, 1948, and Truman to Lehman, November 12, 1948, both in LP, SF, Truman; Lehman to Flynn, November 4, 1948, LP, SF, Flynn.

Chapter 12. "If You Could See the Kind of People in New York City Making Up This Bloc That Is Voting for My Opponent": Lehman and the Election of 1949

1. "The Text of President Truman's Appeal," *NYT*, November 6, 1949, p. 7.

2. "Leaders to Weigh Wagner's Retiring," *NYT*, November 30, 1948, p. 24; "Status of Wagner Again to the Fore," *NYT*, April 30, 1949, p. 18; "Wagner Seen Quitting Senate by July 8 to Force Fall Poll," *NYT*, June 21, 1949, pp. 1, 23; "Senator Wagner Resigns; Fall Election Is Necessary," *NYT*, June 29, 1949, pp. 1, 4; Dulles Appointed Senator; Lehman Weighs Candidacy," *NYT*, July 8, 1949, pp. 1, 11.

3. "Leaders to Weigh Wagner's Retiring," *NYT*, November 30, 1948, p. 24; "Wagner Seen Quitting Senate by July 8 to Force Fall Poll," *NYT*, June 21, 1949, pp.

1, 23; "Liberals Support Lehman for Senate," *NYT*, June 23, 1949, pp. 1, 16; "Lehman Weighing Senate Race Plea," *NYT*, June 30, 1949, pp. 1, 26; "Party Heads Delay Senatorial Choice," *NYT*, July 6, 1949, p. 19; "Lehman's Consent to Run Is Doubted," *NYT*, July 7, 1949, p. 20; Eichelberger to Lehman, July 6, 1949, LP, SF, Eichelberger; Osborne to Lehman, July 7, 1949, LP, SF, Osborne.

4. Lehman to Robert G. A. Jackson, July 11, 1949, LP, SF, Jackson; "Dulles Appointed Senator; Lehman Weighs Candidacy," *NYT*, July 8, 1949, pp. 1, 11.

5. Lehman to Robert G. A. Jackson, July 11, 1949, LP, SF, Jackson; "Dulles Appointed Senator; Lehman Weighs Candidacy," *NYT*, July 8, 1949, pp. 1, 11; "O'Dwyer Now Seen Willing to Run for Mayor Again," *NYT*, July 9, 1949, pp. 1, 28; "O'Dwyer Is Invited to Visit President," *NYT*, July 10, 1949, pp. 1, 39; "New York," *NYT*, July 10, 1949, E-2; "Lehman Hesitancy on Race Is a Hitch in O'Dwyer Draft," *NYT*, July 11, 1949, p. 1. On Liberal opposition to O'Dwyer, see Daniel Soyer, " 'Support the Fair Deal in the Nation; Abolish the Raw Deal in the City': The Liberal Party in 1949," paper delivered at "The World of Governor Lehman: New York City and State in Depression and War," Conference at Columbia University, June 2008, pp. 9–14.

6. Lehman to Robert G. A. Jackson, July 11, 1949, LP, SF, Jackson; "Lehman Hesitancy on Race Is a Hitch in O'Dwyer Draft," *NYT*, July 11, 1949, p. 1; Moscow, *Politics in the Empire State*, pp. 45–46, 120–121; Lehman to Al Smith, May 17, 1935, LP, SF, Smith; "Worthy of Victory," Editorial, *Brooklyn Tablet*, May 11, 1935, LP, SF, Frank Altschul, document 0015_0031 (misdated May 14, 1935, in the list of digital documents in the Lehman Papers); HHLOH, pp. 598–599, 673–674; Carolin Flexner Oral History Transcript, HHLP, CUOHC, pp. 52–53, 66–67; "Many Groups Fight City Ban on Nation," *NYT*, July 14, 1948, p. 25; Spellman to Lehman, July 15, 1948, and Lehman to Spellman, July 21, 1948, both in LP, SF, Spellman; Lehman to Frank Altschul, August 14, 1948, LP, SF, Altschul; Lehman to Frank Altschul, October 11, 1948, and enclosed "An Appeal to Reason and Conscience," Frank Altschul Papers, Catalogued Correspondence, 128b, Herbert H. Lehman, Columbia University Library; "School Ban on Nation Reaffirmed; Open Hearing by Mayor Is Sought," *NYT*, July 20, 1948, pp. 1, 21; Cooney, *The American Pope*, pp. 180–181.

7. Eleanor Roosevelt to Lehman, July 11, 1949, LP, SF, Eleanor Roosevelt; Lash, *Eleanor: The Years Alone*, p. 157.

8. Lehman to Mrs. Roosevelt, July 16, 1949, LP, SF, Eleanor Roosevelt.

9. "Cardinal Calls Mrs. Roosevelt Anti-Catholic on School Bill," *NYT*, July 23, 1949, pp. 1, 26; "Texts of the Cardinal's Letter and of Articles by Mrs. Roosevelt," *NYT*, July 23, 1949, p. 26; "Lehman Condemns Spellman Attack on Mrs. Roosevelt," *NYT*, July 24, 1949, pp. 1, 36; William Liebmann, Interview with Mrs. Herbert Lehman, April 2, 1970, in Joseph Lash Papers, Box 44, FDRL; Lash, *Eleanor: The Years Alone*, pp. 156–162; Pfeffer, *Church, State, and Freedom*, pp. 486–494; Cooney, *The American Pope*, pp. 176–178; "The Shape of Things," *The Nation*, July 30, 1949, p. 97.

10. Lehman to Julius Edelstein, May 21, 1959, LP, SF, Richard Neuberger; Lehman to Irwin Ross, August 7, 1957, and Kirchwey to Lehman, July 12, 1949, both in LP, SF, Spellman; Swope to Lehman, July 14, 1949, LP, SF, Swope; Black to Lehman, July 26, 1949, LP, SF, Black.

11. Lehman to Kirchwey, July 16, 1949, LP, SF, Kirchwey; "O'Dwyer Ready to Run Again After Talking to Truman; May Face Hogan in Primary," *NYT*, July 13,

1949, pp. 1, 22. Former *New York Times* political reporter Warren Moscow wrote years later that O'Dwyer was persuaded to run when President Truman, at the behest of Ed Flynn, promised to appoint O'Dwyer as Ambassador to Mexico in 1950. This would free O'Dwyer from having to serve the full four-year term as Mayor, and his resignation would require another mayoral election in 1950, which Democrats hoped would boost turnout in New York City and improve their chances in the 1950 gubernatorial election. See Moscow, *The Last of the Big-Time Bosses*, pp. 87–88.

    12. "3 Top Democrats Turn Cool to Lehman's Senate Candidacy," *New York Post*, July 25, 1949, pp. 2, 13; "Leaders Fear Lehman Race May Hurt O'D," *New York Daily News*, August 30, 1949, p. 28; Lehman to Irwin Ross, August 7, 1957, LP, SF, Spellman. On the liberalism of the *New York Post* at this time, see Nissenson, *The Lady Upstairs*, pp. x, 97–99, 135; Potter, *Men, Money & Magic*, p. 228; Cooney, *The American Pope*, pp. 203–208; Lash, *Eleanor: The Years Alone*, p. 267.

    13. "Plea for a Liberal Is Sent to Mayor," *NYT*, July 28, 1949, p. 18; Dubinsky to Lehman, July 28, 1949, LP, SF, Dubinsky; "ILGWU Heads Back Morris for Mayor," *NYT*, July 29, 1949, p. 9; Berle to Lehman, August 4, 1949, LP, SF, Berle; "Tammany Accepts Wagner on Ticket," *NYT*, August 5, 1949, pp. 1, 7; Soyer, " 'Support the Fair Deal in the Nation; Abolish the Raw Deal in the City,' " pp. 17–18; Dubinsky and Raskin, *David Dubinsky*, pp. 287–289.

    14. Bingham to Lehman, August 3, 1949, LP, SF, Jonathan and June Bingham.

    15. "Mayor Seeks Peace of Mrs. Roosevelt and the Cardinal," *NYT*, August 4, 1949, pp. 1, 14; Lash, *Eleanor: The Years Alone*, pp. 156–159; Lash, *A World of Love*, pp. 303–304; Moscow, *The Last of the Big-Time Bosses*, p. 122; "Cardinal Gives School Ideas; 'Fair,' Says Mrs. Roosevelt," *NYT*, August 6, 1949, pp. 1, 10; "Pope Sees Dispute Resolved by Cardinal, Mrs. Roosevelt," *NYT*, August 14, 1949, pp. 1, 15; "End of Row Pleases O'Dwyer and Lehman," *NYT*, August 7, 1949, p. 28; "Lehman Decision to Run Averts Democratic Split," *New York Post*, September 1, 1949, pp. 4, 30; Cooney, *The American Pope*, pp. 182–184.

    16. Lash, *A World of Love*, p. 304; Lash, *Eleanor: The Years Alone*, pp. 165; "Cardinal Is Guest of Mrs. Roosevelt," *NYT*, August 25, 1949, p. 25; Drew Pearson, "Merry-Go-Round: Gen. Bradley Hits Defense of Vaughan," *WP*, September 8, 1949, B-15.

    17. "Democratic Leaders Fail to Contact Lehman on Race," *New York Post*, August 8, 1949, p. 6; Leonard Lyons, "The Lyon's Den," *WP*, August 9, 1949, B-13; "Committee Formed to Draft Lehman," *NYT*, August 10, 1949, p. 17; "Lehman to Reply on Senate Bid Soon," *NYT*, August 11, 1949, p. 14; "Movement Under Way to Draft Lehman for the Senate," *NYT*, August 24, 1949, p. 19; Eleanor Roosevelt, "My Day," August 29, 1949, online: http://www.gwu.edu/~erpapers/myday/displaydoc.cfm?_y=1949&_f=md001370.

    18. Henry Modell, Chairman, Citizens Committee to Draft Lehman for U.S. Senate, to the President, August 24, 1949, and Matthew Connelly to Modell, August 25, 1949, both in Truman Papers, PPF 129-A (June–August 1949); "Movement Under Way to Draft Lehman for the Senate," *NYT*, August 24, 1949, p. 19; "The President's News Conference," August 25, 1949, *Public Papers: Truman, 1949*, p. 441; "Truman Hints 1952 Will See Him Retire," *NYT*, August 26, 1949, pp. 1, 2; Truman to Lehman, August 27, 1949, LP, SF, Truman.

19. "Lehman Enters Senate Race; Dulles Likely as GOP Rival," *NYT*, September 1, 1949, pp. 1, 16; "The Shape of Things," *The Nation*, September 10, 1949, p. 241.

20. "The President's News Conference," September 1, 1949, *Public Papers: Truman, 1949*, p. 456; "Lehman to Speak before State CIO," *NYT*, September 2, 1949, p. 13; "Lehman Enters Senate Race; Dulles Likely as GOP Rival," *NYT*, September 1, 1949, pp. 1, 16; Daily Sheet, March 16, 1946, Truman Papers, PSF, Box 69, President's Appointment File, Daily Sheets, March 1946; Truman, *Harry S. Truman*, pp. 540–541.

21. "Dulles in Race for Senate; Attacks 'Trend to Statism,'" *NYT*, September 8, 1949, pp. 1, 22; "Dulles' Statement on Candidacy," *NYT*, September 8, 1949, p. 22; Pruessen, *John Foster Dulles*, pp. 395–403.

22. "The President's News Conference," September 8, 1949, *Public Papers: Truman, 1949*, pp. 471–474; "Truman Can't Define Statism but Still Calls It Scare Word," *WP*, September 9, 1949, pp. 1, 25.

23. "Lehman Is Named for Senate, Vows Civil Rights Fight," *NYT*, September 16, 1949, pp. 1, 22; "Text of Lehman's Acceptance Speech," *NYT*, September 16, 1949, p. 22; "Peekskill, 2nd Round," *NYT*, September 11, 1949, E-2; Duberman, *Paul Robeson*, pp. 364–375. See also the articles in "Paul Robeson: A Centennial Symposium," *Pennsylvania History*, 66: 1 (Winter 1999).

24. "Lehman and O'Dwyer Favor Aid by the U.S. to Parochial Schools," *NYT*, September 16, 1949, pp. 1, 20; "Lehman School Aid Stand Is 'a Switch,' Says Dewey," *NYT*, September 16, 1949, p. 21; "Curran Bids Party to Draft Dewey," *NYT*, September 21, 1949, p. 23. Mrs. Roosevelt made it clear that she, too, had been discussing the general principle of federal aid to education and not endorsing the Braden bill or any other specific proposal. See Roosevelt, "My Day," October 1, 1949, online: http://www.gwu.edu/~erpapers/myday/displaydoc.cfm?_y=1949&_f=md001399.

25. "Dulles Nominated for Senate; Opens Attack on Fair Deal," *NYT*, September 16, 1949, pp. 1, 20; "Text of Speech by Dulles Accepting Republican Senate Nomination," *NYT*, September 16, 1949, p. 21. According to Alonzo Hamby, the Brannan Plan was the Truman administration's proposal to replace "commodity price supports" with "direct income maintenance payments to family farmers," which would have required an "intrusive and expensive bureaucratic monitoring of the precise level of production on every small and medium-size farm in the country." See Hamby, *Man of the People*, pp. 496–497; and Matusow, *Farm Policies and Politics in the Truman Years*, pp. 191–221.

26. "Lehman Says G.O.P. Distorts His Views," *NYT*, October 18, 1949, p. 31; HHLOH, pp. 767–769; Julius C. C. Edelstein Oral History Transcript, HHLP, CUOHC, pp. 8–11.

27. "Truman Asks Law to Force Insuring of Nation's Health," *NYT*, November 20, 1945, pp. 1, 13; "Taft Bolts Hearing on Health Bill After Loud Clash with Murray," *NYT*, April 3, 1946, pp. 1, 21; "Dewey Condemns Social Medicine," *NYT*, October 14, 1949, p. 19; "Lehman Assailed on Medical Stand," *NYT*, October 18, 1949, p. 30; "Doctors to Assist Dulles' Campaign," *NYT*, October 19, 1949, p. 7; Drew Pearson, "The Washington-Merry-Go Round: Ike's Crowd Alienated the AFL," *WP*, September 28, 1952, B-5; Kelley, *Public Relations and Political Power*, pp. 87–99. For more on the Truman administration, the AMA, and national health insurance, see Poen, *Harry S. Truman versus the Medical Lobby*.

28. "Lehman Opposes Truman on Health," *NYT*, October 16, 1949, p. 43; Anna Rosenberg to Edith Lehman, October 20, 1949, LP, SF, Rosenberg; T. Compere to Governor Lehman, Memorandum, "Mailing to Doctors and Dentists in the State," October 21, 1949; and Lehman to Doctors, October 26, 1949, both in LP, Campaign Correspondence and Related Material, 1949, Senate, Publicity, C235-34. On Lehman's retreat from the Fair Deal on this issue, see also Bell, *The Liberal State on Trial*, pp. 169–171.

29. "Lehman Enters Senate Race; Dulles Likely as GOP Rival," *NYT*, September 1, 1949, pp. 1, 16; "Lehman Asserts GOP Chiefs Fight 'Humane' Government," *NYT*, September 11, 1949, pp. 1, 4; "State Labor Joins to Elect Lehman," *NYT*, September 30, 1949, p. 18; "State CIO to Open Drive for Lehman," *NYT*, October 1, 1949, p. 30; "Meany Confident of Lehman Victory," *NYT*, October 15, 1949, p. 32; "Barkley to Speak at Garden Rally," *NYT*, October 9, 1949, p. 41; "Lehman, O'Dwyer Praised by Labor as Its Champions," *NYT*, October 28, 1949, pp. 1, 20; "Green Says Big Issue Is Taft Act Repeal," *NYT*, October 29, 1949, p. 6.

30. Krock, "Clear National Issues Are Shaping Up for '50," *NYT*, September 18, 1949, E-3; "Lehman vs. Dulles," Editorial, *WP*, September 10, 1949, p. 6; "Mr. Dulles Accepts," Editorial, *NYT*, September 8, 1949, p. 28; "Communists Take Full ALP Control," *NYT*, January 8, 1948, pp. 1, 14; "Wallace Refuses to Run for Senate; Blow to ALP, Help to Lehman Seen," *NYT*, September 13, 1949, pp. 1, 33; "ALP to Name No Candidate for Senate or State Judge," *NYT*, September 14, 1949, pp. 1, 36; "Dulles Nominated for Senate; Opens Attack on Fair Deal," *NYT*, September 16, 1949, pp. 1, 20; "Text of Speech by Dulles Accepting Republican Senate Nomination," *NYT*, September 16, 1949, p. 21; "Dulles Says Lehman Pulls Punches in Fight to Bar Communism Spread," *NYT*, September 20, 1949, pp. 1, 21; "Dulles Assails Lehman," *NYT*, September 24, 1949, p. 2; "Communism Top Issue in N.Y. Election," *WP*, September 25, 1949, M-7.

31. Lehman to Mrs. José Ferrer, October 6, 1949, LP, Campaign Correspondence and Related Materials, 1949, Senate, "E-J," C235-18; "Lehman Espouses New and Fair Deal," *NYT*, September 23, 1949, pp. 1, 17; HHLOH, pp. 767–769.

32. "Dewey Bids Anti-Reds Join 'Holy Crusade' to Elect Dulles," *New York Herald Tribune*, October 4, 1949, p. 14; "Dewey Acts 'Shock' Lehman Manager," *NYT*, October 5, 1949, p. 24; "Czech Church Curb an Omen to Dulles," *NYT*, October 6, 1949, p. 26; "Lehman Accuses Rivals of Bigotry," *NYT*, October 7, 1949, p. 21; Arthur Schlesinger, Jr., "India's Nehru Is Viewed as Western Counterpoise of China's Mao: The Week in History," *WP*, October 16, 1949, B-1; Pruessen, *John Foster Dulles*, pp. 398, 402.

33. "Lehman Accuses Rivals of Bigotry," *NYT*, October 7, 1949, p. 21; "Dulles Sees Bias Incited by Lehman," *NYT*, October 11, 1949, p. 37; "Lehman Repeats Charge of Bigotry," *NYT*, October 18, 1949, p. 32; Pruessen, *John Foster Dulles*, p. 402; Julius C. C. Edelstein Oral History Transcript, HHLP, CUOHC, pp. 11–12; Carolin Flexner Oral History Transcript, HHLP, CUOHC, pp. 58(b), 63. On the concern that Lehman was not running a vigorous enough campaign, see Richard Rossbach to Lehman, October 11, 1949, LP, SF, Max J. H. and Mrs. (Mabel Limburg) Rossbach.

34. "Dulles Sees Bias Incited by Lehman," *NYT*, October 11, 1949, p. 37; "Baruch Declares Dulles No Bigot," *NYT*, October 27, 1949, p. 22; "Lehman Repeats Charge of Bigotry," *NYT*, October 18, 1949, p. 32; "17 Negroes Denounce Dulles and

Morris," *NYT*, October 19, 1949, p. 6; "Conviction of Davis Throws N.Y. Political Campaign into Turmoil," *Baltimore Afro-American*, October 29, 1949, p. 5; Independent Citizens' Committee for Election of Herbert H. Lehman, "Sample Three-Minute Speech for Sound Truck," for Immediate Release, October 22, 1949, LP, Campaign Correspondence and Related Materials," 1949, Senate, Dulles (John Foster), C235-17; Dulles to Lehman, October 30, 1949, LP, SF, Dulles; Pruessen, *John Foster Dulles*, p. 402.

35. Dulles to Lehman, October 16, 1949, LP, SF, Dulles; HHLOH, pp. 769–770; "Dulles Rebuffed on Debate Offer," *NYT*, October 17, 1949, p. 29; "Dulles Answers Charge of Bigotry," *NYT*, October 19, 1949, p. 7; "Lehman, Dulles Round Bend for Stretch Race, Mud Flying," *WP*, October 30, 1949, pp. 1, 12.

36. "Catholic Vote Urged on School Aid Fight," *NYT*, September 12, 1949, p. 2; "Lehman Gains Seen in Some Up-State Cities Where Local Issues Hold the Top Interest," *NYT*, October 20, 1949, p. 34; Julius C. C. Edelstein Oral History Transcript, HHLP, CUOHC, pp. 11–12. Auriesville is in Montgomery County, along the Mohawk River, about forty miles west of Albany.

37. Protestants and Catholics United Against the Election of Herbert H. Lehman, "Do You Believe in God?" LP, Campaign Correspondence and Related Materials," 1949, Senate, Dulles (John Foster), C235-17.

38. "Farley in Plea on Air for Lehman Election," *NYT*, November 1, 1949, p. 13; Independent Citizens' Committee for the Election of Herbert H. Lehman as United States Senator, "Text of Radio Address in Behalf of Former Governor Herbert H. Lehman . . . ," For Release November 1, 1949, LP, SF, Farley; "Lehman Election Urged by Wagner," *NYT*, October 21, 1949, p. 14.

39. Sulzberger to Lehman, October 17, 1949, and Lehman to Sulzberger, November 23, 1949, LP, SF, Sulzberger; "The Choice of a Senator," Editorial: *NYT*, October 18, 1949, p. 26. Walter Lippmann endorsed Dulles for similar reasons. See Lippmann, "Today and Tomorrow: Dulles and Lehman," *WP*, October 6, 1949, p. 13.

40. "The President's News Conference," September 8, 1949, in *Public Papers: Truman, 1949*, p. 474; "Fitzpatrick Sees Lehman in by 300,000; Tells Truman He Won't Have to Talk Here," *NYT*, September 20, 1949, p. 21; Truman to Anderson, October 1, 1949, Truman Papers, PPF 2614; "Aid of Truman's Cabinet Is Lent to Cause of Lehman and O'Dwyer," *NYT*, October 3, 1949, p. 12.

41. Eleanor Roosevelt to President Truman, October 6, 1949, document 17, "Eleanor and Harry: The Complete Correspondence of Eleanor Roosevelt and Harry S. Truman," HSTL, online: http://www.trumanlibrary.org/eleanor/1949.html; Lash, *Eleanor: The Years Alone*, pp. 165–166; "Mrs. Roosevelt, Son Franklin, Pledge Aid to the Lehman-Wagner-O'Dwyer Slate," *NYT*, October 7, 1949, p. 19; Memorandum, Imelda Prokopovitsh to Miss Thompson, "Invitation for Mrs. Roosevelt to Speak for Lehman Campaign Program on Tuesday, October 11—Radio Program—2:45 p.m.–3:00 p.m.," October 4, 1949, and Prokopovitsh to Thompson, October 11, 1949, both in Eleanor Roosevelt Papers, 1945–1952, Lehman; "Lehman's Ability Held Senate Need," *NYT*, October 12, 1949, p. 25; "My Day," August 29, 1949, online: http://www.gwu.edu/~erpapers/myday/displaydoc.cfm?_y=1949&_f=md001370; "My Day," October 1, 1949, online: http://www.gwu.edu/~erpapers/myday/displaydoc.cfm?_y=1949&_f=md001399; "My Day," October 7, 1949, online: http://www.gwu.edu/~erpapers/

myday/displaydoc.cfm?_y=1949&_f=md001404; "My Day," November 7, 1949, online: http://www.gwu.edu/~erpapers/myday/displaydoc.cfm?_y=1949&_f=md001430.

42. Truman to Mrs. Roosevelt, October 12, 1949, "Eleanor and Harry," online: http://www.trumanlibrary.org/eleanor/1949.html.

43. "The President's News Conference," October 13, 1949, *Public Papers: Truman, 1949*, p. 511; "Democrats to Dine at $100 a Plate Here," *NYT*, October 12, 1949, p. 23; "Lehman, O'Dwyer Praised by Labor as Its Champions," *NYT*, October 28, 1949, pp. 1, 20; Independent Citizens' Committee for Election of Herbert H. Lehman as United States Senator, Press Release, Text of a Speech Delivered by United States Attorney General J. Howard McGrath, October 28, 1949, LP, SF, McGrath; "Tobin Goes on Air for Lehman Cause," *NYT*, October 25, 1949, p. 17; "Ewing Backs Lehman," *NYT*, October 30, 1949, p. 68.

44. Fitzpatrick to Boyle, October 14, 1949, and Fitzpatrick to Connelly, October 14, 1949, Truman Papers, OF 136-A, April 1949–March 1950.

45. Truman to Lehman, October 20, 1949, LP, SF, Truman; "Truman Sets Issue in Vote for Lehman," *NYT*, October 23, 1949, pp. 1, 3.

46. Lehman to Truman, October 22, 1949, LP, SF, Truman; "Truman Sets Issue in Vote for Lehman," *NYT*, October 23, 1949, pp. 1, 3; "The President's Day," October 23, 1949, Truman Papers, Daily Presidential Appointments; "Truman Assures Lehman He'll Win," *NYT*, October 24, 1949, p. 15.

47. See HST to Matt, handwritten note at the bottom of Fitzpatrick to Connelly, October 14, 1949, Truman Papers, OF 136-A, April 1949–March 1950; "Truman to Back Lehman over Radio on Saturday," *NYT*, October 31, 1949, p. 10; "Truman Aid Called Lehman 'Desperation,' " *WP*, November 1, 1949, p. 3.

48. "Truman Urges Election of Lehman in First Real Test of Fair Deal; . . . President in Plea," *NYT*, November 6, 1949, pp. 1, 6; "The Text of President Truman's Appeal," *NYT*, November 6, 1949, p. 7; Clark Clifford, Memorandum for Mr. Murphy, November 4, 1949, Clifford Papers, Box 40, Presidential Speech File, 1949, November 5, Radio Remarks Endorsing Governor Herbert Lehman for Senator, HSTL.

49. Arthur Krock, "In the Nation: Where 'Bipartisanship' Loses Its Prefix," *NYT*, October 25, 1949, p. 25; Frank Kent, "Politics: The Eyes Turn toward New York as Dulles Battles Lehman in Crucial Election," *Wall Street Journal*, October 3, 1949, p. 4; Mark Sullivan, "Dulles vs. Lehman: New York Race as a National Portent," *WP*, November 5, 1949, p. 7.

50. "5,000,000 Will Vote Today in State and City Elections; U.S. Watches Senate Race . . . Lehman Is Favored," *NYT*, November 8, 1949, pp. 1, 11; "Lehman and O'Dwyer Elected in Sweep, Ex-Governor by 200,000, Mayor 308,430 . . . Dulles Concedes," *NYT*, November 9, 1949, pp. 1, 14; "The Official Count: Lehman by 198,057," *NYT*, December 15, 1949, p. 2; "Democrats' Link to Labor Seen Tightened in Victory; . . . Clinched in State," *NYT*, November 10, 1949, pp. 1, 4; "Liberals and Democrats Claim Credit for Election of Lehman," *NYT*, November 12, 1949, p. 26; "Democrats Sweep," *NYT*, November 13, 1949, E-1; "Dulles Concedes Defeat at 10:45," *NYT*, November 9, 1949, p. 14; "Lehman, O'Dwyer Thank Electorate," *NYT*, November 9, 1949, p. 2; Adolf Berle, Jr., Diary, November 9, 1949, in Berle and Jacobs, eds., *Navigating the Rapids*, p. 589.

51. "Dulles Sends Telegram to Truman: 'You Win,'" *NYT*, November 10, 1949, p. 2; "Democratic Club Honors Trumans," *WP*, November 9, 1949, B-7; "Vote Results Here Hailed by Truman," *NYT*, November 9, 1949, pp. 1, 9.

52. Truman to Lehman, November 9, 1949, and Lehman to Truman, November 11, 1949, both in LP, SF, Truman.

53. "President Upheld, Fitzpatrick Says," *NYT*, November 9, 1949, p. 17; Eleanor Roosevelt, "My Day," November 10, 1949, online: http://www.gwu.edu/~erpapers/myday/displaydoc.cfm?_y=1949&_f=md001433; Humphrey to Lehman, November 9, 1949, LP, SF, Humphrey; Schlesinger to Lehman, November 10, 1949, LP, SF, Schlesinger; Dubinsky to Lehman, November 10, 1949, LP, SF, Dubinsky; Quill and Guinan to Lehman, November 10, 1949, LP, SF, Quill; Leith-Ross to Lehman, November 10, 1949, LP, SF, Leith-Ross; Soyer, "'Support the Fair Deal in the Nation; Abolish the Raw Deal in the City,'" pp. 17–20. The Condon-Wadlin Act was a New York State law that prohibited strikes by public employees.

54. Lehman to Charles Poletti, November 27, 1949, LP, SF, Poletti; Lehman to Barkley, November 11, 1949, LP, SF, Barkley; Lehman to Bethune, November 21, 1949, LP, SF, Bethune; Lehman to Fitzpatrick, November 21, 1949, LP, SF, Fitzpatrick; Lehman to Bowles, November 15, 1949, LP, SF, Bowles.

55. "Vote to Affect '52, Lehman Declares," *NYT*, November 11, 1949, p. 21.

Chapter 13. "I Will Not Compromise with My Conscience": Lehman and McCarthyism, 1950–1952

1. Herbert Lehman quoted in "Name-Calling Jars Senate D.P. Debate," *NYT*, March 8, 1950, p. 15.

2. Mary Van Rensselaer Thayer, "Lehman's Office Prettied Up Like a Debutante; Everybody Calls Him Darling," *WP*, January 5, 1950, B-7.

3. Acheson, *Present at the Creation*, p. 354; "Text of Truman's Address to Jefferson-Jackson Day Dinners," *NYT*, February 17, 1950, p. 3; "Vandenberg Lauds Dulles' Peace Role," *NYT*, October 30, 1949, pp. 1, 57; "The Choice of a Senator," Editorial, *NYT*, October 18, 1949, p. 26; Koen, *The China Lobby in American Politics*, pp. 95–98; Westerfield, *Foreign Policy and Party Politics*, pp. 343–362; Tucker, *Patterns in the Dust*, pp. 12, 161–168, 181–182.

4. "Hoover, Taft Urge U.S. to Aid Formosa by Force if Needed," *NYT*, January 3, 1950, pp. 1, 10; "Truman Bars Military Help for Defense of Formosa; . . . Pacts Recalled," *NYT*, January 6, 1950, pp. 1, 3; "Problem of Asia," *NYT*, January 8, 1950, E-1; "Republicans Angry at Formosa Stand," *NYT*, January 6, 1950, pp. 1, 3; Westerfield, *Foreign Policy and Party Politics*, pp. 363–365.

5. Lehman to Acheson, January 14, 1950, LP, SF, Acheson; "Connally Charges Critics 'Pervert' U.S. China Policy," *NYT*, January 10, 1950, pp. 1, 32; "Acheson Is Firm on Policy; Bars Military Aid," *NYT*, January 11, 1950, pp. 1, 3; "Senator Taft Says State Department Seeks Chiang Fall," *NYT*, January 12, 1950, pp. 1, 11; "Acheson Says U.S. Counts on Chinese Anger at Soviet for Land Seizures in North; Four Areas Listed," *NYT*, January 13, 1950, pp. 1, 2; "Senate Will Query Military Leaders on

Formosa Policy," *NYT*, January 14, 1950, pp. 1, 2; "Acheson to Face New Questioning on Seizure of Peiping Consulate," *NYT*, January 17, 1950, p. 3; James Reston, "Secretary Acheson: A First-Year Audit," *New York Times Magazine*, January 22, 1950, pp. 7–9, 35–38; Acheson, *Present at the Creation*, pp. 354–357; Westerfield, *Foreign Policy and Party Politics*, pp. 328–329.

6. Acheson to Lehman, February 2, 1950, LP, SF, Acheson; 96 *Cong. Rec.* 1554–1560 (February 7, 1950); "Lehman Backs Acheson," *NYT*, February 7, 1950, p. 9. All references to the *Congressional Record* are to the bound volumes.

7. "Hiss Guilty on Both Perjury Counts," *NYT*, January 22, 1950, pp. 1, 50; "Truman Refuses Comment on Hiss," *NYT*, January 28, 1950, p. 6; Acheson, *Present at the Creation*, pp. 250–252, 359–361; HHLOH, pp. 764–765; Goldman, *The Crucial Decade–and After*, pp. 100–137. On the Federal Employee Loyalty Program, see Freeland, *The Truman Doctrine and the Origins of McCarthyism*; and Caute, *The Great Fear*. On HUAC, see Goodman, *The Committee*. On the Hiss case, see Weinstein, *Perjury*; Weinstein and Vassiliev, *The Haunted Wood*; and White, *Alger Hiss's Looking-Glass Wars*.

8. "Lehman Asks Loyalty Tests to Follow Democratic Forms," *WP*, January 28, 1950, pp. 1, 2; "Truman Refuses Comment on Hiss," *NYT*, January 28, 1950, p. 6; "Address by Hon. Herbert H. Lehman, of New York, at Roosevelt Day Dinner," Extension of Remarks of Hon. Hubert H. Humphrey, 96 *Cong. Rec.* A712-713 (February 2, 1950).

9. "McCarthy Insists Truman Oust Reds," *NYT*, February 12, 1950, p. 5; "Acheson Aide Asks '57 Reds' Be Named," *NYT*, February 14, 1950, p. 16; "McCarthy Charges Spy for Russia Has a High State Department Post," *NYT*, February 21, 1950, p. 13; 96 *Cong. Rec.* 1952–1981 (February 20, 1950); Griffith, *The Politics of Fear*, pp. 48–59; Oshinsky, *A Conspiracy So Immense*, pp. 108–114; Reeves, *The Life and Times of Joe McCarthy*, pp. 222–242. On Fuchs, see "British Jail Atom Scientist as a Spy After Tip by F.B.I.; . . . Two Charges Made," *NYT*, February 4, 1950, pp. 1, 2; and "Capital Is Stirred," *NYT*, February 4, 1950, pp. 1, 2.

10. 96 *Cong. Rec.* 1974, 1977 (February 20, 1950); Fried, *Men against McCarthy*, p. 50.

11. "State Department Faces Red Inquiry," *NYT*, February 23, 1950, p. 4; "Lehman Condemns New Bill on D.P.'s," *NYT*, March 2, 1950, p. 8; "Eighteen Senators Offer Eased DP Measure," *WP*, February 28, 1950, B-10; 96 *Cong. Rec.* 2547–2549 (March 1, 1950); Lehman to Dean Acheson, March 27, 1950, LP, SF, Acheson; Lehman to Thomas Finletter, February 28, 1950, LP, SF, Finletter; Bailey and Samuel, *Congress at Work*, pp. 236–261; Dinnerstein, *America and the Survivors of the Holocaust*, pp. 217–245; Ybarra, *Washington Gone Crazy*, pp. 286, 378–381, 463–484.

12. "D.P. 'Treason' Alleged," *NYT*, March 3, 1950, p. 13; "Lehman Sees No Threat in DP Program," *WP*, March 2, 1950, p. 5; "Lehman Defends D.P.'s Screening," *NYT*, March 5, 1950, p. 29; 96 *Cong. Rec.* 2714–2723 (March 3, 1950), and 2803–2812 (March 4, 1950). On Eastland, see Sherrill, *Gothic Politics in the Deep South*, pp. 186–215; and Asch, *The Senator and the Sharecropper*, pp. 132–166. On Jenner, see his vicious attack on General George Marshall in "Congress Votes Marshall Bill in Unusually Bitter Sessions," *NYT*, September 16, 1950, pp. 1, 4.

13. "Name-Calling Jars Senate D.P. Debate," *NYT*, March 8, 1950, p. 15; "Senate Fight over DP Bill May Continue Weeks Longer," *WP*, March 8, 1950, p. 17; 96 *Cong. Rec.* 2910–2916 (March 7, 1950); Bailey and Samuel, *Congress at Work*, p. 263; Julius

Edelstein Oral History Transcript, HHLP, CUPHC, pp. 17–19; HHLOH, p. 783. On McCarran's power in the Senate, see Ybarra, *Washington Gone Crazy*, and Griffith, *The Politics of Fear*, p. 118.

14. "McCarthy Says Miss Kenyon Helped 28 Red Front Groups," *NYT*, March 9, 1950, pp. 1, 5; Dorothy Kenyon to Lehman, June 1, 1936; Kenyon to Lehman, December 19, 1938; Lehman to Kenyon, March 17, 1950; Lehman to Kenyon, March 25, 1950; Kenyon to Mrs. Lehman, December 31, 1963; all in LP, SF, Kenyon; 96 *Cong. Rec.* 3593–3596 (March 20, 1950); "The Texts of Ambassador Jessup's Statement and of the Senator McCarthy Letters," *NYT*, March 21, 1950, p. 24; Henry Stimson, "Methods and Motives of Attack on State Department Questioned," Letter to the Editor, *NYT*, March 27, 1950, p. 22. Senator Ives beat Lehman to the punch in inserting the Stimson letter into the *Congressional Record*. See " 'No Case' Against Lattimore, FBI Chief Hints to Probers; State Dept. Officials Shifted; Accused Man Calls McCarthy's 'Spy' Charge 'Moonshine'; Lawsuit Indicated," *WP*, March 28, 1950, pp. 1, 11.

15. "State Department Denies Harboring 'Top Russian Spy,' " *NYT*, March 24, 1950, pp. 1, 3; "Lattimore Named as 'Top Soviet Spy' Cited by M'Carthy," *NYT*, March 27, 1950, pp. 1, 9; 96 *Cong. Rec.* 4378–4380 (March 30, 1950); Alsop, *The Center*, pp. 8–9; "Truman Calls 3 Senators Saboteurs; . . . M'Carthy Insists He Has Evidence; Assails Lattimore," *NYT*, March 31, 1950, pp. 1, 2; Newman, *Owen Lattimore and the 'Loss' of China*, pp. 214–224.

16. "Wherry Says Acheson Is 'Risk' and 'Must Go,' " *NYT*, March 22, 1950, p. 6; 96 *Cong. Rec.* 3769 (March 22, 1950); "Climax," *NYT*, March 26, 1950, E-1; "Vandenberg Acts to Restore Bipartisan Policy," *NYT*, March 26, 1950, E-3; "Senate G.O.P. Aims Drive at Acheson, Bridges Reports," *NYT*, March 26, 1950, pp. 1, 23; 96 *Cong. Rec.* 4107 (March 27, 1950); " 'Get Acheson' Drive Opened by Bridges," *NYT*, March 28, 1950, pp. 1, 4; Acheson to Lehman, April 7, 1950, LP, SF, Acheson; Fried, *Men against McCarthy*, pp. 69–70.

17. "Vandenberg in Unity Plea; Senator Defends the E.C.A.; Asks 'Unpartisan' Peace Plan," *NYT*, March 26, 1950, pp. 1, 4; "Vandenberg Acts to Restore Bipartisan Policy," *NYT*, March 26, 1950, E-3; "Republican Named to Advise Acheson in London Parleys," *NYT*, March 29, 1950, pp. 1, 20; "Acheson Confers with Vandenberg," *NYT*, March 30, 1950, p. 4; "Cooper Sworn in as Acheson Aide," *NYT*, April 4, 1950, p. 3; 96 *Cong. Rec.* 4387–4391 (March 30, 1950); "Ives Says Acheson Is Hit as Dulles Was," *NYT*, March 31, 1950, p. 18; Marquis Childs, "Bipartisan Policy," *WP*, April 6, 1950, p. 13; "Issues Joined," *NYT*, April 2, 1950, E-1; "Revival of Bipartisanship Is Difficult Task," *NYT*, April 2, 1950, E-3; Acheson, Memorandum of Conversation with the President, April 4, 1950; Memoranda for Files of Telephone Conversations, April 5, 1950; Acheson to Truman, April 5, 1950; and Acheson to Vandenberg, April 10, 1950, all in Acheson Papers, Box 67, Secretary of State Files, Memoranda of Conversations File, April 1950, HSTL; Vandenberg, *The Private Papers of Senator Vandenberg*, pp. 557–561; Gerson, *John Foster Dulles*, pp. 56–59; Pruessen, *John Foster Dulles*, pp. 432–436.

18. Memorandum for Files of Telephone Conversations, April 5, 1950, and Acheson to Truman, April 5, 1950, Acheson Papers, Box 67, Secretary of State Files, Memoranda of Conversations File, April 1950, HSTL.

19. "Is It Dewey and Dulles and (Who) and Lehman?" *NYT*, March 26, 1950, E-10; "Truman Will Name Dulles an Adviser on Foreign Policy," *NYT*, April 6, 1950, pp. 1, 5; Memorandum for Files of Telephone Conversation, April 5, 1950, Acheson

Papers, Box 67, Secretary of State Files, Memoranda of Conversations File, April 1950; "Memorandum of Conversation between Senator Lehman and Secretary Acheson," April 6, 1950, LP, SF, Acheson; Julius Edelstein Oral History Transcript, HHLP, CUOHC, pp. 25–26.

20. "Dulles Named U.S. Adviser to Renew Bipartisan Policy," *NYT*, April 7, 1950, pp. 1, 5; "Memorandum of Conversation between Senator Lehman and Paul Fitzpatrick," April 10, 1950, LP, SF, Fitzpatrick; "Dulles Named as Consultant to Acheson," *WP*, April 7, 1950, pp. 1, 4.

21. "Senate Bloc Seeks to Tag McCarthy as Liar on Floor," *WP*, May 4, 1950, pp. 1, 4; 96 *Cong. Rec.* 6255, 6257 (May 3, 1950); 96 *Cong. Rec.* 7894–7895 (June 1, 1950); "7 Senate Republicans Assail 'Smearing,' Exploiting 'Fear,'" *WP*, June 2, 1950, pp. 1, 21; Doris Fleeson, "Mme. Senator Calls the Turn," June 2, 1950, and Lehman to Fleeson, June 5, 1950, both in LP, SF, Fleeson; Smith, *Declaration of Conscience*, p. 18; Morrison, *Woman of Conscience*, pp. 15–29; Wallace, *A Biography of Margaret Chase Smith*, p. 107.

22. Walter Trohan, "3 Men Called a Government in Themselves," *Chicago Tribune*, May 29, 1950, p. 1; Lehman to Henry Morgenthau, Jr., June 3, 1950, LP, SF, Morgenthau. Trohan later identified his source for the story as "the Latvian-born wife of Loy Henderson," a career diplomat who, as director of the State Department's Office of Near Eastern Affairs, had opposed the creation of the state of Israel and had subsequently been appointed U.S. Ambassador to India. Trohan also claimed in his memoirs that he had been ordered to write this article by Colonel Robert McCormick, owner and publisher of the *Tribune*, and that he had purposely exaggerated the story so that it would be killed by the editors. Despite his denials that he was anti-Semitic, Trohan's allegation that FDR had sneered, "What else can you expect from a Jew" after Lehman had come out against the court-packing plan in 1937, a remark not reported anywhere else and the accuracy of which is highly suspect, suggests at the very least that Trohan agreed with the anti-Semitic sentiments expressed in his *Tribune* article. See Trohan, *Political Animals*, pp. 5–6, 99; Walter Trohan Oral History Transcript, pp. 51–53, HSTL; and chapter 5, n. 16 in the present volume. On anti-Semitism and McCarthyism, see HHLOH, p. 775. On Loy Henderson and Palestine, see Brands, *Inside the Cold War*, pp. 165–192.

23. "Red Charges by M'Carthy Ruled False," *NYT*, July 18, 1950, pp. 1, 17; "The Nation," *NYT*, July 23, 1950, E-1; Excerpt, Drew Pearson Broadcast, September 24, 1950, LP, Senate Subject Files, C205-99, Internal Security—McCarran Bill; Fried, "Electoral Politics and McCarthyism: The 1950 Campaign," p. 192; Griffith, *The Politics of Fear*, pp. 100–101; Hamby, *Beyond the New Deal*, pp. 408–409; Weinstein and Vassiliev, *The Haunted Wood*, pp. 327–334.

24. "Mundt Bill," Editorial, *WP*, July 6, 1950, p. 12; Tanner and Griffith, "Legislative Politics and 'McCarthyism': The Internal Security Act of 1950," pp. 174–178; Thompson, *The Frustration of Politics*, pp. 79–83, 109–110, 113–114, 127–129, 134–135.

25. "M'Naboe's 'Red' Ban Vetoed by Lehman as Peril to Liberty," *NYT*, March 31, 1938, pp. 1, 10; Lehman to Altschul, May 12, 1948, and Lehman to Altschul, July 12, 1950, both in LP, SF, Frank Altschul. Mundt had moved from the House of Representatives to the Senate as a result of the 1948 election.

26. Memorandum, S. K. to J. C. C. E., Delegations on the Mundt-Ferguson Bill, April 19, 1950, LP, Legislative Files, C59-28, Mundt-Ferguson Bill; "Arms Aid

Stalled by Senate Debate on Domestic Issues," *NYT*, June 29, 1950, pp. 1, 5; "Mundt Bill Balked by Senate Recess," *NYT*, July 2, 1950, pp. 1, 10; Richard Spong, "Mundt-Nixon Back from Limbo," Editorial Research Reports, Daily Service, July 21, 1950, LP, Senate Subject Files, C205-104, Internal Security—Miscellaneous Material (2); "Mundt Plans Anti-Red Rider," *NYT*, August 7, 1950, p. 10; Ybarra, *Washington Gone Crazy*, pp. 493–495; "Minutes of Democratic Conference," August 21, 1950, in Ritchie, ed., *Minutes of the Senate Democratic Conference*, pp. 460–465.

27. Michael Quill, President, New York City CIO Council, to Lehman, March 16, 1950, and Lehman to Quill, March 17, 1950, both in LP, SF, Quill; Lehman to Harold Fasick, August 3, 1950, LP, Legislative Files, C60-28a, Mundt-Nixon Bill—Correspondence, I-a.

28. Fried, *Men against McCarthy*, p. 104; "Special Message to the Congress on the Internal Security of the United States," August 8, 1950, *Public Papers: Truman, 1950*, pp. 571–576; "New Power to End Subversive Action Is Asked by Truman," *NYT*, August 9, 1950, pp. 1, 15; Hamby, *Beyond the New Deal*, pp. 410–411.

29. 96 *Cong. Rec.* 11964–11966 (August 8, 1950); "Truman Asks New Curbs on Spies," *WP*, August 9, 1950, pp. 1, 5; Lehman to Jacob Potofsky, August 10, 1950, LP, SF, Potofsky; Ybarra, *Washington Gone Crazy*, pp. 485, 506, 511.

30. S. 4037, 81st Cong, 2d sess., August 10, 1950; 96 *Cong. Rec.* 12145–12146 (August 10, 1950); "New Senate Bill Combines Six Anti-Subversive Measures," *WP*, August 11, 1950, p. 8; S. 4061, 81st Cong., 2d sess., August 17, 1950; 96 *Cong. Rec.* 12693 (August 17, 1950); Lehman to Jacob Potofsky, August 18, 1950, LP, SF, Potofsky; "Minutes of Democratic Conference," August 21, 1950, in Ritchie, ed., *Minutes of the Senate Democratic Conference*, p. 462; U.S., Cong., Senate, Committee on the Judiciary, *Protecting the Internal Security of the United States*, S. Rept. 2369, 81st Cong., 2d sess., August 17, 1950; "Senate Unit Votes New Curb on Reds," *NYT*, August 18, 1950, p. 6; Truman, *Memoirs*, II: 287; Ybarra, *Washington Gone Crazy*, pp. 485–486, 506, 511. The sponsors of the administration-backed bill included Senators Magnuson, Lucas, Myers, Kilgore, Kefauver, Green, Douglas, Humphrey, Graham, and Lehman.

31. 96 *Cong. Rec.* 14189–14194, 14198 (September 5, 1950); "Lehman Attacks Bill to Curb Reds," *NYT*, September 6, 1950, p. 14. FBI Director J. Edgar Hoover later validated Lehman's fears when he requested additional funds for the FBI, asserting that the FBI's job had become more difficult because American Communists had been driven underground. See "Reds Hide Deeper, F.B.I. Chief Warns," *NYT*, March 14, 1951, pp. 1, 36; and "Brownell Combs White Case Files," *NYT*, February 8, 1954, pp. 1, 8.

32. 96 *Cong. Rec.* 14195 (September 5, 1950), 14233–14236 (September 6, 1950), 14442–14444 (September 8, 1950); "Bill Would Permit Reds' Internment," *NYT*, September 7, 1950, p. 34; Ybarra, *Washington Gone Crazy*, pp. 515–516, 518. Lyndon Johnson aide Bobby Baker later said about McCarran: "He thought everybody that had any tendency to be liberal was a communist." See Bobby Baker Oral History Transcript, III, 37, Lyndon Baines Johnson Library (hereinafter LBJL).

33. Memorandum for: Hon. Herbert H. Lehman, September 4, 1950, and attached Memorandum, "The legislative recommendations made by the President in his Internal Security Message of August 8, 1950, to Congress," August 17, 1950, LP, Senate Subject Files, C205-98, Internal Security—Humphrey, Hubert H.; "Pressure on for Law to Check Communists," *NYT*, August 27, 1950, E-10; "Drastic Anti-Red Bill Wins in

House, 354-20; Truman Version Fails; Milder Measure Goal of Administration When Senate Acts; 'Fronts' Are Curbed," *WP*, August 30, 1950, pp. 1, 5. Graham's support for civil rights for African Americans also contributed to his defeat. See Douglas, *In the Fullness of Time*, pp. 238–241; Ashby, *Frank Porter Graham*, pp. 257–271; Burns and Pleasants, *Frank Porter Graham and the 1950 Senate Race in North Carolina.*

34. S. 4130, 81st Cong., 2d sess., September 6, 1950; Memorandum, J. C. C. E. to Senator Lehman, September 4, 1950, and attached Memorandum on Amendment to S. 4061, LP, Senate Subject Files, C205-97, Internal Security—Constitutionality of Bills; "Kilgore Asks Reds Be Held in Camps," *NYT*, September 3, 1950, p. 23; "Bill Would Permit Reds' Internment," *NYT*, September 7, 1950, p. 34; Douglas, *In the Fullness of Time*, p. 306.

35. "The President's Day," September 6, 1950, Truman Papers, Daily Presidential Appointments; "Bill Would Permit Reds' Internment," *NYT*, September 7, 1950, p. 34; "Red Internment Substitute for McCarran Bill Introduced," *WP*, September 7, 1950, p. 13; "The President's News Conference," September 7, 1950, in *Public Papers: Truman, 1950*, p. 620; "Truman Won't Sign Subversive Curb; Red Roundup Ready," *NYT*, September 8, 1950, pp. 1, 13.

36. Douglas, *In the Fullness of Time*, pp. 306–307; William Benton to Chester Bowles, September 13, 1950, LP, SF, Benton; "Senate, 70 to 7, Passes Bill to Register and Intern Reds," *NYT*, September 13, 1950, pp. 1, 6; "November Session Can Be 'Lame Duck' Nightmare," *WP*, September 24, 1950, B-3.

37. 96 *Cong. Rec.* 14627 (September 12, 1950); "Senate, 70 to 7, Passes Bill to Register and Intern Reds," *NYT*, September 13, 1950, pp. 1, 6; Julius Edelstein, "Some Recollections and an Appraisal of Herbert H. Lehman as United States Senator," December 19, 1963, Robert F. Wagner Collection, Speeches Series, Box 060052W, Folder 11, La Guardia and Wagner Archives, online: http://www.laguardiawagnerarchive.lagcc.cuny.edu/FileBrowser.aspx?LinkToFile=FILES_DOC/WAGNER_FILES/06.016.0000.060052W.11.PDF#undefined.

38. 96 *Cong. Rec.* 14628 (September 12, 1950); "Senate, 70 to 7, Passes Bill to Register and Intern Reds," *NYT*, September 13, 1950, pp. 1, 6; William Benton to Chester Bowles, September 13, 1950, and Benton to Lehman, September 13, 1950, both in LP, SF, Benton; "Senate Vote on M'Carran Bill Reflects Hysteria in Nation," *Buffalo Evening News*, September 15, 1950, clipping in LP, Senate Subject Files, C205-105, Internal Security—Printed Matter, Clippings; Excerpt, Drew Pearson Broadcast, September 24, 1950, LP, Senate Subject Files, C205-99, Internal Security—McCarran Bill; Reinhold Niebuhr, "Senator Lehman Commended," Letter to the Editor, *NYT*, September 18, 1950, p. 22; Hartley Howe, "The Making of a Liberal," *The Nation*, October 28, 1950, p. 381. Senators Graham and Taylor had already been defeated in primary elections, Senator Leahy was not running for re-election, and Green, Kefauver, and Murray were not up for re-election in 1950. See "McGrath to Press New Curbs on Reds," *NYT*, September 25, 1950, pp. 1, 10.

39. Lehman, Murray, and Kefauver to the President, September 20, 1950, LP, SF, Truman; "The President's News Conference," September 14, 1950, in *Public Papers, Truman, 1950*, pp. 638–639; "Conferees Pass Red Curbs Bill with Strongest Hill Proposals," *WP*, September 19, 1950, pp. 1, 3; "Congress Passes Bill to Curb Reds by Heavy Margins," *NYT*, September 21, 1950, pp. 1, 13; Ybarra, *Washington Gone Crazy*, pp. 525–526.

40. Truman to Lehman, September 27, 1950, and Truman to the Members of Congress, September 22, 1950, both in LP, SF, Truman; Memorandum, "Political and moral reasons for a Presidential veto of the McCarran anti-subversive bill (H.R. 9490, 81st Congress)," September 20, 1950, Charles Murphy Files, Box 9, President's Speech File, September 22, 1950, Veto Message on Internal Security–McCarran Bill, 2/2, HSTL; "Veto of the Internal Security Act," September 22, 1950, *Public Papers: Truman, 1950*, pp. 645–653; "Red Control Bill Is Vetoed, Repassed at Once by House; . . . . Senate Filibuster," *NYT*, September 23, 1950, pp. 1, 6; Hamby, *Beyond the New Deal*, pp. 413–414; Ybarra, *Washington Gone Crazy*, pp. 526–527.

41. 96 *Cong. Rec.* 15534–15535 (September 22, 1950); Lehman to Connelly, October 1, 1950; Connelly to Lehman, October 23, 1950; Handwritten Note on White House Press Release, September 22, 1950, p. 17; Lehman, Memorandum for the Files, December 30, 1958, all in LP, SF, Truman.

42. "Veto of Anti-Red Bill Overridden by House; Debate Delays Senate, Program for Recess Just After Midnight Is Upset; Filibuster Threat Is Voiced," *WP*, September 23, 1950, pp. 1, 4; "Senate Overrides Veto of Red Controls Bill as Congress Adjourns; Vote Is 57 to 10 After Debate Lasts 20 Hours," *WP*, September 24, 1950, pp. 1, 8; "Red Bill Veto Beaten, 57–10, by Senators," *NYT*, September 24, 1950, pp. 1, 57; 96 *Cong. Rec.* 15726 (September 23, 1950); Douglas, *In the Fullness of Time*, pp. 307–308; Estes Kefauver Oral History Transcript, HHLP, CUOHC, pp. 6–7; Ybarra, *Washington Gone Crazy*, pp. 509, 529–533. On Langer, see Smith, *Langer of North Dakota*; and Barber, "A Diamond in the Rough."

43. "McGrath Denies Blocking Red Law; Studying Act for Changes, He Says," *NYT*, October 16, 1950, pp. 1, 10; *Albertson v. Subversive Activities Control Board*, 382 U.S. 70 (1965); "Nixon Aide Opposes Camps of Detention," *NYT*, December 4, 1969, p. 37; "Agency Asks End of Detention Unit," *NYT*, March 19, 1971, p. 32; "Detention Camps Opposed by House," *NYT*, September 15, 1971, pp. 1, 19; P.L. 92-128, September 25, 1971, 85 *Stat.* 347; "Some Programs to Be Abolished in Move to Reduce Size of Staff," *NYT*, January 30, 1973, p. 20; "Good Riddance," Editorial, *NYT*, March 29, 1973, p. 46; Goldstein, *American Blacklist*, pp. 267–316; Murphy, *The Constitution in Crisis Times*, pp. 372–375, 448–449; Powe, *The Warren Court and American Politics*, pp. 78–85, 149–156, 310–317; Abraham and Perry, *Civil Rights and Liberties in the United States*, pp. 227–231.

44. Julius Edelstein Oral History Transcript, HHLP, CUOHC, p. 8; Joseph and Stewart Alsop, "Parties Weigh November Chances," *WP*, January 29, 1950, B-5; "Democrats About Ready to Rake in GOP's Chips," *WP*, March 26, 1950, B-3; "Dewey Won't Be Candidate; . . . Governor Is Brief," *NYT*, June 18, 1950, pp. 1, 41; "Truman Renames Dulles as U.N. Delegate," *WP*, August 18, 1950, p. 6. On the 1950 Senate race in New York, see also Bailey and Samuel, *Congress at Work*, pp. 12–30.

45. Lehman to Robert G. A. Jackson, May 15, 1950, LP, SF, Jackson; "State C.I.O. Urges Full Term for Lehman," *NYT*, May 26, 1950, p. 16; "State A.F.L. Set to Back Lehman," *NYT*, August 3, 1950, p. 22; "Democrat to Get Liberal Party Aid," *NYT*, June 8, 1950, p. 26; "Liberals Propose Tie to Democrats," *NYT*, August 22, 1950, p. 22.

46. Julius Edelstein, Memorandum of Telephone Conversation Between Senator Lehman and Paul Fitzpatrick, September 1, 1950, LP, SF, Fitzpatrick; "O'Dwyer Will Retire Aug. 31 to Go to Mexico as Envoy; City Votes on Mayor Nov. 7," *NYT*, August 16, 1950, pp. 1, 27; "Flynn Starts Ticket Parleys, Calls Choices 'Wide Open,'" *NYT*,

August 17, 1950, pp. 1, 20; "New York Democrats Hail a 3-In-1 Election," *NYT*, August 20, 1950, E-10; Moscow, *The Last of the Big-Time Bosses*, p. 87.

47. "Democratic Plans Criticized by C.I.O.," *NYT*, August 25, 1950, p. 14; "Conway, Pecora Favored as Ticket by City Democrats," *NYT*, August 31, 1950, pp. 1, 23; "Conway Endorsed by City Democrats," *NYT*, September 1, 1950, pp. 1, 22; Moscow, *The Last of the Big-Time Bosses*, pp. 89–90.

48. "Conway Endorsed by City Democrats," *NYT*, September 1, 1950, pp. 1, 22; "Conway Declares He's Not Candidate for Governorship," *NYT*, September 2, 1950, pp. 1, 9; "New York: Politics Extraordinary," *NYT*, September 3, 1950, E-2; Moscow, *The Last of the Big-Time Bosses*, p. 90.

49. Edelstein, Memorandum of Telephone Conversation between Senator Lehman and Paul Fitzpatrick, September 1, 1950, LP, SF, Fitzpatrick; "Conway Declares He's Not Candidate for Governorship," *NYT*, September 2, 1950, pp. 1, 9; "New York: Politics Extraordinary," *NYT*, September 3, 1950, E-2.

50. "Republicans Here Stay with Hanley," *NYT*, August 15, 1950, p. 20; "Dewey 'Draft' Said to Imperil G.O.P.," *NYT*, August 27, 1950, p. 60; "Hanley Reluctant on Draft of Dewey," *NYT*, August 28, 1950, p. 18; "Aldrich in Move to 'Draft' Dewey," *NYT*, August 31, 1950, p. 35; "Dewey, Hanley in Joint Appearance but Political Status Is Unchanged," *NYT*, September 1, 1950, pp. 1, 22; "Dewey's Nomination Is Seen; Hanley Frees Him of Pledge and Urges Him to Run Again; Reply Due at Once," *NYT*, September 3, 1950, pp. 1, 30; "New York: Politics Extraordinary," *NYT*, September 3, 1950, E-2; "Dewey Runs; for Hanley as Senator," *NYT*, September 5, 1950, pp. 1, 22; "Both Parties Choose Slates, Headed by Dewey and Lynch; Hanley Will Run for Senate; Moore, McGovern, Goldstein Complete Republican Ticket," *NYT*, September 7, 1950, pp. 1, 21; "Republicans Name Dewey and Hanley, Who Score Truman," *NYT*, September 8, 1950, pp. 1, 21; Arthur Krock, "Dewey Raises New Hope and Questions for G.O.P.," *NYT*, September 10, 1950, E-3; "They're Off!," *NYT*, September 10, 1950, E-2; "6-Seat Senate Gain Sure, G.O.P. Is Told," *NYT*, September 15, 1950, p. 21; Smith, *Thomas E. Dewey and His Times*, pp. 561–565.

51. Edelstein, Memorandum of Telephone Conversation between Senator Lehman and Paul Fitzpatrick, September 1, 1950, LP, SF, Fitzpatrick; "Democratic Race Wide Open; Decision Is Expected Tuesday," *NYT*, September 3, 1950, pp. 1, 31; "State Chiefs Agree to Nominate Lynch for Governor Race," *NYT*, September 6, 1950, pp. 1, 6; "Both Parties Choose Slates, Headed by Dewey and Lynch; . . . Pessimism in Air," *NYT*, September 8, 1950, pp. 1, 23; "Texts of Acceptance Speeches by Lynch and Lehman after Nominations; Address by Lehman," *NYT*, September 8, 1950, p. 18; Moscow, *The Last of the Big-Time Bosses*, p. 90.

52. "Texts of Acceptance Speeches by Lynch and Lehman after Nominations; Address by Lehman," *NYT*, September 8, 1950, p. 18; "Hanley Denounces U.S. 'Appeasement,'" *NYT*, October 6, 1950, p. 20; "Lehman Urges End of Anti-Red Law," *NYT*, October 22, 1950, p. 43; "Congress Liberals Asked of Nation," *NYT*, September 24, 1950, p. 59.

53. "Hiss Appeal Heard, Decision Reserved," *NYT*, October 14, 1950, p. 1; Lehman to Hiss, August 6, 1948, LP, SF, Hiss; "Lehman Note Backing Hiss Bared," *New York World-Telegram and Sun*, October 19, 1950, pp. 1, 2; "Dewey for Governor, Hanley for Senator," Editorial, *New York World-Telegram and Sun*, October 25, 1950, p.

30; Carolin Flexner Oral History Transcript, HHLP, CUOHC, p. 59. On Hiss's initial testimony and most people's favorable reaction to it, see Weinstein, *Perjury*, pp. 10–15.

54. Lasky to Lehman, April 11, 1950, and April 26, 1950; and Helen Lehman Buttenwieser to Herbert Lehman, April 14, 1950, all in LP, SF, Hiss; De Toledano and Lasky, *Seeds of Treason*. Lasky later wrote a very critical biography of John F. Kennedy and a spirited defense of Richard Nixon. See Lasky, *J.F.K.*, and Lasky, *It Didn't Start with Watergate*. On Bullitt, see Dunn, *Caught between Roosevelt and Stalin*; Mayers, *FDR's Ambassadors and the Diplomacy of Crisis*; and Gellman, *Secret Affairs*.

55. Lehman to Lasky, May 2, 1950; *New York World-Telegram and Sun* to Lehman, October 23, 1950; and Memo from Mrs. Lehman, October 27, 1950; all in LP, SF, Hiss; "Lehman Note Backing Hiss Bared," *New York World-Telegram and Sun*, October 19, 1950, pp. 1, 2; "Lehman Defends His Letter to Hiss," *NYT*, October 20, 1950, p. 19. On the *World-Telegram and Sun*'s role in publicizing the spy cases, see De Toledano and Lasky, *Seeds of Treason*, pp. 138–139.

56. "Lehman Defends His Letter to Hiss," *NYT*, October 20, 1950, p. 19; "Lehman Won't Answer 2 Hiss Case Questions," *New York World-Telegram and Sun*, October 20, 1950, p. 1; "Lehman Starting Tour, Won't Discuss Hiss," *New York World-Telegram and Sun*, October 21, 1950, p. 3; "Lehman Sees Party as Prosperity Key," *NYT*, October 22, 1950, p. 22.

57. Memo from Mrs. Lehman, October 27, 1950; Peter Hopkins to Lehman, October 30, 1950; and Lehman to Hopkins, November 4, 1950; all in LP, SF, Hiss; "Lehman Remains Deaf to Questions on Hiss," *New York World-Telegram and Sun*, October 24, 1950, p. 8; "Dewey Denounces City Rent Control," *New York Times*, October 21, 1950, pp. 1, 7; "The Nation: Politics Extraordinary; The Lehman Letter," *New York Times*, October 22, 1950, E-2; HHLOH, p. 767. On Dulles and Hiss, see Pruessen, *John Foster Dulles*, pp. 369–373.

58. "Hanley Letter Says He Runs for Senate on Dewey Pledge of Job and Clearing of Debts; Sent to W. K. Macy," *NYT*, October 17, 1950, pp. 1, 34. On questions that were never completely resolved concerning Hanley's debts, see "Senators to Seek Hanley Debt Data," *NYT*, February 4, 1951, p. 42; and "Hanley Story Found False, Ky. Paper Says," *WP*, May 27, 1951, p. 9. President Truman had complained in 1949 about Gannett's conservative and anti-Democratic views. See President Truman to Clinton Anderson, October 1, 1949, Truman Papers, PPF 2614. On Gannett, see also Williamson, *Imprint of a Publisher*.

59. "Party Strife over Leadership Reflected by Hanley Letter," *NYT*, October 17, 1950, pp. 1, 34; "Hanley Letter Used at Spa to Aid Macy," *New York World-Telegram and Sun*, October 18, 1950, pp. 1, 3; "Hanley Letter Stirs Upstate Hopes of Rivals They Can Cut Dewey Lead," *NYT*, October 18, 1950, p. 39; "The Nation: Politics Extraordinary," *NYT*, October 22, 1950, E-1; "Macy Says Dewey Asked Him to Burn the Hanley Letter," *NYT*, April 10, 1951, pp. 1, 22; Smith, *Thomas E. Dewey and His Times*, p. 567.

60. "Hanley Letter Says He Runs for Senate on Dewey Pledge of Job and Clearing of Debts; Sent to W. K. Macy," *NYT*, October 17, 1950, pp. 1, 34; "Not Paid to Quit, Hanley Declares," *NYT*, October 18, 1950, p. 37; "Text of Hanley's Speech on 'Smears,'" *NYT*, October 18, 1950, p. 37; "'Abject Poverty' Cited by Hanley," *NYT*, October 24, 1950, p. 24; Smith, *Thomas E. Dewey and His Times*, pp. 568–569.

61. "Lynch Urges Penal Inquiry into Letter Hanley Wrote," *NYT*, October 18, 1950, pp. 1, 36; "Lehman Cites Rise in Social Security," *NYT*, October 18, 1950, p. 38; "Lehman Says Foes Imperil Security," *NYT*, October 19, 1950, p. 34; "Elections Linked to Fate of World," *NYT*, October 20, 1954, p. 19; "Lehman Says Foes Play 'Phony' Role," *NYT*, October 21, 1950, p. 8; "Lehman Says Hanley Letter Bared 'Startling Situation,'" *NYT*, October 23, 1950, pp. 1, 15; Lynch Is Expected to Win Rochester," *NYT*, October 30, 1950, p. 34; Lehman to Frank and Helen Altschul, November 20, 1950, LP, SF, Frank Altschul; "Hanley Hails Lehman for Clean Campaign," *NYT*, November 9, 1950, p. 36.

62. Lehman to Elbert Thomas, November 6, 1950, LP, SF, Thomas; "The Nation: About Impellitteri," *NYT*, October 29, 1950, E-2; "Impellitteri Puts Lehman to Fore," *NYT*, October 28, 1950, p. 7; "Impellitteri Held Danger to Lehman," *NYT*, October 12, 1950, p. 37; Robert Bendiner, "Outlook for November: VII: New York: No Holds Barred," *The Nation*, November 4, 1950, pp. 408–410; "Mayoral Nominees Long Civic Figures," *NYT*, September 10, 1950, p. 80; Moscow, *The Last of the Big-Time Bosses*, pp. 89–95.

63. "Impellitteri Elected Mayor by 219,527; Senator Lehman and Gov. Dewey Win; . . . State Votes Split," *NYT*, November 8, 1950, pp. 1, 10; "Picking and Choosing," Editorial, *NYT*, November 9, 1950, p. 32; "Election Tables Showing Voting for Governor, Senator, and Mayor; Local Representatives," *NYT*, November 9, 1950, p. 26; "N.Y.: 3 Men, 3 Parties," *NYT*, November 12, 1950, E-1; "Dewey's Plurality Officially 572,668," *NYT*, December 15, 1950, p. 28; "Hanley to Get $16,000 State Job; Dewey Makes Good His Promise," *NYT*, December 17, 1950, pp. 1, 68; "Hanley's State Job Pays Him $22,000, or $6,000 More Than Previously Stated," *NYT*, March 15, 1951, p. 32; Lehman to Dorothy Bernhard, November 20, 1950, LP, SF, Dorothy Lehman Bernhard. An arithmetical or printing error in the December 15, 1950, article in the *New York Times* reported Lehman's final margin as 246,960 votes, but the actual numbers given in the article show a margin of 264,780.

64. "Impellitteri Elected Mayor by 219,527; Senator Lehman and Gov. Dewey Win; Marcantonio Beaten; Taft Easy Victor; Voting Record Set," *NYT*, November 8, 1950, pp. 1, 3; "Republican Senate Gains Held Threat to Major Fair Deal Domestic Plans; Coalition Is Likely," *NYT*, November 9, 1950, pp. 1, 36; "The Voice of the Voters," Editorial, *NYT*, November 9, 1950, p. 32; "Truman Loses," *NYT*, November 12, 1950, E-1; Harold Ickes, "Fear Rides Herd," *New Republic*, November 20, 1950, p. 17; Marquis Childs, "Tough Going for Truman," *WP*, November 10, 1950, p. 22; Truman, Memorandum for John D. Clark, November 18, 1950, Truman Papers, PPF 89, Voting—elections; "The Elections," *The Nation*, November 18, 1950, pp. 451–452; Lehman to June and Jonathan Bingham, November 22, 1950, LP, SF, Bingham; Reeves, *The Life and Times of Joe McCarthy*, pp. 343–346; Griffith, *The Politics of Fear*, pp. 122–131; Fried, "Electoral Politics and McCarthyism," pp. 192–222.

65. Lehman to John Haynes Holmes, March 16, 1954, LP, SF, Holmes; Caute, *The Great Fear*, pp. 39–40; Julius Edelstein to Morris Novik, June 18, 1954, LP, SF, Edelstein; Edith Lehman to Helen and Frank Altschul, August 10, 1954, and Herbert Lehman to Frank Altschul, September 6, 1957, both in LP, SF, Frank Altschul. The August 10, 1954, letter from Edith Lehman to the Altschuls was inadvertently missed when the Lehman Papers Special Files were digitalized and thus it is not available online.

66. "Senators on Side of Mrs. Rosenberg," *NYT*, December 10, 1950, p. 58; Anna Rosenberg Oral History Transcript, HHLP, CUOHC, pp. 8–9; Anna Rosenberg to Lehman, December 5, 1950, and attached Marjorie Shearon, "Challenge to Socialism," IV (November 16, 1950): 36, LP, SF, Rosenberg; Alfred Friendly, "Anna M. Rosenberg: Motives of Some Investigators Unclear," *WP*, January 18, 1951, p. 11; U.S., Cong., Senate, Committee on Armed Services, *Nomination of Anna M. Rosenberg to Be Assistant Secretary of Defense; Hearings* before the Committee on Armed Services, 81st Cong., 2d sess., November–December, 1950, pp. 31, 93, 113–114, 123, 138, 203; Forster and Epstein, *The Trouble-Makers*, pp. 25–61. On Smith, see Jeansonne, *Gerald L. K. Smith*.

67. Benton to Frank Altschul, February 13, 1964, Altschul Papers, Catalogued Correspondence, 128d, Herbert Lehman, Columbia University Libraries; 97 *Cong. Rec.* 865–868 (February 1, 1951); "M'Carthy Is Named to Key Funds Unit," *NYT*, January 31, 1951, p. 15; "Benton Denounces M'Carthy on Floor," *NYT*, February 2, 1951, p. 12; Benton to Lehman, February 17, 1951, LP, SF, Benton; Anna Rosenberg Oral History Transcript, HHLP, CUOHC, p. 8; "M'Carthy's Influence Is Greater in the 82D," *NYT*, January 7, 1951, E-7. McCarthy was bumped from the Appropriations Committee in June 1951 when the death of Senator Vandenberg and his replacement by a Democrat allowed the Democrats to claim an additional seat on the committee. See "Committee Seats Switched by G.O.P.," *NYT*, June 23, 1951, p. 6.

68. 97 *Cong. Rec.* 1218–1220 (February 12, 1951); Drew Pearson to Ivan Nye, March 8, 1953, Pearson Papers, G222, 3 of 3, Personal Papers of Drew Pearson, 34, McCarthy, Joseph (cont.), General, [1] folder 2 of 2, LBJL.

69. "Truman Relieves M'Arthur of All His Posts; Finds Him Unable to Back U.S.-U.N. Policies; . . . President Moves," *NYT*, April 11, 1951, pp. 1, 3; 97 *Cong. Rec.* 3643–3646 (April 11, 1951); "Truman Says He Fired M'Arthur to Avoid Risk of New World War; . . . G.O.P. Hits Ouster," *NYT*, April 12, 1951, pp. 1, 3; "Goal Is to Confine War to Korea, Truman Says; GOP in Congress Assails Ousting of MacArthur, Some Members Discuss Impeaching of President," *WP*, April 12, 1951, pp. 1, 2; Oshinsky, *A Conspiracy So Immense*, pp. 194–195; Spanier, *The Truman-MacArthur Controversy and the Korean War*.

70. "Sens. Capehart, Humphrey, Lehman Scuffle," *WP*, April 21, 1951, p. 1; "Brawling Senators Trade Sound, Fury," *NYT*, April 21, 1951, pp. 1, 8; "Recording Attests Fury of Senators," *NYT*, April 23, 1951, p. 17; "When Reason Departs," Editorial, *WP*, April 22, 1951, B-4.

71. "Brawling Senators Trade Sound, Fury," *NYT*, April 21, 1951, pp. 1, 8; "Sens. Capehart, Humphrey, Lehman Scuffle," *WP*, April 21, 1951, p. 1; "When Reason Departs," Editorial, *WP*, April 22, 1951, B-4; "Recording Attests Fury of Senators," *NYT*, April 23, 1951, p. 17. Hubert Humphrey later minimized his role in the initial pushing and shoving, claiming that his involvement was mostly coming to Lehman's aid. See Hubert Humphrey Oral History Transcript, HHLP, CUOHC, p. 11.

72. 97 *Cong. Rec.* 4229–4233, 4238 (April 24, 1951); "MacArthur Will Testify May 3 Before Senate Quiz," *WP*, April 25, 1951, pp. 1, 4; "M'Arthur Hearing to Be Opened May 3 by Senate Group," *NYT*, April 25, 1951, pp. 1, 6; "The Issues Joined," *NYT*, April 29, 1951, E-1; Lehman to Walter Brown, April 27, 1951, LP, SF, Brown.

73. "Anti-Tydings Drive Held 'Despicable,'" *NYT*, August 4, 1951, pp. 1, 16; 97 *Cong. Rec.* 9498–9500 (August 6, 1951); "Benton Demands M'Carthy Resign," *NYT*,

August 7, 1951, p. 6; Hyman, *The Lives of William Benton*, pp. 452–458; Griffith, *The Politics of Fear*, pp. 152–159; 97 *Cong. Rec.* 9703–9711 (August 9, 1951); "M'Carthy Lists 26 in Loyalty Charge," *NYT*, August 10, 1951, p. 7; "Senator McCarthy Again," *NYT*, August 12, 1951, E-2.

74. 97 *Cong. Rec.* 9711–9712 (August 9, 1951); "M'Carthy Lists 26 in Loyalty Charge," *NYT*, August 10, 1951, p. 7; "M'Carthy at It Again," Editorial, *NYT*, August 11, 1951, p. 8.

75. 97 *Cong. Rec.* 11344–11345 (September 14, 1951); William Shannon, "The Strange Case of Louis Budenz," *New Republic*, October 22, 1951, pp. 9–10; Ybarra, *Washington Gone Crazy*, pp. 569–605.

76. 97 *Cong. Rec.* 11362–11365 (September 14, 1951); "Probe into Alsop Charges Is Blocked by Senators," *WP*, September 15, 1951, p. 1; "Democrats Blaze at Acheson Critics," *NYT*, September 15, 1951, p. 5.

77. 97 *Cong. Rec.* 11936–11940 (September 24, 1951); "Anti-Budenz Charges Laid Before Senate," *WP*, September 25, 1951, p. 8; McGeorge Bundy to Lehman, September 24, 1951, LP, SF, Bundy.

78. "Morals and McCarthy," Editorial, *WP*, January 22, 1952, p. 8; 98 *Cong. Rec.* 2443–2446 (March 18, 1952); "Benton Waives His Immunity; McCarthy Says He Will Sue," *NYT*, March 19, 1952, pp. 1, 16; "M'Carthy Files Suit for Benton 'Libel,'" *NYT*, March 27, 1952, pp. 1, 21; "McCarthy and the Courts," *New Republic*, April 7, 1952, pp. 7–8; "McCarthy Drops Libel Suit Asking 2 Million of Benton," *NYT*, March 6, 1954, pp. 1, 8; Hyman, *The Lives of William Benton*, pp. 467–468, 484–485.

79. S. 2550, 82d Cong., 2d sess., 1952; Wayne Morse Oral History Transcript, HHLP, CUOHC, pp. 4–5; "The New Immigration Bill," Editorial, *NYT*, May 1, 1952, p. 28; "New Immigration Bill Is under Sharp Attack," *NYT*, May 4, 1952, E-10; HHLOH, pp. 203–204; Roger Jones, Memorandum for Mr. David Lloyd, "The McCarran and Walter Omnibus Immigration and Naturalization Bills," February 18, 1952, Richard Neustadt Files, Box 1, Immigration and Nationality Act, 1952, 3 of 4, HSTL; Fowler Harper, "McCarran's Iron Curtain: II: Immigrants: Still Fewer Wanted," *New Republic*, March 3, 1952, pp. 13–15; Ybarra, *Washington Gone Crazy*, pp. 632–636.

80. 98 *Cong. Rec.* 5102, 5109 (May 13, 1952); "Immigration Laws," Editorial, *WP*, March 12, 1952, p. 12; "Immigration and Freedom," Extension of Remarks of Herbert Lehman, April 8, 1952, 98 *Cong. Rec.* A2209–2211.

81. S. 2842, 82d Cong., 2d sess., 1952; 98 *Cong. Rec.* 5103 (May 13, 1952); Lehman to Ernest McFarland, December 20, 1951, and Humphrey, Lehman, et al. to McFarland, April 28, 1952, both in LP, SF, McFarland.

82. 98 *Cong. Rec.* 5088–5100, 5103–5104 (May 13, 1952); "Aliens Bill Stirs Filibuster Charge," *NYT*, May 14, 1952, p. 11; "4 Senators Attack Immigration Bill," *WP*, May 11, 1952, M-9; "Lehman Blasts McCarran on Alien Stand," *WP*, May 14, 1952, p. 10; Julius Edelstein Oral History Transcript, HHLP, CUOHC, pp. 17–19; "cloak and suiters" quoted in Ybarra, *Washington Gone Crazy*, p. 638.

83. "Alien Bill Stirs Filibuster Charge," *NYT*, May 14, 1952, p. 11; "Alien Bill Foes Map Fight for Recommittal," *WP*, May 10, 1952, B-5; "Alien Bill Fight Snarls the Senate," *NYT*, May 15, 1952, p. 17; "Veto Predicted if McCarran Bill Is Passed," *WP*, May 15, 1952, p. 2; "Move for Test Fails on Senate Alien Bill," *NYT*, May 16, 1952, p. 6; "Senate Bars Move to Kill Alien Bill," *NYT*, May 20, 1952, p. 7; "Senate

Rejects Liberal Substitute for McCarran's Immigration Bill," *NYT*, May 22, 1952, pp. 1, 4; "Senate's Vote Barring More Liberal Alien Bill," *NYT*, May 22, 1953, p. 4; "Alien Bill Passed Intact by Senate; Foes Rely on Veto," *NYT*, May 23, 1952, pp. 1, 15; "On Immigration," *NYT*, May 25, 1952, E-2; Ybarra, *Washington Gone Crazy*, pp. 636–639.

84. Lehman to Eleanor Roosevelt, May 23, 1952, LP, SF, Eleanor Roosevelt; Lehman to Robert G. A. Jackson, June 16, 1952, LP, SF, Jackson; "The President's Day," June 5, 1952, and June 9, 1952, Truman Papers, Daily Presidential Appointments; "Conferees Submit Revised Alien Bill," *NYT*, June 10, 1952, p. 11; "Text of Truman's Message to House on Veto of Immigration Bill," *NYT*, June 26, 1952, p. 14; Lehman et al. to Truman, June 25, 1952, LP, SF, Truman; "President Vetoes Immigration Bill as Discriminatory," *NYT*, June 26, 1952, pp. 1, 14.

85. "Congress Enacts Immigration Bill over Truman Veto," *NYT*, June 28, 1952, pp. 1, 10; "Senate Roll-Call Vote to Kill Veto of Alien Bill," *NYT*, June 28, 1952, p. 10; Lehman to John Slawson, June 28, 1952, LP, SF, Slawson; "Humphrey Rips Own Party over Alien Bill," *WP*, June 29, 1952, M-13; Marquis Childs, "Politics and Immigration," *WP*, June 17, 1952, p. 14; Ben H. Brown, Memorandum of Conversation, "Immigration & Naturalization Bill," July 18, 1952, Dean Acheson Papers, Box 70, Secretary of State File, Memoranda of Conversations File, July 1952, HSTL; Hyman, *The Lives of William Benton*, pp. 472–473; Memorandum, Edelstein to Neustadt, June 28, 1952, Neustadt Files, Box 1, Immigration and Nationality Act, 1952, 1 of 4, HSTL; Herbert Lehman, "Travail of Liberalism—," Second Gino Speranza Lecture, April 16, 1958, Columbia University, LP, Speech File; Herbert Lehman, " 'National Origin'—Fraud and Threat," *New Republic*, February 16, 1953, pp. 8–9; Senator John F. Kennedy Press Release, August 2, 1953, Kennedy Pre-Presidential Papers, Box 647, Senate, Legislative Files, 1953–1960, 1953–1955, Immigration, February 26, 1953–May 27, 1955, John F. Kennedy Library (hereinafter JFKL); "Citizens to Press for New Alien Act," *NYT*, January 12, 1954, p. 13; Lehman to Emanuel Celler, March 29, 1954, LP, SF, Celler; Lehman to Hubert Humphrey et al., January 21, 1955, LP, SF, Humphrey; Lehman to Lyndon Johnson, December 2, 1954, and Johnson to Lehman, August 4, 1956, both in LP, SF, Johnson; Lehman to Edward Weinfeld, September 2, 1957, LP, SF, Weinfeld; Lehman to Philip Hart, August 7, 1963, LP, SF, Hart; "Unforgotten Man," Editorial, *New York Post*, October 1, 1965, p. 48; "Notes on Interview with Representative Emanuel Celler, July 1957, HHLP, CUOHC, pp. 1–2; Hubert Humphrey Oral History Transcript, HHLP, CUOHC, pp. 5–6; Julius Edelstein Oral History Transcript, HHLP, CUOHC, p. 14.

Chapter 14. "A Poison Has Begun Spreading Throughout Our Land": Lehman and McCarthyism, 1953–1954

1. Wayne Morse Oral History Transcript, HHLP, CUOHC, p. 26.

2. William S. White, "M'Carthy Senate Power Now Deeply Entrenched," *NYT*, January 18, 1953, E-4; Lehman to Ernest McFarland, November 24, 1952, LP, SF, McFarland; Benton to Lehman, November 29, 1952, LP, SF, Benton; William Benton, "The Big Dilemma: Conscience or Votes," *New York Times Magazine*, April 26, 1959, p. 12; Cabell Phillips, " 'The M'Carthy Problem' in Washington Remains," *NYT*, March

8, 1953, E-10; Hyman, *The Lives of William Benton*, pp. 478–481; Fried, *Men against McCarthy*, pp. 241–242, 246–253; Griffith, *The Politics of Fear*, pp. 194–195.

3. Fried, *Men against McCarthy*, pp. 260–261; Baker, *Wheeling and Dealing*, p. 94; Robert Baker Oral History Transcript, I: 12, LBJL; "Election Issues of '54 Shaping Up in Congress," *NYT*, May 3, 1953, E-3; John Oakes, "Inquiry into McCarthy's Status," *New York Times Magazine*, April 12, 1953, pp. 9, 26–30; Allen Klein, "McCarthy," Letter to the Editor, *New York Times Magazine*, April 19, 1953, p. 6; "Where Responsibility Lies," Editorial, *NYT*, July 15, 1953, p. 24; George Milburn, "Monroney of Oklahoma: Bad Medicine for McCarthy," *The Nation*, August 8, 1953, p. 110.

4. 99 *Cong. Rec.* 2291–2299 (March 25, 1953); Theoharis, *The Yalta Myths*, pp. 165–175; "Bitterness Marks Debate on Bohlen; Taft Defers Vote," *NYT*, March 26, 1953, pp. 1, 6. On Eisenhower's reluctance to tackle McCarthy head-on, see Hughes, *The Ordeal of Power*, p. 92; Oshinsky, *A Conspiracy So Immense*, pp. 258–260.

5. 99 *Cong. Rec.* 2299–2300 (March 25, 1953); "Bitterness Marks Debate on Bohlen; Taft Defers Vote," *NYT*, March 26, 1953, pp. 1, 6.

6. "Address Delivered by Hon. Herbert H. Lehman, of New York, at the New York State Democratic Committee Dinner," Extension of Remarks of Hon. Herbert H. Lehman, July 17, 1953, 99 *Cong. Rec.* A4454–4455; "M'Carthyism Held a Peril by Lehman," *NYT*, April 30, 1953, pp. 1, 36; "Election Issues of '54 Shaping Up in Congress," *NYT*, May 3, 1953, E-3. On the spread of McCarthyism to various aspects of American life, see Caute, *The Great Fear*; Schrecker, *No Ivory Tower*; and Schrecker, *Many Are the Crimes*.

7. 99 *Cong. Rec.* 6386 (June 11, 1953); "M'Carthy, Lehman in Senate Battle," *NYT*, June 12, 1953, pp. 1, 11.

8. 99 *Cong. Rec.* 6387–6388 (June 11, 1953); "M'Carthy, Lehman in Senate Battle," *NYT*, June 12, 1953, pp. 1, 11.

9. 99 *Cong. Rec.* 6389–6391 (June 11, 1953); "M'Carthy, Lehman in Senate Battle," *NYT*, June 12, 1953, pp. 1, 11.

10. "Statement by Senator Herbert H. Lehman in Regard to Senator McCarthy's Floor Criticism," 99 *Cong. Rec.* 6459–6460 (June 15, 1953); "Charges Fly in McCarthy, Lehman Tiff," *WP*, June 12, 1953, p. 5; "Post Office Scans M'Carthy Mailing," *NYT*, June 13, 1953, p. 9. The Post Office eventually sustained Lehman's accusations about McCarthy's improper use of the franking privilege, requiring McCarthy to pay "more than $200" to cover the cost incurred in 1952 in mailing an article recommending his book. See "Cost of Franking Put at $1,700,000," *NYT*, November 29, 1954, p. 14.

11. McCarthy to Lehman, June 30, 1953, in 99 *Cong. Rec.* 8057 (July 7, 1953); "Lehman Reissues Views on M'Carthy," *NYT*, July 7, 1953, p. 12.

12. Lehman to McCarthy, July 6, 1953, in 99 *Cong. Rec.* 8057 (July 7, 1953); "Lehman Reissues Views on M'Carthy," *NYT*, July 7, 1953, p. 12.

13. Langdon Marvin, Jr., to Lehman, June 16, 1953, and Lehman to Marvin, June 19, 1953, both in LP, SF, McCarthy; Lehman to Harriman, June 23, 1953, LP, SF, Harriman; Schlesinger to Lehman, June 16, 1953, LP, SF, Schlesinger; Slawson to Lehman, June 15, 1953, LP, SF, Slawson; Lasky to Lehman, May 28, 1953, LP, SF, Lasky; Theodore Coogan, "McCarthy Stand Upheld," Letter to the Editor, *NYT*, July 27, 1953, p. 18; " 'Liberals' and Communists," Excerpt, *Human Rights*, June 3, 1953, LP, SF, Herbert H. Lehman, document 0530_0184.

14. "The Straitjacket of Fear," Extension of Remarks of Hon. Herbert H. Lehman, June 22, 1953, 99 *Cong. Rec.* A3678–3680; "Lehman Outlines M'Carthy 'Threat,'" *NYT*, June 21, 1953, p. 17.

15. "Address Delivered by Hon. Herbert H. Lehman, of New York, at the New York State Democratic Committee Dinner," Extension of Remarks of Hon. Herbert H. Lehman, July 17, 1953, 99 *Cong. Rec.* A4454; "Monroney Urges Senate to Curb McCarthy in Extension of His Investigating Activities," *WP*, July 14, 1953, p. 11; "Position of M'Carthy in Politics Is Shifting," *NYT*, July 26, 1953, E-8; "The Nation: Senator McCarthy," *NYT*, July 26, 1953, E-2; 99 *Cong. Rec.* 9179 (July 20, 1953); "Velde Group Votes to Hear Matthews," *NYT*, July 21, 1953, pp. 1, 3; George Milburn, "Monroney of Oklahoma: Bad Medicine for McCarthy," *The Nation*, August 8, 1953, pp. 110–112. On Cohn's and Schine's trip to Europe, see Zion, *The Autobiography of Roy Cohn*, pp. 90–96.

16. 99 *Cong. Rec.* 9346–9347, 9352 (July 21, 1953); "Sen. McCarthy Sparks Fiery 'Hill' Debate," *WP*, July 22, 1953, pp. 1, 2; "M'Carthy, Lehman Clash in Senate," *NYT*, July 22, 1953, p. 6; Milburn, "Monroney of Oklahoma: Bad Medicine for McCarthy," *The Nation*, August 8, 1953, pp. 110–112.

17. 99 *Cong. Rec.* 9353 (July 21, 1953); "M'Carthy, Lehman Clash in Senate," *NYT*, July 22, 1953, p. 6. David Oshinsky and Richard Reeves both dismiss the allegation that there was any organized Communist support for McCarthy in the 1946 election. See Oshinsky, *A Conspiracy So Immense*, pp. 47–48; and Reeves, *The Life and Times of Joe McCarthy*, pp. 93–94, 690 (n. 66). Lehman was elected Director General of UNRRA by representatives of forty-four nations, not fifty. See chapter 8.

18. 99 *Cong. Rec.* 9353–9354 (July 21, 1953); "M'Carthy, Lehman Clash in Senate," *NYT*, July 22, 1953, p. 6.

19. Proskauer to Lehman, June 20, 1953, LP, SF, Proskauer; Petegorsky to Lehman, July 23, 1953, LP, SF, Petegorsky; Albert Cohn to Lehman, July 21, 1953, LP, SF, Albert Cohn; Lasky to Lehman, July 23, 1953, LP, SF, Lasky. On Albert Cohn's appointment to the Appellate Division, see Zion, *The Autobiography of Roy Cohn*, pp. 19–21.

20. 100 *Cong. Rec.* 1538–1539 (February 9, 1954); "White House Says G.O.P. Told 'Facts,' Denies Any 'Smear,'" *NYT*, February 10, 1954, pp. 1, 14; "M'Carthy Concessions Laid to Combination of Factors," *NYT*, January 31, 1954, E-5; Fried, *Men against McCarthy*, p. 276. On Lehman's apology to Fulbright, see Woods, *Fulbright*, pp. 183–184.

21. 100 *Cong. Rec.* 2205–2207 (February 24, 1954); "One-Man Inquiries Scored in Senate," *NYT*, February 25, 1954, pp. 1, 9; Jenner quoted in "Fulbright Aids Drive to Censure McCarthy with 6-Count Charge; Fee from Lustron, Attack on Marshall Included; Decision Put Over to Monday," *WP*, August 1, 1954, M-1, 7; Drukman, *Wayne Morse*, pp. 205–206; "Rules That Would Help," Editorial, *WP*, February 27, 1954, p. 10; Senators Kefauver, Morse, Lehman, and Douglas to Senator Russell Long, April 27, 1954, LP, SF, Long; "Democrats Draft Code on Inquiries," *NYT*, May 27, 1954, p. 13; Hubert Humphrey Oral History Transcript, HHLP, CUOHC, pp. 9–10. On McCarthy's grilling of General Zwicker, see Oshinsky, *A Conspiracy So Immense*, pp. 374–377. The *Washington Post* bought the *Washington Times-Herald* on March 17, 1954, and the combined newspaper was called the *Washington Post and Times-Herald* from then until 1973. For consistency, it will continue to be cited herein as *WP*.

22. Lehman to Benton, February 21, 1954, and March 12, 1954, LP, SF, Benton; 100 *Cong. Rec.* 2886 (March 9, 1954); "M'Carthy Strives 'To Shatter' G.O.P., Flanders Asserts," *NYT*, March 10, 1954, pp. 1, 14; "Transcript of Presidential Press Conference, with Comment on the McCarthy Dispute," *NYT*, March 11, 1954, p. 14; Griffith, *The Politics of Fear*, pp. 270–273; Oshinsky, *A Conspiracy So Immense*, pp. 395–397. On Major Irving Peress, the "pink army dentist" discovered by McCarthy, see Oshinsky, *A Conspiracy So Immense*, pp. 365–371.

23. 100 *Cong. Rec.* 4320 (April 1, 1954); Lehman to Alfred Knopf, April 26, 1954, LP, SF, Knopf; Griffith, *The Politics of Fear*, pp. 243–251.

24. 100 *Cong. Rec.* 6260–6262 (May 10, 1954), 6823–6826 (May 19, 1954), 7371 (June 1, 1954); "Monroney Rebuts M'Carthy's View," *NYT*, June 1, 1954, pp. 1, 17; "Lehman Denounces M'Carthy's 'Damage,'" *NYT*, June 13, 1954, p. 39; Lehman to John McClellan, July 5, 1954, LP, SF, McClellan; Lehman to Stuart Symington, July 5, 1954, LP, SF, Symington; Lehman to Henry Jackson, July 5, 1954, LP, SF, Jackson. McCarthy's aides had introduced a photograph during the hearings that seemed to show Secretary of the Army Robert Stevens meeting alone with G. David Schine. In fact, a third person had been cropped out of the photo. McCarthy also introduced a letter purportedly from FBI director J. Edgar Hoover to Army Intelligence, written on January 26, 1951. Hoover denied ever writing such a letter, although he did acknowledge sending a fifteen-page report to Army Intelligence on that date. It was never established how McCarthy got hold of the letter or the longer memorandum on which it was based. On the Army-McCarthy hearings, see Griffith, *The Politics of Fear*, pp. 243–269; Oshinsky, *A Conspiracy So Immense*, pp. 416–471.

25. 100 *Cong. Rec.* 8032–8033 (June 11, 1954); "Flanders Moves in Senate to Strip McCarthy of Posts," *NYT*, June 12, 1954, pp. 1, 8; "Flanders' Motion to Curb M'Carthy Hit by Knowland," *NYT*, June 13, 1954, pp. 1, 36; "Flanders Dispute Disturbs Senate as Both Parties Move Cautiously," *NYT*, June 15, 1954, p. 24; "Flanders Defers M'Carthy Dispute," *NYT*, June 16, 1954, pp. 1, 10. The best account of the Senate's censure of McCarthy remains Griffith, *The Politics of Fear*, pp. 270–317.

26. 100 *Cong. Rec.* 8444–8445 (June 17, 1954); "Lehman Demands Curb on M'Carthy," *NYT*, June 18, 1954, p. 8; "Rules Unit Gets Lehman Move to End McCarthy's Chairmanships," *WP*, June 18, 1954, p. 34; Lehman to Francis Sayre, June 25, 1954, LP, SF, Sayre. On Johnson's strategy on McCarthy, see Caro, *The Years of Lyndon Johnson: Master of the Senate*, pp. 542–556; and Dallek, *Lone Star Rising*, pp. 442, 452–459.

27. "Senate Vote Set on M'Carthy Role," *NYT*, July 14, 1954, pp. 1, 12; "M'Carthy Picks Up Committee Reins, Delays Clean-Up," *NYT*, July 16, 1954, pp. 1, 6; 100 *Cong. Rec.* 10992–11000 (July 20, 1954); "Censure Vote on McCarthy Slated July 30," *WP*, July 21, 1954, p. 6. On Edelstein's involvement with organized anti-McCarthy groups assisting Flanders, see Griffith, *The Politics of Fear*, p. 282.

28. 100 *Cong. Rec.* 12374–12376 (July 28, 1954).

29. Minutes of Meeting—Democratic Policy Committee, July 29, 1954, Lyndon Baines Johnson Senate Papers, Box 364, Papers of the Democratic Leader, Senate Democratic Policy Committee, Minutes of 83d Congress, February 3, 1953–November 9, 1954, LBJL; "Move to Censure McCarthy Up for Senate Debate Today," *NYT*, July 30, 1954, pp. 1, 18. On Johnson, see also the untitled and undated transcript of his

phone conversation with Senator McClellan, which preceded the Policy Committee meeting, in Lyndon Baines Johnson Archives, Box 117, Subject File—Senate, U.S., Integrity of, McCarthy Censure, LBJL.

30. 100 *Cong. Rec.* 12903 (July 31, 1954); "Fulbright Offers Specific Charges against McCarthy," *NYT*, August 1, 1954, pp. 1, 48.

31. Untitled and undated transcript of phone conversation between Senator Johnson and Senator McClellan, LBJ Archives, Box 117, Subject File—Senate, U.S., Integrity of, McCarthy Censure; Minutes of Meeting—Democratic Policy Committee, August 2, 1954, LBJ Senate Papers, Box 364, Papers of the Democratic Leader, Senate Democratic Policy Committee, Minutes of 83d Congress, February 3, 1953–November 9, 1954.

32. "New McCarthy Probe Voted by Senate, 75–12; 6-Man Committee Set Up to Weigh Censure Charges against Senator," *WP*, August 3, 1954, pp. 1, 5; 100 *Cong. Rec.* 12953, 12975–12976 (August 2, 1954); Lehman to Arthur Goodhart, August 5, 1954, LP, SF, Goodhart. The twelve senators who voted against the creation of the special committee were Republicans Ralph Flanders (VT), John Sherman Cooper (KY), and James Duff (PA); and Democrats Herbert Lehman, Dennis Chavez (NM), Paul Douglas (IL), J. William Fulbright (AR), Thomas Hennings (MO), Lister Hill (AL), Hubert Humphrey (MN), Warren Magnuson (WA), and Mike Monroney (OK).

33. 100 *Cong. Rec.* 14102–14105 (August 11, 1954), 14195 (August 12, 1954); " 'Filibuster' Bogs Bill to Curb Reds," *WP*, August 12, 1954, pp. 1, 13; Julius Edelstein to Arthur Schlesinger, Jr., August 23, 1954, LP, SF, Edelstein; Herbert Lehman, "Travail of Liberalism, 1945—," Second Speranza Lecture, April 16, 1958, Columbia University, LP, Speech File.

34. 100 *Cong. Rec.* 14104 (August 11, 1954), 14210 (August 12, 1954); "Senators Outlaw Reds; Bill Curbs Party and Halts Union Infiltration," *WP*, August 13, 1954, pp. 1, 2; "Eisenhower Aides Try to Block Bill Outlawing Reds," *NYT*, August 14, 1954, pp. 1, 5; Julius Edelstein to Arthur Schlesinger, Jr., August 23, 1954, LP, SF, Edelstein; Hubert Humphrey Oral History Transcript, HHLP, CUOHC, pp. 7–9; Solberg, *Hubert Humphrey*, pp. 156–159; McAuliffe, *Crisis on the Left*, pp. 132–139; Griffith, *The Politics of Fear*, pp. 291–294.

35. 100 *Cong. Rec.* 14210, 14227–14229 (August 12, 1954); "Senators Outlaw Reds; Bill Curbs Party and Halts Union Infiltration," *WP*, August 13, 1954, pp. 1, 2; "Senate, by 85 to 0, Votes to Outlaw Communist Party," *NYT*, August 13, 1954, pp. 1, 8; "Eisenhower Aides Try to Block Bill Outlawing Reds," *NYT*, August 14, 1954, pp. 1, 5; Julius Edelstein to Arthur Schlesinger, Jr., August 23, 1954, LP, SF, Edelstein; McAuliffe, *Crisis on the Left*, p. 134.

36. 100 *Cong. Rec.* 14611 (August 16, 1954), 14710–14711, 14727–14728 (August 17, 1954), 15121 (August 19, 1954); Edelstein to Schlesinger, August 23, 1954, LP, SF, Edelstein; "Congress Passes Softened Version of Communist Ban," *NYT*, August 20, 1954, pp. 1, 6; Lehman, "Travail of Liberalism, 1945—," Second Speranza Lecture, April 16, 1958, Columbia University, LP, Speech File; Hubert Humphrey Oral History Transcript, HHLP, CUOHC, p. 7; McAuliffe, *Crisis on the Left*, pp. 141, 183 (n. 54).

37. Edelstein to Schlesinger, August 23, 1954, LP, SF, Edelstein; "Corliss Lamont Defies McCarthy; Senator to Ask Contempt Citation," *NYT*, September 24, 1953, pp. 1, 10; "Witness, on Einstein's Advice, Refuses to Say if He Was Red," *NYT*, December 17, 1953, pp. 1, 25; "M'Carthy Tests Einstein Advice," *NYT*, January 8, 1954, p. 7;

Army Denies Leak to M'Carthy Came from Any Officer," *NYT*, August 12, 1954, pp. 1, 10; "Senate for Citing 3 M'Carthy Foes," *NYT*, August 17, 1954, p. 8; 100 *Cong. Rec.* 14093–14094 (August 11, 1954); 14555–14559, 14586–14589, 14593–14597 (August 16, 1954); "Corliss Lamont Wins Dismissal," *NYT*, July 28, 1955, pp. 1, 17; "Lamont Is Upheld in Appeals Court," *NYT*, August 15, 1956, p. 8; "Lamont Case Dropped," *NYT*, October 16, 1956, p. 67; *U.S. v. Corliss Lamont*, 236 F. 2d 312 (1956); Lehman to Senator Langer, September 28, 1956, LP, SF, Langer. The other Senators who voted against charging Lamont with contempt were William Langer and Dennis Chavez. For more on the Lamont case, see Wittenberg, ed., *The Lamont Case*; and Lamont, *A Lifetime of Dissent*, pp. 93–105. For a critical view of Lamont's left-wing activities, see Shapiro, "Corliss Lamont and Civil Liberties." Coincidentally, Edward Weinfeld, the District Court Judge who dismissed the contempt charge against Lamont and the others, had been appointed to the bench by President Truman in 1950 at Lehman's recommendation. Weinfeld privately commended Lehman in 1953 and 1954 for "waging a magnificent fight" against the "evil" of McCarthyism, which he condemned as "the most divisive influence in American life in our times." See Lehman to President Truman, April 1, 1950; Weinfeld to Lehman, May 27, 1953; and Weinfeld to Lehman, December 11, 1954, all in LP, SF, Weinfeld; Nelson, *In Pursuit of Right and Justice*, pp. 102–106, 114–119, 122–123, 160–161. Lest one think that Weinfeld's friendship with Lehman or his personal opposition to McCarthyism influenced his ruling in the Lamont case, it should be noted that his decisions was upheld unanimously by the U.S. Court of Appeals. See *U.S. v. Corliss Lamont*, 236 F. 2d 312 (1956).

38. 100 *Cong. Rec.* 12983 (August 2, 1954); "Senate Votes 6-Man Panel to Study M'Carthy Censure and Report to This Session," *NYT*, August 3, 1954, pp. 1, 11.

39. Lehman to Arthur Goodhart, August 29, 1954, LP, SF, Goodhart; Edelstein to Lehman, August 27, 1954, and September 3, 1954, both in LP, SF, Edelstein.

40. Edith Lehman to Helen and Frank Altschul, August 10, 1954, LP, SF, Altschul (this document is missing from the digitalized Lehman papers); "Censure of McCarthy Recommended in Special Senate Committee Report; Six Members Unanimous in Decision on Charges," *WP*, September 28, 1954, pp. 1, 5; "Text of Report of Senate Committee That Studied Censure Motion against McCarthy," *NYT*, September 28, 1954, pp. 20–25; "Senate Action on McCarthy Put Off until After Election," *NYT*, September 25, 1954, pp. 1, 16; "Senators Disagree on McCarthy Report," *WP*, September 28, 1954, pp. 1, 5; Lehman to Robert G. A. Jackson, September 30, 1954, LP, SF, Jackson; Griffith, *The Politics of Fear*, p. 295; Caro, *Master of the Senate*, p. 554.

41. Edelstein to John Howe, November 17, 1954, LP, SF, William Benton; Edelstein to Arthur Schlesinger, Jr., November 11, 1954, quoted in Griffith, *The Politics of Fear*, p. 309. There are two letters from Edelstein to Howe dated November 17, 1954. Document 0057_0110 responds to Howe's letter of November 11, and document 0057_0111 responds to Howe's letter of November 12.

42. Lehman to Robert G. A. Jackson, November 15, 1954, LP, SF, Jackson; "M'Carthy Predicts Senate Censure," *NYT*, October 30, 1954, pp. 1, 7; "Text of McCarthy's Speech for Delivery Today in Censure Debate," *NYT*, November 10, 1954, p. 18; "Watkins and Case Assail M'Carthy on 'Red' Innuendo," *NYT*, November 11, 1954, pp. 1, 17; "M'Carthy Ignores Plea for Apology to Avoid Censure," *NYT*, Novem-

ber 12, 1954, pp. 1, 11; "Watkins Demands Senate Enlarge M'Carthy Censure," *NYT*, November 17, 1954, pp. 1, 16. Senator Wallace Bennett was added to the list of McCarthy opponents when he defended Senator Watkins, his fellow Utah Republican, by proposing an amendment to the censure resolution condemning McCarthy's treatment of the Watkins Committee. See "Senate Restricts M'Carthy Debate; Votes Tomorrow; Each Side Limited," *NYT*, November 30, 1954, pp. 1, 21.

43. "Dirksen Will Bid Senators Soften M'Carthy Action," *NYT*, November 18, 1954, pp. 1, 18; 100 *Cong. Rec.* 16133–16135 (November 18, 1954), 16196–16198 (November 30, 1954); "M'Carthy's Injury Brings 10-Day Stop in Censure Debate," *NYT*, November 19, 1954, pp. 1, 13; "McCarthy Better; Recess Irks Critics," *WP*, November 20, 1954, p. 2. On Fulbright's opposition to McCarthy and McCarthyism, see Woods, *Fulbright*, pp. 175–190.

44. 100 *Cong. Rec.* 16154–16155 (November 29, 1954); "Senate Restricts M'Carthy Debate; Votes Tomorrow; Each Side Limited," *NYT*, November 30, 1954, pp. 1, 21; "Senate Accepts Plan for Vote Wednesday on McCarthy Censure; Senator Requests Early Showdown but Remains Firm against Apology," *WP*, November 30, 1954, pp. 1, 10; White, *Citadel*, p. 83; 100 *Cong. Rec.* 16184–16185 (November 30, 1954); "Jenner and Flanders in an Angry Quarrel," *NYT*, December 1, 1954, pp. 1, 25.

45. 100 *Cong. Rec.* 16220–16222 (November 30, 1954).

46. 100 *Cong. Rec.* 16365–16366 (December 2, 1954); "Final Vote Condemns M'Carthy, 67–22, for Abusing Senate and Committee; Zwicker Count Eliminated in Debate; Republicans Split," *NYT*, December 3, 1954, pp. 1, 14; "How the Senate Voted on McCarthy," *NYT*, December 3, 1954, p. 13; "Vote on McCarthy," *NYT*, December 5, 1954, E-1.

47. Lehman to Arthur Goodhart, December 6, 1954, LP, SF, Goodhart; Lehman to Louis Pink, December 15, 1954, LP, SF, Pink; "Remarks by Senator Herbert H. Lehman on Receiving the 'Franklin D. Roosevelt Four Freedoms Award,'" December 13, 1954, LP, SF, Frank Altschul, document 0015_0464; "Lehman Sees Gap in McCarthy Vote," *NYT*, December 14, 1954, p. 22.

48. "Censure Postscript," Editorial, *WP*, December 4, 1954, p. 10; Lehman to Frank Altschul, September 6, 1957, LP, SF, Altschul.

Chapter 15. "The First Duty of Liberals Is Not to Exercise Power, but to Uphold Principle": Herbert Lehman and Lyndon Johnson, 1950–1954

1. Lyndon Johnson to Hubert Humphrey, quoted in Solberg, *Hubert Humphrey*, p. 163.

2. Herbert Lehman, "Travail of Liberalism, 1945—," Second Speranza Lecture, Columbia University, April 16, 1958, LP, Speech File.

3. On Johnson's early life, career, and ambitions, see Steinberg, *Sam Johnson's Boy*; Caro, *The Years of Lyndon Johnson: The Path to Power*; Caro, *The Years of Lyndon Johnson: Means of Ascent*; and Caro, *The Years of Lyndon Johnson: Master of the Senate*. On Lehman's early life, see Nevins, *Herbert H. Lehman and His Era*, pp. 3–41. On

Johnson and Franklin Roosevelt, see also vanden Heuvel, "Franklin Delano Roosevelt and Lyndon Baines Johnson: Architects of a Nation." I am indebted to Ambassador vanden Heuvel for making the text of his remarks available to me.

4. "The mark of a good Senator" in Lehman to Paul Douglas, March 11, 1957, LP, SF, Douglas; Lucas quoted in Nevins, *Herbert H. Lehman and His Era*, p. 354. See also Lehman, "Travail of Liberalism"; White, *Citadel*, pp. 81–94, 107–120; Bobby Baker Oral History Transcript, III: 26, LBJL; McPherson, *A Political Education*, p. 19; George Reedy Oral History Transcript, VII: 13, and VIII: 3, LBJL; and Humphrey, *The Education of a Public Man*, pp. 132–136, 154. On Lehman's growing frustration in the Senate, see Lehman to Isador Lubin, March 11, 1952, Lubin Papers, Box 62, Personal Correspondence, 1935–1971, Lehman, FDRL; and Carolin Flexner Oral History Transcript, HHLP, CUOHC, pp. 56–57. On the conservative coalition controlling Congress, since the late 1930s, see Patterson, *Congressional Conservatism and the New Deal*; Truman, *The Congressional Party*, pp. 61–63; Clark, *The Senate Establishment*; Manley, "The Conservative Coalition in Congress"; and Shelley, *The Permanent Majority*. On Senator Russell, see Fite, *Richard B. Russell, Jr.*; and Caro, *Master of the Senate*, pp. 164–222.

5. Lehman, "Travail of Liberalism"; Lyndon Johnson to Herbert Lehman, August 4, 1956, LP, SF, Johnson; Lyndon Johnson, "Equality of Opportunity," Address on Acceptance of the Distinguished Service Award, Capital Press Club, Washington, D.C., May 18, 1963, in Johnson, *A Time for Action*, pp. 119–120.

6. HHLOH, p. 54; Roy Wilkins Oral History Transcript, HHLP, CUOHC, pp. 1–3. On Lillian Wald and the NAACP, see chapter 1. On Lehman's election to the NAACP's board of directors, see "Lehman Named to Racial Board," *NYT*, November 12, 1929, p. 22. On Lehman's referring to the NAACP as "our organization," see Lehman to Walter White, November 21, 1932, LP, SF, White. On the NAACP's finances, see Walter White to Carolin Flexner, April 19, 1933, and White to Flexner, May 13, 1936, both in LP, SF, White; and "NAACP Reports 1932 as Its Biggest Year," *Baltimore Afro-American*, January 14, 1933, p. 8. On Lehman's financial contributions to the NAACP, see the voluminous correspondence in LP, SF, White; "Fund Raised to Aid Negro," *NYT*, March 10, 1930, p. 18; Roy Wilkins to Lehman, February 17, 1950, and Lehman to Wilkins, February 22, 1950, both in LP, SF, Wilkins; Lehman to White, January 9, 1936, quoted in Report of the Secretary for the Board Meeting of February 1936, in Wilson, ed., *In Search of Democracy*, pp. 170–171; CAF to the Governor, December 3, 1951, LP, SF, Thurgood Marshall; Receipt, NAACP to Lehman, December 28, 1956, LP, SF, Wilkins; Weiss, "Long-Distance Runners of the Civil Rights Movement," in Salzman and West, eds., *Struggles in the Promised Land*, p. 136. On Lehman and the NAACP's Legal Defense and Educational Fund, see Thurgood Marshall to Lehman, March 21, 1940, LP, SF, Marshall; and White to Lehman, March 22, 1941; White to Lehman, December 15, 1941; Lehman, Memorandum for Mr. Brown, May 3, 1941; and Lehman to Walter White, January 6, 1942; all in LP, SF, White.

7. "Governor Lehman Lavish in Praise . . . Promises Continuing to Give Race Jobs," *New York Amsterdam News*, November 5, 1938, p. 12; "Walter White on Board of State School for Boys," *Baltimore Afro-American*, March 18, 1933, p. 3; "Inquiry Board Hits Negro Segregation," *NYT*, November 20, 1936, p. 9; "White Colonel of 369th Inf. Ousted," *Baltimore Afro-American*, March 5, 1938, p. 3; "A Fine Gesture," Editorial, *Baltimore Afro-American*, May 21, 1938, p. 4; "Highest Negro Officer Visits Guard

Unit Here," *NYT*, May 30, 1938, p. 4; "Governor Reviews Harlem Regiment," *NYT*, September 12, 1938, p. 35; "Hooper Commands 369th," *NYT*, November 9, 1940, p. 7; "Insurance Board Named by Lehman," *NYT*, April 29, 1933, p. 5; "N.Y. Governor Signs Anti-J.C. Labor Bill," *Baltimore Afro-American*, March 23, 1935, p. 6; "Schools Getting State Aid Made to Admit All," *Baltimore Afro-American*, May 18, 1935, p. 23; "Lehman Signs Bill to Prohibit Insurance J.C.," *Baltimore Afro-American*, May 18, 1935, p. 7; "N.Y. Passes Antilynch Bill," *Baltimore Afro-American*, March 26, 1938, pp. 1, 2; "N.Y. Antilynch Bill Made Law," *Baltimore Afro-American*, April 16, 1938, p. 6; "N.Y. Outlaws Color Line," *Baltimore Afro-American*, June 17, 1939, pp. 1, 2; "Lehman Submits Harlem Reforms," *NYT*, April 11, 1935, p. 16; "Lehman Backs Negro Aid," *NYT*, March 3, 1937, p. 13; "County Rule Bills Signed by Lehman," *NYT*, June 4, 1937, p. 48; "Named for Urban Negro Inquiry," *NYT*, July 8, 1937, p. 48; Ingalls, *Herbert H. Lehman and New York's Little New Deal*, pp. 114–115; "New York Laundry Workers Aided by Wage Law," *Baltimore Afro-American*, November 5, 1938, p. 17; "Here Are the Facts in Race for Governor," *New York Amsterdam News*, November 5, 1938, p. 4; Haygood, *King of the Cats*, p. 33. On the Harlem Riot in 1935, see Greenberg, "The Politics of Disorder: Reexamining Harlem's Riots of 1935 and 1943."

8. White to Lehman, February 2, 1934, and Lehman to White, February 12, 1934, both in LP, SF, White; "9 Governors, 27 Mayors, 55 Bishops, 92 Editors Sign Resolution to Curb Mobs," *Baltimore Afro-American*, January 5, 1935, p. 2; "Lehman Protests Negro 'Ban' By CCC," *NYT*, April 9, 1937, p. 10; "State Negroes Get 2 New CCC Camps," *NYT*, April 20, 1937, p. 10; "CCC Accepts 269 Negroes," *NYT*, April 21, 1937, p. 13. On the effort to enact a federal anti-lynching law in the 1930s, see Zangrando, *The NAACP Crusade against Lynching*, pp. 98–165. On African Americans and the CCC, see Salmond, *The Civilian Conservation Corps*, pp. 88–101, 188–190.

9. "Text of Governor Lehman's Message Emphasizing Economic Measures for the State," *NYT*, January 15, 1941, p. 16; "Lehman Would End Job Discrimination," *Baltimore Afro-American*, January 25, 1941, p. 5; Elmer Anderson Carter, "Racial Discrimination Seen," Letter to the Editor, *NYT*, February 7, 1941, p. 18; "Lehman Signs Bill Barring Race Curb," *NYT*, April 19, 1941, p. 9; "Lehman Signs Bill to End Racial Ban," *NYT*, May 8, 1942, p. 19.

10. "Keep a Cool Head," Editorial, *New York Amsterdam News*, October 31, 1928, p. 16; "Mr. Tuttle for Governor," Editorial, *New York Amsterdam News*, October 1, 1930, p. 20; "Endorse Lehman and Capper," *Baltimore Afro-American*, October 18, 1930, p. 7; "White Urges Re-Election of Lehman and Sen. Hofstadter," Letter to the Editor, *New York Amsterdam News*, October 22, 1930, p. 13; White to Henry Moskowitz, October 25, 1932, LP, SF, White; "New York City and Up State Vote for Principal National and State Offices," *NYT*, November 9, 1932, p. 4; "New York State Vote for Governor," *NYT*, November 7, 1934, p. 6; "Why We Prefer Lehman," Editorial, *New York Amsterdam News*, October 24, 1936, p. 14; "Big Demonstration to Greet Governor," *New York Amsterdam News*, October 24, 1936, pp. 1, 2; "Acclaim Lehman; Asks F.D. R. Help," *New York Amsterdam News*, October 31, 1936, pp. 1, 2; "Results of the Voting on Candidates and Issues in New York State and City," *NYT*, November 5, 1936, p. 8; "Vote for Lehman," Editorial, *New York Amsterdam News*, November 5, 1938, p. 10; "Here Are the Facts in Race for Governor," *New York Amsterdam News*, November 5, 1938, p. 4; "Results of the Voting for Governor and Other Officers in New York

State," *NYT*, November 9, 1938, p. 6; "Democratic Presidential Memoranda," Opinion, *Baltimore Afro-American*, February 3, 1940, p. 4; "Vote for Senator," *NYT*, November 6, 1946, p. 9; "Czech Church Curb an Omen to Dulles," *NYT*, October 6, 1949, p. 26; "Dulles Answers Charge of Bigotry," *NYT*, October 19, 1949, p. 7; "Conviction of Davis Throws N.Y. Political Campaign into Turmoil," *Baltimore Afro-American*, October 29, 1949, p. 5; "17 Negroes Denounce Dulles and Morris," *NYT*, October 19, 1949, p. 6; "Lehman Promises Aid to Civil Rights," *NYT*, October 31, 1949, p. 10; "Results of Contests for Senator, Mayor, Controller, City Council and Local Judicial Offices," *NYT*, November 9, 1949, p. 6. Numerous articles in the *New York Amsterdam News* in the 1930s make it clear that most of Harlem was in the 19th and 21st Assembly Districts at that time. These were the districts that elected African Americans James Stephens and William Andrews to the Assembly in 1934. See "Stephens and Andrews Win," *New York Amsterdam News*, November 10, 1934, pp. 1, 3. By 1938, the 17th Assembly District also had an African American majority and is included in the votes discussed in the text. See "Harlem Elects Lehman; Governor Polls More Than 2–1 to Win Over Dewey in Biggest Off-Year Vote Drive," *New York Amsterdam News*, November 12, 1938, p. 1. After redistricting in 1944, the 11th, 12th, 13th, and 14th Assembly Districts were located mostly in Harlem. See "City Bill Outlines New Voting Areas," *NYT*, March 30, 1944, p. 14; "Harlem Politicos Grab for Voters," *New York Amsterdam News*, October 19, 1946, pp. 1, 23; "Congressman Survives GOP Dewey Sweep; Four Negro Assemblymen Elected," *New York Amsterdam News*, November 9, 1946, pp. 1, 25. The *Afro-American* was widely distributed and had the largest circulation of any African American newspaper on the East Coast. See Farrar, *The Baltimore "Afro-American."*

11. Caro, *Master of the Senate*, pp. 737–738; Gardner, *Harry Truman and Civil Rights*, pp. 82–83; Miller, *Lyndon*, p. 118. On Johnson's supposed concern for African Americans and Mexican Americans earlier in his career, see Caro, *Master of the Senate*, pp. 711–760.

12. 95 *Cong. Rec.* 2042–2049 (March 9, 1949); Caro, *Master of the Senate*, pp. 212–215; "33 Senators Move to Gag Filibuster," *WP*, March 10, 1949, pp. 1, 2. On the history of the filibuster, see Binder and Smith, *Politics or Principle?* and Douglas, *In the Fullness of Time*, pp. 213–221. On Southern dominance of the Senate and the filibuster, see Caro, *Master of the Senate*, pp. 89–105. On Eastland, see Caro, *Master of the Senate*, pp. 102–103; Sherrill, *Gothic Politics in the Deep South*, pp. 186–215; Asch, *The Senator and the Sharecropper*, pp. 132–166; and Finley, *Delaying the Dream*, p. 76.

13. Caro, *Master of the Senate*, pp. 215–221; Anderson, *Outsider in the Senate*, p. 129; McCoy and Ruetten, *Quest and Response*, pp. 171–187; Berman, *The Politics of Civil Rights in the Truman Administration*, pp. 137–163; 95 *Cong. Rec.* 2724 (March 17, 1949); "Compromise Closure Rule Adopted by Senate, 63 to 23; Filibuster Battle Is Ended," *NYT*, March 18, 1949, pp. 1, 17; "Only Miracle Can Save Civil-Rights Program," *NYT*, March 20, 1949, E-7; Finley, *Delaying the Dream*, pp. 115–121.

14. HHLOH, pp. 770–771; "Senate Democrats Reduce G.O.P. Posts," *NYT*, January 4, 1950, p. 3; Douglas, *In the Fullness of Time*, pp. 206–208; White, *Citadel*, pp. 70–71; Julius Edelstein Oral History Transcript, HHLP, CUOHC, p. 14.

15. "Lehman Will Back 'Careful Economy,' " *NYT*, January 4, 1950, p. 6; "Francis [*sic*] Williams Appointed to Legislative Assistant Post," *Baltimore Afro-American*, January 28, 1950, p. 11; Julius Edelstein Oral History Transcript, HHLP, CUOHC, p. 10;

"President for Revenue Increase; Renews Demands for Fair Deal; Congress Issues Joined; G.O.P. Looses Barbs," *NYT*, January 5, 1950, pp. 1, 11; Minutes of Democratic Conference, January 5, 1950, in Ritchie, ed., *Minutes of the Senate Democratic Conference*, pp. 437–443; "Democrats Move to Speed Session, Merge Fund Bills," *NYT*, January 6, 1950, pp. 1, 10.

16. "Civil Rights Test Will Come on F.E.P.C.," *NYT*, January 8, 1950, E-7; A. Philip Randolph and Roy Wilkins to Lehman, January 4, 1950, and Lehman to Wilkins, January 10, 1950, both in LP, SF, Wilkins; "Civil Rights Group Sees Majority in House," *WP*, January 17, 1950, p. 5; Minutes of Democratic Conference, February 21, 1950, in Ritchie, ed., *Minutes of the Senate Democratic Conference*, pp. 452–454; McCoy and Ruetten, *Quest and Response*, pp. 190–192.

17. 96 *Cong. Rec.* 6793, 6797 (May 10, 1950); "Senate Shunts Civil Rights Issue to Debate Truman N.L.R.B. Plan," *NYT*, May 11, 1950, pp. 1, 25; "F.E.P.C. Is Killed as Senate, 52–32, Defeats Closure," *NYT*, May 20, 1950, pp. 1, 8; Berman, *The Politics of Civil Rights in the Truman Administration*, pp. 173–174.

18. "FEPC Vote Seen Friday in Senate," *WP*, May 17, 1950, p. 2; 96 *Cong. Rec.* 7145–7149 (May 17, 1950); "F.E.P.C. Is Killed as Senate, 52–32, Defeats Closure," *NYT*, May 20, 1950, pp. 1, 8; 96 *Cong. Rec.* 7303–7304 (May 19, 1950); Lehman to Wilkins, May 24, 1950, LP, SF, Wilkins; McCoy and Ruetten, *Quest and Response*, p. 197.

19. "Vote in Senate That Failed to Limit F.E.P.C. Debate," *NYT*, May 20, 1950, p. 8; "Fair Employment Practices Legislation," Extension of Remarks of Hon. Lyndon B. Johnson, May 25, 1950, 96 *Cong Rec.* A4022.

20. Lucas to Lehman, June 15, 1950, LP, SF, Lucas; "G.O.P. to Aid Drive to Close Congress if Program Is Cut," *NYT*, June 15, 1950, pp. 1, 27; "Origin of FEPC Legislation," Extension of Remarks of Hon. Herbert H. Lehman, July 11, 1950, 96 *Cong. Rec.* A5019–5020; 96 *Cong. Rec.* 9981–9982 (July 12, 1950); "F.E.P.C. Bill Dies for This Session as Senate Blocks New Closure Try," *NYT*, July 13, 1950, pp. 1, 18; McCoy and Ruetten, *Quest and Response*, pp. 198–199. On Eastland equating the NAACP and Communism, see Sherrill, *Gothic Politics in the Deep South*, p. 189; and Finley, *Delaying the Dream*, pp. 76–77, 80.

21. "Lehman Asks Ban by Truman on Bias," *NYT*, October 16, 1950, p. 8; "Sen. Lehman Asks Truman Issue New FEPC Directive," *New York Amsterdam News*, October 21, 1950, p. 5; Executive Order 10210, February 2, 1951, online by Gerhard Peters and John T. Woolley, *The American Presidency Project*, http://www.presidency.ucsb.edu/ws/?pid=60785; "Truman Expedites Contract Letting," *NYT*, February 3, 1951, p. 25; Berman, *The Politics of Civil Rights in the Truman Administration*, pp. 179, 184–186.

22. 96 *Cong. Rec.* 13264–13265 (August 24, 1950); "Filibusters Curb Asked by Lehman," *NYT*, August 25, 1950, p. 12; Julius Edelstein to Elbert Thomas, August 2, 1950, LP, SF, Thomas; Lehman to James Murray, August 24, 1950, LP, SF, Murray. The resolution's co-sponsors included Democratic Senators Murray (MT), Thomas (UT), Magnuson (WA), McMahon (CT), Kilgore (WV), Neely (WV), Douglas (IL), Humphrey (MN), and Benton (CT). Republican Senators Ralph Flanders (VT) and Robert Hendrickson (NJ) withdrew their names from the resolution at the last minute. See Lehman to Walter White, September 4, 1950, LP, SF, White.

23. 96 *Cong. Rec.* 8994 (June 21, 1950); "Senate Strikes Out Segregation Plan in Its Bill on Draft," *NYT*, June 22, 1950, pp. 1, 6; Lehman to McCarran, July 7, 1950,

and Lehman to Ida Post, July 7, 1950, both in LP, SF, McCarran; McCoy and Ruetten, *Quest and Response*, pp. 206–208; 96 *Cong. Rec.* 13183–13185 (August 23, 1950); "Senate Notes 24th's Heroism in Korea," *Baltimore Afro-American*, September 2, 1950, p. 13.

24. "DuBois First NY Negro in Senate Race," *New York Amsterdam News*, September 9, 1950, p. 2; "DuBois Outlines Senate Platform," *New York Amsterdam News*, September 30, 1950, p. 5; "Du Bois Tells Harlem Only U.S. Wants War," *NYT*, October 6, 1950, p. 21; "Elmer Raps Adam as Pal of Reds," *New York Amsterdam News*, September 16, 1950, pp. 2, 4; Lehman to Hulan Jack, September 8, 1950, LP, SF, Jack; Tobias to Lehman, September 12, 1950, LP, SF, Tobias; "Text of an Address Delivered by Mrs. Mary McLeod Bethune," October 11, 1950, LP, SF, Bethune; "Radio Discussion between Robert F. Wagner, President of the Borough of Manhattan, and Representative Adam Clayton Powell," October 18, 1950, LP, SF, Powell; "Lehman at Coney Keeps a Tradition," *NYT*, November 6, 1950, p. 35; Randolph to Edward Maguire, October 25, 1950, LP, SF, Randolph; "Lehman Stresses Rent Control Need," *NYT*, October 30, 1950, p. 17; "Candidates Plan Monster Meeting," *New York Amsterdam News*, November 4, 1950, p. 2; "Election Tables Showing Voting for Governor, Senator, and Mayor; Local Representatives," *NYT*, November 8, 1950, p. 16; "City, State Tally," *New York Amsterdam News*, November 11, 1950, p. 6.

25. "Three Defense Bills Voted as 81st Congress Adjourns; M'Farland Is Senate Leader; West-South Chiefs Picked as Fair Dealers Lose by 2-1," *NYT*, January 3, 1951, pp. 1, 19; Steinberg, *Sam Johnson's Boy*, pp. 316–317; Caro, *Master of the Senate*, pp. 364–366; Marquis Childs, "Southerners in the Senate," *WP*, January 5, 1951, p. 20; "Hope for Rights Measures Dim," *Baltimore Afro-American*, January 20, 1951, p. 3; "Fair Deal's Chance Is Slight at Best," *NYT*, January 21, 1951, E-10; McCoy and Ruetten, *Quest and Response*, pp. 284–285.

26. Lehman, Humphrey, and Douglas to Lyndon Johnson, January 4, 1951, Johnson Papers, Senate Papers, Box 362, Senate Office Building Committee, Papers of the Democratic Leader, Lehman, Humphrey, Douglas Telegram, January 4, 1951, LBJL; "Senate Leader Picks His Key Committees," *NYT*, January 5, 1951, p. 11; "Democrats Yield Committee Posts," *NYT*, January 6, 1951, p. 8; "Sparkman, Gillette Given 'Prize' Posts," *WP*, January 6, 1951, p. 6; Paul Douglas Oral History Transcript, HHLP, CUOHC, pp. 15–16; "Senate Democrats Band as Liberals," *NYT*, January 10, 1951, p. 22. Frear had voted the liberal positon on nine of sixteen roll calls tabulated by Americans for Democratic Action in 1950, including voting for cloture on the FEPC bill. See *ADA World*, Congressional Supplement, September 1950, p. 4, online: http://www.adaction.org/media/votingrecords/1950.pdf.

27. "Lehman Appointment to Policy Group Due," *NYT*, April 26, 1951, p. 34; Earle Clements Oral History Transcript, I: 4, and II: 8, LBJL; Evans and Novak, *Lyndon B. Johnson*, p. 53.

28. Minutes of Democratic Conference, February 22, 1951, in Ritchie, ed., *Minutes of the Senate Democratic Conference*, pp. 477–479; 97 *Cong. Rec.* 1649 (February 28, 1951), 2058–2066, 2069–2073 (March 7, 1951); "Army Reactivates 1st Armored Division," *WP*, March 1, 1951, p. 3; Edelstein Oral History Transcript, HHLP, CUOHC, p. 20; "Senate Votes to Limit Armed Forces; 4 Million Ceiling," *NYT*, March 8, 1951, pp. 1, 8; "Senate Kills Move to Protect GIs from Mobs," *Chicago Defender*, March 17, 1951, p. 5; Walter White, "The Chips Are Down; We Must Strike Anti-Negro Lawmakers Where It Hurts," *Chicago Defender*, April 14, 1951, p. 7; Watson, *Lion in*

the Lobby, p. 208; "offer up their lives" quoted from Lehman in 97 *Cong. Rec.* 1649 (February 28, 1951).

29. "6 Senators Seek to End Army's Bias," *Baltimore Afro-American*, March 17, 1951, p. 6; Anna Rosenberg Oral History Transcript, HHLP, CUOHC, pp. 6–7; Rosenberg to Lehman, August 23, 1951, LP, SF, Rosenberg; Lehman and Humphrey to Marshall, June 25, 1951; Marshall to Lehman and Humphrey, July 20, 1951; and Lehman to Marshall, July 28, 1951, all in LP, SF, Marshall; "Army to End Segregation in Asia Command, Closing History of Its Last Negro Regiment," *NYT*, July 28, 1951, p. 2; "Army Race Action Lauded," *NYT*, July 28, 1951, p. 2; "Need for Combat Men Speeded Integration," *Baltimore Afro-American*, August 4, 1951, p. 2; "Urge Ending Jim Crow in Army in U.S.," *Chicago Defender*, August 11, 1951, pp. 1, 2; Nichols, *Breakthrough on the Color Front*; Dalfiume, *Desegregation of the U.S. Armed Forces*, 171, 208–211; and Gardner, *Harry Truman and Civil Rights*, pp. 111–121. Besides Lehman, Senators Benton, Humphrey, Kilgore, Pastore, and Magnuson met with Anna Rosenberg to discuss the slow pace of the Army's desegregation efforts.

30. 97 *Cong. Rec.* 8810 (July 25, 1951); "Clashes in Illinois Bring Out Troops," *NYT*, July 13, 1951, p. 38; "Barbed Wire Bars Rioters in Chicago," *NYT*, July 14, 1951, p. 28; "Incident in Cicero," *NYT*, July 15, 1951, E-2; "Vet Defies 6,000 Rioters," *Baltimore Afro-American*, July 21, 1951, pp. 1, 2. Senator Douglas later addressed the Cicero Riots and their aftermath on the floor of the Senate; see 97 *Cong. Rec.* 12554 (October 3, 1951). On Lehman's concern about prejudice in the North, see also his comments on housing discrimination in New York City in "Lehman, Wagner Aid Urban League," *NYT*, March 19, 1957, p. 22.

31. 97 *Cong. Rec.* 7015 (June 25, 1951); "Offer Civil Rights Bills," *NYT*, June 26, 1951, p. 22; 97 *Cong. Rec.* 2843–2844 (March 22, 1951); "Easier Curb Urged on Senate Debate," *NYT*, March 23, 1951, p. 19; "Antifilibuster Rule," Editorial, *WP*, March 31, 1951, p. 6; Watson, *Lion in the Lobby*, p. 203.

32. U.S., Congress, Senate, Committee on Rules and Administration, *Limitation on Debate in the Senate; Hearings* before the Committee on Rules and Administration, 82nd Cong., 1st sess., October 1951, pp. 1–19; Walter White, "Legislative Freedom Hangs in Balance When Congress Wages War on Filibuster," *Chicago Defender*, September 15, 1951, p. 7; "Limiting Debate," Editorial, *WP*, October 7, 1951, B-4; "Civil Rights Issue Revived in Senate," *WP*, October 3, 1951, p. 2.

33. U.S., Cong., *Limitation on Debate in the Senate*, pp. 125–172, 282–284; Boyle, *The UAW and the Heyday of American Liberalism, 1945–1968*, pp. 110–111; Gould and Hickok, *Walter Reuther*, p. 342; Parrish, *Citizen Rauh*, p. 135. On Rauh and the ADA, see Brock, *Americans for Democratic Action*, pp. 51, 166; and Gillon, *Politics and Vision*, pp. 12, 17.

34. "Senate Unit Acts to Ease Cloture," *NYT*, January 30, 1952, p. 14; "Mild Cloture Change Voted by Rules Unit," *WP*, January 30, 1952, p. 2; Lehman to Kefauver, January 31, 1952, LP, SF, Kefauver; "End to Senate Bog on Rights Is Urged," *NYT*, February 18, 1952, p. 9; U.S., Congress, Senate, Committee on Rules and Administration, *Amending the Cloture Rule with Respect to the Number Required for Adoption of a Cloture Motion*, S. Rept. 1256, 82nd Cong., 2nd sess., March 6, 1952.

35. Lehman to Truman, August 13, 1951, and Truman to Lehman, August 16, 1951, both in Truman Papers, PSF, Box 108, General File, "L"; "'52 Election Spurs M'Farland to Seek a Short Congress," *NYT*, January 5, 1952, pp. 1, 5; "More Mud Than

Measures Will Be Passed on Hill," *WP*, January 6, 1952, B-1, 2; James Carey, Secretary-Treasurer and Chairman, CIO Committee to Abolish Discrimination, to Lyndon Johnson, February 6, 1952, Johnson Senate Papers, Box 227, Legislative Files, 1950–1952, Legislation, Civil Rights; " 'Easy' Rights Bill Talk Dwindles," *Baltimore Afro-American*, May 24, 1952, p. 3; 98 *Cong. Rec.* 7589–7590 (June 19, 1952).

36. S. Res. 3368, 82d Cong., 2d sess., June 20, 1952; 98 *Cong. Rec.* 7665 (June 20, 1952); *Federal Equality of Opportunity in Employment Act*, S. Rept. 2080, 82d Cong., 2d sess., July 3, 1952, p. 2; "Job Rights Bill Approved by Senate Group," *WP*, June 25, 1952, p. 30; "Civil Rights Bill Voted," *NYT*, June 25, 1952, p. 21; S. 3481, 82nd Cong., 2d sess., July 4, 1952; 98 *Cong. Rec.* 9251–9252 (July 4, 1952); "Protecting Soldiers," Editorial, *WP*, August 1, 1952, p. 18; Berman, *The Politics of Civil Rights in the Truman Administration*, pp. 207–208.

37. Robert Albright, "Democrats Face Party-Wrecking Issue," *WP*, October 28, 1951, B-1; "Fair Deal Is Sidetracked for This Congress," *NYT*, January 13, 1952, E-6.

38. "M'Kinney Doubts Truman Will Run," *NYT*, July 15, 1952, pp. 1, 12; "Byrnes Promises Aid if Russell Will Run," *WP*, February 7, 1952, p. 16; "Tammany's Dinner Skips Lehman Talk," *NYT*, June 11, 1952, pp. 1, 14; "Stevenson Still First Choice of Democratic Party Chiefs," *NYT*, May 16, 1952, pp. 1, 11. Senate business prevented Lehman from delivering his speech in person in New York, and Representative Franklin Roosevelt, Jr., agreed to read it in his stead. When the event ran long, however, a recording that Lehman had prepared introducing the speech was played for the attendees, but the speech itself was not read. See "Lehman Speech Cut by Time, Wagner Says," *NYT*, June 12, 1952, p. 24.

39. "Lehman Anti-Filibuster Plan Sought in Civil Rights Plank," *NYT*, July 16, 1952, pp. 1, 14; Lehman quoted in Gardner, *Harry Truman and Civil Rights*, pp. 204–205; Lehman to Benton, July 9, 1952, LP, SF, Benton.

40. "Lehman Anti-Filibuster Plan Sought in Civil Rights Plank," *NYT*, July 16, 1952, pp. 1, 14; Hays, *A Southern Moderate Speaks*, p. 67; "Democrats Tackle Civil Rights Issue," *NYT*, July 18, 1952, p. 8; "Stevenson Is Open to Draft by Party to End a Deadlock," *NYT*, July 17, 1952, pp. 1, 10; "Committee Cool to Direct Voting," *NYT*, July 17, 1952, p. 11.

41. "Civil Rights Peace Fades at Chicago," *NYT*, July 20, 1952, p. 37; "Enter Democrats," *NYT*, July 20, 1952, E-1; "Compromise Sighted in Civil Rights Issue," *NYT*, July 21, 1952, pp. 1, 14; "South's Overture Eases Rights Rift," *NYT*, July 22, 1952, p. 18; "Rights Plank Avoiding Specific Mention of FEPC Is Proposed," *WP*, July 23, 1952, p. 3; David, Moos, and Goldman, eds., *Presidential Nominating Politics in 1952*, I: 111–112; Hays, *A Southern Moderate Speaks*, pp. 67, 72–74; Thurber, *The Politics of Equality*, pp. 80–83; Martin, *Civil Rights and the Crisis of Liberalism*, pp. 108–109; Greene, *The Crusade*, pp. 145–147.

42. "Rights Plank Avoiding Specific Mention of FEPC Is Proposed," *WP*, July 23, 1952, p. 3; "Peace Called Goal of Foreign Policy," *NYT*, July 23, 1952, p. 11; "Strong Civil Rights Plank Ready," *WP*, July 24, 1952, p. 9; Hays, *A Southern Moderate Speaks*, pp. 75–79. To compare the civil rights planks in the 1948 and 1952 platforms, see Porter and Johnson, comps., *National Party Platforms, 1840–1960*, pp. 435, 487.

43. "Strong Civil Rights Plank Ready," *WP*, July 24, 1952, p. 9; "Dawson Guides Rights Plank Through," *Baltimore Afro-American*, August 2, 1952, p. 2; "Powell Threat-

ens a Boycott of Both Parties by Negroes," *NYT*, August 4, 1952, pp. 1, 9; Hays, *A Southern Moderate Speaks*, pp. 79–80; David, Moos, and Goldman, eds., *Presidential Nominating Politics in 1952*, I: 131–132; "General Approval Given to Platform," *NYT*, July 25, 1952, p. 12.

44. "Dawson Guides Rights Plank Through," *Baltimore Afro-American*, August 2, 1952, p. 2; Lehman to Humphrey, September 9, 1952, LP, SF, Humphrey; White quoted in Watson, *Lion in the Lobby*, p. 214; Martin, *Civil Rights and the Crisis of Liberalism*, pp. 108–109. Harlem Congressman Adam Clayton Powell, Jr., denounced Dawson as an "Uncle Tom" for supporting a civil rights plank that failed to mention FEPC by name and for discouraging Lehman from offering a minority report on the floor of the convention. See "Powell Threatens a Boycott of Both Parties by Negroes," *NYT*, August 4, 1952, pp. 1, 9.

45. Stevenson to Lehman, November 6, 1948, Stevenson to Lehman, November 9, 1950, and Lehman to Stevenson, November 15, 1950, all in LP, SF, Stevenson; "Truman Announces He Will Not Run Again; . . . He Bars any Draft," *NYT*, March 30, 1952, pp. 1, 65; "Race Is Wide Open," *NYT*, March 30, 1952, pp. 1, 66; Martin, *Adlai Stevenson of Illinois*, pp. 549–554, 560–562; Martin, *Civil Rights and the Crisis of Liberalism*, pp. 93–100, 105–107; Gillon, *Politics and Vision*, pp. 83–85; "Stevenson Asserts He Couldn't Accept Bid for Presidency," *NYT*, April 17, 1952, pp. 1, 20; "Democratic Race Further Confused," *NYT*, April 17, 1952, pp. 1, 19; David, Moos, and Goldman, eds., *Presidential Nominating Politics in 1952*, I: 33–41, 55–59; Greene, *The Crusade*, pp. 60–70; James Loeb Oral History Transcript, pp. 135–150, HSTL.

46. David, Moos, and Goldman, eds., *Presidential Nominating Politics in 1952*, I: 60–66; David, Moos, and Goldman, eds., *Presidential Nominating Politics in 1952*, II: 166–183; Drew Pearson, "The Washington Merry-Go-Round: Cruel Blows Hit Veep, Harriman," *WP*, July 25, 1952, p. 39; "State's Democrats Seen Uncommitted," *NYT*, April 1, 1952, p. 22; "Truman Lends Aid to Harriman Boom at Party Fete Here," *NYT*, April 18, 1952, pp. 1, 11; "Harriman Backed for the Presidency by 45 County Heads," *NYT*, April 19, 1952, pp. 1, 6; "Harriman Enters Democratic Race; to Make Bid Today," *NYT*, April 22, 1952, pp. 1, 22; "Harriman, Joining Race, Asks Peace and 'a Better America,'" *NYT*, April 23, 1952, pp. 1, 15; Julius Edelstein to Theodore Tannenwald, Jr., April 23, 1952; LP, SF, Harriman; Lehman to Hiram Milton, April 28, 1952, LP, SF, Franklin Roosevelt, Jr.; Edelstein to Edward Maguire, May 27, 1952, LP, SF, Maguire; "Douglas Calls Truman Forces Kefauver Foes, Lehman Boosts Harriman in D.C. Vote Pleas," *WP*, June 14, 1952, pp. 1, 7; Lehman to Robert G. A. Jackson, June 16, 1952, LP, SF, Jackson; "Harriman, Like Truman, Favors FEPC 'With Teeth,'" *Baltimore Afro-American*, June 21, 1952, p. 2; Harriman to Lehman, July 12, 1952, Harriman to Lehman, July 31, 1952, and Lehman to Harriman, August 6, 1952, all in LP, SF, Harriman; Martin, *Adlai Stevenson of Illinois*, pp. 562–564, 570; HHLOH, p. 772–773; Greene, *The Crusade*, pp. 44–46; Abramson, *Spanning the Century*, pp. 485–503; Joseph Rauh, Jr., Oral History Transcript, pp. 83–86, HSTL.

47. "New York Leaning Toward Stevenson," *NYT*, July 22, 1952, pp. 1, 16; "North-South Compromise Drawn; Truman Said to Back Stevenson; Move to Stop Illinoisan Pressed; South Is Amenable," *NYT*, July 23, 1952, pp. 1, 15; "Democratic Party Base Shift to North Seen Liberal Goal," *WP*, July 23, 1952, pp. 1, 4; "Harriman Forces Seek Truman Nod," *NYT*, July 24, 1952, p. 14; "Democrats Vote Today; Southerners

Seated; 3 States Admitted," *NYT*, July 25, 1952, pp. 1, 10; "Democrats Vote Today; Truman Puts His Support Behind Stevenson; Draft Seems Sure," *NYT*, July 25, 1952, pp. 1, 10; "A Big Wind Dies Down," *NYT*, July 25, 1952, p. 10; "Democrats Find Unity in Stormy Convention," *NYT*, July 27, 1952, E-3; "Stevenson Is Nominated on the Third Ballot; . . . Rivals Drop Out," *NYT*, July 26, 1952, pp. 1, 5; Berle and Jacobs, eds., *Navigating the Rapids*, pp. 603–605; Martin, *Civil Rights and the Crisis of Liberalism*, pp. 105–113; Gillon, *Politics and Vision*, pp. 85–88; Martin, *Adlai Stevenson of Illinois*, pp. 592–599; David, Moos, and Goldman, eds., *Presidential Nominating Politics in 1952*, I: 112–154; Greene, *The Crusade*, pp. 145–164; John Stennis to John Kennedy, November 10, 1952, Stennis to Lehman, November 24, 1952, and Lehman to Stennis, December 18, 1952, all in LP, SF, Stennis.

48. "Harriman Bowed to Liberal Cause," *NYT*, July 26, 1952, p. 6; Lehman to Fitzpatrick, August 22, 1952, LP, SF, Fitzpatrick.

49. "Harriman Bowed to Liberal Cause," *NYT*, July 26, 1952, p. 6; "Stevenson Is Nominated on the Third Ballot; . . . Rivals Drop Out," *NYT*, July 26, 1952, pp. 1, 5; "Sparkman Chosen by Democrats as Running Mate for Stevenson; . . . Team Takes Shape," *NYT*, July 27, 1952, pp. 1, 21; "Democrats Expect to Win the South," *NYT*, July 27, 1952, p. 38; "Tapping of Sparkman by Stevenson Follows Huddle with Truman," *WP*, July 27, 1952, M-3; "Sparkman for Veep," Editorial, *WP*, July 27, 1952, B-4; David, Moos, and Goldman, eds., *Presidential Nominating Politics in 1952*, I: 155–156; Fite, *Richard B. Russell, Jr.*, pp. 295–296; Hardeman and Bacon, *Rayburn*, pp. 368–369; Martin, *Adlai Stevenson of Illinois*, pp. 606–607; Watson, *Lion in the Lobby*, p. 216; Dallek, *Lone Star Rising*, pp. 417–418; Woods, *LBJ*, pp. 251–252; Hays, *A Southern Moderate Speaks*, pp. 67–68, 71–75; Thurber, *The Politics of Equality*, p. 83; Greene, *The Crusade*, pp. 38–40, 146–147, 157, 165–168.

50. *ADA World*, October 1951, and August 1952, online: http://www.adaction. org/pages/publications/voting-records.php; "Congressmen Listed Pro and Con by CIO," *WP*, August 17, 1952, M-4.

51. "Sparkman Warned on Rights Plank," *NYT*, July 27, 1952, pp. 1, 20; "Two Negro Leaders Criticize Sparkman," *NYT*, July 27, 1952, p. 31; "Powell Threatens a Boycott of Both Parties by Negroes," *NYT*, August 4, 1952, pp. 1, 9; Berle and Jacobs, eds., *Navigating the Rapids*, p. 604.

52. "16 G.O.P. Leaders Tie F.E.P.C. to Party," *NYT*, August 4, 1952, pp. 1, 10; "Lehman Hits Civil Rights Stand of 16," *WP*, August 6, 1952, p. 2; "Fast Start," *NYT*, August 10, 1952, E-1. For the text of the 1952 Republican platform provisions on civil rights, see Porter and Johnson, comps., *National Party Platforms, 1840–1960*, p. 504.

53. Lehman to Stevenson, August 5, 1952, LP, SF, Stevenson.

54. "Text of Stevenson's Address Accepting Presidential Nomination," *NYT*, July 27, 1952, p. 36; Stevenson to John Battle, August 23, 1952, in Johnson, ed., *The Papers of Adlai E. Stevenson*, IV: 47–48; "Text of Stevenson Addresses at Democratic and Liberal Meetings," *NYT*, August 29, 1952, p. 12; "Stevenson Bids Eisenhower Dismiss 'Gutter' Counselors," *NYT*, August 29, 1952, pp. 1, 12; "Stevenson Leaves; Powell Backs Him; Farley Sees Unity," *NYT*, August 30, 1952, pp. 1, 5; Greene, *The Crusade*, pp. 211–212; Martin, *Adlai Stevenson of Illinois*, pp. 656–657.

55. "Senator Lehman Returns from Europe," *NYT*, September 17, 1952, p. 28; "Stevenson Is Guest of the Cardinal; A.F.L. Speech Today," *NYT*, September 22, 1952,

pp. 1, 13; "Lehman Will Stump for Party's Ticket," *NYT*, October 7, 1952, p. 22; Lehman to Robert G. A. Jackson, December 4, 1952, LP, SF, Jackson; "Campaigners Converge on Critical Northeast," *NYT*, October 26, 1952, E-5; "G.O.P. Tactics Hit by Mrs. Roosevelt," *NYT*, October 6, 1952, p. 13; Earl Brown to Lehman, October 10, 1952, LP, SF, Brown; "Truman, in Harlem, Says G.O.P. Seeks to 'Turn Back Clock' on Civil Rights," *NYT*, October 12, 1952, pp. 1, 78; "Republican Policy on Labor Assailed," *NYT*, October 18, 1952, p. 7; "Lehman Denounces 'Reaction' Coalition," *NYT*, October 26, 1952, p. 70; "Lehman Assails General," *NYT*, October 28, 1952, p. 14; "Lehman Demands America Be Fair," *NYT*, October 30, 1952, p. 22; "Fog Over Airport Delays Stevenson," *NYT*, November 1, 1952, p. 15; Parmet, *The Democrats*, p. 98; Dallek, *Lone Star Rising*, pp. 416–421; Hardeman and Bacon, *Rayburn*, pp. 370–371; Martin, *Adlai Stevenson of Illinois*, pp. 650–652; 682–683; Greene, *The Crusade*, pp. 212–214.

56. Lehman to Rene Cassin, November 2, 1952, LP, SF, Cassin; Lehman to Robert G. A. Jackson, December 4, 1952, LP, SF, Jackson; Monroney to Lehman, November 5, 1952, LP, SF, Monroney.

57. 98 *Cong. Rec.* 9732 (July 7, 1952); Lehman to McFarland, August 12, 1952, LP, SF, McFarland.

58. "2 More Senators Support Johnson," *NYT*, November 13, 1952, p. 24; Drew Pearson, "Merry-Go-Round: Ike Ponders Trip to Latin America," *WP*, November 20, 1952, p. 51; Humphrey, *The Education of a Public Man*, pp. 163–165; Caro, *Master of the Senate*, pp. 474–485; Dallek, *Lone Star Rising*, pp. 421–425; Woods, *LBJ*, pp. 253–256; Fite, *Richard B. Russell, Jr.*, pp. 301–302; "Taft Named Head of G.O.P. in Senate; Martin Is Speaker," *NYT*, January 3, 1953, pp. 1, 8. Dallek and Woods list Lehman, Humphrey, Douglas, Murray, and Hunt as the five who voted for Murray, but Humphrey and Caro report that Johnson was confident that Hunt was going to vote for him despite Hunt's promises to Humphrey and his presence among the liberal delegation that met with Johnson. Caro later states that the fifth vote against Johnson came from Estes Kefauver. See Dallek, *Lone Star Rising*, p. 425; Woods, *LBJ*, p. 255; Humphrey, *The Education of a Public Man*, p. 164; and Caro, *Master of the Senate*, pp. 483, 502.

59. Lehman to Johnson, n.d., but clearly January 6, 1953, based on Johnson to Lehman, January 7, 1953, both in LP, SF, Johnson; Lehman to Arthur Goodhart, January 17, 1953, LP, SF, Goodhart; "Democrats Align Forces in Senate," *NYT*, January 13, 1953, p. 19; Hubert Humphrey Oral History Transcript, HHLP, CUOHC, pp. 16–17; Baker, *Wheeling and Dealing*, pp. 63–64; Bobby Baker Oral History Transcript, VI: 2, 3, LBJL; Anderson, *Outsider in the Senate*, p. 138; Dallek, *Lone Star Rising*, pp. 429–431; Caro, *Master of the Senate*, pp. 488–507.

60. Robert Bendiner, "Battle of Filibuster: New Round Opens," *New York Times Magazine*, September 14, 1952, SM17, 26, 28; "GOP Urges Legislators' Early Return," *WP*, December 28, 1952, M-1, 2; "Senators to Seek Eisenhower Views on Filibuster Plan," *NYT*, December 29, 1952, pp. 1, 12; Paul Douglas Oral History Transcript, HHLP, CUOHC, p. 2; U.S., Congress, Senate, Committee on Rules and Administration, *Limitation on Debate in the Senate; Hearings* before the Committee on Rules and Administration, 82nd Cong., 1st sess., October 1951, pp. 125–172, 282–284; "The Filibuster: A Tool for Good and Bad," *WP*, June 18, 2005, A19.

61. Edelstein Oral History Transcript, HHLP, CUOHC, p. 15; "Senate Rules Fight to Bar Filibustering Set Saturday," *WP*, December 31, 1952, p. 1; "Republicans

Move to Bar Filibuster When Senate Sits," *NYT*, December 31, 1952, pp. 1, 7. Senators Lehman, Humphrey, Douglas, Ives, Anderson, Green, Hunt, Murray, Mansfield, Morse, and Duff attended the meeting, and Senators Smith (NJ) and Magnuson sent members of their staffs. Sine die adjournment means the end of that Congress unless a special session is convened.

62. "Eisenhower Favors a Curb on Filibusters, Lodge Says," *NYT*, August 30, 1952, pp. 1, 4; "GOP Urges Legislators' Early Return," *WP*, December 28, 1952, M-1, 2; "Senators to Seek Eisenhower's Views on Filibuster Ban," *NYT*, December 29, 1952, pp. 1, 12; Arthur Krock, "In the Nation: 'Token' Fight or a Delaying Action," *NYT*, December 29, 1952, p. 18; "Taft to Seek Mid-Summer Hill Recess," *WP*, December 30, 1952, p. 1; Patterson, *Mr. Republican*, pp. 304–305, 429, 443, 509–511.

63. "3 Factions Get Set for Senate Fight on Filibuster," *WP*, January 1, 1953, pp. 1, 9; "Russell Sees Taft on Cloture Issue," *NYT*, January 1, 1953, p. 24; "GOP-Dixiecrat Coalition Set to Block Anti-Filibuster Forces in First Major Test in the New Congress," *Wall Street Journal*, January 3, 1953, p. 2. On Morse, see "GOP Urges Legislators' Early Return," *WP*, December 28, 1952, M-1, 2; and Drukman, *Wayne Morse*, pp. 186–196.

64. "Conference Would Keep Rules Policy in Senate," *WP*, January 3, 1953, pp. 1, 2; "G.O.P. Group Balks Curb on Filibuster," *NYT*, January 3, 1953, p. 9.

65. "Conference Would Keep Rules Policy in Senate," *WP*, January 3, 1953, pp. 1, 2; "G.O.P. Group Balks Curb on Filibuster," *NYT*, January 3, 1953, p. 9; Lehman to Arthur Goodhart, January 2, 1953, LP, SF, Goodhart. The Senators who attended this meeting at Lehman's office included Democrats Humphrey, Douglas, Jackson, Mansfield, Murray, Green, Pastore, Neely, Kennedy, and Anderson; Republicans Ives, Smith (NJ), Duff, and Tobey; and Independent Morse.

66. "Conference Would Keep Rules Policy in Senate," *WP*, January 3, 1953, pp. 1, 2; "G.O.P. Group Balks Curb on Filibuster," *NYT*, January 3, 1953, p. 9; Anderson, *Outsider in the Senate*, pp. 129–131; Douglas, *In the Fullness of Time*, p. 278; Hubert Humphrey Oral History Transcript, HHLP, CUOHC, p. 12; Edelstein to Ives, January 2, 1953, LP, SF, Ives. This is the same Clinton Anderson with whom Lehman had clashed when Anderson had served as Secretary of Agriculture in 1945–1946.

67. 99 *Cong. Rec.* 10–11 (January 3, 1953); "Senate Holds Fire on Filibuster Gag," *NYT*, January 4, 1953, pp. 1, 64; "Senate Puts Off Antifilibuster Battle as Harmony Marks Congress Opening; House Rule Change Unable to Reach Floor," *WP*, January 4, 1953, M-1, 2; "Debate Set for Today in Filibuster Fight," *WP*, January 6, 1953, p. 2; "Senate Rejection of Filibuster Curb Appears Certain," *NYT*, January 6, 1953, pp. 1, 18.

68. 99 *Cong. Rec.* 108, 112–115, 122 (January 6, 1953); "Taft Asks Defeat of Filibuster Curb," *NYT*, January 7, 1953, p. 14; Fite, *Richard B. Russell, Jr.*, p. 304; Watson, *Lion in the Lobby*, p. 358. On Reuther's liberalism, see Boyle, *The UAW and the Heyday of American Liberalism*; Brock, *Americans for Democratic Action*, pp. 51, 73–74, 128; and Gillon, *Politics and Vision*, pp. 13–17, 20–21.

69. 99 *Cong. Rec.* 113, 119, 121–122 (January 6, 1953). On the adoption of the first cloture rule in 1917, see "Senate Adopts Cloture 76 to 3; 'Willful Men' Reply to President; . . . Alters Rule of 100 Years," *NYT*, March 9, 1917, pp. 1, 2; Burdette, *Filibustering in the Senate*, pp. 115–128; Lowitt, "The Armed-Ship Bill Controversy"; and Ryley, *A Little Group of Willful Men*.

70. 99 *Cong. Rec.* 124–128 (January 6, 1953); "Taft Asks Defeat of Filibuster Curb," *NYT*, January 7, 1953, p. 14.

71. 99 *Cong. Rec.* 165–232 (January 7, 1953); "Senate, 70–21, Bars Curb on Filibuster; Rights Bills Mired," *NYT*, January 8, 1953, pp. 1, 24; "Senate Vote That Shelved Move to Curb Filibuster," *NYT*, January 8, 1953, p. 24; Anderson, *Outsider in the Senate*, p. 132. The twenty-one Senators who voted against tabling Anderson's motion included eighteen of the nineteen Senators who had co-sponsored the proposal, plus Democrats Thomas Hennings and Stuart Symington, both of Missouri; and Republican Senator Thomas Kuchel of California. Senator Magnuson, the other co-sponsor of the Anderson motion, did not vote on the motion to table it; instead, he was paired with an absent supporter of the tabling motion.

72. Lehman to Arthur Goodhart, January 8, 1953, January 17, 1953, and February 19, 1953, all in LP, SF, Goodhart; Lehman to Biddle, January 14, 1953, LP, SF, Biddle; 99 *Cong. Rec.* 232 (January 7, 1953); "Senate, 70–21, Bars Curb on Filibuster; Rights Bills Mired," *NYT*, January 8, 1953, pp. 1, 24; "Lehman Sees Ultimate Victory," *NYT*, January 9, 1953, p. 10.

73. "Senate Rejection of Filibuster Curb Appears Certain," *NYT*, January 6, 1953, pp. 1, 18; "Senate, 70–21, Bars Curb on Filibuster; Rights Bills Mired," *NYT*, January 8, 1953, pp. 1, 24; Baker, *Wheeling and Dealing*, p. 65; Johnson in 99 *Cong. Rec.* 11047 and A5311 (August 3, 1953); Anderson, *Outsider in the Senate*, p. 132.

74. Humphrey to Lehman, January 5, 1953, and Lehman to Humphrey, January 9, 1953, LP, SF, Humphrey; Ives to Lehman, December 4, 1953, and Lehman to Ives, December 19, 1953, LP, SF, Ives; "Senate, 70–21, Bars Curb On Filibuster; Rights Bills Mired," *NYT*, January 8, 1953, pp. 1, 24; "Lehman Sees Ultimate Victory," *NYT*, January 9, 1953, p. 10; Burk, *The Eisenhower Administration and Black Civil Rights*; *Brown v. Board of Education*, 347 U.S. 483 (1954); "Segregation in Schools Barred Here Since '38," *NYT*, May 19, 1954, p. 22; Lehman in 100 *Cong. Rec.* 6647 (May 17, 1954); Kluger, *Simple Justice*.

75. On Johnson's leadership: 99 *Cong. Rec.* 11043 (August 3, 1953). On Bohlen: 99 *Cong. Rec.* 2300 (March 25, 1953); "Bohlen Confirmed as Envoy, 74 to 13; Eisenhower Victor," *NYT*, March 28, 1953, pp. 1, 12; "Roll-Call Vote in Senate on Nomination of Bohlen," *NYT*, March 28, 1953, p. 12. On Social Security: 99 *Cong. Rec.* 7751–7760 (July 1, 1953); "Big Change Asked in Social Security," *NYT*, July 2, 1953, p. 12; 100 *Cong. Rec.* 6187 (May 7, 1954); 13008 (August 3, 1954); 14416–14419, 14438–14439 (August 13, 1954) "Widened Pensions Passed by Senate," *NYT*, August 14, 1954, pp. 1, 7. On farm price supports: 100 *Cong. Rec.* 13539–13547, 13553 (August 6, 1954); 13717–13718 (August 9, 1954); "Farm Bill Debate Curbed by Senate," *NYT*, August 7, 1954, p. 5; "Senate Approves President's Plan on Farm Support," *NYT*, August 10, 1954, pp. 1, 10; "Senate Roll-Calls on Farm Bills," *NYT*, August 10, 1954, p. 10; "Senate Votes Bill Giving President His Farm Program," *NYT*, August 11, 1954, pp. 1, 8. On reciprocal trade legislation: "Eisenhower Asks Power on Tariffs for Freer Trade," *NYT*, March 31, 1954, pp. 1, 18; 100 *Cong. Rec.* 7814, 7818–7819 (June 8, 1954); 8838–8839 (June 24, 1954); "Senate Approves Year's Extension of Trade Measure," *NYT*, June 25, 1954, pp. 1, 10; "Senate Vote That Killed 3-Year Trade Act Plan," *NYT*, June 24, 1954, p. 10; Kaufman, *Trade and Aid*, pp. 16–26. On Taft-Hartley

amendments: Johnson to Lehman, May 7, 1954, LP, SF, Johnson; 99 *Cong. Rec.* 4908 (May 14, 1953); "President Gives Farm Plan . . . 15 Taft Act Changes Urged," *NYT*, January 12, 1954, pp. 1, 9; George Meany to Lehman, May 3, 1954, LP, SF, Meany; 100 *Cong. Rec.* 5816–5817, 5829–5830, 5837–5839, 5847, 5947–5953, 5997–6001, 6094, 6200–6203 (May 3–7, 1954); "Broad State Rule over Labor Urged in Senate Debate," *NYT*, May 4, 1954, pp. 1, 35; "Revision Is Likely on Taft Law Plan," *NYT*, May 5, 1954, p. 27; "State Rights Plan on Labor Is Eased," *NYT*, May 7, 1954, p. 16; "Taft Act Changes Killed by Senate; Democrats Solid," *NYT*, May 8, 1954, pp. 1, 11; "Senate Vote to Recommit Labor Bill to Committee," *NYT*, May 8, 1954, p. 11; "Democrats Confident That '54 Is Their Year," *NYT*, May 9, 1954, E-3; Bobby Baker Oral History Transcript, V: 21–23, LBJL; Lee, *Eisenhower and Landrum-Griffin*, pp. 35–39. On statehood for Hawaii and Alaska: 100 *Cong. Rec.* 3068 (March 11, 1954); "Senate Combines Statehood Plans by Vote of 46–43," *NYT*, March 12, 1954, pp. 1, 13; 100 *Cong. Rec.* 3504–3505 (March 18, 1954); "Senate Sets Vote on Statehood Bill," *NYT*, March 31, 1954, pp. 1, 19; 100 *Cong. Rec.* 4324–4325, 4340–4343 (April 1, 1954); "Senate Votes Bill Giving Statehood to Hawaii, Alaska," *NYT*, April 2, 1954, pp. 1, 15; "Roll-Call Vote in Senate Passing Statehood Bill," *NYT*, April 2, 1954, p. 15; "House Unit Kills Statehood Bills for This Session," *NYT*, July 27, 1954, pp. 1, 14; Whitehead, *Completing the Union*.

    76. Hubert Humphrey Oral History Transcript, HHLP, CUOHC, pp. 2–4. In that same interview, Humphrey also expressed his envy of Lehman's freedom from having "to worry about his income," a reflection of Humphrey's insecurities, financial and otherwise. On Humphrey's finances, see Solberg, *Hubert Humphrey*, pp. 44, 52–53, 67–68, 73, 83–84, 88, 147. On Humphrey's growing pragmatism and his political ambitions limiting his liberalism at times, see Lazarowitz, *Years in Exile*, pp. 2–4, 100–101; and Parrish, *Citizen Rauh*, p. 136. On Lyndon Johnson generally during this period, see Caro, *Master of the Senate*, and Dallek, *Lone Star Rising*, pp. 351–591. On Johnson's benefactors in the oil industry, see Caro, *Master of the Senate*, pp. 246–248, 298–300, 406–409; and Dallek, *Lone Star Rising*, pp. 371–377, 404–405. On the offshore mineral rights bill, see 99 *Cong. Rec.* 3109 (April 15, 1953); Lister Hill to Lehman, January 2, 1953, and Lehman to Hill, January 7, 1953, both in LP, SF, Hill; "Senate Bars Move to Delay Debate on Offshore Bill," *NYT*, April 24, 1953, pp. 1, 14; 99 *Cong. Rec.* 2838 (April 8, 1953); "Give-Away in Oil," Editorial, *NYT*, April 10, 1953, p. 20; 99 *Cong. Rec.* 2907 (April 10, 1953), 2968–2982 (April 13, 1953), 3280 (April 18, 1953), 3372—3377 (April 20, 1953), and 3765 (April 24, 1953); "Coastal Oil Bill Wins, 53–35, as Senate Ends Long Debate," *NYT*, May 6, 1953, pp. 1, 23; "Roll-Call Vote in Senate to Pass Offshore Oil Bill," *NYT*, May 6, 1953, p. 23; Eisenhower, *The White House Years: Mandate for Change, 1953–1956*, pp. 203–208; Parmet, *Eisenhower and the American Crusades*, pp. 222–224. On the Dixon-Yates controversy, see "Eisenhower Plans New T.V.A. Study," *NYT*, July 1, 1954, p. 13; 100 *Cong. Rec.* 10155–10156 (July 9, 1954); 10747–10751 (July 17, 1954); 11188–11190 (July 21, 1954); "Lehman Attacks Atom 'Give-Away' on Private Power," *NYT*, July 18, 1954, pp. 1, 39; "Old Power Dispute Is at Root of Atom Row," *NYT*, July 25, 1954, E-7; 100 *Cong. Rec.* 11913–11920, 11932–11933 (July 24, 1954); "Role-Call Vote in Senate Killing A.E.C. Power Ban," *NYT*, July 22, 1954, p. 13; "Roll-Call Vote in Senate on Amending Atomic Bill," *NYT*, July 23, 1954, p. 6; "Senate Filibuster Halted by Recess; End of Tie-Up Seen,"

NYT, July 25, 1954, pp. 1, 56; "Democrats Split, Senate Hopes Rise for Atom Bill Test," *NYT*, July 26, 1954, pp. 1, 9; "Filibuster Sets Campaign Issue," *NYT*, July 28, 1954, pp. 1, 12; 100 *Cong. Rec.* 11938–11942 (July 26, 1954); 12188, 12226 (July 27, 1954); "Senate Ends Its Filibuster, Passes Atom Bill by 57 to 28; Administration Is Victor," *NYT*, July 28, 1954, pp. 1, 12; "Senate Roll-Call to Pass the Atomic Energy Bill," *NYT*, July 28, 1954, p. 12; Lehman to James Carey, July 30, 1954, LP, SF, Carey; Lehman to Mrs. Robert G. A. Jackson, July 28, 1954, LP, SF, Jackson; Lehman to Senator Langer, October 27, 1954, and Langer to Lehman, October 27, 1954, both in LP, SF, Langer; Eisenhower, *The White House Years: Mandate for Change, 1953–1956*, pp. 376–385; Parmet, *Eisenhower and the American Crusades*, pp. 222–224; Evans and Novak, *Lyndon B. Johnson*, pp. 79–81.

77. 99 *Cong. Rec.* 9134 (July 18, 1953); 100 *Cong. Rec.* 1329 (February 4, 1954); 1781 (February 16, 1954); 2372 (February 26, 1954); Lehman to William Benton, February 18, 1954, LP, SF, Benton; Julius Edelstein to Jefferson Fordham, October 3, 1953, LP, SF, Fordham; "Senate Defeats All Plans to Check Treaty Powers; Final Margin Is One Vote," *NYT*, February 27, 1954, pp. 1, 8; Caro, *Master of the Senate*, pp. 527–541; Tananbaum, *The Bricker Amendment Controversy*.

78. 99 *Cong. Rec.* 10105–10108 (July 28, 1953), 10959–10968 (August 3, 1953); "Senate, 63–30, Votes to Let 209,000 Refugees into U.S.," *NYT*, July 30, 1953, pp. 1, 8; S. 2585, 83rd Cong., 1st sess., August 3, 1953; Julius Edelstein to Jefferson Fordham, January 22, 1953, June 10, 1953, and October 3, 1953, all in LP, SF, Fordham; "32 Legislators Begin Fight on Aliens Law," *WP*, August 4, 1953, p. 11; "Revision of the Alien Law," Editorial, *NYT*, August 28, 1953, p. 16; "Pact Bars Change in M'Carran Law," *NYT*, September 24, 1953, p. 17; Drew Pearson, "Washington Merry-Go-Round: McLeod Stalling Refugee Entry," *WP*, November 22, 1953, B-5; "Alien Law Appeal Voiced by Lehman," *NYT*, October 14, 1953, p. 18; Philip Perlman to Harry Truman, June 15, 1954, LP, SF, Perlman; Allan Nevins to Wayne Andrews, December 17, 1962, LP, SF, Nevins; Julius Edelstein Oral History Transcript, HHLP, CUOHC, p. 14; Eisenhower, *Mandate for Change*, pp. 216–218; Ybarra, *Washington Gone Crazy*, pp. 709, 712–715.

79. Lehman to Eisenhower, August 13, 1953, LP, SF, Eisenhower; "Lehman Proposes President Aid Bill," *NYT*, August 16, 1953, p. 34; Memorandum, Edelstein to Stanley Karson, August 13, 1953, and Press Release, August 16, 1953, both in LP, SF, Eisenhower; "Land of Immigrants," Editorial, *WP*, September 3, 1953, p. 14. JTA is the Jewish Telegraphic Agency, a news service that focuses on events and issues of interest to Jews. See http://www.jta.org/about. On Eisenhower's previous criticism of the McCarran-Walter Act, see "Eisenhower Urges Study of Alien Act, Lists 10 Complaints," *NYT*, April 28, 1953, pp. 1, 21; "Text of Letter by Eisenhower," *NYT*, April 28, 1953, p. 21.

80. Wilton Persons to Lehman, August 14, 1953, LP, SF, Eisenhower; Javits to Lehman, September 17, 1953; enclosed press release of August 1, 1953; and Edelstein to Javits, September 28, 1953, all in LP, SF, Javits; Edelstein to Stanley Isaacs, November 25, 1953, LP, SF, Isaacs; Emanuel Celler to Lehman, March 31, 1954, Lehman to Celler, April 2, 1954, and Lehman to Celler, April 15, 1954, all in LP, SF, Celler; "9 to Seek McCarran Act Changes," *WP*, April 12, 1954, p. 2; "G.O.P. Held 'Strong' on Alien Law Issue," *NYT*, September 1, 1953, p. 16; Lyndon Johnson to J. C. Phillips, August 26, 1953, Johnson Papers, Senate, Box 251, Legislative Files, 1953–1954, Immigration, Watkins Bill, S. 1917, 1 of 2; Lehman to Thomas Hennings, May 17,

1954, LP, SF, Hennings; William Langer to Lehman, June 2, 1954, Lehman to Langer, June 24, 1954, and Langer to Lehman, June 25, 1954, all in LP, SF, Langer; Lehman to Theodore Francis Green, June 28, 1954, LP, SF, Green; Irving Engel, "Admitting Aliens," Letter to the Editor, *NYT*, July 6, 1954, p. 22; "House Unit Backs Sheepherder Bill," *NYT*, August 6, 1954, p. 4; "Sheep and Goats," Editorial, *WP*, August 26, 1954, p. 12.

81. Lehman to John Gunther, September 26, 1953, LP, SF, Americans for Democratic Action; Lehman to Walter Reuther, October 27, 1953, and November 6, 1953, both in LP, SF, Reuther; Lehman to Hubert Humphrey, November 7, 1953, LP, SF, Humphrey; Edelstein to Rt. Rev. Monsignor John O'Grady, December 18, 1953, LP, SF, O'Grady; "Lehman Will Ask Alien Act Change," *NYT*, January 11, 1954, p. 10; "Citizens to Press for New Alien Act," *NYT*, January 12, 1954, p. 13; "Immigrant Program Declared in Danger," *NYT*, May 8, 1954, p. 35; Edelstein to Franklin Roosevelt, Jr., May 18, 1954, LP, SF, Franklin Roosevelt, Jr.; Edelstein to Lehman, September 3, 1954, LP, SF, Edelstein; Edelstein to Simon Sobeloff, November 10, 1954, LP, SF, Sobeloff; Edelstein to Thomas Finletter, December 10, 1954, LP, SF, Finletter; "U.S. Entry Quotas Termed Harmful," *NYT*, April 10, 1956, p. 25.

82. Caro, Master of the Senate, p. 807.

Chapter 16. "An Inveterate Crusader": Lehman and Johnson, 1955–1956

1. Douglas, *In the Fullness of Time*, pp. 204–205.

2. Lehman to Mrs. Robert G. A. Jackson, November 15, 1954, LP, SF, Jackson; Minutes of the Senate Democratic Conference, January 4, 1955, in Ritchie, ed., *Minutes of the Senate Democratic Conference*, pp. 495–496; Douglas, *In the Fullness of Time*, pp. 204–205, 234; Lehman to Edelstein, August 26, 1955, LP, SF, Edelstein; McPherson, *A Political Education*, p. 43; Caro, *Master of the Senate*, pp. 564–568, 589–590; Dallek, *Lone Star Rising*, pp. 473–478; Evans and Novak, *Lyndon B. Johnson*, pp. 104–106; Parmet, *The Democrats*, pp. 103–104; Schlesinger, *A Thousand Days*, pp. 10–11.

3. Bobby Baker Oral History Transcript, VI: 3, LBJL; Lehman to Johnson, November 4, 1955, and Johnson to Lehman, November 8, 1955, both in LP, SF, Johnson.

4. Lehman to Johnson, December 2, 1954, and Edelstein, Memorandum to Senator Kilgore, December 10, 1954, both in LP, SF, Johnson; Lehman to Harley Kilgore, December 2, 1954, LP, SF, Kilgore; Lehman to Thomas Hennings, December 2, 1954, LP, SF, Hennings.

5. Johnson to Lehman, December 21, 1954, LP, SF, Johnson; George Reedy Oral History Transcript, VIII: 10, LBJL; Drew Pearson, "The Washington Merry-Go-Round: Leaders Face Test in Congress," *WP*, January 2, 1955, E-5; Dallek, *Lone Star Rising*, pp. 461–462, 470–471; "Barkley Regains Key Senate Posts; Morse Elevated," *NYT*, January 11, 1955, pp. 1, 18.

6. George Reedy, Memorandum to Senator Johnson, December 3, 1954, Lyndon Baines Johnson Archives (hereinafter LBJA), Box 119, Subject File, Senate, U.S., Rules of, Rule XXII, LBJL; Bobby Baker Oral History Transcript, VI: 1–2, LBJL.

7. Lehman to Johnson, January 13, 1955, LP, SF, Johnson. On Johnson's control of the Steering Committee and committee assignments, see Caro, *Master of the Senate*, pp. 563–565. Hubert Humphrey was in error when he claimed in his oral history at the Johnson Library that Johnson agreed to put Lehman on the Judiciary Committee, an error that was then repeated by Robert Mann. See Hubert Humphrey Oral History Transcript, III: 13–14, LBJL; and Mann, *The Walls of Jericho*, p. 132.

8. Johnson to Lehman, January 17, 1955, LP, SF, Johnson. Surprisingly, the liberal *New Republic* agreed that Lehman's not being a lawyer disqualified him from serving on the Judiciary Committee. See "Continuing Influence?" *New Republic*, January 17, 1955, p. 3.

9. Drew Pearson, "The Washington Merry-Go-Round: President's Strategy on Red China," *WP*, February 9, 1955, p. 51; Lehman to Johnson, May 1, 1956, LP, SF, Johnson; "Douglas Placed on Finance Unit," *NYT*, May 19, 1956, p. 40; Douglas, *In the Fullness of Time*, p. 427. On Long and Johnson, see Caro, *Master of the Senate*, p. 572. Pearson was incorrect in claiming that Lehman had been "Governor of New York more terms than anyone in history." Al Smith had also served four terms as Governor, and George Clinton had served seven terms in the late 1700s and early 1800s. See Ellis, Frost, Syrett, and Carman, *A Short History of New York State*, pp. 119, 395.

10. Gunther to Julius Edelstein, December 7, 1954, LP, SF, Americans for Democratic Action; Carey to Lehman, December 29, 1954, LP, SF, Carey; Wilkins to Lehman, January 4, 1955, LP, SF, Wilkins; George Reedy, Memorandum to Senator Johnson, December 3, 1954, LBJA, Box 119, Subject File, Senate, U.S., Rules of, Rule XXII.

11. Douglas to Lehman, November 2, 1958, LP, SF, Douglas; Edelstein to Gunther, December 9, 1954, LP, SF, Americans for Democratic Action; Edelstein Oral History Transcript, HHLP, CUOHC, p. 15; Roy Wilkins Oral History Transcript, HHLP, CUOHC, p. 10; Estes Kefauver Oral History Transcript, HHLP, CUOHC, p. 12.

12. Reedy, Memorandum to Senator Johnson, December 3, 1954, LBJA, Box 119, Subject File, Senate, U.S., Rules of, Rule XXII; "Party Peace Seen on Racial Issue on Hill," *WP*, December 28, 1954, p. 15; Steinberg, *Sam Johnson's Boy*, p. 395. On the Johnson-Humphrey relationship, see Humphrey, *The Education of a Public Man*, pp. 161–165; Solberg, *Hubert Humphrey*, pp. 160–164, 169–171; Mann, *The Walls of Jericho*, pp. 142–148; and Caro, *Master of the Senate*, pp. 439–462, 482–485, 494–499, 600, 699. William S. White of the *New York Times* attributed what he called Humphrey's "zigzag course" on civil rights to "the unyielding facts of life in the Senate." Gary Reichard ascribed Humphrey's retreat from his earlier advocacy of strong civil rights legislation to his political ambitions. See White, *The Citadel*, p. 113; and Reichard, "Democrats, Civil Rights, and Electoral Strategies in the 1950s," pp. 65, 71.

13. Douglas, *In the Fullness of Time*, p. 280; "Filibuster Foes Shift Strategy," *WP*, January 6, 1955, p. 6; Richard Neuberger, "Herbert H. Lehman: A Profile in Courage," *Progressive*, June 1958, reprinted as "Article by Senator Neuberger in Tribute to Ex-Senator Herbert H. Lehman," Extension of Remarks of Hon. Henry M. Jackson, May 29, 1958, 104 *Cong. Rec.* 9863–9864; Wilkins to Lehman, January 6, 1955, LP, SF, Wilkins; Hubert Humphrey Oral History Transcript, HHLP, CUOHC, pp. 12–13; Wayne Morse Oral History Transcript, HHLP, CUOHC, pp. 24–25; Paul Douglas Oral History Transcript, HHLP, CUOHC, p. 3; Roy Wilkins Oral History Transcript,

HHLP, CUOHC, p. 10; Anderson, *Outsider in the Senate*, p. 281; Dallek, *Lone Star Rising*, p. 478; Caro, *Master of the Senate*, p. 600; Thurber, *The Politics of Equality*, pp. 92–93. Paul Sifton, the United Auto Workers' chief Washington lobbyist, believed that Humphrey's abandonment of Lehman and the liberal position on this issue convinced Lehman that the Senate would continue to block civil rights legislation and led in part to Lehman's decision in 1956 not to seek re-election. See Boyle, *The UAW and the Heyday of American Liberalism*, p. 293, n. 13.

14. Paul Douglas Oral History Transcript, HHLP, CUOHC, p. 3; Walter White, Press Release, January 13, 1955, LP, SF, White; Dallek, *Lone Star Rising*, pp. 470–472, 478; Hubert Humphrey Oral History Transcript, HHLP, CUOHC, p. 13; Anderson, *Outsider in the Senate*, p. 138; "Freer Atomic Data for Power Sought," *NYT*, January 13, 1955, p. 3; "Barkley Regains Key Senate Posts; Morse Elevated," *NYT*, January 11, 1955, pp. 1, 18; Caro, *Master of the Senate*, p. 600.

15. 101 *Cong. Rec.* 118–120 (January 6, 1955); "New Drive Begins for Fair Inquiries," *NYT*, January 7, 1955, p. 14; "Liberals Shun Filibuster Fight, but Will Press for Civil Rights," *WP*, January 7, 1955, p. 12.

16. 101 *Cong. Rec.* 118, 120 (January 6, 1955); "Liberals Shun Filibuster Fight, but Will Press for Civil Rights," *WP*, January 7, 1955, p. 12; "Civil Rights Bills Doomed in Capitol," *NYT*, January 8, 1955, pp. 1, 8; Douglas to Lehman, October 10, 1958, LP, SF, Douglas; Douglas, *In the Fullness of Time*, p. 280; "Address by Hon. Herbert H. Lehman, of New York, at Civil Rights Rally of the Conference on Civil Rights," Extension of Remarks of Herbert H. Lehman, 102 *Cong. Rec.* 472–473 (January 12, 1956); Boyle, *The UAW and the Heyday of American Liberalism*, p. 112; Caro, *Master of the Senate*, p. 699.

17. Wayne Morse Oral History Transcript, HHLP, CUOHC, p. 9; "Chiang Foresees War at 'Any Time,'" *NYT*, January 1, 1955, p. 4; "Ike Asks Early Action on Chiang Treaty," *WP*, January 7, 1955, p. 4. There are numerous works on the Formosa crisis of 1955. Eisenhower, *Mandate for Change*, pp. 460–483, and Ambrose, *Eisenhower: The President*, pp. 212–214, 231–245, both present Eisenhower's and Dulles's handling of the situation in a favorable light. More critical are Chang and Di, "The Absence of War in the U.S.-China Confrontation over Quemoy and Matsu in 1954–1955"; Chang, "To the Nuclear Brink: Eisenhower, Dulles, and the Quemoy-Matsu Crisis"; and Brands, "Testing Massive Retaliation: Credibility and Crisis Management in the Taiwan Strait."

18. James Hagerty Diary, January 25, 1955, in Ferrell, ed., *The Diary of James C. Hagerty*, pp. 173–174; Summary of Telephone Call, House Minority Leader Joseph Martin and Speaker of the House Sam Rayburn to President Eisenhower, January 20, 1955, Eisenhower Papers, Diary Series, Box 9, Phone Calls: January–July 1955 (3), Dwight D. Eisenhower Library (hereinafter DDEL); "Eisenhower Asks for Authority to Defend Formosa from Reds," *NYT*, January 25, 1955, pp. 1, 2; Text of Eisenhower's Message to Congress," *NYT*, January 25, 1955, p. 3; Accinelli, "Eisenhower, Congress, and the 1954–55 Offshore Island Crisis," pp. 333–334; H.J. Res. 159, 84th Cong., 1st sess., January 24, 1955; S.J. Res. 28, 84th Cong., 1st sess., January 24, 1955; U.S., Congress, Senate, Committee on Foreign Relations, *Authorizing the President to Employ the Armed Forces of the United States for Protecting the Security of Formosa, the Pescadores, and Related Positions and Territories of That Area*, S. Rept. 13, 84th Cong., 1st sess., January 26, 1955.

19. 96 *Cong. Rec.* 1554–1558 (February 7, 1950); 101 *Cong. Rec.* 925–928 (January 28, 1955).

20. Lehman to Robert G. A. Jackson, February 21, 1955, LP, SF, Jackson; Lehman to La Guardia, January 5, 1934, LP, SF, La Guardia; "Gov. Lehman's Letter," *NYT*, July 20, 1937, p. 1; 101 *Cong. Rec.* 992 (January 28, 1955).

21. 101 *Cong. Rec.* 819–821 (January 27, 1955); 720, 760–769 (January 26, 1955); 981–988 (January 28, 1955); Lehman to C. C. Burlingham, January 31, 1955, LP, SF, Burlingham; Briggs, "Congress and the Cold War," pp. 90–91; Accinelli, "Eisenhower, Congress, and the 1954–55 Offshore Island Crisis," pp. 335–338. On Senator George's key role in the passage of the Formosa Resolution, see Summary of Telephone Call, Dulles to President Eisenhower, January 26, 1955, Eisenhower Papers, Diary Series; James Reston, "Democrats and Islands," *NYT*, April 5, 1955, p. 4; Chalmers Roberts, "Strong Man from the South," *Saturday Evening Post*, 227 (June 25, 1955): 30, 109–112.

22. 101 *Cong. Rec.* 843 (January 27, 1955); 992, 994–995 (January 28, 1955); "Senate Votes Formosa Plan, 85–3," *NYT*, January 29, 1955, pp. 1, 3; Wayne Morse Oral History Transcript, HHLP, CUOHC, pp. 9–15; Drukman, *Wayne Morse*, p. 403. On Langer, see Smith, *Langer of North Dakota*, pp. 60–63.

23. Wayne Morse Oral History Transcript, HHLP, CUOHC, p. 9. The risk of revealing classified information would have been much greater for Morse, who, as a member of the Senate Foreign Relations Committee, had participated in the hearings on the resolution.

24. "Senate Leader to Mayo Clinic," *NYT*, January 19, 1955, p. 25; 101 *Cong. Rec.* 981, 985, 987, 994 (January 28, 1955); Johnson to Styles Bridges, February 2, 1955, LBJA, Congressional File, LBJL, quoted in Gaskin, "Senate Majority Leader Lyndon B. Johnson: The Formosa and Middle East Resolutions," in Firestone and Vogt, eds., *Lyndon Baines Johnson and the Uses of Power*, p. 250. Robert Dallek claims that Johnson was among the congressional leaders with whom Eisenhower consulted before submitting the resolution to Congress, citing a telephone call from the President to Johnson on the morning of January 18, among other sources. However, the summary of the telephone conversation at the Eisenhower Library shows that the purpose of the call was to wish Johnson well if he needed surgery, and the topic of Formosa did not come up. Similarly, in two follow-up letters the President again expressed his concern about Johnson's health and did not mention Formosa or the resolution. See Dallek, *Lone Star Rising*, pp. 469, 479, 681, n. 31; Summary of Telephone Call, Eisenhower to Johnson, January 18, 1955, Eisenhower Papers, Diary Series, Box 9, Phone Calls: January–July 1955 (3); Eisenhower to Johnson, January 22, 1955, and January 27, 1955, Johnson Papers, White House Famous Names, Box 1, Eisenhower. On the Gulf of Tonkin Resolution, see P. L. 88–408, August 10, 1964, 78 *Stat.* 384 (1965); Gibbons, *The U.S. Government and the Vietnam War*, II: 28–342; Dallek, *Flawed Giant*, pp. 143–156; and Mann, *A Grand Delusion*, pp. 342–370.

25. Lehman to Morse, September 23, 1958, LP, SF, Morse; Herbert Lehman, "Against Islands' Defense," Letter to the Editor, *NYT*, September 23, 1958, p. 32; Harry Barnard, "Where Are the Democrats?" *The Nation*, October 4, 1958, pp. 183–186; "Quemoy Policy Backed by Democrats in 1955," *WP*, September 11, 1958, A-16.

26. Lehman to Hubert Humphrey, January 21, 1955, which contains a note that the same letter was sent to Senators Morse, Pastore, Green, Murray, Kennedy, and

Magnuson, LP, SF, Humphrey; Lehman to Clinton Anderson, January 21, 1955, which contains a note that the same letter was sent to Senators Barkley, Chavez, Douglas, Fulbright, Gore, Hennings, Jackson, Kefauver, Kilgore, Mansfield, McNamara, Neely, Neuberger, O'Mahoney, Scott, Symington, Ives, Alexander Smith, Margaret Chase Smith, Clifford Case, Saltonstall, Payne, Langer, Wiley, Aiken, Flanders, Bush, Thye, Duff, Kuchel, Purtell, and Potter, LP, SF, Anderson; S. 1206, 84th Cong., 1st sess., February 25, 1955; 101 *Cong. Rec.* 2093–2101 (February 25, 1955); "Congress Is Pressed to Scrap Alien Act," *NYT*, February 27, 1955, p. 28. Lehman's co-sponsors in 1955 included Senators Chavez, Green, Humphrey, Kefauver, Kennedy, McNamara, Magnuson, Murray, Neuberger, Pastore, Morse, and Langer.

27. 101 *Cong. Rec.* 4996–4998 (April 25, 1955); "Lehman Suggests Ouster of M'Leod," *NYT*, April 24, 1955, p. 15; S. 1794, 84th Cong., 1st sess., April 25, 1955; "Lehman Bids Senate Revamp Relief Act," *NYT*, April 26, 1955, p. 21; "Rescuing the Refugees," Editorial, *WP*, April 26, 1955, p. 20.

28. "Corsi Asks Haste in Refugee Help," *NYT*, April 27, 1955, p. 13; "President Endorses Refugee Act Revision," *NYT*, April 28, 1955, pp. 1, 10; "Transcript of the Presidential Press Conference on Foreign and Domestic Affairs," *NYT*, April 28, 1955, p. 12; "President Offers Refugee Aid Plan and Urges Speed," *NYT*, May 28, 1955, pp. 1, 6; "Text of the President's Refugee Message," *NYT*, May 28, 1955, p. 6. On McLeod, see Bach and Hale, " 'What He Is Speaks So Loud That I Can't Hear What He's Saying.' "

29. "14 GOP Senators Back Ike on Refugees," *WP*, May 29, 1955, A-4; "President Offers Refugee Aid Plan and Urges Speed," *NYT*, May 28, 1955, pp. 1, 6; "Lawyer Named to Refugee Post with Orders to Speed Entries," *NYT*, June 10, 1955, pp. 1, 8; U.S., Cong. Senate, *Amendments to Refugee Relief Act of 1953; Hearings* before the Special Senate Subcommittee to Investigate Problems Connected with the Emigration of Refugees and Escapees from Western European Nations, 84th Cong., 1st sess., June 1955; Langer to Lehman, June 4, 1955, Lehman to Langer, June 13, 1955, Langer to Lehman, June 22, 1955, and Langer to Lehman, July 15, 1955, all in LP, SF, Langer; "Legion, AVC Clash Over Refugees," *WP*, June 9, 1955, p. 11; "New Refugee Bill Faces Fight," *WP*, July 10, 1955, A-2; Langer to Nick Pesch, July 20, 1955, quoted in Barber, "A Diamond in the Rough: William Langer Reexamined," p. 17; "No Accord on Refugee Bill," *NYT*, July 22, 1955, p. 8; 101 *Cong. Rec.* 12284–12291 (July 30, 1955); "Refugee Act Revision Hope Lost," *WP*, August 2, 1955, p. 7; "President Scores U.S. Refugee Act," *NYT*, August 3, 1955, p. 10; "Flailing Tail Hides Immigration Dog," *WP*, May 1, 1955, E-1, 7; Goodman, *The Committee*, pp. 365–366, 397–398, 442–443.

30. 101 *Cong. Rec.* 3786–3788 (March 28, 1955); Lehman to Johnson, March 29, 1955, LP, SF, Johnson.

31. Caro, *Master of the Senate*, pp. 564–569; McPherson, *A Political Education*, p. 43; Parmet, *The Democrats*, pp. 103–104. McPherson also claims that Johnson "had long been a friend of the [Lehman] family," but there is no evidence to support this assertion. See McPherson, *A Political Education*, p. 43.

32. Mooney, *LBJ*, p. 46; Julius Edelstein, "Remarks for Lehman Conference," Roosevelt Library, Hyde Park, NY, November 12, 2004, p. 3. Thanks to Professor Michael Green of the University of Southern Nevada for calling my attention to this passage in Mooney's book. Interviewed years later, Sam Rosenman recalled traveling

with Lehman during his 1928 campaign for Lieutenant Governor and being impressed at how Lehman's sincerity helped him connect with voters even then. See Rosenman's comments in "Herbert H. Lehman: The Making of a Leader," WABC-TV, March 28, 1965, p. 20, copy in LP.

33. "Lyndon Johnson Ill; Out for This Session," *NYT*, July 3, 1955, pp. 1, 22; Telegram, Lehman to Johnson, n.d., but obviously July 1955, LBJA, Congressional File, Box 48, Lehman; 101 *Cong. Rec.* 9834–9837 (July 5, 1955); James Lee, "Senate Pauses to Honor Johnson," *WP*, July 6, 1955, p. 2; Bobby Baker Oral History Transcript, VII: 29, LBJL. On Johnson's heart attack and recovery, see Caro, *Master of the Senate*, pp. 619–640.

34. Lady Bird Johnson to Lehman, July 7, 1955, and July 15, 1955, and Lyndon Johnson to Lehman, September 26, 1955, all in LP, SF, Johnson.

35. Lady Bird Johnson to Lehman, July 25, 1955, LP, SF, Johnson; Humphrey to Allan Nevins, January 14, 1963, LP, SF, Nevins; Hubert Humphrey Oral History Transcript, III: 15, LBJL.

36. "Kilgore Calls Hearings on Immigration Laws," *WP*, September 12, 1955, p. 17; Lehman to Kilgore, August 4, 1955, and September 12, 1955, both in LP, SF, Kilgore; Lehman to Norman Thomas, November 17, 1955, LP, SF, Thomas; 101 *Cong. Rec.* 12284–12291 (July 30, 1955); "Refugee Act Revision Hope Lost," *WP*, August 2, 1955, p. 7; "President Duels with Democrats over His Program," *NYT*, June 30, 1955, pp. 1, 11; "The President's List," Editorial, *NYT*, July 3, 1955, E-6; "Immigration Straddle," Editorial, *WP*, September 14, 1955, p. 16; "Immigration Hearings," Editorial, *NYT*, September 20, 1955, p. 30; "Immigration Act Due for Minor Revisions," *NYT*, November 27, 1955, E-7.

37. "Changes in Aliens Law Unlikely, Lehman Avers," *WP*, November 23, 1955, p. 2; "Alien Act Change Called Unlikely," *NYT*, November 23, 1955, p. 12; "Scrap Alien Law, Senator Pleads," *NYT*, November 21, 1955, p. 29; "Eased Alien Law Urged at Hearing," *NYT*, November 22, 1955, pp. 1, 12; "Revising the M'Carran Act," Editorial, *NYT*, November 22, 1955, p. 34; Lehman to Chester Bowles, November 29, 1955, LP, SF, Bowles; "Hoffman Scores Quota on Aliens," *NYT*, December 1, 1955, p. 16; "Alien Law Scored by Gov. Williams," *NYT*, December 2, 1955, p. 12. These hearings were never printed, but Lehman later inserted his remarks in 102 *Cong. Rec.* 12442–12446 (July 12, 1956).

38. Lehman, Memorandum, November 26, 1955, LP, SF, Johnson; Lehman to G. Mennen Williams, November 23, 1955, LP, SF, Williams; "Alien Law Scored by Gov. Williams," *NYT*, December 2, 1955, p. 12. Hennings suffered from serious alcohol problems and was difficult to find when he was on a bender. See McPherson, *A Political Education*, p. 36; Douglas, *In the Fullness of Time*, p. 290; Anderson, *Confessions of a Muckraker*, pp. 256–260; Baker, *Wheeling and Dealing*, pp. 46, 64; Caro, *Master of the Senate*, pp. 509, 668. Kilgore had also been known to miss or almost miss a vote or two when he had too much to drink. See Tananbaum, *The Bricker Amendment Controversy*, pp. 179–180.

39. "Senate's Roll-Call Vote to Kill Veto of Alien Bill," *NYT*, June 28, 1952, p. 10; Johnson to Friend, Form Letter, February 21, 1956, Johnson Senate Papers, Box 266, Legislative Files, 1955–1956, McCarran-Walter Immigration; "Democrats Held Too Republican," *NYT*, June 6, 1955, p. 12; "Johnson Offers Legislative Plan," *NYT*,

November 21, 1955, p. 27; Baker to Lehman, November 29, 1955, and enclosed Speech of Senator Lyndon B. Johnson, November 21, 1955, LP, SF, Baker; Caro, *Master of the Senate*, pp. 647–648.

40. "Administration to Ask New Immigration Rules," *WP*, December 6, 1955, p. 11; "Text of President Eisenhower's Annual Message to Congress on the State of the Union," *NYT*, January 6, 1956, pp. 10–11; "Eisenhower Asks Civil Right [*sic*] Study," *NYT*, January 6, 1956, p. 13; "Lehman Charges Policy 'Fumbles,'" *NYT*, January 29, 1956, p. 75; "Inflexible Quotas," Editorial, *WP*, January 15, 1956, E-4; "State of the Union," Editorial, *NYT*, January 6, 1956, p. 22; "State of the Union," Editorial, *WP*, January 6, 1956, p. 24.

41. "President Urges Wide Law Change to Aid Immigrants," *NYT*, February 9, 1956, pp. 1, 14; "Ike Urges Letting in 65,000 More Aliens Yearly," *WP*, February 9, 1956, p. 2; "Message by the President Dealing with Immigration," *NYT*, February 9, 1956, p. 14; "Lehman Attacks Immigration Law," *NYT*, February 19, 1956, p. 57.

42. "President Urges Wide Law Change to Aid Immigrants," *NYT*, February 9, 1956, pp. 1, 14; "Ike Urges Letting in 65,000 More Aliens Yearly," *WP*, February 9, 1956, p. 2.

43. "Senator Kilgore, New Dealer, Dies," *NYT*, February 29, 1956, p. 31; "Immigration Act Due for Minor Revisions," *NYT*, November 27, 1955, E-7; "Eastland Slated for Kilgore Post," *NYT*, February 29, 1956, p. 15; "Important Kilgore Post Now Goes to Eastland," *WP*, February 29, 1956, p. 14; White, *The Citadel*, p. 192; Watson, *Lion in the Lobby*, pp. 338–339; "Rights Sold Out, Wilkins Charges," *NYT*, March 5, 1956, p. 16; Robert Spivack, "Watch on the Potomac," *Chicago Defender*, March 7, 1956, p. 4; Humphrey quoted in Thurber, *The Politics of Equality*, p. 275, n. 15; 102 *Cong. Rec.* 3814 (March 2, 1956); Clarence Mitchell, "1. Civil Rights Football," *The Nation*, July 7, 1956, p. 5; Caro, *Master of the Senate*, pp. 783–784; Sherrill, *Gothic Politics in the Deep South*, pp. 193–194; Asch, *The Senator and the Sharecropper*, pp. 155–156. On Neely's pliability, see Caro, *Master of the Senate*, pp. 497–499, 969–970.

44. Eastland Oral History Transcript, I: 3–4, LBJL; 102 *Cong. Rec.* 3814–3822 (March 2, 1956); "Eastland in Judiciary Post; Lehman and Morse Vote No," *NYT*, March 3, 1956, pp. 1, 9; Lehman to Charles Poletti, April 11, 1956, LP, SF, Poletti; Drew Pearson, "The Washington Merry-Go-Round: Morse Urged Not to Fight Eastland," *WP*, March 8, 1956, p. 31.

45. "McCarran Act Changes Sought," *WP*, May 21, 1956, p. 22; Gerald Siegel, "Reasons Why Senate Democratic Leadership Should Back Substantial Immigration Law Revisions in 1956," n.d., Johnson Senate Papers, Box 401, Office Files of Gerald Siegel, Immigration File, 84th Congress, 2/2, LBJL; "Brownell Seeks Wider Alien Law," *NYT*, April 14, 1956, pp. 1, 37; "Brownell Appears at Senate Hearings to Support Immigration Law Changes," *WP*, April 14, 1956, p. 15.

46. Memorandum, S.1794, "To Amend the Refugee Relief Act of 1953," April 13, 1956; Marked-up copy of S. 1794; and Memorandum, Siegel to Johnson, June 6, 1956, all in Johnson Senate Papers, Box 401, Office Files of Gerald Siegel, Immigration File, 84th Congress, 2/2; Julius Edelstein to Irving Engel, May 14, 1956, and Memorandum, Chas to J.C.C.E., May 3, 1956, both in LP, SF, Engel; U.S., Senate, Committee on the Judiciary, *Amending the Act of September 3, 1954*, S. Rept. 2226, 84th Cong., 2nd sess.,

June 13, 1956; Drew Pearson, "The Washington Merry-Go-Round: Stevenson to Add Negroes to Staff," *WP*, June 19, 1956, p. 39. On Johnson's general use of Siegel and the Policy Committee staff to draft compromises acceptable to all Democratic Senators, see Caro, *Master of the Senate*, p. 508.

47. 102 *Cong. Rec.* 10469 (June 18, 1956), 10630–10631 (June 20, 1956), 10805 (June 22, 1956), 13312–13313 (July 18, 1956); "Sheep and Goats," Editorial, *WP*, June 22, 1956, p. 22; "President Signs Foreign Aid Bill; . . . Alien Law Pushed," *NYT*, July 19, 1956, pp. 17. On the previous sheepherder bills, see "Basque Shepherds Prosper on U.S. Ranches," *NYT*, January 9, 1955, p. 79; Ybarra, *Washington Gone Crazy*, pp. 32–33, 465, 631–632, 750.

48. Lehman to Bowles, June 6, 1956, LP, SF, Bowles; "Eisenhower Lists 28 Priority Bills; Hopes for Action," *NYT*, May 25, 1956, pp. 1, 11; Memorandum, Siegel to Johnson, June 6, 1956, Johnson Senate Papers, Box 401, Office Files of Gerald Siegel, Immigration File, 84th Congress, 2/2; "Congress Faces Showdown on Easing of Alien Laws," *NYT*, July 8, 1956, pp. 1, 23. On quota deductions in previous laws, see 101 *Cong. Rec.* 12400–12401 (July 30, 1955).

49. 102 *Cong. Rec.* 10469 (June 18, 1956), 11523 (July 2, 1956), 12790 (July 16, 1956), 13901 (July 23, 1956), 14625 (July 26, 1956), 14999 (July 27, 1956); Siegel, Memorandum, June 25, 1956, Johnson Senate Papers, Box 401, Office Files of Gerald Siegel, Immigration File, 84th Congress, 2/2; "Compromise Offered on Immigration Law," *WP*, July 27, 1956, p. 16; Murrey Marder, "New Alien Law Lost in Rush to Adjourn," *WP*, August 1, 1956, p. 20. On Johnson's frequent use of unanimous consent agreements, see Caro, *Master of the Senate*, pp. 572–580.

50. 102 *Cong. Rec.* 14955–14996 (July 27, 1956); Edelstein to Irving Engel, July 31, 1956, LP, SF, Engel.

51. 102 *Cong. Rec.* 14997–15012 (July 27, 1956).

52. 102 *Cong. Rec.* 14999–15018 (July 27, 1956); "Immigration Bill Passed by Senate," *NYT*, July 28, 1956, p. 35; "New Alien Law Lost in Rush to Adjourn," *WP*, August 1, 1956, p. 20.

53. 102 *Cong. Rec.* 15100–15101 (July 27, 1956).

54. 102 *Cong. Rec.* 14852 (July 26, 1956)).

55. 102 *Cong. Rec.* 15505–15506 (July 27, 1956); "House Kills Alien Bill after Senate Approval," *WP*, July 28, 1956, p. 1; "Random Notes from Washington: Russell Rallies Johnson on Rights," *NYT*, July 30, 1956, p. 8; "New Alien Law Lost in Rush to Adjourn," *WP*, August 1, 1956, p. 20. On Arens, see "House Unit Names Director," *NYT*, May 2, 1956; Ybarra, *Washington Gone Crazy*, pp. 449–450, 479–480, 640–641, 643; Goodman, *The Committee*, pp. 382, 395–396, 399.

56. Edelstein to Irving Engel, July 31, 1956, LP, SF, Engel; Johnson to Lehman, August 4, 1956, LP, SF, Johnson.

57. "Johnson Offers Legislative Plan," *NYT*, November 22, 1955, p. 27. The poll tax was finally abolished in federal elections by the adoption of the 24th Amendment in 1964. See Lawson, *Black Ballots*, pp. 55–85; and Mann, *The Walls of Jericho*, pp. 320–322.

58. "Address by Hon. Herbert H. Lehman, of New York, at Civil Rights Rally of the Conference on Civil Rights," Extension of Remarks of Herbert H. Lehman, 102

Cong. Rec. 472–473 (January 12, 1956); "U.S. Bill of Rights Is Praised at 164," *NYT*, December 16, 1955, p. 33.

59. "Address by Hon. Herbert H. Lehman, of New York, at Civil Rights Rally of the Conference on Civil Rights," Extension of Remarks of Herbert H. Lehman, 102 *Cong. Rec.* 472–473 (January 12, 1956); "U.S. Bill of Rights Is Praised at 164," *NYT*, December 16, 1955, p. 33; Watson, *Lion in the Lobby*, pp. 299–300; "Bias Issue Blocks Reserve Program," *NYT*, May 20, 1955, pp. 1, 8; "Eisenhower Urges Senate to Salvage Reserves Plan," *NYT*, June 9, 1955, pp. 1, 17; Johnson quoted in Caro, *Master of the Senate*, pp. 600–601; N.A.A.C.P. Insists Bias in Guard End," *NYT*, June 28, 1955, p. 14; "Kill Compromise; Powell Halts Reserve Bill Again," *Chicago Defender*, July 2, 1955, p. 7; "Reserve Program Is Voted in House; Bias Rider Loses," *NYT*, July 2, 1955, pp. 1, 6; "Kill Powell Amendment In Congress," *Chicago Defender*, July 9, 1955, pp. 1, 2; 101 *Cong. Rec.* 10518–10524 (July 14, 1955); "New Reserve Bill Passed by Senate," *NYT*, July 15, 1955, pp. 1, 8; Harry McPherson Oral History Transcript, VI: 8, LBJL; Haygood, *King of the Cats*, pp. 134, 207–208; Hamilton, *Adam Clayton Powell, Jr.*, pp. 224–227.

60. "Address by Hon. Herbert H. Lehman, of New York, at Civil Rights Rally of the Conference on Civil Rights," Extension of Remarks of Herbert H. Lehman, 102 *Cong. Rec.* 472–473 (January 12, 1956); Roy Wilkins Oral History Transcript, HHLP, CUOHC, pp. 10–12; HHLOH, pp. 783–785; Wilkins to Lehman, January 24, 1956, LP, SF, Wilkins; 102 *Cong. Rec.* 7053 (April 26, 1956), 10158–10160 (June 13, 1956), 10907–10910 (June 25, 1956); "Lehman to Offer School Bill Rider," *NYT*, June 26, 1956, p. 24; "School Bill Fight Starts in House," *NYT*, January 25, 1956, p. 32; "Powell to Press School-Aid Rider," *NYT*, February 17, 1956, p. 46; "Powell Sees Plot to Kill Bias Plan," *NYT*, May 4, 1956, p. 14; "School Aid First," Editorial, *NYT*, May 6, 1956, E-8; "ADA Criticizes Ike, Democrats," *WP*, May 13, 1956, A-19; "Eisenhower Asks Speed on Schools," *NYT*, May 15, 1956, p. 32; "House Vote Bars Funds to Schools Maintaining Bias," *NYT*, July 4, 1956, pp. 1, 12; "House Vote Kills School Aid Funds for This Session," *NYT*, July 6, 1956, pp. 1, 14; "The School Aid Failure," *NYT*, July 6, 1956, p. 15; "Powell Wins; Bill KO'D," *Chicago Defender*, July 14, 1956, pp. 1, 2; Eisenhower, *Mandate for Change*, p. 552; Haygood, *King of the Cats*, pp. 208–212; Hamilton, *Adam Clayton Powell, Jr.*, pp. 227–235; Watson, *Lion in the Lobby*, pp. 300–316; Burk, *The Eisenhower Administration and Black Civil Rights*, pp. 149–150, 157–159, 164; Anderson, *Eisenhower, Brownell, and the Congress*, pp. 72–81; Hamilton, *Lister Hill*, pp. 214–219.

61. 102 *Cong. Rec.* 4459–4461 (March 12, 1956); "96 in Congress Open Drive to Upset Integration Ruling," *NYT*, March 12, 1956, pp. 1, 19; "Manifesto Splits Democrats Again," *NYT*, March 13, 1956, pp. 1, 14; Hays, *A Southern Moderate Speaks*, pp. 86–96; Finley, *Delaying the Dream*, pp. 138–147; Badger, "The South Confronts the Court."

62. "96 in Congress Open Drive to Upset Integration Ruling," *NYT*, March 12, 1956, pp. 1, 19; "Manifesto Splits Democrats Again," *NYT*, March 13, 1956, pp. 1, 14; Caro, *Master of the Senate*, pp. 785–789; Dallek, *Lone Star Rising*, pp. 496–497; Finley, *Delaying the Dream*, p. 150. The only other Southern Senators not to sign the Manifesto were Tennessee Democrats Estes Kefauver and Albert Gore, who chose not

to sign it partly out of conviction and partly because of their political ambitions. See Finley, *Delaying the Dream*, pp. 148–149.

63. 102 *Cong. Rec.* 4939–4940 (March 16, 1956); "President Scored on Racial Stand," *NYT*, March 17, 1956, pp. 1, 10; Lehman to Clifford Durr, April 18, 1956, LP, SF, Durr.

64. 102 *Cong. Rec.* 4939–4941 (March 16, 1956). On Eisenhower's calls for moderation, see "Eisenhower Asks for 'Moderation' on Segregation," *NYT*, March 15, 1956, pp. 1, 16; "The Transcript of Eisenhower's News Conference on Foreign and Domestic Issues," *NYT*, March 15, 1956, p. 16; Ambrose, *Eisenhower: The President*, pp. 304–307. For more criticism of such calls for moderation, see Carey McWilliams, "The Heart of the Matter," *The Nation*, March 31, 1956, pp. 249–250.

65. "President Offers Civil Rights Plan," *NYT*, April 10, 1956, pp. 1, 20; "Text of Civil Rights Program," *NYT*, April 10, 1956, p. 20; "Ike Rights Plan to Congress," *Chicago Defender*, April 10, 1956, p. 1; "Democrats Map Strategy to Win Passage of Own Civil Rights Bills," *WP*, April 11, 1956, pp. 1, 11; "Brownell's Rights Plan Attacked by Hennings," *WP*, April 13, 1956, p. 26; Drew Pearson, "Washington Merry-Go-Round: A Grueling Session for Brownell," *WP*, June 3, 1956, E-5; Joseph and Stewart Alsop, "Lyndon Gave Adlai Nicest Gift Yet," *WP*, July 29, 1956, E-5; Anderson, *Eisenhower, Brownell, and the Congress*, pp. 14–46; Burk, *The Eisenhower Administration and Black Civil Rights*, pp. 208–216.

66. Murrey Marder, "House Votes Civil Rights Bill, 279–126," *WP*, July 24, 1956, pp. 1, 11; "Civil Rights Bill Passes House; Faces Senate Doom," *Chicago Defender*, July 24, 1956, p. 2; Anderson, *Eisenhower, Brownell, and the Congress*, pp. 40–41, 48, 57–59, 62–63, 66–72, 81–99; Burk, *The Eisenhower Administration and Black Civil Rights*, pp. 215–217.

67. "Rights Bills Put to Eastland Unit," *NYT*, March 4, 1956, p. 83; "N.A.A.C.P. in Protest," *NYT*, June 9, 1956, p. 13; 102 *Cong. Rec.* 12439–12441 (July 12, 1956); "Lehman Scores Rights Bill Delay," *WP*, July 13, 1956, p. 21; Memorandum, Frances Williams to Senator Lehman and Julius Edelstein, June 13, 1956; Lehman to Eastland, June 19, 1956; July 11, 1956; July 12, 1956; and July 12, 1956, all in LP, SF, Eastland; "Rights Manifesto Is Sent to House," *NYT*, July 14, 1956, p. 13; "Senate Hits Snag over Civil Rights," *NYT*, July 18, 1956, p. 17.

68. Caro, *Master of the Senate*, pp. 761–792; Dallek, *Lone Star Rising*, p. 497; Woods, *LBJ*, pp. 304–305; Finley, *Delaying the Dream*, pp. 154–155; Boyle, *The UAW and the Heyday of American Liberalism*, p. 123. On the Emmett Till case, see Whitfield, *A Death in the Delta*.

69. "Cross Is Set Ablaze at Warren's Home," *NYT*, July 15, 1956, pp. 1, 37. On Sobeloff's role in the *Brown* case, see "Arguments Ended on Desegregation," *NYT*, April 15, 1955, pp. 1, 12.

70. Douglas to Lehman, July 12, 1956, LP, SF, Douglas; Douglas, *In the Fullness of Time*, p. 281; Caro, *Master of the Senate*, pp. 792–795.

71. Douglas, *In the Fullness of Time*, pp. 281–282; Miller, *Lyndon*, p. 191; 102 *Cong. Rec.* 13937 (July 23, 1956); Caro, *Master of the Senate*, pp. 792–796; Finley, *Delaying the Dream*, pp. 155–156; Steinberg, *Sam Johnson's Boy*, pp. 435–436; Hamilton, *Lister Hill*, pp. 219–220; Dallek, *Lone Star Rising*, p. 498; "House Votes Civil Rights

Bill, 279–126," *WP*, July 24, 1956, pp. 1, 11; "Civil Rights Bill Passed in House by 279–126 Vote," *NYT*, July 24, 1956, pp. 1, 12. Hennings's frequent absenteeism was the result of his alcoholism. See n. 38 in this chapter.

72. 102 *Cong. Rec.* 13996 (July 23, 1956); Douglas, *In the Fullness of Time*, p. 282; Caro, *Master of the Senate*, pp. 796–797; "Civil Rights Measure Suffers Senate Setback," *WP*, July 25, 1956, p. 11.

73. 102 *Cong. Rec.* 14160–14163 (July 24, 1956); "Civil Rights Measure Suffers Senate Setback," *WP*, July 25, 1956, p. 11; "Civil Rights Debate Is Blocked in Senate," *NYT*, July 25, 1956, pp. 1, 21; Caro, *Master of the Senate*, p. 797; Anderson, *Eisenhower, Brownell, and the Congress*, pp. 101–103.

74. 102 *Cong. Rec.* 14171–14172, 14191, 14194, 14198, 14201–14203, 14205, 14207, 14210, 14212, 14214, 14216 (July 24, 1956); "Hope Fades for Civil Rights Bill Passage," *Chicago Defender*, July 26, 1956, p. 5; "Civil Rights Measure Suffers Senate Setback," *WP*, July 25, 1956, p. 11; Anderson, *Eisenhower, Brownell, and the Congress*, pp. 103–104.

75. 102 *Cong. Rec.* 14228–14229 (July 24, 1956); "Civil Rights Measure Suffers Senate Setback," *WP*, July 25, 1956, p. 11; Douglas, *In the Fullness of Time*, pp. 282–283; Caro, *Master of the Senate*, 798–799; Watson, *Lion in the Lobby*, p. 346; Thurber, *The Politics of Equality*, pp. 97, 276, n. 18.

76. Douglas to Lehman, July 24, 1956, and Lehman to Douglas, July 30, 1956, both in LP, SF, Douglas; Douglas, *In the Fullness of Time*, p. 283.

77. 102 *Cong. Rec.* 14323–14325 (July 25, 1956); "Rights Backers Concede Defeat," *WP*, July 26, 1956, p. 6.

78. 102 *Cong. Rec.* 14744, 14753 (July 26, 1956), 14937 (July 27, 1956); "Senate Gives Civil Rights 'No Hope' Sign," *Chicago Defender*, July 30, 1956, p. 8; "House Approves 3.7 Billion in Aid," *NYT*, July 27, 1956, pp. 1, 41; "84th Congress Adjourns in Spirit of Compromise; House Quits at 11:56 p.m. and Senate at Midnight," *WP*, July 28, 1956, pp. 1, 13; "Civil Rights Measure Suffers Senate Setback," *WP*, July 25, 1956, p. 11.

Chapter 17. "A Symbol of Courage and Conscience in Public Affairs": Herbert Lehman and the Election of 1956

1. "Text of the Announcement by Lehman," *NYT*, August 22, 1956, p. 20.

2. Lehman to Robert G. A. Jackson, December 4, 1952, LP, SF, Jackson; Lehman to Stevenson, November 6, 1952, and November 7, 1952, both in LP, SF, Stevenson.

3. Text of Stevenson's Address on His Party's New Role in Nation," *NYT*, February 15, 1953, p. 67; "Adlai Assails Use of 'Big Stick' on Allies, Says 'Big Deal' May Replace New Deal," *WP*, February 15, 1953, pp. 1, 4.

4. "Stevenson Sees Errors by Rivals Aiding Democrats," *NYT*, October 27, 1954, pp. 1, 22; Julius Edelstein to Lehman, August 27, 1954, September 3, 1954, September 4, 1954, September 11, 1954, and September 16, 1954, all in LP, SF, Edelstein; "Wagner, Lehman Confer in Capital," *NYT*, August 18, 1954, p. 17; "Democrat Chiefs Choose Harriman," *NYT*, September 9, 1954, p. 26; "Roosevelt Silent about Fight on Floor against Harriman," *NYT*, September 10, 1954, pp. 1, 15; "Text of Statements Backing

Harriman," *NYT*, September 10, 1954, p. 15; Lehman to Robert G. A. Jackson, September 30, 1954, and to Mrs. Jackson, November 15, 1954, LP, SF, Jackson; "Harriman Sets Up Democratic Goal," *NYT*, January 15, 1955, p. 8; "Lehman Prefers Stevenson," *NYT*, May 22, 1955, p. 45; "Harriman Urges Race by Lehman," *NYT*, April 22, 1955, pp. 1, 12; "Harriman Spurns 2D Place in 1956," *NYT*, August 6, 1955, p. 7; Julius Edelstein Oral History Transcript, HHLP, CUOHC, p. 23; Sulzberger, *A Long Row of Candles*, p. 1024; Abramson, *Spanning the Century*, pp. 504–515, 532–535; Moscow, *The Last of the Big-Time Bosses*, pp. 123–130.

    5. "Harriman Backed in '56 by New Head of Party in State," *NYT*, July 7, 1955, pp. 1, 13; "De Sapio Queried on Ticket for '56," *NYT*, July 25, 1955, p. 11; "Harriman Guest of Lehman Here," *NYT*, August 9, 1955, p. 17; Stevenson to Mrs. Eugene Meyer, August 12, 1955, in Johnson, ed., *The Papers of Adlai E. Stevenson*, IV: 544–545; "Lehman Off to Europe," *NYT*, August 11, 1955, p. 4.

    6. "Harriman Ready to Compete in '56, Adviser Declares," *NYT*, September 20, 1955, pp. 1, 22; Eric Sevareid, "CBS News Analysis," September 20, 1955, LP, SF, Stevenson; "Backers Envision Gain by Harriman," *NYT*, September 26, 1955, p. 16; "Outlook for Conventions," *NYT*, September 26, 1955, p. 17; "Truman Praises Harriman, but Hedges on '56 Choice," *NYT*, October 9, 1955, pp. 1, 74; "Harriman Denies a Pledge to Back Stevenson in 1956," *NYT*, October 10, 1955, pp. 1, 18; Martin, *Adlai Stevenson and the World*, pp. 214–216; Ambrose, *Eisenhower: The President*, pp. 270–273.

    7. Stevenson to Mrs. Eugene Meyer, August 8, 1955, in Johnson ed., *The Papers of Adlai E. Stevenson*, IV: 544–545; Martin, *Adlai Stevenson and the World*, pp. 215–216, 219–220; Stevenson to Lehman, October 19, 1955, LP, SF, Stevenson; "Stevenson Pays Visit to Lehman," *NYT*, October 19, 1955, p. 25; "Democratic Chiefs Face Possible Split in N.Y.," *WP*, October 20, 1955, p. 2.

    8. Julius Edelstein Oral History Transcript, HHLP, CUOHC, pp. 23–24; "Lehman Backs Stevenson; Blow to Harriman Is Seen," *NYT*, October 21, 1955, pp. 1, 16; "Adlai Drops a Big Tip: He's Going to Run," *Chicago Tribune*, October 21, 1955, p. 1.

    9. Stevenson to Lehman, October 20, 1955, LP, SF, Stevenson; "Adlai Drops a Big Tip: He's Going to Run," *Chicago Tribune*, October 21, 1955, p. 1; "Lehman Backs Stevenson; Blow to Harriman Is Seen," *NYT*, October 21, 1955, pp. 1, 16; "Stevenson and Harriman," *NYT*, October 23, 1955, E-1; Martin, *Adlai Stevenson and the World*, pp. 219–220; "Stevenson Move Stresses State Democratic Division," *NYT*, November 16, 1955, pp. 1, 24; "De Sapio Expects Solid Delegation," *NYT*, November 18, 1955, p. 16; "State Democrats to Back Harriman by 91 of 98 Votes," *NYT*, June 20, 1956, pp. 1, 17; "Mayor and Lehman Win New Convention Seats," *NYT*, August 15, 1956, p. 16; Anna Rosenberg Oral History Transcript, HHLP, CUOHC, p. 13; Drew Pearson, "The Washington Merry-Go-Round: Texas Gas Figure Assists Johnson . . . Democratic Scars," *WP*, August 17, 1956, p. 55.

    10. Robert Spivack, "Watch on the Potomac," *Chicago Defender*, February 13, 1956, p. 4; Martin, *Adlai Stevenson and the World*, pp. 257–259, 267; "Adlai Favors Desegregation, but Gradually," *Chicago Tribune*, February 8, 1956, p. 3; "Bayonets Not Answer to Bias, Stevenson Says," *Los Angeles Times*, February 8, 1956, p. 2; "Adlai Offers Integration Target Date," *WP*, February 8, 1956, p. 2; "Stevenson Backs 'Gradual' Moves for Integration," *NYT*, February 8, 1956, pp. 1, 22. On the racial atmosphere

at this time, see William Bradford Huie, "The Shocking Story of Approved Killing in Mississippi," *Look*, January 24, 1956, pp. 46–49; "Negro Coed Is Suspended to Curb Alabama Clashes," *NYT*, February 7, 1956, pp. 1, 25; Walter Lippmann, "Today and Tomorrow: The Miss Lucy Case," *WP*, February 9, 1956, p. 15; Clark, *The Schoolhouse Door*; Whitfield, *A Death in the Delta*; and Caro, *Master of the Senate*, pp. 761–771. For a more sympathetic account of Stevenson's position on civil rights during the 1956 campaign written by a longtime friend and associate, see Brown, *Conscience in Politics*, pp. 89–111.

11. "Stevenson Backs 'Gradual' Moves for Integration," *NYT*, February 8, 1956, pp. 1, 22; Martin, *Adlai Stevenson and the World*, pp. 259–260, 264; Lehman to Stevenson, February 11, 1956, LP, SF, Stevenson.

12. Lehman to Stevenson, February 11, 1956, LP, SF, Stevenson. Lehman's concern about "gradualism" in civil rights would be echoed seven years later by Martin Luther King, Jr., in his famous Letter from the Birmingham Jail and in his book about the crisis in Birmingham, which he titled *Why We Can't Wait*. See Branch, *Parting the Waters*, pp. 737–745, 804; and King, *Why We Can't Wait*.

13. Lehman to Stevenson, February 11, 1956, LP, SF, Stevenson.

14. Lehman to Stevenson, February 11, 1956, LP, SF, Stevenson.

15. Stevenson to Bernard Sokol, President, The Decalogue Society of Lawyers, February 18, 1956, and Stevenson to Herbert Lehman, February 20, 1956, both in LP, SF, Stevenson; Stevenson to Mrs. Eugene Meyer, February 20, 1956, in Johnson, ed., *The Papers of Adlai Stevenson*, VI: 69–71; Martin, *Adlai Stevenson and the World*, pp. 262–268; Lazarowitz, *Years in Exile*, pp. 101–102; "Stevenson Urges Candidates Ban Integration Issue," *NYT*, February 13, 1956, pp. 1, 15; "Comments by Harriman and Stevenson on Integration," *NYT*, February 13, 1956, p. 14.

16. Entry for February 26, 1956, in Schlesinger, *Journals, 1952–1960*, pp. 41–42; Johnson, ed., *The Papers of Adlai E. Stevenson*, VI: 77–78; "Stevenson Gibes at the President as Inept 'Coach,'" *NYT*, February 26, 1956, pp. 1, 65; "Excerpts from Address by Stevenson," *NYT*, February 26, 1956, p. 64; "Civil Rights and Civil Liberties," Extension of Remarks of Hon. Herbert H. Lehman, 102 *Cong. Rec.* A2206–2208 (March 12, 1956); "Stevenson Calls on North to Drop Own Color Lines," *NYT*, March 3, 1956, pp. 1, 10; Martin, *Adlai Stevenson and the World*, pp. 268–272.

17. Finletter to Lehman, February 7, 1956; March 16, 1956; March 23, 1956; and April 26, 1956; all in LP, SF, Finletter; Stevenson to Lehman, March 26, 1956, and April 27, 1956, both in LP, SF, Stevenson; "Kefauver Arrives with Boost for Home Rule," *WP*, April 23, 1956, pp. 1, 21; "Stevenson Says President Shirks Duty on Integration," *NYT*, April 26, 1956, pp. 1, 18; "Stevenson Sees Harriman In Race," *NYT*, April 27, 1956, p. 20; Martin, *Adlai Stevenson and the World*, pp. 276–316; Thomson and Shattuck, *The 1956 Presidential Campaign*, pp. 37–45.

18. Lehman to De Sapio, June 18, 1956, LP, SF, De Sapio; "Democrats Pick Delegates Today," *NYT*, June 19, 1956, p. 18; "Lehman Step Raises Some Doubt about Race for New Senate Term," *NYT*, July 10, 1956, pp. 1, 22; "Senator Lehman Is Undecided on Whether He'll Run," *WP*, July 11, 1956, p. 2; Drew Pearson, "The Washington Merry-Go-Round: Rooney Knows What 'Cats' Can Do," *WP*, July 29, 1956, E-5; Stewart Alsop, "But It's Only a Dream–So Far," *WP*, June 17, 1956, E-5; Abramson, *Spanning the Century*, pp. 533–542.

19. "Stevenson Expected to Win 3 More Favorite-Son Blocs," *NYT*, August 4, 1956, pp. 1, 34; "Stevenson Stirs Southerners' Ire on Rights Plank," *NYT*, August 8, 1956, pp. 1, 10; "Lehman Endorses Firm Rights Plank," *NYT*, August 10, 1956, p. 8; Martin, *Civil Rights and the Crisis of American Liberalism*, p. 148; Thomson and Shattuck, *The 1956 Presidential Campaign*, pp. 106, 127–129; "South Mollified on 'Rights' Issue," *NYT*, August 9, 1956, p. 16; "Stevenson's Move Left," *NYT*, August 9, 1956, p. 16; "Both Factions Fear Vote Loss on Civil Rights," *Chicago Tribune*, August 11, 1956, p. 2; "Proposed Plank on Rights Avoids Citing Court Ruling," *NYT*, August 11, 1956, pp. 1, 6; Anderson, *Eisenhower, Brownell, and the Congress*, p. 116.

20. "Proposed Plank on Rights Avoids Citing Court Ruling," *NYT*, August 11, 1956, pp. 1, 6; "Fight on Floor Is Threatened on Civil Rights," *Chicago Tribune*, August 13, 1956, p. 4; "Notes of Interview with Representative Emanuel Celler," July 1957, HHLP, CUOHC, pp. 3–4; Eleanor Roosevelt Oral History Transcript, HHLP, CUOHC, pp. 16–17; Hubert Humphrey Oral History Transcript, HHLP, CUOHC, pp. 14–16; Paul Douglas Oral History Transcript, HHLP, CUOHC, pp. 4–5; Anderson, *Eisenhower, Brownell, and the Congress*, pp. 115–116; "Liberals and Conservatives Near an Agreement on Moderate Civil Rights Platform," *NYT*, August 13, 1956, pp. 12; Thomson and Shattuck, *The 1956 Presidential Campaign*, pp. 135–136; Gillon, *Politics and Vision*, p. 101; Scharf, *Eleanor Roosevelt*, pp. 162–163.

21. "Proposed Plank on Rights Avoids Citing Court Ruling," *NYT*, August 11, 1956, pp. 1, 6; "Liberals and Conservatives Near an Agreement on Moderate Civil Rights Platform," *NYT*, August 13, 1956, p. 12; "Fight on Floor Is Threatened on Civil Rights," *Chicago Tribune*, August 13, 1956, p. 4; "Civil Rights Compromise Voted; Northerners Lose Floor Fight; Debate Is Bitter," *NYT*, August 16, 1956, pp. 1, 11; "Civil Rights Plank Wins Adoption," *Los Angeles Times*, August 16, 1956, pp. 1, A, 2; "Dems to Pick Adlai Today; Adopt Majority Plank on Civil Rights; Post-Midnight Battle Climaxes Long Session," *Chicago Tribune*, August 16, 1956, pp. 1, 11; "Liberals Beaten in Floor Fight to Put Teeth into Party's Civil Rights Plank," *New York Post*, August 16, 1956, pp. 3, 42; "Lehman Plea for 'Soul' of Party Set the Tone," *New York Post*, August 16, 1956, p. 42; "A Bad Night for Democrats," Editorial, *New York Post*, August 16, 1956, p. 29; Lehman to Carolin Flexner, August 25, 1956, LP, SF, Flexner; Hays, *A Southern Moderate Speaks*, pp. 101–124; Anderson, *Eisenhower, Brownell and the Congress*, pp. 117–118; Martin, *Civil Rights and the Crisis of American Liberalism*, pp. 150–152; Gillon, *Politics and Vision*, pp. 100–101; Boyle, *The UAW and the Heyday of American Liberalism*, p. 125; Thomson and Shattuck, *The 1956 Presidential Campaign*, pp. 146–149; Porter and Johnson, comps., *National Party Platforms*, pp. 541–542.

22. Harriman to Lehman, July 18, 1956, LP, SF, Harriman; Stewart Alsop, "But It's Only a Dream—So Far," *WP*, June 17, 1956, E-5; "Governor in Race to 'Last Ballot,'" *NYT*, August 1, 1956, pp. 1, 13; "Kefauver Backed for Second Place by His Delegates," *NYT*, August 2, 1956, pp. 1, 12; "Mrs. Roosevelt Aids Stevenson," *NYT*, August 3, 1956, p. 6; "Rosenman Hails Harriman Stand," *NYT*, August 4, 1956, p. 23; Walter Lippmann, "Today and Tomorrow: The Platform and Segregation," *WP*, August 15, 1956, p. 23.

23. "Adlai Thinks Truman Will Stay Neutral," *Chicago Tribune*, August 11, 1956, pp. 1, 3; "Truman Revels in the Suspense," *NYT*, August 12, 1956, p. 60; Leonard Lyons, "Lyons Den," *New York Post*, August 16, 1956, p. 28; Lazarowitz, *Years in Exile*, p.

110; "Truman Backs Harriman on Basis of Experience; Stevenson Is Confident, Johnson in Race," *NYT*, August 12, 1956, pp. 1, 60; "Bowles Helped Win Votes of Williams," *NYT*, August 17, 1956, p. 7; Thomas and Shattuck, *The 1956 Presidential Campaign*, pp. 130–132. The others who appeared on television to demonstrate their continuing support for Stevenson were Senator Humphrey, Senator Sparkman, Governor George Leader of Pennsylvania, Governor Luther Hodges of North Carolina, Democratic National Committeeman Paul Ziffren of California, and public opinion researcher Elmo Roper. See "Seven Democrats on TV Disagree with Truman," *NYT*, August 12, 1956, p. 60.

24. "Virginians Back Johnson of Texas," *NYT*, April 22, 1956, p. 56; "Stevenson Rated as 'Top Candidate,' " *NYT*, October 13, 1955, p. 20; "Johnson Seeking Coalition to Give South Key to '56," *NYT*, October 18, 1955, pp. 1, 41; Arthur Krock, "In the Nation: Maneuvers for Position in the Political Derby," *NYT*, October 28, 1955, p. 24; "Democrats Warm Up," *NYT*, October 30, 1955, E-2; "Stevenson Plans Minnesota Test in March 20 Vote," *NYT*, November 17, 1955, pp. 1, 24; "A Johnson Boom Starts in South," *NYT*, March 12, 1956, pp. 1, 12; "Young Man in a Hurry," *NYT*, March 12, 1956, p. 12; "Kefauver Victory Points to Open Democratic Race; Stevenson to Press Drive; Picture Confused," *NYT*, March 22, 1956, pp. 1, 25; "Now the Dark Horses Are Running," *NYT*, March 25, 1956, E-5; "Dispute in Texas Tests Democrats," *NYT*, March 29, 1956, p. 14; "Johnson Sets Out to Crush Revolt," *NYT*, April 11, 1956, p. 26; "Johnson's Boom Pushed in Texas," *NYT*, May 23, 1956, pp. 1, 32; "Texas Senator Backed," *NYT*, June 30, 1956, p. 9; "They Like Adlai—Except on One Issue," *WP*, May 27, 1956, E-2; George Sokolsky, "These Days: Practical Politics," *WP*, May 30, 1956, p. 25; Caro, *Master of the Senate*, pp. 640–649, 782–804; Dallek, *Lone Star Rising*, pp. 489–502.

25. "Truman Backs Harriman on Basis of Experience; Stevenson Is Confident, Johnson in Race," *NYT*, August 12, 1956, pp. 1, 60; William S. White, "Johnson Neutral as Leading Candidates Court His Favor in Nomination Struggle," *NYT*, August 14, 1956, p. 13; Alfred Friendly, "Truman's Action Puts Johnson in Key Spot," *WP*, August 12, 1956, A-8; Holmes Alexander, "Lone Star of Texas," *Los Angeles Times*, August 13, 1956, B-5; "Sam Rayburn Backs Johnson for President," *WP*, August 12, 1956, A-8; "Byrd Reported Urging Johnson on 1st Ballot," *WP*, August 13, 1956, p. 3; "Stew a la Democrat: Chef Truman's Harriman Soufflé Goes Awry as Convention Opens," *Wall Street Journal*, August 13, 1956, pp. 1, 6; Robert Spivack, "Watch on the Potomac," *Chicago Defender*, August 15, 1956, p. 4; Caro, *Master of the Senate*, pp. 801–830.

26. Thomson and Shattuck, *The 1956 Presidential Campaign*, p. 150; Martin, *Adlai Stevenson and the World*, p. 349; "Remarks of Senator Herbert H. Lehman Seconding the Nomination of Adlai Stevenson, National Democratic Convention, Chicago, Illinois, August 16, 1956," LP, SF, Stevenson.

27. Lehman to Carolin Flexner, August 25, 1956, LP, SF, Flexner; Lehman to Mrs. Roy Wilkins, August 22, 1956, LP, SF, Wilkins.

28. "Stevenson, Here, Charges Rival Risks Loss of Allies," *NYT*, November 1, 1952, pp. 1, 14; "Jewish Educators in Lehman Tribute," *NYT*, December 13, 1953, p. 50; Lehman to Powell, December 21, 1953, LP, SF, Powell; Edelstein to Morris Novik, January 6, 1954, LP, SF, Edelstein.

29. Burlingham to Lehman, January 4, 1955, and Lehman to Burlingham, January 6, 1955, LP, SF, Burlingham; Poletti to Lehman, March 25, 1955, LP, SF, Poletti; "Harriman Urges Race by Lehman," *NYT*, April 22, 1955, pp. 1, 12.

30. Lee Mortimer, "New York Confidential," *New York Daily Mirror*, August 24, 1955, copy enclosed with Frank Altschul to Lehman, August 26, 1955; and Lehman to Altschul, August 29, 1955, all in LP, SF, Frank and Helen Altschul. Lehman was referring to *U.S.A. Confidential*, which Mortimer had co-authored with Jack Lait in 1952. Shortly after the book's publication, Senator Margaret Chase Smith and Representative Augustine Kelley (D-PA) both sued Mortimer and Lait for libel and eventually won apologies and retractions, court costs, and legal fees. See " 'Confidential' Authors Sued by Sen. Smith," *WP*, May 8, 1952, p. 3; "Reply to Suit Renews Attack on Sen. Smith," *Chicago Tribune*, October 16, 1952, A-6; "Senator M. C. Smith Heard in Libel Suit," *NYT*, February 7, 1954, p. 57; "School for Scandal," Editorial, *WP*, October 23, 1956, A-12; "Libel Suit Settled," *NYT*, January 29, 1957, p. 15. On the virulent anti-Communism of the *Daily Mirror*, see Nasaw, *The Chief*, pp. 596–597.

31. George Sokolsky, "These Days: The Woods Are Full," *WP*, October 27, 1955, p. 17; "Wagner 'Hopeful' of Running for Mayor in 1957," *NYT*, December 8, 1955, pp. 1, 42; "Leader in Bronx Chides Stevenson," *NYT*, May 4, 1956, p. 15; Moscow, *What Have You Done for Me Lately?* p. 184; Moscow, *The Last of the Big-Time Bosses*, pp. 106–130.

32. "G.O.P. Sights Set on Senate Seats," *NYT*, November 5, 1955, p. 12; "Javits Hints Entry into Senate Contest," *NYT*, December 19, 1955, pp. 1, 16; "Control of Senate in 1957 Hangs on Election Results in 16 States," *WP*, December 27, 1955, p. 2; "Javits Raps Stevenson on Rights Stand," *Chicago Defender*, February 13, 1956, p. 18; Robert Spivack, "Watch on the Potomac," *Chicago Defender*, March 7, 1956, p. 4, and July 18, 1956, p. 4; Stewart Alsop, "Matter of Fact: Democratic Disarray," *WP*, March 26, 1956, p. 17; "G.O.P. Maps Drive for Negro Votes," *NYT*, June 4, 1956, pp. 1, 18; "Fewer Negro Democratic Votes Seen," *WP*, June 4, 1956, p. 2; "NAACP's Speakers Bid for Votes in November," *WP*, July 1, 1956, B-6; George Sokolsky, "These Days: Stevenson vs. Harriman," *WP*, July 5, 1956, p. 5; Sokolsky, "These Days: The Problem Faces Us," *WP*, August 21, 1956, p. 15; Javits, *Javits*, pp. 91–113, 132–153, 189–219. The other two Democratic Senators targeted by Hall were Warren Magnuson of Washington and Wayne Morse of Oregon.

33. "Lehman Belittles 'Liberals' in G.O.P.," *NYT*, February 4, 1956, pp. 1, 20; "Leader in Bronx Chides Stevenson," *NYT*, May 4, 1956, p. 15.

34. Arthur Corscadden to Mrs. Lehman, March 4, 1956, and Herbert Lehman to Corscadden, March 10, 1956, both in LP, SF, Corscadden; Lehman to Poletti, May 30, 1956, LP, SF, Poletti.

35. 102 *Cong. Rec.* 10805 (June 22, 1956).

36. "Democrats Pick Delegates Today," *NYT*, June 19, 1956, p. 18; "Lehman Step Raises Some Doubt about Race for New Senate Term," *NYT*, July 10, 1956, pp. 1, 22; Lehman to Arthur Corscadden, July 2, 1956, LP, SF, Corscadden.

37. "Lehman Step Raises Some Doubt about Race for New Senate Term," *NYT*, July 10, 1956, pp. 1, 22.

38. Stevenson to Lehman, July 21, 1956, and Lehman to Stevenson, July 31, 1956, both in LP, SF, Stevenson; Lehman to Thomas Finletter, July 3, 1956, LP, SF, Finletter; "Congress Turns Now to Electorate's Votes," *NYT*, July 29, 1956, E-6; "Alfange Making G.O.P. Senate Bid," *NYT*, August 6, 1956, pp. 1, 12; Leonard Lyons, "Lyons Den," *New York Post*, August 20, 1956, p. 28.

39. Irving Engle to Lehman, August 30, 1956, LP, SF, Engle; Drew Pearson to Lehman, September 20, 1956, Pearson Papers, G237, 2 of 3, Lehman, LBJL; "Lehman Still Is Undecided on Whether He Will Seek Another Senate Term," *NYT*, August 18, 1956, p. 9.

40. "Lehman Won't Run Again; Urges Wagner for Senate," *NYT*, August 22, 1956, pp. 1, 20; "Text of the Announcement by Lehman," *NYT*, August 22, 1956, p. 20; "Fete for Lehman Aids Candidates," *NYT*, September 22, 1956, p. 12; Irwin Ross, "Where Do Liberals Go from Here?" *New York Post*, December 23, 1956, pp. 4, 10; Julius Edelstein Oral History Transcript, HHLP, CUOHC, p. 27

41. "Leaders to Urge Lehman Run Again," *New York Post*, August 22, 1956, pp. 2, 13; "To Herbert Lehman," Editorial, *New York Post*, August 22, 1956, p. 47; "Lehman Firm on Decision to Retire," *New York Post*, August 23, 1956, p. 2.

42. Handwritten note on Press Release, "Statement by Senator Herbert H. Lehman regarding his candidacy for re-election to the United States Senate," August 22, 1956, LP, SF, Frank Altschul; Hubert Humphrey Oral History Transcript, HHLP, CUOHC, p. 25; "Notes of an Interview with Representative Emanuel Celler, July 1957, HHLP, CUOHC, p. 4; "Lehman's Wife Sad but Satisfied, Too," *NYT*, August 22, 1956, p. 20.

43. Johnson to Lehman, August 4, 1956, LP, SF, Johnson; Lehman to Rosenman, August 30, 1956, LP, SF, Rosenman; Carolin Flexner Oral History Transcript, HHLP, CUOHC, pp. 56-57; Lehman, "The Travail of Liberalism, 1945—," Second Speranza Lecture, Columbia University, April 16, 1958, LP, Speech File; Parmet, *The Democrats*, pp. 103–104; Boyle, *The UAW and the Heyday of American Liberalism*, p. 293, n. 13; Caro, *Master of the Senate*, pp. 567–572, 591, 792–800.

44. Julius Edelstein Oral History Transcript, HHLP, CUOHC, p. 27; Lehman to Flexner, August 21, 1956, and August 25, 1956, LP, SF, Flexner; Lehman to Morse, August 30, 1956, LP, SF, Morse; Lehman to Corscadden, August 29, 1956, LP, SF, Corscadden; Lehman to Douglas, August 29, 1956, LP, SF, Douglas; Lehman to Thomas Finletter, August 29, 1956, LP, SF, Finletter. William Shannon of the *New York Post* had already tried, with Lehman's cooperation, to write a biography of Lehman, but the project failed in large part because Shannon and Herbert and Edith Lehman could never quite agree on the focus of the book. Shannon wanted to write "a scholarly, documented work," but despite interviewing many of Lehman's friends and colleagues, he found "very little in the way of anecdotes or crisp, dramatic details." The Lehmans believed that "the mere recital of events or activities, important as they are," was "less important than the principles" for which Herbert Lehman had "always fought" and which had "constantly influenced" his work. Unless his "guiding principles and ideals should become apparent" in such a work, Lehman saw "no useful purpose in recording a biography at all." Neither Shannon nor the Lehmans were particularly happy with Shannon's drafts, so the project was abandoned in 1955. See Lehman to William Shannon, August 4, 1953, November 24, 1954, and June 22, 1955; and Shannon to Lehman, May 19, 1955, all in LP, SF, Shannon. Lehman later contracted with Columbia University historian Allan Nevins to write his biography, which was published by Charles Scribner's Sons in 1963 as *Herbert H. Lehman and His Era*.

45. "Mr. Lehman Withdraws," Editorial, *NYT*, August 22, 1956, p. 28; "Conscience of the Senate," Editorial, *WP*, August 23, 1956, p. 16; "Stevenson Extols Sena-

tor," *NYT*, August 22, 1956, p. 20; Kefauver to Lehman, September 3, 1956, LP, SF, Kefauver; Eleanor Roosevelt, "My Day," August 27, 1956, online: http://www.gwu.edu/~erpapers/myday/displaydoc.cfm?_y=1956&_f=md003573; Rosenman to Lehman, August 22, 1956, LP, SF, Rosenman; Graham to Lehman, August 30, 1956, LP, SF, Graham; Langer to Lehman, September 10, 1956, LP, SF, Langer; Lehman to Lyndon Johnson, September 11, 1956, LP, SF, Johnson.

46. Marquis Childs, "Split in New York Plagues Democrats," *WP*, October 30, 1956, A-12; Estes Kefauver Oral History Transcript, HHLP, CUOHC, pp. 10–11; "Javits Is Gaining as Senate Choice," *NYT*, August 22, 1956, p. 21; "State Democrats Face Test in the Selection for the Senate," *NYT*, August 23, 1956, p. 18; "C.I.O. Bids Wagner Seek Senate Seat," *NYT*, August 24, 1956, p. 11; "Wagner Pays Visit to Lehman at Home," *NYT*, August 25, 1956, p. 16; Lehman to De Sapio, August 29, 1956, LP, SF, De Sapio; "Democrats Insist That Wagner Run," *NYT*, August 30, 1956, p. 14; "Wagner Enters Race for Senate; Party Hails Step," *NYT*, August 31, 1956, pp. 1, 5; "Javits Named for Senate by G.O.P.; Wagner Nominated by Democrats; . . . Mayor Confident," *NYT*, September 11, 1956, pp. 1, 24; Anna Rosenberg Oral History Transcript, HHLP, CUOHC, p. 11; Lehman to Stevenson, November 8, 1956, LP, SF, Stevenson; Robert F. Wagner, Jr., to Lehman, December 7, 1956, LP, SF, Wagner; Lehman to Robert G. A. Jackson, November 15, 1956, LP, SF, Jackson; Lehman to Arthur Schlesinger, Jr., September 1, 1956, LP, SF, Schlesinger; "Coattail Caper: Javits Clings to Ike's In New York Race but It May Cost Him Votes," *Wall Street Journal*, November 5, 1956, pp. 1, 10; Javits, *Javits*, pp. 239–251. For some of Lehman's activities during the campaign, see Lehman to Finletter, August 29, 1956, LP, SF, Finletter; Stevenson to Lehman, September 8, 1956; Program, New York Democratic State Committee, "On to Victory Rally," October 23, 1956; and Frank Karelsen to Lehman, October 25, 1956, all in LP, SF, Stevenson; Lehman to Friend, October 25, 1956, LP, SF, Wagner; "Lehman Travels to Back Wagner," *NYT*, October 14, 1956, p. 81; "Lehman Says Nixon Runs Administration," *WP*, October 24, 1956, A-4; "Lehman, Opening Labor Series, Assails Eisenhower and Nixon on Civil Rights," *NYT*, November 1, 1956, p. 29; "Lehman Lays Crisis to Dulles' Policies," *NYT*, November 2, 1956, p. 20. According to figures published by the Senate Elections Subcommittee, Herbert Lehman contributed at least $15,500 to the Stevenson campaign in 1956, and Edith Lehman contributed an additional $2,500. See "List of Contributors of $5,000 or More in 1956 Campaign," *NYT*, February 3, 1957, p. 52.

47. Johnson to Lehman, August 24, 1956, and Lehman to Johnson, September 1, 1956, both in LP, SF, Johnson.

48. "Text of Lehman's Address to Democrats," *NYT*, January 19, 1957, p. 10; "Lehman Upbraids Congress Chiefs," *NYT*, January 19, 1957, pp. 1, 10. Columnist Robert Spivack had offered a similar indictment of the Democratic congressional leadership's "dismal failure" to "make a record" upon which the Democratic presidential candidate could have run. See Spivack, "Watch on the Potomac," *Chicago Defender*, November 15, 1956, p. 4.

49. "Text of Lehman's Address to Democrats," *NYT*, January 19, 1957, p. 10; "Lehman Upbraids Congress Chiefs," *NYT*, January 19, 1957, pp. 1, 10. See also editorial note preceding Adlai Stevenson to Mrs. Eugene Meyer, January 24, 1957, in Johnson, ed., *The Papers of Adlai E. Stevenson*, VI: 431–432.

50. "Lehman Belabors Johnson, Rayburn," *NYT*, March 26, 1958, p. 26.

51. Edelstein to Carey McWilliams, August 27, 1955, and Lehman to Edelstein, August 16, 1955, both in LP, SF, McWilliams; Paul Douglas Oral History Transcript, HHLP, CUOHC, pp. 19–20.

52. On Johnson, McCarran, and other Senators leaving the chamber when Lehman spoke, see Julius Edelstein Oral History Transcript, HHLP, CUOHC, pp. 17–19; and Caro, *Master of the Senate*, p. 568.

Chapter 18. "A Little Less Profile and a Little More Courage": Herbert Lehman and John Kennedy, 1950–1959

1. John Kennedy describing Herbert Lehman, "Remarks of Senator John F. Kennedy," Testimonial Dinner for Herbert H. Lehman, Sponsored by the Jewish Theological Seminary of America, November 23, 1958, LP, SF, Kennedy.

2. Irwin Ross, "Sen. Kennedy," *New York Post*, July 30, 1956, pp. 4, 21; Paul Healy, "The Senate's Gay Young Bachelor," *Saturday Evening Post*, June 13, 1953, pp. 26, 27, 123–129. On Kennedy's appeal to women, see Whalen, *Kennedy versus Lodge*, pp. 83–89. On Lehman's attendance, see Independent Citizens Committee for the Re-Election of Herbert H. Lehman, "Biography of U.S. Senator Herbert H. Lehman," October 1, 1950, and Lehman to Thomas Brunkard, October 8, 1954, both in LP, SF, Herbert H. Lehman, documents 0530_0349 and 0530_0367.

3. Guthman and Shulman, eds., *Robert Kennedy in His Own Words*, p. 432; Dallek, *An Unfinished Life*, pp. 111–147; Parmet, *Jack*, pp. 135–206; Martin and Plaut, *Front Runner, Dark Horse*, pp. 133–147; Burns, *John Kennedy*, pp. 57–79, 85–88; Lehman to President Truman, June 6, 1947, LP, SF, Truman.

4. 95 *Cong. Rec.* 532–533 (January 25, 1949); "China–Statement of Hon. John F. Kennedy of Massachusetts," Extension of Remarks of Hon. George J. Bates, 95 *Cong. Rec.* A993 (February 21, 1949); Dallek, *An Unfinished Life*, pp. 159–160; Parmet, *Jack*, pp. 207–210; Burns, *John Kennedy*, pp. 79–81. On Lehman's defense of the Truman administration's Far Eastern policy, see chapter 13.

5. 96 *Cong. Rec.* 13769 (August 29, 1950), 15297–15298 (September 20, 1950), and 15632–15633 (September 22, 1950); John Mallan, "Massachusetts: Liberal and Corrupt," *New Republic*, October 13, 1952, p. 10. On Lehman and McCarthyism and the McCarran Internal Security Act, see chapter 13. There was considerable controversy over the accuracy of Mallan's article about the Harvard meeting, but James MacGregor Burns interviewed many of those who were present, and his and subsequent accounts agree that Mallan accurately reported the substance of Kennedy's remarks. See "Letters," *New Republic*, November 3, 1952, p. 2; Burns, *John Kennedy*, pp. 133–134, 289; Parmet, *Jack*, pp. 211–214.

6. *ADA World Congressional Supplement*, September 1950, October 1951, and August 1952, online: http://www.adaction.org/pages/publications/voting-records.php; Burns, *John Kennedy*, pp. 94–97, 135–136.

7. 98 *Cong. Rec.* 4441 (April 25, 1952); Lehman to Kennedy, April 28, 1952, LP, SF, John Kennedy. See chapter 13 for a detailed discussion of Lehman's opposition to the McCarran-Walter Act.

8. "Cushing Condemns Immigration Law," *NYT*, October 3, 1952, p. 9; Edelstein to Ted Reardon, September 26, 1952; "Summary of McCarran-Walter Omnibus Immigration Bill (S.2550; H.R.5678)," June 11, 1952; "Extension of Remarks of Hon. Herbert H. Lehman of New York in the Senate of the United States," May 5, 1952; "The Record of the Two Parties on Immigration," n.d., all in John F. Kennedy Pre-Presidential Papers (hereinafter JFK, PPP), Box 108, Nationality Group Files, McCarran-Walter Immigration Bill, John F. Kennedy Library (hereinafter JFKL). On Kennedy and the Jewish vote in 1952, see Whalen, *Kennedy versus Lodge*, pp. 93–97, 160, 184; Parmet, *Jack*, pp. 246–249; Martin and Plaut, *Front Runner, Dark Horse*, pp. 171–174; Bickerton, "Kennedy, the Jewish Community, and Israel," in J. Snyder, ed., *John F. Kennedy*, pp. 100–102; Dallek, *An Unfinished Life*, p. 175. On Kennedy's amendment to the foreign aid bill, see 97 *Cong. Rec.* 10265 (August 17, 1951). Rabbi Nadich had called attention to the deplorable conditions in the displaced persons camps after World War II. See Nadich, *Eisenhower and the Jews*; and "Judah Nadich," Jewish Virtual Library, online: http://www.jewishvirtuallibrary.org/jsource/biography/Nadich.html.

9. Press Release, Sent to Foreign Newspapers, October 2, 1952, JFK, PPP, Box 105, Press Releases, McCarran-Walter Act; "Cong. Kennedy Scores McCarran Immigration Act," *The Jewish Advocate*, October 2, 1952, JFK, PPP, Box 103, Advertisements, Jewish Newspapers. Lodge had been absent but paired supporting the President's veto of the McCarran-Walter Act. See 98 *Cong. Rec.* 8267 (June 27, 1952). On Lodge's efforts to capitalize on Kennedy's absentee record, see Whalen, *Kennedy versus Lodge*, pp. 101–102.

10. "Nationality Groups—Jewish," n.d., and handwritten list of pictures to be obtained, JFK, PPP, Box 109, Jewish: Undated and Articles; Jackson Holtz to Ted Reardon or Sargent Shriver, August 29, 1952; Reardon to Congressman Ribicoff, September 3, 1952; Draft of Proposed Letter From Ribicoff to Congressman Kennedy; Reardon to Scottie Shaw, September 3, 1952; Draft of Proposed Letter from Sabath to Congressman Kennedy; Kennedy to Congressman Sabath, September 12, 1952; Reardon to Congressman Sidney Fine, September 3, 1952; Draft of Proposed Letter from Congressman Fine to Congressman Kennedy; all in JFK, PPP, Box 109, Jewish; Whalen, *Kennedy versus Lodge*, p. 160. For examples of the Lehman letter in Kennedy ads, see "No 5 in a Series of Letters from Fellow Congressmen Hailing CHAMPION OF HUMAN RIGHTS!" *The Jewish Advocate*, October 23, 1952; *Forward*, October 24, 1952; *Forward*, October 30, 1952; *Jewish Times*, October 30, 1952; all in JFK, PPP, Box 103, Ads: Jewish Newspapers.

11. "G.O.P. Group Balks Curb on Filibuster," *NYT*, January 3, 1953, p. 9; 99 *Cong. Rec.* 11 (January 3, 1953); "Senate Holds Fire on Filibuster Gag," *NYT*, January 4, 1953, pp. 1, 64; "Senate, 70–21, Bars Curb on Filibuster; Rights Bills Mired," *NYT*, January 8, 1953, pp. 1, 24; "Senate Vote That Shelved Move to Curb Filibuster," *NYT*, January 8, 1953, p. 24.

12. On Lehman's conception of his role as a Senator, see Lehman to Julius Edelstein, August 16, 1955, LP, SF, Carey McWilliams. On Lehman and the Bricker Amendment, see 99 *Cong. Rec.* 9134 (July 18, 1953); 100 *Cong. Rec.* 1325–1329 (February 4, 1954), 1736, 1739–1746 (February 15, 1954), 1781–1782 (February 16, 1954), 1900–1901 (February 17, 1954), 2043 (February 19, 1954), 2141 (February 20, 1954), 2259–2260 (February 25, 1954), and 2372–2373 (February 26, 1954). On Kennedy, see "The Bricker Amendment," Extension of Remarks of Hon. John F.

Kennedy, 100 *Cong. Rec.* 1075 (February 1, 1954); and 100 *Cong. Rec.* 1231 (February 3, 1954). On the Bricker Amendment, see also "Treaty Amendment Roll Call in Senate," *NYT*, February 27, 1954, p. 2; Kennedy to John Gorman, July 17, 1953, and Kennedy to Anne Pekin, January 25, 1954, both in JFK, PPP, Box 641, Senate Legislative Files, 1953–1960: 1953–1955, Bricker Resolution; and Tananbaum, *The Bricker Amendment Controversy*.

13. Lehman to Kennedy, January 25, 1954, and attached statement, and Kennedy to Lehman, January 27, 1954, all in LP, SF, Kennedy; "Lehman Charges 'Peril' to Liberty," *NYT*, January 25, 1954, p. 13; Burns, *John Kennedy*, p. 136. On Kennedy and the St. Lawrence Seaway, see Savage, *The Senator from New England*, pp. 75–101.

14. On Lehman and McCarthyism in 1950–1952, see chapter 13. On Kennedy and McCarthy during this period, see Parmet, *Jack*, pp. 178–182, 250–251; "Harold Christoffel Decision," Extension of Remarks of Hon. John F. Kennedy, 95 *Cong. Rec.* A4169 (June 29, 1949); Burns, *John Kennedy*, pp. 133–134; Mallan, "Massachusetts: Liberal and Corrupt," *New Republic*, October 13, 1952, p. 10; Whalen, *Kennedy versus Lodge*, pp. 138–146.

15. Burns, *John Kennedy*, pp. 139–143; Kefauver, Morse, Lehman, and Douglas to Kennedy, April 27, 1954, JFK, PPP, Box 641, Senate Files, Legislative Files, 1953–1960: 1953–1955, Bills and Resolutions; S. Con. Res. 64, 83d Cong., 2d sess., February 24, 1954; S. Res 256, 83d Cong., 2d sess., May 27, 1954; 100 *Cong. Rec.* 2205–2212 (February 24, 1954), 7223–7225, 7250–7251 (May 27, 1954); "Code of Fair Investigating Committee Procedures," Extension of Remarks of Hon Herbert H. Lehman, 100 *Cong. Rec.* 9569–9571 (July 1, 1954); Irwin Ross, "Sen. Kennedy," *New York Post*, July 30, 1956, p. 21.

16. Flanders: 100 *Cong. Rec.* 10992–10993 (July 20, 1954); Lehman: 100 *Cong. Rec.* 11000 (July 20, 1954), 12374–12376 (July 28, 1954), 12903 (July 31, 1954), 12953, 12975–12976, 12983 (August 2, 1954); Kennedy: Drew Pearson, "The Washington Merry-Go-Round: Worries of Senator Johnson," *WP*, July 29, 1954, p. 55; Fried, *Men against McCarthy*, p. 296; Sorensen, *Kennedy*, pp. 47–48; 100 *Cong. Rec.* 12962 (August 2, 1954); "New McCarthy Probe Voted by Senate, 75–12; 6-Man Committee Set Up to Weigh Censure Charges against Senator," *WP*, August 3, 1954, pp. 1, 5; Burns, *John Kennedy*, pp. 145–147; Parmet, *Jack*, pp. 304–306; Oshinsky, *A Conspiracy So Immense*, pp. 474, 489–490; Griffith, *The Politics of Fear*, p. 287. On the National Committee for an Effective Congress, see Griffith, *The Politics of Fear*, pp. 224–229, 240–242, 274–291, 301–303.

17. 100 *Cong. Rec.* 16392 (December 2, 1954); Irwin Ross, "Sen. Kennedy," *New York Post*, July 30, 1956, p. 21; T. J. Reardon, Jr., to Nathaniel Bateman, December 14, 1954, JFK, PPP, Box 654, Senate, Legislative Files, 1953–1960: 1953–1955, St. Lawrence Seaway, February 15, 1954–December 14, 1954; Sorensen, *Kennedy*, pp. 48–49; Frank Altschul to Kennedy, May 5, 1960, and Kennedy to Altschul, May 20, 1960, LP, SF, Kennedy; "Notes on the Record of Senator John F. Kennedy on 'McCarthyism' and Civil Liberties," n.d., JFK, PPP, Box 536, Senate Files, General Files, 1953–1960: 1958–1960, POF, Civil Rights, 1960; Parmet, *Jack*, pp. 307–311; Burns, *John Kennedy*, pp. 147–155; Dallek, *An Unfinished Life*, pp. 190–192; Oshinsky, *A Conspiracy So Immense*, pp. 490–491.

18. Kennedy, *Profiles in Courage*; Inscription in *Profiles in Courage*, in "Herbert H. Lehman: Tributes by Authors," LP, SF, Herbert H. Lehman, document 0530_0444; Lehman to Kennedy, January 12, 1956, LP, SF, Kennedy. For examples of the quips about Kennedy needing to show less profile and more courage, see "Random Notes from Washington: 3 Senators Fear for Foreign Aid," *NYT*, August 19, 1957, p. 10; and Wallace, *Between You and Me*, p. 42. In December 1958, Mrs. Roosevelt characterized Kennedy as "someone who understands what courage is and admires it, but has not quite the independence to have it," and a few weeks later, she told Kennedy that her comments were for his own good. She advised that "when blows are rained on one, it is advisable to turn the other profile." See "Mrs. Roosevelt Lauds Humphrey," *NYT*, December 8, 1958, p. 34, and Eleanor Roosevelt to Kennedy, January 29, 1959, quoted in Parmet, *Jack*, p. 464. On the authorship of *Profiles in Courage*, see Parmet, *Jack*, pp. 320–333; and Sorensen, *Counselor*, pp. 144–152.

19. Kennedy, *Profiles in Courage*, pp. 220, 264.

20. Clayton Knowles, "Lehman, Retiring from Senate, Promises He Will Remain Active," *NYT*, December 30, 1956, p. 22.

21. *ADA World Congressional Supplement*, September 1955 and August 1956, online: http://www.adaction.org/pages/publications/voting-records.php; 101 *Cong. Rec.* 1020, 1030–1031 (February 1, 1955) and 1539–1540 (February 15, 1955); "Humphrey Offers Civil Rights Bills," *NYT*, February 2, 1955, p. 14; "Bill Is Filed to Protect MPs on Duty," *WP*, February 16, 1955, p. 14; U.S., Cong., Senate, Committee on the Judiciary, *Civil Rights Proposals; Hearings* before the Committee on the Judiciary, 84th Cong., 2d sess., April 24–July 13, 1956, pp. 341–346. See chapter 16 for the efforts by Lehman and Douglas to force Senate action on a civil rights bill in July 1956. On Kennedy's interest in the Democratic vice presidential nomination in 1956, see Burns, *John Kennedy*, pp. 175, 180–185; Sorensen, *Kennedy*, pp. 80–85; Parmet, *Jack*, pp. 335–364; Dallek, *An Unfinished Life*, pp. 203–206.

22. S. 2585, 83d Cong., 1st sess., August 3, 1953; 99 *Cong. Rec.* 10959 (August 3, 1953); Lehman to Hubert Humphrey, January 21, 1955, with the notation that the same letter was sent to Senators Morse, Pastore, Green, Murray, Kennedy, and Magnuson, LP, SF, Humphrey; S. 1206, 84th Cong., 1st sess., February 25, 1955; 101 *Cong. Rec.* 2093–2101 (February 25, 1955); S. 1794, 84th Cong., 1st sess., April 25, 1955; 101 *Cong. Rec.* 4996–4998 (April 25, 1955); U.S., Cong., Senate, *Amendments to the Refugee Relief Act of 1953; Hearings* before the Subcommittee of the Committee on the Judiciary, 84th Cong., 1st sess., June 1955, pp. 13–26, 280–284 (Lehman), 149–150 (Kennedy); "Kennedy Calls Immigration Act 'Most Blatant Discrimination,'" *WP*, November 21, 1955, p. 2; Kennedy to Harley Kilgore, November 21, 1955, and Draft Press Release, November 21, 1955, both in JFK, PPP, Box 647, Senate Legislative Files, 1953–1960: 1953–1955, Immigration, August 24, 1955–November 28, 1955; "Changes in Aliens Law Unlikely, Lehman Avers," *WP*, November 23, 1955, p. 2; 102 *Cong. Rec.* 14999–15018, 15505–15506 (July 27, 1956); "House Kills Alien Bill after Senate Approval," *WP*, July 28, 1956, p. 1. See chapter 16 for a more detailed discussion of Lehman's efforts to amend the McCarran-Walter and Refugee Relief Acts.

23. "Flooded Plants on Priority List," *NYT*, August 28, 1955, pp. 1, 67; "FHA Studies Backing for Flood Insurance," *WP*, August 31, 1955, p. 2; Kennedy and Salton-

stall to Senator Theodore Francis Green, September 9, 1955, and attached Memorandum on Proposed Federal Flood Insurance Bill; and Edelstein to Kennedy, September 12, 1955, all in LP, SF, Kennedy; "Federal Flood Insurance Plan Similar to Crop Program Is Proposed," *Wall Street Journal*, September 12, 1955, p. 1. On the damage caused by Hurricane Diane, see "Floods Batter the Northeast; 73 Killed, Damage in Billions; 4 States Declare Emergencies," *NYT*, August 20, 1955, pp. 1, 8; "Deluge," *NYT*, August 21, 1955, E-1. On President Eisenhower's response, see "President and Governors Map Speedy Flood Relief; $75,000,000 Fund Is Planned," *NYT*, August 24, 1955, pp. 1, 18; "Text of Eisenhower Appeal," *NYT*, August 24, 1955, p. 18; "100 Million in Flood Grants Sped to States by President," *NYT*, August 25, 1955, pp. 1, 14; "President Allots a Billion in Loans for Flood States," *NYT*, August 26, 1955, pp. 1, 8.

24. "Disaster Aid Hearings Set," *WP*, September 20, 1955, p. 1; U.S., Cong., Senate, Committee on Banking and Currency, *Federal Disaster Insurance; Hearings* before the Committee on Banking and Currency, Part I, 84th Cong., 1st sess., October 31–December 19, 1955; Kennedy and Saltonstall to Lehman, October 14, 1955, in *Federal Disaster Insurance; Hearings*, Part I, p. 429; "Insurance Hearings Urged in Flood Areas," *WP*, October 18, 1955, p. 3; Lehman to Senator Fulbright, October 24, 1955, LP, SF, Fulbright; Fulbright to Lehman, October 28, 1955, in *Federal Disaster Insurance; Hearings*, Part I, p. 29; *Federal Disaster Insurance; Hearings*, Part I, pp. 413–429; Lehman to Kennedy, October 29, 1955, and November 20, 1955, both in LP, SF, Kennedy.

25. "Johnson Offers Legislative Plan," *NYT*, November 22, 1955, p. 27; S. 2768, 84th Cong., 2d sess., January 5, 1956; "Text of President Eisenhower's Annual Message to Congress on the State of the Union," *NYT*, January 6, 1956, p. 10; Bush to Senator, January 3, 1956, LP, SF, Bush; S. 2862, 84th Cong., 2d sess., January 5, 1956; 102 *Cong. Rec.* 73, 75, 97–109 (January 5, 1956); "Congress Pushes Flood Insurance," *NYT*, January 6, 1956, p. 14; "Administration Asks Congress to Authorize $3 Billion 'Experimental' Federal-State Flood Insurance Plan," *Wall Street Journal*, January 6, 1956, p. 2; "$3 Billion Flood Insurance Plan Framed by Kennedy and Lehman," *Boston Globe*, February 6, 1956, p. 5; S. 3137, 84th Cong., 2d sess., February 6, 1956; 102 *Cong. Rec.* 2023–2027 (February 6, 1956). Lehman's co-sponsors, besides Kennedy, included Senators Ervin, Green, Johnston, Morse, Neuberger, Pastore, Scott, and Sparkman.

26. "Problems of Disaster Insurance," *Los Angeles Times*, February 25, 1956, A-4; "Dubious Alternative," *Wall Street Journal*, May 14, 1956, p. 10; "Flood Insurance Held Unfeasible," *NYT*, May 25, 1956, p. 31; "Snows Spur Flood Control," *NYT*, March 25, 1956, E-6; U.S., Cong., Senate, Committee on Banking and Currency, *Federal Disaster Insurance; Hearings* before the Subcommittee on Securities, 84th Cong., 2d sess., Part II, February 16–27, 1956; Lehman to Governor Abraham Ribicoff, March 5, 1956, LP, SF, Ribicoff; U.S., Cong., Senate, Committee on Banking and Currency, Transcript of Proceedings, Subcommittee on Securities, Executive Session on S. 2862 and S. 3137, March 23, 1956; U.S., Cong., Senate, Committee on Banking and Currency, Transcripts of Proceedings, *Flood Insurance*, Executive Sessions, April 10, April 11, April 12, 1956; U.S., Cong., Senate, *Federal Flood Insurance Act of 1956*, S. Rept. 1864, 84th Cong., 2d sess., April 26, 1956; Lehman to Kennedy, April 6, 1956, and May 5, 1956, LP, SF, Kennedy; 102 *Cong. Rec.* 7905–7936 (May 10, 1956); Kennedy to Lehman, May 11, 1956, LP, SF, Kennedy; "5 Billion Flood Insurance Is Voted by Senate, 61 to 7,"

NYT, May 11, 1956, p. 1. ProQuest Congressional now makes it possible to access many congressional committee executive sessions.

27. "House Unit Approves Five-Year 'Experimental' Flood Insurance," *Wall Street Journal*, July 13, 1956, p. 18; U.S., Cong., House, Committee on Banking and Currency, *Federal Flood Insurance Act of 1956*, H. Rept. 2746, 84th Cong., 2d sess., July 17, 1956; Lehman to Hodges, July 18, 1956, LP, SF, Hodges; Lehman to Ribicoff, July 18, 1956, LP, SF, Ribicoff; 102 *Cong. Rec.* 14538–14556 (July 25, 1956); "Flood Insurance Is Voted by House," *NYT*, July 26, 1956, p. 12; U.S., Cong., House, *Federal Flood Insurance*, Conference Report, H. Rept. 2959, 84th Cong., 2d sess., July 27, 1956; 102 *Cong. Rec.* 15104, 15262–15265 (July 27, 1956); "Senate Approves Flood Insurance," *NYT*, July 28, 1956, p. 34; "President Signs Flood Help Bill," *NYT*, August 8, 1956, p. 21; "Federal Flood Insurance Act of 1956," P.L. 1016, August 7, 1956, 70 *Stat.* 1078–1087.

28. 102 *Cong. Rec.* 15104 (July 27, 1956); Harriman to Lehman, August 7, 1956, LP, SF, Harriman; Hodges to Lehman, August 6, 1956, LP, SF, Hodges; "House Bars Funds for a Flood Plan," *NYT*, May 8, 1957, p. 23; "House Again Bars Flood Loss Funds," *NYT*, June 19, 1957, p. 28; "Floods, Minerals Funds Deleted from Money Bill," *WP*, June 20, 1957, A-2; "U.S. Flood Insurance Plan Dies," *WP*, July 2, 1957, A-3; Grossman, "Flood Insurance: Can a Feasible Program Be Created?" Chartered Property Casualty Underwriters Society, Connecticut Chapter, "Flood Insurance and Hurricane Katrina: Evaluation of the National Flood Insurance Program and Overview of the Proposed Solutions"; U.S., Government Accountability Office, *National Flood Insurance Program*, Testimony before the Subcommittee on Housing and Community Opportunity, Committee on Financial Services, House of Representatives, GAO-10-631T, April 21, 2010; U.S., Cong., House, Committee on Financial Services, *Flood Insurance Reform Act of 2011*, H. Rept. 112–102, 112th Cong., 1st sess., June 9, 2011; Michel-Kerjan, "Catastrophe Economics: The National Flood Insurance Plan"; "Flood Insurance Program Extended until July 30," *Insurance Journal*, online: http://www.insurancejournal.com/news/national/2012/05/31/249501.htm.

29. Lehman to Carolin Flexner, August 25, 1956, LP, SF, Flexner; "New York Is Cool to Tennessean," *NYT*, August 18, 1956, pp. 1, 9; "State Democrats Wary on Election," *NYT*, August 19, 1956, p. 62; "Just against Kefauver," *NYT*, August 18, 1956, p. 7; Martin and Plaut, *Front Runner, Dark Horse*, pp. 17–109; Thomson and Shattuck, *The 1956 Presidential Campaign*, pp. 152–163; Martin, *Adlai Stevenson and the World*, pp. 350–351; Martin, *Ballots and Bandwagons*, p. 418. As a delegate at-large, Lehman had one half vote.

30. Lehman to Friend, n.d., but see Eleanor Roosevelt's response to Lehman, December 27, 1956, both in Eleanor Roosevelt Papers, 1953–1956, Lehman; "Lehman Retiring from Senate, Promises He Will Remain Active," *NYT*, December 30, 1956, p. 22; "Biggest Change Will Take Place on V.I.P. Floor," *WP*, December 30, 1956, D-5; Lehman to Lyndon Johnson, January 12, 1957, LP, SF, Johnson.

31. Lehman to John Kennedy, December 27, 1956, JFK, PPP, Box 666, Senate Legislative Files, 1953–1960, 1956–1957, Filibuster, October 19, 1956–December 31, 1956; Press Release, "Text of Letter from Senator Lehman to 51 Senators on Proposed Move to Adopt New Senate Rules Including Change in Anti-Filibuster Rule," December

30, 1956, LP, SF, Langer; "Anti-Filibuster Motion Endorsed by Lehman," *NYT*, December 30, 1956, p. 22.

32. Wilkins to Lehman, December 31, 1956, with handwritten notation "accepted by telegram, 12/31," LP, SF, Wilkins; 103 *Cong. Rec.* 187 (January 4, 1957).

33. 103 *Cong. Rec.* 9–12 (January 3, 1957), 167, 193, 187 (January 4, 1957); "Senate Liberals Prepare New Attack on Filibusters," *NYT*, January 1, 1957, pp. 1, 13; "14 Senators Map Filibuster Fight," *NYT*, January 3, 1957, pp. 1, 18; "Liberals Losing Filibuster Move," *NYT*, January 4, 1957, pp. 1, 11; Anderson, *Outsider in the Senate*, pp. 143–145; "National Grapevine: The Curtain Rise [*sic*]," *Chicago Defender*, January 19, 1957, p. 2; Drew Pearson, "The Washington Merry-Go-Round: Truman Defends Hoover 'Hiring,'" *WP*, January 13, 1957, E-5.

34. 103 *Cong. Rec.* 187 (January 4, 1957).

35. Hennings to Lehman, January 5, 1957, LP, SF, Hennings; 103 *Cong. Rec.* 215 (January 4, 1957); "Senators Block Filibuster Curb by 55-to-38 Vote," *NYT*, January 5, 1957, pp. 1, 8; "14 Senators Map Filibuster Fight," *NYT*, January 3, 1957, pp. 1, 18; "Johnson Opposes Filibuster Limit," *NYT*, November 27, 1956, pp. 1, 24; GER [George Reedy] to Senator, December 16, 1956, and attached Memorandum; GER to Senator, December 17, 1956, and attached memorandum; G. W. Siegel to Senator Johnson, "Senate Rules," December 20, 1956; Siegel to Senator, December 21, 1956, all in Lyndon Johnson Senate Papers, Box 423, Office Files of George Reedy, 1956–1957, Reedy: Rule XXII; Arthur Krock, "In the Nation: The Senate Art of Getting Off the Hook," *NYT*, January 4, 1957, p. 22; "Filibusters Won't Stop Civil Rights Program," *NYT*, January 6, 1957, E-9; Robert Spivack, "Watch on the Potomac," *Chicago Defender*, January 7, 1957, p. 4; Anderson, *Outsider in the Senate*, pp. 144–145; Mann, *The Walls of Jericho*, pp. 182–184; Caro, *Master of the Senate*, pp. 848–861. On the black vote in 1956, see Lawson, *Black Ballots*, pp. 162–163; Moon, "The Negro Vote in the Presidential Election of 1956"; and Lubell, "The Future of the Negro Voter in the United States."

36. Bryant, *The Bystander*, pp. 54–62; 103 *Cong. Rec.* 215 (January 4, 1957); 99 *Cong. Rec.* 11 (January 3, 1953); Kennedy to William Brown, January 8, 1957, JFK, PPP, Box 666, Senate Legislative Files, 1953–1960, 1955–1957, Filibuster, January 1–January 28, 1957; "Record of Senator John F. Kennedy (Dem–Mass.) on Civil Rights and Race Relations," 1958, JFK, PPP, Box 758, Senate Legislative Assistants' Background Files, 1953–1960, Civil Rights (General), Undated; Sorensen, *Kennedy*, p. 471; "Interview with Arthur M. Schlesinger," in Snyder, ed., *John F. Kennedy*, p. 7.

37. "Kennedy Praises Work of Johnson," *NYT*, December 7, 1956, p. 23; "Kennedy Gets Post Sought by Kefauver," *NYT*, January 9, 1957, pp. 1, 24; 103 *Cong. Rec.* 177–178 (January 4, 1957); Caro, *Master of the Senate*, pp. 563–564, 858–859. For more charitable explanations of Kennedy's success in securing the appointment to the Foreign Relations Committee, see "Sen. Kennedy Wins Post from Estes," *Boston Globe*, January 9, 1957, pp. 1, 5; "Sheer Qualifications Won Out for Kennedy," *Boston Globe*, January 10, 1957, pp. 1, 20. According to Doris Kearns Goodwin, Lyndon Johnson later attributed Kennedy's appointment to heavy lobbying by Joe Kennedy on his son's behalf. See Goodwin, *The Fitzgeralds and the Kennedys*, p. 790.

38. "New Move to Curb Filibuster Begun," *NYT*, January 8, 1957, p. 19; "2 Senate Leaders Back Compromise On Closure Rule," *NYT*, January 10, 1957, pp. 1, 21; S. Res. 17, 85th Cong., 1st sess., January 7, 1957; S. Res. 28, 85th Cong., 1st sess.,

January 9, 1957; S. Res. 29, 85th Cong., 1st sess., January 9, 1957; S. Res 30, 85th Cong., 1st sess., January 9, 1957; S. Res. 32, 85th Cong., 1st sess., January 9, 1957; 103 *Cong. Rec.* 247–249 (January 7, 1957), 381–382 (January 9, 1957); Editorial, *Boston Chronicle*, January 12, 1957, JFK, PPP, Box 758, Senate Legislative Assistants' Background File, 1953–1960, Civil Rights (General) January 29, 1954–October 21, 1957. The change to allow two-thirds of Senators present and voting, rather than two-thirds of the Senate, to close off debate was adopted in 1959. See "Senate Approves Filibuster Curb Asked by Johnson," *NYT*, January 13, 1959, pp. 1, 18.

39. "Democrats Set 'Liberal' Goals," *WP*, November 28, 1956, A-2; "Non-Congress Democrats Form Advisory Board," *Boston Globe*, January 5, 1957, p. 2; "Democrats Seek Militant Leaders," *NYT*, January 5, 1957, pp. 1, 8; Harry McPherson Oral History Transcript, VIII: 5–6, LBJL. Mrs. Roosevelt, concerned that formal membership on the DAC might be seen as compromising her objectivity as a newspaper columnist, chose to serve as a consultant to the group rather than a formal member. See "Butler Calls Advisory Group Session Despite Rebuff by Congress Leaders," *WP*, December 19, 1956, A-1, 2. On the DAC, see Cotter and Hennessy, *Politics without Power*, pp. 211–224; Martin, *Adlai Stevenson and the World*, pp. 395–402; Parmet, *The Democrats*, pp. 151–161; Lazarowitz, *Years in Exile*, pp. 119–160; and Sundquist, *Politics and Policy*, pp. 405–410. The DAC began as the Democratic Advisory Committee but soon became the Democratic Advisory Council.

40. "Text of Lehman's Address to Democrats," *NYT*, January 19, 1957, p. 10; "Lehman Upbraids Congress Chiefs," *NYT*, January 19, 1957, pp. 1, 10.

41. Lehman to Paul Douglas, February 7, 1957, LP, SF, Douglas; Lehman to William Benton, February 21, 1957, LP, SF, Benton; "Democrats Meet on Coast Friday," *NYT*, February 10, 1957, p. 58; "Prod Sothern Democrats on 'Rights' Issue," *Chicago Tribune*, February 18, 1957, p. 26. Lehman contributed $10,000 to the DAC. See Lehman to Frank Altschul, June 8, 1957, LP, SF, Frank Altschul; and Parmet, *The Democrats*, pp. 153–154.

42. Sundquist, *Politics and Policy*, p. 409; Parmet, *The Democrats*, p. 159; "Strong Rights Stand Urged on Democrats," *Chicago Tribune*, February 17, 1957, p. 9; Eleanor Roosevelt, "My Day," February 18, 1957, online: http://www.gwu.edu/~erpapers/myday/displaydoc.cfm?_y=1957&_f=md003726a; "Democrats' 'New Look' on Civil Rights Expected," *Los Angeles Times*, February 17, 1957, p. 10; "Democrats Agree on Rights Policy," *NYT*, February 17, 1957, p. 28; "Democrats Press Civil Rights Bills," *NYT*, February 18, 1957, pp. 1, 15; "Text of Statements by Democratic Advisory Council," *NYT*, February 18, 1957, p. 15.

43. "Democrats Name 20 to Chart a Program," *NYT*, December 6, 1956, pp. 1, 31; "Democrats Close Rift over Status of Advisory Unit," *NYT*, January 6, 1957, pp. 1, 57; "Humphrey Backs Lyndon Johnson," *NYT*, December 9, 1956, p. 58; "6 in Senate Seek Filibuster Curb for New Session," *NYT*, November 23, 1956, pp. 1, 31; Thurber, *The Politics of Equality*, p. 100; Solberg, *Hubert Humphrey*, pp. 171–178, 199–200; Mann, *The Walls of Jericho*, pp. 176–180; Parmet, *Jack*, pp. 388, 477; Sundquist, *Politics and Policy*, p. 407; "2 Join Democratic Unit," *NYT*, November 12, 1959, p. 24; Thomas Finletter to Kennedy, November 11, 1959, JFK, PPP, Box 956, 1960 Campaign, Pre-Convention Political Files, 1959–1960, New York Delegates, October 1, 1959–December 28, 1959; Cotter and Hennessy, *Politics without Power*, pp. 215–216.

44. Lehman to Hennings, April 4, 1957, LP, SF, Hennings; 103 *Cong. Rec.* 9145–9146 (June 14, 1957), 9347–9350 (June 17, 1957) and 9826–9827 (June 20, 1957); "Senate, 45 to 39, Sends Rights Bill Straight to Floor," *NYT*, June 21, 1957, pp. 1, 16. On the 1957 Civil Rights Act, see Anderson, *Eisenhower, Brownell, and the Congress*; Anderson, *Outsider in the Senate*, pp. 145–148; Douglas, *In the Fullness of Time*, pp. 285–291; Javits, *Javits*, pp. 323–336; Burk, *The Eisenhower Administration and Black Civil Rights*, pp. 204–226; Watson, *Lion in the Lobby*, 360–399; Mann, *The Walls of Jericho*, pp. 178–224; and Caro, *Master of the Senate*, pp. 863–1012.

45. Lehman to Hennings, August 9, 1957, LP, SF, Hennings; Lehman to Edward Weinfeld, September 2, 1957, LP, SF, Weinfeld; Lehman to Morse, February 18, 1958, LP, SF, Morse. On the Senate's amendments to the civil rights bill, see 103 *Cong. Rec.* 12565 (July 24, 1957) and 13356 (August 1, 1957); "Senate Restricts Civil Rights Bill to The Vote Issue," *NYT*, July 25, 1957, pp. 1, 12; "Senate, 51 to 42, Attaches Jury Trials to Rights Bill in Defeat for President," *NYT*, August 2, 1957, pp. 1, 8.

46. Lehman to Hennings, August 9, 1957, and Hennings to Lehman, August 15, 1957, both in LP, SF, Hennings; Douglas to Lehman, August 10, 1957, LP, SF, Douglas; Caro, *Master of the Senate*, pp. 896–1012; Douglas, *In the Fullness of Time*, pp. 286–291; Watson, *Lion in the Lobby*, pp. 386–394; Mann, *The Walls of Jericho*, pp. 184–224.

47. Kennedy to Alfred Baker Lewis, July 8, 1957 and July 13, 1957, JFK, PPP, Box 439, Senate, Correspondence Copy File, 1953–1960, Pinks, 1957, File 1, "L"; Douglas, *In the Fullness of Time*, p. 255; Kennedy to Herbert Tucker, Jr., June 24, 1957, JFK, PPP, Senate Legislative Files, 1953–1960, 1956–1957, Civil Rights, May 7, 1956–June 29, 1957; 103 *Cong. Rec.* 9793, 9805–9806, 9815 (June 20, 1957); Bryant, *The Bystander*, pp. 65–68; Burns, *John Kennedy*, pp. 200–202; Martin and Plaut, *Front Runner, Dark Horse*, p. 197; Brauer, *John F. Kennedy and the Second Reconstruction*, pp. 20–21; Parmet, *Jack*, pp. 408–410.

48. Kennedy to Alfred Baker Lewis, July 13, 1957, and Kennedy to Mrs. Clifford Lamar, August 1, 1957, JFK, PPP, Box 439, Senate, Correspondence Copy File, 1953–1960, Pinks, 1957, File 1, "L"; Kennedy to Herbert Tucker, Jr., August 2, 1957, JFK, PPP, Box 664, Senate Legislative Files, 1953–1960, 1956–1957, Civil Rights, July 22, 1957–August 9, 1957; Kennedy to David Mayhew, March 22, 1958, JFK, PPP, Box 687, Senate Legislative Files, 1953–1960, 1958, Civil Rights, October 30, 1957–May 22, 1958; 103 *Cong. Rec.* 12467 (July 23, 1957); and 13305–13307 (August 1, 1957); Bryant, *The Bystander*, pp. 63–79; Wilkins, *Standing Fast*, p. 273; Burns, *John Kennedy*, pp. 200–205; Martin and Plaut, *Front Runner, Dark Horse*, pp. 197–198; Brauer, *John F. Kennedy and the Second Reconstruction*, pp. 20–22; Parmet, *Jack*, pp. 408–412; Mann, *The Walls of Jericho*, pp. 214–215, 222, 261; Caro, *Master of the Senate*, pp. 985–986.

49. Lehman to Benton, September 15, 1957, LP, SF, Benton; "President Urges Patience on Crisis," *NYT*, September 11, 1957, p. 25; "President, Faubus Hit by Democratic Council," *Los Angeles Times*, September 16, 1957, p. 11; "Democrats Term President Remiss," *NYT*, September 16, 1957, pp. 1, 21; "Democrats Accused of Politics on Integration," *Los Angeles Times*, September 17, 1957, p. 7; Lehman to Butler, October 22, 1957, LP, SF, Butler; "President Chided for Little Rock," *NYT*, October 22, 1957, p. 23. On the crisis in Little Rock, see Hays, *A Southern Moderate Speaks*, pp. 130–194, and Bartley, *The Rise of Massive Resistance*, pp. 251–269. On the Eisenhower administration's lack of enthusiasm and effort in implementing the *Brown* decision, see

"Little Rock Delay Hinted; School Tilts Hit Democrats," *Christian Science Monitor*, September 17, 1957, p. 1; Burk, *The Eisenhower Administration and Black Civil Rights*, pp. 147–203; Ambrose, *Eisenhower: The President*, pp. 414–423; and Duram, *A Moderate among Extremists*.

50. "Kennedy Hits Mob Violence," *Pittsburgh Courier*, October 12, 1957, A-5; "Senator Kennedy Courts Southern and Northern-Liberal Support," *Atlanta Daily World*, October 23, 1957, pp. 1, 4; "Staking Out the Claims," Editorial, *Boston Globe*, October 22, 1957, p. 18; Carroll Kilpatrick, "Kennedy, the Moderate," *WP*, October 24, 1957, A-13; Parmet, *Jack*, pp. 412–414; Bryant, *The Bystander*, pp. 81–87.

51. "Lehman Calls Harlem a Rebuke to the North," *WP*, June 4, 1956, p. 17; "Sen. Lehman Cites Harlem as North Rights Problem," *Hartford Courant*, June 4, 1956, p. 4; "City Officials Mum on Lehman Remarks," *New York Amsterdam News*, June 9, 1956, pp. 1, 34; Lehman to Wagner, June 13, 1956, LP, SF, Wagner; "Housing Bias Bill Backed at Parley," *NYT*, October 23, 1957, p. 26.

52. Lehman to Wayne Morse, March 7, 1958, LP, SF, Morse. Hubert Humphrey inserted the text of Lehman's remarks in 104 *Cong. Rec.* 3370–3372 (March 4, 1958). On Eisenhower's attempt to portray himself as a moderate following a middle course between extremists, see Duram, *A Moderate among Extremists*.

53. 104 *Cong. Rec.* 3372 (March 4, 1958); "She Asks for an Answer," *WP*, February 25, 1958, A1. Interestingly, different newspapers focused on different themes in Lehman's speech in their reports. The *Washington Post and Times-Herald* highlighted Lehman's praise for the courage and bravery of black children integrating Southern schools and his discussion of the Vietnamese girl's letter to that paper's editors, while the *New York Times* concentrated on Lehman's criticism of President Eisenhower's failure to bring moral suasion and effective leadership to the fight for civil rights. The *Pittsburgh Courier*, one of the nation's leading African American newspapers, stressed Lehman's attack on "gradualism," and his call for leadership and federal action to end segregation. See "Lehman in Howard Talk Extols Negro Children," *WP*, March 4, 1958, A15; "President Is Cited on Bias by Lehman," *NYT*, March 4, 1958, p. 59; " '300 Years of Waiting,' " *Pittsburgh Courier*, March 15, 1958, A4.

54. 104 *Cong. Rec.* 3370 (March 4, 1958); Wilkins to Lehman, April 1, 1958, LP, SF, Wilkins.

55. Eisenhower, *The White House Years: Waging Peace, 1956–1961*, pp. 292–304; "Text of Eisenhower Speech on Taiwan Situation," *NYT*, September 12, 1958, p. 2; "President Says Nation Must Fight if Necessary to Bar Quemoy Fall; Sees No War; Urges Negotiations," *NYT*, September 12, 1958, pp. 1, 2; Stolper, *China, Taiwan, and the Offshore Islands*, pp. 114–131; Ambrose, *Eisenhower: The President*, pp. 482–485; Chang, *Friends and Enemies*, pp. 182–199; Young, *Negotiating with the Chinese Communists*, pp. 3–134. On the U.S. policy of "Strategic Ambiguity" toward China, see Tucker, "Strategic Ambiguity or Strategic Clarity?" in Tucker, ed., *Dangerous Strait: The U.S.-Taiwan-China Crisis*, pp. 186–211.

56. "Text of Eisenhower Speech on Taiwan Situation," *NYT*, September 12, 1958, p. 2; "Letters on China Issue Exchanged by Eisenhower and Green," *NYT*, October 5, 1958, p. 12; Press Releases from the Office of Senator Wayne Morse (Democrat-Oregon), August 25, 1958, and August 29, 1958, attached to Morse to Lehman, October 3, 1958, LP, SF, Morse; "Democratic Brass Outlines '58 Issues," *Christian Science Monitor*,

September 11, 1958, p. 16; Edelstein to Lehman, September 3, 1958 and September 6, 1958, both in LP, Special Subject Files, New York State Democratic Convention, 1958; "Not One Life for Quemoy, Lehman Plea," *Chicago Tribune*, September 20, 1958, p. 2; "Lehman Opposes U.S. Risk," *Findlay (OH) Republican-Courier*, September 20, 1958, p. 1; Herbert Lehman, "Against Islands' Defense," Letter to the Editor, *NYT*, September 23, 1958, p. 32; "Lehman: Quemoy Not Worth a War," Letter to the Editor, *New York Herald Tribune*, September 23, 1958, p. 20; Lehman to Benjamin Cohen, September 23, 1958, LP, SF, Cohen.

57. Kennedy to Lehman, September 20, 1958, and Lehman to Kennedy, September 25, 1958, LP, SF, Kennedy.

58. Lehman to Kennedy, September 25, 1958, and Kennedy to Lehman, October 2, 1958, both in LP, SF, Kennedy; Feldman to Bert Doering, October 7, 1958, and Kennedy to Professor Kahin, October 9, 1958, both in JFK, PPP, Box 692, Senate Legislative Files, 1953–1960, 1958, Foreign Policy: Formosa, October 5–October 10, 1958. On Kennedy's position on the Lehman amendment and the final text of the Formosa Resolution in 1955, see 101 *Cong. Rec.* 987, 994 (January 28, 1955).

59. Lehman to James Marshall, October 14, 1958, LP, SF, Marshall. On the end of the Formosa crisis, see Young, *Negotiating with the Chinese Communists*, pp. 160–198; and Stolper, *China, Taiwan, and the Offshore Islands*, pp. 130–131. On Formosa in the 1960 campaign, see chapter 19, and see Democratic National Committee Research Division, "The Issue of Quemoy and Matsu," Fact Sheet RD 60-24, October 1960, JFK, PPP, Box 1030, 1960 Campaign, Press and Publicity, Speeches, Statements, and Sections, Foreign Affairs—Quemoy and Matsu.

60. "2 Senate Leaders Back Compromise on Closure Rule," *NYT*, January 10, 1957, pp. 1, 21; "Filibuster Curb Voted by 'Hill' Unit," *WP*, March 27, 1958, C12; U.S. Senate, Committee on Rules and Administration, *Proposed Amendments to Rule XXII of the Standing Rules of the Senate*, S. Rept. 1534, 85th Cong., 2nd sess., April 30, 1958; 104 *Cong. Rec.* 7682 (April 30, 1958), 7842 (May 1, 1958), 17536 (August 14, 1958), 18077 (August 18, 1958), 19356 (August 23, 1958); Hennings to Lehman, December 19, 1958, LP, SF, Hennings; 104 *Cong. Rec.* 15428 (July 29, 1958); Javits, *Javits*, p. 258.

61. "48 Million Slated to Vote Tuesday; Off-Year Record," *NYT*, November 2, 1958, pp. 1, 54; "Election: Pocketbook Big Issue," *NYT*, November 2, 1958, E5; "Democrats Gain 13 Senate Seats," *NYT*, November 6, 1958, pp. 1, 16; Chalmers Roberts, "Voters Respond . . . Republicans Erred on Issues," *WP*, November 7, 1958, A17; "The News of the Week in Review: Now for '60," *NYT*, November 9, 1958, E1; "Erratic Big Wind Picked Them by Personality," *WP*, November 9, 1958, E1; Foley, *The New Senate*, pp. 25–26; Mann, *The Walls of Jericho*, p. 236. On the Sherman Adams scandal, see Edward Weinfeld to Lehman, July 14, 1958, LP, SF, Weinfeld; and Parmet, *Eisenhower and the American Crusades*, pp. 518–523. On Landrum-Griffin, see Lee, *Eisenhower and Landrum-Griffin*.

62. Julius Edelstein, Memorandum to Senator Lehman September 25, 1958, LP, SF, Edelstein; Lehman to Eleanor Roosevelt, October 23, 1958, LP, SF, Eleanor Roosevelt; Lehman to Mike Monroney, July 18, 1958, LP, SF, Monroney; Lehman to Albert Gore, July 19, 1958, and Lehman to Julius, July 23, 1958, both in LP, SF, Gore; Parmet, *Jack*, pp. 449–464. The 1958 elections in New York will be discussed in more detail in the next chapter.

63. " 'Right-to-Work' Boomerang," Editorial, *WP*, November 8, 1958, A8; "New Group to Fight the 'Right-to-Work,' " *NYT*, July 10, 1958, p. 28; "N.Y. Ex-Sen. Lehman Raps Right to Work," *Los Angeles Times*, October 22, 1958, p. 9; Meany to Lehman, December 11, 1958, LP, SF, Meany; Reuther to Lehman, January 21, 1959, LP, SF, Reuther; "5 of 6 States Beat 'Work' Proposals," *NYT*, November 6, 1958, p. 19; "Foes of Work Law Went Democratic," *NYT*, November 9, 1958, p. 72; Joseph Alsop, "A Fantasy Called 'Right to Work,' " *WP*, November 9, 1958, E-5; Miller and Ware, "Organized Labor in the Political Process: A Case Study of the Right-to-Work Campaign in Ohio"; Davies, *Defender of the Old Guard*, pp. 195–204; author's interview with Senator Bricker, Columbus, OH, June 26, 1975.

64. Lehman to Allan Nevins, November 8, 1958, LP, SF, Nevins; Lehman to Paul Douglas, November 10, 1958, LP, SF, Douglas; Allen Drury, "The Vote: What Kind of Congress?" *NYT*, November 9, 1958, E5; "Democrats View Gains as Mandate for Action; Ike to Battle Spenders; Victors Expect to Increase Big Lead on 'Hill,' " *WP*, November 6, 1958, A1, A12; "Democrats Gain 13 Senate Seats," *NYT*, November 6, 1958, pp. 1, 16; "Senate Vote Hits G.O.P. Right Wing," *NYT*, November 6, 1958, p. 24; "The National Picture," Editorial, *NYT*, November 6, 1958, p. 36; "Erratic Big Wind Picked Them by Personality," *WP*, November 9, 1958, E1; "Douglas Sees Mandate to Push Civil Rights," *WP*, November 9, 1958, A2; "Filibuster Curb Chances Brighten," *WP*, November 9, 1958, A2; Foley, *The New Senate*, pp. 26–30; Mann, *The Walls of Jericho*, pp. 236–238.

65. "4 Senators Pledge to Seek Curb on 'Veto Power' of Filibusters," *WP*, September 23, 1958, A17; Lehman to Douglas, October 1, 1958; Douglas to Lehman, October 10, 1958; Lehman to Douglas, October 21, 1958; Douglas to Lehman, November 2, 1958; and Frank McCulloch to Lehman, October 6, 1958; all in LP, SF, Douglas.

66. Douglas, *In the Fullness of Time*, p. 213; William S. White, "Filibuster Fight Coming," *Washington Evening Star*, November 19, 1958, reprinted in *Syracuse Herald-Journal*, November 20, 1958, p. 38.

67. Herbert Lehman, "On the Senate Filibuster Rule," *Washington Evening Star*, December 1, 1958, copy in LP, SF, Douglas. Lehman also rejected White's assertion in *The Citadel: The Story of the U.S. Senate*, that compromise and accommodation with the "inner club" were necessary to be a good Senator. See Lehman to Paul Douglas, March 11, 1957, LP, SF, Douglas; and White, *The Citadel*, pp. 111, 115.

68. Herbert Lehman, "On the Senate Filibuster Rule," *Washington Evening Star*, December 1, 1958, copy in LP, SF, Douglas.

69. Ibid.

70. Lehman to John Kennedy, December 11, 1958, LP, SF, Kennedy; Lehman to Douglas, December 20, 1958, and Douglas to Lehman, December 16, 1958, both in LP, SF, Douglas; Proxmire to Lehman, December 16, 1958, LP, SF, Proxmire; Engle to Lehman, December 18, 1958, LP, SF, Engle; Williams to Lehman, December 24, 1958, LP, SF, Williams. All the Senators discussed in this paragraph voted for the Douglas proposal. See 105 *Cong. Rec.* 439 (January 12, 1959).

71. Chavez to Lehman, December 23, 1958, LP, SF, Chavez; Allott to Lehman, December 23, 1958, LP, SF, Allott; Lausche to Lehman, December 15, 1958, LP, SF, Lausche; Jackson to Lehman, December 17, 1958, LP, SF, Jackson; O'Mahoney to Lehman, December 19, 1958, LP, SF, O'Mahoney. All five Senators discussed in this

paragraph voted for the Anderson motion in 1957 but against the Douglas proposal in 1959. See 103 *Cong. Rec.* 215 (January 4, 1957) and 105 *Cong. Rec.* 439 (January 12, 1959).

72. Lehman to Roy Wilkins, January 2, 1959, LP, SF, Wilkins; Lehman to Hubert Humphrey, December 15, 1958, and Humphrey to Lehman, December 22, 1958, both in LP, SF, Humphrey; "Rallies Senators to Modify Filibuster," *Chicago Defender,* January 5, 1959, p. 4; "Dixiecrats See Rights Stalemate," *Chicago Defender,* January 5, 1959, A2; "Douglas Doubts Filibuster Curb," *NYT,* January 5, 1959, p. 18; "Showdown Charted on Filibuster," *Hartford Courant,* January 7, 1959, 11B; "Anti-Filibuster Leaders See Victory Chance," *Boston Globe,* January 7, 1959, pp. 1, 3; Roy Wilkins, "Race Relations in the U.S. 1958," *New York Amsterdam News,* January 3, 1959, p. 3; Lawson, Memorandum to Senator Kennedy Re: Revision of Rule 22, n.d., but probably January 6, 1959, JFK, PPP, Box 536, Senate Files, General Files, 1953–1960, 1958–1960, Civil Rights, 1957–1959; Lehman to Richard Neuberger, December 16, 1958, LP, SF, Neuberger. On Marjorie Lawson and Kennedy, see Bryant, *The Bystander,* p. 90, and Parmet, *Jack,* pp. 453–456.

73. Lehman to Neuberger, December 16, 1958, LP, SF, Neuberger; Lawson, Memorandum to Senator Kennedy Re: Revision of Rule 22, n.d., but probably January 6, 1959, JFK, PPP, Box 536, Senate Files, General Files, 1953–1960, 1958–1960, Civil Rights, 1957–1959; "The Filibuster Issue," Editorial, *WP,* January 5, 1959, A10; "Johnson Mum as Filibuster Fight Begins," *WP,* January 7, 1959, A1, A10; "Senate Liberals Map Battle Plan," *NYT,* January 7, 1959, pp. 1, 25.

74. Lehman to John Sherman Cooper, January 9, 1959, LP, SF, Cooper; "New Senators Yoo-Hoo to Friends in Gallery," *Hartford Courant,* January 8, 1959, 9B; 105 *Cong. Rec.* 6–11 (January 7, 1959). S. Res. 5, 86th Cong., 1st sess., January 7, 1959, was co-sponsored by Johnson; Carl Hayden (D-AZ), the senior-most Democrat in the Senate and the head of the Appropriations Committee; Minority Leader Everett Dirksen of Illinois; Democratic Whip Mike Mansfield of Montana; Leverett Saltonstall of Massachusetts, the chairman of the Republican Conference; and Styles Bridges of New Hampshire, the chairman of the Republican Policy Committee. See 105 *Cong. Rec.* 8 (January 7, 1959). The only member of the leadership of either party who did not co-sponsor the resolution was Republican Whip Thomas Kuchel of California, who supported the Anderson motion on changing the rules and the Douglas proposal for majority cloture.

75. 105 *Cong. Rec.* 6–11 (January 7, 1959); "Congress Opens with Rules Fight; . . . Liberals Lose Round In Senate," *WP,* January 8, 1959, A1, A17; "Filibuster Foes Set Back; Filibuster Fight Begins In Senate," *NYT,* January 8, 1959, pp. 1, 11; "Filibuster Wrangle Headed Off," *Chicago Tribune,* January 8, 1959, p. 4; Doris Fleeson, "Two Political Virtuosos," *Boston Globe,* January 9, 1959, p. 32; Lehman to Paul Douglas, January 16, 1959, LP, SF, Douglas; Javits, *Javits,* pp. 258–259; Dallek, *Lone Star Rising,* p. 547; Mann, *The Walls of Jericho,* p. 239. The co-sponsors of the Anderson motion included Democrats Anderson, Douglas, Humphrey, Carroll, Clark, Symington, Neuberger, McNamara, Magnuson, Jackson, Kennedy, Lausche, Morse, Hennings, Proxmire, Pastore, Engle, Cannon, Hart, McCarthy, Muskie, and Williams (NJ); and Republicans Case, Javits, Kuchel, Smith, Bush, Allott, Cooper, Beall, Keating, Prouty, and Scott. See 105 *Cong. Rec.* 10 (January 7, 1959).

76. 105 *Cong. Rec.* 126 (January 8, 1959), 295 (January 9, 1959); Lehman to Clinton Anderson, January 28, 1959, LP, SF, Anderson; "Rule XXII," Editorial, *NYT,* January 9, 1959, p. 26; "Foes of Filibuster Defeated, 60–36; Johnson Is Victor," *NYT,* January 10, 1959, pp. 1, 8.

77. 105 *Cong. Rec.* 95–99, 103, 129, 131–132 (January 8, 1959), 296–299 (January 9, 1959); Douglas to Lehman, January 19, 1959, and Lehman to Douglas, January 23, 1959, both in LP, SF, Douglas; Hollander to Lehman, January 15, 1959, LP, SF, Americans for Democratic Action; "Rules Plan Faces Test Today; Senate to Vote on Motion to Block Liberals' Move; Lawmakers Argue Filibuster Curb for Second Day," *WP,* January 9, 1959, A1, A2; "Filibuster Foes Face a Setback in Voting Today," *NYT,* January 9, 1959, pp. 1, 14.

78. 105 *Cong. Rec.* 207–208 (January 9, 1959), 439, 446, 490, 494 (January 12, 1959); "Senate Approves Filibuster Curb Asked by Johnson," *NYT,* January 13, 1959, pp. 1, 18.

79. Lehman to John Sherman Cooper, January 9, 1959, LP, SF, Cooper; Lehman to Douglas, January 16, 1959, and January 23, 1959, both in LP, SF, Douglas; Lehman to Anderson, January 28, 1959, LP, SF, Anderson; Hart to Lehman, January 14, 1959, LP, SF, Hart. On Lehman's campaign contributions in 1958, see J.C.C.E., Memorandum to Senator Lehman, September 25, 1958, LP, SF, Edelstein; and Lehman to Eleanor Roosevelt, October 23, 1958, LP, SF, Eleanor Roosevelt. On the Senators' votes on the various measures, see "Senate Approves Filibuster Curb Asked by Johnson," *NYT,* January 13, 1959, pp. 1, 18; "Senate Roll-Call on Rules," *NYT,* January 10, 1959, p. 8; "Senate's Roll-Call Votes on Filibuster," *NYT,* January 13, 1959, p. 18. On Johnson's influence and the power of committee assignments, see Drew Pearson, "The Washington Merry-Go-Round: Johnson Swings Filibuster Votes," *WP,* January 14, 1959, B21. An article in the *Washington Post and Times-Herald* erroneously asserted that "Democratic committee assignments . . . showed no freshman was punished for opposing the leadership on the filibuster rules fight." In fact, Edmund Muskie was relegated to the Banking, Public Works, and Government Operations Committees for crossing Johnson, while Howard Cannon, who voted to table the Anderson motion even though he was one of its co-sponsors, received the appointment he wanted to the Armed Services Committee. Prized seats on the Appropriations Committee went to Senators Byrd and McGee, who voted with Johnson throughout the controversy, and Senator Dodd, who voted with Johnson to table the Anderson motion. Dodd was also appointed to the Judiciary and the Space and Astronautics Committees. See "House GOP Fires a Broadside at Red Probe Unit's Opponents," *WP,* January 15, 1959, A2; "Cannon Says He'll Reverse Sen. Malone," *WP,* December 6, 1958, A2; Robert Byrnes, "Washington Report: Dodd Gets Major Committee Posts; Appropriations, Judiciary, Space," *Hartford Courant,* January 15, 1959, p. 2; 105 *Cong. Rec.* 671 (January 14, 1959); Evans and Novak, *Lyndon B. Johnson,* pp. 200–202; Steinberg, *Sam Johnson's Boy,* p. 495; Dallek, *Lone Star Rising,* pp. 547–548. Lehman continued to be "deeply disappointed at the performance of some of our liberal friends in whom I had placed great confidence," telling Wayne Morse in July 1959 that "the attitude of some liberals certainly has not been edifying nor what I had expected from the last campaign." See Lehman to Morse, July 26, 1959, LP, SF, Morse.

80. Kennedy to Mrs. William Lam, November 17, 1958, JFK, PPP, Box 687, Senate Files, Legislative Files, 1953–1960, 1958, Civil Rights, May 28–December 31,

1958; Marjorie Lawson, Memorandum to Senator Kennedy, "Strategy on Rule 22," December 2, 1958, JFK, PPP, Box 544, Senate General Files, 1953–1960, 1958–1960, POF, "L"; Lehman to Kennedy, December 11, 1958, LP, SF, Kennedy. On Marjorie Lawson, see Parmet, *Jack*, pp. 387, 453–456; and Bryant, *The Bystander*, pp. 91, 94–95, 101, 105–106, 109–111.

81. Kennedy to Dr. Thomas Plaut, January 7, 1959; Kennedy to Thomas Gallagher, January 16, 1959; and Hollander to Kennedy, January 26, 1959, all in JFK, PPP, Box 714, Senate Legislative Files, 1953–1960, 1959, Cloture; Marjorie Lawson, Memorandum to Senator Kennedy Re: Strategy on Rule 22, December 2, 1958, JFK, PPP, Box 544, Senate General Files, 1953–1960, 1958–1960 POF, "L;" Lawson, Memorandum to Senator Kennedy Re: Revision of Rule 22, n.d., JFK, PPP, Box 536, Senate General Files, 1953–1960, 1958–1960, Civil Rights, 1957–1959.

82. "State of World 'Alarms' Lehman," *NYT*, December 12, 1956, p. 21; Philip Perlman to Lehman, August 14, 1957, Lehman to Perlman, August 27, 1957, and Perlman to Lehman, August 30, 1957, all in LP, SF, Perlman; Julius Edelstein Oral History Transcript, HHLP, CUOHC, p. 14; Ralph Dungan Oral History Transcript, p. 28, JFKL.

83. 103 *Cong. Rec.* 8347–8349 (June 5, 1957), 10457 (June 27, 1957), 16176–16177 (August 27, 1957), 16719–16720 (August 30, 1957); Walter quoted in "Compromise Set on Immigration," *NYT*, August 16, 1957, p. 3; Kennedy to Reverend Bishop Anson Phelps Stokes, Jr., June 19, 1957, and Press Release from the Office of Senator John F. Kennedy, June 27, 1957, both in JFK, PPP, Box 670, Senate Legislative Files, 1953–1960, 1956–1957, Immigration Legislation, June 19–July 8, 1957; "Immigration Rise in 1957 Is Doubted," *NYT*, February 2, 1957, p. 6; "Legislative Prospects—I: Refugee Bills Still Blocked," *WP*, April 30, 1957, A-13; "Kennedy Files Immigration Bill to Admit 72,000," *Boston Globe*, June 28, 1957, p. 10; "Democrats Back Easing of Curbs On Alien Quotas," *NYT*, July 4, 1957, pp. 1, 11; "Immigrant Rule Eased in House," *WP*, August 13, 1957, A-2; "A Refugee Bill Gains in Senate," *NYT*, August 21, 1957, p. 13; "Senate Votes Relief of Alien Hardships," *NYT*, August 22, 1957, pp. 1, 5; "Immigration Bill Passed by Senate," *NYT*, August 30, 1957, p. 17; John F. Kennedy, Memorandum, August 1957, JFK, PPP, Box 670, Senate Legislative Files, 1953–1960, 1956–1957, Immigration Legislation, August 12–August 20, 1957; Ralph Dungan to Rev. Z. K. Vipartas, September 20, 1957, JFK, PPP, Box 670, Senate Legislative Files, 1953–1960, 1956–1957, Immigration Legislation, September 20–September 27, 1957; Lehman to Edward Weinfeld, September 2, 1957, LP, SF, Weinfeld. For speculation that Lyndon Johnson had designated Kennedy to play the lead role among the Democrats on immigration reform in the Senate to boost the chances of a Johnson-Kennedy ticket in 1960, see "Johnson Plugs Kennedy as '60 Running Mate," *Chicago Tribune*, August 18, 1957, p. 2.

84. William Korey to Ralph Dungan, April 29, 1958, JFK, PPP, Box 767, Senate Files, Legislative Assistants' Background Files, 1953–1960, Immigration, September 17, 1956–July 11, 1958, and Undated; Parmet, *Jack*, p. 479; Kennedy, *A Nation of Immigrants*, p. 37.

85. "Walter Confident of Plan Support," *Christian Science Monitor*, January 5, 1959, p. 2; "Walter's Grip Imperils Immigration Reform," *WP*, December 11, 1958, A21; "Rep. Walter Asks New Committee," *Los Angeles Times*, December 18, 1958, p. 12; *Watkins v. United States*, 354 U.S. 178 (1957); "Court Pondering Power of Inquiry,"

NYT, March 8, 1957, p. 11; "High Court, Releasing Watkins, Restricts Congress on Privacy; . . . Union Aide Victor," *NYT*, June 18, 1957, pp. 1, 20; "Inquiry Reform Seen Inevitable," *NYT*, June 19, 1957, p. 16; "Walter Deplores Decision on Reds," *NYT*, June 19, 1957, p. 18; "The Nation: Watkins Aftermath," *NYT*, July 14, 1957, E2; Alan Barth, "Warren Court vs. Vinson Court," *WP*, January 18, 1959, E3; Goodman, *The Committee*, pp. 358–361, 411–413.

86. "Lehman Opposes House Unit Shift," *NYT*, January 3, 1959, p. 7; "Lehman Fears Calamity," *NYT*, January 5, 1959, p. 17; Goodman, *The Committee*, pp. 372, 394–398.

87. Herbert Lehman, "The Test before the House," *WP*, January 6, 1959, A10.

88. Lehman, Memorandum for the Files, December 30, 1958, LP, SF, Truman.

89. "Security Suzerainty," Editorial, *WP*, December 19, 1958, A12; "House Red Probers Plan to Reorganize," *Hartford Courant*, December 21, 1958, 30A; "The Un-American Activities Committee should be abolished, not reorganized and expanded," advertisement, *WP*, January 7, 1959, A8; Herblock, "The Idea Is to Set It Up in a Quick Change, See?" *WP*, January 5, 1959, A10; Lehman to Herbert Block, January 8, 1959, LP, SF, Block.

90. "Rayburn Blocks Alien-Laws Shift," *NYT*, January 6, 1959, p. 18; Lehman to Richard Neuberger, January 6, 1959, LP, SF, Neuberger; Lehman to Truman, January 7, 1959, LP, SF, Truman; Goodman, *The Committee*, p. 413. It is not clear if Truman actually did anything to help kill Walter's plan. Records at the Truman Library do not show any meeting or correspondence on this matter between Truman and Rayburn during the week between Lehman's phone call and the Speaker's announcement, but it is possible that Truman discussed it with Rayburn on the telephone. Truman might well have followed through, for he shared Lehman's dislike for HUAC. A few months later, Truman denounced the committee as "the most un-American thing in the country today." See email from Randy Sowell, Archivist, Truman Library, to this author, July 11, 2012; and "Truman Day Here: Talk, Walk, Talk," *NYT*, April 30, 1959, p. 17.

91. 104 *Cong. Rec.* 5744 (March 31, 1958); Kennedy to Lehman, March 28, 1958, and Lehman to Kennedy, October 20, 1958, LP, SF, Kennedy; Kennedy to Lehman, April 1, 1958, JFK, PPP, Box 456, Senate Files, Correspondence, Correspondence Copy Files, 1953–1960, Yellows: 1958, File 2: Sorensen, Political, "L"; "Mr. Lehman's 80 Good Years," Editorial, *NYT*, March 28, 1958, p. 24; Lehman to Kennedy, April 15, 1957, JFK, PPP, Box 521, Senate Files, General Files, 1953–1960, 1956–1957, L(2); "Senator and Cleric Get Amity Awards," *NYT*, May 27, 1957, p. 30; Kennedy to Ira Guilden, October 6, 1958, JFK, PPP, Box 457, Senate Files, Correspondence, Correspondence Copy Files, 1953–1960, Yellows: 1958, File 2: October–December, 1958; Benjamin Swig to Kennedy, August 11, 1958, JFK, PPP, Box 536, Senate Files, General Files, 1953–1960, 1958–1960, POF, Committees, Honorary, 1957–1958; Swig to Kennedy, October 21, 1958, JFK, PPP, Box 611, Senate Files, Invitations, 1953–1958, Invitations Accepted, November 1958.

92. "Remarks of Senator John F. Kennedy," Testimonial Dinner for Herbert H. Lehman, Sponsored by the Jewish Theological Seminary of America, November 23, 1958, LP, SF, Kennedy; Kennedy to Dr. Louis Finkelstein, December 15, 1958, JFK, PPP, Box 457, Senate Files, Correspondence, Correspondence Copy Files, 1953–1960, Yellows: 1958, File 2: October–December, 1958.

93. Telegram, Lehman to Kennedy, November 1958, JFK, PPP, Box 544, Senate Files, General Files, 1953–1960, 1958–1960, POF "L," Lauback-Levy; Kennedy to Lehman, November 15, 1958, LP, SF, Kennedy. On Kennedy's re-election in 1958 over Vincent Celeste, see Parmet, *Jack*, pp. 449–458. On liberal doubts about Kennedy, see Parmet, *Jack*, pp. 460–464; Dallek, *An Unfinished Life*, pp. 232–239.

Chapter 19. "You Weren't Double—Crossed, I Was": Herbert Lehman, John Kennedy, and the Bosses, 1961–1963

1. Moynihan, "'Bosses' and 'Reformers,'" p. 467.

2. HHLOH, pp. 273–274; Marquis Childs, "Split in New York Plagues Democrats," *WP*, October 30, 1956, A12; "Kennedy Assures New York Chiefs," *NYT*, July 15, 1960, pp. 1, 10. On Lehman's battle with Tammany to secure the nomination for Governor in 1932, see chapter 2. On De Sapio, see Moscow, *The Last of the Big-Time Bosses*; Connable and Silberfarb, *Tigers of Tammany*, pp. 295–333; and Allen, *The Tiger*, pp. 261–277. On De Sapio, Wagner, and the mayoral elections of 1953 and 1957, see McNickle, *To Be Mayor of New York*, pp. 91–121. On the connections between the early New York City Democratic reform movement and the Stevenson campaigns, see Moscow, *The Last of the Big-Time Bosses*, pp. 137–138; Moynihan, "'Bosses' and 'Reformers,'" p. 462; Costikyan, *Behind Closed Doors*, pp. 18–19, 25–26, 77–79, 344–345; Eleanor Roosevelt, *On My Own*, pp. 172–173; Wilson, *The Amateur Democrat*, pp. 22, 52–57; Anthony Akers Oral History Transcript, p. 10, JFKL; McNickle, *To Be Mayor of New York*, pp. 89, 114–116. I am indebted to Steven Petrus for pointing me to many of the key sources and improving my understanding of the reform movement in New York Democratic politics in the late 1950s and early 1960s. See Steven Petrus, "To Break Down Walls: The Politics and Culture of Greenwich Village, 1955–1965," PhD Dissertation, City University of New York Graduate Center, 2010, pp. 45–46, 51–52.

3. "Lehman, Hailed at Birthday Fete, Urges a Liberal Democrat for Senate," *NYT*, March 30, 1958, pp. 1, 41; "Finletter Gets Lehman Backing in Democratic Race for Senate," *NYT*, May 8, 1958, p. 34; "Finletter Picked for Albany Post," March 28, 1958, p. 18; "Search for Candidates Is on in the State," *NYT*, March 30, 1958, E6; Moynihan, "'Bosses' and 'Reformers,'" pp. 465–466; Abramson, *Spanning the Century*, pp. 553–554; Edelstein, Memorandum to Senator Lehman, August 29, 1958, LP, Special Subject Files (hereinafter SSF), New York State Democratic Convention, 1958.

4. "Finletter Enters Race for Senate," *NYT*, July 24, 1958, pp. 1, 13; Lehman to Edward Weinfeld, August 2, 1958, LP, SF, Weinfeld; Memorandum, Julius Edelstein to Lehman, March 20, 1958, LP, SF, Edelstein.

5. Lehman to Wagner, August 7, 1958; Lehman to Harriman, August 10, 1958; Edelstein to Lehman, August 14, 1958; Edelstein to Lehman, August 18, 1958; Edelstein to Lehman, August 22, 1958; Lehman to Harriman, August 24, 1958; Lehman to Finletter, August 24, 1958; Edelstein to Lehman, August 27, 1958; and Edelstein, Memorandum to Senator Lehman, August 29, 1958; all in LP, SSF, New York State Democratic Convention, 1958; Finletter to Lehman, August 11, 1958, LP, SF, Finletter; "Harriman Backs Finletter; Murray Is Second Choice," *NYT*, August 15, 1958, pp. 1, 14; "Democratic Chiefs Weigh Choice for Senate Contest," *NYT*, August 25, 1958,

pp. 1, 12; "Democrats Pick Hogan for Senate over Murray after a Party Split," *NYT*, August 27, 1958, pp. 1, 20; "Harriman Seeks Democrats' Unity after Hogan Rift," *NYT*, August 28, 1958, pp. 1, 14; "New York's Election May Turn on 'Bossism,'" *NYT*, August 31, 1958, E-4; Berle and Jacobs, eds., *Navigating the Rapids*, p. 688; Costikyan, *Behind Closed Doors*, pp. 159–162; Moynihan, "'Bosses' and 'Reformers,'" pp. 465–466; Moscow, *The Last of the Big-Time Bosses*, pp. 139–158; Connable and Silberfarb, *Tigers of Tammany*, pp. 330–331; Abramson, *Spanning the Century*, pp. 552–569; McNickle, *To Be Mayor of New York*, pp. 124–130, 137–138. Columnist Robert Spivack speculated that De Sapio wanted to remove the "scrupulously honest" Hogan from the District Attorney's office to protect the mob's influence in Tammany Hall, while liberal activist Arthur Schlesinger, Jr., believed that De Sapio's preference for Hogan over Finletter represented De Sapio's "capitulation to the Know-Nothing elements in the lower rungs of the party organization," reflecting "a revolt of the low-level professional within the party organization against the New Deal and post–New Deal leadership of the Democratic Party." Edward Costikyan, De Sapio's successor as the leader of New York County Democrats, attributed De Sapio's actions to "an ego that led him to place himself farther and farther out front," and his fondness for delaying decisions so he could "spring things at the last minute." Longtime reporter and De Sapio biographer Warren Moscow argued that De Sapio wanted to demonstrate his control over the state convention in 1958 to enhance his influence in the selection of the Democratic presidential nominee in 1960. See Robert Spivack, "Watch on the Potomac," *Chicago Defender*, September 8, 1958, A-4; Arthur Schlesinger, Jr., "Death Wish of the Democrats," *New Republic*, September 15, 1958, pp. 7–8; Costikyan, *Behind Closed Doors*, p. 315; and Moscow, *The Last of the Big-Time Bosses*, pp. 145–146.

6. Lehman to Edward Weinfeld, September 9, 1958, LP, SF, Weinfeld; Lehman to Robert Wagner, Jr., September 2, 1958, LP, SF, Wagner; "Liberals Pushing Finletter Choice," *NYT*, August 22, 1958, pp. 1, 42; "Liberals Choose Finletter for Senate, but Could Shift," *NYT*, August 27, 1958, pp. 1, 22; "Finletter Bars Race as Liberal," *NYT*, August 29, 1958, pp. 1, 46; Lehman to Alex Rose, September 2, 1958; Edelstein to Lehman, September 3, 1958; Lehman to Dubinsky, September 3, 1958; and Hogan to Lehman, September 5, 1958, all in LP, SSF, New York State Democratic Convention, 1958; "Lehman Counsels Liberals to Back Hogan for Senate," *NYT*, September 4, 1958, pp. 1, 19; "Hogan Is Backed by the Liberals," *NYT*, September 5, 1958, pp. 1, 19; Berle and Jacobs, eds., *Navigating the Rapids*, p. 688; Moscow, *The Last of the Big-Time Bosses*, pp. 152–153.

7. Lehman to Richard Neuberger, September 18, 1958, LP, SF, Neuberger; "Rockefeller Sets De Sapio as Issue," *NYT*, August 29, 1958, p. 24; "Rockefeller Hits at De Sapio Again," *NYT*, August 30, 1958, p. 16; "Keating Attacks Hogan on Bossism," *NYT*, October 3, 1958, p. 14; "Keating Attacks De Sapio's Role," *NYT*, October 17, 1958, p. 21; "Rockefeller Says Tammany's Chief 'Rules' Harriman," *NYT*, October 17, 1958, pp. 1, 17; "Keating for Senator," Editorial, *NYT*, October 17, 1958, p. 28; Lehman to Paul Douglas, October 21, 1958, LP, SF, Douglas; George Backer to Lehman, October 31, 1958, LP, SF, Backer; Independent Citizens Committee for Harriman-Hogan advertisement for "Today on Radio: Herbert H. Lehman on Rockefeller—Prisoner of Reaction?" *NYT*, October 28, 1958, p. 70; "3 State Democrats Make TV Records," *NYT*, October 28, 1958, p. 26; Herbert Lehman, Letter to the Editor, "Harriman

Defended," *NYT*, October 28, 1958, p. 34; Citizens for Rockefeller-Keating, "De Sapio Bossism Shocks . . . Democrats . . . Liberals . . . Labor," *NYT*, October 3, 1958, p. 22; "Lehman Protests Ad," *NYT*, October 7, 1958, p. 23; "20,000 in the Garment District Hear Democratic-Liberal Candidates," *NYT*, October 31, 1958, pp. 1, 18; "Democrats Ask Mandate to Finish Work 'in the Liberal Tradition,'" *NYT*, November 4, 1958, pp. 1, 21; Smith, *On His Own Terms*, pp. 281–291.

8. "Rockefeller Wins by 560,000 Margin; Harriman Routed," *NYT*, November 5, 1958, pp. 1, 32; "Keating Wins Senate Post, Beating Hogan by 160,000," *NYT*, November 5, 1958, pp. 1, 30; "Mr. De Sapio Downgraded," Editorial, *NYT*, November 6, 1958, p. 36; "Democrats Gain 13 Senate Seats," *NYT*, November 6, 1958, pp. 1, 16; Lehman to Allan Nevins, November 8, 1958, LP, SF, Nevins; Abramson, *Spanning the Century*, pp. 563–568; Moscow, *The Last of the Big-Time Bosses*, pp. 152–158. On Rockefeller's effectiveness as a campaigner, see Reich, *The Life of Nelson A. Rockefeller*, pp. 733–752 and 765–767; Boyd and Holcomb, *Oreos and Dubonnet*, pp. 1–2, 5–11, 63–75; Smith, *On His Own Terms*, pp. 265–291. While Harriman lost to Rockefeller by 557,000 votes, Hogan ran a much closer race, losing to Keating by 131,000 votes, and Warren Moscow asserts that "Hogan would have done better, could have even won, if his campaign had not been sabotaged in his own headquarters and at the polls by the reformers." According to Moscow, "De Sapio, in his eagerness to heal party wounds, had turned over the actual management of the Harriman-Hogan joint campaign to the reformers when he appointed Finletter chairman of the Citizens Committee for Harriman-Hogan," and Moscow details instances that he witnessed where the Hogan campaign was allegedly undermined by its own campaign committee. Moscow never explains, however, why De Sapio would have allowed such actions to continue, especially since De Sapio's own reputation was at stake in the elections, or why the party organization didn't counter such tactics by stepping up its own efforts on Hogan's behalf. Moscow does not mention Herbert Lehman when discussing this alleged sabotage of the Hogan campaign, and he notes Lehman's crucial role in helping Hogan obtain the Liberal Party nomination. See Moscow, *The Last of the Big-Time Bosses*, pp. 152–153, 158; and "Complete Vote for Governor and Senator; Results of State and Local Contests," *NYT*, November 6, 1958, p. 28.

9. Moscow, *The Last of the Big-Time Bosses*, pp. 123–124, 152–153, 160; Lehman to Edward Weinfeld, September 9, 1958, LP, SF, Weinfeld; McNickle, *To Be Mayor of New York*, pp. 137–138; Eleanor Roosevelt, "My Day," October 17, 1958, online: http://www.gwu.edu/~erpapers/myday/displaydoc.cfm?_y=1958&_f=md004252; "Mrs. Roosevelt Wary on Hogan," *NYT*, October 27, 1958, p. 21; "Mrs. Roosevelt Supports Hogan," *NYT*, October 30, 1958, p. 24; Lash, *Eleanor: The Years Alone*, pp. 274–276.

10. "Harriman Meets 3 Top Democrats on Party's Policy," *NYT*, November 15, 1958, pp. 1, 24; Edelstein, Memorandum to Senator Lehman, November 21, 1958; Liz to Senator, November 24, 1958; and Lehman, Memorandum for the Files, December 30, 1958, all in LP, SF, Harriman; Alistair Cooke, "White House Manoeuvres," *Manchester Guardian*, November 19, 1958, p. 6; McNickle, *To Be Mayor of New York*, pp. 138–139; Draft Announcements by Governor Harriman, Mayor Wagner, Former Senator Lehman, and Controller Levitt, December 6, 1958, and December 27, 1958, both in LP, SSF, New York City Reform Politics, 1957–January 1959. Although no public announcement of such a committee was ever made, the draft announcements reflect Lehman's concern

about being associated with party leaders. The original draft announcement asserted that this State Democratic Advisory Committee was being established at the suggestion of State Chairman Prendergast. The second draft omitted any mention of Prendergast. Prendergast did appoint a State Democratic Advisory Committee chaired by Harriman in June 1959. Lehman, having already launched his public challenge to the party organization, refused to participate. See "Democrats Plan Fight for State," *NYT*, June 28, 1959, p. 28. On Prendergast's background, see Moynihan, "'Bosses' and 'Reformers,'" p. 467; on Prendergast's subservience to De Sapio, see Moscow, *The Last of the Big-Time Bosses*, pp. 149, 164. On George Backer, see Abramson, *Spanning the Century*, pp. 506–507.

11. "Texts of Two Democratic Statements," *NYT*, January 23, 1959, p. 12; Edelstein, Memorandum to the Senator, January 15 [1959], LP, SSF, New York City Reform Politics, 1957–January 1959; Moynihan, "'Bosses' and 'Reformers,'" pp. 461–466; Moscow, *The Last of the Big-Time Bosses*, p. 160; Petrus, "To Break Down Walls," pp. 57–58.

12. Moscow, *The Last of the Big-Time Bosses*, pp. 160–161; "Democratic Liberals Open Drive to Remove De Sapio," *NYT*, January 23, 1959, pp. 1, 12; Texts of Two Democratic Statements," *NYT*, January 23, 1959, p. 12; McNickle, *To Be Mayor of New York*, pp. 139–140.

13. "Young Democrats Hail Reform Move," *NYT*, January 25, 1959, p. 21; "George Backer, Harriman Aide, Hails Group Opposing De Sapio," *NYT*, January 29, 1959, p. 15; "Anti-De Sapio Reform," Editorial, *NYT*, January 24, 1959, p. 18; "The Nation: Against De Sapio," *NYT*, January 25, 1959, E2; Tom O'Hara, "Anti-De Sapio Candidates to Get Funds," *New York Herald Tribune*, February 11, 1959, clipping in LP, SSF, New York City Reform Politics, February 1959; "Lecture on Unity," Editorial, *Chicago Tribune*, September 21, 1959, p. 16; "Democrats Mixed on Reform Call," *NYT*, January 24, 1959, p. 8; "Finletter Doubts Harriman Report," *NYT*, February 9, 1959, p. 19; "Wagner Supports De Sapio Against Ouster Attempts," *NYT*, February 10, 1959, pp. 1, 23; Eleanor Roosevelt, "My Day," February 11, 1959, online: http://www.gwu.edu/~erpapers/myday/displaydoc.cfm?_y=1958&_f=md004352; "De Sapio Upheld by Party Chiefs on Bossism Issue," *NYT*, February 15, 1959, pp. 1, 46; Lehman to Douglas, January 23, 1959, LP, SF, Douglas.

14. On Lehman's contributions and fund-raising for the CDV, see "Notes for Remarks at Fund Raising Dinner of New York Committee for Democratic Voters," March 5, 1959, LP, SSF, New York City Reform Politics, March 1959; Patty Lewis, Memorandum to Sam Harris, "Contributions Received to Date by the Committee," March 13, 1959, LP, SSF, New York City Reform Politics, 11–30 September 1959; Backer to Lehman, March 10, 1959, LP, SF, Backer; Lehman to Finletter, April 2, 1959, LP, SF, Finletter; Moscow, *The Last of the Big-Times Bosses*, p. 161. On Lehman's February 21 meeting with the insurgents, see Lehman to Nevins, February 23, 1959, LP, SF, Nevins; Press Release, "Excerpts from Remarks of Honorable Herbert H. Lehman at Meeting with Reform Leaders," February 21, 1959, LP, SSF, New York City Reform Politics, February 1959; "Lehman Renews Fight on 'Bosses,'" *NYT*, February 22, 1959, p. 64; Catherine Hemenway to Thomas Finletter, March 1, 1959, LP, SF, Finletter. On Lehman's interviews and speeches, see "Wagner's Stand Puzzles Lehman," *NYT*, March 2, 1959, p. 18; "Remarks of Former Senator Herbert H. Lehman at Women's National Democratic Club Dinner, Washington, D.C., March 19, 1959," Extension of Remarks of Hon. Samuel S. Stratton, May 14, 1959, 105 *Cong. Rec.* A4077–A4079; "Lehman

Attacks Idea of City Boss," *NYT*, March 20, 1959, p. 16. On Lehman's speech to the FDR-Woodrow Wilson Independent Democrats, see Helen Gahagan Douglas to Allan Nevins, April 10, 1959, LP, SF, Helen Gahagan Douglas; "Remarks of Former Senator Herbert H. Lehman at Meeting of F.D.R.-Woodrow Wilson Independent Democrats," March 30, 1959, LP, SSF, New York City Reform Politics, March 1959; "A Free Judiciary Asked by Lehman," *NYT*, March 31, 1959, p. 32. On Lehman's meeting with Costikyan and McCabe, see Paul Bragdon, Memorandum to Senator Lehman, March 26, 1959, LP, SSF, New York City Reform Politics, March 1959; and Costikyan to Lehman, April 8, 1959, LP, SF, Backer. On Lehman's comments before leaving for Europe, see "Lehman Sees Fight for District Posts," *NYT*, April 9, 1959, p. 18; and Lehman to George Backer, April 13, 1959, LP, SF, Backer. On the New York press corps ditty, see "Politicians Get a Ride in Rhyme," *NYT*, March 8, 1959, p. 75.

15. "Foes of De Sapio Talk in Village," *NYT*, June 12, 1959, p. 18; Petrus, "To Break Down Walls," p. 61; "Prendergast on Lehman's List for Ouster in 'Bossism' Fight," *NYT*, June 18, 1959, p. 15; "Lehman Assails Ban on Political Ideals," *NYT*, June 30, 1959, p. 23; "Lehman Cancels Appointments," *NYT*, July 1, 1959, p. 15.

16. "Remarks of Honorable Herbert H. Lehman at 6th Assembly District Motorcade Rally," September 8, 1959, and "Remarks of Honorable Herbert H. Lehman at 7th Assembly District Rally Sponsored by Riverside Democratic Club," September 10, 1959, both in LP, SSF, New York City Reform Politics, 1–10 September 1959; William Fitts Ryan and Shirley Kaye to Lehman, October 16, 1959, LP, SF, Ryan; "7 Primary Fights Arouse West Side," *NYT*, September 7, 1959, p. 11; " 'New Blood' Urged By Lehman," *NYT*, September 13, 1959, p. 16; "Lehman Warns 'Village' Voters," *NYT*, September 10, 1959, p. 28.

17. "Stakes Are High in De Sapio Race," *NYT*, September 11, 1959, p. 18; "De Sapio Is Victor in Close Primary as Key Aides Lose," *NYT*, September 16, 1959, pp. 1, 34; McNickle, *To Be Mayor of New York*, pp. 144–145; Petrus, "To Break Down Walls," p. 62. The *Chicago Tribune*, which had proclaimed Thomas Dewey the winner over Harry Truman in 1948, exaggerated when it reported that De Sapio had "crushed an insurgent challenge to his power in the September primary." See "De Sapio Rule to Get Test in Bench Ballot," *Chicago Tribune*, November 2, 1959, A6. The incumbent district leaders re-elected with CDV support included William Fitts Ryan, Edward Costikyan, Jean Baltzell, and Millard Midonick.

18. "Foes of De Sapio Threaten to Sue to Unseat Him," *NYT*, September 17, 1959, pp. 1, 26; "The Nation: De Sapio's Setback," *NYT*, September 20, 1959, E2; Lehman to Robert G. A. Jackson, October 5, 1959, LP, SF, Jackson. Chris McNickle argues that the growing strength of the reform movement also reflected the growing power of Jews in the Democratic Party at the expense of the Irish and Italian Catholics who had previously predominated. See McNickle, *To Be Mayor of New York*, pp. 141–144. James Q. Wilson emphasizes that in addition to being Jewish, many of the reformers were highly educated, young, middle-class professionals who welcomed women into their ranks. See Wilson, *The Amateur Democrat*, pp. 13–15.

19. "Basic Text of Informal Remarks of Hon. Herbert H. Lehman at Victory Reception for Reform Leaders," September 28, 1959, LP, SSF, New York City Reform Politics, 11–30 September 1959; "Mayor Seeks Unity," *NYT*, September 21, 1959, p. 4; "Lehman Presses Fight on 'Bosses,' " *NYT*, September 29, 1959, p. 29.

20. Press Release, "Broadened Executive Committee to Direct Democratic Party Reform Effort," December 29, 1959, JFK, PPP, Box 956, 1960 Campaign, Pre-Convention Political Files, 1959–1960, New York, Organization, April 1, 1957–February 26, 1960 and undated material; "Reform Democrats Widen Attack Here," *NYT*, December 30, 1959, pp. 1, 13. On the reorganization process, see "Remarks by Hon. Herbert H. Lehman at Meeting of the New York Young Democratic Club, Inc.," October 21, 1959, LP, SSF, New York City Reform Politics, October–December 1959; "Lehman Reports Insurgent Drive," *NYT*, October 22, 1959, p. 31. On Lehman's long association with Engel, see the voluminous correspondence between them in LP, SF, Engel.

21. "Remarks of Former Senator Herbert H. Lehman at Meeting of F.D.R.–Woodrow Wilson Independent Democrats," March 30, 1959, LP, SSF, New York City Reform Politics, March 1959; New York Committee for Democratic Voters, "A Statement of Principles," July 1959, LP, SSF, New York City Reform Politics, 1957–January 1959.

22. Lehman to Altschul, March 20, 1959, LP, SF, Humphrey, document 0425_0232; Lehman to Neuberger, May 5, 1959, LP, SF, Neuberger; "Prendergast on Lehman's List for Ouster in 'Bossism' Fight," *NYT*, June 18, 1959, p. 15; " 'Whispering' Scored," *NYT*, June 1, 1959, p. 28; New York Committee for Democratic Voters, "A Statement of Principles," July 1959, LP, SSF, New York City Reform Politics, 1957–January 1959; "Lehman Warns Democrats on '60," *NYT*, August 26, 1959, p. 22; George Sokolsky, "These Days . . . 1960 Politics," *WP*, May 21, 1959, A21; Louis Harris and Associates, "A Study of Presidential Preferences in New York City," April 1959, JFK, PPP, Box 816, Senate Files, Polls, Polls of Political Opinion, 1954–1960, p. 13. On Mrs. Roosevelt's reservations on Kennedy, see "Kennedy Disputes Mrs. Roosevelt on Softness toward 'McCarthyism,' " *Boston Globe*, March 31, 1958, p. 4; Lash, *Eleanor: The Years Alone*, pp. 280–282; Parmet, *Jack*, pp. 462–464; Scharf, *Eleanor Roosevelt*, pp. 168–170; and Fuchs, "The Senator and the Lady."

23. "State Democrats Will Back Wagner for Vice President," *NYT*, August 21, 1959, pp. 1, 22; "De Sapio's Close Victory Weakens His 1960 Position," *NYT*, September 20, 1959, E-7; Roscoe Drummond, "1960 Picture Changes," *WP*, September 27, 1959, A18; Moscow, *The Last of the Big-Time Bosses*, pp. 165–166. For the contrary view that De Sapio's narrow victory meant that "Carmine is in; Mrs. Roosevelt is out. And that means that at the 1960 Democratic Convention, an anti-Stevenson delegation will come from New York," see George Sokolsky, "These Days: A Little Politics," *WP*, September 25, 1959, A-13.

24. George Martin to Evelyn Lincoln, January 8, 1959, and Kennedy to Martin, January 14, 1959, both in JFK, PPP, Box 956, Pre-Convention Political Files, 1959–1960, New York, Delegates, January 14–September 29, 1959; "Kennedy Hailed in Buffalo Visit," *NYT*, May 22, 1959, p. 10; Kennedy to Schlesinger, June 17, 1959, John Kennedy Papers, President's Office Files, Box 32, Special Correspondence, Reference Copies, Schlesinger, April 28–November 15, 1959; Schlesinger, *A Thousand Days*, pp. 15–16; Parmet, *Jack*, pp. 474–475; "Meeting at: Hyannisport, Massachusetts," October 18, 1959, Robert Kennedy Papers, Pre-Administration Political Files, Box 39, 1960 Campaign and Transition, General Subject Files, 1959–1960, Memos: Robert Kennedy, Outgoing, October 28, 1959–April 30, 1960.

25. Schlesinger to Kennedy, June 22, 1959, JFK, President's Office Files, Box 32, Special Correspondence, Reference Copies, Schlesinger, April 28–November 15, 1959;

Peggy Lynch Gerstle, Lexington Democratic Club, to Steve Smith, October 22, 1959; Mary Bancroft to Kennedy, July 14, 1959, and October 31, 1959, and attached clipping, "In the Backrooms," *New York Post*, October 31, 1959, all in JFK, PPP, Box 1040, 1960 Campaign, Press and Publicity, Press Secretary's State Files, 1958–1960, New York, May 14–November 30, 1959; John Stillman to John Saltonstall, September 4, 1959, JFK, PPP, Box 956, 1960 Campaign, Pre-Convention Political Files, 1959–1960, New York Delegates, January 14–September 29, 1959; Kennedy to Finletter, October 27, 1959, and Finletter to Kennedy, October 31, 1959, both in JFK, PPP, Box 540, Senate, General Files, 1953–1960, 1958–1960 Personal Office Files, Finletter. On the Lexington Democratic Club, see Moscow, *The Last of the Big-Time Bosses*, pp. 136–137. In addition to being an old friend of JFK, Mary Bancroft was a former debutante, author, O.S.S. agent, and paramour of O.S.S. director Allen Dulles during World War II. See Bancroft, *Autobiography of a Spy*, and Kinzer, *The Brothers*, pp. 70–71, 74.

    26. Schlesinger to Kennedy, November 13, 1959, JFK, President's Office Files, Box 32, Special Correspondence, Reference Copies, Schlesinger, April 28–November 15, 1959; "The Nation: The Democratic Way," *NYT*, December 13, 1959, E-2; Finletter to Kennedy, November 11, 1959, JFK, PPP, Box 956, 1960 Campaign, Pre-Convention Political Files, 1959–1960, New York, Delegates, October 1–December 28, 1959; "2 Join Democratic Unit," *NYT*, November 12, 1959, p. 24; "Democrats Add Kennedy As Speaker," *WP*, November 18, 1959, B8; Kennedy to Finletter, November 18, 1959, JFK, PPP, Senate, General Files, 1953–1960, 1958–1960 Personal Office Files, Finletter; "Kennedy Joins Party Council," *Chicago Defender*, November 23, 1959, p. 10; "Democrats Ready for '60 'Kick-Off,'" *NYT*, November 27, 1959, p. 23.

    27. "Democrats Ask 'Peace Agency,'" *WP*, December 6, 1959, A2; "Mrs. Roosevelt Disputes Truman on Liberals' Role," *NYT*, December 8, 1959, pp. 1, 53; Lehman to Hubert Humphrey, November 30, 1959, LP, SF, Humphrey; G. Mennen Williams to Lehman, December 10, 1959, LP, SF, Williams; Phillip Perlman to Lehman, December 13, 1959, LP, SF, Perlman; Edmund Brown to Lehman, December 15, 1959, LP, SF, Brown.

    28. Kennedy to Lehman, December 28, 1959, and "Statement of Senator John F. Kennedy," January 2, 1960, both in LP, SF, Kennedy; "Kennedy in Race; Bars Second Spot in any Situation," *NYT*, January 3, 1960, pp. 1, 44.

    29. George Sokolsky, "These Days: The Ordeal of Adlai," *WP*, January 7, 1960, A-19; Lehman to Frank Altschul, March 20, 1959; Lehman to Altschul, April 3, 1959; Humphrey to Lehman, March 31, 1959; Humphrey to Lehman, November 3, 1959; Humphrey to Lehman, November 17, 1959; Humphrey to Lehman, November 24, 1959; Lehman to Humphrey, November 30, 1959; Humphrey to Lehman, December 29, 1959; "Statement by Senator Hubert H. Humphrey," December 30, 1959; Lehman to Humphrey, January 2, 1960; Humphrey to Lehman, January 6, 1960; and Humphrey to Edith Lehman, January 19, 1960, all in LP, SF, Humphrey; Edith Lehman to Maurine Neuberger, February 25, 1960, LP, SF, Richard Neuberger; "Humphrey Enters Presidency Race; Sees Uphill Fight," *NYT*, December 31, 1959, pp. 1, 10. On Stevenson's noncandidacy during this period, see Martin, *Adlai Stevenson and the World*, pp. 464–471; and White, *The Making of the President, 1960*, pp. 46–49.

    30. "Prendergast Urges Party to Unite Here," *NYT*, November 23, 1959, p. 20; Lehman to Eleanor Roosevelt, January 14, 1960, Eleanor Roosevelt Papers, Box 3583,

1957–1962, Lehman; Press Release, Letter from Lehman, Eleanor Roosevelt, Thomas Finletter, Lloyd Garrison, and Francis Adams to Michael Prendergast, January 16, 1960, LP, SF, Prendergast; "Elect Delegates, Democrats Urged," *NYT*, January 17, 1960, p. 74.

31. Prendergast to Lehman, January 29, 1960, LP, SF, Prendergast; "Peace Bid Made by Prendergast to Reform Group," *NYT*, January 31, 1960, pp. 1, 43.

32. Lehman to Prendergast, for Release February 1, 1960, LP. SF, Prendergast; "Prendergast's Plea Spurned by Lehman," *NYT*, February 1, 1960, pp. 1, 21.

33. "Democrats Snub Lehman's Faction on Delegate Plan," *NYT*, February 5, 1960, pp. 1, 14; "Political House Divided," *NYT*, February 8, 1960, p. 20; Irving Engel to Democratic State Committee, February 9, 1960, and New York Committee for Democratic Voters, Press Release, February 11, 1960, "Reform Democrats Urge Democratic State Committee to Reject De Sapio–Prendergast Proposal on Convention Delegates," both in LP, SSF, New York City Reform Politics, January–February 1960; "Kennedy Appeals for Support Here," *NYT*, February 14, 1960, pp. 1, 48. Only ten of the approximately 240 votes cast at the Democratic State Committee meeting supported Lehman's position that the additional delegates should be elected rather than appointed.

34. "Kennedy Appeals for Support Here," *NYT*, February 14, 1960, pp. 1, 48; "$100 Event in City to Hear Kennedy," *NYT*, January 21, 1960, p. 19; "De Sapio and Prendergast Act to Assure Delegation Control," *WP*, January 23, 1960, A6.

35. Lehman to Nevins, February 1, 1960, LP, SF, Nevins.

36. "Stevenson Again, Lehman Expects," *NYT*, April 18, 1960, p. 24; Lehman to Nevins, April 29, 1960, LP, SF, Nevins.

37. "Lehman Favors Stevenson Race," *NYT*, May 17, 1960, p. 28; Lehman to Morse, June 9, 1960, LP, SF, Morse; Lehman to Tom O'Hara, June 19, 1961, LP, SF, John Kennedy. On the U-2 incident, the collapse of the summit, and the impact of the international situation on the campaign, see White, *The Making of the President, 1960*, pp. 115–149.

38. Anthony Akers Oral History Transcript, pp. 10–12; John Bailey Oral History Transcript, pp. 113–115; John English Oral History Transcript, p. 12; Myer Feldman Oral History Transcript, p. 233, all in JFKL; Joseph Alsop, "Kennedy's Big Gamble," *Boston Globe*, January 22, 1960, p. 14; "State Democrats Unmoved by Vote," *NYT*, April 7, 1960, pp. 1, 29; "Kennedy Gain Seen," *NYT*, April 28, 1960, p. 21; "Senator Sways Democrats in New York and Jersey," *NYT*, May 12, 1960, pp. 1, 22; "Kennedy Cheered Here as He Seeks Leaders' Backing," *NYT*, May 13, 1960, pp. 1, 23; Frank Altschul to Kennedy, May 5, 1960, and Kennedy to Altschul, May 20, 1960, both in LP, SF, Kennedy; Richard Sachs to Senator Kennedy, June 13, 1960, William Walton Papers, Box 5, Personal–New York Campaign, JFKL; Robert Spivack, "Watch on the Potomac," *Chicago Defender*, June 13, 1960, A-10, and June 28, 1960, p. 10; John Stillman to Steve Smith, January 5, 1960; John Stillman to Theodore Sorensen, February 23, 1960; Sorensen to Stillman, March 2, 1960; and Stillman to Franklin D. Roosevelt, Jr., February 29, 1960, all in JFK, PPP, Box 956, 1960 Campaign, Pre-Convention Political Files, 1959–1960, New York Delegates, January 4, 1960–March 31, 1960; Stillman to Theodore Sorenson [*sic*], January 29, 1960, JFK, PPP, Box 956, 1960 Campaign, Pre-Convention Political Files, 1959–1960, New York Clubs, November 10, 1958–January 29, 1960; and Stillman to Sorenson [*sic*], April 8, 1960, and Statement by John S. Stillman, April 13, 1960, both in JFK, PPP, Box 956, 1960 Campaign,

Pre-Convention Political Files, 1959–1960, New York Delegates, April 2, 1960–April 30, 1960; Stillman to Patricia Burke, May 6, 1960, and attached clipping, "N.Y. Delegates Swing to Kennedy Banner," *New York World-Telegram and Sun*, May 11, 1960, p. 1; and Stillman to Sorenson [*sic*], May 17, 1960, all in JFK, PPP, Box 956, 1960 Campaign, Pre-Convention Political Files, 1959–1960, New York Delegates, May 2, 1960–October 22, 1960, and Undated Material; Swanson, "The Presidential Convention as a Stage in the Struggle for Political Leadership," in Tillett, ed., *Inside Politics*, pp. 202–203; White, *The Making of the President, 1960*, pp. 139–141; Moynihan, " 'Bosses' and 'Reformers,' " pp. 463–464; Moscow, *The Last of the Big-Time Bosses*, pp. 166–167; Guthman and Shulman, eds., *Robert Kennedy in His Own Words*, p. 356.

39. Press Release, March 21, 1960, LP, SSF, New York City Reform Politics, March 1960; "Insurgents Gain Tammany Accord," *NYT*, March 15, 1960, p. 40.

40. Edelstein, Memorandum to Senator Lehman, March 13, 1960, LP, SSF, New York City Reform Politics, March 1960; Lash, *A World of Love*, p. 515; Draft Minutes, Administrative Committee Meeting, April 13, 1960, LP, SSF, New York City Reform Politics, April 1960; "Liberals Oppose Reform Leader," *NYT*, March 24, 1960, p. 21; "Rally!! Come Hear Senator Herbert H. Lehman, William F. Ryan, Reform Candidate for Congress," May 23, 1960, LP, SSF, New York City Reform Politics, May–July 1960; "Lehman Backs Rubin's Nomination in Race for Congressman," *New York Amsterdam News*, May 28, 1960, p. 23; "Teller and Ryan List Primary Costs," *NYT*, June 30, 1960, p. 10; "Party Challenge Seen by Lehman," *NYT*, April 9, 1960, p. 10; "Lehman Stumps for Insurgents," *NYT*, May 5, 1960, p. 28; Petrus, "To Break Down Walls," pp. 62–64. On Buckley's control in the Bronx, see "Boss in the Bronx," *NYT*, May 12, 1960, p. 22.

41. "Two De Sapio Men Lose in Primary on the West Side," *NYT*, June 8, 1960, pp. 1, 33; Lehman to Maurine Neuberger, June 9, 1960, LP, SF, Richard Neuberger; "De Sapio Candidates Routed in Key Manhattan Districts," *New York Herald Tribune*, June 8, 1960, clipping in LP, SF, Frank Altschul; "Tammany Candidates Beaten by Insurgents," *WP*, June 8, 1960, A2; "De Sapio Setback," *NYT* June 12, 1960, E2; "Voters Hit Tammany Hard," *Christian Science Monitor*, June 8, 1960, p. 10; Petrus, "To Break Down Walls," pp. 63–64; Ryan supporter and Wilson quote from Wilson, *The Amateur Democrat*, pp. 336–337.

42. "Voters Hit Tammany Hard," *Christian Science Monitor*, June 8, 1960, p. 10; White, *The Making of the President, 1960*, p. 141; "Lehman Ousted as a Delegate," *New York Herald Tribune*, June 17, 1960, and "Lehman Blasts 'Boss' Steamroller," *New York Post*, June 17, 1960, clippings in LP, SF, Frank Altschul; "Lehman Is Denied Delegate's Role by State Leaders," *NYT*, June 17, 1960, pp. 1, 18; Swanson, "The Presidential Convention as a Stage in the Struggle for Political Leadership," pp. 197–198; Moscow, *The Last of the Big-Time Bosses*, pp. 164–165; Petrus, "To Break Down Walls," p. 64.

43. Lehman to Frank Altschul, June 19, 1960; "Statement of Herbert H. Lehman on His Rejection as Delegate-at-Large by Democratic State Committee," June 16, 1960; Press Release, "Statement by Irving M. Engel on Democratic State Committee Action," June 16, 1960; "Not So Bright to Snub Mr. Lehman," Editorial, *New York Herald Tribune*, June 18, 1960, all in LP, SF, Frank Altschul; Lehman to Fleeson, June 20, 1960, LP, SF, Fleeson; "Lehman Is Denied Delegate's Role by State Leaders," *NYT*, June 17, 1960, pp. 1, 18; "A Party's Little Men," Editorial, *NYT*, June 21, 1960, p. 32. Lehman was disappointed that it took the *New York Times* almost a week to run an editorial

commenting on the State Committee's rejection of him as a delegate to the national convention, complaining that the *Times*, "a great newspaper, should have been in the forefront in the fight against bossism." See Lehman to Frank Altschul, June 19, 1960, LP, SF, Altschul.

44. "Lehman Ousted as a Delegate," *New York Herald Tribune*, June 17, 1960, clipping in LP, SF, Frank Altschul; "Lehman Is Denied Delegate's Role by State Leaders," *NYT*, June 17, 1960, pp. 1, 18; "Mayor Supports Kennedy to Spur Bandwagon Move," *NYT*, June 21, 1960, pp. 1, 20; William vanden Heuvel, "Banning Lehman Protested," Letter to the Editor, *NYT*, June 22, 1960, p. 34; Anna Rosenberg to Prendergast, June 22, 1960, LP, SF, Rosenberg; "Delegates Offer Places to Lehman," *NYT*, June 22, 1960, p. 21; Moynihan, " 'Bosses' and 'Reformers,' " p. 467.

45. "Prendergast Rebuffs Bid to Aid Lehman," *NYT*, June 23, 1960, p. 12; "Mayor Supports Kennedy to Spur Bandwagon Move," *NYT*, June 21, 1960, pp. 1, 20; "Memo of Telephone Conversation between Mayor Robert F. Wagner and Governor Herbert H. Lehman," June 22, 1960, LP, SF, Wagner; Franklin D. Roosevelt, Jr., to Lehman, June 21, 1960, LP, SF, Franklin D. Roosevelt, Jr.; "Delegates Offer Places to Lehman," *NYT*, June 22, 1960, p. 21; Joseph Sharkey Oral History Transcript, pp. 36–40, JFKL; Stark to Lehman, June 24, 1960, LP, SF, Stark; Swanson, "The Presidential Convention as a Stage in the Struggle for Political Leadership," pp. 198–199; Moscow, *The Last of the Big-Time Bosses*, p. 165.

46. "Lehman Offered Delegate's Post as Leaders Shift," *NYT*, June 24, 1960, pp. 1, 12; "Memo of Telephone Conversation between Mayor Robert F. Wagner and Governor Herbert H. Lehman," June 22, 1960, LP, SF, Wagner; Prendergast to Lehman, June 24, 1960, and Lehman to Prendergast, June 24, 1960, both in LP, SF, Prendergast; "Lehman Accepts Delegate's Post; Asserts Freedom," *NYT*, June 25, 1960, pp. 1, 18; Eleanor Roosevelt, "Are Political Conventions Obsolete?" unpublished article, 1960, in Black, ed., *What I Hope to Leave Behind*, pp. 470–471; Lehman to Anna Rosenberg, June 27, 1960, LP, SF, Rosenberg; Lehman to Lithgow Osborne, June 25, 1960, LP, SF, Osborne; Lehman to Abe Stark, June 29, 1960, LP, SF, Stark; Douglas Dales, "About-Face on Lehman," *NYT*, June 27, 1960, p. 16; Murray Kempton, "The Titans," *New York Post*, July 7, 1960, p. 45; "Lehman Is Elected Convention Delegate," *NYT*, June 30, 1960, p. 15; Moscow, *The Last of the Big-Time Bosses*, p. 165.

47. White, *The Making of the President, 1960*, pp. 141; "Kennedy Claims 710 of 761 Votes," *NYT*, June 17, 1960, p. 19; "Kennedy Sidesteps N.Y. Row," *WP*, June 18, 1960, A-2; "Democrats Here Praise Kennedy," *NYT*, June 18, 1960, p. 10.

48. "Democrats Here Praise Kennedy," *NYT*, June 18, 1960, p. 10; "Early Support of Kennedy Asked of State Delegation," *NYT*, June 20, 1960, pp. 1, 21; "Mayor Supports Kennedy to Spur Bandwagon Move," *NYT*, June 21, 1960, pp. 1, 20; Alistair Cooke, "Climbing on Kennedy's Band-Wagon," *Manchester Guardian*, June 21, 1960, p. 9; "Kennedy Is Victor in State Caucus," *NYT*, June 24, 1960, p. 12; Anthony Akers Oral History Transcript, p. 11, JFKL; Moscow, *The Last of the Big-Time Bosses*, pp. 165–167; Schlesinger, *Robert Kennedy and His Times*, p. 204; Swanson, "The Presidential Convention as a Stage in the Struggle for Political Leadership," pp. 202–204.

49. "Mrs. Roosevelt for Stevenson, with Kennedy as Running Mate," *NYT*, June 10, 1960, p. 14; "A Stevenson Group Will Back Kennedy," *NYT*, June 8, 1960, pp. 1, 27; "Reason for Shift," *NYT*, June 8, 1960, p. 27; Roosevelt, *The Autobiography of Eleanor*

Roosevelt, pp. 422–423; Eleanor Roosevelt, "My Day," June 11, 1960, online: http://www.gwu.edu/~erpapers/myday/displaydoc.cfm?_y=1960&_f=md004769; "Stevenson: Not Candidate; Mrs. Roosevelt: Yes, He Is," *NYT*, June 13, 1960, pp. 1, 19; Joseph Alsop, "Adlai's Friends Are Trying to Stop Kennedy," *Boston Globe*, June 15, 1960, p. 18; Eleanor Roosevelt, "My Day," June 16, 1960, online: http://www.gwu.edu/~erpapers/myday/displaydoc.cfm?_y=1960&_f=md004773; "Mrs. Roosevelt Analyzes Trend," *NYT*, June 20, 1960, p. 16; Lehman to Mrs. Eugene Meyer, June 17, 1960, LP, SF, Meyer; "Draft Stevenson Move Just Keeps Simmering," *Los Angeles Times*, June 23, 1960, p. 6; Philip Hart to Lehman, July 2, 1960, LP, SF, Hart; "Coordinator Is Named," *NYT*, June 24, 1960, p. 13; "Stevenson Rally Set," *NYT*, June 26, 1960, p. 41; Lehman to William Haddad, June 29, 1960, LP, SF, Haddad; Stevenson to James Warburg, November 4, 1963, in Johnson, ed., *The Papers of Adlai E. Stevenson*, VIII: 465–466; James Doyle Oral History Transcript, p. 9, JFKL; Lash, *Eleanor: The Years Alone*, pp. 285–292; White, *The Making of the President, 1960*, pp. 121–122. On the role of the deteriorating situation in foreign affairs on Mrs. Roosevelt's decision to come out for Stevenson at this time, see "The Non-Candidates: Can They Make It?" *NYT*, June 19, 1960, E-5; John Harris, "Foreign Policy Is the Big Issue Now," *Boston Globe*, June 19, 1960, 2A; "Mrs. Roosevelt Says Truman Backs Johnson," *Los Angeles Times*, June 20, 1960, p. 13. Historian and Lehman biographer Allan Nevins was among the academics who had supported Stevenson in 1956 but now endorsed Kennedy. See "Stevenson Group Backing Kennedy," *NYT*, June 17, 1960, p. 18.

50. "Poll Favoring Adlai Withheld, Lehman Says," *WP*, July 6, 1960, A2; "Prendergast Cites Poll Showing New York Swing to Kennedy Due," *NYT*, June 26, 1960, p. 41; "Stevenson Seen Injured by Nixon," *NYT*, June 28, 1960, p. 17; Swanson, "The Presidential Convention as a Stage in the Struggle for Political Leadership," pp. 203–204; "Stevenson Draft Gets Recognition," *NYT*, July 1, 1960, p. 5; "Butler Denies Rigging Kennedy Nomination," *WP*, July 1, 1960, A1, A17; Associated Stevenson for President Committees of California, "America Wants Adlai Stevenson," *Los Angeles Times*, July 6, 1960, B9; "Stevenson Edges Near Candidacy," *NYT*, July 9, 1960, pp. 1, 8; "Adlai Gives Lift to Team's Hopes," *Boston Globe*, July 9, 1960, pp. 1, 2; Martin, *Adlai Stevenson and the World*, p. 521; Lehman quoted in William Osten, Letter to the Editor, *New York Post*, July 10, 1960, Magazine, p. 8.

51. "Lehman Arrives amid Chants for Stevenson," *Los Angeles Times*, July 9, 1960, p. 4; "Bailey, Others Interviewed on CBS Network," *Hartford Courant*, July 10, 1960, 17A; "Lehman Fails to Get State Caucus Bid," *New York Post*, July 11, 1960, p. 3; "Bostonian on the First Ballot Is Prendergast—De Sapio View," *NYT*, July 11, 1960, p. 18; "Kennedy in Rights Talk Applauded and Booed," *WP*, July 11, 1960, A9.

52. "Lehman Fails to Get State Caucus Bid," *New York Post*, July 11, 1960, p. 3; Lehman to Agnes Meyer, July 4, 1960, LP, SF, Eugene and Agnes Meyer; Lehman to Allan Nevins, July 23, 1960, LP, SF, Nevins; Swanson, "The Presidential Convention as a Stage in the Struggle for Political Leadership," pp. 206–207. On the geography of the convention and the hotels, see the map in "Scene of Democratic Convention," *NYT*, July 10, 1960, p. 48.

53. "Kennedy Assures New Yorkers He'd Confer on Vice President," *NYT*, July 12, 1960, p. 22; White, *The Making of the President, 1960*, p. 164; "State Delegation

Aids Nomination," *NYT*, July 14, 1960, p. 17; Edwin Weisl, Jr., Oral History Transcript, pp. 20–21, LBJL; Swanson, "The Presidential Convention as a Stage in the Struggle for Political Leadership," pp. 207–210; Eleanor Roosevelt, "My Day," July 13, 1960, online: http://www.gwu.edu/~erpapers/myday/displaydoc.cfm?_y=1960&_f=md004796. Mrs. Roosevelt erroneously credited Lehman with securing four and a half votes for Stevenson in the New York delegation, one more than the actual number.

54. Mrs. Lehman quoted in Lash, *Eleanor: The Years Alone*, p. 296; "Last-Ditch Move on to Unite Behind Stevenson," *New York Post*, July 12, 1960, p. 3; White, *The Making of the President, 1960*, p. 161; Orville Freeman Oral History Transcript, p. 9, JFKL; "Platform Wins After Clashes on Civil Rights; South the Loser," *NYT*, July 13, 1960, pp. 1, 18; Mike Monroney to Lehman, August 15, 1960, LP, SF, Monroney; Swanson, "The Presidential Convention as a Stage in the Struggle for Political Leadership," pp. 209–210.

55. "Platform Wins after Clashes on Civil Rights; South the Loser," *NYT*, July 13, 1960, pp. 1, 18; "Powell Is Supporting Kennedy but Doubts That Bostonian Could Carry New York; Sees Opposition by Negro Voters," *NYT*, July 13, 1960, p. 22. On the drafting of the Democratic platform in 1960, especially the civil right section, see Mann, *The Walls of Jericho*, pp. 272–274; Parrish, *Citizen Rauh*, pp. 142–143; Brauer, *John F. Kennedy and the Second Reconstruction*, pp. 35–36; Bryant, *The Bystander*, pp. 143–145. For the text of the platform provisions on immigration and civil rights, see "Democratic Platform of 1960," in Porter and Johnson, comps., *National Party Platforms*, pp. 577–578, 599–600.

56. Lehman to Agnes Meyer, July 4, 1960, LP, SF, Eugene and Agnes Meyer; "Highlights and Chronology of Nominating Session of the Democratic Convention," *NYT*, July 14, 1960, p. 18; "State Delegation Aids Nomination," *NYT*, July 14, 1960, p. 17; Martin, *Adlai Stevenson and the World*, p. 526.

57. "Lehman Wins Banner Tug-of-War," *New York Post*, July 14, 1960, p. 7; "Stevenson Given a Wild Reception," *NYT*, July 14, 1960, pp. 1, 15. On Wagner's role as nominal leader of the New York delegation, see "Kennedy Facing New York Split," *NYT*, July 18, 1960, pp. 1, 13; "Wagner Planning 'Real' Leadership of Party in State," *NYT*, July 19, 1960, pp. 1, 18; and Swanson, "The Presidential Convention as a Stage in the Struggle for Political Leadership," pp. 200–202, 208, 211–212.

58. Eleanor Roosevelt, "My Day," July 15, 1960, online: http://www.gwu.edu/~erpapers/myday/displaydoc.cfm?_y=1960&_f=md004798; Lehman to Robert G. A. Jackson, August 9, 1960, LP, SF, Jackson; John Bailey Oral History Transcript, p. 46, JFKL; Schlesinger, *A Thousand Days*, pp. 58–59; Schlesinger, *Journals, 1952–2000*, pp. 77–78; Lehman to Kennedy, July 15, 1960, LP, SF, John Kennedy.

59. Lehman to Johnson, July 15, 1960, LP, SF, Johnson; "Johnson Choice Hailed by South, *NYT*, July 15, 1960, p. 8; "Kennedy's Key Problem: N.Y. Liberals Lukewarm," *New York Post*, July 15, 1960, p. 2; Herbert Lehman, Personal Memorandum, July 15, 1960, LP, SF, John Kennedy. On liberal opposition to Johnson, see Violet Gunther, Americans for Democratic Action, to All Chapters and Board Members, "Lyndon Johnson's Voting Record," April 6, 1960, LP, SF, Johnson; "Nominee Problems: Democrats Must Pacify Unions, Negroes, Avoid Alienating the South," *Wall Street Journal*, July 18, 1960, pp. 1, 15. On Kennedy's choice of Johnson and the latter's acceptance of the second spot on the ticket, see Dallek, *Lone Star Rising*, pp. 574–582; Dallek, *An*

Unfinished Life, pp. 267–274; Shesol, *Mutual Contempt*, pp. 41–56; and Caro, *The Years of Lyndon Johnson: The Passage of Power*, pp. 109–143.

60. James Landis to Robert Kennedy, June 24, 1960, Robert Kennedy Papers, Pre-Administration Political Files, Box 33, 1960 Campaign and Transition, General Subject Files, 1959–1960, After Convention File, June 13–June 27, 1960. On Landis and the Kennedys, see Parmet, *Jack*, passim.

61. Robert Kennedy to James Landis, June 27, 1960, Robert Kennedy Papers, Pre-Administration Political Files, Box 33, 1960 Campaign and Transition, General Subject Files, 1959–1960, After Convention File, June 13–June 27, 1960; "Kennedy Assures New York Chiefs," *NYT*, July 15, 1960, pp. 1, 10.

62. Lehman, Personal Memorandum, July 15, 1960, LP, SF, John Kennedy.

63. Lehman, Personal Memorandum, July 15, 1960, LP, SF, John Kennedy; "Stevenson Role Seen by Kennedy," *NYT*, July 16, 1960, pp. 1, 6; "Kennedy Facing New York Split," *NYT*, July 18, 1960, pp. 1, 13; "Kennedy Favors a Citizens' Group for Drive in City," *NYT*, July 20, 1960, pp. 1, 17.

64. "Kennedy Favors a Citizens' Group for Drive in City," *NYT*, July 20, 1960, pp. 1, 17; Julius Edelstein to Lehman, July 20, 1960, LP, SF, John Kennedy; "Citizens for Kennedy," *NYT*, July 25, 1960, p. 12; "Prendergast Challenges Wagner; State Chief Firm," *NYT*, July 26, 1960, pp. 1, 17; "Kennedy Accepts Prendergast Bid," *NYT*, July 27, 1960, p. 15.

65. "Reform Democrats Get Campaign Role," *NYT*, July 29, 1960, pp. 1, 13; "Democrats: Little Brother Is Watching," *Time*, October 10, 1960, pp. 23ff; "Kennedy Sets Up Citizen Unit Here," *NYT*, August 2, 1960, pp. 1, 21; "Mayor Wins Unity on Campaign Role," *NYT*, July 30, 1960, pp. 1, 8; "Robert Kennedy Eases Split Here," *NYT*, July 28, 1960, pp. 1, 16; Pierre Salinger to Jay Schulman, August 1, 1960, JFK, PPP, Box 1041, 1960 Campaign, Press and Publicity, Press Secretary's State Files, 1958–1960, New York, July 20–August 16, 1960; "Democrats Name A Campaign Chief," *NYT*, August 7, 1960, p. 57; Anthony Akers Oral History Transcript, pp. 1–6, 15–18, JFKL; Parmet, *The Democrats*, pp. 179–180.

66. Lehman to Sidney Yates, July 28, 1960, LP, SF, Yates; "Kennedy Sets Up Citizens Unit Here," *NYT*, August 2, 1960, pp. 1, 21; Akers Oral History Transcript, pp. 17–19, JFKL; "Kennedy Appeals for Minority Vote on Visit to City," *NYT*, August 6, 1960, pp. 1, 8; Lehman to Kennedy, August 6, 1960, LP, SF, Kennedy; "State Democrats Foresee Harmony," *NYT*, August 11, 1960, p. 12; "Mrs. Roosevelt for Rights Stay," *NYT*, August 18, 1960, p. 16. On Stevenson, see Lehman to Robert G. A. Jackson, August 9, 1960, LP, SF, Jackson; and Martin, *Adlai Stevenson and the World*, p. 530. On Eleanor Roosevelt's concerns and her delay in agreeing to serve as an honorary chairman of the Citizens for Kennedy Committee, see Eleanor Roosevelt to Mary Lasker, August 15, 1960, online: http://www.gwu.edu/~erpapers/mep/displaydoc.cfm?docid=jfk10; Mrs. Roosevelt to John Kennedy, August 16, 1960, online: http://www.gwu.edu/~erpapers/mep/displaydoc.cfm?docid=jfk11; Eleanor Roosevelt, "My Day," August 17, 1960, online: http://www.gwu.edu/~erpapers/myday/displaydoc.cfm?_y=1960&_f=md004826; Kennedy to Mrs. Roosevelt, August 26, 1960, online: http://www.gwu.edu/~erpapers/mep/displaydoc.cfm?docid=jfk13; "Mrs. Roosevelt Asks Party Drive," *NYT*, August 20, 1960, p. 10; Fuchs, "The Senator and the Lady"; Lash, *Eleanor: The Years Alone*, pp. 297–299; Leuchtenburg, *In the Shadow of FDR*, p. 93; Parmet, *JFK*, pp. 35–36.

67. Sayre to Lehman, July 29, 1960, and Lehman to Sayre, August 8, 1960, both in LP, SF, Sayre. It would later be revealed that the rumors about Kennedy's womanizing were true, but there was no reason for Herbert Lehman to know that in 1960. On Kennedy's philandering after his marriage, see Dallek, *An Unfinished Life*, pp. 194–195, 281–282.

68. Schlesinger to Kennedy, August 30, 1960, JFK, President's Office Files, Box 32, Special Correspondence, Reference Copy, Schlesinger, Jr., April 26, 1960–January 23, 1961, and undated; Brock, *Americans for Democratic Action*, pp. 186–191; Schlesinger, *A Thousand Days*, p. 66; "A.D.A. for Kennedy, Silent on Johnson," *NYT*, August 28, 1960, p. 37.

69. Schlesinger to Kennedy, August 26, 1960, and August 30, 1960, both in JFK, President's Office Files, Box 32, Special Correspondence, Reference Copy, Schlesinger, Jr., April 26, 1960–January 23, 1961, and undated.

70. Memorandum, Senator Kennedy to Bobby, September 3, 1960, Robert Kennedy Papers, Pre-Administration Political Files, Box 39, 1960 Campaign and Transition, General Subjects, 1959–1960, JFKL; Louis Harris and Associates, Inc., "A Study of the 1960 Presidential Election in New York State," September 19, 1960, JFK, PPP, Box 816, Senate Files, Polls, Polls of Political Opinion, 1954–1960, Harris: The 1960 Presidential Election in New York State; Robert F. Wagner, Jr. (the son of Mayor Wagner), quoted in McNickle, *To Be Mayor of New York*, p. 137.

71. William Walton Oral History Transcript, p. 128, JFKL; Robert Kennedy to Lehman, September 19, 1960, and October 17, 1960, both in LP, SF, Robert Kennedy; New York Citizens for Kennedy and Johnson, "Welcome Senator John F. Kennedy," *NYT*, September 14, 1960, p. 39; Lehman to Frank Altschul, September 12, 1960, Frank Altschul Papers, Catalogued Correspondence, 128c, Herbert Lehman; "Kennedy Spells Out Credo of Liberalism," *WP*, September 15, 1960, A2; "Kennedy Stumps City for 8 Hours; Sees U.S. Drifting," *NYT*, September 15, 1960, pp. 1, 29; Lehman to John Kennedy, September 20, 1960, LP, SF, Kennedy.

72. "City's Catholics Split on Election; Lean to Kennedy," *NYT*, September 20, 1960, pp. 1, 42; Louis Harris and Associates, Inc., "A Study of the 1960 Presidential Election in New York State," September 19, 1960, JFK, PPP, Box 816, Senate Files, Polls, Polls of Political Opinion, 1954–1960, Harris: The 1960 Presidential Election in New York State; "Protestant Groups' Statements," *NYT*, September 8, 1960, p. 25; "Transcript of Kennedy Talk to Ministers and Questions and Answers," *NYT*, September 13, 1960, p. 22; Zeitz, *White Ethnic New York*, p. 140; "1910 Strike Marked by Garment Union," *NYT*, September 18, 1960, p. 58; "Mrs. Roosevelt and Lehman Meet Johnson and Back Him," *NYT*, October 7, 1960, p. 23; "Lehman Deplores Campaign Bigotry," *NYT*, October 25, 1960, p. 26. On Kennedy and the religious issue in the campaign, see Parmet, *JFK*, pp. 37–44; and Dallek, *An Unfinished Life*, pp. 282–284.

73. Johnson to Lehman, September 16, 1960; Lehman to Johnson, September 26, 1960; and Johnson to Lehman, October 3, 1960, all in LP, SF, Johnson; Johnson to Tom Finletter, September 16, 1960, Johnson Papers, Senate Political Files, Box 199, LBJ For Vice President, New York Correspondence, LBJL; "Transcript of Recorded Remarks Made At Coffee," October 6, 1960, Statements, Box 44, October 6, 1960, Remarks Made at Democratic Coffee, LBJL; "Mrs. Roosevelt and Lehman Meet Johnson and Back Him," *NYT*, October 7, 1960, p. 23.

74. "Address of John F. Kennedy Upon Accepting the Liberal Party Nomination for President," September 14, 1960, online: http://www.jfklibrary.org/Research/Research-Aids/JFK-Speeches/Liberal-Party-Nomination-NYC_19600914.aspx; "Eisenhower Lacks Leadership on Civil Rights, Kennedy Group Says," *Los Angeles Times*, October 12, 1960, p. 6; "Civil Rights Lag Laid to President," *NYT*, October 12, 1960, pp. 1, 33; "Remarks of Senator John F. Kennedy at National Conference on Constitutional Rights And American Freedom," October 12, 1960, online: http://www.jfklibrary.org/Research/Research-Aids/JFK-Speeches/Constitutional-Rights-Conference-NYC_19601012.aspx; "Excerpts of Remarks of Senator John F. Kennedy, Public Rally, Hotel Theresa," October 12, 1960, in U.S., Cong., Senate, Committee on Commerce, *Freedom of Communications*, Part 1, *The Speeches, Remarks, Press Conferences, and Statements of Senator John F. Kennedy, August 1 through November 7, 1960*, S. Rept. 994, 87th Cong., 1st sess., September 13, 1961, pp. 580–583; Kennedy to Lehman, n.d., 1960, LP, SF, Kennedy, document 0473-0100; Jerry Hoeck, Advertising Department for States, Democratic National Committee, October 17, 1960, William Walton Papers, Box 5, Personal, New York Campaign, JFKL; "Tune In to the 'Fight for Civil Rights,'" *Los Angeles Sentinel*, November 3, 1960, C-3; Louis Harris and Associates, Inc., "A Study of the 1960 Presidential Election in New York State," September 19, 1960, JFK, PPP, Box 816, Senate Files, Polls, Polls of Political Opinion, 1954–1960, Harris: The 1960 Presidential Election in New York State; Brauer, *John F. Kennedy and the Second Reconstruction*, pp. 42–46; Bryant, *The Bystander*, pp. 159–178, 188. On the Conference on Constitutional Rights, see also Press Release of Senator John F. Kennedy, September 24, 1960, in *Freedom of Communications*, S. Rept. 994, 87th Cong., 1st sess., September 13, 1961, Part 1, p. 358; undated memo from John Seigenthaler, Robert Kennedy Papers, Pre-Administration Political Files, Box 34, 1960 Campaign and Transition, General Subject File, 1959–1960, Civil Rights: Campaign Strategy, October 1960–November 1960 and undated; "Constitution Day Conference," September 17, 1960, Robert Kennedy Papers, Pre-Administration Files, Box 48, 1960 Campaign and Transition, General Subject File, 1959–1960, Speakers Bureau, September 17–October 28, 1960; Eleanor Roosevelt, "My Day," October 19, 1960, online: http://www.gwu.edu/~erpapers/myday/displaydoc.cfm?_y=1960&_f=md004865; "Kennedy Promises Rights Bill," *New York Amsterdam News*, October 15, 1960, pp. 1, 39; "Top Democrats Hold National Meeting on Civil Rights Program; Kennedy Outlines Program," *Los Angeles Sentinel*, October 20, 1960, A-1, 4; Wofford, *Of Kennedys and Kings*, pp. 63–65.

75. Louis Harris and Associates, "Summary of Key Group Voting Patterns," October 1960, JFK, PPP, Box 816, Senate Files, Polls, Polls of Political Opinion, 1954–1960, Harris: (New York City by Ethnic Group); "Letter from Senator John F. Kennedy to Hon. Herbert H. Lehman," November 2, 1960, in *Freedom of Communications*, S. Rept. 994, 87th Cong., 1st sess., September 13, 1961, Part 1, p. 1232; "Just Suez Solution Urged by Kennedy," *NYT*, November 3, 1960, p. 27.

76. "Speech of Senator John F. Kennedy, Democratic Women's Luncheon," September 14, 1960, in *Freedom of Communications*, S. Rept. 994, 87th Cong., 1st sess., September 13, 1961, Part 1, p. 233; "Text of Kennedy's Speech to Democratic Dinner on the Offshore Chinese Islands," *NYT*, October 13, 1960, p. 24; "Nominees Clash over Arbitration," *NYT*, October 14, 1960, p. 22; Democratic National Committee, "Facts for Victory in '60: The Issue of Quemoy and Matsu," October [1960], JFK, PPP, Box 1030, 1960 Campaign, Press and Publicity, Speeches, Statements, and Sections, Foreign Affairs—Quemoy and Matsu; "National Affairs: Quemoy and Matsu," *Time*, October

24, 1960; "Quemoy Key Issue in 3d Debate?" *New York Post*, October 13, 1960, p. 3; "The Quemoy-Matsu Debate: Just a Matter of Life and Death," Editorial, *New York Post*, October 13, 1960, p. 30; "Debate Shows Quemoy Is Big Issue," *New York Post*, October 14, 1960, p. 3.

77. "Lehman Cites Nixon's Vote on Immigration Quota Law," *New York Post*, October 11, 1960, p. 40; "Lehman Scores Nixon's Record," *NYT*, October 11, 1960, p. 36; "Nixon Is Assailed on Civil Liberties," *NYT*, October 21, 1960, p. 25; "Remarks of Herbert H. Lehman at Ceremony Commemorating 74th Anniversary of Statue of Liberty Dedication," October 29, 1960, copy in David Stowe Papers, Box 17, 1960 Presidential Campaign File, Statue of Liberty Dedication—74th Anniversary—Speech—Herbert H. Lehman—New York–October 29, 1960, HSTL; "Laws on Aliens Hit by Kennedy, Lehman," *NYT*, October 30, 1960, p. 56.

78. "Democrats Here Get Working Agreement," *New York Post*, August 2, 1960, p. 3; "Akers Maps Reform—De Sapio Truce," *New York Post*, August 19, 1960, p. 5; Lehman to Frank Altschul, August 27, 1960, LP, SF, James Farley, document 0286_0408 (this document was obviously in the wrong file when it was digitalized); "City Is 'Scouted' by Kennedy Team," *NYT*, October 11, 1960, p. 50; "Kennedy to Make His Final Drive Here Today," *NYT*, November 5, 1960, p. 15; New York Citizens for Kennedy and Johnson, "Meet Jack Kennedy," Advertisement, *New York Post*, November 4, 1960, p. 56; Ronnie Eldridge Oral History Transcript, pp. 19–20, JFKL; Anthony Akers Oral History Transcript, pp. 23–26, JFKL; O'Donnell and Powers, *"Johnny, We Hardly Knew Ye,"* pp. 218–219; "Kennedy Tours City Area, Crowds Greet Him in Rain," *NYT*, November 6, 1960, pp. 1, 67.

79. "Kennedy Here: Torchlight Parade; Final N.Y. Rally," *New York Post*, November 6, 1960, p. 1; Anthony Akers Oral History Transcript, pp. 24–27, JFKL; Moscow, *The Last of the Big-Time Bosses*, pp. 167–168; "N.Y. Democrats in Trouble with Kennedy," *Boston Globe*, November 13, 1960, p. 33; "Kennedy Said to Bypass De Sapio over Patronage," *NYT*, November 18, 1960, pp. 1, 16; William Walton Oral History Transcript, pp. 129–130, JFKL; John English Oral History Transcript, pp. 11–12, JFKL; O'Donnell and Powers, *"Johnny, We Hardly Knew Ye,"* pp. 219–220; "Kennedy Tours City Area, Crowds Greet Him in Rain," *NYT*, November 6, 1960, pp. 1, 67; "Kennedy Pledges Strong Leadership; . . . Spells Out Concept of Presidency," *WP*, November 6, 1960, A-1, 12.

80. Akers to Lehman, November 6, 1960, and Lehman to Akers, November 8, 1960, both in LP, SF, Akers.

81. "Kennedy Is Apparent Victor; . . . City Lead 791,333," *NYT*, November 9, 1960, pp. 1, 26; Edith and Herbert Lehman to John Kennedy, November 9, 1960, LP, SF, Kennedy; Edith and Herbert Lehman to Lyndon Johnson, November 9, 1960, LP, SF, Johnson; Lehman to Allan Nevins, November 11, 1960, LP, SF, Nevins; Lehman to Paul Douglas, November 22, 1960, LP, SF, Douglas.

Chapter 20. "To Free This City . . . from the Shackles of the Boss System": Herbert Lehman and the Bosses, 1961–1963

1. Lehman to Allan Nevins, August 13, 1962, LP, SF, Nevins.

2. "Democrats Halt Their Truce Here," *NYT*, November 9, 1960, p. 26; "Reform Fight Is on Again," *New York Post*, November 9, 1960, p. 4.

3. "Democrats Here Split in Victory; Lehman Assailed," *NYT*, November 10, 1960, pp. 1, 43; "De Sapio Statement on Lehman," *NYT*, November 10, 1960, p. 43.

4. Press Release, Dictated over the Phone to Senator Lehman's Secretary, November 10, 1960, LP, SF, De Sapio; "De Sapio Plans Full-Scale Battle in Primary Elections to Oust Reform Faction; Upstate Leaders Try to Avoid Feud," *NYT*, November 11, 1960, p. 24; "Election Showing Spurs Hopes of Liberal Party," *New York Post*, November 11, 1960, p. 2; "Statement Issued by Senator Lehman on Behalf of Reform Leaders in Manhattan," [November 28, 1960] LP, SSF, New York City Reform Politics, August–November 1960; "Lehman Summons Reform Leaders," *NYT*, November 24, 1960, p. 37; "Foes of De Sapio Unite to Oust Him," *NYT*, November 29, 1960, p. 30; "County Rules Hit by Reform Group," *NYT*, December 21, 1960, p. 27; "Reform Leaders Meet with Mayor," *NYT*, December 22, 1960, p. 21; Lehman to Nevins, December 16, 1960, LP, SF, Nevins.

5. Robert Kennedy to Lehman, December 27, 1960, LP, SF, Robert Kennedy; "N.Y. Democrats in Trouble With Kennedy," *Boston Globe*, November 13, 1960, p. 33; "Kennedy Said to Bypass De Sapio over Patronage," *NYT*, November 18, 1960, pp. 1, 16; "Kennedy to Seek Party Peace Here," *NYT*, December 3, 1960, pp. 1, 12; "Kennedy Confers on State Leader," *NYT*, December 9, 1960, pp. 1, 26; "New York: Democratic Problems," *NYT*, December 11, 1960, E-2; "Prendergast Out, Democrats Hear," *NYT*, December 16, 1960, p. 36; Drew Pearson, "The Washington Merry-Go-Round: Why the Word Came to De Sapio," *WP*, December 18, 1960, E-5; George Sokolsky, "These Days: Looking to 1962," *WP*, January 28, 1961, A-9; Schlesinger, *A Thousand Days*, pp. 118–119.

6. "Kennedy and New York," *NYT*, January 8, 1961, E8; "Kennedy Confers with Chiefs Here," *NYT*, January 9, 1961, pp. 1, 22; "Kennedy Backing Wagner's Moves," *NYT*, January 11, 1961, p. 22.

7. Lehman to John Kennedy, January 10, 1961; Invitation, "In honor of Mrs. Franklin D. Roosevelt, the Honorable Herbert H. Lehman, and Mrs. Lehman," n.d.; Inaugural Committee, Invitation, n.d.; Telegram, Lehman to John Kennedy, n.d., and Telegram, Lehman to John Kennedy, January 21, 1961, all LP, SF, John Kennedy, documents 0473_0141, 0473_0131, 0473_0128, and 0473_0143; "Pre-Inaugural Program," *NYT*, January 19, 1961, p. 20; Lehman to Philip Hart, February 3, 1961, LP, SF, Hart; Lehman to William Fitts Ryan, January 17, 1961, LP, SF, Ryan; Lehman to Robert Kennedy, January 24, 1961, LP, SF, Robert Kennedy; "Preparations Crowd Kennedy Out of Home," *WP*, January 19, 1961, A4; "Weather Limits Crowds at Fetes," *NYT*, January 21, 1960, pp. 1, 14.

8. "Democrats Seat Bailey as Leader," *NYT*, January 22, 1961, pp. 1, 47; "Finletter Given NATO Envoy Post," *NYT*, January 29, 1961, pp. 1, 47; "Jonathan Brewster Bingham," *NYT*, January 29, 1961, p. 47; "Always at the Top: Jonathan Brewster Bingham," *NYT*, March 14, 1961, p. 4; "Snub by President," *NYT*, January 30, 1961, p. 14; George Sokolsky, "These Days: Appointments," *WP*, February 2, 1961, A-23; "Prendergast Hits Move to Oust Him as Slap at Party," *NYT*, February 12, 1961, pp. 1, 59; "City Democrats Are Rebuffed by Robert Kennedy on Patronage," *NYT*, March 9, 1961, p. 18; "Federal Patronage Pipeline to New York City Still Clogged," *WP*, March 13, 1961, A6; "Prendergast Due for Test Today," *NYT*, March 23, 1961, p. 22; "Bailey Predicts New State Chief," *NYT*, March 24, 1961, pp. 1, 18; "Bailey Is Defied

by Prendergast," *NYT*, March 26, 1961, pp. 1, 43; "Mrs. Roosevelt Asks Party Drive," *NYT*, August 20, 1960, p. 10; June Bingham to Herbert Lehman, November 11, 1960, LP, SF, Bingham; "Shift Is Reported on U.S. Attorney," *NYT*, March 21, 1961, p. 24; "Robert Morgenthau to Get Post as U.S. Attorney for This Area," *NYT*, March 29, 1961, pp. 1, 19; "Morgenthau Named," *NYT*, April 6, 1961, p. 19; Eleanor Roosevelt to President Kennedy, April 18, 1961, JFK, President's Office Files, Box 32, Special Correspondence, Reference Copy, Eleanor Roosevelt, January 17, 1961–December 27, 1961; Al Sostchen, "Political Postscripts," *New York Post*, March 8, 1961, p. 58; Sostchen, "Political Postscripts," *New York Post*, March 22, 1961, p. 62; Sidey, *John F. Kennedy, President*, pp. 87–89; Schlesinger, *A Thousand Days*, pp. 118–119; Schlesinger, *Robert Kennedy and His Times*, pp. 370–373.

    9. "Prendergast Out, Democrats Hear," *NYT*, December 16, 1960, p. 36; "Patronage Offer to State Is Hinted," *NYT*, March 8, 1961, p. 25; "Crotty Appears Kennedy Choice as State Leader," *NYT*, March 14, 1961, pp. 1, 22; "De Sapio vs. Wagner," Editorial, *NYT*, February 14, 1961, p. 36; "Politics and the City," Editorial, *NYT*, May 17, 1961, p. 36; "Warming Up the Wrong Man," Editorial, *New York Post*, March 15, 1961, p. 44.

    10. "Prendergast Out, Democrats Hear," *NYT*, December 16, 1960, p. 36; Arthur Massolo, Oliver Pilat, and Edward Katcher, "In the Backrooms," *New York Post*, March 19, 1961, p. 4; "Mayor Criticized by Foe of De Sapio," *NYT*, April 1, 1961, p. 18; "Crotty Appears Kennedy Choice as State Leader," *NYT*, March 14, 1961, pp. 1, 22; "Reform Chiefs Taking Crotty on Approval," *New York Post*, March 23, 1961, p. 7; "Lehman Bids Reform Hold Fire on Crotty," *New York Post*, March 29, 1961, p. 4; "Crotty Is Opposed by Tammany Foes," *NYT*, March 30, 1961, p. 20; "Reform Group Bolts, Votes 'No' on Crotty," *New York Post*, March 30, 1961, p. 2. On Lehman's illness and his spending time in Florida with his grandchildren, see "Lehman Overcoming Illness," *NYT*, March 6, 1961, p. 21; and Lehman to Nevins, March 6, 1961, LP, SF, Nevins.

    11. Oliver Pilat, "Lehman Chides Reform Group for Ignoring Advice on Crotty," *New York Post*, n.d.; Memorandum, Edelstein to Lehman, "Approach to Board of Advisors," April 8, 1961; and Tom O'Hara, "Political Offbeat: Hotheads among Foes of De Sapio Snub Advice of Their Boss: Lehman," *New York Herald Tribune*, April 2, 1961, all in LP, SSF, New York City Reform Politics, January–April 1961; Oliver Pilat, "Reform Group Bolts, Votes 'No' on Crotty," *New York Post*, March 30, 1961, p. 2; "Lanigan Is Selected in 'Village' to Oppose De Sapio as Leader," *NYT*, March 30, 1961, p. 21; "Reform's Rough Road," Editorial, *New York Post*, April 2, 1961, Magazine, p. 8. On Lanigan, see "An Ivy Leaguer in Tammany Hall?" *Los Angeles Times*, September 10, 1961, F3; Moscow, *The Last of the Big-Time Bosses*, pp. 180–181.

    12. Engel to Lehman, March 8, 1960, LP, SF, Engel; Lehman to Allan Nevins, November 22, 1960, LP, SF, Nevins. On Lehman's reverence for the late Senator Robert F. Wagner, see Murray Kempton, "Conscript," *New York Post*, June 20, 1961, p. 53; Bob Wagner to Lehman, April 16, 1962, LP, SF, Wagner; and Lehman to Nevins, November 20, 1962, LP, SF, Nevins. On Wagner, see also "Deliberate Mayor: Robert Ferdinand Wagner," *NYT*, June 23, 1961, p. 16. On Wagner and De Sapio, see Moscow, *The Last of the Big-Time Bosses*, pp. 106–120, 134–135, 169–170; Connable and Silberfarb, *Tigers of Tammany*, pp. 323–325; McNickle, *To Be Mayor of New York*, pp. 94–98,

102–121, 148–179. The CDV and the NYCDV were the same entity; only the name was changed.

13. "Fight on De Sapio Nears Showdown," *NYT*, December 2, 1960, pp. 1, 15; Eleanor Roosevelt, "My Day," December 5, 1960, online: http://www.gwu.edu/~erpapers/myday/displaydoc.cfm?_y=1960&_f=md004885; "Hulan Jack Is Convicted on 3 Counts at 2D Trial; Will Lose Borough Post," *NYT*, December 7, 1960, pp. 1, 36; "Mayor Held Ready to Act on De Sapio," *NYT*, December 15, 1960, p. 48; "Reform Leaders Meet with Mayor," *NYT*, December 22, 1960, p. 21; "Mayor Ignores Tammany on Borough Presidency," *NYT*, December 29, 1960, pp. 1, 19; "Wagner vs. De Sapio," *NYT*, January 1, 1961, E2; "Mayor Discusses Ousting De Sapio," *NYT*, January 6, 1961, pp. 1, 10; Moscow, *The Last of the Big-Time Bosses*, pp. 173–174.

14. "Reform Dems Launch Stop Wagner Drive," *Village Voice*, January 12, 1961, clipping in LP, SSF, New York City Reform Politics, January–April, 1961; "Brown Ruled Out as Borough Head," *NYT*, January 26, 1961, p. 19; Petrus, "To Break Down Walls," p. 67; Costikyan, *Behind Closed Doors*, pp. 28–29. On the Village Independent Democrats, see Petrus, "To Break Down Walls," chap. 2.

15. "Reform Dems Launch Stop Wagner Drive," *Village Voice*, January 12, 1961, clipping in LP, SSF, New York City Reform Politics, January–April, 1961; "Mayor Demands De Sapio Resign; Gets 'A Loud No,'" *NYT*, February 4, 1961, pp. 1, 9; "Lehman to Oppose a De Sapio Choice," *NYT*, February 19, 1961, pp. 1, 46; Petrus, "To Break Down Walls," pp. 66–67.

16. "Reform Group Split on Wagner 3d Term," *New York Post*, March 6, 1961, p. 4; "Prendergast Ouster Near, Bailey Hints," *New York Post*, March 24, 1961, p. 6; "Dudley Asks Care in Charter Moves," *NYT*, March 12, 1961, p. 64; "Foes of De Sapio Silent on Mayor," *NYT*, March 11, 1961, p. 10; "Democratic Unit Divided on Mayor," *NYT*, April 6, 1961, p. 22; "Democratic Bloc Delays City Stand," *NYT*, April 11, 1961, p. 41; "Lehman Calls Buildup First Aim of Reform," *New York Post*, April 11, 1961, p. 19.

17. "Notes for General Committee Meeting," April 20, 1961, LP, SSF, New York City Reform Politics, January–April 1961; "Reform 'Realism' Urged by Lehman," *NYT*, April 21, 1961, p. 23. On Lehman's prestige and its crucial role in building support for the reform movement, see Wilson, *The Amateur Democrat*, pp. 59–60, 335–337.

18. "Minutes of the Special General Committee Meeting," April 20, 1961, LP, SSF, New York City Reform Politics, January–April 1961; "Reform 'Realism' Urged by Lehman," *NYT*, April 21, 1961, p. 23.

19. Memorandum, Edelstein to Senator Lehman, n.d., LP, SSF, New York City Reform Politics, May 1961.

20. "Should Mayor Wagner Run Again?" Editorial, *New York Post*, June 14, 1961, p. 1; New York Committee for Democratic Voters, "Minutes of the General Committee Meeting," May 18, 1961; New York Committee for Democratic Voters, "Resolution, May 12, 1961: Document A of the Appendix to the Minutes of the Meeting of the General Committee of May 18, 1961," May 23, 1961; New York Committee for Democratic Voters, "Report of the Committee on City-Wide Elections: Document B of the Appendix to the Minutes of the Meeting of the General Committee of May 18, 1961," May 18, 1961, all in LP, SSF, New York City Reform Politics, May 1961; "Reform 'Realism' Urged by Lehman," *NYT*, April 21, 1961, p. 23; Oliver Pilat and

Edward Katcher, "In the Backrooms," *New York Post*, May 7, 1961, p. 4; "Big Questions about a Big Job," Editorial, *New York Post*, May 9, 1961, p. 28; "Democratic Unit Delays on Mayor," *NYT*, May 23, 1961, p. 35; Arthur Massolo, Oliver Pilat, and Edward Katcher, "In the Backrooms," *New York Post*, May 28, 1961, p. 4; "Liberals Demand Wagner Decision," *NYT*, June 8, 1961, pp. 1, 32; "Reform Group, Liberal Party: Wagner, if . . . ," *New York Post*, June 8, 1961, p. 4; Costikyan, *Behind Closed Doors*, pp. 28–29. Not all reformers fell into line behind Lehman and Wagner. The West Brooklyn Independent Democrats adopted a resolution in late May "urging its officers to oppose any proposal to give the Mayor factional support." See "Stark and Gerosa Winning Support," *NYT*, May 25, 1961, pp. 1, 28. See also the anti-Wagner letters in "Mayor Wagner . . . Yes and No," Letters to the Editor, *New York Post*, June 12, 1961, p. 26. On the negotiations on Lehman's role in the CDV, see Memorandum, Arnold Fein et al. to the Board of Advisors, "Relationship between Board of Advisors and General Committee," April 27, 1961; New York Committee for Democratic Voters, "Draft Resolution," n.d.; Lehman to Arnold Fein, May 1, 1961; New York Committee for Democratic Voters, "Draft Resolution," n.d.; and New York Committee for Democratic Voters, "Minutes of Executive Committee Meeting," May 1, 1961, all in LP, SSF, New York City Reform Politics, May 1961.

21. Program Transcript, *New York Forum*, May 14, 1961, WCBS-TV, copy in Robert Wagner Documents Collection, Julius Edelstein (Wagner Staff) Series, Subject Files III Sub Series, Box 060300, Folder 23: "Lehman—Endorsement," May 1961–August 1961, La Guardia and Wagner Archives, online: http://www.laguardiawagnerarchive.lagcc.cuny.edu/FileBrowser.aspx?LinkToFile=FILES_DOC/WAGNER_FILES/06.020.0059.060300.23.PDF#undefined; "Lehman Outlines His Price to Back Wagner: 'Reform,'" *NYT*, May 15, 1961, pp. 1, 20; "News from CBS Radio," *Let's Find Out*, May 21, 1961, copy in Robert Wagner Documents Collection, Julius Edelstein (Wagner Staff) Series, Subject Files III Sub Series, Box 060301, Folder 2: "Lehman—Statements on Wagner (1)," May 21, 1961, La Guardia and Wagner Archives, online at http://www.laguardiawagnerarchive.lagcc.cuny.edu/FileBrowser.aspx?LinkToFile=FILES_DOC/WAGNER_FILES/06.020.0059.060301.2.PDF#undefined; "Javits Would Ask Eisenhower Here," *NYT*, May 22, 1961, p. 15.

22. Lehman to Tom O'Hara, June 19, 1961, LP, SF, John Kennedy. The alleged quote to which Lehman was responding was published in Tom O'Hara's "Off-Beat New York Politics" column in the *New York Herald Tribune* on June 18, 1961, and later repeated in Victor Lasky's highly critical biography of Kennedy, *J.F.K.: The Man and the Myth*, p. 400. On Lehman's meeting with Kennedy after the convention, see Herbert Lehman, Personal Memorandum, July 15, 1960, LP, SF, John Kennedy. On the reformers' difficulties in winning support among Catholics, see Moynihan, "'Bosses' and 'Reformers'"; Wilson, *The Amateur Democrat*, pp. 14, 302–304; and McNickle, *To Be Mayor of New York*, pp. 175–177.

23. "Stark Threatens Primary Contest if He Is Dropped," *NYT*, June 21, 1961, pp. 1, 25; "Wagner Announces He Will Run, Proposes Screvane-Stark Slate; Gerosa Dropped," *NYT*, June 23, 1961, pp., 1, 16; "Party Chiefs May Oppose Ticket; De Sapio Is Silent," *NYT*, June 23, 1961, pp. 1, 17; "Gerosa Enters Mayoralty Race; Stark Won't Join Wagner Slate; Reply by Mayor," *NYT*, June 27, 1961, pp. 1, 22; "Reform Group, Liberal Party: Wagner if . . . ," *New York Post*, June 8, 1961, p. 4; Anthony Massolo,

Oliver Pilat, and Edward Katcher, "In the Backrooms," *New York Post*, June 11, 1961, p. 4; "The Gerosa Problem," *NYT*, June 12, 1961, p. 23; "Wagner Decision to Run Indicated; New Slate Seen," *NYT*, June 15, 1961, pp. 1, 33; "Wagner Attempt to Choose Slate Irks Party Heads," *NYT*, June 19, 1961, pp. 1, 12; "Mayor Seeing Lehman, May Name Slate," *New York Post*, June 20, 1961, p. 4; "Wagner Looks to '62 and '64," *NYT*, June 25, 1961, E10; Moscow, *The Last of the Big-Time Bosses*, pp. 175–177.

24. "Levitt to Oppose Wagner; White House Appeal Fails to Avert Primary Battle," *NYT*, July 8, 1961, pp. 1, 8.

25. "Lehman Foresees De Sapio as 'Boss' if Levitt Is Victor," *NYT*, July 10, 1961, pp. 1, 16; News Release, "Statement of Hon. Herbert H. Lehman at Press Conference, 820 Park Avenue, New York City, Sunday, July 9, 1961," LP, SSF, New York City Reform Politics, July 1961; "Wagner Set to Roll with Lehman Aid," *New York Post*, July 10, 1961, pp. 3, 7.

26. "Mayor Proposes Party Reforms," *NYT*, July 19, 1961, p. 18; "The New Battle of New York," Editorial, *New York Post*, July 12, 1961, p. 38; "Wagner Courting Reform Leaders," *New York Post*, July 14, 1961, p. 5; "Wagner Says He Will End Boss Control," *New York Post*, July 18, 1961, p. 5; "Mr. Prendergast Rides Again," Editorial, *New York Post*, July 21, 1961, p. 32; "Reform Group Delays Vote on Wagner, *New York Post*, July 21, 1961, p. 4; Al Sostchen, "Political Postscripts," *New York Post*, July 21, 1961, p. 50; "City Labor Backs Wagner; Will Seek Place on Ballot," *NYT*, July 21, 1961, pp. 1, 11; "Manpower for Wagner," *NYT*, July 24, 1961, p. 12; "Wagner Moves to Win over Two Top Reform Groups," *New York Post*, July 24, 1961, p. 5; "Buckley Aides Bolt to Mayor," *New York Post*, July 25, 1961, p. 5; "Two Big Points for a Big Change," Editorial, *New York Post*, July 25, 1961, p. 26; "Mayor Endorsed by Lehman Group; Gets Primary Aid," *NYT*, July 26, 1961, pp. 1, 18; "Wagner Gets 2 Big Boosts in Campaign," *New York Post*, July 26, 1961, p. 4; Murray Kempton, "Comic Marriage," *New York Post*, July 26, 1961, p. 39; Costikyan, *Behind Closed Doors*, p. 29; Petrus, "To Break Down Walls," p. 69.

27. Lehman to Robert G. A. Jackson, August 9, 1961, and Lehman to Barbara Ward Jackson, August 19, 1961, both in LP, SF, Jackson; Citizens for Wagner, Screvane, and Beame, Press Release, August 11, 1961, LP, SSF, New York City Reform Politics, 1–23 August 1961; "Lehman Assails 'Bosses' in City," *NYT*, August 11, 1961, p. 11.

28. "Lehman Assails 'Bosses' in City," *NYT*, August 11, 1961, p. 11; McNickle, *To Be Mayor of New York*, pp. 166, 171; New York Committee for Democratic Voters, "Reform Democrats Support Wagner for Mayor Because . . . ," n.d.; and Citizens Committee for Wagner, Beame, and Screvane, "Transcript of TV Broadcast by Mayor Wagner and Senator Lehman," for Release August 23, 1961, both in LP, SSF, New York City Reform Politics, 24 August–October 1961; Memorandum, Edelstein to Stan Lowell, August 20, 1961; and Memorandum, Lowell to Cavanaugh, Beame, Screvane, Lehman, and Edelstein, August 23, 1961, both in LP, SSF, New York City Reform Politics, 1–23 August 1961; Lehman to Allan Nevins, September 27, 1961, LP, SF, Nevins; "Group She Helped Found in '17 Keeps Mrs. Lehman's Days Full," *NYT*, April 25, 1965, p. 80; "Wagner Stumps East Side Slums," *NYT*, August 28, 1961, p. 19; "Mayor Says Foes Plan to Use Bias," *NYT*, September 4, 1961, p. 1; "Mayor and Lehman Shed Coats on Hot 6-Hour Tour of Beaches," *NYT*, September 4, 1961, p. 13; "Footnote about

a Happy Warrior," Editorial, *New York Post*, September 5, 1961; Zeitz, *White Ethnic New York*, p. 173.

29. Citizens for Wagner-Beame and Screvane, for Immediate Release, August 27, 1961; and Citizens for Wagner, Beame, and Screvane, "Excerpts from Remarks of Hon. Herbert H. Lehman in Course of Tour of West Side with Mayor Wagner, Monday, August 28," for Release August 29, both in LP, SSF, New York City Reform Politics, 24 August–October 1961; "Mayor Says Buckley Club Mailed 'Scurrilous' Attack," *NYT*, September 7, 1961, pp. 1, 24. On Helen Buttenwieser helping post bail for Soblen, see "Soblen Set Free on Bail of $100,000," *WP*, August 29, 1961. Mrs. Buttenwieser's involvement in Alger Hiss's defense had been raised as an issue when Lehman had run for re-election to the Senate in 1950. See chapter 13.

30. "Wagner Announces He Will Run, Proposes Screvane-Stark Slate; Gerosa Dropped," *NYT*, June 23, 1961, pp. 1, 16; "Levitt Accuses Mayor's Forces of Anti-Semitism," *NYT*, September 1, 1961, pp. 1, 15; "Levitt Demands Bigotry Inquiry," *NYT*, September 2, 1961, pp. 1, 8; "Statement of Herbert H. Lehman," August 31, 1961, LP, SSF, New York City Reform Politics, 24 August–October 1961; Max Lerner, "Wagner's Battle," *Pittsburgh Courier*, September 16, 1961, A-9; Zeitz, *White Ethnic New York*, p. 173; Moscow, *The Last of the Big-Time Bosses*, pp. 178–180; McNickle, *To Be Mayor of New York*, pp. 171–175.

31. Moscow, *The Last of the Big-Time Bosses*, pp. 180–183; "Lehman Bids Foes of De Sapio Unite," *NYT*, August 22, 1961, p. 22; Lehman to My Dear Fellow Democrats, August 21, 1961, LP, SSF, New York City Reform Democrats, 1–23 August 1961; Lanigan to Lehman, September 7, 1961, LP, SF, Lanigan; Petrus, "To Break Down Walls," pp. 68–73.

32. "Wagner Defeats Levitt in Reform Sweep; Margin Is 159,516," *NYT*, September 8, 1961, pp. 1, 24; "De Sapio Is Upset by Lanigan; 'Village' Vote Big," *NYT*, September 8, 1961, pp. 1, 25; Lehman to Jonathan Bingham, September 12, 1961, LP, SF, Bingham; Edelstein, Memorandum to Senator Lehman, September 10, 1961, LP, SSF, New York City Reform Politics, 24 August–October 1961; Moscow, *The Last of the Big-Time Bosses*, pp. 183–184; Connable and Silberfarb, *Tigers of Tammany*, pp. 332–333; Petrus, "To Break Down Walls," pp. 76–77.

33. "Mayor Was Aided by Diverse Staff," *NYT*, September 9, 1961, p. 10; "Wagner Defeats Levitt in Reform Sweep; Margin Is 159,516," *NYT*, September 8, 1961, pp. 1, 24; Garrison to Lehman, September 9, 1961, LP, SF, Garrison; Eleanor Roosevelt, "My Day," September 11, 1961, online: http://www.gwu.edu/~erpapers/myday/displaydoc. cfm?_y=1961&_f=md005001; "Mayor Wagner's Great Victory," Editorial, *The Day— Jewish Journal*, September 9, 1961, p. 6, LP, SSF, New York City Reform Politics, 24 August–October 1961; Akers to Lehman, September 20, 1961, LP, SF, Akers; Humphrey to Lehman, September 11, 1961, LP, SF, Humphrey; Shannon to Lehman, September 14, 1961, LP, SF, Shannon; Edelstein, Memorandum to Senator Lehman, September 10, 1961, LP, SSF, New York City Reform Politics, 24 August–October 1961.

34. Lehman to Allan Nevins, September 27, 1961; August 8, 1962; and September 21, 1962, all in LP, SF, Nevins; "Lehmans Give City Zoo for Children," *NYT*, June 16, 1960, p. 35; "Noah's Ark for City Kids," *New York Times Sunday Magazine*, October 8, 1961, SM18; "Tenants for the Zoo," Editorial, *Chicago Tribune*, June 20,

1960, p. 16; "New Zoo Begun," *NYT*, November 19, 1960, p. 24; Lehman to James Rosenberg, July 29, 1961, LP, SF, Rosenberg; "18-Cubit Noah's Ark Launched at Central Park Children's Zoo," *NYT*, June 27, 1961, p. 35; "Arrival of Whale in Central Park Greeted by Delighted Youngsters," *NYT*, August 4, 1961, p. 23; "Zoo for Children Is Opened in Park," *NYT*, September 28, 1961, p. 43; Lehman to Edward Coe Embury, September 30, 1961, LP, SF, Embury; Lehman to Robert G. A. Jackson, October 21, 1961, LP, SF, Jackson; "Millionth Visitor to Children's Zoo Is an Old-Timer," *NYT*, September 22, 1962, p. 27; Newbold Morris to Mrs. Lehman, February 14, 1963, and Mrs. Lehman to Morris, February 21, 1963, both in LP, SF, Morris; Eleanor Roosevelt to Lehman, September 28, 1961, LP, SF, Eleanor Roosevelt; Sonny Sloan, "Zoo Story," Letter to the Editor, *New York Times Sunday Magazine*, October 15, 1961, SM12; Nevins, *Herbert H. Lehman and His Era*, p. 407. See the lovely photographs of the Children's Zoo in Scheier, *The Central Park Zoo*, pp. 117–122. The Children's Zoo that the Lehmans had created closed in the early 1990s and was subsequently demolished. It was replaced in 1997 by the Tisch Children's Zoo. See "At the 1961 Children's Zoo, A Last Goodbye to Jonah and Friends," *NYT*, August 11, 1996, p. 33; and "Where the Wild Things Meet," *NYT*, September 21, 1997, p. 41.

35. Lehman to Robert G. A. Jackson, October 21, 1961, LP, SF, Jackson; "A New Mayor for New York," Editorial, *NYT*, October 19, 1961, p. 34; Herbert Lehman, "Lehman Praises Wagner," Letter to the Editor, *NYT*, October 21, 1961, p. 20; Lehman to Allan Nevins, October 25, 1961, LP, SF, Nevins.

36. "Lefkowitz Scores 'Shakedowns'; Wagner Calls Him Conservative; Mayor Vows Liberalism," *NYT*, October 26, 1961, pp. 1, 29; "Mayor Sees Race as National Test," *NYT*, November 1, 1961, pp. 1, 31; "Lehman Attacks Lefkowitz 'Pose,'" *NYT*, November 3, 1961, p. 26; Citizens Committee for Wagner, Beame, Screvane, "'Lehman Exposes Lefkowitz Record," *NYT*, November 4, 1961, p. 4; "Lefkowitz Vows Drive on Addicts," *NYT*, November 4, 1961, pp. 1, 10; "Lefkowitz Predicts Vote of the 'Angry' Will Defeat Mayor," *NYT*, November 5, 1961, pp. 1, 79.

37. "Wagner Wins by 397,980 in a Party Sweep; . . . City Vote Heavy," *NYT*, November 8, 1961, pp. 1, 24; "Text of Wagner's Victory Statement to Supporters," *NYT*, November 8, 1961, p. 24; Eleanor Roosevelt, "My Day," November 10, 1961, online: http://www.gwu.edu/~erpapers/myday/displaydoc.cfm?_y=1961&_f=md005027; Beame to Lehman, November 9, 1961, LP, SF, Beame; Butler to Lehman, November 8, 1961, LP, SF, Butler; Fitzpatrick to Lehman, November 15, 1961, LP, SF, Fitzpatrick.

38. Lehman to John Slawson, November 15, 1961, LP, SF, Slawson; Lehman to Louis Finkelstein, November 16, 1961, LP, SF, Finkelstein.

39. Edelstein, Memorandum to Senator Lehman, September 10, 1961, LP, SSF, New York City Reform Politics, 24 August–October 1961; Lehman to John Slawson, November 15, 1961, LP, SF, Slawson; Press Release, "Statement by Herbert H. Lehman," November 27, 1961, Eleanor Roosevelt Papers, Box 3583, 1957–1962, Lehman; "Kennedy Chooses Wagner to Direct State Patronage," *NYT*, November 14, 1961, pp. 1, 27; "Lehman Resigns as Chief Adviser of Reform Group," *NYT*, November 27, 1961, pp. 1, 16.

40. Lehman to Friends, General Committee, N.Y. Committee for Democratic Voters, November 25, 1961, and Press Release, "Statement by Herbert H. Lehman," November 27, 1961, both in Eleanor Roosevelt Papers, Box 3583, 1957–1962, Lehman;

"Lehman Resigns as Chief Adviser of Reform Group," *NYT*, November 27, 1961, pp. 1, 16.

41. Press Release, "Statement by Herbert Lehman," November 27, 1961, Eleanor Roosevelt Papers, Box 3583, 1957–1962, Lehman; "Lehman Resigns as Chief Adviser of Reform Group," *NYT*, November 27, 1961, pp. 1, 16; "Lehman Sounds Note of Caution," *Christian Science Monitor*, November 27, 1961, p. 5; "The Lehman Contribution," Editorial, *NYT*, November 28, 1961, p. 36; Edelstein to Lehman, December 6, 1961, and Edelstein to Governor, December 12 or 13, 1961 (date is not completely legible, but placement in the folder suggests either December 12 or 13), both in Robert Wagner Documents Collection, Julius Edelstein (Wagner Staff) Series, Subject Files III Sub Series, Box 060300, Folder 22: "Lehman—Correspondence," December 1961, La Guardia and Wagner Archives, online: http://www.laguardiawagnerarchive.lagcc.cuny.edu/ FileBrowser.aspx?LinkToFile=FILES_DOC/WAGNER_FILES/06.020.0059.060300.22. PDF#undefined; "Mayor Dismisses Chief of Markets," *NYT*, December 29, 1961, pp. 1, 8; "Julius C. C. Edelstein," *NYT*, December 29, 1961, p. 8.

42. "Lehman Resigns as Chief Adviser of Reform Group," *NYT*, November 27, 1961, pp. 1, 16; "Wagner Cool to 2 in Tammany Race," *NYT*, November 28, 1961, p. 30; "Kennedy Invites Buckley to Game," *NYT*, December 1, 1961, p. 23; "Sharkey to Fight Mayor's Plan to Oust Him from Two Posts," *NYT*, December 6, 1961, p. 52; "Mayor Asks Jones to Be Coordinator of City Democrats," *NYT*, December 8, 1961, pp. 1, 30; "Regulars to Ask Mayor for Jones," *NYT*, January 8, 1962, p. 19. On Jones's role in Wagner's campaign, see Murray Kempton, "The Master," *New York Post*, July 21, 1961, p. 33; Walter, *The Harlem Fox*, pp. 150–161; Connable and Silberfarb, *Tigers of Tammany*, pp. 343–344; Wilson, *The Amateur Democrat*, pp. 279–282; McNickle, *To Be Mayor of New York*, pp. 154, 177–178. On African American support for Wagner in the primary, see Edelstein to Lehman, September 1, 1961, LP, SF, Edelstein; "Where We Stand," Editorial, *New York Amsterdam News*, September 2, 1961, p. 1; Earl Brown, "A 'Good Thing!'" *New York Amsterdam News*, September 2, 1961, p. 11; and Edelstein, Memorandum to Senator Lehman, September 10, 1961, LP, SSF, New York City Reform Politics, 24 August–October 1961. Jones and his wife attributed her appointment to Jones's support for Lyndon Johnson's bid for the Democratic presidential nomination in 1960 rather than seeing it as an attempt to resolve the county leader dispute. See Walter, *The Harlem Fox*, pp. 10–11.

43. "Sharkey to Fight Mayor's Plan to Oust Him from Two Posts," *NYT*, December 6, 1961, p. 52; "Lehman Opposes Jones as Leader," *NYT*, December 10, 1961, p. 71; "Jones Visits Lehman to Request Support in Leadership Contest," *NYT*, December 11, 1961, p. 34; Walter, *The Harlem Fox*, p. 160.

44. "Wagner Cool to 2 in Tammany Race," *NYT*, November 28, 1961, p. 30; "One Vote," Editorial, *New York Amsterdam News*, December 9, 1961, p. 12; C. Sumner Stone, Jr., to Lehman, December 12, 1961, LP, SF, Raymond Jones; "Powell Attacks City Reformers," *NYT*, December 17, 1961, p. 65; "Powell Charges 'Lynching,'" *New York Amsterdam News*, December 23, 1961, pp. 1, 13; "Jones' Chances Seem Slim," *Pittsburgh Courier*, December 23, 1961, A-7; "Jackie Robinson Says," *Chicago Defender*, February 24, 1962, p. 2; "Jackie Robinson Says: What Is a Liberal?" *Chicago Defender*, March 31, 1962, p. 8; Edelstein to Lehman, December 5, 1961; Edelstein to Lehman, December 6, 1961; and Edelstein to Lehman, December 13, 1961, all in Robert Wagner

Documents Collection, Julius Edelstein (Wagner Staff) Series, Subject Files III Sub Series, Box 060300, Folder 22: "Lehman–Correspondence," December 1961, La Guardia and Wagner Archives, online: http://www.laguardiawagnerarchive.lagcc.cuny.edu/ FileBrowser.aspx?LinkToFile=FILES_DOC/WAGNER_FILES/06.020.0059.060300.22. PDF#undefined. On Robinson's support for Nixon and Rockefeller, see "Robinson Says Nixon Is Better for Negro," *NYT*, September 5, 1960; and Jackie Robinson, "Rockefeller and the Negro Vote," *New York Amsterdam News*, September 29, 1962, p. 11.

45. Kenneth Clark, Hubert Delany, Thomas Dyett, and Edward Lewis to Lehman, December 29, 1961; Lehman to Clark, Delany, Dyett, and Lewis, January 5, 1962; and Clark, Delany, Dyett, and Lewis to Lehman, January 15, 1962, all in LP, SF, Raymond Jones; Walter, *The Harlem Fox*, pp. 160, 246; Connable and Silberfarb, *Tigers of Tammany*, pp. 344–346.

46. Frederick Weaver to Lehman, January 15, 1962; Lehman to Weaver, January 19, 1962; Lehman to Thomas Sinclair, Jr., June 22, 1963; Lehman to J. Raymond Jones, August 8, 1963; and Jones to Lehman, October 1, 1963, all in Lehman Papers, SF, Raymond Jones; "Ray Jones Dinner Shows His Power," *New York Amsterdam News*, June 9, 1962, pp. 1, 2; "Democrats Split in Harlem Battle," *NYT*, July 1, 1963, p. 24; "Jones Gets Campaign Aid," *NYT*, August 23, 1963, p. 50; Walter, *The Harlem Fox*, p. 165. Jones did become the New York County Democratic Leader in December 1964. See "Democrats Name Jones, A Negro, Manhattan Chief," *NYT*, December 4, 1964, pp. 1, 30; Walter, *The Harlem Fox*, pp. 246–247; Connable and Silberfarb, *Tigers of Tammany*, p. 353; McNickle, *To Be Mayor of New York*, pp. 183–184.

47. "Wagner Cool to 2 in Tammany Race," *NYT*, November 28, 1961, p. 30; "Mayor's Next Job: Choice of Leader," *NYT*, January 22, 1962, p. 15; "Wagner Pressed to Pick a Leader," *NYT*, January 26, 1962, p. 16; "Democrats Set March 2 as Date to Choose De Sapio Successor," *NYT*, February 16, 1962, p. 17; "Democrats to Name McKeon State Chief," *NYT*, February 27, 1962, pp. 1, 20; "Democrats Oust Prendergast; McKeon Elected but Faces Suit," *NYT*, March 2, 1962, pp. 1, 12; "Democrats Here Name Costikyan as County Chief," *NYT*, March 3, 1962, pp. 1, 9; Costikyan, *Behind Closed Doors*, pp. 30–34; Walter, *The Harlem Fox*, pp. 160–161; Petrus, "To Break Down Walls," p. 80; Connable and Silberfarb, *Tigers of Tammany*, pp. 346–347.

48. "Gerosa Is Backed by Prendergast; Wagner Assailed," *NYT*, November 2, 1961, pp. 1, 31; "Democrats to Name McKeon State Chief," *NYT*, February 27, 1962, pp. 1, 20; "Democrats Oust Prendergast; McKeon Elected but Faces Suit," *NYT*, March 2, 1962, pp. 1, 12; McKeon to Lehman, March 8, 1962, LP, SF, McKeon.

49. "Farley Is Opposed by Reform Group," *NYT*, June 18, 1962, p. 19; "Reform Leaders Appeal on Farley," *NYT*, June 19, 1962, p. 19; "Convention Role Asked for Farley," *NYT*, June 25, 1962, p. 20; "Lehman Endorses Regular Democrat," *NYT*, August 30, 1962, pp. 1, 30; "Mayor Endorses Reformers' Rival in Race in Village," *NYT*, August 31, 1962, pp. 1, 46; Lehman to Nevins, September 1, 1962, LP, SF, Nevins; "Cracks Show in N.Y. Reform Movement," *Christian Science Monitor*, August 31, 1962, p. 1; "Wagner Draws a Line," *NYT*, September 3, 1962, p. 12; "Lanigan Resigns from Reform Club," *NYT*, September 5, 1962, pp. 1, 33; William Honan, "Ed Koch: The Man behind the Mayor," *New York Times Sunday Magazine*, February 1, 1981, SM21; Koch, *Politics*, pp. 22–23, 34–38; Petrus, "To Break Down Walls," pp. 81–84; Soffer, *Ed Koch and the Rebuilding of New York City*, pp. 45–46.

50. "Lehman Endorses Regular Democrat," *NYT*, August 30, 1962, pp. 1, 30; "Mayor Endorses Reformers' Rival in Race in Village," *NYT*, August 31, 1962, pp. 1, 46; Koch to Mrs. Roosevelt, quoted in Soffer, *Ed Koch and the Rebuilding of New York City*, p. 46; Koch quoted in Koch, *Politics*, p. 23.

51. JCCE, Memorandum to Governor Lehman, December 19, 1961, Robert Wagner Documents Collection, Julius Edelstein (Wagner Staff) Series, Subject Files III Sub Series, Box 060300, Folder 22: "Lehman—Correspondence," December 1961, La Guardia and Wagner Archives, online: http://www.laguardiawagnerarchive.lagcc.cuny.edu/ FileBrowser.aspx?LinkToFile=FILES_DOC/WAGNER_FILES/06.020.0059.060300.22. PDF#undefined; Lehman to Robert G. A. Jackson, March 27, 1962, LP, SF, Jackson; "Governor Assays Impact of Divorce," *NYT*, February 15, 1962, p. 20; "Mrs. Rockefeller Receives Divorce; 2 Sons with Her," *NYT*, March 17, 1962, pp. 1, 14; "State Party Is Set by Conservatives," *NYT*, February 14, 1962, p. 20; "McKeon Favors Renomination of Levitt for State Controller," *NYT*, March 20, 1962, p. 32; "Poll Finds Mayor Leads Governor," April 20, 1962, pp. 1, 16; "Mayor Rules Out Governor Race; Decision 'Final,'" *NYT*, April 29, 1962, pp. 1, 74; "Rockefeller Poll Encourages G.O.P.," *NYT*, May 1, 1962, pp. 1, 30; Costikyan, *Behind Closed Doors*, pp. 213–214; McNickle, *To Be Mayor of New York*, pp. 186–187; Smith, *On His Own Terms*, pp. 363–365, 370–379. On the formation of the New York State Conservative Party, see Mahoney, *Actions Speak Louder*.

52. Lehman to Robert G. A. Jackson, June 27, 1962, LP, SF, Jackson; "Capital Proposes Party Plan Here," *NYT*, July 6, 1962, p. 12; "Another Lehman," Editorial, *Newsday*, July 9, 1962, p. 35; "N.Y. Democrats Eye Stable," *Christian Science Monitor*, July 10, 1962, p. 5; "Democrats Consider Robert Morgenthau," *NYT*, August 16, 1962, pp. 1, 17; "Interest in Morgenthau," *NYT*, August 20, 1962, p. 14; "Morgenthau Gets Backing in Party," *NYT*, August 23, 1962, p. 26; "Kennedy Stays Neutral," *NYT*, August 23, 1962, p. 26; "Morgenthau Support Builds," *Christian Science Monitor*, August 28, 1962, p. 12; "Morgenthau the Man?" Editorial, *NYT*, August 28, 1962, p. 25; "Who Needs a Convention?" Editorial, *NYT*, August 30, 1962, p. 23; "Lehman Endorses Regular Democrat," *NYT*, August 30, 1962, pp. 1, 30; "Morgenthau Bids for Nomination; Resigns U.S. Post," *NYT*, September 5, 1962, pp. 1, 33; "Kennedy Aids Hopes of Morgenthau in N.Y.," *Los Angeles Times*, September 6, 1962, p. 4; "Morgenthau Opens Drive; Hits Rockefeller's Record," *NYT*, September 6, 1962, pp. 1, 20; "Wagner, Lehman Declare Support for Morgenthau," *NYT*, September 13, 1962, pp. 1, 24; "Text of Wagner and Lehman Statements," *NYT*, September 13, 1962, p. 24; Lehman to Nevins, September 13, 1962, LP, SF, Nevins; McNickle, *To Be Mayor of New York City*, pp. 184–185; Smith, *On His Own Terms*, p. 379.

53. Sulzberger to Lehman, September 17, 1962, LP, SF, Sulzberger; "Stratton Promises a Fight on 'Bossism' at Convention," *NYT*, September 16, 1962, pp. 1, 43; "Democrats Open N.Y. State Convention; Morgenthau Seen Choice for Governor," *WP*, September 18, 1962, A-8; "Morgenthau Nominated to Oppose Rockefeller; Victor on Second Ballot," *NYT*, September 18, 1962, pp. 1, 30; "Democrats Name Dudley, a Negro, to State Ticket; Donovan to Oppose Javits," *NYT*, September 19, 1962, pp. 1, 26; "Democrats Start Job of Healing Convention Scars," *NYT*, September 19, 1962, p. 27; "N.Y. Democrats Fight Doubts," *Christian Science Monitor*, September 19, 1962, p. 5; Lehman to Mrs. Roosevelt, September 19, 1962, LP, SF, Eleanor Roosevelt;

Costikyan, *Behind Closed Doors*, pp. 163–165; Schlesinger, *Robert Kennedy and His Times*, pp. 370–371; Smith, *On His Own Terms*, p. 379.

54. Herbert and Edith Lehman to Morgenthau, September 18, 1962, and Morgenthau to Lehman, October 12, 1962, both in LP, SF, Morgenthau; Lehman to Mrs. Roosevelt, September 19, 1962, LP, SF, Eleanor Roosevelt; Morgenthau in Libo, ed., *Lots of Lehmans*, p. 251; Lehman to Allan Nevins, October 6, 1962, LP, SF, Nevins; "Morgenthau Pays a Visit to Coney," *NYT*, October 22, 1962, pp. 1, 23; "Morgenthau Is Heading Upstate, Shorn of Cabinet Members' Aid," *NYT*, October 25, 1962, p. 29; "Summing Up Given by Morgenthau," *NYT*, November 5, 1962, p. 24; "Morgenthau Sees Big Switch to Him," *NYT*, November 6, 1962, p. 25.

55. McNickle, *To Be Mayor of New York City*, p. 185; "N.Y. Democrats Fight Doubts," *Christian Science Monitor*, September 19, 1962, p. 5; "Text of Morgenthau's Acceptance Speech, Assailing Rockefeller's Record," *NYT*, September 19, 1962, p. 26; Victor Riesel, "Kennedy and Aides Plan to Crack the Solid-as-a-Rockefeller Image," *Los Angeles Times*, September 27, 1962, A5; "Kennedy Aids State Tickets in Tours of City and Jersey," *NYT*, October 13, 1962, pp. 1, 9; "Morgenthau Is Heading Upstate, Shorn of Cabinet Members' Aid," *NYT*, October 25, 1962, p. 29; Marquis Childs, "Trial Balance for Rockefeller," *WP*, November 5, 1962, A-16; Lehman to Nevins, October 26, 1962, LP, SF, Nevins; " 'Regrets' Barred by Morgenthau," *NYT*, November 7, 1962, p. 16; Smith, *On His Own Terms*, pp. 380–384.

56. "Re-Election of Governor and Javits Is Predicted," *NYT*, November 5, 1962, pp. 1, 25; "Gov. Rockefeller and Morgenthau Both See Victory," *NYT*, November 6, 1962, pp. 1, 25; "Rockefeller, Javits, and Levitt Win; Lefkowitz Victor," *NYT*, November 7, 1962, pp. 1, 16; " 'Regrets' Barred by Morgenthau, *NYT*, November 7, 1962, p. 16; "Rocky Got the Job; Morgy Got the Cheers," *Newsday*, November 7, 1962, p. 4; "Rockefeller Edge Spurs '64 Hopes," *NYT*, November 8, 1963, pp. 1, 23; "Ethnic Divisions in Vote Analyzed," *NYT*, November 14, 1962, p. 32; A. M. Sonnabend, "Jewish Vote Denied," Letter to the Editor, *NYT*, July 17, 1962, p. 24; Costikyan, *Behind Closed Doors*, pp. 214–215; Moscow, *What Have You Done For Me Lately?* pp. 126–127; McNickle, *To Be Mayor of New York City*, pp. 185–186; Smith, *On His Own Terms*, p. 384; Mahoney, *Actions Speak Louder*, pp. 117–118; Javits, *Javits*, pp. 365–366.

57. Morgenthau to Lehman, December 6, 1962, and Lehman to Morgenthau, December 10, 1962, both in LP, SF, Morgenthau, "Rocky Got the Job; Morgy Got the Cheers," *Newsday*, November 7, 1962, p. 4; "Morgenthau Reappointed to Post as U.S. Attorney," *NYT*, November 23, 1962, pp. 1, 20; "Morgenthau Trounces Kuh in D.A. Race," *NYT*, November 6, 1974, pp. 1, 30; "Morgenthau Heads for Door, Legacy Assured," *NYT*, February 28, 2009, A-1, A-18.

58. "De Sapio Will Run for District Leader," *NYT*, June 20, 1963, pp. 1, 40; "Koch Regrets Denouncing Wagner and Lehman in '62," *NYT*, July 22, 1963, p. 36; Lehman to Lloyd Garrison, May 24, 1963, and June 12, 1963, both in LP, SF, Garrison; "Lehman Endorses Rival of De Sapio," *NYT*, August 11, 1963, p. 29; "Koch Said to Use Outsiders' Help," *NYT*, August 29, 1963, p. 11; "De Sapio Beaten; Koch Is Elected by 41-Vote Edge," *NYT*, September 6, 1963, pp. 1, 17; Newfield and Barrett, *City for Sale*, p. 114; Costikyan, *Behind Closed Doors*, p. 216; Soffer, *Ed Koch and the Rebuilding of New York City*, p. 48; Petrus, "To Break Down Walls," pp. 86–89; Moscow, *The Last of the Big-Time Bosses*, pp. 185–186.

Chapter 21. "To Inspire Men and Women of All Generations": Herbert Lehman and President Kennedy, 1961–1963

1. John Kennedy to Robert Benjamin on the occasion of the Annual Dinner Concert of the America-Israel Cultural Foundation, which was honoring Herbert Lehman, January 16, 1962, LP, SF, John Kennedy.

2. Lehman to Robert G.A. Jackson, December 29, 1960, and April 3, 1961, both in LP, SF, Jackson; Joseph Proskauer to Lehman, November 11, 1960, and Lehman to Proskauer, November 15, 1960, both in LP, SF, Proskauer; Lehman to Bowles, December 12, 1960, LP, SF, Bowles; Lehman to John Kennedy, December 12, 1960, and Kennedy to Lehman December 15, 1960, LP, SF, Kennedy; Lehman to Stevenson, December 12, 1960, and Stevenson to Lehman, December 29, 1960, LP, SF, Stevenson; Lehman to Schlesinger, January 27, 1961, LP, SF, Schlesinger. On opposition to Fulbright's possible appointment as Secretary of State, see Woods, *Fulbright*, pp. 255–260. On Stevenson's appointment as U.S. Ambassador to the U.N., see Martin, *Adlai Stevenson and the World*, pp. 551–565; and Dallek, *An Unfinished Life*, pp. 313–316.

3. Lehman to Guy Gillette, December 20, 1960, LP, SF, Gillette; Lehman to Eleanor Roosevelt, July 23, 1961, LP, SF, Eleanor Roosevelt; Lehman to John Kennedy, January 10, 1961; Lehman to Kennedy, December 4, 1961; and Ralph Dungan to Lehman, December 13, 1961, all in LP, SF, John Kennedy; Edelstein to Governor Lehman, December 5, 1961, Robert Wagner Documents Collection, Julius Edelstein (Wagner Staff) Series, Subject Files III Sub Series, Box 060300, Folder 22, "Lehman–Correspondence," December 1961, La Guardia and Wagner Archives, online: http://www.laguardiawagnerarchive.lagcc.cuny.edu/FileBrowser.aspx?LinkToFile=FILES_DOC/WAGNER_FILES/06.020.0059.060300.22.PDF#undefined; Jerome Udell to Harold Linder, November 5, 1949; Benjamin Lazrus to Linder, October 8, 1950; Linder to Lehman, February 6, 1961; and Bertha and Harold Linder to Mrs. Lehman, December 6, 1963, all in LP, SF, Linder; "Kennedy Chooses Trade Bank Chief," *NYT*, February 1, 1961, p. 6; Lehman to Robert Kennedy, January 24, 1961, LP, SF, Robert Kennedy; Edelstein to John Kennedy, December 4, 1960, JFK, White House Name File, Edelstein; Lehman to Anthony Akers, April 28, 1961, LP, SF, Akers; "Finletter Given NATO Envoy Post," *NYT*, January 29, 1961, pp. 1, 47; Al Sostchen, "Political Postscripts," *New York Post*, August 3, 1960, p. 18; "Snub by President," *NYT*, January 30, 1961, p. 14. On Frank Altschul, see Roberts, "Frank Altschul, Lazard Frères, and the Council on Foreign Relations."

4. Lehman to Allan Nevins, March 14, 1961, LP, SF, Nevins; "President Asks Restraint in Education-Aid Dispute," *NYT*, March 16, 1961, pp. 1, 23; Lehman to Hubert Humphrey, January 31, 1963, LP, SF, Humphrey. On Kennedy's difficulties in getting his education bill through Congress, see Bernstein, *Promises Kept*, pp. 218–245; and Graham, *The Uncertain Triumph*, pp. 11–52. On Kennedy's lack of success in getting his legislative program passed by Congress, see "Democrats Keep Congress Strength; 50 Million Vote," *NYT*, November 7, 1962, pp. 1, 42; Dallek, *An Unfinished Life*, pp. 328–336, 377–388; Caro, *The Passage of Power*, pp. 454–455.

5. John Kennedy to Robert Benjamin, January 16, 1962, and Lehman to the President, May 10, 1962, both in LP, SF, John Kennedy; "Cultural Centers Planned For Israel," *NYT*, January 17, 1962, p. 20; "Premier of Norway Here To See Kennedy," *NYT*, May 9, 1962, p. 16; "Kennedy To Join Fund Rally Here," *NYT*, April 3, 1962, pp. 1,

23; "Kennedy, at 'Salute' Here, Asks Voters to Back Party," *NYT*, May 20, 1962, pp. 1, 63; Arthur Krim to Richard Maguire, May 28, 1962; Kennedy to Lehman, June 1, 1962; and Alan Emory to President Kennedy, August 13, 1962, all in JFK, White House Name File, Lehman; Lehman to Kennedy, June 5, 1962, President's Office Files, Box 11, General Correspondence, Reference Copy, 1962, LE; Lehman to Arthur Goldberg, August 30, 1962, LP, SF, Goldberg; Lehman to Robert Kennedy, October 12, 1962, LP, SF, Robert Kennedy.

    6. Krim to Lehman, August 6, 1962; Lehman to Krim, August 9, 1962; and Memorandum of Telephone Call from Governor Lehman to Mr. Arthur Krim, October 4, 1962, all in LP, SF, Edward Kennedy. It is not clear which Senate candidate outside of New York Lehman endorsed in 1962, but it was probably either Congressman Sidney Yates in Illinois or Senator Ernest Gruening in Alaska. Lehman contributed generously to both of their campaigns. See Gruening to Lehman, October 22, 1962, LP, SF, Gruening; and Yates to Lehman, October 19, 1962, LP, SF, Yates.

    7. From Press Office, "Senator John F. Kennedy, Immigration and Naturalization Laws," Hyannis Inn Motel, Hyannis, Mass., August 6, 1960, in *Freedom of Communications*, S. Rept. 994, 87th Cong., 1st sess., September 13, 1961, Part 1, pp. 7–8; "Lehman Scores Nixon's Record," *NYT*, October 11, 1960, p. 36; "Remarks of Herbert H. Lehman at Ceremony Commemorating 74th Anniversary of Statue of Liberty Dedication," October 29, 1960, David Stowe Papers, Box 17, 1960 Presidential Campaign Files, Statue of Liberty Dedication–74th Anniversary–Speech–Herbert H. Lehman, New York, October 29, 1960, HSTL; "Laws On Aliens Hit By Kennedy, Lehman," *NYT*, October 30, 1960, p. 56.

    8. "Address by the Honorable Herbert H. Lehman at 77th Annual Meeting of United HIAS Services," Extension of Remarks of Hon. Philip A. Hart, 107 *Cong. Rec.* A1869–A1870 (March 16, 1961).

    9. Edelstein to Feldman, February 7, 1961, JFK, White House Name File, Lehman; "The President's News Conference of August 10, 1961," Document 318, *Public Papers of the Presidents: Kennedy, 1961*, p. 560; "Kennedy Signs Refugee Aid Bill Allowing Non-Quota Admissions," *NYT*, June 29, 1962, p. 3; "Walter Plans Immigration Policy Study," *WP*, June 28, 1962, A-23; H. Res. 56, 87th Cong., 1st sess., 107 *Cong. Rec.* 2003 (February 9, 1961); 108 *Cong. Rec.* 11967–11968 (June 27, 1962); Congressional Research Service, *U.S. Immigration Law and Policy, 1952–1979: A Report Prepared at the Request of Senator Edward M. Kennedy*, 96th Cong., 1st sess., 1979, pp. 44–45; Schwartz, *The Open Society*, pp. 22–34, 112–113; Bennett, *American Immigration Policies*, pp. 240–275, 286–290. On Walter's influence in limiting significant immigration reform, see "Frustrated Reform," Editorial, *NYT*, September 18, 1961, p. 28.

    10. John Kennedy, "Letter to the President of the Senate and to the Speaker of the House of Representatives on Revision of the Immigration Laws," July 23, 1963, Document 311, *Public Papers of the Presidents: Kennedy, 1963*, pp. 594–597; "President Urges Repeal of Quotas For Immigration," *NYT*, July 24, 1963, pp. 1, 13; "The Nation: The Huddled Masses," *NYT*, July 28, 1963, E2; Lehman to Hart, August 7, 1963, and Hart to Lehman, August 19, 1963, LP, SF, Hart; "Rep. Francis Walter, 69, Dies; Wrote Immigration Restrictions," *NYT*, June 1, 1963, p. 16; Schwartz, *The Open Society*, pp. 113–116. Walter's position as chairman of the House Judiciary Subcommittee on Immigration was filled by Representative Michael Feighan, a conservative Democrat from

Ohio, who opposed any loosening of the nation's immigration policies. See "Several in House Are Expected to Share Four Positions That Walter Held," *NYT*, June 2, 1963, p. 36; Schwartz, *The Open Society*, pp. 18–20, 58–66, 116–119, 122–124.

11. John Kennedy, *A Nation of Immigrants*, Revised and Enlarged edition; John Kennedy, "With Clean Hands and a Clear Conscience," *Saturday Evening Post*, October 3, 1964, pp. 21–23; Congressional Research Service, *U.S. Immigration Law and Policy, 1952–1979*, pp. 48–51; "Herbert H. Lehman," Editorial, *WP*, December 6, 1963, A16; Robert Segal, "As We Were Saying," *American Israelite*, December 19, 1963, pp. 1, 11; "Publishers Hear Kennedy, Keating," *Boston Globe*, September 16, 1964, p. 26; Public Law 89–236, 79 *Stat.* 911, October 3, 1965. For a critical view emphasizing the Johnson administration's retreat from Kennedy's vision and the immigration bill's original provisions, see Schwartz, *The Open Society*, pp. 1–21, 117–125.

12. Eleanor Roosevelt, "My Day," January 30, 1961, online: http://www.gwu. edu/~erpapers/myday/displaydoc.cfm?_y=1961&_f=md004906; "Award to Dr. Martin Luther King," 107 *Cong. Rec.* 3328–3329 (March 7, 1961). On Senator Kennedy and civil rights, see chapter 18.

13. Lehman to Weaver, January 9, 1961, LP, SF, Weaver; "Judaism's Status in U.S. Acclaimed," *NYT*, January 14, 1961, p. 48; "Weaver's Fight on Bias Firm but Well-Tempered," *WP*, January 1, 1961, A-4; "A Good Man for the Job," Editorial, *NYT*, January 1, 1961, E-6; Pritchett, *Robert Clifton Weaver and the American City*, pp. 136, 171–192, 203–220; Lehman to Marshall, September 29, 1961, and September 19, 1962, LP, SF, Marshall; Schlesinger, *Robert Kennedy and His Times*, p. 308; Rowan, *Dream Makers, Dream Breakers*, pp. 272–273, 279–283; Tushnet, *Making Constitutional Law*, pp. 9–13; Zelden, *Thurgood Marshall*, pp. 125–131.

14. Lehman to Morse, March 10, 1961, LP, SF, Morse; "Meriwether Approved in 5-to-4 Vote," *WP*, March 3, 1961, A-1, A-4; "Ground for Doubt," Editorial, *WP*, March 3, 1961, A-12; "Senate Test Survived by Meriwether," *WP*, March 8, 1961, A1, A2; "Wrong Man for the Wrong Job," Editorial, *Chicago Defender*, March 8, 1961, p. 10; "Meriwether Gets Senate Approval," *NYT*, March 9, 1961, pp. 1, 18; Robert Spivack, "Watch on the Potomac," *Chicago Defender*, March 9, 1961, p. 14; Doris Fleeson, "Meriwether Episode Lesson for Kennedy," *Boston Globe*, March 12, 1961, p. 24. Paul Douglas and Hubert Humphrey were among the liberals who voted to confirm Meriwether. See "Senate Roll-Call Vote on Meriwether's Post," *NYT*, March 9, 1961, p. 18. On Kennedy's appointment of Southern racists to federal positions, see Brauer, *John F. Kennedy and the Second Reconstruction*, pp. 86–87, 120–125; and Bryant, *The Bystander*, pp. 218–219.

15. Wilkins to Lehman, June 14, 1961, and August 8, 1961, both in LP, SF, Wilkins. On Lehman's service on the NAACP Board of Directors, see "Negroes to Fight Labor Union Bans," *NYT*, January 7, 1930, p. 21; "Herbert H. Lehman—Biographical Outline," n.d., LP, SF, Herbert Lehman, document 0530_0308; "NAACP Sees No Letup," *New York Amsterdam News*, January 19, 1963, p. 2. On Attorney General Robert Kennedy's petition to the ICC, see "Robert Kennedy Asks I.C.C. to End Bus Segregation," *NYT*, May 30, 1961, pp. 1, 7; Schlesinger, *Robert Kennedy and His Times*, p. 300; Branch, *Parting the Waters*, p. 478.

16. Lehman to Kennedy, October 24, 1961, JFK, President's Official Files, Box 3 (Overflow), General Correspondence, 1961, La–Le, Reference Copy. On disappointment

with the Kennedy administration's civil rights record in its first year, see Wofford, *Of Kennedys and Kings*, pp. 124–164; Mann, *The Walls of Jericho*, pp. 300–316, 334–335; Watson, *Lion in the Lobby*, pp. 450–461; Bryant, *The Bystander*, pp. 225–242; Dallek, *An Unfinished Life*, pp. 380–388.

17. Kennedy to Lehman, November 3, 1961, and attached "Summary of Civil Rights Progress in the Last Nine Months," November 1, 1961, JFK, President's Official Files, Box 3 (Overflow), General Correspondence, 1961, La–Le, Reference Copy. On this "Summary," see Dallek, *An Unfinished Life*, p. 383.

18. "Robert Kennedy Bids Club End Ban," *NYT*, May 17, 1961, p. 23; "Duke Protests Metropolitan's Ban on Africans in Capital," *NYT*, August 9, 1961, p. 12; "Robert Kennedy Quits Social Club," *NYT*, September 21, 1961, p. 22; "Gov. Is Member of Jim Crow Club," *New York Amsterdam News*, October 14, 1961, pp. 1, 13; Mayor Wagner's Aide in 'Lily-White' Club," *New York Amsterdam News*, October 21, 1961, pp. 1, 13; "A Big, BIG Man!" *New York Amsterdam News*, October 21, 1961, p. 1; James Hicks, "Now We Know!" *New York Amsterdam News*, October 21, 1961, p. 12; W. J. DuBose to Lehman, November 18, 1961, LP, SF, Herbert Lehman, document 0530_0220; Schlesinger, *Robert Kennedy and His Times*, p. 290; Bryant, *The Bystander*, p. 223.

19. Martin Luther King, Jr., and Wyatt Walker to Lehman, May 2, 1962, and attached Petition, LP, SF, King; "Race Group to Stress Gandhi Non-Violence," *WP*, May 18, 1962, A-2; Jackie Robinson, "Kennedy Is No Lincoln," *New York Amsterdam News*, May 26, 1962, p. 11.

20. Lehman to King and Walker, May 11, 1962, LP, SF, King.

21. Robert Kennedy to Lehman, March 17, 1962; Lehman to Kennedy, May 21, 1962; and Kennedy to Lehman, May 28, 1962, all in LP, SF, Robert Kennedy; "Robert Kennedy Asks Vote Equity," *NYT*, May 6, 1962, p. 75. On the Senate's rejection of legislation banning literacy tests in federal elections, see Brauer, *John F. Kennedy and the Second Reconstruction*, pp. 132–137; Bryant, *The Bystander*, pp. 302–307. On Lehman receiving the AJC's American Liberties Medallion, see Lehman to Samuel Leidesdorf, October 18, 1956, LP, SF, Leidesdorf.

22. Lehman to John Kennedy, October 2, 1962; and Kennedy to Lehman, October 22, 1962, both in LP, SF, Kennedy; Lehman to Allan Nevins, October 6, 1962, LP, SF, Nevins. On the Kennedy administration's handling of James Meredith's admission to the University of Mississippi, see Dallek, *An Unfinished Life*, pp. 514–518; Brauer, *John F. Kennedy and the Second Reconstruction*, pp. 180–204; Schlesinger, *Robert Kennedy and His Times*, pp. 317–327.

23. "N.A.A.C.P. to Ask Courts to End Union Racial Bars," *NYT*, August 6, 1962, pp. 1, 22; "ILGWU Inquiry Called Frame-Up," *NYT*, August 19, 1962, pp. 1, 41; U.S., Congress, House, Committee on Education and Labor, *Investigation of the Garment Industry; Hearings* before the Ad Hoc Subcommittee on Investigation of the Garment Industry, 87th Cong., 2d sess., August 17, 18, 23, 24, and September 21, 1962, p. 111; "Negro Defends I.L.G.W.U. on Bias," *NYT*, August 23, 1962, p. 30; "Dubinsky Scores House Inquiry; Denies Bias in Garment Union," *NYT*, August 25, 1962, pp. 1, 10; "Liberal Attacks Garment Inquiry," *NYT*, August 11, 1962, p. 42; "Zelenko Assailed on Garment Inquiry," *NYT*, August 14, 1962, p. 25; "Race Bias Denied in Garment Union," *NYT*, August 18, 1962, p. 17; Jonas, *Freedom's Sword*, pp.

238–279; Dubinsky and Raskin, *David Dubinsky*, pp. 15–16, 326–327; Parmet, *Master of Seventh Avenue*, pp. 300–307; Marshall, *The Negro and Organized Labor*, pp. 53–85; Foner, *Organized Labor and the Black Worker, 1619–1973*, pp. 342–345. Hill, who was also working as a special consultant to the subcommittee, published his accusations against the ILGWU as "The ILGWU Today," and they were inserted by Representative Thomas Curtis (R-MO) in 109 *Cong. Rec.* 1569–1572 (January 31, 1963). The black press, in reporting on the controversy, was very critical of the ILGWU. See "NAACP Proves Bias in Garment Union," *New York Amsterdam News*, August 25, 1962, pp. 1, 38; "Union Policies Said to Restrict Minority Earning," *Atlanta Daily World*, August 29, 1962, p. 2; "Garment Union Colonialism," Editorial, *Pittsburgh Courier*, September 1, 1962, pp. 1, 12. The Liberal Party had endorsed Representative William Fitts Ryan, a leader of the reform Democratic movement, who defeated Zelenko in the September primary after redistricting had placed them in the same district, and Mae Watts, who was challenging Powell. See "Powell Sets Open Hearings on Garment Industry," *NYT*, August 8, 1962, p. 20. On Dubinsky and the Liberal Party, see Dubinsky and Raskin, *David Dubinsky*, pp. 262–317; and Parmet, *The Master of Seventh Avenue*, pp. 188–199, 206–224, 249–257, 282–287.

24. Dubinsky to Lehman, October 19, 1962; Hannah Haskel to Lehman, October 19, 1962, and attached "Resolution on ILGWU by NAACP Board of Directors," all in LP, SF, Dubinsky; "NAACP Hits ILGWU Prejudice; Dudley and Dubinsky in Clash," *New York Amsterdam News*, October 13, 1962, pp. 1, 2; Parmet, *Master of Seventh Avenue*, pp. 307–308; Jonas, *Freedom's Sword*, pp. 271–272. While Dubinsky engaged in McCarthy-like red-baiting in some of his allegations against Hill, other ILGWU officials charged that Hill was practicing McCarthyism in constantly changing the number of blacks and Puerto Ricans in one of the union's locals and using "the anonymous smear." Despite the fact that Hill was Jewish (and white), ILGWU officials also accused him of anti-Semitism. See Tyler, "The Truth about the ILGWU," pp. 9, 10, 17.

25. Lehman to Wilkins, October 23, 1962, LP, SF, Wilkins.

26. Wilkins to Lehman, October 30, 1962, LP, SF, Wilkins.

27. Wilkins to Lehman, October 30, 1962, LP, SF, Wilkins.

28. Lehman to Dubinsky, November 2, 1962, LP, SF, Dubinsky; Tyler, "The Truth about the ILGWU," p. 7; "Meany Denounces Aide of N.A.A.C.P.," *NYT*, November 10, 1962, pp. 1, 13; Hill, "The ILGWU—Fact and Fiction," p. 7; "NAACP Hits Back at George Meany," *New York Amsterdam News*, November 17, 1962, pp. 1, 42; "No Let Up in NAACP Bias Drive," *New York Amsterdam News*, December 15, 1962, p. 54; "Wilkins Scores Unions' Inaction," *NYT*, May 18, 1965, p. 12; Parmet, *Master of Seventh Avenue*, pp. 308–311; Watson, *Lion in the Lobby*, p. 526; Goulden, *Meany*, p. 323; Foner, *Organized Labor and the Black Worker*, pp. 344–377; Boyle, *The UAW and the Heyday of American Liberalism*, pp. 161–184; and Green, "Blacks, Jews, and the 'Natural Alliance.'" On the growing antagonism between organized labor and the civil rights movement at this time, see Jackie Robinson, "David Dubinsky and the People," *New York Amsterdam News*, November 10, 1962, p. 13; Alistair Cooke, "Labour and the Negro," *Manchester Guardian*, November 12, 1962, p. 10; "TULC Backs Herbert Hill," *Pittsburgh Courier*, November 17, 1962, p. 28; James Hicks, "Union Activities," *New York Amsterdam News*, December 1, 1962, p. 10. Hill remained with the NAACP until 1977,

when he left to become a professor of Industrial Relations and Afro-American Studies at the University of Wisconsin. See "Herbert Hill, a Voice against Discrimination, Dies at 80," *NYT*, August 21, 2004, A-13. On the partnership and conflict between blacks and Jews, see *Black Anti-Semitism and Jewish Racism*; Hill, "Black-Jewish Conflict in the Labor Context: Race, Jobs, and Institutional Power," in Franklin, Grant, Kletnick and McNeil, eds., *African Americans and Jews in the Twentieth Century*, pp. 264–292; Salzman, Black, and Sorin, eds., *Bridges and Boundaries*; Weisbord and Stein, *Bittersweet Encounter*; Harris and Swanson, *Black-Jewish Relations in New York City*; Podair, *The Strike That Changed Everything*; and Greenberg, *Troubling the Waters*.

29. Lehman to Humphrey, January 31, 1963, LP, SF, Humphrey; Lehman to David Morse, May 14, 1963, LP, SF, Morse; "Filibuster Foes Defeated, Drop Senate Fight in '63," *NYT*, February 8, 1963, pp. 1, 6; Brauer, *John F. Kennedy and the Second Reconstruction*, p. 213; Bryant, *The Bystander*, p. 366.

30. Lehman to David Morse, May 14, 1963, LP, SF, Morse; "Kennedy Statement," *NYT*, May 13, 1963, p. 25; Lehman to President Kennedy, June 7, 1963, JFK, White House Name File, Lehman. On the crisis in Birmingham, see Branch, *Parting the Waters*, pp. 673–802. On Kennedy's televised address on June 11, see "Kennedy Sees 'Moral Crisis' In U.S.; President in Plea," *NYT*, June 12, 1963, pp. 1, 20; "Transcript of the President's Address," *NYT*, June 12, 1963, p. 20; Brauer, *John F. Kennedy and the Second Reconstruction*, pp. 259–264.

31. Lehman to Wilkins, August 29, 1963; and Wilkins to Lehman, September 24, 1963, both in LP, SF, Wilkins. On the March on Washington, see Wilkins, *Standing Fast*, pp. 291–293; Branch, *Parting the Waters*, pp. 816–817, 839–841, 846–850, 871–887; Dallek, *An Unfinished Life*, pp. 640–646.

32. Robert Kennedy to Lehman, October 29, 1963, LP, SF, Kennedy; William vanden Heuvel to Author, August 16, 2013; "Prince Edward Negroes Given Wide Support for Free Schools," *NYT*, October 20, 1963, p. 85; Smith, *They Closed Their Schools*, pp. 236–241; Schlesinger, *Robert Kennedy and His Times*, p. 345; Titus, *Brown's Battleground*, pp. 133–159; Bonastia, *Southern Stalemate*.

33. Lehman to Robert Kennedy, January 3, 1963; and Kennedy to Lehman, January 18, 1963, both in LP, SF, Robert Kennedy; "Capital Awaits Kennedy Trio Act," *Christian Science Monitor*, January 2, 1963, p. 1.

34. Lehman to Robert Kennedy, January 31, 1963; Lehman to the President of the Bar Association of the City of New York, January 31, 1963; Kennedy to Lehman, February 11, 1963; Kennedy to Lehman, March 13, 1963; the Attorney General to the President, March 6, 1963; White House Press Release, March 8, 1963; and Lehman to Kennedy, March 16, 1963, all in LP, SF, Robert Kennedy; Lehman to Emanuel Celler, January 31, 1963, LP, SF, Celler; Schlesinger, *Robert Kennedy and His Times*, pp. 392–393; P.L. 88-455, 78 *Stat.* 552–554 (1964).

35. Doris Fleeson, "The Target," *New York Post*, May 25, 1961, Magazine p. 2; Lehman to Tractors for Freedom Committee, May 29, 1961, Eleanor Roosevelt Papers, Box 3583, 1957–1962, Lehman; Eleanor Roosevelt to Lehman, May 31, 1961, LP, SF, Eleanor Roosevelt; Lehman to Robert G. A. Jackson, August 9, 1961, and March 27, 1962, both in LP, SF, Jackson; Lehman to Kennedy, June 7, 1961; Kennedy to Lehman, June 12, 1961; Lehman to Kennedy, July 26, 1961; Kennedy to Lehman, August 1, 1961; and Kennedy to Lehman, September 28, 1961, all in LP, SF, Kennedy; Lehman

to Allan Nevins, September 27, 1961, LP, SF, Nevins; Lehman to Lithgow Osborne, November 6, 1962, LP, SF, Osborne; Lehman to Stevenson, October 26, 1962, LP, SF, Stevenson. On the Bay of Pigs, the Vienna Summit, the Berlin Wall, and the Cuban Missile Crisis, see Beschloss, *The Crisis Years*, pp. 104–134, 193–231, 231–248, 255–290, 412–575; and Dallek, *An Unfinished Life*, pp. 356–371, 401–425, 535–574. For the text of Kennedy's speeches, see "Radio and Television Report to the American People on Returning from Europe," June 6, 1961, Document 231; "Radio and Television Report to the American People on the Berlin Crisis," July 25, 1961, Document 302; and "Address in New York City before the General Assembly of the United Nations," September 25, 1961, Document 387, *Public Papers of the Presidents, Kennedy, 1961*, pp. 441–446, 533–540, 618–626.

36. Dungan to Lehman, October 30, 1961, LP, SF, John Kennedy; Frank Church to Lehman, October 18, 1961, LP, SF, Church; "President Goes to People on Aid," *NYT*, July 11, 1961, pp. 1, 2; Humphrey to Lehman, August 18, 1961; Lehman to Humphrey, August 23, 1961; and Lehman to Humphrey, August 23, 1961 (there are two letters from Lehman to Humphrey dated August 23, 1961), all in LP, SF, Humphrey; John McCloy to Lehman, August 21, 1961, LP, SF, McCloy; McGovern to Lehman, October 30, 1961; and Lehman to McGovern, November 2, 1961, both in LP, SF, John Kennedy; "Group to Combat Hunger in World," *NYT*, November 23, 1961, pp. 1, 17. Humphrey later revealed that the President had given him the green light to proceed on the bill to establish the Arms Control and Disarmament Agency after he and Kennedy had discussed the matter while skinny-dipping in the White House pool. See Humphrey, *The Education of a Public Man*, pp. 251–252. On the creation of the Arms Control and Disarmament Agency, see "Letter to the President of the Senate and to the Speaker of the House Proposing the Establishment of a United States Disarmament Agency," June 29, 1961, Document 262; and "Remarks in New York City upon Signing Bill Establishing the U.S. Arms Control and Disarmament Agency," September 26, 1961, Document 388, *Public Papers of the Presidents: Kennedy, 1961*, pp. 486–488, 626–627; Schlesinger, *A Thousand Days*, pp. 472–473; Bird, *The Chairman*, pp. 513–514.

37. Lehman to President Kennedy, July 27, 1963; and Kennedy to Lehman, August 6, 1963, both in LP, SF, Kennedy; Lehman to Barbara Ward Jackson, July 29, 1963, LP, SF, Robert and Barbara Ward Jackson; Citizens Committee for a Nuclear Test Ban to President Kennedy, August 7, 1963, JFK, White House Central Files, Subject Files, Box 661, PC 1, August 3, 1963–August 16, 1963; "Kennedy to Send Test Ban Treaty to Senate Today," *NYT*, August 8, 1963, pp. 1, 2; "Radio and Television Address to the American People on the Nuclear Test Ban Treaty," July 26, 1963, Document 316, *Public Papers of the Presidents: Kennedy, 1963*, pp. 601–606; Seaborg, *Kennedy, Khrushchev, and the Test Ban*, pp. 264–265; Abramson, *Spanning the Century*, pp. 594–599; Beschloss, *The Crisis Years*, pp. 618–638; Dallek, *An Unfinished Life*, pp. 612–630; William Burr and Hector Montford, eds., "The Making of the Limited Test Ban Treaty, 1958–1963," National Security Archive, online: http://www.gwu.edu/~nsarchiv/NSAEBB/NSAEBB94/index2.htm.

38. Lehman to Edward Weinfeld, June 4, 1949, LP, SF, Weinfeld; Elihu Elath to Lehman, August 18, 1949, LP, SF, Elath; "Lehman Honored in Israel," *NYT*, April 22, 1959, p. 66; "Informal Meeting in Israel," *NYT*, April 30, 1959, p. 5; Lehman to Ogden Reid, June 9, 1959, LP, SF, Reid; Lehman to David Ben Gurion, May 6, 1959,

LP, SF, Ben Gurion. Lehman's annual contributions to UJA ranged from $50,000 in 1948 to $75,000 for 1963. See Lehman to Sam Leidesdorf, February 28, 1948, and Leidesdorf to Lehman, December 20, 1962, both in LP, SF, Leidesdorf; "U.J.A. Opens Drive for World Relief," *NYT*, March 13, 1959, p. 20.

39. "Non-Zionist Unit Chides Goldmann," *NYT*, May 9, 1961, p. 17. On the AJC's concern about "dual loyalties," see Proskauer, *A Segment of My Times*, pp. 196–215, 229–261; Cohen, *Not Free to Desist*, pp. 305–306, 312–315.

40. S. Res. 298, 84th Cong., 2d sess., June 27, 1956; S. Res. 323, 84th Cong., 2d sess., July 25, 1956; 102 *Cong. Rec.* 11052, 11057–11072 (June 27, 1956), 11324 (June 29, 1956), 14330 (July 25, 1956), 14731–14734 (July 26, 1956); "U.S. Policy Scored on Arab Visa Curbs," *WP*, June 28, 1956, p. 29; "Senate Scores Bias in Religion Abroad," *NYT*, July 28, 1956, p. 36; "Democratic Party Platform of 1960," in Porter and Johnson, comps., *National Party Platforms*, pp. 578, 579, 597; "Letter to Rabbi Israel Goldstein by Senator John F. Kennedy," August 10, 1960, in *Freedom of Communications*, S. Rept. 994, 87th Cong., 1st sess., September 13, 1961, Part 1, pp. 962–963; "Kennedy Says Middle East Goal Is End of 'War' against Israel," *NYT*, August 18, 1960, p. 16; Sarna, *Boycott and Blacklist*, pp. 81–83. In a brief article noting Senator Lehman's August 1956 decision not to seek re-election, the *Jerusalem Post* cited only one specific action of Lehman's: that he "was the man directly responsible for the most recent Senate resolution condemning Saudi Arabia for its anti-Jewish policy towards the American armed forces." See "Senator Lehman Retiring from Politics," *Jerusalem Post*, August 23, 1956, p. 1.

41. Sarna, *Boycott and Blacklist*, pp. 83–84; Section 108, Public Law 86–704, September 2, 1960, 74 *Stat.* 779; Section 102, Public Law 87–194, September 1, 1961, 75 *Stat.* 425; Abba Schwartz to Kenneth O'Donnell, December 27, 1961; O'Donnell, Memorandum for Mike Feldman, January 8, 1962; and Meeting with the President, April 30, 1962, all in JFK, White House Name File, Lehman; Schwartz to Feldman, March 8, 1962, JFK, White House Central Files, Subject Files, Box 791, PR 8-1, American F-K; H.R. 10787, 87th Cong., 2d sess., March 15, 1962; H.R. 10856, 87th Cong., 2d sess., March 21, 1962; 108 *Cong. Rec.* 4299, 4326 (March 15, 1962), 4754 (March 21, 1962); "Congress Asked to Bar Aid to Nations Which Discriminate," *Atlanta Daily World*, March 28, 1962, pp. 1, 6; "Aid Ban Is Pressed," *NYT*, March 27, 1962, p. 70. On the AJC's long interest in this issue, see American Jewish Committee, "The Assault on American Citizenship," included with the remarks of Senator Paul Douglas in 102 *Cong. Rec.* 11839–11842 (July 5, 1956); James Marshall, Vice President, American Jewish Committee, "Arab Boycott Assailed," Letter to the Editor, *NYT*, July 20, 1961, p. 26.

42. S [John Slawson] to Lehman, Blaustein, Engel, and Caplan, May 11, 1962, and attached "Meeting with President John F. Kennedy," April 30, 1962, LP, SF, Kennedy; "A Jewish Group Talks to Kennedy on Rights," *NYT*, May 1, 1962, p. 20; "JFK AJC Talk," *Chicago Defender*, May 2, 1962, p. 10.

43. S [John Slawson] to Lehman, Blaustein, Engel, and Caplan, May 11, 1962, and attached "Meeting with President John F. Kennedy," April 30, 1962; and Lehman to President Kennedy, May 2, 1962, all in LP, SF, Kennedy; Spiegel, *The Other Arab-Israeli Conflict*, p. 94; Bass, *Support Any Friend*, p. 56. On Feldman, see Spiegel, *The Other Arab-Israeli Conflict*, p. 100; and Bass, *Support Any Friend*, pp. 57–59.

44. Memorandum from the President's Deputy Special Counsel (Feldman) to the National Security Council Executive Secretary (Smith), May 29, 1962, Document 280; Paper Prepared in the Bureau of Near Eastern and South Asian Affairs," June 30, 1962, Document 314; both in *FRUS, 1961–1963*, XVII: 687–688, 762, 766–769; Memorandum of Conversation, October 5, 1962, Document 71, *FRUS, 1961–1963*, XVIII: 162–167.

45. "Saudi Arabia Lets Jews in U.S. Units Serve on Her Soil," *NYT*, June 10, 1963, pp. 1, 4; "U.S. Says Jews Serve in Arabia Despite a Denial from Mecca," *NYT*, June 14, 1963, p. 4; Hart, *Saudi Arabia and the United States*, p. 199; Editorial Note, Document 270, *FRUS, 1961–1963*, XVIII: 581–583; "U.S.-Saudi Air Exercise Shrouded in Sensitivity," *WP*, June 30, 1963, A1; Bass, *Support Any Friend*, pp. 130–132.

46. John Kennedy to A. M. Sonnabend, May 14, 1963; Lehman to President Kennedy, June 7, 1963, and attached "Statement on the Middle East," May 19, 1963, all in JFK, White House Name File, Lehman; "U.S. Will Supply Israel Missiles in Policy Change," *NYT*, September 27, 1962, pp. 1, 3; Bass, *Support Any Friend*, pp. 64–185. It was Robert Komer, who handled Middle Eastern matters for the National Security Council, who referred to Nasser as "the Mister Big of the Arab World." See n. 1 of McGeorge Bundy to the Secretary of State, National Security Action Memorandum 105, October 16, 1961, document 128, *FRUS, 1961–1963*, XVII: 303.

47. Feldman to Lehman, June 15, 1963, LP, SF, John Kennedy; Steve Smith to Mike [Myer Feldman], August 8, 1963, JFK, White House Name File, Lehman. On Feldman's role, see Bass, *Support Any Friend*, pp. 57–59.

48. Feller to Lehman, December 17, 1946; Lehman to Feller, December 23, 1946; and Lehman to Feller, March 22, 1947, all in LP, SF, Feller; Jessup to the Overbook [*sic*] Press, March 12, 1947; Lehman to Jessup, March 29, 1947; and Jessup to Lehman, April 7, 1947, all in LP, SF, Jessup; Osborne to Lehman, February 14, 1947; Osborne to Lehman, May 28, 1947; Osborne to Lehman, June 24, 1947; Lehman to Osborne, June 25, 1947; Haakon Lie to Osborne, June 27, 1947; Osborne to Lehman, July 22, 1947; and Lehman to Osborne, July 25, 1947, all in LP, SF, Osborne; "Nobel Awards Studied," *NYT*, March 15, 1947, p. 11; "Quakers Win Nobel Peace Prize; Units Here and in Britain Honored," *NYT*, November 1, 1947, pp. 1, 17. Many of the awards and medals that Lehman did receive are on display at the Herbert H. Lehman Center for American History at Columbia University.

49. "Italian Awards Planned to Outdo Nobel Prizes," *Los Angeles Times*, April 3, 1961, p. 25; Tarchiani to Herbert Lehman, March 26, 1946; Tarchiani to Herbert Lehman, April 30, 1946; Mrs. Lehman to Tarchiani, October 4, 1961; Tarchiani to Mrs. Lehman, October 19, 1961; and Tarchiani to Mrs. Lehman, October 24, 1961, all in LP, SF, Tarchiani; "Nobel Group Wins a New Peace Prize," *NYT*, March 2, 1962, p. 6.

50. Stevenson to Morse, April 19, 1962, LP, SF, Stevenson; Bunche to Morse, April 19, 1962, LP, SF, Bunche; Goldberg to Morse, April 20, 1962, LP, SF, Goldberg; Meany to Morse, April 25, 1962, LP, SF, Meany; Wilkins to Morse, April 18, 1962, LP, SF, Wilkins; Johnson to Morse, May 1, 1962, LP, SF, Johnson; Lehman to Morse, May 14, 1963, LP, SF, Morse; "Pope John Receives Balzan Peace Award of $230,000," *NYT*, May 11, 1963, pp. 1, 16. On Lehman and Morse, see Morse to Lehman, February 18, 1942; Lehman to Morse, February 23, 1942; Mrs. Lehman to U.S. Civil Service

Commission, October 23, 1944; Morse to Lehman, August 22, 1945; and Lehman to Morse, March 3, 1947, all in LP, SF, Morse.

51. "President Kennedy Leads Nation in Expressing Sorrow at Death of Mrs. Roosevelt," *NYT*, November 8, 1962, p. 34; Edith and Herbert Lehman to Franklin D. Roosevelt, Jr., November 8, 1962, and Edith and Herbert Lehman to Anna Halsted, November 8, 1962, both in LP, SF, Eleanor Roosevelt; Schlesinger, *A Thousand Days*, pp. 676–677; Berle and Jacobs, eds., *Navigating the Rapids*, pp. 776–777. Berle and FDR's other advisors from Columbia University and elsewhere were originally called the Brains Trust, but the name was soon changed to Brain Trust. See Leuchtenburg, *Franklin D. Roosevelt and the New Deal*, p. 32.

52. Schlesinger, Memorandum for Fred Holborn, January 26, 1963, JFK, WHCF, Subject Files, Box 534, ME 1-2/L*; "Lehman Fractures Hip in Fall at Palm Springs," *NYT*, February 12, 1963, p. 5; Mrs. Lehman to Mayor Wagner, February 16, 1963, LP, SF, Wagner; Lehman to Mike Monroney, March 23, 1963, LP, SF, Monroney; George Dixon, "Washington Scene . . . Partying at 85," *WP*, March 25, 1963, A-15; John Kennedy to Lehman, February 16, 1963, and March 27, 1963, and Lehman to Kennedy, March 30, 1963, all in LP, SF, John Kennedy; Lehman to David Morse, April 4, 1963, LP, SF, Morse.

53. "Lehman to Be Honored with 'Day' on 85th Birthday," *NYT*, March 27, 1963, p. 6; "Herbert Lehman at 85," Editorial, *NYT*, March 28, 1963, p. 6.

54. "State Party United for Kennedy Fete," *NYT*, April 14, 1963, p. 64; "President Given Birthday Party," *NYT*, May 24, 1963, p. 14; Kenneth O'Donnell to Lehman, November 8, 1963; Edith and Herbert Lehman to President Kennedy, May 29, 1963; Edith and Herbert Lehman to President and Mrs. Kennedy, August 10, 1963; and John Kennedy to Governor and Mrs. Lehman, August 26, 1963, all in LP, SF, John Kennedy; "Kennedys Mourning Baby Son; Funeral Today Will Be Private," *NYT*, August 10, 1963, pp. 1, 44.

55. John Kennedy, "Remarks at Amherst College upon Receiving an Honorary Degree," October 26, 1963, Document 439, *Public Papers of the Presidents: Kennedy, 1963*, p. 816; White House Press Release, February 22, 1963, JFK, WHCF, Subject Files, Box 513, MA2-10, Presidential Medal of Freedom; "President Sets Up Highest Civil Honor," *NYT*, February 23, 1963, pp. 1, 4; Memorandum, Stanley Karson to Hubert Humphrey, March 7, 1963, JFK, WHCF, Subject Files, Box 534, ME1-2/L*. On Humphrey's role, see also Lehman to Humphrey, August 31, 1963, LP, SF, Humphrey. On Karson, see "Chronicle: Reunion for Senator Lehman's Staff," *NYT*, October 13, 1994, B-28. On the decision to revive the Presidential Medal of Freedom, see "Proposal for a Civil Honors System," December 28, 1962; Fred Holborn, Memorandum for the President, January 3, 1963; Daniel Patrick Moynihan, Memorandum for the President, January 3, 1963; Frederick Holborn to the Attorney General, January 18, 1963; Holborn, Memorandum for Ralph Dungan, February 6, 1963; Arthur Focke to Robert Kennedy, February 21, 1963; Nobert Schlei, Memorandum Re: Proposed Executive Order entitled "The Presidential Medal of Freedom," February 21, 1963; Schlei to the President, February 21, 1963, all in JFK, WHCF, Subject Files, Box 513, MA2-10, Presidential Medal of Freedom; Schlesinger, *A Thousand Days*, p. 733; Sorensen, *Kennedy*, p. 384.

56. John Macy, Jr., to Robert Kennedy, March 5, 1963; Macy to Robert Kennedy, April 2, 1963; Macy to Robert Kennedy, April 4, 1963; Macy to Robert Kennedy, April

18, 1963, all in Robert Kennedy Papers, Attorney General's General Correspondence, Box 46, President's Medal of Freedom, February 19, 1963–February 1964, JFKL; "Public Affairs," n.d. and "Medal of Freedom with Special Distinction; 6 Names Submitted to President," n.d., both in Robert Kennedy Papers, Attorney General's General Correspondence, Box 46, President's Medal of Freedom: Nominations; John Kennedy to Lehman, July 1, 1963, LP, SF, John Kennedy. For the full list of the members of the Distinguished Civilian Service Awards Board and the recipients, see "President Names 31 for Freedom Medal," *NYT*, July 5, 1963, pp. 1, 10; and "An American Honors List," *New York Times Magazine*, July 14, 1963, pp. 16–17.

57. Lehman to John Kennedy, July 1, 1963, LP, SF, John Kennedy; Lehman to Arthur Goodhart, July 9, 1963, LP, SF, Goodhart; Lehman to Humphrey, August 31, 1963, LP, SF, Humphrey.

58. Frederick Holborn to R. Ginsberg, August 15, 1963, JFK, WHCF, Subject Files, Box 513, MA2-10, Presidential Medal of Freedom; Kenneth O'Donnell to Herbert Lehman, November 8, 1963, LP, SF, John Kennedy; Holborn, Memorandum for the President, November 15, 1963, JFK, WHCF, Subject Files, Box 512, MA2-10, Presidential Medal of Freedom; Edith and Herbert Lehman to Mrs. Kennedy, n.d., LP, SF, Jacqueline Kennedy Onassis, document 0702_0004; Edith and Herbert Lehman to Robert Kennedy, November 23, 1963, and December 2, 1963, both in LP, SF, Robert Kennedy; "Rockefeller and Wagner Order a 30-Day Period of Mourning," *NYT*, November 23, 1963, p. 7; Max Freedman, "Kennedy Remembered as Man Who Walked to Far Horizons," *Los Angeles Times*, December 1, 1963, M2.

Chapter 22. "We Mourn That He Is Gone but Glad That He Had Lived": Herbert Lehman and President Johnson, 1963–1964

1. Citation on the Presidential Medal of Freedom which Herbert Lehman was to be presented on December 6, 1963, *NYT*, December 6, 1963, p. 29.

2. See for example Johnson to Lehman, November 27, 1962, Johnson Papers, Vice President Files, 1961–1963, Box 604, Congressional File, "L," LBJL; Johnson to Herbert Lehman, February 12, 1963, and Edith Lehman to Johnson, February 14, 1963, LP, SF, Johnson. On Lehman and Johnson in the Senate, see chapters 15 and 16. On Lehman and Johnson and the 1960 election, see chapter 19. On liberal "crazies," see Caro, *Master of the Senate*, p. 807.

3. Lehmans to Johnson, November 23, 1963; Lehman to Johnson, November 27, 1963; and Johnson to Lehman, December 2, 1963, all in LP, SF, Johnson. On Johnson's address to the Joint Session of Congress, see "Johnson Bids Congress Enact Rights Bill with Speed; Asks End of Hate and Violence," *NYT*, November 28, 1963, pp. 1, 20; "Transcript of President Johnson's Address before the Joint Session of Congress," *NYT*, November 28, 1963, p. 20; Caro, *The Passage of Power*, pp. 425–436.

4. Lehman to Allan Nevins, March 6, 1961; Lehman to Nevins, March 14, 1961; Lehman to Nevins, May 11, 1962; Lehman to Nevins, July 16, 1962; Lehman to Nevins, July 27, 1962, all in LP, SF, Nevins; Lehman to William Benton, April 24, 1962; Lehman to Benton, May 31, 1962; Lehman to Benton, July 26, 1962, all in LP, SF, Benton; "Lehman Fractures Hip in Fall at Palm Springs," *NYT*, February 12, 1963,

p. 5; Edith Lehman to Robert and Martha Morgenthau, February 15, 1963, LP, SF, Morgenthau; Edith Lehman to Mayor Wagner, February 16, 1963, LP, SF, Wagner; Herbert Lehman to Mike Monroney, March 23, 1963, LP, SF, Monroney; Lehman to Hubert Humphrey, August 31, 1963, and Lehman to Humphrey, October 25, 1963, both in LP, SF, Humphrey; Dr. Isadore Rosenfeld quoted in Libo, ed., *Lots of Lehmans*, pp. 252–253; "Herbert Lehman, 85, Dies; Ex-Governor and Senator," *NYT*, December 6, 1963, pp. 1, 29. In addition to being Lehman's physician, Dr. Rosenfeld was married to Edith Lehman's niece, Camilla Master Rosenfeld. See Libo, ed., *Lots of Lehmans*, p. 311.

    5. Lehman to Hubert Humphrey, August 31, 1963, LP, SF, Humphrey; "Herbert Lehman, 85, Dies; Ex-Governor and Senator," *NYT*, December 6, 1963, pp. 1, 29; Benton to Edith Lehman, December 6, 1963, LP, SF, Benton; Lyndon Johnson to Mrs. Lehman, December 5, 1963, LP, SF, Johnson; Libo, ed., *Lots of Lehmans*, p. 253. On Johnson's emphasis on continuity and stability, see Tom Wicker, "Johnson Acts to Build a Broad Base of National Support; His Procedure: President Has Adopted the Program and Approach of His Predecessor," *NYT*, December 8, 1963, E-3; Dallek, *Flawed Giant*, pp. 49–59; Caro, *The Passage of Power*, pp. xv, 329–434.

    6. Hubert Humphrey in 109 *Cong. Rec.* 23712 (December 6, 1963); "Lehman Is Extolled as Humanitarian and Statesman," *NYT*, December 6, 1963, p. 29; "Top Leaders Pay Tribute to Lehman," *Newsday*, December 6, 1963, p. 5; "Gov. Lehman Mourned by All New Yorkers," *New York Amsterdam News*, December 14, 1963, p. 8; "Herbert H. Lehman," Editorial, *NYT*, December 6, 1963, p. 33; "Herbert H. Lehman," *Chicago Defender*, December 11, 1963, p. 13; "Deaths," *NYT*, December 6, 1963, p. 35; December 7, 1963, p. 22; and December 8, 1963, p. 87; "fearless champion" quoted from Hadassah tribute to Herbert Lehman, "Deaths," *NYT*, December 6, 1963, p. 35.

    7. Cliff Carter, Memorandum to the President, 5:25 p.m., n.d., but probably December 5, 1963, WHCF, Name File, Box 131, Lehman, H-K, LBJL; Floral Arrangement for Lehman from President and Mrs. Johnson, Universal Funeral Chapel, December 7, 1963, LP, SF, Johnson, document 0453_0109; Schlesinger, Memorandum for William Moyers, Herbert Lehman Funeral, December 6, 1963; Larry O'Brien, Memoranda to Bill Moyers Re: Governor Lehman's Funeral, December 6, 1963 and December 7, 1963; Information from Mr. Desautels, Mr. O'Brien's Office, n.d.; Office of the Air Force Aide, "Passenger List," 8 December 1963; President Johnson to Arthur Schlesinger, Jr., December 8, 1963, all in President's Appointment File [Diary Backup], Box 2, December 8, 1963, Governor Lehman's Funeral, LBJL; "Johnson Invited Justices to Attend Lehman Rites," *NYT*, December 10, 1963, p. 31; Dallek, *Flawed Giant*, p. 124.

    8. Schlesinger, Memorandum for William Moyers, Herbert Lehman Funeral, December 6, 1963, President's Appointment File [Diary Backup], Box 2, December 8, 1963, Governor Lehman's Funeral, LBJL; Joseph Rauh to Lyndon Johnson, December 9, 1963, and Johnson to Rauh, December 11, 1963, WHCF, TR2, Box 10, New York City, December 8, 1963; James Wechsler, "Plane Drama," *New York Post*, December 10, 1963, p. 30; "Lyndon Johnson and the Civil Rights Revolution: A Panel Discussion," in Firestone and Vogt, eds., *Lyndon Baines Johnson and the Uses of Power*, p. 186; Parrish, *Citizen Rauh*, pp. 159–160; Evans and Novak, *Lyndon B. Johnson*, p. 351; Watson, *Lion in the Lobby*, p. 591; Oberdorfer, *Senator Mansfield*, p. 213.

    9. Chalmers Roberts, "Political Pot Boiling after a Brief Pause," *WP*, December 9, 1963, A-1, A-8; Bernard Nossiter, "Johnson Flies to Rites for Lehman in N.Y. under

Heavy Guard," *WP*, December 9, 1963, A-1, A-10; Doris Fleeson, "Washington Calling," *Newsday*, December 10, 1963, p. 48; Walter Trohan, "Report from Washington: Johnson Starts Building Image for '64 Race," *Chicago Tribune*, December 11, 1963, p. 2; Douglas, *In the Fullness of Time*, p. 295.

10. Transcript of Telephone Conversation, Edith Lehman to President Johnson, December 6, 1963, 2:40 p.m., White House Tape Recording K6312.04, PNO 17, LBJL; "Johnson Insisted On Journey Here," *NYT*, December 8, 1963, pp. 1, 48; J.V., "John Lehman called . . . ," December 6, 1963, 5:50 pm, and D. F. Barbee, Memorandum for Captain Shepard, December 7, 1963, both in President's Appointment File [Diary Backup], Box 2, December 8, 1963, Governor Lehman's Funeral.

11. "Johnson to Attend Lehman's Funeral in City Tomorrow," *NYT*, December 7, 1963, pp. 1, 14; "Johnson Insisted on Journey Here," *NYT*, December 8, 1963, pp. 1, 48; "Leaders of the Nation, State and City Attend the Rites at the Temple," *NYT*, December 9, 1963, p. 30.

12. "Johnson to Attend Lehman's Funeral in City Tomorrow," *NYT*, December 7, 1963, pp. 1, 14; "Johnson at Lehman Rites; 2,000 Guard Him on Visit; Service Is at Emanu-El," *NYT*, December 9, 1963, pp. 1, 30; "President in City 2 Hours," *NYT*, December 9, 1963, pp. 1, 30; Johnson Guarded by 2,000 in N.Y.," *Chicago Tribune*, December 9, 1963, pp. 1, 14; Larry O'Brien Oral History Transcript, VII: 6, LBJL; D.F. Barbee, Memorandum for Captain Shepard, December 7, 1963; and Lem Johns, no title, both in President's Appointment File [Diary Backup], Box 2, December 8, 1963, Governor Lehman's Funeral.

13. "Johnson at Lehman Rites; 2,000 Guard Him on Visit," *NYT*, December 9, 1963, pp. 1, 30; "Funeral Service for Hon. Herbert H. Lehman," December 8, 1963 (Stamford, CT: Overbrook Press, 1964), pp. 1–2, copy in Special Collections, Lehman College Library. A manuscript copy of the funeral service, with a different pagination, is in LP, SF, Herbert Lehman, document 0530_0012.

14. "Johnson at Lehman Rites; 2,000 Guard Him on Visit; Service Is at Emanu-El," *NYT*, December 9, 1963, pp. 1, 30; "Don't Hide Faith, Lehman Told Boy," *NYT*, December 9, 1963, p. 30; "Funeral Service for Hon. Herbert H. Lehman," pp. 2–3. Lehman had offered similar advice to Abe Ribicoff when Ribicoff had wondered whether being Jewish would hurt him if he ran for Governor of Connecticut, a state with a Jewish population of only 4 percent. As Ribicoff later recalled, Lehman had told him: "I have never found that my religion hurt me or helped me. People take you for what you are." See Drew Pearson, "The Lehman Legacy: Religion and Politics Mix Just Fine," *WP*, December 15, 1963, E-7. In his oral history interview in 1957, Lehman expressed similar views, asserting that although prejudice and anti-Semitism still existed, he did "not think it's as widespread as lots of people think it is," and he "certainly did not have the feeling that it was exercised against" him "to any considerable extent." See HHLOH, pp. 773–775.

15. Nelson, *In Pursuit of Right and Justice*, p. 210.

16. "Johnson at Lehman Rites; 2,000 Guard Him on Visit; Service Is at Emanu-El," *NYT*, December 9, 1963, pp. 1, 30; "Funeral Service for Hon. Herbert H. Lehman," pp. 4–6.

17. "Johnson at Lehman Rites; 2,000 Guard Him on Visit; Service Is at Emanu-El," *NYT*, December 9, 1963, pp. 1, 30; "Funeral Service for Hon. Herbert H. Lehman," p. 5.

18. "Johnson at Lehman Rites; 2,000 Guard Him on Visit; Service Is at Emanu-El," *NYT*, December 9, 1963, pp. 1, 30; "Funeral Service for Hon. Herbert H. Lehman," pp. 6–7. On Edith Lehman, see also Libo, ed., *Lots of Lehmans*, pp. 259–282.

19. "Johnson at Lehman Rites; 2,000 Guard Him on Visit; Service Is at Emanu-El," *NYT*, December 9, 1963, pp. 1, 30; "Funeral Service for Hon. Herbert H. Lehman," p. 8.

20. "Johnson at Lehman Rites; 2,000 Guard Him on Visit; Service Is at Emanu-El," *NYT*, December 9, 1963, pp. 1, 30; "Funeral Service for Hon. Herbert H. Lehman," pp. 9–11.

21. "Johnson at Lehman Rites; 2,000 Guard Him on Visit; Service Is at Emanu-El," *NYT*, December 9, 1963, pp. 1, 30; Mrs. Lehman to Dr. Mark, December 26, 1963, LP, SF, Mark; Lem Johns, December 8, 1963, and Johnson to Arthur Schlesinger, Jr., December 8, 1963, both in President's Appointment File [Diary Backup], Box 2, December 8, 1963, Governor Lehman's Funeral.

22. "Johnson at Lehman Rites; 2,000 Guard Him on Visit; Service Is at Emanu-El," *NYT*, December 9, 1963, pp. 1, 30; Edith Lehman to Johnson, December 9, 1963, and Johnson to Mrs. Lehman, December 18, 1963, both in LP, SF, Johnson.

23. Frank Altschul to James Linen, December 12, 1963, Altschul Papers, Catalogued Correspondence, 128g, Herbert Lehman, Columbia University Library; "The Highest Form," *Time*, December 13, 1963, p. 35.

24. White House Press Release, "Remarks of the President and George W. Ball, Under Secretary of State, Presentation of Medal of Freedom Awards," December 6, 1963, p. 3, August Heckscher Files, White House Papers, White House Staff Files, Box 40, Recognition Awards, Medal of Freedom, December 5, 1963–December 6, 1963, and undated, JFKL; "Freedom Medal Honors Kennedy," *NYT*, December 7, 1963, pp. 1, 14.

25. "Johnson State of Union Address Provides Budget of $97.9 Billion, War on Poverty, Atomic Cutback," *NYT*, January 9, 1964, pp. 1, 17; "Texts of Johnson's State of the Union Message and His Earlier Press Briefing," *NYT*, January 9, 1964, p. 16; Edith Lehman to President Johnson, January 7, 1964, WHCF, Subject File, Gen SP 2-4/1964/Pro/L, Box 136; Caro, *The Passage of Power*, pp. 537–551. On Johnson's Great Society, see Mackenzie and Weisbrot, *The Liberal Hour*; and Zelizer, *The Fierce Urgency of Now*. Mrs. Lehman's letter to President Johnson is obviously misdated; since the President delivered his speech on January 8, she could not have congratulated him on it on January 7. There are also a few minor transcription errors in the typescript file copy of this handwritten note in LP, SF, Johnson.

26. "John Lehman called . . . ," December 6, 1963, 5:50 p.m., President's Appointment File [Diary Backup], Box 2, December 8, 1963, Governor Lehman's Funeral; Weisl to the President, January 8, 1964, Johnson Papers, WHCF, MA2-10, Box 11, Presidential Medal of Freedom, November 22, 1963–August 31, 1964. On Weisl as Johnson's "'eyes and ears' in New York," see "Friend of President Replacing De Sapio in State Party Post," *NYT*, August 23, 1964, pp. 1, 81. On Johnson, Edwin Weisl, and Bobby Lehman, see Robert Lehman to Lyndon Johnson, January 14, 1953, LBJA, Box 117, Subject File, Senate, U.S., Leadership–Minority, 1953; Johnson to Robert Lehman, April 6, 1960, and June 7, 1960, both in Lyndon Johnson Papers, U.S. Senate, 1949–1961, Box 111, Master File Index, LEE–LEI, 1960; Arthur Krim Oral History Transcript, I: 8, 25, 27; and Edwin Weisl, Sr., Oral History Transcript,

pp. 24–25, both in LBJL; Caro, *Master of the Senate*, p. 1022; and Caro, *The Passage of Power*, pp. 408–409.

27. See the notation on the bottom of Weisl to the President, January 8, 1964, indicating that the letter "was seen by the President"; Moyers to Weisl, January 14, 1964; Weisl to Moyers, January 20, 1964; and Kenneth O'Donnell to Weisl, January 22, 1964, all in WHCF, MA2-10, Box 11, Presidential Medal of Freedom, November 22, 1963–August 31, 1964; List of Attendees for Medal of Freedom Presentation to Mrs. Lehman, January 28, 1964, attached to "The President's Appointments," Tuesday, January 28, 1964; and C. V. Clifton, Memorandum for the President, "Presentation of the Lehman Medal," January 28, 1964, all in President's Appointment File [Diary backup], Box 3, January 28, 1964; "Remarks of the President at Presentation of Medal of Freedom Award to Mrs. Herbert H. Lehman," LP, SF, Johnson, document 0453_0114; "Johnson Recalls Lehman Prayer as He Presents Medal to Widow," *NYT*, January 29, 1964, p. 17.

28. "Remarks of the President at Presentation of Medal of Freedom Award to Mrs. Herbert H. Lehman," LP, SF, Lyndon Johnson; "Johnson Recalls Lehman Prayer as He Presents Medal to Widow," *NYT*, January 29, 1964, p. 17.

29. "Remarks of the President at Presentation of Medal of Freedom Award to Mrs. Herbert H. Lehman," LP, SF, Lyndon Johnson; "Johnson Recalls Lehman Prayer as He Presents Medal to Widow," *NYT*, January 29, 1964, p. 17.

30. Mrs. Lehman to the President, January 29, 1964, LP, SF, Johnson.

31. White, *The Making of the President, 1964*, p. 282; Goldman, *The Tragedy of Lyndon Johnson*, p. 190; Humphrey, *The Education of a Public Man*, p. 305; Dallek, *Flawed Giant*, pp. 122–124, 160–161.

32. On Johnson's obsession with Robert Kennedy, see Beschloss, ed., *Taking Charge*, pp. 467–541; Schlesinger, *Robert Kennedy and His Times*, pp. 646–654, 657–665; Dallek, *Flawed Giant*, pp. 135–142; and Shesol, *Mutual Contempt*, pp. 176–221. On the Mississippi Freedom Democrats, see Branch, *Pillar of Fire*, pp. 448–476; Holt, *The Summer That Didn't End*, pp. 152–183; Boyle, *The UAW and the Heyday of American Liberalism*, pp. 193–196; comments by James Farmer and Joseph Rauh in "Lyndon Johnson and the Civil Rights Revolution: A Panel Discussion," in Firestone and Vogt, eds., *Lyndon Baines Johnson and the Uses of Power*, pp. 178, 186–187; and Parrish, *Citizen Rauh*, pp. 164–174. On Humphrey's involvement and his selection as Johnson's running mate, see Humphrey, *The Education of a Public Man*, pp. 289–304; Solberg, *Hubert Humphrey*, pp. 240–256; and Mann, *The Walls of Jericho*, pp. 433–441. The quote about "a place named 'at-large'" is from Holt, *The Summer That Didn't End*, p. 170. On the scheduling of the film tribute to JFK, see Mary McGrory, "Democrats Harried by Too Many Stars," *Boston Globe*, July 22, 1964, p. 22; "Democrats Delay Movie on Kennedy," *NYT*, July 31, 1964, p. 9; Arthur Krim Oral History Transcript, I: 15, LBJL.

33. Mary McGrory, "Democrats Harried by Too Many Stars," *Boston Globe*, July 22, 1964, p. 22; "Senator Pastore Named Keynoter for Democrats," *NYT*, July 30, 1964, p. 8; Memorandum, Douglas Cater to Bill Moyers, July 31, 1964, WHCF, EX PL1, Box 78, Conventions, November 22, 1963–July 20, 1964; Memorandum, Toi [Toinette Bachelder] to Bill [Moyers], August 5, 1964, WHCF, EX PL1, Box 78, Conventions, July 21, 1964–August 16, 1964.

34. Johnson to Mrs. Lehman, February 18, 1964; Mrs. Lehman to Walter Jenkins, August 26, 1964; Mayor Wagner to President Johnson, August 5, 1964; and Stanley

Karson to Walter Jenkins, August 18, 1964; all in WHCF, Name File, Box 131, Lehman, H-K; Myer Feldman for Mr. Moyers, August 17, 1964, WHCF, PL1, Box 79, August 4, 1964–August 14, 1964; Transcript of Telephone Conversation, Edith Lehman to President Johnson, August 20, 1964, 9:00 a.m., Tape WH6408.28, PN 27, LBJL. On the President's Club, see "Johnson Pledges Israel Water Aid with Atom Power," *NYT*, February 7, 1964, pp. 1, 17; White, *The Making of the President, 1964*, p. 258; and Arthur Krim Oral History Transcript, I: 7–14, 20–23, LBJL. Representative Charles Goodell (R-NY) inserted into the *Congressional Record* in 1966 a list of contributors to the President's Club that showed that Mrs. Lehman had contributed $2,000 to Johnson's campaign between August 4, 1964 and May 31, 1966. See 112 *Cong. Rec.* 21404, 21412 (August 31, 1966).

35. Transcript of Telephone Conversation, Edith Lehman to President Johnson, August 20, 1964, 9:00 a.m., Tape WH6408.28, PN 27, LBJL.

36. Ibid.

37. Ibid.

38. Transcript of Telephone Conversation, President Johnson to Hubert Humphrey, August 20, 1964, 9:20 a.m., Tape WH6408.29, PN 02, and Tape WH6408.29, PN 03, LBJL. On Cliff Carter at the DNC, see White, *The Making of the President, 1964*, p. 246; and Goldman, *The Tragedy of Lyndon Johnson*, p. 221.

39. "The Convention Schedule," *NYT*, August 23, 1964, p. 81; "The Convention Schedule," *NYT*, August 27, 1964, p. 21; Robert F. Wagner, "Text of Speech to the Democratic National Convention," August 27, 1964, Robert Wagner Papers, Speeches, Box 060018W, Folder 4, Text of Speech—Democratic National Convention, La Guardia and Wagner Archives, online: http://www.laguardiawagnerarchive.lagcc.cuny.edu/FileBrowser.aspx?LinkToFile=FILES_DOC/WAGNER_FILES/06.016.0000.060018W.4.PDF#undefined.

40. Democratic National Committee, *Official Report of the Proceedings of the Democratic National Convention, 1964*, pp. 112–113; Robert F. Wagner, "Text of Speech to the Democratic National Convention," August 27, 1964, La Guardia and Wagner Archives, online: http://www.laguardiawagnerarchive.lagcc.cuny.edu/FileBrowser.aspx?LinkToFile=FILES_DOC/WAGNER_FILES/06.016.0000.060018W.4.PDF#undefined. Arthur Schlesinger, Jr., noted specifically in his journal Wagner's moving memorial tribute to Herbert Lehman, implying that Wagner did deliver his planned tribute to Lehman. But none of the New York newspapers or other accounts of the convention's proceedings that night, including the DNC's official account, suggest that Wagner delivered his prepared remarks honoring Lehman. See Schlesinger, August 29, 1964, *Journals, 1952–2000*, p. 232.

Conclusion. "Consistently Liberal": Herbert Lehman and Liberalism

1. Bartley Crum to Herbert Lehman, April 14, 1958, LP, SF, Crum.

2. Hartley Howe, "The Making of a Liberal," *The Nation*, October 28, 1950, p. 381; Eleanor Roosevelt Oral History Transcript, HHLP, CUOHC, p. 6; James Wechsler, "The Big One," *New York Post*, November 6, 1961.

3. HHLOH, p. 54; Herbert Lehman, "Triumph of Liberalism," First Speranza Lecture, Columbia University, April 9, 1958, LP, Speech Files.

4. Ickes, *The Secret Diary of Harold L. Ickes*, II: 166–168, 171, 232–233, 282, 326; "The Shape of Things," *The Nation*, July 24, 1937, p. 85; "The Week," *New Republic*, July 28, 1937, pp. 317–318; Steve Early to the President, August 26, 1937; President Roosevelt to Early, August 29, 1937; Early to Missy, March 3, 1938; and F.D.R. to S.T.E., March 4, 1938, all in Franklin Roosevelt Papers, PPF 93, Herbert Lehman, 1936–1939, FDRL; "Garner and Ickes Raise 1940 Campaign Banners," *NYT*, December 24, 1939, p. 39.

5. Delton, *Rethinking the 1950s*, p. 2; Plotke, *Building a Democratic Political Order*, pp. 1, 267–270; Brinkley, "The New Deal and the Idea of the State," in Fraser and Gerstle, eds., *The Rise and Fall of the New Deal Order, 1930–1980*, pp. 85–121; Boyle, *The UAW and the Heyday of American Liberalism*, pp. 44–46.

6. Herbert Lehman, "Travail of Liberalism," Second Speranza Lecture, Columbia University, April 16, 1958, LP, Speech Files; Irwin Ross, "Where Do Liberals Go from Here?" *New York Post*, December 23, 1956, pp. 4, 10; Hubert Humphrey Oral History Transcript, HHLP, CUOHC, pp. 3–4; Lazarowitz, *Years in Exile*, pp. 1–6.

7. Mackenzie and Weisbrot, *The Liberal Hour*.

8. Zelizer, *The Fierce Urgency of Now*, p. 303; Schlesinger, *A Thousand Days*, pp. 58–59.

Bibliography

Manuscript Sources

Columbia University
    Frank Altschul Papers
    Edith Lehman Papers
    Herbert Lehman Papers
    United Nations Relief and Rehabilitation Administration Papers (microfilm)
Dwight D. Eisenhower Library
    Dwight Eisenhower Papers
Houghton Library, Harvard University
    Jay Pierrepont Moffat Papers
Lyndon B. Johnson Library
    Lyndon Johnson Papers
    Drew Pearson Papers
    George Reedy Files
    Gerald Siegel Files
John F. Kennedy Library
    August Heckscher Files
    Frederick Holborn Files
    John Kennedy Papers
    Robert Kennedy Papers
    Arthur Schlesinger, Jr., Papers
    David Stowe Papers
    White House Staff Files
    William Walton Papers
La Guardia and Wagner Archives
    Julius Edelstein Files
    Robert Wagner Papers
Leonard Lief Library, Lehman College
    Herbert Lehman Materials, Special Collections
Library of Congress
    James Farley Papers

New York City Municipal Archives
    Robert Wagner Papers
Franklin D. Roosevelt Library
    Democratic Party National Committee Papers
    Mary Dewson Papers
    Edward Flynn Papers
    Joseph Lash Papers
    Isadore Lubin Papers
    Henry Morgenthau, Jr., Papers
    Leland Olds Papers
    Eleanor Roosevelt Papers
    Franklin Roosevelt Papers
    Samuel Rosenman Papers
    Myron Taylor Papers
Harry S. Truman Library
    Dean Acheson Papers
    Clinton Anderson Papers
    Oscar Chapman Papers
    Will Clayton Papers
    Clark Clifford Papers
    Matthew Connelly Files
    Oscar Ewing Papers
    Katherine Fite Lincoln Papers
    David Lloyd Files
    Frank McNaughton Papers
    Charles Murphy Files
    David Niles Papers
    Richard Neustadt Files
    Harold Smith Papers
    David Stowe Papers
    Harry Truman Papers
Online
    "Eleanor and Harry: The Complete Correspondence of Eleanor Roosevelt and Harry S. Truman." Online: http://www.trumanlibrary.org/eleanor/
    Eleanor Roosevelt. "My Day." Online: http://www.gwu.edu/~erpapers/myday/
    "Hoover and Truman: A Presidential Friendship." Online: https://www.truman-library.org/hoover/
Author's Interview
    John Bricker, Columbus, Ohio, June 26, 1975

Oral Histories

Columbia University Oral History Collections
    Benjamin Buttenwieser
    Herbert Lehman
    Frances Perkins

Herbert Lehman Project, Columbia University Oral History Collections:
    Emanuel Celler
    Paul Douglas
    Julius Edelstein
    James Farley
    Carolin Flexner
    Hubert Humphrey
    Estes Kefauver
    George Meany
    Henry Morgenthau, Jr.
    Wayne Morse
    Charles Poletti
    Eleanor Roosevelt
    Anna Rosenberg
    Samuel Rosenman
    Rabbi Marc Tanenbaum
    Roy Wilkins
Lyndon B. Johnson Library
    Robert (Bobby) Baker
    Earle Clements
    James Eastland
    Hubert Humphrey
    Arthur Krim
    Harry McPherson
    Lawrence O'Brien
    George Reedy
    Edwin Weisl, Jr.
    Edwin Weisl, Sr.
John F. Kennedy Library
    Anthony Akers
    John Bailey
    John Cogley
    James Doyle
    Ralph Dungan
    Ronnie Eldridge
    John English
    Myer Feldman
    Orville Freeman
    Joseph Sharkey
    William Walton
Harry S. Truman Library
    Nathan Becker
    James Loeb
    Joseph Rauh, Jr.
    Walter Trohan
    C. Tyler Wood

Newspapers and Periodicals

ADA World
American Israelite
Atlanta Constitution
Atlanta Daily World
The Atlantic Monthly
Baltimore Afro-American
Boston Globe
Buffalo Evening News
Chicago Defender
Chicago Tribune
Christian Science Monitor
Hartford Courant
Jerusalem Post
Life
Look
Los Angeles Sentinel
Los Angeles Times
Manchester Guardian
The Nation
New Republic
New York Amsterdam News
New York Daily News
New York Herald Tribune
New York Journal and American
New York Post
New York Times
New York World
New York World-Telegram
New York World-Telegram and Sun
Newsday
Pittsburgh Courier
Progressive
Saturday Evening Post
Syracuse Herald-Journal
Time
Wall Street Journal
Washington Post
Washington Post and Times-Herald
Westchester Journal News

Government Documents

(Documents in this section are arranged chronologically by year, and then by subject within a year.)

U.S. Congress. *Congressional Record.*

U.S. Department of State. *Department of State Bulletin.*

U.S. Department of State. *Foreign Relations of the United States.*

Public Papers of the Presidents.

U.S. Statutes at Large.

State of New York. *Proceedings of the Court for the Trial of Impeachments: The People of the State of New York by the Assembly Thereof against William Sulzer as Governor.* 2 Vols. Albany: J. B. Lyon, 1913.

Public Papers of Franklin D. Roosevelt, Forty-eighth Governor of the State of New York. 4 Vols. Albany: J. B. Lyon, 1930–1939.

Public Papers of Herbert H. Lehman, Forty-ninth Governor of the State of New York. 10 Vols. Various publishers, 1934–1949.

Public Papers and Addresses of Franklin D. Roosevelt. 13 Vols. Comp. by Samuel Rosenman. New York: Russell & Russell, 1938–1950.

U.S. Congress. House. Committee on International Relations. Selected Executive Session Hearings of the Committee, 1943–1950. *Problems of World War II and Its Aftermath; Part 1: Postwar International Organization, Relations with Italy.* Historical Series, 1976.

U.S. Congress. House. Committee on International Relations. Selected Executive Session Hearings of the Committee, 1943–1950. *Problems of World War II and Its Aftermath; Part 2: The Palestine Question, Problems of Postwar Europe.* Historical Series, 1976.

U.S. Congress. House. Committee on Foreign Affairs. *To Enable the United States to Participate in the Work of the United Nations Relief and Rehabilitation Administration. Hearings* before the Committee on Foreign Affairs on H.J. Res. 192, 78th Cong., 1st and 2d sess., December 1943–January 1944.

U.S. Congress. House. Committee on Foreign Affairs. *Authorizing the United States to Participate in the Work of the United Nations Relief and Rehabilitation Administration.* H. Rept. 994, 78th Cong., 2d sess., January 17, 1944.

U.S. Congress. Senate. Committee on Foreign Relations. *United Nations Relief and Rehabilitation Organization. Hearings* before the Committee on Foreign Relations on H.J. Res. 192, 78th Cong., 2d sess., February 1944.

U.S. Congress. House. Committee on Appropriations. *Foreign Economic Administration Appropriation Bill, 1945—Including Defense Aid (Lend-Lease) and Participation by the United States in the United Nations Relief and Rehabilitation Administration.* H. Rept. 1591, 78th Cong., 2d sess., June 2, 1944.

U.S. Congress. House. Committee on Foreign Affairs. *Message from the President of the United States Transmitting the Third Quarterly Report on United States Participation in Operations of UNRRA.* H. Document 251, 79th Cong., 1st sess., June 30, 1945.

U.S. Congress. House. Committee on Appropriations. *Communication from the President of the United States Transmitting Estimate for the Appropriation of $550,000,000 for the United Nations Relief and Rehabilitation Administration.* H. Document 305, 79th Cong., 1st sess., October 4, 1945.

U.S. Congress. House. Committee on Foreign Affairs. *Message from the President of the United States Transmitting Fourth Report to Congress on United States Participation in Operations of UNRRA.* H. Document 309, 79th Cong., 1st sess., October 11, 1945.

U.S. Congress. House. Committee on Appropriations. *Additional Appropriation, Fiscal Year 1946, for United Nations Relief and Rehabilitation Administration.* H. Rept. 1166, 79th Cong., 1st sess., October 30, 1945.

U.S. Congress. House. Committee on Foreign Affairs. *Further Participation in Work of UNRRA.* Hearings before the Committee on Foreign Affairs on H.R. 4649, 79th Cong., 1st sess., November 1945.

U.S. Congress. House. Committee on Appropriations. *United Nations Relief and Rehabilitation Administration, 1946.* Hearings before the Subcommittee of the Committee on Appropriations, 79th Cong., 1st sess., November 1945.

U.S. Congress. Senate. Committee on Appropriations. *United Nations Relief and Rehabilitation Administration, 1946.* Hearings before the Subcommittee of the Committee on Appropriations, 79th Cong., 1st sess., November 1945.

U.S. Congress. Senate. Committee on Appropriations. *United Nations Relief and Rehabilitation Administration Participation Act, 1946.* S. Rept. 798, 79th Cong., 1st sess., November 26, 1945.

U.S. Congress. House. Committee on Foreign Affairs. *Further Participation in Work of UNRRA.* H. Rept. 1311, 79th Cong., 1st sess., November 27, 1945.

U.S. Congress. Committee on Rules. *Consideration of H.R. 4649.* H. Rept. 1332, 79th Cong., 1st sess., December 4, 1945.

U.S. Congress. House. Committee on Appropriations. *United Nations Relief and Rehabilitation Administration Participation Bill, 1946.* H. Rept. 1355, 79th Cong., 1st sess., December 10, 1945.

U.S. Congress. House. Committee on Appropriations. *Communication from the President of the United States Transmitting Estimate for the Appropriation of $1,350,000,000 for the United Nations Relief and Rehabilitation Administration.* H. Document 384, 79th Cong., 1st sess., December 11, 1945.

U.S. Congress. Senate. Committee on Foreign Relations. *Enabling the United States to Further Participate in the Work of the United Nations Relief and Rehabilitation Administration.* S. Rept. 856, 79th Cong., 1st sess., December 13, 1945.

U.S. Congress. Senate. Committee on the Judiciary. *Protecting the Internal Security of the United States.* S. Rept. 2369, 81st Cong., 2d sess., August 17, 1950.

U.S. Congress. Senate. Committee on the Judiciary. *Protecting the Internal Security of the United States.* S. Rept. 2369, Part 2, "Minority Views," 81st Cong., 2d sess., August 28, 1950.

U.S. Congress. Senate. Committee on Armed Services. *Nomination of Anna M. Rosenberg to Be Assistant Secretary of Defense.* Hearings before the Committee on Armed Services, 81st Cong., 2d sess., November 29–December 14, 1950.

U.S. Congress. Senate. Committee on Rules and Administration. *Limitation on Debate in the Senate.* Hearings before the Committee on Rules and Administration, 82d Cong., 1st sess., October 1951.

U.S. Congress. Senate. Committee on Rules and Administration. *Amending the Cloture Rule with Respect to the Number Required for Adoption of a Cloture Motion.* S. Rept. 1256, 82d Cong., 2d sess., March 6, 1952.

U.S. Congress. Senate. Committee on Labor and Public Welfare. *Federal Equality of Opportunity in Employment Act.* S. Rept. 2080, 82d Cong., 2d sess., July 3, 1952.

U.S. Congress. Senate. Committee on Foreign Relations. *Authorizing the President to Employ the Armed Forces of the United States for Protecting the Security of Formosa, the Pescadores, and Related Positions and Territories of That Area.* S. Rept. 13, 84th Cong., 1st sess., January 26, 1955.

U.S. Congress. Senate. *Committee on the Judiciary. Investigation on Administration of Refugee Relief Act.* Hearings before a Subcommittee of the Committee on the Judiciary, 84th Cong., 1st sess., April–May 1955.

U.S. Congress. Senate. Committee on the Judiciary. *Amendments to Refugee Relief Act of 1953.* Hearings before a Subcommittee of the Committee on the Judiciary, 84th Cong., 1st sess., June 1955.

U.S. Congress. Senate. Committee on Banking and Currency. *Federal Disaster Insurance.* Hearings before the Committee on Banking and Currency, 84th Cong., 1st sess., November–December 1955.

U.S. Congress. Senate. Committee on Banking and Currency. *Federal Disaster Insurance.* Staff Study for the Committee on Banking and Currency, 84th Cong., 1st sess., November 30, 1955.

U.S. Congress. Senate. Committee on Banking and Currency. *Federal Disaster Insurance.* Hearings before a Subcommittee of the Committee on Banking and Currency, 84th Cong., 2d sess., February 1956.

U.S. Congress. Senate. Committee on Banking and Currency. *Transcript of Proceedings,* Committee on Banking and Currency, Subcommittee on Securities, 84th Cong., 2d sess., Executive Session, March 23, 1956.

U.S. Congress. Senate. Committee on Banking and Currency. *Transcript of Proceedings, Flood Insurance,* Committee on Banking and Currency, 84th Cong., 2d sess., Executive Session, April 10, 1956.

U.S. Congress. Senate. Committee on Banking and Currency. *Transcript of Proceedings, Flood Insurance,* Committee on Banking and Currency, 84th Cong., 2d sess., Executive Session, April 11, 1956.

U.S. Congress. Senate. Committee on Banking and Currency. *Transcript of Proceedings, Flood Insurance, Housing Bills,* Committee on Banking and Currency, 84th Cong., 2d sess., Executive Session, April 12, 1956.

U.S. Congress. Senate. Committee on Banking and Currency. *Federal Flood Insurance Act of 1956.* S. Rept. 1864, 84th Cong., 2d sess., April 26, 1956.

U.S. Congress. House. Committee on Banking and Currency. *Federal Flood Insurance Act of 1956.* H. Rept. 2746, 84th Cong., 2d sess., July 17, 1956.

U.S. Congress. House. Committee of Conference. *Federal Flood Insurance.* H. Rept. 2959, 84th Cong., 2d sess., July 27, 1956.

U.S. Congress. Senate. Committee on the Judiciary. *Civil Rights Proposals.* Hearings before the Committee on the Judiciary, 84th Cong., 2d sess., April–July 1956.

U.S. Congress. Senate. Committee on the Judiciary. *Amending the Act of September 3, 1954.* S. Rept. 2226, 84th Cong., 2d sess., June 13, 1956.

U.S. Congress. Senate. Committee on the Judiciary. *Certain Revisions of the Immigration and Nationality Laws.* S. Rept. 1057, 85th Cong., 1st sess., August 20, 1957.

U.S. Congress. Senate. Committee on Rules and Administration. *Proposed Amendments to Rule XXII of the Standing Rules of the Senate (Relating to Cloture).* S. Rept. 1509, 85th Cong., 2d sess., April 30, 1958.

U.S. Congress. Senate. Committee on Commerce. *Freedom of Communications*. S. Rept. 994, Part 1, "The Speeches, Remarks, Press Conferences, and Statements of Senator John F. Kennedy, August 1 through November 7, 1960," 87th Cong., 1st sess., September 13, 1961.

U.S. Congress. Senate. Committee on Commerce. *Freedom of Communications*. S. Rept. 994, Part 3, "The Joint Appearances of Senator John F. Kennedy and Vice President Richard M. Nixon and Other 1960 Campaign Presentations," 87th Cong., 1st sess., December 11, 1961.

U.S. Congress. House. Committee on Education and Labor. *Investigation of the Garment Industry. Hearings* before the Ad Hoc Subcommittee on Investigation of the Garment Industry, 87th Cong., 2d sess., August–September 1962.

U.S. Congress. Senate. Committee on the Judiciary. *Prohibiting Detention Camps. Hearings* before Subcommittee No. 3 of the Committee on the Judiciary, 92d Cong., 1st sess., March 18, 1971.

U.S. Congress. Senate. Committee on the Judiciary. *Administration of the Internal Security Act of 1950*. Prepared for the Subcommittee to Investigate the Administration of the Internal Security Act and Other Internal Security Laws, 94th Cong., 1st sess., July 1975.

U.S. Congress. Senate. Committee on the Judiciary. *U.S. Immigration Law and Policy, 1952–1979: A Report Prepared at the Request of Senator Edward M. Kennedy by the Congressional Research Service*, 96th Cong., 1st sess., 1979.

Ritchie, Donald, ed. *Minutes of the Senate Democratic Conference: Fifty-eighth Congress through Eighty-eighth Congress, 1903–1964*. S. Doc. 105-20, 105th Cong. 2d sess., 1998.

U.S. Government Accountability Office. *Testimony before the Subcommittee on Housing and Community Opportunity, Committee on Financial Services, House of Representatives, on National Flood Insurance Program: Continued Actions Needed to Address Financial and Operational Issues, Statement of Orice Williams Brown, Director Financial Markets and Community Investment*, GAO-10-631T, April 21, 2010.

U.S. Congress. House. Committee on Financial Services. *Flood Insurance Reform Act of 2011*. H. Rept. 112–102, 112th Cong., 1st sess., June 9, 2011.

Books, Articles, Dissertations, and Presentations

Abels, Jules. *Out of the Jaws of Victory*. New York: Henry Holt, 1959.

Abraham, Henry, and Barbara Perry. *Freedom and the Court: Civil Rights and Liberties in the United States*. Lawrence: University Press of Kansas, 2003.

Abramson, Rudy. *Spanning the Century: The Life of W. Averell Harriman, 1891–1986*. New York: William Morrow, 1992.

Accinelli, Robert. "Eisenhower, Congress, and the 1954–55 Offshore Island Crisis." *Presidential Studies Quarterly*, XX, 2 (Spring 1990): 329–348.

Acheson, Dean. *Present at the Creation: My Years in the State Department*. New York: Norton, 1969.

Allen, Oliver. *The Tiger: The Rise and Fall of Tammany Hall*. Reading: Addison-Wesley, 1993.

Allen, Robert, and William Shannon. *The Truman Merry-Go-Round*. New York: Vanguard Press, 1950.

Allswang, John. *The New Deal and American Politics: A Study in Political Change*. New York: John Wiley & Sons, 1978.

Alsop, Stewart. *The Center: People and Power in Political Washington*. New York: Harper & Row, 1968.

Alterman, Eric. *Why We're Liberals: A Political Handbook for Post-Bush America*. New York: Viking Press, 2008.

Ambrose, Stephen. *Eisenhower: The President*. New York: Simon & Schuster, 1984.

"The American Medical Association: Power, Purpose, and Politics in Organized Medicine." *Yale Law Journal*, LXIII, 7 (May 1954): 937–1022.

Anderson, Clinton, with Milton Viorst. *Outsider in the Senate: Senator Clinton Anderson's Memoirs*. New York: World, 1970.

Anderson, J. W. *Eisenhower, Brownell, and the Congress: The Tangled Origins of the Civil Rights Bill of 1956–1957*. University: University of Alabama Press, 1964.

Anderson, Jack, with James Boyd. *Confessions of a Muckraker: The Inside Story of Life in Washington during the Truman, Eisenhower, Kennedy and Johnson Years*. New York: Random House, 1979.

Asbell, Bernard. *The F.D.R. Memoirs*. Garden City: Doubleday, 1973.

Asch, Chris Myers. *The Senator and the Sharecropper: The Freedom Struggles of James O. Eastland and Fannie Lou Hamer*. New York: New Press, 2008.

Ashby, Warren. *Frank Porter Graham: A Southern Liberal*. Winston-Salem: John F. Blair, 1980.

Auerbach, Jerold. *Are We One? Jewish Identity in the United States and Israel*. New Brunswick: Rutgers University Press, 2001.

Bach, Morten, and Korcaighe Hale. "'What He Is Speaks So Loud That I Can't Hear What He's Saying': R. W. Scott McLeod and the Long Shadow of Joe McCarthy." *The Historian*, LXXII, 1 (Spring 2010): 67–95.

Badger, Anthony. "The South Confronts the Court: The Southern Manifesto of 1956." *Journal of Policy History*, XX, 1 (2008): 126–142.

Bailey, Stephen, and Howard Samuel. *Congress at Work*. New York: Henry Holt, 1952.

Baker, Bobby, with Larry King. *Wheeling and Dealing: Confessions of a Capitol Hill Operator*. New York: Norton, 1978.

Baker, Leonard. *Back to Back: The Duel between FDR and the Supreme Court*. New York: Macmillan, 1967.

Bancroft, Mary. *Autobiography of a Spy*. New York: William Morrow, 1983.

Barber, Charles. "A Diamond in the Rough: William Langer Reexamined." *North Dakota History*, LXV, 4 (Fall 1998): 2–18.

Barnard, John. *Walter Reuther and the Rise of the Auto Workers*. Boston: Little, Brown, 1983.

Bartley, Numan. *The Rise of Massive Resistance: Race and Politics in the South during the 1950s*. Baton Rouge: Louisiana State University Press, 1969.

Baruch, Bernard. *Baruch: The Public Years*. New York: Holt, Rinehart & Winston, 1960.

Bass, Warren. *Support Any Friend: Kennedy's Middle East and the Making of the U.S.-Israel Alliance*. New York: Oxford University Press, 2003.

Bauer, Yehuda. *My Brother's Keeper: A History of the American Jewish Joint Distribution Committee, 1929–1939*. Philadelphia: Jewish Publication Society of America, 1974.

Bayor, Ronald. *Neighbors in Conflict: The Irish, Germans, Jews, and Italians of New York City, 1929–1941*. Urbana: University of Illinois Press, 1988.

Bell, Jonathan. *The Liberal State on Trial: The Cold War and American Politics in the Truman Years*. New York: Columbia University Press, 2004.

Bell, Jonathan, and Timothy Stanley, eds. *Making Sense of American Liberalism*. Urbana: University of Illinois Press, 2012.

Bellush, Bernard. *Franklin D. Roosevelt as Governor of New York*. New York: Columbia University Press, 1955.

Bellush, Jewel. "Roosevelt's Good Right Arm: Lieut. Governor Herbert H. Lehman." *New York History*, XLI, 4 (1960): 423–443.

Bellush, Jewell. "Milk Price Control: History of Its Adoption, 1933." *New York History*, XLIII, 1 (1962): 79–104.

Bellush, Jewel. "The Politics of Liquor." *New York History*, XLV, 2 (1964): 114–134.

Bennett, Marion. *American Immigration Policies: A History*. Washington, DC: PublicAffairs Press, 1963.

Bentley, Amy. *Eating for Victory: Food Rationing and the Politics of Domesticity*. Urbana: University of Illinois Press, 1998.

Berle, Beatrice Bishop, and Travis Beal Jacobs, eds. *Navigating the Rapids 1918–1971: From the Papers of Adolf A. Berle*. New York: Harcourt Brace Jovanovich, 1973.

Berman, Daniel. *A Bill Becomes a Law: Congress Enacts Civil Rights Legislation*. New York: Macmillan, 1966.

Berman, William. *The Politics of Civil Rights in the Truman Administration*. Columbus: Ohio State University Press, 1970.

Bernstein, Barton. "The Postwar Famine and Price Control, 1946." *Agricultural History*, XXXVIII, 4 (October 1964): 235–240.

Bernstein, Barton. "Clash of Interests: The Postwar Battle between the Office of Price Administration and the Department of Agriculture." *Agricultural History*, XLI, 1 (January 1967): 45–57.

Bernstein, Irving. *The Lean Years: A History of the American Worker, 1920–1933*. Boston: Houghton Mifflin, 1972.

Bernstein, Irving. *Promises Kept: John F. Kennedy's New Frontier*. New York: Oxford University Press, 1991.

Beschloss, Michael. *The Crisis Years: Kennedy and Khrushchev, 1960–1963*. New York: Edward Burlingame Books, 1991.

Beschloss, Michael. *Taking Charge: The Johnson White House Tapes, 1963–1964*. New York: Simon & Schuster, 1997.

Beschloss, Michael. *Presidential Courage: Brave Leaders and How They Changed America, 1789–1989*. New York: Simon & Schuster, 2007.

Best, Gary Dean. *Herbert Hoover: The Postpresidential Years, 1933–1964*. 2 Vols. Stanford: Stanford University Press, 1983.

Biles, Roger. *A New Deal for the American People*. DeKalb: Northern Illinois University Press, 1991.

Biles, Roger. *Crusading Liberal: Paul H. Douglas of Illinois.* DeKalb: Northern Illinois University Press, 2002.

Binder, Sarah, and Steven Smith. *Politics or Principle? Filibustering in the United States Senate.* Washington, DC: Brookings Institution Press, 1997.

Biondi, Martha. *To Stand and Fight: The Struggle for Civil Rights in Postwar New York City.* Cambridge: Harvard University Press, 2003.

Bird, Kai. *The Chairman: John J. McCloy—The Making of the American Establishment.* New York: Simon & Schuster, 1992.

Birmingham, Stephen. *"Our Crowd": The Great Jewish Families of New York.* New York: Harper & Row, 1967.

Black, Allida, ed. *What I Hope to Leave Behind: The Essential Essays of Eleanor Roosevelt.* Brooklyn: Carlson, 1995.

Black, Allida. *Casting Her Own Shadow: Eleanor Roosevelt and the Shaping of Postwar Liberalism.* New York: Columbia University Press, 1996.

Black Anti-Semitism and Jewish Racism. Introduction by Nat Hentoff. New York: Richard W. Baron, 1969.

Bloom, Sol. *The Autobiography of Sol Bloom.* New York: G. P. Putnam's Sons, 1948.

Blum, John Morton. *From the Morgenthau Diaries; Volume II: The Years of War, 1941–1945.* Boston: Houghton Mifflin, 1967.

Blum, John Morton. *The Price of Vision: The Diary of Henry A. Wallace, 1942–1946.* Boston: Houghton Mifflin, 1973.

Bonastia, Christopher. *Southern Stalemate: Five Years without Public Education in Prince Edward County, Virginia.* Chicago: University of Chicago Press, 2012.

Bowen, Michael. "Communism vs. Republicanism: B. Carroll Reece and the Congressional Elections of 1946." *Journal of East Tennessee History,* LXXIII (2001): 39–52.

Bowles, Chester. *Promises to Keep: My Years in Public Life, 1941–1969.* New York: Harper & Row, 1972.

Boyd, Joseph H., Jr., and Charles Holcomb. *Oreos and Dubonnet: Remembering Governor Nelson A. Rockefeller.* Albany: State University of New York Press, 2012.

Boyle, Kevin. *The UAW and the Heyday of American Liberalism, 1945–1968.* Ithaca: Cornell University Press, 1995.

Bracey, John H., Jr., August Meier, and Elliott Rudwick, eds. *Black Workers and Organized Labor.* Belmont: Wadsworth, 1971.

Branch, Taylor. *Parting the Waters: America in the King Years, 1954–63.* New York: Simon & Schuster, 1988.

Branch, Taylor. *Pillar of Fire: America in the King Years, 1963–65.* New York: Simon & Schuster, 1998.

Brands, H. W., Jr. "Testing Massive Retaliation: Credibility and Crisis Management in the Taiwan Strait." *International Security,* XII, 4 (Spring 1988): 124–151.

Brands, H. W. *Inside the Cold War: Loy Henderson and the Rise of the American Empire, 1918–1961.* New York: Oxford University Press, 1991.

Brands, H. W. *The Strange Death of American Liberalism.* New Haven: Yale University Press, 2001.

Brauer, Carl. *John F. Kennedy and the Second Reconstruction.* New York: Columbia University Press, 1977.

Breitman, Richard, and Alan Kraut. *American Refugee Policy and European Jewry, 1933–1945*. Bloomington: Indiana University Press, 1987.

Breitman, Richard, Barbara McDonald Stewart, and Severin Hochberg, eds. *Advocate for the Doomed: The Diaries and Papers of James G. McDonald, 1932–1935*. Bloomington: Indiana University Press, 2007.

Breitman, Richard, Barbara McDonald Stewart, and Severin Hochberg, eds. *Refugees and Rescue: The Diaries and Papers of James G. McDonald, 1935–1945*. Bloomington: Indiana University Press, 2009.

Breitman, Richard, and Allan Lichtman. *FDR and the Jews*. Cambridge: Belknap Press of Harvard University Press, 2013.

Briggs, Philip. "Congress and the Cold War: U.S.-China Policy, 1955." *China Quarterly*, LXXXV (March 1981): 80–95.

Brinkley, Alan. "The New Deal and the Idea of the State." In *The Rise and Fall of the New Deal Order, 1930–1980*, ed. Steve Fraser and Gary Gerstle. Princeton: Princeton University Press, 1989.

Brinkley, Alan. "AHR Forum: The Problem of American Conservatism." *American Historical Review*, XCIX, 2 (April 1994): 409–429.

Brinkley, Alan. "AHR Forum: Response to the Comments of Leo Ribuffo and Susan Yohn." *American Historical Review*, XCIX, 2 (April 1994): 450–452.

Brinkley, Alan. *The End of Reform: New Deal Liberalism in Recession and War*. New York: Knopf, 1995.

Brinkley, Alan. *Liberalism and Its Discontents*. Cambridge: Harvard University Press, 1998.

Brock, Clifton. *Americans for Democratic Action: Its Role in National Politics*. Washington, DC: PublicAffairs Press, 1962.

Brown, Stuart Gerry. *Conscience in Politics: Adlai E. Stevenson in the 1950s*. Syracuse: Syracuse University Press, 1961.

Browne, Arthur, Dan Collins, and Michael Goodwin. *I, Koch: A Decidedly Unauthorized Biography of the Mayor of New York City, Edward I. Koch*. New York: Dodd, Mead, 1985.

Bryant, Nick. *The Bystander: John F. Kennedy and the Struggle for Black Equality*. New York: Basic Books, 2006.

Burdette, Franklin. *Filibustering in the Senate*. New York: Russell & Russell, 1965. Originally published by Princeton University Press, 1940.

Burk, Robert Fredrick. *The Eisenhower Administration and Black Civil Rights*. Knoxville: University of Tennessee Press, 1984.

Burner, David. *The Politics of Provincialism: The Democratic Party in Transition, 1918–1932*. New York: Knopf, 1970.

Burns, Augustus, III, and Julian Pleasants. *Frank Porter Graham and the 1950 Senate Race in North Carolina*. Chapel Hill: University of North Carolina Press, 1990.

Burns, James MacGregor. *Roosevelt: The Lion and the Fox*. New York: Harcourt, Brace, & World, 1956.

Burns, James MacGregor. *John Kennedy: A Political Profile*. New York: Harcourt, Brace, 1960.

Burns, James MacGregor. *Roosevelt: The Soldier of Freedom*. New York: Harcourt Brace Jovanovich, 1970.

Burr, William, and Hector Montford, eds. "The Making of the Limited Test Ban Treaty, 1958–1963." National Security Archive. Online: http://www2.gwu.edu/~nsarchiv/NSAEBB/NSAEBB94/index2.htm.

Burrow, James. *AMA: Voice of American Medicine*. Baltimore: Johns Hopkins University Press, 1963.

Butler, Susan, ed. *My Dear Mr. Stalin: The Complete Correspondence Between Franklin D. Roosevelt and Joseph V. Stalin*. New Haven: Yale University Press, 2005.

Byrnes, James. *Speaking Frankly*. New York: Harper & Brothers, 1947.

Byrnes, James. *All in One Lifetime*. New York: Harper & Brothers, 1958.

Campbell, Thomas, and George Herring, eds. *The Diaries of Edward R. Stettinius, Jr., 1943–1946*. New York: Franklin Watts, 1975.

Campion, Frank. *The AMA and U.S. Health Policy since 1940*. Chicago: Chicago Review Press, 1984.

Capeci, Dominic J., Jr. *The Harlem Riot of 1943*. Philadelphia: Temple University Press, 1977.

Caro, Robert. *The Power Broker: Robert Moses and the Fall of New York*. New York: Knopf, 1974.

Caro, Robert. *The Years of Lyndon Johnson: The Path to Power*. New York: Knopf, 1982.

Caro, Robert. *The Years of Lyndon Johnson: Means of Ascent*. New York: Knopf, 1990.

Caro, Robert. *The Years of Lyndon Johnson: Master of the Senate*. New York: Knopf, 2002.

Caro, Robert. *The Years of Lyndon Johnson: The Passage of Power*. New York: Knopf, 2012.

Carson, Clayborne. *In Struggle: SNCC and the Black Awakening of the 1960s*. Cambridge: Harvard University Press, 1995.

Carter, Hodding, III. *The South Strikes Back*. Garden City: Doubleday, 1959.

Case, Josephine Young, and Everett Needham Case. *Owen D. Young and American Enterprise: A Biography*. Boston: David R. Godine, 1982.

Caute, David. *The Great Fear: The Anti-Communist Purge under Truman and Eisenhower*. New York: Simon & Schuster, 1978.

Chace, James. *1912: Wilson, Roosevelt, Taft and Debs: The Election That Changed the Country*. New York: Simon & Schuster, 2004.

Chafe, William, ed. *The Achievement of American Liberalism: The New Deal and Its Legacies*. New York: Columbia University Press, 2003.

Chandler, Alfred D., Jr., and Louis Galambos, eds. *The Papers of Dwight David Eisenhower*: VI: *Occupation, 1945*. Baltimore: Johns Hopkins University Press, 1978.

Chang, Gordon. "To the Nuclear Brink: Eisenhower, Dulles, and the Quemoy-Matsu Crisis." *International Security*, XII, 4 (Spring 1988): 96–123.

Chang, Gordon. *Friends and Enemies: The United States, China, and the Soviet Union, 1948–1972*. Stanford: Stanford University Press, 1990.

Chang, Gordon, and He Di. "The Absence of War in the U.S.-China Confrontation over Quemoy and Matsu in 1954–1955: Contingency, Luck, Deterrence?" *American Historical Review*, XCVIII, 5 (December 1993): 1500–1524.

Chen, Anthony. " 'The Hitlerian Rule of Quotas': Racial Conservatism and the Politics of Fair Employment Legislation in New York State, 1941–1945." *Journal of American History*, XCII, 4 (March 2006): 1238–1264.

Chartered Property Casualty Underwriters Society, Connecticut Chapter. "Flood Insurance and Hurricane Katrina: Evaluation of the National Flood Insurance Program and Overview of the Proposed Solutions." *CPCU eJournal* (September, 2006): 1–21.

Chernow, Ron. *The Warburgs: The Twentieth-Century Odyssey of a Remarkable Jewish Family*. New York: Random House, 1993.

Citino, Nathan. *From Arab Nationalism to OPEC: Eisenhower, King Saud, and the Making of U.S.-Saudi Relations*. Bloomington: Indiana University Press, 2002.

Clark, E. Culpepper. *The Schoolhouse Door: Segregation's Last Stand at the University of Alabama*. New York: Oxford University Press, 1993.

Clark, Joseph. *The Senate Establishment*. New York: Hill and Wang, 1963.

Cohen, Michael. *Truman and Israel*. Berkeley: University of California Press, 1990.

Cohen, Naomi. *Not Free to Desist: The American Jewish Committee, 1906–1966*. Philadelphia: Jewish Publication Society of America, 1972.

Cohen, Naomi. *American Jews and the Zionist Idea*. New York: KTAV, 1975.

Cohodas, Nadine. *Strom Thurmond and the Politics of Southern Change*. New York: Simon & Schuster, 1993.

Collingham, Lizzie. *The Taste of War: World War Two and the Battle for Food*. London: Allen Lane, 2011.

Connable, Alfred, and Edward Silberfarb. *Tigers of Tammany: Nine Men Who Ran New York*. New York: Holt, Rinehart and Winston, 1967.

Connolly, Harold. *A Ghetto Grows in Brooklyn*. New York: New York University Press, 1977.

Costikyan, Edward. *Behind Closed Doors: Politics in the Public Interest*. New York: Harcourt, Brace & World, 1966.

Cooney, John. *The American Pope: The Life and Times of Francis Cardinal Spellman*. New York: Times Books, 1984.

Cotter, Cornelius, and Bernard Hennessy. *Politics without Power: The National Party Committees*. New York: Atherton Press, 1964.

Creel, George. *Rebel at Large: Recollections of Fifty Crowded Years*. New York: G. P. Putnam's Sons, 1947.

Crespino, Joseph. *Strom Thurmond's America*. New York: Hill and Wang, 2012.

Dalfiume, Richard. *Desegregation of the U.S. Armed Forces: Fighting on Two Fronts, 1939–1953*. Columbia: University of Missouri Press, 1969.

Dallek, Robert. *Franklin D. Roosevelt and American Foreign Policy, 1932–1945*. New York: Oxford University Press, 1979.

Dallek, Robert. *Lone Star Rising: Lyndon Johnson and His Times, 1908–1960*. New York: Oxford University Press, 1991.

Dallek, Robert. *Flawed Giant: Lyndon Johnson and His Times, 1961–1973*. New York: Oxford University Press, 1998.

Dallek, Robert. *An Unfinished Life: John F. Kennedy, 1917–1963*. Boston: Little, Brown, 2003.

Daniels, Doris Groshen. *Always a Sister: The Feminism of Lillian D. Wald*. New York: Feminist Press at the City University of New York, 1989.

David, Paul, Malcolm Moos, and Ralph Goldman, eds. *Presidential Nominating Politics in 1952: Vol. I: The National Story*. Baltimore: Johns Hopkins University Press, 1954.

David, Paul, Malcolm Moos, and Ralph Goldman, eds. *Presidential Nominating Politics in 1952: Vol. II: The Northeast*. Baltimore: Johns Hopkins University Press, 1954.

Davies, Richard. *Defender of the Old Guard: John Bricker and American Politics*. Columbus: Ohio State University Press, 1993.

Davis, Allen. *Spearheads for Reform: The Social Settlements and the Progressive Movement, 1890–1914*. New York: Oxford University Press, 1967.

Davis, Kenneth S. *FDR: The Beckoning of Destiny, 1882–1928*. New York: G. P. Putnam's Sons, 1972.

Davis, Kenneth S. *FDR: The New York Years, 1928–1933*. New York: Random House, 1985.

Davis, Kenneth S. *FDR: The New Deal Years, 1933–1937*. New York: Random House, 1986.

Davis, Kenneth S. *FDR: Into the Storm, 1937–1940*. New York: Random House, 1993.

De Toledano, Ralph, and Victor Lasky. *Seeds of Treason: The True Story of the Hiss-Chambers Tragedy*. New York: Funk & Wagnalls, 1950.

Delton, Jennifer. *Rethinking the 1950s: How Anticommunism and the Cold War Made America Liberal*. New York: Cambridge University Press, 2013.

Democratic National Committee. *Official Report of the Proceedings of the Democratic National Convention, 1964: Resulting in the Nomination of Lyndon B. Johnson of Texas for President and in the Nomination of Hubert H. Humphrey of Minnesota for Vice President*. Washington, DC: Democratic National Committee, 1968.

Derickson, Alan. "Health Security for All? Social Unionism and Universal Health Insurance, 1935–1958." *Journal of American History*, LXXX, 4 (March 1994): 1333–1356.

Diner, Hasia. *In the Almost Promised Land: American Jews and Blacks, 1915–1935*. Westport: Greenwood Press, 1977.

Dinnerstein, Leonard. *America and the Survivors of the Holocaust*. New York: Columbia University Press, 1982.

Divine, Robert. *American Immigration Policy, 1924–1952*. New Haven: Yale University Press, 1957.

Divine, Robert. *Second Chance: The Triumph of Internationalism in America during World War II*. New York: Atheneum, 1967.

Divine, Robert. *The Illusion of Neutrality*. Chicago: Quadrangle Books, 1968.

Divine, Robert. *Foreign Policy and U.S. Presidential Elections, 1940–1948*. New York: Franklin Watts, 1974.

Dobney, Fredrick, ed. *Selected Papers of Will Clayton*. Baltimore: Johns Hopkins University Press, 1971.

Donahoe, Bernard. *Private Plans and Public Dangers: The Story of FDR's Third Nomination*. Notre Dame: University of Notre Dame Press, 1965.

Donaldson, Gary. *Truman Defeats Dewey*. Lexington: University Press of Kentucky, 1999.

Donaldson, Gary. *The First Modern Campaign: Kennedy, Nixon, and the Election of 1960*. Lanham: Rowman & Littlefield, 2007.

Donovan, Robert. *Conflict and Crisis: The Presidency of Harry S Truman, 1945–1948*. New York: Norton, 1977.

Donovan, Robert. *Tumultuous Years: The Presidency of Harry S Truman, 1949–1953*. New York: Norton, 1982.

Dorough, C. Dwight. *Mr. Sam*. New York: Random House, 1962.

Dorwart, Jeffery. *Eberstadt and Forrestal: A National Security Partnership, 1909–1949*. College Station: Texas A&M University Press, 1991.

Douglas, Helen Gahagan. *A Full Life*. Garden City: Doubleday, 1982.

Douglas, Paul. *In the Fullness of Time: The Memoirs of Paul H. Douglas*. New York: Harcourt Brace Jovanovich, 1972.

Drukman, Mason. *Wayne Morse: A Political Biography*. Portland: Oregon Historical Society Press, 1997.

Duberman, Martin. *Paul Robeson*. New York: Knopf, 1989.

Dubinsky, David, and A. H. Raskin. *David Dubinsky: A Life with Labor*. New York: Simon & Schuster, 1977.

Duffus, R. L. *Lillian Wald: Neighbor and Crusader*. New York: Macmillan, 1938.

Dulles, Foster Rhea. *The American Red Cross: A History*. New York: Harper & Brothers, 1950.

Dulles, Foster Rhea. *The Civil Rights Commission: 1957–1965*. East Lansing: Michigan State University Press, 1968.

Dunn, Dennis. *Caught between Roosevelt and Stalin: America's Ambassadors to Moscow*. Lexington: University Press of Kentucky, 1998.

Dunn, Susan. *Roosevelt's Purge: How FDR Fought to Change the Democratic Party*. Cambridge: Belknap Press of Harvard University Press, 2010.

Duram, James. *A Moderate among Extremists: Dwight D. Eisenhower and the School Desegregation Crisis*. Chicago: Nelson-Hall, 1981.

Eagleton, Thomas, and Diane Duffin. "Bob Hannegan and Harry Truman's Vice Presidential Nomination." *Missouri Historical Review*, XC, 3 (April 1996): 265–283.

Edelstein, Julius. "Remarks for Lehman Conference." Roosevelt Library, November 2004.

Eisenhower, Dwight. *The White House Years: Mandate for Change, 1953–1956*. Garden City: Doubleday, 1963.

Eisenhower, Dwight. *The White House Years: Waging Peace, 1956–1961*. Garden City: Doubleday, 1965.

Ellis, David, James Frost, Harold Syrett, and Harry Carman. *A Short History of New York State*. Ithaca: Cornell University Press, 1957.

Emery, Edwin. *The Press and America: An Interpretative History of the Mass Media*. 3rd edition. Englewood Cliffs: Prentice-Hall, 1972.

Evans, Rowland, and Robert Novak. *Lyndon B. Johnson: The Exercise of Power*. New York: New American Library, 1966.

Ewen, Stuart. *PR! A Social History of Spin*. New York: Basic Books, 1996.

Farley, James. *Behind the Ballots: The Personal History of a Politician*. New York: Harcourt, Brace, 1938.

Farley, James. *Jim Farley's Story: The Roosevelt Years*. New York: McGraw-Hill, 1948.

Farrar, Hayward. *The Baltimore "Afro-American": 1892–1950*. Westport: Greenwood Press, 1998.

Feingold, Henry. *The Politics of Rescue: The Roosevelt Administration and the Holocaust, 1938–1945*. New Brunswick: Rutgers University Press, 1970.

Feld, Marjorie. *Lillian Wald: A Biography*. Chapel Hill: University of North Carolina Press, 2008.

Felt, Jeremy. *Hostages of Fortune: Child Labor Reform in New York State*. Syracuse: Syracuse University Press, 1965.

Fenberg, Steven. *Unprecedented Power: Jesse Jones, Capitalism, and the Common Good*. College Station: Texas A&M University Press, 2011.

Ferrell, Robert, ed. *The Diary of James C. Hagerty: Eisenhower in Mid-Course, 1954–1955*. Bloomington: Indiana University Press, 1983.

Ferrell, Robert. *Choosing Truman: The Democratic Convention of 1944*. Columbia: University of Missouri Press, 1994.

Finan, Christopher. *Alfred E. Smith: The Happy Warrior*. New York: Hill and Wang, 2002.

Finley, Keith. *Delaying the Dream: Southern Senators and the Fight against Civil Rights, 1938–1965*. Baton Rouge: Louisiana State University Press, 2008.

Firestone, Bernard, and Robert Vogt, eds. *Lyndon Baines Johnson and the Uses of Power*. New York: Greenwood Press, 1988.

Fite, Gilbert. *Richard B. Russell, Jr., Senator from Georgia*. Chapel Hill: University of North Carolina Press, 1991.

Flade, Roland. *The Lehmans: From Rimpar to the New World—A Family History*. Second enlarged edition. Wurzburg: Konigshausen & Neumann, 1999.

Flynn, Edward. *You're the Boss*. New York: Viking Press, 1947.

Foley, Michael. *The New Senate: Liberal Influence on a Conservative Institution, 1959–1972*. New Haven: Yale University Press, 1980.

Foner, Philip. *Organized Labor and the Black Worker, 1619–1973*. New York: Praeger, 1974.

Fones-Wolf, Elizabeth. *Selling Free Enterprise: The Business Assault on Labor and Liberalism, 1945–60*. Urbana: University of Illinois Press, 1994.

Ford, Edwin, and Edwin Emery, eds. *Highlights in the History of the American Press: A Book of Readings*. Minneapolis: University of Minnesota Press, 1954.

Forster, Arnold, and Benjamin Epstein. *The Trouble-Makers: An Anti-Defamation League Report*. Westport: Negro Universities Press, 1970. Originally published by Doubleday, 1952.

Fossedal, Gregory. *Our Finest Hour: Will Clayton, the Marshall Plan, and the Triumph of Democracy*. Stanford: Hoover Institution Press, 1993.

Fox, Grace. "The Origins of UNRRA." *Political Science Quarterly*, LXV, 4 (December 1950): 561–584.

Franklin, V. P., Nancy Grant, Harold Kletnick, and Genna Rae McNeil, eds. *African Americans and the Jews in the Twentieth Century: Studies in Convergence and Conflict*. Columbia: University of Missouri Press, 1998.

Fraser, Steve, and Gary Gerstle, eds. *The Rise and Fall of the New Deal Order, 1930–1980*. Princeton: Princeton University Press, 1989.

Fraser, Steven. *Labor Will Rule: Sidney Hillman and the Rise of American Labor*. New York: Free Press, 1991.

Freedman, Max, ed. *Roosevelt and Frankfurter: Their Correspondence, 1928–1945*. Boston: Little, Brown, 1967.

Freedman, Robert, ed. *Israel and the United States: Six Decades of US-Israeli Relations*. Boulder: Westview Press, 2012.

Freeland, Richard. *The Truman Doctrine and the Origins of McCarthyism: Foreign Policy, Domestic Politics, and Internal Security, 1946–1948*. New York: New York University Press, 1985.

Freeman, Joshua. *Working-Class New York: Life and Labor since World War II*. New York: New Press, 2000.

Freiberger, Steven. *Dawn over Suez: The Rise of American Power in the Middle East, 1953–1957*. Chicago: Ivan R. Dee, 1992.

Freidel, Frank. *Franklin D. Roosevelt: The Apprenticeship*. Boston: Little, Brown, 1952.

Freidel, Frank. *Franklin D. Roosevelt: The Ordeal*. Boston: Little, Brown, 1954.

Freidel, Frank. *Franklin D. Roosevelt: The Triumph*. Boston: Little, Brown, 1956.

Freidel, Frank. *Franklin D. Roosevelt: Launching the New Deal*. Boston: Little, Brown, 1973.

Freidel, Frank. *Franklin D. Roosevelt: A Rendezvous with Destiny*. Boston: Little, Brown, 1990.

Fried, Richard. "Electoral Politics and McCarthyism: The 1950 Campaign." In *The Specter: Original Essays on the Cold War and the Origins of McCarthyism*, ed. Robert Griffith and Athan Theoharis. New York: New Viewpoints, 1974.

Fried, Richard. *Men against McCarthy*. New York: Columbia University Press, 1976.

Fried, Richard. *Nightmare in Red: The McCarthy Era in Perspective*. New York: Oxford University Press, 1990.

Friedman, Jacob. *The Impeachment of Governor William Sulzer*. New York: AMS Press, 1968. Originally published by Columbia University Press, 1939.

Friedman, Murray, with the assistance of Peter Binzen. *What Went Wrong? The Creation and Collapse of the Black-Jewish Alliance*. New York: Free Press, 1995.

Fuchs, Lawrence. *The Political Behavior of American Jews*. Glencoe: Free Press, 1956.

Fuchs, Lawrence. *John F. Kennedy and American Catholicism*. New York: Meredith Press, 1967.

Fuchs, Lawrence. "The Senator and the Lady." *American Heritage*, XXV, 6 (October 1974): 57–83.

Furman, Bess. *Washington By-Line: The Personal History of a Newspaperwoman*. New York: Knopf, 1949.

Gallup, George. *The Gallup Poll: Vol. I: Public Opinion, 1935–1971*. New York: Random House, 1972.

Ganin, Zvi. *Truman, American Jewry, and Israel, 1945–1948*. New York: Holmes & Meier, 1979.

Gardner, Michael. *Harry Truman and Civil Rights: Moral Courage and Political Risks*. Carbondale: Southern Illinois University Press, 2002.

Garrett, Charles. *The La Guardia Years: Machine and Reform Politics in New York City*. New Brunswick: Rutgers University Press, 1961.

Garrow, David. *Bearing the Cross: Martin Luther King, Jr., and the Southern Christian Leadership Conference*. New York: Vintage Books, 1988.

Gaskin, Thomas. "Senate Majority Leader Lyndon B. Johnson: The Formosa and Middle East Resolutions." In *Lyndon Baines Johnson and the Uses of Power*, ed. Bernard Firestone and Robert Vogt. New York: Greenwood Press, 1988.

Gellman, Irwin. *Secret Affairs: Franklin Roosevelt, Cordell Hull, and Sumner Welles*. Baltimore: Johns Hopkins University Press, 1995.

Gerson, Louis. *John Foster Dulles: Vol. XVII: The American Secretaries of State and Their Diplomacy*. Ed. Robert Ferrell and Samuel Flagg Bemis. New York: Cooper Square, 1967.

Gerstle, Gary. "The Protean Character of American Liberalism." *American Historical Review*, XCIX, 4 (October 1994): 1043–1073.

Gerstle, Gary. "Race and the Myth of the Liberal Consensus." *Journal of American History*, LXXXII, 2 (September 1995): 579–586.

Gibbons, William Conrad. *The U.S. Government and the Vietnam War: Executive and Legislative Roles and Relationships, Part II: 1961–1964*. Princeton: Princeton University Press, 1986.

Gibbs, Nancy, and Michael Duffy. *The Presidents Club: Inside the World's Most Exclusive Fraternity*. New York: Simon & Schuster, 2012.

Gibson, James. *Jacko, Where Are You Now? A Life of Robert Jackson, Master of Humanitarian Relief, the Man Who Saved Malta*. Richmond: Parsons, 2006.

Gillon, Steven. *Politics and Vision: The ADA and American Liberalism, 1947–1985*. New York: Oxford University Press, 1987.

Glazer, Nathan, and Daniel Patrick Moynihan. *Beyond the Melting Pot: The Negroes, Puerto Ricans, Jews, Italians, and Irish of New York City*. 2nd ed. Cambridge: MIT Press, 1970.

Gold, Bela. *Wartime Economic Planning in Agriculture: A Study in the Allocation of Resources*. New York: Columbia University Press, 1949.

Goldman, Eric. *The Crucial Decade—And After: America, 1945–1960*. New York: Vintage Books, 1960.

Goldman, Eric. *The Tragedy of Lyndon Johnson*. New York: Knopf, 1969.

Goldstein, Robert. *American Blacklist: The Attorney General's List of Subversive Organizations*. Lawrence: University Press of Kansas, 2008.

Goodhart, Philip. *Fifty Ships That Saved the World: The Foundation of the Anglo-American Alliance*. Garden City: Doubleday, 1965.

Goodman, Walter. *The Committee: The Extraordinary Career of the House Committee on Un-American Activities*. New York: Farrar, Straus and Giroux, 1968.

Goodwin, Doris Kearns. *The Fitzgeralds and the Kennedys*. New York: Simon & Schuster, 1987.

Gordon, Colin. *Dead on Arrival: The Politics of Health Care in Twentieth-Century America*. Princeton: Princeton University Press, 2003.

Gosnell, Harold. *Truman's Crises: A Political Biography of Harry S. Truman*. Westport: Greenwood Press, 1980.

Gould, Jean, and Lorena Hickok. *Walter Reuther: Labor's Rugged Individualist*. New York: Dodd, Mead, 1972.

Goulden, Joseph. *Meany*. New York: Atheneum, 1972.

Graham, Hugh Davis. *The Uncertain Triumph: Federal Education Policy in the Kennedy and Johnson Years*. Chapel Hill: University of North Carolina Press, 1984.

Green, Nancy. "Blacks, Jews, and the 'Natural Alliance': Labor Cohabitation and the ILGWU." *Jewish Social Studies*, IV (Fall 1997): 79–104.

Greenberg, Cheryl. "The Politics of Disorder: Reexamining Harlem's Riots of 1935 and 1943." *Journal of Urban History*, XVIII, 4 (August 1992): 395–441.

Greenberg, Cheryl. *Troubling the Waters: Black-Jewish Relations in the American Century*. Princeton: Princeton University Press, 2006.

Greene, John Robert. *The Crusade: The Presidential Election of 1952*. Lanham: University Press of America, 1985.

Griffith, Robert. *The Politics of Fear: Joseph R. McCarthy and the Senate*. New York: Hayden, 1970.

Griffith, Robert, and Athan Theoharis, eds. *The Specter: Original Essays on the Cold War and the Origins of McCarthyism*. New York: New Viewpoints, 1974.

Grossman, David. "Flood Insurance: Can a Feasible Program Be Created?" *Land Economics*, XXXIV, 4 (November 1958): 352–357.

Guthman, Edwin, and Jeffrey Shulman, eds. *Robert Kennedy in His Own Words: The Unpublished Recollections of the Kennedy Years*. New York: Bantam Books, 1988.

Hacker, Jacob. *The Divided Welfare State: The Battle over Public and Private Social Benefits in the United States*. New York: Cambridge University Press, 2002.

Hacker, Louis, and Mark Hirsch. *Proskauer: His Life and Times*. University: University of Alabama Press, 1978.

Hahn, Peter. *The United States, Great Britain, and Egypt, 1945–1956: Strategy and Diplomacy in the Early Cold War*. Chapel Hill: University of North Carolina Press, 1991.

Hall, Helen. *Unfinished Business in Neighborhood and Nation*. New York: Macmillan, 1971.

Hamby, Alonzo. "The Liberals, Truman, and FDR as Symbol and Myth." *Journal of American History*, LVI, 4 (March 1970): 859–867.

Hamby, Alonzo. *Beyond the New Deal: Harry S. Truman and American Liberalism*. New York: Columbia University Press, 1973.

Hamby, Alonzo. *Liberalism and Its Challengers: From F.D.R. to Bush*. New York: Oxford University Press, 1992.

Hamby, Alonzo. *Man of the People: A Life of Harry S. Truman*. New York: Oxford University Press, 1995.

Hamilton, Charles. *Adam Clayton Powell, Jr.: The Political Biography of an American Dilemma*. New York: Atheneum, 1991.

Hamilton, Virginia Van der Veer. *Lister Hill: Statesman from the South*. Chapel Hill: University of North Carolina Press, 1987.

Hand, Samuel. *Counsel and Advise: A Political Biography of Samuel I. Rosenman*. New York: Garland, 1979.

Handlin, Oscar. *Al Smith and His America*. Boston: Little, Brown, 1958.

Handlin, Oscar. *A Continuing Task: The American Jewish Joint Distribution Committee, 1914–1964*. New York: Random House, 1964.

Hardeman, D. B., and Donald Bacon. *Rayburn: A Biography*. Houston: Gulf, 1987.

Hardy, Henry, ed. *Letters, 1928–1946: Isaiah Berlin*. New York: Cambridge University Press, 2004.

Hareven, Tamara. *Eleanor Roosevelt: An American Conscience*. Chicago: Quadrangle Books, 1968.

Harris, Louis, and Bert Swanson. *Black-Jewish Relations in New York City*. New York: Praeger, 1970.

Hart, Parker. *Saudi Arabia and the United States: Birth of a Security Partnership*. Bloomington: Indiana University Press, 1998.

Hartmann, Susan. *Truman and the 80th Congress*. Columbia: University of Missouri Press, 1971.

Hartzell, Karl Drew. *The Empire State at War: World War II*. Albany: New York State War Council, 1949.

Hassett, William. *Off the Record with F.D.R., 1942–1945*. New Brunswick: Rutgers University Press, 1958.

Haygood, Wil. *King of the Cats: The Life and Times of Adam Clayton Powell, Jr.* Boston: Houghton Mifflin, 1993.

Hays, Brooks. *A Southern Moderate Speaks.* Chapel Hill: University of North Carolina Press, 1959.

Heinrichs, Waldo. *Threshold of War: Franklin D. Roosevelt and American Entry into World War II.* New York: Oxford University Press, 1988.

Henry, Richard. *Eleanor Roosevelt and Adlai Stevenson.* New York: Palgrave Macmillan, 2010.

Hero, Alfred O., Jr. *American Religious Groups View Foreign Policy: Trends in Rank-and-File Opinion, 1937–1969.* Durham: Duke University Press, 1973.

Hill, Herbert. "The ILGWU Today: The Decay of a Labor Union." *New Politics,* I, 4 (Summer 1962): 6–17.

Hill, Herbert. "The ILGWU: Fact and Fiction." *New Politics,* II, 2 (Winter 1963): 7–27.

Hill, Herbert. "Black-Jewish Conflict in the Labor Context." In *African Americans and Jews in the Twentieth Century: Studies in Convergence and Conflict,* ed. V. P. Franklin, Nancy Grant, Harold Kletnick, and Genna Rae McNeil. Columbia: University of Missouri Press, 1998.

Hirschmann, Ira. *The Embers Still Burn: An Eye-Witness View of the Postwar Ferment in Europe and the Middle East and Our Disastrous Get-Soft-with-Germany-Policy.* New York: Simon & Schuster, 1949.

Hogan, Michael. *The Marshall Plan: America, Britain, and the Reconstruction of Western Europe, 1947–1952.* New York: Cambridge University Press, 1987.

Holt, Len. *The Summer That Didn't End.* New York: William Morrow, 1965.

Hoover, Herbert. *An American Epic, Volume IV: The Guns Cease Killing and the Saving of Life from Famine Begins, 1939–1963.* Chicago: Henry Regnery, 1964.

Horwitz, Morton. *The Warren Court and the Pursuit of Justice.* New York: Hill and Wang, 1998.

Hughes, Emmet John. *The Ordeal of Power: A Political Memoir of the Eisenhower Years.* New York: Atheneum, 1963.

Hull, Cordell. *The Memoirs of Cordell Hull.* 2 Vols. New York: Macmillan Company, 1948.

Humphrey, Hubert. *The Education of a Public Man: My Life and Politics.* Ed. Norman Sherman. Garden City: Doubleday, 1976.

Hutchins, Mason, ed. *The New York Red Book, 1940: An Illustrated State Manual.* Albany: J. B. Lyon, 1940.

Hutchinson, E. P. *Legislative History of American Immigration Policy, 1798–1965.* Philadelphia: University of Pennsylvania Press, 1981.

Huthmacher, J. Joseph. *Senator Robert F. Wagner and the Rise of Urban Liberalism.* New York: Atheneum, 1968.

Hyman, Sidney. *The Lives of William Benton.* Chicago: University of Chicago Press, 1969.

Ickes, Harold. *The Secret Diary of Harold L. Ickes, Volume I: The First Thousand Days, 1933–1936.* New York: Simon & Schuster, 1953.

Ickes, Harold. *The Secret Diary of Harold L. Ickes, Volume II: The Inside Struggle, 1936–1939.* New York: Simon & Schuster, 1954.

Ickes, Harold. *The Secret Diary of Harold L. Ickes, Volume III: The Lowering Clouds, 1939–1941.* New York: Simon & Schuster, 1954.

Ingalls, Robert. *Herbert H. Lehman and New York's Little New Deal.* New York: New York University Press, 1975.

Isaacs, Stephen. *Jews and American Politics.* Garden City: Doubleday, 1974.

Jack, Robert. *History of the National Association for the Advancement of Colored People.* Boston: Meador, 1943.

Jackson, Kenneth. *The Ku Klux Klan in the City, 1915–1930.* New York: Oxford University Press, 1967.

Jackson, Robert. *That Man: An Insider's Portrait of Franklin D. Roosevelt.* Ed. John Barrett. New York: Oxford University Press, 2004.

Jacobs, Meg. " 'How About Some Meat?' The Office of Price Administration, Consumption Politics, and State Building from the Bottom Up." *Journal of American History*, LXXXIV, 3 (December 1997): 910–941.

Jacobson, Gary. "The Effects of the George W. Bush Presidency on Partisan Attitudes." *Presidential Studies Quarterly*, XXXIX, 2 (June 2009): 172–209.

Janken, Kenneth. *White: The Biography of Walter White, Mr. NAACP.* New York: New Press, 2003.

Javits, Jacob, with Rafael Steinberg. *Javits: The Autobiography of a Public Man.* Boston: Houghton Mifflin, 1981.

Jeansonne, Glen. *Gerald L. K. Smith, Minister of Hate.* New Haven: Yale University Press, 1988.

Johnson, Evans. *Oscar W. Underwood: A Political Biography.* Baton Rouge: Louisiana State University Press, 1980.

Johnson, Lyndon. *A Time for Action: A Selection from the Speeches and Writings of Lyndon B. Johnson, 1953–64.* New York: Atheneum, 1964.

Jonas, Gilbert. *Freedom's Sword: The NAACP and the Struggle against Racism in America, 1909–1969.* New York: Routledge, 2007.

Jones, Maldwyn. *American Immigration.* Chicago: University of Chicago Press, 1992.

Josephson, Matthew. *Sidney Hillman: Statesman of American Labor.* Garden City: Doubleday, 1952.

Josephson, Matthew, and Hannah Josephson. *Al Smith: Hero of the Cities—A Political Portrait Drawing on the Papers of Frances Perkins.* Boston: Houghton Mifflin, 1969.

Kahn, E. J., Jr. *The World of Swope.* New York: Simon & Schuster, 1965.

Kahn, E. J., Jr. *The China Hands: America's Foreign Service Officers and What Befell Them.* New York: Viking Press, 1975.

Kaufman, Burton. *Trade and Aid: Eisenhower's Foreign Economic Policy, 1953–1961.* Baltimore: Johns Hopkins University Press, 1982.

Kaufman, Jonathan. *Broken Alliance: The Turbulent Times between Blacks and Jews in America.* New York: Charles Scribner's Sons, 1988.

Kelley, Stanley, Jr. *Professional Public Relations and Political Power.* Baltimore: Johns Hopkins University Press, 1956.

Kellogg, Charles. *NAACP: A History of the National Association for the Advancement of Colored People: Vol. I: 1909–1920.* Baltimore: Johns Hopkins University Press, 1967.

Kelly, Frank. *The Fight for the White House: The Story of 1912.* New York: Thomas Y. Crowell, 1961.

Kemper, Donald. *Decade of Fear: Senator Hennings and Civil Liberties.* Columbia: University of Missouri Press, 1965.

Kenen, I. L. *Israel's Defense Line: Her Friends and Foes in Washington*. Buffalo: Prometheus Books, 1981.

Kennedy, David. *Freedom from Fear: The American People in Depression and War, 1929–1945*. New York: Oxford University Press, 1999.

Kennedy, John. *Profiles in Courage*. New York: Harper & Brothers, 1956.

Kennedy, John. *A Nation of Immigrants*. New York: Anti-Defamation League of B'nai B'rith, 1958.

Kennedy, John. *A Nation of Immigrants*. Revised and enlarged ed. New York: Harper & Row, 1964.

Kennedy, Susan Estabrook. "Herbert Hoover and the Two Great Food Crusades of the 1940s." In *Understanding Herbert Hoover: Ten Perspectives*, ed. Lee Nash. Stanford: Hoover Institution Press, 1987.

Kessner, Thomas. *Fiorello H. La Guardia and the Making of Modern New York*. New York: McGraw-Hill, 1989.

Khrushchev, Nikita. *Khrushchev Remembers: The Last Testament*. Trans. Strobe Talbott. Boston: Little, Brown, 1974.

Kimball, Warren. *The Juggler: Franklin Roosevelt as Wartime Statesman*. Princeton: Princeton University Press, 1991.

King, Martin Luther, Jr. *Why We Can't Wait*. New York: New American Library, 1964.

Kinzer, Stephen. *The Brothers: John Foster Dulles, Allen Dulles, and Their Secret World War*. New York: St. Martin's Griffin, 2013.

Kluger, Richard. *Simple Justice: The History of Brown v. Board of Education and Black America's Struggle for Equality*. New York: Knopf, 1977.

Knight, Amy. *How the Cold War Began: The Igor Gouzenko Affair and the Hunt for Soviet Spies*. New York: Carroll & Graf, 2006.

Koch, Edward, with William Rauch. *Politics*. New York: Simon & Schuster, 1985.

Koen, Ross. *The China Lobby in American Politics*. New York: Harper & Row, 1974.

Kotlowski, Dean. "With All Deliberate Delay: Kennedy, Johnson, and School Desegregation." *Journal of Policy History*, XVII, 2 (2005): 155–192.

Krock, Arthur. *Memoirs: Sixty Years on the Firing Line*. New York: Funk & Wagnalls, 1968.

Krock, Arthur. *The Consent of the Governed and Other Deceits*. Boston: Little, Brown, 1971.

LaCerra, Charles. *Franklin Delano Roosevelt and Tammany Hall of New York*. Lanham: University Press of America, 1997.

Lamont, Corliss. *A Lifetime of Dissent*. Buffalo: Prometheus Press, 1988.

Larrabee, Eric. *Commander in Chief: Franklin Delano Roosevelt, His Lieutenants, and Their War*. New York: Harper & Row, 1987.

Lash, Joseph. *Eleanor Roosevelt: A Friend's Memoir*. Garden City: Doubleday, 1964.

Lash, Joseph. *Eleanor and Franklin: The Story of Their Relationship, Based on Eleanor Roosevelt's Private Papers*. New York: Norton, 1971.

Lash, Joseph. *Eleanor: The Years Alone*. New York: Norton, 1972.

Lash, Joseph. *Love, Eleanor: Eleanor Roosevelt and Her Friends*. Garden City: Doubleday, 1982.

Lash, Joseph. *A World of Love: Eleanor Roosevelt and Her Friends, 1943–1962*. Garden City: Doubleday, 1984.

Lasky, Victor. *J.F.K.: The Man and the Myth*. New York: Macmillan, 1963.

Lasky, Victor. *It Didn't Start with Watergate.* New York: Dial Press, 1977.

Lasser, William. *Benjamin V. Cohen: Architect of the New Deal.* New Haven: Yale University Press, 2002.

Lawson, Steven. *Black Ballots: Voting Rights in the South, 1944–1969.* New York: Columbia University Press, 1976.

Lay, Shawn. *Hooded Knights on the Niagara: The Ku Klux Klan in Buffalo, New York.* New York: New York University Press, 1995.

Lazarowitz, Arlene. *Years in Exile: The Liberal Democrats, 1950–1959.* New York: Garland, 1988.

Lee, R. Alton. *Eisenhower and Landrum-Griffin: A Study in Labor-Management Politics.* Lexington: University Press of Kentucky, 1990.

LeMay, Michael. *Guarding the Gates: Immigration and National Security.* Westport: Praeger Security International, 2006.

Leuchtenburg, William E. *Franklin D. Roosevelt and the New Deal, 1932–1940.* New York: Harper & Row, 1963.

Leuchtenburg, William E. *In the Shadow of FDR: From Harry Truman to Ronald Reagan.* Revised and updated ed. Ithaca: Cornell University Press, 1989.

Leuchtenburg, William E. *The Supreme Court Reborn: The Constitutional Revolution in the Age of Roosevelt.* New York: Oxford University Press, 1995.

Leuchtenburg, William E. "New Faces of 1946." *Smithsonian,* XXXVII, 8 (November 2006): 48–54.

Lewinson, Edwin. *Black Politics in New York City.* New York: Twayne, 1974.

Lewis, Alfred Allan. *Man of the World: Herbert Bayard Swope—A Charmed Life of Pulitzer Prizes, Poker and Politics.* Indianapolis: Bobbs-Merrill, 1978.

Libo, Kenneth, ed. *Lots of Lehmans: The Family of Mayer Lehman of Lehman Brothers, Remembered by His Descendants.* New York: Center for Jewish History, 2007.

Lichtman, Allan. *Prejudice and the Old Politics: The Presidential Election of 1928.* Chapel Hill: University of North Carolina Press, 1979.

Lifflander, Matthew. *The Impeachment of Governor Sulzer: A Story of American Politics.* Albany: State University of New York Press, 2012.

Lippman, Theo, Jr. *The Squire of Warm Springs: F.D.R. in Georgia, 1924–1945.* Chicago: Playboy Press, 1977.

Lowitt, Richard. "The Armed-Ship Bill Controversy; A Legislative View." *Mid-America,* XXXXVI, 1 (January 1964): 38–47.

Lubell, Samuel. "The Future of the Negro Voter in the United States." *Journal of Negro Education,* XXVI, 3 (Summer 1957): 408–417.

"Lyndon Johnson and the Civil Rights Revolution: A Panel Discussion." In *Lyndon Baines Johnson and the Uses of Power,* ed. Bernard Firestone and Robert Vogt. New York: Greenwood Press, 1988.

MacDuffie, Marshall. *The Red Carpet: 10,000 Miles through Russia on a Visa from Khrushchev.* New York: Norton, 1955.

Mackenzie, G. Calvin, and Robert Weisbrot. *The Liberal Hour: Washington and the Politics of Change in the 1960s.* New York: Penguin Books, 2009.

Mahoney, J. Daniel. *Actions Speak Louder.* New York: Arlington House, 1968.

Malsberger, John. *From Obstruction to Moderation: The Transformation of Senate Conservatism, 1938–1952.* Selinsgrove: Susquehanna University Press, 2000.

Manley, John. "The Conservative Coalition in Congress." *American Behavioral Scientist*, XVII (1973): 223–247.

Mann, Arthur. *La Guardia Comes to Power, 1933*. Philadelphia: J. B. Lippincott, 1965.

Mann, Robert. *The Walls of Jericho: Lyndon Johnson, Hubert Humphrey, Richard Russell, and the Struggle for Civil Rights*. New York: Harcourt Brace, 1996.

Mann, Robert. *A Grand Delusion: America's Descent into Vietnam*. New York: Basic Books, 2001.

Markowitz, Norman. *The Rise and Fall of the People's Century: Henry A. Wallace and American Liberalism, 1941–1948*. New York: Free Press, 1973.

Marshall, Ray. *The Negro and Organized Labor*. New York: John Wiley & Sons, 1965.

Martin, George. *Madam Secretary: Frances Perkins*. Boston: Houghton Mifflin, 1976.

Martin, John Bartlow. *The Deep South Says "Never."* Westport: Negro Universities Press, 1970. Originally published by Ballantine Books, 1957.

Martin, John Bartlow. *Adlai Stevenson of Illinois: The Life of Adlai E. Stevenson*. Garden City: Doubleday, 1976.

Martin, John Bartlow. *Adlai Stevenson and the World: The Life of Adlai E. Stevenson*. Garden City: Doubleday, 1977.

Martin, John Frederick. *Civil Rights and the Crisis of Liberalism: The Democratic Party, 1945–1976*. Boulder: Westview Press, 1979.

Martin, Ralph. *Ballots and Bandwagons*. Chicago: Rand McNally, 1964.

Martin, Ralph, and Ed Plaut. *Front Runner, Dark Horse*. Garden City: Doubleday, 1960.

Matthews, Donald. *U.S. Senators and Their World*. Chapel Hill: University of North Carolina Press, 1960.

Mattson, Kevin. *When America Was Great: The Fighting Faith of Postwar Liberalism*. New York: Routledge, 2006.

Matusow, Allen. *Farm Policies and Politics in the Truman Years*. Cambridge: Harvard University Press, 1967.

Matz, Johan. "Sweden, the United States, and Raoul Wallenberg's Mission to Hungary in 1944." *Journal of Cold War Studies*, XIV, 3 (Summer, 2012): 97–148.

Mayers, David Allan. *FDR's Ambassadors and the Diplomacy of Crisis: From the Rise of Hitler to the End of World War II*. New York: Cambridge University Press, 2013.

McAuliffe, Mary Sperling. *Crisis on the Left: Cold War Politics and American Liberals, 1947–1954*. Amherst: University of Massachusetts Press, 1978.

McCarthy, Joe. *The Remarkable Kennedys*. New York: Dial Press, 1960.

McCoy, Donald, and Richard Ruetten. *Quest and Response: Minority Rights and the Truman Administration*. Lawrence: University Press of Kansas, 1973.

McJimsey, George. *Harry Hopkins: Ally of the Poor and Defender of Democracy*. Cambridge: Harvard University Press, 1987.

McKenna, Marian. *Franklin Roosevelt and the Great Constitutional War: The Court-Packing Crisis of 1937*. New York: Fordham University Press, 2002.

McLellan, David. *Dean Acheson: The State Department Years*. New York: Dodd, Mead, 1976.

McNickle, Chris. *To Be Mayor of New York: Ethnic Politics in the City*. New York: Columbia University Press, 1993.

McPherson, Harry. *A Political Education: A Washington Memoir*. Boston: Houghton Mifflin, 1988.

Michel-Kerjan, Erwann. "Catastrophe Economics: The National Flood Insurance Program." *Journal of Economic Perspectives*, XXIV, 4 (Fall 2010): 165–186.

Miller, Merle. *Lyndon: An Oral Biography*. New York: G. P. Putnam's Sons, 1980.

Miller, Glen, and Stephen Ware. "Organized Labor in the Political Process: A Case Study of the Right-to-Work Campaign in Ohio." *Labor History*, IV (Winter 1963): 51–67.

Millis, Walter, ed., with the collaboration of E. S. Duffield. *The Forrestal Diaries*. New York: Viking Press, 1951.

Miroff, Bruce. *The Liberals' Moment: The McGovern Insurgency and the Identity Crisis of the Democratic Party*. Lawrence: University Press of Kansas, 2007.

Mitchell, Franklin. *Harry S. Truman and the News Media: Contentious Relations, Belated Respect*. Columbia: University of Missouri Press, 1998.

Moon, Henry Lee. *Balance of Power: The Negro Vote*. Garden City: Doubleday, 1949.

Moon, Henry Lee. "The Negro Vote in the Presidential Election of 1956." *Journal of Negro Education*, XXVI, 3 (Summer, 1957): 219–230.

Mooney, Booth. *LBJ: An Irreverent Chronicle*. New York: Thomas Y. Crowell, 1976.

Moreira, Peter. *The Jew Who Defeated Hitler: Henry Morgenthau Jr., FDR, and How We Won the War*. Amherst: Prometheus Books, 2014.

Morgan, Ted. *Reds: McCarthyism in Twentieth-Century America*. New York: Random House, 2003.

Morgenthau, Henry, III. *Mostly Morgenthaus: A Family History*. New York: Ticknor & Fields, 1991.

Morrison, Dennis. *Woman of Conscience: Senator Margaret Chase Smith of Maine*. St. James: Brandywine Press, 1994.

Moscow, Warren. *Politics in the Empire State*. New York: Knopf, 1948.

Moscow, Warren. *What Have You Done for Me Lately? The Ins and Outs of New York City Politics*. Englewood Cliffs: Prentice-Hall, 1967.

Moscow, Warren. *The Last of the Big-Time Bosses: The Life and Times of Carmine De Sapio and the Rise and Fall of Tammany Hall*. New York: Stein and Day, 1971.

Moynihan, Daniel. " 'Bosses' and 'Reformers': A Profile of the New York Democrats." *Commentary*, XXXI, 6 (June 1961): 461–470.

Mudd, Roger. *The Place to Be: Washington, CBS, and the Glory Days of Television News*. New York: PublicAffairs, 2008.

Murphy, Paul. *The Constitution in Crisis Times, 1918–1969*. New York: Harper & Row, 1972.

Murray, Robert. *The 103rd Ballot: Democrats and the Disaster in Madison Square Garden*. New York: Harper & Row, 1976.

Nadich, Judah. *Eisenhower and the Jews*. New York: Twayne, 1953.

Nasaw, David. *The Chief: The Life of William Randolph Hearst*. Boston: Houghton Mifflin, 2000.

Nelson, William. *In Pursuit of Right and Justice: Edward Weinfeld as Lawyer and Judge*. New York: New York University Press, 2004.

Nevins, Allan. *Herbert H. Lehman and His Era*. New York: Charles Scribner's Sons, 1963.

Newfield, Jack, and Wayne Barrett. *City for Sale: Ed Koch and the Betrayal of New York*. New York: Harper & Row, 1988.

Newman, Robert. *Owen Lattimore and the "Loss" of China*. Berkeley: University of California Press, 1992.

Nicholas, H. G., ed. *Washington Despatches, 1941–1945: Weekly Political Reports from the British Embassy*. Chicago: University of Chicago Press, 1981.

Nichols, Lee. *Breakthrough on the Color Front*. New York: Random House, 1954.

Nissenson, Marilyn. *The Lady Upstairs: Dorothy Schiff and the New York Post*. New York: St. Martin's Press, 2007.

Nixon, Edgar, ed. *Franklin D. Roosevelt and Foreign Affairs*. 3 Vols. Cambridge: Belknap Press of Harvard University Press, 1969.

Noble, George Bernard. *Christian A. Herter: Vol. XVIII: The American Secretaries of State and Their Diplomacy*. Ed. Robert Ferrell and Samuel Flagg Bemis. New York: Cooper Square, 1970.

Oberdorfer, Don. *Senator Mansfield: The Extraordinary Life of a Great American Statesman and Diplomat*. Washington, DC: Smithsonian Books, 2003.

O'Connor, Richard. *The First Hurrah: A Biography of Alfred E. Smith*. New York: G. P. Putnam's Sons, 1970.

O'Donnell, Kenneth, and David Powers, with Joe McCarthy. *"Johnny, We Hardly Knew Ye": Memories of John Fitzgerald Kennedy*. Boston: Little, Brown, 1972.

O'Dwyer, William. *Beyond the Golden Door*. Ed. Paul O'Dwyer. Jamaica: St. John's University, 1987.

O'Neill, Tip, with William Novak. *Man of the House: The Life and Political Memoirs of Speaker Tip O'Neill*. New York: Random House, 1987.

Oshinsky, David. *A Conspiracy So Immense: The World of Joe McCarthy*. New York: Free Press, 1983.

O'Sullivan, Christopher. *Harry Hopkins: FDR's Envoy to Churchill and Stalin*. Lanham: Rowman & Littlefield, 2015.

Overacker, Louise. *Money in Elections*. New York: Macmillan, 1932.

Ovington, Mary White. *The Walls Came Tumbling Down*. New York: Harcourt, Brace, 1947.

Ovington, Mary White. *Black and White Sat Down Together: The Reminiscences of an NAACP Founder*. Ed. Ralph Luker. New York: Feminist Press at the City University of New York, 1995.

Parmet, Herbert. *Eisenhower and the American Crusades*. New York: Macmillan, 1972.

Parmet, Herbert. *The Democrats: The Years after FDR*. New York: Macmillan, 1976.

Parmet, Herbert. *Jack: The Struggles of John F. Kennedy*. New York: Dial Press, 1980.

Parmet, Herbert. *JFK: The Presidency of John F. Kennedy*. New York: Penguin Books, 1984.

Parmet, Herbert, and Marie B. Hecht. *Never Again: A President Runs for a Third Term*. New York: Macmillan, 1968.

Parmet, Robert D. *Master of Seventh Avenue: David Dubinsky and the American Labor Movement*. New York: New York University Press, 2005.

Parrish, Michael. *Citizen Rauh: An American Liberal's Life in Law and Politics*. Ann Arbor: University of Michigan Press, 2010.

Patterson, James. *Congressional Conservatism and the New Deal: The Growth of the Conservative Coalition in Congress, 1933–1939*. Lexington: University of Kentucky Press, 1967.

Patterson, James. *Mr. Republican: A Biography of Robert A. Taft*. Boston: Houghton Mifflin, 1972.

"Paul Robeson: A Centennial Symposium." *Pennsylvania History*, LXVI, 1 (Winter 1999).

Pemberton, William. *Harry S. Truman: Fair Dealer and Cold Warrior*. Boston: Twayne, 1989.

Peres, Shimon. *David's Sling*. London: Weidenfeld and Nicolson, 1970.

Perry, Elisabeth Israels. *Belle Moskowitz: Feminine Politics and the Exercise of Power in the Age of Alfred E. Smith*. New York: Oxford University Press, 1987.

Peters, Charles. *Five Days in Philadelphia: 1940, Wendell Willkie, and the Political Convention That Freed FDR to Win World War II*. New York: PublicAffairs, 2005.

Petrus, Stephen. "To Break Down Walls: The Politics and Culture of Greenwich Village, 1955–1965." PhD Dissertation, Graduate Center of the City University of New York, 2010.

Pfeffer, Leo. *Church, State, and Freedom*. Boston: Beacon Press, 1953.

Phillips, Cabell. *The Truman Presidency: The History of a Triumphant Succession*. New York: Macmillan, 1966.

Plesur, Milton. "The Republican Congressional Comeback of 1938." *Review of Politics*, XXIV, 4 (October 1962): 525–562.

Plotke, David. *Building a Democratic Political Order: Reshaping American Liberalism in the 1930s and 1940s*. New York: Cambridge University Press, 1996.

Podair, Jerald. *The Strike That Changed New York: Blacks, Whites, and the Ocean Hill-Brownsville Crisis*. New Haven: Yale University Press, 2002.

Poen, Monte. *Harry S. Truman versus the Medical Lobby: The Genesis of Medicare*. Columbia: University of Missouri Press, 1979.

Polenberg, Richard. "Franklin Roosevelt and the Purge of John J. O'Connor." *New York History*, XLIX (July 1968): 306–326.

Porter, Kirk, and Donald Bruce Johnson, compilers. *National Party Platforms, 1840–1960*. Urbana: University of Illinois Press, 1961.

Porter, Stephen. "Humanitarian Diplomacy after World War II: The United Nations Relief and Rehabilitation Administration." In *Foreign Policy Breakthroughs: Cases in Successful Diplomacy*, ed. Robert Hutchings and Jeremi Suri. New York: Oxford University Press, 2015.

Potter, Jeffrey. *Men, Money and Magic: The Story of Dorothy Schiff*. New York: Coward, McCann & Geoghegan, 1976.

Powe, Lucas A., Jr. *The Warren Court and American Politics*. Cambridge: Harvard University Press, 2000.

Price, Charles, and Joseph Boskin. "The Roosevelt 'Purge': A Reappraisal." *Journal of Politics*, XXVIII (August 1966): 660–670.

Pritchett, Wendell. *Brownsville, Brooklyn: Blacks, Jews, and the Changing Face of the Ghetto*. Chicago: University of Chicago Press, 2002.

Pritchett, Wendell. *Robert Clifton Weaver and the American City: The Life and Times of an Urban Reformer*. Chicago: University of Chicago Press, 2008.

Proskauer, Joseph. *A Segment of My Times*. New York: Farrar, Straus, 1950.

Pruessen, Ronald. *John Foster Dulles: The Road to Power*. New York: Free Press, 1982.

Quadagno, Jill. *One Nation Uninsured: Why the U.S. Has No National Health Insurance*. New York: Oxford University Press, 2005.

Redding, Jack. *Inside the Democratic Party*. Indianapolis: Bobbs-Merrill, 1958.

Reeves, Thomas. *The Life and Times of Joe McCarthy: A Biography*. New York: Stein and Day, 1982.

Reeves, Thomas. *A Question of Character: A Life of John F. Kennedy*. New York: Free Press, 1991.

Reich, Cary. *The Life of Nelson A. Rockefeller: Worlds to Conquer, 1908–1958*. New York: Doubleday, 1996.

Reichard, Gary. "Divisions and Dissent: Democrats and Foreign Policy, 1952–1956." *Political Science Quarterly*, LXXXXIII, 1 (Spring 1978): 51–72.

Reichard, Gary. "Democrats, Civil Rights, and Electoral Strategies in the 1950s." *Congress and the Presidency*, XIII, 1 (March 1986): 59–81.

Reinisch, Jessica. "Introduction: Relief in the Aftermath of War." *Journal of Contemporary History*, XLIII, 3 (July 2008): 371–404.

"Relief in the Aftermath of War." Special Issue. *Journal of Contemporary History*, XLIII, 3 (July 2008).

Reynolds, David. *From Munich to Pearl Harbor: Roosevelt's America and the Origins of the Second World War*. Chicago: Ivan R. Dee, 2004.

Reznikoff, Charles, ed. *Louis Marshall, Champion of Liberty: Selected Papers and Addresses*. 2 Vols. Philadelphia: Jewish Publication Society of America, 1957.

Ribuffo, Leo. "AHR Forum: Why Is There So Much Conservatism in the United States and Why Do So Few Historians Know Anything about It?" *American Historical Review*, LXXXXIV, 2 (April 1994): 438–449.

Roberts, Priscilla. "Frank Altschul, Lazard Frères, and the Council on Foreign Relations: The Evolution of a Transatlantic Thinker." *Journal of Transatlantic Studies*, I, 2 (September 2003): 175–213.

Roberts, Sam. *The Brother: The Untold Story of the Rosenberg Case*. New York: Random House, 2001.

Roche, John, and Leonard Levy. *The Congress*. New York: Harcourt, Brace & World, 1964.

Roll, David. *The Hopkins Touch: Harry Hopkins and the Forging of the Alliance to Defeat Hitler*. New York: Oxford University Press, 2013.

Roosevelt, Eleanor. *This I Remember*. New York: Harper & Brothers, 1949.

Roosevelt, Eleanor. *On My Own*. New York: Harper & Brothers, 1958.

Roosevelt, Eleanor. *The Autobiography of Eleanor Roosevelt*. New York: Harper & Brothers, 1961.

Roosevelt, Elliott, ed. *F.D.R.: His Personal Letters, 1928–1945*. New York: Duell, Sloan and Pearce, 1950.

Rosenman, Samuel. *Working with Roosevelt*. New York: Harper & Brothers, 1952.

Rosenman, Samuel, and Dorothy Rosenman. *Presidential Style: Some Giants and a Pygmy in the White House*. New York: Harper & Row, 1976.

Ross, Joyce. *J. E. Spingarn and the Rise of the NAACP, 1911–1939*. New York: Atheneum, 1972.

Rourke, John. *Congress and the Presidency in U.S. Foreign Policymaking: A Study of Interaction and Influence, 1945–1982*. Boulder: Westview Press, 1983.

Rowan, Carl. *Dream Makers, Dream Breakers: The World of Justice Thurgood Marshall*. Boston: Little, Brown, 1993.

Ryley, Thomas. *A Little Group of Willful Men: A Study of Congressional-Presidential Author-ity.* Port Washington: Kennikat Press, 1975.

Sachar, Howard. *A History of the Jews in America.* New York: Vintage Books, 1993.

Salmond, John. *The Civilian Conservation Corps, 1933–1942: A New Deal Case Study.* Durham: Duke University Press, 1967.

Salzman, Jack, ed., with Adina Back and Gretchen Sullivan Sorin. *Bridges and Boundaries: African Americans and American Jews.* New York: George Braziller, 1992.

Salzman, Jack, and Cornel West, eds. *Struggles in the Promised Land: Toward a History of Black-Jewish Relations in the United States.* New York: Oxford University Press, 1997.

Sarna, Aaron. *Boycott and Blacklist: A History of Arab Economic Warfare Against Israel.* Totowa: Rowman & Littlefield, 1986.

Savage, Sean. *Roosevelt: The Party Leader, 1932–1945.* Lexington: University Press of Kentucky, 1991.

Savage, Sean. *Truman and the Democratic Party.* Lexington: University Press of Kentucky, 1997.

Savage, Sean. *JFK, LBJ, and the Democratic Party.* Albany: State University of New York Press, 2004.

Savage, Sean. *The Senator from New England: The Rise of JFK.* Albany: State University of New York Press, 2015.

Schapsmeier, Edward, and Frederick Schapsmeier. *Prophet in Politics: Henry A. Wallace and the War Years, 1940–1965.* Ames: Iowa State University Press, 1970.

Scharf, Lois. *Eleanor Roosevelt: First Lady of American Liberalism.* Boston: Twayne, 1987.

Scheier, Joan. *Images of America: The Central Park Zoo.* Charleston: Arcadia, 2002.

Schlesinger, Arthur M., Jr. *The Age of Roosevelt: Vol. I: The Crisis of the Old Order, 1919–1933.* Boston: Houghton Mifflin, 1956.

Schlesinger, Arthur M., Jr. *The Age of Roosevelt: Vol. II: The Coming of the New Deal.* Boston: Houghton Mifflin, 1958.

Schlesinger, Arthur M., Jr. *The Age of Roosevelt: Vol. III: The Politics of Upheaval.* Boston: Houghton Mifflin, 1960.

Schlesinger, Arthur M., Jr. *The Politics of Hope.* Boston: Houghton Mifflin, 1962.

Schlesinger, Arthur M., Jr. *A Thousand Days: John F. Kennedy in the White House.* Boston: Houghton Mifflin, 1965.

Schlesinger, Arthur M., Jr. *Robert Kennedy and His Times.* Boston: Houghton Mifflin, 1978.

Schlesinger, Arthur M., Jr. *Journals: 1952–2000.* Ed. Andrew Schlesinger and Stephen Schlesinger. New York: Penguin Press, 2007.

Schmidt, Karl. *Henry A. Wallace: Quixotic Crusade 1948.* Syracuse: Syracuse University Press, 1960.

Schrecker, Ellen. *No Ivory Tower: McCarthyism and the Universities.* New York: Oxford University Press, 1986.

Schrecker, Ellen. *Many Are the Crimes: McCarthyism in America.* Princeton: Princeton University Press, 1998.

Schwartz, Abba. *The Open Society.* New York: William Morrow, 1968.

Schwarz, Jordan. *The Speculator: Bernard M. Baruch in Washington, 1917–1965.* Chapel Hill: University of North Carolina Press, 1981.

Schwarz, Jordan. *Liberal: Adolf A. Berle and the Vision of an American Era*. New York: Free Press, 1987.

Scroop, Daniel. *Mr. Democrat: Jim Farley, the New Deal, and the Making of Modern American Politics*. Ann Arbor: University of Michigan Press, 2006.

Seaborg, Glenn, with the assistance of Benjamin Loeb. *Kennedy, Khrushchev, and the Test Ban*. Berkeley: University of California Press, 1981.

Shapiro, Edward. "Corliss Lamont and Civil Liberties." *Modern Age*, XLII, 2 (Spring 2000): 158–175.

Shelley, Mack C., II. *The Permanent Majority: The Conservative Coalition in the United States Congress*. University: University of Alabama Press, 1983.

Shephard, Ben. *The Long Road Home: The Aftermath of the Second World War*. New York: Knopf, 2011.

Sherrill, Robert. *Gothic Politics in the Deep South: Stars of the New Confederacy*. New York: Grossman, 1968.

Shesol, Jeff. *Mutual Contempt: Lyndon Johnson, Robert Kennedy, and the Feud that Defined a Decade*. New York: Norton, 1997.

Shesol, Jeff. *Supreme Power: Franklin Roosevelt vs. the Supreme Court*. New York: Norton, 2010.

Shogan, Robert. *Prelude to Catastrophe: FDR's Jews and the Menace of Nazism*. Chicago: Ivan R. Dee, 2010.

Sidey, Hugh. *John F. Kennedy, President*. New edition. New York: Atheneum, 1964.

Sitkoff, Harvard. *A New Deal for Blacks: The Emergence of Civil Rights as a National Issue, Volume I: The Depression Decade*. New York: Oxford University Press, 1978.

Slayton, Robert. *Empire Statesman: The Rise and Redemption of Al Smith*. New York: Free Press, 2001.

Sleeper, Jim. *The Closest of Strangers: Liberalism and the Politics of Race in New York*. New York: Norton, 1990.

Smith, Alfred E. *Up to Now: An Autobiography*. New York: Viking Press, 1929.

Smith, Bob. *They Closed Their Schools: Prince Edward County, Virginia, 1951–1964*. Chapel Hill: University of North Carolina Press, 1965.

Smith, Glenn. *Langer of North Dakota: A Study in Isolationism, 1940–1959*. New York: Garland, 1979.

Smith, Margaret Chase. *Declaration of Conscience*. Ed. William C. Lewis, Jr. Garden City: Doubleday, 1972.

Smith, Richard Norton. *Thomas E. Dewey and His Times*. New York: Simon & Schuster, 1982.

Smith, Richard Norton. *An Uncommon Man: The Triumph of Herbert Hoover*. New York: Simon & Schuster, 1984.

Smith, Richard Norton. *On His Own Terms: A Life of Nelson Rockefeller*. New York: Random House, 2014.

Snetsinger, John. *Truman, the Jewish Vote, and the Creation of Israel*. Stanford: Hoover Institution Press, 1974.

Snyder, J. Richard, ed. *John F. Kennedy: Person, Policy, Presidency*. Wilmington: SR Books, 1988.

Soffer, Jonathan. *Ed Koch and the Rebuilding of New York City*. New York: Columbia University Press, 2010.

Solberg, Carl. *Hubert Humphrey: A Biography.* New York: Norton, 1984.

Solomon, Burt. *FDR v. the Constitution: The Court-Packing Fight and the Triumph of Democracy.* New York: Walker & Company, 2009.

Sorensen, Ted. *Counselor: A Life at the Edge of History.* New York: Harper, 2008.

Sorensen, Theodore. *Kennedy.* New York: Harper & Row, 1965.

Souhami, Diana. *Edith Cavell.* London: Quercus, 2010.

Soyer, Daniel. "'Support the Fair Deal in the Nation; Abolish the Raw Deal in the City': The Liberal Party in 1949." Unpublished paper delivered at "The World of Governor Lehman: New York City and State in Depression and War." Columbia University, 2008.

Spanier, John. *The Truman-MacArthur Controversy and the Korean War.* Cambridge: Harvard University Press, 1959.

Spiegel, Steven. *The Other Arab-Israeli Conflict: Making America's Middle East Policy, from Truman to Reagan.* Chicago: University of Chicago Press, 1985.

Steinberg, Alfred. *Mrs. R: The Life of Eleanor Roosevelt.* New York: G. P. Putnam's Sons, 1958.

Steinberg, Alfred. *Sam Johnson's Boy: A Close-Up of the President from Texas.* New York: Macmillan, 1968.

Stevenson, Adlai. *The Papers of Adlai E. Stevenson, Volume IV: "Let's Talk Sense to the American People," 1952–1955.* Ed. Walter Johnson. Boston: Little, Brown, 1974.

Stevenson, Adlai. *The Papers of Adlai E. Stevenson, Volume VI: Toward a New America, 1955–1957.* Ed. Walter Johnson. Boston: Little, Brown, 1976.

Stevenson, Adlai. *The Papers of Adlai E. Stevenson, Volume VIII: Ambassador to the United Nations, 1961–1965.* Ed. Walter Johnson. Boston: Little, Brown, 1979.

Stolper, Thomas. *China, Taiwan, and the Offshore Islands: Together with an Implication for Outer Mongolia and Sino-Soviet Relations.* Armonk: M. E. Sharpe, 1985.

Sulzberger, C. L. *A Long Row of Candles: Memoirs and Diaries, 1934–1954.* New York: Macmillan, 1969.

Sundquist, James. *Politics and Policy: The Eisenhower, Kennedy, and Johnson Years.* Washington, DC: Brookings Institution, 1968.

Swanson, Bert. "The Presidential Convention as a Stage in the Struggle for Political Leadership: The New York Democratic Delegation." In *Inside Politics: The National Conventions, 1960,* ed. Paul Tillett. Dobbs Ferry: Oceana, 1962.

Syrett, John. "Roosevelt vs. Farley: The New York Gubernatorial Election of 1942." *New York History,* LVI, 1 (January 1975): 51–81.

Tananbaum, Duane. "Not for the First Time: Antecedents and Origins of the War Powers Resolution, 1945–1970." In *Congress and United States Foreign Policy: Controlling the Use of Force in the Nuclear Age,* ed. Michael Barnhart. Albany: State University of New York Press, 1987.

Tananbaum, Duane. *The Bricker Amendment Controversy: A Test of Eisenhower's Political Leadership.* Ithaca: Cornell University Press, 1988.

Tananbaum, Duane. "'I Can Leave the Combination of My Safe to Colonel Lehman': Herbert Lehman and Franklin Roosevelt: Working Together to Improve the Lives of New Yorkers and People All Over the World." *New York History,* LXXXVII, 1 (Winter 2006): 88–133.

Tananbaum, Duane. "Allies and Adversaries: Herbert Lehman and Robert Moses." Unpublished paper presented at "Robert Moses: New Perspectives on the Master Builder." Columbia University, 2007.

Tananbaum, Duane. *Drawn to Public Service: Political Cartoons from the Papers of Herbert H. Lehman.* New York: Columbia University Libraries, 2009.

Taubman, William. *Khrushchev: The Man and His Era.* New York: Norton, 2003.

Theoharis, Athan. *The Yalta Myths: An Issue in U.S. Politics, 1945–1955.* Columbia: University of Missouri Press, 1970.

Thompson, Francis. *The Frustration of Politics: Truman, Congress, and the Loyalty Issue, 1945–1953.* Rutherford: Fairleigh Dickinson University Press, 1979.

Thomson, Charles, and Frances Shattuck. *The 1956 Presidential Campaign.* Washington, DC: Brookings Institution, 1960.

Thurber, Timothy. *The Politics of Equality: Hubert H. Humphrey and the African American Freedom Struggle.* New York: Columbia University Press, 1999.

Tillett, Paul, ed. *Inside Politics: The National Conventions, 1960.* Dobbs Ferry: Oceana, 1962.

Titus, Jill. *Brown's Battleground: Students, Segregationists, and the Struggle for Justice in Prince Edward County, Virginia.* Chapel Hill: University of North Carolina Press, 2011.

Trattner, Walter. *Crusade for the Children: A History of the National Child Labor Committee and Child Labor Reform in America.* Chicago: Quadrangle Books, 1970.

Trohan, Walter. *Political Animals: Memoirs of a Sentimental Cynic.* Garden City: Doubleday, 1975.

Truman, David. *The Congressional Party: A Case Study.* New York: John Wiley & Sons, 1959.

Truman, Harry. *Memoirs: Volume I, Year of Decisions.* Garden City: Doubleday, 1955.

Truman, Harry. *Memoirs: Volume II, Years of Trial and Hope.* Garden City: Doubleday, 1956.

Truman, Harry, and Dean Acheson. *Affection and Trust: The Personal Correspondence of Harry S. Truman and Dean Acheson, 1953–1971.* Ed. Ray Geselbracht and David Acheson. New York: Knopf, 2010.

Truman, Margaret. *Harry S. Truman.* New York: William Morrow & Company, 1973.

Tucker, Nancy Bernkopf. *Patterns in the Dust: Chinese-American Relations and the Recognition Controversy, 1949–1950.* New York: Columbia University Press, 1983.

Tucker, Nancy Bernkopf, ed. *Dangerous Strait: The U.S.-Taiwan-China Crisis.* New York: Columbia University Press, 2005.

Tugwell, Rexford. *The Democratic Roosevelt: A Biography of Franklin D. Roosevelt.* Garden City: Doubleday, 1957.

Turck, Nancy. "The Arab Boycott of Israel." *Foreign Affairs,* LV, 3 (April 1977): 472–493.

Tushnet, Mark. *Making Constitutional Law: Thurgood Marshall and the Supreme Court, 1961–1991.* New York: Oxford University Press, 1991.

Tyler, Gus. "The Truth about the ILGWU." *New Politics,* II, 1 (Fall 1962): 6–17.

Tyler, Robert. "The American Veterans Committee: Out of a Hot War and into the Cold." *American Quarterly,* XVIII, 3 (Autumn 1966): 419–436.

Urofsky, Melvin. *American Zionism from Herzl to the Holocaust*. Garden City: Doubleday, 1975.

Urofsky, Melvin. *We Are One! American Jewry and Israel*. Garden City: Doubleday, 1978.

Vanden Heuvel, William. "Franklin Delano Roosevelt and Lyndon Baines Johnson: Architects of a Nation." Unpublished address delivered at the LBJ Presidential Library, March 2000.

Vandenberg, Arthur, Jr., ed., with the collaboration of Joe Alex Morris. *The Private Papers of Senator Vandenberg*. Boston: Houghton Mifflin, 1952.

Vernetti, Michael. *Senator Howard Cannon of Nevada: A Biography*. Reno: University of Nevada Press, 2008.

Von Hoffman, Nicholas. *Citizen Cohn*. New York: Doubleday, 1988.

Vorspan, Albert. *Giants of Justice*. New York: Union of American Hebrew Congregations, 1961.

Voss, Carl Hermann, ed. *Stephen S. Wise, Servant of the People: Selected Letters*. Philadelphia: Jewish Publication Society of America, 1970.

Wald, Lillian. *The House on Henry Street*. New York: Henry Holt, 1915.

Wald, Lillian. *Windows on Henry Street*. Boston: Little, Brown, 1934.

Wallace, Mike, with Gary Paul Gates. *Between You and Me: A Memoir*. New York: Hyperion, 2005.

Wallace, Patricia Ward. *Politics of Conscience: A Biography of Margaret Chase Smith*. Westport: Praeger, 1995.

Waller, Douglas. *Wild Bill Donovan: The Spymaster Who Created the OSS and Modern American Espionage*. New York: Free Press, 2011.

Walter, John. *The Harlem Fox: J. Raymond Jones and Tammany, 1920–1970*. Albany: State University of New York Press, 1989.

Warburg, James. *The Long Road Home: The Autobiography of a Maverick*. Garden City: Doubleday, 1964.

Ward, Geoffrey. *A First-Class Temperament: The Emergence of Franklin Roosevelt*. New York: Harper & Row, 1989.

Watson, Denton. *Lion in the Lobby: Clarence Mitchel, Jr.'s Struggle for the Passage of Civil Rights Laws*. New York: William Morrow, 1990.

Weinstein, Allen. *Perjury: The Hiss-Chambers Case*. New York: Vintage Books, 1979.

Weinstein, Allen, and Alexander Vassiliev. *The Haunted Wood: Soviet Espionage in America, The Stalin Era*. New York: Modern Library, 2000.

Weisbord, Robert, and Arthur Stein. *Bittersweet Encounter: The Afro-American and the American Jew*. Westport: Negro Universities Press, 1970.

Weiss, Nancy. *Charles Francis Murphy, 1858–1924: Respectability and Responsibility in Tammany Politics*. Northampton: Smith College, 1968.

Weiss, Nancy. *The National Urban League, 1910–1940*. New York: Oxford University Press, 1974.

Weiss, Nancy. *Farewell to the Party of Lincoln: Black Politics in the Age of FDR*. Princeton: Princeton University Press, 1983.

Weiss, Nancy. "Long-Distance Runners of the Civil Rights Movement: The Contribution of Jews to the NAACP and the National Urban League in the Early Twentieth Century." In *Struggles in the Promised Land: Toward a History of Black-Jewish Rela-*

tions in the United States, ed. Jack Salzman and Cornel West. New York: Oxford University Press, 1997.

Welles, Benjamin. *Sumner Welles: FDR's Global Strategist: A Biography*. New York: St. Martin's Press, 1997.

Werner, M. R. *Tammany Hall*. Garden City: Doubleday, Doran, 1928.

Wesser, Robert. "The Impeachment of a Governor: William Sulzer and the Politics of Excess." *New York History*, LX, 4 (October 1979): 407–438.

Wesser, Robert. *A Response to Progressivism: The Democratic Party and New York Politics, 1902–1918*. New York: New York University Press, 1986.

Westerfield, H. Bradford. *Foreign Policy and Party Politics: From Pearl Harbor to Korea*. New Haven: Yale University Press, 1955.

Whalen, Thomas. *Kennedy versus Lodge: The 1952 Massachusetts Senate Race*. Boston: Northeastern University Press, 2000.

White, G. Edward. *Alger Hiss's Looking-Glass Wars: The Covert Life of a Soviet Spy*. New York: Oxford University Press, 2004.

White, Graham. *FDR and the Press*. Chicago: University of Chicago Press, 1979.

White, Theodore. *The Making of the President, 1960*. New York: Atheneum, 1961.

White, Theodore. *The Making of the President, 1964*. New York: Atheneum, 1965.

White, William S. *Citadel: The Story of the U.S. Senate*. New York: Harper & Brothers, 1957.

White, William S. *The Professional: Lyndon B. Johnson*. Boston: Houghton Mifflin, 1964.

Whitehead, John. *Completing the Union: Alaska, Hawai'i, and the Battle for Statehood*. Albuquerque: University of New Mexico Press, 2004.

Whitfield, Stephen. *A Death in the Delta: The Story of Emmett Till*. Baltimore: Johns Hopkins University Press, 1991.

Williams, Francis. *A Prime Minister Remembers: The War and Post-War Memoirs of the Rt. Hon. Earl Attlee*. London: Heinemann, 1961.

Williams, Mason. *City of Ambition: FDR, La Guardia, and the Making of Modern New York*. New York: Norton, 2013.

Williamson, Samuel. *Imprint of a Publisher: The Story of Frank Gannett and His Independent Newspapers*. New York: R. M. McBride, 1948.

Wilson, James. *The Amateur Democrat: Club Politics in Three Cities*. Chicago: University of Chicago Press, 1962.

Wilson, Sondra Kathryn, ed. *In Search of Democracy: The NAACP Writings of James Weldon Johnson, Walter White, and Roy Wilkins, 1920–1977*. New York: Oxford University Press, 1999.

Wise, Stephen. *As I See It*. New York: Jewish Opinion, 1944.

Wise, Stephen. *Challenging Years: The Autobiography of Stephen Wise*. New York: G. P. Putnam's Sons, 1949.

Wittenberg, Philip, ed. *The Lamont Case: History of a Congressional Investigation*. New York: Horizon Press, 1957.

Wofford, Harris. *Of Kennedys and Kings: Making Sense of the Sixties*. New York: Farrar, Straus, Giroux, 1980.

Wolf, Thomas, William Pederson, and Byron Daynes, eds. *Franklin D. Roosevelt and Congress: The New Deal and Its Aftermath*. Vol. II. Armonk: M. E. Sharpe, 2001.

Woodbridge, George, ed. *UNNRA: The History of the United Nations Relief and Reha-bilitation Administration*. 3 Vols. New York: Columbia University Press, 1950.

Woods, Randall. *Fulbright: A Biography*. New York: Cambridge University Press, 1995.

Woods, Randall. *LBJ: Architect of American Ambition*. Cambridge: Harvard University Press, 2006.

Wyman, David. *Paper Walls: America and the Refugee Crisis, 1938–1941*. Amherst: University of Massachusetts Press, 1968.

Wyman, David. *The Abandonment of the Jews: America and the Holocaust, 1941–1945*. New York: Pantheon Books, 1984.

Ybarra, Michael. *Washington Gone Crazy: Senator Pat McCarran and the Great American Communist Hunt*. Hanover: Steerforth Press, 2004.

Yohn, Susan. "AHR Forum: Will the Real Conservative Please Stand Up? Or, The Pitfalls Involved in Examining Ideological Sympathies: A Comment on Alan Brinkley's 'Problem of American Conservatism.' " *American Historical Review*, XCIX, 2 (April 1994): 430–437.

Young, James. *Reconsidering American Liberalism: The Troubled Odyssey of the Liberal Idea*. Boulder: Westview Press, 1996.

Young, Kenneth. *Negotiating with the Chinese Communists: The United States Experience, 1953–1967*. New York: McGraw-Hill, 1968.

Zangrando, Robert. *The NAACP Crusade Against Lynching, 1909–1950*. Philadelphia: Temple University Press, 1980.

Zelden, Charles. *Thurgood Marshall: Race, Rights, and the Struggle for a More Perfect Union*. New York: Routledge, 2013.

Zeitz, Joshua. *White Ethnic New York: Jews, Catholics, and the Shaping of Postwar Politics*. Chapel Hill: University of North Carolina Press, 2007.

Zelizer, Julian. *The Fierce Urgency of Now: Lyndon Johnson, Congress, and the Battle for the Great Society*. New York: Penguin Press, 2015.

Zion, Sidney. *The Autobiography of Roy Cohn*. Secaucus: Lyle Stuart, 1988.

Index